EXPLORERS
and
DISCOVERERS
of the
WORLD

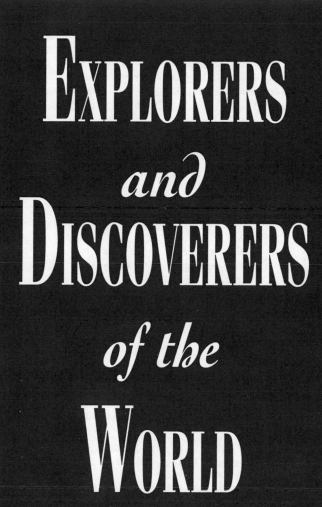

EXPLORERS

and

DISCOVERERS

of the

WORLD

EDITED BY

DANIEL B. BAKER

Gale Research Inc.

DETROIT • WASHINGTON DC • LONDON

Daniel B. Baker, *Editor*

Gale Research Inc. staff

Linda Metzger, *Coordinating Editor*
Victoria A. Coughlin, *Associate Editor*
Special thanks to Paula Cutcher-Jackson, Shelley Dickey, Kenneth Estell, Louise Gagne,
Monica M. Hubbard, Prindle LaBarge, and David Oblender

Jeanne A. Gough, *Permissions Manager*
Margaret Chamberlain, *Permissions Supervisor*
Pamela Hayes, *Permissions Associate*
Amy Lynn Emrich, Karla Kulkis, Nancy M. Rattenbury, Keith Reed, *Permissions Assistants*

Mary Beth Trimper, *Production Director*
Evi Seoud, *Assistant Production Manager*
Mary Kelley, *Production Assistant*

Cynthia Baldwin, *Art Director*
Mary Krzewinski, *Graphic Designer*

Cover Photo/NASA

The paper used in this publication meets the minimum requirements of American National Standard for Information Sciences—Permanence Paper for Printed Library Materials, ANSI Z39.48-1984.

LC 92-055094

ISBN: 0-8103-5421-7
Printed in the United States of America
Published simultaneously in the United Kingdom
by Gale Research International Limited
(An affiliated company of Gale Research Inc.)

059732

Contents

Preface xi
Introduction xiii
Chronology of Exploration xvii
Area Maps xxv
Glossary 599
Bibliography 601
List of Explorers by Area Explored 605
List of Explorers by Place of Birth 611
Index 615

Preface

Explorers and Discoverers of the World presents biographical information on more than 320 world explorers. Beginning with early Greek scholars and travelers and extending to 20th-century underwater and space exploration, *Explorers and Discoverers of the World* also expands coverage beyond the standard well-known explorers to include the contributions of women and non-Europeans for whom information isn't always readily available.

Selection Criteria and Research Methods

Knowing that one aim of this book was to include women and non-Europeans as well as the traditional explorers, a master list of potential listees was sent to an advisory board of school and public librarians who assisted in determining the final grouping. Once subjects were selected, a search of secondary sources further refined the list. *Explorers and Discoverers of the World* synthesizes our present state of knowledge of the field of exploration. Certainly more research will be done and more can be learned as additional primary documents are examined.

Special Features

Entries provide biographical portraits of the listees and examine the historical significance and consequences of their discoveries or explorations. Political, economic, and religious contexts are explored. *Explorers and Discoverers of the World* serves those interested in history as well as tells exciting and inspiring real-life stories. Many explorers' lives and expeditions were intertwined. A name in **bold-face type** within the body of an entry indicates that there is also an entry for that individual elsewhere in the book.

In addition, the following types of data are available throughout the volume:

Selected Bibliographies—Provided at the end of each entry, an explorer-specific list of readings serves as a basis for further research. Effort has been made to include autobiographical accounts of expeditions within the bibliographic citations.

Photographs and Maps—These visual aids spark additional interest in the material. Area maps give broad overviews of major regions while maps within specific entries pinpoint the geographic details discussed and help readers trace an explorer's route.

Chronology—Arranged by geographical area explored, significant expeditions are highlighted and help the reader put the entries in sharper focus by highlighting sequential and concurrent discoveries.

General Bibliography and Glossary—These useful features provide additional assistance to the student, researcher, teacher, and others.

Subject Index, List of Explorers by Place of Birth, and List of Explorers by Area Explored—The index and two lists guide users to the exact profiles they need. Whether finding the explorer by name of ship (e.g., *Challenger*), grouping explorers by nationality (e.g., Chinese), or concentrating on a specific part of the world (e.g., Antarctica) or geographic feature (e.g. the Niger River), the user can easily locate the information of interest.

Acknowledgments

The editor would like to extend two special acknowledgments of appreciation. The first is to Linda Metzger, the editor at Gale Research, who has been infinitely patient during what has proven to be a time-consuming and difficult process, and to Richard Deagle, graphic artist, who has produced such easily-read and useful maps.

Suggestions Are Welcome

Your comments on this work are welcome. Please write: Editor, *Explorers and Discoverers of the World*, Gale Research Inc., 835 Penobscot Bldg., Detroit, MI 48226-4904; or call toll-free 800-347-4253.

Introduction

What Is Exploration and Discovery?

"Exploration" in this book is defined as *systematic investigation* while "discovery" means *to make known*, especially to make known to the wider world. Discovery does not mean that the explorers presented here were the first humans to have seen a place, as was rarely the case. Even if an explorer were the first from his nation or continent to step foot on a new land, many of the lands discovered during the great European periods of exploration were already occupied, and the land's existence had often been recognized by other people. Among the last areas of the world to be explored were Antarctica, the Arctic Ocean, the interior of Greenland, and a few isolated islands in the world's oceans.

However, the great explorers did supply a systematic knowledge about how all the parts related to each other, which was their important contribution to the rest of humankind. Although even the first humans migrated and travelled, they either did not pass on the knowledge they gained to succeeding generations or other peoples, or they imparted that knowledge in an imperfect manner. The advent of literacy allowed past knowledge to be recorded, stored, used again, and compared with the experiences of other travelers. Literacy, therefore, became a pre-condition for "discovery"—making known to the outside world through some form of publication the discoverer's written records of his journey. These records played an important role in humankind's understanding of ourselves and our world and are stressed in the bibliographies in this volume.

Exploration as a Reflection of Society

Exploration reflects the social climate in which it is carried out. An obvious consequence of this is the role women have played in exploration and how that role has been recorded by history. It would have been unthinkable, for example, for a woman to have captained a ship in 15th- or 16th- century Spain. Therefore, it is futile to search for a female **Christopher Columbus** or **Ferdinand Magellan**. When a woman did play an important role in the explorations of that period, such as Ysabel Barrato on the voyage of **Alvaro de Mendaña**, she was universally portrayed in stereotypical terms: in this case, as a shrew who was responsible for the voyage's failure. On the other hand, one should not forget that Malinche in the case of **Hernán Cortés** and Inés Suarez in the case of **Pedro de Valdivia** are given credit for saving the male discoverers' lives and careers.

Later, as Western society changed, women began to be recognized for their individual accomplishments. At the end of the 18th and beginning of the 19th centuries, a few remarkable women, such as **Lady Hester Stanhope** and **Ida Pfeiffer**, broke away from societal roles and accomplished some remarkable journeys. By the end of the century, the number of female adventurers increased. However, the accomplishments of these pioneering women probably did not receive the recognition they deserved, and only in recent years has extensive work been done on rescuing many of them from obscurity.

That said, however, many of these journeys were remarkable, not because they had never been accomplished before, but because they had never been accomplished by a woman before. When **Delia Akeley** became the first woman known to cross Africa, she followed the first men (**Pedro João Baptista** and **Amaro José**) by 115 years and the first European man (**David Livingstone**) by 70 years. **Annie Smith Peck**, on the other hand, climbed peaks that no one had ever climbed before and was constantly being held back or disappointed by the male colleagues she insisted on dragging along after her. Her archrival, **Fanny Bullock Workman**, always accompanied Mr. Workman.

When we reach the age of aviation in the first part of the 20th century, women were truly at the forefront of exploration. **Amelia Earhart**, **Amy Johnson**, **Beryl Markham**, and other aviators not included in this book had just as many "firsts" as their male colleagues and rivals. This makes it all the more inexplicable that when the age of space exploration began in the 1950s, women were long denied a role. **Sally Ride**'s first voyage in space in 1983 came 21 years after **John Glenn** became the first American to orbit the earth. The U.S.S.R. did somewhat better in this regard: **Valentina Tereshkova** made the fourth Soviet space journey, two years after that of **Yuri Gagarin**. However, many Americans dismissed Tereshkova's flight as a propaganda stunt and it was not until 1982 that another Soviet woman flew in space.

Explorers in Their Social Context

The presentation of this book, a series of biographies of individual explorers, reinforces a popularly-held view of exploration—that as a group explorers were "loners" who went out on their own against all odds. This is not entirely true. Obviously, the fact that they succeeded implied that they had the ability to be cut off from familiar surroundings, adapt themselves to entirely new circumstances, and still survive. (Interestingly, one of the most common survival mechanisms was to vilify the new human cultures they came into contact with.)

But explorers were almost never "alone." By the nature of things they were generally surrounded by other people. In some cases, such as **Charles Montagu Doughty** and **Heinrich Barth**, they might be the only Western members of an African or Arab caravan, but they were part of a group with a planned destination.

More commonly, the explorers profiled here themselves led large expeditions. Often the use of the explorer's name is merely shorthand for the achievements of the expedition as a whole. When writing this volume, it was sometimes difficult to know when to write "they" and when to write "he." Columbus "discovered" America along with 90 other European men. **Robert Edward Peary** was the first man to reach the North Pole—along with **Matthew A. Henson**, Egingwah, Seeglo, Ootah, and Ooqueah. It has been suggested more than once that Peary purposely chose an African-American and four Inuit rather than well-known ship captain **Bob Bartlett** because, given the social attitudes of the time, this would assure that Peary would receive sole credit for reaching the North Pole.

Probably the only truly one-man show to reach an historically significant place with no financial or other support from anyone else was the explorer **René Caillié**, who was the first Westerner to travel to the fabled city of Timbuktu and return alive. Otherwise, most of the significant explorations were systematic, generally quite organized, and reflected the outward-looking tendencies of their home societies.

The Spanish and Portuguese states organized and supported the voyages of Columbus, **Vasco da Gama,** and the conquistadores of the 16th century. **Prince Henry the Navigator** sponsored the series of expeditions down the coast of West Africa. The popes of Rome sent out envoys to negotiate with the Mongol khans. The Hudson's Bay Company, in its search for fur, was largely responsible for the exploration of Canada. **Sir Joseph Banks** and the Royal Geographical Society were the great sponsors of African exploration in the 19th century. In our own age, two super-powers—the United States and the former Soviet Union—carried out the systematic exploration of space. The list is long and indicative of the fact that exploration has been less a matter of individual enterprise and more an organized social effort. In fact, many of the explorers in this book were military officers (both army and navy) who were acting on official orders, or they were government officials (da Gama and **Peter Warburton**, to take two very different examples).

Therefore, exploration was not a haphazard enterprise but an organized effort by a society. Commenting that the British were pre-eminent in 19th-century exploration does not presuppose that British men were somehow more suited to exploration; Great Britain was simply the strongest country in the world at the time and had the technological, financial, and organizational skills to carry out the systematic investigation of the whole world. Even the Indian Pundits, such as **Nain Singh**, were employees of the British government, and their reports were first published by the Royal Geographical Society. Britain's main 19th-century competitors in exploration were other similarly organized states—France and Russia—and later the United States and Germany.

Ongoing Reassessment

Our own social climate affects our understanding and appreciation of exploration and discovery. The present viewpoint tends to stress the negative impact that European societies had on the existing societies they found in other parts of the world. The explorer, as the forerunner of Western expansionism and influence, is therefore often viewed in a negative light. This contrasts greatly with the 19th-century view that the explorers were exemplary men who brought a higher civilization to lesser peoples elsewhere. In our own day, Columbus has been transformed almost overnight from being a great hero to being a villain.

In fact, many writers confuse the consequences of the explorers' actions with the explorers themselves. In the case of Columbus, his voyages had gigantic consequences; therefore, if we believe a biographer like Samuel Eliot Morison, Columbus necessarily becomes a gigantic man himself. (This does not appear to be true. Columbus did, after all, return from his third voyage in chains because his contemporaries found him difficult and capricious.) On the other hand, the more recent study by Kirkpatrick Sale takes the opposite tack: the consequences of the Columbian voyages were bad therefore he himself must have been a rascal.

This book attempts to present "objectively" what the explorers did, with a minimum of judgment on the consequences of their actions.

Chronology of Exploration

As an aid to the reader who wishes to trace the history of exploration or the explorers active in a particular location, the major expeditions within a geographical area are listed below in chronological order.

Africa; across the continent

1802-1814	Pedro João Baptista & Amaro José
1854-1856	David Livingstone
1858-1864	David Livingstone
1871-1875	Verney Lovett Cameron
1872-1873	David Livingstone
1873-1877	Henry Morton Stanley
1877-1880	Hermenegildo de Brito Capelo & Roberto Ivens
1884-1885	Hermenegildo de Brito Capelo & Roberto Ivens
1888-1890	Henry Morton Stanley
1890-1892	Emin Pasha
1896-1898	Jean-Baptiste Marchand
1924-1925	Delia Akeley

Africa; coast

500 B.C.	Hanno
1416-1460	Prince Henry the Navigator
1434-1436	Gil Eannes
1455-1456	Alvise da Cadamosto
1485	Diogo Cão
1486	Diogo Cão
1487-1488	Bartolomeu Dias

Africa; east (See also Nile River)

1848	Johannes Rebmann
1848-1849	Ludwig Krapf
1848-1849	Johannes Rebmann
1849	Johannes Rebmann
1851	Ludwig Krapf
1857-1859	Sir Richard Burton & John Hanning Speke
1860-1863	John Hanning Speke & James Augustus Grant
1880	Gaetano Casati
1883-1884	Joseph Thomson
1891	May French Sheldon
1905-1906	Delia Akeley
1909-1910	Theodore Roosevelt
1909-1911	Delia Akeley

Africa; south

1825	Robert Moffat
1849	David Livingstone
1850	David Livingstone
1850	Carl Johan Andersson
1851-1852	David Livingstone
1853-1854	Carl Johan Andersson
1857-1858	Robert Moffat
1858	Carl Johan Andersson

Africa; west (See also Niger River)

1856-1860	Paul Du Chaillu
1863	Paul Du Chaillu
1867	Paul Du Chaillu
1875-1878	Pierre Savorgnan de Brazza
1879	Henry Morton Stanley
1879-1881	Pierre Savorgnan de Brazza
1883-1885	Pierre Savorgnan de Brazza
1888-1889	Louis-Gustave Binger
1891-1892	Pierre Savorgnan de Brazza
1893	Mary Kingsley
1894	Mary Kingsley

Amazon Basin see South America; interior

Antarctica

1819-1821	Fabian Gottlieb von Bellingshausen
1831-1832	John Biscoe
1837-1840	Jules-Sébastien-César Dumont d'Urville
1839-1840	Charles Wilkes
1839-1841	James Clark Ross
1841-1842	James Clark Ross
1842-1843	James Clark Ross
1897-1899	Frederick Albert Cook
1901-1904	Robert Falcon Scott
1903-1904	Jean-Baptiste Charcot
1907-1909	Ernest Shackleton
1908-1910	Jean-Baptiste Charcot
1910-1912	Roald Amundsen
1910-1912	Robert Falcon Scott
1911-1914	Douglas Mawson
1914-1916	Ernest Shackleton
1921-1922	Ernest Shackleton
1928	Sir (George) Hubert Wilkins
1928-1929	Richard Evelyn Byrd
1929	Sir (George) Hubert Wilkins
1929-1931	Douglas Mawson
1933-1934	Lincoln Ellsworth
1933-1935	Richard Evelyn Byrd
1935-1936	Lincoln Ellsworth

1937	Lincoln Ellsworth
1939-1940	Richard Evelyn Byrd
1946-1947	Richard Evelyn Byrd
1956	Richard Evelyn Byrd
1956-1958	Sir Vivian Fuchs
1960-1962	Wally Herbert
1989-1990	Will Steger

Arabia

25 B.C.	Aelius Gallus
1502-1508	Ludovico di Varthema
1587-1595	Pedro Paez
1761-1764	Carsten Niebuhr
1812-1813	Lady Hester Stanhope
1812-1815	Jean Louis Burckhardt
1834-1835	James Wellsted
1854-1855	Sir Richard Burton
1876-1878	Charles Montagu Doughty
1877-1878	Lady Anne Blunt & Sir Wilfrid Scawen Blunt
1879-1880	Lady Anne Blunt & Sir Wilfrid Scawen Blunt
1913	Gertrude Bell
1917	Harry St. John Philby
1932	Harry St. John Philby
1945-1946	Wilfred Thesiger
1946-1947	Wilfred Thesiger
1948-1950	Wilfred Thesiger

Arctic (*See also* North America; Northwest Passage)

1827	Sir (William) Edward Parry
1871	Charles Francis Hall
1872-1873	(Nils) Adolf Erik Nordenskjöld
1879-1881	George Washington De Long
1893-1896	Fridtjof Nansen
1902	Robert Edward Peary
1905-1906	Robert Edward Peary
1907-1909	Frederick Albert Cook
1908-1909	Robert Edward Peary
1925	Roald Amundsen
1925	Richard Evelyn Byrd
1926	Roald Amundsen & Umberto Nobile
1926	Louise Arner Boyd
1926	Richard Evelyn Byrd
1926-1927	Sir (George) Hubert Wilkins
1928	Louise Arner Boyd
1928	Umberto Nobile
1928	Sir Hubert Wilkins
1931	Sir Hubert Wilkins
1940	Louise Arner Boyd
1955	Louise Arner Boyd
1958	U.S.S. Nautilus
1968-1969	Wally Herbert
1986	Will Steger

Asia; interior

1847-1848	Ida Pfeiffer
1866-1868	Francis Garnier
1870-1872	Nikolai Przhevalsky
1876	Nikolai Przhevalsky
1883-1885	Nikolai Przhevalsky
1887	Sir Francis Younghusband
1889	Sir Francis Younghusband
1890-1891	Sir Francis Younghusband
1893	Sir Percy Sykes
1893-1895	Sven Hedin
1894-1897	Sir Percy Sykes
1895-1897	Isabella Bird
1897-1901	Sir Percy Sykes
1899	Fanny Bullock Workman
1899-1901	Sven Hedin
1900	Sir Aurel Stein
1902-1906	Sir Percy Sykes
1903-1905	Sven Hedin
1906	Fanny Bullock Workman
1906-1908	Sir Aurel Stein
1913-1915	Sir Aurel Stein
1927-1933	Sven Hedin
1934-1936	Sven Hedin
1935-1936	Ella Maillart
1953	Sir Edmund Hillary
1977	Sir Edmund Hillary

Asia/Europe; link *see* Europe/Asia; link

Asia, south/China; link

645-689 B.C.	I-Ching
629-645 B.C.	Hsüan-Chuang
399-414 B.C.	Fa-Hsien
138-126 B.C.	Chang Ch'ien
1405-1407	Cheng Ho
1407-1409	Cheng Ho
1409-1411	Cheng Ho
1413-1415	Cheng Ho
1417-1419	Cheng Ho
1421-1422	Cheng Ho
1433-1435	Cheng Ho

Australia

1605-1606	Willem Janszoon
1606	Luis Vaez de Torres
1642	Abel Janszoon Tasman
1644	Abel Janszoon Tasman
1688	William Dampier
1699-1701	William Dampier
1770	James Cook
1798-1799	Matthew Flinders
1801-1802	Matthew Flinders
1802-1803	Matthew Flinders

1813	Gregory Blaxland
1817	John Oxley
1818	John Oxley
1823	Allan Cunningham
1824-1825	(Alexander) Hamilton Hume
1827	Allan Cunningham
1828-1829	Charles Sturt
1829-1830	Charles Sturt
1831	Thomas Livingstone Mitchell
1835	Thomas Livingstone Mitchell
1836	Thomas Livingstone Mitchell
1839	Edward John Eyre
1840-1841	Edward John Eyre
1844-1846	Ludwig Leichhardt
1844-1846	Charles Sturt
1845-1846	Thomas Livingstone Mitchell
1847-1848	Edmund Kennedy
1848	Edmund Kennedy
1848	Ludwig Leichhardt
1855	Sir Augustus Gregory
1857-1858	Sir Augustus Gregory
1858	John McDouall Stuart
1858	Peter Warburton
1860	John McDouall Stuart
1860-1861	Robert O'Hara Burke & William John Wills
1860-1861	John McDouall Stuart
1861-1862	John McDouall Stuart
1869	John Forrest
1870	John Forrest
1872	Ernest Giles
1873	Ernest Giles
1873-1874	Peter Warburton
1874	John Forrest
1875-1876	Ernest Giles

Aviation

1927	Charles A. Lindbergh
1928	Amelia Earhart
1930	Beryl Markham
1930	Amy Johnson
1931	Amy Johnson
1931	Wiley Post
1932	Amelia Earhart
1932	Amy Johnson
1933	Wiley Post
1935	Amelia Earhart
1936	Amelia Earhart
1936	Beryl Markham
1947	Charles E. Yeager
1986	Dick Rutan & Jeana Yeager

China/south Asia; link *see* Asia, south/China; link

Conquistadores

1513-1514	Vasco Nuñez de Balboa

1518-1522	Hernán Cortés
1523-1526	Pedro de Alvarado
1524-1525	Francisco Pizarro
1526-1527	Francisco Pizarro
1530-1531	Diego de Ordaz
1531-1541	Francisco Pizarro
1533-1534	Pedro de Alvarado
1535-1538	Diego de Almagro
1536-1538	Gonzalo Jiménez de Quesada

Ethiopia

1490-1526	Pero da Covilhão
1603-1622	Pedro Paez
1768-1773	James Bruce
1857	Sir Richard Burton
1930	Wilfred Thesiger

Europe/Asia; link

520 B.C	Scylax of Caryanda
454-443 B.C.	Herodotus
401-399 B.C.	Xenophon
334-323 B.C.	Alexander the Great
325-324 B.C.	Nearchus
310-306 B.C.	Pytheas
1159-1173	Benjamin of Tudela
1180-1186	Pethahiah of Regensburg
1245-1247	Giovanni di Piano Carpini
1252-1255	William of Rubruck
1253-1269	Nicolò & Maffeo Polo
1271-1295	Marco Polo
1280-1290	Rabban Bar-Sauma
1291-1328	John of Monte Corvino
1317-1327	Odoric of Pordenone
1321-1340	Jordanus of Séverac
1338-1353	John of Marignolli
1487-1490	Pero da Covilhão
1492-1493	Christopher Columbus
1497-1499	Vasco da Gama
1500-1501	Pedro Alvares Cabral
1502-1503	Vasco da Gama
1506-1515	Afonso de Albuquerque
1537-1558	Fernão Mendes Pinto
1549-1551	St. Francis Xavier
1558-1559	Anthony Jenkinson
1561-1564	Anthony Jenkinson
1583-1592	Jan Huygen van Linschoten
1595-1597	Cornelius Houtman
1598-1599	Cornelius Houtman

Greenland

982	Erik (the Red)
1612	William Baffin
1870	(Nils) Adolf Erik Nordenskjöld
1886	Robert Edward Peary

1888	Fridtjof Nansen
1891-1892	Robert Edward Peary
1893-1895	Robert Edward Peary
1931	Louise Arner Boyd
1931-1934	Jean-Baptiste Charcot
1933	Louise Arner Boyd
1936	Jean-Baptiste Charcot
1937	Louise Arner Boyd
1938	Louise Arner Boyd

Muslim world

915-917	al Mas'udi
918-928	al Mas'udi
921-922	Ibn Fadlan
943-973	Abu al-Kasim Ibn Ali al Nasibi ibn Hawkal
966-987	Muhammed ibn-Ahmad al-Muqaddasi
1120-1150	Abu Abd-Allah Muhammed al-Sarif al-Idrisi
1182-1185	Abu al-Hasan Muhammed Ibn Jubayr
1189-1191	Abu al-Hasan Muhammed Ibn Jubayr
1217	Abu al-Hasan Muhammed Ibn Jubayr
1325-1349	Abu Abdallah Ibn Battuta

New Guinea

1606	Luis Vaez de Torres
1876	Luigi Maria D'Albertis
1877	Luigi Maria D'Albertis
1930	Michael J. Leahy
1931	Michael J. Leahy
1932-1933	Michael J. Leahy
1933-1939	Evelyn Cheesman

Niger River

1789-1791	Daniel Houghton
1795-1799	Mungo Park
1805	Mungo Park
1822-1824	Hugh Clapperton
1825-1826	Alexander Gordon Laing
1825-1828	Hugh Clapperton
1827-1828	René Caillié
1830-1832	Richard Lander
1841-1842	Samuel Adjai Crowther
1854	William Balfour Baikie
1857-1864	William Balfour Baikie

Nile River; source

1768-1773	James Bruce
1857-1859	Sir Richard Burton & John Hanning Speke
1860-1863	John Hanning Speke & James Augustus Grant
1862-1863	Alexine Tinné
1862-1864	Samuel White Baker & Florence Baker
1865-1871	David Livingstone
1868-1871	Georg August Schweinfurth
1870-1873	Samuel White Baker & Florence Baker
1871-1873	Henry Morton Stanley

1874-1875	Charles Chaillé-Long
1888-1889	Emin Pasha

North America; coast

1001-1002	Leif Eriksson
1493-1496	Christopher Columbus
1497	John Cabot
1498	John Cabot
1500	Gaspar Corte-Real
1501	Gaspar Corte-Real
1502	Miguel Corte-Real
1502-1504	Christopher Columbus
1508	Sebastian Cabot
1513	Juan Ponce de León
1524	Giovanni da Verrazzano
1534	Jacques Cartier
1535-1536	Jacques Cartier
1541-1542	Jacques Cartier
1542-1543	Juan Rodriguez Cabrillo
1583	Sir Humphrey Gilbert
1584	Sir Walter Raleigh
1585-1586	Sir Walter Raleigh
1587-1589	Sir Walter Raleigh
1603	Samuel de Champlain
1604-1607	Samuel de Champlain
1606-1609	John Smith
1608-1610	Samuel de Champlain
1609	Henry Hudson
1610	Samuel de Champlain
1614	John Smith
1792-1794	George Vancouver

North America; Northwest Passage

1576	Sir Martin Frobisher
1577	Sir Martin Frobisher
1578	Sir Martin Frobisher
1585	John Davis
1586	John Davis
1587	John Davis
1610-1613	Henry Hudson
1615	Robert Bylot
1616	Robert Bylot
1616	William Baffin
1631	Luke Fox
1631-1632	Thomas James
1776-1779	James Cook
1818	Sir John Ross
1819-1820	Sir (William) Edward Parry
1821-1823	Sir (William) Edward Parry
1824-1825	Sir (William) Edward Parry
1829-1833	James Clark Ross
1829-1833	Sir John Ross
1836-1837	Sir George Back
1845-1847	Sir John Franklin
1848-1849	James Clark Ross

1850-1851	Sir Francis Leopold McClintock
1850-1851	Sir John Ross
1850-1854	Sir Robert McClure
1852-1854	Sir Francis Leopold McClintock
1857-1860	Sir Francis Leopold McClintock
1903-1906	Roald Amundsen
1969	S.S. Manhattan

North America; sub-Arctic

1654-1656	Médard Chouart des Groseilliers
1668	Médard Chouart des Groseilliers
1668	Pierre-Esprit Radisson
1670	Pierre-Esprit Radisson
1679	Louis Jolliet
1682-1683	Médard Chouart des Groseilliers
1684	Pierre-Esprit Radisson
1685-1687	Pierre-Esprit Radisson
1689	Louis Jolliet
1694	Louis Jolliet
1770-1772	Samuel Hearne
1789	Sir Alexander Mackenzie
1795	Alexander Andreyevich Baranov
1799	Alexander Andreyevich Baranov
1819-1822	Sir John Franklin
1819-1822	Sir George Back
1822-1827	Sir George Back
1825-1827	Sir John Franklin
1833-1835	Sir George Back
1860-1862	Charles Francis Hall
1864-1869	Charles Francis Hall
1906-1907	Vilhjalmur Stefansson
1908-1909	Vilhjalmur Stefansson
1910-1912	Vilhjalmur Stefansson
1913-1918	Vilhjalmur Stefansson

North America; west

1527-1536	Alvar Núñez Cabeza de Vaca
1538-1543	Hernando de Soto
1540-1542	Francisco Vázquez de Coronado
1611-1612	Samuel de Champlain
1613-1615	Samuel de Champlain
1615-1616	Samuel de Champlain
1615-1616	Etienne Brûlé
1621-1623	Etienne Brûlé
1634-1635	Jean Nicollet
1657	Pierre-Esprit Radisson
1659-1660	Médard Chouart des Groseilliers
1659-1660	Pierre-Esprit Radisson
1669-1670	René-Robert Cavelier de La Salle
1672-1674	Louis Jolliet
1678-1683	René-Robert Cavelier de La Salle
1684-1687	René-Robert Cavelier de La Salle
1685-1686	Henri de Tonty
1689-1690	Henri de Tonty

1695-1696	Henri de Tonty
1698-1703	Henri de Tonty
1731-1734	Pierre de la Vérendrye
1736-1737	Pierre de la Vérendrye
1738-1739	Pierre de la Vérendrye
1769-1771	Daniel Boone
1775	Daniel Boone
1792-1794	Sir Alexander Mackenzie
1792-1797	David Thompson
1797-1799	David Thompson
1800-1802	David Thompson
1804-1806	Meriwether Lewis & William Clark
1805-1806	Zebulon Pike
1805-1808	Simon Fraser
1806-1807	Zebulon Pike
1807-1808	John Colter
1807-1811	David Thompson
1809-1810	John Colter
1811-1813	Wilson Price Hunt & Robert Stuart
1817	Stephen Long
1819	Stephen Long
1820	Stephen Long
1823	Stephen Long
1823-1825	Jedediah Smith
1824-1825	William Henry Ashley
1824-1825	Peter Skene Ogden
1825-1826	Peter Skene Ogden
1826-1827	Peter Skene Ogden
1826-1828	Jedediah Smith
1828-1829	Peter Skene Ogden
1829-1830	Peter Skene Ogden
1832-1834	Joseph Reddeford Walker
1832-1835	Benjamin Louis Eulalie de Bonneville
1842	John Charles Frémont
1843-1844	John Charles Frémont
1845-1848	John Charles Frémont
1848-1849	John Charles Frémont
1850-1851	Jim Beckwourth
1853-1855	John Charles Frémont
1857-1860	John Palliser

North Pole *see* Arctic

Northeast Passage

1553-1554	Richard Chancellor
1555-1556	Richard Chancellor
1594-1595	Jan Huygen van Linschoten
1594-1596	Willem Barents
1607	Henry Hudson
1613-1614	William Baffin
1725-1729	Vitus Bering
1740-1741	Vitus Bering
1878-1879	(Nils) Adolf Erik Nordenskjöld
1918-1920	Roald Amundsen
1931	Lincoln Ellsworth

Northwest Passage *see* **North America; Northwest Passage**

Oceans

1872-1876	Challenger
1925-1927	S.S. Meteor
1942-1943	Jacques(-Yves) Cousteau
1948	Auguste Piccard
1954	Auguste Piccard
1960	Jacques Piccard
1968-1980	Glomar Challenger
1969	Jacques Piccard

Pacific; south

1519-1522	Ferdinand Magellan
1525-1536	Andrés de Urdaneta
1527-1529	Alvaro de Saavedra y Cerón
1564-1565	Andrés de Urdaneta
1567-1569	Alvaro de Mendaña
1577-1580	Sir Francis Drake
1595-1597	Alvaro de Mendaña
1605-1606	Pedro Fernandez de Quiros
1606-1607	Luis Vaez de Torres
1615-1617	Willem Schouten & Jacob le Maire
1642-1643	Abel Janszoon Tasman
1721-1722	Jacob Roggeveen
1764-1766	John Byron
1766-1768	Samuel Wallis
1766-1769	Philip Carteret
1767-1769	Louis Antoine de Bougainville
1768-1771	James Cook
1772-1775	James Cook
1776-1779	James Cook
1785-1788	Jean François de Galaup, Comte de la Pérouse
1791	George Vancouver
1791-1793	Joseph-Antoine Raymond Bruni d'Entrecasteaux
1826-1829	Jules-Sébastien-César Dumont d'Urville
1834-1836	Charles Darwin
1838-1839	Jules-Sébastien-César Dumont d'Urville
1838-1842	Charles Wilkes
1852	Ida Pfeiffer
1854-1862	Alfred Russell Wallace

Patagonia

1831-1834	Charles Darwin
1869-1870	George Chaworth Musters

Sahara Desert; crossing

1352-1353	Abu Abdallah Ibn Battuta
1797-1800	Friedrich Hornemann
1850-1855	Heinrich Barth
1858-1861	Henri Duveyrier
1865-1867	Gerhard Rohlfs

1869	Alexine Tinné
1869-1871	Gustav Nachtigal
1880	Paul-Xavier Flatters
1880-1881	Paul-Xavier Flatters
1898-1900	Fernand Foureau

Siberia

1581-1585	Yermak Timofeyev
1643-1646	Vasily Danilovich Poyarkov
1648-1650	Semyon Ivanovich Dezhnev
1649-1650	Yerofey Pavlovich Khabarov
1650-1653	Yerofey Pavlovich Khabarov
1697-1699	Vladimir Vasilyevich Atlasov
1719-1727	Daniel Gottlieb Messerschmidt
1787	Jean François de Galaup, Comte de la Pérouse
1848-1849	Gennady Ivanovich Nevelskoy
1849-1850	Gennady Ivanovich Nevelskoy
1851-1855	Gennady Ivanovich Nevelskoy

South America; coast

1498-1500	Christopher Columbus
1499-1500	Alonso de Ojeda
1499-1500	Amerigo Vespucci
1500	Vicente Yáñez Pinzón
1501-1502	Amerigo Vespucci
1502	Alonso de Ojeda
1502-1504	Vicente Yáñez Pinzón
1505	Alonso de Ojeda
1508-1509	Vicente Yáñez Pinzón
1509-1510	Alonso de Ojeda
1515-1516	Juan Díaz de Solís
1519-1520	Ferdinand Magellan
1526-1530	Sebastian Cabot
1527	Giovanni da Verrazzano
1528	Giovanni da Verrazzano
1591	John Davis
1594	Sir Walter Raleigh
1595	Sir Walter Raleigh
1617-1618	Sir Walter Raleigh

South America; interior

1500	Vicente Yáñez Pinzón
1540-1544	Alvar Núñez Cabeza de Vaca
1541-1542	Francisco de Orellana
1569-1571	Gonzalo Jiménez de Quesada
1637-1639	Pedro de Teixeira
1648-1652	Antônio Raposo Tavares
1735-1745	Charles-Marie de la Condamine
1760-1762	José Celestino Mutis
1769-1770	Isabel Godin des Odonais
1777-1778	José Celestino Mutis
1777-1778	Hipólito Ruiz
1782-1792	José Celestino Mutis
1799-1803	Alexander von Humboldt

1835-1836	Sir Robert Hermann Schomburgk
1836-1839	Sir Robert Hermann Schomburgk
1841-1843	Sir Robert Hermann Schomburgk
1844-1847	Francis de la Porte, Comte de Castelnau
1848-1852	Alfred Russell Wallace
1848-1859	Henry Walter Bates
1849-1864	Richard Spruce
1877-1882	Jules Crevaux
1884	Karl von den Steinen
1887	Karl von den Steinen
1900-1906	Cândido Rondon
1903	Annie Smith Peck
1904	Annie Smith Peck
1906-1907	Cândido Rondon
1908	Annie Smith Peck
1909-1910	Cândido Rondon
1911	Hiram Bingham
1912	Hiram Bingham
1913-1914	Theodore Roosevelt
1915	Hiram Bingham
1925	Percy Fawcett

Space

1957	Sputnik
1958-1970	Explorer
1959-1972	Luna
1961	Yuri Gagarin
1962	John Glenn
1962-1975	Mariner
1963	Valentina Vladimirovna Tereshkova
1967-1972	Apollo
1969	Neil Armstrong
1975-1983	Viking
1977-1990	Voyager 1 & 2
1983	Sally Ride

Tibet

1624-1630	Antonio de Andrade
1626-1628	João Cabral
1631-1632	João Cabral
1631-1632	Francisco de Azevado
1661-1664	Johann Grüber
1714-1721	Ippolito Desideri
1811-1812	Thomas Manning
1844-1846	Evariste Régis Huc
1865-1866	Nain Singh
1867-1868	Nain Singh
1871-1872	Hari Ram
1872-1873	Kishen Singh
1873-1874	Hari Ram
1878-1882	Kishen Singh
1879-1880	Nikolai Przhevalsky
1880-1884	Kintup
1885-1886	Hari Ram
1892-1893	Annie Royle Taylor
1898	Susie Carson Rijnhart
1901	Sven Hedin
1903-1905	Sir Francis Younghusband
1915-1916	Alexandra David-Neel
1923-1924	Alexandra David-Neel

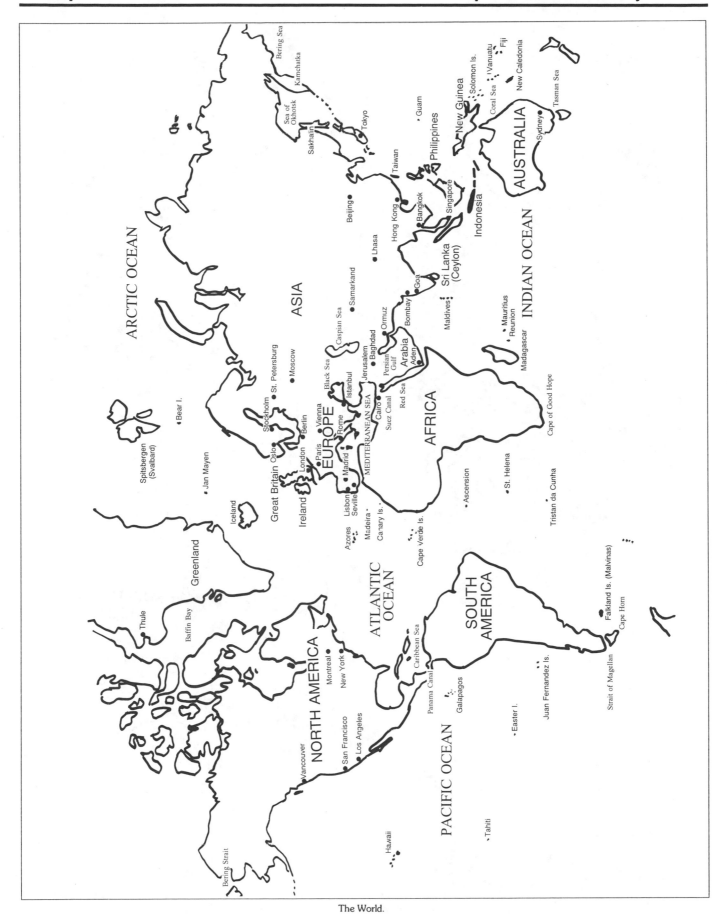

The World.

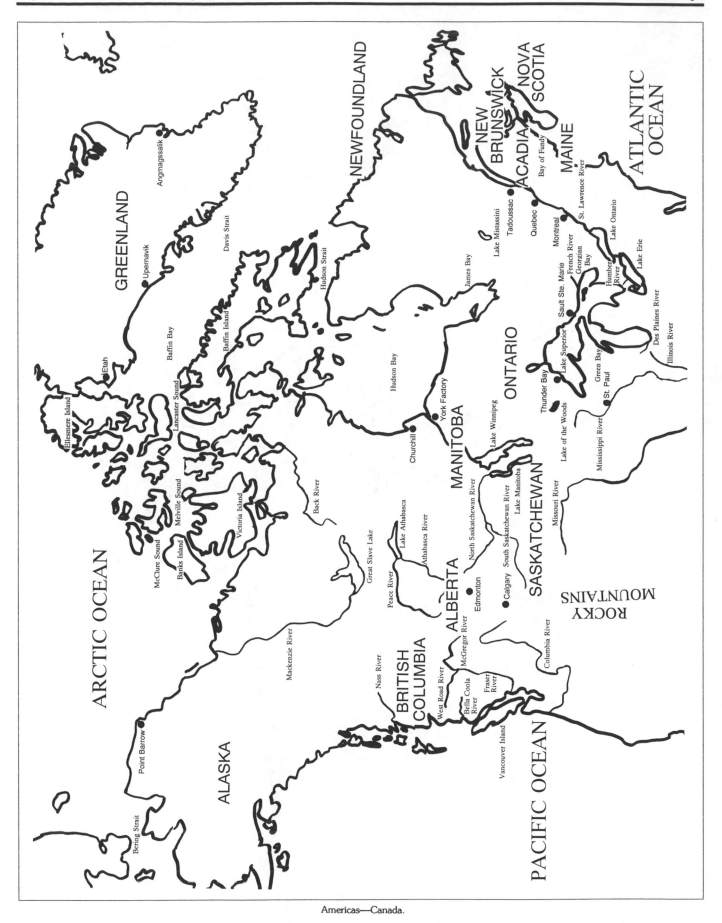

Americas—Canada.

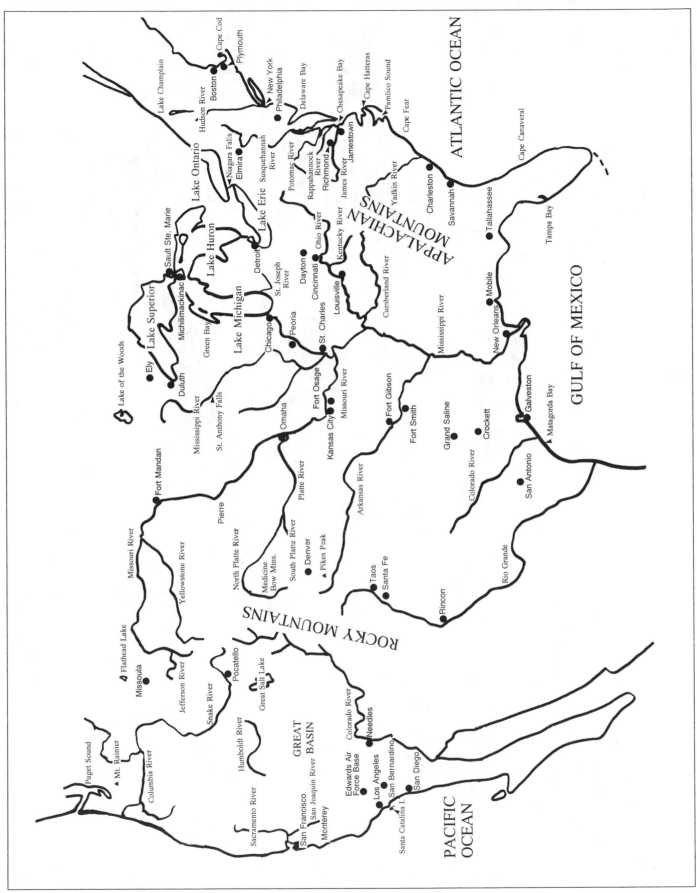

Americas—United States of America.

Americas—Mexico and Central America.

Margarita Island Gulf of Paria

Cartagena Lake Maracaibo Caracas

Magdalena River **Venezuela**

CUNDINAMARCA **Guyana** Berbice River

Colombia Orinoco River Demerara River Devil's Island

Meta River Mount Roraima ▲ Cayenne

Buenaventura Uraricoera River Paramaribo **French Guiana**

Bogota Maroni River

Guavaiare River **RORAIMA** Courantyne River Itany River

ESMERALDAS Casiquiare Canal Rio Branco Jari River

Aguarico River Rio Negro Amazon River

Quito Andoas Manaus Belem

Ecuador Napo River Amazon River Parintins

Guayaquil Iquitos Tefe (Ega) Sao Luis

Maranon River Leticia Madeira River Tapajos River **MARANHAO**

Huallaga River Acre River Juruena River Xingu River Cabo Sao Roque

Mt. Husacaran ▲ Abuna River Roosevelt River Paranatinga Recife

Callao Urubamba River **RONDONIA** Araguaia River **Brazil**

Lima Guapore River Tocantins River Bahia

Machu Picchu Cuzco Cuiaba

Arequipa La Paz **Bolivia** Goias Brasilia

Mt. Illampu **MATO GROSSO**

Sucre **MINAS GERAIS**

Tarma Potosi Paraguay River

Andes Mountains **GRAN CHACO** Ouro Preto

Pilcomayo River Sao Paulo Rio de Janeiro

Atacama Desert Asuncion

Copiapo **Paraguay** Encarnacion

Pacific Ocean **RIO GRANDE DO SUL**

Coquimbo Parana River

Argentina **Uruguay**

Valparaiso ▲ Mt. Aconcagua

Santiago Buenos Aires **Atlantic Ocean**

Chile Rio de la Plata

Concepcion Rio Colorado

Arauco Rio Negro

Lake Musters

Lake Colhue Huapi

PATAGONIA

Punta Arenas Falkland Islands (Malvinas)

Americas—South America.

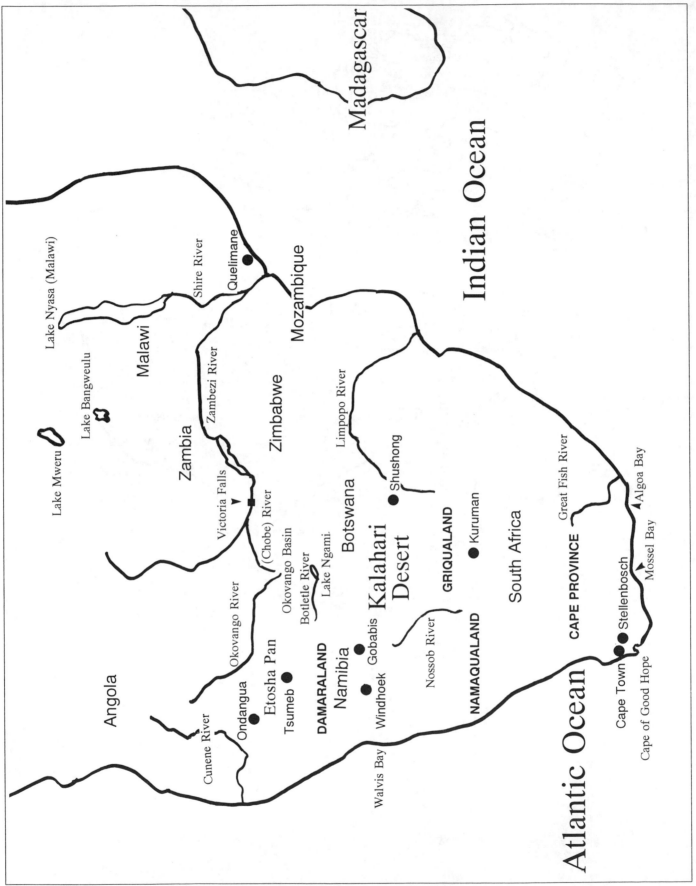

Africa and the Middle East—Southern Africa.

Africa and the Middle East—Eastern Africa.

Africa and the Middle East—Northwest Africa.

Africa and the Middle East—The Middle East and Arabia.

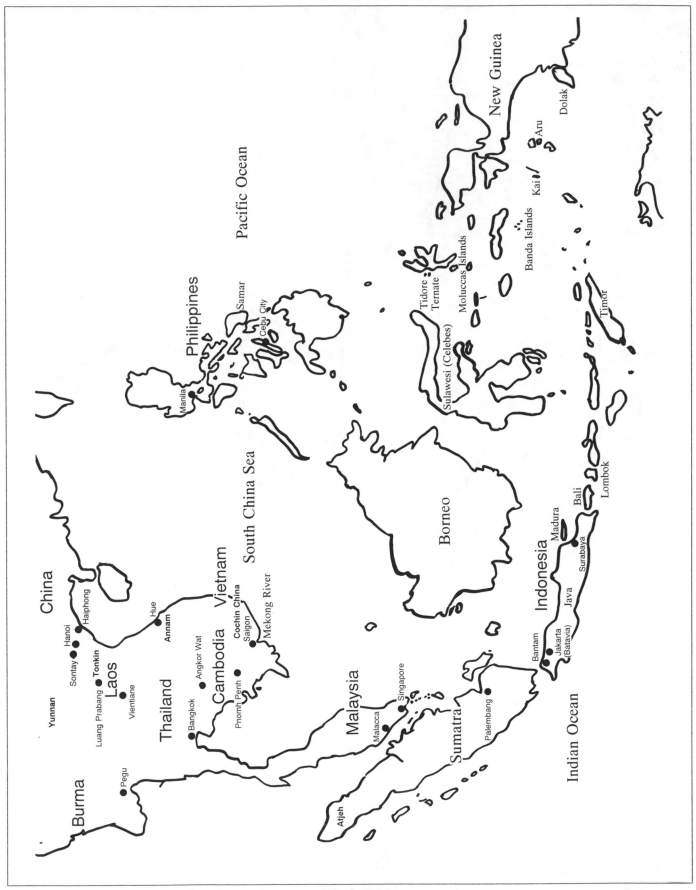

Asia—Southeast Asia.

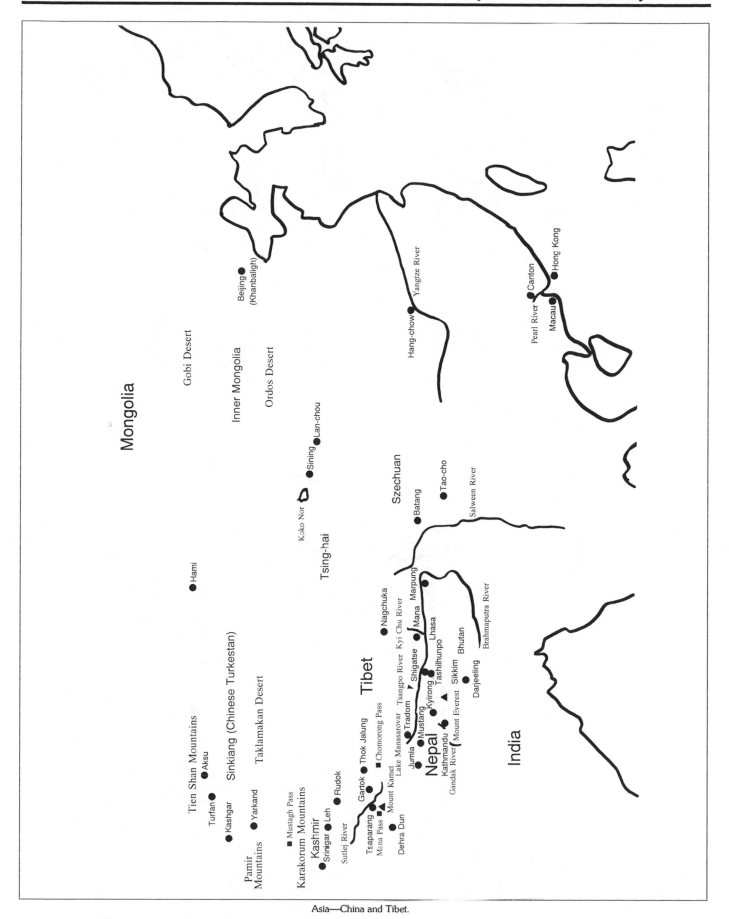

Asia—China and Tibet.

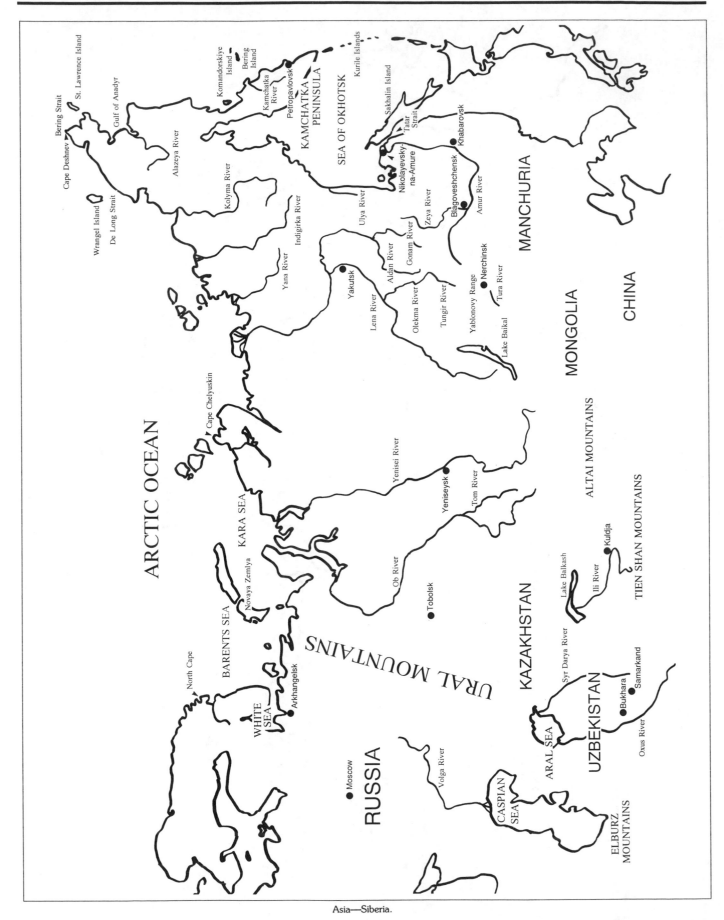

Asia—Siberia.

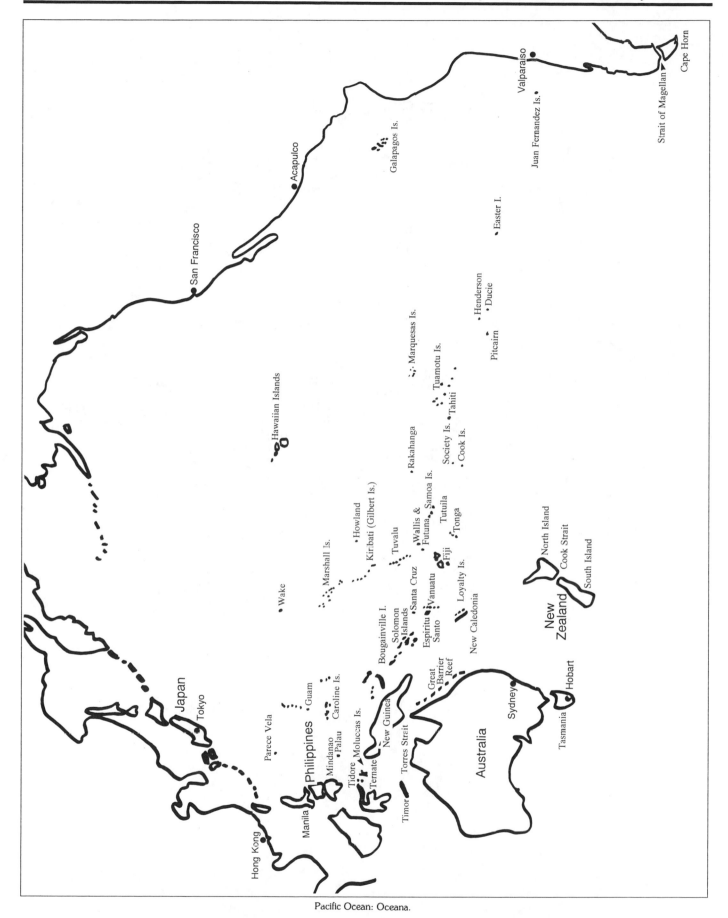

Pacific Ocean: Oceana.

Pacific Ocean: Australia.

Pacific Ocean: New Guinea.

Arctic Region.

Antarctic Region.

EXPLORERS

and

DISCOVERERS

of the

WORLD

Delia Akeley

(1875 - 1970)

Delia Akeley was an American who made several trips to Africa, where she was one of the first Westerners to study the Pygmy tribes of Zaire. She was the first woman to cross Africa.

Delia Akeley was born on a farm in Beaver Dam, Wisconsin on December 5, 1875, the daughter of Irish immigrants. She ran away from home at the age of thirteen and went to Milwaukee. There she was taken in by a barber, who married her the following year when she was only fourteen. They were divorced some time later and on December 23, 1902, when she was 27, she married Carl Akeley. He was a taxidermist who had helped the Milwaukee Public Museum mount exhibitions of wild life.

Carl Akeley had experimented with various techniques to make animal displays more realistic, and he changed the science of taxidermy completely. As a result, he was appointed to the prestigious Field Museum of Natural History in Chicago. He had gone on an expedition to Africa in 1896 to find specimens for the museum. After their marriage he took Delia Akeley with him on his next trip in 1905.

The Akeleys went to the Athi plains in Kenya not far from the capital at Nairobi. They stayed in Kenya for a year and a half collecting specimens. Delia was as good a shot as her husband and killed a bull elephant on August 31, 1906 that is still on display in the Field Museum. As a result of their successes they were invited by the American Museum of Natural History in New York to undertake another expedition in 1909. Along the way they met up with former president **Theodore Roosevelt** and his son Kermit.

During this second expedition Carl became ill, and they had great difficulty in finding a bull elephant to take back to New York. By this time, the elephant population of Kenya was already being wiped out by hunters. One of the Akeley's main concerns was to capture animals and preserve them for later study before it was too late. They finally shot a large bull but were almost charged and killed by the wounded animal before a lucky shot from Carl's rifle saved them.

After this incident they moved their camp to higher ground, which was more comfortable for Carl who was still ill. One evening while Delia was in camp two porters arrived to say that Carl had been injured by a charging elephant and was helpless some miles away. Leading a group of unwilling porters she traveled through the night to reach him. When they got near the next morning, the porters could not remember where they had left him. It was only by frantic searching and firing signals with her gun that she was able to find Carl, who was severely injured: he had several head injuries and several ribs had been broken, some of them cutting into his lung. Delia was able to save him.

The Akeleys remained in camp for three months while Carl recovered, and Delia took over the responsibilities of shooting game for food, managing the camp and nursing her husband, who also came down with malaria. During the period of Carl's recuperation Delia adopted a pet monkey that she took back to New York with her and who became the tyrant of their household; the pet threw jealous rages whenever Delia gave any of her attention to anyone else.

The Akeleys returned to New York in 1911, and Carl took over mounting his African exhibitions. The Akeley African Hall still exists at the American Museum of Natural History. Delia went to Europe in July 1918 to work in canteens for American servicemen during World War I. After she returned, the Akeleys divorced on March 22, 1923. Carl remarried and then died on an expedition to Zaire in 1926.

Soon after her divorce Delia Akeley started out on her greatest adventure. She was commissioned by the Brooklyn Museum to travel to Africa to collect specimens. The newspapers headlined "Woman to Forget Marital Woe by Fighting African Jungle Beasts." She left New York on August 23, 1924 and traveled to Mombasa in Kenya. She left Mombasa on October 16 by traveling up the Tana River into the interior. It took ten weeks for her canoes to reach the post of San Kuri at the head of the Tana; from there she started out by camel across the Somali Desert but was forced to turn back by an insurrection of Somali warriors.

Akeley then turned southwest and headed to Meru at the foot of Mt. Kenya and continued by truck to Nairobi where she sent her specimens back to Brooklyn. From Nairobi she took the train to Kisumu on Lake Victoria Nyanza and then a boat to Uganda. She went by truck and bus from Jinja to Lake Albert and then by car to Zaire, then the colony of the Belgian Congo. Her goal was to travel to the remote forests of the Ituri River where she wanted to visit Pygmy tribes. She crossed the Ituri River at the modern town of Nduye and headed for the post of Wamba.

At Wamba Akeley met up with members of a Pygmy village and was taken to their lands in the tropical rain forest. Many of the Pygmy villages had never been visited by Europeans, and it was only 50 years previously that **Georg Schweinfurth** had confirmed their existence, which had been a source of myth for centuries. She stayed in the village for several weeks and then headed north to the Bomokandi River and the town of Bafuka in June 1925 where she spent a month waiting for supplies that she had ordered. At that point her detailed diary stops because she became ill with fever.

After her recovery she traveled by bus to Kisangani and from there by riverboat down the Congo River to Kinshasa. She reached the Atlantic Ocean at Boma on September 3, 1925. She was the first woman known to have crossed Africa.

Akeley went to Africa one more time. She went to Port Sudan on the Red Sea in November 1929 and then to Khartoum where she took a steamer up the Nile River and crossed over into Zaire. She spent five months among the Pygmy tribes. During that time she took over 1500 photos and collected a large number of examples of the material culture of the Pygmies. On her return to the United States, the *New York Times* published a full-page photo spread of her pictures from the Pygmy village.

After that trip Akeley remained in the United States where she wrote and lectured about her experiences in Africa. She remarried at the age of 64 and then retired later to Florida where she died at the age of 95.

Where to learn more

This account is largely based upon *Women of the Four Winds* by Elizabeth Fagg Olds (Boston: Houghton Mifflin, 1985), an excellent book that gives extensive treatment to four woman explorers. It is based on original research and interviews and includes a complete bibliography. There are two other collections of biographies of women explorers that include information about Akeley: Marion Tinling, *Women into the Unknown* (New York: Greenwood Press, 1989) and Mignon Rittenhouse, *Seven Women Explorers* (Philadelphia: J.B. Lippincott Company, 1964).

Akeley herself did not write a great deal. Her only books were *"J.T., Jr.."*: *The Biography of an African Monkey* (New York: Macmillan, 1929) and *Jungle Portraits* (New York: Macmillan, 1939), a collection of photographs. She also wrote a chapter called "My First Elephant" in *All True: The Record of Actual Adventures That Have Happened to Ten Women of Today* (New York: Brewer, Warren & Putnam, 1931).

Afonso de Albuquerque

(1453? - 1515)

Afonso de Albuquerque traveled throughout the Indian Ocean, establishing the basis for Portuguese power in the region. He was the Portuguese equivalent of the Spanish conquistadores of the Americas.

Afonso de Albuquerque was the second son of Gonçalo de Albuquerque, the feudal lord of the Portuguese town of Vila Verde dos Francos. He was related to the Portuguese royal family and grew up in the court of King Afonso V. He fought in the Battle of Arzila in 1471 against the Muslims of Morocco and then served in the garrison that guarded the North African city for the Portuguese for the next ten years. He returned to Portugal and served as an adviser to King João II when he was planning the voyage of **Vasco da Gama** that led the Portuguese to India.

Albuquerque made his first trip to India in 1503 along with his cousin Francisco de Albuquerque in command of a small fleet

Afonso de Albuquerque. The Bettman Archive.

that founded a Portuguese fort at the south Indian trading center of Cochin. He returned to Portugal in 1504 and presented to King Manuel a strategic plan for gaining control of the Indian Ocean by capturing the key points that guarded access to it—Aden, Ormuz, and Malacca—and a trading center in the south of India. King Manuel approved Albuquerque's plan and sent him back to India with secret instructions to take over as Viceroy of India from Francisco de Almeida after an interval of three years.

Albuquerque left Portugal in 1506. He commanded part of a fleet that was under the overall command of Tristan da Cunha. Albuquerque's instructions were to aid da Cunha in the capture of the island of Socotra and then to proceed on his own to capture Ormuz, the main Persian port on the Persian Gulf. In 1507 da Cunha and Albuquerque fulfilled the first part of their instructions by taking the island of Socotra at the mouth of the Gulf of Aden, one of the pressure points that Albuquerque had talked about in his plan.

From Socotra Albuquerque proceeded to the Persian Gulf where he sacked the city of Muscat in Oman. He then blockaded Ormuz, which was ruled by a petty king subject to the Shah of Persia. Albuquerque destroyed the ships that lay in the harbor of Ormuz and got the king to sign a treaty that gave overlordship to the King of Portugal. He had to abandon the building of a Portuguese fort, however, because he ran short of supplies and some of his captains wanted to go immediately to India.

Albuquerque arrived in India, at the fort of Cochin (now known as Kozhikode), in 1508. Initially Almeida refused to turn over command to Albuquerque. However, a fleet from Portugal under Fernando Coutinho, a relative of Albuquerque's, arrived and backed up Albuquerque's claims. Almeida relinquished his office and returned to Portugal but was killed in a skirmish with Africans along the coast of South Africa. In the meantime, Coutinho insisted that Albuquerque help in an attack on the Indian city of Calicut. The attack went badly and Coutinho was killed, but Albuquerque was able to extricate the Portuguese without too many losses.

On his return to Cochin, Albuquerque was approached by a supporter of one of the factions that was trying to win control of the city of Goa, a major port on the south Indian coast that was ruled by Muslims. Albuquerque offered his aid and captured the city in March 1510. The Portuguese were forced out shortly thereafter, but Albuquerque returned in November 1510 and recaptured it definitively. He took his revenge by massacring every Muslim man, woman, and child living in the city. He then began construction of a new Portuguese city, and this became the center for Portuguese rule in Asia for the next 450 years.

Albuquerque then turned his attentions to the east—to the city of Malacca on the Malay Peninsula that guarded the narrow Strait of Malacca between Sumatra and Malaysia. It was and is the main route between the Indian Ocean and the Far East. The Portuguese had set up a small trading post there in 1509 but had later been driven out. Albuquerque arrived there in May 1511 with a force of 1,400 men and 18 ships. With the aid of some troops from the Indonesian island of Java he stormed and captured the city. He built a Portuguese fort there. When the Javanese prince came under suspicion of treachery, Albuquerque took him and all the male members of his family and executed them publicly in the main square of Malacca. From Malacca Albuquerque sent three ships under the command of Antonio de Abreu to the Moluccas. These were the first Europeans to travel directly to the "Spice Islands," the source of the spices that had brought the Portuguese to the East in the first place.

Returning to India, Albuquerque's ship, *Flor de la Mar*, was wrecked on the coast of Sumatra with the loss of much valuable cargo. In order to get back to Goa the remaining ships had to seize local vessels for their water and supplies. On his return to Goa, Albuquerque found the city encircled by an Indian army aided by renegade Portuguese. Albuquerque defeated the army, just before it was about to be reinforced, and then tortured and killed the Portuguese deserters.

In February 1513 Albuquerque headed for the port of Aden on the southwestern coast of Arabia. Aden would be a much better way to control access to the Red Sea than the island of Socotra, if the Portuguese could capture it. Albuquerque's assault on Aden failed because the Portuguese attackers ran out of water. Leaving the city behind, Albuquerque sailed into the Red Sea, the first European to command ships there. On his return to India he stopped at the port of Diu and established a Portuguese trading post there. He then returned to Goa and spent the year 1514 on administrative and diplomatic tasks intended to strengthen the Portuguese position there.

Albuquerque then turned his attention back to Ormuz. The Portuguese fort that he had started had never been completed, and the new ruler of Ormuz was making noise about renouncing his agreement with the Portuguese. Albuquerque sailed for Ormuz on February 21, 1515 with all the resources at his command, captured the city and then executed the new chief minister in front of the new king, who was still a child. He then completed the building of the fortress.

Albuquerque headed back for Goa after completing these tasks, although by this time he was very ill. Before he reached Goa, an Indian ship stopped alongside to give him the news that a new Portuguese convoy had reached Goa, including his replacement as Viceroy. As Albuquerque's ship entered the harbor of Goa on December 16, 1515, he spent his time writing a long letter to King Manuel justifying and explaining his actions and requesting help for his only child, an illegitimate son. He died before the ship docked.

Where to learn more

Three volumes of Afonso d'Albuquerque's own writings, *The Commentaries of the Great Afonso D'Albuquerque, Second Viceroy of India* were published in London by the Hakluyt Society in 1876-1880.

The best recent book for the whole story of Portuguese expansion is C.R. Boxer's *The Portuguese Seaborne Empire, 1415-1825* (London: Hutchinson, 1969). Another is Gerald Rae Crone's *The Discovery of the East* (London: Hamish Hamilton, 1972).

A very important book about the interaction between Europe and Asia, which contains a discussion of Albuquerque, is Donald Lach's *Asia in the Making of Europe*, vol. 1: *The Century of Discovery* (Chicago: The University of Chicago Press, 1965).

Still considered the best introductions to the story of Portuguese power in India are two books that are long out of print but can be found in some libraries: R.S. Whiteway, *The Rise of Portuguese Power in India, 1497-1550* (London: 1899) and F.C. Danvers, *The Portuguese in India: Being a History of the Rise and Decline of Their Empire* (London: W.H. Allen, 1894).

Alexander the Great

356 - 323 B.C.

Alexander the Great was the King of Macedonia who led a great military expedition as far east as the Indus River and expanded the knowledge of Westerners about the civilized world.

Alexander was born in 356 B.C. to the first wife of King Philip II of Macedonia. As a teenager Alexander was educated by the Athenian philosopher Aristotle. By the year 337 B.C. all of the Greek city-states had been conquered or forced into an alliance by King Philip II. He was planning to lead their joint forces in an invasion of the Persian Empire when he was assassinated in 336 B.C. at the wedding of Alexander's sister to the king of one his vassal states. Alexander succeeded to the throne of Macedonia at the age of 19. The unhappy Greeks immediately revolted but were quickly put down by Alexander who quickly showed his genius as a military leader. Having subdued all of Greece, he picked up his father's plan and headed east to fight the Persians.

Alexander's army crossed the Hellespont—now called the Dardanelles—in the spring of 334 B.C. He stopped at the site of the ancient Greek city of Troy, scene of Homer's *Iliad*. He met the Persians in battle for the first time on the Granicus River, which flows into the Sea of Marmara, and smashed the opposing army. Alexander himself narrowly missed being killed during the battle. Following this victory, Alexander pressed on through Asia Minor, being checked briefly by the Persians at the city of Miletos. He was near present-day Iskenderun in southern Turkey when he learned that the newly-crowned King Darius III of Persia and his army were at Issos, to his north.

Alexander encountered Darius at Issos in October 333 B.C. Alexander's army attacked while the Persians were trying to retreat to the sea in order to escape. He cut them off and inflicted a crushing defeat with an enormous number of Persian dead. Darius fled. Alexander then turned south and invaded Syria and Phoenicia, intending to take the Mediterranean ports where the Persian fleet had its bases. It took a siege of eight months to conquer the Phoenician city of Tyre, on an island of the coast of Lebanon. It is said that in the final battle in July 332 B.C. 8,000 of the inhabitants were killed and 30,000 were taken as slaves.

During the siege, Alexander received an offer of peace from Darius. The terms were seemingly so favorable that Alexander's second-in-command, Parmenio, is said to have said that he would accept them if he were Alexander. "That," replied Alexander, "is what I should do were I Parmenio."

Alexander then turned south and took the fortress of Gaza, with a Persian garrison inside, after a siege of two months. He crossed over into Egypt, where he was welcomed as a liberator from the hated Persians. He founded the port city of Alexandria in place of the old Greek trading port of Naukratis. This was the largest of the 70 cities that Alexander founded during the course of his conquests. He visited the ancient oracle of Zeus Ammon. Alexander never revealed what the oracle told him, but his soldiers spread the rumor that he had said that Alexander was destined to rule the world.

Alexander left Egypt with an army of 400,000 foot soldiers and 7,000 cavalry. He crossed the Euphrates and entered Mesopotamia where in 331 B.C. he met the Persian king once more at Gaugamela, east of the Tigris River. In spite of the fact that his army was smaller than that of the Persians, Alexander's superior tactics won the field, and Darius was forced to flee again. By this victory he effectively won the war, although much more fighting was necessary before the Persian Empire finally disappeared. It took three years to subdue all of eastern Iran.

After the Battle of Gaugamela, Alexander entered the ancient city of Babylon as a conqueror. From there he moved on to the great cities of the Persian Empire: Susa, Persepolis, and Pasargadae. In 330 B.C. he defeated an army that was guarding the narrow pass known as the Persian Gates by finding a track that led around it and attacking from the rear. This gave him entrance to the Persian capital of Persepolis, where he and his men went on an orgy of destruction and burned down the palace of Xerxes.

Having penetrated this far into modern-day Iran, Alexander's army was now in country that was unmapped by and virtually unknown to the Greeks. Still pursuing Darius, he turned northwest toward Ecbatana (modern Hamadan) then northeast to Rhagae (near Teheran). Darius had been taken hostage by Bessus, the ruler of the province of Bactria. Alexander caught up with him as he was dying. Alexander had his body taken back to Persepolis to be buried in the royal tombs. At the death of the Persian king, Alexander adopted the title of Lord of Asia—as the ruler of the Persian Empire was called.

When Alexander learned that Bessus had adopted the title of Great King and was leading a revolt in the eastern provinces of the empire, Alexander led his army toward Bactria. The Greek army crossed the Hindu Kush mountains north of Kabul by the Khawak Pass, which lies more than 11,500 feet above sea level. When the army descended into Bactria they learned that Bessus had devastated the countryside and fled north, over the Oxus River (Amu Darya). By the time Alexander's men overtook him,

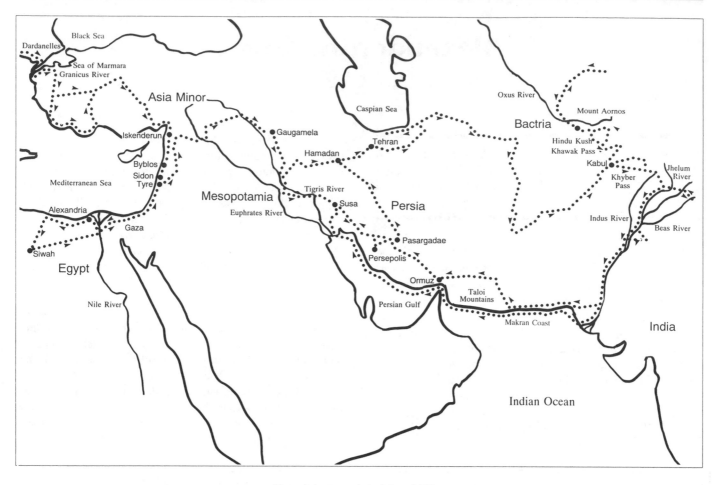

Alexander's conquests in Asia and Africa.

he had already been overthrown. Alexander had him formally tried for the murder of Darius and had his nose and ears cut off and then sent him to Ecbatana where he was publicly put to death by crucifixion.

By this time Alexander was becoming more and more despotic. He killed his own foster brother, Clitus, in a drunken brawl after Clitus had insulted him. He antagonized many of his Greek and Macedonian followers by marrying a Persian princess, Roxane. When a plot was discovered to murder him, he had his old teacher and historian Callisthenes put to death. Alexander spent the year 328 B.C. subjugating Bactria and in early summer 327 B.C. recrossed the Hindu Kush to the south headed for India. Sending half of the army ahead by way of the Khyber Pass with orders to build a boat bridge across the Indus River, Alexander himself fought his way to the river through the hills north of the pass. He spent the winter fighting the local hill tribes.

His greatest accomplishment in this campaign was in scaling and taking Mount Aornos (Pir-Sar), which was supposed to be unconquerable. Following this victory, Alexander led his army to the banks of the Indus where they rested until spring. They then crossed the river and marched three days to the city of Taxila,

where he was greeted by the king with much pomp and ceremony. He then continued on to the Hydaspes (Jhelum) River, where he met and defeated King Porus in what was to be his last great battle. He pushed on to the east, but on the banks of the Hyphasis (Beas) River—his army rebelled. They were tired after the long years of war and were anxious to see their families back in Greece. Alexander could not persuade them otherwise and after sulking in his tent for two days agreed to lead them back home.

Alexander shared the classical belief that the Indus and Nile Rivers were the same. He resolved to test this theory and see whether he could return to the Mediterranean that way. On the Hydaspes River, he constructed a large number of boats in which part of his force sailed downstream. The remainder were divided into three groups and made the journey by land. They departed in November 326 B.C. Going downstream Alexander engaged in constant warfare. The Indians would not supply his troops without a fight. At a city that is thought to be present-day Multan, Alexander climbed a ladder to lead the attack and was badly wounded. For several days it seemed as though he would die, and his men went berserk destroying everything and everyone who got in their way. They reached the mouths of the Indus in the summer of 325 B.C. Alexander explored both arms of the river and proved that it was not connected to the Nile.

Before the expedition had reached the Indian Ocean, Alexander sent Craterus, one of his senior officers, back to Persia with the largest part of the army. He instructed **Nearchus** to wait until the monsoon in October and then to sail along the coast to the Persian Gulf to find a sea route back to the mouth of the Euphrates. Alexander and the remainder of the expedition made their way along the unexplored Makran coast of what is now Pakistan. He intended to follow the coastline and set up supply depots for the ships along the way, but the Taloi Mountains forced him to turn inland. Nearchus and the fleet were left to find their own supplies along a very desolate shore.

Alexander's journey through what he called the Gedrosia Desert in the months of August, September, and October 325 B.C. was among the most difficult he made. The expedition, including many women and children, had to walk over the waterless desert at night to avoid the intense heat by day. They did not have enough food or water, and many of them died before they reached Pura, the capital of the province of Gedrosia. Alexander then went to Kerman where he was met by Craterus and his forces. It was another six months before Alexander and Nearchus met at the Persian port of Ormuz.

Alexander's army reached the Persian city of Susa in the spring of 324 B.C. Alexander adopted more and more of the customs of the Asian despots, taking a second wife and integrating non-Greeks into his army. These measures alarmed his Greek and Macedonian veterans, and they voiced their discontent. Alexander discharged them and many headed back to Europe. During this time, however, Alexander laid the basis for future expeditions. He sent Heraclides to explore the Caspian Sea, to find out whether it was joined to the ocean that was supposed to circle the world. He also planned to send a fleet under Nearchus to sail around Arabia, hoping to discover a route between India and the Red Sea. He seems to have had plans to conquer Arabia as well. All of these projects were abandoned, however, when Alexander became ill at a banquet on June 1, 323 B.C. He died on June 13 at the age of 32, possibly as a result of having been poisoned.

Where to learn more

Writers have been writing about Alexander from the time he started his conquests, and there is an enormous literature on his life. Any library is likely to have several books about him. Some recent works that can be recommended are two by Robin Lane Fox—*Alexander the Great* (New York: Dial Press, 1974) and *The Search for Alexander* (Boston: Little, Brown & Co., 1980)—as well as A.B. Bosworth's *Conquest and Empire: The Reign of Alexander the Great* (New York: Cambridge University Press, 1988). Peter Green's *Alexander the Great* was originally published in 1970 (New York: Praeger Publishers). It has now been revised and is appearing in two volumes. The first came out in 1991: *Alexander of Macedon, 356-323 B.C.* (Berkeley: University of California Press).

A work about Alexander's travels that includes some of the earliest writings about him is by John Watson M'Crindle, *The Invasion of India by Alexander the Great*. It was originally published in 1896 but was reprinted in New York by AMS Press in 1972. A contemporary account by Arrian is available as a Penguin paperback. Another book specifically about his travels is Harold Lamb's *Alexander of Macedon, the Journey to World's End* (Garden City, N.Y.: Doubleday, 1946).

A very good fictionalized account of Alexander's life was written by the pseudonymous British author Mary Renault in three volumes: *Fire from Heaven* (New York: Pantheon Books, 1969), *The Persian Boy* (New York: Pantheon Books, 1972), and *Funeral Games* (New York: Pantheon Books, 1981). In addition to this popular series, Renault wrote a non-fiction book about Alexander called *The Nature of Alexander* (New York: Pantheon Books, 1975).

Diego de Almagro

(1475? - 1538)

Diego de Almagro was a Spanish conquistador *who took part in the conquest of Peru and then led the first Spanish expedition to Chile.*

Diego de Almagro was born in the village of Almagro in the western Spanish province of Extremadura. Like many of the Spanish adventurers who conquered the Americas he came from a very poor family; he, himself, was of illegitimate birth. In 1514 he traveled to Panama with the new governor and got caught up in the schemes of **Francisco Pizarro** to conquer the lands of the Incas in South America. He took part in the two scouting expedition that Pizarro led along the Pacific coast of South America from 1524 to 1528. In 1525 Almagro lost an eye and several fingers in a fight with Native Americans.

Following Pizarro's initial expeditions Almagro became his associate in planning the next major one to Peru. Almagro arrived on the coast of Peru with about 200 men in April 1533. By this time Pizarro had already defeated the Incas and had captured their ruler. Pizarro refused to share any of his spoils with Almagro, who did, however, participate in later campaigns. As a result, he was named Governor of Cuzco in what is now southern Peru in December 1534. Soon afterwards, an order came from the King of Spain instructing Almagro to "discover, conquer, and settle the lands and provinces which are along the coast of the South Sea" to the south of the area controlled by Pizarro. Almagro was to become governor of this new territory, which was to be called Nuevo Toledo. Pizarro and Almagro disagreed over whether Cuzco, the former capital of the Incas, was part of Almagro's new province or not.

Almagro sent out an advance party of 570 Spanish soldiers and several thousand Native Americans to his new territories and then followed himself in mid-July 1535 with about 200 Spaniards and a former Inca prince as hostage. Almagro headed south along the old Inca highway that went through the Andes rather than following the coastal route, which would have been easier. He skirted Lake Titicaca, which is now on the border of Peru and Bolivia, into the *altiplano*, the high Andean plateau. It was winter in the southern hemisphere, and the route was very difficult. It is estimated that 150 Spaniards, 10,000 Native Americans and 30 horses died before they reached the Salta Valley in what is now northern Argentina. They waited there until summer when they crossed through the high San Francisco pass

Diego de Almagro. The Granger Collection, New York.

into Chile. It was so cold traveling through the pass that a further 1,500 Indians, 150 Blacks, and 2 Spaniards died. It is said that six years later another Spanish traveller came across the frozen body of one of Almagro's Black servants and his horse; both were still standing and frozen solid.

Almagro reached the Copiapó Valley in northern Chile, where he and his soldiers subdued the inhabitants. He then headed south to the center of present-day Chile as far as the Maule River, which marked the southern boundary of the Inca Empire. He sent out parties of soldiers to explore the surrounding country and to try to find gold and other precious metals, always the first goal of the *conquistadores*. They quickly learned that Chile was not as rich in these metals as Peru. With the news that civil war had broken out in Peru, Almagro returned there to try to stake his claim to the city of Cuzco. This time he traveled along the Pacific coast, having to pass through the extremely dry Atacama Desert.

He and his men reached Arequipa in southern Peru in early 1537.

Once Almagro got back to Cuzco he found that it was being attacked by an Inca leader. Almagro defeated the Incas and took possession of the city. He then proclaimed himself governor. This claim was immediately disputed by Pizarro. Almagro and his men were defeated in the Battle of Las Salinas outside of Cuzco on April 26, 1538. Almagro was captured and executed several weeks after the battle. Pizarro then sent **Pedro de Valdivia** south to take control of Chile.

Where to learn more

A book that specifically discusses the Spanish in Chile is H.R.S. Pocock, *The Conquest of Chile* (New York: Stein & Day, 1967). An excellent book by John Hemming, *The Conquest of the Incas* (New York: Harcourt, Brace, Jovanovich, 1970) elaborates on the relation between Pizarro and Almagro. There are many books that deal with the conquest of the Incas. One of the earliest to be published in English, and still very entertaining, is by the great American historian, William H. Prescott. His classic history *The Conquest of Peru* is available in many editions. Also recommended are: *The Conquistadors* by Jean Descola, translated by Malcolm Barnes, (London: Allen & Unwin, 1954) and Frederick A. Kirkpatrick's *The Spanish Conquistadores* (Cleveland: World Publishing Co., 1962), which has been called "the best general account."

Pedro de Alvarado

(1485 -1541)

Pedro de Alvarado was a Spanish conquistador *who played a major part in the conquest of Mexico and then subdued the Mayas of Guatemala and El Salvador and traveled to Peru.*

Pedro de Alvarado was born in the town of Badajoz in the Spanish province of Extremadura. He traveled to America in 1510 and settled first in Santo Domingo and then in Cuba. He took part in an expedition led by Juan de Grijalva that went to the Yucatan Peninsula in 1518. Grijalva sent Alvarado back to Cuba with reports of a rich kingdom in the center of Mexico. The Spanish governor, Diego Velásquez, sponsored an expedition led by **Hernán Cortés** to conquer Mexico. Alvarado sailed with Cortés in February 1519.

The Spanish under Cortés entered the Mexican capital of Tenochtitlan (on the site of Mexico City) on November 8, 1519.

Pedro de Alvaredo. The Granger Collection, New York.

After he had been in the city for six months, Cortés received word that a rival, Pánfilo de Narvaez, had landed on the Caribbean coast with the aim of displacing Cortés as the Spanish leader. Cortés left Tenochtitlan for the coast immediately to defeat Narvaez, leaving Alvarado in charge of 140 Spanish soldiers in Tenochtitlan. During the absence of Cortés, the Aztec rulers celebrated an important religious ceremony in the city's main square. Either because he thought that this was a prelude to a massacre of the Spanish or because he thought it offered a unique opportunity, Alvarado blocked off the entrances to the square and then attacked the Aztecs, killing 200 nobles. He and his soldiers were set upon by an infuriated mob and forced to retreat to the palace of Axayácatl, where they were besieged.

When Cortés returned, he was allowed back into the city but was then attacked by the inhabitants. He was forced to retreat on the night of June 30, 1520 with Alvarado in charge of the rearguard. Alvarado became renowned among his Spanish colleagues during this exit when he made an incredible leap across a wide gap in the causeway that led out of the city across Lake Texcoco. When the Spanish returned in May 1521, Alvarado played a major role in the attacks that finally resulted in a Spanish victory on August 21, 1521.

Following the subjugation of the Aztecs, Alvarado was sent in 1522 to defeat the Mixtecs and Zapotecs south of Mexico City, and he left a party of Spaniards to establish the town of Oaxaca in what is now the far south of Mexico. He was sent by Cortés in late 1523 to conquer the former Mayan territory of Guatemala. In campaigns that lasted for two years, he had to fight several bloody campaigns with the Native Americans there, but was eventually able to subdue what are now the countries of Guatemala and El Salvador. In 1526 he returned to Spain to report on his conquests, and he was made Governor and Captain General of the new Spanish territories. He went back to Guatemala to take up his posts.

However, Alvarado was much more interested in adventure and conquest than he was in governing and managing. He built a fleet with the aim of sailing out across the Pacific to see if he could reach Asia. In 1532, however, he heard about the incredible victories that **Francisco Pizarro** was winning over the Incas in Peru, and he decided to use his boats to sail there instead. He left Guatemala in 1533 with 500 Spanish soldiers, 3,000 Guatemalan slaves, and 227 horses. He landed at Puerto Viejo in Ecuador and then set out to reach the Inca city of Quito. Traveling over the Andes proved to be extremely difficult, and 80 Spaniards and at least 2,000 of the Guatemalans died in the extreme cold. It took Alvarado six months to reach the Inca highway that traversed the mountains, only to find that a lieutenant of Pizarro's had already conquered the area. On August 26, 1534 Alvarado turned his soldiers and arms over to Pizarro, who paid him 100,000 gold pesos. Alvarado himself returned to Guatemala, where in 1536 he also took over the command of Honduras.

In 1540 Alvarado renewed his attempt to sail to the Spice Islands in what is now Indonesia. He sailed along the west coast of Mexico with a fleet of 13 ships intending to sail westward from there. However, the Viceroy of Mexico persuaded him to delay his trip in order to take part in the search that was being led by **Francisco Vázquez de Coronado** to find the fabled Seven Cities of Cibola in what is now New Mexico. In Jalisco, Alvarado became involved in helping to put down a revolt by the Zacatecas Indians. He led a cavalry attack a Zacatecas stronghold on the top of a mountain. Three times the Spanish were pushed back and then they panicked and fled from the pursuing Native Americans. Alvarado was on foot and was crushed when a horse climbing up the side of a ravine fell on him. He was taken to the city of Guadalajara where he died 11 days later.

Where to learn more

There is one full-scale biography of Alvarado in English: John E. Kelly, *Pedro de Alvarado, Conquistador* (Princeton: Princeton University Press, 1932).

The story of the conquest of Mexico has been often told. The classic account in English is by the American historian William H. Prescott, *History of the Conquest of Mexico*, available in many editions. Alvarado's involvement in the conquest of Peru is discussed in John Hemming's *The Conquest of the Inca* (New York: Harcourt, Brace, Jovanovich, 1970).

Roald Amundsen

(1872 - 1928)

Roald Amundsen was a Norwegian explorer who was the first man to sail the Northwest Passage, the first man to travel to the South Pole, and the first man to reach both Poles.

Roald Amundsen. Norwegian Information Service.

Roald Amundsen was born in the Norwegian town of Borge near Oslo. His father was a shipbuilder who died when Roald was 14. At the age of 15 he read about the Arctic explorations of **Sir John Franklin** and decided that he wanted to be an Arctic explorer himself. He prepared himself by hard physical exercise, including skiing, and by keeping the window in his bedroom open at night no matter what the weather. His mother wanted him to study to become a doctor. She died when he was 21, and he immediately turned his attention away from studying medicine to prepare himself to travel to the Arctic. He later wrote, "I had been struck by one fatal weakness common to many of the preceding Arctic expeditions. This was that the commanders of these expeditions had not always been ships' captains." Amundsen resolved to become an experienced navigator.

Amundsen's first job was as a deckhand on a sealing ship that spent five months in the Arctic Ocean north of Norway. On another occasion he bicycled across France and Spain to catch up with a ship that was sailing to Florida. Returning to Europe the ship stopped in Grimsby in northern England where Amundsen spent all the money he had to buy a secondhand copy of a book of memoirs by Arctic voyagers.

In 1897 Amundsen was chosen to be first mate on the *Belgica*, the ship carrying the first Belgian Antarctic expedition under the command of Adrien de Gerlache. Also on the ship was the American **Frederick Albert Cook**. The *Belgica* got caught in the ice off of Graham's Land and was the first ship to winter in the Antarctic. When all of the ship's crew became ill with scurvy, Amundsen saved the day by digging in the snow around the ship for seal carcasses and forcing the men to eat the meat.

On his return to Norway in 1899, Amundsen was able to get his skipper's license and immediately began making plans for his own expedition with the assistance of the famous Norwegian explorer **Fridtjof Nansen**. His aim was to go to the North Magnetic Pole, which had first been located by **James Clark Ross**, and then to try to traverse the Northwest Passage. In 1900 he spent a couple of months studying magnetism at the German Marine Observatory in Hamburg. On his return to Norway he raised money and recruited a crew for his expedition. He borrowed money from his brothers and bought a small ship, the *Gjöa*. The boat was so small that it only needed a crew of six. It left at midnight on June 16, 1903 from Oslo harbor in the middle of a heavy rainstorm in order to get away before Amundsen's creditors could confiscate the boat.

On August 22, 1903 the *Gjöa* arrived off the south coast of Devon Island, which is north of Lancaster Sound, the entrance to the Northwest Passage. It then headed around Somerset Island down Peel Strait and Franklin Strait in the direction that the compass said the Magnetic Pole should be. On August 31 the engine room caught on fire (the *Gjöa* had one mast and a 13-horsepower engine), but it was put out before it could spread to the reserve tanks of oil. The next day the boat hit a reef and was damaged, and the *Gjöa* floated free only after some of the deck cargo was thrown overboard. In early September they were caught in the winter's first storm, which threatened to sink the ship. On September 12 the *Gjöa* anchored in a little harbor on

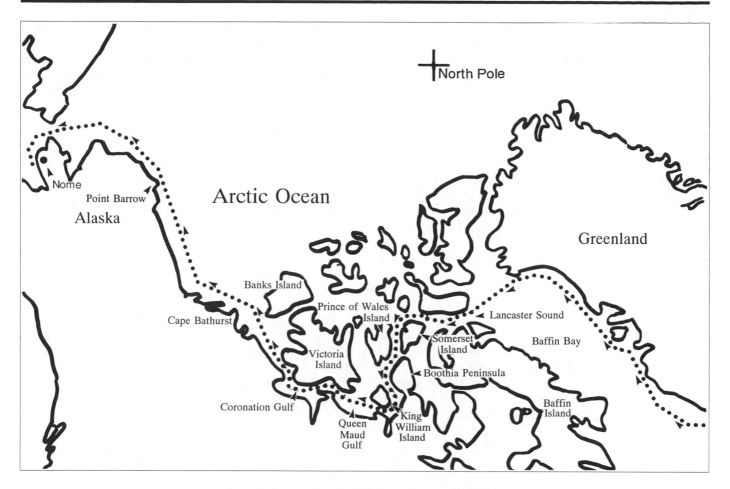

Amundsen's voyage through the Northwest Passage, 1903-1906.

the south coast of King William Island that Amundsen named Gjöa Haven.

Amundsen and his crew stayed two winters at Gjöa Haven. On land they built two buildings for magnetic observations, an astronomical observatory, a supply hut and a small hut where two of the crew members lived. They were soon joined by a large band of members of the Netsilik tribe of Inuit who settled down in a camp next to the Norwegians. During the time he spent with the Inuit, Amundsen learned many of the techniques for survival in the Arctic that he was to put to use in later years.

During the spring and summer of 1904 Amundsen and the other members of the expedition made trips to map the surrounding areas and to locate the North Magnetic Pole. When Amundsen got to the spot where Ross had found the Pole in 1831, he found that it had moved 30 miles away. That was one of the most important results of his expedition—the realization that the Magnetic Poles were not fixed positions.

On August 12, 1905 the *Gjöa* left Gjöa Haven and sailed westward through Simpson Strait into a large body of water that Amundsen named Queen Maud Gulf after the Queen of Norway and then anchored in Cambridge Bay on August 1905. Cam-

bridge Bay had been approached from the west by Captain Richard Collinson in 1852. By reaching it, Amundsen had closed the last unknown gap in the Northwest Passage. However, he had also shown that it was so narrow and shallow and full of reefs and hidden rocks that it would never be navigated by any but the smallest ships. On the other hand, the more open northern route through Parry Channel was so clogged with ice that only the largest and strongest icebreaking ships, like the **S.S. Manhattan**, could make their way through it.

The *Gjöa* continued its way westward south of Victoria Island until it reached open water in an area later named Amundsen Gulf. On August 26 Amundsen met another ship, an American sailing vessel that traded in Arctic waters. The ship's captain knew about Amundsen and greeted him by saying, "I am exceedingly pleased to be the first one to welcome you on getting through the North West Passage."

West of the Mackenzie River delta the *Gjöa* became trapped in ice near Herschel Island. During the winter of 1905-1906 Amundsen traveled overland by dog team to the nearest telegraph station at Eagle, Alaska, on the Yukon River to send word of his success back to Norway. When he got back to his ship in March 1906, he found that one of the crew members had died from a ruptured appendix and was buried at King Point on the north coast of Canada. By August 10 the ice had melted sufficiently for the *Gjöa* to continue its voyage. It fought its way past two masses of ice off Point Barrow and reached Nome, Alaska, in early September 1906. The entire town turned out to welcome them, and the nephew of the Norwegian explorer Otto Sverdrup, who was there at the time, played the Norwegian national anthem as the ship pulled into the dock. Amundsen broke into tears.

Amundsen stayed with the ship until it reached Seattle and then returned to Oslo from there. The *Gjöa* itself made it as far as San Francisco where it was on exhibit at Golden Gate Park until 1973 when it was returned to Oslo and placed in the national ship museum. When Amundsen got back to Norway, he was received as a hero and addressed several European geographical societies and wrote a book about his expedition.

Following this success, Amundsen decided to try to be the first person to reach the North Pole itself. He wanted to test Nansen's theory that it would be possible to follow the Arctic currents and drift aboard a ship as far as the Pole. He got Nansen to lend him the *Fram*, the ship that Nansen had specially constructed and had used in his own attempt to reach the Pole. While Amundsen was preparing for his expedition, news arrived in September 1909 that **Robert Edward Peary** and **Matthew A. Henson** and three Inuit companions had reached the North Pole by dogsled. Amundsen secretly resolved to change his goal to the South Pole but did not tell anyone because he did not want to lose any of his backers. On August 9, 1910 the *Fram* left Oslo with the announced purpose of sailing to the South Atlantic and around Cape Horn and then through the Pacific to the Bering Strait into the Arctic Ocean. When they reached Funchal on the island of Madeira on September 9, 1910, Amundsen told the crew about his real destination and telegraphed back to Nansen and the King of Norway to let them know about his change of plans.

In the meantime, the British naval officer **Robert Falcon Scott** had left England at the head of an expedition to reach the South Pole. When he arrived in Melbourne, Australia, he was surprised to receive a telegram: "Beg leave to inform you proceeding Antarctica. Amundsen." There was now a race between the British and the Norwegians to see who could reach the South Pole first. The *Fram* proceeded much more quickly, and Amundsen had already set up his base on the Bay of Whales at the edge of the Ross Ice Shelf when Scott arrived at McMurdo Sound, which was 60 miles farther from the Pole.

Four weeks after landing, on February 10, 1911, Amundsen left camp to set up his first supply depot at latitude 80°. On their return their dog teams achieved a record performance of 90 miles in two days. The other runs to set up depots did not go so smoothly, but Amundsen had them all established by the time winter set in. An April blizzard allowed the Norwegians to construct a series of tunnels and rooms underneath a massive snow drift, and they were able to live and work there until the spring thaw. As the thaw began, Amundsen set out for the Pole at the end of August 1911. But it was too early: he and his companions were overwhelmed by cold and blizzards. They were forced to turn back, and Amundsen, apparently for the only time, lost his nerve and outran his colleagues in getting back to the base at "Franheim."

They set out again on October 20, 1911: Helmer Hanssen, Oskar Wisting, Olav Bjaaland, and Sverre Hassel out in front leading dog teams, with Amundsen following behind on skis. They had four dogsleds and 52 dogs. Amundsen and Bjaaland had ingeniously modified the sleds to reduce their weight. Amundsen had also learned from his contact with the Inuit to adopt warm, loose-fitting, and lightweight fur garments. (His British rivals wore wool clothes that got wet and froze.) They reached the first supply depot in four days and rested there for two days. They made it to the last advance depot, just south of latitude 85°, on November 3.

From the last advance base the snow was so smooth that Amundsen and his four colleagues were able to travel by wearing skis and tying themselves to the dogsleds to be pulled along by the dogs. "And there I stood," wrote Amundsen, "until we reached 85°05' S—34 miles. Yes, that was a pleasant surprise. We had never dreamed of driving on skis to the Pole." On November 17 they left the Ross Ice Shelf and started up Axel Heiberg Glacier (named by Amundsen after one of his sponsors) to get over the Transantarctic Mountains. The dog teams had difficulty making it up the steep glacier, and they had to retrace their steps several times when their way was blocked by massive blocks of ice. At the top they set up camp at a place they called Butcher Shop: by now many of the dogs were no longer needed to carry the lighter loads (they had been consuming their supplies along the way), and the excess ones were shot and either fed to the other dogs or to the explorers. Amundsen stayed in his tent while the killing went on outside.

On December 7, Amundsen achieved a new record when they passed the previous farthest south that had been reached by **Ernest Shackleton**. They then had to cross the "Devil's Ballroom"—a double dome of ice over a vast crevasse. The sleds kept falling through, but they made it to the other side safely. As they came within 15 miles of the Pole on December 13, Amundsen stuck a Norwegian flag on the leading dogsled. Amundsen later wrote that night he had the "same feeling that I can remember as a little boy of the night before Christmas Eve— an intense expectation of what was going to happen."

The next day, December 14, 1911, at three o'clock on a sunny afternoon, the Norwegians raised their country's flag over the spot their calculations told them was the South Pole. They celebrated their achievement with double rations. On December 17 they headed back north. This time they detoured most of Axel Heiberg Glacier, and following an uneventful trip reached their base at 4:00 a.m. on January 25, 1912. They had covered 1,860 miles in 99 days. They reboarded the *Fram* at the end of January and sailed to Hobart in Australia. When Scott's British expedition arrived at the Pole on the morning of January 18, 1912, they found the Norwegian flag flying over it. On the way back they all died.

Following his return to Norway, Amundsen once again took up his goal of drifting to the North Pole. He designed and constructed a ship named the *Maud*. Between 1918 and 1921, Amundsen sailed in the *Maud* but did not drift to the North Pole. Instead, he ended up navigating the Northeast Passage along the northern coasts of Europe and Asia to Nome, Alaska. He was the second person in history, following **A. E. Nordenskjöld**, to make this voyage.

Disappointed that he had still not made it to the North Pole, Amundsen then came up with the idea of trying to get there by airplane. Following a lecture in New York City, he met the American explorer and millionaire **Lincoln Ellsworth** who offered to finance a flying expedition to the Pole. In 1925 they

Amundsen's trek to the South Pole.

made two unsuccessful attempts to fly over the icepack and to land at the North Pole using Junkers and Curtiss aircraft. They then fitted out two Dornier-Wal flying boats with twin Rolls-Royce engines of 360 horsepower each. Amundsen and Ellsworth flew from the island of Spitsbergen on May 21, 1925. With half of their fuel gone, one of the planes developed engine trouble, and they were forced to land in open water at 87°43′ N. The "lead" they were on rapidly iced over and crushed one of the planes. They then had to repair and modify the remaining plane so that it could take off from the ice. (It was a "flying boat," designed to take off and land on water). They constructed a makeshift runway and on June 15 they were able to take off, just clearing the runway. They were able to glide to a landing in open water off of Spitsbergen and were rescued by a sealing ship.

The Pole was finally reached by plane by **Richard Evelyn Byrd** in May 1926. On his return to Spitsbergen, Byrd met Amundsen who was about to try again, this time in a dirigible named the *Norge*. The *Norge* had been designed by the Italian engineer and pilot **Umberto Nobile**. It was equipped with two 250-horsepower engines that allowed it to travel up to 50 miles per hour, and it carried seven tons of fuel. On May 11, two days after Byrd's flight, the *Norge* left the ground at 8:55 a.m. in a temperature of -49°F in almost windless conditions. At 1:15 p.m. they were over the Pole and threw down the Italian, Norwegian, and American flags. After leaving the Pole, they ran into a number of difficulties: the propellers threw ice against the side of the airship and put a hole in the canvas, fog reduced visibility to almost zero, and the radio stopped working. They reached Point Barrow, Alaska on May 14, having flown 3,400 miles from Europe to Alaska.

Amundsen's flight, which had crossed previously unknown territory, added important new information about the Arctic and made Amundsen the first man to travel to both of the Poles. The acclaim that he received for this inspired jealousy on the part of Nobile, who had designed and flown the *Norge*, but claimed that he had not been given due credit for the achievement. He received support from Mussolini's Italian government to build another dirigible and to fly it over the Pole.

On May 23, 1928 Nobile took the *Italia* on his second Arctic flight. Nothing was heard from the expedition for six weeks. Amundsen was attending a banquet in his and Ellsworth's honor in Oslo when a telegram was handed to him, telling him that the *Italia* had been officially declared lost. Amundsen, at the age of 56, said, "I am ready to go at once." Two search parties went out. One of them found the crashed *Italia*, whose survivors included Nobile. Amundsen left the northern Norwegian city of Tromsö headed for Spitsbergen on June 8, 1928 in a French seaplane with Lieutenant Commander Guilbaud and a crew of three. They never arrived in Spitsbergen, and it was only some time later that the plane's wreckage was spotted from the air.

Where to learn more

Amundsen told his own life story in *My Life As an Explorer* (Garden City: Doubleday, Page & Co., 1928). A biography is *Amundsen* by Bellamy Partridge (London: Robert Hale Ltd., 1953).

For the story of sailing through the Northwest Passage see L.H. Neatby, *Conquest of the Last Frontier* (Athens: Ohio University Press, 1966) and Pierre Berton, *The Arctic Grail: The Quest for the North West Passage and the North Pole, 1818-1909* (New York: Viking, 1988) as well as Amundsen's own record, *The North West Passage*, 2 vols. (London: Archibald Constable & Co., 1908)

For the exciting narrative of the race to the South Pole see Amundsen's *The South Pole*, 2 vols. (London: John Murray, 1912) as well as L.P. Kirwan, *A History of Polar Exploration* (New York: W.W. Norton & Company, 1960); Roland Huntford, *Scott and Amundsen* (London: Hodder & Stoughton, 1979); and John Maxtone-Graham, *Safe Return Doubtful: The Heroic Age of Polar Exploration* (New York: Charles Scribner's Sons, 1988).

The best version of the flight over the North Pole is John Grierson's *Heroes of the Polar Skies* (New York: Meredith Press, 1967).

Carl Johan Andersson

(1827 - 1867)

Carl Johan Andersson was a Swedish hunter and explorer who was the first European to visit many areas of northern Namibia and Botswana.

Carl Johan Andersson was born in the town of Vänersborg in Sweden. He was the son of a Welsh hunter and author named Llewellyn Lloyd and a Swedish farm woman named Kajsa Andersdotter. His mother and father were never married, and he adopted his mother's family name. He entered the University of Lund in Sweden in 1847 to study zoology but was forced to leave after a year because of financial difficulties. He worked as a professional hunter in Sweden for two years and then decided to travel to Africa to hunt there. In order to finance his trip he went to England to sell some zoological specimens and two live bears that he had captured.

In England Andersson met Francis Galton, an English hunter. Andersson decided to travel with Galton to southwestern Africa to try to reach Lake Ngami, in what is now Botswana, which had been discovered in 1849 by **David Livingstone**. They arrived at Walvis Bay, the only natural harbor on the coast of Namibia, at the end of 1850. They set out by wagon into the interior of Namibia with the aim of opening up a trade route to Lake Ngami. They traveled through the Okahandja region and then to the land of the Ovambos, who are today the largest ethnic group in Namibia, which had never been visited by Europeans before. They stopped at the artesian wells at the eastern end of the swamp area called the Etosha Pan and reached Tsumeb on May 26, 1851 and then turned south and headed back to the coast. They never made it as far as Lake Ngami.

During the winter of 1851 Andersson and Galton set out on another trading expedition, reaching the site of Windhoek, the present-day capital of Namibia on August 30, 1851 and going as far as Gobabis on the western edge of the Kalahari Desert. On their return to the coast, Galton decided to return to England but gave Andersson financial support to continue his explorations. In April 1853 Andersson reached the Nossob River and then traveled to Gobabis and on to the Kalahari Dessert. Traveling through the Kalahari he made it as far as the western shore of Lake Ngami by the end of June. He spent several weeks there collecting biological specimens and studying the customs of the local Tswana tribe.

From Lake Ngami Andersson traveled back to Walvis Bay and then to Cape Town in South Africa where he presented his biological specimens to the local museum. He also became engaged to Sarah Jane Aitchison, whose brother was postmaster-general of the British Cape Province. In Cape Town he learned that his father had become ill so he decided to make a trip to Sweden to visit him. Along the way, he stopped in London in November 1854 and gave a lecture to the Royal Geographical Society on the results of his search for a route to Lake Ngami. He was introduced to **Charles Darwin** and presented him with notes about his expedition.

Following the recovery of his father, Andersson returned to South Africa in 1857 and took charge of a mine at Walvis Bay. After the mine failed, he took up exploring again. In 1859 he traveled north to try to reach the Cunene River, which now forms the boundary between Angola and Namibia. Along the way he became the first European to see and describe the course of the Okovango River, which flows eastward to disappear in a large depression in northern Botswana called the Okovango Basin. While along the shore of the Okovango River Andersson was attacked by a rhinoceros that gored his thigh. As a result, he was forced to stay in camp for several months to recover.

After his recovery Andersson traveled back to Cape Town where he got married in July 1860. He then returned to Namibia where he supported himself by supplying elephant hunters and by trading in ivory and cattle. Living in northern Namibia Andersson became a friend of the local Herero tribe. However, he quarreled with the Nama tribe, who were the enemies of the Herero. Andersson was made a chief of the Hereros and, following a raid by the Namas, led the Hereros in battle on June 6, 1864. In the fight known as "Andersson's Battle" the Hereros were victorious but Andersson was hit by five bullets, one of which smashed his right leg below the knee. It was nine months before he was able to travel again, and during this time he made a systematic study of the birds of Damaraland in central Namibia.

Andersson and his wife left Namibia in May 1865 to travel to Europe to get medical advice. He decided against surgery and then returned to Cape Town where he stayed at his brother-in-law's seaside house and wrote a scientific description and catalog of the birds of Namibia. Although he was still not totally recovered, Andersson left Cape Town in May 1866 and traveled to Walvis Bay and then north into Namibia to collect and sell ivory, cattle, and ostrich feathers. He was successful but lost part of his supplies in a raid by Nama warriors. He then decided to go farther north to trade with the Portuguese north of the Cunene River. Along the way he became ill from his old wounds and died at the village of Ondangua in northern Namibia on July 7, 1867.

Andersson's specimens of birds and other animals were sent to museums in Europe and South Africa where they served as the basis for several studies on the animal life of Namibia. The scientific names of several birds that he identified, such as *Tephrocorys anderssoni*, a lark, were named in his honor.

Where to learn more

Andersson wrote several books about his travels in Namibia and Botswana. The first was published in 1856 (New York: Harper & Brothers) as *Lake Ngami: or, Explorations and Discoveries during Four Years' Wanderings in the Wilds of South-western Africa*. His discovery of the Okovango River is recounted in *The Okavango River: A Narrative of Travel, Exploration, and Adventure* (New York: Harper & Brothers, 1861). After his death a collection of Andersson's writings and travel diaries was published in London in 1873 (*The Lion and the Elephant*). The diary of his last trip to the north was published as *Notes on Travel in South Africa* (London, 1875). It was reprinted by C. Struik Ltd. of Cape Town in 1969.

There is not much secondary source material available on Andersson. There is an interesting chapter on him in a nineteenth-century work, *Africa: The History of Exploration and Adventure* by Charles H. Jones (New York: Henry Holt & Co., 1875) that was reprinted in 1970 by Negro Universities Press of Westport, Connecticut.

Antonio de Andrade

(1580 - 1634)

Antonio de Andrade was a Portuguese missionary who was the first European to travel over the Himalayas into Tibet.

Following the first Portuguese expeditions to India in the early 1500s, the Roman Catholic Church had established several missions that achieved some success in converting Indians to Christianity. The most successful were those founded by the Jesuit Order. In 1615 the Jesuit missions were placed under the leadership of Father Antonio de Andrade, a native of Portugal. There were rumors circulating among the Jesuit missions that there were Christian communities in the Kingdom of Tibet, north of the Himalayas. Andrade determined to discover the truth.

In March 1624 Andrade and a lay brother named Manuel Marques joined the entourage of the Mogul Emperor Jehangir and traveled from the capital at Agra to Delhi. In Delhi they adopted disguises and attached themselves to a caravan of Hindu pilgrims headed for Kashmir, in the far north of the country. Crossing through the Himalayas the two Jesuits reached the province of Garhwal where they were discovered and forced to explain their presence. Andrade said that he was a Portuguese merchant on his way to Tibet to visit his brother who was sick. After a week's detention they were allowed to proceed.

Andrade and Marques traveled through the narrow paths of the Himalayas and crossed the headwaters of the Ganges River several times on "bridges formed by frozen snow." In May or early June 1624 they reached the holy Hindu shrine of Badrinath high in the Himalayas. They were the first Europeans to reach the shrine—and the last ones for another 200 years.

At the town of Mana on the border with Tibet, they were stopped and forbidden to continue on their journey. Marques stayed in the town to deal with the authorities, but Andrade continued on his journey. At the crest of the mountains, he was stopped once again, and his guide returned to Mana. Andrade tried to soldier on alone, but he was faced by such heavy snowfall and extreme cold that he was forced to turn back and set up a camp lower on the slopes. There, Marques caught up with him and the two waited for better weather and then finally crossed through the Mana Pass into Tibet. They were the first Europeans in the country since the visit of **Odoric of Pordenone** 300 years before.

In early August 1624 Andrade reached Tsaparang, the capital of a Tibetan kingdom in the southwestern part of the country. He had decided that he would have to return to India before the autumn snows began, but the King of Tsaparang liked him so much that he could only get permission to leave if he promised to return the following year. The King gave him a letter saying that the two Jesuits could count on his full protection and indicated his interest in learning about the Christian religion.

Andrade returned to Goa in November 1624 to write up his report and then headed back to Tsaparang, arriving there in August 1625. He built a church in Tsaparang with money donated by the King, and three other Jesuits joined Andrade and his two companions to help in the mission's work. The king was baptized by Andrade in 1630. The ceremony had been delayed because the king had not wished to give up his many mistresses, which Andrade demanded.

Andrade left Tsaparang to become the Jesuit superior in the main Portuguese base at Goa in 1630. Shortly after his departure, the Buddhist subjects of the King of Tsaparang rebelled under the leadership of the king's brother, the Chief Lama. The King was taken prisoner, and many of the 400 converts to Christianity were enslaved. The church was destroyed, but none of the missionaries were hurt although they were forced to leave the country. The following year news of these developments reached Andrade in Goa, and he sent **Francisco de Azevado** to Tsaparang to find out what had happened.

Azevado was able to obtain some temporary success, and Andrade was so encouraged by this that he sought permission to resign as head of the Jesuits in India and to go back and work as a missionary in Tsaparang. But his death in 1634 kept him from fulfilling this wish. His death gave rise to rumors that he had been poisoned by enemies who disliked the harsh way he was carrying out the Inquisition in Goa.

Where to learn more

The best source in English about European contacts with Tibet is John MacGregor, *Tibet: A Chronicle of Exploration* (London: Routledge & Kegan Paul, 1970), which was the chief source for this account. MacGregor used two main sources for his discussion of Andrade: a letter written by Andrade dated November 8, 1624 that was published in Lisbon in 1626 as *Novo descrobrimento do Gran Cathayo ou Reinos de Tibet* and a book by C. Wessels, *Early Jesuit Travellers in Central Asia, 1603-1721* (the Hague: Martinus Nijhoff, 1924).

Apollo

(1957 - 1972)

The Apollo program was the effort made by the United States to send manned spacecraft to and from the surface of the Moon. It succeeded in making a total of six lunar landings.

On May 25, 1961 President John F. Kennedy made a speech to Congress in which he challenged the nation to land a human on the Moon and return him safely to earth before the end of the decade. In fact, planning was well under way to achieve such a goal, having started in April 1957. The name "Apollo," (the Greek god of the Sun) was proposed by Abe Silverstein, the Director of Space Flight Development, at a conference on July 28-19, 1960.

In the following years the necessary equipment was developed and tested. The lift-off from Earth was achieved by a three-stage Saturn 5 rocket developed by Dr. Werner von Braun and his colleagues. After the first two stages of the rocket had dropped off, the third stage of the rocket put the spacecraft into Earth orbit. It was then refired to send the rocket at a speed of 25,000 miles an hour toward the Moon. Along the way, the command module at the top of the rocket separated and docked with the

Apollo 11 on the launch pad. NASA.

lunar module that was nested inside the Saturn. The third stage of the rocket then dropped away.

The spacecraft itself consisted of a command module where the astronauts were housed and a service module that contained the electrical power and fuel. The service module powered the command module back to Earth and then dropped away just prior to re-entry into the Earth's atmosphere.

The lunar module was a funny-looking contraption 23 feet high that weighed 15 tons. It had its own spider-like legs that supported the vessel on landing and then served as the platform for the take off from the Moon's surface. It had no heat shields and could only operate in the vacuum of space. Once it was fired from the Moon, it would go into lunar orbit and dock with the command module, which would then readjust its course to head back to Earth.

The entire Apollo program was delayed by a fire that took place on the Apollo 1 spacecraft on January 27, 1967. Three astronauts, Virgil "Gus" Grissom, Edward White, and Roger Chaffee, had entered the spacecraft at 1:00 p.m. for a "plugs-out" test. The test continued routinely through the afternoon. At 6:31 p.m. the technicians in the control room heard "There's a fire in here." It was caused by a short circuit near Grissom's seat. It took five minutes to open the hatch: the three astronauts were dead, having been suffocated within a matter of seconds by lethal fumes. They were not burned because their spacesuits protected them.

The next few Apollo missions were unmanned flights to test the safety of the equipment. The next manned flight was Apollo 7, which took place from October 11-22, 1968. It was commanded by Walter "Wally" Schirra, who had flown on Mercury 5 and Gemini 6, and who thus became the first American to make three flights in space. The crew members were Donn Eisele and Walter Cunningham. The aim of the mission was to test the service module, whose engines were fired eight times during the 11 days that the astronauts were in space. The crew members all came down with colds during the flight. When the spacecraft landed in the Pacific Ocean off the coast of Baja California, it flipped over. There was no radio contact with the crew for 20 minutes, but they all emerged unharmed.

The Apollo 8 mission was the first one to fly to the Moon. It took off on December 21, 1968 from Cape Canaveral with Frank Borman, James Lovell, and William Anders on board. As they entered lunar orbit on December 24, they were out of voice contact with Earth since they were on the far side of the moon.

They were able to broadcast live pictures of the Moon's surface starting at 7:00 a.m. on Christmas Eve. That night the crew members read the first 10 verses of the Book of Genesis from the Bible. After making ten orbits, they headed back to Earth on Christmas morning, December 25. On their return to Earth on December 27, Borman, referring to an old folk myth, said of the moon, "It's not made of green cheese, it's made of American cheese."

The aim of the Apollo 9 mission was to fire and recover the lunar module in space. On board were James McDivitt, David Scott, and Russell Schweickart. The Saturn 5 rocket took off on March 3, 1969 from Cape Canaveral. With Scott controlling the command module, the lunar module was fired by McDivitt with Schweickart in the module with him. There were a few problems getting the lunar module up to speed. Schweickart's job was to walk in space from the lunar module to test his spacesuit. However, he had vomited twice during the mission, and it was decided that it was too dangerous to send him out. He stood on the doorway of the spacecraft with Scott in the open hatch. Schweickart did not get sick. The two vehicles were separated for six hours and then re-united. This was a crucial test because no one knew how much "kick" would occur when the lunar module docked.

The Apollo 10 mission nicknamed the command module *Charlie Brown* and the lunar module *Snoopy* after the cartoon characters. The mission was a final test run before the landing on the Moon. It left on May 18, 1969 with Thomas Stafford, John Young, and Eugene Cernan on board. Apollo 10 made 31 orbits of the Moon. The lunar module practiced flying close to the surface of the Moon and came within 50,000 feet, the distance

a commercial jet flies over the surface of the Earth. They returned on May 26, 1969, and the National Aeronautics and Space Administration declared that a lunar landing was possible.

The Apollo 11 mission commanded by **Neil Armstrong** and backed up by Michael Collins and Edwin "Buzz" Aldrin left the space center on July 16, 1969. The lunar module with Armstrong and Aldrin on board descended to the surface of the Moon on July 20, 1969 and stayed for 15 hours. They were the first humans to reach the surface of the Earth's only satellite.

The success of the Apollo 11 mission did not mean the end of the program. Further missions were planned to actually explore the surface of the Moon. Apollo 12 left on November 14, 1969 with Pete Conrad, Richard Gordon, and Alan Bean on board. Watched by President Richard M. Nixon, the rocket was hit by lightning as it took off. Despite initial fears, there was no significant damage and the mission proceeded. It was targeted to land near the site where an unmanned Surveyor III probe had landed in 1967. It landed 535 feet away (Apollo 11 had been four miles from its target), in the Ocean of Storms, 955 miles west of where Apollo 11 had landed. Conrad and Bean took two walks on the surface, one for 3 hours and 56 minutes, the second for 3 hours and 49 minutes. They returned safely to Earth on November 24.

Apollo 13 was the only aborted mission in the Apollo program. Astronauts James Lovell, John Swigert, and Fred Haise took off from Cape Canaveral on April 11, 1970 at 1:13 p.m. At 10:13 p.m. on April 13 an oxygen tank in the service module behind the crew exploded, eliminating oxygen, electricity, light, and water from the command module. The crew had to transfer

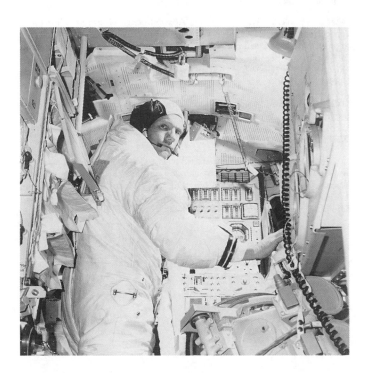

Neil Armstrong training for the Apollo 11 mission. NASA.

Alan Shepard, commander of Apollo 14. NASA.

to the cramped quarters of the lunar module, which was designed for 45 hours of use. They were forced to stay there for 90 hours. Inside, the temperature dropped to 38°F, and frost formed on the inside of the windows. The crew was able to make necessary course corrections to return to Earth, jettisoning the damaged service module just before re-entering the Earth's atmosphere on April 17.

Apollo 14 was commanded by Alan Shepard, who had been the first American in space in 1961 when he had made a sub-orbital Mercury flight that preceded **John Glenn**'s first orbit of the Earth. He had not flown since then because of an inner ear problem that affected his balance. He had undergone a secret operation to correct the disability and had been restored to flight status. Shepard was accompanied by Stuart Roosa and Edgar Mitchell. They took off on January 31, 1971, and Shepard and Mitchell landed on the Moon at 4:18 a.m. on February 5, 1971. They made two "moonwalks" in the Fra Mauro Highlands not far from the landing site of Apollo 12. They were equipped with a little cart like a rickshaw that they pulled after them to collect lunar soil and rocks. They returned to Earth on February 9. As with the previous astronauts who had made lunar landings, they were subjected to a long quarantine period to see if any viruses or other diseases developed. When they did not, it was decided that quarantines were no longer necessary.

Apollo 15 was the first mission to land in mountainous terrain. It took off on July 26, 1971 with David Scott (from the Apollo 9 mission), Alfred Worden, and James Irwin on board. Scott and Irwin landed in the Appenine Mountains about 465 miles north of the lunar equator. The mountains are higher than any found on earth. For the first time, the astronauts were equipped with a powered vehicle, the Lunar Rover, that gave them much greater mobility than previous missions. They made three trips to collect geological specimens and were out of the lunar module for a total of about 18½ hours. They performed a demonstration of Galileo's discovery that objects will fall at the same speed no matter what their weight by dropping a hammer and a falcon feather onto the Moon's surface. Irwin then accidentally stepped on the feather, and it got lost in the Moon dust and never made it back to Earth. One of Apollo 15's major discoveries was a moon rock that was 4.1 billion years old, later dubbed the Genesis Rock.

Apollo 16 took off on April 16, 1972. It was commanded by John Young (who had been on the Apollo 10 mission) with

Thomas Mattingly and Charles Duke as crew members. They landed on the Moon at an elevation of 25,688 feet in the Descartes Mountains. Traveling around in the Lunar Rover, Young and Duke covered 22.4 miles and set a lunar speed record of 11.2 miles per hour. They brought back 213 pounds of lunar rock and soil for analysis. As they landed, Duke's microphone cord got mixed up with the tube that had been devised to supply orange juice during the moonwalk and squirted the inside of his helmet with sticky liquid. When they blasted off they left the Lunar Rover behind with a television camera attached to it. It relayed live pictures of the blast-off of the lunar module back to Earth.

The last Apollo mission to the Moon was Apollo 17, which left the Earth on December 7, 1972 and returned on December 19. The lunar module, with astronauts Eugene Cernan and Harrison Schmitt aboard, touched down in the Valley of Taurus-Littrow at 2:54 p.m. on December 11. Ronald Evans remained in the command module. The two lunar astronauts spent 75 hours on the surface of the Moon, and spent 22 hours outside the module. They returned with 250 pounds of lunar material. They left the Moon at 5:50 p.m. on December 14, 1972. Gene Cernan was the last human to walk on the Moon. As he left he made a little speech saying that humans would return one day and left a plaque recording the event, similar to the one left by Apollo 11 when it made the first lunar landing.

Where to learn more

Of all the books to appear about the Apollo missions, probably the best to date is Charles Murray and Catherine Bly Cox, *Apollo: The Race to the Moon* (New York: Simon & Schuster, 1989). Peter Ryan's, *The Invasion of the Moon, 1957-1970* (London: Penguin Books, 1971) has very good diagrams to help visualize exactly how the lunar landings took place and gives an almost minute-by-minute account of the Apollo 11 mission.

Other good books are: Richard S. Lewis, *Appointment on the Moon* (New York: Viking Press, 1968); Dale Carter, *The Final Frontier: The Rise and Fall of the American Rocket State* (London: Verso, 1988), which gives a critical analysis of the American space program; and Bruce Murray, *Journey Into Space: The First Thirty Years of Space Exploration* (New York: W.W. Norton & Company, 1989).

NASA has published two official histories that contain many remarkable photographs: Edgar M. Cortright, *Apollo Expeditions* (Washington, D.C.: NASA, 1975) and *Chariots for Apollo: A History of Manned Lunar Spacecraft* (Washington, D.C.: NASA, 1979).

Two books have appeared that are based on interviews with the astronauts who made the historic flights: Douglas MacKinnon and Joseph Baldanza, *Footprints* (Washington, D.C.: Acropolis Books, Ltd., 1985), which includes verbatim interviews with the 12 astronauts that walked on the moon, and Harry Hurt III, *For All Mankind* (New York: Atlantic Monthly Press, 1988).

Neil Armstrong

(1930 -   )

Neil Armstrong is an American astronaut who was the first human to walk on the surface of the Moon.

Neil Armstrong was born in Wapakoneta, Ohio on August 5, 1930. He started learning to fly at age 14 and got his wings two years later, paying the $9.00 an hour fee for his flying lessons by doing odd jobs. After he graduated from high school, he entered Purdue University to study aeronautical engineering on a Navy scholarship. After two years of college he was called to active duty and flew 78 combat missions from the aircraft carrier *Essex* during the Korean War. He was shot down once but managed to parachute to safety. He was awarded three air medals.

After the Korean War Armstrong returned to Purdue and received his B.Sc. degree in 1955. He was then hired as a civilian

Neil Armstrong. NASA

research pilot flying experimental planes out of Edwards Air Force Base in California. In 1962 he was one of the second group of astronauts chosen by NASA (the National Aeronautics and Space Administration) and the first civilian. He made his first space flight on March 16, 1966 as commander of the Gemini 8 mission. During this flight, he accomplished the first successful docking of two orbiting spacecraft when he linked up with an Agena target vehicle. Half an hour after the link-up the two vessels starting spinning out of control. Armstrong thought that it was the Agena that was causing the problem and disengaged. In fact, one of the thrusters on his own spacecraft was malfunctioning, and he had to end the mission.

In January 1969 Armstrong was named commander of the Apollo 11 mission that was to be the first attempt to land humans on the Moon. On July 16, 1969, Armstrong and his colleagues Edwin "Buzz" Aldrin and Michael Collins took off from the Cape Canaveral space center on a Saturn rocket. Aboard the spacecraft were small sections of the wing and propeller of the Wright Brothers airplane that had first flown from Kitty Hawk, North Carolina on December 17, 1903. The Saturn entered lunar orbit on July 19. The next day, Sunday the 20th, Armstrong and Aldrin entered the lunar module named *Eagle* that was to separate from the command module *Columbia,* with Collins in charge. After about five hours of tests *Eagle* separated from *Columbia* and entered its own orbit. After less than two hours in orbit Armstrong fired the engines that steered the landing craft to the surface of the Moon, 300 miles below.

It took about 12 minutes to make the descent. As they were about to land Armstrong saw that their course would take them right into the middle of a boulder-strewn crater and was able to delay the touchdown to a flatter area in the Sea of Tranquillity, about four miles from the originally targeted landing point. At 4:17 p.m. (EST) on July 20, 1969, Armstrong radioed to mission control in Florida: "Houston, Tranquillity base here, the *Eagle* has landed." At about the same time a Soviet Luna rocket was only 10 miles above the surface of the Moon, but it later crashed into the Sea of Crises.

A little less than seven hours later, after eating a meal and waiting for the cabin to depressurize, the two astronauts opened the hatch of the landing craft, and Armstrong climbed out onto the ladder. He climbed down the nine steps, and at 10:56 p.m. became the first human to reach the surface of the Moon. "That's one small step for a man, one giant leap for mankind" were the words he spoke on the historic occasion. Aldrin joined him shortly thereafter. As Aldrin climbed down the ladder, he radioed to Armstrong, "Now I want to partially close the hatch, making sure not to lock it on my way out." Armstrong replied, "A good thought." The two of them spent the next two hours and 37 minutes collecting samples of the rocks and soil around the landing craft, setting up scientific instruments, and planting the American flag. (NASA had wanted to put up a flag of the United Nations, but that had been blocked by the U.S. Congress.) They also set up a plaque telling about their achievement: "We came in peace for all mankind." All the while they were able to transmit live television pictures back to Earth, and President Richard Nixon placed a telephone call to them from the White House.

Armstrong and Aldrin then returned to the landing module, where they ate another meal and rested for eight hours before firing the rocket boosters that launched the landing craft off the surface of the Moon. The ascent rocket burned itself out seven minutes later after putting the spacecraft in an orbit about 50 miles above the lunar surface. *Eagle* docked with *Columbia* about two hours after it reached orbit. When they docked the aim was slightly inaccurate and the impact set the two craft spinning, but the astronauts were able to use their thrusters to control the spin. The crew then unloaded their equipment from the *Eagle* onto the *Columbia* and jettisoned the *Eagle*. The *Columbia* set off for Earth during its 31st orbit of the Moon. It took about 60 hours to cover the 236,642 miles from the Moon to the Earth.

The three men splashed down in the Pacific Ocean on July 24 and were met by Navy frogmen from the aircraft carrier *Hornet*. Special precautions were taken to prevent contamination with any germs imported from space. Armstrong, Aldrin, and Collins were placed in quarantine for 18 days while the ship traveled to Hawaii. From there the astronauts were flown to Houston, where they received an enormous welcome. Armstrong went on to address a joint session of the U.S. Congress on September 16, 1969.

Following the flight to the Moon, Armstrong was appointed Deputy Associate Administrator of NASA for Aeronautics. He left the agency in 1971 to become professor of aerospace engineering at the University of Cincinnati. In 1979 he founded his own computer systems company and has been president of that company ever since. He has continued to serve as adviser to the U.S. space program and in 1986 was the vice-chairman of the Presidential Commission appointed to investigate the *Challenger* space shuttle disaster.

Where to learn more

The three astronauts who traveled to the Moon collaborated on a book about their flight: *First on the Moon*, written with Gene Farmer & Dora Jane Hamblin (Boston: Little, Brown & Co, 1970). Michael Collins wrote an autobiography, *Carrying the Fire: An Astronaut's Journeys*, first published in 1974 (New York: Farrar, Straus & Giroux) and then in a new edition in 1989. Buzz Aldrin also wrote about his life in collaboration with Malcolm McConnell, *Men From Earth* (New York: Bantam, 1989). There are interviews with all twelve of the astronauts who flew to the Moon in *Footprints* by Douglas MacKinnon & Joseph Baldanza (Washington, D.C.: Acropolis Books, Ltd., 1985). However, Armstrong did not give a live interview and his quotations are from previously published interviews.

A day-by-day, hour-by-hour, and sometimes minute-by-minute account of the historic flight is given in Peter Ryan's *The Invasion of the Moon, 1957-1970* (London: Penguin Books, 1971).

William Henry Ashley

(1778 - 1838)

William Henry Ashley, one of the organizers of the American fur trade, led an exploring expedition to the Green River in Wyoming and Utah.

William Henry Ashley was born in Powhatan County, Virginia, west of Richmond. He moved west and settled in Missouri sometime between 1803 and 1805. He went into the mining business and prospered selling saltpeter (needed to make gunpowder) during the War of 1812. He took on a series of local posts and was elected Lieutenant Governor of Missouri when the state entered the Union in 1820.

Always looking for a profit, in 1822 Ashley and his partner Andrew Henry went into the fur-trading business that was just beginning in the newly opened lands of the Louisiana Purchase. They sent a large group of men, including **Jedediah Smith**, up the Missouri River as far as where it meets the Yellowstone River in extreme western North Dakota. On their way back with a large supply of furs this party was attacked by members of the Arikara tribe, and fourteen of the trappers were killed and most of the furs were lost.

Trying to recoup their losses Ashley and Henry sent out another party led by Henry that traveled from Fort Kiowa in southern South Dakota to the Yellowstone River but was once again met with hostility from Native Americans and accomplished little. Another group led by Smith went south of this area to the Green River in western Wyoming and reported better prospects. Ashley, who was $100,000 in debt by this time, determined to follow up on Smith's findings himself. He left from Fort Atkinson on the Missouri River north of present-day Omaha on November 3, 1824 with a party of 25 men, 50 pack horses and a number of horse-drawn wagons. They traveled south of the Platte River in the dead of winter and had to abandon the wagons and many of the horses along the way. They would have died of starvation if they had not been welcomed by Pawnee tribesmen near the fork of the North and South Platte Rivers in western Nebraska.

After resting in the Pawnee village, Ashley and his men went up the South Platte to the Rocky Mountains and crossed the Front Range in three days. They then crossed the Medicine Bow Mountains in southern Wyoming and went north around the Red Desert to the Big Sandy River and followed it to the Green River, which they reached on April 15, 1825. They then became the first Westerners to navigate the Green River by building boats out of buffalo hides and floating downstream through its turbulent waters. Ashley himself could not swim and almost drowned when his boat capsized in a whirlpool. Legend has it that he was rescued by **Jim Beckwourth**, although there are doubts as to whether Beckwourth's account is strictly true.

Ashley and his party followed the Green River through Red Canyon (where he wrote his name on the mountain wall), Flaming Gorge, Lodore Canyon, and Split Mountain Gorge, all of which are modern day national forest, recreation or wilderness areas. They met up with a party of French trappers and joined forces with them. Together they traveled as far as the Uinta River in northeastern Utah and then went up that river to its source in the Uinta Mountains where they traded for furs with members of the Ute tribe. They traveled overland to the north to the point where Henry's Fork meets the Green River in southern Wyoming.

Ashley had set this point as the rendezvous for all of the trapping parties he had sent out along the way plus the French party and the deserters from **Peter Skene Ogden**'s Hudson's Bay Company expedition. This was the origin of the annual fur rendezvous which was to be the main feature of the fur trade in the United States for as long as it lasted. Every year at a set time and place trappers and traders from all over the West met to trade and socialize (where many of them lost all their money gambling).

From the rendezvous point Ashley took his valuable supply of furs and headed north to the Yellowstone River and from there down the Missouri. This time he was not worried by attacks from the Native Americans because he had received word that he would be met by a U.S. Army expedition under Colonel Leavenworth. He made it home to St. Louis safely and the profit he made from selling his furs got him out of debt and started him on the road to a new fortune. The following year he traveled to the rendezvous on the Cache River and there he sold his fur-trading business to Jedediah Smith and other trappers. He returned to St. Louis to continue his political career.

Ashley lost a race for governor in 1824 and one for senator in 1829. He was elected to the House of Representatives in 1831 to fill a vacancy left by a member who had been killed in a duel. Ashley represented his district in Congress until 1837. During this time he served on the House Committee on Indian Affairs where he was one of the loudest voices urging the government to pursue a vigorous policy in pushing the Native Americans off their land. He retired in poor health in 1837 and returned to Missouri where he died from pneumonia on March 26, 1838.

Where to learn more

A good general introduction to the history of western exploration, which includes a section on Ashley, can be found in William H. Goetzmann, *Exploration and Empire* (New York: William Morrow & Co., 1966).

More specific information on Ashley is presented in: Dale L. Morgan, ed. "The Diary of William H. Ashley," *Missouri Historical Society Bulletin*, vol. 11 (1954-1955), pp. 9-40, 158-186, 279-302; Harrison C. Dale, ed. *The Ashley-Smith Explorations and the Discovery of a Central Route to the Pacific,* *1822-1829* (Glendale, California: Arthur H. Clark Co., 1941); Dale L. Morgan, *The West of William H. Ashley* (Denver: The Old West Publishing Co., 1964); Richard M. Clokey, *William H. Ashley: Enterprise and Politics in the Trans-Mississippi West* (Norman: University of Oklahoma Press, 1980). There is also a chapter on Ashley by Harvey L. Carter, a Professor of History at Colorado College, in *Mountain Men and Fur Traders of the Far West*, edited by LeRoy R. Hafen, in a paperback edition published by the University of Nebraska Press in 1982.

Vladimir Vasilyevich Atlasov

(? - 1711)

Vladimir Vasilyevich Atlasov was a Russian Cossack who explored the Kamchatka Peninsula and claimed it for the Russian tsar.

As the Russians expanded eastward through Siberia to the Pacific Ocean, the main routes of exploration lay generally north because the northern areas were the sources of the best furs, the main economic motive pushing the Russians on. As part of this movement east the Russians had built a fort in 1656 on the Anadyr River, which flows into the Pacific Ocean at the far northern Barents Sea. In their trade with local tribes they heard about a great peninsula to the south—an area called Kamchatka.

In 1695 a Cossack peasant from the Russian town of Ustyug, Vladimir Vasilyevich Atlasov, was made manager of the Anadyr fort. Atlasov sent one of his men, Luka Morozko, to the northern part of Kamchatka in 1696, and then led a major expedition there himself in 1697.

Atlasov, at the head of a group of 120 men, started down the western side of the peninsula, demanding tribute from the Koryaks, the people who inhabited that part of Kamchatka. He then crossed over the mountain range that makes up the central spine of the peninsula and headed down the Pacific side. He proclaimed the Russian annexation of Kamchatka in 1697 by erecting a cross on the Krestovka River, a tributary of the Kamchatka River.

At this point in his trip, Atlasov ran into trouble. His force was made up of Russians and of Yukagirs, the native people of the area around Anadyrsk. The Yukagirs on the expedition heard that their kinsmen back home had revolted against Russian rule, and they themselves turned against Atlasov. They killed three Russians and wounded Atlasov and fourteen others before they were subdued by another party of Russians led by Morozko.

Following these difficulties, Atlasov crossed and recrossed the peninsula until he discovered the Kamchatka River on the eastern side, where there were numerous settlements of another people, the Kamchadals. Atlasov estimated their population at 25,000. The Kamchadals did not have metal tools of any kind, but they did have some wooden lacquered articles, which they had gotten from tribes to the south. We now know that these had come from Japan.

Some of the Kamchadals were friendly, some were not, but Atlasov was able to exact tribute from all of them. On his return to a base camp he discovered that his reindeer had been stolen by a party of Koryak marauders. He chased them and fought a pitched battle that left 150 Koryaks dead.

Atlasov continued south on the west coast. Here he made two interesting discoveries. One was reports of the Ainu, a people of Caucasian origin who were the original inhabitants of Japan and who lived as far north as the Kurile Islands and the southern tip of Kamchatka. The other was the first Russian encounter with a Japanese.

The Japanese man had been captured by Kurile Islanders. The Russians were struck by this first representative they met from the civilization of Japan, and Atlasov wrote a long report about him and his "Hindu" writings. He was so struck that he took the man, Denbei, back with him to Anadyrsk and then sent him as a gift to Tsar Peter I in St. Petersburg, where he lived from 1701 until his death in 1705.

Atlasov made it almost to the southern tip of Kamchatka where he could see the northernmost of the Kurile Islands, which has been named for him—Atlasov Island. On his way back north he founded the fort of Verkhne-Kamchatsk on the Kamchatka River. He returned to Anadyrsk on July 2, 1699.

Atlasov went to Yakutsk to report on his expedition, which the governor considered so important that he sent him all the way to Moscow to tell his story in person. He arrived there in February 1701. He was made the officer in charge of Kamchatka and was sent back to take over the government of the new territory. Along the way, however, he and his party of ten men attacked and robbed a Russian merchant who was on his way back from China. The crime was discovered and Atlasov was thrown into prison in Yakutsk.

In the meantime, other Cossacks attempted to control Kamchatka but their methods were so harsh that the local peoples revolted. Atlasov was released from prison in 1707 and ordered to take charge of the Kamchatka situation. His own methods were so cruel that his Cossacks revolted and imprisoned him at Verkhne-Kamchatsk. He escaped to the newer fort at Nizhne-Kamchatsk, at the mouth of the Kamchatka River. However, a rebel band of Cossacks searched him out there and killed him in his sleep in February 1711.

Where to learn more

The best account in English, and the one on which this account is based, of the Russian penetration of Siberia is by George V. Lantzeff and Richard A. Pierce, *Eastward to Empire: Exploration and Conquest on the Russian Open Frontier, to 1750* (Montreal: McGill-Queen's University Press, 1973).

Francisco de Azevado

(1578 - 1660)

Francisco de Azevado was a Portuguese Jesuit missionary who made a trip to Tibet and Ladakh to try to establish Christian missions there.

Francisco de Azevado was a native of Portugal who entered a Jesuit seminary as a young man. After his ordination as a Roman Catholic priest, he was sent to southern India in 1610 to work as a missionary. He gained the trust of his superiors, and in 1630 was sent by the head of the Jesuits in Goa, **Antonio de Andrade**, to Tsaparang in the Himalayas to find out why the Jesuit mission there had been closed.

Traveling north to Kashmir, at the city of Srinigar, Azevado met Brother Manuel Marques, Andrade's co-worker, on his way back from Mana, on the Tibetan border, to get supplies and to send Andrade a report on the Tsaparang situation. They were forced to stay for a while in Srinigar to witness the funeral of the recently deceased Rajah, including the ritual death of 60 of his widows. Together Azevado and Marques began the journey to Tsaparang.

Once he got to Tsaparang on August 25, 1631, Azevado found that the situation there had changed greatly since the departure of Andrade. It was now ruled by the King of Ladakh (a region in the northeastern part of Kashmir), who was represented in Tsaparang by a governor who hated the Christians. Faced with this situation, Azevado decided to travel to Leh, the capital of Ladakh, to appeal to the new king to allow the work of the Catholic mission to continue. He was able to join a caravan of horse dealers who were traveling to Leh in October 1631.

It took Azevado 21 days to travel from Tsaparang to Leh. He was the first European to visit the remote city. Immediately after his arrival, he was presented to the King and Queen in order to present his presents, but it was four days before he was allowed to discuss any business. Once he was able to make his request, the King listened sympathetically and gave orders that the missionaries could continue their work. He even gave Azevado a gift—a broken-down old horse.

Azevado then returned to India in order to report his good news. He left Leh at the beginning of November, and winter had already set in. It was already late in the year, and the mountain passes were so cold and icy that he wore out his shoes and crippled himself. He had to be carried in a litter during the last part of the trip.

Azevado reached Agra, the capital city of the Mogul Empire in India on January 3, 1632. His journey had been successful, but the results were not very long-lived. The Buddhists in Tsaparang continued to be hostile to the Jesuits, and they were forced to abandon the mission there for good in 1635. It was to be another thirty years after Azevado's trip that the Jesuits **Johann Grüber** and Albert d'Orville were to travel to Tibet to try once again to establish Christianity north of the Himalayas.

Where to learn more

John MacGregor, *Tibet: A Chronicle of Exploration* (London: Routledge & Kegan Paul, 1970) is the best available source in English of the entire field of Tibetan exploration. One earlier source is C. Wessels, *Early Jesuit Travellers in Central Asia, 1603-1721* (the Hague: Martinus Nijhoff, 1924).

Sir George Back

(1796 - 1878)

Sir George Back was a British naval officer who took part in four expeditions to the Canadian Arctic and was the first European to see and travel down the Great Fish River, later renamed the Back River.

George Back was born in the town of Stockport in the English county of Cheshire. He entered the Royal Navy as a midshipman in 1808. During the war with Napoleon's France he was captured and taken prisoner at the age of 13 in 1809. He was held at the French fortress of Verdun where he studied mathematics, French and drawing. Following the end of the war he traveled across France by foot during the winter of 1813-1814 to get back to England. He then served on a British ship off the coast of North America that was hit by a hurricane and almost sank in 1815.

In 1818 Back volunteered to serve with **Sir John Franklin** on the *Trent* that was sent to survey the Arctic Ocean north of

Sir George Back. The Granger Collection, New York.

Spitsbergen. In 1819 he agreed to accompany Franklin on the first overland expedition to the Coppermine River in northern Canada. He traveled 1,204 miles during the winter of 1820-1821 to bring supplies from Fort Chipewyan, an outpost of the Hudson's Bay Company, to the makeshift headquarters that Franklin had constructed and named Fort Enterprise. It was only because of Back's efforts that the expedition did not starve to death. During the long winter, Back and his fellow midshipman on the expedition, Robert Hood, both fell in love with a 15-year-old Native American girl named Greenstockings and were prepared to fight a duel over her until one of the other members of the expedition removed their pistols.

Once the expedition reached the Coppermine River, they were deserted by the native Canadian *voyageurs* who served as guides and porters. Back was sent back to Fort Enterprise to find them. He found it deserted and continued his search farther. He returned to Fort Enterprise on November 7, 1821 with a party of Native Americans to find the remnants of the Franklin expedition. He arrived in time to save all of the British explorers except for his old rival Hood who had committed suicide. But during the course of the expedition one Inuit and nine Canadian *voyageurs* had died from starvation and overexertion.

On his return to England, Back was promoted to lieutenant and served for a year on a ship in the Caribbean. He was then chosen by the Admiralty to go on a second Franklin overland expedition even though Franklin did not want him. Traveling overland from New York, they left the Great Slave Lake in late June 1826 and reached the mouth of the Mackenzie River on July 27, 1826. On the return of the expedition to England in 1827, Back was promoted to commander.

Unable to get a ship to command, Back spent the next few years in Italy studying art. There he received the news that an expedition was to be sent out to try to find **Sir John Ross**, who had been missing for four years. Back volunteered his services and was accepted by the Royal Geographical Society with a grant from the government. He set out in June 1833 with a party numbering 20, including a medical officer, Dr. Richard King. They spent the winter of 1833-1834 at a post called Fort Reliance that they had constructed near the Great Slave Lake.

On his earlier expeditions, Back had heard rumors of a river that flowed northeastward east of the Great Slave Lake through the tundra. In spite of doubts among Hudson's Bay Company traders, he set out to find it. He reached the headwaters of the Great Fish River in early 1834. There he received word that Ross had returned safely, and he was able to devote his time to exploring the river. He sailed down it during the summer of 1834, traversing or going around its numerous falls and rapids. The river was later renamed in his honor. He saw the Boothia Peninsula but could not determine whether it was an island or not. He did not explore any farther but turned back the way it came. He reached a Hudson's Bay post in August 1835 and returned to England in October of that year.

Back was promoted to captain and given the Gold Medal of the Royal Geographical Society. Back was sent back in the ship *Terror* in 1836 with orders to winter at Repulse Bay and to cross the Melville Peninsula to see what was on the other side. One the officers on the ship was **Sir Robert McClure**, who would later return as an Arctic explorer in his own right. The expedition was a disaster. The ship was caught in the ice off Cape Comfort in the Frozen Channel for ten months and almost destroyed. For three days in July it was forced by the ice onto its side, but finally righted itself. Heading back to England, Back was forced to beach the ship in Lough Swilly in Ireland on September 3, 1837, just as it was sinking.

This was Back's last expedition. He was an invalid for the next six years and was unable to resume his Navy duties. He received two medals from the Royal Geographical Society in 1837 and was knighted in 1839. He later carried out some administrative duties for the Navy and was made an admiral in 1857 as well as receiving other honors. He died on June 23, 1878.

Where to learn more

Back wrote two books about his experiences. The first, published in London in 1836, was *A Narrative of the Arctic Land Expedition to the Mouth of the Great Fish River in 1834 and 1835*. It was reprinted in 1970 (Edmonton, Alberta: Hurtig). The second was *Narrative of an Expedition in Her Majesty's Ship Terror in the Years 1836 and 1837* (London: John Murray, 1838).

An excellent modern source for the history of the exploration of the Canadian Arctic is *The Arctic Grail: The Quest for the North West Passage and the North Pole, 1818-1909* (New York: Viking, 1988) by the popular Canadian author Pierre Berton. It is available in a paperback edition by Penguin Books.

William Baffin

(1584?-1622)

William Baffin was an English pilot who made two trips to the Canadian Arctic to try to find the Northwest Passage to Asia.

William Baffin was born near London, probably in 1584. We know nothing about his early life except that he was self-educated in navigation and mathematics.

In 1612 Baffin sailed as chief pilot on the expedition of Captain James Hall to Greenland. Hall was killed by the native Inuit of Greenland, and Baffin returned to England to write an account of the expedition, which includes important astronomical observations and descriptions of Greenland.

In 1613 and 1614 Baffin sailed north of Scandinavia with ships of the Muscovy Company to hunt for whales near the Spitsbergen Islands, and he explored along the coasts of those islands. As a result of his experience in the Arctic, Baffin was chosen to be chief pilot for an expedition commanded by **Robert Bylot** to explore Hudson Bay, discovered in 1611 by **Henry Hudson**, to see if it led to the Northwest Passage around North America. They sailed from England on March 15, 1615.

Bylot's voyage in his ship the *Discovery* was made famous by Baffin's navigational and geographical observations which were found to be amazingly accurate by later explorers. The 19th-century explorer **William Edward Parry** named Baffin Island after the pilot because he was so impressed with his work. The expedition however could not enter Hudson Bay because of heavy ice conditions in the fall of 1615. Baffin concluded, correctly, that there was no entrance to the Northwest Passage from the Bay.

On March 26, 1616 Baffin and Bylot sailed once again from England in the *Discovery*. This time they sailed around the great body of water known as Baffin Bay between Greenland and Baffin Island. They sailed farther north than any European had been before in North America, and their record was not matched for another 236 years. In fact, although Baffin's observations were very accurate, future generations did not even believe in the existence of Baffin Bay, and it disappeared from maps until **Sir John Ross** confirmed it in 1818. But the men on *Discovery* were not able to find a way out of the Baffin Bay into the Northwest Passage.

When Baffin returned to England, he decided he would try to find the Passage by approaching it from the other side—from Asia. He sailed on a ship of the East India Company on February 4, 1617 and reached India in September. From there he went to the Persian Gulf before returning to India without even getting near the Pacific. He sailed again on March 25, 1620 in a fleet that was sent to attack Portuguese possessions in the Indian Ocean. He was killed in a battle off the port of Ormuz in the Persian Gulf on January 20, 1622, "as he was trying his mathematical projects and conclusions."

Where to learn more

The original record of Baffin's voyages are found in Clements K. Markham, ed. *The Voyages of William Baffin, 1612-1622* (London: Hakluyt Society, 1881). A good summary of early Arctic exploration is Tryggvi J. Olesen, *Early Voyages and Northern Approaches 1000-1632* (Toronto: McClelland and Stewart Ltd., 1963).

William Balfour Baikie

(1825 - 1864)

William Balfour Baikie was a Scottish doctor who led an exploring expedition up the Niger River and then returned to become the first European to set up permanent headquarters in the interior of Africa.

William Balfour Baikie was born in the Orkney Islands off the northern coast of Scotland on August 27, 1825, the son of a Royal Navy officer. He graduated with a medical degree from the University of Edinburgh in 1848 and became a doctor on a Royal Navy ship. In 1851 he became the assistant surgeon at a hospital in London and then used his influence to get appointed surgeon on board a ship being sent to the Niger River.

In 1852 the British Foreign Office decided to send a Royal Navy ship to meet **Heinrich Barth** who was on the upper Niger River. The British Admiralty constructed a specially designed ship named the *Pleiad* and sent it up to the Bight of Biafra on the coast of Nigeria in 1854. The ship's captain died along the way and command was turned over to Baikie who was the ship's doctor and naturalist. Baikie pioneered the use of quinine on

William Balfour Baikie. The Granger Collection, New York.

board the *Pleiad* to prevent malaria, and as a result none of the ship's crew of 12 Europeans and 54 Africans died.

The *Pleiad* headed up the Niger in June 1854. Along the way it stopped to trade for ivory and in a single day bought as much as 620 pounds of ivory. The ship reached the confluence of the Niger with the Benue River in central Nigeria but did not find Barth. He had already headed west to Timbuktu and then traveled over the Sahara Desert to Tripoli. The ship, under Baikie's command, penetrated 250 miles farther up the Niger than any previous expedition. The *Pleiad* returned to England in February 1855 without having lost any men and with a valuable cargo of ivory. The way was now open for the British to exploit the Niger valley without the great human losses that had always deterred European imperialists in the past.

In order to take advantage of this opportunity Baikie returned to Nigeria in May 1857 in the steamer *Dayspring*. He established a trading post at the mouth of the Niger and another at the confluence of the Niger and Benue. By these posts, the British were able to tap the trade of the great city of Kano, which previously had traded mainly to the north via the Sahara caravans, a journey of 14 months. The *Dayspring* stayed for three weeks at the confluence setting up the trading post and then headed upriver. On October 7, 1857 it ran into a hidden rock in the river and sank. The expedition consisting of Baikie, 15 Europeans and 38 Africans was stranded on the east bank of the Niger for 364 days until a British relief vessel arrived to pick them up. Once again, they all survived.

While they were stranded Lieutenant Glover, Baikie's second in command traveled 700 miles along the Niger and reached the Bussa rapids where **Mungo Park** had died. He bought Park's nautical almanac from a the chief of a nearby village. When the relief steamer arrived, Baikie traveled with it to the confluence where he set up a farm and began a term as British consul. He became the first British settler in west Africa and the precursor of British rule of Nigeria.

Baikie stayed at the place he named Lokoja for five years. He adopted local customs and cultivated native African plants. He set up house with a local woman; they had several children. He translated the Book of Genesis and the Anglican Book of Common Prayer into Hausa, the language spoken by millions of inhabitants in Nigeria's north and northeast, and collected vocabularies of several other languages. He cleared 100 acres of farmland, built houses and often worked 14-hour days. All of this went a long way toward proving that Europeans could live and work in Africa, or any of the world's other tropical regions for that matter. He also worked to break the power of the slave trade in the region and bought many slaves himself in order to set them free. He served as an adviser to the local ruler, the Emir of Nupe.

In 1861 the British Foreign Office drafted instructions to recall Baikie as a cost-cutting measure. The order did not reach him for a year and he then was able to keep delaying his departure for another two years. However, after suffering what Baikie said was 100 bouts of fever, his health was impaired and he left Lokoja in October 1864 on a paddle-steamer that brought out a new British official to serve as consul. Baikie got as far as Sierra Leone on the west coast of Africa, where he died of dysentery on December 12, 1864. Queen Victoria wrote a personal letter to the Emir of Nupe on July 20, 1865 to inform him of Baikie's death and to request his assistance in stamping out the slave trade.

Where to learn more

Baikie's story of his first expedition is told in *Narrative of an Exploring Voyage up the . . . Niger and Isadda* (London, 1856). Excerpts from this book are included in Margery Perham & J. Simmons, *African Discovery: An Anthology of Exploration* (Chicago: Northwestern University Press, 1963).

Later books about Baikie are: A.C.G. Hastings, *Voyage of the Dayspring* (London: 1926) and Duran-Reynals, *The Fever Tree* (Paris: 1960). A very well-researched and readable book about the history of Niger River exploration includes material on Baikie: Sanche de Gramont, *The Strong Brown God* (Boston: Houghton Mifflin Company, 1975).

Samuel White Baker

(1821 - 1893)

Florence Baker

(1841 - 1916)

Samuel White Baker was a British explorer in the southern Sudan and, accompanied by his future wife, Florence, was the first European to see Lake Albert.

Samuel White Baker was born in the county of Gloucestershire in England on June 8, 1821. His father was a wealthy sugar merchant who owned estates in the Caribbean and on the island of Mauritius in the Indian Ocean. He was educated at home and then sent to Frankfurt in Germany to complete his studies. He helped manage one of his father's estates on Mauritius for a while and then made a trip to Sri Lanka in 1846. He was very attracted to the island and returned there the following year with his wife and 18 other settlers to found a farming colony in the Sri Lankan highlands.

Baker stayed in Sri Lanka for nine years. The colony was a success, and he spent much of his time exploring the island and hunting. He wrote about his experiences in two books—*The Rifle and Hound in Ceylon*, published in 1854, and *Eight Years' Wanderings in Ceylon*, published in 1855. Baker, however, suffered from tropical diseases and was forced to return to England in 1855. His wife died from typhus fever shortly after their return.

At loose ends, in 1858 Baker agreed to accompany a young Indian maharajah, Duleep Singh, who was being educated in England on a trip to Constantinople (now Istanbul) in Turkey. Along the way they stopped at a port on the Danube River called Widdin (now Vidin in Bulgaria). At that time all of the Balkan Peninsula was ruled by the Ottoman Turks, and slavery still existed in the Ottoman Empire. Baker and Duleep Singh attended a slave auction in Widdin, and there Baker bought a young

Samuel White Baker. The Granger Collection, New York.

Florence Baker. The Granger Collection, New York.

ethnic German woman, whom he named Florence. She had been born in what is now the Romanian province of Transylvania on August 6, 1841 into a German family named Sass. Her family had been killed in an uprising in 1848, and she was adopted by an Armenian merchant named Finnian who later put her on the auction block. From these facts, Baker later concocted a false tale that Florence was the daughter of a wealthy German named Herr Finian von Saas.

In the meantime, it was impossible for Baker to return to England with Florence. He therefore took a job with a British company that was building a railroad to the Romanian port of Constanta on the Black Sea. He and Florence stayed there until the end of 1860. In the meantime, **John Hanning Speke** had returned from his expedition with **Richard Burton** and reported the discovery of Lake Victoria in east Africa, which he believed to be the source of the Nile River. In order to prove his theory, Speke returned to Africa in April 1860 with **James Augustus Grant**. White decided that he would travel south up the Nile River and meet Speke and Grant as they emerged from the sources of the Nile in what is now Uganda.

Baker and Florence left Cairo on April 15, 1861. They traveled up the Nile to what is now northern Sudan. Since Speke was not expected to emerge until 1863, Baker decided to spend some time exploring the tributaries of the Nile that originated in the highlands of Ethiopia. He traveled up the Atbara, Setit, Bahr-el-Salam, and Angareb Rivers before continuing on the journey to Khartoum, which he reached on June 11, 1862. Khartoum, now the capital of Sudan, was the last outpost of Egyptian rule and was also a major slave-trading center. Baker and Florence arrived there at the same time as the Dutch explorer **Alexine Tinné**.

In Khartoum Baker met the British consul John Petherick who had been officially delegated to proceed south and meet Speke and Grant. Petherick was being very slow in his preparations however, and Baker decided to head out on his own. Unable to get official backing, he assembled his own little army, whose uniforms he designed and paid for. They left Khartoum on December 18, 1862. They reached Gondokoro, a slave emporium and last known spot coming from the north, on February 2, 1863. Speke had not yet arrived.

They only had a short wait. Speke and Grant showed up in the company of an Arab slaving expedition on February 15. Speke and Baker were acquainted, but Speke had no idea that it would be Baker who came to meet him, shouting "Hurrah for Old England." Speke had been expecting Petherick, who did not arrive until February 20. Speke thought that the delay had been caused by Petherick misusing the funds that had been raised for Speke. On his return to England, he had Petherick removed from office, and his reputation was ruined.

Baker was disappointed when he learned that Speke had indeed found the source of the Nile River. But Speke also told him about another large lake, the Luta N'zige, which was supposed to be connected to the Nile system but which remained unexplored. Baker decided to investigate this report, and he started out with Florence and part of their original party in March 1863. In order to proceed, they were forced to attach themselves to a slave trader's caravan. They did not reach the Kingdom of Bunyoro until January 1864. The ruler of the kingdom, Kamurasi, wanted to keep Florence for one of his numerous wives and tried to force Baker to give her up in return for an escort to the Luta N'zige.

Baker talked his way out of that situation, and the two of them left Kamurasi's capital together. However, along the way, Florence was overcome by heat and went into a coma that lasted for several days. After she came out of the coma, she was subject to delirium for a time. But nothing would stop Baker, and he had her tied to a litter and transported with him to find the lake. Finally, on March 14, 1864 they reached Luta N'zige, which Baker renamed Lake Albert in honor of Queen Victoria's consort. They were able to get some canoes and paddled to where the Nile enters the lake. A short distance from there they came upon one of the world's greatest waterfalls, which they named Murchison Falls, in honor of the president of the Royal Geographical Society.

Baker was awarded the Gold Medal of the Royal Geographical Society even before his return to England, and in 1866 he received a knighthood. It was only on his return to England in October 1865 that he secretly married Florence before introducing her to his family and to English society. The next few years Baker spent quietly at an estate he acquired in Norfolk county. In 1869 he was asked to accompany the Prince of Wales on a trip to Egypt. As a result of this trip, the Khedive (ruler) of Egypt appointed him Governor of the Equatorial Nile basin on April 1, 1869. At this time Egypt was nominally part of the Turkish Ottoman Empire but was in fact more and more a ward of the British Empire. Baker's appointment was one of the first in which the two countries collaborated to found what was to become known as the Anglo-Egyptian Sudan.

Baker and Florence (now known as Lady Baker) left Cairo on December 1, 1870 and reached Gondokoro on April 15, 1871 and took possession of it in the name of Egypt on May 26, 1871. They then headed south to the regions they had explored in 1863 and 1864. However, the Africans were not at all anxious to be annexed to Egypt, and he met hostility everywhere. In May 1872 Baker was drugged by servants of the young king Kabrega who had succeeded his father Kamrasi, and the expedition was attacked. They had to fight their way back north, abandoning their supplies along the way. When they reached the post of Faliko they were attacked by one of the Arab slave traders and had to fight him as well. Upon reaching Gondokoro on April 1, 1873 Baker relinquished his command and returned to Cairo.

Following this retreat, Lady Baker refused to allow her husband to ever return to the Sudan again. But Baker stayed in touch with Sudanese affairs and was largely responsible for having General Charles ("Chinese") Gordon sent to Khartoum as governor. Gordon's presence stirred up a religious uprising, and Gordon and all of his troops were killed by troops of a popular

Muslim leader known as the Mahdi. Baker himself occupied his time with traveling and big game hunting: elephants in Africa and Sri Lanka, seven trips to India to shoot tigers, deer-stalking in Japan, bear shooting in the Rocky Mountains of the United States. He died quietly at home on December 30, 1893. Florence lived on without him until 1919.

Where to learn more

Baker's own story of his two African expeditions was published as *Albert N'yanza, Great Basin of the Nile*, 2 vols. (London: Macmillan, 1866) and *Ismailia, a Narrative of the Expedition to Central Africa for the Suppression of the Slave Trade Organized by Ismail, Khedive of Egypt*, 2 vols. (London: Macmillan, 1874; reprinted, New York: Negro Universities Press, 1969). Ex-

cerpts from these can be found in *East African Explorers*, edited by Charles Richards and James Place, London: Oxford University Press, 1960).

Of the several biographies of Baker, the one by Dorothy Middleton, *Baker of the Nile* (London: The Falcon Press, 1949) is one of the best. Much of the information about the relationship between Baker and Florence was superseded by Richard Hall in *Lovers on the Nile* (London: Collins, 1980), who searched out the truth about Florence's obscure background and told an exciting and romantic story about the couple. There is a good chapter on Baker by Robert O.Collins in Robert I. Rotberg, ed. *Africa and Its Explorers: Motives, Methods, and Impact* (Cambridge: Harvard University Press, 1970).

Florence Baker's life is discussed in Marion Tinling, *Women into the Unknown* (New York: Greenwood Press, 1989). Her diary has been published by Anne Baker, *Morning Star: Florence Baker's Dairy of the Expedition to Put Down the Slave Trade on the Nile, 1870-1873)* (London: Wm. Kimber, 1972).

Vasco Nuñez de Balboa

(1475 - 1519)

Vasco Nuñez de Balboa was a Spanish explorer who crossed the isthmus of Panama and was the first European to see the Pacific Ocean from its eastern shore.

Vasco Nuñez de Balboa was born in the town of Jerez de los Caballeros in the Spanish province of Extremadura. Coming from a family of impoverished gentry, he served as a page to a Spanish nobleman, Don Pedro Puertocarrero. In 1501 he left Spain in the expedition of Rodrigo de Bastidas, who had been inspired by reports of **Christopher Columbus** to look for pearls on the northern coast of Venezuela.

The expedition was a success. Bastidas and Balboa were able to trade their European goods for a large quantity of pearls and gold. They sailed from the Gulf of Maracaibo to the mouth of the Magdalena River in what is now Colombia. Farther west, they found the harbor that they named Cartagena, which was later to become the main Spanish port in northern South America. They followed the shoreline until it turned southward to the Gulf of Urabá. Their ship was leaking so they headed north to the island of Hispaniola where they were forced to abandon the ship on the south coast. There their goods were confiscated by the governor and Balboa was left penniless.

Balboa tried to make a living as a farmer in the new Spanish colony of Santo Domingo, but he fell into debt and was unable to pay his creditors. In order to get out of his situation, in 1510 he stowed away with his dog Leoncico on board a ship in Santo Domingo harbor. It turned out to be one of two commanded by Martín Fernandez de Enciso who was taking relief supplies to the Darien Peninsula (Panama) for the settlement of San Sebastián founded by **Alonso de Ojeda**. Ojeda had given up and had relinquished command of the garrison to **Francisco Pizarro**. Once discovered on the ship, Balboa proved to be a great help to Enciso who turned out to be an ineffective leader.

When they reached San Sebastián, they found that it had been burned down by Native Americans. Balboa then convinced the group to follow him to another spot that he had seen on his earlier expedition. He took them to the Gulf of Urabá and there founded the town of Santa Maria de la Antigua del Darién, next to a native village. Quarreling with Enciso, Balboa arrested him and sent him back to Spain and assumed the offices of Captain-General and Governor himself.

Balboa then went exploring in the neighboring region of Coiba. He made friends with a local chief, Careta, and married the chief's daughter. He arranged an alliance between the Spaniards and another powerful chief, Comogre. Comogre's oldest son saw how avid the Spanish were to get gold, and he offered to lead them to the other side of the Peninsula if they would help defeat one of his tribe's enemies. The Spanish agreed and set out with 190 Spanish soldiers and 810 Native Americans under Balboa's command on September 1, 1513. They sailed across the Gulf to the Darien Peninsula.

Part of Balboa's expedition remained behind, while he led a group through some of the roughest terrain and densest rain forest in the world. Even today, there is no road that traverses it. Balboa's party fought the enemy tribesmen in the Sierra de Quareca and won a complete victory. They then massacred the Native Americans and destroyed their village before resting. It is said that they killed 600.

Vasco Nuñez de Balboa.

Because many of the men were ill, Balboa left most of them in the village and set out with a small party of 67 to cross the mountains in the center of the peninsula. Legend has it that on the morning of Sunday, September 25, 1513, accompanied only by his dog, Balboa climbed a peak and became the first European to look out on the Pacific Ocean from its eastern shore. The other Spaniards, including Francisco Pizarro, then joined him and erected a pile of stones and a cross, knelt and sang a Catholic hymn of thanksgiving. They then marched on to arrive at the Ocean's shore and formally take possession of it in the name of the King and Queen of Spain. Twenty-six of the men witnessed this act on September 29, St. Michael's Day, and Balboa named the place Bahía San Miguel (St. Michael's Bay).

The Spanish spent a month on the Pacific shore collecting gold and pearls and visiting the Islas de las Perlas (the Pearl Islands). Crossing the isthmus by another route, they conquered more native chiefs and took even more gold. They returned to the settlement of Darien on January 19, 1514 without the loss of any Spanish lives.

On his return, however, Balboa learned that Enciso had made unfavorable reports of his actions back in Spain and that King Ferdinand of Spain was sending out a new governor. The new governor, Pedro Arias de Avila, when he arrived, developed a great hatred towards Balboa and spent several years spinning plots against him. In the meantime, Balboa spent his time crossing the Isthmus of Panama and building a fleet of four ships, at a great loss of life of the Native American laborers, with which he intended to sail south to Peru. Eventually, Arias de Avila was able to make up charges against him and sent Francisco Pizarro to arrest him. Balboa was tried and convicted of treason and publicly beheaded sometime between January 13 and 21, 1519.

Where to learn more

The basic documentary source for our information about Balboa is a book by an Italian priest, Pietro Martire d'Anghiera, usually referred to as Peter Martyr. The first English translation of his book, *The Decades of the Newe World, or West Indies* appeared in 1555. There was another translation by F.A. MacNutt in 1912. It was reprinted in New York in 1970 under the title *De Orbe Novo: The Eight Decades of Peter Martyr D'Anghiera.*

There are two good recent biographies of Balboa in English: Charles Loftus Grant Anderson, *Life and Letters of Vasco Nuñez de Balboa* (New York: Fleming H. Revell Co, 1941; reprinted, Westport, Connecticut: Greenwood Press, 1970); and Kathleen Romoli, *Balboa of Darien: Discoverer of the Pacific* (Garden City, N.Y.: Doubleday, 1953).

Sir Joseph Banks

(1743 - 1820)

Sir Joseph Banks was a British scientist who sailed with James Cook on his first voyage around the world and later became President of the Royal Society, in which post he sponsored explorations in Africa, Australia, and the Arctic.

Sir Joseph Banks. The Granger Collection, New York.

Joseph Banks was born in London on February 13, 1743. His father was a rich landholder who owned a large estate in the English county of Lincolnshire. On his father's death, Banks inherited the estate and a large fortune at the age of 18. According to Banks, in a story that he told in later years, the great transformation in his life occurred while he was a student at Eton at the age of 14. One summer evening he was walking back to school after swimming in a local pond when he looked around and saw the profusion of flowers along the lane. He decided then and there that he would devote the rest of his life to the study of nature. He studied botany at Eton and then went on to Oxford University. When he learned that the only Professor of Botany at Oxford did not give lectures, he went to Cambridge University and hired a professor to come back with him to Oxford to teach him.

Banks graduated from Oxford in December 1763. In February 1764 he came of age and took over his inheritance. Already well known for his knowledge of the natural sciences, in May 1766 Banks was made a fellow of the Royal Society, the leading British institution for the study of science. Later that year he sailed on a Fisheries Protection ship called the *Niger* to visit Newfoundland and Labrador to bring back plant specimens. On his return to England he learned, through his connections at the Royal Society, about the planned expedition of **James Cook** to the South Pacific and got the Society's backing to accompany the explorer as on-board naturalist, agreeing to pay for all his own expenses plus those of his staff.

Captain Cook's first expedition on the ship *Endeavour* left England in 1768. It stopped first in Brazil and then sailed to Tierra del Fuego at the tip of South America, where two of Banks' servants went ashore and got drunk and froze to death. They then went to Tahiti in the South Pacific, where Banks became one of the first Europeans to be tattooed by the Polynesian artists and is said to have had a romantic attachment to one or more of the Tahitian women. They then went on to New Zealand and Australia. Banks brought back with him to England 1,000 new species of plants, 500 fish, and 500 birds and "insects innumerable." On his return to England, Banks was lionized by English society. He was received by King George III, and the two remained friends for the rest of the King's life. The great Swedish naturalist Linnaeus wrote a highly complimentary tribute.

Following his first highly successful voyage, Cook set out again in 1772. Banks always intended to be a part of the voyage. In fact, he began to think of it as *his* voyage. He hired 15 people to accompany him, including two horn players. In order to accommodate all of them it was necessary to build cabins on the deck of the ship. When it became obvious that the ship could not sail with these new constructions, Cook ordered them torn down. Banks refused to cut down the members of his party or to compromise his comfort, and it is said that he stamped his feet in rage on the dockside when he could not get his way. But Cook sailed without him, to Banks' lifelong regret.

Banks consoled himself by sailing to Iceland in August 1772 where he stayed for six weeks. It was his last journey abroad. Six years later, on November 30, 1778, when Banks was 35, he was elected President of the Royal Society, probably the most prestigious scientific post in the world at that time. In that position Banks pursued an enormous number of interests. He started a library that is now kept in a separate room of the British Museum and contains a valuable collection of travel books, and he initiated a series of expeditions to collect plant specimens from around the world that are now on view at the famous Kew Gardens. It was Banks who suggested that Captain William Bligh be sent to Tahiti in the *Bounty* to collect seedlings of the breadfruit tree so that they could be grown in the West Indies to supply food for the slaves in the cane fields.

Above all, Banks was interested in exploration. He became interested in Africa at an early age and interviewed **James Bruce** on his return from Ethiopia in 1774. At a meeting in a London tavern of a group of English gentlemen on June 9, 1788 Banks proposed and had adopted a resolution to form an "Association for Promoting the Discovery of the Inland Parts of Africa," usually called the African Association. It set as its first goal the discovery of the source and flow of the Niger River. It did not waste any time—the first explorer was on his way within a month of the memorable June 9 dinner. This was John Ledyard, a 37-year-old American who had attended Dartmouth College for a short time, had been a midshipman on Captain Cook's last expedition and then made a trip into Russia and Siberia. Following that trip Ledyard showed up at Banks' door in Soho Square, in rags and without any money. Banks recommended him to the selection committee of the African Association. Ledyard made it as far as Cairo where he died after drinking a stomach remedy.

After the initial missions in 1788, Banks urged the recruitment of more explorers. As a result, **Daniel Houghton** was hired in July 1790. He also failed to return. Banks knew a gardener named James Dickson, who had written several works on botanical subjects. Dickson's Scottish wife had a younger brother named **Mungo Park**, who was studying medicine at the University of Edinburgh and wanted to travel. Banks sent him off to Africa.

Banks had tried three approaches to the Niger: from Tripoli with Simon Lucas; from Cairo with Ledyard and **Friedrich Hornemann**; and from the Gambia with Houghton and Park. He now decided that it might be worthwhile to try to approach the river from the south. In 1804, while Park was preparing for his second expedition, the African Association recruited an explorer named Henry Nicholls to start from one of the trading stations on the Gulf of Guinea and head north to find the Niger.

Nicholls arrived at the mouth of the Cross River, which, unknown to him, was just east of the Niger delta on January 14, 1805, but he died of fever in April.

Following the death of Nicholls, the African Association's most active period came to an end. Between 1805 and 1831 it sent out only two more explorers. Its membership and financial resources dwindled, and Banks was hampered by ill health and his other responsibilities from taking an active role. Eventually, in 1831, the African Association was absorbed by the newly-founded Royal Geographical Society. Banks was also actively interested in the colonization of Australia. In 1801 he sponsored the voyage of **Matthew Flinders** that sailed around Australia, paying for much of the necessary equipment out of his own pocket, and he encouraged **Gregory Blaxland** to move to the new British colony.

Banks was also involved in the renewed attempts by the British to try to find a Northwest Passage from the Atlantic to the Pacific Ocean. These efforts started in 1817 following the end of the Napoleonic Wars. For years Banks had been in communication with the whaling captain William Scoresby who had written to him about his Arctic experiences and observations. Scoresby returned from a voyage in 1817 to report that for the first time that anyone knew of the east coast of Greenland was free of ice. Banks was also visited by a furloughed naval captain **William Edward Parry**, who advocated an aggressive attempt at northern exploration. This combination of events led to the first explorations of Parry and **Sir John Ross**.

By this time Banks was getting old. He suffered increasingly from gout and had not been able to walk since 1804, having to be carried in a sedan chair or pushed around in a wheelchair. He died on June 19, 1820.

Where to learn more

The most important of Banks' papers are found in Warren R. Dawson, editor, *The Banks Letters* (London: British Museum, 1958). The important journal that Banks kept of his voyage around the world with Cook was never published in his lifetime. It was published later in the nineteenth century in a very truncated version. The definitive edition had to wait until the work of the distinguished Pacific scholar J.C. Beaglehole: *The Endeavour Journal of Joseph Banks, 1768-1771* (Sydney: Angus and Robertson, 1962). A very interesting book that discusses Banks' relationship with Cook is *The Fatal Impact* by Alan Moorehead (New York: Harper & Row, 1966).

There have been several biographies of Banks. Two fairly recent ones are Hector Charles Cameron, *Sir Joseph Banks: The Autocrat of the Philosophers* (London, Batchworth Press, 1952) and Patrick O'Brian, *Joseph Banks: A Life* (London: Collins Harvill, 1987). A very beautiful book that contains engravings of the botanical drawings that Banks and his assistants made during their voyage with Cook is *The Flowering of the Pacific: Being an Account of Joseph Banks' Travels* by Brian Adams (London: British Museum (Natural History), 1986).

Pedro João Baptista & Amaro José

(early 19th century)

Pedro João Baptista and Amaro José were two Angolans of color who made the first recorded trip across the A.ican continent.

With establishments on the west (Angola) and east (Mozambique) coasts of Africa since the sixteenth century, the Portuguese had long dreamed of signing trade agreements with the central African chiefs and establishing a trade route between the two settlements. Francisco José de Lacerda attempted this in 1798, when he left from the large Portuguese trading center of Tete on the Zambezi River in interior Mozambique and headed west. He died along the way, however, and the remains of his expedition returned to Tete.

At the time of Lacerda's mission, the Captain-General of Angola, Fernando de Noronha, made a similar search for a route through Africa from the west. He instructed Francisco Honorato da Costa, commandant of the frontier post of Kasanje, to send an expedition eastward to Tete. Honorato da Costa chose two *mestiço* (part African and part European) frontiersmen, or *pombeiros* (traveling agents, from the Angolan Portuguese word *pombo*, "road"), named Pedro João Baptista and Amaro José to carry out this mission. Baptista had some education and wrote a journal of their expedition.

Baptista and José left Kasanje in November 1802. Their route led them through the territory of a chief named Mawata Yamvo who lived south of Kasanje. In order to get his authorization, Honorato da Costa sent word that the two *pombeiros* were coming to look for the remains of the Lacerda expedition. However, not believing their story, the chief held them captive for two years, only eight days' march from Kasanje. They started out again in 1805, going as far as the Kingdom of Lovale where they found guides who took them to the north around the Cassai River. After 39 days of travel they reached the court at Muropue, the center of the Ovimbundu Kingdom. They left there on May 22, 1806 equipped with the king's authorization to travel and led by guides.

They traveled westward through Katanga (now in the country of Zaire) and into the large kingdom of Kazembe in what is now southeastern Zaire and northern Zambia. They met and were well received by the ruler of the kingdom, the Muata Kazembe, and described his gorgeous costume and impressive retinue. However, they had to stay four years in Kazembe, partly because of a revolt against the Muata Kazembe's rule. Africans from Tete finally escorted them out.

After 57 days of travel they arrived in Tete on February 2, 1811. The next day Baptista delivered a letter from the Angolan governor to the local commandant and one of Lacerda's former companions, Gonçalo Pereira. Baptista and José wanted to return at once to Angola, but they were delayed because Pereira would not provide them with the goods they needed to trade their way back across Africa.

While in Tete, however, Baptista recorded his observations about the town: "The trade of the town of Tete consists in ivory and gold dust called money, which the traders from Mozambique, Senna and Quelimane came to buy with Indian stuffs. There is not a large trade carried on there in slaves, the price not being good enough to pay the traders. In former times they were worth more, but not at present."

Finally reaching an agreement with Pereira, Baptista and José left Tete in May 1811 and were back at Kasanje in 1814, after spending another nine months with the Muata Kazembe. They left Kazembe, however, without the means to buy food for the rest of the trip. Most of the slaves they had brought from Tete either starved to death or escaped on the return trip. They were forced to pitch camp by a river for two months "to fatten up the people who were lean and sick of hunger: the same was true of us."

The successful completion of their trip meant that Baptista and José were the first persons known to have crossed the African continent, and they did it in both directions. The Captain-General at Luanda, the capital of Angola, was so pleased that he sent Baptista (José seems to have died) to make a report to the Portuguese Court, which because of the Napoleonic Wars was then in Rio de Janeiro in Brazil. An announced plan of sending a yearly trading mission from Angola to Tete with Baptista at its head was never carried out.

Baptista's journal was published in Portuguese in 1843, and an English translation appeared two years later, sponsored by the Royal Geographical Society. It was the only source of knowledge in Europe about central Africa until **David Livingstone** started writing of his explorations in 1865.

Where to learn more

The only recent narrative in English of Baptista and Amaro's journey is found in Charles E. Nowell, *The Rose-Colored Map: Portugal's Attempt to Build an African Empire from the Atlantic to the Indian Ocean* (Lisbon: Junta de Investigações Científicas do Ultramar, 1982).

Alexander Andreyevich Baranov

(1746 - 1819)

Alexander Andreyevich Baranov was Russian trader and administrator who was responsible for much of the exploration of the coast of Alaska.

Alexander Andreyevich Baranov was born in the village of Kargopol in northern Russia near the Finnish border. His father was a poor itinerant merchant. At the age of 15, Alexander ran away to Moscow where he witnessed the coronation of the Empress Catherine the Great. He went to work for a German merchant who taught him German and accounting. In 1780 he moved to Siberia to become a trader, sending his wife and daughter to stay in Kargopol. Using the capital he had saved from his trading, Baranov started a small glass factory in the city of Irkutsk on the shores of Lake Baikal.

In 1787 Gregory Shelekhov, the founder of Russian trading posts in Alaska, asked Baranov to take charge of his operations. Baranov thought that he could do better on his own and turned

Alexander Andreyevich Baranov. The Granger Collection, New York.

him down. In the years 1789-1790 he and his brother Peter traded for furs in the Chukchi Peninsula of far northeastern Siberia. They had collected a large quantity when they were robbed by a party of Chukchis. Baranov went to the Siberian port of Okhotsk to get help in recovering his valuable stores. The local military governor refused to give him any assistance. Faced with a catastrophe (he was heavily in debt to pay for his trade goods), Baranov's only option was to accept Shelikhov's offer.

Baranov left from Okhotsk on August 30, 1790 and sailed to the island of Unalaska in the Aleutian Islands off the southwestern coast of Alaska. The ship was wrecked on the night of October 8 in a small port on Unalaska. Baranov and his crew were forced to spend the winter there. In the spring, they constructed three whaleskin boats to sail to Kodiak, which was the center of Russian trading operations. During the long sea passage, Baranov became ill and was carried unconscious into the small Russian fort when they landed at Kodiak on July 8, 1791. He had recovered by mid-August and started traveling in the neighborhood of the Russian settlement.

In the spring of 1792 Baranov moved the Russian settlement to the other side of the island of Kodiak. In the summer he led an expedition to Prince William Sound on the south coast of Alaska to look for a place to set up a new trading post. While there, he met an English ship whose captain told him about Spanish settlements in California and the situation in Hawaii. In the summer of 1793 he went to Cook Inlet (where Anchorage is now located) and encountered the ships of British captain **George Vancouver**. He and Vancouver did not actually talk because Baranov kept putting him off. He did not want the English to get too much information about the Russian operations. In the summer of 1794 the chief of the tribe at Prince William Sound visited Baranov and offered him his daughter in ''marriage.'' Baranov gave her the Russian name of Anna Grigorievna, and they had two children together.

In the summer of 1795 Baranov sent the *Phoenix*, a ship that he had constructed the previous year from local materials, to Okhotsk with a load of furs. He himself made an expedition to Yakutat Bay on the south coast of Alaska, where he built a Russian fort, and then headed south through the Alexander Archipelago. He discovered Sitka Island, which was later renamed Baranof Island in his honor. He returned to Kodiak in the middle of September 1795.

For the next four years, Baranov directed the affairs of the colony from Kodiak. In 1799 he traveled to Sitka, where he started building the fort of New Archangel. It was completed on

Easter Sunday 1800. Baranov then returned to Kodiak where he learned that the Native Americans were refusing to trade with the Russians because of their brutality, that one of his local trading ships had been wrecked, and that the *Phoenix* had disappeared on its return from Okhotsk. By the end of the year the Aleuts of Kodiak were in full revolt, led by priests of the Russian Orthodox Church. Baranov thereupon arrested all of the priests on the island and had them imprisoned in a small hut. He spent the following years managing the affairs of the colonies to regain the trust of the Native Americans on which it depended.

In the spring of 1802 Baranov received word that he had been named Governor of Russian America by the Tsar. However, this news was quickly marred by word that on June 20, 1802 the fort at Sitka had been attacked and destroyed by members of the Tlingit-Haida tribe. Baranov led an expedition there in 1804 in the company of Yuri Lisiansky who was making a trip around the world in the *Neva*. They recaptured the site and rebuilt Fort New Archangel, which he then made the center of Russian America.

Baranov's goal was to establish Russian control all the way down the coast as far as San Francisco. From New Archangel he sent trading and exploring expeditions along the west coast to California. He sent the first trading party to California in 1804. In 1812 he sent his assistant I.A. Kuskov to found Fort Ross 50 miles north of San Francisco. He tried to work out a trading arrangement with John Jacob Astor's fur-trading company out of Astoria, Oregon, but the agreement fell apart during the War of 1812. In 1815 he sent another assistant to Hawaii in order to take over the islands for Russia. The Russians annexed the island of Kauai but were driven out by King Kamehameha in 1817.

Because Baranov's ambitious plans were not succeeding but were costing the Russians a lot of money, he was relieved of his position on January 23, 1818. Following his resignation, he attended the wedding of his Alaskan daughter Irina to a young Russian officer from a Ukrainian noble family. Baranov left Alaska on December 1, 1818. His ship traveled to Batavia (Jakarta) in the Dutch East Indies, where it stayed for a month trading. It is said that during that time Baranov stayed in his hotel room drinking. He contracted malaria and died on board the ship as it was passing through Sunda Strait west of Java on April 13, 1819.

Where to learn more

There are two full-scale biographies of Baranov in English: Hector Chevigny, *Lord of Alaska: Baranov and the Russian Venture* (New York: 1942) and K.T. Khlebnikov, *Baranov*, translated by Colin Beirne, (Kingston, Ontario: Queen's University Press, 1973). For the story of the Russian trading ventures in Alaska, see S.B. Okun, *The Russian American Company*, translated by Carl Ginsburg, (Cambridge: Harvard University Press, 1951). The history of the attempt to take over Hawaii is in Richard Pierce's *Russia's Hawaiian Adventure, 1815-1817* (Berkeley: University of California Press, 1965).

Willem Barents

(1550? - 1597)

Willem Barents was a Dutch navigator who led several Dutch expeditions in search of the Northeast Passage and died in the Arctic Ocean north of Russia.

A t the end of the sixteenth century, the merchants of the country we now call the Netherlands were the most enterprising in the world. Their chief interest was in breaking the monopoly of trade with Asia that was held by the Portuguese, who controlled the route around Africa, and the Spanish, whose galleons sailed between the Philippines and Mexico.

While trying to force their way through the southern route, they reasoned that there must be a way north as well. Therefore they started a series of voyages designed to sail north of Eurasia to the northeast tip of Asia and then south into the Pacific Ocean. While their theory was certainly correct, they seriously underestimated the difficulties in accomplishing it.

In 1594, the Dutch merchants of Amsterdam commissioned Willem Barents to lead an expedition to China via Novaya Zemlya, a large island off the Arctic coast of European Russia. Barents (or Barentszoon, or Barent's son, as he was known at the time) was a native of the island of Ter Schelling off the coast of Friesland in the northern Netherlands. He moved to Amsterdam and became a burgher of that city. He sailed from the island of Texel north of Amsterdam on June 4, 1594 and headed through the North Sea. He sailed north of Norway through the sea that is now named after him and made it as far as the northern tip of Novaya Zemlya but could proceed no farther because of floating ice.

In the meantime a companion voyage by **Jan van Linschoten** was able to make it to the Kara Sea east of Novaya Zemlya by sailing south of the island. So, the following year it was by Linschoten's route that Barents and Linschoten sailed. The ice was bad, and they only reached Vaigach Island, which is in the straits between Novaya Zemlya and the mainland.

On May 13, 1596 Barents set out again, this time as pilot for an expedition of two ships led by Jacob van Heemskerk. They discovered Svalbard and Bear Island, north of Norway, and rounded the northern tip of Novaya Zemlya. One of the ships turned back to Amsterdam, but van Heemskerk and Barents stayed behind. On the north coast of Novaya Zemlya the ice closed in and gradually crushed the little Dutch ship. The men used the timber from the boat to build a shelter on the island.

Building a wooden house for winter. The Granger Collection, New York.

There they spent a terrible winter, which was so cold that the sheets froze on the beds, the wine froze, and they almost suffocated from the smoke of the fire they had to keep going all the time.

Almost all of the Dutchmen survived but when spring came they realized they would have to head back to Holland. They took the longboats from the ship and headed to the Russian mainland. Five days after they left, Barents, weakened by the long winter, died in the open boat. Most of his companions made it back home, but this was the last attempt the Dutch made to find a northeast passage.

Barents' story was not quite over. In 1871 a Norwegian expedition under Captain Carlsen found Barents' winter quarters undisturbed after 274 years. And in 1875 another explorer found part of his journal, so we have a good record of the first winter spent in the Arctic by Europeans.

Where to learn more

The history of Barents' expeditions is found in Gerrit de Veer, *The Three Voyages of William Barents to the Arctic Regions, 1594, 1595 and 1596* (London: Hakluyt Society, 1876; reprinted in New York, no date, by Burt Franklin, Publisher).

Rabban Bar-Sauma

(1225? - ?)

Rabban Bar-Sauma was a Nestorian Christian monk from Beijing who made a pilgrimage to Persia and Iraq and was sent on a diplomatic mission to the rulers of Western Europe.

We know most about those Medieval travelers who journeyed from Europe to Asia. However, the traffic was not all one way. Unfortunately, the Asian travelers to Europe either did not write narratives of their trips or they have remained undiscovered. There was one important exception—a Nestorian priest from Beijing, China, who traveled all the way to western France.

This man, the Rabban Bar-Sauma, belonged to a Christian sect known as the Nestorians. The Nestorians were followers of the Patriarch Nestorius of Constantinople who split off from the main branch of Christianity at the Council of Ephesus in 431. The Nestorians became the most important Christian sect in present-day Iraq and Iran before these countries were conquered by the Muslims. Missionaries were sent throughout Asia, including an important Nestorian colony in China starting in 635, which was later suppressed. However, the religion continued to flourish among the Turkic-speaking Uighur tribes who lived in the province of Sinkiang.

Following the conquest of Beijing by the Mongols under Genghis Khan in 1215, the Nestorians returned to China and restarted their missionary work with the support of influential Nestorians among the Khans, including Kublai Khan's mother. One of these Nestorians was the Rabban Bar-Sauma, who was born in Khanbaligh (capital of the Mongols, which later regained its Chinese name of Beijing) about 1225 into a well-to-do Uighur family.

At the age of 20 Bar-Sauma became a monk and went to live in a cave, where he became renowned for his preaching. One of the people who was attracted by his preaching was a young monk named Mark. Sometime after 1275 and 1280 Bar-Sauma and Mark set off to make a pilgrimage to Jerusalem. They were furnished with a letter of recommendation from the Nestorian bishop of Khanbaligh and a travel permit from Kublai Khan. They made their way through Sinkiang and the Uighur regions to Central Asia with great difficulty since there was an armed rebellion against the Khan's rule going on at the time. They arrived at Khurasan in eastern Persia (Iran) and then made their way to Maragheh in what is now Iranian Azerbaijan. There they were welcomed by the Catholicus, the head of the Nestorian church and the Patriarch of the East.

From Azerbaijan they went on into Iraq, visiting Baghdad and stopping at a monastery in the northern part of the country. They were sent by the Catholicus on a mission to the court of the Il-Khan, the Mongol ruler of Persia. On their return they traveled by way of Christian Armenia. Back in Baghdad, the Catholicus asked them to return to China as his emissaries. In 1280 he named Mark a bishop and created him Metropolitan of part of north China. They could not make the return trip immediately because of fighting along the route. In the meantime the Catholicus died. At the meeting of bishops to name a successor, Mark was chosen, chiefly because of his knowledge of the Mongol language and customs since most Nestorians were under Mongol rule.

Following the election, Mark and Bar Sauma traveled to Azerbaijan to have the selection confirmed by Abaga, the Il-Khan. The Il-Khan dynasty was the branch of the Mongol ruling family descended from Genghis Khan's grandson Hulegu that ruled over Persia. In 1284 Arghun, Abaga's son took over the throne. Arghun was friendly toward the Nestorians, and he was also ambitious. He had the idea of driving the Muslims out of Syria and Palestine, and thought that he could gain the help of the Christian Europeans in doing so. This was at the end of the epoch of the crusades, and there were still Crusader kingdoms in what is now Israel and Lebanon. Arghun sought the advice of the Catholicus, who recommended sending his old teacher to travel to Europe to seek Christian support.

Bar-Sauma left Iraq in 1287 and headed north through Armenia to the Black Sea. He sailed from the Greek trading city of Trebizond on the north coast of Asia Minor to Constantinople. He met the Byzantine Emperor Andronicus II and visited the enormous cathedral of Hagia Sophia. It took him two months to sail through the Mediterranean to Naples. He passed by Sicily where he saw an eruption of Mount Etna. Bar-Sauma arrived in Rome at a time when there was no reigning Pope, and he became involved in theological disputes with the cardinals at the Holy See. From Rome he went north to Tuscany (*Thuzkan* as Bar-Sauma called it) and Genoa (*Ginuha*).

From northern Italy Bar-Sauma went to Paris, where he had a meeting with King Philip IV of France (*Frangestan*) and then on to Gascony in southwestern France, which was then ruled by the kings of England (*Alanguitar* from the French word *Angleterre*). He met King Edward I of England in Bordeaux.

On his return to Rome Bar-Sauma received communion from the new Pope, Nicholas IV, on Palm Sunday, 1288. He returned to Persia by the same route he had taken out and reported back to the Il-Khan that the Western powers were well disposed to efforts to combine against the Muslims. This alliance never took place, but it did set the stage for diplomatic missions from the West, including those of **John of Monte Corvino** and Galfridus of Langele.

Where to learn more

Jeannette Mirsky includes a chapter on Bar-Sauma in her book on early Chinese explorers, *The Great Chinese Travelers: An Anthology* (New York: Pantheon Books, 1964), based upon Bar-Sauma's writings. The traditional source on medieval travel is Arthur Percival Newton, *Travel and Travellers of the Middle Ages*, originally published in 1926, reprinted in 1962 (Freeport, N.Y.: Books for Libraries Press). There is a specialized scholarly work on Bar-Sauma: J.A. Montgomery, ed. *The History of Yaballaha III and His Vicar, Bar-Sauma*, first published in 1927 and reprinted in New York in 1966.

Heinrich Barth

(1821-1865)

Heinrich Barth was a German explorer employed by the British government who made a five-year expedition to Africa that took him across the Sahara to Lake Chad and Timbuktu and then back north to the Mediterranean.

Heinrich Barth was born in the north German port of Hamburg. His father was an orphan who had come to Hamburg as a youth and had made himself into a wealthy merchant. Barth was sent to the best private schools in the city. Precocious, by the time he was 11 he could read Latin and Greek and was studying Arabic on his own. He entered the University of Berlin and studied archaeology and geography. He wrote his senior thesis in 1844 on the commercial history of the city of Corinth in ancient Greece. Following his graduation, he traveled for three years in the eastern Mediterranean, going to North Africa, Egypt, Palestine, Asia Minor, and Greece. On his return to Germany he got a position as a lecturer at the University of Berlin. It is said that he was such a poor speaker that his class was empty after the third lecture.

In 1849 the British government appointed James Richardson, who had already traveled to the Sahara in 1845, to lead an expedition to explore the caravan routes south from Tripoli across the Sahara. Richardson wanted his expedition to contain men with scientific knowledge to accompany him. A German mapmaker that he knew spoke to the Prussian ambassador in London who contacted Karl Ritter, the leading geographer of the day and a professor at the University of Berlin. Ritter suggested Barth, who was offered a place in the expedition if he would contribute the money to pay for his own expenses.

Barth eagerly accepted the offer, partly, it is said, to forget an unhappy love affair. While traveling in North Africa, he had met a Hausa slave from the great city of Kano, now in northern Nigeria, who had read his palm and prophesied, "Please God, you shall go and visit Kano." A third member of the expedition was recruited, a young German geologist named Adolf Overweg. Barth and Overweg arrived in Tunis in December 1849 and traveled to Tripoli, where they met up with Richardson. The expedition left Tripoli on March 24, 1850 and headed into the Sahara. They carried with them great quantities of stores, equipment, scientific instruments, and a large wooden boat in which they planned to sail across Lake Chad. The boat was in cut up into four sections to make it easier to carry, but even so was a major encumbrance on the trip. The fourth European member of the expedition was a British sailor brought along to manage the boat.

Unfortunately, Richardson, who was a fervent Christian, and Barth, who adopted the name Abd el Kerim, quickly came to dislike each other intensely. The party split up into two groups: the two Germans rode ahead while Richardson and the British sailor followed at a distance. The two groups pitched separate camps at night. When they reached the oasis of Marzuq in the beginning of May 1850 the sailor was sent back to Tripoli. They had to wait in Marzuq while they were trying to get safe conducts to Ghat, their next stop.

In mid-July, about 300 miles out of Marzuq, as they approached Ghat, Barth decided to climb Mount Idinen, believed by local Tuareg tribesmen to be inhabited by demons. He reached the top of the mountain but had drunk all of his water. He got lost trying to find his way back to camp. With nothing to drink, he cut open a vein and drank his own blood. He then collapsed into semi-consciousness. When he awoke he heard the sound of a camel. One of the expedition's guides had gone out looking for him and carried him back to camp, where he was well enough travel the next day.

From Ghat the expedition traveled through the Tassili-n-Ajjer where Barth saw rock carvings of bulls and buffaloes that led him to conjecture, correctly, that the Sahara had not always been a desert. After passing through the Air Mountains, Barth set out on his own to visit the ancient city of Agadez, which had once been one of the major trading centers of the Sahara. Barth entered the city on October 15, 1850. He attended the coronation of a new sultan and investigated the history of the city. He caught up with his companions at the end of October at the oasis of Tintellust. Barth wanted to continue but the other two wanted to wait until the beginning of December to catch the great salt caravan heading south. They joined the caravan in December and crossed the edge of the desert on January 6, 1851. They then separated on January 10, with Richardson heading for Zinder, Overweg to Gobir, and Barth to Kano.

Barth entered Kano on February 2, 1851. He noted that it was a wealthy trading center and could one day serve as the hub for a large part of Africa. Barth left the city in early March because the three explorers had made plans to meet at Kukawa on the western shores of Lake Chad in April. As Barth entered the Kingdom of Bornu on March 24, he was informed by a messenger that Richardson had died of malaria in Kukawa and his property had been seized. On his arrival in Kukawa Barth was able have Richardson's property restored. Overweg did not show

View of Timbuktu.

up until May and he was also suffering from malaria. Barth later came down with the disease, but the two explorers recovered enough to explore Lake Chad in the boat they had brought. Barth explored the territory to the south and east of the lake, and discovered that the Benue River, a major tributary of the Niger did not flow from Lake Chad.

The British government eventually heard of the death of Richardson and appointed Barth in his place. At the beginning of 1852, Overweg became ill with malaria again. Barth traveled on his own and had many adventures. At one point, he was put in irons and held prisoner for four days until an African friend got him released. At another time he joined a slave caravan, where he saw 170 men massacred, many of them bleeding to death when their legs were cut off. He returned to Kukawa in August 1852 where Overweg was still sick. In September they went on a hunting trip to Lake Chad. Richardson got wet retrieving a bird he had shot and the next day was delirious. He died at the age of 29 on September 27, 1851.

Following Overweg's death, Barth stayed for a year in Kukawa, making it his base for several expeditions in the area. He then left Kukawa on November 25, 1852 and headed west. He arrived at the city of Katsina at the end of January 1853, where he found a consignment of sugar that had been sent to him by the British government. At the bottom of the box of sugar was $1,000. He reached Sokoto in March and was shown the house where the explorer **Hugh Clapperton** had died in 1827. Barth crossed the Niger River at the town of Say in June 1853. From there he set off overland to Timbuktu, disguising himself as a Tuareg.

Barth had estimated that it would take two years to travel to Timbuktu. In fact, he made it there in ten months, arriving on September 7, 1853, the first European to visit the legendary city since **René Caillié** 25 years before. He was forced to stay there for seven months, being accused of being a spy and being caught in the middle of a local power struggle. It is said that he was saved several times by demonstrating the ability of his Colt revolver to fire six shots in succession. Barth was finally allowed to leave on May 18, 1854 and traveled back to Kukawa. In Sokoto he heard that another German explorer, Dr. Edward Vogel, had been sent out to look for him by the British government. Amazingly enough, the two ran into each other by accident on December 1, 1854 in the forest west of Kukawa. The news was relayed back to London—"the rumour of Dr. Barth's death has most happily proved unfounded."

Vogel stayed on in Africa, and was killed on the orders of the Sultan of Wadai on February 8, 1865. When that news was received in England, the Foreign Minister wrote in the margins of the report: "This is very melancholy." Back in Kukawa, Barth made plans to return home. He left in May 1855 and took the regular caravan trading route, east of his earlier route, back to Tripoli, where he arrived on August 28, 1855. He took a Turkish steamer to Malta and reached London on September 16.

Barth was received by the British foreign minister and was awarded the Order of Bath by Queen Victoria. But he felt that his travels did not receive the recognition they deserved. He felt that he was being upstaged by other explorers, such as **Sir Richard Burton** and **David Livingstone**, simply because they were British. He made a brief visit to Germany and then returned to England to write up the history of his expedition. He then moved back to Germany in 1857. He was very disappointed when he was rejected for membership in the Berlin Academy of Sciences. Later he was elected president of the Prussian Geographical Society and in 1863 he was appointed Professor of Geography at the University of Berlin. These honors do not seem to have made him any happier, and he lived as a recluse. He died on

November 24, 1865 at the age of 44 from a stomach perforation caused by ulcers he had contracted while in Africa.

Where to learn more

Barth's own narrative was published in the United States as *Travels and Discoveries in North and Central Africa in the Years 1849-1855* in three volumes (New York: Harper and Brothers, 1857-1859). A noted British historian of West African exploration, Anthony Kirk-Greene has edited the journal for modern readers: *Barth's Travels in Nigeria: Extracts from the Journal of Heinrich Barth* (London: Oxford University Press, 1982). Kirk-Greene also wrote a chapter entitled "Heinrich Barth: An Exercise in Empathy" in Robert I. Rotberg, ed., *Africa and Its Explorers: Motives, Methods, and Impact* (Cambridge: Harvard University Press, 1970).

A book that discusses the whole story of the European exploration of the Niger valley and Timbuktu, and which was helpful in writing this account of Heinrich Barth, is *The Strong Brown God: The Story of the Niger River* by Sanche de Gramont (Boston: Houghton Mifflin Company, 1975) and is available in a paperback edition. A German historian of exploration, Paul Herrmann, presents a psychological interpretation of Barth in *The Great Age of Discovery* (New York: Harper & Brothers, 1958). Other books about the exploration of West Africa give considerable space to discussions of Barth, including A. Adu Boahen, *Britain, the Sahara, and the Western Sudan, 1788-1861* (Oxford: Clarendon Press, 1964) and Christopher Hibbert, *Africa Explored: Europeans in the Dark Continent, 1769-1889* (London: Allen Lane, 1982).

Bob Bartlett

(1875 - 1946)

Bob Bartlett was a native of Newfoundland who became known as the best Arctic sea captain of his time. He accompanied Robert Peary on his attempts to reach the North Pole and was the captain of the first Canadian Arctic Expedition.

Bob Bartlett was born in the small Newfoundland fishing village, or outpost, of Brigus on August 15, 1875, the oldest of 10 children. At the age of 15 he left Brigus to attend boarding school in St. John's, the capital of Newfoundland. He was unhappy there and after two years convinced his parents to let him go to sea aboard a sealing ship. He quickly earned a reputation for efficiency in killing seals, which was a major form of livelihood for the Newfoundland population at the time.

In 1898 Bartlett was hired by an uncle to serve as first mate on the *Windward*, used by **Robert Peary** in his first attempt to reach the North Pole. After a winter in the far north, Bartlett and the *Windward* returned south in the spring of 1899, leaving Peary, who spent four years in the Arctic.

In 1905 Peary purchased the *Roosevelt* as his Arctic exploration ship and asked Bartlett to captain it. Bartlett agreed only if he were allowed to accompany Peary to the Pole. They sailed north through the narrow strait between Greenland and Ellesmere Island and reached Cape Sheridan at the northern end of Ellesmere Island (near present-day Alert) on September 5, 1905. Starting in February 1906, Bartlett led parties of Inuit to the north to cut trails and set up supply depots. He reached his farthest north on April 21 at 85°12′ and was stopped by a large expanse of open sea that he called the "Big Lead." Peary tried to sledge farther but was stopped by the open body of water. During this time he claimed to have sighted a large landmass that he named Crocker Land after one of his financial backers.

They could go no farther that year, and on July 4 Bartlett took the *Roosevelt* south. Along the way, sea ice almost crushed the ship, destroying the rudder and making a big hole in the bottom. It took 75 days to steam to Etah in northern Greenland. There, they made some temporary repairs and continued on. Off the coast of Greenland they were hit by several storms but made it to Cape Breton Island in Nova Scotia, where Peary got off and took a train back to New York. Bartlett continued to sail the disabled ship down the coast until it reached New York Harbor on December 24, 1906, 99 days after leaving Etah.

In the following years, Peary worked to get financing to repair the *Roosevelt* and to pay for another assault on the North Pole. Bartlett returned to Newfoundland to captain sealing ships. In June 1908 he got a telegram from Peary saying that the *Roosevelt* was ready to sail again and calling him to New York. They set sail on July 7, 1908, from Oyster Bay, New York, where the ship's namesake, **Theodore Roosevelt**, came to see them off.

The expedition reached Cape Sheridan on September 5. During the winter the members of the expedition set up supply drops to the north. On February 28, 1909 Bartlett left the main base and headed north to break the main trail. As other support parties turned back, Bartlett continued on, coming to within 150 miles of the Pole. Peary set out along this route on March 14. On March 31 Peary and **Matthew Henson** caught up with Bartlett. The next day Peary informed Bartlett, totally unexpectedly, that he was taking Henson with him to the Pole and that Bartlett would have to return to the main base. In a later account that he gave to a newspaper, Bartlett said, "It was a bitter disappointment. I got up early the next morning while the rest were asleep, and started north alone. I don't know, perhaps I cried a little. I guess perhaps that I was just a little crazy then."

There has always been speculation that Peary did not take Bartlett because he did not want to share credit for reaching the North Pole with another white man. (Henson, an African-American, and their three Inuit colleagues did not "count.") There have also been accusations that Peary did not take Bartlett because he knew that he could not reach the Pole and that Bartlett, an experienced navigator, would know this. Henson and the three Inuit did not know how to take latitude and longitude readings.

Bartlett left the advance camp on April 1, 1909 before Peary and Henson were awake. It took him 18 days to get back to the main camp. At one point he fell through the ice but was rescued by his Inuit colleagues. When Peary returned, Bartlett congratulated him on his success, and they sailed to Labrador to telegraph the news to the world. In 1910 Bartlett went on a lecture tour of Europe talking about the expedition. He was then hired by a couple of American millionaires to go hunting for polar bear in Greenland and northern Baffin Island. On this expedition they captured the first adult male polar bear ever taken alive and donated it to the Bronx Zoo.

In 1913 **Vilhjalmur Stefansson** convinced the Canadian government to sponsor an expedition to the Arctic, partly to reinforce Canada's uncertain claims to that region. The government bought an old wooden sailing ship, the *Karluk*, and hired Bartlett to be its captain. It sailed from the port of Victoria in British Columbia in July 1913. Its destination was Herschel Island, west of the Mackenzie River delta in far northwest Canada. The ship encountered a storm off the Alaska coast on August 9 and could proceed no farther. By August 12 it was frozen in.

Stefansson left the ship on September 19 with a small party, including his photographer, **Hubert Wilkins**. He said he was going to hunt caribou and would return within 10 days. In fact, he headed for Herschel Island and then carried out his originally-planned explorations during the next five years. Bartlett and 25 people, including an Inuit woman and her young daughter and son, were left on board the *Karluk*. Shortly after Stefansson left, the ship was hit by a storm, and the ice parted. The ship was caught in a patch of clear water in a large sheet of ice about 1-2 miles square. This ice pan began drifting to the west pushed by heavy winds and ocean currents. The *Karluk* was nearly crushed by floes as it passed north of Bering Strait.

By October 10 the *Karluk* was north of Siberia near where the *Jeannette*, commanded by **George Washington De Long**, had been lost in 1879. In order to avoid the same fate, Bartlett had his crew and passengers move everything possible off the ship onto the ice floe. They built igloos on the ice. This turned out to be wise because on January 10, 1914 the *Karluk* was crushed by the ice and sank. Bartlett stayed on board till the last minute playing music on the wind-up record player.

On January 20 Bartlett sent a small party of four men south to a rock named Herald Island to see whether it could possibly serve as a base. They were never heard from again. Soon after, a group of the expedition's scientists set out on their own to try to reach the mainland. They also disappeared. Bartlett, in the meantime, systematically sent out small parties to blaze a trail and to set up food depots. This was accomplished over a period of six weeks, and on February 19 the survivors left "Shipwreck Camp." At one point Bartlett spent four days hacking a passage through a wall of ice ridges.

Bartlett and his group of survivors reached Wrangel Island on March 12. Once a camp had been set up, Bartlett left with an Inuit hunter and headed for the mainland. They reached it and were taken in by a party of Chukchi hunters. They then headed for the Bering Strait, where they met a Russian trader who got word of the *Karluk* disaster to the outside world. Bartlett found a ship to take him to Alaska, which he reached on May 28. He spent the next two months trying to find a ship that would take him back to Wrangel Island. He found an American sailing ship that was willing to try and it got within 20 miles of the island before being forced to turn back on August 24. On September 7, a Russian schooner was able to make it all the way to the island and remove the survivors, three more of whom had died.

Following the return, there was an investigation that found Bartlett partially responsible for the *Karluk* disaster. Many people realized that this was unfair, but it caused great bitterness on Bartlett's part. During World War I he moved to the United States and became an American citizen. During the war he carried out routine assignments for the U.S. Navy. In 1917 he commanded the ship sent north by the Crocker Land Expedition to try to discover the large landmass that Peary had claimed to see. There is no such land, and the expedition returned to announce its negative results. In the following years Bartlett promoted several schemes for Arctic exploration but found no backers.

During these discouraging years Bartlett began to drink heavily. In the winter of 1924 he was drunk and was hit by a wagon as he tried to cross New York's 44th Street. He spent three weeks in the hospital. He then resolved never to drink again. In 1925 a millionaire friend bought Bartlett a sailing schooner, the *Effie M. Morrissey*. He used this ship to make 20 voyages to the Canadian Arctic, collecting a large amount of scientific data.

Bartlett made his first exploring expedition in the *Morrissey* under the auspices of publisher George M. Putnam (who was later to marry **Amelia Earhart**). They carried supplies to Danish explorer Knud Rasmussen at Thule, Greenland. Putnam brought along his 12-year-old son David, who wrote a book about his adventures.

In 1927 and 1933, expeditions led by Bartlett explored Foxe Channel and Basin and the Fury and Hecla Strait between Baffin Island and the mainland. In 1930 he made his first visit to northeast Greenland and returned there in 1931 and 1939, sponsored by eight different scientific organizations as well as collecting oceanic and atmospheric data for the U.S. Navy. From 1932 to 1941 he made eight trips to Ellesmere Island and northwest Greenland. He wrote articles about these trips for a variety of publications, including the *National Geographic*, and published two books about his experiences. During World War II he made several trips to northern Canada and Greenland, setting up and supplying military bases for the Allied war effort. After the war, he returned to live in New York. He caught pneumonia there and died in a hospital on April 28, 1946. The *Effie M. Morrissey* was later put on display at Mystic Seaport in Connecticut.

Where to learn more

Bartlett wrote three books about his exploits: *Northward Ho!: The Last Voyage of the Karluk* (Boston: Small, Maynard & Co., 1916); *The Log of Bob Bartlett* (New York: G.P. Putnam's Sons, 1928); and *Sails Over Ice* (New York: Scribner's, 1934).

There is an excellent biography of Bartlett that served as the basis for this account: Harold Horwood, *Bartlett: The Great Canadian Explorer* (Garden City, N.Y.: Doubleday & Co., 1977). There is a detailed and fascinating history of the *Karluk* disaster in William Laird McKinlay, *Karluk* (London: Weidenfeld and Nicolson, 1976).

George P. Putnam wrote about his explorer friend in *Mariner of the North* (New York: Duell, Sloan and Pierce, 1947), and his son David wrote about his exciting summer in the Arctic in *David Goes to Greenland* (New York: G.P. Putnam's Sons, 1927).

Henry Walter Bates

(1825 - 1892)

Henry Walter Bates was a British entomologist who spent 11 years along the Amazon River collecting specimens of insects.

Henry Walter Bates was born into a modest family in the Midlands of England. He served as an apprentice in a textile company and then as a clerk in a brewery. During this time he attended what would now be called night school and studied on his own. He developed a passionate interest in the study of insects, entomology, and spent his free time in the forests near his home collecting specimens.

He met **Alfred Russell Wallace** who was teaching at a nearby school, and the two friends spent a great deal of time discussing the works of **Charles Darwin** and other naturalists and the developing theories of evolution. They read a book titled *A Voyage Up the River Amazon*, by William H. Edwards and decided that the Amazon River offered the best undeveloped field for studying insect evolution.

Bates and Wallace left England on April 26, 1848 and traveled to the Brazilian port of Pará, now known as Belém, near the mouth of the Amazon. Since they had very little money, their plan was to collect duplicates of all their specimens and send one of each back to England to sell for about three pennies each. That is what they did, and Bates even made a small profit from these sales over the several years he was in South America.

The two men spent 18 months collecting specimens around Belém. They also traveled by canoe up the great Tocantins River, the third largest of the tributaries of the Amazon. In July 1849 they were joined by Wallace's younger brother Herbert and soon afterward they headed up the Amazon to the town of Santarém. There they met another British naturalist who was to become famous for his work in the Amazon valley — **Richard Spruce**. It was Spruce who took rubber plants back to England where they were eventually transplanted to Southeast Asia to form the basis of a giant industry.

After a few months in Santarém, Bates and the two Wallaces went farther upstream to the town of Manaus, the center of the Brazilian Amazon. Here they split up, "finding it," as Wallace wrote, "more convenient to explore separate districts and collect independently." Bates headed up the main tributary of the Amazon, known as the Solimôes. He spent a year at the village of Ega (now known as Tefé). During that year he collected specimens of more than 7,500 insect species — an amazing total.

After a year in Ega, Bates had become very lonely and depressed and had also been robbed. He therefore returned to Belém where he met Herbert Wallace, who had become ill with yellow fever. Bates nursed Wallace during his illness, but he died and then Bates himself became ill. After his recovery, he returned to Santarém in November, 1851 and spent the next three years collecting in that area. He met up with Wallace in June 1852, who was on his way back to England. He also explored up the Tapajos and Cuparí Rivers.

In spite of his previous experiences, Bates returned to Ega in 1855, where he spent the next four years. This stay became famous among botanists for the numerous discoveries he made, including 550 different species of butterflies. During this time he planned to travel to the headwaters of the Amazon but made it only as far as the village of São Paulo de Olivença, when illness

Henry Walter Bates. The Granger Collection, New York.

forced him to return. In February, 1859 he returned to England, bringing with him 14,000 species of insects, 8,000 of which were unknown.

By the time Bates returned to England, Charles Darwin had written his famous book *On the Origin of the Species*, and many of Bates discoveries were used to confirm Darwin's theories. On his own, Bates introduced the theory of "mimicry" by which different species will develop the same or similar characteristics in response to similar environmental constraints. Bates also wrote a book, published in 1863, about his experiences called *A Naturalist on the Amazons*, which was called the best work of natural history travels published in England.

After his return to England Bates applied to become head of the Zoological Department of the British Museum, but he was turned down in favor of a poet who knew nothing about zoology.

Bates then became the Assistant Secretary, or main administrative officer, of the Royal Geographical Society. He stayed in that job for 28 years, where he was responsible for sponsoring many great expeditions and for publishing the results. He died from bronchitis in London on February 16, 1892.

Where to learn more

Bates only wrote one book about his experiences, which has been called a classic of scientific and geographical literature: *The Naturalist on the River Amazons*, 2 vols. (London: 1863; reprinted in 1 vol., Berkeley: University of California Press, 1962).

A book that puts Bates in context with the other natural scientists of the nineteenth century is Paul Russell Cutright, *The Great Naturalists Explore South America*, vol. 1, (New York: Macmillan, 1940). There is one full-scale biography of Bates: George Woodcock, *Henry Walter Bates, Naturalist of the Amazons* (London: 1969).

Jim Beckwourth

(1800? - 1866)

Jim Beckwourth was an African-American fur trapper and trader who became a war chief of the Crow tribe and discovered one of the main entry routes into northern California from the east.

Jim Beckwourth was born near Fredericksburg, Virginia sometime around the year 1800. His father was Sir Jennings Beckwith, the scion of a prominent Virginia family. His mother has commonly been known as "Miss Kill," although it is not clear whether that was her real name or not. She was one of the Beckwith's slaves. Beckwourth's father moved to Missouri in 1806 and took Jim and his mother with him. They settled on a large farm where the Missouri and Mississippi Rivers meet near the town of St. Charles. Jim's father sent him to school in St. Louis from about 1810 until 1814. He was then appren-

James Beckwourth. The Granger Collection, New York.

ticed to a blacksmith in St. Charles. Beckwourth fought with the blacksmith and returned to his father's farm. He was set free on his nineteenth birthday, but it appears that he remained on his father's farm for a while after that. At some point he adopted his own version of the family name.

Although he may have made an earlier trip west, the first definite knowledge we have is that he joined **William Henry Ashley**'s trapping and trading expedition to the Far West in 1824. At one point in that journey, Beckwourth was sent ahead to buy horses from the Pawnee tribe. Not finding them and without sufficient food, he made a desperate trip back to a trading post and would have starved to death if he had not been found by a friendly band of Native Americans. Beckwourth later wrote an account of the journey that casts himself in a favorable light and plays up his own role in the expedition. This tendency to exaggerate has led many later writers to discount the truth of his accounts, but quite often there seems to be a core of reality about them. The most famous incident is one in which Beckwourth claims to have saved Ashley from drowning, although it was later shown that it could not have happened the way he described. However, a similar incident did occur, and Beckwourth seems to be very familiar with it.

Beckwourth continued to trap and worked for William Sublette who was one of the buyers of Ashley's fur trading business. In 1827 he "married" a woman from the Blackfoot tribe. In 1829 he found himself unable to pay a debt, so he took refuge among his friends of the Crow tribe, where he married again. Beckwourth says he married eight women while staying with the Crow. He soon led a successful raiding party against another tribe and was made a chief of the Crow. In later years, Beckwourth led the Crow in a great battle against their Blackfoot enemies in which he claimed that all the Blackfoot were killed and the Crow lost thirty or forty warriors. During this time Beckwourth continued to trap and sold his furs to the American Fur Company of St. Louis. In 1837, however, he was dropped from the Company's books and decided to look elsewhere for a livelihood.

Beckwourth found employment as a scout and mule driver for the U.S. Army in its war against the Seminole tribe of Florida. He took part in the Battle of Okeechobee that was fought on December 25, 1837, but after the war settled into routine, Beckwourth became bored and returned to Missouri and the fur trade. He was offered employment by Andrew Sublette, the younger brother of William. He took a trading party down the Santa Fe trail to Taos, New Mexico, where married a local Mexican woman. In October 1842, Beckwourth and his bride headed north to what is now Colorado and opened a trading post on the Arkansas River that eventually grew into the city of Pueblo.

In 1843 Beckwourth left Pueblo with a trading party of 15 and headed for California, then a part of Mexico. They arrived in Los Angeles in January 1844. When the local residents rebelled against the Mexican officials, Beckwourth joined their side in the "Battle" of Cahuenga in 1845. He then left California for New Mexico and traded along the Santa Fe Trail until August 1848. He was hired as a guide by an official of the U.S. War Department, and their party traveled to Los Angeles, where they arrived on October 25, 1848. From there they went north to Monterey, the capital of California at the time. He took on a job as a courier to a ranch near the present-day city of Santa Maria, north of Los Angeles. On his way there he came upon the massacre of the Reed family who were living in the old Mission of San Miguel and led the posse that apprehended the murderers.

When gold was discovered in northern California, Beckwourth joined the California Gold Rush. He did not actively pan for gold but gambled and traded horses and made his living among the prospectors. In the spring of 1850 he traveled to the remote mining areas of the Sierra Nevada in the region of the present-day Lassen Volcanic National Park. One day he saw what looked like a low pass to the west. At the end of April he led three men to this pass, which was subsequently named Beckwourth Pass. It is just to the west of the California-Nevada border about 30 miles north of Reno. Beckwourth immediately saw that it could be a major entrance from the east into the goldmining region, and he and his companions spent the summer and fall of 1850 opening a road through the pass. During the spring of 1851 he actively promoted his "New Emigrant Route" and got capital from the merchants of Marysville, California to develop it. Beckwourth guided the first wagon train through the Pass in late July or early August 1851. When it arrived in Marysville in September 1851, there was so much celebration that the town almost burned down.

At about that time Beckwourth met T.D. Bonner. Bonner was the former president of the New Hampshire Temperance Society who had been forced to emigrate to California when he started drinking again. He became a justice of the peace in Butte County, California where Beckwourth met him. In the spring of 1852, Beckwourth had decided to settle in the "pleasant valley" that lay to the west of Beckwourth Pass. There he built a house and hotel for the travelers coming through the Pass. It developed into one of the main entry points for pioneers coming to California. In October 1854 Bonner came to live in Beckwourth's hotel, and he contracted to write Beckwourth's "autobiography." By June of 1855 Bonner was back east and had signed a contract with Harper and Brothers in New York to publish it. When it came out in 1856 its tall tales and exciting adventures made it a bestseller, and Beckwourth became an instant celebrity.

Beckwourth stayed at his ranch (now Beckwourth, California) until November 1858. He then headed back east to Missouri, and the St. Louis and Kansas City newspapers recorded the visit of the famous mountain man. He moved to Denver, Colorado, where he married once again and settled down as the manager of a general store. He and his wife had a daughter who died in infancy. After her death, the marriage broke up, and Beckwourth moved in with a Crow woman. He became involved in various scrapes with the law, including a charge of manslaughter from which he was acquitted on the grounds of self-defense. He then joined the U.S. Army as a scout and took part in several actions against the Cheyenne tribe. In September 1866 he went to visit a Crow village on a mission for the Army. He died there, sometime around September 25, 1866.

Where to learn more

T.D. Bonner's life of Beckwourth, which was supposed to have been taken from Beckwourth's own dictation, was first published in 1856: *The Life and Adventures of James P. Beckwourth, Mountaineer, Scout, Pioneer and Chief of the Crow Nation* (New York: Harper and Brothers). There was an edition published in 1931 by Alfred A. Knopf, Inc. of New York that included an introduction by noted Western historian Bernard De Voto. The most recent reprinting was by the University of Nebraska Press in Lincoln in 1972.

Most of this account is based on a book by Elinor Wilson entitled *Jim Beckwourth: Black Mountain Man and War Chief of the Crows* (Norman: University of Oklahoma Press, 1972). Wilson spent a great deal of time tracking down sources and tries to separate fact from fiction in the numerous stories of Beckwourth's life.

Gertrude Bell

(1868 -1926)

Gertrude Bell was an English woman who became the best known traveler in the Middle East and Arabia in the years before World War I.

Gertrude Bell was born in county Durham, in England, on July 14, 1868 into a wealthy family. Her father owned an iron works. Her mother died in childbirth two year after Bell's birth, and she was raised by a stepmother. At sixteen she attended Queens College and then went to Lady Margaret Hall, a women's college at Oxford University. She graduated with high honors in history.

Bell traveled to the Middle East for the first time in 1892 to visit her uncle who was the British ambassador to Tehran in Persia (now Iran). There she met a young diplomat and wrote to her parents asking for permission to marry him. They ordered her home instead (the young man died nine months later). She wrote a book about her experiences called *Persian Pictures, A Book of Travels* that was published in 1894.

In 1899 Bell went to Jerusalem and studied Arabic there. She went during the spring of 1900 to visit the Druse in the

Gertrude Bell. The Granger Collection, New York.

mountains of southern Lebanon. She also visited Palmyra, the ruins of a Roman city in Jordan. She described it as "a white skeleton of a town, standing knee-deep in the blown sand." She then went mountain climbing in the Alps and took two trips around the world with her brother.

In January 1905 Bell made her first extended trip to the Middle East. She traveled through Syria to Cilicia and Konya in Asia Minor (Turkey). She traveled alone except for Arab servants and stayed in tents as well as in the houses of the wealthy, where her family could provide her with introductions. At the city of Alexandretta in southern Turkey she hired a servant, Fattuh, who was to stay with her the rest of her life. She visited many ruins along the way and became interested in archeology. She wrote about her experiences in *Syria: The Desert and the Sown*, published in 1907.

In 1907 Bell herself returned to Asia Minor with the British archeologist Sir William Ramsay to help excavate early Christian churches, and the two of them collaborated on a picture book of their discoveries. In 1909 she left from Aleppo in Syria and traveled through the valley of the Euphrates River to Baghdad, visiting Babylonian sites along the way. She also went to the Shi'ite (a Muslim sect) holy city of Karbala. Along the way Bell was robbed of her money and, most importantly, her notebooks. The whole countryside turned out to try to find the thieves, but the objects reappeared on a rock above her camp. Meanwhile when the Turkish soldiers of the Ottoman government arrived, they found a nearby village deserted, the inhabitants having fled for fear of retribution. Bell blamed herself for having been careless and causing all the difficulty.

Bell returned in 1911 to revisit the great castle at Kheidir and crossed the desert between Damascus and Baghdad. She then returned to England where she joined in the movement *against* giving votes to women. She also had an unhappy love affair with a married man, and decided to return to Arabia to forget her unhappiness.

This time she traveled to the city of Ha'il in the center of Arabia that had rarely been visited by Westerners. There, in 1913 she was virtually held prisoner and her money was taken from her until she finally prevailed and was released. However, Arab hostility forced her to cut her journey short rather than continuing to Riyadh as she had originally intended. She returned to Damascus in May 1914, having gained an unprecedented knowledge about the deserts of northern Arabia and the ruined cities that are found there.

This knowledge was suddenly to be of great value. War broke out in Europe in August 1914, and in November 1914 Turkey, which then ruled all of the Middle East, joined Germany in the fight against Great Britain. Bell was hired by the Arab intelligence bureau in Cairo as an advisor on Arabia. There she became friends with T.E. Lawrence (the famous "Lawrence of Arabia") and helped formulate the British strategy of encouraging the Arabs to revolt against the Turks.

In 1916 Bell was sent to Basra in Iraq as an assistant political officer and then was transferred to Baghdad in 1917, where she made her home for the rest of her life. She was very involved in the political negotiations that divided up the Arab world into new countries and established British political influence in the Middle East. She also started and directed the Iraq Museum. She died of an overdose of drugs on the night of July 11-12, 1926 at her home in Baghdad.

Where to learn more

Bell wrote a number of works about her various travels. These include *Persian Pictures*, several editions, the most recent being 1928 (New York: Boni & Liveright); *Amurath to Amurath* (London: William Heinemann, 1911); *The Desert and the Sown* (London: William Heinemann, 1919; reprinted, Boston: Beacon Press, 1985). There are two volumes of her letters: Lady Florence Bell, ed. *The Letters of Gertrude Bell* (London: E. Benn, 1927; reprinted, 1947) and Elsa Richmond, ed. *The Earlier Letters of Gertrude Bell* (New York: Liveright, 1937).

Of the several biographies of Bell, the most prominent are Josephine Kann, *Daughter of the Desert: The Story of Gertrude Bell* (London: Bodley Head, 1956); Anne Tibble, *Gertrude Bell* (London: A. & C. Black, 1958); Elizabeth Burgoyne, *Gertrude Bell, from Her Personal Papers*, 2 vols. (London: E. Benn, 1958 & 1961); H.V.F. Winstone, *Gertrude Bell* (London: Jonathan Cape, 1978), which includes an extensive bibliography; and Susan Goodman, *Gertrude Bell* (Leamington Spa, England: Berg, 1985).

Several of the collections of biographies of women explorers includes chapters on Bell, including Dea Birkett, *Spinsters Abroad: Victorian Lady Explorers* (London: Basil Blackwell, 1989) and Marion Tinling, *Women into the Unknown* (New York: Greenwood Press, 1989).

Fabian Gottlieb von Bellingshausen

(1779 - 1852)

Fabian Gottlieb von Bellingshausen was an Estonian serving in the Russian navy who made a circumnavigation of the Antarctic continent and may have been the first person to see the Antarctic mainland.

Fabian Gottlieb von Bellingshausen was born on Ösel Island in the Baltic Sea into the class of German gentry that had long been prominent landholders and merchants in Estonia. At that time Estonia was part of the Russian Empire. (His name in Russian is given as Faddei Faddeevich Bellingshausen.) Bellingshausen entered the Russian Naval Academy at Kronstadt outside of St. Petersburg and then served as a junior officer on the ship commanded by Adam Johann von Krusenshtern that made the first Russian voyage around the world from 1803 to 1806. From 1810 to 1819 Bellingshausen carried out hydrographical surveys in the Black Sea.

In May 1819 Bellingshausen was summoned to St. Petersburg to learn that he had been chosen to lead an expedition ordered by Tsar Alexander I to explore Antarctica. At the same time a counterpart expedition was being sent out under Commander Vasilev to explore the possibility of finding the Northwest Passage north of Alaska. Bellingshausen had only a short time to prepare for his voyage—he left Kronstadt on July 16, 1819 with two ships, the recently constructed *Vostok* (East) and a smaller and slower transport, the *Mirnyi* (Peaceful) commanded by Mikhail Lazarev.

Bellingshausen stopped first in Copenhagen where he was supposed to take on two German naturalists. The Germans, however, backed out at the last minute. Sailing to England, Bellingshausen met with **Sir Joseph Banks** in an attempt to find a British naturalist willing to sail with the expedition, but he was unsuccessful. Bellingshausen and his two ships then started south, stopping at Rio de Janeiro on the way and then heading for the sub-Antarctic island of South Georgia. Bellingshausen mapped the south coast of South Georgia to complete the work that **James Cook** had done on the north coast in 1775. (Bellingshausen was a great fan of Cook's and kept his works close at hand.)

On January 27, 1820 Bellingshausen's ships crossed the Antarctic Circle, the first to do so since Cook in 1773. The next day he sighted distant mountains in what is now called Princess Martha Coast on the Antarctic mainland. This may have been the first sighting of the Antarctic mainland. Bellingshausen recorded seeing ice cliffs again on February 17 and 18 and "ice-covered" mountains on the 19th. However, he did not realize that these were parts of a large continent and never claimed to have seen "Antarctica." At almost exactly the same time, the British naval captain Edward Bransfield and the American sealing captain Nathaniel Palmer sighted similar phenomena and today it is not clear who really saw the continent first.

A heavy storm on February 22, 1820 forced the ships to turn northward at about the longitude of Cape Town, South Africa. Bellingshausen sailed east to Australia, where the *Vostok* arrived in Sydney harbor on April 11 and the *Mirnyi* eight days later. They remained there until May repairing and refitting the ships and taking on supplies. During the southern winter he sailed among the islands of Polynesia, stopping at New Zealand along the way. He sailed among the islands of the Tuamotu Archipelago and was the first European to see some of them. He also discovered and named the small, uninhabited and isolated island of Vostok. Returning through the central Pacific where he fixed the location of many islands, Bellingshausen reached Sydney in September 1820 and left for the last time on November 11.

Spending a few days on isolated Macquarie Island south of Australia, Bellingshausen encountered many sealing ships and accurately forecast that the seal population would soon be destroyed. On January 21, 1821, Bellingshausen reached his farthest point south, 69.5°S, in what is now the Bellingshausen Sea, off Ellsworth Land, a coast so heavily surrounded by ice that no ship has ever reached it. The following day Bellingshausen discovered an island that he named after the tsar who had founded the Russian navy—Peter I Island.

On January 28, 1821 Bellingshausen sighted a large mass of mountains that he named Alexander I Land—actually an island in the great bend of the Antarctic Peninsula. Sailing north to the South Shetland Islands, the Russians met eight sealing ships. The captain of one of them, Nathaniel Palmer, came aboard to visit Bellingshausen. According to an American account published 12 years later, Palmer told Bellingshausen that he had discovered the mainland of a continent, which the Americans called the Palmer Peninsula—the northern tip of the Antarctic Peninsula. The Russian account makes no mention of this claim.

From the South Shetlands, Bellingshausen sailed north, reaching Rio de Janeiro in March 1821 and arriving in Kronstadt on August 4, 1821. Upon his return, Bellingshausen's discoveries were largely ignored. The publication of his report was delayed for several years, and the Russian Empire never sent another expedition to Antarctica. The Soviet Union became actively involved in Antarctic affairs starting with the International Geophysical Year in 1957 and then put forward the claim that Bellingshausen was the first man to see the continent of Antarctica.

After writing the results of his expedition, Bellingshausen returned to active duty in the Russian navy. He fought in the Russo-Turkish War of 1828-1829 with the rank of rear admiral. In 1831 he was promoted to admiral and in 1839 was made military governor of Kronstadt, where he served until his death in 1852.

Where to learn more

Bellingshausen's report of his voyage has been translated and published in English by Frank Debenham, editor, *The Voyage of Captain Bellingshausen to the Antarctic Seas, 1819-1821*, 2 vols. (London: Hakluyt Society, 1945). Two good accounts of his expedition can be found in L.P. Kirwan, *A History of Polar Exploration* (New York: W.W. Norton, 1960) and *Antarctica: Great Stories from the Frozen Continent* (Sydney: Reader's Digest, 1988). A discussion of the implications of Bellingshausen's discoveries is in E.W. Hunter Christie, *The Antarctic Problem: An Historical and Political Study* (London: Allen & Unwin, 1951).

Benjamin of Tudela

(12th century)

Benjamin of Tudela was a medieval Jewish rabbi from Spain who traveled to the Middle East and wrote a description of the countries and the state of the Jewish communities he visited.

Throughout the Middle Ages, the Jews of Western Europe were persecuted and in some cases forced to leave their homes and countries. Partly this was the result of a Christian prejudice that labeled the Jews "the murderers of Christ," partly it was jealousy because some Jews had become wealthy by lending money and by trading in foreign goods.

Until they were expelled in 1492, the Iberian peninsula, or Spain, had a large and prosperous Jewish population, even though they suffered much discrimination. In the second half of the twelfth century the rabbi Benjamin from the Spanish town of Tudela, on the Ebro River in the northern region of Navarre, made an extensive journey throughout the Mediterranean and to the Holy Land and the city of Baghdad. On his return, he wrote an extremely valuable *Record* of his travels, which shows that one of his main motives was to report on the status of Jewish communities throughout the Mediterranean and Middle East, potentially as places of refuge if the Jews were forced to leave Spain.

Benjamin's travels started around the year 1159 from the port city of Barcelona. He went north from there into France to the cities of Montpellier and Marseilles, where he noted the presence of large Jewish settlements and the beginnings of the Albigensian heresy which was to bring much warfare to the south of France. He took a ship from Marseilles to Genoa and from there to Pisa. He found almost no Jews in either of these cities but did find some in prominent positions once he reached Rome.

He headed south through Naples and into Sicily, which was then ruled by the Normans from northern France whose ancestors had come from Scandinavia. In Greece Benjamin found a large Jewish colony in Thebes, where there were 2,000 Jewish dyers and silk-workers and where the learning of the rabbis was unsurpassed anywhere in the world. He reached the city of Constantinople in December 1161, where he viewed the festivities surrounding the marriage of the emperor Manuel Comnenus. He also described the church of Saint Sophia, the largest in the world, and the bustle of endless nationalities trading at the port.

For all its size and wealth, Constantinople suffered in Benjamin's eyes because it segregated its Jews in a distant suburb, forbade them to ride horses (except for the imperial physician),

and often set upon and ridiculed the Jewish population. From Constantinople Benjamin voyaged through the islands of the Aegean to Cyprus where he was shocked to find a heretical Jewish sect that did not even observe the Sabbath.

Sometime in the year 1163 Benjamin reached the great city of Antioch in Syria, which was ruled by a French prince who led a Crusader army. He traveled south through Lebanon and reported on the Assassins, a non-orthodox Muslim sect who specialized in the murder of their enemies. From there, he entered the Holy Land, where he found many nationalities living in Jerusalem, including about 200 Jews. He visited Hebron where he found the Samaritans, the remnants of an early Jewish sect.

In Damascus Benjamin estimated that there were 3,000 Jews and a continuing tradition of Jewish education. He was overwhelmed by the beauty of the city's chief mosque. From Damascus, Benjamin visited the ruins of Baalbek in what is now Lebanon. From northern Syria he crossed over into Mesopotamia and eventually reached Baghdad, the capital of the caliph of all Islam and probably the largest city in the world at that time. He reported on the high status of the Jews of the city and the respect enjoyed by the Jewish leader—"the Prince of the Captivity". The year of his visit was probably 1164, almost a full century before Baghdad was destroyed by the invading Mongols.

Benjamin visited the ruins of the old city of Babylon and then proceeded into the western parts of Persia as far north as the Caspian Sea. Along the way he found numerous Jewish settlements. He then turned westward and reached Egypt sometime during the year 1171, describing Alexandria and the Greek monasteries in the Sinai Desert. He embarked from the port of Damietta to Messina in Sicily and then made his way back to Spain. On his return to his hometown of Tudela in 1173, he wrote a narrative of his travels, describing all the things he had seen.

Where to learn more

The complete text of Benjamin of Tudela's narrative can be found in M.N. Adler, *The Travels of Benjamin of Tudela* (London: 1907), which also contains the Hebrew original, and in a later edition, *The Itinerary of Benjamin of Tudela: Travels in the Middle Ages*, introduction by Michael A. Signer (New York: Joseph Simon Publisher, 1983).

The most accessible modern versions are in Michael Komroff, ed. *Contemporaries of Marco Polo* (reprinted, New York: Dorset Press, 1989) and Elkan Nathan Adler, ed. *Jewish Travelers: A Treasury of Travelogues from Nine Centuries* (London: George Routledge & Sons, 1930; 2nd edition, New York: Hermon Press, 1966). The best discussion of Benjamin's travels is in a very important book, which is unfortunately long out of print: C. Raymond Beazley, *The Dawn of Modern Geography*, vol. 2 (London: John Murray, 1901; reprinted, New York: Peter Smith, 1949).

Vitus Bering

(1681-1741)

Vitus Bering was a Danish navigator who sailed in the service of the Russian tsar, proving the existence of a passage between Asia and North America.

Vitus Bering was born at Horsens in Denmark. In his youth he sailed with a Dutch fleet to the East Indies. Later, he joined other foreigners who were recruited by the Russian tsar, Peter the Great, to serve in his newly-formed navy. He came to the tsar's attention because of his bravery during the Great Northern War with Sweden from 1700-1721. In 1725, the year of his death, Peter commissioned Bering to lead an expedition to travel across the Sea of Okhotsk to Kamchatka and to round the northeast tip of Asia.

In the previous century the Cossack Deshnev had actually sailed through the straits between Asia and North America, but his discoveries were by now merely legends and Peter wanted to establish the relationship between the two continents definitively.

Vitus Bering. The Granger Collection, New York.

Bering and his men left St. Petersburg in February 1725 and traveled overland across Siberia with the supplies for the expedition and the materials to build a boat. They built the boat and sailed across the Sea of Okhotsk in July 1727. They then sledded across the Kamchatka Peninsula and built another boat, the *Gabriel*, on the east coast of Kamchatka.

Sailing in July, 1728 he sailed up the east coast of Kamchatka. He followed the coast northward, sighting a large island out to sea which he named St. Lawrence, which is now part of Alaska. Finally, the mainland started to trend westward, and Bering was convinced that he had come as far as the tip of Asia. He could go no farther because of the rising ice.

Bering spent the winter of 1728-29 in Kamchatka and then sailed back across the Sea of Okhotsk, taking time along the way to plot the latitude and longitude of the southern tip of the peninsula. He traveled back overland to St. Petersburg and made his report to the Imperial Court and tried to interest it in opening up northwestern North America by way of Siberia.

Bering requested permission from Empress Anna to lead a second expedition. In 1733 he was made commander of the "Great Northern Expedition", charged with exploring the Arctic coast of Siberia and the Kurile Islands, as well being named leader of a Second Kamchatka Expedition. Bering was not able to leave Okhotsk until September 1740 on his voyage to North America. This time he took several scientists with him to investigate various aspects of the new lands. He sailed in two ships, the *St. Paul* and the *St. Peter*, the second ship being commanded by Alexei Ilyich Chirikov who had been a member of Bering's first voyage.

The expedition spent the first winter at a base they established on the east coast of Kamchatka at a place they named Petropavlovsk after their two ships. Today, it is the largest Russian city in Kamchatka. On June 5, 1741 the two ships sailed towards North America but were almost immediately separated. Chirikov's ship made it to the mainland of North America, but he lost the ship's two boats that he sent out to reconnoiter. His crew suffered greatly from scurvy, and he was lucky to get back to Petropavlovsk in October.

Bering was much less lucky. He initially sailed south but then turned east. On July 17 Bering sighted Mt. St. Elias on the American mainland and landed briefly on Kayak Island off the south coast of Alaska. On his return he sighted the Kenai Peninsula and many of the Aleutian Islands. Bering and his men became very ill from scurvy and as the winter neared they were wrecked on a small island off the east coast of Kamchatka. This island has since been named Bering Island; it is part of the Komandorskiye Group and is only 300 miles from Petropavlovsk. The men suffered intensely on the barren island, and Bering and most of his men died during the winter. Bering died on December 8, 1741. The few survivors built a new boat from the wreckage of the old in order to sail to Petropavlovsk, which they reached on August 27, 1742.

Where to learn more

A very good recent book that includes extensive research in Russian-language sources is Raymond H. Fisher's *Bering's Voyages: Whither and Why* (Seattle: University of Washington Press, 1977). In 1922 the American Geographical Society published a two-volume account of Bering's explorations by F. A. Golder that included his log books and official reports. It was reprinted in 1968 by Octagon Books, Inc. of New York: *Bering's Voyages: An Account of the Efforts of the Russians to Determine the Relation of Asia and America.* The University of Alaska Press in Fairbanks recently published (1986) a translation of one of the major sources for Bering's voyages—the account in German of Gerhard Friedrich Müller that was originally published in 1758, called in English *Bering's Voyages: The Reports from Russia.* Another was published by Stanford University Press in 1988: Georg Wilhelm Steler, *Journal of a Voyage with Bering, 1741-1742*, edited by O.W. Frost.

Louis-Gustave Binger

(1856 - 1936)

Louis-Gustave Binger was leading French colonialist who led an expedition to West Africa that explored much unknown territory and discovered the source of the Volta River.

Louis-Gustave Binger was born in the French city of Strasbourg on October 14, 1856, the son of a factory owner. During the Franco-Prussian War of 1870 Strasbourg and its region, Alsace, were captured and then annexed by the Germans. Binger's family escaped to French-held territory, and he joined the French army in the Norman city of Rouen in 1874. He was sent to officers' school in 1879 and was sent as a junior lieutenant to Senegal at the end of 1880.

While in Senegal Binger took part in an expedition to the Casamance region in the south of the country, and then was sent on several mapping expeditions, first in Senegal and then to what is now Mali. He returned to France and was put in charge of drafting the first map of Senegal. He also wrote a book on the Bambara language, one of the major languages of West Africa.

At the end of 1886 Binger was sent back to Senegal at his request and was put in charge of an expedition to travel to the Niger River. He left in charge of a small military column of 10 men and 18 mules from Dakar, the capital of Senegal, on February 20, 1887. He crossed through the land of the African leader Samory who was trying to organize resistance to France's imperialist efforts to control West Africa. Binger laid siege to the town of Tieba in August 1887 and then traveled on to Kong in what is now northern Ivory Coast on February 20, 1888. Welcomed by the ruler of that region, he then traveled up the Volta River to its source in what is now Burkina Faso. He reached Ouagadougou, then the capital of the Mossi people and now the capital of Burkina Faso, in July 1888.

From Burkina Faso Binger went south to Salaga and then back to Kong in January 1889. He went south to the small port of Grand-Bassam, near present-day Abidjan, in March 1889. He and his small group of men had traveled about 2,500 miles in two years through interior parts of West Africa never before visited by Europeans. He published the results of his trip in 1890 in a book called *From the Niger to the Gulf of Guinea*. The Binger expedition laid the foundation for the future colony of French West Africa.

Following this successful mission Binger's career proceeded rapidly. He was put in charge of a French national colonial conference in 1889-1890 and then was sent as the French representative to negotiate the boundaries between the Ivory Coast and the Ashante tribe in what is now Ghana. He was named the administrator of the new colony of Ivory Coast in 1892. He returned to France as the director of African affairs for the Ministry of Colonies in 1896. He was later put in charge of fixing the boundaries between the French and the British and German colonies in West Africa. He reached the rank of Governor General of West Africa before retiring in 1907. He made one last trip to Africa in 1927 before his death in a French country retreat on November 10, 1936.

Where to learn more

There is very little available about Binger in English. The account of his expedition was published only in French as *Du Niger au golfe de Guinée* in two volumes, the first being a short summary of the complete record found in volume 2, in Paris in 1890 and 1892. His autobiography, *Une vie d'explorateur* (The Life of an Explorer) was published in Paris in 1938.

Hiram Bingham

(1875 - 1956)

Hiram Bingham was an American explorer who discovered the famous Inca ruins of Machu Picchu and other important Inca sites.

Hiram Bingham was born in Honolulu, Hawaii, on November 19, 1875, the son of retired missionaries from an old Hawaii family. He graduated from Yale University and then returned to Hawaii for a short time. He decided on an academic career and received his M.A. degree from the University of California at Berkeley and then a Ph.D. at Yale in Latin American history.

In 1905 Bingham made his first trip to South America, following the route of the Liberator, Simón Bolivar, from Caracas, Venezuela to Bogotá, Colombia. He wrote about the journey in *The Journal of an Expedition Across Venezuela and Colombia*. He returned in 1908 and 1909 and retraced the old Spanish trade route from Buenos Aires to Lima. While in Peru, in February, 1909, he visited Choqquequirau, a recently discovered Inca site that had once been thought to be the last refuge of the Inca rulers after they were defeated by **Francisco Pizarro**. This visit inspired him with the desire to find the legendary "lost city of the Incas."

In 1911 Bingham went back to Peru with two goals: to climb Mount Coropuna to see whether it was higher than Mount Aconcagua and to seek out the last capital of the Incas, the almost mystical city of Vilcabamba. Arriving in Arequipa in Peru in June 1911, he decided that it would not be wise to try to make the climb in winter and instead decided to look for ruins in the valley of the Rio Urubamba. According to legend, the last Inca ruler, Manco II, had established his capital, Vitcos, in the Vilcabamba range. Various stories of ruins circulated, but the best opinions fixed the capital somewhere in the valleys of the Vilcabamba and Urubamba rivers.

Setting out with a mule train, Bingham left Cuzco in July 1911. He traveled through the terraces of the valley of Yucay and past the gardens of Ollantaitambo. At Salapunco in the Urubamba valley he saw the ruins of a small fortress of pre-European origin. One night, Bingham camped between the road and the Urubamba River. The owner of a nearby hut, Melchor Arteaga, came out to see who the stranger was and told him about some nearby ruins called Machu Picchu. On the next morning, July 24, 1911, Bingham persuaded Arteaga to take him there. After a walk of 45 minutes, they left the main road, crossed the rapids of the Urubamba River on a rickety bridge, and climbed up a rough path through the forest. They ate lunch in the hut of some Native Americans who were farming on some ancient Inca terraces.

Leaving the hut, Bingham spent an hour and twenty minutes climbing to the top of row upon row of terraces almost 1,000 feet high. He crossed the terraces, went through a nearby forest, and came upon a vast complex of granite houses constructed with extremely careful stonework. There he also saw a three-sided temple that rivaled any that had ever been found in Peru. This was Machu Picchu, the most famous of all the Inca ruins.

Bingham did not stay long at Machu Picchu because he felt that he could still find the capital city of Vitcos, which was supposed to be marked by a white boulder over a spring of water. At Huadquiña Bingham learned of "important ruins" a few days' journey down the Urubamba River. They turned out to be merely the ruins of a small Inca storehouse. He then traveled up the Vilcabamba River to the village of Lucma, where he consulted Evaristo Morovejo, the sub-prefect of the village. Morovejo's brother was supposed to have found some ruins while hunting for buried treasure in 1884.

Morovejo took Bingham to the small village of Puquiura, three miles from Lucma. The ruins they saw were of a Spanish mill. However, on a hill above Puquiura, called Rosaspata by the locals, there were more ruins that Bingham went to investigate. They turned out to be the remains of a fortress containing 14 rectangular Inca buildings, including a "long palace" that had 15 doors along one side. Bingham was convinced that this was Vitcos. On the second day, August 8, 1911, Morovejo showed him a white boulder and, some distance away, a spring. Bingham followed the stream to an open spot where he saw what he had been looking for: a gigantic white boulder with Inca carvings on its side overlooking a pool near the ruins of an Inca temple. Bingham had found Vitcos.

From Vitcos, Bingham went to the small Spanish town of Vilcabamba, named after, but not the same as, the Inca city of Vilcabamba. He traveled from there into the surrounding jungle lowlands and reached a remote sugar plantation on August 15, 1911. Its owner took him on a two-day trip into the forest to a spot called Espíritu Pampa (the Plain of the Spirits). Here they found more Inca ruins, which later turned out to be those of a large town. Bingham's guides and porters were impatient, however, and he was not able to stay long at the site.

After these incredible discoveries within the space of a few weeks, Bingham's climb up Mount Coropuna was anticlimactic. He made the climb with an American mountaineer, H.L. Tucker, a British naturalist, an American astronomer, and a Peruvian guide. The astronomer was injured and forced to return to Arequipa. Since they were going to altitudes not previously scaled, their guide was not much help, and the muleteers demanded extra pay before they would climb past the snow line. The Native American guide went with Tucker and Bingham to the peak, which they reached from a base camp they had set up at 17,300 feet. They were clothed warmly enough that they did not have to worry about frostbite, but they did suffer from *soroche*, the illness caused by lack of oxygen. The three men reached the summit on October 14 after a climb of six and a half hours. The mountain turned out to have three peaks, and it was only by chance that they had climbed the highest one. Once they got to the top and made their measurements, Bingham was disappointed to learn that it was not as high as Aconcagua. He left feeling that he had conquered the second highest peak in the Andes. In later years, however, it was established that Coropuna is only the nineteenth highest peak in the Andes.

Bingham led expeditions back to the Vilcabamba region in 1912 and 1915 to clear the ruins he had discovered and to make further explorations and scientific studies in the area. These expeditions found many small Inca ruins in the hills near Machu Picchu, and traces of Inca roads and buildings at various places along the mountain range. As a result of these expeditions, Bingham became more and more convinced that Machu Picchu was the lost city of Vilcabamba and supported this view until his death. More recent expeditions and interpretations make it seem more likely that Vilcabamba should be identified with Bingham's other great discovery at Espíritu Pampa.

Following the 1915 expedition, Bingham made no further exploring trips to South America. He volunteered to serve in World War I and became the chief of air personnel in the air service after learning how to fly. He then entered Republican politics and was elected lieutenant governor of Connecticut in 1922. He ran for governor in 1924 and won that race as well. However, he served for only one day. During the election campaign, one of the Connecticut senators committed suicide, and a special election was held to replace him. Bingham entered the race and won once again. He served as United States senator from 1925 to 1933.

While in the Senate, Bingham became involved in a scandal when it was revealed that he was using a paid lobbyist to help him draft legislation and had taken him to closed committee meetings as a staff member. He was censured by the Senate and lost the following election. He spent the following years writing and serving on the boards of several large corporations. He was recalled to Washington by President Truman and put in charge of the Loyalty Review Board of the Civil Service Commission in 1951. This was during the "Red Scare" of the early 1950s, and the Board's job was to search out possibly disloyal employees. Bingham carried out his distasteful job with notable zeal. He left the board in 1953 and died three years later on June 6, 1956 in Washington, D.C.

Where to learn more

Bingham wrote several accounts of his expeditions: *Across South America* (Boston: Houghton Mifflin, 1911), which discusses his travels before discovering Machu Picchu; "In the Wonderland of Peru," *National Geographic Magazine*, vol. 24 (April 1913), an account of his Inca discoveries that takes up the entire issue of the magazine; *In the Wonderland of Peru: The Work Accomplished by the Peruvian Expedition of 1912, under the Auspices of Yale University and the National Geographic Society* (Washington: The National Geographic Society, 1913), an expanded version of the preceding; and *Inca Land: Explorations in the Highlands of Peru* (Boston: Houghton Mifflin Co., 1922), which includes the discovery of Machu Picchu as well as the results of the 1915 expedition.

In 1989 two biographies of Bingham were published by relatives that made use of documentary source material and family photographs: Alfred M. Bingham, *Portrait of an Explorer: Hiram Bingham, Discoverer of Machu Picchu* (Ames: Iowa State University Press) and Woodbridge Bingham, *Hiram Bingham: A Personal History* (Boulder, Colorado: Bin Lan Zhen Publishers). There is also a fictionalized account of Bingham's discovery of the Inca ruins: Carter Wilson, *Treasures on Earth* (New York: Alfred A. Knopf, 1981).

The greatest help for writing this account came from two sources: John Hemming, *The Conquest of the Incas* (New York: Macmillan, 1970) and Edward J. Goodman, *The Explorers of South America* (New York: Macmillan, 1972).

Isabella Bird

(1831 - 1904)

Isabella Bird was an English traveler who made a remarkable series of journeys at the end of the 19th century.

Isabella Bird was born in the English county of Yorkshire on October 15, 1831. Her father was an Anglican clergyman and her mother was the daughter of a clergyman. Bird was a small woman and suffered from several ailments during her childhood. In 1850 she had an operation to remove a tumor from her spine. The operation was only partially successful, and she suffered from insomnia and depression. He doctor recommended that she travel, and in 1854 her father gave her £100 and told her she was free to go wherever she wanted. She used it to travel to North America and stayed for several months in eastern Canada and the United States. On her return she used the letters she had written to her sister, Hennie, as the basis for her first book, *The Englishwoman in America*.

Bird's father died in 1858 and she and her sister and mother moved to Edinburgh in Scotland, where she lived for the rest of her life. She took other short trips during the following years, including three to North America and one to the Mediterranean. However, the turning point in her life came in 1872 when she traveled to Hawaii. She had taken a ship from San Francisco headed for New Zealand, but decided to get off in Hawaii and stayed there for six months. During that time she learned how to ride a horse astride, which ended the backaches she suffered from riding sidesaddle, and she climbed up to the top of Hawaii's volcanic peaks. Later, she wrote about her pleasure in "visiting remote regions which are known to few even of the residents, living among the natives, and otherwise seeing Hawaiian life in all its phases." She recorded her happy visit in *Six Months in the Sandwich Islands*, published in 1875.

Leaving Hawaii, Bird went to the west coast of the United States. From San Francisco she traveled alone by horse to Lake Tahoe and then to the Rocky Mountains and Colorado. During that trip she had many adventures, including riding alone through a blizzard with her eyes frozen shut, spending several months snowed in a cabin with two young men, and being wooed by a lonely outlaw. All these tales she told in her book *A Lady's Life in the Rocky Mountains*, published in 1879.

From San Francisco Bird went to Japan, where she hired a young Japanese man of 18 to be her translator. They traveled together to the northern part of Hokkaido, the northernmost part of the country, where she stayed among members of the Ainu tribe, the original, non-Japanese, inhabitants of the islands. Her

experiences formed the basis for her book *Unbeaten Tracks in Japan*, published in 1880. From Japan she traveled to Hong Kong, Canton, Saigon, and Singapore. From Singapore she traveled among the Malay states of the Malayan Peninsula for five weeks.

When Bird returned to England she was famous for her books about Hawaii and the Rocky Mountains. However, shortly after her return her sister died from typhoid. Bird married the doctor who had taken care of her, Dr. John Bishop, in 1881. They were happy together, but he died only five years after the marriage.

Following Bishop's death, Bird set out again on her travels. In 1888 she left for India. While there she established the Henrietta Bird Hospital in Amritsar and the John Bishop Memorial Hospital in Srinigar. She traveled to Kashmir and to Ladakh in the far north on the border with Tibet. During her travels one of her horses lost its footing while crossing a river. The horse drowned and Bird suffered two broken ribs. On her return to Simla in northern India she met up with Major Herbert Sawyer who was on his way to Persia (Iran). The two traveled together through the desert in mid-winter and arrived in Tehran half-dead. After depositing the major at his new duty station, Bird set out alone and spent the next six months traveling at the head of her own caravan through northern Iran, Kurdistan, and Turkey.

On her return to England, Bird spoke out against the atrocities that were being committed against the Armenians in the Middle East and met with Prime Minister Gladstone and addressed a Parliamentary committee on the question. By this time she was extremely well known in her native land and was made a fellow of the Royal Scottish Geographical Society and the first woman fellow of the Royal Geographical Society. However, she was not happy being still and in 1894 she set out again.

Bird traveled first to Yokohama in Japan and from there into Korea. She spent several months in that country and then was forced to leave at the outbreak of the Sino-Japanese War that was to lead to the occupation of Korea by Japan. She went to Mukden in Manchuria and photographed Chinese soldiers headed for the front. She then went back into Korea to view the devastation of the war. From Korea she went to the Yangtze River in China in January 1896. She traveled by sampan up the river as far as she could go and then went overland into the province of Sichuan. There she was attacked by a mob that called her a "foreign devil" and trapped her in the top floor of a house, which they then set on fire. She was rescued at the last minute by a detachment of soldiers. At another place she was stoned and knocked unconscious. She then traveled into the mountains bordering Tibet before returning home in 1897.

Back in Britain she wrote *The Yangtze Valley and Beyond*, which was published in 1900. She made her last trip to Morocco in 1901. On her return she became ill and died in Edinburgh on October 7, 1904.

Where to learn more

Isabella Bird (or Isabella Bird Bishop as she became known after her marriage) wrote several travelogues: *The Englishwoman in America* (London: Murray, 1856); *The Hawaiian Archipelago* (London: Murray, 1875), reprinted as *Six Months in the Sandwich Islands* in a paperback edition by the University of Hawaii Press in 1964; *A Lady's Life in the Rocky Mountains* (London: Murray,

1879); *Unbeaten Tracks in Japan* (London: Murray, 1880); *The Golden Chersonese and the Way Thither* (London: Murray, 1883); *Among the Tibetans* (New York: Revell, 1894); *The Yangtze Valley and Beyond* (London: Murray, 1900), reprinted as a paperback in 1985 (Boston: Beacon Press).

There is a collection of her writings edited by Cicely Paalser Haveley entitled *This Grand Beyond: Travels of Isabella Bird Bishop* (London: Century, 1984) and a fairly recent biography, Pat Barr, *A Curious Life for a Lady: The Story of Isabella Bird, a Remarkable Victorian Traveler* (Garden City, N.Y.: Doubleday, 1970).

There are chapters on Bird in Mignon Rittenhouse, *Seven Women Explorers* (Philadelphia: Lippincott, 1964); Dea Birkett, *Spinsters Abroad: Victorian Lady Explorers* (London: Basil Blackwell, 1989); and Marion Tinling, *Women into the Unknown* (New York: Greenwood Press, 1989).

John Biscoe

(1794 - 1849)

John Biscoe was an English sealing captain who made a circumnavigation of Antarctica and discovered several parts of the continent.

John Biscoe was born in Middlesex County in England, which is now part of Greater London. He joined the Royal Navy in 1812 and fought in the war against the United States (the War of 1812) until July 1815. After leaving the Navy he sailed on merchant ships to the Caribbean and to Asia. He then went to work for the firm of Enderby Brothers as the captain of a sealing ship.

Enderby Brothers had been founded as a commercial shipping line by Samuel Enderby. When his American trade was cut off by the American Revolution, Enderby turned to sealing—the capture of seals in the southern oceans to supply sealskins and seal oil for markets in Europe and China. Enderby was very interested in the discoveries made by his sealing captains, and this was even more true of one of his sons, Charles Enderby, one of the founders of the Royal Geographical Society in London. Samuel Enderby died in 1829, and the firm was taken over by Charles and his two brothers.

In 1830 Charles Enderby sent Biscoe south with instructions to search for land in the far south, east of the meridian of Greenwich, or 0° of longitude. He was put in charge of two small ships, the *Tula* and the *Lively*. They left England on July 14, 1830 and reached the Falkland Islands (Malvinas) in the South Atlantic in early November. Not finding any seals in the vicinity, Biscoe headed south and crossed the Antarctic Circle on January 22, 1831. He reached his farthest south on January 29 at 69°3'S when he was forced to turn back north. He then sailed eastward along the edge of the ice pack. On February 24 he was the first person to sight land in the Indian Ocean sector of Antarctica, probably at a place now called Casey Bay. Biscoe had himself lowered into the ship's boat and tried to row ashore but was forced to turn back after only half an hour.

Still sailing eastward, Biscoe sighted land more clearly in the following days in an area he called Enderby Land. He saw a mountain peak, which he called Cape Ann and which is now named Mount Biscoe. On March 3 the ships were hit by a storm and were separated. The *Tula* was blown 120 miles to the northwest and could only head back south on March 16. Biscoe sighted Mount Biscoe again on March 17. On April 3 he gave up his voyage along the coast of Antarctica and sailed north. By then, many of the crew were sick from scurvy and several died

before they reached port at Hobart, Tasmania. There the *Tula* was reunited with the *Lively*, whose crew had been reduced to three men by deaths from scurvy.

While in Hobart, Biscoe repaired his two ships and tried to return his men to good health. He set sail again on October 10, 1831. Still unable to find seals, he turned south and headed for the South Shetland Islands, off the Antarctic Peninsula, which had been discovered in 1819 by other British sealing captains. On February 15, 1832 Biscoe sighted land and named it Adelaide Island after the Queen of England. He sailed along the western coast of the Peninsula discovering many island groups, including those named the Biscoe Islands. On February 21, 1832 Biscoe rowed ashore and took possession of the land in the name of King William IV of Great Britain. He named the area that he saw Graham Land, which is still used for the southern part of the Antarctic Peninsula. If, as he thought, Biscoe had landed on the mainland, it is possible that he was the first man to do so. However, it is considered more likely that he had reached Anvers Island off the coast.

Still having found few seals, Biscoe headed north and reached the Falkland Islands. He had completed the third circumnavigation of Antarctica, following **James Cook** and **Fabian von Bellingshausen**. In the Falkland Islands, the *Lively* was wrecked in July 1832, and the crew had to transfer to the *Tula*. However, when Biscoe announced his attention of continuing to hunt for seals, most of the crew deserted. By September 29 he was left with only four men and three boys to sail his ship and was to return to England, where he arrived in January 1833. The log of his voyage was presented to the newly formed Royal Geographical Society, and Biscoe was awarded its Gold Medal. In 1837 Biscoe moved to Sydney in Australia and then on to Hobart. By then, he was in poor health and was unable to work. There was a request for a public subscription for funds to send him back to England. He died on the voyage back, in 1843, and was buried at sea. He left a widow and four children with no income. In 1850 a number of prominent persons, including the explorers **Sir Edward Parry** and **Sir George Back** sponsored a public appeal to raise money to support them.

Where to learn more

One of the best books about the exploration of Antarctica has been published by Reader's Digest of Australia with the name *Antarctica: Great Stories from the Frozen Continent* (Sydney: 1988). The editors went to a great deal of trouble to track down often obscure information about sealers such as John Biscoe, and much of the above narrative is based on their research. Another helpful book for putting Biscoe's voyage into perspective with those of other sealing captains of the era is the *Chronological List of Antarctic Expeditions and Related Historical Events*, by R. K. Headland of the Scott Polar Research Institute of the University of Cambridge, published by the Cambridge University Press in 1989.

Gregory Blaxland

(1778 - 1853)

Gregory Blaxland was an Australian rancher who was the first person to find a way through the mountains west of Sydney.

Gregory Blaxland was born in the English county of Kent on June 17, 1778, the son of a local mayor and large property owner. In 1799 he married the daughter of another prosperous farmer. The Blaxlands were friends of **Sir Joseph Banks**, who encouraged them to emigrate to Australia as a way of increasing the free settler element in that British penal colony, founded in 1788. They left England on September 1, 1805. Once in Australia Blaxland bought 4,000 acres of pasture land and hired 40 convict laborers and immediately became one of the colony's most prominent citizens. He continued to expand his landholding and became an outspoken opponent of the administration.

For the first twenty-odd years of its existence the colony of New South Wales had been limited to a very small area around the settlement at Sydney. Starting in 1810 there was a severe drought that threatened to wipe out the herds of livestock on which the colony depended. Blaxland decided that he would try to take his herd to new grazing areas rather than stand by and watch them die. On May 11, 1813 he left his ranch at South Creek, near the present-day town on St. Mary's, about 25 miles east of Sydney. He took with him Lieutenant William Lawson, a surveyor, and another sheep rancher, William Charles Wentworth, and four convicts as well as his herd of sheep. At the time the expedition seemed to have been a joint one, and it was only later that Blaxland claimed to be its instigator and leader.

The exploring party did a very smart thing: rather than follow the valleys, which previous trips had shown ended in dead-ends, they went to the top of the ridges and followed them between the river valleys. Although they only covered two miles a day Blaxland's methods worked, and he made it into the Blue Mountains and the valley of the Warragamba River. At Mount York, about 70 miles from Sydney, on May 28, 1813 the party looked down on a wide stretch of pasture land. He reported on

his return that there was "enough grass to support the stock of the colony for thirty years." He went into the valley, and on the shores of the Lett River, a few miles south of the present town of Lithgow, the members of the expedition feasted on kangaroo and fish while the animals were able to fill themselves on grass.

Blaxland continued on a little farther, to Mount Blaxland, and then returned to Sydney to give his important news to the governor. Governor Macquarie immediately sent out his surveyor, George William Evans, who followed Blaxland's route and then continued on to the Fish River on the other side of the Blue Mountains. The route that Blaxland pioneered is the route of the Great Western Highway, the main road between Sydney and the west.

On his return to Sydney, Blaxland was not allowed to exploit his new-found lands and thereafter became a harsh critic of the colonial government. He lost much of his wealth in the continuing drought. He settled down on one of his farms in 1819 and experimented with raising various crops, of which the most successful was grapes for making wine. In 1822 he took a sample of his wine to England and was awarded a silver medal for it. While in England he wrote the account of his exploring expedition. His wife died in 1826, and Blaxland spent the next few years dealing with his creditors and criticizing the government. He was sufficiently prominent to be sent by a group of settlers to London in 1829 with a petition asking for trial by jury and some form of representative government for the colony. He then retired from public view and settled on his property in what is now the Sydney suburb of North Parramatta on the site of the Parramatta Psychiatric Centre. He hanged himself on January 1, 1853.

Where to learn more

Gregory Blaxland's own account of his expedition, *A Journal of Discovery Across the Blue Mountains, New South Wales in 1813*, was published in London in 1823. It was reprinted in vol. 23 (1937) of the *Journal of the Royal Australian Historical Society*. Excerpts were published in *Australian Explorers: A Selection from their Writings with an Introduction* by Kathleen Fitzpatrick (London: Oxford University Press, 1958). The best account of Blaxland's expedition, which does not necessarily accept Blaxland's own view of his prominence in it, is by Arthur Jose in *Builders and Pioneers of Australia* (London: J.M. Dent & Sons, 1928).

Lady Anne Blunt

(1837 - 1917)

Sir Wilfrid Scawen Blunt

(1840 - 1922)

Lady Anne and Sir Wilfrid Scawen Blunt were an English couple who made a trip to the Bedouin tribes of Iraq and another into central Arabia. Lady Anne Blunt was the first European woman to travel in Arabia.

Lady Anne Noel was a granddaughter of Lord Byron, the famous English poet. She was born into a noble family and spent most of her childhood in Europe where she learned to speak several languages and learned how to draw and play the violin (she owned two Stradivarius violins and practiced five hours every day). Wilfrid Blunt was born into a wealthy landholding family in the county of Sussex. His father died when he was two years old and he spent an unhappy childhood traveling with his mother and being sent away to boarding schools. He joined the British Foreign Service at the age of 18 and spent 12 years at various posts in Europe and South America.

Anne and Wilfrid met in Florence, Italy, and were married in London on June 8, 1869. Following their marriage, Anne suffered a series of miscarriages. However, in 1873 she gave birth to a daughter, their only child. Wilfrid inherited his father's title and estates in 1872, and they used the opportunity that this provided to travel.

In 1873 the Blunts traveled to Constantinople and Asia Minor. The following year they went to Algeria and journeyed into the Sahara. In 1875-1876 they went to Egypt. Both of the Blunts had a desire to see Arabia, and they made that their next destination. They left England in November 1877 and landed at Alexandretta at the eastern end of the Mediterranean and then traveled to Aleppo in Syria. Staying in Aleppo for a month, they discussed their plans with the British consul there, a distant relation of Anne's. He encouraged them to make a systematic trip to the Bedouin tribes of the Tigris and Euphrates River valleys, about whom little was known in the outside world. They assembled a small caravan and set out from Aleppo on January 9, 1878 through the Syrian Desert.

The Blunts met their first party of Bedouins about a week later. On January 17 they were held in the town of Deyr by Turkish officials, who were the rulers of the country and who suspected the Blunts of being spies. They were released a week later and traveled on to Baghdad. They did not like the city and left on February 24 heading north. They traveled from one Bedouin encampment to another and adopted Arab clothes and rode on Arabian stallions, which they found more comfortable than camels. In mid-March they reached the camp of Faris, one of the two great sheikhs of the Shammar tribe. Faris became quite fond

Lady Anne and Sir Wilfrid Blunt. The Granger Collection, New York.

of them and adopted Wilfrid as his "blood brother" in an impressive ceremony.

Leaving the Shammar tribe the Blunts headed back to Deyr, where they were once again threatened by the Turks and then turned toward the ruins of Palmyra, earlier visited by **Lady Hester Stanhope**. They met the son of a local sheikh, Muhammad Ibn Aruk, who served as their guide to Palmyra and then led them south to the camp of the Anazeh tribe and the enormous tent city of the Rowallah tribe with 20,000 tents and 150,000 camels. From there they headed north to Damascus. On the last night of their trip Muhammad and Wilfrid became blood brothers, and the sheikh's son offered to take them on a trip to Arabia the following year. On their arrival in Damascus they were shocked at the manners of a group of visiting English tourists and decided they liked the ways of the desert better.

The Blunts took back six Arabian mares with them to England and started a breeding farm for racehorses that was to become world famous. While they were in England Anne wrote the story of their visits to the Bedouin tribes. They returned to Damascus in November 1878 to begin their journey to the Najd, the central region of the Arabian peninsula. There they met up with Muhammad ibn Aruk and headed south on the pilgrimage route towards Mecca on December 13, 1878. On January 3, 1879 they were surrounded by a Bedouin raiding party but were left unharmed when Muhammad said that they were under his protection.

The first large town that the Blunts came to was Al-Jawf on the northern edge of the Nafud Desert, which had been conquered by the people of the city of Ha'il. South of Al-Jawf they met distant relatives of Muhammad, and Wilfrid led in the negotiations to arrange a marriage for the young man. They then crossed the red sands of the Nafud Desert, a journey that lasted from January 12-24, 1879. The end of their trip was at the city of Ha'il.

At Ha'il the Blunts were received by the local emir, and they had a fascinating stay. Anne was invited to visit the harem, and she wrote about the boredom of the life there. One evening at a banquet they were shown a telephone, which had only been invented three years earlier by Alexander Graham Bell and which the Blunts had never seen. At one time through a series of misunderstandings they lost their favored positions and seemed threatened, but it was quickly cleared up. Wilfrid spent his time studying the traditional methods of Arab government, which he was to write about on his return. They went for a ride in the desert in which all the emir's horses, the most famous in Arabia, took part.

The Blunts left Ha'il on February 2, 1879 with a party of Persians returning to Iran after having made the pilgrimage to Mecca. Along the way the caravan ran out of food, and they traveled the last 170 miles in six days with nothing to eat. They reached Baghdad on March 6 in the middle of a heavy rainstorm. Anne was the first European woman to have traveled in Arabia.

Although Anne wanted to return to England at that point, Wilfrid had agreed to travel on to India in order to make a report about the possibility of building a railroad from the Tigris River to the Persian Gulf. The trip was a disaster, Wilfrid almost dying of dysentery along the way. Anne later characterized it as "disagreeable, difficult, dangerous and all but disastrous . . . disappointing and disheartening. She wrote in a letter that "Wilfrid will *never* want to go on any hard journey again, I will swear to that!"

Anne and Wilfrid Blunt reached the Persian Gulf port of Bushire on April 25, 1879 after a journey of 2,000 miles. They were probably the first Europeans in modern times to travel all the way from the Mediterranean to the Persian Gulf. When they arrived at the door of the British consul, the guards refused to allow them in because they could not believe that the two vagabonds were really English. They were finally admitted and then traveled on to India and back to England.

On their return to England, Wilfrid took up the cause of Arabian nationalism and was unhappy about the wave of Western imperialism that was engulfing western Asia. He ran for a seat in Parliament but lost. His strong anti-colonial feelings led him to be shunned by many of his former friends. He was jailed in 1888 for a short time for advocating the right of the Irish to rule themselves. In 1882 the Blunts returned to Egypt and bought a large estate named Sheykh Obeyd in the desert outside of Cairo near the pyramids. Over the years it became Anne's principal residence, and she generally spoke Arabic rather than English. Wilfrid, who had always had a reputation as a "womanizer," continued to have a series of affairs outside of his marriage. In 1906 his mistress moved in with him in his estate in England. This caused a separation from Anne, and he never returned to Sheykh Obeyd. She died there on December 15, 1917. He died in England on September 10, 1922 and was buried on the grounds of his estate in a Bedouin ceremony.

Where to learn more

Lady Anne Blunt wrote the accounts of the two trips that the Blunts made to the Arab world. The first, *Bedouin Tribes of the Euphrates*, was published in 1879 (London: Cass; New York: Harper). The second, *A Pilgrimage to Nejd, the Cradle of the Arab Race* was first published by Murray in London in 1881. It was then reprinted by Cass in 1968 and then appeared in a paperback edition in 1985 (London: Century).

There are several books about the experiences of Europeans in Arabia that include interesting chapters about the Blunts. The best are Kathryn Tidrick, *Heart-Beguiling Araby* (Cambridge: Cambridge University Press, 1981); James C. Simmons, *Passionate Pilgrims: English Travelers to the World of the Desert Arabs* (New York: William Morrow and Company, 1987); and Zahra Freeth and H.V.F. Winstone, *Explorers of Arabia* (New York: Holmes & Meier, 1978).

There are several full-length biographies of Sir Wilfrid Blunt (but none for Lady Anne). The best and most recent is Elizabeth Longford's *A Pilgrimage of Passion: The Life of Wilfrid Scawen Blunt* (London: Weidenfeld and Nicolson, 1979). An interesting analysis of Wilfrid Blunt's amorous adventures can be found in Mark Girouard's *The Return to Camelot: Chivalry and the English Gentleman* (New Haven: Yale University Press, 1981).

Sidi Mubarak Bombay

(1820? - 1885)

Sidi Mubarak Bombay was a freed African slave who served as a leader of caravans in the expeditions of Richard Burton and John Hanning Speke, Speke and James Augustus Grant, Henry Morton Stanley, and Verney Lovett Cameron in Africa.

Sidi Mubarak (his Muslim name) was a member of the Yao tribe of east Africa, whose homeland is around Lake Nyasa (or Lake Malawi). At the age of 12 he was taken by Swahili traders to the port of Kilwa and then shipped to the island of Zanzibar where he was sold as a slave to an Arab merchant. His Arab owner moved to the city of Bombay in India and took Sidi Mubarak with him. On his death the slave was freed and adopted the name of Bombay.

Bombay returned to Zanzibar and became a soldier in the army of the Sultan of Zanzibar who claimed a large part of the African mainland. He was posted to the small garrison of Chokwe, about seven miles from the coast. On February 8, 1857 the British explorers **Sir Richard Burton** and **John Hanning Speke** arrived in Chokwe following a visit to the German missionary **Johannes Rebmann** in Mombasa. They were preparing an expedition into the interior of Africa to look for the source of the Nile River. They were recruiting porters and soldiers to accompany them on the trip, and they paid the commander of the garrison at Chokwe for the services of six soldiers, including Bombay, a guide, and five slaves. They made a short expedition into the interior. The two Englishmen formed a high opinion of Bombay's ability and contracted with the commander to employ him for a longer period. Speke, in particular, became attached to Bombay because they could converse in Hindi, which Speke had learned while he was an officer in the Indian Army. Burton had a natural talent for languages and could speak several fluently, and Speke had often felt excluded from conversations.

When the expedition in search of the Nile source began on June 16, 1857, Bombay was one of eight soldiers on the march. He proved to be the most loyal of all of Africans and Asians who were engaged on the journey, and he and his "brother" Mabruki sometimes carried Burton and Speke when they were too ill to walk. They reached the Arab emporium of Kazé (Tabora) in the center of what is now Tanzania on November 7, 1857. They stayed there for several weeks to recover. When they left on December 15, Bombay did not follow immediately, but he caught up with the expedition. When they reached Lake Tanganyika on February 13, 1858, both Burton and Speke were almost blind, and it was Bombay who first sighted the great body of water.

From Lake Tanganyika, the expedition returned to Tabora. Burton stayed there to recuperate while Speke went in search of the large Lake Ukerewe that they had heard about to the north. Bombay accompanied Speke and was responsible for negotiations along the way to obtain food and managed the porters and soldiers to keep the expedition moving. They reached the lake on August 3, 1858. Speke named it Lake Victoria, after the Queen of England, and was convinced that it was the source of the Nile. They only stayed a couple of days and returned to Tabora on August 25. Burton, incorrectly, did not believe that the lake was the Nile source and blamed the misunderstanding on Bombay's faulty translation from Swahili.

On the return trip, Speke became very ill with fever and was cared for by Bombay. They reached Zanzibar in early March 1858 and Burton and sailed from there on March 22, with Bombay on the dock waving goodbye. He then found a job working for the British consul in Bombay. Following their return to England, the argument between Burton and Speke broke out into public, and Speke was sent back to Africa by the Royal Geographical Society to verify his claims. When he and **James Augustus Grant** arrived in Zanzibar on August 17, 1860, Bombay was at the dock to meet them.

Bombay helped Speke and Grant outfit their expedition and left with them from Bagamoyo on the mainland on September 25, 1860. It took them 71 marching days to travel the approximately 500 miles to Tabora, and they arrived there on January 23, 1861. Speke found that the free labor that Bombay had hired in Zanzibar was much more efficient than the slaves and soldiers he had contracted for and wrote that without their support he never could have achieved his goal. Setting out from Tabora the expedition was delayed by illness and a local war. Speke sent Bombay back to Tabora to hire more porters. He then served as emissary to the King of Karagwe and, later, to the King of Buganda. In January 1862 Bombay and Speke got involved in a serious argument, and Bombay quit the expedition for a while but was persuaded to come back.

The expedition reached the place where the Nile flows out of Lake Victoria on July 21, 1862. They were blocked from going farther by King Kamurasi of Bunyoro. Once again, Bombay was chosen to lead the negotiations, and eventually they were allowed to proceed on November 9. They reached Gondokoro in what is now the southern Sudan on February 15, 1863, where they were met by **Samuel** and **Florence Baker**. They reached Khartoum on March 30. When they arrived in Cairo there were 18 of the original African supporters left. These men (nicknamed "Speke's Faithful") had their photograph taken in Cairo as part of the round of excursions and entertainments they had there. They parted with Speke on July 1, 1863 and were each given an extra year's wages and a $10 dowry to take back with them. They sailed on a British ship that was supposed to stop in Zanzibar, but it sailed to Mauritius instead. They had to wait another month to catch a ship home. They were taken care of there by the Inspector-General of Police, who took them to a circus. In a later letter, Speke wrote that Bombay was "the life and success of the expedition." As a result, Bombay was awarded the Silver Medal of the Royal Geographical Society, and the remainder of the "Faithful" were given bronze medals.

Following his return to Zanzibar, Bombay settled on the nearby island of Pemba. On January 6, 1871 **Henry Morton Stanley** arrived in Zanzibar to begin his expedition to search for **David Livingstone**. He hired Bombay to help him outfit the expedition. When the expedition left from the coast in March 1871, Bombay was in charge of the 12 soldiers. Stanley and Bombay had an argument in May that seems to have led to Bombay's demotion. They reached Tabora on June 23 and stayed until July 29, with Bombay unwilling to leave since he had moved in with a local woman. Leaving Tabora, they got involved in a battle between Arabs and Africans, in which Bombay protected Stanley. They were forced to return to Tabora and then set out again on September 20 by a different route. In October when Stanley refused to allow the men an additional day of rest, they mutinied for a short while. Stanley blamed Bombay for the troubles, and briefly had him put in chains. He was released after a short period and restored to his post.

When the expedition reached Ujiji on the shores of Lake Tanganyika on November 10, 1871, they were met by David Susi, who led them to Livingstone. After a few days Livingstone and Stanley and their African supporters set off across Lake Tanganyika, with Bombay serving as one of the rowers. On the return trip, Bombay was put in charge of one of the groups of men. It took them six weeks to get to Tabora, and they reached Zanzibar on May 7, 1872. Stanley paid Bombay a $50 bonus for his work.

Bombay was shortly to go to work again. In January 1874 he was hired by **Verney Lovett Cameron** to be his caravan leader on an expedition sent out to bring Livingstone out of Africa. The expedition was in Tabora when **James Chuma** arrived with the news that Livingstone had died. Cameron continued on with the aim of exploring Lake Tanganyika and finding its outlet. They reached the lake on February 21, 1875. With Bombay in command of one of the two canoes, they started exploring the lake on March 13. During the first part of the voyage, Cameron was sick and was cared for by Bombay. They reached the Lukuga River, the lake's only outlet, on May 4 and returned to Ujiji on May 9. By this time Bombay had been almost all the way around the lake.

The expedition crossed to the western side of Lake Tanganyika and set out from there to find the Congo River. They were met by Tippu Tib on August 19, 1875. The expedition made it all the way across Africa, reaching the Atlantic Ocean on November 11, 1875 and marching into Luanda, in Portuguese Angola, on November 21. Of the 54 members who reached the Atlantic, 49 of them had been recruited by Bombay in Zanzibar and had come the entire distance. In Luanda, Cameron bought a schooner and sent Bombay and the rest of his crew back to Zanzibar on February 8, 1876.

Back in Zanzibar, Bombay was visited by the Reverend W. Salter Price on May 5, 1876 of the Church Missionary Society and asked to lead a caravan to Uganda with the aim of opening a mission there. Bombay led a preliminary trip to Bagamoyo on the mainland, but in August he was informed that he had been awarded a life pension by the Royal Geographical Society and decided to retire. He died in Zanzibar on October 12, 1885.

Where to learn more

The only scholarly work about the role of Africans in the exploration of east Africa is Donald Simpson, *Dark Companions: The African Contribution to the European Exploration of East Africa* (New York: Harper & Row, 1976), upon which this résumé of Bombay's life is based. Simpson's history is based upon the journals of the various explorers, which are listed under their separate entries.

Benjamin Louis Eulalie de Bonneville

(1796 - 1878)

Benjamin Louis Eulalie de Bonneville was a U.S. Army officer who went on what was supposed to be a private exploring and fur-trading trip to the American West, but was apparently sponsored by the American government as part of a policy of expansion.

Benjamin Louis Eulalie de Bonneville was born in Paris, France in 1796. His father was a prominent French revolutionary and Thomas Paine, the American radical, had lived in his house for a number of years. Forced by the rise of Napoleon to leave France, the Bonneville family left France and migrated to the United States in August 1803. Thanks to family connections Benjamin was admitted to the West Point Military Academy at the age of 15 and graduated from there in December 1815.

Following his graduation Bonneville was assigned to various military posts throughout the United States and in 1820 helped build the military road being constructed between Washington, D.C. and New Orleans. In 1821 he was assigned to Fort Smith, Arkansas and then to Fort Gibson, Oklahoma. In 1825 he was

sent east to accompany the Marquis de Lafayette on his visit to the United States and then returned to Fort Gibson in 1826.

While serving at Fort Gibson, Bonneville saw the financial rewards that men were gaining in the fur trade in the Rocky Mountains. He decided that he wanted to participate as well and asked for and was granted a leave of absence from the army. He was financed by an associate of John Jacob Astor, the famous American fur-trading entrepreneur. It appears, however, that Bonneville's purpose was not strictly commercial. Although he was supposed to be on a private expedition, he was furnished with a set of instructions from the War Department in Washington that indicated that he was to look for the best routes westward to California and to report on the military capacities of the various Native American tribes he encountered. Bonneville was being used as an agent for American expansion.

Bonneville and his large party of 110 men left Fort Osage, Missouri on May 1, 1832. They traveled via the South Platte River to the Little Sandy River in western Wyoming and then down to the Green River. There he built a fort that was of little use as a fur-trading depot but was a good place for a potential military post. Bonneville and his men spent the winter of 1832-1833 trapping in the Rockies. At the fur-trading rendezvous in 1833 Bonneville sent **Joseph Reddeford Walker** out on the expedition that was to find the easiest route to California.

During the winter of 1833-1834 Bonneville traveled over the Rocky Mountains to the Columbia River to the Hudson's Bay Company trading post at Walla Walla. The British commander in charge of the post refused to let him proceed farther, and he was forced to turn back to the junction of the Snake and Portneuf Rivers near present-day Pocatello, Idaho. He traveled back to Walla Walla in 1834. He also visited the Willamette Valley in eastern Oregon and was the first American to report on its potential as a farming area. Apparently, Bonneville's aim was to assess British strength in the Pacific Northwest. At that time the area was disputed between Great Britain and the United States and was not awarded to the United States until 1846.

During the winter of 1834-1835 Bonneville encamped on the Bear River in northern Utah. During this period he organized exploring missions to the Great Salt Lake and the desert west of it and visited the salt flats that are named for him in western Utah. He attended the annual fur rendezvous at the forks of the Wind River in June and July 1835. He then traveled to the lands of the Crow tribe in Montana before heading back east.

Benjamin Louis Eulalie de Bonneville. The Granger Collection, New York.

On his return to the United States, Bonneville submitted his maps and reports to the Army. One of his maps is apparently the first one to show the Great Basin of Nevada. He was ordered to explain to a committee of the U.S. Senate why he had overstayed his leave of absence. As a result of his testimony, Washington Irving, the author, wrote a book entitled *The Adventures of Captain Bonneville* that became a best-seller and made Bonneville a national hero.

Bonneville was reinstated in the Army and spent the rest of his career serving in various posts. He fought in Mexico during the Mexican War and was promoted to lieutenant colonel and then to full colonel in 1855. He served during the Civil War and, in spite of a period of disability, was promoted to brigadier general in 1865. He retired in 1866 and moved to Fort Smith, Arkansas. He married a young woman there at the age of 74 and lived until the age of 82, dying peacefully at home.

Where to learn more

The legend of Benjamin Bonneville was made by the history by Washington Irving, *The Adventures of Captain Bonneville*, first published in 1837. It was reprinted in 1961 in an edition edited by Edgeley W. Todd (Norman: University of Oklahoma Press, 1961).

There is a chapter on Bonneville by Professor Todd of Colorado State University in LeRoy R. Hafen & Harvey L. Carter, eds., *Mountain Men and Fur Traders of the Far West* (Lincoln: University of Nebraska Press, 1982). Several of the histories of the American West discuss Bonneville. Two of the most important are Bernard DeVoto, *Across the Wide Missouri* (Boston: 1947) and William H. Goetzmann, *Exploration and Empire* (New York: Alfred A. Knopf, 1966).

Daniel Boone

(1734 - 1820)

Daniel Boone was an American frontiersman who was one of the first to explore what is now Kentucky and founded the first American settlement west of the Appalachian Mountains.

Daniel Boone was born about 11 miles from Reading, Pennsylvania, the son of Squire and Sarah Morgan Boone. When he was 15 his family moved to the Yadkin Valley in western North Carolina. He fought briefly in the French and Indian War, serving as a wagon driver in General Braddock's expedition to Pittsburgh in 1755. There he met a hunter named John Finley who told him about Kentucky, the land on the far slope of the Appalachians, west of Virginia. When Braddock's army was defeated on July 9, 1755, Boone was able to escape on one of the horses pulling the wagons.

Daniel Boone.

Returning to North Carolina, Boone married Rebecca Bryan on August 14, 1755. They built a log cabin, began farming, and had two sons. A raid by Native Americans drove them off the farm, and Boone found employment as a wagoner for a tobacco plantation in Virginia. He joined an expedition of volunteers against the Cherokee tribe in Tennessee. The defeat of the Cherokees allowed the Boone family to return to their farm in North Carolina. Boone began to spend more time hunting and trapping and made a notable trip as far south as Florida in 1765. He tried to convince his wife to move to Pensacola, then the capital of the new British colony of West Florida, but she refused.

Boone made his first trip to Kentucky in the winter of 1767-1768, getting as far as present-day Floyd County in the mountains of eastern Kentucky. In the winter of 1768, Finley showed up at Boone's farm, and the two planned a new expedition. They left the Yadkin Valley on May 1, 1769 with a small party of four. Provisioned by Judge Richard Henderson of North Carolina, a land speculator and an acquaintance of Boone's, they traveled up the Watauga River valley to the crest of the mountains and then descended the valley of the South Fork of the Holston River in what is now extreme northeastern Tennessee. They climbed over ridges to reach the Clinch and Powell Rivers and then attained the Cumberland Gap, where they descended into Kentucky. They traveled as far as Station Camp Creek in present Estill County, when they split up into two groups.

Reaching the South Fork of the Kentucky River in what is now the Daniel Boone National Forest, in December 1769 Boone and his companion were captured by a Shawnee raiding party but were able to escape after a week but lost most of their supplies and ammunition. They were then reunited with Boone's brother, Squire, and the fourth member of the party. The winter of 1769-1770 was very cold and difficult. One of the men did not return from a lone hunting trip and another returned home. In the spring of 1770 Boone's brother returned to North Carolina for a several weeks to get more ammunition. Boone traveled by himself through the Kentucky and Licking River valleys and explored the Ohio River down to the falls near present Louisville. On the return of his brother, they spent the summer hunting along the Kentucky River and the winter of 1770-1771 trapping furs in the Green and Cumberland valleys.

In March 1771 Boone and his brother headed back to North Carolina with a large supply of furs. Near the Cumberland Gap the brothers met a band of Cherokee tribesmen, who took their horses, supplies, and furs. They returned on foot to the Yadkin Valley with nothing.

Boone told his neighbors about the fertile lands of Kentucky and in 1773 convinced a group of settlers to accompany him back over the mountains. They were attacked at the Cumberland Gap in October 1773 by Native Americans, who killed Boone's oldest son James, who was 16 years old, and five others. Against Boone's advice, the rest of the party returned to North Carolina. Boone and his family spent the winter in an abandoned cabin in the Clinch River valley, and then they too recrossed the mountains and went home.

Back in North Carolina, the wealthy Judge Henderson decided that Kentucky offered great opportunities for land speculation, and he organized the Transylvania Company (without a charter) to purchase land from the Native American tribes. He hired Boone to negotiate such a purchase from a faction of the Cherokee tribe in an agreement known as the Watauga Treaty. In March 1775, Henderson sent Boone with a party of 28 to mark a trail across Cherokee territory to Cumberland Gap and into Kentucky as far as the south bank of the Kentucky River. This was the beginning of the famous Wilderness Road. On April 1, 1775, Boone began building a fort on the Kentucky River that was to become Boonesborough, in present-day Madison County.

Henderson tried to organize a separate government for his Kentucky settlements, but the Continental Congress then meeting in Philadelphia disapproved. George Rogers Clark arrived to annex Kentucky as part of Virginia, and Boone was appointed captain of the local militia and a justice. He spent the following years hunting and guiding parties of settlers to the new territory.

In February 1778 he was captured by a party of the same Shawnee warriors he had escaped from in 1769. He was first taken to Detroit, a British outpost, and then moved to a camp at Chillicothe, Ohio. He escaped on the night of June 16, 1778 and made his way back to Boonesborough. When he arrived, he learned that his wife had given him up for dead and had returned to North Carolina. Boone warned the settlers of an impending attack, and they spent the summer strengthening the defenses of Boonesborough. The attack did not come until September and after much fighting and efforts at negotiation was finally beaten off. Boone returned to North Carolina to find his wife. He returned to Kentucky in October 1779 with a new party of settlers that included Abraham Lincoln's grandmother and grandfather.

Since the government had not accepted Henderson's claims to Kentucky, the deeds that the settlers had from him were no longer valid. Therefore, the Kentucky settlers got together and raised $20,000 that they gave to Boone. He was to return to Richmond, the capital of Virginia, and purchase new land warrants for the settlers. A few days out of Boonesborough he was robbed of the entire amount. On his return, he moved his home to the west to a place named Boone's Station. From there he was elected to the Virginia legislature in April 1781. The American Revolution was still being fought, and the legislature was forced to meet in Charlottesville. In June 1781 the town was raided by a party of British cavalry, and Boone and a couple of other legislators were captured and held for a few days.

When Boone returned to his remote farm, he was attacked one day by a group of Native Americans and his brother Edward was killed. In the defense of an outpost named Bryan's Station, near Lexington, his son Israel was killed. These attacks led to a major campaign against the Native Americans by George Rogers Clark that removed them as a threat to the Kentucky settlements.

In spite of holding many local offices, Boone had always been inattentive about registering his own land claims. These were increasingly challenged, and he eventually lost all of the land he had ever settled. In the spring of 1786 he and his wife moved to Maysville on the Ohio River above Cincinnati where they ran a tavern and a store for travelers coming down the river. They then moved on in the fall of 1788 to Point Pleasant in present-day West Virginia where the Kanawha and Ohio Rivers meet. In 1791 Boone was chosen to represent his county in the first Virginia legislature formed after the adoption of the new constitution of the United States. At home, his wife kept the family store, and Boone hunted and trapped in the Kanawha valley.

Boone's son, Daniel Morgan Boone, founded a settlement called Femme Osage in 1796 in what was then the Spanish territory of Louisiana and is now the state of Missouri, near the town of St. Charles north of the Missouri River. In 1799 Boone and his wife moved there. He was appointed a magistrate in the Spanish administration and served until the territory was taken over by the Americans in 1804. His title to Missouri lands was contested but was finally confirmed by an Act of Congress in 1814. In 1810 Boone traveled back to Kentucky to pay off his debts there. It is said that this gave him enormous satisfaction but left him with 50 cents in his pocket. His wife died on March 18, 1813, and he went to live with his son Nathan until his death on September 26, 1820 at the age of 85.

Where to learn more

The first book about Daniel Boone was written in 1784 by a schoolmaster from Lexington, Virginia, named John Filson. Called *The Discovery, Settlement, and Present State of Kentucke*, it was the beginning of the making of the Boone legend. The British poet Lord Byron wrote about him in his famous poem *Don Juan* in 1823, and he became world famous. Two fairly recent biographies can be recommended. One, by John Bakeless, *Daniel Boone, Master of the Wilderness*, was originally published in 1939 but was reprinted in 1989 by the University of Nebraska Press in Lincoln and is available in paperback. The other is by Lawrence Elliott, *The Long Hunter: A New Life of Daniel Boone* (New York: Reader's Digest Press, 1976).

Louis Antoine de Bougainville

(1729-1811)

Louis Antoine de Bougainville was a French officer who led the first French circumnavigation of the globe, which also included the first circumnavigation by a woman. He sighted many Pacific islands and gave them exact locations.

Louis Antoine de Bougainville was a French nobleman born in Paris in 1729. During the Seven Years' War (called the French and Indian War in North America), Bougainville was the aide-de-camp to General Montcalm, who was killed during the English attack on Quebec in 1756. Bougainville returned to Europe and fought in the French Army in Germany until the war ended in 1763.

The main results of the Seven Years' War were that France lost all of its possessions in North America and India to the British. There was much talk in France of starting a new empire in other parts of the world, and Bougainville, as a loyal officer of the king, offered to lead one such expedition. In 1765 he sailed with a group of colonists to the Falkland Islands in the South Atlantic, islands that the French called the Malouines after the French port of Saint-Malo. The colony lasted only one year because the King of Spain, who owned the colonies that later became Argentina, said that the islands were his. Since Spain was France's most important ally, King Louis XV of France backed down and turned them over to Spain, who changed the French name slightly and called them the Malvinas.

Interestingly enough, at the very same time that Bougainville was establishing the French colony, the British captain **John Byron** was in the western part of the islands claiming them for England. This claim was directly counter to the one inherited by Argentina, and this antagonism eventually led to the Falklands War of 1982.

In any case, Bougainville was ordered to go back to the Falklands in 1766 and take the Frenchmen off the island. He reached the settlement of Port Louis on April 1, 1767 and took the colonists to Rio de Janeiro from which they made their way back to France. In the meantime, Bougainville had been ordered to continue around the world. Aboard his ship was a young astronomer named Pierre Antoine Véron who was able to use new instruments to calculate the correct longitude of the places they visited for the first time, an important scientific advance.

Bougainville commanded two ships, the *Boudeuse* and the *Etoile*, which sailed from Brazil in November 1767 and passed through the Straits of Magellan into the Pacific Ocean on January 26, 1768. It took 52 days to sail through the Straits, one of the longest times on record. Once in the Pacific, they sailed to the traditional stopping place at the Juan Fernandez Islands, but the winds blew them off course, and they sailed on to the Tuamotu Islands. They passed many small islands where it was not possible to anchor until they reached the much bigger and mountainous island of Tahiti.

Bougainville and his men were the second group of Europeans to reach Tahiti. The British captain **Samuel Wallis** had been there the year before—in June and July 1767. Bougainville landed in another part of the island on April 4, 1768. He stayed only two weeks, but his reports echoed those of Wallis that the island was paradise on earth. In general, the Frenchmen and the Tahitians got along all right, and Bougainville was entertained by the local chief. When he left, he took a brother of the chief with him who said he wanted to see France. (The Tahitian reached France, but it is not known if he ever made it back home to Tahiti.)

Louis Antoine de Bougainville. The Granger Collection, New York.

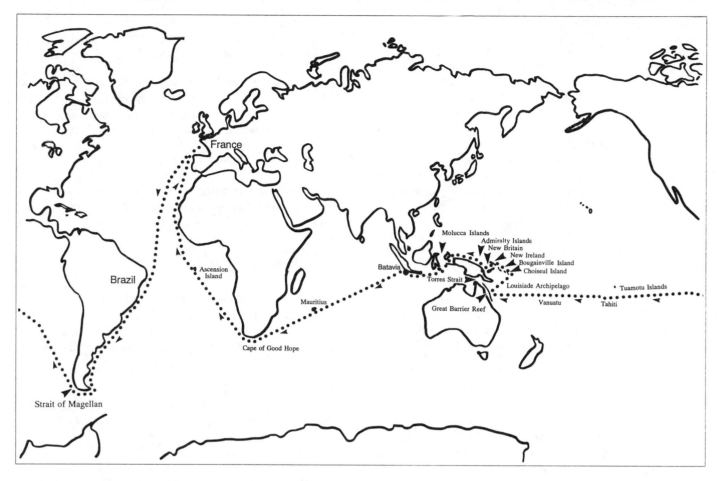

Bougainville's voyage around the world.

While he was in Tahiti, Bougainville was surprised by one discovery. One of the members of his crew was a woman. Before the ships left France, one of the officers, Commercon, who also served as botanist on the expedition, had been approached by a young man named Bare who was looking for a job as a servant on the expedition. He was hired. When the crew came on shore in Tahiti, the Tahitians recognized what the French had not—Bare was not a man. Confessing, Bare revealed that she was an orphan who had first disguised herself as a boy to get employment as a valet. Later when she learned about Bougainville's expedition, she decided to continue the disguise in order to carry out an adventure that would have been impossible if she were known to be a woman. She was the first woman known to have circled the globe.

From Tahiti Bougainville sailed west to Samoa. At that point he made an important decision. Previous navigators had sailed northwestward from those parts in order to get around the northern part of New Guinea. Bougainville decided to sail directly westward and see if he could find the great southern continent, which many geographers thought existed in the southern hemisphere. As a result, he sailed right into the middle of the islands of Vanuatu (the New Hebrides) that **Pedro Fernandez de Quiros**

had discovered in 1605 and that had not been seen by Europeans since that date. Bougainville confirmed what Quiros had found and gave the islands an accurate location.

There was still a question of whether these islands were part of the great southern continent, and Bougainville continued to sail west to see if that were true. There is in fact quite a stretch of sea between Vanuatu and Australia, and Bougainville continued across it until he was almost wrecked during the night of June 4, 1768, on the Great Barrier Reef off the shore of northern Australia. He could not see the land of the vast continent behind the reef, but tried for several days to sail north around the reef. He finally gave up and headed eastward. If he had continued north he would have come upon the Torres Strait that separates Australia from New Guinea. This strait had been discovered by the Spanish navigator **Luis Vaez de Torres** in 1605. But his information had never been published, and it was thought that New Guinea and Australia were all part of the same landmass.

Once Bougainville turned eastward he entered the Louisiade Archipelago (which he named), a maze of small islands and coral reefs that scared the French captain and his crew because they seemed to be almost constantly about to run aground. They finally emerged June 20, 1768 and headed eastward to the Solomon Islands.

The Solomon Islands had been discovered by the Spanish explorer **Alvaro de Mendaña** in 1567, but his locations had been so inexact that no Europeans had been able to find them since that time, and many had decided that they were mere legends. The same group had been stumbled upon by the English captain **Philip Carteret** immediately before Bougainville's arrival—in August 1767. However, neither Carteret nor Bougainville believed that he had rediscovered the Solomons. Bougainville did however give many of these islands the names they have to this day—Buka, Choiseul and Bougainville itself.

Bougainville headed north through the Solomons to the large island of New Britain, where he landed on July 7, 1768 to get fresh water and provisions. Amazingly enough, in the whole vast Pacific, he had landed next to the same tiny cove where Carteret had rested in September of the previous year. One of Bougainville's men found a plaque that the English had hammered to a tree. While in the cove the scientist Véron observed a solar eclipse and was able to use the information to calculate the width of the Pacific Ocean for the first time.

The two French ships sailed north and west along the coast of New Ireland, the Admiralty islands and New Guinea until they reached a Dutch settlement in the Moluccas Islands (or Spice Islands) on September 1, 1768. While in the Moluccas, Bougainville carried out a secret instruction that he had been given—to collect specimens of clove and nutmeg plants to take to the French colony of Mauritius in the Indian Ocean where they could be cultivated and thus destroy the monopoly that the Dutch had on the spice trade. From the Moluccas, the French ships continued on to the capital of the Dutch East Indies at Batavia (present-day Jakarta), which they reached on September 28, just four weeks after Carteret had sailed.

Bougainville left Batavia on October 18 and reached the island of Mauritius on November 8, where he stayed until January 1769 so that his men could recover from the scurvy they had gotten on their long sea journey and from the fever they had caught in the East Indies. He went on to the Cape of Good Hope and finally overtook Carteret off the coast of Ascension Island.

Bougainville sailed into the harbor of Saint-Malo on March 16, 1769, the first Frenchman to circumnavigate the globe, and with the loss of only seven lives, a record for the time.

Following his great voyage, Bougainville continued to serve his country. He fought in the French navy during the American Revolution when France was allied with the young United States. He was made a field marshal in the French Army in 1780, and then retired during the years of the French Revolution to write scientific papers. After Napoleon came to power he became a senator, a count of the empire, and was awarded the Legion of Honor, the highest French decoration.

Where to learn more

By far the best book about Bougainville and the other Pacific explorers is *The Exploration of the Pacific* by J.C. Beaglehole (Palo Alto: Stanford University Press, 1966). Bougainville's own account of his voyage was published in Paris in 1771 as *Voyage autour du monde*. It was translated into English as *A Voyage round the World* in London in 1772. Other good books are *French Explorers in the Pacific* by John Dunmore, a student of Beaglehole's (Oxford University Press, 1965) and *The Discovery of the Pacific Islands* by Andrew Sharp (Oxford University Press, 1960). An entertaining book by Derek Wilson, *The Circumnavigators* (New York: M. Evans and Company, 1989), gives some valuable information, such as the odyssey of Bare, that the others leave out.

Louise Arner Boyd

(1887 - 1972)

Louise Arner Boyd was an American who financed and led several expeditions to the Arctic and became an expert on the fiords and glaciers on the east coast of Greenland.

L ouise Arner Boyd was born in San Rafael, California, north of San Francisco, on September 16, 1887. She came from a wealthy family, her grandfather having made a fortune in the California Gold Rush. Both of Boyd's brothers were sickly and died in childhood; her parents were also not well and traveled frequently for their health. Her mother died in 1919 and her father in 1920, leaving her with the family fortune. She succeeded her father as president of the Boyd Investment Company in San Francisco.

Before this Boyd had traveled to Europe and Egypt and had worked as a nurse during the influenza epidemic of 1918. After her parents' death she returned to Europe with a woman friend and then went there again in 1924. On that trip she traveled on a

Louise Arner Boyd. UPI/Bettmann.

Norwegian ship past North Cape, the northernmost point in Europe. As a result of that trip she developed an interest in exploring the Arctic.

She made her first trip to the Arctic in the summer of 1926 when she traveled to Franz Josef Land, a group of islands north of Siberia, with a group of friends to go hunting for polar bears. She chartered the ship that had been the supply ship for the explorers **Roald Amundsen** and **Lincoln Ellsworth**. She returned with thousands of feet of film, 700 photographs, and a great desire to return.

Boyd returned to the Arctic in 1928 and chartered the same ship. She got there just at the time that a search was underway for **Umberto Nobile**, the Italian aviator whose airship had crashed on the polar ice. Nobile was rescued, but in the search operations Amundsen was lost and never found. Boyd offered her ship to the search operations for Amundsen and spent four months with her crew looking for him. They were unsuccessful, but as a result of her efforts she was presented with a medal by the King of Norway.

Boyd set out again in 1931, and this time she hired several scientists to go with her to make the trip a scientific venture as well as satisfying her longing for adventure. The expedition sailed up the east coast of Greenland, and later part of that coast was named Louise Boyd Land. This expedition began Boyd's association with the American Geographical Society, which sponsored her expedition in the summer of 1933 to Jan Mayen Island in the North Atlantic and to the fiord region of the east coast of Greenland. The expedition included several scientists, but the botanists became ill and Boyd took on the job of collecting plant specimens. She undertook expeditions to the same area in 1937 and 1938.

As a result of her increasing knowledge of these areas, in 1934 Boyd was chosen by several American learned societies to represent them at international conferences in Europe. The knowledge she had gained about the east coast of Greenland became very valuable after World War II broke out, and she was asked by the United States government not to publish the book she had in preparation. Instead she was sent at the head of an expedition to investigate magnetic and radio phenomena in the Arctic in 1940. Her book, *The Coast of Northeast Greenland*, was published after the war in 1948. During the remainder of the war Boyd worked on secret assignments for the U.S. Department of the Army.

By the time the war was over, Boyd was almost 60 and did not take part in any further Arctic expeditions. She did, however, charter a private plane and flew across the North Pole in 1955, the first woman to do so. She died on September 14, 1972, having spent most of her fortune to finance her Arctic explorations.

Where to learn more

Several books that deal with women explorers have included chapters on Louise Arner Boyd. These include *Seven Women Explorers* by Mignon Rittenhouse (Philadelphia: J.B. Lippincott Company, 1964); *Women into the Unknown* by Marion Tinling (Westport, Connecticut: Greenwood Press, 1989); and *Wayward Women: A Guide to Women Travellers* by Jane Robinson (Oxford: Oxford University Press, 1990). The most complete account can be found in *Women of the Four Winds* by Elizabeth Fagg Olds (Boston: Houghton Mifflin, 1985).

Boyd wrote several articles and books about her trips to Greenland. The two most important books were *The Fiord Region of East Greenland* (New York: American Geographical Society, 1935) and *The Coast of Northeast Greenland*, published by the American Geographical Society in 1948.

Pierre Savorgnan de Brazza

(1852 - 1905)

Pierre Savorgnan de Brazza was an Italian nobleman in the service of France who explored along the Ogowe and Congo Rivers in West Africa and founded a French colony there.

Pierre Savorgnan de Brazza was born in Rome on January 25, 1852. His father was an Italian nobleman who was prominent in Italian nationalist and cultural circles. At an early age Pierre developed an interest in a career at sea and in joining the navy. At that time Rome was governed by the Popes and had no navy of its own. At the age of 13 Brazza met a French admiral who was visiting his family and begged him to take him into the French navy. Later, when Brazza had reached the appropriate age, Admiral Montaignac, his mentor, was able to get him an appointment to the French naval academy.

Brazza was not a particularly brilliant student at the French school for naval officers, but he developed an intense love of France and requested to become a French citizen. He served in the French navy during the Franco-Prussian War and then was sent on a ship of the South Atlantic fleet that visited the west coast of Africa. It was at that time that Brazza conceived his plan to lead an expedition into the interior of Gabon from the French trading posts established on the coast. He wrote a letter dated June 23, 1874 to Admiral Montaignac, who was then Minister of Marine, asking to be put in charge of such an expedition.

Brazza's proposals were reviewed by experts at the Ministry and his proposal was accepted as well as his request for naturalization. He was given a small budget and the right to choose his subordinates. Brazza was only 23 years old when he started out on his expedition from Bordeaux in August 1875. He stopped at Dakar to pick up a contingent of Senegalese sailors and then traveled to the mouth of the Ogowe River in Gabon. From there he took a river steamer as far as Lambaréné, a trading post that was later to become famous as the site of Dr. Albert Schweitzer's hospital.

Brazza and three French companions and ten Senegalese left Lambaréné in January 1876. Upriver they ran into difficulties with the African tribes and in the village of Lope rescued the German scientist Oskar Lenz who had been held captive by the Africans for a year. Brazza became ill in Lope and stayed there for two months. They did not reach the territory of the Adouma tribe, beyond any previous expedition, until March 1877. There one of Brazza's French colleagues turned back. Brazza and the remainder of the party did not reach the headwaters of the Ogowe until August 1877. He had hoped that it would lead far inland to the heart of Africa. In fact, although it is the largest river on the west coast of Africa between the Niger and the Congo, it only travels about 500 miles inland.

After reaching the source of the Ogowe Brazza continued on to the head of the Alima River, a tributary of the Congo. He hoped to reach the Congo and travel down it but was forced to turn back in July 1878 by the hostility of the Apfouru tribe. He returned the way he came and reached France again in December 1878, where he was welcomed as a hero.

In the meantime, while Brazza had been on his expedition, **Henry Morton Stanley** had led an expedition on behalf of the King of the Belgians that had claimed vast parts of the Congo basin. The French were very unhappy about these developments, and the government decided to sent Brazza back to Africa to try to forestall Stanley. It wanted him to gain possession of the territory in the region of Stanley Pool, a large natural lake on the lower Congo.

Pierre Savorgnan de Brazza. The Granger Collection, New York.

Brazza left France on his second expedition on December 27, 1879 with a small force of 11 Senegalese sailors. He rapidly made his way up the Ogowe and set up a French post at a place on the upper Ogowe where it is joined by the Passa River, that he named Franceville. He left there in June 1880 and then rapidly crossed the watershed to the river the local tribes called the Olumo, which turned out to be the Congo. Along the way he had each of the local chiefs acknowledge French sovereignty, although it is very doubtful that they understood the implications of what they were doing. The most important of these agreements was with the important chief Makoko. Talks with Makoko began on August 28, 1880 and a treaty was signed on September 10, 1880. This accord gave France part of the right bank of the Congo and the adjacent territory. Brazza then went to the village of N'Tamo and set up a post under his Senegalese sergeant, Malamine. This was to grow into the city of Brazzaville, today the capital of the Republic of Congo.

From the new post Brazza traveled down the Congo and met Stanley at the village of Vivi near the mouth of the Congo on November 7, 1880. Brazza had beaten Stanley and the two famous explorers did not get along very well. Stanley finally reached Stanley Pool (which he had discovered in 1877 coming downstream on the Congo) to find that Malamine had established his, and France's, authority on the west side of the river. Brazza continued along the coast back to Libreville in Gabon. He traveled back up the Ogowe and established supply posts and reinforced France's claim to the territory. In 1881, however, he was recalled to France. King Leopold of the Belgians had prevailed on the French government to leave the Congo to Belgium. On his way back to France Brazza was stranded without any money in the English city of Portsmouth. When the French consul there wired for instructions, the Ministry of Marine wrote back to send him home, "the cheapest way possible."

Back in France Brazza immediately started a campaign to get the French government and public to realize the potential value of colonies along the Congo. King Leopold invited him to Brussels and in an interview on September 12, 1882 tried to get him to leave France and come to work for him. Brazza refused and soon after, on October 20, he attended a dinner in Paris in honor of Henry Morton Stanley at which the two explorers exchanged insults. Brazza's standing up for France's honor caught the imagination of the French public and, with a change of government, Brazza's treaty with Makoko was confirmed by the French parliament in December 1882 and money was voted for a new Brazza expedition.

Brazza left Paris on his third expedition on March 10, 1883 and reached Libreville in April. This was a much larger affair than his previous expeditions and the purpose was clearly to establish French occupation. Brazza started out by making a trip to what is now the Atlantic coast of the Republic of Congo to sign treaties of annexation with the chiefs there. He then traveled up the Ogowe once again and traveled to visit Chief Makoko on the Congo River, reaching there in April 1884. Brazza sent his brother

Jacques and another Italian, Attilio Pecile, north to the Bangui River on a secret mission to annex that area. The Great Powers of Europe met in Berlin in November 1884 and divided up the African continent. As a result of Brazza's activities what is now Gabon, Congo, and the Central African Republic were awarded to France. King Leopold was given a vast territory known as the Congo Free State (now Zaire) as his personal territory.

Brazza returned to France in 1885. As a tribute to his achievements, he was appointed governor of the new French colony of the Congo in April 1886. He reached Libreville in March 1887 and served in his post for the next ten years. During that time he tried to develop the colony without trampling on the rights of the Africans. Brazza's administration was not a success. The French government did not spend enough money to make any real development in the infrastructure of the new colony, and French merchants were not successful in opening up trade. They looked in envy across the Congo River where King Leopold gave commercial companies vast concessions that left them as the real rulers of large areas of the country. Finally, in 1897 **Jean-Baptiste Marchand** claimed Brazza's lack of cooperation was the reason his march to Fashoda had failed. In face of this opposition Brazza was recalled in January 1898.

Following Brazza's departure the French adopted Leopold's policy of giving concessions to large commercial companies to see if the Congo could be developed by private interests. Brazza retired to Algiers in North Africa, but was very troubled by reports that came out of the Congo. The concessionary companies were basically making a profit by extorting goods and labor out of the African population. In 1904 the situation in both the Congo Free State and the French Congo became international scandals when enterprising journalists and public servants like Edmund Morel and Roger Casement revealed how the Africans were being brutalized and even murdered for profit. The French government called Brazza out of retirement to lead a commission to investigate.

Brazza arrived in Libreville for the last time on April 29, 1905. He traveled to Brazzaville and elsewhere in the colony over a period of four months. He became ill with dysentery along the way and left Brazzaville on August 29. On the return trip to France he became progressively sicker and was taken off the ship at Dakar to be moved to a hospital. He died there the next day, on September 14, 1905. He had time to write his report, which damned the administration of the French Congo. After it was read back in Paris, the French parliament voted in February 1906 not to release it because it was considered to be too damaging to the prestige of France.

Where to learn more

There is a complete biography of Brazza in English by Richard West, *Brazza of the Congo: European Exploration and Exploitation in French Equatorial Africa* (London: Jonathan Cape, 1972). The best biography in French is by noted colonial historian Henri Brunschwig, *Brazza Explorateur* (Paris: 1966).

James Bruce

(1730 - 1794)

James Bruce was a Scottish traveler who visited the highlands of Ethiopia and the source of the Blue Nile River.

James Bruce was born in 1730 into an aristocratic Scottish family at Kinnaird House in Stirlingshire. His mother died when he was three years old, and his father sent him first to a private tutor in London and then to Harrow School and Edinburgh University. His father forced him to study law, but he hated it and instead spent his time studying languages and art. In 1752 he married the daughter of a wealthy wine merchant and entered his wife's family business. However, she died nine months after the marriage while carrying their first child.

To recover from his unhappiness, Bruce spent the following years traveling throughout Europe, including time studying Arabic manuscripts in the Escorial Palace in Spain. His father died in 1758, and he returned for a while to London, where he began studying Ge'ez, the classic language of Ethiopia. His study of

Ethiopia gave him the desire to travel there and to find the sources of the Nile River. This was furthered when he was able to procure an appointment as the British Consul-General in Algiers. He arrived there in June 1762 and spent two difficult years at the court of the Bey of Algiers, who was most noted for preying on European ships in the Mediterranean. Leaving Algiers, he spent the following years traveling along the Mediterranean coasts of North Africa and the Middle East. He visited Roman ruins in Algeria, Tunis, and Tripoli and made careful drawings of the sites. He also continued his studies of Arabic and Ge'ez.

In 1768 Bruce was in Cairo in Egypt accompanied by an Italian named Luigi Balugani who acted as his art assistant and secretary. In Cairo he practiced as a doctor and, as a result, was able to make the acquaintance of various influential people, including the Patriarch of Ethiopia, who gave him a letter of introduction to the Greek Christians in Ethiopia. Equipped with this letter, he set out up the Nile, and made it as far as Aswan, where he was stopped by a local war.

From Aswan Bruce and Balugani went a short ways back down the Nile and then cut across the desert to reach the Red Sea port of Al-Kusayr. They sailed across the Red Sea to the port of Jiddah in Arabia and from there to Massawa, in what is now Eritrea. The two Europeans arrived there in September 1769 but were not able to leave for the interior until November, when they set off with a guide and a party of about 20 porters. They traveled to Aduwa, later the site of an Ethiopian triumph over Italian invaders, and to Axum, which was the ancient capital of Ethiopia (or Abyssinia as it was then called). Bruce later recounted an incident that took place along the route: he saw three Ethiopians capture a cow, cut two pieces of meat off of the buttocks and then reclose the wound and send the animal on its way.

Bruce arrived in Gondar, the then-capital of Abyssinia in the middle of February 1770. He was received by the Empress Iteghe. On their return to the city, he was welcomed by the young Emperor Tecla Haimanot and by the 70-year-old Ras Michael of Tigre, who was the real ruler of the country. Bruce wrote about the various court intrigues going on a the time and reported on the ruthless manner in which Ras Michael dealt with his enemies. He did not, however, forget about the reason for his journey and was very pleased when Ras Michael asked him to accompany him on an expedition to the Little Abbai River, which was thought to be the source of the Blue Nile. Bruce reached the river at the Tississat Falls (previously visited by **Pedro Paez**), near the river's exit from Lake Tana 6,000 feet up in the mountains. He used his scientific instruments to measure the position of the falls accu-

James Bruce. The Granger Collection, New York.

rately. He was forced to return to Gondar with Ras Michael's army before he could travel to the source of the Little Abbai.

Bruce set out from Gondar again in October 1770 accompanied by Balugani. This time he was able to reach the source of the Little Abbai on November 4, 1770—a series of springs that flowed into a tiny stream. Bruce was ecstatic, thinking he had found the source of the Nile and not knowing that Paez had already been there in 1618. Forced to stay in the country because of civil unrest among the Galla (or Oromo) tribes, Bruce accompanied the army of Ras Michael on various expeditions.

He was thus able to visit large parts of northern Ethiopia and the region to the south of Lake Tana. He and Balugani kept a detailed diary, made accurate drawings of the things they saw, and made measurements of many locations. Bruce also collected an entire library of Ethiopic manuscripts, which he took with him when he left Abyssinia. These later became one of the main sources for European knowledge about Ethiopian history. The main body of these valuable documents is now kept in the Bodleian Library of Oxford University.

In the course of the military actions Balugani died from dysentery, and Ras Michael was finally driven out of Gondar. Bruce became very tired of the constant warfare and in December 1771 was given permission to leave the country. He traveled overland to the town of Sennar on the Blue Nile in what is now Sudan. Sennar was the center of a Muslim state, and Bruce stayed there for four months taking note of the life of the inhabitants. He lost most of his possessions in Sennar.

Leaving Sennar in September 1772, Bruce followed the Blue Nile to the place where it met the White Nile. There, at what was later to be the site of Khartoum, he noticed that the White Nile was a deeper river, but he still believed that the Blue Nile was the more important of the two. He reached Aswan at the end of November 1772 and Cairo early in 1773.

Bruce traveled from Egypt to France and from there to Italy. He had received word that his fiancée, whom he had left in Scotland 12 years before, had married an Italian marchese. He confronted the Italian aristocrat and accused him of stealing his intended wife. The Italian had never even heard of Bruce before, and the Scottish woman thought that Bruce had long since been dead. He traveled on to Paris where he was given an enthusiastic reception by the world of learning. It was here that he learned from the cartographer d'Anville that Paez had already been to the source of the Nile before him.

Bruce finally returned to London in 1774. At first he was well received, but then people began to doubt his tall tales. He was received in an audience by King George III but otherwise received no official recognition of his journey and the vast amounts of information that he had brought back. He was particularly offended when the famous intellectual Dr. Samuel Johnson let it be known that he found Bruce unreliable.

Suffering from hurt pride, Bruce retired to his estate at Kinnaird House. There he married a woman 24 years younger than he was and lived happily in the role of local lord until her sudden death in 1788. This seems to have spurred him to try to regain his reputation, and he traveled to London to spend a year writing up the results of his travels. His book was published in 1790. Once again, however, his critics disbelieved him, and he was labeled a Baron Munchhausen—a notorious liar. In fact, modern scholarship has confirmed that most of what he wrote was quite accurate. He retired once again to Kinnaird House. He died a few years later when he fell down a flight of stairs while on his way to escort a lady to her carriage.

Where to learn more

Bruce's account of his travels in Ethiopia was published as *Travels to Discover the Source of the Nile in the Years 1768, 1769, 1770, 1771, 1772 and 1773*. The first edition was published in five volumes in Edinburgh in 1790; the second edition in London by Longman & Rees in 1804; and the third edition in eight volumes in Edinburgh in 1813.

The first biography of Bruce was F.B. Head, *The Life of Bruce* (London: Murray, 1836). There is a much more recent full-scale biography by J.M. Reid entitled *Traveller Extraordinary: The Life of James Bruce of Kinnaird* (New York: W.W. Norton & Company, 1968).

Much of this account is based upon Alan Moorehead's *The Blue Nile* (New York: Harper & Row, 1962), which gives a good summary of Bruce's travels in the context of the history of European involvement with the Blue Nile and Ethiopia.

Etienne Brûlé

(1592? - 1633)

Etienne Brûlé was a Frenchman who went to live among Native Americans in order to serve as an interpreter and made several notable journeys in the region of the Great Lakes, New York and Pennsylvania.

Etienne Brûlé was born near Paris probably in the year 1592. He went to Quebec in 1608. In 1610 he requested permission from **Samuel de Champlain** to live among the Algonquins so that he could learn their language and serve as interpreter between the French and the Native Americans. This request was granted, and he traveled to the Ottawa River to live among the Iroquet tribe. Along the way, he achieved local fame by being the first European to shoot the Lachine Rapids just upstream of Montreal. Brûlé returned to Quebec on

Etienne Brûlé with members of the Huron tribe. The Granger Collection, New York.

June 13, 1611, having mastered the language and gained the confidence of his hosts. In the next four years, he most likely traveled up the Ottawa River into Lake Nipissing, the French River, and Georgian Bay. If so, he pioneered the main route for the fur trade to the west.

In 1615 the French and the Huron tribe were preparing a campaign against their mutual enemies the Iroquois. They decided to send a delegation to the Susquehannahs, also enemies of the Iroquois, to try to get them as allies. Brûlé asked to go along. They traveled from Lake Simcoe in present-day Ontario, down the Humber River, across the western end of Lake Ontario and then up the Niagara and Genesee Rivers to the headquarters of the Susquehannah at Carantouan, between Elmira and Binghamton in upstate New York. The mission was a success but by the time the Susquehannahs arrived the Hurons had already been defeated by the Iroquois and had retreated. The Susquehannahs then decided to return home, and Brûlé went with them. He spent the next fall and winter visiting neighboring tribes and went down the Susquehannah River as far as Chesapeake Bay, which had been visited in 1608 by **John Smith**. By making this journey, Brûlé became the first European to set foot in what is now Pennsylvania.

On his return to Canada, Brûlé was captured by the Senecas, a member of the Iroquois confederation. He claims that he was tortured by them, but this cannot be proven, and he left on good terms with the promise to work for peace with the French. Most of Brûlé's voyages are difficult to document, but it seems probable that in 1621-1623 he became the first European to see Lake Superior and to traverse it as far as the site of Duluth, Minnesota. He is also thought to have been the first European to have seen Lake Erie. If so, he can be counted as the discoverer of four of the Great Lakes.

In spite of his exploits, Brûlé was not well liked by Champlain who thought that he had adopted too many of the customs of the Native Americans that he lived among for so long and who resented Brûlé working for the British during their brief occupation of Quebec. On the return of the French, he left and went to live once again among the Hurons. For reasons that remain unknown he was killed by one of the Huron clans in 1633.

Where to learn more

There is a biography of Brûlé, which is unfortunately out of print: C.W. Butterfield, *History of Brûlé's Discoveries and Explorations, 1610-1626* (Cleveland: 1898). For an extensive history of the relations between Brûlé and Champlain, see Morris Bishop, *Champlain: The Life of Fortitude* (New York: 1948; reprinted in paperback, Toronto: McClelland and Stewart, 1963).

Jean Louis Burckhardt

(1784-1817)

Jean Louis Burckhardt was a Swiss explorer who was hired by a British group to travel to the Niger River. He never made it there but spent several years exploring the Middle East and Arabia.

Jean Louis Burckhardt was born into a well-to-do family in Lausanne, Switzerland in 1784. He studied at the University of Göttingen in Germany. (He is sometimes known by his German name of Johann Ludwig.) He went to England in 1805 where one of his professors at the University had furnished him with an introduction to **Sir Joseph Banks**, one of the founders of the Association for Promoting the Discovery of the Interior Parts of Africa. Burckhardt offered to travel to Africa for the Association in order to explore the Niger River, where **Mungo Park** had recently died.

The Association gave Burckhardt a grant to attend Cambridge University for a year to study Arabic and other subjects that would help him on his travels. The Association proposed to send Burckhardt to North Africa to see whether it was possible to approach the Niger from that direction. He traveled first to Aleppo in Syria, where he arrived in July 1809. He stayed there

Jean Louis Burckhardt. Etching by Angelica Clarke.

for the next two and a half years perfecting his knowledge of Arabic and of Islamic customs. In the spring of 1810 he went into the surrounding country and lived with a nomadic Turkish tribe. Later that year he reached the ruins of the ancient Arabic city of Palmyra in the Syrian Desert. He is thought to be the first Westerner to have seen the city since ancient times.

Starting in the autumn of 1810, Burckhardt began to travel to other Arabic countries. He used the name Sheikh Ibrahim ibn Abdullah but would admit to being a Westerner if questioned. He claimed to have converted to Islam and was able to display a good knowledge of the Koran. In June 1812 he traveled to Egypt by way of the Jordan Valley and across the Sinai Peninsula. On August 22, 1812 he arrived at one of the ancient site of the temple-tomb known as the Pharaoh's Treasure, which stands more than 60 feet high and was carved from living (uncut) red rock. He visited the ruins of the city of Petra, the capital of the ancient Nabateans, now in southern Jordan.

Burckhardt arrived in Cairo on September 3, 1812. From there he took a boat up the Nile River. Early in 1813, he left Esne in Upper Egypt and went south as far as a place named Tinareh, north of the Third Cataract on the east bank of the Nile. From here, he became, on March 22, the first Westerner to see another of the great wonders of the ancient Egyptians—the great rock temple of Abu Simbel with its four 60-foot figures of Rameses II.

Back at Esne, Burckhardt became ill with an eye infection. He had hoped to be able to catch a caravan traveling across the desert to the Niger River. When he realized that would not be possible for him that year, he wrote a letter to the African Association in May 1813 saying that he planned to make the pilgrimage to Mecca in the meantime. Burckhardt set out in a caravan that reached the great trading center of Shendi on April 17, 1814. There he bought an African slave boy for 11 Spanish dollars. From Shendi he joined another caravan that took him to the port of Suakin on the Red Sea in what is now Sudan.

Burckhardt reached Suakin at the end of June 1814. He caught a boat filled with African pilgrims from there to Jeddah, the main port on the west coast of Arabia. On his arrival he tried to get money on a letter of credit that he had arranged in Cairo, but it was out of date. He became ill with fever and could have died. He was befriended by a Greek ship captain, however, who took care of him. Desperate, he asked the Greek to sell his slave for him. The sea captain did so—for $48, giving Burckhardt a profit of $32 on his dealings.

At the time of Burckhardt's visit, Jeddah and the Muslim holy cities were under the control of an Egyptian army commanded by Mehemet Ali Pasha, the Turkish viceroy of Egypt. Burckhardt had previously had some dealings with the Pasha's court in Cairo. He now traveled to the Pasha's headquarters at the city of Ta'if south of Mecca to seek help in resolving his monetary difficulties. Not only was he given a loan, but he received the Pasha's permission to visit Mecca, apparently having convinced him that he was a Muslim. He set out for Mecca on the morning of September 7. Once in the holy city, he performed the required Muslim rituals. He was not the first Westerner to visit Mecca (that was probably **Ludovico de Varthema**).

Burckhardt returned to Jeddah on September 15 to buy supplies and then settled in at Mecca for a stay of several weeks. He was there during the pilgrimage season and wrote one of the earliest and most accurate accounts of this major pillar of the Islamic religion. He stayed in Mecca until December 1 when he left for Jeddah and stayed on board an English ship for a couple of weeks. He then returned to Mecca and arranged a trip to Medina, leaving on January 15, 1815. After a trip of 12 days he visited the tomb of the prophet Mohammed, the main attraction of the city.

Following his arrival in Medina, Burckhardt turned over his supply of quinine to Mehemet Ali Pasha's physician. Two days later he himself came down with malaria and was desperately sick until April. He left Medina on April 21 and traveled to the port city of Yenbu. From there, it took him 20 miserable days to cross the Red Sea to the Sinai Peninsula. On his return to Cairo on June 24, 1815, he spent his time writing about his travels and observations in Arabia. He stayed there for two more years but was never able to find a caravan that could take him across the desert to the Niger. In October 1817 he became ill with dysentery, and he died during the night of October 15.

Where to learn more

Burckhardt wrote about his various journeys in a series of books, which were all published after his death: *Travels in Nubia* (London: 1819); *Travels in Syria and the Holy Land* (London: 1822); *Travels in Arabia* (London: 1829); *Arabic Proverbs, or the Manners and Customs of the Modern Egyptians* (London: 1830); *Notes on the Bedouins and Wahabys* (London: 1831).

There is an excellent biography of Burckhardt: Katharine Sim, *Desert Traveller: The Life of Jean Louis Burckhardt* (London: Gollancz, 1969). There is also a good summary of his Arabian travels in Zahra Freeth and H.V.F. Winstone, *Explorers of Arabia: From the Renaissance to the End of the Victorian Era* (London: George Allen & Unwin, 1978).

Robert O'Hara Burke

(1820-1861)

William John Wills

(1834-1861)

Robert O'Hara Burke and William John Wills, two Australian explorers, were the first to cross Australia from south to north but died on the return trip.

By the 1860s most of the habitable parts of the Australian continent had been explored. However, these had not been linked together. In an effort to do so, the South Australian government offered a reward to anyone who could find a north-south route to build a telegraph line from Adelaide to the north coast. This was the incentive that sent **John McDouall Stuart** on his expeditions. Not to be outdone, the rich gold-mining state of Victoria sponsored its own expedition to travel from Melbourne to the north coast.

Two inexperienced men were chosen to lead this expedition: the largest and most expensive ever mounted in Australia. The leader was Robert O'Hara Burke, who was born in County Galway in Ireland, educated in Belgium, served in the Austrian army (1840), joined the Irish Constabulary (1848), and emigrated to Australia in 1853. He became a police inspector in Victoria. His deputy was William John Wills who had studied medicine and then became a surveyor and meteorologist in Victoria.

The expedition started out with great fanfare from Melbourne on August 20, 1860. Public contributions and government subsidies had provided ample funds. Twenty-five camels and three drivers had been brought from India, and what seemed to be very careful preparations were arranged for a journey from Menindee on the Darling River north to the Gulf of Carpentaria.

The members of the expedition started to quarrel even before they reached Menindee. George Landells, the second in command, resigned and Wills took his place. Burke recruited a local man, William Wright, to show them a short cut to Cooper's Creek.

At this point not all of the intended men had arrived at Menindee. Burke became impatient and he had Wright guide him and Wills and three other men—John King, Charles Gray, and William Brahe—to Cooper's Creek 400 miles to the northwest

and then to go back for the others. They left on October 19, 1860 and arrived at Cooper's Creek 23 days later. Wright was given instructions to follow as soon as the remaining men and supplies reached Menindee. For various reasons, he actually ended up delaying his departure for three months.

In the meantime Burke became impatient again and began his dash for the north coast. He left on December 16, resolved to "dash into the interior and cross the continent at all hazards." Mounted on his gray horse, he took with him Wills, Gray, and King, who all rode camels. Brahe stayed behind at Cooper's Creek with orders to wait there for three months or until the supplies ran out.

The route that Burke had chosen was easier to cross than the desert that Stuart attempted. Much of it skirted the desert and crossed land already occupied by sheep and cattle stations. They actually made good progress at first, but then the rainy season began and the land became a morass of mud. It took them eight weeks to reach the coast. Eventually they were forced to leave the animals behind, and Burke and Wills walked on by themselves, reaching the mouth of the Flinders River at the Gulf of Carpentaria on February 9, 1861. They could see the effects of the tide on the river, but they were unable to see the ocean because of the mangrove swamps. Figuring that it would take another two days to cut their way through the swampland, they decided that they could not afford the supplies to do so. So, after their difficult journey they left without seeing their goal.

Burke and Wills calculated that they had supplies enough to last five weeks and that the trip back would take eight. It actually took ten. They left the coast on February 13 in a thunderstorm, and it rained constantly for the following weeks. They all became ill with dysentery and other diseases. They ate one of the horses, and four of the six camels died. On March 25 Gray was discovered stealing rations, and Burke gave him a beating. Gray died on April 17. The three survivors reached the camp at Cooper's Creek on the evening of April 21. There was no one there. Brahe had waited six weeks longer than he had been instructed to, but he had finally given up and left just eight hours earlier. He left a message carved on a tree telling them where to dig to find provisions and the letter telling them of his departure.

Robert O'Hara Burke. The Granger Collection, New York.

William John Wills. The Granger Collection, New York.

Wills recorded his disappointment: "Arrived the depot this evening just in time to find it deserted. A note left in the plant by Brahe communicates the pleasing information that they have started today for the Darling: their camels and horses all well and in good condition."

Before starting out again, Burke wrote a note and left it in the tree at Cooper's Creek: "The return party from Carpentaria, consisting of myself, Wills, and King (Gray dead), arrived here last night, and found that the depot party had only started the same day. We proceed on tomorrow slowly down the creek towards Adelaide by Mount Hopeless, and shall endeavor to follow Gregory's track; but we are very weak. The two camels are done up, and we shall not be able to travel faster than four or five miles a day. Gray died on the road from exhaustion and fatigue. We have all suffered much hunger. Greatly disappointed at finding the party here gone. Robert O'Hara Burke, Leader. April 22, 1861. P.S. The camels cannot travel and we cannot walk, or we should follow the other party. We shall move very slowly down the creek."

Wills and King wanted to follow Brahe, who was by then only 14 miles away, along their old route to Menindee. Burke, however, was convinced that they would never catch up and insisted that they follow a tributary of Cooper's Creek called Strzelecki Creek to the south in an attempt to reach a cattle ranch at Mount Hopeless 150 miles away. They rested for five days before setting out. Along the way, friendly Aborigines gave them some food—freshwater, fish, rats, and nardoo, the seeds of a fern that was pounded to make a kind of flour.

By May 17 the three men had killed their last two camels. They wandered aimlessly and by May 28 were back near the camp at Cooper's Creek, where they had started out a month before. In the meantime, on May 8 Brahe had returned to the camp after meeting up with Wright who was at last making his way up from Menindee, but the camp looked exactly as he had left it. Burke, Wills, and King had carefully covered all signs of their visit so that the Aborigines would not be attracted to the depot and destroy the note they had left behind (which Brahe did not find anyway). Brahe rode away, not bothering to look in the hole where he had left provisions to see if they were still there.

The three men attached themselves to a group of Aborigines in order to stay alive. However, they became weaker and weaker and were no longer able to gather nardoo. The constantly wandering Aborigines moved on, leaving Burke, Wills, and King behind. King was the strongest of the three, and he tried to supply the other two with food. In their desperate situation it was decided that King and Burke would try to find the band of Aborigines. They left Wills behind with eight days' supply of food. Two days after setting out, Burke collapsed. King made him a last meal from a crow that he had shot and some nardoo flour. "I hope you will remain with me till I am quite dead," Burke said. "It is a comfort to know that someone is by." He died at 8:00 a.m. on the morning of June 30, 1861.

King went back to where they had left Wills and found that he had also died. His last journal entry reads: "I am weaker than ever although I have a good appetite and relish the nardoo much, but it seems to give no nutriment. I may live four or five days if the weather continues warm. Starvation on nardoo is by no means very unpleasant but for the weakness one feels and utter inability to move oneself."

King was able to catch up with the band of Aborigines, who tolerated his presence and gave him food. In return, he shot crows and hawks for them. In the meantime, four different rescue parties had been sent out to find the survivors of the disastrous Burke-Wills expedition. One of them, led by Alfred Howitt, finally found King on September 18, 1861. Howitt wrote that King was "wasted to a shadow, and hardly to be distinguished as a civilized human being but by the remnants of the clothes upon him."

The bodies of Burke and Wills were carried back to Melbourne where there was a tremendous funeral parade for them.

Where to learn more

The best and most exciting account of the doomed Burke and Wills expedition is Alan Moorehead's *Cooper's Creek* (New York: Harper & Row, 1963). A profusely illustrated history of the expedition can be found in Max Colwell, *The Journey of Burke and Wills* (Sydney: Paul Hamlyn, 1971). Extracts from the journals of the expedition can be found in Kathleen Fitzpatrick, ed. *Australian Explorers: A Selection from Their Writings* (London: Oxford University Press, 1958).

Sir Richard Burton

(1821 - 1890)

Richard Burton was an English soldier and writer who led an adventurous life that took him into the Muslim holy city of Mecca and on an expedition to discover the source of the Nile River.

Richard Burton was born in the English port of Torquay on March 19, 1821, the son of a retired Anglo-Irish colonel in the British Army. Soon after his birth, his parents moved to a castle in the Loire Valley of France, where Burton spent his early childhood with little formal education. Then followed several years of wandering in England, France, and Italy. His father wanted him to become a clergyman in the Anglican Church and sent him to Oxford University. Burton hated it there and arranged to have himself expelled by breaking a rule that forbade students to attend the local racetrack. While at Oxford, however, he began to study Arabic; he was eventually to master 29 languages. He also started to read about Eastern mysticism, which was to be a theme throughout his life.

In 1842, Burton joined the army that was maintained by the East India Company to protect its possessions in India. Even before leaving England he began to study Hindi. He later became a scholar of the language and translated many of its classic texts into English. He arrived in Bombay on October 27, 1842. His first duty post was in the city of Baroda, where he followed the custom of many of the other British officers and took an Indian mistress. In November 1843 he was transferred to the province of Sind in what is now Pakistan. There he began to wear Indian clothes. He also adopted Islam and had himself circumcised, which is required of all Muslim men. In later years, he wrote about falling in love with a "Persian lady" and that the affair ended tragically; it is even possible that the woman was killed because of her liaison with a Westerner.

Because of Burton's command of Indian languages and his ability to disguise himself, he became a spy for British army intelligence. His adventures were the basis of Rudyard Kipling's famous novel *Kim* and other stories about the "Great Game"— the struggle for control of central Asia. After seven years in India Burton became quite ill and returned to Europe in 1849 to recuperate. He settled down in the French port of Boulogne and wrote four books about his Indian experiences. There he met his future wife, Isabel Arundell, then 19 years old, from a prominent English Catholic family. Arundell later wrote that when she saw Burton for the first time she realized it was her destiny to marry him.

Sir Richard Burton. The Granger Collection, New York.

In 1852 Burton traveled to London and proposed to the Royal Geographical Society that they sponsor him on a journey to Arabia, where he wanted to fulfill his religious duty as a Muslim by making the pilgrimage to Mecca and to add to the geographical knowledge about Arabia. The Society agreed to his request, and he left England in April 1853. He disguised himself as an Indian-born Afghan doctor and traveled via Alexandria, Cairo and Port Suez in Egypt to the Arab port of Yenbu, where he arrived on July 18, 1853.

Along the way Burton had cut his foot on a sea urchin; it had become infected and he could not walk. Joining a caravan with his servants, he reached the holy city of Medina on July 24, where he visited the tomb of the Prophet Mohammed. On August 31, he set off with a caravan for Mecca along the Darb-al-Shakri, the inland road that crosses fields of lava. On September 7 he reached the valley of the El Zaribah, where pilgrims prepare for the entry into Mecca, which he did on September 11, 1853.

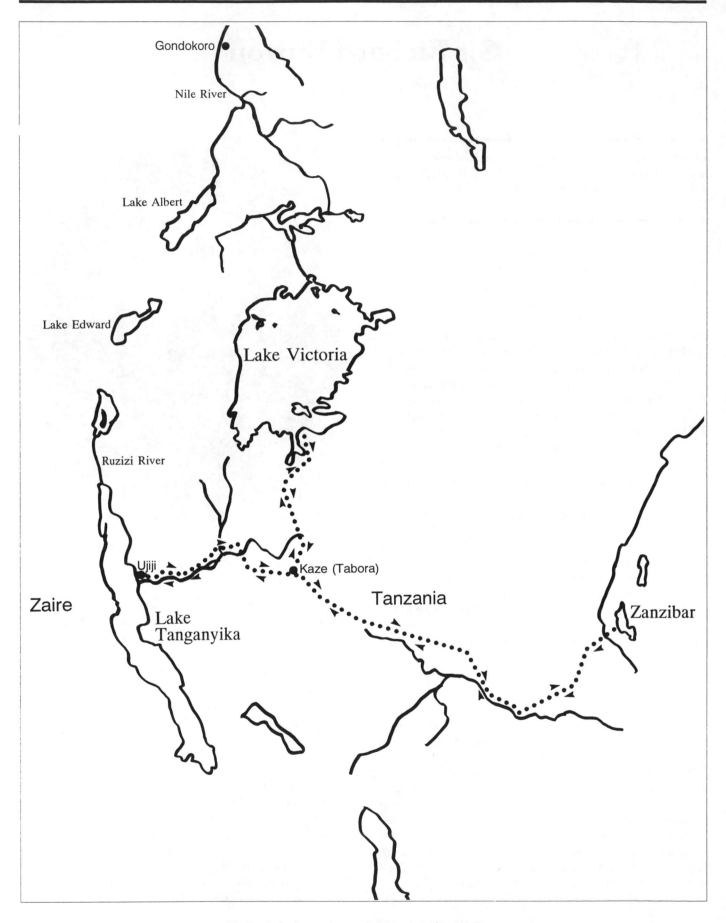

The Burton-Speke expedition to find the source of the Nile River.

Burton made the required walk around the holiest spot in Islam, the Ka'abah, a huge building in the shape of a cube that contains a chunk of black rock, probably a meteorite. On the day of Id-al-Khabir, he took part in a ceremony in which pilgrims throw stones to commemorate the way the patriarch Abraham drove away the Devil. In his description of what he saw and did, Burton often quoted the writings of **Jean Louis Burckhardt**, a previous Western visitor to Mecca. Typically, Burton spent the three hours of a boring sermon flirting with a young Arab woman, whose face was covered with a thin veil. Short of money, Burton did not continue his proposed trip to eastern Arabia but traveled to the Red Sea port of Jeddah and took a ship to Egypt. He settled at Shepheard's Hotel in Cairo and wrote a book about his pilgrimage.

While in Cairo, Burton met **Ludwig Krapf**, a German missionary who had been one of the first Europeans to explore in east Africa. Krapf told him about stories he had heard of a large inland lake from which flowed the Nile River. This was the beginning of Burton's obsession to find the source of the Nile. By now, his leave of absence from the Indian Army had expired and, against his will, he was forced to return to Bombay. There, he bombarded his superiors and the Royal Geographical Society with ideas about mounting an expedition to discover the source of the Nile.

Instead, Burton was given the task of exploring the northern coast of Somalia, whose port of Berbera would make an excellent stopping point for British ships sailing from Suez to India. Once again disguised, Burton sailed from the new British colony of Aden in southern Arabia on October 29, 1854. On January 3, 1855 he reached Harar, now in eastern Ethiopia, a "forbidden holy city" that had allegedly never been visited by a Westerner before. He returned to the coast where he met up with other members of the expedition, including **John Hanning Speke**, an Indian Army officer on leave whom Burton had met in Aden. After reporting back to Aden, Burton and Speke returned to Somalia in April. Their camp was attacked by Somalis: Burton had a javelin thrust through the lower part of his face while Speke was captured but managed to escape with eleven wounds, some serious. They returned to England to recover.

While in England, Burton renewed his acquaintance with Isabel Arundell. He was sent to join the British army for a short while in Turkey during the Crimean War. On his return, he was finally able to convince the Royal Geographical Society to sponsor an expedition to search for the Nile source. He invited Speke to join him. They sailed to Bombay in November 1856 and from there to Zanzibar in December. They made a short reconnaissance trip to the mainland where they solicited information from **Johannes Rebmann** and hired **Sidi Mubarak Bombay** as caravan leader. On June 16, 1857 they left Zanzibar and crossed over to the mainland.

The Burton and Speke expedition followed one of the traditional routes of Arab slave traders into the interior. They were able to travel about 10 miles a day, but both of the two Englishmen quickly became ill and were often too weak to walk and could barely sit on their donkeys. They reached the trading center of Kazé (modern Tabora), some 500 miles inland, on November 7, 1857.

They stayed in Tabora for five weeks, recuperating and reorganizing their expedition. Soon after they set off again, Burton was struck by paralysis and partial blindness, and Speke went almost totally blind. They did not give up, however, and on February 13, 1858 they climbed a hill so steep that it killed Speke's donkey. Since both Burton and Speke were unable to see, it was Bombay who first sighted the body of water called the Sea of Ujiji, now known as Lake Tanganyika. Burton and Speke were the first Europeans to see it, insofar as they could.

Burton hoped that Lake Tanganyika would turn out to be the source of the Nile, and he speculated that a large river in the north, the Ruzizi, that he had heard about was in fact the Nile. Although very sick, the two explorers traveled by canoe to the north end of the lake, where they heard from Arab traders that the Ruzizi flows into the lake, not out of it. "I felt sick at heart," Burton later wrote.

They left the lake on May 26, 1858, with Speke now ill from an ear infection as well. In June 1858 they were back at Tabora, where they both recovered somewhat. There they heard stories of a great lake to the north, which might prove to be the Nile source. Here the accounts diverge. Speke says that Burton was ill and did not want to explore the northern lake. Burton says that he had more important things to do and sent Speke to verify the rumors. In any case, Speke, accompanied by Bombay, did go north and visited the large lake which he named after Queen Victoria on August 3, 1858. He decided that it was indeed the source of the Nile. On his return to Tabora on August 25, Burton refused to believe him.

The relationship between the two men had been strained; now it broke down entirely. By the time they reached Zanzibar on March 4, 1859, they were barely on speaking terms. Speke arrived in London 12 days ahead of Burton and told the president of the Royal Geographical Society that he had discovered the source of the Nile. By the time Burton arrived, Speke had already given a public lecture on the expedition and had become a popular hero.

Burton was furious and the two began a public quarrel. Speke received backing from the Royal Geographical Society to return to Africa along with **James Augustus Grant**. They traveled from Lake Victoria Nyanza to Gondokoro in the southern Sudan, where they were met by **Samuel** and **Florence Baker** on the upper Nile, thereby proving Speke's theory. However, he was unable to travel along the river for a stretch of some 60 miles. Burton used this as the excuse to claim that Speke's claim was unproven. Geographers were divided into rival camps, some believing Speke had found the source, others supporting Burton's counterclaim that the Nile originates in another river flowing out of Lake Tanganyika. Finally, it was arranged for the two rivals to confront one another at a public meeting in the resort city of Bath, England. But on September 16, 1864, the morning of the meeting, Speke went out to shoot partridges and shot himself in the chest while climbing over a low wall and died shortly thereafter.

In spite of the official verdict that the death was accidental, many people thought that it had been suicide. It was felt that the inarticulate Speke was afraid to debate Burton. But, in fact, Speke was right and Burton was wrong.

In the meantime, after his return from east Africa, Burton had renewed his courtship of Isabel Arundell. When her family refused to allow her to marry him, he disappeared suddenly and made a trip to North America in April 1860. He returned at Christmas and told Arundell that if they did not marry he would return to India. In spite of her mother's disapproval they were married in a Catholic church on January 22, 1861. At the wedding reception, one of the guests asked, "Now, Burton, tell me, how do you feel when you have killed a man?" "Oh, quite jolly, doctor! how do you?" he replied. (There is no reason to think Burton ever killed anyone.)

In 1861 Burton was appointed British consul on the island of Fernando Po in the Gulf of Guinea. While there, he led a British diplomatic mission to the African kingdom of Dahomey (now Benin). He also traveled to Gabon to try to find the gorillas that had recently been written about by **Paul Du Chaillu**. He returned to England in the summer of 1864 shortly after Speke's return and accepted the challenge of taking part in the fateful debate.

Thanks to his wife's lobbying, Burton was then appointed consul in Santos in Brazil, where the couple went in October, 1865. In August 1868, Isabel returned to England and Burton traveled to Buenos Aires (sometimes in the company of **Sir Wilfrid Scawen Blunt**) and over the Andes to Lima, where he learned that he had been appointed British consul in Damascus, Syria. He served there until 1872 when he was transferred to the port of Trieste on the Adriatic Sea. It was there that Burton translated the *Kama Sutra*, an erotic Indian classic. Burton's home was in Trieste for the rest of his life, but he wandered ceaselessly all over Europe and farther afield.

In 1875 Burton went searching for diamonds in India, stopping in Egypt on the return. In 1876-1878 he visited what is now Jordan, and he went looking for gold in Ghana in 1882. His translation of the *Arabian Nights* appeared in 1886. He was unexpectedly knighted in 1886 (thus becoming *Sir* Richard Burton). In 1889 he made his last trip, to North Africa. He then returned home to Trieste, where he died on October 20, 1890. Following his death, Isabel burned many of his writings, and there has always been much speculation as to what they contained. She wrote a sanitized version of his life before her own death in 1896.

Where to learn more

There is an enormous bibliography on the life of Sir Richard Burton. Burton himself wrote some 50 books, not to mention innumerable smaller articles, reviews and published letters.

Burton's books that directly relate to the explorations discussed above are: on the trip to Arabia, *Personal Narrative of a Pilgrimage to El-Medinah and Meccah*, 3 vols. (London: Longman, Brown, Green, and Longmans, 1855-1857); on the expedition to Somalia, *First Footsteps in East Africa; or, an Exploration of Harar*, 2 vols. (London: Longmans Green, 1856); on the search for the source of the Nile, *The Lake Regions of Central Africa*, 2 vols. (London: Longman, Green, Longman, and Roberts, 1860) and, with James M'Queen, *The Nile Basin* (London: Tinsley Brothers, 1864), which was published only a few months after Speke's death.

Any trip that Burton made was worth a weighty volume or two, including: *The City of the Saints and Across the Rocky Mountains to California* (London: Longman, Green, Longman, and Roberts, 1861); *Abeokuta and the Cameroons Mountains: An Exploration*, 2 vols. (London: Tinsley Brothers, 1863); *Wanderings in West Africa from Liverpool to Fernando Po*, 2 vols. (London: Tinsley Brothers, 1863); *A Mission to Gelele, King of Dahome*, 2 vols. (London: Tinsley Brothers, 1864); *The Highlands of Brazil*, 2 vols. (London: Tinsley Brothers, 1869); *Unexplored Syria*, 2 vols. (London: Tinsley Brothers, 1872); *Zanzibar, City, Island and Coast*, 2 vols. (London: Tinsley Brothers, 1872); and *Two Trips to Gorilla Land and the Cataracts of the Congo*, 2 vols. (London: Sampson Low, Marston, Low & Searle, 1876).

The first biography of Burton to appear after his death was the one by his wife: Isabel Arundell Burton, *The Life of Captain Sir Richard F. Burton*, 2 vols. (London: Chapman and Hall, 1893). One of Burton's cousins so objected to this work that she immediately wrote another biography to counter his wife's version: Georgiana M. Sisted, *True Life of Capt. Sir Richard Burton* (London: Nichols, 1896).

Since these two biographies appeared, there have been many others. They include two fairly recent ones—Lesley Blanch, *The Wilder Shores of Love* (London: Murray, 1954) and Fawn Brodie, *The Devil Drives: A Life of Sir Richard Burton* (New York: W.W. Norton & Co., 1967)—that discuss his life from a psychoanalytical point of view.

There are two excellent biographies that have appeared recently in paperback editions. The first, Byron Farwell's *Burton: A Biography of Sir Richard Francis Burton* (New York: Holt, Rinehart and Winston, 1963; paperback, New York: Penguin, 1987) is particularly strong on Burton's various travels. The second, Edward Rice's *Captain Sir Richard Francis Burton* (New York: Charles Scribner's Sons, 1990; paperback, New York: HarperCollins, 1991) is an excellent overall synthesis of Burton's life.

Various specialized aspects of Burton's travels have been the subject of studies in their own right. Seton Dearden has published two books on Burton in Arabia: *Burton of Arabia* (New York: Robert McBride & Co., 1937) and *The Arabian Knight* (London: Barker, 1953). A recent book discusses Burton's less well-known trips to North and South America: Frank McLynn, *From the Sierras to the Pampas: Richard Burton's Travels in the Americas, 1860-69* (London: Century, 1991).

There is a feature-length movie about Burton's east African explorations that also deals with his relationships to Speke and to his wife: *The Mountains of the Moon* (Carolco Pictures, 1989).

Robert Bylot

(voyaged 1610 - 1616)

Robert Bylot was an Englishman who made four voyages to Hudson Bay and the area north of it searching for a Northwest Passage.

Little is known about the life of Robert Bylot except that he played a crucial role in the four earliest voyages to the Canadian Arctic and the search for the Northwest Passage. He was mate on board the *Discovery* that was captained by **Henry Hudson** in 1610-1611 that first explored Hudson Bay. Although Bylot later claimed not to have been involved in the mutiny that put Hudson adrift in the bay, he was chosen second in command to the leader of the mutiny, Henry Greene, on the return trip to England. After Greene's death it was Bylot who piloted the ship back to England, and it was this feat that secured his pardon.

Bylot sailed again on an expedition in 1612 with Sir Thomas Button. They left England in April of that year with two ships, the *Resolution* and the *Discovery*. They explored the entrance to Hudson Bay and found Resolution Island named after one of the ships. They then sailed to the west coast of the bay the mouth of a river that was named the Nelson, after one of the ships' officers. They spent the winter of 1612-1613 on shore, and many of the men died. In the spring they traveled north to the strait between Southampton Island and the mainland that was later named Sir Thomas Roe's Welcome. In August 1613 they explored another large island, Mansel Island, at the entrance to Hudson Bay and then returned to England.

Bylot set out again in 1615 as the captain of the *Discovery* with **William Baffin** as pilot. They sailed to the north of Southampton Island and proved that there was no passageway to the west there. The same two men voyaged together again in 1616. This time they sailed to the north of what was named Baffin Island and explored the large body of water known as Baffin Bay. On this voyage they sailed 300 miles farther north than **John Davis** had done 30 years before and set a record that lasted for more than two centuries. They found the entrance to the three large sounds that flow into Baffin Bay and named them for their financial sponsors—Smith, Jones, and Lancaster. One of these, Lancaster Sound, does in fact provide entrance to the only usable Northwest Passage, but neither Baffin nor Bylot recognized that. Their discoveries were forgotten until 200 years later when search for the Northwest Passage started again.

Nothing is known about the life of Bylot either before or after these voyages. Baffin wrote up the results of their two expeditions and testified that Bylot was very skilled at navigating through icy waters.

Where to learn more

The original records of Baffin's expeditions were published by the Hakluyt Society in 1881: Clements K. Markham, ed. *The Voyages of William Baffin, 1612-1622* (London: 1881). The best account of these early Arctic voyages can be found in Tryggvi J. Olesen, *Early Voyages and Northern Approaches, 1000-1632* (Toronto: MacClelland and Stewart, 1963).

Richard Evelyn Byrd

(1888 - 1957)

Richard Evelyn Byrd was an American naval pilot who was the first man to fly over the North Pole and the South Pole and who led several American expeditions to Antarctica.

R ichard Evelyn Byrd was born in Winchester, Virginia on October 25, 1888 into one of the most prominent Virginia families. At the age of 14 he went on a trip by himself to the Philippines. There he stayed with a family friend who had been appointed a judge in the new American administration of the Philippines, conquered in the Spanish-American War in 1898. He stayed for a year and then continued on his own around the world by taking a British tramp steamer to India, Suez, England, and New York. On his return Byrd wrote in his diary, at the age of 15, that he intended to be the first man to reach the North Pole, but he was beaten by **Robert Edward Peary** and **Matthew A. Henson** in 1909.

Byrd started his university career at the University of Virginia where he was intended for a legal career, but he found that he was not suited for life in an office and transferred to the U.S. Naval Academy to prepare to become a naval officer. At Annapolis Byrd excelled at athletics but broke his right ankle twice in accidents—once in football and once in gymnastics. He received his commission in 1912 and served as a gunnery officer on U.S. Navy ships. In 1916, however, he broke his ankle again, and this time it was so serious that he was invalided out of the Navy.

Byrd was forced to stay out of the Navy for only two months. As the United States geared up for its participation in World War I, he was taken back into the services as a training officer. He was then able to use his influence and enthusiasm to convince the Navy that he was sufficiently recovered to learn how to fly. He was sent to the Naval flight school at Pensacola, Florida and got his wings. He then worked on a plan to send flying boats (a type of amphibious airplane) across the Atlantic to Europe. Byrd developed two important navigational tools as part of the preparations. However, the planned trip never took place. There was a successful flight after the war in 1919, but Byrd was not on board.

Following the war, Byrd worked at administrative tasks for the Navy, including setting up its Bureau of Aeronautics. In 1925 he made his first trip to the Arctic when he participated in an expedition sponsored by the National Geographic Society with joint Army-Navy participation. Byrd was the first person to fly over the interior of Ellesmere Island and over the Greenland Ice Cap.

Richard Evelyn Byrd. U.S. Navy Department.

This trip made Byrd determined to be the first person to fly over the North Pole. At the time, other explorers, including **Roald Amundsen**, were attempting to do the same thing, and he knew he would have to hurry. He got financial support from John D. Rockefeller and Edsel Ford, the son of Henry Ford. He flew to Spitsbergen Island in the *Josephine Ford* on April 29, 1926, and then flew on to the North Pole, reaching it a 9:02 a.m. on May 9, 1926 in spite of a difficult take-off and an oil leak in one of the engines of the Fokker monoplane with three 200-horsepower engines. He was accompanied by warrant officer Floyd Bennett, and they were met by Amundsen on their return to Spitsbergen.

On his return to the United States, Byrd was welcomed as a hero. He then set out to fly non-stop across the North Atlantic but his trip was dimmed by the solo flight of **Charles A.**

Lindbergh. Byrd flew with a three-man crew in June 1927 but crashed on the coast of France at Ver-sur-Mer.

Byrd then transferred his ambitions to Antarctica where he set out to become the first to fly over the South Pole. He sailed for Antarctica on August 25, 1928 and set up his base camp at a place he named Little America, which was to become the main scientific camp for American expeditions. One of the two planes he took with him was wrecked in a storm. The other plane

(named the *Floyd Bennett* in tribute to Byrd's earlier co-pilot who had died in a crash), a Ford tri-motor, ran into problems in reaching the required altitude and had a forced landing that damaged the engine. At 3:29 p.m. on November 28, 1929, however, Byrd set out with four other men with himself as navigator. At one point they were forced to throw 250 pounds of emergency rations out of the plane in order to gain the 20 feet needed to clear Liv's Glacier. After that they had smooth flying and reached the Pole at 1:14 a.m. on November 29. They circled

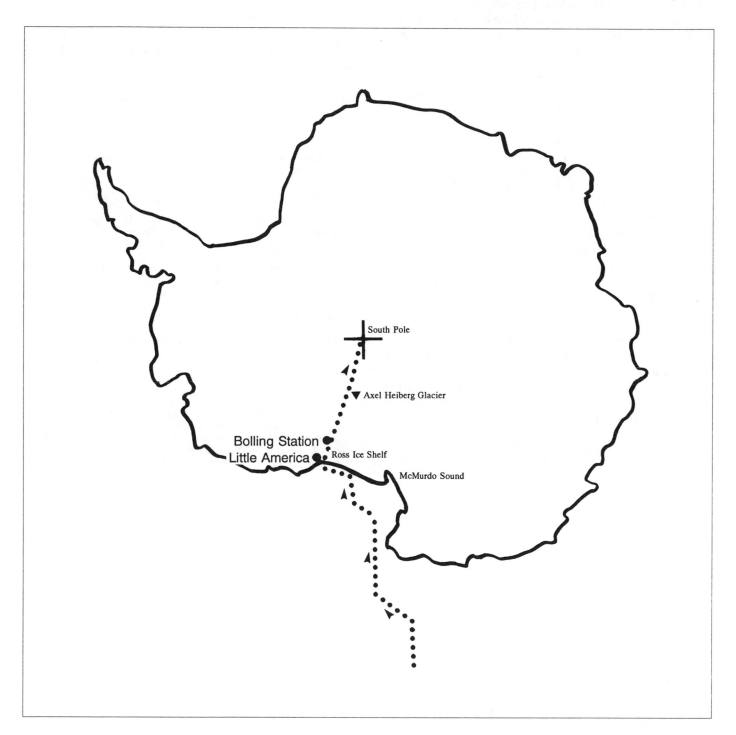

Byrd's bases in Antarctica and his route to the South Pole.

the Pole twice and landed back at the base 18 hours and 39 minutes after they left, having covered 1,500 air miles.

Following this first expedition to Antarctica, Byrd returned to New York on February 19, 1930. He set out again in 1933 at the head of a major scientific expedition to Little America that included four airplanes as part of its equipment. A major goal was to establish a small advance weather post, the Bolling Advanced Weather Station, which was built 125 miles south of Little America in a tiny prefabricated hut buried in the snow. The only entry was by way of a hatch that would not close properly, and it was heated by a stove that turned out to be defective. Byrd left by himself to man the little "station" in March 1934.

In May 1934, Byrd was caught outside the hut during a blizzard and was almost unable to get back in. In his book *Little America*, Byrd wrote "It is more than just wind, it is a solid wall of snow moving at gale force, pounding like surf . . . you can't see, you can't hear, you can hardly move." He was somehow able to find a shovel and to dig his way to the hatch and get it open.

Starting in May, Byrd's radio transmissions back to Little America became increasingly irrational: he was being poisoned by carbon monoxide from the defective stove. In July, Dr. Poulter, the second in command, decided to send out a rescue mission, but they did not reach Byrd until August 10, 1934. By that time Byrd was seriously ill, and it took two months of nursing before they were able to take him back to Little America. The expedition left Little America on February 7, 1935 with much valuable scientific information.

Byrd's third Antarctic expedition was in November 1939 right after the outbreak of World War II. Its aim was to map parts of the continent in case the United States decided to join other countries in claiming Antarctic territory. It set up two new bases, and Byrd returned to the United States at the end of 1940. During World War II Admiral Byrd helped plan U.S. strategy in the Pacific.

After the war, in 1946, Byrd commanded the largest expedition sent to Antarctica up to that time. Called Operation Highjump, it was made up of 4,100 men (including 300 scientists), 13 ships, 19 airplanes, four helicopters, and a submarine. The large expedition was divided up into different task forces to accomplish various goals. In addition to serving as overall leader of the expedition, Byrd took part in a two-plane flight over the South Pole and unknown land beyond it. They were the second and third planes to reach the Pole. Byrd returned to the United States in March 1947. Operation Highjump explored much new territory and mapped and photographed 1,400 miles of the coast of Antarctica.

During the International Geophysical Year of 1957-1958, Admiral Byrd was put in charge of the U.S. program and made one last flight over the South Pole on January 8, 1956. He died peacefully at home on March 11, 1957 at the age of 68.

Where to learn more

Byrd wrote several books about his polar expeditions: *Skyward* (New York: G.P. Putnam's Sons, 1928); *Little America* (New York: G.P. Putnam's Sons, 1930); *Discovery* (New York: G.P. Putnam's Sons, 1935); and *Alone* (G.P. Putnam's Sons, 1938).

There is a fairly recent biography of Byrd that tells the whole story of his adventurous life: Edwin P. Hoyt, *The Last Explorer: The Adventures of Admiral Byrd* (New York: The John Day Company, 1968).

A good summary of Byrd's activities can be found in John Grierson, *Heroes of the Polar Skies* (New York: Meredith Press, 1967 and in George Simmons, *Target Arctic: Men in the Skies at the Top of the World* (Philadelphia: Chilton Books, 1965. The important role that Byrd played in the American exploration of Antarctica is discussed in Kenneth J. Bertrand, *Americans in the Antarctic* (New York: American Geographical Society, 1971) and George J. Dufek, *Operation Deepfreeze* (New York: Harcourt Brace, 1957). An excellent book about Antarctic exploration, including many photographs and maps is *Antarctica: Great Stories from the Frozen Continent* (Sydney: Reader's Digest, 1988).

There are two recent books about Byrd's early Antarctic explorations. The first is a memoir by a naval officer who accompanied Byrd: Norman D. Vaughan, with Cecil B. Murphey, *With Byrd at the Bottom of the World: The South Pole Expedition of 1928-1930* (Harrisburg, Pennsylvania: Stackpole Books, 1990). The second is an excellent academic study that includes an extensive bibliography: Eugene Rodgers, *Beyond the Barrier: The Story of Byrd's First Expedition to Antarctica* (Annapolis, Maryland: Naval Institute Press, 1990).

John Byron

1723 - 1786

John Byron was an English naval captain who laid claim to the Falkland Islands for Great Britain and then completed a voyage around the world.

John Byron was the second son of the fourth Lord Byron. He went to sea at the age of 14 as an "able seaman" on a Royal Navy ship escorting merchant vessels between Lisbon and Newfoundland. At the age of 16, he was chosen to be midshipman on the *Wager*, a small British warship that was part of a British squadron commanded by Commodore George Anson. The squadron was sent to capture the Chilean port of Valdivia during the "War of Jenkins' Ear," which had broken out between Great Britain and Spain in October 1739. The squadron left England in September 1740. The ships reached Cape Horn in March 1740, and it took a month to pass around Cape Horn and into the Pacific because of the stormy weather. The *Wager* was severely injured and was wrecked on the desolate shore of southern Chile early in the morning of May 14, 1740.

Once ashore, the survivors among the crew were in very bad shape, and they had difficulty finding anything to eat. Desperate, some of them decided to take the ship's longboat and try to sail through the Straits of Magellan to Brazil. In defiance of the captain's orders, they left the "Gulf of Affliction" in October. Some of the officers and men, including Byron, stayed with the captain, and they tried to sail north in a small canoe in December, 1740. Unable to make any progress against the heavy seas, they were forced to return to Wager Island. They were rescued by a small party of Native Americans who took them overland to the nearest Spanish settlement at Chiloe Island in a trip that lasted three months. They stayed on Chiloe until the beginning of January 1743 before being taken to the port of Valparaiso, where they were thrown in prison. From Valparaiso they were taken to Santiago. They were treated well but were forced to stay there until the end of December 1744. They did not get back to England until March 1746, where survivors of the group that had sailed through the Straits also trickled in.

Having acquitted himself well during the course of this odyssey, Byron was given command of a frigate in 1746 and then commanded various ships after peace was declared. When war broke out again between Great Britain and France in 1756, Byron was in command of a warship that led an attack that destroyed a French convoy carrying troops and supplies for the relief of Quebec City, which was being besieged by the troops of General Wolfe.

After the end of the Seven Years' War (called the French and Indian War in North America) in 1763, both England and France had the opportunity to send out expeditions to try to discover unknown parts of the world. Byron commanded one such expedition that was sent out with some rather grandiose instructions. He was supposed to sail to the South Atlantic and take possession of the Falkland Islands or the nearby "Pepys Island" to be used as a British base to control the access to the Pacific Island. He was then directed to sail up the west coast of the Americas to the New Albion (California) that **Sir Francis Drake** had discovered in 1587. From there he was to head north and try to find the elusive northwest passage across the northern part of North America into Hudson Bay. (It was hoped that this might be more easily discovered approaching from the west.) If this proved not to be possible, he was supposed to sail westward to China and the Dutch East Indies.

Byron carried out the first part of these instructions reasonably well. He left England with two ships, the *Dolphin* with 190 men and the *Tamar* with 115 on July 3, 1764. They reached the Patagonian coast of South America in November. In southern Patagonia, Byron went ashore and encountered a large group of Native Americans. Patagonia had been named from a corruption of Portuguese words meaning "big feet." Early explorers had claimed to see giant footprints in the dirt. Byron's own descriptions, which were mirrored by members of the crew, seemed to indicate that the Patagonians he met were unusually large. This was later magnified by popular writers in England to talk about giants that were anywhere from eight to twenty feet tall. These descriptions were much ridiculed in England, and, indeed, later visitors have never seen any trace of these giant humans.

From the coast of Patagonia, Byron sailed westward to the Falklands, decided that they were the same thing as Pepys Island (which they were), and took formal possession of them on January 12, 1765. While he was there he surprised to see a French ship in the same waters. In fact, this was the French explorer **Louis Antoine de Bougainville** who had come to start a French colony. The British have based their claim to the Falkland Islands on Byron's voyage while the French claim was turned over to Spain and then passed to Argentina when that country became independent. The Falkland Islands War in 1982 was the result of these conflicting claims, and of the two passing ships in 1765.

Byron sailed back to Patagonia and encountered a British supply ship that had been sent out with fresh provisions. When that ship returned to England, Byron sent a letter saying that his ships were too disabled to make the trip northward and that he was going to head west across the Pacific to try to find the Solomon Islands that **Alvaro de Mendaña** had found in 1567.

To get to the Pacific from Patagonia, Byron had to sail through the Straits of Magellan. Because of bad weather, this short sail took seven weeks and two days. Since his crew and his ships were in bad shape by this time, he headed northwestward towards the Juan Fernandez Islands. He missed these and ended up on June 7, 1765 in the Tuamotu islands where **Jacob Roggeveen** had been in 1722. In fact, he found remnants of one of Roggeveen's boats that had been wrecked on the island of Takaroa.

With his crew sick from being at sea so long, Byron could not afford to spend much time trying to make new discoveries, so he sailed west past some of the smaller islands of the Society and Tokelau archipelagoes. At some of these he was able to stop and get fresh water and food. He then turned north and passed through the southern islands of Kiribati and on July 31 reached the island of Tinian in the Mariana chain, which was under the loose control of Spaniards from Guam. The expedition ships stayed there for nine weeks while the crew recovered from scurvy and repairs were made to the ships.

From Tinian Byron took the fastest route home, reaching Batavia in the Dutch East Indies in December 1765 and England on May 9, 1766. It had taken him 22 months to travel around the world, which was very quick for those years. However, he had only carried out a part of his mission —visiting and claiming the Falkland Islands.

On his return to England, Byron acted as an adviser to the British Admiralty in mounting other expeditions to the South Pacific. He was appointed Governor of Newfoundland in 1769 and served there for three years. He was promoted to rear admiral in 1775 and vice-admiral in 1778. He was given command of a fleet that was sent out on June 8, 1778 to defeat the French fleet that was supporting the Americans during the Revolution. By this time, Byron had been nicknamed "Foul Weather Jack" because of his seeming tendency to run into bad weather wherever he went. The nickname turned out to be appropriate in this case, and his fleet was dispersed by a series of storms off the coast of North America. He had to retreat to Halifax, leaving the French in control. He then headed for the Caribbean where he was defeated on July 6, 1779 by the French Admiral D'Estaing in an engagement off the island of Grenada.

Suffering from a "nervous fever," Byron returned to England and retired. He had married Sophia Trevanion in 1748, and they had two sons. He later gained some notoriety in English society by setting up his wife's maid in a house of her own and "visiting there frequently." He died on April 10, 1786. The older of his two sons, John, was nicknamed "Mad Jack Byron" and was a notorious rake. By his second wife, "Mad Jack" had a son named George Gordon, generally known as Lord Byron, the poet. The elder John Byron's second son, George Anson Byron, followed in his father's footsteps and pursued a naval career. He played a major role in defeating a French fleet in the Battle of The Saints between Guadeloupe and Dominica on April 8, 1782, helping to retrieve some of the family honor lost by his father's defeat a few years earlier.

Where to learn more

Byron told his own account of the *Wager* disaster in *The Narrative of the Honourable John Byron containing an Account of the Great Distresses Suffered by Himself and His Companions. . . .* (London: 1768). The story has been retold with an accounting of all of the survivors of the shipwreck in Peter Shankland's *Byron of the Wager* (New York: Coward, McCann & Geogheghan, 1975).

Byron's narrative of his voyage around the world can be found in Robert E. Gallagher, ed. *Byron's Journal of His Circumnavigation, 1764-1766* (Cambridge: Cambridge University Press for the Hakluyt Society). A modern retelling is in Derek Wilson, *The Circumnavigators* (New York: M. Evans & Company, 1989).

Alvar Núñez Cabeza de Vaca

(1490 - 1556?)

Alvar Núñez Cabeza de Vaca was a Spanish explorer who spent many years in what is now Texas after being shipwrecked and who traveled overland to Mexico. He also explored along the Paraguay River in South America.

Alvar Núñez Cabeza de Vaca ("Cow's Head") was born into a noble family in the Spanish town of Jerez de la Frontera, the center of sherry production. His family had got its name and title of nobility in the year 1212 when a peasant ancestor had used the skull of a dead cow to mark a route for a Christian army that defeated the Muslim Moors in battle. Cabeza de Vaca fought in the army of the Spanish king in Italy and Navarre (in northern Spain) and against rebels in the city of Toledo in 1520-1521. In 1527 he was appointed royal treasurer on an expedition to North America commanded by Pánfilo de Narváez.

The expedition of Narváez included 600 men and five ships. It made stops in Santo Domingo and Cuba and then crossed over to Florida, where it landed in Tampa Bay on April 14, 1528. Narváez decided to follow up on reports he heard from the local Native Americans of an abundance of gold at a place called Apalachen (near modern-day Tallahassee). In the meantime, the ships sailed northward to look for a port that the pilots said they knew. They were not seen again, and it was later learned that they had sailed back to Mexico.

With a force of approximately 250 to 300 Spaniards, Narváez set out for Apalachen. When they arrived there, they found large stores of corn but no gold. They left Apalachen about a month later with the Native Americans shooting arrows at them as they left. Having lost hope of contacting the ships, the members of the party decided to try to reach the Spanish settlement of Pánuco in northeastern Mexico by sailing along the coast of the Gulf of Mexico.

In order to construct barges, the Spaniards melted down their metal for nails, made sails out of clothing, wove horsehair into ropes and used horse hides to make water containers. A total of 242 men set sail in five barges on September 22, 1528 from a bay that could be one of several in what is now the Florida panhandle. The Spanish named it the Bay of the Horses because they had killed and eaten the last of their horses there. They sailed west, keeping close to the shore and suffering greatly from lack of water. They passed the mouth of the Mississippi River, where the wind and heavy current separated the five barges.

Alvar Núñez Cabeza de Vaca. The Granger Collection, New York.

On November 6, Cabeza de Vaca's barge was cast ashore on Galveston Island. A few days later he was joined by another barge commanded by Alonso de Castillo and Andres Dorantes. The other three barges all sank at sea. A total of 80 Spaniards made it to shore. They found themselves among a group of Native Americans who subsisted by hunting and gathering and had no surplus to help the Europeans, although they were not hostile to them. During the winter, the weather was so severe that many of the Spaniards died: by the spring there were only 15 left. In the spring of 1529 these remaining Spaniards left Galveston Island and headed for the Texas mainland. Cabeza de Vaca, however, was left behind because of illness.

When he was well enough to travel, Cabeza de Vaca crossed over to the mainland and then headed west, trying to get to Pánuco overland. For several years, he lived among the various tribes of eastern Texas as a trader, traveling inland and along the coast. He also acted as a healer and gained a considerable reputation among his Native American hosts. During his travels, he became the first European to see the North American bison, or buffalo. At the beginning of the winter of 1533, he met Castillo and Dorantes and the Muslim slave **Estevanico** along the Colorado River of Texas, where the Native Americans gathered every year to feast on the pecan harvest. They reported that they were the only survivors of the party that had left Cabeza de Vaca in 1529 and that they had spent the following years as slaves of various tribes.

The four men agreed to meet the following summer at a place where the tribes gathered to eat prickly pears. They would then attempt to reach Mexico together. They did meet up as planned near the site of the modern city of San Antonio and were able to break away in September 1534. They traveled north and spent the following winter with a tribe they called the Avavares. They continued their westward journey in the summer of 1535, with Native Americans as guides. Depending on their reputations as medicine men, the four Spaniards were conducted from one tribe to the next and were able to maintain the goodwill of all of them. Cabeza de Vaca even reports that "it was very tiresome to have to breathe on and make the sign of the cross over every morsel they (the Native Americans) ate or drank."

The four Spanish survivors crossed the Rio Grande at what is now Rincon, New Mexico. Near there, they saw items of Spanish origin on members of the Yaqui tribe, who told them how they had been driven off their land by the Europeans. Cabeza de Vaca and his three companions headed south into the modern Mexican state of Sonora. They made their first contacts with other Spaniards near the city of Culiacán in early 1536. They rested for several weeks and then continued on to Mexico City, which they reached in the summer of 1536.

The news of Cabeza de Vaca's travels had generated a lot of interest in Mexico, and the travelers were warmly welcomed by Viceroy Antonio de Mendoza. In response to their reports, the Viceroy sent out an expedition under Fray Marcos de Niza that was guided by Estevanico, who was killed in one of the pueblos along the way. On the return of Marcos, a larger expedition under **Francisco Vázquez de Coronado** was sent out.

Cabeza de Vaca left for Spain in 1537, stopping at Santo Domingo along the way. While there, he submitted a report written along with Castillo and Dorantes which is called the *Joint Report* and is one of the two main sources about their trip. (The other is a book written by Cabeza de Vaca and published in Spain in 1542 with the title *Relación de los Naufragios*—The Story of the Ship-Wrecked Ones). Back in Spain, Cabeza de Vaca turned down the chance to return to Florida with the expedition of **Hernando de Soto**.

On March 8, 1540 Cabeza de Vaca was named captain-general and adelantado of Spanish settlements on the Río de la Plata, headquartered at Asunción in what is now Paraguay. He left Spain with three ships on November 2, 1540 and landed on the island of Santa Catarina, Brazil, on March 29, 1541. He left there on November 2 and traveled overland to Asunción with a force of about 280 men.

The Spanish force survived by bartering with the villages of the Guaraní tribe, and Cabeza de Vaca was so honest in his dealings that they were able to maintain good relations all along the way. In early January 1542, they became the first Europeans to see the Iguaçu Falls. The only casualty of his expedition was a man lost by drowning while trying to cross the river below the falls. Cabeza de Vaca continued by river down the Paraná to where it meets the Paraguay River. Part of the expedition went upstream on rafts while Cabeza de Vaca marched by land to Asunción, where he arrived on March 11, 1542, to the great joy of the inhabitants who thought they had been abandoned.

In September 1543 Cabeza de Vaca decided to open up a route between the settlements on the Paraguay River and the rich mines and cities of Peru. He led about 400 Spaniards and 800 members of the Guaraní tribe up the Paraguay to a place he called Puerto de los Reyes (Port of the Kings). He traveled a short way into the interior but was forced to return by his followers who did not want to risk the hazards of the forest.

Two weeks after his return to Asunción in April 1544, Cabeza de Vaca was thrown out of his office of Governor by a group of Spaniards who were unhappy with his rule. In 1545 he was sent to Spain for trial on a variety of charges, including one that he had tried to assume the authority of the King. After years of trial, he was eventually found guilty. He appealed the decision. It was upheld, but his punishment was lightened. He died in poverty sometime after the year 1556.

Where to learn more

Cabeza de Vaca's *Relación*, mentioned above, was published in English as *The Narrative of Cabeza de Vaca*, translated by Buckingham Smith, in F.W. Hodge, ed. *Spanish Explorers of the Southern United States* (New York: 1907).

There are several books that recount the story of Cabeza de Vaca's journey across Texas and the southwest: Morris Bishop, *The Odyssey of Cabeza de Vaca* (New York: The Century Co., 1933); Cleve Hallenbeck, *Alvar Núñez Cabeza de Vaca: The Journey and Route of the First European to Cross the Continent of North America* (Glendale, California: 1940); John Upton Terrell, *Journey into Darkness* (New York: William Morrow & Company, 1962); and Maia Rodman, *Odyssey of Courage: The Story of Alvaro Núñez Cabeza de Vaca* (London: Burns & Oates, 1965).

The story of Cabeza de Vaca's adventures in South America can be found in: Robert B. Cunninghame Graham, *The Conquest of the River Plate* (London: William Heinemann, 1924) and Frederick A. Kirkpatrick, *The Spanish Conquistadores* (London: A.C. Blade, 1934). A good summary can be found in Edward J. Goodman, *The Explorers of South America* (New York: Macmillan, 1972).

John Cabot

(1451? - 1498)

John Cabot, an Italian navigator in the service of the King of England, was the first European known to have reached the mainland of North America following the Vikings.

John Cabot was probably from the Italian port city of Genoa. In 1476 he was granted citizenship in Venice. Venice was then the major trading center for all of the Mediterranean, and Cabot worked as a merchant and navigator. It is thought that from 1490 to 1493 he lived in the Spanish city of Valencia and may have been there in April 1493 when **Christopher Columbus** traveled through the city on the way to report on his successful voyage to America to the King and Queen of Spain.

Cabot, however, did not believe that Columbus had reached Asia because he felt that the distance was much greater than that traveled by Columbus. He did believe that it was possible to reach Asia, however, by sailing around the northern end of the body of land that Columbus had found. This was the beginning of the search for the Northwest Passage that was to lead to many voyages of exploration for the next 350 years.

In 1495 Cabot went to England to try to sell his plan of discovery to King Henry VII. On March 5, 1496 the king issued "letters of patent" that granted to "John Cabotto, Citezen of Venice" the right to sail with five ships "to all parts, countries and seas of the East, of the West, and of the North" where he was to "discover and find whatsoever isles, countries, regions or provinces of heathens and infidels, in whatsoever part of the world they be, which before this time were unknown to all Christians."

Cabot made a first attempt to sail to North America in 1496 but was forced to turn back because of shortage of food, bad weather, and problems with the crew. On May 20, 1497 he sailed again from the port of Bristol in a small ship named the *Matthew* with a crew of 20 that included his son **Sebastian Cabot**. They sailed south of Ireland for 35 days until they sighted land on June 24, St. John the Baptist's Day. Cabot went ashore and saw signs of human habitation but did not meet anyone. He then sailed on for 300 leagues from west to east before turning back and heading for Ireland. It took him 15 days to cross the Atlantic to Brittany and from there to Bristol, where he landed on August 6. He reported to the King in London on August 11, who gave him a reward, and was back home in Bristol with his family by August 23.

Ever since then people have argued about where Cabot actually went. The most likely itinerary is that he touched land somewhere on the coast of Maine and then headed north along the coast of Nova Scotia and Cape Breton Island as far as Cape Race in Newfoundland, and from there sailed back to Europe.

Having found land that was previously unknown to Europeans, Cabot was able to get backing from the king for a new expedition. This time he commanded five ships and a much larger crew. The ships sailed from Bristol in May 1498 and were never heard of again.

Some evidence that was obtained by later explorers seems to indicate that this second expedition reached the coast of Newfoundland. Some of the ships or survivors may have fallen into the hands of the Spanish because later explorers such as **Gaspar Corte-Real** and **Alonso de Ojeda** seem to have sailed with some knowledge of previous discoveries made by the English.

Where to learn more

The documentary sources for the voyages of the Cabots are found in J.A. Williamson, *The Cabot Voyages and Bristol Discovery under Henry VII* (London: Hakluyt Society, 1962). The best modern discussion of the voyages of John Cabot is in the works of the eminent American historian Samuel Eliot Morison, especially *The European Discovery of America: The Northern Voyages* (New York: Oxford University Press, 1971), which is available in a paperback edition. There is a good chapter on Cabot in Tryggvi J. Olesen, *Early Voyages and Northern Approaches, 1000-1632* (Toronto: McClelland and Stewart, 1963) and J.M. Scott, *Icebound: Journeys to the Northwest Sea* (Toronto: Gordon & Cremonesi, 1977).

Sebastian Cabot

(1484 - 1557)

Sebastian Cabot was a navigator of Venetian origin who explored the coast of North America for the King of England and named and sailed up the Río de la Plata in the service of the King of Spain.

Sebastian Cabot was born in Venice sometime around the year 1484, the second son of the explorer **John Cabot**. He went with his father to England in 1495 and then accompanied him on his voyage to North America in 1497. On his father's death, he was given an annual income by King Henry VII in recognition of his services.

Sometime during the spring of 1508 Cabot was sent out on an exploring expedition north of where his father had gone to try to discover the northern passage around North America that every-

Sebastian Cabot.

one of the age hoped, and believed, existed. Cabot himself did not write about his voyage so we have to rely on the accounts of others written at a later date. The first and probably the most accurate was written by an Italian monk named Peter Martyr in 1516: "He equipped two ships at his own cost in Britain, and with three hundred men steered first for the north, until even in the month of July he found great icebergs floating in the sea and almost continuous daylight, yet with the land free by the melting of the ice. Wherefore he was obliged, as he says, to turn and make for the west. And he extended his course furthermore to the southward owing to the curve of the coastline, so that his latitude was almost that of the Straits of Gibraltar and he penetrated so far to the west that he had the island of Cuba on his left hand almost in the same longitude with himself."

If this account is accurate it would seem to mean that Cabot sailed from England to Iceland and southern Greenland to the coast of Labrador and north along it until his crew refused to sail farther and then headed south along the coast of North America. From maps that Cabot drew later in his life it also seems possible that he found the entrance to Hudson Bay and thought that this was the way to Asia.

After Cabot returned to England he found work in southern France and in 1512 settled in Spain, where he was appointed Pilot Major to the Spanish king, in succession to **Juan Diaz de Solís**. This meant that he was responsible for keeping the records of all the Spanish voyages of discovery. He became involved in plans for voyages to the New World in 1516 and again, with English support, in 1521, but both of these fell through.

In 1524, however, the Spanish king and a group of Seville merchants decided to invest in a voyage to South America to test Cabot's theory that there was an easier passage to the Pacific Ocean than the one found by **Ferdinand Magellan** in 1520. He was to find the new passage and sail to the Spice, or Moluccas, Islands. The expedition left Spain with four ships and about 200 men on April 3, 1526. They stopped at the Canary and Cape Verde Islands and landed at Recife on the north coast of Brazil, near the "hump" that sticks out toward Africa, on June 3, 1526.

At Recife, Cabot picked up an abandoned sailor who reported on the results of a previous Spanish expedition to the interior of South America that had returned with a large supply of silver, most of which had been lost in a shipwreck. Several of the sailor's companions were also rescued by Cabot farther south, and they also told tales of "a mountain two hundred leagues inland containing many mines of gold and silver and other metals."

These stories were actually the first Spanish knowledge of the Inca Empire and its large mineral wealth. Influenced by these reports, Cabot changed the goal of his expedition toward Argentina. He named the great estuary there the Río de la Plata, or Silver River, and it has kept that name till today.

Cabot explored the two large rivers, the Uruguay and Paraná, that make up the Río de la Plata and in 1527 built a small fort, called Sancti Spiritus, near the present-day city of Rosario. From there exploring parties traveled up the Paraná and as far as the foothills of the Andes. They never found any silver. The local Native Americans were antagonized by the actions of the Spaniards and during one of Cabot's absences they destroyed the fort of Sancti Spiritus. At a meeting on October 6, 1529, it was decided to return to Spain, and what was left of the expedition, one ship and 24 men, arrived there on July 22, 1530.

As a result of the way he had led this expedition Cabot was put on trial and sentenced to four years of banishment. However, the Spanish king, Charles V, pardoned him, and he resumed his activities as Pilot Major in 1532. In this position he was responsi- ble for the publication of several important maps and charts and became involved in the disputes going on at the time on how to determine longitude.

Cabot was not happy in Spain, and in 1548 he returned to work for the king of England. In 1553 he became the governor of the Muscovy Company, which was charged with trading with Russia and with finding a Northeast Passage to China. As such he drew up the instructions for the Company's first voyage under **Richard Chancellor**. He died sometime before December 1557.

Where to learn more

There is a long out-of-print book that presents a complete history of both of the two Cabots: Henry Harrisse, *John Cabot, the Discoverer of North America, and Sebastian, His Son* (London: 1896). Cabot's northern voyage is discussed in Tryggvi J. Olesen, *Early Voyages and Northern Approaches* (Toronto: McClelland and Stewart, 1963) and in J.M. Scott, *Icebound: Journeys to the Northwest Sea* (London: Gordon & Cremonesi, 1977). A very good history of the whole field of South American exploration by Edward J. Goodman, *The Explorers of South America* (New York: Macmillan, 1972), includes an account of the voyage to the Río de la Plata.

João Cabral

(1599 - 1669)

João Cabral was a Portuguese missionary in India who was the first European to travel to Bhutan and Nepal.

In 1625, during the second visit of the Jesuit missionary **Antonio de Andrade** to Tsaparang in western Tibet, merchants from China had told him about Utsang, a province of southeastern Tibet whose capital was Shigatse. Andrade thought that Utsang held potential for Christian missionary work and sent a letter to the head of the Catholic missions in Bengal asking him to send priests to Shigatse. In fact, the Provincial, presumably acting on previous communications, had already chosen Fathers João Cabral and Estevão Cacella to go to Utsang. They were initially accompanied by an Italian lay brother who died along the way.

Cabral and Cacella started their journey from the city of Hooghly on the Ganges delta where there was a Jesuit mission. They left Hooghly on August 2, 1626. Making their way northeast across the Brahmaputra, they turned west through the Kingdom of Cooch Behar. They were forced to wait there for four months during the worst of the winter storms before they could begin their ascent of the Himalayas in February 1627.

Cabral and Cacella were the first Europeans to visit the Kingdom of Bhutan, which even today restricts the number of foreigners it allows into the country. The ruler of Bhutan, was, however, pleased to have his Western visitors and tried to convince them to stay in his kingdom. One reason he wanted them to stay was that he feared that Christian support to the rival state of Utsang would upset the local balance of power. Afraid that they would be trapped in Bhutan, Cacella snuck out while the king was on a hunting trip; three weeks later he reached Shigatse. The king then allowed Cabral to follow after him, and he traveled to Shigatse in the dead of winter of 1627 and was reunited with Cacella in January 1628. There the two priests were given a house, food, and permission to preach.

Cabral and Cacella arrived in Tibet during a time when there was much internal friction between competing Buddhist sects. Cabral wanted to go back to India to report on the situation but was afraid of returning by way of Bhutan. Instead, leaving Shigatse in January 1628, he headed for Nepal. He was the first European to travel in the high passes of the Himalayas between Tibet and Nepal.

After delivering his report in Hooghly, Cabral set out once again for Shigatse. He had written to Cacella asking him to send an escort. Cacella in the meantime had tried to go to Tsaparang and did not get Cabral's letter. However, he was not able to get through to Tsaparang and turned south to head for India. There, he met Cabral at a small village on the border between Bhutan and India called Cocho.

In September 1629 Cacella headed back to Shigatse, leaving Cabral behind to guard their supplies. Cacella did not reach Shigatse until the end of the following April. By the time he got there he was seriously ill and died the week after his arrival. The King of Utsang sent for Cabral, who, after several delays, returned to Shigatse in 1631. Cabral tried one last time to set up a communications route with Tsaparang. He did not succeed, and his superiors back in India decided that the mission was too difficult to supply and ordered him to leave the country. Cabral went back to Hooghly in 1632 and then took up a new post in Malabar in the south of India. The Shigatse and Tsaparang missions were both officially closed in 1635.

Where to learn more

The history of the early Jesuit missions to the Himalayas and Tibet was lost to history for many years. It was rediscovered by a Jesuit priest, C. Wessels, who discovered the information while doing research in the early archives of the Jesuits in India. His book, *Early Jesuit Travellers in Central Asia, 1603-1721* (The Hague: Martinus Nijhoff, 1924), brought their accomplishments to the attention of the world. A more recent book, John MacGregor, *Tibet: A Chronicle of Exploration* (London: Routledge & Kegan Paul, 1970) gives a good survey of the whole field of Tibetan exploration and discusses the exploits of the early Jesuit missionaries.

Pedro Alvares Cabral

(1467 - 1519?)

Pedro Alvares Cabral led the second Portuguese expedition to India and along the way discovered Brazil.

Pedro Alvares Cabral was born in the village of Belmonte, in the center of Portugal near the Spanish border, in 1467. At the age of 17 he was sent to serve at the Portuguese court and seems to have risen rapidly in the esteem of the two monarchs he served.

It was during Cabral's years at court that the Portuguese were making the great discoveries that were to open up the ocean routes between Europe and Asia. **Bartolomeu Dias** had rounded the Cape of Good Hope at the southern tip of Africa in 1488, and **Vasco da Gama** reached India in 1498. On da Gama's return to Portugal in September 1498, the Portuguese king decided to send out another expedition immediately to India to take advantage of the new trading opportunities that had been opened up. Although da Gama would have been the logical choice to lead such a venture, he apparently still needed to recover from his recent voyage and, perhaps at his suggestion, Cabral was chosen instead.

Cabral left Lisbon on March 9, 1500 at the head of a fleet of 13 ships, much larger than that of da Gama. They reached the Cape Verde Islands off the coast of Africa on March 22. On da Gama's advice Cabral then sailed farther westward to avoid the doldrums and contrary currents that had plagued the earlier expedition. As a result, on April 22, the Wednesday before Easter, he sighted land—Brazil.

On the day after this landfall Cabral sent a boat ashore, and the Portuguese took possession of what was to become the major colony of their empire and one of the world's great nations. Because of this, Cabral is generally credited with the discovery of Brazil in spite of the fact that the Spanish explorers **Alonso de Ojeda, Amerigo Vespucci**, and **Vicente Yañez Pinzón** had sighted land along what is now the north coast of the Republic of Brazil. Cabral's claim depends on the fact that he sighted land in what was to become the center of the country (in the present-day state of Bahia), that it was not an extension of the northern coast already visited by several explorers, and that he and his men actually went ashore.

What is much less certain is whether Cabral was surprised to find land where he did. In fact, the land he found had already been given to Portugal. Shortly after the return of **Christopher Columbus**, Spain and Portugal had signed the Treaty of Tordesillas

in June 1494 that divided the new discoveries they were making between them. It split the world in half: Portugal essentially got Africa and Asia, and Spain took the Americas. But the dividing line was set at a point 370 leagues west of the Cape Verde Islands. Because of the hump that Brazil makes, it was actually in the Portuguese sphere. Did the Portuguese already know that? Had Cabral been sent to find land that the Portuguese already knew existed? There is no definitive answer, but the consensus seems to be that his discovery was accidental.

Cabral stayed on the coast of Brazil from April 22, 1500 to May 2. The ceremony taking possession actually took place on May 1, and Cabral named the land Vera Cruz, the land of the True Cross. It quickly became known as Brazil because its earliest export was brazilwood, a forest product that was used to make red dye. When Cabral left on May 2, he left behind two

Cabral taking possession of Brazil in the name of Portugal. The Granger Collection, New York.

Portuguese convicts who were supposed to stay and report on the land and the people. They were never heard of again.

After Cabral left Brazil, his fleet was hit by a storm on May 24 in the South Atlantic that sank four of his ships, including one captained by Bartolomeu Dias. The rest were separated and sailed for 20 days in stormy weather, unable to raise their sails. Cabral sailed south of the Cape of Good Hope and finally touched land at Sofala, in Mozambique with only two other ships remaining in his fleet. They met up with three more on July 20 at the port of Mozambique. They then sailed up the east coast of Africa, stopping at the trading ports of Kilwa on July 26, 1500 (where they were treated like pirates) and Malindi on August 2 (where they were welcomed).

From Malindi the Portuguese fleet sailed across the Indian Ocean to the small island of Anjediva on the southwest coast of India. They reached there on August 22 and stayed for 15 days, resting and repairing their ships. They then headed south for the great trading center of Calicut (Kozhikode), where they arrived on September 13.

The merchants of Calicut were not at all pleased at the arrival of the Portuguese, because the new trade route threatened the monopoly they had on the spice trade with Europe. After the Portuguese built a trading post on land, it was attacked and 50 men were killed. Cabral then seized 10 Arab ships and bombarded the city with his guns. Since he had still not traded for the goods he wanted, he sailed south to the port of Cochin (present-day Kozhikode). Cochin was an enemy of Calicut, so its inhabi-

tants were happy to receive the Portuguese traders. They were able to fill up their ships with merchandise and left the town in early January 1501.

On the return voyage, one of Cabral's ships lost off the coast of Africa, and they met up with another ship that had been separated during the Atlantic storm. The ships in Cabral's expedition drifted back into Lisbon harbor during June and July 1501. The merchandise they brought back was extremely valuable, and the expedition had proved that there was a way to trade with Asia via the Atlantic and Indian Oceans. The king sent out another expedition in February 1502, this time once again under the command of Vasco da Gama.

Cabral retired to manage a small estate near the Portuguese city of Santarém. He married in 1503 and had six children. He died, probably in 1519, and was buried in a monastery in Santarém.

Where to learn more

The documentary records of Cabral's voyage have been published in W.B. Greenlee, ed. *The Voyage of Pedro Alvares Cabral to Brazil and India* (London: Hakluyt Society, 1937).

The American historian of the early maritime exploration of the Americas, Samuel Eliot Morison, discusses Cabral in *Portuguese Voyages to America in the Fifteenth Century* (Cambridge: Harvard University Press, 1940). Other books about the early Portuguese voyages to India naturally include chapters on Cabral: Edgar Prestage, *The Portuguese Pioneers* (London: Adam & Charles Black, 1933; reprinted 1966); G.R. Crone, *The Discovery of the East* (London: Hamish Hamilton, 1972); Christopher Bell, *Portugal and the Quest for the Indies* (New York: Harper & Row, 1974).

Juan Rodriguez Cabrillo

(? - 1543)

Juan Rodriguez Cabrillo was a Portuguese in the service of Spain who was the first European to explore the coast of California.

Juan Rodriguez Cabrillo was born in Portugal. The first word we have of him dates from 1520 when he is known to have been a soldier under the command of Panfilo de Narvaez during the conquest of Mexico by **Hernán Cortés**. Later, he went to Guatemala, probably at the same time as **Pedro de Alvarado**. Following its conquest, he stayed in Guatemala and seems to have done well there.

In the meantime, the first Spanish viceroy of New Spain (Mexico), Antonio de Mendoza, began to send out exploring expeditions in various directions—a fleet across the Pacific to the Philippines and the overland expeditions of Fray Marcos and **Francisco Vázquez de Coronado** into what is now the southwestern part of the United States. Mendoza chose Cabrillo to lead an expedition of two ships north along the Pacific coast of Mexico to see if he could find a passage between the Atlantic and the Pacific Oceans.

Cabrillo left from the Mexican port of Navidad on June 27, 1542. He sailed along the outer coast of the southern part of California, or Baja California, which was already known to the Spanish as the result of several expeditions sent out by Cortés. They had named the region California after the name of a mythical island that was ruled by the Queen of the Amazons, Queen Califia, in a popular Spanish tale written by Garci-Rodriguez de Montalvo that had been published in about 1510.

On September 2, 1542 Cabrillo sailed into San Diego harbor. From there, he continued north along the California coast, stopping frequently. The first Native Americans he met were fishermen, and they told him about the people who lived on the mainland and subsisted by growing corn (maize). All the Native Americans he met were friendly. Just north of present-day Los Angeles he saw a large village and landed and took possession of the country in the name of the King of Spain.

From this place, Cabrillo sailed in October through the Santa Barbara Channel, visiting Santa Catalina and other islands. He then regained the mainland at Point Conception. There the two Spanish ships ran into heavy storms. They continued north, but because of the bad weather they missed seeing both Monterey Bay and San Francisco Bay, places where they could have found shelter from the storms. The ships turned south and anchored at San Miguel, one of the islands in the Santa Barbara Channel, where they decided to wait for better weather. Cabrillo died there on January 3, 1543 after a fall.

The captain of the second ship, Bartolomé Ferrelo, took command of the expedition. He decided to try sailing north again. He made his first attempt on January 19 but was forced to turn back by bad weather. He stayed among the Channel Islands for another month. When he set out again, he headed some ways out to sea before turning north. He spotted land at Point Arena, about 100 miles north of San Francisco. Ferrelo and his two ships rounded Cape Mendocino and then went as far north as the mouth of the Rogue River in southern Oregon, which they reached on March 1, 1543.

Heading south, the two ships ran into more bad weather. They were separated for a while, but eventually met up again and sailed safely into Navidad harbor on April 14, 1543.

Cabrillo's discoveries had no immediate results in either New Spain or Spain itself. It was not until the next century that Spanish friars began to push up the coast of California and to effectively bring that part of the world into the Spanish empire. Cabrillo Point at the entrance to San Diego harbor is named in honor of the explorer.

Where to learn more

Although Cabrillo's expedition was not very important at the time and the documentary evidence about it is fairly fragmentary, it later generated enormous interest because it was the first European contact with a part of the world that was later to become of great importance in the history and economy of the United States and of the world. The documentary evidence can be found in Herbert Dugene Bolton, editor, *Spanish Exploration in the Southwest, 1542-1706: Original Narratives of Early American History* (New York: Charles Scribner's Sons, 1925).

A recent book has examined all the source material and presents everything we are likely to know about Cabrillo's voyage: Harry Kelsey, *Juan Rodriguez Cabrillo* (San Marino, California: Huntington Library, 1986).

Earlier works that include discussions of Cabrillo include Henry R. Wagner, *Spanish Voyages to the Northwest Coast of America in the Sixteenth Century* (San Francisco: 1929) and John Bartlet Brebner, *The Explorers of North America, 1492-1606* (New York: Macmillan, 1933).

Alvise da Cadamosto

(1432 - 1488)

Alvise da Cadamosto was a Venetian explorer who entered the service of Prince Henry the Navigator of Portugal and traveled along the west coast of Africa as far as present-day Guinea-Bissau.

Alvise da Cadamosto was a Venetian sailor and merchant who took part in various trading voyages throughout the Mediterranean and Western Europe. On August 8, 1454 he left Venice as part of a Venetian convoy to Flanders, in what is now Belgium. However, his ship was wrecked at Cape Saint Vincent on the south coast of Portugal, near the headquarters of **Prince Henry the Navigator**. Prince Henry was actively recruiting experienced seamen and convinced Cadamosto to work for him.

Prince Henry's strategy was to push down the west coast of Africa by incremental steps with the ultimate goal of finding a sea route to Asia. There had been a period from 1446 to 1455 when little progress was made because of internal problems in Portugal and the necessity to consolidate the discoveries already made. Now, Prince Henry decided to renew the push onward with Cadamosto in charge.

Cadamosto left on his first voyage from Lisbon on March 22, 1455 accompanied by another Venetian merchant, Antoniotto Usodimare. On the trip south they stopped at the fort of Arguim that Henry had established in about 1445. This fort was on the Atlantic Ocean just south of Cabo Blanco in what is now Mauritania. It was designed to tap the trans-Sahara trade of the western part of Africa. According to Cadamosto, many ships visited it every year, trading for gold, slaves, silk, and cotton, in exchange for corn, cloth, and horses.

Cadamosto also stopped in the Canary Islands and on the island of Madeira. Madeira was, in effect, Europe's first colonial territory, having been settled by Portuguese and Flemings (from Flanders) in about 1425. Cadamosto found four settlements with about 800 persons, who exported wood, wax, honey and sugar.

Of these products the most valuable was sugar, which had been grown in southern Portugal at least as early as the beginning of the century and was introduced into Madeira by 1433. In Cadamosto's day the production was already about 2,000 tons. This production set the pattern for sugarcane production in the West Indies and Brazil, which in centuries to come was to be one of the main sources of wealth for the European imperial powers

On this first trip Cadamosto reached as far as the mouth of the Gambia River, but did not travel upstream, before returning to Portugal. He left Lisbon again in May 1456 and sailed up the Gambia River to trade with an African tribe. On this second voyage, Cadamosto also continued as far south as the Geba River which is now in the country of Guinea-Bissau. He also explored the Bijagos islands off the coast; these two discoveries were the beginning of Portuguese involvement with this part of Africa that eventually resulted in the colony of Portuguese Guinea, which remained Portuguese until 1974.

In the account he wrote of his travels, Cadamosto also says that he visited the Cape Verde Islands, but it is not clear whether he was the first European to reach this island group. In any case, he visited four of the islands of the archipelago—Boavista, Santiago, Maio, and Sal. Cadamosto returned to Lisbon in October 1456 and stayed there, as a merchant, until February 1, 1463, when he returned to Venice. He died in his native city on July 18, 1488.

Besides advancing the Portuguese farther down the African coast, Cadamosto's chief importance is his remarkably detailed narrative of his voyages, published in Italy in 1507. He was the first European to describe the peoples and wildlife of West Africa.

Where to learn more

Cadamosto's narrative has been translated and edited by Gerald R. Crone in *The Voyages of Cadamosto* (London: Hakluyt Society, 1937). The best account of Cadamosto's voyages can be found in *The Portuguese Pioneers* by Edgar Prestage (London: Adam & Charles Black), originally published in 1933 and reprinted in 1966.

René Caillié

(1799-1838)

René Caillié was a Frenchmen who was the first European to reach the fabled city of Timbuktu and to return.

René Caillié was the son of a poor Parisian baker. He started reading travel books at an early age and decided that he wanted to be an explorer as well. At the age of 16 he got a job as a servant on a French ship sailing to Senegal and was able to travel some distance inland. He made a return trip to Senegal eight years later in 1824 and lived there until 1827.

In 1826 the French Geographical Society announced a prize of 10,000 francs to the first European who could travel to the fabled city of Timbuktu. Caillié wrote in his journal, "Dead or alive, the prize shall be mine." Convinced that the local inhabitants would kill any Christian they found, Caillié started the preparations for his trip by spending nine months in a Muslim tribe on the Senegal River where he studied the Koran and learned to speak Arabic.

In March 1827 he traveled to the town of Freetown in Sierra Leone and then went north in a coastal vessel to the Rio Nunez where he joined a caravan to the interior. He told his companions that he was from Cairo and had been taken as a child by Frenchman to Senegal. While it is doubtful that his story was entirely believable, Caillié was so poor that no one bothered to rob him or keep him from making his way into the interior.

In June the caravan reached the town of Kouroussa and Caillié joined another caravan traveling to the important trading town of Djenné. Along the way he became ill with malaria and scurvy and rested for five months in the town of Tieme where one of the local women nursed him back to health. He reached Djenné on the shores of the Niger River in March 1828 and took a boat from there to Timbuktu. Because he was so poor, he had to take passage in the slave quarters below decks where he suffered from the great heat during the 500-mile journey. The boat was boarded by Tuareg pirates and had to pay tribute at every Tuareg camp it passed. On April 20 Caillié reached Timbuktu to find that it did not meet his expectations:

"I had formed a totally different idea of the grandeur and wealth of Timbuctoo. The city presented, at first view, nothing but a mass of ill-looking houses, built of earth. Nothing was to be seen in all directions but immense plains of quicksand of a yellowish white colour. The sky was a pale red as far as the horizon: all nature wore a dreary aspect, and the most profound

René Caillié. The Granger Collection, New York.

silence prevailed; not even the warbling of a bird was to be heard. Still, though I cannot account for the impression, there was something imposing in the aspect of a great city, raised in the midst of sands, and the difficulties surmounted by its founders cannot fail to excite admiration."

Timbuktu, now in Mali, had been founded in the 12th century and for many centuries had been the center of the trade across the Sahara desert. Its reputation as a magnificent city had been gained when **Abu Abdullah Ibn Battuta** wrote about it in the 14th century. Since that time, it had become much less important, was subject to raids by the Tuareg, and there were only two functioning mosques at the time of Caillié's visit. Caillié stayed for two weeks in Timbuktu. He stayed in a house across from where **Alexander Gordon Laing** had been in 1826. He began to worry that the inhabitants would find out that he was a Christian and that he would be murdered as Laing had been.

Caillié then joined a great caravan of 1,400 camels and 400 men that headed north from Timbuktu on May 4, 1828. Four days out of the city his companions pointed out the spot where Laing had been killed, worrying Caillié even more. However, it was not the members of the caravan that he needed to worry about but the great desert itself. He suffered from the great heat and the constant thirst: "My throat was on fire and my tongue clove to the roof of my mouth. I thought only of water—rivers, streams, rivulets were the only ideas that presented themselves to my mind." The members of the caravan were allowed only one drink at the end of the day: "It is difficult to describe with what impatience we longed for this moment. To enhance the pleasure which I expected from my portion, I thrust my head into the vessel, and sucked up the water in long draughts. When I had drunk, I had an unpleasant sensation all over me, which was quickly succeeded by fresh thirst."

The caravan reached the Atlas Mountains in Morocco in mid-June and then it took Caillié six more weeks to get to Fez and the city of Tangier on the Mediterranean. In Tangier Caillié went to see the French consul to ask help in getting back to France. At first, the consul refused to believe Caillié's story but later smug-gled him on a ship bound for the French port of Toulon. Once he reached Toulon the French Geographical Society sent him a small sum of money to get to Paris where a special commission was set up to examine his claims. It eventually decided that he was telling the truth and awarded him the Legion of Honor, a gold medal, and an annual pension. He wrote a book about his travels that was more popular in England than in France. There were still doubts about his honesty, and the pension was stopped in 1833. Suffering from ailments he had contracted during his travels, he died in poverty in 1838. It was only later that his story was confirmed.

Where to learn more

Caillié's own story, *Travels through Central Africa to Timbuktoo* was published in Paris (in French) and London in 1830. There is an excellent full-scale biography in English: Galbraith Welch, *The Unveiling of Timbuctoo: The Astounding Adventures of Caillié* (New York: William Morrow & Co., 1939). Paul Herrmann in *The Great Age of Discovery* (New York: Harper & Brothers, 1958) gives an exciting retelling of Caillié's story as does Christopher Hibbert in *Africa Explored: Europeans in the Dark Continent, 1769-1889* (London: Allen Lane, 1982).

Verney Lovett Cameron

(1844 - 1894)

Verney Lovett Cameron was a British explorer who was sent out to find David Livingstone. Following Livingstone's death, he set out on his own and made the first east-west crossing of Africa by a European.

Verney Lovett Cameron was born in the small village of Radipole in the county of Dorset in the west of England. His father was a clergyman. Cameron entered the Royal Navy at the age of 13 and served in the Mediterranean Sea, the West Indies, the Red Sea, and on the east coast of Africa. While in the Indian Ocean he was involved in stopping slaving ships, and this led to a lifelong hatred of slavery and its evils. In 1870 he was assigned to shore duty in England.

Shortly after his return to England, Cameron volunteered to lead an expedition sponsored by the Royal Geographical Society to Africa to search for **David Livingstone**. His offer was at first refused, and the American journalist **Henry Morton Stanley** "found" Livingstone in 1871. However, Livingstone did not return with Stanley to the east coast of Africa. A couple of years later the Royal Geographical Society sent out another expedition to meet up with the famous explorer, and this time Cameron was put in charge.

Cameron was instructed by the Society to find Livingstone and to offer him any assistance that he might need. Apparently, he also had it in his mind to carry out some explorations on his own. Cameron and the three European members of his expedition reached Zanzibar in January 1873. There he hired the famous African caravan leader **Sidi Mubarak Bombay** to organize his caravan. They left from Bagamoyo on the coast of East Africa in March 1873. Robert Moffat, Livingstone's nephew, died along the way of fever. The rest of the expedition reached Unyanyembe in early August, where the three remaining Europeans became ill.

"It was on the 20th of October, as I lay on my bed prostrate, listless, and enfeebled from repeated attacks of fever, my mind dazed and confused with whirling thoughts and fancies of home and those dear ones far away, that my servant, Mohammed Malim, came running into my tent with a letter in his hand." The letter had been brought by Livingstone's companion **James Chuma** and announced that the explorer had died. His body arrived a few days later, and it was decided that Cameron would continue into the interior while his two European colleagues would accompany the corpse to Zanzibar.

Cameron continued on to Livingstone's headquarters at Ujiji on the shores of Lake Tanganyika. He arrived there on February

Verney Lovett Cameron. The Granger Collection, New York.

21, 1874 and recovered Livingstone's books and papers, which he packed up and sent to England. Leaving Ujiji on March 13, Cameron set out to explore Lake Tanganyika. He found 96 rivers that flowed into the lake but only one, the Lukuga, that flows out. The Lukuga leaves the enormous lake in about the middle of its western shore. Cameron could not travel down it, however, because the entrance was blocked with vegetation. He returned to Ujiji.

Cameron wanted to continue west to try to find the sources of the Congo River. He set out on May 31, 1874 in the company of an Arab trader. He traveled to Nyangwe on the Lualaba River, which he wanted to explore to find its relation to the Congo. (In fact, it flows many miles to the north before joining the Congo in northern Zaire.) However, at Nyangwe he was unable to find the canoes necessary to make the trip.

In August he met up with the famous slave trader and explorer Tippu Tib and accompanied him to his headquarters. Following his advice, Cameron decided to head toward the Atlantic Ocean by a more southerly route. This route entailed many hardships.

He crossed the Cuanza River in October, but by then he and most of his porters and guides were ill. He decided to make a dash to the coast with a smaller band of followers. They undertook a forced march of five and a half days that got them to the Atlantic coast north of Benguela in Angola on November 7, 1875. He was greeted by a French trader who "instantly opened a bottle to drink to the honour of the first European who had ever succeeded in crossing tropical Africa from east to west."

The rest of the expedition caught up with Cameron on November 11, and Cameron bought cloth to make them new uniforms so that they could march triumphantly into the Angolan capital of Luanda on November 21, 1875. He then chartered a ship to take the African members of the expedition back to Zanzibar while he traveled on to England. He returned home on April 2, 1876, where he received a hero's welcome.

Cameron was awarded a medal for his exploit by the Royal Geographical Society in 1876. That same year, he was chosen as a British delegate to the conference on Africa that was being sponsored by King Leopold II of the Belgians. From that time he was regarded as an expert on Africa and spoke out frequently against the slave trade that was still being carried on in the interior of Africa. He also made an overland trip to India to investigate the possibility of a rail line between Istanbul and Baghdad. He returned briefly to Africa in 1882 with **Sir Richard Burton** to look into mining concessions in Ghana. He died in 1894 from a hunting accident.

Where to learn more

Cameron wrote the story of his transcontinental trip in *Across Africa*, 2 vols. (London: Daldy, Isbister & Co., 1877; reprinted, New York: Johnson Reprint Corp., 1971). Excerpts from it can be found in *East African Explorers*, edited by Charles Richards and James Place (London: Oxford University Press, 1960).

There is one full-scale biography: W.R. Foran, *African Odyssey: The Life of Verney Lovett-Cameron* (London: 1937). A more recent biographical essay can be found in James R. Hooker, "Verney Lovett Cameron: A Sailor in Central Africa" in Robert Rotberg, ed. *Africa and Its Explorers* (Cambridge: Harvard University Press, 1970).

There is a chapter on Cameron and the role played by Africans in his expedition in Donald Simpson, *Dark Companions: The African Contribution to the European Exploration of East Africa* (New York: Barnes & Noble, 1976).

Diogo Cão

(1450?-1486)

Diogo Cão was a Portuguese navigator who sighted the Congo River and advanced almost all the way down the west coast of Africa.

In 1481, a new king ascended to the throne of Portugal—King John II. He was an enthusiastic supporter of the voyages of exploration, and in the year after his accession he commissioned his first expedition. Its leader, Diogo Cão was an experienced seaman who had taken part in trips to Guinea on the west coat of Africa.

When he set out from Lisbon in 1485, Cão's ships carried *padrões*, stone pillars surmounted by a cross and the arms of Portugal, that were to be used as markers and proofs of Portuguese discoveries. Cão sailed south past Cape St. Catherine, now in Gabon, which was the southernmost point that the Portuguese had reached, and continued to the mouth of a great river, which he called the Zaire, but which is today generally known as the Congo. There, he set up his first *padroa*. On Cape St. Mary, still farther south in Angola, he set up a second padroa.

He heard about a powerful chief in the interior, and sent a delegation to visit him. When his party did not return, Cão left for Lisbon taking several Africans with him and promised to return with them the following year. He lived up to his promise, and the reports brought back by the Africans convinced the great chief, the "Manicongo," to seek conversion to Christianity and friendship with the Portuguese. This was the start of the Portuguese empire in Angola.

On this second voyage, Cão erected two more padrôes in 1485, one on Monte Negro, north of the Cunene River in Angola, and the other on Cape Cross, about halfway down the coast of Namibia. There is also evidence that Cão traveled up the Congo River during this voyage. Cão is thought to have died somewhere south of Cape Cross, but most of the members of his expedition made it back to Lisbon.

Cão's padrôes survived for centuries. The one that he placed at the mouth of the Congo served as an object of worship for the local inhabitants until 1859 when some British sailors dropped it overboard while trying to salvage it. The ones in Angola were brought to Lisbon in 1892, while the fourth one on Cape Cross was carried to Germany.

Where to learn more

There are chapters or discussions of Cão's voyages in several books that deal with early Portuguese voyages: Björn Landström, *The Quest for India* (New York: Doubleday, 1964); Edgar Prestage, *The Portuguese Pioneers* (London: Adam & Charles Black, 1933; reprinted, 1966); Eric Axelson, *Congo to Cape: Early Portuguese Explorers* (New York: 1973); and Christopher Bell, *Portugal and the Quest for the Indies* (New York: Harper & Row, 1974).

Hermenegildo de Brito Capelo

(1841 - 1917)

Roberto Ivens

(1850 - 1898)

Hermenegildo de Brito Capelo and Roberto Ivens were Portuguese naval officers who explored much of northern Angola and then tried to establish an overland link between Angola and Mozambique.

Hermenegildo de Brito Capelo was a Portuguese naval officer who had served in Portugal's African colonies of Angola and Mozambique when he was asked by the Portuguese government to accompany an army major, Alexandre Alberto da Rocha de Serpa Pinto, on an exploring mission to the interior of Angola. Capelo suggested as the third member of the expedition Roberto Ivens, a young naval lieutenant who was a former colleague of Capelo's.

The year was 1877, at the beginning of what was later called by historians "The Scramble for Africa." Western European countries had long held trading posts along the coasts of Africa, but it was only in the second half of the nineteenth century that they expanded into the interior, conquering African tribes and dividing up the continent into separate colonies. The European country with the longest history of exploitation in Africa was Portugal. Portuguese nationalists wanted to unite their settlements on the west coast (Angola) with those on the east coast (Mozambique) into a broad band of territory cutting across the middle of Africa.

The expedition led by Capelo and Serpa Pinto was one of the first efforts by the Portuguese to achieve that goal. However, the aims of the expedition were not clearly laid out, and the members ended up quarreling about what they should attempt to achieve. Capelo and Serpa Pinto left Lisbon on July 5, 1877 and traveled to Luanda, the capital of Angola, where Ivens met them on September 1. They received little cooperation from the Portuguese governor and had a difficult time recruiting African porters and guides. They met **Henry Morton Stanley** who was just completing his trans-Africa trip that included a descent of the Congo River. Because of his success, the three Portuguese decided to concentrate their efforts farther south.

The Portuguese explorers set out for the port of Benguela south of Luanda and headed inland from there at the end of

October 1877 to the Bié plateau. When Serpa Pinto left the expedition to try to find more African porters, Capelo and Ivens went on ahead. By this time, Serpa Pinto was ill, and he was very angry with his partners for what he saw as a desertion. When they were reunited at the small Portuguese outpost of Belmonte, they decided to split up permanently.

Capelo and Ivens went north from Bié and spent two years exploring the regions of Kassange and Malange as well as the upper parts of the Cuango River. They made extensive scientific observations and were the first Europeans to explore what is now northeastern Angola systematically. They returned to Lisbon in February 1880 and addressed the Society of Geography of Lisbon and were invited to London to speak to the Royal Geographical Society. They published a book about their experiences in Portuguese that was also translated and published in English in 1882.

As a result of their successful trip Capelo and Ivens were called upon by a new Portuguese government to undertake a more important mission in 1883: to travel across Africa from Angola to Mozambique. In other words, they were to lay the groundwork for Portugal's imperialistic goal of uniting their two African colonies. A similar trip, the first across Africa, had been made by two Angolan *mestiços*, **João Baptista** and **Amaro José**, early in the century but it had not led to any further expeditions.

Capelo and Ivens set out on their mission on January 6, 1884. They traveled to the southern Angolan port of Moçâmedes and then went inland from there through little-known territory. They reached the last Portuguese outpost at Huila on May 3, 1884. They then traveled to the headwaters of the Cunene River, sending back their last report before disappearing into the interior.

Capelo and Ivens hiked overland to the African village of Handa on the Cubango River. They then traversed an uninhabited region to the upper part of the Zambezi River at Libongo. They found little food in this region, and they and their party were near starvation when they were met by representatives of King Lewanika of the upper Zambezi, or Liambai, region. With the gifts furnished by the king they were able to revive themselves and cross the Zambezi on October 13.

At this point the two Portuguese explorers could have made a much easier trip by heading straight down the Zambezi River to the Mozambique settlements. Instead, they turned north in order to try to map the headwaters of the Zambezi and Congo Rivers since no one knew where the two systems started. At the end of October, they reached the town of chief Muene N'Tenke who quickly became their friend and replenished their food supplies and tried to get them to marry two young women from the town. Ivens went off to the town of Bunkeya to meet the king of the area, M'Siri. This was the farthest point north reached by the expedition—the center of the modern Zairean province of Shaba near the mining towns of Kolwezi, Likasi, and Lubumbashi. They were the first Europeans in this part of Africa.

Capelo and Ivens then headed east to the Luapula River, one of the main tributaries of the Congo, which they reached on February 1, 1885. By this time they were ill from scurvy and malaria and were anxious to reach their destination. Along the way, they did see and report on the Mambirima Falls of the Luapula. From there they headed across central Zambia to the farthest Portuguese outpost on the Zambezi, a little fort called Zumbo. They arrived in Zumbo on May 4 and spent 19 days recuperating. They reached the larger town of Tete on June 4. When they arrived in Quelimane on the coast, they learned that Capelo's wife had died in his absence.

From Quelimane the two Portuguese naval officers traveled to the port of Mozambique where they telegraphed the results of their expedition back to Portugal. They returned to Lisbon on September 15, 1885. They had shown that it was possible to travel overland between Angola and Mozambique, but Portugal lacked the resources to follow up on their explorations. Great Britain, a much wealthier and more powerful country, was able to block the Portuguese corridor by establishing the colonies of Southern Rhodesia (Zimbabwe) and Northern Rhodesia (Zambia) by pushing up from the south.

On their return to Portugal, Capelo and Ivens were received by King Luis of Portugal. Capelo became an important official, serving as vice-president of the Portuguese Overseas Institute and aide-de-camp for King Luis and his son King Carlos. He died in Lisbon in 1917. Ivens remained in the Navy and died off the coast of Africa on board the ship he was captaining on January 28, 1898.

Where to learn more

The only accessible source in English about the expeditions of Capelo and Ivens is Charles E. Nowell, *The Rose-Colored Map: Portugal's Attempt to Build an African Empire from the Atlantic to the Indian Ocean* (Lisbon: Junta de Investigaçoes Científicas do Ultramar, 1982). Capelo and Ivens wrote two book in Portuguese about their expeditions: *De Angola a Contre Costa* (Lisbon, 1886) and *De Benguelle as terras de Iacca* (Lisbon, 1888).

Giovanni di Piano Carpini

(1182? - 1252)

Giovanni di Piano Carpini was a Franciscan monk who was charged by the Pope with a diplomatic mission to the court of the Great Khan in China, the first one sent from Europe.

The rise and conquests of the Mongol tribesmen from the steppes of northern Central Asia is one of the great chapters of world history. Under their leader Genghis Khan, who became Great Khan in 1206, the Mongols captured Beijing in 1215 and Bukhara, thousands of miles to the West in Central Asia, in 1220. Under Genghis's son Ögedei, all of China was conquered by 1234. The Mongols then turned westward and took Moscow in 1238, Kiev in 1240, and then advanced as far as Vienna and the Adriatic Sea. In April 1241 the Mongols defeated two large Christian armies, one at Liegnitz in Silesia, in what is now western Poland, and one in Mohi in Hungary. They could have conquered all of Europe when they suddenly turned back during the winter of 1242-1243 on receiving news of the death of Ögedei.

The next Mongol ruler, Möngkhe, concentrated his attacks on the Muslim lands of the Middle East and invaded Persia and captured Baghdad in 1258. It looked as though all of the Arab-ruled lands would fall, but once again the Mongols turned when Möngkhe died in 1260. His successor was Khublai Khan, who ruled from the city of Khanbaligh (now called by its Chinese name of Beijing) from 1260 to 1294. Khublai was the Great Khan during **Marco Polo**'s visit to China.

These invasions obviously frightened all of the countries of Eurasia, and many leaders sent diplomats to the court of the Khans to try to deflect their attacks onto other targets. Among the most important of these was one sent by Pope Innocent IV in 1245 headed by Giovanni di Piano Carpini.

Carpini had been born in the village of Piano del Carpini near the city of Perugia in Tuscany. He was a contemporary of the founder of the Franciscan order of monks, St. Francis Assisi, and became one of its earliest members. He had been sent on missions to Germany, Spain, Czechoslovakia, Hungary, Poland, and Scandinavia. He was almost 65 years old when he was chosen by the Pope to lead the mission to the Mongols. He was also very fat and could not walk well, often having to be carried by a donkey. However, he never complained about his own sufferings during his long journey.

Carpini and his companions left Lyons in France, where a Catholic Council was being held, on Easter Sunday, April 16,

1245, and traveled by way of Bohemia (in Czechoslovakia), Poland and Ukraine to the encampment of the Mongol general Batu on the banks of the Volga River, where they arrived on April 6, 1246. Much to Carpini's surprise, the Mongols were unimpressed by his Papal letters and paid no attention to his appeals for peace, his desire to send missionaries to convert the Mongols to Christianity, and his requests that they cease their attacks on the West.

In fact, the Western visitors were subject to demands for gifts and were forced to undergo a purification ceremony in which they had to walk between two great fires. The only food they were given was some boiled millet and melted snow to drink.

In April 1246 Batu sent the Carpini mission on to the court of the Great Khan, and Carpini states that "most tearfully we set out, not knowing whether it was for life or for death." They traveled through the plains of southern Russia and the desert regions north of the Caspian Sea to the Syr Darya River. By then, Carpini was in lands inhabited by Muslims, all of whom had been conquered by the Mongols. He headed eastward to Lake Alakol, which is now in the easternmost part of Kazakhstan. He then had to traverse the Altai Mountains, where the party encountered snow and high winds even at the end of June.

Finally, on July 22, 1246, Carpini and his fellow travelers reached the court of the Great Khan near Karakorum, which are now ruins in north central China near the Mongolian border. They arrived just at the time that the Mongols were engaged in electing Güyük as Great Khan to succeed Ögedei who had died five years previously. Carpini was not allowed to see the new Khan until after the election took place, but he joined in the festivities along with "more than 4,000 ambassadors" from all over Asia, the Middle East, and eastern Europe who had come to recognize the new ruler.

Carpini was present at the enthronement of the Great Khan on August 24 and reported on the multitudes in attendance, the rich clothes of the Mongol leaders, the obeisance and lavish gifts given to the new ruler, and the feasting and drunkenness that followed the coronation. During the ceremonies, one of the other visitors, Prince Yaroslav of Suzdal in Russia, was poisoned and died, apparently at the hands of the new Khan's mother. Carpini was no doubt alarmed when he was instructed to stay in the court of this woman, the Empress Töregene.

The mission from the Latin Pope was finally allowed to present its letters. These were translated, and in November 1246 a response was drafted from the Khan for them to take back to

Rome. Güyük's letter was later found in the Vatican archives; it insultingly demands that the Pope travel to Khanbaligh himself and submit to the Khan. Carpini was able, however, to resist an offer to take back ambassadors from Güyük, thinking they would be spies and might seek to come up with excuses for war.

Carpini left Mongolia on November 13, 1246 and suffered much hardship while traveling through the mountains and steppes during the winter. Carpini wrote about sleeping on the ground at night and waking to find himself covered in snow. He returned to the court of Batu on May 9, 1247, where, now under the protection of the Great Khan, he was received with greater honor than on his way out. The mission arrived in the Christian city of Kiev on June 9, where they were received "with great joy." Carpini made it back to give his report to the Pope in Lyons on November 18, 1247.

In 1248 Carpini was sent as Papal Legate (ambassador) to the court of King Louis IX of France (later named Saint Louis) to try (unsuccessfully) to convince the King to delay his Crusade to the Middle East. He was then named Bishop of Antivari on the coast of Dalmatia. His appointment was disputed by the local archbishop, however, and he was forced to return to Italy, where he died on August 1, 1252.

Where to learn more

There are several versions of Carpini's report, *Historia Mongalorum quos nos Tartaros appellamus* ("A description of the Mongols, whom we call Tartars").

The basic documents were translated into English at the beginning of the 20th century: W. Woodville Rockhill, *The Journey of William of Rubruck to the Eastern Parts of the World, 1253-55, as Narrated by Himself, with Two Accounts of the Earlier Journey of John of Pian de Carpini* (London: Hakluyt Society, 1900) and C. Raymond Beazley, *The Text and Versions of John de Plano Carpini and William de Rubruquis* (London: Hakluyt Society, 1903) and *On a Hitherto Unexamined Manuscript of John de Plano Carpini* (London: Hakluyt Society, 1903).

These texts are included in Christopher Dawson, ed. *The Mongol Mission: Narratives and Letters of the Franciscan Missionaries in Mongolia and China in the 13th and 14th Centuries* (London: Sheed and Ward, 1955), which has been reprinted under the title of *The Mission to Asia* (Toronto: University of Toronto Press for the Mediaeval Academy of America, 1986). There is a selection of Carpini's narratives in Manuel Komroff, ed. *Contemporaries of Marco Polo* (New York: 1928; reprinted, New York: Dorset Press, 1989).

Summaries of Carpini's journey can be found in: C. Raymond Beazley, *The Dawn of Modern Geography*, vol. 2 (London: John Murray, 1901); Leonardo Olschki, *Marco Polo's Precursors* (Baltimore: The Johns Hopkins Press, 1943; reprinted, New York: Octagon Books, 1972); and I. de Rachewiltz, *Papal Envoys to the Great Khans* (Stanford: Stanford University Press, 1971).

One of the reports about Carpini's mission was written by a Franciscan friar, C. de Bridia, who interviewed the members of the mission as they traveled through Poland on their way back to Lyons. He wrote an account, which was later called the "Tartar Relation." There is a controversial book by R.A. Skelton, Thomas E. Marston and George D. Painter: *The Vinland Map and the Tartar Relation* (New London: Yale University Press, 1965) that attempts to show that the "Tartar Relation" was the main source for European knowledge of Asia in the Late Middle Ages.

Philip Carteret

(1734 - 1796)

Philip Carteret was a British naval officer who commanded a leaky ship in a voyage around the world. He was the first European to see many of the Pacific islands, including Pitcairn.

When **John Byron** made his trip around the world in 1764-1766, one of the officers on board was Philip Carteret who had served as first lieutenant on both of the ships in the expedition. On his return to England, he almost immediately embarked on a new expedition under the command of **Samuel Wallis**, charged with finding the great southern continent. Carteret was given command of the *Swallow*, which turned out to be a leaky old vessel with few repair facilities on board and that was almost impossible to navigate.

The *Swallow* followed Wallis's ship, the *Dolphin*, south through the Atlantic to the Straits of Magellan. Because of the extremely bad weather, it took the two ships four months just to get through the straits. On the day that the two ships emerged into the Pacific, April 11, 1767, they became separated, and the *Dolphin* sailed on without the *Swallow*. In his log of the voyage, Carteret seems to feel that Wallis purposely sailed on without him in order not to be burdened by the *Swallow*.

Despite having a ship that was almost unsailable, Carteret bravely wrote in his journal, "I determined at all events to perform . . . in the best manner I was able." He headed north to the Juan Fernandez Islands in the middle of a storm in which his sails were split and his rigging carried away. He reached Juan Fernandez on May 8 to find that the Spanish had occupied the island and would not let him land. He sailed westward to a smaller island, Masafuera, where he was able to load water and make some repairs.

In spite of very bad weather, Carteret sailed due west looking for the continent that did not exist. The first land he saw was the tiny, isolated island of Pitcairn, which was named after one of the crewmen who had sighted it for the first time. The island was uninhabited—it was settled 23 years later by the *Bounty* mutineers.

From Pitcairn the *Swallow* sailed northwestward and passed some of the small uninhabited islands of the Tuamotus. Further north towards the equator, the ship finally encountered favorable winds, and it proceeded due west. By this time all of the men had become ill with scurvy, the ship could not be steered, and it had

sprung a leak below the water line. At the last minute, Carteret and his crew sighted the Santa Cruz islands that had last been seen by Westerners under **Alvaro de Mendaña** 200 years before.

On one of these islands, Carteret sent one of the other two officers to land in one of the boats attached to the ship. At first the people on the island were friendly, but then the officer started to cut down a coconut tree even though the inhabitants kept trying to stop him. They attacked, and the landing party returned to the ship with the officer and three other men dead and the rest wounded. There were now only two officers, Carteret and his first lieutenant, left alive who knew how to navigate the ship.

The ship stayed at anchor long enough to repair the leak, and an armed party went ashore to get fresh water. However, it was now impossible to trade with the natives for any other provisions. Carteret then headed west and came into the Solomon Islands, which Mendaña had discovered and which seamen had been looking for ever since. However, the Spaniards had given such bad locations that Carteret did not realize that he had refound the lost islands.

From the Solomons, Carteret sailed north to the large island of New Britain, where he found a cove in which he could anchor to make further repairs and take on some fresh supplies. From there he coasted along the island of New Ireland and then sailed west, where he discovered and named the Admiralty Islands. Passing the north coast of New Guinea, he eventually reached the island of Sulawesi in the Dutch East Indies (now Indonesia). In spite of some difficulties with the Dutch he was allowed to stay from December 21, 1767 to May 22, 1768, when he moved on to Batavia to make repairs to the *Swallow*. The ship was in such bad condition that the Dutch carpenters were convinced that it would never make it back to England.

However, Carteret sailed on—leaving Batavia in September 1768 and reaching the Cape of Good Hope at the end of November, where he stayed for six weeks. Three weeks after passing the island of Ascension, the *Swallow* was overtaken by a French ship, which turned out to be the *Boudeuse*, commanded by **Louis Antoine de Bougainville**, returning from its circumnavigation. Bougainville knew about the *Swallow*: Wallis had long since returned to England and had reported the ship missing. When the French ship sailed away, "she shot by us as if we had been at anchor, notwithstanding we had a fine fresh gale and all our sails set."

The *Swallow* faced one further storm in which it lost one of its sails, but on May 20, 1769, it anchored off Portsmouth in England "to our great joy." Following his return, Carteret was promoted. During the American Revolution he commanded ships in the Caribbean but missed the naval engagements that took place during the war. By the end of the war, he was in poor health and returned to England in 1781. He retired from active service in 1794 and died in the port of Southampton on July 21, 1796, where his obituary said that he had "long been afflicted with loss of speech."

Where to learn more

Carteret's *Journal* of his voyage around the world was published in London in 1773 and was republished in an edition edited by Helen Wallis for the Hakluyt Society in 1965, *Carteret's Voyage Round the World, 1766-1769*, 2 vols. (Cambridge: Cambridge University Press, 1965). The best historian of the exploration of the Pacific is J.C. Beaglehole, whose book, *The Exploration of the Pacific* (Stanford: Stanford University Press, 1966) includes a chapter on Carteret. An informative and entertaining book by Derek Wilson, *The Circumnavigators* (New York: M. Evans and Company, 1989) includes a chapter on Carteret based upon his journal. The history of the efforts to refind Mendana's Solomon Islands is told in Colin Jack-Hinton, *The Search for the Islands of Solomon, 1567-1838* (Oxford: Clarendon Press, 1969).

Jacques Cartier

(1491 - 1557)

Jacques Cartier was a French explorer who made three voyages to Canada and discovered the Gulf of St. Lawrence and the St. Lawrence River.

Jacques Cartier was a navigator from the French port of Saint-Malo in the province of Brittany. We do not know anything about his early life, but it is clear that he made several sea voyages. There has even been a suggestion that he was a crew member in **Giovanni da Verrazzano**'s expeditions to America in 1524 and 1528.

In 1532 the Bishop of Saint-Malo proposed to King François I of France that he sponsor an expedition to the New World and that Cartier be chosen to lead it since he had, according to the Bishop, already been to Brazil and Newfoundland. The King

Jacques Cartier. The Granger Collection, New York.

accepted this nomination, and on April 20, 1534 Cartier set off from Saint-Malo with two ships and 61 men charged "to discover certain islands and lands where it is said that a great quantity of gold, and other precious things, are to be found." It was clear from the start that Cartier was supposed to find mineral wealth.

Cartier and his ships sailed to the northern tip of the island of Newfoundland to the Strait of Belle-Isle, which was known to lead to open waters beyond. Cartier sailed along what is now called the North Coast of Quebec, naming many of the rivers and harbors that he saw. Along the way they encountered a French fishing ship that was lost and directed it how to get out of the Strait of Belle-Isle. He then traveled down the west coast of Newfoundland to what is now called Cabot Strait. He did not enter Cabot Strait so he did not find out that it separates Newfoundland from Cape Breton Island and is a better route to enter the Gulf of St. Lawrence than by way of Belle-Isle far to the north.

In the course of exploring the Gulf of St. Lawrence, Cartier was the first European to report on the Iles de la Madeleine, Prince Edward Island, the Bay of Gaspé, and Anticosti Island. He did not travel far enough beyond Anticosti to discover the St. Lawrence River. While anchored off the Gaspé Peninsula, Cartier went ashore and claimed the land for France. There he encountered the Iroquois chief Donnacona. When he left, he took two of the chief's sons with him to France as guests. He returned to Saint-Malo on September 5, 1534, where he received a great welcome even though he had not found any gold.

The following year Cartier was provided with three ships to return to Canada. He left Saint-Malo on May 15, 1535 and took with him the two Native Americans who had learned French in order to serve as translators. This was Cartier's most important voyage: guided by the Iroquois he sailed west from Anticosti and entered the great estuary of the St. Lawrence on August 13. This was to be the main gateway for the French into North America for the next two centuries.

Cartier sailed up the St. Lawrence past the Saguenay River to the village of Stadacona, on the site of present-day Quebec City. He met with Donnacona there and then traveled farther up the river to the village of Hochelaga on the site of Montreal. After planting a cross there, he returned to Stadacona where the Iroquois were becoming less and less friendly. Cartier reached the village in October and settled there for the winter. He and his men were the first Europeans to spend the winter in Canada, and they were surprised at how cold it became.

The Frenchmen suffered from scurvy during the winter and were saved only when the Iroquois taught them how to make a tea out of white cedar, which was a source of vitamin C. Cartier left Stadacona on May 6, 1536, and this time he took Chief Donnacona back with him to France, where they arrived on July 16.

Cartier's second voyage had been a big success: he had found a great waterway that might be the sought-after route to Asia and he even brought back a few pieces of gold. The French king wanted to send him back again, but war broke out between France and the Habsburg Empire. Cartier was not able to leave until May 1541. In the meantime, the rights to colonize Canada had been given to a French nobleman, the Sieur de Roberval, and Cartier was supposed to be doing reconnaissance work for Roberval's voyage the following year.

On this third voyage, Cartier reached Stadacona on August 23, 1541. Donnacona had died in France, but this probably made it easier for Cartier to deal with his successor, Agona, who now did not have to worry about his rival. Cartier built a camp at the present-day town of Charlesbourg, north of Quebec and found some stones there that he thought were diamonds. He traveled back to Hochelaga and then returned to spend the winter at Charlesbourg. Once again, the Frenchmen suffered through a harsh winter. By spring they were faced with the hostility of the Iroquois and decided to leave the camp and head back to France.

Cartier left Stadacona in June 1542 and traveled to the port of St. John's, Newfoundland, where he met Roberval. Cartier was instructed to sail back with Roberval and help him to found the new colony. However, in the dark of night he slipped away and traveled on to Saint-Malo, leaving Roberval to fend for himself. When he arrived back in France he found that the "gold" he was carrying was iron pyrite and the "diamonds" were quartz crystals. He was not punished for leaving Roberval behind, but he was never given another expedition to command. He retired to Saint-Malo where he became a prosperous businessman and died there on September 1, 1557.

Where to learn more

Cartier's own version of events can be found in H.P. Biggar, ed. *Documents Relating to Jacques Cartier and the Sieur de Roberval* (London: Hakluyt Society, 1903-1905; reprinted, including French originals, Ottawa: Public Archives of Canada, 1930). The article on Cartier by French-Canadian historian Marcel Trudel in vol. 1 of the *Dictionary of Canadian Biography* (Toronto: University of Toronto Press, 1967) is quite complete and is a careful review of all available source material. The only book-length English-language biography of Cartier is H.P. Biggar, *The Voyages of Jacques Cartier* (Ottawa: Public Archives of Canada, 1924). Samuel Eliot Morison devotes his usual careful attention to Cartier in *The European Discovery of America: The Northern Voyages* (New York: Oxford University Press, 1971) and its abridgement, *The Great Explorers: The European Discovery of America* (New York: Oxford University Press, 1978; paperback edition, 1986).

Gaetano Casati

(1838 - 1902)

Gaetano Casati was an Italian army officer and geographer who explored in the Nile and Congo basins and became an assistant to the German explorer Emin Pasha.

Gaetano Casati was born in the town of Ponte d'Albiate in northern Italy (near Milan) where his father was a doctor. He entered the University of Pavia in 1859 to study mathematics but gave it up to join the fight for Italian unification. He stayed in the army and advanced to captain and served as an instructor and then helped draw up military maps of Italy. He retired in 1877 and joined the editorial staff of an Italian geographical magazine called *The Explorer* which was seeking to promote Italy's participation in the "Scramble for Africa."

In 1879 the explorer Romolo Gessi wrote to the Italian publisher of the magazine asking him to recommend a cartographer who could help map the Bahr-el-Ghazal region of the Sudan. Casati was the logical choice, and he left for Africa on December 12, 1879. He arrived in Khartoum at the end of February 1880 and eventually traveled up the Nile River to meet Gessi on August 26, 1880. Casati became ill with fever and returned to Khartoum in September. Following his recuperation he returned to the southern Sudan, but by that time Gessi had left to return to Europe (where he died along the way).

On his own, Casati now began a series of explorations that took him to the valley of the Rohl River and to the divide between the Nile and Congo Rivers. He explored the Uele River in what is now northern Zaire and visited the notorious Niam-Niam tribe that had first been contacted by the German explorer **Georg August Schweinfurth**. Along the way, he met Wilhelm Junker, and they traveled through these regions together. During this time there was no news of Casati back in Italy, and it was feared that he had died or been killed. In early 1883, however, some of his letters made their way back to Milan, where the information about his travels caused great interest.

In 1883 Casati traveled to Lado in the southern Sudan where he met the German **Emin Pasha**. He joined Emin Pasha's staff and traveled with him through the southern province that Emin Pasha was administering in the name of the Khedive of Egypt. In 1885, however, the Mahdist revolt in the Sudan succeeded in capturing Khartoum and killing the British general Charles Gordon. Emin Pasha and Casati were cut off from the north and from communications to the outside. They headed south to the town of Wadelai, about 65 miles north of the northern shore of Lake Albert and fortified it. Casati was put in charge of negotiations with King Kabarega of Bunyoro to the south (now in Uganda), designed to keep the King friendly to the Europeans. Casati traveled to Bunyoro to meet with the King in May 1886 and stayed there for 18 months.

By the beginning of 1888, King Kabarega was growing tired of Casati and had him beaten up and tied to a tree. He even threatened him with death. Casati, however, escaped and managed to make his way across Lake Albert almost naked and with none of his weapons or other possessions. He was met by Emin Pasha. In the meantime the "Emin Pasha Relief Expedition" led by **Henry Morton Stanley** made its way from the Atlantic coast into the interior of Africa. Stanley met up with Emin Pasha and Casati on April 29, 1888, neither of whom wanted to leave their stronghold, where they were the effective rulers of their little kingdom, to "escape." However, the Mahdists continued to make their way south, and Casati was put in charge of negotiating with them in December 1888.

Although Casati and Stanley were not friends, he accepted the American's ultimatum to leave with him in early 1889. Stanley, Casati and Emin Pasha left Lado on April 10, 1889. Following a difficult march to the coast, during which Casati became gravely ill, they reached Bagamoyo on the Indian Ocean in December 1889. Casati went to Zanzibar where he stayed until April 5, 1890 and then continued on to Egypt via Aden. He had been appointed the personal representative to report to the Khedive on Emin Pasha, who stayed behind and later returned to the interior of Africa.

When Casati arrived in Egypt, he was welcomed with great ceremony and celebration by the Khedive, who still saw himself as the legitimate ruler of the Sudan. Casati, who was not a good public speaker, insulted the Khedive by mistake and ruined his own welcome. He then traveled to Rome where he delivered several lectures about his adventures. He retired to his estate in northern Italy to write about the 10 years that he had spent in Africa. When his book came out in 1891, he was awarded the Gold Medal of the first Italian Geographical Congress. Casati's book was distinguished by the sympathy that he had for the Africans he encountered and his ability, not shared by men like Stanley, to put aside his European viewpoint and prejudices. Casati brought back with him six Africans, all of whom died of respiratory illness except for one girl, whom he adopted and made his heir. He lived quietly in retirement and died at his estate on March 7, 1902.

Where to learn more

Casati's own book about his adventures is entitled *Ten Years in Equatoria and the Return with Emin Pasha*, 2 vols. (London: Frederick Warne & Co., 1891). Excerpts from it are in Charles Richards and James Place, eds. *East African Explorers* (London: Oxford University Press, 1960). Alan Moorehead's excellent book on east African exploration, *The White Nile* (New York: Harper & Row, 1960) contains information on Casati.

Francis de la Porte, Comte de Castelnau

(1812 - 1880)

Francis de la Porte, Comte de Castelnau was a French aristocrat who led an expedition to South America that covered more of that continent than any other scientific expedition.

Francis de la Porte, Comte de Castelnau was born in London in 1812, where his family had sought asylum from the regime of Napoleon in France. Following Napoleon's defeat and overthrow they returned to Paris where they were prominent supporters of the Orleanist regime that took over France under King Louis Philippe in 1830.

The young Castelnau made a voyage to North America that lasted five years, from 1837 to 1841. While in the United States, he made friends with prominent Americans who suggested that he take up a diplomatic position in South America as a representative of the United States. On his return to France, the King's brother and heir to the throne, the Duke of Orleans, chided Castelnau for wanting to work for a foreign government and instead offered him the opportunity to head a French scientific expedition to South America. This he immediately accepted.

It took a long time to equip the large expedition that was being planned and several times it looked like it would be abandoned, especially after the death of the Duke of Orleans in a carriage accident. But Castelnau left France on a French navy ship on April 30, 1843. His companions were two botanists, Eugene d'Osery and Hugues Weddell, and a taxidermist, Emile Deville. They arrived in Rio de Janeiro on June 17, 1843. From Rio they traveled inland into the state of Minas Gerais, where they visited the old mining center of Ouro Preto, and on to Goiás, which is in the center of the country. It is now the site of the capital city of Brasilia, but at the time of Castelnau's visit it was largely unknown.

Castelnau and his party left Goiás on May 3, 1844 and traveled down the Araguaia River to the Tocantins River. They reached the last Brazilian outpost, Salinas, on May 14. They put together a crew of Xavantes Indians and started downstream on the Tocantins on June 11. They canoed on the righthand stream around the great island of Bananal and arrived in the territory of the Chamboia tribe who had never seen Europeans before. They reached a military post farther downstream where they packed up their scientific specimens and sent them on to the port of Belém to be shipped back to France. They then turned around and headed up the Tocantins and back overland to Goiás. From Goiás they traveled westward to Cuiabá and from there north to find the sources of the Paraguay and Tapajós Rivers. They took the Paraguay downstream to Asunción, the capital of Paraguay.

From Asunción the French explorers traveled in the flat Gran Chaco region west of the Paraguay River and then crossed the Xarayes swampland that had not previously been on any map. Once in Bolivia the expedition split up, with Weddell traveling around the Republic of Bolivia while Castelnau went on to Sucre and Potosí in the Andes and then to the capital of La Paz. From there he descended the Andes to the port of Arequipa and took a ship to Callao and Lima, where Weddell caught up with the party.

Castelnau and the members of his expedition traveled throughout the Peruvian Andes and then went to the eastern cordillera where they set out down the Urubamba River. At one camp they were suddenly abandoned by all of their porters and guides and were left on their own. Worried about the biological specimens and notes that they had in their possession, Castelnau decided to send Osery back to Lima with that valuable material. Along the way, he was killed by his new guides and the material was destroyed.

Castelnau and his group continued on in canoes to the mission at Sarayacu and then crossed the Pampa del Sacramento to reach the headwaters of the Amazon. They floated down the Amazon at a leisurely pace and studied its biology and the various tribes that they encountered along the way. From Belém at the mouth of the Amazon, they caught a boat to Cayenne in the French colony of Guiana and then made their way back to France in 1847. Castelnau's expedition had covered more territory in South America than any previous one, except perhaps that of **Antonio Raposo Tavares** in the 17th century.

In 1849 Castelnau was made French consul in the Brazilian port of Bahia. He worked on the official record of the expedition which was constructed without the material lost by Osery's death. It was published in 14 volumes from 1850 to 1859. In 1858 Castelnau was appointed consul in Cape Town, South Africa and then in Singapore. In 1862 he was made French Consul General in Melbourne, Australia. He served there until his retirement in 1877 but stayed in Melbourne where he died on February 4, 1880.

Where to learn more

Castelnau's record of his expedition, *Expédition dans les parties centrales de l'Amérique du Sud*, 14 vols. (Paris: P. Bertrand, 1850-1859) was published only in French. The major source for this account is Edward J. Goodman, *The Explorers of South America* (New York: Macmillan, 1972).

Charles Chaillé-Long

(1842 - 1917)

Charles Chaillé-Long was an American adventurer who was the first to travel the entire course of the upper Nile River.

Charles Chaillé-Long was born on the Eastern Shore of Maryland on July 2, 1842, the descendant of French Huguenots. The American Civil War broke out while he was still a student. He quit school and enlisted in the United States infantry. He was promoted to captain and served throughout the war. At the end of the war, he sought to take advantage of his military experience and obtained an appointment as an officer in the Egyptian army.

On February 19, 1874 Chaillé-Long was commissioned chief of staff to the British General Charles ("Chinese") Gordon who had been jointly appointed by the Egyptian and British governments to serve at the head of an army to suppress the slave trade in Sudan. Gordon sent Chaillé-Long via the Red Sea and then up the Nile to Gondokoro, which was then the center of the Arab slave traders. From there his instructions were to continue south to meet with Mutesa, the King of Buganda, who had been contacted by **John Hanning Speke** on his expedition to discover the source of the Nile.

Leaving Gondokoro in July 1875, Chaillé-Long traveled all along the Nile, including the 60 miles of waterway that Speke had not been able to traverse, thus proving once and for all that the Nile did flow out of Lake Victoria in spite of assertions made by **Sir Richard Burton**. Once he reached Mutesa's capital at Rubaga, he was warmly welcomed, and it is said that the King sacrificed thirty humans in his honor.

From Rubaga Chaillé-Long went from the source of the Nile at Lake Victoria to Karuma Falls and discovered Lake Kyoga along the way. On his return to Gondokoro, Chaillé-Long traveled west-southwest along the divide between the Congo and Nile river basins and discovered the relation of the Bahr-el-Ghazal system to those two great river systems. On his return to Gondokoro, he came down with fever and had to be sent back to Khartoum to recover. He wrote about his experiences in a book entitled *Naked Truths of Naked People*, published in 1876.

Back in Egypt, Chaillé-Long was recruited by the Khedive of Egypt to take part in an expedition to try to stop the slave trade from the coast (as well as put it under Egyptian rule). In September 1875 he sailed with four ships and 550 Egyptian troops to the port of Barawa on the coast of Somalia. But the forces were too small to accomplish anything and returned to Egypt after four months.

Following this expedition, Chaillé-Long left Egypt and returned to the United States where he attended Columbia University and graduated with a law degree in 1880. He then entered the American consular service and was sent to Alexandria in Egypt, where he organized the rescue of Westerners threatened by outraged Egyptians after a British bombardment of the city. He practiced international law in Paris for five years and was then appointed American consul-general in Korea. While in Korea he took part in a scientific expedition to the island of Cheju-do.

Where to learn more

Chaillé-Long wrote about his east African experiences in *Central Africa: Naked Truths of Naked People* (London: Sampson Low, Marston, Searle & Rivington, 1876; reprinted, Farnborough, England: Gregg International Publishers, Ltd., 1968). His autobiography is *My Life in Four Continents* (London: Hutchinson, 1912).

Chaillé-Long's role in east African exploration and his relationship with General Gordon is discussed in Alan Moorehead, *The White Nile* (New York: Harper & Row, 1960).

Challenger

(1872 - 1876)

The Challenger *expedition was the first scientific expedition to explore the world's oceans.*

The idea for an expedition to travel the oceans of the world and investigate their physical and biological properties came from two British naturalists, William B. Carpenter and Charles Wyville Thomson. They had already dredged in the North Atlantic off the coasts of Britain and realized that there was a wealth of information that could be learned about the world's oceans if they were examined in a systematic way.

Prompted by Carpenter, the major British scientific society, the Royal Society, requested the British Admiralty to supply a ship and a crew to make such a voyage. The request was granted. Naval command was given to Sir George Nares, while Thomson was put in charge of scientific research. The instructions given to these men were to "investigate the physical condition of the deep sea throughout the three great ocean basins."

The ship provided, the *Challenger*, set sail from British naval harbor at Portsmouth on December 21, 1872. It was a 226-foot-long combination steam and sailing vessel. During the course of the expedition, it stopped every 200 miles and stayed in place to record ocean depths, dredge for animal life, and take temperatures of the oceans at different depths. It performed these operations at 362 stations. It dredged to depths of up to 5,486 meters.

The voyage covered 69,000 miles, traveled to every ocean except the Arctic, and crossed the equator six times. The expedition took a two-month break in Australia in March and April 1874, and the scientists spent their time ashore studying freshwater biology. While cruising in the Pacific in 1875, the ship encountered ocean depths greater than had been thought possible, and the thermometers used to measure temperatures at various depths broke under the unexpected pressure. Returning to the Atlantic in 1876, the varying measurements of the ocean floor convinced the geologists of a revolutionary idea—that there were mountain ranges under the sea. The *Challenger* returned to England on May 24, 1876 carrying "a great freight of facts." It added 715 new genuses to man's knowledge of marine zoology and 4,417 new species. It found life at depths much deeper than ever before suspected. It revealed the physical and chemical nature of the ocean floor, obtained seawater for chemical analy-

Challenger. The Granger Collection, New York.

sis, and added much information about the circulation of the ocean currents. The results of the expedition required 50 volumes to be published.

Where to learn more

The results of the *Challenger* expedition were published as *Report on the Scientific Results of the Voyage of H.M.S. Challenger During the Years 1873-1876*, edited by C. Wyville Thomson and John Murray. The *Narrative* appeared in 1885 (London: H.M.S.O.). Thomson also wrote a 2-volume account called *The Voyage of the Challenger* (London: 1877). There is a biography of Thomson: Silvanus P. Thompson, *The Life of William Thomson, Baron Kelvin of Largs*, 2 vols. (London: 1910). Other members of the expedition also wrote their own volumes, including: George S. Nares, *H.M.S. Challenger: Reports of Captain G.S. Nares, R.N.* (London: Admiralty, 1873); Henry Nottidge Moseley, *Notes by a Naturalist: An Account of Observations Made During the Voyage of H.M.S. Challenger* (London: 1892); William J.J. Spry, *The Cruise of H.M.S. Challenger* (London: 1884); and John James Wild, *At Anchor: A Narrative of Experiences Afloat and Ashore During the Voyage of H.M.S. Challenger from 1872 to 1876* (London: 1878).

A good summary of the *Challenger* voyage can be found in Margaret Deacon, *Scientists and the Sea, 1650-1900: A Study of Marine Science* (New York: Academic Press, 1971) and in Eric Linklater, *The Voyage of the Challenger* (Garden City, N.Y.: Doubleday, 1972).

Samuel de Champlain

(1570? - 1635)

Samuel de Champlain was a Frenchman who explored much of eastern North America and was involved in the founding of French colonies in Acadia and Quebec.

Samuel de Champlain was born in the small seaport of Brouage on the west coast of France in about the year 1570. He was probably born a Protestant but at some point converted to Catholicism. This was the period when the Protestants and Catholics in France fought to control the government.

Champlain went to sea at an early age and learned the art of navigation and of drafting maps and charts. He fought as a sergeant on the side of Henri IV until 1598 and made a voyage of two and a half years to the West Indies. In 1603 he joined the expedition of François Gravé Du Pont to Canada.

This expedition landed at Tadoussac at the place where the Saguenay River runs into the St. Lawrence on May 26, 1603. Champlain wrote about the customs of the Native Americans he met and made a trip up the Saguenay River. He sailed with the rest of the expedition up the St. Lawrence past the sites of

Samuel de Champlain.

Quebec, Trois-Rivières and Montreal. While on this voyage he first formed the idea that these lands could be colonized and made a source of wealth for the French king. He also learned about the existence of the Great Lakes and thought that these might be the Northwest Passage to Asia.

After the return of the expedition to Tadoussac in July it then sailed around the Gaspé Peninsula into a region that Champlain called Acadia, probably originally Arcadia, a mythical paradise of the ancient Greeks. On his return to France in September 1603 Champlain wrote about his travels and began to propagandize for exploration of Acadia, which he said had rich mines and could lead to the Northwest Passage.

As a result of these efforts, Champlain was chosen to be geographer on an expedition led by Lieutenant-General Pierre de Monts to Acadia, which left France in March 1604. They landed first on the east coast of what is now Nova Scotia and then went round to the other side to the Bay of Fundy. They visited the site of Port-Royal, or Annapolis Royal, which was later to be the center of settlement for the French Acadians. They then sailed down the coast of New Brunswick and built a fort on a small island in the Saint Croix River, which is now almost exactly on the border between the United States and Canada.

During this time Champlain went off on exploring missions of his own along the coast of Maine and as far as 150 miles inland. The expedition spent the winter of 1604-05 on the island in the Saint Croix, but when spring came they set off to find a more suitable location. They sailed down the coast of New England as far as Cape Cod. The same area was then being explored by Englishmen and this would eventually lead to the settlement of Plymouth Colony in 1620. However, Champlain was the first European to give a detailed account of the area.

The Frenchmen did not find a spot they particularly liked, and they returned to Acadia to build a fort at Port Royal. De Monts returned to France but Champlain spent the following two winters in Acadia. In September 1606 he made another exploring trip to the south that went as far as Rhode Island. During the winter of 1606-07 the Frenchmen made the best of their isolated situation by forming the Order of Good Cheer which sponsored banquets and games and amateur shows. However, in 1607 de Monts had his trading privileges taken away by the French king, and the whole colony was forced to return to France. Before he left Champlain charted the whole coast of Nova Scotia.

Champlain now convinced de Monts to consider sponsoring a colony along the St. Lawrence River, and he was chosen as de

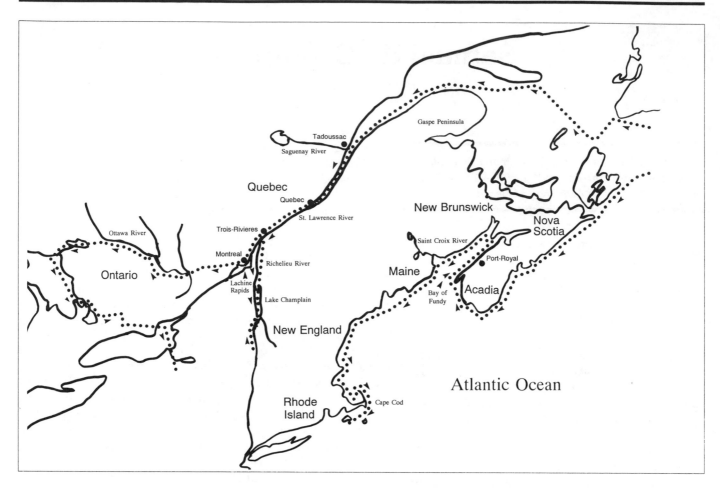

Champlain's explorations in eastern Canada and New England.

Monts' lieutenant on that expedition. He left France on April 13, 1608, and on July 3 started building the fort at Quebec City. In the spring of 1609 he headed up the St. Lawrence River and then up the Richelieu River to Lake Champlain. On July 29, 1609 he fought a great battle with the Iroquois tribes that was to lead to 150 years of hostility between the French and the Iroquois. At almost exactly the same time **Henry Hudson** was coming up the Hudson River to a spot not far south of where Champlain turned back.

Champlain returned to France to report on his new base at Quebec, and it was decided to make it the center for French fur trading in North America. He returned there in April 1610. He only stayed until the fall during which time he fought another battle with the Iroquois. Back in Canada in spring 1611, Champlain sailed up the St. Lawrence as far as the site of Montreal and shot the rapids of Lachine in a canoe by himself. Returning to France he got involved in who had the rights to the fur trade in North America but was finally chosen to be the King's lieutenant in New France. He also published the story of his adventures, called the *Voyages*.

Champlain returned to Quebec in March 1613, where he stayed only briefly before traveling once again up the St. Law-

rence. This time he went as far as the Ottawa River and explored the route that was to be the main river road to the Great Lakes for the next two centuries. By now the fur trade was becoming a prosperous business, and Champlain could afford to spend time on other aspects of governing the colony. In 1615 he returned from France with the first Catholic missionaries who came to convert the Native Americans to Christianity. During the summer of 1615 he traveled into what is now Ontario and saw the Great Lakes for the first time.

By this time the French had made allies with many of the native tribes, including the Hurons. Together they attacked an Iroquois fort in October 1615 but were not successful, and Champlain was badly wounded. He spent that winter among the Hurons. On his return to France in 1616 he found that politics at court had endangered his position, and he lost his title of lieutenant in North America. In order to regain his position he proposed an ambitious plan to colonize Quebec, establish agriculture there and to look for the Northwest Passage. He gained the king's support and spent part of 1618 in the new colony.

Champlain's problems had not ended, however, and on his return to France he became involved in various law suits and political maneuvers. Once again, however, he received the King's support and left in 1620 with his young wife to live in Quebec. He was now officially commander of the colony and spent the next few years trying to strengthen it. In 1627 the most powerful man in the French government, the Cardinal de Richelieu, formed the Company of the 100 Associates to rule New France with Champlain in charge.

Things were going well until 1629 when a party of Englishmen under the Kirke brothers attacked the fort at Quebec and forced Champlain to surrender on July 24. Forced to return to France, he spent the next four years arguing about the importance of New France and in writing various accounts of his life. When a peace treaty was signed between England and France in 1632 Quebec was returned to France, and Champlain was once again sent out to be its governor.

By this time Champlain was becoming older and infirm. After returning to Quebec in May 1633, he was stricken with various health problems and died there on December 25, 1635.

Where to learn more

Champlain's own records are found in *Narrative of a Voyage to the West Indies and Mexico in the Years 1599-1602* (London: Hakluyt Society, 1859) and H.P. Biggar, ed. *The Works of Samuel de Champlain*, 6 vols. (Toronto: The Champlain Society, 1927-1935). There are two excellent biographies of Champlain available in English: Morris Bishop, *Champlain, the Life of Fortitude* (New York: Alfred A. Knopf, 1949; reprinted in paperback, Toronto: McClelland & Stewart, 1963) and Samuel Eliot Morison, *Samuel de Champlain: Father of New France* (Boston: Little, Brown & Co., 1972), which contains an extensive bibliography.

Richard Chancellor

(? - 1556)

Richard Chancellor was an English merchant who opened up a trading route between England and Russia through the Arctic Ocean.

Richard Chancellor grew up in the household of an important English nobleman, Sir Henry Sidney (the father of Sir Philip Sidney, a famous English poet). Through his connections, he was chosen as "pilot-general" of Sir Hugh Willoughby's expedition in search of a northeast passage to China and India. The three ships steered north, but north of the Lofoten Islands, on the northwest coast of Norway, they were separated in a storm.

Willoughby, in one of the ships, landed in the vicinity of Vardöhus, where he had arranged to meet Chancellor. They did not meet, and he sailed on, probably going as far as Novaya Zemlya. But on the return voyage the ship was wrecked off Lapland and all aboard were lost. Their remains were found by Russian fishermen the following year.

The second of the expedition's three ships disappeared completely. Chancellor, after waiting seven days in Vardöhus, proceeded alone in his ship the *Edward Bonaventure* into the White Sea, and then landed at the seaport of Arkhangelsk, to discover that he was in Muscovy, as the English then called Russia. He travelled overland to the court at Moscow, where he met Tsar Ivan IV (the Terrible) who encouraged the English to begin trading with his country.

In the spring of 1554 Chancellor returned to the White Sea and sailed home to England, where his reports led to the establishment of what came to be known as the Muscovy Company. So pleased were the English at Chancellor's achievement that in 1555 they sent him to Moscow again. On this trip he was able to obtain a trade monopoly in the White Sea for the Muscovy Company from the tsar. During this trip Chancellor also learned about what had happened to Willoughby and was able to recover his papers.

Chancellor left Moscow on this second trip in July 1556. He made it safely to Archangelsk and through the northern seas, but on November 10 his ship was wrecked off the northeast coast of Scotland at Aberdour Bay, Aberdeenshire. Some of the crew were saved, but Chancellor was killed.

Where to learn more

The original source for information on Chancellor's voyages is Richard Hakluyt's *The Principal Navigations, Voyages, Traffiques, and Discoveries of the English Nation*, which was first published in 1598-1600 and was reprinted by the Hakluyt Society in 1903-1905.

The best modern source for information about Chancellor is Lloyd E. Berry and Robert O. Crummery, eds. *Rude and Barbarous Kingdom: Russia in the Accounts of Sixteenth-Century English Visitors* (Madison: University of Wisconsin Press, 1968). There are discussions of Chancellor in two good summaries of Arctic exploration: Jeanette Mirsky, *To the Arctic!: The Story of Northern Exploration from Earliest Times to the Present* (New York: Alfred A. Knopf, 1948) and L.P. Kirwan *A History of Polar Exploration* (New York: W.W. Norton & Co., 1960).

Chang Ch'ien

(160? - 107 B.C.)

Chang Ch'ien was a Chinese diplomat who made the first recorded trip of a Chinese into Central Asia and opened up the "Silk Road" trade route with Rome.

Wu-Ti, a member of the Han dynasty, became the emperor of China in 140 B.C. At that time, China was threatened by the Hsiung-nu (Hun) "barbarians" on its northern borders. The new emperor tried to deal with this threat by organizing military alliances against the Hsiung-nu. He asked for volunteers to carry out a diplomatic mission to the Yueh-chih nomads in Central Asia. This challenge was accepted by Chang Ch'ien, a young court official from the city of Hanzhong. The Yueh-chih were Indo-Scythian tribesmen (ancestors of modern Afghans and Tajiks) who had taken over control of Central Asia after the disintegration of the empire of **Alexander the Great**.

Chang Ch'ien and his entourage, which included a Tatar slave named Kan Fu, traveled west through the Chinese province of Gansu in 138 B.C. They were captured by members of the Hsiung-nu tribe and taken to their headquarters in the Altai Mountains. Chang Ch'ien was kept in captivity for 10 years (where he married and had a son) until he was able to escape and make his way southward. He traveled through Fergana, in what is now Uzbekistan, and Sogdiana to Bactria, in present-day Afghanistan, and northern Pakistan around the city of Peshawar, which was then ruled by the Yueh-chih. He finally reached the goal of his mission at the Yueh-chih capital of Heyuchi. He learned, however, that the Yueh-chih did not want to join with the Chinese in fighting the Huns.

Leaving Bactria, Chang Ch'ien headed home by a more southerly route, hoping to avoid the Hsiung-nu. He went south of the Kunlun Mountains to the lake at Lop Nor and then to the Tsaidam Depression. But once again he was captured. This time he escaped after only one year and returned to the Emperor's court in 126 B.C., bringing with him his wife and Kan Fu. He reported to the Emperor not only about the countries he had visited but also about places he had heard of, including India, the Caucasus Mountains, Persia, Mesopotamia, and the Roman provinces in Asia. He proposed setting up trading relations with India via the Chinese province of Szechuan. The Emperor tried to do this, but all four of the missions he sent out failed.

Chang Ch'ien was given a title of nobility and took part in a campaign against the Huns in 122 B.C. He failed, however, to come to the aid of his commander during an attack. For this dereliction he was fined and reduced to the rank of private. In the following year, the Chinese inflicted a major defeat on the Huns, and Chang Ch'ien was restored to the Emperor's favor.

Chang Ch'ien then proposed to head another diplomatic mission. He went to Wusun in the valley of the Ili River in what is now Chinese Turkestan and Kazakhstan. Once again, the mission failed diplomatically. However, it did have one important result. While in Wusun, Chang Ch'ien sent out missions to neighboring countries that carried gifts of silk produced in China. These silks gradually found their way to the West and opened up what is called the Silk Road—the overland trade route through Central Asia between China and the Roman Empire. This route traveled from Merv (in Turkmenistan) through northern Iran to Ecbatana. From there it went to the dual city of Seleucia-Ctesiphon (near Baghdad) through northern Mesopotamia and Syria to the port of Antioch, 6,000 miles from China.

Following his mission to Wusun, Chang Ch'ien returned to China, where he was appointed the head of the Office of Foreign Affairs. He died the following year.

Where to learn more

Our knowledge of Chang Ch'ien comes from an account by the Chinese historian Ssu-ma Ch'ien that was written in about the year 100 B.C. It was translated by Friedrich Hirth in the *Journal of the American Oriental Society*, vol. 37, 1917, pp. 89-116. Excerpts from it can be found in Jeannette Mirsky, *The Great Chinese Travelers* (New York: Random House, 1964).

Jean-Baptiste Charcot

(1867 - 1936)

Jean-Baptiste Charcot was a French doctor and scientist who led two expeditions to unexplored parts of the coast of Antarctica and several expeditions to the North Atlantic.

Jean-Baptiste Charcot was born in the suburbs of Paris on July 15, 1867. During the Franco-Prussian War in 1870-1871 he took refuge with his family in London. His father was a famous doctor, and Charcot followed in his footsteps. He got his medical degree in 1895 and practiced in a hospital in Paris. He married Victor Hugo's granddaughter in 1896. During his vacations he pursued his hobby of sailing and made a trip to the Mediterranean and Nile with the American millionaire Cornelius Vanderbilt in 1897 and sailed around Ireland in the summer of 1900.

In 1901 Charcot entered the Arctic regions for the first time when he sailed to the Faeroe Islands in the North Atlantic and carried out scientific research there. He returned in the summer of 1902 to study Jan Mayen Island.

Jean-Baptiste Charcot. The Granger Collection, New York.

During the early years of the twentieth century expeditions from several countries were headed toward Antarctica. Charcot wanted France to be among them. In 1903 he prepared a 250-ton polar vessel, the *Français*, at the French port of St. Malo, using money that he earned from the sale of a painting by the famous French artist Honoré Fragonard. His original intention had been to come to the rescue of Otto Nordenskjöld's Swedish expedition, which had not been heard from for several months. When he learned that it had been rescued, he decided to go ahead anyway. The ship left the dock at St. Malo on August 15, 1903 but had to return immediately when a sailor on board was killed by a broken piece of equipment two minutes after setting sail.

The *Français* explored the west coast of the Graham Peninsula and Alexander Land in Antarctica. Prominent among its discoveries was what is now know as the Loubet Coast of Graham Land, a mountainous coast with long spurs descending from a snow-capped plateau. It was named in honor of President Emile Loubet of France who had helped raise money to pay for the expedition. Following bad storms and engine problems, Charcot anchored off Wandel Island (now called Booth Island) in March 1904. The ship was iced in for the winter, and the crew spent the time carrying out scientific investigations and making exploratory visits to nearby areas.

The *Français* was able to leave the ice on December 26, but while sailing north on January 15, 1905 it hit a submerged rock. In order to keep the ship afloat, the crew had to man the pumps constantly even though their fingers froze to the handle. They made it to an Argentine port in February, where Charcot learned that his wife was divorcing him on grounds of desertion. Charcot was able to sell his damaged ship to the Argentine government.

In August 1908 Charcot set out on another expedition mainly financed by the French Government. This time he took his second wife, Marguerite, with him. He sailed from Le Havre in an 800-ton steamer, the *Pourquoi-Pas?* (Why Not?), that was also rigged to serve as a sailing vessel if necessary. The ship was specially constructed and equipped with the most modern innovations—a motor launch, searchlight and telephones. It even carried electric cables so that the ship could be used as a power source for land stations. Charcot conducted his exploration in a highly civilized way, carrying French wines on board and including a library of 1,500 books.

From Punta Arenas on Magellan Strait (where Marguerite Charcot left the ship), Charcot took the *Pourquoi-Pas?* to Wiencke Island in the Palmer Archipelago, where it hit a rock, doing serious damage to the keel. The crew was able to make enough repairs to keep the ship afloat. They found that the land west of the Antarctic Peninsula, between Palmer Archipelago and Alexander Island and named after Queen Adelaide by **John Biscoe** in 1832, was in fact an island. They spent the winter anchored at Port Circumcision on Petermann Island, where they passed the time writing a romantic novel called *The Typist's Lover*.

During the summer of 1909-1910, Charcot discovered the Fallières Coast, in shore of Marguerite Bay on the Antarctic peninsula. On January 11, 1910 he sighted Charcot Land, off Alexander Island, which he named after his father. When he returned to France on June 4, 1910 he had mapped over 2,000 kilometers of previously unknown coastline.

During World War I Charcot served in the French Navy, devising ways of combatting German submarine warfare. In the years following the war he led a scientific expedition into the North Atlantic every summer. He went to Rockall, a small island northwest of Ireland in 1921 to study its geology. In 1926 he went to Scoresby Sound on the northeastern coast of Greenland to rescue a Danish expedition. In 1929 when the Italian aviator

Umberto Nobile crashed on the polar ice, Charcot led one of the expeditions sent out to find him. Starting in 1931 Charcot helped establish a French scientific base at Scoresby Sound and traveled there in 1932 and 1933. In 1934 he went to Angmagssalik on the east coast of Greenland and in 1935 returned to Jan Mayen.

In the summer of 1936 Charcot returned to Angmagssalik for his annual expedition. The boiler on the ship exploded and had to be repaired in Reykjavik, Iceland. Leaving that port it ran into a bad storm and was thrown against the rocks in western Iceland in the early morning hours of September 16. Charcot and all but one of the crew members were killed.

Where to learn more

A very good book about Antarctic exploration that includes several photos from Charcot's expeditions is *Antarctica: Great Stories from the Frozen Continent* (Sydney: Reader's Digest, 1988). Charcot's story of his second expedition was published in English in London in 1911, *The Voyage of the 'Why Not' in the Antarctic* (Hodder & Stoughton). There is also a translation into English of a biography by M. Oulie, *Charcot of the Antarctic* (London: 1938).

Evelyn Cheesman

(1881 - 1969)

Evelyn Cheesman was a British scientist who traveled to remote islands in the South Pacific collecting insect specimens.

E velyn Cheesman was born in a small village in the English county of Kent. She came from a prosperous family but received only the conventional education of a young woman at the end of the nineteenth century. She had wanted to be a veterinarian, but women were not admitted to veterinary school. During World War I she worked as a clerk in a government department, from which she transferred to the London Zoo. There she found her real love, entomology (the study of insects) and took over the Insect House, arranging its exhibits and conducting school tours.

As a result of this job, she was offered the position of clerk on a government scientific expedition that was going to the South Pacific in 1923. She readily agreed and left London with £10 in her purse. When the expedition reached Tahiti she received a letter from one of her brothers that contained £100. This prompted her to resign from the expedition and go collecting on her own. She roomed with an old sea captain on Tahiti and traveled to Bora Bora and some of the other islands in French Polynesia. She returned to England with a collection of 500 specimens that she donated to the British Museum of Natural History.

In 1928 the British Museum gave Cheesman a grant to collect insects in Vanuatu (then called the New Hebrides) in the South Pacific. This island group was almost entirely unknown scientifically, and she was the first natural scientist to go there. Her first visit was to the large island of Malekula. Accompanied by the manager of a coastal plantation she traveled inland to the land of the Big Nambas, a remote group who had had only minimal contact with Europeans. She was the first European woman, and possibly the first European, to have visited the Nambas. She was well received and made some valuable additions to her collections. From Malekula Cheesman traveled to both the northern and southern islands of Vanuatu, including a trip to Aneityum, a small, seldom-visited island in the south. After two years, she became ill and was forced to return home via Australia.

In 1933 Cheesman traveled to the island of New Guinea. She went to inland areas of the Australian colony of Papua New Guinea and to the Dutch-ruled western half of the island. This part of the island was very little known, and parts of it were only visited by Europeans during and after World War II. Cheesman went to the Cyclops Mountains and to Waigeo and Japen Islands off the west coast of the island. When the Japanese invaded New Guinea in 1942, Cheesman was on the last boat to leave the island.

During World War II Cheesman worked on various projects for the British government including supplying information about the South Pacific islands she had visited. She was injured in a train accident near the end of the war and was unable to walk for a while. After she recovered, she went to New Caledonia in the South Pacific and climbed the long mountain chain that makes up the central spine of the island, collecting more specimens. She also visited the island of Lifou in the Loyalty Islands.

In June 1953 Cheesman had an operation to correct the problems caused by her earlier accident and then returned to Vanuatu and the island of Aneityum. She was often alone on the island and had to radio for a patrol boat when she was ready to leave. During all this time, Cheesman lived very modestly—she did not get any salary from the British Museum in her role as "honorary associate." Her only income was from the books and lectures she wrote about her adventures. Any extra that she earned she spent on "a gift-book to a young naturalist or a microscope to a government department." In 1953, however, the government granted her a small pension, and she lived quietly in London until her death on April 15, 1969 at the age of 88.

Where to learn more

Cheesman wrote two autobiographical works: *Things Worth While* (London: Hutchinson, 1957) and *Time Well Spent* (London: Hutchinson, 1960).

Each of her various expeditions were the subject of books that Cheesman wrote during her career: *Islands Near the Sun: Off the Beaten Track in the Far, Fair Society Islands* (London: F. & G. Witherby, 1927); *Hunting Insects in the South Seas* (London: P. Allan, 1932); *Backwaters of the Savage South Seas* (London: Jarrolds, 1933); *The Two Roads of Papua* (London; Jarrolds, 1935); *The Land of the Red Bird* (London: H. Joseph, 1938); *Camping Adventures in New Guinea* (London: Harrap, 1948); *Camping Adventures on Cannibal Islands* (London: Harrap, 1948); *Marooned in Du-bu Cove* (London: Bell, 1949); *Six-Legged Snakes in New Guinea: A Collecting Expedition to Two Unexplored Islands* (London: Harrap, 1949); *Who Stand Alone* (London: G. Bles, 1965).

The best biography of Cheesman can be found in Marion Tinling's *Women into the Unknown* (New York: Greenwood Press, 1989), which served as the basis for this account.

Cheng Ho

(1371 - 1434?)

Cheng Ho was a Chinese admiral who led seven large naval expeditions from China to Southeast Asia, India, Arabia, and the east coast of Africa.

C heng Ho was born into a Muslim family in the city of Kunyang in Yunnan province in southwestern China at the beginning of the Ming dynasty. In 1381 the Chinese put down a rebellion by the Muslims of Yunnan, and Cheng Ho was one of the local children who were selected to be castrated to become eunuchs in the service of the Chinese emperor. He became a servant to one of the princes, Chu Ti, who later became emperor under the name Yung-lo. Cheng Ho accompanied Chu Ti in various campaigns against the Mongols on the northern border and became one of the prince's most valued military leaders and advisers.

Chu Ti led an insurrection against the state that led to his being crowned emperor in 1402. When he became emperor, Yung-lo put Cheng Ho in charge of several naval expeditions that he sent out to foreign lands. The Chinese chronicles say, "In the third year of the Yung-lo reign the Imperial Palace Eunuch Cheng Ho was sent on a mission to the Western Oceans. The Emperor, under the suspicion that the previous Chien-Wen Emperor might have fled beyond the seas commissioned Cheng Ho and others to pursue his traces."

Cheng Ho's first voyage began in 1405 from the mouth of the Yang-tse River with an enormous fleet that was said to contain 65 large and 255 small vessels and a total crew of 27,800. They sailed south across the South China Sea and anchored at Qui Nhon in what is now Vietnam. He met the famous Chinese pirate Chen Tsu-i, who ruled Sumatra, in battle. Cheng Ho defeated Chen Tsu-i and sent him as a prisoner back to Nanjing to be executed. Cheng Ho continued on to Sri Lanka and the port of Calicut (today called Kozhikode) in south India, returning to China in 1407.

In the same year, Cheng Ho set out on his second voyage. His goal was to once again reach Calicut, which was the center of the spice trade in southern India. Returning from Calicut, Cheng Ho's expedition stopped in Thailand and Java before returning home in 1409. During the third voyage (1409-1411), which reached the same destination as the second, excursions were made to Thailand, Malacca (on the coast of Malaya), Sumatra, and Sri Lanka. There was some trouble with the King of Sri Lanka, and he was taken prisoner and brought back to China.

The fourth voyage (1413-1415) took the fleet even farther. It divided up into several squadrons and some sailed to Sri Lanka and Bengal while others made stops at the Maldive Islands off the southwest coast of India, Ormuz (the main port of Persia), and the south coast of Arabia and the port of Aden.

On the fifth voyage (1417-1419) the fleet went to the Ryukyu Islands between Japan and Taiwan, Brunei on the north coast of Borneo, Java. Squadrons continued on to the shores of East Africa, including Mogadishu, Brava, and Juba in Somalia; Malindi and Mombasa in Kenya; the island of Zanzibar and ports in Tanzania and Mozambique. The sixth expedition (1421-1422) expanded upon the previous one, visiting states between Brunei and Zanzibar, including the ports of Brava and Mogadishu in present-day Somalia.

Before the return of the sixth expedition, Cheng Ho lost his major supporter when Emperor Yung-lo died. Bureaucrats at the court began to lobby to stop Cheng Ho's voyages, believing that they were unnecessary and wasteful and that the "Middle Kingdom" had nothing to gain by dealing with other countries. However, one last voyage was approved by the new emperor, Chu Chan-chi, in 1431. Between 1433 and 1435 this final expedition revisited many places on the coast of Africa and went as far as Ormuz. It brought back gifts and tributes from many rulers to the Chinese emperor. Cheng Ho himself died in Calicut in about 1434, but his body was brought back to be buried in Nanjing.

According to a monument (discovered in 1937) that was erected by Cheng Ho in a Taoist temple in 1431, he had "gone to more than thirty countries large and small. We have traversed more than one hundred thousand *li* (a *li* is about one-third of a mile) of immense water spaces and have beheld in the ocean huge waves like mountains rising sky-high, and we have set eyes on barbarian regions far away hidden in a blue transparency of light vapors." In many ways Cheng Ho anticipated the voyages of **Vasco da Gama** and the other Portuguese and European navigators who were to start sailing in the same waters about 70 years later. One of the great questions of history is why the Chinese did not follow up on the explorations of Cheng Ho and what would have happened if they had.

Where to learn more

The texts of two monuments describing Cheng Ho's accomplishments are found in J.J.L. Duyvendak, *China's Discovery of Africa* (London: Arthur Probsthain, 1949). There are excerpts in Jeannette Mirsky, *The Great Chinese Travelers* (New York: Random House, 1964). See also Kuei-sheng Chang, "The Ming Maritime Enterprise and China's Knowledge of Africa Prior to the Age of Great Discoveries," *Terrae Incognitae*, vol. 3, 1971, pp. 33-44.

James Chuma

(1850? - 1882)

James Chuma was a freed African slave who worked as a servant to David Livingstone and helped to carry his body out of Africa and then served as caravan leader for several European expeditions, including those of Joseph Thomson.

Chuma (or Juma) was a member of the Yao tribe who lived around Lake Malawi (or Lake Nyasa). His father was a fisherman named Chimilengo; his mother was named Chinjeriapi. During local wars, he was captured and eventually sold to a Portuguese slave trader. He was rescued from slavery by a fellow Yao named Wekotani. They attended the mission school founded by Anglican Bishop Charles Frederick Mackenzie at Magomero before his death in 1862.

Wekotani and Chuma were hired by **David Livingstone** to be his servants on his return from an expedition to the Zambezi River in 1864. Livingstone sailed his ship, the *Lady Nyassa*, from Zanzibar to Bombay in India and took the two Africans with him. He left them in Bombay in June 1864 in a Protestant mission school. Livingstone returned to Bombay in September 1865 and found the two Africans there. Chuma was in good health and had done well in school, being able to read and write English. He was baptized with the name James Chuma on December 10, 1865, and he and Wekotani sailed with Livingstone on January 5, 1866.

On his next expedition, Livingstone left from the Mozambique port of Quelimane in March 1866 and reached Lake Nyasa on August 8. Back among his own people, Wekotani announced his desire to stay behind and marry. At about this time, Chuma was relieved of his duties as cook, but he remained loyal to Livingstone. In September many of the Africans deserted, leaving only nine of the original 36, including Chuma. Early in October, he met a woman who claimed to be his aunt, but Livingstone doubted the relationship and convinced him to give her only a few trade goods.

Livingstone and his remaining followers took up with a party of Arabs in January 1867 and traveled with them for more than a year. During this time, they went to Lake Mweru, on the border between Zambia and Zaire, and then headed toward Lake Bangweulu. In April 1867 Chuma and several others mutinied, saying they feared going to Kazembe (now in eastern Zambia), which was a notorious haunt of slave traders. Livingstone reached Kazembe in May and Lake Bangweulu on July 18. Chuma and

David Susi returned to join him on November 13. They went to Ujiji, on the east shore of Lake Tanganyika, and Bambarre, where they stayed until October 1868. Livingstone wanted to explore the Lualaba River, which flows out of Lake Tanganyika, but only Chuma, Susi, and one other of his supporters were willing to go along.

Livingstone went back to Ujiji with no trade goods to barter for food in October 1871. It was there that he had his famous meeting with **Henry Morton Stanley** on November 10. The two Europeans went exploring on Lake Tanganyika with Chuma, Susi and **Sidi Mubarak Bombay** as rowers. They then traveled to the town of Tabora (now in central Tanzania) where Chuma was on hand to see Stanley off on March 14, 1872. There, also, Chuma married one of Livingstone's cooks, Ntaoeka, on June 2, 1872. Supplies sent by Stanley arrived on August 14, and they set off into the interior once again.

James Chuma and David Susi.

In January 1873 Livingstone and his supporters headed back to Lake Bangweulu. Chuma was put in charge of the advance party. By April, Livingstone was too weak to walk and had to be carried by Chuma, Susi and some of the others. The Scots explorer was found dead in his hut by Susi on the morning of May 1, 1873. Chuma was put in charge of negotiations with local chiefs to try to extricate themselves from their situation. The group decided to carry Livingstone's body as well as his papers, maps, and instruments back to Zanzibar. His heart and other internal organs were cut out and buried at the site of his death. The party of about 60 Africans then loaded up Livingstone's body and started out around May 5, 1873.

In the long walk to the coast, both Susi and Chuma became ill. They encountered a hostile tribe at Wausi, at which a pitched battle took place and the expedition captured two villages. From there, they entered known territory and came to the town of Kumba Kumba, the brother of Tippu Tib. They met a friendly Arab caravan that told them that a relief expedition sent out to find Livingstone was at Tabora. Chuma was sent ahead with a letter to **Verney Lovett Cameron** informing him of Livingstone's death.

The expedition arrived in Tabora on October 20, 1873. Cameron decided to continue on into the interior, and Dr. Dillon was sent along to accompany Livingstone's body to the coast. Becoming ill, however, Dr. Dillon killed himself on November 18, and Chuma had to bury him before they could continue. Once again, Chuma was sent ahead to report, and he reached Zanzibar on February 3, 1874. The British consul returned with Chuma to claim Livingstone's body. They also brought supplies for the Africans and paid the bearers their back wages. From Zanzibar, Jacob Wainwright, another of Livingstone's supporters, was sent with the body to England where it was buried with great pomp at Westminster Abbey. The tombstone reads: "Brought by faithful hands over land and sea here rests David Livingstone . . .".

Following the funeral, Chuma and Susi and their wives were brought to England at the expense of a friend of Livingstone's. Among others, they met with Livingstone's son and with well-known Africanist Horace Waller who wrote, "I found them actual geographers of no mean attainments." They attended a meeting of the Royal Geographical Society on June 1, 1874. At the anniversary meeting a few weeks later that commemorated Livingstone's accomplishments, they were presented with special medals by the Society. They stayed with Waller for four months telling him the history of their expedition. Chuma made a model of Livingstone's grass hut and presented it to the Livingstone family. They returned to Zanzibar on October 20. The Royal Geographical Society made up 60 silver medals that were inscribed "Faithful to the End" and presented them to Chuma and as many of the others that could be found at a ceremony in Zanzibar on August 17, 1875.

Following his return to Zanzibar, Chuma was recruited in August 1875 by the Universities Mission to lead several caravans to the interior. The first of these set off on November 1, 1875, followed by another in June 1876. In October 1876, with 70 porters under his command, Chuma helped to establish a mission station at Masasi. He returned to Zanzibar twice for supplies and led a new party to Masasi in June 1877. On his return to Zanzibar in December, Chuma had a meeting with the British consul where he gave him an assessment of the situation in the interior.

On January 5, 1879, Keith Johnston and **Joseph Thomson** arrived in Zanzibar to explore a route between Dar es Salaam and Lake Nyasa. They hired Chuma as caravan leader and set out on May 14 with 150 porters and guides. Johnston died on June 28, but Thomson decided to continue. Chuma served as commander of the caravan and chief negotiator with the tribes they encountered. They reached Lake Nyasa on September 20, 1879 and traveled to its northern end. They continued on to Lake Tanganyika, where they arrived on November 3, 1879. Once along the way, Thomson, who was ill, and Chuma got into an argument, but Thomson realized he needed Chuma and they quickly made up. In fact, Thomson, who was only 21 years old at the time, was so dependent on Chuma that he was nicknamed "Chuma's white man." They arrived back in Zanzibar in July 1880. Chuma was given another silver medal by the Royal Geographical Society, which was presented to him on a return trip by Thomson in June 1881.

By the time the medal was presented to him, Chuma was ill. He made out his will on September 25, 1882 and died in the mission hospital in Zanzibar sometime shortly thereafter.

Where to learn more

The story of the expedition to bring Livingstone's body to the coast, as told by Chuma and Susi, is found in Horace Waller, ed. *The Last Journals of David Livingstone*, 2 vols. (London: 1874). The other sources for the life of Chuma are the records of the other expeditions. These have been collected and assimilated in an important book by Donald Simpson, *Dark Companions: The African Contribution to the European Exploration of East Africa* (New York: Harper & Row, 1976), which served as the source for this account.

Hugh Clapperton

(1788 - 1827)

Hugh Clapperton was a British naval officer who made two trips to the interior of West Africa to find the Niger River. He succeeded on his second trip but died along the way, in the city of Sokoto.

Hugh Clapperton was one of 21 children of a doctor who practiced in the little town of Annan in southern Scotland near the English border. Clapperton had an elementary education under a local schoolmaster until the age of 13. He then became an apprentice on board a trading ship to the West Indies. He was impressed (kidnapped) onto a warship of the Royal Navy. Fortunately, he met an uncle who was a Royal Navy officer and who was able to use his influence to get Clapperton an appointment as a midshipman, or junior officer. He served in the East Indies during the Napoleonic Wars and in Canada during the War of 1812 with the United States.

In 1817 Clapperton was retired from active duty with the rank of lieutenant and put on half-pay. In 1820 he moved to

Hugh Clapperton. The Granger Collection, New York.

Edinburgh and became a neighbor and friend of Walter Oudney, a retired naval surgeon. Oudney volunteered to head an expedition to search for the Niger River, and he enlisted Clapperton to accompany him. The third member of what was called the Bornou Mission was Major Dixon Denham, an officer at the Royal Military College at Sandhurst.

Clapperton and Oudney went to Tripoli in October 1821. Denham arrived soon afterwards. From the beginning, Denham and Clapperton did not get along, and Denham spent a good deal of his time writing reports accusing Clapperton of bad conduct. The Bornou Mission traveled across the Sahara in a caravan and reached Lake Chad, a great lake in the center of Africa on February 4, 1823.

The desert crossing had been very difficult, and the men were sick by the time they got to Lake Chad. They split up, with Denham heading off to the southeast to the Chari River in the present-day Central African Republic while Clapperton and Oudney went west to the great trading center of Kano, which is now in northern Nigeria. Oudney died before they reached Kano. Clapperton entered Kano on January 20, 1824 and gave the following description:

"At eleven o'clock we entered Kano, the great emporium of the kingdom of Haussa, but I had no sooner passed the gates than I felt grievously disappointed; for from the flourishing description of it given by the Arabs, I expected to see a city of surprising grandeur: I found on the contrary, the houses nearly a quarter of a mile from the walls, and in many parts scattered into detached groups, between large stagnant pools of water. I might have spared all the pains I had taken with my toilet; for not an individual turned his head round to gaze at me, but all, intent on their own business, allowed me to pass by without notice or remark."

Clapperton continued on from Kano to the city of Sokoto to the northwest, at which point he was only 150 miles from the Niger River. However, he could not find a guide to take him farther, and he was forced to turn back. He met up again with Denham, and they took the caravan north to Tripoli. They reached England in June 1825. Denham was appointed governor of Sierra Leone and died soon after arriving there in 1828. The editor of his journal wrote: "it remains difficult to recall in the chequered history of geographical discovery—a vocation that has attracted many very odd characters—a more odious man than Dixon Denham."

Clapperton came back to England determined to find the mouth of the Niger. He was afraid that another explorer, **Alexander Gordon Laing**, would beat him to it. Therefore, he set out again almost immediately. He left Portsmouth on August 17, 1825. This time he took with him a young man he had hired as a servant, **Richard Lander**. They landed at Badagri on the coast of Nigeria near present-day Lagos in November 1825 and traveled north through the homeland of the Yoruba people. All the members of the party became ill with malaria and dysentery but they struggled on, Clapperton having succumbed on March 12. He saw the Niger for the first time at the town of Bussa on March 31, 1826. This was the place where **Mungo Park** had died in 1806. By this time, Clapperton was feeling better, and in the village of Wawa he accepted the advances of a rich widow named Zuma, who had first tried to seduce Lander without success.

On April 10, 1826 Clapperton and Lander crossed the Niger River at Komie. They reached Kano on July 20, where they were forced to stay for five weeks while Clapperton recovered. He then went on alone to Sokoto, which was the seat of Sultan Bello. Clapperton aimed to continue on from there back to the Niger and then follow it downstream to its mouth. He became involved in tedious negotiations with the Sultan, however, and suffered a relapse. He summoned Lander, who arrived on December 23.

Lander tried to nurse Clapperton back to health but without success. He died in Sokoto on April 18, 1827. In his history of the expedition, Lander records Clapperton's funeral: "The body was then taken from the camel's back, and placed in a shed, whilst the slaves were employed in digging the grave. Their task being speedily accomplished, the corpse was borne to the brink of the pit, and I planted the flag close to it; then, uncovering my head, and opening a prayer-book, amidst showers of tears, I read the impressive funeral service of the Church of England over the remains of my valued master—the English flag waving slowly and mournfully over them at the same moment. Not a single soul listened to this peculiarly distressing ceremony, for the slaves were quarrelling with each other the whole of the time it lasted."

Where to learn more

The record of the Bornou Mission was written by Denham: *The Narrative of Travels and Discoveries in Northern and Central Africa in the Years 1822, 1823 and 1824, by Major Denham, Captain Clapperton and the Late Doctor Oudney* to which Clapperton appended his "Journal of an Excursion to Soccatoo" (London: 1826). Additional material, diaries and letters, was published much later by E. W. Borill, ed. *Missions to the Niger*, vols. 2-4 (Cambridge: Cambridge University Press for the Hakluyt Society, 1966). It is this material which reveals Denham's treacherous conduct.

Following Clapperton's death, Lander retrieved his diary, which was published as a *Journal of a Second Expedition into the Interior of Africa from the Bight of Benin to Soccatoo by the Late Commander Clapperton of the Royal Navy. To Which is Added the Journal of Richard Lander from Kano to the Sea-Coast, Partly by a More Eastern Route* (London: John Murray, 1829; reprinted, London: Frank Cass and Company, Ltd., 1966). Lander then published his own account as *Records of Captain Clapperton's Last Expedition to Africa*, 2 vols. (London: Henry Colburn & Richard Bentley, 1830; reprinted, London: Frank Cass and Company, Ltd., 1967).

Excerpts from all these original sources can be found in Margery Perham and J. Simmons, *African Discovery: An Anthology of Exploration* (London: Faber and Faber, 1957; reprinted, Chicago: Northwestern University Press, 1963).

There are several good books about the history of the exploration of the Niger that include accounts of Clapperton's two expeditions: A. Adu Boahen, *Britain, the Sahara, and the Western Sudan, 1788-1861* (Oxford: Clarendon Press, 1964); Christopher Lloyd, *The Search for the Niger* (London: Collins, 1973); Sanche de Gramont, *The Strong Brown God: The Story of the Niger River* (Boston: Houghton Mifflin Company, 1975; reprinted in paperback, 1991).

John Colter

(1774? - 1813)

John Colter was an American fur trapper who was the first Westerner to see the area of present-day Yellowstone and Grand Teton parks.

John Colter was born near Staunton, Virginia in 1774 or 1775, the son of a farmer. Following the American Revolution, he joined the tide of Americans heading west and moved into Kentucky and Tennessee. He enlisted as a private in the company of **Meriwether Lewis** and **William Clark** at Louisville, Kentucky, on October 15, 1803. Colter worked as a hunter during the Lewis and Clark expedition and is often mentioned in the leaders' journals. As the expedition returned back down the Missouri in 1806, Colter requested that he be allowed to join Joseph Dickson and Forrest Hancock to go fur-trapping in the Rocky Mountains. The three men left the Lewis and Clark encampment on August 16, 1806.

Colter and his two partners trapped for furs during the winter and spring of 1806-1807. He then returned alone down the Missouri. Along the way, he met a fur trading expedition led by Manuel Lisa at the mouth of the Platte River. Lisa convinced Colter to go to join them. They went as far as the Yellowstone River and its juncture with the Bighorn River (in present-day Montana), where, on November 21, they started building Fort Raymond, the first American fur-trading post in the Louisiana Territory. Colter was sent out alone to scout and to tell the Native Americans that Lisa wanted to trade for furs.

Colter's route during that winter is not exactly known. It is thought that he headed upstream on Pryor's Fork of the Yellowstone and then went westward across the Pryor Mountains, along the Clark's Fork of the Yellowstone, across the upper Big Horn Basin to the Sunlight Basin on what is now the eastern edge of Yellowstone Park. From there, he headed southeastward to the Shoshone River. In the canyon of the North Fork of the Shoshone River he saw the tar pits, thermal springs, geysers and sulfur vents that later trappers named "Colter's Hell." He crossed the continental divide at Togwotee Pass and looked down on the valley that is now called Jackson Hole. He then traveled through the area of Grand Teton National Park in northwestern Wyoming, leaving a stone marked "1808" at Pierre's Hole. He continued north through present-day Yellowstone Park past Yellowstone Lake back to the Shoshone River and Fort Raymond.

In the summer of 1808 Colter was sent to the Three Forks of the Missouri River, east of what is now Butte, Montana. The area

was controlled by the Blackfoot tribe. Colter joined a group of Crows and Flatheads who were attacked by the Blackfeet. Colter was injured during the battle and could not walk. Stretched out in a pile of bushes, his accurate shooting was able to fight off the Blackfeet and win the battle for his allies.

In October 1808 Colter set out to trap with another member of Lisa's company, John Potts. Foolishly, they returned to the Three Forks area, where they were able to amass almost a ton of fur. However, at Jefferson Fork they were attacked by Blackfeet who shot and killed Potts and took the furs. Colter was captured and given a chance to live. He was stripped naked and given 30 seconds' headstart to run for his life. Colter outran all of them except for one. When they were the only two left, Colter turned upon him and killed the man with his own spear. Colter ran for five miles across a rocky plain between the Jefferson and Madison Forks.

Once he reached the Madison River, he dived under a mass of logs and beaver lodges and hid in an air pocket in the icy water until nightfall. He went six miles downstream and climbed up a sheer cliff. He walked, still without any clothes, the 250 miles to Fort Raymond, where he arrived after 11 days.

In the winter of 1808-1809 Colter went back to the Three Forks area to recover his traps. Once again he was attacked by Native Americans and narrowly escaped. He traveled down the Yellowstone and Missouri Rivers to the mouth of the Knife River, where he stayed at the Hidatsa village there in order to recover. There he met an expedition of the St. Louis Missouri Fur Trading Company heading upriver. He was persuaded to return with them.

Colter and a party of 32 men went back to the Three Forks area to build a fort. They arrived there on April 3, 1810. Nine days later they were attacked by Blackfeet, and five men were killed. Over the next few days more of the Americans were killed, and Colter decided that he had finally had enough. On about April 21, he and two others left the post and went back to Fort Raymond. The rest of the trappers and traders also dispersed, with one small group heading west and setting up the first American post west of the Rockies. Colter built himself a small dugout canoe out of a cottonwood tree and traveled 2,000 miles alone down the Missouri River, reaching St. Louis before the end of May.

Back in Missouri, Colter took up a farm near Dundee, not far from where **Daniel Boone** had settled. He married a young woman and settled down. However, a couple of years later he became ill, either from "jaundice" (hepatitis) or smallpox, and died in November 1813.

Where to learn more

Colter did not himself write about any of his exploits. The earliest sources we have are Henry M. Brackenridge, *Views of Louisiana, Together with a Journal of a Voyage up the Missouri River in 1811* (Pittsburgh: 1814); John Bradbury, *Travels in the Interior of America in the Years 1809, 1810, and 1811* (Liverpool, England: 1817; 2nd edition, London: 1819); Thomas James, *Three Years Among the Indians and Mexicans* (New York: 1846).

The best overall history of the fur trade is now somewhat out of date: Hiram M. Chittenden, *A History of the American Fur Trade of the Far West*, 2 vols. (New York: 1902; reprinted, Stanford, California: Academic Reprints, 1954).

An excellent modern biography of Colter, which details the route through Yellowstone Park outlined above, is Burton Harris, *John Colter: His Years in the Rockies* (New York: Charles Scribner's Sons, 1952). There is a biographical sketch of Colter by Aubrey L. Haines in volume 8 of *The Mountain Men and the Fur Trade of the Far West*, edited by LeRoy R. Hafen (Glendale, California: Arthur H. Clark Company, 1965-1972). His relations with Manuel Lisa are discussed in Richard E. Oglesby, *Manuel Lisa and the Opening of the Missouri Fur Trade* (Norman: University of Oklahoma Press, 1963).

Christopher Columbus

(1451 - 1506)

Christopher Columbus was an Italian mariner who sailed in the service of the King and Queen of Spain and made four voyages to the Caribbean and South America between 1492 and 1504.

Christopher Columbus was born in the city of Genoa in Italy some time in the fall of 1451. His family had lived in Genoa for at least as far back as three generations and were engaged in the manufacture and trading of woolen fabrics. Nothing more is known about Columbus's early life until he was in his early twenties when, in letters written much later, he described his career as a mariner sailing on merchant and war ships in the Mediterranean.

In May 1476 Columbus was a crew member of a convoy of ships that left the Greek island of Chios bound for Lisbon, England and Flanders. The convoy was attacked by a French and Portuguese war fleet near the southern Portuguese port of Lagos. Columbus's ship was wrecked, and he made it to shore. He then went to Lisbon where his younger brother Bartholomew already lived.

Once settled in Lisbon, Columbus took advantage of the opportunity to learn mathematics and astronomy. According to a note written much later by his son Ferdinand, he took part in a voyage in February 1477 that sailed to Iceland and even farther north. In 1478 he was captain of a merchant ship that sailed to the island of Madeira on an unsuccessful trading mission. In that same year, he married the widow of the captain of Porto Santo in Madeira and settled there where his son Diego was born.

Sometime in the early 1480s Columbus made a voyage to the Portuguese trading fortress of São Jorge da Mina in what is now Benin on the west coast of Africa. On his return from that trip Columbus began to push his "great idea": that it would be faster and easier to get to Asia by sailing westward across the Atlantic than by trying to sail around Africa into and across the Indian Ocean as the Portuguese were then trying to do. Contrary to legend, all educated Europeans knew that the earth was a sphere. In theory, Columbus's idea would work, but no one had any idea about the size of the globe. In making his arguments, Columbus used guesses by others and his own speculation that made the distance much smaller than it actually is. For example, he claimed that the distance from Lisbon to Japan would prove to be about 2,400 nautical miles. It is actually more than 10,000.

Starting in 1484, Columbus tried to sell his idea to the Portuguese king and court. He received a hearing from King João II who referred the matter to his court advisers. They concluded that Columbus's estimates of distance were way too small. By this time, Columbus's wife had died, and he took his small son Diego and left Portugal. They traveled by ship to the Spanish port of Palos de la Frontera near the Portuguese border. There, Columbus put his son in a boarding school run by Franciscan monks at the monastery of La Rábida while he traveled around Spain trying to sell his idea to the Spanish court. As it happened, the Franciscans were interested in the possibility of foreign missions and gave Columbus a letter of introduction to an influential Spanish nobleman, the Count of Medina Celi.

Columbus traveled to the city of Córdoba in January 1496 but missed the Spanish king and queen who had moved on. He stayed there and found support among the Genoese colony in the city. He met a young peasant woman named Beatriz Enriquez who became his mistress, and in 1488 they had a son named

Christopher Columbus.

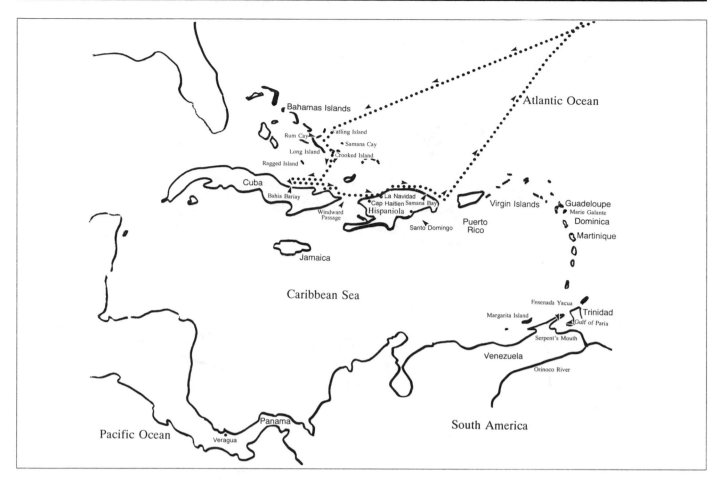

Columbus's discovery of the New World, 1492.

Fernando. The Spanish monarchs returned to Córdoba, and on May 1, 1486 Columbus was received by Queen Isabella. He explained his idea, and she appointed a royal commission to study its practicality.

This commission, called the Talavera Commission, could not come to any decision, but it thought enough of Columbus's idea to give him a modest annual retainer to support him while it made its deliberations. In the meantime, he continued to try to get support for his plans from other monarchs. He wrote to the Portuguese king in early 1488, who invited him back to Lisbon. He went there later in the year, only to be present in December 1488 for the return of **Bartolomeu Dias** from having rounded the Cape of Good Hope at the southern end of Africa. The Portuguese had finally found the passageway to India and were no longer interested in Columbus. Columbus's brother Bartholomew sold his business and traveled to England and France to try to get support there—without success.

In late 1490 the Talavera Commission issued a report that said that Columbus's idea was unsound: the world was much larger than he thought, and there was no way that a ship could sail that far. Columbus went back to the monastery of La Rábida, where the monks urged him to try once more with the Queen. She

consented to see him, and in December 1491 he traveled to her court outside the city of Granada where the Spanish were engaged in the last battle to defeat the Muslim Moors who then ruled southern Spain.

There followed a new commission and a new recommendation by the Royal Council. The commission said that Columbus should be allowed to try, but the Council recommended refusal because Columbus had upped his demands: he now wanted to be Admiral and viceroy of any lands he discovered. The Queen reluctantly concurred with this recommendation, and in January 1492 Columbus made plans to leave Spain and try his luck in France. Four miles outside of the Spanish camp a messenger caught up with Columbus and told him that thanks to the intervention of a court official, Luis de Santangel, the Queen had changed her mind: she would sponsor the voyage.

In April 1492 Queen Isabella and King Ferdinand of Spain signed an agreement with Columbus called the Capitulations that agreed to sponsor him on a voyage of exploration. He would be named Admiral, become the governor of any lands he discovered, and would have the right to 10 percent of any merchandise obtained in the new lands free of taxes, and these rights would be hereditary in his family.

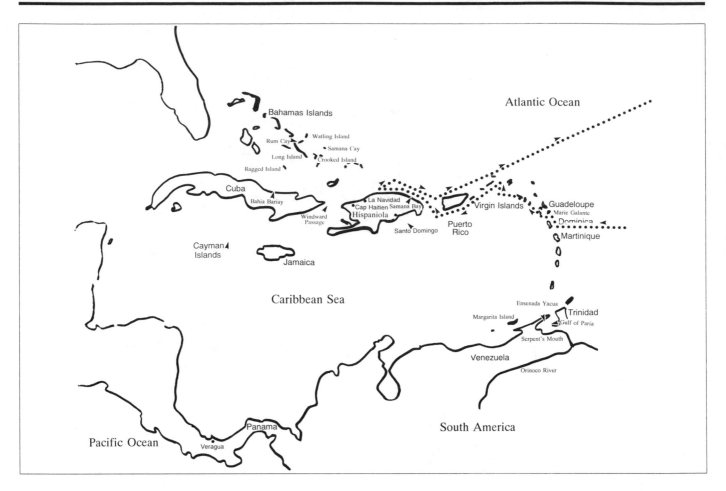

Columbus's second voyage in the Caribbean Sea, 1493-1496.

Columbus returned to the little port of Palos and obtained three ships: the *Santa Maria* with himself as captain and Juan de la Cosa (who would later make a famous map of the discoveries) as master; the *Pinta*, with Martín Alonso Pinzón as captain; and the *Niña*, with **Vicente Yañez Pinzón** as captain. The total crew of the three ships was about 90 men and boys. The fleet sailed on Friday morning, August 3, 1492. At the same time that it was leaving it passed ships of Jews who were being expelled from Spain. The three ships passed the entrance to the Tinto River at 8:00 a.m. on the morning of the 3rd.

Columbus sailed first to the Canary Islands off the coast of Africa. In previous sailing in that latitude he had noticed that the winds blew from the east, and it was also the same latitude as where he expected Japan to be. The *Pinta* had to undergo some repairs at Las Palmas, the main port of the Canaries. They left Las Palmas on September 6 and because of still winds were not out of sight of the Canaries until the 9th.

After that day, Columbus's three ships had remarkably good winds and were able to make very good time, traveling as much as 150 miles a day and made 182 miles on one day. On September 16 they came to the edge of the giant seaweed fields that were later named the Sargasso Sea. On September 17 the crew noticed that for the first time the North Star was east of where their compasses said that north should be. Columbus explained this, correctly, to his crew that "it appears that the Star moves like other stars, and the compasses always point true." Starting on September 19, they had 10 days of light winds and were only able to travel 234 miles over the next five days.

By this time, if Columbus's original theories had been right, they should have been in sight of land. In fact, at one point the crew members thought they spotted land, but it turned out to be a low-lying cloudbank. The wind picked up on the 26th and they were able to travel a further 382 miles by October 1. The wind increased further, and they traveled 710 miles between October 2 and October 6. On October 10 the crew began to become mutinous and wanted to turn back, but on October 11 signs of land became apparent—branches with green leaves and flowers floating in the water—and the crew calmed down. At about 10 p.m. on the night of October 11 Columbus thought he saw firelight on the horizon. At about 2 a.m. on the morning of October 12 the lookout on the *Pinta*, Rodrigo de Triana, saw white cliffs in the moonlight and called out "Tierra! tierra!" (Later

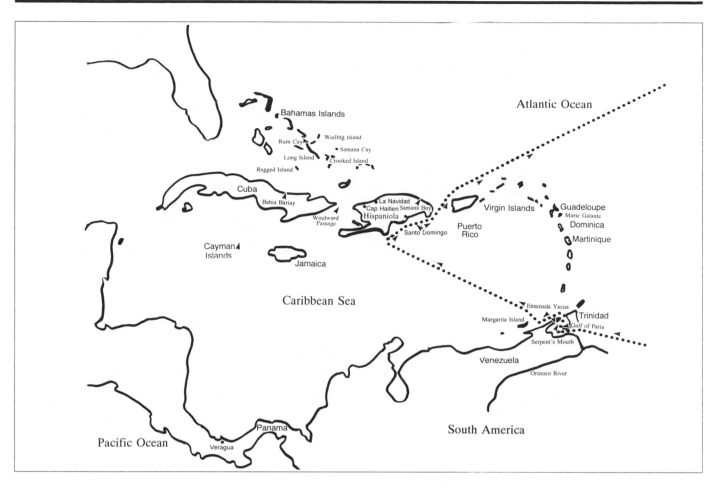

Columbus's third voyage, 1498.

Columbus awarded himself the bonus for being the first to sight land because he had seen the firelight in the distance.)

Columbus had landed on a small island in the Bahamas. The natives called it Guanahani; Columbus renamed it San Salvador (Holy Savior); and the general consensus has been that it was the island later known as Watling. However, recent evidence has shown that a small island farther south, Samana Cay, may be a likelier location. Columbus stayed on the island for two days. He met with members of the Taino tribe who were the inhabitants. Not knowing where he was, and always assuming that he had reached Asia, the "Indies," he called them Indians.

From San Salvador Columbus spent several days roaming around the Bahamas, visiting Rum Cay, Long Island, Crooked Island, Hog Cay, etc. None of them fulfilled the visions of wealth and material civilization that he had imagined. The Native Americans told him about another much larger island named Colba (Cuba), which he decided must be part of China or Japan. He left his anchorage at Ragged Island on October 17 and on the morning of October 28 he sighted Bahía Bariay on the north coast of Cuba. For the next month, Columbus sailed along the north coast of Cuba. Always looking for gold, he sent two of his men into the interior to visit the reputed capital of the land, which

he thought would be the city of the Great Khan (Beijing). They actually found a small village but brought back the first specimens of the tobacco plant that Europeans had ever seen.

While Columbus's ships were sailing along the northern coast of Cuba, Martín Alonso Pinzón suddenly left in the *Pinta* without telling Columbus to sail eastward to Great Inagua Island to follow up on a rumor of gold. Columbus with the *Santa Maria* and *Niña* left the coast of Cuba on December 5, 1492 and sailed across the Windward Passage to another large island which he named Hispaniola because it reminded him so much of Spain. The first landfall was at what is now the Haitian town of Môle St. Nicolas, named by Columbus because he landed there on December 6, the feast day of St. Nicholas.

Sailing eastward along the north coast of Hispaniola on December 17, Columbus was rewarded for all his troubles. He was met by a young chief, or *kaseke* (*cacique*) who was wearing gold ornaments, which he was very willing to trade for European goods. Farther east he met a more important chief who had even larger pieces of gold. Columbus entertained him and his people on board the *Santa Maria* on Christmas eve not far from the modern Haitian city of Cap Haïtien. After the festivities, everyone, including Columbus, went to sleep and the *Santa Maria* hit

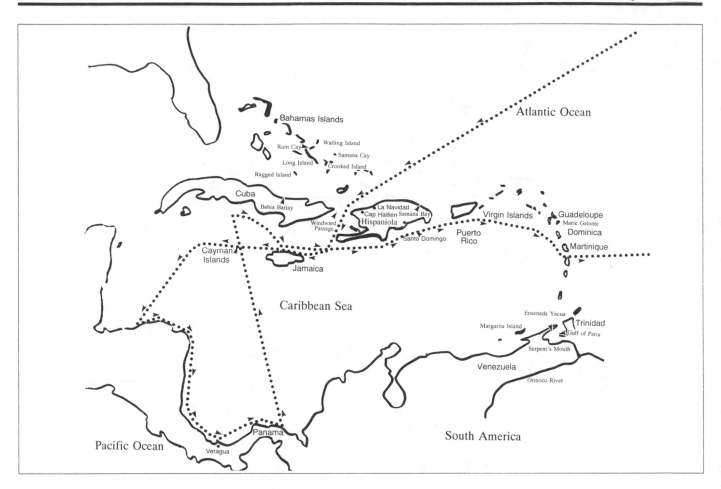

Columbus's final voyage to the New World, 1502-1504.

a coral reef. In spite of efforts to save her, the ship began to founder. Helped by the *cacique* and his followers, the Spanish were able to unload most of the goods that were on the ship and carry them to shore. Making the best of a bad situation, Columbus founded the first European settlement in the Americas. He named it La Navidad after the birthday of Christ; it was on a small bay where the Haitian village of Limonade-Bord-de-Mer now stands.

Columbus sailed from La Navidad on January 4, 1493 in the *Niña*. He left 21 men behind under the command of Diego de Harana, the cousin of his mistress. Two days later he encountered Pinzón in the *Pinta*, and the two ships sailed along the north coast of the Dominican Republic until they reached Samaná Bay on the eastern end of the island. They left from there for Spain three hours before dawn on January 18. He sailed north and then east, which unknown to him took him into the best prevailing winds. They had good weather and made good time until they reached the Azores where they ran into a bad storm that separated the two Spanish ships. Columbus anchored off the Portuguese island of Santa Maria, where most of his men were put in jail for a few days by the local governor who thought they were returning from an illicit voyage to west Africa.

Once Columbus left the Azores on February 24, he was hit by storms again and driven northward where he saw the mainland at Cabo da Roca at the mouth of the Tagus River in Portugal. He was summoned by King João II, who therefore received the first report of the discovery of America before Queen Isabella of Castile. After repairing the *Niña*, he sailed from Portugal on March 14 and returned to Palos in Spain the next morning.

Columbus had already sent a report of his voyage to Queen Isabella and King Ferdinand while he was in Portugal. In case it had not reached them, he sent another copy from Palos. On April 7 he got a letter back from them expressing their pleasure at his accomplishments and asking him to meet them in Barcelona and to start immediate preparations for a new voyage. He reached the court at Barcelona on April 20. He stayed there for three months during which time news of his discoveries began to travel through Europe. He was given various titles and honors by the King and Queen, detailed plans were made for a second voyage, negotiations were begun to divide the world into a Spanish and a Portuguese sphere, and the Native Americans who came back with Columbus began to spread syphilis in Europe, much as the Europeans spread smallpox and measles to the Americas.

Columbus's second voyage to America was much larger than the first. There were seventeen ships, the flagship was once again named the *Santa Maria*, but it was considerably larger than its namesake on the first voyage, and there were about 1,200-1,500 men (no women) aboard. They left the Spanish port of Cadiz on September 25, 1493. They stopped for ten days in the Canary Islands during the first part of October and then sighted land on the morning of November 3. Because it was Sunday, Columbus named this island Dominica.

Columbus did not land on Dominica but headed north to the small flat island of Marie Galante (now part of the French department of Guadeloupe). He anchored the next day off the large island of Guadeloupe, where he encountered the first Caribs, a Native American people different from the Arawaks he had met in the Bahamas and Hispaniola and who had a reputation for warlike fierceness. On the island of St. Croix in the Virgin Islands, a group of Spaniards in a boat were attacked by a group of Native Americans in a canoe. One of the Spaniards and one of the Caribs were killed; the other Caribs were captured and taken to Spain as slaves. Columbus's fleet reached Puerto Rico on the 19th and anchored off the west coast at Añasco Bay for three days.

Sailing from Puerto Rico the Spanish reached their goal—the settlement at La Navidad—on the night of November 27. When they went ashore the next morning, they found it in ruins and the unburied bodies of the Spanish were everywhere. No one knows what had happened, although it was supposed that either the demands that the Spanish had made on the Arawaks had turned them against the Europeans or the Spanish had fought among themselves, or it had been a combination of the two. Abandoning the site, Columbus took his new colonists 75 miles to the east to a small, shallow bay where he built a trading fort called Isabela, in what is now the Dominican Republic. It turned out not to be a good location, but Columbus laid out a main square with a church and "royal palace" and constructed 200 huts for the settlers.

Four days after landing at Isabela, Columbus sent **Alonso de Ojeda** into the interior mountains where he did in fact find gold. Columbus then sent a load of it and what he thought were spices with most of the ships back to Spain with the good news. He kept only five of the seventeen ships with him. After the main fleet had returned to Spain and he had led an expedition into the interior, on April 24, 1494 Columbus took three of the ships and went exploring. He sailed to the south coast of Cuba and then south to the island of Jamaica and then back north to Cuba, where he coasted along the entire south shore to the western end of the island. On June 12 a curious incident occurred. Columbus gathered all his men together and made them swear to an oath that the land they had been traveling along was not an island but part of the mainland of Asia. He was still convinced or was trying to convince himself that he had found the "Indies."

On his way back, Columbus revisited Jamaica and sailed along the south coast of Hispaniola. He intended to visit Puerto Rico, but he became ill and was forced to return to Isabela on September 29, 1494. When he reached there, he found that his brother Bartholomew had arrived from Spain. By this time the Arawak natives of Hispaniola had realized that the arrival of the Spanish meant their destruction, and they had collected a large force to try to drive them off the island. Columbus, Bartholomew, and Ojeda led a force into the interior that utterly defeated the Native Americans at the end of March 1495. After that time they were enslaved and became subject to European diseases and quickly died out. In the meantime news had traveled back to Spain that the colonists at Isabela were not doing well, and Columbus returned to Spain on March 10, 1496 to explain the situation to Ferdinand and Isabella. He left Bartholomew in charge, who quickly abandoned Isabela and moved the Spanish headquarters to the south side of the island at Santo Domingo.

Columbus traveled back to Spain on the *Niña* once again, accompanied by one other small ship. When he landed in Cadiz he did something that historians have not been able to explain. He adopted the coarse dress of a Franciscan friar and stayed at austere monasteries. Columbus lived that way for two years while in Spain, trying to convince Ferdinand and Isabella to send him out on a third voyage of discovery. He visited them sometime during the summer or early fall of 1496. They agreed to put him in charge of a small provisioning fleet to Hispaniola in mid-1497. The fleet did not actually leave until May 30, 1498, because Columbus had had trouble in finding ships and supplies.

On this trip Columbus decided to take a more southerly course, and he landed on the island of Trinidad on August 1. The next day he sailed into the Gulf of Paria that separates Trinidad from Venezuela. He passed the mouth of the great Orinoco River and seems to have realized almost at once that he had reached a continental land mass: this was his first view of the mainland of the Americas. On August 4 the Spanish ships were almost sunk by a tidal wave or tidal bore, and Columbus decided to leave the entrance to the Gulf of Paria as fast as possible. He named the spot the *Boca del Sierpe*, the Serpent's Mouth.

From there Columbus went north to a little bay on the mainland called the Ensenada Yacua, and there he and his officers went ashore, the first Europeans since **Leif Eriksson** to actually set foot on the mainland of America. He then sailed along the coast of Venezuela, which he declared to be the Terrestrial Paradise. He also observed from his observations of the North Star that the world was not a perfect hemisphere, the first person to note that. The Spanish also discovered the pearl fisheries off Margarita Island. Columbus then turned north and reached the south coast of Hispaniola near Santo Domingo on August 21, where he was greeted by his brother Bartholomew. He then stayed on the island and administered the gold mines that had been found in the interior.

In the meantime, the Spanish King and Queen had been hearing unfavorable reports about the administration of Hispaniola by the Columbus brothers. In July 1500 they sent Francisco de Bobadilla to replace Columbus and become the new governor. When he arrived in Santo Domingo, he found the Spanish inhabitants in a state of rebellion and immediately arrested Christopher, Diego, and Bartholomew Columbus. He sent them back to Spain in chains, where they arrived at the end of October 1500. Columbus stayed in chains for five weeks after his return until he was ordered released by Ferdinand and Isabella on December 12. He was ordered to report to the court at Granada, where he was received on December 17.

Columbus explained his side of the story and requested restoration of all his titles, including that of Governor. The King and Queen said they would make a judgment, which was not announced until September 1501. Columbus was allowed to keep his title of Admiral of the Ocean Sea, but a new governor, Nicolás de Ovando, was appointed and sent out to Santo Domingo with a great fleet.

The humbled Columbus asked to be allowed to lead another voyage of exploration, and this request was granted on February 26, 1502. Columbus sailed from Cadiz on May 9, 1502 with four small ships and a total of 143 men and boys, including his younger son Fernando and his brother Bartholomew. Columbus called this his "high voyage" because he traveled so far and encountered so many places unknown to the Europeans. He arrived in Santo Domingo on June 29 in the middle of a hurricane, but Governor Ovando would not let him enter the harbor. He then sailed across the Caribbean to the coast of Honduras where he ran into another storm. Columbus sailed southward along the coast of Central America looking for a passageway west. Of course by the time he reached Panama, he was very near the Pacific, but it was to be a few years until **Vasco Nuñez de Balboa** would actually cross the isthmus. By this time, Columbus realized that he had found a continent different from Asia, and that the as-yet-unnamed Americas stood between him and the "Indies" he had been searching for.

Columbus tried to found a new colony at a place called Veragua in western Panama. It was highly unsuitable: it is one of the rainiest places in the world and the Native Americans were definitely hostile. He left there on Easter Sunday, April 16, 1503 and sailed eastward to what he thought was the longitude of Santo Domingo. He then turned north but ended up in the Cayman Islands and on May 12 on the western end of Cuba. By now Columbus's two remaining ships were in very bad condition, leaky and missing sails. It took them until June 10, 1503 to fight their way eastward across the south coast of Cuba. Then, Columbus decided that if he was to make any progress before his ships sank, he would have to put out into the open sea. However, they started leaking so badly that he was forced to turn to Jamaica and run both ships aground on June 23, 1503.

Columbus and his 116 remaining crew members were forced to spend a year at St. Ann's Bay in Jamaica. They were rescued by sending one of the crew members, Diego Mendez, by canoe across the Jamaica Channel to Hispaniola. He reached Santo Domingo in August 1503, but Governor Ovando would not let him charter a rescue ship. While he was away, Columbus was faced with a mutiny on New Year's Day 1504, when a group of men tried to leave on their own but were forced to return. On February 28, 1504 Columbus frightened the Native Americans by correctly predicting a lunar eclipse and used that as a tool to make them supply the Spaniards with food.

At the end of March 1504 a passing Spanish ship revealed that Governor Ovando knew of Columbus's predicament but refused to let him be rescued. This led to a pitched battle between Columbus's followers and the mutineers on May 29. But Diego Mendez was finally able to charter a vessel and reached Jamaica at the end of June 1504. It was a small caravel that leaked so badly that it took six and a half weeks to get back to Santo Domingo. There, Columbus chartered another boat and left for Spain on September 12, 1504. He did not arrive until November 7.

Columbus was ill by this time and retired to a house in Seville. He received word of Queen Isabella's death on November 26. He was actually financially well off as a result of the share he got of Spain's newfound gold in Hispaniola. He stayed in Seville and recovered and was received by King Ferdinand at Segovia in May 1505. He tried to get the king to allow him to lead another expedition but had no success. He followed the court as it traveled around Spain and moved into a house in the city of Valladolid in April 1506. There he made his last will on May 19, making his son Diego his principal heir. He died the following day.

Where to learn more

The documentary records on Columbus's voyages can be found in Samuel Eliot Morison, ed. *Journals and Other Documents on the Life and Voyages of Christopher Columbus* (New York: Heritage, 1963).

There is an enormous amount of literature on Columbus, and with the 500th anniversary of his first voyage this is increasing exponentially. Any library will have several books dealing with Columbus. A good place to start is with two excellent books that present exactly contradictory viewpoints of the explorer. The first is Samuel Eliot Morison's *Admiral of the Ocean Sea* (Boston: Little, Brown & Co., 1942; reprinted Boston: Northeastern University, 1983), which presents the "traditional" view of Columbus—that he was a great hero who changed the course of human history. Morison's vast research and inspired writing can also be found in *The Great Explorers: The European Discovery of America* (New York: Oxford University Press, 1978; reprinted in paperback, 1986).

The "revisionist" viewpoint is best summarized in a book by Kirkpatrick Sale that caused great controversy when it was published: *The Conquest of Paradise: Christopher Columbus and the Columbian Legacy* (New York: Knopf, 1990; reprinted in paperback, New York: Penguin, 1991). His picture of Columbus is that of a bumbling fool whose greed and brutality started a process that upset the world's ecological and human balance. Both Morison and Sale include extensive bibliographies to back up their arguments.

The recent evidence that Columbus's first landfall was on Samana Cay is presented in Joseph Judge, "Where Columbus Found the New World," *National Geographic* (November 1986, pp. 566-599). The January 1992 edition of the *National Geographic* magazine started off the anniversary year with articles about Columbus's life and the excavation of the site of Isabela.

Frederick Albert Cook

(1865 - 1940)

Frederick Albert Cook was an American doctor who went on expeditions in both the Arctic and Antarctic and then claimed to have been the first man to reach the North Pole, although it is likely that he never went there at all.

Frederick Albert Cook was born on June 10, 1865 in Callicoon in Sullivan County in upstate New York, one of five children of a German immigrant. He worked his way through medical school by working as a milkman and took up the practice of surgery in Brooklyn. Thrilled by tales of polar exploration, in 1891 Cook answered an ad in the Brooklyn *Standard-Union* calling for volunteers to join **Robert Edward Peary** on a trip to the Far North. To Cook's amazement he was accepted. He served as doctor and ethnologist on Peary's expedition to Inglefield Gulf in Greenland in 1891.

Frederick Albert Cook.

Following Cook's return he tried to get the resources together to mount an American expedition to the Antarctic. He was not successful and sailed instead as a doctor with a Belgian expedition under the command of Adrien de Gerlache in 1897 on the *Belgica*, which had **Roald Amundsen** as first mate. Landings were made on the Palmer Archipelago in January 1898 and important geological and zoological investigations were carried out there. In February they sailed to Alexander Island.

Then, in early March 1898 at 71°30'S, the *Belgica* was trapped by the ice and drifted for a year to the south of Peter I Island. It was the first ship to spend the winter in the Antarctic, and Cook and the other members of the expedition were the first to live through that experience. The sun disappeared for a period 70 days on May 15, and the crew suffered from anemia, due to the unsuitable rations, and from depression. Daylight returned in July, but it was another six months before the ship could get free to start home in the spring of 1899. During this time Cook showed much ingenuity: he dug in the snow around the ship for seal carcasses for food, sewing warm clothing into blankets, and making a mattress of seal skins to protect the ship's sides from the ice.

In 1906 Cook made a trip to Alaska and claimed to be the first person to have climbed Mt. McKinley, which at 20,320 feet is the tallest mountain in North America. In later years this claim was shown to be false when his Alaskan guide came forth and said that they had, in fact, climbed a nearby peak that was only 8,000 feet high and had then faked photographs and Cook's diary.

On his return from Alaska, Cook was invited by a millionaire friend, John R. Bradley, to accompany him on his private yacht on an expedition to hunt polar bears in northern Greenland. Once they reached their base at Anoatok, near Etah in northern Greenland, Cook suddenly announced that he was going to make an assault on the North Pole from there, without any prior preparations at all. With the onset of winter Bradley left Cook behind with one volunteer, Rudolph Franke, at Anoatoak. During the winter the 250 Inuit who lived in the village helped Cook prepare for the coming journey by sewing fur garments, making sledges, and storing pemmican, the dried meat that was the chief food of polar explorers. They also constructed a collapsible boat.

In February 1908 Cook, Francke, nine Etah Inuit, 103 dogs and 11 sledges carrying 4,000 pounds of supplies crossed Smith Sound and then set off across Ellesmere Island and then westward to Cape Thomas Hubbard, the most northerly point of Axel Heiberg Island, a bluff about 1,600 feet high with a gravel beach in front of it, which they reached on March 8. Up to this point, the party succeeded in living off the land by hunting.

Here, Cook sent back the majority of his support group, including Franke, and with two Inuit named Ahwelahtea and Etukishook, 26 dogs, and the collapsible boat set off for the Pole on March 18, 1908. Twelve days later he claimed to have sighted land to the west at 84°50′N, which he named Bradley Land (no such land exists).

On April 21, according to Cook, he reached the Pole, after the usual hazards associated with crossing the Arctic ice. He stayed there 24 hours and then returned by way of the Ringnes Islands to the Grinnell Peninsula on North Devon Island, having gotten lost in fog on the way. They used the collapsible boat to travel through Jones Sound and reached Cape Sparbo on the north coast of North Devon by early September. There they took refuge in an abandoned Inuit village and a cave that the Inuit had carved out of a hillside. They lived in the cave for five months and were able to survive by killing small game with bows and arrows and muskoxen with lassos. They were pursued by polar bears who practically held them prisoner in their cave until the polar night set in on November 3, and the bears went into hibernation.

Cook and his two companions set off from North Devon on February 18 when the temperature reached -40°F. They were able to sledge their way across Baffin Bay and up the coast of Ellesmere Island until they were opposite Greenland. They had to travel farther north to a place where the ice formed a bridge between Ellesmere and Greenland. They lived off rotten seal carcass until that was gone and then they gnawed their sealskin boots and lashing. When they got back to Anoatoak in the spring of 1909 they found that Robert Peary had been through the village and had taken possession of Cook's storehouse that he had left in the charge of Rudolf Franke. This led to much recrimination later.

From Anoatoak Cook headed south to the Danish settlement at Upernavik so that he could tell the world about his trip to the Pole. He left all his instruments and papers behind at Anoatoak. He left Anoatoak in the third week of April 1909 and reached Upernavik in late May. His story was radioed to the world. He left Upernavik on June 20 on a Danish boat that sailed down the coast of Greenland and then took another one headed for Copenhagen. When Cook arrived in Denmark on September 4 he was a world hero and was besieged by the press. Peary regained contact with the outside world after his trip to the North Pole in a fishing village in Labrador on September 6.

Almost immediately Cook and Peary and their supporters began slinging accusations at each other. It was not clear at the time whether each or both of them was telling the truth, and there were partisans of every possible case—that either both had reached the Pole, neither had or one had and the other had not. As it turns out Cook was almost surely lying. He was never able to produce any proof of his journey, and the book that he claimed he left at Anoatoak with the records of the trip turned out to contain only scientific instruments—no diary.

Cook's two Inuit companions later claimed that they were never out of sight of Axel Heiberg Island. When the Canadian explorer **Vilhjalmur Stefansson** began making explorations in the same area in 1913-1918, he found numerous discrepancies in Cook's story. He believed that Cook and the two Inuit left Cape Thomas Hubbard and then traveled south along the west coast of Axel Heiberg Island. They then passed the winter in Jones Sound and returned to Greenland just as he later recounted. This was a remarkable journey of itself and would have earned Cook a place in the history of Polar exploration, but it was not a trip to the North Pole.

At first Cook's story was believed, but as more and more evidence came out he was widely perceived as a fraud, and the publication of his book, *My Attainment of the Pole* in 1911 did nothing to change that. By the time Peary died in 1920, it was widely acknowledged that he had been the first man to reach the North Pole. Cook's reputation was further damaged when he was convicted of stock fraud in Fort Worth, Texas in 1923 and spent seven years in jail. He spent the following years fighting libel suits against his critics. President Franklin Roosevelt granted him a full pardon for his stock fraud conviction just before his death from a stroke on August 5, 1940.

Where to learn more

Cook wrote about his expedition on the *Belgica* in *Through the First Antarctic Night* (London: William Heinemann, 1900). The North Pole escapade is recounted in *My Attainment of the Pole, Being a Record of the Expedition Which First Reached the Boreal Center, 1907-1909* (New York: Polar Publishing Co., 1911).

There are lots of books and articles on the question of what Cook did and why he did it. See, for example: Andrew Freeman, *The Case for Doctor Cook* (New York: Coward-McCann, 1961); Theon Wright, *The Big Nail: The Story of the Cook-Peary Feud* (New York: The John Day Company, 1970); Hugh Eames, *Winner Lose All: Dr. Cook and the Theft of the North Pole* (Boston: Little, Brown & Co., 1973);

Two excellent histories of Arctic exploration give interesting, and entertaining, histories of the Cook story: Jeannette Mirsky, *To the Arctic!: The Story of Northern Exploration from Earliest Times to the Present* (New York: Alfred A. Knopf, 1948) and Pierre Berton, *The Arctic Grail: The Quest for the North West Passage and the North Pole, 1818-1909* (New York: Viking, 1988; paperback edition, New York: Penguin, 1989).

James Cook

(1728 - 1779)

James Cook was an English mariner who led three expeditions to the Pacific Ocean, Antarctica, and the Arctic that were responsible for increasing human knowledge of the world's geography more than those of any other explorer.

James Cook was born on October 27, 1728 in the village of Marton, near Whitby in northern England, the son of a Scottish farm laborer. He received some education in the village school but left at an early age to do farm work. At the age of 17 he was sent to a coastal town to work as a grocer's assistant. Recommended by his employer, the following year he was apprenticed to a Whitby shipowner named Walker whose business was shipping coal from the mines of northern England to London and across the North Sea to Europe. Encouraged by Walker, Cook spent his spare time studying mathematics and navigation. At the end of his three-year apprenticeship, he sailed on various Whitby ships and in 1752 returned to work for Walker as a mate on one of his ships.

In 1755 hostilities started between Britain and France in their on-going struggle for control of North America. The British government began to gear up for war. Cook took advantage of this opportunity to join the Royal Navy even though it meant serving as an ordinary sailor. In doing so, he gave up the chance to be captain of one of Walker's colliers (a ship transporting coal). His ability was quickly recognized, however, and by 1757 he had risen to the rank of master, or warrant officer.

Cook served on board a ship that was involved in the siege of Quebec, which culminated in the capture of the capital of New France by James Wolfe in 1759. Following the British victory, Cook stayed in North America until 1762 as master of a ship engaged in mapping the coasts of eastern Canada. Cook's exceptional skill as a navigator and surveyor began to be recognized at this time. Some of his charts were used for over a century. In 1763 Cook returned to England and married Elizabeth Batts, who came from a family that made its living along the Thames waterfront in London. They bought a house on the outskirts of London, and over the next few years they had six children, three of whom died in childhood.

Following the end of the Seven Years' War in 1763, Cook accepted an appointment from the Governor of Newfoundland to survey and chart the coasts of that British colony. He spent each summer until 1767 carrying out that task, returning to London in the winter. In 1766 he witnessed a solar eclipse and wrote a paper about it for the Royal Society, the leading British

Captain James Cook.

scientific society. This was an unheard-of honor for a non-commissioned officer. The Governor of Newfoundland recommended Cook for his first command, of the schooner *Grenville*. He used it for his surveying work and sailed it back to England during the winter of 1767-1768.

In 1768 the Royal Society asked the British government to send a ship to the Pacific to study the transit of Venus across the sun, which would take place on June 3, 1769. It was thought that observations of this phenomenon from different locations could help to calculate the distance from the sun to the Earth. One of the places that the Royal Society wanted to observe from was the island of Tahiti, first visited by **Samuel Wallis** in 1767. The British Admiralty supported the voyage to Tahiti but were also interested in using it as an opportunity to investigate the Great Southern Continent that was thought to exist in the South Pacific.

Because of his demonstrated ability as a surveyor and navigator, Cook was chosen to command the expedition. He was

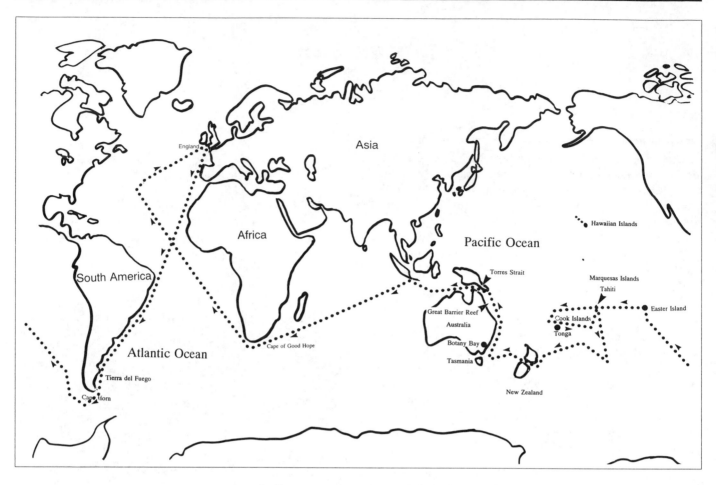

Cook's voyage on the *Endeavour*, 1768-1771.

therefore promoted to lieutenant at the age of 40. The ship he was named to command was a converted collier of the type that he had sailed on in Whitby. It was flat-bottomed and could maneuver well along tidal coasts. It was very sturdy and had a large storage capacity but compensated for these qualities by being very slow. The ship was refitted and renamed the *Endeavour*. Provisioned for 18 months, it carried 94 men on board, of whom 11 were civilians. Among the civilians was **Sir Joseph Banks**, an enthusiastic naturalist who was later to become President of the Royal Society. He paid for himself and several assistants to make various scientific observations during the course of the voyage. He brought with him two botanists, an astronomer, an artist, and four servants. Before they left, Cook was given an unpublished book by Alexander Dalrymple, who had discovered **Luis Vaez de Torres**'s report of a strait between Australia and New Guinea that had remained unknown for 150 years.

The *Endeavour* sailed from Plymouth on August 26, 1768. The ship stopped at Madeira and Rio de Janeiro. It reached Tierra del Fuego on January 11, 1769 and rounded Cape Horn, at the southern tip of South America. Even though it was mid-summer in the southern hemisphere, two of Banks's servants froze to death when they went ashore to collect specimens on

Tierra del Fuego. After leaving the coast of South America, Cook sailed the *Endeavour* generally west (rather than north along the coast as previous navigators had done) in hopes of spotting the Great Southern Continent. He found nothing before reaching Tahiti on April 11, 1769. At that time there was still no accurate way of calculating longitude, and Cook had to find the island by reaching its latitude and then sailing west until he ran into it.

Cook and the crew of the *Endeavour* spent three months at Tahiti, the first prolonged contact between the two peoples. Cook built a little fort, called Fort Venus, at the eastern side of Matavai Bay. The naturalists spent their time collecting samples of the local plants and animals. The artist made sketches of the biological specimens and of the landscape and the Tahitians. Cook had instructed everyone under his command to treat the population "with every imaginable humanity," and there were no serious difficulties during the visit. The major source of friction occurred when the Tahitians took some of the scientific instruments, and the Europeans had to put them back together again since the parts had been distributed.

The transit of Venus was observed (although the observations did not help in making the desired calculations), the coast of the island was charted, and the *Endeavour* sailed from Tahiti on July

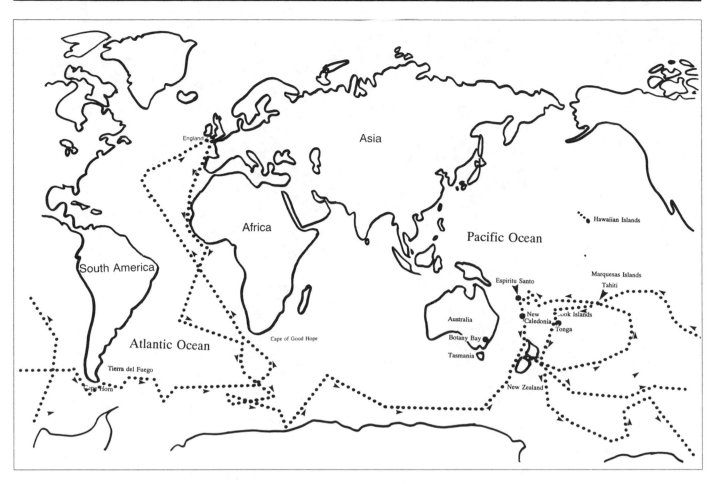

Cook's search for a southern continent, 1772-1775.

13, 1769. On board was a Tahitian chief named Tupia who proved very useful as a pilot and interpreter. On his advice, Cook visited the neighboring islands, which he named the Society Islands in honor of the Royal Society. Following his instructions, he sailed south as far as 40° without seeing any large landmass. He then took a zigzag course to the west until he sighted the east coast of New Zealand's North Island on October 6, 1769. He was the first European to see the land since **Abel Janszoon Tasman** in 1643.

Cook's relations with New Zealand Maoris were not as successful as with the Tahitians. On the third day after dropping anchor, he sent a boat ashore but it was driven away. On the third attempt, the Maori canoes would not stop after the Englishmen fired shots over their heads, and four Maoris were killed in the resulting struggle. Cook was very distressed that these first contacts had ended so badly.

Cook headed north along the east coast, meticulously charting the coastline. He did not reach the northern tip of New Zealand until the end of the year. Along the way, relations with the Maori improved but were always tenuous. Sailing south along the west coast, Cook came to the strait between the North Island and the South Island, which Tasman had spotted but had not sailed

through. Cook did so, showing that New Zealand is made up of two large islands. The strait was named Cook Strait. He spent a month at a large sheltered bay on the north tip of South Island, which he named Queen Charlotte's Sound, repairing his ship.

It took six months for the *Endeavour* to make its complete 2,500-mile circumnavigation of the islands, proving that they were not part of a continental landmass. On April 1, 1770 Cook left New Zealand and headed home. He chose the route around the Cape of Good Hope because it was safer than going around the Horn, and his ship had already been at sea for 18 months. On April 19, 1770 he sighted the southeast corner of mainland Australia, missing the island of Tasmania, which had been his goal. Sailing north for 10 days along the coast, Cook found an anchorage at Botany Bay, south of Sydney. There he had his first meeting with the Aborigines, who avoided all contact with the Europeans. Banks collected specimens of many species that were very different from anything known in Europe. The *Endeavour* left Botany Bay on May 7, 1770.

Cook continued northward, missing the entrance to Sydney harbor but naming Moreton Bay, the site of Brisbane, on May 17. Soon the *Endeavour* was within the treacherous waters of the Great Barrier Reef. The farther north that Cook sailed, the more

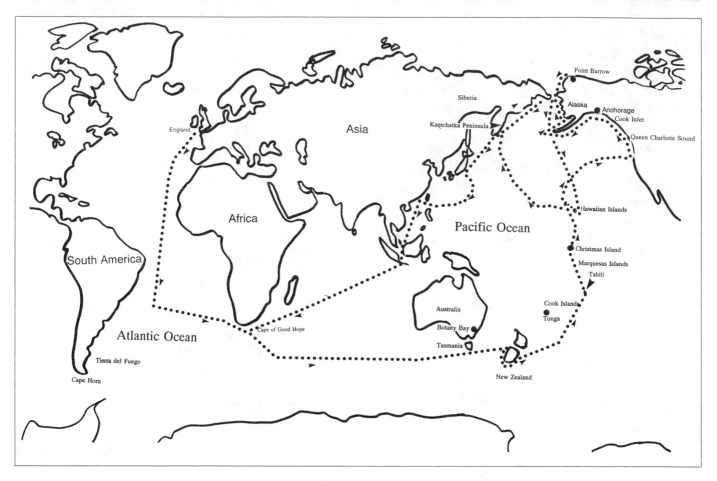

Cook's final voyage in search of the Northwest Passage, 1776-1780.

dangerous the waters became. For weeks the *Endeavour* moved very slowly while boats were sent ahead to take soundings, and men on yardarms tried to spot the reefs from above. They made it successfully through almost 1,000 miles when the ship struck a reef on the night of June 11, 1770. The ship was stuck for a night and a day. When the second high tide floated it off, it was necessary to work all of the pumps constantly in order to keep the ship from sinking from all the water it was taking on. Cook was forced to "fother" the vessel, a procedure by which a sail filled with rags, wool, rope ends, and dung is passed under the ship to plug the hole. It has been compared to putting a giant band-aid on the ship.

The ship sailed north until it reached the mouth of a small river where there was a secure anchorage. It was later named the Endeavour River and is the site of Cooktown in northern Queensland. There, the *Endeavour* was beached, and it was discovered that there was a large piece of coral caught in the hole, which had probably saved the ship. Cook and his men stayed there for six weeks, until August 6, 1770, repairing the ship. During that time they saw such typical Australian animals as the kangaroo and dingo for the first time.

Once the ship was repaired, Cook found a passage through the reef to the open sea. But the strong current and winds kept threatening to throw it back on the reef. At one point it looked as though it would certainly be wrecked against a large wall of coral when a small gust of wind blew it out to sea for a minute. Cook then spotted an opening in the reef and sailed back into the protected sea behind it. In his log, he wrote, "It is but a few days ago that I rejoiced at having got without the reef; but that joy was nothing when compared with what I now felt at being safe at an anchor within it."

The *Endeavour* therefore had to continue on its painstaking way north through the barrier reef. On August 21, 1770 the ship reached the northern end of Australia, and Cook was able to confirm that there was a strait between Australia and New Guinea, just as Torres had written. The English ship sailed through it and headed west for the Dutch East Indies, arriving in Batavia on October 10, 1770, where three months were spent in making repairs. Many of the men got sick from malaria and dysentery and died there or on the way across the Indian Ocean. Tupia was one of the casualties. The *Endeavour* reached England on July 12, 1771, not quite three years after leaving.

In spite of the fact that Cook's voyage had seemed to show that there was no large southern continent, it had not proven this conclusively. Cook therefore proposed that he lead another expedition in order "to put an end to all diversity of opinion about a matter so curious and important." This time he asked for two ships in case he encountered the kind of difficulties he had run into in the Great Barrier Reef and one of the ships was lost. The Admiralty approved and, following a recommendation of King George III who had met with Cook in August 1771, promoted him to commander. The *Endeavour* was no longer seaworthy, and, at Cook's request, two new Whitby colliers were bought and refitted: the 462-ton *Resolution* and the 340-ton *Adventure*.

Once again, Banks was scheduled to accompany Cook as the leader of the scientific party. This time he increased the number of his entourage and had a special deck and cabin constructed on the *Resolution* in order to house them. When Cook saw what he had been done, and how it affected the seaworthiness of his ship, he ordered it taken down. This infuriated Banks, who then declined to make the trip at all. (The two later made up and remained friends until Cook's death.) A German naturalist, Johann Reinhold Forster, was substituted in his place. William Wales served as astronomer, and a Swedish botanist, H. Sparrman, joined the expedition in Cape Town.

The two ships sailed from Plymouth on July 13, 1772 and reached Cape Town by the end of October. From there they sailed south toward Antarctica to look for a land that the French navigator Bouvet de Lozier said that he had spotted in 1739. Cook found nothing, and indeed the land was not part of a continental landmass but a small island that has since been named Bouvet Island. The ships sailed into seas that had many icebergs and ice floes. On January 17, 1773 Cook wrote: "At ¼ past 11 o'clock we crossed the Antarctic Circle, and are undoubtedly the first and only ship that ever crossed that line." In fact, he was the first navigator to have even come close to the circle, much less being the first one to cross it.

On February 8, 1773 the two ships lost each other in a fog, and Captain Tobias Furneaux, commander of the *Adventure*, headed immediately for the designated rendez-vous point in New Zealand. Cook, however, lingered in the Antarctic waters and did not turn northeastward until March 16, 1773. He looked for the Kerguelen and Crozet Islands that had previously been spotted by the French navigators of the same names, but he did not find them. He did prove that there was no landmass anywhere north of 60°S between the longitudes of Greenwich and New Zealand. Cook sailed more than 11,000 miles after leaving Cape Town, most of it where no human had ever been before.

Cook met up with Furneaux at Queen Charlotte's Sound in mid-April. Furneaux had spent some time at Tasmania, and he convinced Cook, erroneously, that it was part of the mainland of Australia and did not warrant further investigation. Therefore, on June 7, 1773 both ships headed out from New Zealand in an east-northeast direction to see if they could find any land. They went halfway to South America without seeing anything at all.

They then turned north and sailed among the islands of the Tuamotu Archipelago until they reached Tahiti on July 16, where they stayed for six weeks.

In September, the *Resolution* and *Adventure* left Tahiti and sailed west to the Tonga Islands, which had last been visited by a European when Tasman had gone there in the previous century. Because of the warm welcome he received, Cook named them the "Friendly Islands." Heading south to New Zealand, the two ships were separated in a storm. The *Adventure* was pushed far to the east and did not reach New Zealand until after Cook had already headed south towards Antarctica. Cook left a message in a bottle for the *Adventure*, but the two did not meet up again.

Cook explored the southern latitudes between New Zealand and South America, fighting his way through the ice much of the time. On January 30, 1774 the *Resolution* touched latitude 71°10′, about 1,250 miles from the South Pole. This was the farthest point south any ship had ever been, and the record stood until the explorations of whaling captain James Weddell 49 years later. As the ship headed south, midshipman **George Vancouver**, then 16 years old, hung from the bowsprit of the ship, yelling, "I am the farthest south man in the world!"

After he had finished these investigations, Cook was convinced that there was no southern continent north of the polar ice. "I will not say that it was impossible to get farther to the South," he wrote, "but the attempting of it would have been a dangerous and rash enterprise and what I believe no man in my situation would have thought of."

Rather than continuing on to Cape Horn, Cook turned north in early February to look for islands in the Pacific. He himself became dangerously ill, but, to the unanimous relief of the crew, he recovered. During the next six months the *Resolution* traveled to Easter Island; the Marquesas, whose last European visitor had been **Alvaro de Mendaña** in 1595; Tahiti, where the Englishmen stayed from the last week of April to mid-May 1774; and Espiritu Santo in Vanuatu. Cook charted the islands of the Vanuatu archipelago. On the way south to New Zealand, he spent 10 days on the island of New Caledonia, which he was the first European to see.

Cook returned to Queen Charlotte's Sound on October 18, 1774. He saw that Furneaux had removed his message but had left no reply so Cook had no idea where he had gone. In fact, he had headed east in the *Adventure* north of the latitudes where Cook was voyaging and had gone around Cape Horn to the Cape of Good Hope and then back to England, thereby becoming the first person to sail around the world in an eastward direction.

The *Resolution* stayed in New Zealand until November 11, 1774 and sailed to the east, staying in the range of 54°-55°S in one final attempt to find land between New Zealand and Cape Horn. There was none. The ship arrived at Tierra del Fuego a week before Christmas and spent the following two weeks surveying its south shores. Christmas was celebrated in a cove off Tierra del

Fuego, eating goose pie and drinking Madeira. On December 28 Cook rounded Cape Horn. Sailing into the South Atlantic, he looked for and found an island that had been spotted by a previous Spanish navigator. He named it South Georgia in honor of King George. He then went farther south and found the South Sandwich Islands, which he named after the First Lord of the Admiralty. Heading north, he wrote: "I was sick of these high latitudes where nothing is to be found but ice and thick fogs."

Cook reached Cape Town in March 1775, stayed there a month, and then took three months to sail north to England, arriving in Portsmouth on July 29, 1775. The most remarkable thing about the trip was that due to Cook's precautions not a single person on his ship died of scurvy, an unheard-of record. As a result of this accomplishment, he was elected to the Royal Society, which presented him with its gold medal. He was granted an audience by the King and was promoted to captain. In addition, he was given a position at Greenwich Hospital that allowed him the time to write his narrative of the voyage. It also allowed the chance to spend some time with his family for the first time in many years.

In fact, Cook did not enjoy this luxury for very long. In 1776 the British Admiralty decided that the answer to finding the long-sought-after Northwest Passage around North America was to approach the problem from the opposite direction—to look for it from the Pacific side. The First Lord consulted with Cook in February 1776, and he volunteered to lead the expedition himself, even though he was in poor health. The *Resolution* was refitted, and a new Whitby collier was commissioned as the *Discovery*, to be commanded by Captain Charles Clerke, who first had to be rescued from debtors' prison.

Cook sailed from England in the *Resolution* on July 12, 1776. His officers included Vancouver and William Bligh, who was later to become notorious as the captain of the *Bounty*. The *Resolution* arrived in Cape Town on October 18 and stayed there until the end of November, repairing some defects in the ships caused by the poor workmanship of the Naval dockyards. The two ships then headed south into the Indian Ocean and this time found Prince Edward, Marion, Crozet, and Kerguelen Islands. Cook landed in Tasmania on January 24, 1777 and from there went to New Zealand, where he stayed during February. Heading north, he became the first European to sight the Cook Islands. He spent two months on Tonga, where he heard about Fiji and Samoa but did not travel to those places.

Cook reached Tahiti for the last time in August 1777 and delivered some horses, cows and other domestic animals that were gifts from King George. He was suffering greatly from rheumatism, and a group of Tahitian women demonstrated their traditional techniques of massage therapy that greatly reduced the pain.

From Tahiti, Cook headed north toward Alaska, where he was to investigate possible routes east. Along the way, he found Christmas Island on December 25, 1777 and then made one of his most significant discoveries on January 18, 1778—the Hawaiian Islands, which he named the Sandwich Islands, in honor of his patron, the Earl of Sandwich, First Lord of the Admiralty. Cook did not linger in Hawaii on this occasion but continued his way northward.

Once in Alaska, Cook tried various routes to see if they connected with a passageway around America. The most promising was Cook Inlet, which is a large bay where the city of Anchorage now stands. However, like all his other investigations along the coast this one inevitably led nowhere. He sailed through the Aleutian chain and as far north as 70°44', near Point Barrow on the north coast of Alaska. He saw no way around either North America or Siberia south of the Arctic Ocean.

Cook decided to return to Hawaii to spend the winter. On the morning of January 17, 1779, Cook stepped ashore at Kealakekua Bay on the west coast of the "Big Island" of Hawaii. About 1,500 canoes had surrounded the two ships, and the islanders had come out to welcome Cook. They thought that he was the reincarnation of Lono, the god of harvests and happiness. Cook was unaware of this, but he treated the ceremony with the same solemnity and dignity as the Hawaiians.

Cook stayed on Hawaii until February 4, 1779. When he announced his departure it was obvious that his hosts were relieved. The presence of the foreigners, especially since they were gods and could be denied nothing, had been a strain on the society. Two days after they departed, the two English ships ran into a storm, and one of the masts on the *Resolution* was damaged. They were forced to return to Kealakekua Bay in order to make repairs. This time the Hawaiians were not happy to see the Europeans. When one of the sailors died, he was buried on shore, and the islanders learned that the Europeans were mortal. During the day of February 13, there was a confrontation on the shore when some of the Europeans' possessions were taken, and a chief was injured in the ensuing fight.

During the night of February 13, 1779, the small sailboat that was attached to the *Discovery* was stolen. The next morning, February 14, Cook went ashore, escorted by ten marines, to announce that he intended to take the local chief hostage until the boat was returned. A crowd began to form to prevent the chief from being taken. When they learned that one of their canoes had been fired on by the English ship, they became openly hostile and began to throw stones. Cook decided that he had to retreat and tried to make his way back down the beach to his boats. His men fired warning shots, and then the men off shore also opened fire even though Cook yelled at them to stop. As he turned to call out to them, he stumbled and the infuriated mob fell upon him. He was stabbed and clubbed, and his dismembered body was taken back to the village. Four of the marines were also killed. After a few days, the Hawaiians returned Cook's remains, and they were buried in the bay on February 22.

Following Cook's death, the two English ships sailed north during the spring and summer of 1779 to the Kamchatka

Peninsula and the coast of Siberia. Finding no passage, they sailed for home and reached England on October 4, 1780.

Where to learn more

When Cook returned from his first voyage, the Admiralty felt that he was not sufficiently "literary" to write the narrative of the expedition. Therefore, it commissioned Dr. John Hawkesworth to use Cook's journals as the basis for the official report, which was published as part of *An Account of the Voyages Undertaken by the Orders of His Majesty for Making Discoveries in the Southern Hemispehre and Successively Performed by Commodore byron, Captain Carteret, Captain Wallis and Captain Cook in the Dolphin, the Swallow, and the Endeavour*, 3 vols. (London: W. Strahan & T. Cadell, 1774). Cook's own journal was not published until 1893: W.J.L. Wharton, ed. *Captain Cook's Journal During His First Voyage Round the World* (London: E. Stock, 1893). Cook did write the narrative of his second voyage: *A Voyage Towards the South Pole and Round the World*, 2 vols. (London: W. Strahan, 1777). The account of the third voyage was written by Captain James King from Cook's journal and was completed by him: *A Voyage to the Pacific Ocean*, 3 vols. (London: G. Nicol & T. Cadell, 1784). Cook's journals from all three voyages were edited by J.C. Beaglehole: *The Journals of Captain James Cook on His Voyages of Discovery*, 3 vols. (Cambridge: Cambridge University Press for the Hakluyt Society, 1955, 1961 & 1967).

Cook was not the only person to keep and publish journals of his expeditions: Sir Joseph Banks, *The Endeavour Journal of Joseph Banks*, 2 vols., edited by J.C. Beaglehole (Sydney: 1962); Sydney Parkinson, *A Journal of a Voyage to the South Seas, in His Majesty's Ship the Endeavour* (London:1773); George Forster (Johann Reinhold Forster's son), *A Voyage Round the World*, 2 vols. (London: B. White, 1777); John Kenneth Munford, ed. *John Ledyard's Journal*

of Captain Cook's Last Voyage (Corvallis, Oregon. Oregon State University Press, 1963).

The first biography of Cook was written soon after his death by Andrew Kippis: *The Life of Captain James Cook* (London: G. Nicol and G.G.J. & J. Robinson, 1788). Since then, there have been many others: Arthur Kitson, *Captain James Cook* (London: 1907); Sir Joseph Carruthers, *Captain James Cook* (London: 1930); R.T. Gould, *Captain Cook* (London: 1935); Hugh Carrington, *Life of Captain Cook* (London: Sidgwick & Jackson, 1939); and Rear-Admiral J.R. Muir, *Captain James Cook* (London: 1939). One small volume that gives a useful summary of Cook's life and was very helpful in writing this account is James A. Williamson, *Cook and the Opening of the Pacific* (London: Hodder & Stoughton, 1946) as was Alan Villiers, "Captain Cook, the Man Who Mapped the Pacific," *National Geographic*, September 1971.

The pre-eminent Cook scholar is Professor J.C. Beaglehole, and his biography of Cook, *The Life of Captain James Cook* (Stanford: Stanford University Press, 1974) can be considered to be the best and most definitive ever published.

In addition to general biographies, there are studies of individual voyages: John Gwythir, *First Voyage* (London: Andrew Melrose, 1954) and Richard Hough, *The Last Voyage of Captain James Cook* (New York: William Morrow & Company, 1979). Alan Moorehead has written an interesting study of the effect of Cook's voyages on the native peoples of the Pacific and Australia: *Fatal Impact* (New York: Harper & Row, 1966).

General studies of Pacific exploration necessarily devote important sections to Cook and his voyages. Three of the most interesting and useful are: J.C. Beaglehole, *The Exploration of the Pacific* (Stanford: Stanford University Press, 1966); Andrew Sharp, *The Discovery of the Pacific Islands* (Oxford: Oxford University Press, 1960); and O.H.K. Spate, *Paradise Lost and Found* (Minneapolis: University of Minnesota Prss, 1988).

Francisco Vázquez de Coronado

(1510? - 1554)

Francisco Vázquez de Coronado was a Spanish official who led the first European expedition to the southwestern United States.

Francisco Vázquez de Coronado was born in Salamanca, Spain, into a family of the minor nobility. He arrived in Mexico in 1535 as a member of the party of Antonio de Mendoza, the first viceroy of New Spain, as Mexico was then called. He married Beatriz de Estrada, the wealthy heiress of the former treasurer of New Spain. He took part in putting down an uprising in the royal mines and in October 1538 was named governor of New Galicia, a province on the west coast of Mexico. As governor he had jurisdiction over Spanish explorations on the northern frontier.

Soon after taking over his new duties, Coronado was involved in outfitting **Estevanico**, a "Moorish" slave, and Fray Marcos de Niza, a Franciscan friar. They were headed north to verify reports of the fabulous "Seven Cities of Cibola" that had been brought to Mexico by Estevanico, who had been a companion of **Alvar Nuñez Cabeza de Vaca**.

Francisco Vázquez de Coronado, from a painting by Newell Convers Wyeth. The Bettman Archive.

Fray Marcos left the town of Culiacan on March 7, 1539. He returned alone about five and a half months later, Estevanico having been killed at the Zuni pueblo of Hawikuh. Fray Marcos said that he had seen the very rich and very large city of Cibola from a distance. Since there was no such place and since his own journal is contradictory, it is generally thought that Fray Marcos made the whole story up. Coronado, however, was impressed enough to travel with Fray Marcos to Mexico City to report to Mendoza.

Mendoza had long been interested in exploring north of Mexico and was convinced by the friar's stories. He decided to equip an expedition at royal expense and named Coronado to head it. Coronado assembled a force of about 300 Spaniards and nearly 1,000 Native Americans at the west coast town of Compostela. Mendoza traveled to Compostela to review the expedition in person before it started out on February 25, 1540. The Viceroy also sent two ships up the Gulf of California under the command of Hernando de Alarcón to support the expedition from the sea. These ships lost contact with Coronado but traveled 200 miles up the Colorado River.

Coronado traveled with his army to the town of Culiacán, the present-day capital of Sinaloa state. From there, he left on April 22 with an advance force of about 100 Spaniards, a number of Native Americans, and four friars. They traveled up the Yaqui River valley, where they founded the town of San Gerónimo, and Coronado left Melchor Díaz in charge. Díaz later went up the Colorado to try to find Alarcón and his ships. He did find a letter left behind by Alarcón but not the ships. He crossed the Colorado near Yuma, Arizona, and traveled four days in what is now California, the first European to do so. Meanwhile, Coronado and his men crossed the Gila River, and entered the Colorado Plateau. They reached Hawikuh in what is now western New Mexico on July 7, 1540. The Spanish had no difficulty in capturing the town but once inside they realized that it did not come close to matching Fray Marcos's glowing description. As a result, the friar was sent back to Mexico in disgrace—"such were the curses that some hurled at Fray Marcos that I pray God may protect him from them."

On July 15, 1540, Coronado sent Pedro de Tovar and Fray Juan de Padilla to the northwest to a province that was called Tusayan. They found the ancient Hopi villages in what is now northern Arizona. There they heard about a great river to the west. On August 25, 1540 Garcia Lopez de Cárdenas led a small group of Spaniards to find this river. They saw the Colorado from the edge of the Grand Canyon, the first Europeans to see the

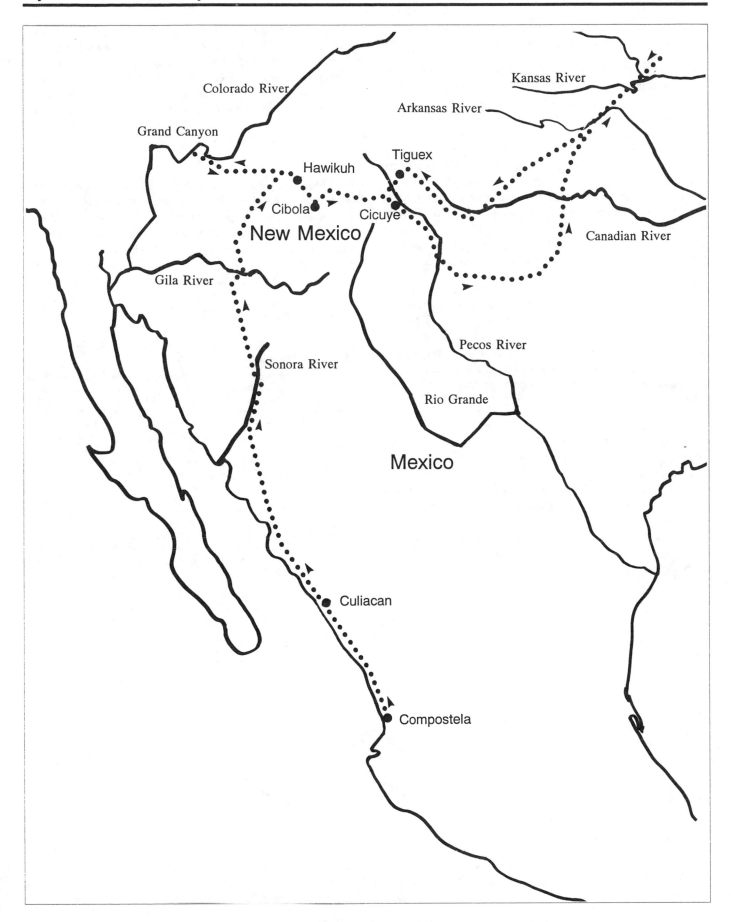

Coronado's expeditions to the American Southwest.

natural wonder. They spent three days trying to climb down the cliffs to the river but were forced to turn back.

On August 29, 1540, Coronado sent out another party to the east under the command of Hernando de Alvarado. He reached the pueblo of Acoma, perched high on a rock, where the inhabitants gave the Spaniards food. Alvarado then went to Tiguex in the Rio Grande valley north of Albuquerque, near present-day Bernalillo. He reported back that Tiguex had plenty of food supplies, and Coronado decided to make his headquarters there. During the winter of 1540-1541, the demands of the Spaniards for supplies and friction over women led to hostilities between the Europeans and Native Americans, the "Tiguex War." After capturing one pueblo, the Spanish burnt 200 of their captives alive. Several Spaniards were also killed during various engagements, and Coronado was wounded many times.

Alvarado had traveled to the east to Cicuye (on the Pecos River), where he had captured a Plains Indian (perhaps a Pawnee), whom the Spanish named "the Turk." The Turk told stories of the land of Quivira to the east that was ruled by a powerful king and where there was abundant gold. On April 23, 1541 Coronado left Tiguex to find Quivira and headed eastward into the Great Plains, where the Spanish saw enormous herds of buffalo.

As they saw the meager material possessions of the nomadic Plains tribes, the Spanish realized that they had been duped once again. Coronado sent his main force back to the Rio Grande with large supplies of buffalo meat. He then took command of a small detachment that headed north and east for 42 days, probably reaching central Kansas near the present-day town of Lyons. "Neither gold nor silver nor any trace of either was found." The Turk confessed that he had lied in order to draw the Spaniards into the interior, and the Spaniards strangled him to death. (It is said that Coronado opposed his execution.)

Coronado returned to Tiguex on October 2, 1541. Shortly after, he was seriously injured in a riding accident, being near death for some time. By then, the Spaniards were ready to return to Mexico. They left Tiguex in April 1542 and arrived in Mexico City in the late autumn. Mendoza was angry that the expedition had not found any wealth but gradually came to the view that Coronado had done the best he could. He reappointed him governor of New Galicia in 1544-1545.

In May 1544 a royal judge began a formal investigation of accusations of that Coronado was guilty of brutality to the Native Americans. He was relieved of his duties as governor but was cleared of all charges on February 19, 1546. He then became an official in the municipal government of Mexico City. In 1547 he testified in favor of Mendoza during an investigation of the Viceroy's rule. He was given a land grant in 1549 in reward for his services. His health declined, however, and he died in Mexico City on September 22, 1554.

Where to learn more

The main source for Coronado's journey (from which the quotes in the text above come) is the narrative called the *Relación de la Jornada de Cíbola*, written by Pedro de Castañeda, a soldier on the expedition. It can be found, along with other documents, including letters from Coronado to Mendoza and the King of Spain, in George Parker Winship, ed. *The Journey of Coronado, 1540-1542* (New York: 1904; 2nd edition, New York: 1922); Frederick W. Hodge and I.H. Lewis, eds. *Spanish Explorers in the Southern United States, 1528-1543* (New York: 1907); and George P. Hammond and Agapito Rey, *Narratives of the Coronado Expedition* (Albuquerque: University of New Mexico Press, 1940).

Several good, scholarly books have been written about Coronado's expedition: Carl O. Sauer, *The Road to Cibola* (Berkeley: University of California Press, 1932); A. Grove Day, *Coronado's Quest* (Berkeley: University of California Press, 1940; reprinted, 1964); Herbert E. Bolton, *Coronado: Knight of the Pueblos and Plains* (Albuquerque: University of New Mexico Press, 1949; reprinted, 1964); and Stephen Clissold, *The Seven Cities of Cíbola* (London: Eyre & Spottiswoode, 1961).

Gaspar Corte-Real

(1455? - 1501)

Miguel Corte-Real

(1450? - 1502)

Gaspar and Miguel Corte-Real were Portuguese noblemen who crossed the North Atlantic and explored the coast of Newfoundland.

G aspar and Miguel Corte-Real were two of the three sons of João Vaz Corte Real, a nobleman of Portugal who served as captain of the island of Terceira in the Azores. His sons also served in the Azores, and the family seems to have been much esteemed by King Manuel I.

Gaspar, the youngest son, served in the King's court. After his father's death in 1496, he moved to Terceira where he served as deputy captain of the island under his older brother Miguel. In a document dated May 12, 1500, King Manuel I authorized Gaspar to make a voyage of exploration and gave him property and trading rights over any lands that he discovered. The document mentions that he had previously made a voyage at his own expense, but nothing is known about its results, if any. On this new voyage, Corte-Real came upon a land that he named Terra Verde. This is thought to be the island of Newfoundland although some researchers think that it may have been Cape Farewell at the southern tip of Greenland (Terra Verde means "green land" in Portuguese). Corte-Real sailed back to Lisbon in the autumn of 1500.

Gaspar appears to have been anxious to follow up on his initial discoveries because the following year, in May 1501, he set out once more across the Atlantic. Two of the three caravels from this expedition returned to Portugal in October 1501, but the third ship, which had been captained by Gaspar, never returned.

The survivors reported that they had once again been to Terra Verde. There have been disagreements whether the land they visited was Labrador or Newfoundland and/or someplace farther south. They did bring back 57 Native Americans whom they had kidnapped. According to some accounts, these people seem to have come from two different regions.

Gaspar's brother Miguel obtained permission from the King to go search for his brother. He left Lisbon in May 1502 with three ships. Exploring along the coast of North America, they were supposed to rendez-vous at a place that may have been St. John's, Newfoundland. Only two of the ships showed up. The flagship, with Miguel Corte-Real on board, disappeared. King Manuel refused permission for the third son, Vasco Annes, to go look for his two lost brothers.

The voyages of the Corte-Real brothers did not lead the King of Portugal to press forward in exploring the North Atlantic. They were, however, the pioneering trips for an industry that became and still is very important to the Portuguese economy and diet—fishing for cod off the coast of Newfoundland.

Where to learn more

At the beginning of the twentieth century, Canadian historian Henry P. Biggar studied much of the documentary evidence about the voyages of the Corte-Reals and proposed theories about the lands they visited. He presented the results in *The Voyages of the Cabots and of the Corte-Reals to North America and Greenland, 1497-1503* (Paris: 1903) and *The Precursors of Jacques Cartier, 1497-1534* (Ottawa: 1911). Since then, the major work on the two Portuguese explorers has been that of Samuel Eliot Morison, who discusses them in *Portuguese Voyages to America in the Fifteenth Century* (Cambridge: Harvard University Press, 1940) and *The European Discovery of America: The Northern Voyages, A.D. 500-1600* (New York: Oxford University Press, 1971).

Hernán Cortés

(1485 - 1547)

Hernán Cortés was a Spanish conquistador *who conquered Mexico and sponsored many exploring expeditions in the Americas.*

Hernán Cortés was born into a family that belonged to the minor nobility in the town of Medellín in the Spanish province of Extremadura. At the age of 14 he was sent to the University of Salamanca to study law, but he stayed there for only two years. In 1504 his family raised the money to send him to the new Spanish colony of Santo Domingo, first visited by **Christopher Columbus** only 12 years earlier. On his arrival, Cortés was given a small land grant and named the public notary in the town of Azua, about 50 miles west of Santo Domingo. He stayed there seven years.

In 1511 the governor of Santo Domingo sent out Diego Velázquez to conquer the nearby island of Cuba. Cortés was engaged as Velázquez's secretary. Cortés and Velázquez quar-

Hernan Cortés.

reled, and Cortés was held in prison for a while. They were reconciled, and Cortés married Catalina Xuárez, the sister of Velázquez's mistress. He was appointed mayor of Santiago in the eastern part of the island and prospered mining gold and raising livestock.

In 1517 Velázquez sponsored a voyage by Francisco Hernández de Córdoba to the Yucatan Peninsula on the American mainland. This force was met by armed Maya warriors and suffered heavy casualties but brought back reports of a highly civilized people. In April 1518 Velázquez sent out his nephew Juan de Grijalva with a larger expedition to investigate the reports. Grijalva landed on the island of Cozumel at the eastern end of Yucatan and then sailed along the coast to a place about 50 miles from the modern city of Veracruz. There he was met by emissaries sent by Montezuma, the Aztec ruler of Mexico. Grijalva sent one of his lieutenants, **Pedro de Alvarado**, to report to Cuba and to carry back some of the gold they had found. Grijalva followed in November.

During Grijalva's absence, Velázquez had recruited Cortés to lead the next expedition to the mainland. As reports came back from Mexico, Cortés had no trouble in recruiting his countrymen to join the venture. At his headquarters in Santiago he assembled a large company of men (and one Spanish woman) and a great quantity of supplies. Velázquez began to worry about Cortés's intentions, but before he could do anything, Cortés left Santiago on November 18, 1518. He sailed along the south coast of Cuba to the port of Trinidad where he enlisted Alvarado and other soldiers. His final force consisted of about 550 soldiers, 100 sailors, 14 cannon, and 16 horses.

Cortés followed Grijalva's lead and sailed to Cozumel. There, he learned about two castaways from a Spanish ship that had been wrecked on the coast of Yucatan in 1511. He was able to locate one of the men, Jerónimo de Aguilar, who acted as Cortés's interpreter. The Spaniards then sailed along the coast to Tabasco, near the mouth of the Grijalva River. When the inhabitants of the local town resisted Cortés's demands for supplies, he attacked and captured it. On the sixth day, the Native Americans from the area massed in a large army and tried to push the Europeans off their shores, but they were defeated by the European artillery and cavalry.

As part of the reparations they were forced to pay to the Spanish, the Tabascoans turned over a number of slaves, including a young woman named Malinche, whom the Spaniards called Doña Marina. She was from a chiefly family in a neighboring area and spoke Nahuatl, the language of the Aztecs. She served as

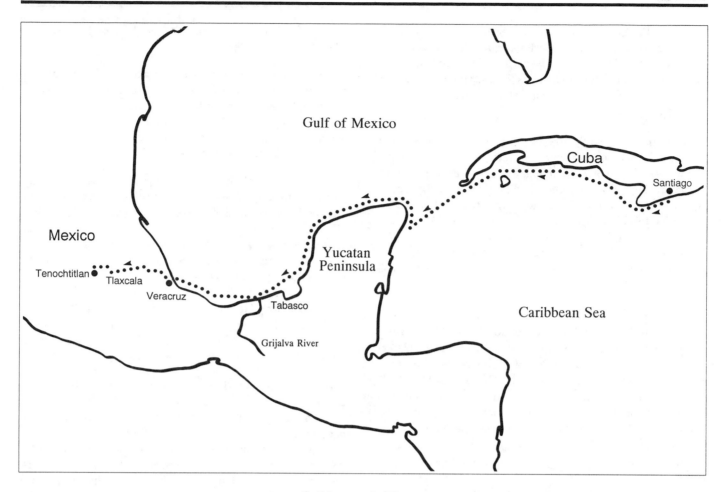

Cortés's conquest of Mexico.

translator from Nahuatl into Maya for Aguilar. She later became Cortés's mistress and, oftentimes, his spy.

Cortés and his army made their second landing farther west, near present-day Veracruz. He anchored there on the Christian holiday of Good Friday and was met by a large contingent of the local dignitaries on Easter Sunday, 1519. It was then that Cortes heard about the legends concerning the Aztec god Quetzalcoatl and of his expected return from over the sea. He also received his first embassy from the Aztec king Montezuma. Montezuma thought that Cortes was Quetzalcoatl. He was also worried about some recent grim omens that his astrologers said were predictions about the fall of the Aztec dynasty. He forbade the Spaniards to come to his capital of Tenochtitlan (on the site of today's Mexico City).

Cortés decided that he needed a base camp and so built the town of Veracruz. He received word that Velázquez had been named commander of any mainland settlements that were founded. To counter this, Cortes loaded one ship with all the treasure he had captured thus far and sent it back to Spain, putting himself under the direct rule of the King of Spain. He then had the remaining ships destroyed. By these means he showed his followers, many of whom were unhappy, that they would have to find their destiny in Mexico because they could not return to Cuba.

Cortés left Veracruz on August 15, 1519. He was accompanied by 300 foot soldiers and 15 cavalry. His route led onto the plateau of Mexico via Jalapa, Xocotla, and Tlaxcala. Cortes succeeded in forming an alliance with the independent state of Tlaxcala, and 6,000 Tlaxcalan volunteers went with him on his march to Tenochtitlan. As he pushed on through Mexico, he received more embassies from Montezuma. They brought rich gifts that made the Spaniards even more greedy, but they always tried to keep Cortes from advancing. But he was all the more eager to go on.

At Cholula, Cortes narrowly escaped a plot to destroy his force. Doña Marina found out about the conspiracy, and Cortés forestalled it by gathering 6,000 Cholulan warriors in the main square and then mowing them down with gunfire. From there, the Spanish force climbed the mountains through the snowy pass between the spectacular volcanoes of Popocatépetl and Iztaccíhuatl to look down upon the Valley of Mexico and the great city of Tenochtitlan, which they entered on November 8, 1519.

At first, the Spanish were welcomed by Montezuma, but their position seemed precarious. Cortés decided that he would be safer if he took Montezuma as hostage, and he was installed in the Spanish quarters, where he was effectively made a prisoner. He lived with the Europeans and gave them many gifts, including much gold.

Montezuma apparently believed that Cortés was indeed a god and that he had to obey him. However, in April 1520 the Spaniards took over an Aztec temple and turned it into a shrine to the Virgin Mary. Montezuma then told Cortés that the Aztec gods had told him that he must kill Cortés but advised him to leave the city before this happened. At just this time, in early May 1520, Cortes heard that Pánfilo de Narváez had been sent to Mexico by Velázquez to arrest him. Cortés decided to leave for the coast but, in agreement with Montezuma, left Alvarado behind with a small force.

At Veracruz Cortés fought and won a battle with Narváez and convinced most of the defeated soldiers to join him. On his return to Tenochtitlan, he found that Alvarado had made the population very angry by attacking an unarmed and peaceful religious procession. In order to calm them down, Cortés forced Montezuma to appear before them, but the angry crowd stoned him to death. Cortés and his men then left the city in the early morning of July 1, 1520, an event the Spanish called the *Noche Triste*, the "Sorrowful Night." As they left over the causeway that led out of the city, the Spaniards were attacked and at least 450 were killed. At the town of Otumba the Spanish turned and fought back and were able to drive off their attackers.

The Spanish retreated to Tlaxcala where they found that their allies were still loyal. There, the Europeans recuperated. In the meantime, smallpox, a disease introduced from the West, broke out and decimated the Aztec forces. Montezuma's successor died during the epidemic and was replaced by the war chief Cuauhtemoc. Spanish reinforcements continued to arrive from Cuba. At the end of December 1520 Cortés left Tlaxcala and headed back to the Valley of Mexico. He captured the small towns around the capital and cut off its supplies of water and food. Thousands of Aztecs died from hunger and disease. Several pitched battles took place, and the Spaniards gradually advanced on the city. By July 25, 1521 Cortés had taken the central square and controlled most of the city. Cuauhtemoc surrendered on August 21, 1521. He was later tortured to reveal where there was supposedly hidden treasure.

Cortés immediately started on the task of rebuilding Tenochtitlan, which became the Spanish city of Mexico. His wife arrived unexpectedly from Cuba in June 1522. She died "in mysterious circumstances" three months later. On October 22, 1522, Cortés's exploits were rewarded by King Charles V, who named him governor and captain general of New Spain, as the newly conquered region was called. Even though he now had major administrative tasks, Cortés remained committed to exploration and, in particular, to the search for a strait between the Atlantic and Pacific Oceans, a subject in which the King was also interested.

Several expeditions were sent to explore both coasts of New Spain. In October 1524 Cortés himself traveled all the way to Honduras to track down a rebellious lieutenant, Cristóbal de Olid. He took Cuauhtemoc with him as insurance against an uprising during his absence. Informed that the Aztec leader was plotting against him, Cortés had him hanged.

Cortés was away from Mexico for a year and nine months. On his return, he found that the government was being taken over more and more by royal officials sent out from Spain. On March 17, 1528 Cortés left Veracruz to visit Spain to try to convince King Charles V to make him viceroy of New Spain. He was received with great honors and was given the title of Marques del Valle de Oaxaca, with extensive rights over a large section of central Mexico, but he made no headway with his efforts to be given real power. He returned to Mexico in July 1530 with his newly-married second wife. His position continued to deteriorate, and in 1535 Spain's first viceroy, Antonio de Mendoza, arrived.

As part of his reward from the King, Cortés had been put in charge of exploration in the South Sea (Pacific Ocean) and promised a share of any riches that were found there. He occupied himself more and more with these matters. Already in 1527 he had sent out an expedition under **Alvaro de Saavedra y Cerón** that had crossed the ocean to the Philippines. In 1534 he sent out an expedition that sailed across the Gulf of California and landed in La Paz Bay in Baja California, where it found a pearl fishery.

Cortés decided to look into this new possibility of wealth in person. He sailed from the port of Sinaloa on April 18, 1535 with three ships and about 170 men. He landed in La Paz Bay on May 3 and claimed the country for Spain. It turned out to be poor desert land with little water or food. Cortés stayed for a year but then gave it up and returned to Mexico. In 1539 he sponsored a voyage by Francisco de Ulloa that sailed around the tip of Baja California and up the west coast, showing that it was a peninsula and not an island. In 1540 Cortés wanted to lead the expedition to find the Seven Cities of Cíbola, but Mendoza gave the commission to **Francisco Vázquez de Coronado** instead.

Still unhappy with his position, Cortés traveled back to Spain in 1540. The King, who was also Emperor Charles V of the Holy Roman Empire, was not there, and Cortés was unable to present his petition personally. In October 1541, he and two of his sons (including one by Doña Marina) took part in a Spanish expedition against the city of Algiers in North Africa. The Spanish fleet was destroyed in a violent storm. Cortés escaped, but his pride was mortally wounded when he was not asked to take part in the war councils. From then on, he spent his time writing letters to the King asking for the honors he felt were his due. He died in the little town of Castilleja de la Cuesta outside of Seville on December 2, 1547.

Where to learn more

There is considerable documentary source material available on Cortés and the conquest of Mexico. Cortés himself wrote five long letters to King Charles V telling him about his exploits and accomplishments. The most recent edition of these is *Hernan Cortes: Letters from Mexico*, translated and edited by A.R. Pagden (New York: Grossman Publishers, 1971). There is also a 2 volume reprint of an earlier edition: Francis Augustus MacNutt, translator and editor, *Fernando Cortes: His Five Letters of Relation to the Emperor Charles V* (Cleveland: A.H. Clark Co., 1908; reprinted, Glorieta, New Mexico: The Rio Grande Press, 1977).

A second important documentary source is a biography of Cortés written by his secretary in his last years in Spain, Francisco López de Gómara, that was printed as the *Istoria de la conquista de Mexico* in Zaragoza, Spain in 1552. There is an excellent modern English edition: *Cortés: The Life of the Conqueror by His Secretary*, translated and edited by Lesley Bird Simpson (Berkeley: University of California Press, 1964).

López de Gómara's narrative is by someone who did not actually take part in the events he recorded, unlike the history written by Bernal Díaz del Castillo. Díaz del Castillo was a soldier in Cortés's army from the very beginning, and his is an important eyewitness account. An English translation of this was published early in this century: A.P. Maudslay, trans. *The True Story of the Conquest of New Spain*, 5 vols. (London: The Hakluyt Society, 1908-1916). An edited version appeared much later: *The Discovery and Conquest of Mexico, 1517-1521* (New York: Farrar, Straus and Cudahy, 1956; reprinted, 1966). Another version

is *The Bernal Díaz Chronicles: The True Story of the Conquest of Mexico*, translated and edited by Albert Idell (Garden City, N.Y.: Doubleday & Co., 1956). Díaz del Castillo is an important character in his own right and has merited an interesting biography: Herbert Cerwin, *Bernal Diaz: Historian of the Conquest* (Norman: University of Oklahoma Press, 1963). The memoirs of other participants can be found in Patricia de Fuentes, ed. *The Conquistadors* (New York: Orion Press, 1963).

One of the monuments of American historiography is William H. Prescott's *History of the Conquest of Mexico*, which was first published in 1843 and is available in many editions.

As one might expect, there are numerous biographies of Cortés. One classic one in English is Salvador de Madariaga, *Hernán Cortés: Conqueror of Mexico* (New York: Macmillan, 1941). One good scholarly study about the early part of his life is Henry R. Wagner, *The Rise of Fernando Cortés* (Berkeley: The Cortés Society, Bancroft Library, 1944). A more recent study is Jon Manchip White, *Cortés and the Downfall of the Aztec Empire* (New York: St. Martin's Press, 1971). Two short biographies that can be recommended are: Maurice Collis, *Cortés and Montezuma* (New York: Harcourt, Brace & Co., 1954) and William Weber Johnson, *Cortés* (London: Hutchinson, 1977).

An important book because it gives the story of the conquest from the position of the Native Americans who lost the campaign is: Miguel León-Portilla, ed., trans. by Lysander Kemp, *The Broken Spears: The Aztec Account of the Conquest of Mexico* (Boston: Beacon Press, 1972).

Jacques(-Yves) Cousteau

(1910 -   )

Probably the world's most noted underwater explorer, Jacques (-Yves) Cousteau is a former French naval officer who invented the aqualung and designed the first underwater habitats.

Jacques (-Yves) Cousteau was born in the small village of Saint-André-de-Cubzac (his parents' ancestral home) in the south of France on June 11, 1910. His father was actually a lawyer working in Paris, and Cousteau spent most of his youth in the capital. His father represented rich American businessmen in Europe, and, as a result, the family lived in New York from 1920 to 1922. Cousteau was a tinkerer from an early age and especially loved photography—at the age of 13 he bought one of the first home movie cameras sold in France and from then on was constantly making films. He went to a French high school, or *lycée*, in Paris but was an indifferent student and was expelled for breaking 17 windows with rocks one night. He was sent to a boarding school in Alsace. There his grades improved enough for him to be admitted to the French Naval Academy in 1930.

Cousteau graduated second in his class with a degree in engineering in 1932. He then joined a naval voyage around the world that included a stop in Los Angeles, where Cousteau filmed movie stars Mary Pickford and Douglas Fairbanks greeting the French officers. He served for a while in Shanghai in China and returned to Europe via the trans-Siberian railroad with a sidetrip by car to Afghanistan.

Cousteau wanted to become an airplane pilot and was accepted at the French naval aviation school. He had made his first solo flight and was a few weeks' away from graduation when he was injured in an automobile accident. On a lonely mountain road at night, his car spun out of control and Cousteau was seriously hurt—his right arm was paralyzed. He was forced to drop out of aviation school, and it was only after many years of physical therapy that he was able to regain full use of his arm.

When he was sufficiently recovered, Cousteau was assigned to the cruiser *Dupleix* stationed in the port of Toulon on the Mediterranean. In Toulon a fellow officer suggested to Cousteau that he take up swimming as a way of rehabilitating his arm. In the summer of 1936 he began to spend all his spare time at the beach in the company of two friends. He started using goggles as a way of seeing underwater and adapted his camera so that he could film the fish.

Cousteau began to think about the problem of breathing underwater. Ever since man had started making deep sea dives in the 1870s, the only way to supply oxygen was by way of an air line coming from the boat, and this greatly restricted mobility under the sea. (One such device was invented by **Auguste Piccard**.) Cousteau started thinking and tinkering until he eventually developed a contraption he called the aqualung. The aqualung was made up of an air canister containing compressed air, a demand regulator that could supply a constant flow of oxygen at the same pressure as the water the diver was in, and a mouthpiece for the diver to breathe through. The U.S. Navy later called the invention "scuba" for "Self-Contained Underwater Breathing Apparatus."

In 1937 Cousteau married Simone Melchior, whom he had met at a party in Paris. She later became his partner on most of his sea voyages. They had two sons: Jean-Michel, born in 1938, and Philippe, born in 1940 and killed in an airplane crash in Lisbon in 1979.

Following the defeat of France in 1940, the Cousteaus stayed in Toulon where the French Navy was interned. It was there in 1942-1943 that he developed the aqualung with the help of an uncle who was a director in a French company that produced compressed air and other industrial gases. During the war, Cousteau's older brother Pierre stayed in Paris and worked on a newspaper sponsored by the Nazis. After the war, Pierre Cousteau was convicted of collaboration and spent many years in prison.

At the conclusion of World War II, Cousteau convinced the French Navy that there was a way to put his new invention to an immediate practical use. He organized diving crews to remove the mines that were blocking southern French ports. Cousteau remained in the French Navy until 1956 and continued experimentation with underwater photography and with testing and improving his equipment in order to make ever-deeper dives. He developed an underwater camera that could descend to 600 meters below the surface, which he used to make some of the first photographs and films of life undersea.

In 1951 Cousteau commissioned the first of his famous exploring ships, the *Calypso*, and began to systematically investigate the world's oceans, the first trip being one to the Red Sea in 1952. Following this voyage, he published a book that included many startling photographs. The English edition, *The Silent World*, sold 500,000 copies in the first year. In 1955 he made the film *The World of Silence* with director Louis Malle. It won numerous international film awards, including an Oscar as best documentary.

In 1957 Cousteau was made director of the Oceanographic Museum of Monaco, and he used this position and the *Calypso* to start several new scientific explorations. The most innovative of these involved more than just extending the depths to which humans could go beneath the sea. He began to look for ways to actually live beneath the sea. Cousteau's *Conshelf* stations developed in the 1960s were the first underwater living environments. In them, it was possible for divers to live and work for weeks at a time. Somewhat later, the United States Navy began a similar series of experiments that it called *Sealab*.

Cousteau's first Conshelf project was started in 1962. Two men stayed for a week in a small chamber that was sunk 33 feet into the Mediterranean Sea. Conshelf Two took place the following year in the Red Sea off the coast of Egypt and involved more complicated experiments. In Conshelf Two there were five men sunk to the same depth of 33 feet, but this time they lived in a more complex underwater settlement. It was equipped with full living and working facilities, and the five-man crew stayed there for a month. Conshelf Three followed in 1965, by which time Cousteau was thinking of setting up semi-permanent stations, similar to a space station, where people could live indefinitely.

Starting in 1960, when he opposed the French government's decision to dump nuclear waste in the Mediterranean, Cousteau

became a spokesman for environmental causes. He has used his platform as the world's most notable underwater explorer to lobby for greater awareness of the environmental dangers faced by the world's oceans. He has done this mostly with several series of television films. In 1970 he produced 12 one-hour programs on the *The Undersea Odyssey of the Calypso* and followed this with six more with the same title in 1973. In 1984 he did a series on the underwater exploration of the Amazon River and then 22 one-hour programs on the world's oceans starting in 1985.

Cousteau has been the recipient of numerous awards both in France and other countries. He was given the Medal of Freedom by the United States in 1985 and was elected to the very prestigious Académie Française in 1988.

Where to learn more

Cousteau is the author of a great many books as well as articles for the National Geographic and other magazines and cinematic and television films. The following books have appeared in English: *The Silent World* (New York: Harper Brothers, 1953); *Book of Fishes* (Washington, D.C.: National Geographic Society, 1958); *Captain Cousteau's Underwater Treasury* (New York: Harper, 1959); *The Living Sea* (New York: Harper & Row, 1962); *The Shark: Splendid Savage of the Sea* (Garden City, N.Y.: Doubleday, 1970); *Life and Death in a Coral Sea* (Garden City, N.Y.: Doubleday, 1971); *Diving for Sunken Treasure* (Garden City, N.Y.: Doubleday, 1972); *The Whale: Mighty Monarch of the Sea* (Garden City, N.Y.: Doubleday, 1972); *Octopus and Squid: The Soft Intelligence* (Garden City, N.Y.: Doubleday, 1973); *Three Adventures: Galapagos,*

Jacques Cousteau and associate. ABC Press Relations.

Titicaca, the Blue Holes (Garden City, N.Y.: Doubleday, 1973); *The Ocean World*, 20 volumes (New York: World Publishing, vols. 1-7, and Abrams, vols. 8-20); *Diving Companions: Sea Lion, Elephant Seal, Walrus* (Garden City, N.Y.); *Dolphins* (Garden City, N.Y.: Doubleday, 1975); *Cousteau's Calypso* (New York: Abrams, 1980); *A Bill of Rights for Future Generations* (New York: Myrin Institute, 1980); *The Cousteau Almanac of the Environment: An Inventory of Life on a Water Planet* (New York: Doubleday, 1981); *Cousteau's Amazon Journey* (New York: Abrams, 1984).

There have been two biographies of Cousteau: Genie Iverson, *Jacques Cousteau* (New York: G.P. Putnam's Sons, 1976) and Axel Madsen, *Cousteau: An Unauthorized Biography* (New York: Beaufort Books Publishers, 1986), which served as the main source for this account.

Pero da Covilhão

(1450 - 1545)

Pero da Covilhão was a Portuguese nobleman who made a journey to East Africa and India that confirmed that it was possible to sail to India around Africa and then was the first Westerner to visit Abyssinia (Ethiopia).

In August 1487 **Bartolomeu Dias** started out on the journey that was to lead him to round the Cape of Good Hope at the southern tip of Africa. A little earlier, in May 1487, another Portuguese, Pero da Covilhão, headed for the east coast of Africa by traveling overland from the north. Together, the information they supplied enabled **Vasco da Gama** to make his epic voyage around Africa to India a few years later.

Covilhão was born in a village of the same name in Portugal. As a youth, he went to Spain and served seven years in the household of the Duke of Medina Sidonia in Andalusia. He then returned to Portugal and became a member of the court of King Alfonso. Because of his ability to speak Spanish, the King sent him back to Spain to spy on dissident Portuguese who lived in the neighboring country. On his return, he went to North Africa where he served as both a diplomat and commercial agent in Morocco. As a result of this experience he became fluent in Arabic.

Covilhão was called back to Portugal where he was introduced to Afonso de Paiva, a man from the Canary Islands, who also spoke Arabic. The two men were entrusted with an important mission by the King: to visit all the ports of importance on the route to India, India itself, and the east coast of Africa, and to make contact with Prester John, a mythical Christian king living somewhere in the East. The details of the journey were worked out with Jose Vizinho and Master Rodrigo (who was the King of Portugal's physician). These two men had been present when the King had turned down **Christopher Columbus**'s request for Portuguese help in making his projected voyage.

On May 7, 1487 Covilhão and de Paiva received their final instructions from the King, who gave them 400 gold cruzados to pay for their journey. The cruzado was a pure gold coin made from gold earned in trade with the west coast of Africa. It was first minted in 1457 and was the first gold coin to be circulated in Portugal for nearly 200 years. The two travelers entrusted part of the money to a Florentine banker who gave them a letter of credit that they later redeemed in Naples.

They left from the town of Santarem, and their departure was witnessed by the King's cousin, who later became King Manuel "the Fortunate." They were provided with a "map for navigating, taken from the map of the world . . . and a letter of credence for all the countries and provinces of the world."

In addition to looking for the land of Prester John, the main object of their journey, they were to inquire "what were the principal markets for the spice and particularly the pepper trade in India; and what were the different channels by which this was conveyed to Europe; whence came the gold and silver, the medium of this trade; and above all they were to inform themselves distinctly, whether it was possible to arrive in India by sailing round the Southern promontory of Africa."

Covilhão and de Paiva left immediately for Barcelona and from there went to Naples. They then went to the Greek island of Rhodes where they disguised themselves as Muslim merchants and bought a stock of honey to sell in Egypt, but in Alexandria they fell ill with fever, and the local governor impounded it. After they recovered, they bought a fresh stock of goods and pushed on to Cairo. They stayed there for some time until they met some pilgrims from Morocco traveling to Mecca. In 1488 they sailed with the pilgrims through the Red Sea to Aden at the entrance to the Indian Ocean in a small Arab vessel. They stopped at El Tor in Sinai (until recently a quarantine station for pilgrims to Mecca) and at Suakin, then the chief port in the Sudan. The voyage took about two months.

At Aden the two Portuguese separated. De Paiva was supposed to go to Abyssinia, as Ethiopia was then known, and find Prester John. Covilhão went across the Indian Ocean to Cannanore, a port on the Malabar Coast of southwest India. From here he visited Calicut (now Kozhikode), which was the center for the spice trade. At Goa (Panjim), 300 miles to the north, Covilhão took a ship to Ormuz on the south coast of Persia opposite Arabia. It was the principal port of the Persian Gulf at that time. He then journeyed down the coasts of Arabia and Africa to Sofala, an important Arab port in what is now Mozambique, opposite Madagascar. The trip to Sofala convinced him that Africa could be circumnavigated, and he returned to Cairo in 1490 with this valuable information, stopping at the ports of Kilwa, Mombasa, and Malindi along the way. When he got to Cairo, he learned that de Paiva had died.

Covilhão was on the brink of returning to Portugal to deliver his information when he met up with two Portuguese Jews, Rabbi Abraham de Beja and Joseph de Lamego, who were searching for him to deliver letters they were carrying from the

King of Portugal. They had been sent to learn about the trade of Ormuz. When they found out that Covilhão had already been there, Lamego agreed to carry his reports back to Portugal.

Apparently, Covilhão was instructed to concentrate on the search for Prester John. He and Rabbi Abraham sailed to Aden and Ormuz, where Covilhão left the Rabbi behind. He then sailed to Jeddah on the west coast of Arabia and from there went to the Muslim holy cities of Mecca and Medina. He went back to Sinai and found a ship sailing down the Red Sea that left him off at the port of Zeila, in what is now Somalia.

When Covilhão reached Zeila, he learned that Emperor Iskander of Abyssinia was nearby, engaged in a war with a Muslim king. Covilhão was able to meet up with the Emperor and accompanied him back to his stronghold of Shoa in the Ethiopian highlands. The Emperor was greatly pleased with Covilhão and treated him well. He was told that at some time in the future "he would send him to his country with much honor." However, before this could happen, Iskander was killed in a battle, and Covilhão was stuck at the Abyssinian court.

On one occasion, Covilhão was given permission to leave and had started off with many presents accompanied by a large band of retainers. However, the members of his escort became involved in a confrontation with local residents along the way, and the Emperor recalled the whole party back to his court at Tegulet. Covilhão settled down in Abyssinia and where he married a noblewoman and was given an official position and valuable lands. He was allowed to write to the King of Portugal but was not permitted to leave the country.

Covilhão's letters to the King of Portugal aroused immense interest in Europe. A Portuguese named Fernão Gomez was sent by the King of Portugal in the fleet of **Afonso de Albuquerque** to support Covilhão. He got to Abyssinia in 1508 but, like Covilhão, was not allowed to leave. In 1520 the King of Portugal sent an official mission to Abyssinia under Rodrigo da Lima. Da Lima found both Covilhão and Gomez still living there.

The chronicle of the da Lima mission was written by Francisco Alvarez, who in fact got most of his information from Covilhão. According to Alvarez, Covilhão was "a man who knows all the languages that can be spoken, both of Christians, Moors and Gentiles, and who knows all the things for which he was sent; moreover, he gives an account of them as if they were present before him."

When the da Lima mission left Abyssinia in 1526, they took an Ethiopian envoy with them back to Portugal. However, Covilhão either did not want to or was not allowed to depart, and he stayed in his adopted country until his death in 1545.

Where to learn more

Our knowledge of Covilhão comes from the writings of Alvarez. These have been translated and published in English as *Narrative of the Portuguese Embassy to Abyssinia during the Years 1520-1527 by Father Francisco Alvarez*, translated by Lord Stanley of Alderley (London: The Hakluyt Society, 1881; reprinted, New York: Burt Franklin, 1970).

A 19th-century Portuguese history of Covilhão's travels has recently been reprinted in a beautiful edition: Francisco Manuel de Melo, Conde de Ficalho, *Viagens de Pero da Covilho* (Lisbon: Imprensa Nacional-Casa da Moeda, 1988).

Jules Crevaux

(1847 - 1883)

Jules Crevaux was a French doctor who made several expeditions to the Amazon basin and was killed by an Indian tribe that feared European exploitation.

Jules Crevaux was born in the village of Lorquin in northeastern France on April 1, 1847, the son of an innkeeper. He started his medical studies at the University of Strasbourg and then transferred to the French Navy's medical school at Brest. He was appointed a medical assistant in 1868 and served on board a ship that went to Senegal, the French West Indies, and French Guiana. When the Franco-Prussian War broke out in 1870, he volunteered to serve as a marine in the Loire valley. He was wounded and captured by the Germans on December 17, 1870. He escaped and then was assigned to the front line, where he was again wounded on January 24, 1871.

At the end of the war, Crevaux finished his medical studies and was awarded his M.D. degree in 1872. He then saw duty at the naval hospital in Brest and on board a French warship. In 1876 he was assigned to the French colony of French Guiana on the northern coast of South America. Leaving France on December 7, 1876, he stopped at the notorious penal colony on Devil's Island off the coast of French Guiana and helped to care for prisoners who were suffering from yellow fever.

Once in French Guiana, Crevaux wanted to travel into the little-known interior. French Guiana had never been an economic success and consisted largely of penal colonies and small trading villages on the coast and an almost empty interior, with some Native American settlements. On July 8, 1877 Crevaux headed up the Maroni River on the colony's western border and stopped at the villages of the Galibi tribe. He then stayed at the village of the Bonis, an African people who had escaped from slavery in the neighboring colony of Suriname and re-established themselves in the interior out of the reach of the Europeans.

Crevaux traveled up the Itany River, a tributary of the Maroni, visiting the Roucouyenne tribe and then followed a trail of the Emerillon tribe to the summit of the Tumuc Humac Mountains, which form the southern border of French Guiana, on September 21, 1877. He went down the opposite side of the mountains and reached the Jari River, a tributary of the Amazon. By this time he had used or lost most of his belongings and was practically naked, but he continued down the Jari and the Amazon until he made it to the Brazilian city of Belém, on the Atlantic coast at the mouth of the Amazon. The Brazilians thought that he was an escaped French prisoner and refused to give him any assistance. Finally, a fellow Frenchman took pity on him and bought him passage on a boat sailing to France. On his return, Crevaux gave a lecture on his journey to the French Geographical Society on April 17, 1878 and was made a "knight" of France's Legion of Honor.

Not having had enough, Crevaux left France for Guiana once again on July 7, 1878 and arrived there on August 24. He immediately traveled up the Oyapock River on the colony's eastern border. He went up the Oyapock to its source and then climbed the Tumuc Humac Mountains again to a spot now known as Crevaux Peak. He descended the other side and headed down to the Jari River, which he reached on October 10, 1878. Not wanting to repeat his previous journey, he went west to the headwaters of the Paru River and canoed down it to the Amazon. After 41 days of travel he arrived in Belem, where he received a better welcome than on his first visit.

There were no scheduled steamboats to France from Belém for a while, so Crevaux came up with the idea of traveling up the Amazon and exploring the Japura River. He went as far as Manaus and, realizing he could not make the larger expedition, he opted instead to canoe up the Ica River to the town of Concepción in Colombia. He crossed over to the Japura and headed back down until he reached the Amazon on July 8, 1879. He carried a great number of biological specimens back with him to France. As a result of this trip, Crevaux was awarded the Gold Medal of the French Geographical Society.

Following these two successful journeys, Crevaux was sent out on an expedition with a pharmacist and three other scientists to collect botanical specimens in northern South America. They left France on August 6, 1880 and traveled up the Magdalena River in Colombia, crossed the Andes and then descended the Guavaiare River to the Orinoco in Venezuela and from there to the Atlantic Ocean. The expedition spent 161 days traveling up or down these rivers. On March 25, 1881 he returned to France, where he was made an officer of the Legion of Honor.

Crevaux was then requested by France's Department of Public Instruction to lead another scientific expedition to explore the divide between the Amazon and Paraguay river basins. The party arrived in Buenos Aires in December 1881. There Crevaux met with the president of the Argentine Geographical Institute and representatives of the Bolivian government. They urged him to explore the unknown upper course of the Pilcomayo River, which rises in Bolivia and then forms part of the boundary between Paraguay and Argentina. Crevaux accepted the challenge.

Crevaux and his colleagues were given free transportation by the Argentine government and a marine escort. They reached the Bolivian border on January 16, 1882, where they were set upon by bandits but were able to fight them off. By March 8 they were in the Bolivian town of Tarija where a Catholic missionary offered to accompany them to a mission station on the Pilcomayo river. He also introduced them to Yalla Petrona, a young girl from the Toba tribe who offered to guide them to her people's territory.

When they reached the settlement of Caíza, they learned that the people of Caíza had gone to war with the Tobas. The missionary urged Crevaux not to proceed any farther. On March 30, 1882 a war party of Caíza people returned with the news that they had killed 12 allies of the Tobas and captured seven children. Crevaux sent the oldest of the girl captives back to the Tobas with Yalla Petrona as an emissary to tell them that the Frenchmen were coming and had only peaceful intentions.

After Yalla Petrona had departed, there was news of a Toba attack on another mission station, but Crevaux decided to push on. His canoes were ready by April 18, and he left Caíza on the 19th. On April 27, 1882 a party of Tobas invited them to come ashore to eat. Once on land the Frenchmen were surrounded and clubbed to death.

When news of the fate of the Crevaux expedition got back to France, another explorer, Arthur Thouar, was directed to go to the Pilcomayo to investigate. He took with him a force of 200 Bolivian soldiers. He reached Toba country in August 1883, where he found traces of the Crevaux expedition. He occupied an abandoned mission station and fortified it. On October 3 he was attacked by 1,000 Tobas but was able to repel them and to conclude an armistice with the chief. Thouar then proceeded up the Pilcomayo, crossed over to the Paraguay River and then descended to Paraguay and Argentina.

In 1885 Thouar returned to Bolivia to map the Pilcomayo River. There he met, in early 1887, Yalla Petrona who told him that she had told her Toba kinsmen that Crevaux was there to take away their land and fishing rights and that he was coming without a Bolivian army escort. It was this report that had caused the attack that resulted in the death of the French scientists.

Where to learn more

Crevaux wrote about his trips to Guiana in *Voyage dans la Guyane et le bassin de l'Amazone* (Paris: 1880). Following his death two other books were written about his earlier expeditions based on his notes: *Voyages dans l'Amérique du Sud* (Paris: 1882) and *Fleuves de l'Amérique du Sud* (Paris: 1883). The story of the last expedition and the attempts to find out what had happened is told by Arthur Thouar in *Explorations dans l'Amérique du Sud* (Paris: Hachette, 1891). There is one book-length biography of Crevaux in French: L. Boudet, *La Vie et la mort de Jules Crevaux* (Paris: 1934).

The only readily available account in English of the explorations of Crevaux is found in the excellent survey of South American exploration by Edward J. Goodman, *The Explorers of South America* (New York: Macmillan, 1972).

Samuel Adjai Crowther

(1811 - 1892)

A Yoruba from what is now Nigeria, Samuel Adjai Crowther was an Anglican missionary who took part in two expeditions to explore the Niger River.

Adjai was the son of a chief of the Yoruba people, who lived in what is now southwestern Nigeria. At the age of 11 he and his mother were kidnapped by a party of Portuguese slave traders and put on a Portuguese slave ship bound for America. The third day out, the ship was captured by the British naval vessel *Myrmidon* captained by H.J. Leake. The British government had outlawed the slave trade, and Royal Navy ships were active in pursuing any slavers they found on the west coast of Africa.

The British ship took Adjai and the other liberated Africans to the new colony of Freetown in Sierra Leone, which had been established as a home for freed slaves. There, Adjai was baptized into the Christian religion and given the new name of Samuel Crowther. He was sent to a mission school and did so well that in 1826 he was sent to England for further education. He returned to Sierra Leone to teach in the mission school. He met and married a young woman named Susan Thompson.

In 1841 the British government sent out the First Royal Niger Expedition under the command of H. Dundas Trotter, William Allen and Bird Allen. They left England on March 23, 1841, and the occasion was marked by the first public speech of Prince Albert, Queen Victoria's new husband. When the three ships stopped in Sierra Leone, the Church Missionary Society requested that it take two missionaries along with them. Crowther was one of the two who were chosen.

The Niger expedition entered the Niger River at one of its mouths on August 13, 1841. The crews of the ships remained healthy while they traveled through the river's extensive delta. As they traveled upstream on the main course of the Niger, however, many of the Europeans became ill from malaria. By the time the ships reached the confluence with the Benue River many of the crew members had died and all but three had become ill. By the time the last of the three ships left the Niger on July 2, 1842 and headed home, more than one-third of the Europeans had died. Crowther, however, remained healthy and wrote a valuable account of the voyage.

On Crowther's return to England, his work received widespread acknowledgment. He completed his theological studies at the Church Missionary Society Training College and was ordained a priest in the Anglican church in 1843.

Crowther returned to Nigeria to teach and minister and was there reunited with his mother, after a separation of 20 years. In 1851 he returned to England and was granted a private audience with Queen Victoria to discuss the suppression of slavery and the slave trade in Africa. He also spoke at Cambridge University as well as addressing several organizations about the commercial possibilities of opening up Africa for trade.

As a result, the government sent out a second expedition to Nigeria with the financial backing of Macgregor Laird, a rich Liverpool businessman. Crowther was once again a member as was **William Balfour Baikie**, who became head of the expedition when the original leader died on the island of Fernando Poo. Crowther was indispensable to the expedition because he was able to speak all the local languages. His journal is particularly valuable for the details it gives about the people of the Benue valley, the major tributary of the Niger. Crowther set up his first mission station at Igbobi, near the confluence of the Benue and Niger Rivers, near Lokoja where Baikie had set up his post.

On Crowther's return to England, he was nominated to become a bishop of the Anglican church, the first African to have reached such a position. He was consecrated on June 29, 1864 in Canterbury Cathedral and named Bishop of the Niger. In the audience was Admiral Leake, who had commanded the ship that had rescued Crowther when he was a young boy.

Crowther was made the head of the Anglican church for a 1,000 miles of the coast of West Africa. He was responsible for sending out many missionaries into the field and for training many young Africans in his religion. He faced an uphill fight in trying to put down the slave trade because this threatened the revenues of many of the chiefs. At one point, he was kidnapped by one chief and held for ransom before he was able to escape.

The various difficulties that Crowther faced made progress in spreading Christianity along the Niger very slow. The mission did not achieve the hoped-for results, and many of the missionaries led less than exemplary lives. Eventually, a commission of inquiry was sent out from London, and, while it found Crowther himself innocent of any charges, it also discovered many problems in the diocese. The strain of this investigation hastened Crowther's death in Lagos on January 9, 1892.

Where to learn more

Crowther wrote several important books about his exploring trips: *Journals of the Rev. James Frederick Schön and Mr. Samuel Crowther, Who, with Her*

Majesty's Government, Accompanied the Expedition of the Niger in 1841, on Behalf of the Church Missionary Society* (London: 1842; reprinted, London: Frank Cass & Co., 1970); *Journal of the Expedition up the Niger in 1841* (London: 1854; reprinted, London: Frank Cass & Co., 1970); and *Journal of an Expedition up the Niger and Tshadda Rivers Undertaken by Macgregor Laird in Connection with the British Government in 1854* (London: 1855; reprinted, London: Frank Cass & Co., 1970).

There is one biography of Crowther: Jesse Page, *The Black Bishop* (London: 1900). There are biographical sketches in several books: Georgina Anne Gollock, *Lives of Eminent Africans* (London: Longmans, Green & Co., 1928); J.A. Rogers, *World's Great Men of Color*, vol. 1 (New York: 1946; reprinted, Macmillan, 1972); Sir Rex Niven, *Nine Great Africans* (New York: Roy Publishers, 1964); Robert W. July, *The Origins of Modern African Thought* (Washington, D.C.: Frederick A. Praeger, 1967); Florence T. Polatnick and Alberta L. Saletan, *Shapers of Africa* (New York: Julius Messner, 1969).

Books about European exploration of the Niger which include information on Crowther: A. Adu Boahen, *Britain, the Sahara, and the Western Sudan, 1788-1861* (Oxford: Clarendon Press, 1964); E.W. Bovill, *The Niger Explored* (Cambridge: Cambridge University Press, 1968); Christopher Lloyd, *The Search for the Niger* (London: Collins, 1973); Sanche de Gramont, *The Strong Brown God: The Story of the Niger River* (Boston: Houghton Mifflin, 1975).

Allan Cunningham

(1791 - 1839)

Allan Cunningham was an English botanist who made several expeditions west and north of Sydney, opening up some of Australia's most productive territory for British settlement.

Allan Cunningham was born on July 13, 1791 in Wimbledon, England, not far from London. He came from a well-to-do family and was educated at a private school. He worked as a law clerk for a while, but found his true vocation in 1808 when he was appointed to a position at England's famous Royal Botanical Gardens at Kew. On the recommendation of **Sir Joseph Banks**, he was given the job of botanist on an expedition to Brazil. He left London in October 1814 and stayed in South America for two years. From there he was sent to the new British colony of New South Wales in Australia.

Cunningham arrived in Sydney on December 10, 1816. In 1817 he accompanied **John Oxley** on the first of his expeditions into the interior of New South Wales. On his return, Cunningham sailed on December 21, 1817 on an expedition led by P.P. King that traveled to the north and northwest coasts of Australia. Cunningham made extensive collecting expeditions in Arnhem Land in what is now the Northern Territory and on Melville Island before returning to Sydney on July 29, 1818. He returned with 300 botanical specimens, including several unknown species. In 1819 he made a trip to Tasmania and another one to the northwest coast. He made additional trips to the same area in 1820 and 1821. He returned to Sydney in April 1822 and spent his time until January 1823 collecting specimens near the modern city of Bathurst west of Sydney.

On his second expedition in 1818 Oxley had found a fertile region in the northern part of the colony, the Liverpool Plains, but the round-about route he took was not suitable for large-scale movements of people. Therefore, in early 1823 Governor Thomas Makdougall Brisbane summoned Cunningham to Sydney and put him in charge of an expedition to find a better route to Liverpool Plains. Cunningham set out from Bathurst in June 1823 and in the course of the next eleven weeks covered 500 miles of difficult terrain testing one possibility after another. He finally found Pandora's Pass through the Liverpool Range, thus opening up new territory for settlement.

Following his return, Cunningham made several trips into the country around Bathurst and Sydney, including one with the French explorer **Jules-Sébastien-César Dumont d'Urville**, who stopped in Sydney in 1823. He went to New Zealand in 1826, returning in January 1827.

In May 1827 the new Governor, Ralph Darling, sent Cunningham on another mission—to explore the country in the far north of the present-day state of New South Wales. He crossed the Liverpool Range to the Plains and headed north to discover the Namoi, Gwydir, Dumaresq, and Macintyre rivers. On June 8 from a hill above the Macintyre he looked down on a vast expanse of fertile land. He named the area in honor of his patron—the Darling Downs. Today this vast plain is by far the most important agricultural area in the state of Queensland, producing more than half of its crops and a large part of its livestock. Through the Darling Downs, Cunningham headed east and found a pass through the Great Dividing Range to the coast—Cunningham's Gap. This led down to Moreton Bay, the site of the present-day city of Brisbane, capital of Queensland. Cunningham opened the way to the founding of the state of Queensland, which is today the third largest in Australia.

On his way back to Sydney, Cunningham took a route farther east than on the way out. This brought him across the New England Plateau in northern New South Wales, which is also a rich agricultural area. Cunningham is therefore responsible for opening up more economically-valuable land than any other explorer in Australian history.

Cunningham traveled to Moreton Bay by sea in July and August 1828, and in May 1829 he explored the upper course of the Brisbane River. In November 1830 he was granted permission to return to England. He left Sydney in February 1831 and arrived in London in July. He spent the following years arranging his collections and writing up scientific reports on his explorations. He recommended his younger brother Richard for the post of Colonial Botanist in New South Wales. Richard was killed in a skirmish with Aborigines in April 1835, and the government asked Cunningham to take up his brother's post. He agreed and returned to Sydney in February 1837. When he learned that his new duties meant that he was supposed to grow vegetables for the Governor's dinner table, he resigned. He sailed to New Zealand in April 1838. When he returned in October, he was sick with tuberculosis. He died in Sydney on June 27, 1839 and was buried in the Sydney Botanical Gardens.

Where to learn more

Cunningham never published a book about his various explorations. The story of his 1823 trip to the Liverpool Plains is contained in a chapter entitled "Journal of a Route from Bathurst to Liverpool Plains" in Barron Field, ed. *Geographical Memoirs on New South Wales by Various Hands* (London: 1825). His paper "Brief View of the Progress of Interior Discovery in New South Wales" was published in the *Journal of the Royal Geographical Society* in 1832. It is reprinted in Kathleen Fitzpatrick, ed. *Australian Explorers: A Selection from their Writings* (London: Oxford University Press, 1958).

There is a fairly recent biography of Cunningham: W.G. McMinn, *Allan Cunningham, Botanist and Explorer* (Melbourne: 1970). General histories of Australian exploration that discuss Cunningham are: I. Lee, *Early Explorers in Australia* (London: 1925) and E.H.J. Feeken, G.E.E. Feeken, and O.H.K. Spate, *The Discovery and Exploration of Australia* (London: 1970).

Vasco da Gama

(1460? - 1524)

Vasco da Gama was a Portuguese nobleman who led the first European expedition around Africa to India.

Little is known about the early life of Vasco da Gama. He was born around 1460 in the Portuguese seaport of Sines, in the southern region of Alentejo. His father, Estevão da Gama, was governor of the town. He probably received the usual upbringing and education of a young nobleman of his time and at some point went to serve in the court of King João II. In 1492 da Gama was entrusted with important duties during a dispute with the King of France, which he carried out successfully. Otherwise, nothing is known about him until he took command of the first Portuguese expedition to the East.

King Manoel I came to the Portuguese throne in 1495 at the age of 26. By the time of his accession, **Bartolomeu Dias** had

Vasco da Gama.

rounded the southern tip of Africa in 1488 and **Christopher Columbus** had sailed to the Americas in 1492. As a result of these efforts, the Portuguese and the Spaniards decided to divide the world between themselves. The Spanish would take the western half—the "New World"—and the Portuguese would take Africa and the East. This was confirmed by the Treaty of Tordesillas signed between King João II and the Spanish King and Queen, Ferdinand and Isabella, in 1494.

Once he became King, Manoel decided to take advantage of the provisions of the treaty to send an expedition all the way around Africa to India. He selected da Gama to lead it and to serve as his ambassador to the rulers of India. It is not known why he chose da Gama, although some of the chronicles indicate that the command was originally intended for his father who had died before he could depart and/or that it was offered to Vasco's older brother Paulo who had turned it down.

Da Gama spent several months planning and equipping the expedition. His fleet consisted of four ships: the flagship *São Gabriel*, commanded by Gonçalo Alvares; the *São Rafael*, commanded by da Gama's brother Paulo; the *Berrio*; and a storeship. Estimates of the size of the crew vary in different accounts from 118 to 170 men. Of these, several were convicts, who were regarded as expendable, and they were used to perform particularly dangerous tasks. When all the preparations had been made, da Gama traveled to Manoel's court at the town of Montemór. There was a formal court ceremony in which da Gama pledged his loyalty and received his final instructions from the King.

Da Gama and his officers returned to Lisbon at the beginning of July 1497. On the night of July 7, they went to a chapel on the banks of the Tagus River that had been built by **Prince Henry the Navigator**. They spent the night there praying for the success of their mission. The next morning, July 8, 1497, there was a solemn mass in the chapel and then a large procession accompanied the sailors to the wharf where the ships were docked. Unlike many other voyages of exploration, this one was a major state occasion and was accompanied by much pomp and ceremony.

The four ships set sail, accompanied by a fifth one under Bartolomeu Dias who was on his way to take command of the Portuguese fortress of Elmina on the Gulf of Guinea. From the Tagus, da Gama's ships reached the Canary Islands on July 15 and then rendezvoused in the Cape Verde Islands, where they stayed from July 26 to August 3. Then they continued south until they were off the coast of what is now Sierra Leone. At that point,

Dias split off. Da Gama, rather than following the coastline south, sailed directly into the South Atlantic and was out of sight of land until November 4, when the ships reached the coast of South Africa at St. Helena Bay about 150 miles north of the Cape of Good Hope. This route took advantage of the prevailing winds and became the main route south for all succeeding sailing vessels.

The Portuguese remained at St. Helena Bay until November 16, taking on food and water. There they had their first contact with the Hottentot people of South Africa, which began in a friendly manner but later became hostile. Adverse winds kept them from rounding the Cape of Good Hope until November 22. They reached Mossel Bay on November 25. This was the place that Dias had named the "Cowboys' Bay," and once again the Portuguese were able to barter with the Hottentots for cattle. They bought a black ox that they found "as toothsome as the beef of Portugal."

While at Mossel Bay, da Gama erected a *padrão* (stone marker) to mark the progress of the expedition. However, by the time he left, relations with the Africans had turned sour, and he saw them destroy the *padrão* as he sailed out of the harbor. At this point, the storeship was broken up and its goods were shared out among the three remaining ships. Setting sail on December 8, they passed the Great Fish River, where Dias had erected his last *padrão*, on December 16. On December 25, they named the land they were passing Natal, in honor of the birth of Christ. On January 11 they anchored at the mouth of a river that they named the Copper River because the Bantu people who lived there had a large quantity of copper tools and ornaments. The people were very friendly and supplied the Europeans with food and water. Da Gama named the country the "Land of the Good People."

On January 25, 1498 the three Portuguese ships arrived at the Kilimane River, on the coast of Mozambique. This was the southern limit of Muslim influence, which had spread down the coast of East Africa in the wake of Arab traders. Da Gama erected a *padrão* at Kilimane, and he and his men rested there for a month while they repaired their ships and took on supplies. During this time, many of the men became sick with scurvy, and several of them died.

From Kilimane the Portuguese sailed to the port of Mozambique, where they arrived on March 2. The people of the city assumed that the visitors were Muslims like themselves. The Sultan of Mozambique came on board the flagship and dined with da Gama. After a few days, he began to realize that he was dealing with the hated and despised Christians. In order to get rid of the unwanted guests, he supplied da Gama with two pilots to guide him through the East African waters. When they learned that their new employers were Christians, they both tried to escape, one of them successfully. Relations with the Sultan deteriorated and ended in armed hostility before the Portuguese left on March 30.

At Mombasa, which had the best harbor on the coast of East Africa and was an important trading center, news of the approaching Christians preceded da Gama. The local sheikh tried to capture the Portuguese fleet, and the remaining pilot was able to escape. Da Gama tortured some Arab captives with boiling oil to make them reveal the Mombasans' "plot."

The next port of call was Malindi, where da Gama arrived on April 15, Easter Sunday, 1498. The ruler of Malindi was the chief rival of Mombasa, and he received the Portuguese very openly, hoping to gain an ally in his struggle with the neighboring port. Da Gama stayed there a week and left with a renowned local pilot on board, Ahmad Ibn Majid, who was to guide the ships to India.

Da Gama left Malindi with favorable monsoon winds and sailed quickly across the Indian Ocean, reaching the port of Calicut on May 20, after sailing for only 23 days out of sight of land. Calicut (now known as Kozhikode) was the most important city on the Malabar Coast of southwestern India and was a major trading emporium. The city was ruled by a Hindu king called the *samudrin raja*, which was corrupted to "Zamorin" by the Portuguese. Its trade was in the hands of Muslim merchants, both Indians and Arabs, who immediately resented the Portuguese as potential rivals.

The Zamorin was away in a nearby town when da Gama arrived, but he returned to greet the Portuguese visitors. On May 28, 1498 da Gama came ashore and was received by the Zamorin with great ceremony and was taken to a Hindu temple, which the Portuguese thought, for some reason, belonged to a Christian sect. Da Gama tried to negotiate a trading agreement, but the Zamorin did not want to alienate the local merchants and, in any case, the goods that the Portuguese wanted to trade had little appeal.

What the Portuguese had to offer seemed so shoddy that the Zamorin refused to accept da Gama's gifts, saying they were not worthy of him. This led to a deterioration in relations. Da Gama's goods sat unbought in a storehouse while the Portuguese sailors spent their time as tourists in the city. This stalemate lasted for two months. Da Gama decided that he was not going to get anywhere and announced his departure. The Zamorin told him that he had to pay a heavy tax in order to depart and seized the Portuguese goods as collateral. Da Gama, in turn, took several hostages. Finally, the Portuguese departed on August 29, 1498 after part of the merchandise was returned and all but five of the hostages were released. Despite the hostility, da Gama left a *padrão* with the Zamorin to be erected to mark his visit, and he carried back a letter in which the Zamorin promised to trade spices and gems if the Portuguese could furnish gold, silver, coral, and scarlet cloth.

The Portuguese headed north along the Indian coast until they reached the Anjedive Islands, where they stayed for two weeks repairing their ships. While there, they were approached by a renegade Venetian who had converted to Islam and worked for the King of Goa. Da Gama took him back to Portugal where he

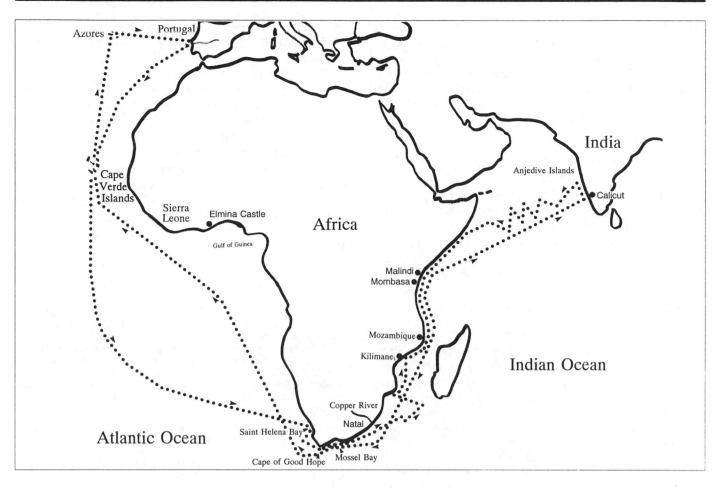

Da Gama's route around Africa and across the Indian Ocean.

was renamed Gaspar da Gama or Gaspar da India. He went out on the next several Portuguese voyages to the East, serving as a very valued interpreter.

The Portuguese left the Anjedive Islands at the wrong time of the year to take advantage of the winds, and it took them from October 2, 1498 to January 2, 1499 to cross to Mogadishu on the African coast, during which time many of the men died of scurvy. Da Gama and his ships arrived back in Malindi on January 7. The *São Rafael* had been damaged in a storm and the crew members were so reduced that da Gama ordered it destroyed and redistributed the crew between the two remaining ships.

From Malindi, the *São Gabriel* and the *Berrio* sailed south, rounding the Cape of Good Hope on March 20. A month later the two ships were separated by a storm, and the *Berrio* reached Lisbon on July 10, 1499. Da Gama, on board the *São Gabriel*, had stopped on the island of Terceira in the Azores because his brother Paulo was dying of tuberculosis. He was buried there, and da Gama returned to Lisbon at the end of August or early in September.

Da Gama was received as a hero in Portugal. King Manoel awarded him with titles and gave him a large annual income. In 1502 he was created Admiral of the Indian Seas and in 1519 he was made Count of Vidigueira. King Manuel himself adopted a new title, calling himself "Lord of Guinea and of the Conquest, Navigation, and Commerce of Ethiopia, Arabia, Persia, and India." In fact, the material benefits of the voyage had been very slight, but the possibilities were enormous. The King began to pursue these opportunities immediately by sending out a new voyage under the command of **Pedro Alvarez Cabral** in 1500.

On Cabral's return, da Gama was sent out on a second voyage. He left February 10, 1502 in command of two squadrons that totaled 15 ships, which were later joined by another five ships. It was necessary to send out a strong fleet because the Portuguese had generated much hostility along the Malabar coast. On the way out, da Gama visited the port of Sofala in what is now Mozambique and Kilwa in Tanzania. In the latter place, he took the local ruler hostage and made him swear loyalty to the King of Portugal. He was prevented by contrary winds from landing in Malindi.

On this voyage, da Gama sailed closer to shore and went around the northern end of the Arabian Sea and then down the coast of India, stopping briefly at the Gulf of Cambay, Goa, and the Anjedive Islands before anchoring off the port of Cannanore.

There, da Gama awaited the return of a ship carrying pilgrims from Mecca. When the *Meri* came into sight, the Portuguese overtook it and forced it to stop. The merchandise was taken onto the Portuguese ships, and the 380 passengers were locked in the hold below. The ship was then set on fire. The fire kept being put out, and da Gama kept ordering his men to restart it. It took four days for the ship to finally sink, killing all of the men, women, and children aboard.

Da Gama arrived at Calicut on October 30, 1502. Faced with the large Portuguese fleet, the Zamorin said that he was willing to sign a treaty. Da Gama told him that he would have to banish every Muslim from his kingdom. In order to impress the Zamorin, he captured 38 fisherman who had come alongside the Portuguese ship to sell their catch. They were hanged from the yardarms of the Portuguese ship. That night the Portuguese took them down and cut off their heads, hands, and feet and floated the limbs and the dismembered corpses onto the shore. Da Gama then began to bombard the city with his guns.

Da Gama sailed to Cochin where he took more hostages and loaded his ships with spices. Attacked by a fleet of the Rajah of Cannanore on February 12, 1503, the Portuguese easily defeated the Arabs. After this demonstration of Portuguese power, da Gama set sail from Cannanore on February 20, catching the favorable monsoon winds to Mozambique. From there he sailed around the Cape back to Portugal, where he arrived on October 11, 1503.

Following his return from his second voyage, da Gama lived in semi-retirement, quarreling with King Manoel as to the value of his accomplishments. He even asked permission to leave Portugal and offer his services to another country. The King wrote him a letter on August 17, 1518 refusing his request. It was soon after that da Gama was made lord of Vidigueira, which seems to have been designed as an inducement to get him to stay. The King died during an epidemic in December 1521, and his son ascended to the throne as João III. Da Gama marched in the coronation procession.

The new King appointed da Gama Viceroy of Portuguese India in February 1524. He went out to take his new post accompanied by his two sons and a fleet of 14 ships that carried 3,000 men, including soldiers and government officials. The fleet stopped in Mozambique on its way to India. Off the coast of India on September 8, 1524, the ships were rocked by a submarine earthquake.

Shortly after, da Gama arrived in Goa, which had become the capital of Portuguese India. On his arrival, he ordered three women who had hidden themselves on the ships in Lisbon to be publicly flogged. By this time, da Gama was quite ill, but he traveled to Cochin to see the retiring governor (and to order his arrest for corruption). He died there in the early morning hours of December 24, 1524. His remains were taken back to Portugal and were eventually buried in the chapel where he had prayed the night before leaving on his first voyage.

Where to learn more

The record of da Gama's first voyage was made by one of the members of the expedition, probably a man named Alvaro Velho. The Portuguese version was first published in 1838 and was translated by E.G. Ravenstein as *A Journal of the First Voyage of Vasco da Gama* (London: Hakluyt Society, 1898). A record of the second voyage was made by an anonymous Dutch sailor, which is known as the "Flemish account." It was translated by Jean Philibert Berjeau as *Calcoen: A Dutch Narrative of the Second Voyage of Vasco da Gama to Calicut* (London: 1874). Another account of da Gama's three voyages was written somewhat later by Gaspar Correa. It is considered to be less reliable than the others. It appeared in English as *Three Voyages of Vasco da Gama, and His Viceroyalty*, translated by Lord Stanley of Alderley (London: Hakluyt Society, 1869). Selections can be found in Charles D. Ley, ed. *Portuguese Voyages, 1498-1663* (London: Everyman's Library, 1947).

Two exhaustive and comprehensive histories of the Portuguese in India were written at the end of the 19th century: Frederick C. Danvers, *The Portuguese in India: Being a History of the Rise and Decline of Their Eastern Empire*, 2 vols. (London: 1894) and Richard S. Whiteway, *The Rise of Portuguese Power in India, 1497-1550* (London: 1899).

A detailed history of da Gama is Kingsley G. Jayne, *Vasco da Gama and His Successors, 1460-1580* (London: 1910). A more recent study and one that can be recommended in spite of the author's tendency to put thoughts in his characters' head and to retail his own prejudices is Henry H. Hart, *Sea Road to the Indies* (New York: Macmillan, 1950). It includes an extensive bibliography.

Summaries of da Gama's voyages can be found in: Edgar Prestage, *The Portuguese Pioneers* (London: Adam & Charles Black, 1933; reprinted, 1966); Mary Seymour Lucas, *Vast Horizons* (New York: Viking, 1943); Boies Penrose, *Travel and Discovery in the Renaissance, 1420-1620* (Cambridge: Harvard University Press, 1952); Gilbert Renault, *The Caravels of Christ*, trans. by Richmond Hill (New York: G.P. Putnam's Sons, 1959); G.R. Crone, *The Discovery of the East* (London: Hamish Hamilton, 1972); and Christopher Bell, *Portugal and the Quest for the Indies* (New York: Harper & row, 1974).

A very important "source" is the *Lúsiadas*, written by Luis de Camoens and first published in 1572. It is an epic poem about the opening of the trade routes to India by the Portuguese and is the national epic. It is available in many editions.

Luigi Maria D'Albertis

(1841 - 1901)

Luigi Maria D'Albertis was an Italian naturalist who made three expeditions up the Fly River into the island of New Guinea.

By the close of the nineteenth century most of the great regions of the world had been at least superficially explored, and their general characteristics were known. There was one great exception, however—the large tropical island of New Guinea. Although the New Guinea coast had been known since the earliest days of the Spanish and Portuguese explorers to the East Indies, practically nothing was known about its interior, where a combination of tropical rainforest and unwelcoming tribes had deterred all visitors.

As the Europeans encroached on more and more of the planet, it was inevitable that New Guinea should not remain untouched. It is perhaps appropriate that the first systematic assault was made by a man with great romantic fantasies, who seems to have attempted the feat more from bravado than for any other reason. He travelled up one of the world's great tropical rivers singing operatic arias and, unfortunately, shooting at any hapless inhabitants who got in his way.

Luigi Maria D'Albertis was born in the coastal town of Voltri not far from the great port of Genoa on November 21, 1841. Left an orphan, he was raised by a pious uncle who sent him to a Jesuit school. There he was influenced by a priest, who later became a missionary in Tibet, to study far-away and unexplored places. D'Albertis was one of the famous "Thousand" led by Giuseppe Garibaldi who invaded the Kingdom of the Two Sicilies in 1860, which led to the unification of the Kingdom of Italy in 1861.

On his return to Genoa, D'Albertis started studying at the Museum of Natural History. In the company of another naturalist he left Genoa on November 25, 1871 and reached the Vogelkop (Bird's Head) Peninsula in western New Guinea on April 9, 1872. He collected specimens of exotic birds and headhunting trophies in the Arfak Mountains at the extreme western end of the island. Ill, D'Albertis moved to Sydney in Australia and then went back to Europe from April 1874 until the end of the year. He returned to Yule Island, which is in the Torres Strait between Australia and New Guinea, in March 1875. This tiny bit of land had become the headquarters for Westerners trying to learn more about the great island to the north.

D'Albertis used the small island as a base to travel along the New Guinea coast and collect specimens. He also felt called upon to terrorize the local population: "I appeared at the window and repeated the order to leave, upon which they insulted me. I then fired at them and, judging from the way in which they fled, I fancy some of them were peppered."

On one expedition to New Guinea, he joined the riverboat *Ellengowan* which started up the Fly River, one of the great rivers emptying into the south coast of New Guinea. The boat went 150 miles upstream before turning back. D'Albertis was convinced that this river held the key to penetrating New Guinea, and he was very disappointed at the decision to turn around: "I said within myself 'Farewell, Fly River! We shall meet again, and soon! Now I repeat, in the solitude of my hut, 'I will return to the Fly; I will go to its source!' A voice within me asks, 'Wilt thou succeed?' I answer, 'We shall see.'"

D'Albertis was able to convince the government of the colony of New South Wales to pay for a riverboat, the *Neva*, to make the expedition. He set off with a crew of nine from all over the world on May 23, 1876. On his first night out he set off fireworks to let the local inhabitants know that he was on his way. Within eight days he had passed the point reached on his earlier trip. He went relentlessly on in spite of hostile tribes that he scared off by firing guns, shortage of food, and dissension among the crew, who seemed to spend most of their time fighting. D'Albertis himself was happily occupied collecting specimens of plants and animals hitherto unknown to the Western world.

The *Neva* eventually made it 580 miles from the mouth of the Fly on June 27, 1876. This was by far the farthest that Westerners had ever penetrated into the island. In fact, it was the farthest they got for several decades. At this point, the river was too narrow to proceed further, but they were within sight of the great mountain chain that runs through the center of the island, which D'Albertis named after King Victor Emmanuel of Italy (which has since been renamed the Star Mountains). He also stole two skeletons from a burial platform in a deserted village ("Exclaim, if you will against my barbarity—say that I have sacrilegiously violated the grave! I shall turn a deaf ear; I am too delighted with my prize to heed reproof!").

On its return trip, the *Neva* turned up one of the tributaries of the Fly, which D'Albertis named the Alice River. However, they struck ground on July 4 and had to wait for a rainstorm to set them free. By this time most of the crew, including D'Albertis, were sick with fever, and they turned back on July 6, stopping along the way to shoot at tribesmen who had had the nerve to turn their backsides to the explorers. Going downstream, it only took ten days to reach the mouth of the river.

The expedition was considered to be a great success and certainly came back with a large number of exotic specimens. However, D'Albertis did run into much criticism for his methods when he went to Sydney the following year to get support for another voyage. He was able to mount a second *Neva* expedition in 1877, but this turned out to be a serious mistake. D'Albertis merely repeated the voyage of the previous year without opening up any new territory; in fact, he ended fifty miles short of where he had gone in 1876. In addition, he encountered serious problems along the way.

The local tribes were uniformly hostile after their prior experiences with D'Albertis, and he was forced to fight his way both up and down the river. River conditions were much less favorable, and it took six months to accomplish a voyage that had taken two months the year before. His new crew was even less disciplined than the previous one; all except one were either killed, deserted or became too sick to work. This experience seems to have ended D'Albertis' taste for adventure, and he returned home to Italy.

D'Albertis spent the following years in writing up the histories of his expedition, which were published in Italy and in England in 1880. After that, he became a recluse and moved to the island of Sardinia, where he spent most of his time hunting. He died in the Sardinian town of Sassari on September 2, 1901. He left his estate to the hospital of his native town of Voltri and his anthropological and biological specimens to museums in Florence and Rome.

Where to learn more

D'Albertis wrote about his explorations in *New Guinea: What I Did and What I Saw*, 2 vols. (London: Sampson Low, 1880). The best general history of the exploration of New Guinea, which includes the story of D'Albertis' three voyages is Gavin Souter, *New Guinea: The Last Unknown* (New York: Taplinger Publishing Co., 1967).

William Dampier

(1651-1715)

William Dampier was an English adventurer who made two expeditions to the west coast of Australia.

William Dampier was born on June 8, 1652 in the village of East Coker in Somerset County, England, the son of a tenant farmer. He went to sea as a young boy and sailed to Newfoundland, the Dutch East Indies, fought in a war against the Dutch, worked on a plantation in Jamaica, and cut timber on the Yucatan peninsula in Mexico. In 1683 he became a buccaneer, a pirate that raided ships on the "Spanish Main" off the coast of central America. He sailed in the West Indies and in the eastern Pacific, lived for a while in Virginia, went to the west coast of Africa, and then went through the Straits of Magellan and up the Pacific coast of the Americas as far as Mexico.

In 1686, Dampier joined a pirate ship called the *Cygnet* in Mexico and sailed with it to the Philippines, Indochina, Taiwan and the island of Timor in Indonesia. The pirates decided to see what they could find on the western coast of Australia, which had been named New Holland by the Dutch sailors who had been visiting there since 1616. These first Englishmen in Australia landed on January 4, 1688 at a bay in the northwestern corner of Australia (Cygnet Bay), surrounded by the many islands of Buccaneer Archipelago. They stayed until March but reported back that the land was very desolate and the Aborigines they met were unfriendly. This view corresponded with that of the Dutch, who had never seen any reason to set up a base in this "New Holland."

From Australia the *Cygnet* sailed to the Nicobar Islands off the coast of India, where Dampier and seven others left the pirate ship and went in a small canoe to Sumatra in Indonesia. He roamed around southeast Asia for a while and then returned to England in September 1691.

In spite of his years as a buccaneer, Dampier returned home with only one item of value—the journal he had kept of his many adventures and wanderings. A summary of the diary was published in 1697 as a *New Voyage Round the World*, and Dampier immediately became a famous man. He was much praised for the acuteness and detail of his observations, and he was consulted by the government on various navigational matters. He was asked to suggest a voyage to the British Admiralty that would be of benefit to the nation. Dampier proposed to return to New Holland and from there see if it was linked to the great southern continent, the *Terra Australis incognita*, that men of that age thought existed.

Dampier's idea was accepted and he was named captain of a ship sent out to investigate Australia. He was, however, given inadequate resources to carry out this task. He was supplied with an old ship, the *Roebuck*, whose wooden timbers were rotten, and an untrained crew that was too small to effectively man the ship. In any case, he set out on January 14, 1699. In his original plan, Dampier had wanted to sail around the southern tip of South America and then to head west for Australia. This was something that had never been attempted before, and if successful would have given humankind a picture of the world that it would not actually have for another century. However, the conditions under which he had to sail convinced Dampier to follow the safer, and well-known, course of sailing eastward from the Cape of Good Hope.

From the very beginning of his voyage, Dampier had trouble with his crew, who were mutinous and incompetent. In Brazil, he turned his second in command, Lieutenant Fisher, over to a Portuguese prison. He reached western Australia on July 31, 1699 and stayed at a place called Dirk Hartog's Island, discovered by that Dutchman in 1616. The *Roebuck* sailed northward along the coast of western Australia, where it discovered Dampier's Archipelago and Roebuck Bay. Dampier had two aims—to find a passage to the east and a source of fresh water for his crew. Unfortunately, he found neither and in desperate straits was forced to call off the search after five weeks and head for the island of Timor in the East Indies.

After getting fresh provisions on Timor, Dampier sailed eastward to New Guinea, which he sighted on January 1, 1700. He sailed around the western tip of that large island and then headed east as far as the islands of New Hanover, New Ireland, and New Britain. He sailed around the eastern end of these islands and then through Dampier Strait, which separates New Britain from New Guinea. This was the first proof that the islands were not all part of one larger landmass, and Dampier was the first European to visit the large island of New Britain.

Dampier would have liked to go farther east and try to see if there was a passage between New Guinea and Australia, but the condition of his crew and his ship made this impossible. He headed back along the northern coast of New Guinea to Timor and then to Batavia, the capital of the Dutch East Indies, where his ship was repaired.

The *Roebuck* left Batavia on October 17, 1700 and traveled on till it reached Ascension Island in the mid-Atlantic on February 22, 1701. There, the ship was so rotten that it sprung a leak and sank off the coast of the small island. Dampier and the crew made it safely to shore where they had to wait five weeks, living on turtles and wild goats, for English ships to stop and take them home.

When Dampier got back to London, he found that the Lieutenant Fisher that he had left behind in Brazil had made his way back to England and had started legal proceedings against his former captain. Eventually Dampier was found guilty of improper procedure and fined all his pay.

Dampier then took up his old profession of buccaneer and made two trips to the Pacific to prey on Spanish ships. In the first of these, from 1703 to 1707, he served as captain of one of two ships. He lost his ship in the Pacific, and the voyage did not make money. It had a special note of interest in that the master of the other ship, Alexander Selkirk, was left ashore on Juan Fernandez Island and stayed there alone for more than four years. His story served as the model for Daniel Defoe's *Robinson Crusoe*, written in 1720. Dampier himself was accused of brutality, drunkenness, and cowardice on this voyage. The angry book he wrote on his return—the *Vindication*—did nothing to restore his reputation.

Dampier's last voyage was as navigator for a buccaneer ship commanded by Captain Woodes Rogers from 1708 to 1711. Rogers' ship picked up Alexander Selkirk from his exile. This voyage was very successful and captured the Manila silver galleon, but Dampier did not get the part of the profit that he thought was his due. He died in poverty in England in March 1715.

Dampier is today highly regarded for the clear-headed ("scientific") way in which he recorded his observations during his travels, unlike those of many of his contemporaries who easily mixed fact with legend. His record of the winds and currents of the Pacific Ocean proved to be accurate and served navigators for many years.

Where to learn more

Dampier wrote four books about his voyages: *A New Voyage Round the World* (London: James Knapton, 1697); *Voyages and Descriptions* (London: James Knapton, 1699); *Voyage to New Holland &c. in the Year 1699* (London: James Knapton, 1703; with a Supplement published in 1709); and *Captain Dampier's Vindication of his Voyage to the South Seas in the Ship St. George* (London: 1707). A collection of his voyages was published by James Knapton in 1729 in four volumes.

Much of Dampier's modern reputation rests upon an edition of the these works that was edited by the famous English poet John Masefield: *Dampier's Voyages* (London: Grant Richards, 1906). Masefield also wrote a romantic account of one of Dampier's journeys in *On the Spanish Main* (New York: 1906).

The only full-scale twentieth century biography of Dampier is long out of print: Clennel Wilkinson, *Dampier, Explorer and Buccaneer* (New York: 1929). There are also two shorter studies. The first, Willard Hallam Bonner, *Captain William Dampier, Buccaneer-Author* (Stanford: Stanford University Press, 1934), discusses Dampier as a writer and his influence on such noted English authors as Daniel Defoe and Jonathan Swift. The other, Joseph C. Shipman, *William Dampier: Seaman-Scientist* (Lawrence, Kansas: The University of Kansas Libraries, 1962) discusses the scientific tone and method of his journals.

There are discussions of Dampier in Vilhjalmur Stefansson, *Great Adventures and Explorations* (New York: 1947); J.C. Beaglehole, *The Exploration of the Pacific* (Stanford: Stanford University Press, 1966); and Derek Wilson, *The Circumnavigators* (New York: M. Evans & Co., 1989).

Charles Darwin

(1809 - 1882)

Charles Darwin was an English scientist who made one great trip around the world that led him to develop his theories of evolution.

Charles Darwin.

Charles Darwin was born in Shrewsbury, England, on February 12, 1809 at almost exactly the same hour as Abraham Lincoln. Darwin's father was a doctor; his mother was the daughter of Josiah Wedgwood, the founder of the famous pottery firm. His grandfather (already dead) was a famous botanist, Erasmus Darwin. Darwin's mother died when he was eight years old. He was not a very successful student, but as a teenager he became interested in natural science and started various collections. He went to Edinburgh University to study medicine but did not do well. He transferred to Cambridge University with the idea of studying theology and becoming a clergyman. There he met Professor John Henslow, a botanist, who became his mentor and persuaded him to study geology. He also read **Alexander von Humboldt**'s book, *A Personal Narrative*, about his travels in South America, which greatly inspired him.

Darwin got his B.A. degree from Cambridge in June 1831. During the summer he traveled with a geology professor to study rock formations in Wales. On his return to Shrewsbury on August 29, he found a letter waiting for him from Henslow. Henslow had recommended Darwin for a job as naturalist on board a Royal Navy ship, the *Beagle*, under the command of Captain Robert Fitzroy. The ship was going on a long trip to survey the southern coasts of South America. Darwin's father was initially opposed because he felt that this would keep him from starting his career in the church. With the help of his Wedgwood relatives, Darwin was able to get his father's permission.

The *Beagle* left England on December 27, 1831. It was a small ship, only 90 feet long, with a crew of 74. Darwin's laboratory was a small space at the end of the chartroom, where he also had his hammock for sleeping. Not only was his space cramped, but Darwin suffered miserably from seasickness every day that the ship was at sea. He tried to remedy this by spending as much time ashore as possible and often traveled overland to meet up with the ship at another port.

From England the *Beagle* sailed to the Cape Verde Islands and then to the Brazilian port of Bahia, where it arrived on February 29, 1832. Darwin spent much of his time there collecting specimens from the surrounding forests. He also got into a violent quarrel with Fitzroy on the subject of slavery (a major

question in Brazil at the time) to which Darwin was adamantly opposed. Reaching Rio de Janeiro in early April, Darwin met an Irishman and traveled with him by horseback for seven days to his coffee plantation in the interior. Along the way, he collected specimens of the teeming insect life.

In July and August 1832 Darwin and the *Beagle* were in Montevideo in Uruguay. During this first visit, the ship's crew did not have many opportunities to go ashore because of civil unrest. On August 19, the *Beagle* headed south to begin surveying the coast of Patagonia in southern Argentina. On September 23 near Bahia Blanca, Darwin made a highly significant discovery—the bones of "numerous gigantic extinct Quadrupeds." There were remains of several different species, none of which existed any longer, and they were covered with seashells. The fact that these creatures had been alive "whilst the sea was peopled with most of its present inhabitants" was an important revelation.

In January 1833, the *Beagle* sailed into the Beagle Channel south of the large island of Tierra del Fuego. It was hit by a storm

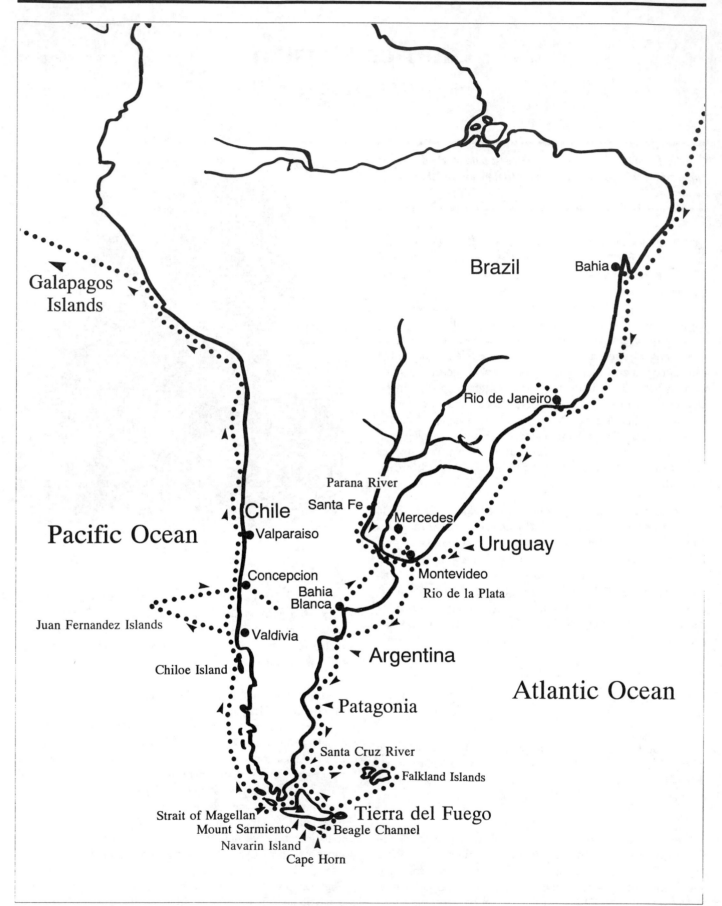

Brazil

Bahia

Galapagos
Islands

Pacific Ocean

Chile
• Valparaiso

Parana River

Santa Fe

Mercedes

Uruguay

Montevideo

Rio de Janeiro

Concepcion

Bahia
Blanca

Rio de la Plata

Juan Fernandez Islands

Valdivia

Argentina

Atlantic Ocean

Chiloe Island

Patagonia

Santa Cruz River

Falkland Islands

Strait of Magellan

Tierra del Fuego

Mount Sarmiento

Beagle Channel

Navarin Island

Cape Horn

Voyage of the *Beagle* and Darwin's inland treks.

that lasted 24 days and at one point almost overturned the ship. Darwin was seasick for most of the time. The aim in going to Tierra del Fuego was to return three native Fuegians that Fitzroy had taken on board during a previous voyage. With them went a missionary, sent to convert the Fuegians to Christianity. On their arrival, one of the Fuegians did not want to return home, and the ship had to return a week later to pick up the missionary who had been threatened with his life by the Native Americans on the island. Soon after, they almost lost the ship's boats when a glacier "calved" and created giant waves that almost washed the boats out to sea.

In March and April 1833 the *Beagle* spent five weeks in the Falkland Islands, which had just been claimed by Great Britain. It spent the southern winter in the harbor in Montevideo. In August 1833 Fitzroy left Darwin ashore at the little town of Carmen de Patagones while the ship carried out routine surveying chores. Darwin rode overland to Bahia Blanca where he re-examined the fossil remains and thought about their significance. By the time he left on September 8, 1833 he had begun to doubt the accepted view that the species were unchangeable and had existed in their current form ever since the Creation. His entire outlook on the nature of life had changed. He was careful, however, not to share his views with Fitzroy, who remained a firm "Creationist" all his life.

From Bahia Blanca Darwin traveled north across the Argentine pampas (plains) accompanied by gauchos (cowboys) who hunted with *bolas* and *lazos* (a kind of weighted lasso). Along the way he met the Argentine dictator, Juan Manuel Rosas, who was engaged in a war of extermination against the Native Americans of the pampas. He saw flocks of rheas, a form of ostrich, which were flightless but could outrun most horses. Darwin found the remains of an unknown species of rhea that he sent back to England and which was named after him—*rhea darwinii.*

After reaching Buenos Aires and resting a few days at the home of an English merchant, Darwin traveled up the Paraná River to the port city of Santa Fe, where he saw some more fossils. He then made a trip from Mercedes to Montevideo in Uruguay, where he met up with the *Beagle* on December 6, 1833. In March 1834, after having visited the Falkland Islands once again, the *Beagle* went back to Tierra del Fuego where they met up with one of the returned Fuegians. In April they sailed up the coast of Patagonia, putting into the mouth of the Santa Cruz River to carry out some repairs.

On April 18, 1834 Fitzroy and Darwin with 23 men and three whaleboats set off on a three-week journey of exploration up the Santa Cruz River. They saw continual signs of Native Americans but never met up with any in the cold desert region of southern Patagonia. They traveled to the foothills of the Andes and came within a few miles of the river's source at Lago Argentino without realizing it. Along the way, Darwin shot a condor that had a wing span of eight feet. To Darwin's disappointment they were forced to turn back because of low supplies. The others were uncomfortable and grumbled, but Darwin remained cheerful: "Almost every

one is discontented with this expedition, much hard work, and much time lost and scarcely anything seen or gained . . . To me the cruize has been most satisfactory, from affording so excellent a section of the great tertiary formations of Patagonia."

At the end of May 1834 the *Beagle* entered the Straits of Magellan for the last time and then exited into the Pacific. Stormy weather made sailing slow, and they put in on Chiloé Island to wait for better weather. The ship's purser died there. They reached Valparaiso, the chief port of Chile, on July 23, 1834. An old acquaintance from Shrewsbury was living there, and Darwin stayed as a guest in his house. Like many of his shipmates, he was ill for the first few weeks of his stay. In fact, it appears as though Fitzroy suffered a nervous breakdown in Valparaiso, and this delayed their departure. Darwin used the extra time to set out on an expedition across the Andes to the Argentine town of Mendoza. In November 1834 Fitzroy took the *Beagle* south again to Chiloé Island. Darwin was able to get a specimen of the very rare Chilotan fox by walking up behind it while it was observing two British officers take measurements and hitting it on the head with his geological hammer. On February 20, 1835 at Valdivia on the coast of Chile, they experienced the strongest earthquake that anyone in the area had experienced, which destroyed the city of Concepción farther north. When they reached Concepción, Darwin found that the earthquake had permanently raised the land and saw evidence of such uplift from previous quakes as well.

When the *Beagle* returned to Valparaiso in March 1835 Darwin arranged with Fitzroy to leave the ship and travel overland through the Andes by way of the dangerous Portillo Pass into Peru. Once again, he found evidence of the changing geological history of the earth—"It is an old story, but not the less wonderful, to hear of shells, which formerly were crawling about at the bottom of the sea, being now elevated nearly 14,000 feet above its level." Darwin rejoined his ship at the Peruvian port of Copiapó on July 5, 1835. They left from there on September 6 to go to the Galápagos Islands.

On September 15, 1835 the *Beagle* reached Chatham Island in the Galápagos Archipelago. The ship stayed among the islands for five weeks. Darwin wrote, "the natural history of this archipelago is very remarkable: it seems to be a little world within itself, the greater number of its inhabitants, both vegetable and animal, being found nowhere else." Of the 26 species of land birds that he looked at, only one, a kind of finch, was known to exist anywhere else. He was fascinated by the giant tortoises and the other varieties of reptiles that he saw. While in the Galápagos Darwin did not come up with any answers as to why the forms of life were so different in those remote islands from the rest of the world. But he did begin to ask himself some questions. This later became the basis for his famous theories. A couple of years later, in 1837, he wrote the following entry in his *Journal:* "In July opened first notebook on Transmutation of Species. Had been greatly struck from about the month of previous March on character of South American fossils, and species on Galapagos

Archipelago. These facts (especially the latter) are the origin of all my views."

The trip homeward from the Galápagos was relatively uneventful. The *Beagle* stopped for ten days in Tahiti, where Darwin took two hikes into the interior. The expedition spent Christmas 1835 at a mission station on the North Island of New Zealand. Darwin compared the New Zealand Maoris, who had been subject to more Western influence, unfavorably to the Tahitians. He praised the work of the missionaries, however. In New Zealand he heard stories about the giant moa, a flightless bird between 10 and 12 feet tall that had only recently become extinct.

Stopping at Sydney in Australia, Darwin took a 12-day riding trip to the town of Bathurst, traveling part of the time with a group of Aborigines. The *Beagle* sailed via Tasmania and King George Sound in southwestern Australia to the Cocos Islands in the Indian Ocean, where Darwin investigated several natural phenomena. One of these was that the island's vegetation had mostly originated in Java and Sumatra, some 600 miles away; seeds and plants had been driven there by winds and currents and had taken root. Darwin was also fascinated by the coral formations that make up the Cocos Islands. He discovered that the coral polyps can only build a reef at a maximum depth of between 20 and 30 fathoms. Any coral reef or island that extended deeper than that below the water, and there are many, must have been created over millions of years as the original ground surface sank.

The *Beagle* continued on to Mauritius; Cape Town, where Darwin had dinner with the famous astronomer Sir John Herschel; St. Helena, where he slept near Napoleon's tomb; and Ascension Island. At Ascension several letters from home reached him, and he learned that some of his reports had been read at the Geological Society in London and received universal praise. The last ports of call were Bahia, Brazil and the Azores. The *Beagle* reached Falmouth, England on October 2, 1836, and Darwin left to go home to Shrewsbury, "having lived on board the little vessel very nearly five years."

The voyage of the *Beagle* constituted Darwin's lifetime field research. He never went abroad again. It was only after he was back in England and began to reflect on what he had seen that he started to develop his ideas on evolution. He began to publish the results of these reflections soon after his return, the first being on the nature of coral formations. The rest of his life was spent on research and writing.

Darwin's most important work, *The Origin of the Species*, only appeared in 1859. In it he put forth the theory of evolution that has guided scientists ever since—that living organisms change by a series of random permutations, which are "naturally selected" insofar as they are adapted to their environment. These ideas were not entirely new. Thomas Malthus had already presented similar ideas, and Darwin's friend **Alfred Russell Wallace** was working towards the same conclusion indepen-

dently. As a result of the *Beagle* voyage, however, Darwin was able to back up his ideas with concrete evidence.

Following his return to England, Darwin spent the next few years living as a bachelor in London. On November 11, 1838 ("the day of days"), he proposed to his cousin Emma Wedgwood and she accepted. They were married in January 1839; together they had 10 children, three of whom died in childhood. Darwin was elected to the prestigious Royal Society a few days before his marriage. In September 1842 he and his family moved to Down House in the English county of Kent, where he spent the rest of his life. Darwin suffered from increasing ill health over the years. Many theories have been put forth as to the nature of his illness. One that is widely held is that he suffered from Chagas' disease, a tropical ailment that affects the nervous system, as the result of a bite he got in Brazil. Other theories hold that the illness was essentially psychosomatic, with a wide range of possible causes. He died at the age of 73 at Down House on April 19, 1882.

Where to learn more

There is an enormous volume of literature about Darwin. There is even an encyclopedia of Darwiniana: R.B. Freeman, *Charles Darwin: A Companion* (Folkestone, England: Dawson, Anchor Books, 1978). The obvious place to start is with Darwin's own works, which are all very readable. His account of the *Beagle* voyage is *Journal of Researches into the Natural History and Geology of the Countries Visited During the Voyage of H.M.S. Beagle Round the World* (London: Henry Colburn, 1839). The best known is the second edition (London: John Murray, 1845). There is a paperback abridgement that can be recommended: Janet Browne and Michael Neve, editors, *Voyage of the Beagle* (New York: Penguin Books, 1989). Darwin's actual shipboard diary was published many years later: Richard Keynes, ed. *Charles Darwin's Beagle Diary* (Cambridge: Cambridge University Press). Darwin's account was originally published as volume 3 of the official record of the expedition. Captain Robert Fitzroy wrote the first two volumes: *Narrative of the Surveying Voyages of HMS Adventure and Beagle Between 1826 and 1836* (London: 1839).

Darwin's other works include: *On the Origin of the Species* (London: John Murray, 1859; many subsequent editions, including a facsimile reprint with an introduction by Ernst Mayr, Cambridge: Harvard University Press, 1964); *The Descent of Man, and Selection in Relation to Sex*, 2 vols. (London: John Murray, 1871; many subsequent editions); Francis Darwin, ed. *Life and Letters of Charles Darwin*, 3 vols. (London: John Murray, 1887); Francis Darwin and A.C. Seward, *More Letters of Charles Darwin*, 2 vols. (London: John Murray, 1903). The *Complete Correspondence of Charles Darwin* is in the process of being edited by Frederick Burckhardt and Sydney Smith, published by Cambridge University Press. The first four volumes were published from 1985 to 1988. Frederick Burckhardt also edited *Darwin's Scientific Diaries 1836-1842* (Cambridge: Cambridge University Press, 1987).

Darwin's granddaughter, Nora Barlow, has edited three important volumes: *Charles Darwin and the Voyage of the "Beagle"* (London: Pilot Press, 1945); *The Autobiography of Charles Darwin*, which he wrote between 1872 and his death but which was not published during his lifetime (London: Collins, 1958); and *Darwin and Henslow: The Growth of an Idea. Letters, 1831-1860* (London: John Murray, 1967).

Of books about Darwin, several can be recommended: H.E.L. Mellersh, *Charles Darwin: Pioneer of the Theory of Evolution* (London: 1964); Julian Huxley, *Charles Darwin and His World* (London: 1965); Benjamin Farrington, *What Darwin Really Said* (London: 1966). There is a good account of the *Beagle* voyage in Victor Wolfgang von Hagen, *South America Called Them* (Boston: Little, Brown & Company, 1955). Particularly enjoyable to read, and with copious illustrations, is Alan Moorehead, *Darwin and the Beagle* (New York: Harper & Row, 1969; reprinted New York: Crescent Books, 1983).

On the subject of Darwin's illness, there is quite a lot of research, including Ralph Colp, Jr., *To Be an Invalid: The Illness of Charles Darwin* (Chicago: Chicago University Press, 1977) and John Bowlby, *Charles Darwin: A New Life* (New York: W.W. Norton & Co., 1990). The latter of these is a complete biography, with emphasis on the medical aspects of Darwin's life.

Alexandra David-Neel

(1868 - 1969)

Alexandra David-Neel was a noted French authority on Buddhism who was the first European woman to travel to Lhasa, the capital of Tibet.

Alexandra David was born in the Paris suburb of Saint-Mandé on October 24, 1868. Her father was a French journalist and her mother was a Belgian. They had an unhappy marriage and David-Neel spent a lonely childhood. She ran away from home several times and spent much of her time reading about Eastern religions and philosophy.

In pursuit of her desire to learn more about non-Christian religions, she traveled to India in 1891. But she was unable to afford a lengthy stay and returned to France where she got a job in 1894 as a singer in a traveling opera company under the stage name of Mademoiselle Myrial. Traveling with the opera company she went to French colonies in Indochina and to Greece and Tunis. In Tunis in 1904 she met and married a French engineer

Alexandra David-Neel. UPI/Bettmann.

named Philippe-François Neel. He adored her and financed her subsequent travels although they spent most of their married years apart.

Following her marriage, David-Neel (the name she adopted after her marriage) returned to Paris and began to study Oriental religions systematically and to lecture on comparative religions. In 1910 the French Ministry of Education sent her to India to continue her research. In 1911 she learned that the Dalai Lama, the chief spiritual and political leader of Tibet, had fled his country because of a Chinese invasion and was staying in Bhutan. She went to visit him there and was the first European woman admitted to his presence. She returned to say good-bye to him when he returned to Lhasa (the capital of Tibet) in 1912.

From Bhutan David-Neel traveled to the nearby kingdom of Sikkim where she started her studies of Tibetan. She stayed at the monastery of Podang. There she was given a 15-year-old Sikkimese student lama, Yongden, as a companion. In order to experience the life of a Buddhist nun, David-Neel went to a remote cave in Sikkim and spent the winter of 1914-1915 meditating in the cave. Yongden and other servants lived a short distance away and brought her one meal a day. Leaving the cave, she left Sikkim and traveled for a short way into Tibet to the monastery of Tashilhumpo, where the Panchen Lama, the second-ranking Tibetan lama, lived.

As a result of her unauthorized visit, David-Neel was kicked out of Sikkim and returned to India. She (always accompanied by Yongden) made two short trips into Tibet during the summers of 1915 and 1916 and then traveled to Burma and Japan and China. In northern China she stayed in a Buddhist monastery for 2½ years translating Tibetan texts. In the winter of 1922-1923 she and Yongden traveled across the Gobi Desert in southern Mongolia and tried to enter Tibet from the north. Her disguise was discovered, and she was escorted out of the country.

In the summer of 1923 David-Neel and Yongden tried to get to Lhasa once more. This time they traveled from the extreme southeastern part of Tibet with a group of Buddhist pilgrims. David-Neel dressed as a Tibetan woman and claimed to be the mother of Yongden. Yongden was able to travel freely because of his status as a lama. They traveled leisurely through the Tibetan countryside, stopping to visit monasteries and areas of natural beauty. Yongden sprained his ankle and David-Neel had to carry him for a while. They got lost and were almost attacked by robbers until they scared them away with gunshots. They reached Lhasa during the Buddhist New Year in early 1924. Still in her disguise, David-Neel roamed throughout the city and had a tour of the Potala, the mighty palace of the Dalai Lama.

Leaving Lhasa, she and Yongden traveled to a Catholic mission at Podang in the Himalayas on the Indian side of the border. There she wrote to her husband who had had no news of her for two years. She and Yongden went to France in May 1925 where she wrote about her experiences as the first European woman to have traveled to Lhasa. Her articles were serialized in a magazine and then made into a book, which was a great success. She used the proceeds from the sales to buy a house in 1928 in the south of France, which she named Samten Dzong (Fortress of Meditation), in the town of Digne. She also convinced her husband to legally adopt Yongden, whose new name became Arthur David-Neel. The two of them lived together in Digne while her husband stayed in North Africa.

In 1936 David-Neel and Yongden traveled back to China. By that time, the country was in turmoil because of civil war and Japanese invasion. They took refuge in a monastery on the Tibetan border and stayed there for six years until the end of World War II. There she received word of her husband's death in 1941. With the end of the war, David-Neel and Yongden fled south into French Indochina and were evacuated from there to India and then back to France. They returned to Digne, where Yongden died from alcoholism in 1955. David-Neel lived on until September 8, 1969, when she died peacefully in her sleep at the age of 100.

Where to learn more

David-Neel was the author of several works about her travels and her studies of Buddhist mysticism. Those that have been translated into English that deal specifically with her travels are: *My Journey to Lhasa* (New York: Harper & Brothers, 1927; paperback reprint, Boston: Beacon Press, 1986) and *Tibetan Journey* (London: Lane, 1936).

David-Neel's unusual life has generated much interest in recent years. An excellent biography was published by Barbara M. Foster and Michael Foster, *Forbidden Journey: The Life of Alexandra David-Neel* (New York: Harper & Row, 1987; paperback edition, 1989). Another biography, emphasizing her Buddhist studies and writings is Ruth Middleton, *Alexandra David-Neel: Portrait of an Adventurer* (Boston: Shambhala Publications, 1989). There are shorter biographies in Lurie Miller, *On Top of the World: Five Women Explorers in Tibet* (London: Paddington, 1976); Marion Tinling, *Women into the Unknown* (New York: Greenwood Press, 1989); and Dea Birkett, *Spinsters Abroad: Victorian Lady Explorers* (London: Basil Blackwell, 1989).

John Davis

(1550-1605)

John Davis was an English navigator who made three important voyages to Greenland and Baffin Island, discovered the Falkland Islands, and later sailed to the East Indies.

John Davis was born in the English county of Devon in what is known as the West Country, where many of England's great navigators and seamen came from. He was a childhood friend of **Sir Humphrey Gilbert** and **Sir Walter Raleigh**. He had only a grammar school education but became a highly skilled navigator.

Like both Gilbert and Raleigh, Davis believed in a Northwest Passage around North America to Asia. In 1585 he was able to convince backers to sponsor a voyage to look for the passage. He left Dartmouth, England on June 7, 1585 with two ships—the *Sunneshine* and the *Mooneshine*. He sailed to the west coast of Greenland which had been settled by Vikings but had then lost contact with Europe in the thirteenth century. Davis was the first European to see the coast of Greenland since that time. From Greenland he sailed across what is now called Davis Strait to land on the west coast of Baffin Island. He returned to England on September 30, 1585.

After this trip Davis was convinced that the entrance to the Northwest Passage could be found either up Cumberland Sound on the east coast of Baffin Island or farther up Davis Strait. He left England again on May 7, 1586 with his original two ships plus the *Mermayde* and the *North Starre*. This time the ice conditions were less favorable than on his previous voyage, and he was forced to turn back some ways up Davis Strait. He replenished his supplies off the coast of Labrador and then returned to England on October 14, 1586.

Davis set out again on May 19, 1587. This year ice conditions were much better, and he was able to sail up Davis Strait to about 72° north on the west coast of Greenland to a spot he named Hope Sanderson after one of his backers. He could not proceed to the west because the currents kept pushing him south. He went along the coast of Baffin Island and found Frobisher Bay and Hudson Strait, the entrance into Hudson Bay. He went down the coast of Labrador and discovered the fjord that now has his name—Davis Inlet. He provided the first descriptions of the Inuit and his log book became a model for other explorers. He reached England on September 15, 1587.

This was Davis's last trip to the Arctic. He joined the expedition of Thomas Cavendish that set out from England on August 26, 1591 with the aim of sailing around the world. The plan was that once they had gone through the Straits of Magellan, Davis was supposed to separate off and head up the west coast of the Americas and look for the Northwest Passage from that side. The expedition never made it through the Straits. Forced back into the Atlantic, Davis with two small ships put into Puerto Deseado on the coast of Argentina, leaving Cavendish alone with one ship in the Atlantic. Cavendish accused Davis of desertion ("that villain that hath been the death of me"), which Davis strenuously denied. He made three further attempts to sail through the Straits, with no success. Davis's ship *Desire* was driven off course in "a sore storm" and on August 14, 1592 was "driven in among certaine isles never before discovered . . . lying fiftie leagues or better from the ashore east and northerly from the streights." As far as is known, he was the first person to have seen the Falkland Islands.

In 1595 Davis published a book called *The worldes hydrographical discription*, which is the most accurate description of geographical knowledge at that time. He then became a pilot for various expeditions to the East Indies: from 1598 to 1600 on the second Dutch expedition. When Davis offered his services to the Dutch he made much of the fact that he felt slighted by the English because they refused to sponsor another expedition to find the Northwest Passage. It made a convincing story, but it became apparent after the trip that Davis had had another reason for wanting to go on the Dutch expedition to the Indies.

Just three days after his return in 1600, Davis wrote a letter to the Earl of Essex, an important official in Queen Elizabeth's court, saying "According to those directions which your Lordship gave me in charge at my departure; when it please You to employ me in this voyage for the Discovering of these Eastern Ports of the World, to the service of Her Majesty and the good of our Country." Enclosed with the letter was his journal of the trip. Before the end of 1600 the English had formed their own East India Company and in 1603-1604 Davis was the pilot of the first English expedition to the East Indies.

In December 1604 Davis left England once again as the pilot of the ship *Tiger* sailing to the Indies. He charted the west coast of Sumatra. Off the coast of Malaya the ship captured a Japanese pirate ship. On December 27, 1605 the Japanese prisoners escaped and killed Davis as their first victim.

Where to learn more

Davis's own works are included in Richard Hakluyt's *Principal Navigations, Voyages, Traffiques and Discoveries of the English Nation* (London: Hakluyt Society, 1903-1905) and in *Hakluyt's Collection of the Early Voyages, Travels, and Discoveries of the English Nation*, 5 vols., edited by R.H. Evans (London: 1812).

There are two biographies of Davis: A.H. Markham, *The Voyages and Works of John Davis* (London: Hakluyt Society, 1880) and C.R. Markham, *A Life of John Davis, the Navigator, 1550-1605, Discoverer of Davis Straits* (London: 1889).

More recent discussions of Davis can be found in: Jeannette Mirsky, *To the Arctic!: The Story of Northern Exploration from Earliest Times to the Present* (New York: Alfred A. Knopf, 1948); Tryggvi J. Olesen, *Early Voyages and Northern Approaches, 1000-1632* (Toronto: McClelland and Stewart, 1963); and J.M. Scott, *Icebound: Journeys to the Northwest Sea* (London: Gordon & Cremonesi, 1977).

George Washington De Long

(1844-1881)

George Washington De Long was an American explorer who died trying to prove that it was possible to sail all the way to the North Pole by sailing north through Bering Strait.

G eorge Washington De Long was an American naval officer, born in New York City. In 1873 he took part in a voyage to search for the ship *Polaris*, which under Captain **Charles Francis Hall** had set out to reach the North Pole by sailing up the west coast of Greenland. Hall had died (probably from poisoning by his own crew) in northern Greenland and his ship had been broken up in the ice, although most members of the expedition were saved.

This experience gave De Long the polar bug, and he decided to try to reach the Pole himself. De Long heard about the theories of a German scientist named August Petermann. Petermann, without any evidence at all, felt that on the Pacific entrance to the Arctic Ocean a warm current of water led to a basin of clear water at the top of the world—in other words that it was possible to sail to the North Pole.

At this time in the United States, there was fierce competition among the many newspapers for circulation. One of the devices they used was to sponsor newsworthy "stunts" to which they would have exclusive rights. A newspaper had, for example, sent **Henry Morton Stanley** to find **David Livingstone**. De Long was able to convince the publisher of the New York *Herald* to pay for the costs of his expedition through the Bering Strait to the North Pole.

De Long left San Francisco on July 8, 1879 in a coal-burning steamer also equipped with sails, the *Jeannette*. The ship sailed

Sinking of the *Jeanette*.

George Washington De Long. The Granger Collection, New York.

was wrong in thinking it part of a larger body of land, through a body of water that has since been named for him—Proliv Longa—and past a group of small islands—Ostrova De Longa.

At this point, in June 1881, the *Jeannette* was crushed by the pack ice, and De Long and his crew of 33 men were forced to abandon the ship in three lifeboats. The boats were separated: one disappeared in a storm; one, with De Long on board, made it to the mainland of Siberia, but then all its crew died from starvation and exhaustion; the last one made it to the mainland and was rescued. De Long had traveled 300 miles by sledge and boat to the Siberian coast, but did not survive the ordeal. He had found out that the theory of an open-water route to the Pole was, as he wrote in his diary that was recovered, "a delusion and a snare."

There was an interesting sequel to De Long's trip. Three years after the *Jeannette* broke up, some materials from it, including a pair of oilskin breeches marked with the name of one of the sailors and a hat, turned up off the southwest coast of Greenland, 2,900 miles away. This proved that the polar ice was in motion, and the Norwegian **Fridtjof Nansen** began to speculate whether it might not be possible to float on that ice to the Pole.

Where to learn more

The records of De Long's expedition were edited and published by his wife: Emma De Long, ed. *The Voyage of the "Jeannette"*, 2 vols. (Boston: Houghton Mifflin Company, 1883).

The definitive account on the expedition is Leonard F. Guttridge's *Icebound: The Jeannette Expedition's Quest for the North Pole* (Annapolis, Maryland: Naval Institute Press, 1986). It includes an extensive bibliography and several photographs.

There are interesting accounts of the voyage of the *Jeannette* in Jeannette Mirsky, *To the Arctic!: The Story of Northern Exploration from Earliest Times to the Present* (New York: Alfred A. Knopf, 1948) and John Maxtone-Graham, *Safe Return Doubtful: The Heroic Age of Polar Exploration* (New York: Charles Scribner's Sons, 1988).

through the Bering Strait and then headed for Wrangel Island, north of the eastern end of Siberia, which De Long thought to be part of a larger landmass. Short of Wrangel Island, the *Jeannette* became trapped in ice and was never able to escape. The ice carried the ship northwestward for the next 22 months. De Long and his men saw Wrangel Island pass by, proving that De Long

Ippolito Desideri

(1684 - 1733)

Ippolito Desideri was an Italian missionary who traveled to Tibet from India and stayed in that country for four years.

Ippolito Desideri was born into an aristocratic family in the town of Pistoia north of Florence. He joined the Jesuit order at the age of 16 in 1700. He left Genoa on November 22, 1712 headed for India. He traveled through the Straits of Gibraltar to Lisbon and then embarked on a Portuguese ship traveling around the Cape of Good Hope. He stopped in Mozambique before arriving in Goa on the coast of India on September 20, 1713. He then went to the port of Surat near present-day Bombay and then overland to the city of Delhi, capital of the Mughal emperor, which he reached on May 10, 1714. In Delhi he became friends with an influential Portuguese woman, Dona Juliana Diaz da Costa, who financed his trip to Tibet. There he also met a Portuguese priest, Father Emmanuel Freyre, who had 20 years' experience as a missionary in India.

Desideri and Freyre set out from Delhi on September 24, 1714 to travel to Tibet to open a mission station there. On November 13 they reached Srinigar, the capital of Kashmir. Winter was setting in, the mountain passes were closed, and Desideri was weak and ill from dysentery and bleeding in his lungs. They therefore spent the winter in Srinigar. Desideri liked the city, which is called the Venice of India because it is crisscrossed with canals, but Freyre hated it.

Forty days after leaving Srinigar in May 1715, Desideri and Freyre reached Leh, the capital of the Kingdom of Ladakh. The King of Ladakh welcomed them, hoping that they would settle in Leh, but the hardships of the trip had made Freyre determined to return home. Since he would not return by the route they had come, Desideri convinced him to travel via Tibet. On August 17, 1715 the two missionaries set out again, this time on horseback. They also had guides to help them on their journey, but at Gartok they joined a caravan bound for Lhasa led by a Tartar princess.

The route followed by Desideri and Freyre from Gartok was unknown to Europeans, and would not be followed by another European until 1904 when members of **Sir Francis Young-husband**'s expedition traveled that way. Their route went around Mount Kailas, which Desideri called the Mountain of Urghien, one of the most sacred places in Buddhist Tibet. Tibetan legaend said that Urghien, the founder of the Tibetan Lamaist religion, had lived as a hermit on this mountain. At the time that Desideri visited it, it was the site of many pilgrimages and had a temple and a monastery.

Early in December 1715 they passed Lake Mansarowar. Desideri thought that it was the source of both the Indus and Ganges Rivers. This is not quite accurate. It is near the source of the Ganges and is the source of the Sutlej, one of the major tributaries of the Indus. They reached Lhasa on March 18, 1716, after having been delayed for a month because of the illness of the Tartar princess. Freyre stayed in Lhasa only a few days before returning to India. Desideri was the only European in Lhasa after Freyre's departure, and he was granted permission to teach about Christianity. He learned the Tibetan language and by January 1717 was able to present the Mongol king (who had replaced the last Dalai Lama, or religious leader) a report on Christianity written in Tibetan. He was the first European to learn Tibetan.

For four months during 1717 Desideri stayed in a monastery and studied the sacred works of Lamaism. In August he went to the University of Sera outside Lhasa to continue his studies. He was in Sera when the Mongols invaded Tibet and burned Lhasa. Unharmed, Desideri moved to the province of Takpo-Khier, eight days' journey from the capital. From December 1717 he stayed in a monastery at a place called Trong Gnee. Apart from a few months at Lhasa, he remained at Takpo-Khier until April 1721. In that month he was ordered to leave Tibet because of the arrival of Capuchin monks. These priests belonged to a different order from the Jesuits, and they were given the right to preach in Tibet by the Pope in Rome. As a result Desideri left Lhasa on April 25, 1721.

Following his departure from Tibet, Desideri spent five more years in India and became one of the highest-ranking Jesuits in that country. He then returned to Europe by sea. He reached Rome in 1728, where he stayed until his death in April 1733 at the age of 49.

Desideri left a lengthy account of his journey to Lhasa including a geographical description of Tibet. It was the most complete account for 200 years. But it was not known until 1875 when it was discovered by an Italian nobleman in the city of Pistoia. It was not published until 1904.

Where to learn more

The major source for information on Desideri is Filippo de Filippi, trans. & ed. *An Account of Tibet: The Travels of Ippolito Desideri of Pistoia, S.J., 1712-1727* (London: George Routledge & Sons, 1931; revised edition, 1937). It is well summarized in John Macgregor, *Tibet: A Chronicle of Exploration* (London: Routledge & Kegan Paul, 1970).

Hernando de Soto

(1500 - 1542)

Hernando de Soto, a Spaniard, led the first European expedition to the southeastern United States. He died along the way.

Hernando de Soto was born in the Spanish province of Extremadura near the Portuguese border. In 1524 de Soto joined Francisco Hernandez de Córdoba on an expedition to Nicaragua and took part in founding the city of Granada. He later took the side of Pedro Arias in a dispute with Córdoba that ended with Córdoba's death. De Soto stayed in Nicaragua and prospered, partly by engaging in slave trading. He was enlisted by **Francisco Pizarro** to take part in his third expedition to Peru.

Arriving in Peru in December 1531, the Spaniards traveled into the Andes to the city of Cajamarca where Atahualpa, the ruler of the Incas was encamped. On the day of their arrival, November 15, 1532, Pizarro sent de Soto into the city to meet with Atahualpa. The next day Pizarro invited Atahualpa to dinner, where the Inca was taken prisoner. In spite of continued uprisings, Pizarro was thereafter the master of Peru. During one revolt, Pizarro had Atahualpa executed even though de Soto argued against it. In 1533 de Soto joined Pizarro in the conquest of Cuzco, the capital of the Inca domains, and almost lost his life in a Peruvian ambush.

In 1536 de Soto returned to Spain. His participation in the conquest of Peru had made him a very wealthy man. He asked the King of Spain to grant him the governorship of one of the newly conquered realms in the Americas. In April 1537 he was named governor of Cuba and granted the right to conquer and colonize Florida, the still vaguely defined land north of Cuba on the mainland of North America, first visited by **Juan Ponce de León** in 1513.

While de Soto was preparing his expedition to Florida, **Alvar Núñez Cabeza de Vaca** returned to Spain after his odyssey in the American southwest. His reports of stories that he had heard about the "Seven Cities of Cíbola" encouraged de Soto to think that he might find vast wealth in his new territory, even though Cabeza de Vaca's personal experiences were less than hopeful. De Soto left Spain on April 7, 1538 with about 600 men and 200 horses. They reprovisioned in Cuba and landed at Tampa Bay on May 27, 1539.

The Spaniards reached the town of Apalachen, near modern Tallahassee, Florida, on October 6, 1539. They stayed there for the following winter in spite of the hostility of the Native Americans. They left Apalachen on March 3, 1540 to try to find a place called Cofitachequi, which was reputed to be ruled by a great and wealthy queen. They reached Cofitachequi, about 75 miles from the mouth of the Savannah River in eastern Georgia, on April 30. It was ruled by a queen, but the only treasure was a few freshwater pearls.

The expedition left Cofitachequi on May 13 and headed north to the land of Chiaha that was supposed to be rich in gold. They crossed the Appalachian Mountains and reached Chiaha, which turned out to be an island (Burns Island) in the middle of the Tennessee River, on June 6. Once again, the reports of gold turned out to be false. From there, the Spaniards went south, meeting with the great chief Cosa on the Coosa River north of Childersburg, Alabama, and another important chief, Tuscaloosa, in a village along the shores of the Alabama River.

Hernando de Soto. The Bettmann Archive.

Route of de Soto's expedition through the southwestern United States.

At Mabila (perhaps near Choctaw Bluff, Alabama), de Soto got news that his ships had sailed up the Gulf to meet him. But the Spaniards got involved in a fierce battle with a group of Native Americans, and on November 17, 1540 they were forced to head to the north and west. They set up their winter camp about 125 miles east of the Mississippi River near present-day Pontotoc, Mississippi. On March 4, 1541, they were attacked by members of the Chickasaw tribe, and 12 Spaniards were killed.

De Soto and his men left their winter camp at the end of April 1541. They reached the Mississippi on May 8 south of modern Memphis, Tennessee. They built barges and crossed the river on June 18. De Soto heard reports of the Ozark Mountains and headed in that direction, always hoping to find gold and silver. He spent several months traveling through what is now the state of Arkansas and made his winter camp near Camden. They left camp on March 6, 1542. By then, they were in desperate straits. Juan Ortiz had died along with many others and most of the horses. De Soto decided to head back to the Mississippi and then sail down it to the sea. They reached the river and pillaged a Native American village in order to have a secure place to build their boats. In the meantime, however, de Soto had come down with fever and died during the night of May 21, 1542.

The survivors were led by Luis de Moscoso. They built seven barges and set out down the Brazos river on July 5, 1543. They made it to the mouth of the Mississippi and then sailed along the Gulf coast until they reached the settlement of Panuco in northwestern Mexico on September 10, 1543. A total of 311 men (out of the original 600) had survived.

Where to learn more

There are several primary sources for the de Soto expedition. The most famous is by "a gentleman from Elvas." The most recent edition is Jerald T. Milanich, ed. *The Hernando de Soto Expedition*, vol. 11 in *Spanish Borderlands Sourcebooks* (New York: Garland, 1991). It also contains two other sources—the diary of Rodrigo Ranjel, Soto's secretary, and "the Cañete fragment." Another source was written later in the 16th century by Garcilaso de la Vega, based on the reminiscences of a member of the expedition. A complete translation can be found in *The Florida of the Inca*, trans. and edited by John Grier Varner and Jeannette Johnson Varner (Austin: University of Texas Press, 1951). The report of the De Soto Commission, which traced de Soto's route, is John R. Swanton, ed. *The Final Report of the United States De Soto Expedition Commission* (Washington, D.C.: U.S. Government Printing Office, 1939). A very good recent biography with an extensive bibliography is Miguel Albornoz, *Hernando de Soto: Knight of the Americas*, trans. by Bruce Boeglin (New York: Franklin Watts, 1986).

Semyon Ivanovich Dezhnev

(1605?-1673?)

Semyon Ivanovich Dezhnev was a Russian adventurer who was the first person to sail through what we now call the Bering Strait.

Semyon Ivanovich Dezhnev was a Cossack in the service of the Russian tsar who served in Tobolsk and Yeniseysk, in western Siberia, and from 1638 in Yakutsk, the main Russian post on the great Lena River in eastern Siberia. In 1640-1641 he was on the Yana River, still farther east. In the winter of 1641-1642 he was part of the expedition of Mikhail Stadukhin that went overland to the upper Indigirka River. He traveled down the Indigirka to its mouth in 1643 and sailed through the Arctic Ocean to the mouth of the Alazeya River, always a little farther to the east.

In about 1644 Dezhnev traveled to the lower Kolyma River, which also flows into the Arctic Ocean, where Stadukhin had built a Russian fort. Dezhnev was asked to take part in an expedition in 1647 led by Fyodor Alekseyev Popov that aimed to travel by sea from the mouth of the Kolyma to the mouth of the Anadyr River, which flows into the Pacific Ocean. In other words, they were going to round the eastern tip of Siberia. They were forced to turn back by the heavy ice.

In 1648 Dezhnev and Popov set out again. They started out with seven boats and over a hundred men. Along the way, four of the boats disappeared in the Arctic Ocean. In August, 1648, the other three boats rounded the easternmost tip of Eurasia, now called Cape Dezhnev. One boat was lost, and when the remaining two went ashore, they were attacked by Chuckchis, the people who live at the far northeastern corner of the continent. Popov was wounded, and Dezhnev became leader of the expedition. Popov's boat later disappeared at sea.

When he finally landed south of the Anadyr River, Dezhnev was left with one boat and twenty-five men. These men had therefore become the first Westerners to sail between Siberia and North America and were in effect the discoverers of the "Bering" Strait. However, they themselves were unaware of what they had done, and the results of their voyage were never generally known. It was not until almost one hundred years later, in 1741, that **Vitus Bering** sailed into the strait that is now named for him.

Some of the remaining men in Dezhnev's party died trying to travel up the Anadyr River during the winter. Dezhnev and the twelve survivors built a boat and went up the river during the summer, stopping to built a camp halfway up the river. This became the fort of Anadyrsk, the center for the Russian advance into far eastern Siberia. In the meantime, after several unsuccessful tries, Stadukhin was able to cross over to the Anadyr River by land from his post on the Kolyma, where he met Dezhnev in 1650. Stadukhin was jealous that Dezhnev was already collecting tribute from the local people, and the two parties got into a big fight.

In 1652 Dezhnev went down the Andayr River to the Gulf of Anadyr, where he discovered a large heap of walrus tusks. It was rumors of this vast supply of ivory that had originally led the Russians to search for the mouth of the Anadyr River, so Dezhnev's trials were eventually crowned with success. He stayed in the Anadyr region until 1662, and then went back to Yakutsk. In about 1664, he arrived in Moscow with the valuable proceeds of his travels. From 1665-1671 he served once again as a Cossack leader in Yakutsk. He then returned to Moscow, where he died in 1672 or 1673.

Where to learn more

The records of Dezhnev's trip through Bering Strait have been published in Raymond H. Fisher, ed. *The Voyage of Semen Dezhnev in 1648: Bering's Precursor* (London: Hakluyt Society, 1981). This account is based on George V. Lantzeff and Richard A. Pierce, *Eastward to Empire: Exploration and Conquest on the Russian Open Frontier, to 1750* (Montreal: McGill-Queen's University Press, 1973), which remains the only generally accessible summary in English of the exploration of Siberia.

Bartolomeu Dias

(1450? - 1500)

Bartolomeu Dias was the first European to round the southern tip of Africa.

As a result of the voyages of **Diogo Cão**, Portuguese ships had sailed almost to the southern tip of Africa. King John II was convinced that it was possible to sail around the continent. He decided to send out a new expedition under the command of Bartolomeu Dias, a knight of the royal household, who was descended from an old seafaring family and who had headed many trading voyages to Guinea on the west coast of Africa. He was put in charge of two caravels and a supply-ship. The supply-ship was the solution to the problem of supplying long-distance journeys: it was to set up a camp along the way so that the ships would be able to re-provision on the return trip.

The expedition left Lisbon in August 1487 and reached Walvis Bay, in what is now Namibia, without much difficulty by December. South of Walvis Bay the ships encountered very strong headwinds, which drove them out to sea, away from the sight of land. They headed south for 13 days before they were able to turn and head eastward to regain the shore. But they did not find the shoreline they expected. In a sudden burst of inspiration, Dias is said to have realized that they must have sailed beyond the southern tip of Africa and that in order to regain it they would have to head north. This they did, and on February 3, 1488 he sighted land, land that was heading northeastward, proof that they had rounded the cape.

The Portuguese saw African herdsmen and cows, and Dias named his new discovery the Bahia dos Vaqueiros, Cowboy Bay. It is now called Mossel Bay on the south coast of South Africa. Dias insisted on continuing eastward but only made it as far as the Great Fish River, where the South African coast starts heading north before his worried crew forced him to turn back.

On the way home, Dias passed the great cape that is the southern tip of the African continent. He named it Stormy Cape, but the new king, Manoel I, with a better sense of advertising, called it the Cape of Good Hope, because it presented hope of reaching India.

Dias stopped and took on the provisions that had been left behind with the store-ship on the coast of Angola. He returned to Lisbon in December, 1488 after an absence of 17 months and 17 days. Dias continued in the service of the King. On March 4, 1493 he was sent over in a rowboat to talk to the captain of a

Bartolomeu Dias. The Granger Collection, New York.

Spanish ship that had anchored in Lisbon harbor. It turned out to be **Christopher Columbus**, who reported to Dias on the new land he had found on the other side of the Atlantic.

The Portuguese, however, were more interested in the possibilities opened up by Dias's expedition to the south: it was possible to sail around Africa to get to India. This information led King Manoel to send out the expedition under **Vasco da Gama** that was to fulfill the promise of Dias's voyage.

Following da Gama's return, King Manoel immediately sent out a large expedition of thirteen ships under the command of a young nobleman, **Pedro Alvarez Cabral**, that left Lisbon on March 9, 1500. Bartolomeu Dias captained one of the ships in this expedition. Cabral's ships sailed much farther west than those of da Gama and were rewarded on April 22 by the sight of a new land—the coast of Brazil. After spending some time there,

Cabral headed east and ran into very bad weather on his way around the Cape of Good Hope. During this storm, three of his ships were sunk, including the one commanded by Bartolomeu Dias.

Where to learn more

There are numerous books on the Portuguese voyages of exploration at the end of the 15th century. Recommended are Edgar Prestage, *The Portuguese Pioneers* (London: 1933) and "The Search for the Sea Route to India" in Arthur Percival Newton, ed. *Travel and Travellers of the Middle Ages* (New York: Alfred A. Knopf, 1930); Mary Seymour Lucas, *Vast Horizons* (New York: The Viking Press, 1943); Boies Penrose, *Travel and Discovery in the Renaissance, 1420-1620* (Cambridge: Harvard University Press, 1952); and Gerald R. Crone, *The Discovery of the East* (London: Hamish Hamilton, 1972).

Probably the best account of Dias's voyage is in Eric Axelson, *Congo to Cape: Early Portuguese Explorers* (New York: 1974).

Charles Montagu Doughty

(1843 - 1926)

Charles Montagu Doughty was an English writer who made a two-year long trip to western and northern Arabia and wrote a book about his adventures that is now considered to be a classic.

Charles Montagu Doughty. The Granger Collection, New York.

Charles Montagu Doughty was born in the English county of Suffolk, the son of a clergyman. He attended Cambridge University, where he studied geology, and then went to Oxford University to study early English literature. In 1870 Doughty left England to travel around southern Europe and the Mediterranean. While in Greece in 1874 he decided that he wanted to study the ancient ruins of the Middle East.

Doughty traveled via Turkey to Egypt. His first exploring trip was a three-month camel journey through the Sinai Peninsula, accompanied by a Bedouin guide. He then visited the ruins of the city of Petra, in Jordan not far from the modern city of Ma'an. From his guides at Petra Doughty learned about the ruins of the city of Meda'in Salih, which had never been visited by Europeans. He resolved to make that his next goal.

Doughty returned to Europe to try to get financial backing for his journey. Unsuccessful, he decided to do it on his own. He returned to Damascus where he spent a year learning Arabic. He adopted the Arabic name of Khalil and started wearing Arab robes, but refused to disguise his British nationality or his Christian faith. On November 12, 1876 he joined the great pilgrimage caravan that left Damascus headed for Mecca, having made it clear that he did not intend to go as far as the Islamic holy city.

The caravan reached Meda'in Salih in northwestern Arabia on December 4. At first Doughty was refused permission to travel to the ruins, but then he became friends with a local sheikh, Zeyd el-Sbeychan, and the two visited the ruins together. Meda'in Salih was a pre-Islamic Arab town that had been carved out of rock and had once been prosperous as a center for trade in frankincense, cinnamon, and gold between the Mediterranean and southern Arabia. Doughty spent two months there recording what he saw and sketching the ruins.

Doughty's original plan had been to catch the pilgrimage caravan on its return to Damascus. But when it passed through Meda'in Salih on February 5, 1877, Doughty had become so curious about the lives of the Bedouin, the nomadic Arabs, that he decided to stay behind with his friend Zeyd. This was the beginning of his travels in Arabia, which he told about in his book *Travels in Arabia Deserta*, which is written in an idiosyncratic kind of English influenced by Doughty's studies of medieval literature.

The English traveler stayed with Zeyd's band until the summer of 1877 recording the aspects of their daily life: "The Bedouins coming near a stead where they will encamp, Zeyd returned to us; and where he thought good there struck down the heel of his tall horseman's lance *shelfa* or *romhh*. stepping it in some sandy desert bush: this is the standard of Zeyd's fellowship—they that encamp with him, and are called his people."

After leaving his friend, Doughty passed from one Bedouin group to another. He had very little money, and he depended upon the hospitality of the Arabs to survive: once they had accepted him into their tents they were obliged to take care of him. That did not mean that they were happy to do so and often he was threatened and was given only a small quantity of food.

In the town of Tayma the inhabitants thought that the non-believer Doughty had made a well collapse, and he received several threats. From there, he went to the city of Ha'il, the capital of northern Arabia. After being received by the local emir, Doughty's welcome wore out. After a stay of several weeks, he was beaten by the emir's guard and expelled from the city. As he left Ha'il for Khaybar, farther west, he stopped to buy dates from a poor family, "These poor folk, disinherited of the world, spoke to with human kindness. . . . The women, of their own thought, took from my shoulders and mended my mantle which had been rent yesterday in Hail."

The town of Khaybar is in the highlands of the western Arabian province of Hejaz. At the time of Doughty's visit, it was ruled by the Ottoman Turks. The local Turkish governor thought Doughty was a spy and relieved him of his travel documents and his money and made him wait in the town until he received instructions from his superior in Medina. Doughty was there from November 1877 until mid-March 1878. He returned to Ha'il while the emir was away, and the inhabitants were no happier about seeing him than when he had left. He departed once again in the company of two Bedouin guides, whom he overheard plotting to kill him.

The Bedouin guides abandoned Doughty, and he had to make it on his own to the town of Buraydah, where he was once again beaten and robbed. However, in the nearby town of Unayzah he was befriended by a local merchant who cashed a check for him (which took a year to clear his bank in London) and put him on a caravan headed for the port city of Jidda.

As this caravan approached Mecca, Doughty was threatened by a fanatical camel driver who almost shot him until he was rescued by a servant of the governor of Mecca. By this time his clothes were torn and he was forced to beg for food, but he made it to Jidda. There he was welcomed by the governor and turned over to the British consulate, which arranged for him to travel back to England.

Once home, it took Doughty a long time to recover from his travels. He then spent ten years writing *Travels in Arabia Deserta*. The rest of his life he devoted to writing epic poetry in the vein of the medieval classics. This work is totally forgotten now, but his book on Arabia has been considered to be the best book ever written by a European about Arabia. He died in England on January 20, 1926 at the age of 82.

Where to learn more

The basic source for studying Doughty's travels is, of course, *Travels in Arabia Deserta*. It was first published by Cambridge University Press in 1888. A new edition was published in 2 volumes in London by Jonathan Cape in 1936, and in a paperback edition in 1964. It is also available in paperback from Dover.

There is only one full-scale biography of Doughty: D.G. Hogarth, *The Life of Charles M. Doughty* (New York: Doubleday, 1929).

Professor Stephen Tabachnik has made extensive studies of the literary aspects of *Travels in Arabia Deserta*. These can be found in *Charles Doughty* (Boston: Twayne, 1981) and *Explorations in Doughty's Arabia Deserta* (Athens: University of Georgia Press, 1987).

Several books that give profiles of European travelers in Arabia discuss Doughty: Thomas J. Assad, *Three Victorian Travellers* (London: Routledge & Kegan Paul, 1964); Zahra Reeth and H.V.F. Winstone, *Explorers of Arabia: From the Renaissance to the End of the Victorian Era* (London: George Allen & Unwin, 1978);Kathryn Tidrick, *Heart-Beguiling Araby* (Cambridge: Cambridge University Press, 1981); and James C. Simmons, *Passionate Pilgrims: English Travelers to the World of the Desert Arabs* (New York: William Morrow & Co., 1987), which was particularly useful in writing this survey.

Sir Francis Drake

(1543 - 1596)

Sir Francis Drake was an English seaman and pirate who made the second voyage around the world and later led the English in defeating the Spanish Armada.

Francis Drake was born in the town of Tavistock in Devonshire in the west of England. He was one of 12 sons in a modest family, almost all of whom went to sea. Drake himself was apprenticed to a shipmaster engaged in the coasting trade. In 1566 he was employed as a seaman on voyages that went to the west coast of Africa and to the Caribbean. In 1567 he sailed with a relative, John Hawkins, to Africa where they traded for slaves and then to the Caribbean in order to sell them to plantation owners there. The Spanish did not allow foreigners to trade in their colonies, and they attacked

Sir Francis Drake.

the ship at Veracruz in Mexico, where Drake narrowly escaped being captured.

On his return to England in 1569 Drake made a report about his adventures to Sir William Cecil, one of Queen Elizabeth I's closest advisers. He then made several voyages to the Caribbean to attack Spanish ships either as a pirate or a privateer. The difference between the two was that the pirate operated entirely on his own while a privateer was commissioned by the government of one country to attack the ships of another country and got to keep part of the proceeds.

In May 1572 Drake provisioned two small ships, the *Pasha* and the *Swan*, with a total of 73 men, and traveled to Central America. He attacked the Spanish city of Nombre de Dios in Panama on July 29 and almost succeeded in capturing the Spanish treasure fleet. He burned the town of Porto Belo and then destroyed many Spanish ships. He crossed the Isthmus of Panama to its highest point so that he could look out on the Pacific Ocean. There, he "besought Almighty God of his goodness to give him life and leave to sail once in an English ship in that sea." Drake arrived back in England on August 9, 1573 where he became a popular hero.

In 1577 Drake fitted out the *Pelican* of 100 tons, the *Elizabeth* of 80 tons, and three smaller vessels. He sailed from the port of Plymouth on December 13, 1577 on his quest to see the Pacific. He sailed to Brazil, the mouth of the Río de la Plata in Argentina, and Patagonia. He entered the Straits of Magellan on August 20, 1578. By then he had only three ships: two had burned. Once into the Pacific, the little fleet was hit by a fierce storm that lasted for 52 days and drove him far to the south. One of the remaining ships was sunk with all hands on board, and the other returned home. Drake renamed his ship the *Golden Hind* and continued on his way.

Drake sailed up the coast of South America, provisioning himself with supplies captured from Spanish storehouses in Valparaiso, Chile and with several Spanish ships captured en route. In 1579 he anchored near Coos Bay, Oregon, and then repaired his ship in Drake's Bay, California, where a celebrated brass plaque of his was found in the 1930s. He did not, however, find San Francisco Bay. He then headed out into the Pacific and did not sight land for 68 days until he reached Palau in the southwestern part of Micronesia. He refitted his ship in Java, sailed to the Cape of Good Hope and arrived in England on September 26, 1580, where he was knighted by Queen Elizabeth I on April 4, 1581. He was the second person to lead an expedition around the world and the first Englishman to do so.

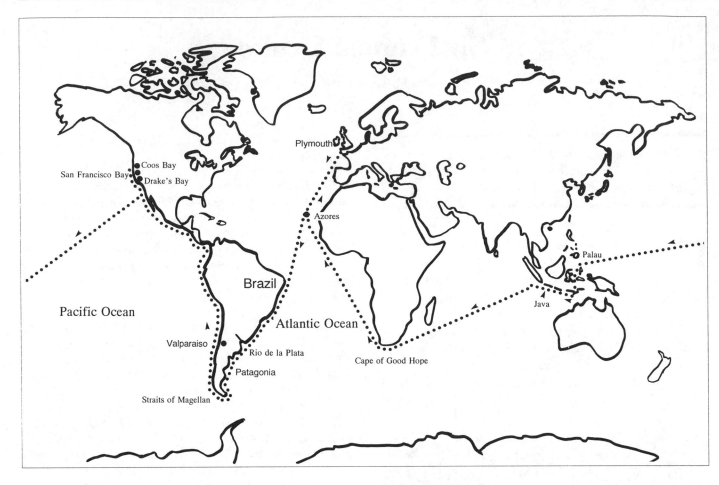

Drake's voyage around the world, 1577-1580.

In 1585 Drake led an expedition to attack the Spanish in the Caribbean, including Santo Domingo, Cartagena in Colombia, and Florida. Early in 1587 he set sail with a strong squadron and entered the Spanish port of Cadiz, destroyed 33 ships and returned unharmed with an enormous amount of gold and silver. He then sailed to the Azores and captured a Portuguese ship returning with a rich cargo from the East Indies.

By this time the Spanish were determined to put a stop to the English raids and mounted the Great Armada. Drake was put in charge of the English fleet. The battle began on July 19, 1588 and lasted for a full week. After they disengaged Drake attacked again on July 29 and decisively defeated the Spanish. They were forced to travel home via the North Sea and the north coast of Scotland, and all the Spanish ships were destroyed in storms. It was the moment when England replaced Spain as the greatest sea power on earth.

In the spring of 1589 Drake led an expedition against Spanish and Portuguese ports. He did not have much success, and many of his crew died from sickness and hunger. Drake returned to England. In August 1595 he came out of retirement to lead an expedition to Panama. He died on board his ship off the town of Porto Belo, Panama on January 28, 1596 from dysentery.

Where to learn more

A very early narrative of Drake's voyage around the world was published by Richard Hakluyt, the famous English chronicler of exploration. In his original edition of *Principall Navigations* in 1589, there is a section on "The Famous Voyage of Sir Francis Drake into the South Sea, and There Hence About the Whole Globe of the Earth, 1577." The Hakluyt Society later published contemporary records of the circumnavigation: W.S.W Vaux, editor, Sir Francis Drake, *The World Encompassed* (London: The Hakluyt Society, 1854). The Argonaut Press published a beautiful edition of the work in 1928 and this is available on microfilm: *The World Encompassed by Sir Francis Drake Carefully Collected Out of the Notes of Master Francis Fletcher* (London: Nicholas Bourne, 1628; edited by N.M. Penzer, London: Argonaut Press, 1926; available on University Microfilms, Ann Arbor, Mich, 1966). The Hakluyt Society has also published other records pertaining to Drake's career: Zelia Nuttall, ed. *New Light on Drake: A Collection of Documents Relating to His Voyage of Circumnavigation, 1577-1580* (London: Hakluyt Society, 1945); Kenneth R. Andrews, ed. *The Last Voyages of Drake and Hawkins* (Cambridge: Cambridge University for the Hakluyt Society, 1972); Mary Rear Keeler, ed. *Sir Francis Drake's West Indian Voyage, 1585-1586* (London: Hakluyt Society, 1981).

Other contemporary accounts are: Henry R. Wagner, *Sir Francis Drake's Voyage Around the World: Its Aims and Achievements* (San Francisco: John Howell, 1926); Derek Wilson, *The World Encompassed: Drake's Great Voyage, 1577-1580* (New York: Harper & Row, 1977); and Norman T. W. Thrower, *Sir Francis Drake and the Famous Voyage, 1577-1580* (Berkeley: University of California Press, 1984).

Paul Du Chaillu

(1831? - 1903)

Paul Du Chaillu was an American of French origin who made three trips to Gabon in west Africa and was the first Westerner to write about the gorilla.

Paul Du Chaillu was always very mysterious about his origins, sometimes claiming to have been born in Paris, sometimes in New York, and sometimes in New Orleans. According to English writer Edward Clodd, quoted by J.A. Rogers in *World's Great Men of Color*, Du Chaillu was the son of a French trader on the Indian Ocean island of Réunion and his part-African mistress. His father set up a trading post on the coast of Gabon in West Africa in 1845 and Paul joined him there in 1848. According to some stories, he was rescued by American missionaries when his canoe upset, and they painted such a glowing picture of their country that he decided to travel there. In the United States, he took up the study of natural science and adopted American citizenship.

Du Chaillu wanted to return to Gabon and explore the interior of that country's dense tropical forest. He was able to convince the Philadelphia Academy of Natural Sciences to back him, and in 1855 he set off again for Gabon. He spent the next four years there travelling throughout the country alone and with only very modest supplies.

In his book about his experiences, *Explorations and Adventures in Equatorial Africa*, he wrote, "I travelled—always on foot and unaccompanied by other white men—about 8,000 miles. I shot, stuffed and brought home over 2,000 birds, of which more than 60 are new species, and I killed upwards of 1,000 quadrupeds, of which 200 were stuffed and brought home, with more than 80 skeletons . . . I suffered 50 attacks of the African fever, taking, to cure myself, more than fourteen ounces of quinine. Of famine, long-continued exposures to the tropical rains, and attacks of ferocious ants and venomous flies, it is not worthwhile to speak." He then went on to speak about them.

Du Chaillu traveled up the Ogowe River as far as the site of Lambaréné, the place where Albert Schweitzer would later build his famous hospital. He reported that the main commercial activity of the whole country was the selling of slaves, and he told many stories of the evil effects of the slave trade on the inhabitants. He described one camp as "an immense enclosure defended by a wall of 12-foot-high stakes that contained a large

Paul Du Chaillu in Africa. The Granger Collection, New York.

number of barracks surrounded by trees under which slept enough people to make up a large African village."

Du Chaillu's great discovery was to be the first European to see and report on the gorilla. In the N'tem Highlands of Gabon he stayed with members of the Fan tribe who hunted gorillas and elephants as sources of meat. Du Chaillu went on a number of these hunting expeditions, and told about one in which the gorilla won the contest. "He [Du Chaillu's African friend] stood his ground, and as quickly as he could reloaded his gun. Just as he raised it to fire the gorilla dashed it out of his hands, the gun going off in the fall, and then in an instant, and with a terrible roar, the animal gave him a tremendous blow with an immense open paw, frightfully lacerating the abdomen, and with this single blow laying bare part of the intestines. As he sank, bleeding, to the ground, the monster seized the gun, and the poor hunter thought he would have his brains dashed out with it. But the gorilla seemed to have looked upon this also as an enemy, and in his rage flattened the barrel between his strong jaws."

During his time in Gabon, Du Chaillu killed several gorillas. In June 1859 he returned to the United States to write about his adventures and about the gorillas. Unfortunately, the two live baby gorillas that he brought back with him died en route. His book contained so many adventurous tales that, even though they were true, many people refused to believe him. In particular, his stories about the gorillas were looked upon as fantasies, like that of other mythical creatures like unicorns. At a lecture that he gave at the London Ethnological Society in July 1861, he was practically accused of being a liar, and he and his adversary almost came to blows.

To prove he was telling the truth, Du Chaillu returned to Gabon in 1863 with a larger expedition. On this expedition he encountered many difficulties, including the loss of his scientific instruments, and was attacked by members of the Ashango tribe. He had learned photography before embarking for Africa, and the photos that he took and the specimens that he collected convinced the skeptics. The book that he wrote about his experiences, *A Journey to Ashongo Land*, was well received, and his reputation was restored. In this book, he gave the first reports by a Westerner of life in a pygmy tribe. He appeared before the Royal Geographical Society in London and was endorsed by the membership.

This was Du Chaillu's last trip to Africa. He retired to the Marlborough Hotel in New York and spent most of his time writing children's books as "Uncle Paul." Many of the books were based on his experiences in Africa. He also traveled frequently. In 1871 he made a trip to Scandinavia and wrote a book about his experiences there. In 1901 he went to Russia. He became ill there and died in St. Petersburg on April 30, 1903.

Where to learn more

Du Chaillu's accounts of his two African trips are: *Explorations and Adventures in Equatorial Africa* (New York: Harper & Brothers, 1861; reprinted, New York: Negro Universities Press, 1969) and *A Journey to Ashango-Land* (New York: D. Appleton & Co., 1867). The succeeding books of stories include: *Stories of the Gorilla Country* (London: 1868); *Wild Life Under the Equator* (London: 1869); *Lost in the Jungle* (New York: Harper and Brothers, 1869); *The Country of the Dwarfs* (London: Sampson Low Son & Marston, 1872; reprinted, New York: Negro Universities Press, 1969). His trip to Scandinavia is documented in *The Land of the Midnight Sun* (London: 1881).

There is one full-scale biography of Du Chaillu: Michel Vaucaire *Paul Du Chaillu: Gorilla Hunter* (New York: Harper and Brothers, 1931). See also K. David Patterson, "Paul B. Du Chaillu and the Exploration of Gabon, 1855-1865," *The International Journal of African Historical Studies,* vol. 7 (1975), pages 647-667 and chapters on Du Chaillu in J.A. Rogers, *World's Great Men of Color,* vol. 1 (New York: Macmillan, 1972; also available in paperback) and Richard West, *Brazza of the Congo* (London: Jonathan Cape, 1972).

Jules-Sébastien-César Dumont d'Urville

(1790 - 1842)

Jules-Sébastien-César Dumont d'Urville was a French naval officer who made a number of important scientific expeditions to the Pacific and was the first Frenchman to explore Antarctica.

Jules-Sébastien-César Dumont d'Urville was born in the village of Condé in Calvados in Normandy. He entered the French Navy in 1807 and studied at the naval base at Toulon on the Mediterranean, where he graduated at the head of the class of 1811. In early 1817 he was serving aboard a French ship in the Aegean Sea off the coast of Greece. While on the island of Milos he was responsible for identifying and purchasing the famous statue known as the "Venus de Milo," which is now in the Louvre Museum in Paris. For this exploit King Charles X awarded him the French Legion of Honor and he was promoted.

In August 1822 Dumont d'Urville started out on his first voyage of exploration, as an officer of the Duperrey Expedition

Jules-Sebástien-César Dumont d'Urville. The Granger Collection, New York.

that explored the Gilbert and Caroline islands in the central Pacific. He occupied himself collecting specimens of unknown plants and insects. When the ship returned to Toulon on May 22, 1825, Dumont d'Urville had with him a remarkable collection. He used this as the basis for a number of scientific articles and a book that he wrote in the following years.

On his return Dumont d'Urville proposed to make an expedition to search for the remains of the **Comte de La Pérouse** and to study the Pacific islands. His plan was approved in December 1825, and he set out on April 25, 1826 on the *Astrolabe*. In his search for La Pérouse, Dumont d'Urville ran into a piece of good luck. While he was at Sydney in Australia, an English merchant captain brought back reports of finding remains of La Pérouse's ships on the island of Vanikoro in the Santa Cruz Islands, now part of the Republic of the Solomon Islands.

Dumont d'Urville reached Vanikoro in the *Astrolabe* in 1828 and wrote later in his account of the expedition: "Lying at the bottom of the sea, three or four fathoms below the surface, our men saw anchors, cannons, shot and a huge quantity of lead plates." Further exploration established that these were indeed the remains of the La Pérouse expedition, and he was able to get the story of the wreck from the islanders: About 30 of the men had succeeded in getting ashore but had been massacred. Others, who were better armed, had managed to stay alive for seven months, after which they had set sail for the north (and were never heard of again).

In the course of this voyage around the world, Dumont d'Urville's expedition amassed the largest collection of scientific material that had so far been brought to Europe.

He charted various islands in the island groups of Melanesia and charted the New Zealand coast, including Cook Strait that separates the North from the South Island. He brought back 1,600 plant specimens, 900 rocks and 500 insects as well as an enormous amount of drawings.

On his return to France on March 25, 1829 Dumont d'Urville did not receive the recognition that he expected. Some deprecated the extent of his scientific work, and he was much criticized for the death rate on his ship—29 crew members were lost. He took a desk job at Toulon where he wrote two books about his expedition. These books were very successful and restored his reputation. In 1835 his only daughter was killed in a cholera epidemic. (His older son had died ten years earlier).

In 1836 Dumont d'Urville put forward proposals for another expedition to the Pacific, which were accepted by the French

Admiralty. However, the King of the French, Louis-Philippe, had become interested in Antarctica following the voyages of the Englishman James Weddell. So he suggested that Dumont d'Urville redirect his expedition and head for the Weddell Sea off the coast of Antarctica and try to make it farther south than Weddell had done. Dumont d'Urville badly wanted to make the expedition so he agreed to the new instructions. Partly crippled with gout, he sailed from Toulon on September 7, 1837 with two ships, the *Astrolabe* and *Zelée*, both designed for tropical rather than polar exploration.

The two ships reached the Straits of Magellan in early December 1837 and had to spend some time making repairs. They headed south on January 8, 1838 and encountered their first ice a few days later. The pack ice was very heavy that year, and they could not get very far. They were forced to turn back north on January 23, considerably short of where Weddell had been in 1823. They rested in the South Orkney Islands and tried again in February.

On February 2 the two ships entered an inlet in the ice and the next morning they were iced in. They did not escape until February 9. They landed on Weddell Island and continued westward. Dumont d'Urville sighted the northern part of the Graham Peninsula, which he named Louis Philippe Land, and the islands of d'Urville and Joinville, which he called Joinville Land. Both these areas had, however, already been sighted before. He did accomplish a lot of good cartographic work in the Falkland Islands, the South Orkney Islands, and the South Shetlands.

By this time many members of the crew were ill with scurvy, and Dumont d'Urville headed north to reprovision at Valparaiso, Chile. He then sailed out into the Pacific, which is where he had wanted to go all along. From May 1838 until December 1839 the two French ships crisscrossed the Pacific, visiting Tahiti, Tonga, Fiji, Vanuatu, the Solomons, the Caroline Islands, the Dutch East Indies, and New Guinea. When he reached Hobart, Tasmania in Australia on December 12, 1839 many of the men on the two ships were sick from fever and dysentery. More than 20 men died.

In Hobart Dumont d'Urville heard about **James Clark Ross**'s expedition to try to find the South Magnetic Pole, and he decided to go look for it himself. He left from Hobart on January 2, 1840.

On January 20, 1840 Dumont d'Urville's ships were close to the Antarctic Circle, and the following day the members of the expedition awoke to find themselves in a calm sea facing a coastline of vertical ice-cliffs, about 120 feet high. Behind them, rising from 3,000-4,000 feet, lay a vast land completely covered with ice and snow. Dumont d'Urville named this forbidding terrain Adélie Land after his wife. He was never able to find a gap in the ice where he could go ashore although one boat did land on a small islet.

On January 29, while in a fogbound sea, the Frenchmen sighted another ship approaching them. It hoisted the American colors: it was the *Porpoise*, one of the ships of **Charles Wilkes**'s Antarctic expedition, the first great maritime exploration by the United States. The two ships passed each other but did not exchange signals or any other greeting. On January 30 Dumont d'Urville ran into the icepack, and the following day he took his ship northwards towards Hobart.

On his way back to Europe from Hobart, Dumont d'Urville stopped to explore the Loyalty Islands off New Caledonia and the Louisiade Archipelago off the southeast coast of New Guinea. He sailed into Toulon on November 6, 1840. This time, in spite of some criticism once again about the number of men lost, he was promoted to admiral and awarded a gold medal by the French Geographical Society. While working on the account of the expedition, he and his wife and only remaining son were all killed in a train wreck at Versailles on May 8, 1842.

Where to learn more

Dumont d'Urville's own accounts of his voyages are available only in French: *Voyage de la corvette l'Astrolabe exécuté par ordre du Roi, pendant les années 1826, 1827, 1828, 1829, sous le commandement de M. J. Dumont d'Urville,* 22 vols. and 7 atlases (Paris: 1830-1835) and *Voyage au Pôle Sud et dans l'Océanie sur les corvettes l'Astrolabe et la Zélée, exécuté par ordre du Roi pendant les années 1837, 1838, 1839, 1840, sous le Commandement de M. J. Dumont d'Urville,* 23 vols., 4 atlases (Paris: 1843). Excerpts from this account can be found in Olive Wright, translator and editor, *The Voyage of the Astrolabe, 1840* (Wellington, N.Z.: 1955).

The best summary in English can be found in John Dunmore, *French Explorers in the Pacific,* vol. 2 (Oxford: Clarendon Press, 1969).

Henri Duveyrier

(1840 - 1892)

Henri Duveyrier was a Frenchman who traveled to North Africa and the Sahara and was the first European to live with and write about the Tuareg people.

Henri Duveyrier was born in Paris on February 28, 1840. His father was a well-known French playwright. Duveyrier studied at schools in France and Germany. During the years 1855 to 1857 he went to a school in Leipzig in Germany, where he studied Arabic. He returned to Paris and started studying Chinese but quickly gave that up in order to make a trip to Algeria. He stayed there from February to April 1857, living among the Berber people and studying their language. On his return, he visited London where he met the famous German explorer **Heinrich Barth**. Barth encouraged Duveyrier to return to Africa in order to visit the Sahara and study its peoples.

Therefore, on May 8, 1859, Duveyrier set out for the Mediterranean coast of North Africa. He joined a caravan going into the Sahara Desert and visited the Mzab region, El Goléa, Metlili, Touggourt, Ouargla and returned to Algiers via Gabès in Tunisia and the city of Biskra. He set out again in 1860 in order to make contact with Tuareg tribesmen. The Tuareg were a little-known warrior tribe who controlled the Sahara trade routes from their stronghold in the Ahaggar Mountains in the middle of the Sahara.

Duveyrier traveled from Tripoli to the large inland town of Ghadamès and from there to Ghat on the edge of the Ahaggar. He was the first Westerner to have any prolonged contact with the Tuareg, who speak a Berber language. Although Muslims, they were in almost constant warfare with the Arabs who controlled the coastal regions of North Africa. The Tuareg had a fearsome reputation throughout the region as being exceedingly warlike and hostile to strangers.

Duveyrier was initially received with much hostility himself, but he was able to win the trust of the Tuareg and was able to live with them for almost two years. He wrote about their habit of covering themselves in blue garments that, in the case of the men, almost completely covered their faces so that even their friends never saw their naked face. The women, on the other hand, unlike the Arabs, were unveiled. The Tuareg lived by raiding the possessions of their neighbors, but were extremely poor. Their poverty, however, was matched by their pride, which made them behave as though the whole desert belonged to them.

The French explorer was himself much impressed by the Tuareg. He reported back to the outside world that they were brave, hospitable, faithful, patient, tolerant, industrious, charitable, and magnanimous. He described them as being full of dignity and physically attractive: "The torso of both the men and the women is well developed. The arms and legs, elongated, muscular, end in small and well-formed hands and in feet which would also be beautiful were it not for the big toe, which has an ugly protrusion caused by the sandals they wear. . . . The men are strong, robust, tireless." Duveyrier's appreciation of the Tuareg was not necessarily shared by later Europeans who were often subject to attack by these warriors of the desert.

Duveyrier returned to France in 1861, seriously ill from his sojourn in the desert. In 1864 he published his famous study— *The Tuareg of the North*. He wanted to return to North Africa but was prevented by illness from doing so. He was conscripted during the Franco-Prussian War in 1870 but was forced to leave the service because of bad health. He rejoined toward the end of the war and was captured and sent to a prison camp in Germany. His knowledge of German and his acquaintance with German academics assured him a relatively painless imprisonment.

On Duveyrier's return to France in 1871, he published several studies on Africa and was elected president of the French Geographical Society in 1884. His reputation as a scholar made him the most consulted French expert on the Sahara for many years. However, he never had a happy personal life. He continued to be in bad health and never married. He earned little from his writing. In addition, his reputation suffered as a result of the failure of the expedition of **Paul-Xavier Flatters**, which Duveyrier had helped to initiate. On April 27, 1892 he went for a walk in the woods near Paris and shot himself in the head with a revolver.

Where to learn more

Duveyrier wrote all of his books in French: *Exploration du Sahara: Les Touaregs du Nord* (Paris: 1864); *Livingstone et ses explorations dans l'Afrique orientale* (Paris: 1874); *La Tunisie* (Paris: 1881); *La Confrérie musulmane de Sidi Mohamed Ben' Ali Es-Senoûsi et son domaine géographique* (Paris: 1884); *Journal d'un voyage dans la province d'Alger*, edited by Charles Maunoir (Paris: 1900); *Sahara algérien et tunisien: Journal de route de Henri Duveyrier*, edited by Charles Maunoir and Henri Schirmer (Paris: 1905).

Likewise, the only full-length study of Duveyrier is in French, written by a noted scholar of the Sahara: Raymond Pottier, *Un prince saharien méconnu: Henri Duveyrier* (Paris: 1938). There is a very good book about the history of the French penetration of the Sahara that includes information about Duveyrier: Douglas Porch, *The Conquest of the Sahara* (New York: Alfred A. Knopf, 1984).

Gil Eannes

(15th century)

Gil Eannes was a Portuguese navigator who succeeded in passing Cape Bojador, the farthest south that men had sailed along the coast of Africa.

In 1420, about the time that **Prince Henry the Navigator** began sponsoring voyages of exploration, the known southern limit of the Atlantic Ocean and West African coast was in the region of Cape Bojador, just below latitude 27° north, in what is now the Western Sahara. This cape projects twenty-five miles westward from the mainland. The cape had long been dreaded by mariners. It is subject to violent waves and currents on its northern side, shallows toward the coast, and frequent fogs and mist. Because of prevailing winds it is difficult to return north once the cape has been passed. For all these reasons, Portuguese mariners believed stories told by Arab geographers that said that beyond Cape Bojador lay the "Green Sea of Darkness," from which there was no return.

It is thought that Prince Henry sent out some 15 expeditions south during the years from 1424 to 1434. Some of his ships sailed to Madeira and to the Canary Islands, and by 1432 Gonçalo Cabral had reached the Azores. But no one had been able to venture beyond the dreaded cape.

Gil Eannes was a native of the town of Lagos in the southern Algarve region of Portugal, near where Prince Henry had his court. He served as a squire in Henry's household. In 1433 Henry sent him on a voyage south, but he only got as far as the Canary Islands, where he took a few captives and returned to Portugal. In 1434 Henry sent him out again, this time telling him to pay no heed to the many legends he had heard about the cape. "Make the voyage from which, by the grace of God, you cannot fail to derive honor and profit."

Eannes persisted and did round the cape on this voyage. He found a calm sea on the other side and landed on the desert coast in a small boat. The only living things that he found were some small plants, known in Portugal as "Saint Mary's roses." He collected a bunch and brought them back to Henry as proof of his accomplishment.

Eannes returned to Henry's court at Sagres to be welcomed as a hero—and with some reason. His voyage south of Cape Bojador was small in terms of discovery, but it had a major effect. Once he had shown that the cape could be rounded, the way was open for others to journey south. He had broken the psychological barrier that had prevented Europeans from sailing down the west coast of Africa.

In 1435 Eannes made another voyage, landing on the African coast about 50 leagues south of Cape Bojador. There, he and Alfonso Gonçalves Baldaya saw tracks of men and camels. In 1436 Henry sent Baldaya south to meet these men. He found a large bay, which he thought was the River of Gold, the Senegal, and named it Rio de Ouro, though he was in fact only half way there. Two boys from his ship went ashore and saw 19 armed men, who ran away when confronted by the Europeans. Baldaya sailed farther south to Cabo Blanco, and he returned home with thousands of sealskins, the first commercial cargo to be brought to Europe from that part of Africa.

The last mention that we have of Eannes is that he participated in the great armada of 14 caravels that left Portugal on August 10, 1445 under the command of Admiral Lançarote to conquer the island of Tidra off the coast of what is now Mauritania. The Muslim inhabitants of the island had attacked a party of Portuguese sailors, and their countrymen wanted revenge. There was a pitched battle, which the Portuguese won, taking 57 captives. Some of the ships from this fleet sailed even farther south, going as far as Cape Verde in Senegal, the westernmost point of Africa.

Where to learn more

The knowledge that we have of Eannes comes from a Portuguese chronicle known as the *Crónica dos Feitos da Guiné* ("Chronicle of Guinea") by Diogo Gomes. The story of Eannes' voyage is basically an episode in the history of Prince Henry the Navigator's explorations. There are many books about Henry that discuss Eannes, including: Edgar Prestage, *The Portuguese Pioneers* (London: Adam & Charles Black, 1933; reprinted 1966); Ernle Bradford, *A Wind from the North: The Life of Henry the Navigator* (New York: Harcourt, Brace & Co., 1960); and John Ure, *Prince Henry the Navigator* (London: Constable, 1977).

Amelia Earhart

(1898 - 1937)

Amelia Earhart was an American aircraft pilot who set numerous records, including being the first woman to fly solo across the Atlantic. She disappeared mysteriously in the Pacific during a pioneering flight around the world.

Amelia Earhart was born in Atchison, Kansas, the daughter of a lawyer who worked for a railroad company. Until the age of 12 she lived with her sister and grandparents in Atchison, and then she moved with her parents to various cities where her father was working until he was dismissed from the railroad company for alcoholism. In 1918, at the age of 20, she went to visit her sister in Toronto, Canada. This was during World War I and after seeing wounded servicemen on the streets of Toronto, she volunteered to work as a nurse's aide at a local military hospital. She also visited a local airfield and decided then that she wanted to learn how to fly.

For a short time after the war, Earhart took a medical course at Columbia University in New York. She then joined her family in Los Angeles and persuaded her father to spend $10 to send her up on a joyride at an airshow. After she landed, she decided that she was going to take flying lessons immediately. She hired Neta Snook, the first woman instructor to graduate from the Curtiss School of Aviation, to teach her. She paid for the first lessons by driving a sand and gravel truck. After only 2½ hours of instruction, she decided that she wanted to buy her own plane. She bought a small experimental plane that cost $2,000 with money advanced by her mother and took a job at a local telephone company sorting mail to help pay for it.

Earhart made her first solo flight in 1922 and shortly afterward set a new altitude record of 14,000 feet in her plane. This record was shortly broken by someone else, and Earhart immediately set out to remake it. She ran into dense fog at 12,000 feet, in a plane with no instruments at all, and almost crashed but was finally able to land safely. In 1924 Earhart's parents divorced, and she bought a yellow roadster to drive her mother back to the east coast. In order to pay for the car, she sold her plane to a young man who took off while she watched and promptly crashed it and killed himself. In Boston, Earhart resumed her medical studies for a short while and then went to work in 1926 as a social worker in a settlement house in Boston.

After going to work in the settlement house, Earhart's flying became a hobby although she tried to fly as often as she had time for and could afford on her small salary. In April 1928, she received an unexpected invitation to travel to New York to be

Amelia Earhart. U.S. Information Agency.

interviewed by a committee headed by the publisher and publicist George Palmer Putnam to select the first woman to travel, as a passenger, on a plane across the Atlantic. Earhart was selected and left with a male pilot and navigator on June 3, 1928 in the *Friendship*, the same plane that **Richard Evelyn Byrd** had flown across the North Pole. Putnam released the news to the press, and the *Christian Science Monitor* headlined "Boston Woman Flies Into Dawn on Surprise Atlantic Trip." This news was not exactly accurate since fog forced them to land in Newfoundland and wait there until June 17. They took off that morning with the pilot drunk and landed in a bay in Wales 20 hours and 40 minutes later. They were greeted with great enthusiasm, and Earhart became the center of international attention because she was the first woman to have flown over the ocean even though she had only been a passenger.

On her return to the United States, Earhart was suddenly looked upon as a spokesperson for women aviators, and with George Putnam as her manager undertook an extensive series of lecture tours and was hired to write a column on aviation for

Cosmopolitan magazine. She also was hired to endorse several commercial products. In September 1928, she flew across the country to visit her father in Los Angeles and then flew back to New York. This made her the first woman to fly both ways solo across the country.

In 1929 the Lockheed Company presented Earhart with a brand-new Vega, a new type of single-wing plane that was also flown by **Amy Johnson** and **Beryl Markham**. She flew the Vega in the first Women's Air Derby across the United States and came in third. In July 1930 she set a new speed record for women and in 1931 she made a tour of the United States in an autogiro, a forerunner of the helicopter, in which she set an altitude record.

In February 1931 Earhart married George Putnam, who had recently divorced. They both pursued their careers, but he used his great abilities as a publicist to make her one of the best-known personalities in America. In 1932 Earhart decided to fly solo across the Atlantic in order to earn the fame that she had been unjustly given in 1928. She took off from Harbor Grace, Newfoundland on the evening of May 20, 1932. For the first few hours everything went well. Then she began to run into difficulties. She ran into a violent electrical storm, the altimeter failed, the wings iced up and sent the plane into a tailspin for 3,000 feet. Finally, the exhaust manifold caught on fire. In the face of the problems, Earhart decided to land in Ireland rather than continuing on to Paris as she had originally planned. She landed in a pasture outside of Londonderry in Northern Ireland 14 hours and 56 minutes after she had left Newfoundland. Once again she became the center of public adulation, and this time she felt she had earned it. She was feted throughout Europe and then returned to New York to a giant ticker-tape parade.

In the following years, Earhart was able to profit from her fame by expanding her circle of friends, including flying over Washington with Eleanor Roosevelt and joyriding with her around the White House grounds in a race car. She also undertook interesting professional assignments, including becoming a visiting faculty member at Purdue University. She endorsed numerous products, including her own design for traveling clothes and Amelia Earhart luggage, still being sold today. She loved daredevil stunts such as jumping off a metal tower with a parachute and piloting a one-person submarine.

But during these years Earhart also continued to set flying records. In January 1935 she became the first person to fly from Hawaii to the American mainland. In April 1935 she set a speed record on a solo flight from Los Angeles to Mexico City and then set another record from Mexico City to New York. Writing about her flight from Hawaii, she said "After midnight the moon set and I was alone with the stars. I have often said that the lure of flying is the lure of beauty, and I need no other flights to convince me that the reason flyers fly, whether they know it or not, is the aesthetic appeal of flying."

Stimulated by her Hawaii flight, Earhart set herself a new goal, to fly around the world at (or near) the Equator, something never before attempted. Purdue University purchased a new twin-engine Lockheed Electra that was specially modified for the flight. The test plane was first flown on July 22, 1936 and was then presented to Earhart on her 39th birthday. She announced her world trip at a press conference in New York in February 1937 and then left from San Francisco in the early morning of March 17 when all but one member of the accompanying press corps was asleep. The flight to Hawaii set a new record of just under 16 hours. However, as she was leaving Hawaii, the heavily laden plane crashed on take-off. It took $50,000 and five weeks of work to repair the plane and to reschedule the flight. The cost was donated by a number of private individuals.

Because of the delay, Earhart decided to reverse the original course of her flight by flying from west to east to take advantage of changed weather patterns and air currents. She also replaced the original navigator with Fred Noonan. They took off on June 1, 1937 from Miami, Florida and headed for Brazil. They flew across the Atlantic to Africa and then across the Red Sea to Arabia and on to Karachi, Pakistan, Calcutta and Burma. They reached Lae in New Guinea on June 30. This was to be the most dangerous leg, to land on Howland Island, a tiny speck only 2½ miles long in the middle of the Pacific Ocean.

Earhart and Noonan never reached Howland Island, and to this day no one knows what happened to their plane. There was much speculation then and now that part of Earhart's mission was to spy on the Japanese-mandated Pacific islands. According to this theory, the Japanese knew this, and intercepted her plane and took her captive. There has never been any substantiation for this theory. In 1992, an expedition found certain objects (a shoe and a metal plate) on the small atoll of Nikumaroro south of Howland, which could have been left by Earhart and Noonan.

Where to learn more

Given the accomplishments of her career and the mysteries surrounding her disappearance, it is inevitable that there are a large number of works about Earhart. Her own books are: *20 Hrs. 40 Min.* (New York: G.P. Putnam's Sons, 1928); *The Fun of It* (New York: Brewer, Warren and Putnam, 1932); and *Last Flight* (New York: Harcourt, Brace and World, 1937), edited by her husband, George Putnam, who went on to write *Soaring Wings: A Biography of Amelia Earhart* (New York: Harcourt, Brace and World, 1939).

Other biographies include: Doris Shannon Garst, *Amelia Earhart: Heroine of the Skies* (New York: Messner, 1950); Adele Louise DeLeeuw, *Story of Amelia Earhart* (New York: Grosset & Dunlap, 1955); Fred Goerner, *The Search for Amelia Earhart* (New York: Doubleday, 1966); John Burke, *Winged Legend— The Story of Amelia Earhart* (London: Arthur Barker, 1970); Dick Strippel, *Amelia Earhart: The Myth and the Reality* (New York: Exposition Press, 1972); Burke Davis, *Amelia Earhart* (New York: G.P. Putnam's Sons, 1972); Jean Backus, *Letters from Amelia* (Boston: Beacon Press, 1982); Oliver Knaggs, *Amelia Earhart: Her Last Flight* (Cape Town: Timmins Publishers, 1983); Vincent Loomis, *Amelia Earhart* (New York: Random House, 1985); Muriel Morrissey, *Amelia Earhart* (Santa Barbara, California: Bellerophon, 1985); Roxane Chadwick, *Amelia Earhart: Aviation Pioneer* (Minneapolis: Lerner, 1987); Muriel Morrissey and Carol Osborne, *Amelia, My Courageous Sister* (Santa Clara, California: Osborne Publishers, 1988); Mary S. Lovell, *The Sound of Wings: The Life of Amelia Earhart* (New York: St. Martin's Press, 1989; also available in paperback).

There are several good books about women aviators that include short biographies of Earhart: Wendy Boase, *The Sky's the Limit: Women Pioneers in Aviation* (New York: Macmillan, 1979); Valerie Moolman, *Women Aloft* (New York: Time-Life Books, 1981); and Judy Lomax, *Women of the Air* (New York: Dodd, Mead & Co., 1987).

Lincoln Ellsworth

(1880 - 1951)

Lincoln Ellsworth was an American aviator who took part in several flying expeditions over the Arctic and then became the first person to fly across Antarctica.

Lincoln Ellsworth was born in Chicago on May 12, 1880. His father was a wealthy mining engineer. Lincoln himself was educated in the same profession and spent the first part of his career working in Canada and Alaska. From 1914 to 1917 he worked as a naturalist collecting specimens for the United States Biological Survey. When World War I broke out he went to France as a volunteer pilot even though he was over age. During the war he met **Roald Amundsen** in Paris, and that started him thinking about polar exploration.

In the early 1920s Ellsworth took part in a scientific expedition to South America. On his return to New York he met Amundsen again who told him about his scheme to fly over the North Pole in a lighter-than-air craft. Ellsworth prevailed upon his father to help finance the expedition. In the preparations for the flight, Ellsworth was instrumental in rescuing two crew members who crash landed in an airplane and was awarded a medal by the King of Norway. Ellsworth was aboard the airship *Norge* designed and piloted by **Umberto Nobile**, with Amundsen as leader of the expedition, that flew over the North Pole on May 12, 1926. The expedition was jointly financed by Ellsworth and the Norwegian government.

Following the success of the *Norge* Ellsworth then became involved in efforts by **Sir George Hubert Wilkins** to sail a submarine under the North Pole. Once again, he provided money for the expedition but did not participate in the expedition itself, which soon ended unsuccessfully. Ellsworth then accepted a German invitation to fly in the huge dirigible the *Graf Zeppelin* along the Arctic coast of Siberia. The airship left Leningrad on July 26, 1931 and arrived back on July 31, after a trip of 5,000 miles. The expedition cleared up several questions in Arctic geography, including discovering that two islands drawn on maps did not really exist.

Up to then Ellsworth had helped finance several expeditions but had never actually led one of his own. He therefore came up with the idea of being the first person to fly across Antarctica. Ellsworth purchased a plane and hired Bernt Balchen, the pilot who had flown with **Richard Evelyn Byrd**. They left New Zealand in December 1933 and arrived at Little America in January 1934. One night the ice that the plane was parked on began to break up, and the next morning it sank.

Ellsworth did not give up, however. He returned to the United States, bought a new plane, and returned with Balchen to Antarctica. Hubert Wilkins accompanied them to handle logistics on the ground. This time Ellsworth proposed attacking the problem from the other side—flying from Deception Island off the Graham Peninsula to Little America. After some initial test flying, Ellsworth and Balchen set off on January 3, 1935. But after an hour's flying Balchen suddenly turned back, claiming the weather was too bad. The attempt had to be abandoned once again.

Ellsworth returned to Antarctica in November 1935 with a new pilot, a Canadian, Herbert Hollick-Kenyon. They flew in a Northrop monoplane, the *Polar Star*, from Dundee Island, southwest of Joinville Island. They flew first on November 21,

Lincoln Ellsworth. The Granger Collection, New York.

1935, discovering a new range of mountains, which Ellsworth named the Eternity Mountains, but were forced to turn back after 11 hours because of bad weather. They tried again on November 22. They landed four times along the way to rest and check their position and each time were forced to wait for clearer skies. When they were ready to leave the last time, it took them two days to dig the plane out from under the snow. They ran out of fuel and were forced to land at a point about 60 miles from the Ross Sea on December 5. They reached Little America II at the Bay of Whales on foot on December 15. The base was not occupied at the time, and they had to wait until January 14 to be picked up by a British ship. By the time it arrived, Ellsworth was very ill with a gangrenous left leg and frostbite.

Ellsworth returned to Antarctica once more in 1937 and made a flight of 305 miles into the interior of Enderby Land and claimed 105,000 square miles of territory for the United States, which was never recognized by the government. He died in New York in 1951.

Where to learn more

Ellsworth told the story of his exploits in the Arctic in *Search* (New York: G.P. Putnam's Sons, 1932). and in *Beyond Horizon* (New York: Doubleday, 1938). There is a chapter on Ellsworth in John Grierson, *Heroes of the Polar Skies* (New York: Meredith Press, 1967). A good summary of Ellsworth's flights can be found in *Antarctica: Great Stories from the Frozen Continent* (Sydney: Reader's Digest, 1988).

Emin Pasha

(1840 - 1892)

Emin Pasha was a German who converted to Islam and entered the service of the Government of Egypt. He explored the area of the headwaters of the Nile River and was the object of a famous rescue expedition by Henry Stanley.

Emin Pasha was born Eduard Karl Oskar Theodor Schnitzer on March 28, 1840 in the Prussian town of Oppeln (now the Polish town of Opole) of Jewish parents. They moved to the nearby town of Neisse (Nysa) when Eduard was two years old, and his father died there three years later. His mother was remarried to a Lutheran, in which church Eduard was baptized. He studied medicine at the Universities of Breslau and Berlin. On graduation, he had problems in getting his medical certification (possibly because of his Jewish parentage). In frustration, he left Germany and moved in December 1864 to the port of Scutari (now Shkodër in Albania), which was then in the Ottoman Turkish empire. He returned to his hometown only once in the following years.

Once in Turkey, Schnitzer adopted a Turkish name (which evolved into Emin Pasha) and the Muslim faith. He became a quarantine officer for the Turkish government and then took on a variety of government posts in various parts of the Ottoman Empire—Trebizond, Epirus, Anatolia, Syria, and Cairo. He learned to speak several European and Asiatic languages and studied various branches of the natural sciences. Emin Pasha entered the service of the Khedive of Egypt, and in 1876 he was hired by Charles "Chinese" Gordon, who had been appointed Governor of the new colony of the Anglo-Egyptian Sudan. Gordon appointed him medical officer of the Equatorial Province in the far south of the Sudan and emissary to King Mutesa of Buganda. In July 1878 Emin Pasha became Governor of Equatorial Province with its capital at Gondokoro.

During the next several years, Emin administered the province and tried to cut off the slave trade that flowed to the east coast of Africa. He also spent his time investigating the country around him and wrote letters and papers that he sent to Europe on the anthropology, zoology, botany, and meteorology of central Africa. He also sent valuable collections of plant and animal specimens to Western museums. He made explorations on the Nile-Congo watershed and around the headwaters of the White Nile River.

In 1883, there was a strong reaction to the exploitation of their country by the Sudanese people. Under the command of a religious leader, the Mahdi, they began a campaign to drive the

Emin Pasha.

Egyptians and Europeans out of their country. Starting in the east of the country, they drove the foreign garrisons out of Kordofan Province in January 1883 and overran the Bahr-el-Ghazal, just north of Equatoria, in April 1884. Gordon (who had returned to the Sudan to organize its defense after being away for several years) was trapped in the capital city of Khartoum and killed in January 1885 just before a British relief column reached the city.

Emin Pasha was now cut off from the outside world. He moved his headquarters south to Wadelai on Lake Albert in what is now Uganda and positioned his troops to prepare for an escape via Buganda to the south if necessary. There he was visited at the end of 1885 by the German explorer Wilhelm Junker. Junker traveled back to Europe and told the world about Emin's plight and quoted him as saying, "We shall hold out until we obtain help, or until we perish."

Several private supporters and the Egyptian government got together the resources to send a mission to the rescue of Emin Pasha. Chosen to lead it was **Henry Morton Stanley**, the man who had "found" David Livingstone. The Emin Pasha Relief Expedition was also supported by King Leopold II of the Belgians who used it as a cover for his imperialistic designs on central Africa. Because of Leopold's involvement, the relief expedition did not travel to Emin the easy way via the island of Zanzibar on the east coast but went inland via the Congo River on the west coast instead. In addition to several regular officers, Stanley's expedition included two English volunteers--A.J. Mounteney Jephson and James S. Jameson, who was part of the "Rear Column."

After traveling to Zanzibar to hire porters, Stanley traveled around Africa and set out from the Atlantic coast on June 28, 1887. They reached Lake Albert Nyanza at the village of Kavalli on December 13, 1887. There, Stanley became ill and was unable to travel farther. In April 1888 he received a letter from Emin telling of his whereabouts. On April 23, Stanley sent out Jephson, who met up with Emin and **Gaetano Casati** on April 27. Together they went back to Stanley's camp, where the two famous men met on April 29. They drank six half-bottles of champagne to celebrate the occasion. Stanley proposed to take Emin out of Africa by way of Zanzibar. He also wanted Emin to turn over his possessions to King Leopold.

Emin returned to Wadelai with Jephson and Casati to think over Stanley's propositions. Along the way, they were taken prisoner in the town of Dufile on August 18, 1888 by a local rebel. They were held there until November 16. Given this turn of events, and Stanley's determination to make his expedition a success, Emin agreed to accompany Stanley to the coast. They set out on April 10, 1889.

Along the way to Zanzibar, Emin and Stanley saw Lake Edward, previously unknown to Europeans, and the Ruwenzori Mountains, the famous "Mountains of the Moon" that had first been mentioned by the Greek geographer Ptolemy. They reached Bagamoyo on the Indian Ocean in December 1889. There, Emin found that Bagamoyo and Dar-es-Salaam had been occupied by the German East Africa Company, which had set up its own "German Emin Pasha Expedition" under the command of Hermann von Wissman. Stanley had never revealed that the Germans had been trying to reach their countryman from the east.

Stanley left the coast to go to Zanzibar and then back to England. Emin stayed in Bagamoyo where he accepted an offer from the German Kaiser to work for him in expanding German influence in east Africa. Accompanied by the German explorer Stuhlman, he set off to return to his headquarters at Wadelai. However, the Arabs and Swahilis working from Zanzibar had undermined his authority in his absence, and he was not welcomed there. He then set off with Stuhlmann to try to cross over to the west coast of Africa, but his throat was slit one night in the Manyema country west of Lake Tanganyika in what is now Zaire in October 1892.

Where to learn more

Emin Pasha and the Emin Pasha Relief Expedition were great media events of the 1880s. The major participants all wrote accounts of the expedition. The foremost of these is, of course, Stanley's: *In Darkest Africa, or the Quest, Rescue and Retreat of Emin, Governor of Equatoria*, 2 vols. (London: Sampson Low, Marston, Searle & Rivington, 1890). Others are: Thomas Heagle Parke, *My Personal Experiences in Equatorial Africa as Medical Officer of the Emin Pasha Relief Expedition* (New York: Charles Scribner's Sons, 1891; reprinted, New York: Negro Universities Press, 1969); James S. Jameson, *The Story of the Rear Column of the Emin Pasha Relief Expedition* (New York: John W. Lovell Company, 1890; reprinted, New York: Negro Universities Press, 1969); A.J. Mounteney-Jephson, *Emin Pasha and the Rebellion at the Equator: A Story of Nine Months' Experiences in the Last of the Soudan Provinces* (London: Sampson Low, Marston, Searle & Rivington, 1890). Jephson's diary was later edited and published: Dorothy Middleton, ed. *The Diary of A.J. Mounteney Jephson: Emin Pasha Relief Expedition 1887-1889*.

The first biography of Emin Pasha came out soon after his death based largely on his own diaries and letters: Georg Schweitzer, *Emin Pasha: His Life and Work*, 2 vols. (London: Archibald Constable & Co., 1898). Since then, there have been numerous studies. The most entertaining is Olivia Manning, *The Reluctant Rescue* (Garden City, N.Y.: Doubleday, 1947; reprinted as *The Remarkable Expedition: The Story of Stanley's Rescue of Emin Pasha from Equatorial Africa* (New York: Atheneum, 1985). Others include: Jain R. Smith, *The Emin Pasha Relief Expedition, 1886-1890* (Oxford: Clarendon Press, 1972); Roger Jones, *The Rescue of Emin Pasha: The story of Henry M. Stanley and the Emin Pasha Relief Expedition, 1887-1889* (London: Allison and Busby, 1972); Alan Caillou (pseudonym for Alan Lyle-Smyth), *South from Khartoum: The Story of Emin Pasha* (New York: Hawthorn Books, 1974); Tony Gould, *In Limbo: The Story of Stanley's Rear Column* (London: Hamish Hamilton, 1979).

Joseph-Antoine Raymond Bruni d'Entrecasteaux

(1739-1793)

Entrecasteaux was a French naval officer who was sent out to find the missing La Pérouse and who collected much valuable information while he was in the South Pacific.

Joseph-Antoine Raymond Bruni d'Entrecasteaux was born at Aix in the southern province of Provence in France, the son of a prominent family. He joined the navy at the age of 15 so that he could fight in the Seven Years' War then being fought between France and Great Britain. Following the war, he served in the Mediterranean and in the Indian Ocean where he studied hydrography and came to be recognized as an expert in that field. In 1786 he was made commander of the Indian Station of the French navy. In that position he made an exploratory trip to China aboard the ship *La Révolution*. He pioneered a new route via the Sunda Strait and the Molucca Island in the eastern part of the East Indies that could be used in the monsoon season.

Entrecasteaux was next appointed governor of the two French islands of Ile de France (now Mauritius) and Ile Bourbon (now Réunion) in the Indian Ocean. Entrecasteaux was a success in this job, and he was looked upon with favor by the French government back in Paris.

In January 1788 the great French exploring expedition under **Comte de La Pérouse** had left Australia and had disappeared. Once the French government became aware of the disappearance, it was very anxious to try to find the men. Therefore, Entrecasteaux was called back to France and charged with the command of an expedition to search for them. He sailed from the port of Brest on September 28, 1791 with two ships, *La Recherche* and *L'Espérance*. He had orders to sail via the Cape of Good Hope to southwestern Australia, then along the south coast of Australia into the Pacific. In addition to looking for La Pérouse, he was charged with making scientific surveys along the way and to check the accuracy of the charts of the Indian and South Pacific Oceans. He was accompanied by a number of scientists, including a hydrographer, an astronomer, an artist, and a botanist.

While he was at the Cape of Good Hope, Entrecasteaux learned that clothes and objects of French origin had been seen in the Admiralty Islands, off the northern coast of New Guinea. He reached Recherche Bay on the south coast of Tasmania on April 23, 1792. While there he made detailed surveys and charts of the southern coast of Tasmania. He discovered that Bruny Island (named after him) was not part of the mainland by sailing through the channel (Entrecasteaux Channel) that separates it from the mainland.

The expedition then headed for New Caledonia, whose coast was also thoroughly explored. While there, the captain of *L'Espérance*, Huon de Kermadec, a noteworthy explorer in his own right, died. Entrecasteaux then traveled north to Bougainville Island in the Solomons and to the Admiralty Islands where he hoped to find traces of La Pérouse, but without any success. He sailed westward along the northern coast of New Guinea and put in at the Dutch trading fort at Amboina in the Molucca Islands.

Entrecasteaux left Amboina on October 14, 1792 and sailed to the southwest coast of Australia so that he could carry out his instructions of charting the south coast of the continent. The two ships sighted land near Cape Leeuwin, the southwestern point of Australia, on December 5, 1792 near St. Allouarn Island, which had been discovered by French ships in 1772. The expedition then sailed eastward past Point Entrecasteaux to Esperance Bay and the Archipelago of the Recherche along the shores of the Great Australian Bight to Entrecasteaux Reef. By now they were desperately short of water, and they gave up the exploration of the coast to head once again for Tasmania.

Entrecasteaux and his two ships remained there from January 21 to February 28, 1793, completing the work they had started earlier. Coincidentally, the day that they arrived in Tasmania was the day that the sponsor of the expedition, King Louis XVI, was beheaded in Paris.

Entrecasteaux sailed from Tasmania to New Zealand to investigate the coast there. He then headed north to look for La Pérouse once again in the island groups of Melanesia. He traveled via Tonga and New Caledonia and then north. On this part of the voyage he surveyed the Santa Cruz Islands. On May 19 both of the ships almost ran into the reefs off Vanikoro Island in the Santa Cruz group, where La Pérouse had, in fact, been wrecked. They sailed within a few miles of their quarry without being aware of it. It was not until 1828 that **Jules-Sébastien-César Dumont d'Urville** was to find the wreckage.

While in this part of the Pacific, Entrecasteaux made many valuable discoveries including islands in the Louisiade Archipelago, the Entrecasteaux Islands, and the Trobriand Islands, all off the southeast coast of New Guinea, as well as islands in the Solomon Islands and the Bismarck Archipelago. By this time Entrecasteaux and many of his men were sick with scurvy and dysentery. He therefore headed east, planning to rest once again on Amboina. But Entrecasteaux never made it—he died off the northeast coast of New Guinea on July 20, 1793.

The command of the two ships was taken over by two of the other officers in the expedition: d'Auribeau of *L'Espérance* and de Rossel of *La Recherche*. When they reached Surabaya in eastern Java, they learned from the Dutch that war had broken out between France and Holland, and some of the more important members of the expedition were imprisoned for several months. D'Auribeau, however, who was a royalist sympathizer, was able to negotiate special terms for himself. On the other hand, de Rossel, who had charge of the records of the expedi-

tion, was released by the Dutch only to be captured by the British on his way back to France. He was held captive in London for several months. All the documents and charts from the voyage were taken from him and were not returned until the end of the war in 1797, when de Rossel began work on the official account of the expedition.

Where to learn more

De Rossel's narrative, *Voyage de d'Entrecasteaux envoyé à la recherche de Lapérouse*, was published in Paris in two volumes in 1807. The best and most accessible source in English is John Dunmore, *French Explorers in the Pacific*, vol. 1, *The Eighteenth Century* (Oxford: Clarendon Press, 1965).

Erik (the Red)

(950? - 1004?)

Erik the Red was a Norseman from Iceland who was the first European to land on and settle in Greenland.

Erik the Red was born in Norway near the town of Stavanger. His father, Thorvald Asvaldsson, became involved in a blood feud and killed a man. As was usual for the time, he was sentenced to exile in Iceland, which had first been settled by the Norwegians starting in the 870s. The family moved to a remote part of western Iceland. After he was grown and married, Erik moved to another part of Iceland where he too became involved in a blood feud and killed two of his enemy's sons. As punishment, he was banished overseas for a period of three years.

Erik had heard about the voyages of a man named Gunnbjörn Ulfsson who had found a group of small islands west of Iceland and said that he had seen a much larger land beyond that. Erik announced that he was going in search of Ulfsson's land. With a group of retainers he sailed due west from the peninsula called Snaefellsnes in the year 982. He sighted Gunnbjörn's Skerries, thought to be off Cape Dan in eastern Greenland near the modern town of Angmagssalik, and then touched land on the shore of eastern Greenland at a place he named Midjökull (Middle Glacier).

Because of the way the currents flow, eastern Greenland has a much harsher environment than western Greenland, and Erik did not linger where he first landed. He sailed south down the coast and rounded the southern tip at Cape Farewell. He landed along the southwest coast at an area that was to become known as the Eastern Settlement (Eystribygd, in the region of modern Julianehåb or Qaqortoq). He spent the winter on an island he named "Erik's Island." The next spring (983) he sailed up the nearby fjord that he also named after himself. The next winter he spent on the southern tip of Greenland and then sailed up the east coast in the spring of 984. He returned to spend the following winter on Erik's Island.

By this time, the term of Erik's banishment from Iceland was complete. He sailed around the southern tip of Greenland and returned safely to Breidafjörd in Iceland in the summer of 985. On his return, the blood feud with his neighbors started up again. Erik then began to promote the colonization of his new found land, calling it "Greenland," thinking that would make it more appealing. He left Iceland in 986 with 14 ships that carried 400-500 people as well as domestic animals and household goods.

Erik settled at a place he named Brattahlid (now a trading station named Qagssiarssuk) at the head of Erik's Fjord, which became the center of the Eastern Settlement. The Western Settlement (around present-day Godthåb or Nuuk) was about 180 miles farther up the coast. There was a smaller settlement between the Eastern and Western Settlements.

In the year 999 Erik's son, **Leif Eriksson**, pioneered the first direct route to Norway from Greenland. While in Norway, Leif converted to Christianity and brought back the first missionary with him to Greenland. This did not please Erik, who remained true to the old Viking religion. When Leif made his trip to Vinland in 1001 or 1002, Erik wanted to go with him but fell off his horse on the way to the ship and injured his leg.

Erik died sometime during the winter of 1003-1004. Ironically, he was buried on the grounds of what became the Christian cathedral at Brattahlid. He left behind three sons—Leif, Thorvald, and Thorsteinn—and an illegitimate daughter named Freydis, noted for her disputatious manner. She married a man named Thorvard, and they became the richest but least popular couple in the Greenland settlement.

The Norse Greenland settlements prospered for a while, but then they were afflicted by a changing climatic pattern that made the weather much colder and no longer suitable for European farming practices. The increased ice in the ocean also made communication with Iceland more difficult. The last recorded voyage between Iceland and Greenland was made in 1410, although it is probable that there were some later trips. The Inuit advancing from the north are thought to have overwhelmed the Western Settlement around 1350. The last Norsemen in the Eastern Settlement probably disappeared sometime in the early 16th century. By the time **Sir Martin Frobisher** saw the coast of Greenland in 1576, the former European population had disappeared.

Where to learn more

The basic documentary source for our knowledge of the Norse exploration and colonization of Greenland is the Icelandic sagas, especially *Eiriks saga rauda* ("The Saga of Erik the Red") and the *Groenlendinga saga* ("The Saga of the Greenlanders"). The other source of information is from archaeological excavations done at Norse sites in southern Greenland. Books on the subject include: Fridtjof Nansen, *In Northern Mists: Arctic Exploration in Early Times* (London: W. Heinemann, 1911; New York: F.A. Stokes, 1911); G.M. Gathorne-Hardy, *The Norse Discoverers of America* (Oxford: Oxford University Press, 1921); Poul Nörlund, *Viking Settlers of Greenland* (London: 1936);, Gwyn Jones, *The Norse Atlantic Saga* (Oxford: Oxford University Press, 1965); Knud J. Krogh, *Viking Greenland* (Copenhagen: The National Museum, 1967); Finn Gad, *The History of Greenland*, vol. 1 (Montreal: McGill-Queen's University Press, 1971); and G.J. Marcus, *The Conquest of the North Atlantic* (New York: Oxford University Press, 1981).

Leif Eriksson

(970s - 1020?)

Leif Eriksson was a Norseman who sailed from Greenland and landed at four places on the coast of North America around the year 1000.

Leif Eriksson was born in Iceland in the late 970s. He was the son of **Erik the Red** who founded the Norse settlement in Greenland. Eriksson moved with his family to Greenland in 985 or 986, settling at a place called Brattahlid on the southwest corner of the island along the Eiriksfjord.

Eriksson is said in the Icelandic sagas to be "tall and strong and very impressive in appearance. He was a shrewd man and always moderate in behavior."

In the Icelandic saga called *Erik the Red's Saga*, written sometime after 1250, Eriksson is credited with bringing Christianity to Greenland and with being the first European to see North America. This version is no longer accepted as true. Greater weight is now given to the more complicated series of events related in the *Greenlanders' Saga*, written in about 1200.

According to this saga, North America was first sighted by Bjarni Herjolfsson who was driven off course on his way from Iceland to Greenland in 985 or 986. However, he did not go ashore. Eriksson, who was the first Norseman to make the direct voyage from Norway to Greenland, decided to follow up on Herjolfsson's sightings and sailed west.

Eriksson left Greenland with a crew of 35 in 1001. He landed first at a place that he named Helluland, "the Land of Flat Stone," which is thought to be on the southern end of Baffin Island. From there he went to "Markland" (Forest Land) which is considered to be somewhere on the coast of Labrador. He then landed on an unnamed island, which is possibly Belle Isle in the Strait of Belle Isle that separates Labrador from the island of Newfoundland. "There was dew on the grass, and the first thing they did was to get some of it on their hands and put it to their lips, and to them it seemed the sweetest thing they had ever tasted."

Eriksson and his companions reached Vinland (the land of the vine or Wineland or, possibly, pastureland) in the fall of 1001. They landed at the mouth of a river on the west of a large peninsula of land pointing north. They followed the river upstream to a lake. This was the only geographical description given of Vinland, but the astronomical readings show that it was south of Greenland. From the description given, the site could be that of L'Anse aux Meadows on the northeastern tip of Newfoundland, where remains of a Norse settlement were found in the 1960s. The expedition spent the winter in Vinland and built several dwellings at a place they named Leifrsbudir (Leif's Booths). They then returned to Greenland in the spring of 1002 with a supply of timber and "grapes."

The year following Eriksson's voyage, in 1003, his brother Thorvald returned to Leifrsbudir. He spent the winter of 1003-1004 there. The next spring and summer he went exploring in Vinland, which he found to be beautiful and well-wooded. He went back to Leifrsbudir to spend the winter of 1004-1005 and then headed north to Markland the following spring. There, the Norsemen encountered and clashed with a group of Native Americans, whom they called "Skraelings." Thorvald was killed by an arrow. His crew went back to Leifsbudir to spend the winter and then sailed back to Greenland in 1006.

On the news of Thorvald's death, his brother Thorstein tried to sail to Markland to recover his body but ran into storms and was driven into the North Atlantic. Thorstein died on his return to Greenland.

In 1010 Thorfinn Karlsefni, who had married Thorstein's widow, Gudrid, sailed from Greenland with 160 men and some women on board three ships to found a settlement in Vinland. They built houses at Leifrsbudir, and in the summer of 1011 Gudrid gave birth to a son, Snorri. At first, the Norsemen traded for furs with the Skraelings. Relations worsened, however, and warfare broke out in the winter of 1011-1012. The Norsemen returned to Greenland in 1013.

Following the return of Thorfinn Karlsefni, Erik the Red's illegitimate daughter Freydis went into partnership with two brothers, Helgi and Finnbogi, to trade for furs and wood in Vinland. Once in Leifrsbudir, Freydis had her supporters murder Helgi and Finnbogi and their followers. The saga said that when the men in her party refused to kill the women, she did it herself. She then confiscated her enemies' goods and returned home, where she was rich from the profits of the voyage.

Back in Greenland, Leif Eriksson had inherited his father's estate at Brattahlid and his position as leader of the colony. When confronted with the news of Freydis's crimes, he could not bring himself to punish his half-sister. On Eriksson's death in about 1020 the estate came into the possession of his son, Thorkell.

Where to learn more

Trying to reconstruct the history of Norse encounters with America has been a favorite occupation of scholars for years. There are two starting points from which all theories then diverge. The first is the Icelandic sagas. English translations of the relevant ones can be found in Gwyn Jones, *The Norse Atlantic Saga* (Oxford: Oxford University Press, 1986). The second source is the archeological evidence: Anne Stine Ingstad, *The Discovery of a Norse Settlement in America: Excavations at L'Anse aux Meadows, Newfoundland, 1961-1968* (Oslo: Universitetsforlaget, 1977).

Important secondary sources are: Fridtjof Nansen, *In Northern Mists: Arctic Exploration in Early Times* (London: W. Heinemann, 1911; New York: F.A. Stokes, 1911); G.M. Gathorne-Hardy, *The Norse Discoverers of America* (Oxford: Oxford University Press, 1921); Tryggvi J. Olesen, *Early Voyages and Northern Approaches, 1000-1632* (Toronto: McClelland and Stewart, 1963); Samuel Eliot Morison, *The European Discovery of America: The Northern Voyages, A.D. 500-1600* (New York: Oxford University Press, 1971); and E. Guralnick, ed. *Vikings in the West* (Chicago: University of Chicago Press, 1982).

Estevanico

(1500? - 1539)

Estevanico, often called "the Black," was a Moroccan slave who accompanied Cabeza de Vaca on his odyssey through the southwestern United States and was then the forerunner of Coronado in visiting the "Seven Cities of Cibola."

Estevanico (also known as Estevan and Estebanico) was born sometime around the beginning of the 16th century in the town of Azemmour on the west coast of Morocco. During that time the Arabs of Morocco were in constant warfare with their Spanish and Portuguese neighbors to the north. At some point, Estevanico was captured and sold as a slave in Spain. He was often called Estevanico the Black, and it may well be that he was African or part-African in descent, since there were many years of contact between the Arabs and Berbers of North Africa and the Blacks who lived south of the Sahara.

Estevanico (which is a Spanish diminutive for "Stephen") came into the possession of Andres Dorantes de Carranca, a nobleman of the Extremadura region of Spain. Dorantes joined the expedition to North America led by Panfilo de Narvaez that included **Alvar Nuñez Cabeza de Vaca**. They landed in Florida in April 1528. Disregarding the advice of his captains, Narvaez abandoned his ships and marched into the interior on May 1 in search of gold. The history of the succeeding trek comes from the report that Cabeza de Vaca made after his return to Spain. At first, there is no mention of Estevanico.

Narvaez's expedition was attacked by Native Americans near the modern city of Tallahassee. The Spaniards went to a bay on the Gulf of Mexico and constructed five boats with which to sail along the coastline to a Spanish base in Mexico. They set sail on September 22, 1528; Estevanico was in the third boat, commanded by Dorantes. In November they were hit by storms and Dorantes' boat and the one captained by Cabeza de Vaca were wrecked on Galveston Island off the coast of Texas. In the spring of 1529 only 15 men were still alive. Thirteen of them, including Estevanico, left Galveston to try to get to Mexico overland. Cabeza de Vaca was too sick to travel and was left behind.

The party commanded by Dorantes headed west and south. Several died along the way, and the rest were captured by Native Americans at San Antonio Bay. By the autumn of 1530 only Dorantes, Estevanico, and Alonzo del Castillo Maldonado were still alive. They were harshly treated by their captors. Dorantes escaped and went inland to a village of the Mariame tribe, where his life was easier. In the spring of 1532 Estevanico and Castillo also got free and made it to Dorantes' village. In the spring of 1533 they were surprised to see Cabeza de Vaca, who was working as a trader among the various tribes, turn up. The four men were forced to separate but agreed to meet the following autumn at the annual festival to celebrate the harvest of prickly pears.

They did meet in the fall of 1533 but were unable to escape. They returned with their different captors and met again in the fall of 1534 at which time they were able to escape. They came to a camp of the Avavares tribe where they were warmly welcomed as medicine men. Estevanico joined the others in healing the Indians, and was especially noted for his ability to learn to speak other languages and to use sign language. They stayed with the Avavares until the spring of 1535. Their reputation as healers preceded them, and they were welcomed wherever they went.

As the four men went farther west, they saw evidence of different cultures. They saw a metal bell and medicine gourds made by the Pueblo tribes of New Mexico. Estevanico took one of these gourds and used it in his healing act. The four Westerners reached the Rio Grande River at the end of 1535, and Castillo and Estevanico headed upstream. There they came upon the permanent towns or "pueblos" of the Jumano tribe. When the others caught up with them, they found Estevanico surrounded by Indians, who treated him like a god. Along the way, the men heard tales of a group of rich cities in the interior, which they called the Seven Cities of Cibola.

From the Rio Grande, Estevanico and the three Spaniards traveled into what is now the Mexican state of Chihuahua. As they traveled, they saw more and more evidence of contact with Europeans. They met up with a party of Spaniards in March 1536 and entered Mexico City on July 24, 1536. The four men, including Estevanico, were well received by Viceroy Antonio Mendoza, who was intrigued by their tales of wealthy cities to the north.

Cabeza de Vaca returned to Spain while Castillo and Dorantes married and settled down in Mexico. Dorantes sold or gave Estevanico to Viceroy Mendoza. Mendoza wanted to send an expedition north and eventually accepted the offer of a Spanish friar, Fray Marcos de Niza, to lead it. He appointed Estevanico to be his guide. They went north to the town of Culiacan in the autumn of 1538, where **Francisco Vázquez de Coronado** had recently been appointed governor. Estevanico and Fray Marcos left Culiacan on March 7, 1539. On March 21 Fray Marcos sent Estevanico ahead to scout the trail. Four days later, Native American messengers returned to Fray Marcos to report that Estevanico had heard news that he was 30 days' march from Cibola and asked Fray Marcos to join him.

Fray Marcos headed northward, but Estevanico did not wait for him. As the friar entered each new village, he found a message from Estevanico saying that he had continued on. Fray Marcos chased after him for weeks but was unable to catch up. Estevanico headed through the large desert region of the Mexican state of Sonora and southern Arizona; he was the first Westerner to enter what are now Arizona and New Mexico. Wherever he traveled, Estevanico sent his medicine gourd ahead of him to announce his arrival. In May he reached the Zuni pueblo of Hawikuh, the first of the "Seven Cities of Cibola." There he showed his magic gourd, but the chief threw it down in anger and told Estevanico to leave the town. The chief took away all his possessions and put him in a house on the edge of the town without food or water. The next morning he was attacked by a band of warriors and killed.

Several of the Native American escorts escaped and returned to tell Fray Marcos the news of Estevanico's death. In his report to Mendoza, Fray Marcos said that he continued to travel north until he could see Hawikuh, or Cibola, but did not enter the pueblo. In his report he said that it was a rich place that was even bigger than Mexico City. Since it is in fact only a small pueblo, it seems as though Fray Marcos did not make the trip he claimed. However,

his report inspired Mendoza to send out the ill-fated Coronado expedition. When they reached the small village of Hawikuh they learned that Fray Marcos had been lying. They also found that the chief had appropriated Estevanico's green dinner plates, his greyhound dogs, and his metal bells.

When asked why they had killed Estevanico, the Zuni said that he had claimed that there was a huge army coming behind him with many weapons. The chiefs met in council and decided that he was a spy and that it was safer to kill him. Once dead, they cut up his body into little pieces and distributed the parts among the chiefs.

Where to learn more

The original source materials that we have on Estevanico are the *Joint Report*, written by Cabeza de Vaca, Dorantes, and Castillo; Cabeza de Vaca's *Relation*; and the reports sent back to Mendoza by Fray Marcos. Fray Marcos's account is available in a new edition along with a study of his journey: Adolph F. Bandelier, *The Discovery of New Mexico by the Franciscan Monk Friar Marcos de Niza in 1539*, translated by Madeleine Turrell Rodack (Tucson: University of Arizona Press, 1981).

These original documentary sources have been used to construct a narrative of Estevanico's adventures by John Upton Terrell in *Estevanico the Black* (Los Angeles: Westernlore Press, 1968), which served as the basis for this account. Terrell includes an extensive bibliography of the original sources and selected secondary sources that discuss the role of Estevanico.

Explorer

(1958 - 1970)

Explorer 1 was the first U.S.-made artificial satellite to orbit the earth.

The United States first publicly indicated its intention of exploring space on July 29, 1955, when President Eisenhower announced that he had approved "the launching of small unmanned Earth-circling satellites" as part of America's contribution to the International Geophysical Year in 1958. The program had problems from the very beginning. Rather than work on the basis of existing military rockets as the carrier vehicle, the United States decided to develop its small experimental weather rockets.

The development of this new rocket was called the Vanguard project and was run by the U.S. Navy as a continuation of its earlier Viking program. The decision to use this small rocket is hard to explain, especially since the Army's Jupiter-C rocket, based on the earlier Redstone missile, had a very successful firing on September 20, 1956, when it sent a payload 3,400 miles across the Atlantic reaching an altitude of 600 miles. The Jupiter rocket had been developed by famed German rocket scientist Wernher von Braun. He resented the decision to go ahead with the Vanguard project and continued experiments with his own design at the Army Ballistic Missile Station in Huntsville, Alabama. Fearing that he might go ahead on his own, the Defense Department instructed von Braun not to use the Jupiter to launch his own satellite.

Project Vanguard was officially inaugurated on September 9, 1955, soon after Eisenhower's speech. The final design of the

Explorer 1 launch, January 31, 1958. NASA.

Vanguard missile was approved in March 1956, and production began immediately. The first Vanguard was launched from Cape Canaveral on October 23, 1957. It carried a 4,000-pound payload on a 109-mile-high, 335-mile-long trajectory. The next two Vanguards were supposed to put an artificial satellite into orbit. They exploded on launch in December 1957 and February 1958, respectively. British newspapers nicknamed the flights "Kaputnik" and "Flopnik."

Vanguard TV-4 ("TV" stood for "test vehicle") succeeded in putting a 3.25 pound satellite (the smallest ever) into orbit on March 17, 1958 with two radio transmitters aboard. It was immediately named *Vanguard 1*. By then, however, it was too late to be a "first." **Sputnik** 1 had been launched on October 14, 1957, and there was also another American satellite already in orbit.

Vanguard was upstaged not only by the Soviets but by another American program. Once the Sputnik was launched, the U.S. government was galvanized into action. It ordered von Braun to ignore its recent orders and to get a satellite into the air as quickly as possible. Fortunately, von Braun had the instrument at hand. He had developed a rocket named Juno 1 which was very similar to the Jupiter C except that it had four stages instead of three. The Secretary of the Army said that it would be possible to launch a satellite using the Juno 1 four months after the order was given. A government commission endorsed this plan on October 25, 1957, and the Secretary of Defense gave the order on November 8. A few days later the target date was advanced to January 30, 1958.

Under von Braun's direction six Juno 1 rockets were constructed in record time. Eventually, three of them launched satellites into orbit. The first was *Explorer 1*, the first United States satellite, which was launched on January 31, 1958—only one day later than the revised schedule. *Explorer 1* was 80 inches long and 6 inches in diameter and weighed 31 pounds, of which 18 pounds were scientific instruments.

America's first three satellites, *Explorer 1*, *Vanguard 1*, and *Explorer 2* (launched in March 1958), were all much smaller than the Sputniks. However, they did have the advantage of having carefully-engineered miniaturized instruments that were able to gather large amounts of data. The most interesting information that they recorded was that the Earth is surrounded by a large zone of radiation. This was named for the University of Iowa scientist who discovered it, James van Allen. *Explorer 1* re-entered the earth's atmosphere and disintegrated on March 31, 1970 after having spent 12 years in orbit.

Where to learn more

Although *Explorer 1* was America's first satellite, there is little written specifically on it. However, most early books dealing with America's space program mention it to one degree or another. You might consider looking at Richard S. Lewis, *Appointment on the Moon: The Full Story of Americans in Space from Explorer 1 to the Lunar Landing* (New York: Ballantine Books, 1969); David Fishlock, *A Guide to Earth Satellites* (New York: American Elsevier, 1971); and T.M. Wilding-White's *Janes Pocket Book of Space Exploration* (New York: Collier Books, 1977).

A good book that presents an overview of space exploration thus far is Wernher von Braun and Frederick I. Ordway III, *Space Travel: A History* (New York: Harper & Row, 1985). It served as the main source for this account.

Edward John Eyre

(1815-1901)

Edward John Eyre was an English explorer who was one of the first persons to begin the exploration of central Australia and made the first overland trip across Australia.

Edward John Eyre. The Granger Collection, New York.

Edward John Eyre was the son of a Yorkshire clergyman who emigrated to Australia at the age of 17, arriving in Sydney on March 20, 1833. He used the capital he had brought to Australia to buy a sheep ranch. However, he had problems with diseased sheep, and in 1837 he turned to a new profession: taking livestock overland from settled areas to pioneer country. He made profitable trips taking stock from Sydney to Melbourne, from Melbourne to Adelaide, and from Sydney to Adelaide.

Eyre moved to Adelaide in 1838 and used that as a base for exploring the interior. In May 1839 he went north of Spencer Gulf, a large body of water on the south coast of Australia and discovered a mountain range, the Flinders Ranges, and a large interior lake, Lake Torrens, that was usually dry. Later in the same year he went to the west side of Spencer Gulf and explored the Eyre Peninsula, which was named after him.

In January 1840 Eyre took a shipment of cattle from Albany on the south coast of Western Australia to the Swan River (where the city of Perth is now) on the west coast. This inspired him to come up with his most ambitious scheme—to find a route overland where cattle could be driven from Adelaide to the west coast of Australia. Receiving financial support from the colonists in South Australia, he set out with a party of eight men from the head of Spencer Gulf in June 1840. At first he went north but could not find a way through the dried-up lake beds that make up this part of Australia. He did, however, discover the largest of these, Lake Eyre.

Eyre then headed due west and came out at place called Streaky Bay on the west side of the Eyre Peninsula in November 1840. Ahead of him stretched an enormous desert, the Nullarbor Plain (Nullarbor means "no-trees"), one of the driest places in the world. Foolhardily, Eyre decided to cross the desert by a series of forced marches. To do so, he sent back all of the members of the exploring party except for his assistant, John Baxter, and three Aborigines. He wrote in his journal that he was determined "either to accomplish the object I had in view, or perish in the attempt."

Throughout the entire trip, Eyre and his companions were plagued by the extreme scarcity of water and the blowing sand that slowed them down. They passed the last waterhole on March 12, 1841 at a place which is now called Eucla on the border of Western and South Australia. The only reason they survived was because the Aborigines knew how to get water out of the roots of trees and from wells dug in the sand. By the middle of April they were very short on food, and the southern winter was starting, which made the nights very cold. Miserable, two of the Aborigines killed Baxter on the night of April 28-29 and left with the remaining provisions.

Eyre and the remaining Aborigine boy, Wylie, were all alone. Eyre pressed on, however, and was rewarded with rain to drink, and he killed one of his two horses in order to have something to eat. On June 2, they reached Esperance Bay on the south coast of Western Australia, where they met a French whaling ship at anchor. After resting on the boat for several days, Eyre insisted on completing his journey overland, and he finally made it to Albany on July 7, 1841.

Eyre was the first person to cross Australia. However, rather than finding a way to drive livestock overland, he had proved just the opposite—that there was no practical way of doing so. On his return to Adelaide, Eyre was appointed magistrate for a large unsettled part of the colony of South Australia and wrote up the history of his explorations.

Eyre returned to England in 1844. In 1846 he was appointed Lieutenant Governor of New Zealand; in 1854, the Governor of St. Vincent; in 1860, the Governor of the Leeward Islands in the Caribbean; and, in 1862, the Governor of Jamaica. While he was Governor of Jamaica, there was a rebellion by the Jamaicans. He put it down very harshly, and in particular declared martial law and had a member of the local legislature condemned to death. For this, he was heavily censured in England and was recalled. He was put on trial three times, and his case became a major public issue in Victorian England. Eyre was supported by important literary figures, such as Thomas Carlyle and Alfred, Lord Tennyson, while others, such as John Stuart Mill, led the criticism against him. He was finally exonerated and retired to a country manor where he lived until his death on November 30, 1901.

Where to learn more

Eyre's own story of his journeys was published in London in 1845: *Journals of Expeditions of Discovery into Central Australia and Overland from Adelaide to King George's Sound in the Years 1840-1*, 2 vols. Extracts can be found in Kathleen Fitzpatrick, ed. *Australian Explorers: A Selection from Their Writings* (London: Oxford University Press, 1958).

There is one modern biography: Geoffrey Dutton, *The Hero as Murderer: The Life of Edward John Eyre* (London: Wm. Collins, 1967). The story of the explorations is told in Malcolm Uren and Robert Stephens, *Waterless Horizons* (Melbourne: Robertson & Mullens, 1941). There is an interesting section on him in Alan Moorehead's excellent book, *The Fatal Impact* (New York: Harper & Row, 1966). The story of the famous trials is in B. Semmel, *The Governor Eyre Controversy* (London: 1962).

Fa-Hsien

(374? - 462?)

Fa-Hsien was a Chinese Buddhist monk who made an epic voyage to and from India to collect religious texts.

Fa-Hsien, whose original family name was Kung, was born in the village of Wu-yang in China's Shansi province. His three older brothers all died in childhood and, as a way of safeguarding his life, Fa-Hsien's father had him dedicated to a Buddhist society. He went to live in a Buddhist monastery at the age of 3. At the age of 10 his father died, and his uncle urged him to return to the family home. He refused and only visited his home for a short time a few years later when his mother died. He became a full monk at the age of 20.

The original texts of Buddhism are written in Sanskrit, the ancient holy language of India. Fa-Hsien felt that the Chinese translations then in use were inadequate, and at about the age of 25 he set out for India to bring back original manuscripts from which new translations could be made.

Fa-Hsien set out in the year 399. He traveled across North China via the cities of Xi'an and Xining, the westernmost city in China. He then went along the south side of the Nan Shan Mountains to Dunhuang and then to the dried lakebed of Lop Nor. He followed the Tarim and Khotan Rivers around the great Takla Makan desert to the Buddhist kingdom of Khotan centered on the present-day town of Hetian. It took him 25 days to go to the caravan town of Yarkand and then another month to get to Kashgar which is in the westernmost part of what is now Chinese Turkestan.

From Kashgar Fa-Hsien followed a difficult route through the Pamir Mountains and headed for the headwaters of the Indus River. He passed through mountains that were covered with snow all year round. "There are also among them venomous dragons, which, when provoked, spit forth poisonous winds, and cause showers of snow and storms of sand and gravel. Not one in ten thousand of those who encounter these dangers escapes with his life." He went through Gilgit and then down the Kabul River to the great city of Peshawar and across the Punjab plains into the heartland of India. In the holy city of Magadha (near modern Patna) he spent three years collecting and copying Buddhist texts. He then traveled down the Ganges, visiting the holy sites along the way, to the port of Tamralipti where he spent another two years.

Leaving India, Fa-Hsien traveled by sea to Sri Lanka, which was an important center of Buddhism, where he spent another two years. He set out for home by sea from Sri Lanka, but his ship was wrecked on a small island off the coast of Sumatra in Indonesia. He made it to Java, where he stayed for five months waiting for a ship to China. The ship he took got blown off its course headed for Canton in South China and drifted for 70 days. Finally, it turned northward and touched land on the Shantung Peninsula in northern China. He reached there in 414, after an absence of 15 years.

On his return, Fa-Hsien went to the capital of China (then at Nanjing) and worked translating some of the texts he had brought back. He then retired to a monastery in the province of Hupei, where he wrote the story of his travels. It was called the *Fo-Kwe-Ki* (Memoirs of the Buddhist Realms) and told future Chinese pilgrims of the way to India overland and by sea. Fa-Hsien stayed in the monastery until his death at the age of 88.

Where to learn more

The Western work on Fa-Hsien all dates from the 19th century. The first translation of the *Fo-Kwe-Ki* was made into French by M. Abel-Rémusat in 1836. This was translated into English by a Mr. Laidlay. The first direct translation into English was made by Samuel Beal, a chaplain in the Royal Navy and student of Buddhism who later became professor of Chinese at the University of London: *Travels of Fah-Hian and Sung-Yun, Buddhist Pilgrims from China to India* (London: Trübner, 1869; reprinted, London: Susil Gupta, 1964.) A revised version of this translation appeared with other texts in Samuel Beal, *Buddhist Records of the Western World*, 2 vols. (London: Kegan Paul, Trench, Trübner & Co., 1884; reprinted, New York: Paragon Books, 1968). Another translation was made by Herbert A. Giles, a British diplomat in China, *The Travels of Fah-hsien* (London: 1877; reprinted, Cambridge: 1923). A third version was made by James Legge, of Oxford University, *A Record of Buddhistic Kingdoms: Being an Account by the Chinese Monk Fa-Hien of His Travels in India and Ceylon (A.D. 399-414) in Search of the Buddhist Books of Discipline* (Oxford: Clarendon Press, 1886; reprinted, New York: Paragon, 1965). Legge's is the most readable version.

Percy Fawcett

(1867-1925)

Percy Fawcett was a British explorer who surveyed the borders of several South American countries and disappeared while looking for lost civilizations in the Amazon forest.

Percy Fawcett was born in Torquay, England in 1867. He joined the British army at the age of nineteen and spent the next twenty years as an army officer, including service in Sri Lanka and Hong Kong. He studied surveying and in 1906 was offered the job of surveying the boundary between Bolivia and Peru and Brazil.

On his first expedition to South America in 1906 and 1907, he surveyed the Madeira, Abuna, and Acre Rivers, which formed part of the disputed boundaries. In spite of the difficulties involved in this exploration, Fawcett loved this life of adventure, and he accepted a new commission from the Bolivian government to survey the unknown Verde River in the eastern part of the country on the border with Brazil. This trip in 1908 was so difficult that five of his porters died during the expedition. In his account, Fawcett wrote, "For nearly three weeks we lived upon occasional palm tops. We were eaten by insects; were drenched by a succession of violent storms with a southerly wind, bitterly cold for wet and blanketless people."

In 1909 Fawcett returned to the Verde River with the boundary commissions of Bolivia and Brazil to lay out the boundary he had surveyed. He was then commissioned by the Bolivian government to explore the Heath River between Bolivia and Peru. He undertook this assignment on two trips in 1910 and 1911. At this point, he was forced to resign his commission in the British army because they would no longer release him for his boundary work.

At the end of his second expedition to the Heath River, Fawcett returned to the Bolivian capital of La Paz in December, 1911 to find that the Bolivians and Peruvians were quarrelling over the new boundary. He quit his job in disgust and began to make explorations on his own. In the course of his boundary work, he had heard numerous stories or legends about mysterious light-skinned people and fabulous cities in the interior of South America. Although such stories had been heard ever since Europeans first arrived in South America, Fawcett believed they were true and set out to prove their existence.

In 1913 and 1914 Fawcett traveled in northern Bolivia, but he returned to England in September 1914 after the First World War broke out. He fought in the British army until the end of the war

and rose to the rank of colonel. When the war ended, he wanted to go back to South America to continue his search for lost civilizations. He was able to get backing from the Brazilian government for a trip to the Mato Grosso region of western Brazil in 1920. On both that and a follow-up trip in 1921 he was forced to turn back because the other members of the expedition could not stand up to the hazards and rigors of the trip.

Fawcett was determined not to give up, and in 1925 he set out on another expedition with the financial backing of the North American Newspaper Alliance, which had rights to his story. This time he chose as his traveling companions his 21-year-old son Jack and a friend of Jack's named Raleigh Rimell. Their aim was to find the lost city of "Z" that Fawcett was convinced existed in the Amazon basin of Brazil. They set out from the town of Cuiabá on the edge of the Mato Grosso on April 20, 1925, and by May 20 they had reached a place that Fawcett named Dead Horse Camp near the headwaters of the mighty Xingu River. From there he planned to go east to the Araguaia River and then down the Araguaia, where Fawcett thought they would find "Z".

By the time Fawcett and the two young men reached Dead Horse Camp, they had already experienced difficulties. They had been devoured by insects, and it turned out that Rimell was highly allergic to their stings and was no longer able to walk. From Dead Horse Camp, Fawcett wrote a letter to his wife that he sent by messenger back to Cuiabá. That was the last that was ever heard of him.

When it was realized that Fawcett was not coming back, his sponsors sent out an expedition under George Dyott in 1928 to find out what had happened. Dyott found Dead Horse Camp and followed Fawcett's route from there for a while, finding some objects left behind and some Native Americans who remembered the party. Dyott was convinced that Fawcett had been killed by the Native Americans, and this is the most likely explanation. However, he had no proof of this, and, as a result, a series of legends grew up that Fawcett was still alive in the Brazilian forest. For years there were various reports of sightings of unknown Europeans, but they all turned out to be unfounded rumors. The famous English writer Evelyn Waugh used these stories as the basis for the ending of his novel *Decline and Fall*.

Where to learn more

The complete story of all of Fawcett's expeditions can be found in *Lost Trails, Lost Cities* (New York: Funk & Wagnalls, 1953), which includes his records and letters selected and arranged by his son Brian. The story of the search for traces of the lost party can be found in George Dyott, "The Search for Col. Fawcett," *Geographical Journal*, vol. 72 (1928), pp. 443-448 and vol. 74 (1929), pp. 513-540, and in a book by G. Cummins, *The Fate of Colonel Fawcett* (London: 1955).

Paul-Xavier Flatters

(1832 - 1881)

Paul-Xavier Flatters was a French soldier who led two expeditions into the southern Sahara of Algeria.

Paul-Xavier Flatters was born in Paris on September 16, 1832, the son of a well-known French sculptor. Both his parents died when he was young, and his guardians sent him to the French military academy of St-Cyr where he graduated in 1853. He was immediately sent to Algeria, then a French colony, and spent most of the rest of his career there, with only brief tours of duty in France. He did return to France to fight in the Franco-Prussian War in 1870 and was captured by the Germans. After his release from a prisoner of war camp, he helped the French army put down the popular uprising in Paris known as the Commune in 1871.

Flatters returned to Algeria where he received the command of a garrison near the Sahara Desert, which was not then under French control. He became interested in the possibility of building a trans-Saharan railroad and was chosen by the Paris-based Trans-Saharan Committee to lead an expedition into the desert to scout out possible routes. He was sent out with only eight French companions, four of them soldiers, to the land of the Tuareg, declared enemies of the French. He headed into the Sahara on March 5, 1880 and made it as far as the rocky hills of the Tassili-n-Ajjer. Along the way, he alienated most of his companions and refused to accept advice from his African advisers, which made the trip unnecessarily difficult. Following his return to Algeria on June 3, he traveled to Paris where he made an optimistic report about the possibility of constructing the railroad.

The Trans-Saharan Committee almost immediately sent Flatters back to the desert to continue his investigation. This time he had a larger group of men but was still unable to manage them effectively. He left in October 1880 and reached the town of Amguid at the western end of the Tassili-n-Ajjer on January 18, 1881. At that point he accepted as guides a group of Tuareg sent out by the ruler of the Ahaggar region. They set out on February 11, but on the 16th the guides claimed to have lost their way. They went ahead to scout out the path and returned later in the day. They then offered to lead the Frenchmen to a source of water in the Ahaggar Mountains. There, a detachment of Tuaregs attacked Flatters. He was knocked out, cut by sabres, thrust into by lances, and his body was dismembered. His second in command and the expedition's doctor were also killed.

The remaining Frenchmen formed a column to head back to Algeria, but their camels and supplies were taken by the Tuareg who followed the column through the desert. Along the way, the Frenchmen and their Algerian supporters were either killed, starved or died of thirst. On two separate occasions, stragglers were attacked and killed by their own companions and their flesh was eaten. When the remnants of the column reached the town of Ouargla on the edge of the desert, it consisted of 12 Arabs out of the total of 112 Arabs and Frenchmen who had started out. The calls for revenge in France against the destruction of the Flatters expedition was to be one of the main reasons for French expansion into the Sahara in the following years.

Where to learn more

There are several books in French about Flatters: J. Mélia, *Le drame de la mission Flatters* (Paris: 1942) and R. Pottier, *Flatters* (Paris: 1948). The best account in English can be found in Douglas Porch, *The Conquest of the Sahara* (New York: Alfred A. Knopf, 1984).

Matthew Flinders

(1774-1814)

Matthew Flinders was an English navigator who established that Tasmania is an island, charted the south coast of Australia, and was the first person to sail around Australia.

Matthew Flinders was born on March 16, 1774 at Donington, Lincolnshire, in England. Influenced by reading *Robinson Crusoe*, he decided that he wanted to go to sea, and he entered the navy in 1789 at the age of fifteen. He was a midshipman on a ship commanded by Captain William Bligh that sailed to Tahiti, and he fought with Admiral Horatio Nelson's forces against the French. He was then sent to the new colony of New South Wales in Australia.

Flinders arrived in Sydney in 1795 as a junior officer on the *Reliance*. On the voyage from England, he had become friends with George Bass, the ship's surgeon, who was also an enthusiastic amateur explorer. Together they began, on their own initiative, to explore the dangerous coast of Australia. For this purpose

Matthew Flinders. The Granger Collection, New York.

they bought the *Tom Thumb*, a boat only eight feet long. Their first exploration came soon after their arrival in Sydney when they went south to Botany Bay and rowed up the Georges River. After the *Reliance* made a brief excursion to Norfolk Island, the two British officers made another trip south in 1796 and explored Lake Illiwarra, a large lagoon on the coast south of Sydney where the city of Wollongong is now located.

Flinders was sent to the Cape of Good Hope to bring back cattle for the colony. In 1798, he was promoted to lieutenant. In February of that year he was entrusted with task of rescuing some stranded sailors and explored the Furneaux Islands north of Tasmania and then made a second to Norfolk Island.

In the meantime Bass had traveled south to Tasmania and came back with the belief that it was an island, not a part of the mainland. This was confirmed when he and Flinders traveled south on the *Norfolk* from October 7, 1798 to January 12, 1799. They sailed westward through the strait that separates Tasmania from the mainland and then went completely around Tasmania in a counter-clockwise direction. The strait was named Bass Strait, marking the surgeon's last exploring trip. Following their return, Flinders made a trip northwards to what is now Queensland.

In March 1800 Flinders returned to England on the *Reliance* and while he was there wrote an account of the explorations that he and Bass had accomplished. Also, while he was in England, he married a young woman from his native Lincolnshire and requested permission to take her back with him to Australia. This was refused, and they did not see each other for nine years.

On July 18, 1801, Flinders left England as captain of the 334-ton sloop *Investigator*. Thanks to the recommendations of **Sir Joseph Banks** he was entrusted with the task of surveying the southern coast of Australia. He sighted land at Cape Leeuwin in extreme southwestern Australia on December 6, 1801 and then sailed to King George Sound (site of the town of Albany), which had been discovered by **George Vancouver**. Following the coast of the Great Australian Bight, he sailed eastward until February 20, 1802 when he reached Spencer Gulf, a large indentation in the south coast that extends far into the interior of Australia. This was an important discovery because no one had any idea what the interior of Australia was like, and Flinders thought it possible that this was a great bay that cut all the way into the middle of the continent or even divided it into separate islands.

The possibility of finding a passageway into the interior of Australia was an exciting one, which Flinders recorded by saying that he had the "prospect of making an interesting discovery." However, he was quickly disappointed: the gulf rapidly narrows and only stretches for some 200 miles into what is now the state of South Australia. As he had done all along the coast, he named the main geographical features after Royal Navy colleagues and supporters and place names from his home in Lincolnshire.

When he reached the upper end of Spencer Gulf, Flinders took the ship's boat to explore the shoreline, along with William Westall, a landscape draftsman, Ferdinand Bauer, who painted specimens of the local plants and animals, and Robert Brown, the expedition's biologist, who was able to collect specimens of nearly 4,000 species during the course of the expedition. North of the modern town of Port Augusta they went ashore and climbed to the top of Mount Brown in the Flinders Range.

Sailing south out of Spencer Gulf Flinders sighted a large island, across the Investigator Strait. It had no human inhabitants but had a large population of seals and kangaroos. The British sailors killed enough kangaroos to furnish meat for the expedition for four months. In their honor Flinders named the island Kangaroo Island. He then sailed into Gulf St. Vincent, where the city of Adelaide is now located; once again this did not prove to be a route to the interior.

On April 8, Flinders sighted the sails of another ship—that of a rival French expedition commanded by Nicolas Baudin. Baudin's expedition had similar aims to those of Flinders', and he had been working his way westward along the south coast. The meeting was friendly in spite of the tensions between the two countries, and Flinders and Baudin had breakfast together. Flinders named the spot where they met Encounter Bay. The two expeditions then continued on their separate ways: Flinders to Sydney and Baudin to Kangaroo Island and then west to Spencer Gulf.

Flinders reached the site of Melbourne on April 26, 1802 (which had actually been seen by another British captain some 10 weeks earlier) and entered Sydney Harbor on May 9, 1802. Remarkably for that era, none of his crew were sick with scurvy when they arrived.

Flinders only stayed in Sydney for a short while before setting out again in the *Investigator* on July 22, 1802. He headed north with the aim of completing **James Cook**'s nautical chart of the east coast of Australia. Unlike Cook, Flinders was able to find a passage through the Great Barrier Reef at the northern end, and he sailed through the Torres Strait (between Australia and New Guinea) to the Gulf of Carpentaria. At this point the *Investigator* was leaking badly, and it turned out that many of the timbers were rotten. Since he could not fight his way back against the wind down the east coast, Flinders decided to travel west all the way around Australia. He returned to Sydney on June 9, 1803, the first person to circumnavigate Australia.

The *Investigator* was found to be beyond repair, so Flinders set sail as a passenger on the *Porpoise*, a Spanish prize, with a greenhouse erected on its deck to hold his plant collection, which was being sent to the Royal Botanical Gardens at Kew, England. Seven days out of Sydney, the *Porpoise* hit a reef and sank. Flinders used his great navigational skills to sail the ship's boat back to Sydney through 700 miles of open sea. He then started out for England again in a very small ship, the *Cumberland*. It began to leak in the Indian Ocean, and Flinders was forced to land on the French island of Mauritius on December 17, 1803.

By the time Flinders landed, war had broken out between Great Britain and France, and the French governor refused to recognize the authority of Flinders' letter of protection from the Emperor Napoleon on the grounds that it applied only to the *Investigator*. In spite of efforts in England and orders from Paris, the unreasonable governor kept Flinders for six and a half years. During this time he worked on the journals of his expedition.

Finally, right before Mauritius was captured by the British, Flinders was released on June 14, 1810 and reached England on October 23, 1810. By now, his health was ruined, and he was only able to work on seeing the account of his voyage published. It was published the day before he died on July 19, 1814.

Where to learn more

Flinders book, *A Voyage to Terra Australis Undertaken for the Purpose of Completing the Discovery of that Vast Country*, was published in London in 1814.

The best fairly recent book on Flinders is K.A. Austin, *The Voyage of the Investigator 1801-1803* (Adelaide: 1958). There is an out-of-print biography by Ernest Scott, *The Life of Captain Matthew Flinders* (Sydney: 1914), who also wrote a general survey, *Australian Discovery by Sea* (London: Dent, 1929), and a book about the parallel French expedition under Baudin, *Terre Napoléon* (London: Methuen, 1910).

John Forrest

(1847-1918)

John Forrest was a Western Australian surveyor who made three expeditions into the interior of Australia, becoming the first person to cross the western half of the continent from west to east.

John Forrest was born in Bunbury on the south coast of Western Australia on August 22, 1847. His parents were Scottish immigrants who had come to Australia as servants and had saved to buy a farm. Forrest started school at Bunbury and then transferred to a private high school in the capital city of Perth when he was 13. In 1863 he became apprenticed to a Bunbury surveyor, and in 1866 he joined the staff of the Western Australia Surveyor-General's Office.

In 1869 the government heard about some bones in the interior and decided to send an expedition to see if these might be the remains of the disastrous expedition led by **Ludwig Leichhardt** in 1848. Forrest was chosen to be second-in-command, and, when the proposed leader backed out, he was put in charge. He found the bones, which turned out to be those of runaway horses from an 1854 expedition. Between April and August 1869, Forrest traveled from Perth to the edge of the Great Victoria Desert near Mount Weld in the very center of Australia. He crossed over more than 2,000 miles of territory, a lot of which had never been mapped.

On his return, Forrest was given command of a party of six men charged with crossing from Perth to Adelaide in South Australia in order to blaze a route between the two population centers. He followed a parallel route to that of **Edward John Eyre** in 1841, who had crossed from east to west. Forrest left Perth on March 30, 1870 and arrived in Adelaide on August 27. Like Eyre before him, he found that the country was mostly barren desert although he did discover some good grazing land. Later, in 1877, the route he pioneered was chosen for the cross-continent telegraph line, and the present-day highway across the Nullarbor Plain also follows Forrest's route.

Following these successes, Forrest was put in charge of all the surveying in the northern part of Western Australia. As part of his responsibilities he headed an expedition that left Perth on March 18, 1874 with his brother Alexander and four other men and twenty packhorses. They headed north to explore the headwaters of the Murchison River, which flows out of central Australia to end in the Indian Ocean about halfway up the coast of Western Australia. From there they went due east and explored the land between the Gibson Desert on the north and the Great Victoria Desert on the south. Crossing the Gibson Desert the group of men almost died from lack of water, and they were attacked by Aborigines on several occasions. Only four of the horses survived. On September 30, 1874, they reached the Overland Telegraph Line that had been built from Adelaide to Darwin in 1872 following the route opened up by **John McDouall Stuart**. They followed the telegraph line south to Adelaide, which they reached on November 3, 1874 to a triumphant welcome.

Rewarded with a land grant of 5,000 acres for his discoveries, Forrest published the story of his explorations in 1875. He then started on what turned out to be a highly successful political career. He became deputy Surveyor General in 1876, Surveyor General in 1883, and the first Premier of Western Australia from 1900-1901. In that capacity he negotiated the terms for joining the Australian Federation, which were less favorable than what he had hoped for. He then entered the federal Australian parliament when it was set up in 1901 and became successively Postmaster General, Minister for Defence, for Home Affairs, and Treasurer. He was one of the founders of what was to become the National Party, and he was acting Prime Minister for a few months in 1907 while Alfred Deakin was away in London. He was disappointed several times, however, when he tried to become Prime Minister in his own right.

Later in his career, in 1917 Forrest had the satisfaction of being on the first train that crossed Australia from east to west, which had been one of the things he had wanted when Western Australia joined the federation. In February 1918 it was announced that King George V had named him 1st Baron Forrest of Bunbury, the first Australian to receive such an honor. He resigned from the government the following month and left with his wife in July to travel to England to seek medical treatment for cancer and to receive his baronetcy. He died along the way, on September 3, 1918, off the coast of Sierra Leone in west Africa.

Where to learn more

Forrest wrote the narrative of his three explorations in *Explorations in Australia* (London: Sampson Low, Marston, Low & Searle, 1875; reprinted, Adelaide: Libraries Board of South Australia, 1969). Excerpts from this can be found in Kathleen Fitzpatrick, *Australian Explorers: A Selection from their Writings* (London: Oxford University Press, 1958). There is a full-scale biography of Forrest, of which the first volume contains the story of his early years as an explorer: F.K. Crowley, *Forrest 1847-1918*, vol. 1: *1847-91: Apprenticeship to Premiership* (St. Lucia, Queensland: University of Queensland Press, 1971). Crowley has written a long biographical essay on Forrest in the *Australian Dictionary of Biography*.

Fernand Foureau

(1850 - 1914)

Fernand Foureau was a French explorer who made eleven trips into the northern part of the Sahara and then was put in charge of the French expedition that fought its way across the Sahara and conquered Chad for the French Empire.

Fernand Foureau was a Frenchman from Paris who left his comfortable middle-class life in France in 1876 after the Franco-Prussian War to settle in Algeria, then a French colony. He started out as a farmer, but this was not successful, and he took up another profession—that of explorer. For the next 22 years he made a total of 11 expeditions into the Sahara Desert from his base at El Goléa at the extreme limits of French control. Unlike earlier explorers, he did not set out to make one grand trip across the desert but limited his goals and obtained important results by making a series of smaller expeditions. As a result, he successfully reached the Tademait Plateau, the Great Eastern Erg, and the northern fringes of the Tassili Mountains.

After the failure of the expedition of **Paul-Xavier Flatters** in 1881 the French imperialists were even more determined to control the Sahara and thereby link up their colonies in North Africa with those expanding inland from the coasts of West Africa. As always, the barrier to this expansion was the hostility of the various Tuareg tribes who controlled the Sahara trade routes. Foureau knew from his own experience that the Tuareg would never agree to French occupation without putting up a fight. Any new French expedition would have to be strong enough to fight its way across the Sahara.

In 1896 a small expedition led by a French adventurer, the Marquis de Morès, was annihilated at the oasis of Ghadamès. This goaded the French to send out a more powerful force led by Foureau, who had become the acknowledged French expert on the Sahara. In charge of the large military force was Major François Lamy, who had had experience in Algeria and several other French colonies and was serving as chief military aide to French President Felix Faure. Foureau and Lamy met in Paris in August 1897 to plan their expedition, and the budget was approved in March 1898. Lamy left in September for Algeria to put together the military force of about 300 Algerian soldiers and 40 French officers and non-commissioned officers. Although it was supposed to be a "scientific" expedition, there were only four civilians besides Foureau.

The Foureau-Lamy Mission left the French outpost of Blida on September 20, 1898. It went south to Ouargla with a total of 1,004 camels to carry the men and supplies. Loading the final supplies, they left Ouargla on October 23 to march to Lake Chad, 2,000 miles away. From the beginning they had difficulty with inexperienced camel handlers, and the overloaded camels began to sicken and die. By December they were on short rations and were forced to buy rotten dates from the Tuareg who followed the caravan. They brought out supplies they had saved in order to celebrate Christmas Day and New Year's in the valley of Tikhamnar. They reached the wells of Tadent on January 8, 1899 on the eastern edge of the Hoggar Massif. Lamy led a small party to visit the site where Flatters had been killed.

When they reached the plateau of Ténéré, they built a small fort at In Azaoua and left most of the men there while Foureau and Lamy went ahead on February 11, 1899 to the plains of Air. They reached the small town of Iferouane with only half of their camels still alive. They stayed there for three months while they tried to buy more camels from the Tuareg. Instead, they were attacked on the morning of March 12 by Tuareg warriors. The better-armed French were victorious, and they were able to capture a large number of Tuareg camels. They then sent back for the men left at In Azaoua and the remaining supplies. They camped at Iferouane for a further two months recuperating and trying to purchase camels from the south.

The Tuareg hoped to destroy the French by letting them rot at Iferouane, but the French finally realized their predicament and sent out a series of raiding parties to capture the camels they could not buy. Even so, when they left Iferouane on June 8 they had to leave most of the supplies behind. By this time, the men and the camels were beginning to die, and there was practically nothing left to eat. They did not reach the town of Agadez until June 27, by which time they were desperate. It took a show of force before the local sultan would give them any supplies. They stayed there until August 10 and marched east but soon got lost and had to return to Agadez on August 18.

Foureau and his men were stuck at Agadez for two more months trying to negotiate for guides and camels. Finally, they had to surround the town's well and threaten to cut off the water supply unless they got what they wanted. This worked, and they were able to leave on October 17. The last of the original camels died on October 28.

The French reached the town of Zinder (in what is now southern Niger not far from Nigeria) on November 2. They were out of the desert and in the area of plains called the Sahel. At Zinder they heard of the defeat by the local sultan Rabih of another French column coming from the south, which had been headquartered on the Chari River near Lake Chad. The Foureau column headed east and reached Lake Chad on January 21, 1900. They were inevitably disappointed by the lake, which fluctuates greatly in size and depth according to the rains. At the time Foureau arrived, it was a shallow marsh. He and the rest of the expedition traveled around the north end of the lake to reach Rabih's capital of Kousseri south of the lake where the Logone River meets the Chari. On the morning of March 3 the French attacked and overran the city.

Following this victory, Foureau left Lamy in charge and went south via the Congo River to try to get reinforcements and to pass the word that a new town had become part of the French Empire. (Kousseri was renamed Fort-Lamy and became the capital of the French colony of Chad; it is now called Ndjamena.) During Foureau's absence, Lamy attacked Rabih's force outside of the city on April 22, 1900. Rabih counterattacked, and in the fierce battle both Lamy and Rabih were killed. It took another year for the French to subdue the whole area. Once this was accomplished, the Algerian soldiers who had traveled all the way across the Sahara were paddled down the Congo River to the Atlantic and sent home via Bordeaux in France.

Where to learn more

The most accessible and complete source in English on the Foureau-Lamy Mission is Douglas Porch, *The Conquest of the Sahara* (New York: Alfred A. Knopf, 1984), which served as the source for this account. Another good book is A.S. Kanya-Forstner, *The Conquest of the Western Sudan: A Study in French Military Imperialism* (Cambridge: Cambridge University Press, 1969).

Luke Fox

(1586 - 1635)

Luke Fox was an English navigator who sailed along the west coast of Hudson Bay and proved that it did not lead to a Northwest Passage.

Luke Fox was born on October 20, 1586 in Yorkshire in the north of England. He gained experience as a mariner sailing out of the port of Hull and trading across the North Sea. He was reputed to be very skilled at mathematics and navigation. He became interested in the search for a Northwest Passage between America and Asia. In 1629 he requested permission from King Charles I to lead an expedition to follow up on **Henry Hudson**'s discoveries in Hudson Bay, to see if there was a passage to the west. Having the support of several noblemen at the court, this permission was granted.

Fox left the port of Deptford on May 5, 1631 in a small ship named the *Charles* and a crew of 23. This was two days after the departure of **Thomas James** on a similar expedition. Fox traveled north along the coast of England and then headed west from the Orkney Islands off the north coast of Scotland. He reached Hudson Strait on June 22 and entered Hudson Bay. He then traveled down the entire west coast of Hudson Bay searching for a possible exit out. There was none.

Fox met James on July 29 at Cape Henrietta Maria. From there he turned to the north and traveled out of the bay. He then discovered Foxe Channel and Foxe Basin off the north coast of the mainland of Canada. (These features were named for him; his name is sometimes spelled Foxe.) On September 22 he reached Cape Dorchester, which he named "Fox his farthest," and went slightly beyond the Arctic Circle, the farthest point to be reached by navigators for many years.

Fox's voyage was very significant because it proved that there was no need to continue looking for the Northwest Passage in Hudson's Bay. If it existed at all, it would have to be farther north. This information slowed down Arctic exploration for almost 200 years.

On his return, Fox wrote a narrative of his voyage that he called *North-West Fox*. It is one of the most important sources on early Arctic exploration and includes much information on tides, ice formations, ocean depths, and the animal and plant life of northern Canada. It also includes descriptions of the native peoples of the region. He named 27 localities, and eight of these names are still in use.

Following his voyage, Fox seems to have spent the rest of his life in poverty, "having received neither sallery, wages, or reward." He died shortly after publication of his book in 1635.

Where to learn more

The main source for Fox's voyage is Miller Christy, ed. *The Voyages of Captain Luke Foxe of Hull, and Captain Thomas James of Bristol in Search of a North-West Passage, in 1631-32* (London: Hakluyt Society, 1894). It contains Fox's narrative, *North-West Fox*.

There are discussions of Fox's voyage in: Sir Clements Markham, *The Lands of Silence* (Cambridge: Cambridge University Press, 1921); Jeannette Mirsky, *To the Arctic!: The Story of Northern Exploration from Earliest Times to the Present* (New York: Alfred A. Knopf, 1948); Ernest Dodge, *Northwest by Sea* (New York: 1961); and Tryggvi J. Olesen, *Early Voyages and Northern Approaches 1000-1632* (Toronto: McClelland and Stewart, 1963).

Sir John Franklin

(1786 - 1847)

Sir John Franklin was a British naval officer put in charge of three expeditions to the Canadian Arctic. The first two of these were overland; he disappeared on the third.

John Franklin was born in the village of Spilsby in Lincolnshire in England. He entered the Royal Navy as a volunteer at the age of 14 in 1800. He fought in the Battle of Copenhagen during the Napoleonic Wars. He then served on the *Investigator* commanded by **Matthew Flinders** in his expedition to the coast of Australia. During this expedition the ship was abandoned; the ship that rescued Franklin and his comrades was then shipwrecked and the next ship was attacked by the French. Franklin reached England in 1804 when he was still only 18 years old.

On his return Franklin served on a ship that was involved in the Battle of Trafalgar and in ships off the coast of South America and in the North Sea. He was promoted to lieutenant in 1808. In

Sir John Franklin.

1814 he served on a ship that took part in the attack on New Orleans as part of the War of 1812 between Britain and the United States. At the end of the Napoleonic Wars Franklin was put on half-pay and not given any new assignments.

This semi-retirement ended in 1818 when Franklin was chosen to be second-in-command to Captain David Buchan on an expedition to the Arctic Ocean to try to find a passage from Spitsbergen (north of Norway) to northern Canada. No such passage exists, and the expedition got no farther than Spitsbergen where it was locked in ice for three weeks before returning to England.

As part of its efforts to find a Northwest Passage north of Canada, the British Admiralty then sent Franklin along with two midshipmen, two sailors, and a naturalist to explore the land side of the north coast of Canada from the Coppermine River to Hudson Bay. They left England on May 23, 1819 on a Hudson's Bay Company ship. They landed at York Factory in what is now Manitoba and traveled overland with various fur-trading parties to the northwest. They entered unknown territory north of the Great Slave Lake in the summer of 1820, and built a base camp at Fort Enterprise on Winter Lake near the Coppermine River.

On July 14, 1821 they set out to the north coast with a party of trappers. The aid the trappers were able to supply was inadequate, and Franklin was able to go only a short distance along the coast eastward until winter set in, and he was forced to return to Fort Enterprise. Along the return trip half of the trappers died of starvation, and one of the others killed a British officer. When they reached Fort Enterprise they found that Native Americans had raided the fort and stripped it of its supplies. One of the midshipman, **George Back**, made contact with a party of Native Americans and was able to barter enough to keep the remainder of the expedition alive. Franklin and the others then stayed one more winter in the north.

In spite of the mediocre results of this expedition, Franklin was looked upon as a hero when he returned to England. He was promoted to captain and made a member of the prestigious Royal Society. He almost immediately began planning his next expedition.

Franklin set out again for the Canadian north on February 16, 1825, this time traveling with his own team of canoers and porters. His aim was to travel to the delta of the Mackenzie River explored by **Alexander Mackenzie** and to travel east of there. This time he traveled to Great Bear Lake and built a supply fort at

Franklin's expeditions in the Canadian Arctic, 1819-1822, 1825-1826, 1845-1847.

a place called Fort Franklin on the western shore. They set off from there on June 22, 1826. At the Mackenzie delta, the party split up. Two members headed east to the Coppermine River, which they reached without difficulty. Franklin and George Back headed west with the aim of reaching Point Barrow, Alaska, but were forced to turn back about halfway. Franklin and his party returned to England in September 1827, this time without the loss of any lives.

On his return to England Franklin was knighted in April 1828. In November of that year he married Jane Griffin, his second wife (the first having died in 1825 after only two years of marriage). He toured the Mediterranean from 1830 to 1834. In 1836 he was appointed governor of Tasmania in Australia. He arrived there in January 1837 and stayed for six years. During that time he fought constantly with the island's colonists and with the Colonial Office, and his term was not a success.

On Franklin's return to England in 1844 he was asked by the Admiralty to make plans for an exploration of the Northwest Passage. Even though he was now 58 years old, he approached the idea enthusiastically. The expedition sailed from London on May 19, 1845. It consisted of 129 men and two ships, the *Erebus* (commanded by Franklin) and the *Terror* and was

provisioned for three years. The expedition was last seen at the end of July 1845 by whalers in northern Baffin Bay.

From notes of the expedition that were later found by **Francis McClintock**, we have a general picture of where Franklin went. He wintered at Beechey Island in 1845-1846. He then traveled around Cornwallis Island and sailed through Peel Sound and Franklin Strait to the northwest of King William Island. The expedition wintered there during the winter of 1846-1847, and Franklin himself died there in June 1847. Unable to float their ship, the rest of the party headed down the west and south coast to try to get to the mainland at the Back River, which they could use to travel south to Hudson Bay and, with any luck, find trappers and traders along the way. All of the survivors of Franklin's expedition died during this overland march.

It was only in 1848 that the Admiralty began to worry about Franklin's fate. Urged on by Lady Jane Franklin, it sent out the first expedition to search for him in May 1848 under the command of **Sir James Clark Ross**. Several other expeditions followed, including those commanded by Horatio Austin, **Sir John Ross**, Richard Collinson, **Sir Robert McClure**, and Sir Edward Belcher. In April 1854 Dr. John Rae got the first news of Franklin's party from some Inuit he encountered while exploring in the Boothia Peninsula. The remains of Franklin's expedition were finally found in 1859 by Francis McClintock in a private search sponsored by Franklin's widow.

Where to learn more

Franklin wrote the histories of his two overland expeditions: *Narrative of a Journey to the Shores of the Polar Sea in the Years 1819, 20, 21 and 22* (London: John Murray, 1823) and *Narrative of a Second Expedition to the Shores of the Polar Sea in the Years 1825, 1826 and 1827* (London: John Murray, 1828).

The life of Franklin was told in Henry Duff Traill, *The Life of Sir John Franklin, R.N.* (London: John Murray, 1896) and by Paul Nanton, *Arctic Breakthrough: Franklin's Expeditions, 1819-1847* (Toronto: Clarke Irwin, 1970).

The fate of the final, fatal expedition has been the subject of much research and speculation ever since it happened. See Richard King, *The Franklin Expedition from First to Last* (London: John Churchill, 1855); Joseph Henry Skewes, *Sir John Franklin: The True Secret of the Discovery of His Fate* (London: Bemrose & Sons, 1889); Richard J. Cyriax, *Sir John Franklin's Last Arctic Expedition; A Chapter in the History of the Royal Navy* (London: Methuen, 1939); Roderic Owen, *The Fate of Franklin* (London: Hutchinson, 1978); and John Geiger, *The Fate of the Franklin Expedition* (London: Bloomsbury, 1987).

The history of the search for Franklin properly belongs under the headings of the various explorers who took part. There are, however, some general histories of the search that are very useful: Noel Wright, *Quest for Franklin* (London: Heinemann, 1959) and Leslie Neatby, *The Search for Franklin* (London: Arthur Barker, 1970).

Lady Jane Franklin is almost as important to the history of Polar exploration as her husband because she inspired and motivated the numerous searches to find out what had happened to him. She is the subject of two biographies: Edith Mary Gell, *John Franklin's Bride* (London: John Murray, 1930); Frances J. Woodward, *Portrait of Jane: A Life of Lady Franklin* (London: Hodder & Stoughton, 1951).

A recent book that gives a very informative and readable survey of the whole Franklin saga is Pierre Berton, *The Arctic Grail: The Quest for the North West Passage and the North Pole, 1818-1909* (New York: Viking, 1988; reprinted in paperback, New York: Penguin, 1989).

Simon Fraser

(1776 - 1862)

Simon Fraser was an American-born Canadian who discovered the Fraser River and opened up British Columbia to European trade and settlement.

Simon Fraser was born into a family of Roman Catholic Scottish immigrants who settled in Vermont in 1774. His father fought on the Loyalist side in the American Revolution, was captured and died in a prison in Albany, New York in 1778. Fraser's family moved to Montreal, which remained part of the British Empire.

At the age of 16, Fraser was apprenticed to the North West Company, which was one of the major companies involved in the fur trade that was the main economic activity of Canada. Nothing is known of his activities in the following years, but he apparently turned out to be a successful fur trader because in 1802, at the age of 25, he was made a partner in the company.

The North West Company was interested in opening up the country west of the Rocky Mountains both as a potential fur-trapping region and as a possible way of opening up the Pacific as a supply and trading route. **Alexander Mackenzie** had tried to find a route to the coast in 1789 but instead had discovered the Mackenzie River that flows into the Arctic Ocean. He did reach the Pacific in 1793 but by a route that was so difficult that it was thought to be useless.

In 1805 Fraser was given the job of exploring a more practicable route to the Pacific. In the fall of that year he built a supply base on the Peace River in northern Alberta and then headed up the Peace and its tributaries to found a small fort at Fort McLeod—the first European settlement in Canada west of the Rockies.

During the winter of 1805-1806 Fraser and his lieutenant, John Stuart, heard about a lake, Stuart Lake, that was in territory inhabited by the Carrier tribe and which emptied into a river flowing south. On May 20, 1806 Fraser led an expedition to the lake, which he reached on July 26. He founded a trading post there known as Fort St. James. His supplies were very low, and he had to wait until the fall of 1807 until he received a shipment from the east. That meant that he could not make any major explorations until the spring of 1808, although he and his men did build two other posts—Fort Fraser and Fort George (now the town of Prince George, British Columbia).

On May 28, 1808 Fraser and his men left Fort George, which is at the site where the great Fraser River turns south, and headed downstream. The Fraser River is full of rapids and falls, and they had an extremely difficult time. Near the present-day town of Lillooet they abandoned their canoes and went overland. They reached the mouth of the Fraser, the site of the future cities of New Westminster and Vancouver, in the first week of July. By his diplomatic skills Fraser was able to maintain good relations with the Native Americans en route and to keep his sometimes difficult men together. They arrived safely back at Fort George on August 6, 1808.

Fraser had discovered a great river that was to become the center for the Canadian province of British Columbia. At the time, however, he was disappointed: he had hoped that the river he explored would be the Columbia (which empties into the Pacific much farther south). Also, the journey had proven so difficult that it did not seem like a practicable route for fur traders to reach the Pacific. He did not appreciate the importance his discovery was to have.

After Fraser left the Rocky Mountains, he went back east and managed a fur trading region for the North West Company. He became involved in disputes between the fur traders and colonists along the Red River in what is now Manitoba. This eventually led to a trial in Ontario, but he was acquitted of all charges. He then retired to a farm in Stormont County in eastern Ontario. During the Canadian rebellion of 1837-1838 he served as a captain of militia and was severely injured. This prevented him from working, and he lived out the last 24 years of his life in poverty.

Where to learn more

The basic source material on Fraser's career is in W. Kaye Lamb, ed. *The Letters and Journals of Simon Fraser, 1806-1808* (Toronto: Macmillan, 1960).

There is no full-scale biography of Fraser. A brief biographical sketch is given in Corday MacKay, "With Fraser to the Sea," *The Beaver* (the magazine of the Hudson's Bay Company), December 1944.

Information about Fraser's explorations can be found in general histories of the Canadian fur trade and Western exploration, including: L.J. Burpee, *The Search for the Western Sea: The Story of the Exploration of Northwestern America* (Toronto: 1908); Bruce Hutchison, *The Fraser* (Rivers of America series) (Toronto: Clarke, Irwin, 1950); Margaret A. Ormsby, *British Columbia: A History* (Toronto: Macmillan, 1958); Frank Rasky, *The Taming of the Canadian West* (Toronto: McClelland and Stewart, 1967); Peter C. Newman, *Caesars of the Wilderness*, vol. 2 of *Company of Adventurers* (New York: Viking, 1987); and Jean Barman, *The West Beyond the West: A History of British Columbia* (Toronto: University of Toronto Press, 1991).

John Charles Frémont

(1813-1890)

John Charles Frémont was an American surveyor who was known as "The Pathfinder" for opening up large parts of the American West for settlement.

John Charles Frémont was born in Savannah, Georgia in 1813. His father was a French immigrant who eloped with Frémont's mother even though she was still married at the time. He died when Frémont was six. His mother moved to Charleston, South Carolina, where Frémont grew up. In 1829 he entered the College of Charleston, where he showed an aptitude for mathematics but did not graduate, allegedly because of a romantic scandal. In 1833 he was appointed teacher of mathematics on a U.S. Navy ship, where he taught until 1835 while the ship traveled around South America. He then joined a team surveying a railway route between Charleston and Cincinnati, Ohio, and discovered that surveying was what he wanted to do.

Frémont received his degree in 1836, and in 1838 he was commissioned a second lieutenant in the Topographical Corps of the U.S. Army. The Topographical Corps had the responsibility of surveying the unmapped parts of the United States, and Frémont was quickly given an important assignment. He accompanied Jean Nicholas Nicollet in making a survey of the upper Mississippi and Missouri rivers. On his return in 1841, he was sent out to survey the Des Moines River, a tributary of the Mississippi in the present-day state of Iowa.

On his return from this expedition, Frémont married Jessie Benton, the daughter of Thomas Hart Benton, senator from Missouri and one of the leading advocates of the "Manifest Destiny" of the United States—the doctrine that his country was destined to occupy all of North America. By this marriage, Frémont gained an important sponsor, and he himself became one of Benton's tools for American imperialism.

By this time, American settlers were moving to the Oregon Country, and in 1842 Frémont requested to be put in charge of an expedition to survey a route from the Mississippi to South Pass, Wyoming, which was used by American settlers crossing through the Rocky Mountains. During this expedition, Frémont hired as his guide the famous Mountain Man Kit Carson for $100 a month. During this expedition, Frémont climbed Fremont Peak in the Wind River Range of Wyoming, which he thought (wrongly) was the highest peak in the Rockies. On his return, he wrote a glowing report about the possibilities of the region that he had traveled through, contradicting **Zebulon Pike**'s view that it was the "Great American Desert." His report increased the flow of pioneers westward.

Inspired by Benton, Frémont next undertook an expedition in 1843 to travel west of South Pass to explore the land in the Great Basin region. He set out from Kansas City with 39 men and met up with Kit Carson at Bent's Fort (near Pueblo, Colorado) in July 1843. His party towed a twelve-pound brass howitzer (cannon) after them to ward off unfriendly Indians. He surveyed the northern shores of the Great Salt Lake, and his report encouraged the Mormons under Brigham Young to settle there four years later. On this expedition Frémont traveled north to the Snake River and then to the Columbia River, which he followed to its mouth on the Pacific at Fort Vancouver (Vancouver, Washington).

Returning from the Pacific in mid-winter, he was forced to turn south. He headed south over the Sierra Nevada Mountains into the Mexican province of California, finding a pass through the mountains with the help of a Native American guide. He reached Sutter's Fort on the Sacramento River in March, 1844 and then traveled south through the San Joaquin Valley and around the

John Charles Frémont.

southern end of the Sierra Nevada to the site of Las Vegas, Nevada in May 1844.

Along the way occurred a famous incident. The Americans encountered a group of Mexicans who had had their horses stolen by Native Americans. Carson and another guide, Alexis Godey, pursued them and surprised them in their camp. They captured two and scalped them while they were still alive. When one of the Native Americans tried to escape, Carson shot him in the back. They returned to Frémont's camp with the two scalps and some of the horses after traveling 100 miles in 30 hours. Frémont described the affair with great admiration for Carson. Later writers have been less complimentary.

From southern Nevada, Frémont and his party went through the southern part of the Great Basin back into Utah, where he described Utah Lake, mistaking it for the southern part of the Great Salt Lake. He returned to Bent's Fort in July 1844 and traveled on to St. Louis in August, where he received a hero's welcome. His enthusiastic report encouraged even more Americans to head west, and it also pinpointed the weakness of the Mexicans in California, encouraging American imperialists.

Frémont was soon sent west again, in March 1845. This time there was a threat of war with Mexico, and he was sent at the head of a large Army contingent that included **Joseph Reddeford Walker** as guide. He surveyed the southern end of the Great Salt Lake, crossed the Great Basin and the Sierra Nevada and reached Sutter's Fort in December. Because of the tension between the United States and Mexico over the annexation of Texas by the United States, the Mexicans ordered Frémont to leave. He retreated to Oregon (which was part of the United States), where he and Kit Carson beat off an attack by members of the Klamath tribe. While in Oregon, he was overtaken by a messenger with secret orders from Washington. He returned to California and led a group of American settlers in their revolt against Mexico and set up the "Bear Flag Republic."

Frémont was chosen as Governor of the new territory, but his authority was quickly revoked by a regular Army force under General Stephen Kearny. When Frémont refused to give up his post, he was arrested and sent back east as a prisoner. There he was found guilty of mutiny and disobedience at a court martial, but President James K. Polk remitted the sentence. Frémont, however, was furious at his treatment and quit the Army.

After leaving the Army, Frémont made another trip to the West to survey a route for a possible railroad that he and Senator Benton had an interest in. This time his guide was another famous Mountain Man, "Old Bill" Williams. Unwisely, Frémont's expedition tried to cross the Sangre de Cristo Mountains of Colorado in mid-December 1848 but was forced back after eleven men had died. There was much recrimination later about who was responsible for the disaster.

The exploring party split up and Frémont headed south, finally making it to California by following a route through New Mexico

and Arizona. On his arrival at Sutter's Fort in 1849, he received word of the discovery of gold that was to transform California. Frémont himself had purchased a large amount of land at the foot of the Sierra Nevada Mountains, which turned out to be gold-bearing. The discovery made him a very rich man. In 1850 the Californians elected him to the U.S. Senate.

In 1853 the U.S. government decided to survey a route to California for a trans-continental railroad. When he was not chosen to lead the expedition, Frémont sponsored his own expedition which took him from the Arkansas River to the Colorado River through the southern part of the Great Basin and into California. The fame that he gained from making this exploration led the newly-formed Republican Party to nominate him as its first candidate for President of the United States in 1856. He lost to the Democrat, James Buchanan. During the campaign one of his political opponents said that Frémont had every requirement for genius except talent.

When the Civil War broke out in 1861, Frémont was in Europe, and he purchased arms and ammunition for the Federal forces on his own authority. He returned to the United States to rejoin the U.S. Army as a Major-General and was put in charge of the department of the West, with headquarters in St. Louis. He was not a success, and President Abraham Lincoln reassigned him to Kentucky. He was unhappy there and resigned once again in 1862. In 1864 he was the choice of certain dissident Republicans to be a candidate against Lincoln, but he eventually stepped aside in Lincoln's favor.

Following the war, Frémont continued his railroad projects, but these were never very successful; he was even convicted of fraud by a French court in connection with his fundraising activities for the Southern Pacific Railroad. In 1878 he was appointed Governor of the Arizona Territory, where he served for five years. He then retired to California but died while on a visit to New York City in 1890.

Because of Frémont's numerous trips to the American Far West that preceded widespread settlement, he earned the nickname "The Pathfinder" during his lifetime. This is not entirely accurate since he was generally following routes that had already been discovered earlier by other explorers, trappers, and traders. However, it was the accurate surveys that he made and the exciting reports that he wrote that opened up large parts of the American West for settlement.

Where to learn more

Frémont's report on his first expedition was published by the United States government in Washington, D.C. in 1845: *Report of the Exploring Expedition to the Rocky Mountains*. This was then popularized by his *Narrative of the Exploring Expedition to the Rocky Mountains in the Year 1842 and to Oregon and California in the Years 1843 and 1844* (New York, 1846). A German cartographer, Charles Preuss, who was on these two expeditions wrote an account of them that has been translated and edited by Erwin G. and Elizabeth K. Gudde as *Exploring with Fremont* (Norman: University of Oklahoma Press, 1958).

The documents relating to Frémont's 1848-1849 journey were edited by LeRoy R. and Ann W. Hafen as *Frémont's Fourth Expedition* (Glendale, CA: Arthur H. Clark Company, 1960). A narrative of that expedition is in William Brandon, *The Men and the Mountain: Frémont's Fourth Expedition* (New York: 1955).

Frémont's reports and journals were re-edited by Allan Nevins as *Narratives of Exploration and Adventure* (New York: 1957). The collected papers are found in Donald Jackson and Mary Lee Spence, eds., 3 vols. *The Expeditions of John Charles Frémont* (Urbana: University of Illinois Press, 1970). Frémont published his autobiography shortly before his death: *Memoirs of My Life* (Chicago: Belford, Clarke & Company, 1887).

Frederick S. Dellenbaugh, *Frémont and '49* (New York: G.P. Putnam's Sons, 1914), presents a general account of his explorations. The most favorable view of

Frémont can be found in a biography by Allan Nevins, 2 vols., *Frémont: The West's Greatest Adventurer* (New York: Harper & Brothers, 1928), which was edited into a single volume as *Frémont, Pathmarker of the West* (New York: 1939) and reprinted in 1955. This was reissued in paperback by the University of Nebraska Press in 1992. A less complimentary biography is Cardinal Goodwin, *John Charles Frémont: An Explanation of His Career* (Stanford: Stanford University Press, 1930). The same topic of Frémont's motivations is discussed by Andrew Rolle in "Exploring an Explorer: Psychohistory and John Charles Frémont," *Pacific Historical Review* 51 (May 1982). A more recent biography is Ferol Egan, *Frémont, Explorer for a Restless Nation* (Garden City, N.Y.: Doubleday, 1977).

Sir Martin Frobisher

(1539-1594)

Sir Martin Frobisher was one of the first Englishmen to look for the Northwest Passage and led three expeditions to Frobisher Bay in the Canadian Arctic.

Martin Frobisher was born into an influential family in England—his uncle was the director of the English mint. As a teenager he went on two trading voyages to West Africa. During the second one he was held as a hostage for several months by an African chief.

After his adventures in Africa, Frobisher fought in the English army in Ireland and then became a privateer—a pirate who was commissioned by the Queen to take ships from enemy countries and who was allowed to keep a certain part of the profits. Frobisher was very successful at this and became famous for capturing French and Spanish merchant ships. At some point during his privateering career, Frobisher became interested in the tales of the Northwest Passage—the supposed route north of America that led from Europe to Asia.

In 1575 Frobisher was able to convince the directors of the Muscovy Company, which had a monopoly on trade between England and Russia, to invest in a voyage to search for the Northwest Passage. Frobisher left England on June 7, 1576 in command of two small ships with a total crew of only 35. They sailed northwestward and sighted the coast of Greenland. In a storm off the coast of Greenland the two ships were separated. One of them returned to England and reported that the other, the one with Frobisher on board, had been lost.

In fact, Frobisher continued to sail westward and on July 28 sighted Resolution Island off the south coast of Baffin Island. He then sailed into the great inlet on Baffin Island that has since been named Frobisher Bay. He was convinced that this was the passageway to Asia. While exploring in this bay, Frobisher and his men encountered a group of Inuits. Trying to interpret their signals, Frobisher wishfully thought they were indicating the route to follow to the west. When five of his crewmen accompanied these Native Americans to shore they were never seen again.

Frobisher spent some time looking for the sailors but finally decided that he had to return to England. On the way out of Frobisher Bay he captured an Inuit and his kayak. When the ship returned to England on October 9, 1576, there was much excitement both because he had been thought dead and because

of the sights he reported on. The Inuit was a great curiosity until he died from a cold about a month after his arrival.

One of the things that Frobisher brought back with him was mineral samples. Most of the goldsmiths who saw them thought that they were pyrites, or "fool's gold." But some believed that they indicated deposits of real gold and on this flimsy evidence Frobisher was able to get backing for another trip. In order to do this, he formed the Cathay Company (Cathay was the contemporary name for China and indicated his hopes of reaching Asia by sailing west) with himself as "high admiral." Queen Elizabeth herself invested money in this company and supplied it with a ship.

On May 31, 1577 Frobisher set off again. This time he had three ships and about 120 men. He was given explicit instructions to look for gold. He sighted Greenland once again and sailed on to Frobisher Bay which he reached on July 17, 1577. He loaded about 200 tons of ore onto his ships and captured an Inuit man, woman, and child to take back to England. Like the earlier captive, they also died within a short time of reaching Europe.

On Frobisher's return his partners realized that the mineral ore that he had brought back was worthless, but they decided to send out an even larger expedition to bring back further samples. So, on May 31, 1578 Frobisher left England at the head of a large expedition of 15 ships. This time he was supposed to mine for ore and look for a passage to the west. While sailing south of Baffin Island, they entered what is now called Hudson Strait. Frobisher was convinced that this was the route to Asia, but ice, wind and currents would not allow him to enter. He returned once again to Frobisher Bay and mined ore. He also built a stone house on shore whose remains were found almost three hundred years later, in 1862, by the American explorer **Charles Francis Hall**.

The ships in Frobisher's expedition returned to England in August. Metal workers tried to refine the ore into gold but had to admit failure, and the Cathay Company collapsed. Frobisher continued in the English navy and as a privateer. He was one of the main commanders in the fight against the Spanish Armada in 1588. He was wounded in a fight against the Spanish and died of his wound in the English seaport of Plymouth on November 22, 1594.

Where to learn more

The original text of Frobisher's narratives of his voyages can be found in Vilhjalmur Stefansson, ed. *The Three Voyages of Martin Frobisher in Search*

---

of a Passage to Cathay and India by the North-West, A.D. 1576-8. From the Original 1578 Text of George Best, 2 vols. (London, 1938).

The biography of the mariner is William McFee's *The Life of Sir Martin Frobisher* (New York: 1928). The noted Norwegian explorer Fridtjof Nansen gave a history of early Arctic voyages in *In Northern Mists, Arctic Exploration in Early Times* (New York: F.A. Stokes, 1911). Jeannette Mirsky discusses Frobisher in *To the Arctic!: The Story of Northern Exploration from Earliest Times to the Present* (New York: Alfred A. Knopf, 1948), and there is a chapter on him in Tryggvi J. Olesen, *Early Voyages and Northern Approaches 1000-1632* (Toronto: McClelland and Stewart, 1963). The noted historian Samuel Eliot Morison gives details of Frobisher's voyages that included revisiting the sites Frobisher saw in *The European Discovery of America: The Northern Voyages, A.D. 500-1600* (New York: Oxford University Press, 1971).

Alan Cooke has written a detailed biography of Frobisher that takes into account the original sources in the *Dictionary of Canadian Biography*, vol. 1 (Toronto: University of Toronto Press, 1967).

Sir Vivian Fuchs

(1908 -   )

Vivian Fuchs led the British expedition that was the first to cross Antarctica from coast to coast.

Vivian Fuchs was born in the English county of Kent, the son of a farmer of German origin. He was educated at Cambridge University, where he studied geology. Between the years 1929 and 1938 he went on four geological expeditions to East Africa. During World War II he was a major in the British Army and served in West Africa and Germany and received several medals for bravery.

After the war, Fuchs was put in charge of the Falkland Islands Dependencies Survey in 1947. The Dependencies were a group of islands near Antarctica and included Britain's claim to part of the mainland of Antarctica. Fuchs set up scientific bases on the Graham Peninsula and was marooned in one of them for a year when the supply ship could not land because of weather conditions. During that time he conceived of a plan to fulfill **Ernest Shackleton**'s dream of crossing Antarctica from coast to coast.

Fuchs' plan was carried out by the British Commonwealth Trans-Antarctic expedition as part of the activities of the International Geophysical Year in 1957-1958. The plan involved two parties. One, led by Fuchs, left Shackleton Base on the Filchner Ice Shelf on November 24, 1957. In the meantime, a New Zealand team headed by **Sir Edmund Hillary** was establishing supply bases of food and fuel starting from McMurdo Sound on the other side of the continent.

Fuchs made slow progress in very bad conditions, with his heavy new Sno-Cat and Weasel vehicles frequently getting stuck in the snow. The British party had to cross a very dangerous region of crevasses at the place where the ice-shelf joined the Antarctic continent. Dog teams had to be sent ahead to find a safe route for the tractors, which were always in danger of falling into one of the crevasses. Furthermore, Fuchs's party was engaged in making seismic and gravity soundings all along their route, in order to determine the nature of the land underneath the Antarctic ice cap. This was extremely slow work although it was also extremely valuable. It showed, for example, that the ice reached depths of 9,000 feet and that there was a great valley at the South Pole. Establishing this information had been one of the main goals of the International Geophysical Year.

While Fuchs was engaged in this work, Hillary's teams made much faster progress. Originally, the New Zealand team had intended to go only as far as a place called Depot 700, 500 miles from the Pole, but Hillary continued on and reached the South Pole on January 3, 1958. He had made such good progress that he saw the possibility of completing the crossing himself. Early in January 1958, he radioed to London headquarters and to Fuchs to have Fuchs turn back in the face of the coming winter. This Fuchs refused to do. He carried on to the South Pole, which he reached on January 19, 1958. He was greeted enthusiastically by Hillary and the Americans who were stationed there at the Amundsen-Scott Base.

From the South Pole, Fuchs and Hillary continued on their very difficult trek as winter approached. They reached McMurdo Sound on March 2, 1958. It had taken Fuchs 90 days to cover the 2,180 miles from one side of Antarctica to the other. When they reached Scott Base in Victoria Land, Fuchs received word that he had been knighted as a result of his accomplishment. He and Hillary collaborated on writing the story of the expedition.

Fuchs was appointed Director of the British Antarctic Survey in 1958 and headed it until his retirement in 1977.

Where to learn more

The joint history of the Fuchs-Hillary expedition is *The Crossing of Antarctica* (London: Cassell, 1958). Fuchs later wrote a book about British activities in Antarctica and discussed his work there: *Of Ice and Men: The Story of the British Antarctic Survey, 1943-73* (London: Anthony Nelson, 1982). There is a good account of the Fuchs-Hillary expedition in Gerald Bowman, *Men of Antarctica* (New York: Fleet Publishing Corp., 1965) and in C.E.Fogg and David Smith, *The Explorations of Antarctica: The Last Unspoilt Continent* (London: Cassell, 1990).

Yuri Gagarin

(1934 - 1968)

Yuri Gagarin was a Soviet cosmonaut who was the first human to travel in space, making one complete orbit of the earth on April 12, 1961.

Yuri Gagarin was born on March 9, 1934 in the village of Klushino, 100 miles west of Moscow, near the town of Gzhatsk (now renamed Gagarin). His mother and father worked on a collective farm. Gagarin started school in 1941, but was forced to quit soon after when the Germans invaded the Soviet Union. For a while the Gagarins were forced to live in a dugout shelter because their house was occupied by German soldiers. When the Germans retreated, they took two of Gagarin's sisters with them as forced laborers, but they were able to return home after the war.

When he finished school in Gzhatsk in 1950, Gagarin went to a school in a suburb of Moscow where he worked in a steel factory and learned how to be a foundryman. After a year, however, he was accepted into a four-year technical college in the Russian city of Saratov on the Volga River. There was a flying school and airfield near the school, and during his fourth year Gagarin took aviation courses at night. He made a parachute jump and got his first ride in an airplane. In 1955 he graduated from the technical college with honors and also got his ground school diploma from the flying school. In the summer of that year, he went to an aviation camp where he learned how to fly.

Gagarin was then accepted for training at the Orenburg Pilot Training School and graduated two years later. He then joined the Soviet Air Force. He was the shortest one in his class and had to take a cushion with him on the planes so he could reach the controls. While in Orenburg, Gagarin met his future wife, Valentina, a nursing student. Gagarin volunteered for a difficult assignment in the Russian Arctic while Valentina finished her nurse's training in Moscow. They were married in 1957 and had their first child, a daughter in 1958.

In 1959 Gagarin volunteered for the cosmonaut training school and after passing a series of tests was accepted on March 9, 1960. He then joined the Communist Party that summer. Gagarin's second daughter was born in March 1961, and at that time he told his wife that he was in training to go into space (his assignment was a secret before then) and that he had been chosen to be the first man in space.

The Soviets had been preparing for the first manned space-flight since May 1960 when they launched a series of Vostok

Yuri Gagarin. Novosti Press Agency, Moscow.

rockets. These tests were initially unsuccessful. The first rocket had not been able to return to earth, and the second one blew up in midair. The third one succeeded in launching two dogs into space and returning them back to Earth. In December 1960, however, two rockets crashed with dogs on board. The program was then shut down for three months while redesign work was done. Sputnik 9 was launched on March 9, 1961 and Sputnik 10 on March 25; both were successful. It was decided to go ahead with the manned flight.

The final assembly of the rocket took place on April 5, 1961. It took place at the Soviet space center of Tyuratam in the Republic of Kazakhstan. As part of a plan of deception, the Soviets always referred to it as the Baikonur Space Center, but Tyuratam is actually located 200 miles southwest of Baikonur on a spur of the main railroad line between Moscow and Tashkent. Gagarin was officially chosen as the first cosmonaut to enter space on April 8;

Gherman Titov was to be his back-up. This was announced only to the other cosmonauts and not to the public at large. On April 10 at 4 p.m. the Soviet State Commission on Space approved the final plans for launch. At 5 a.m. on April 11 the rocket was towed to the launch pad.

At 1 p.m. on April 11, 1961 Gagarin was driven to the launch pad. He was accompanied by Sergei Korolov, the chief architect of the Soviet space program. (At that time, Korolov's name had never been released. The Americans, jealous of the success of the Soviets, called him the "Chief Designer.") Gagarin was presented to the assembly workers, and he and Korolov spent an hour going through the final checks and procedures. The next morning, Gagarin and Titov were awakened at 5:30 a.m., and sensors were attached to their bodies to monitor pulse, blood pressure, etc. Gagarin arrived at the spaceship at 7:30 a.m. Before getting into the space craft, he made a little speech: "Am I happy, setting out on this space flight? Of course I am. In all times and epochs the greatest happiness for man has been to take part in new discoveries."

After Gagarin was in the spacecraft, he had to wait an hour and a half for final countdown to take place. He would have no control over the rocket himself; it was all done by ground control. If there was a malfunction, he had an envelope to be opened that contained a code that would allow him to operate the controls manually. (The code was 1-4-5, but he never had to use it.) Gagarin took off at 9:07 a.m. on April 12, 1961. His first recorded words were: "Poyekhali!" (Let's go!). He reached the maximum pressure nine minutes into the flight when it reached 6 g's (six times the pull of gravity). The flight was officially announced on Radio Moscow at 10:00 a.m.

During the flight Gagarin went in an orbit that took him across Siberia, Japan, southeastward to the tip of South America, then northeastward across west Africa. As he passed over various countries, he radioed greetings from the Soviet people. Gagarin described his flight: "I saw for the first time the spherical shape of the Earth. You can see its curvature when looking to the horizon. It is unique and beautiful." He was the first human to actually see the roundness of the earth.

Gagarin made one complete orbit of the earth in a flight that lasted 108 minutes and reached an altitude of 327 kilometers. While in orbit, he experienced weightlessness and ate and drank to test man's ability to do those things in space. At 10:25 a.m. as he passed over West Africa, retro-rockets fired to send him back into the earth's atmosphere. He lost radio contact with the earth

for a while, and his body was subjected to 8-10 g's of force. At an altitude of 8,000 meters, the hatch on the Vostok blew off and he was fired from his ejector seat and the parachutes unfolded. He landed in a potato field near the village of Smelovka not far from the city of Saratov. The first person he saw was a woman planting potatoes with her 6-year-old daughter. "I must report my return to earth!" he yelled to her. (It was years before the Soviets detailed whether he landed after being ejected or was inside the spacecraft with the parachutes attached to the craft.)

After he landed, Gagarin was taken to the nearest airstrip where Titov arrived in a plane to greet him. He was then flown to a villa on the Volga to rest and celebrate. On April 14, he flew to Moscow where he was greeted by Nikita Khrushchev, leader of the Soviet Union, and an enormous crowd. He was named a Hero of the Soviet Union and awarded the Order of Lenin. His arrival was broadcast live throughout the world, another engineering first. His mother and father came from their village to greet him: he wore a carpenter's cap and she had on her best shawl.

In the following years, Gagarin spent a lot of time traveling around the world and acting as a goodwill ambassador for the Soviet Union. He also carried out responsibilities in the Soviet space program, being named commander of the cosmonaut team in 1963. He was elected to the Supreme Soviet. In August 1966 he began training as a back-up for Soyuz I, which was launched on April 23, 1967. (The cosmonaut who actually flew was killed during re-entry.) There were rumors that he had been chosen to head the first Soviet landing on the Moon. On March 27, 1968 he flew on a training flight in a two-seat MiG 15 jet with another pilot. The plane crashed at 10:08 a.m. about 30 miles east of Moscow. At the time, it was said that his ashes were buried in the Kremlin wall. In 1984 it was revealed that his body had never been found.

Where to learn more

Gagarin's own story of his historic flight is *Road to the Stars* (Moscow: Foreign Languages Publishing House, 1961). For a critical view of the Soviet space program, see Leonid Vladimirov, *The Russian Space Bluff*, translated by David Floyd (London: Tom Stacey, Ltd., 1971). At about the same time an American reporter, who later was the object of a diplomatic crisis between Moscow and Washington, wrote a more complimentary view of Soviet space achievements: Nicholas Daniloff, *The Kremlin and the Cosmos* (New York: Alfred A. Knopf, 1972) as did Evgeny Riabchikov, *Russians in Space*, translated by Gary Daniels and edited by Nikolai Kamanin (Garden City, N.Y.: Doubleday, 1971). A few years later it was possible to take a more long-range view of the American-Soviet competition: Brian Harvey, *Race Into Space: The Soviet Space Programme* (London: Ellis Howard, Ltd., 1988).

Aelius Gallus

(about 25 B.C.)

Aelius Gallus was a Roman soldier who led an expedition to the south of Arabia.

During the period of classical Greece and the Roman Republic, nothing was known about Arabia other than the trading centers on the northern edges. The Greeks and Romans knew that there were caravan routes that went from Aqaba at the head of the Red Sea to southern Arabia and from the Euphrates to the Hadhramaut, in what is now Yemen. It was known that there was a central desert, but there was no knowledge of the great inland plateau.

The expedition of Aelius Gallus sent out by the Emperor Augustus was therefore important, not so much for what it accomplished but because it represented a systematic effort to gather information about a part of the world of which there was only scanty information. Gallus was the Roman governor of Egypt. He was put in charge of a military expedition of 10,000 troops that was supposed to travel to the land of the Himyarites, the pre-Arab inhabitants of south Arabia. Our knowledge of the expedition comes from the writings of the Roman historian Strabo.

Gallus's army consisted of Egyptian troops, Jews, and Nabataean allies of the Romans who came from the trading city of Petra. The force was assembled around 25 B.C. at Cleopatris in the Gulf of Suez and then sailed down the Gulf of Suez and the northern part of the Red Sea to the port of El Haura in northern Arabia (or Leuke Kome as it was known in classical times). They were forced to stay there through the following summer and winter because many of the troops became ill eating contaminated food and drinking polluted water. They set out into the desert in the spring of the following year, using camels to carry the water supplies.

Gallus and his troops traveled for 30 days through the lands of the friendly Areta tribe and then 50 more through a desert region that was ruled by the Bedouin king Sabos. At the end of this journey, they reached Najran in what is now the southwestern part of Saudi Arabia. This was a fertile part of the peninsula, and the Roman soldiers stayed there long enough to conquer some of the nearby towns and replenish their supplies.

The army went as far south as the town of Mar'ib in the interior of Yemen. However, their siege of the town was unsuccessful because they ran out of water. Gallus heard that he was only two days' march from what he called the Aromatic region, the source of frankincense and myrrh, which is now the Hadhramaut region of Yemen. He hired a guide named Syllaeus, who then proceeded to spend six months getting the Romans lost in the desert. Gallus blamed all of his problems on the treachery of Syllaeus. By this time many of his troops had died from hunger, thirst, and disease. Gallus was forced to return to Najran.

The return trip to the port of Egra on the Red Sea only required 60 days. The army crossed over to Egypt and returned home. It is said that only seven men were lost in battle, but it is clear that many more died from hunger or disease, although there is no record of how many. Gallus brought back some information on the Himyarites and the rest of Arabia but otherwise his expedition was a failure. As a result, the Romans gave up any ideas of expanding their empire in that direction. They later created a province in northern Arabia centered on the city of Petra, and they pursued peaceful relations with the Arabs through trading caravans out of Palmyra and Petra and by voyages along the coasts of the peninsula.

Where to learn more

The best source for information about ancient Greek and Roman travel is M. Cary and E.H. Warmington, *The Ancient Explorers* (London: Methuen, 1929, reprinted in paperback, Baltimore, Maryland: Penguin: 1963).

Francis Garnier

(1839 - 1873)

Francis Garnier was a French naval officer who led the first European expedition up the Mekong River in Southeast Asia.

Francis Garnier was born in the French city of St. Etienne on July 25, 1839. His family was strongly monarchist and traditionalist. He attended the Lycée in Montpellier and then went to the French Naval Academy, where he graduated in 1857. The following year he took part in a French naval cruise that went to Brazil, Uruguay, Cape Horn, Chile, and Tahiti.

War had broken out between China and the two main Western imperialist powers, Great Britain and France, over the attempts of the Europeans to secure advantageous trade treaties. Garnier was assigned to a French warship, the *Suffren*, which left France on January 9, 1860 to take part in the hostilities. During the voyage Garnier distinguished himself by saving a sailor who had fallen overboard. As a result, he was promoted and attached to the personal staff of the admiral in charge of the French fleet. Once in China, Garnier was put in charge of building gunboats to ascend the Pei Ho River to attack Beijing. He was present when the Imperial Palace in Beijing was captured by the Western allies in October 1860.

From China Garnier was sent to Vietnam. France had established the colony of Cochin China, which consisted of the southernmost part of what is now Vietnam with its capital at Saigon. It was constantly engaged in hostilities and negotiations with Vietnam, or Annam as it was then called, to increase its influence in the rest of the country. Garnier took part in two small campaigns in early 1861 and then returned to France in November. Bored with garrison life in France, he requested another assignment in Cochin China and was sent out in January 1863 to take over a position as "inspector of native affairs" in Cholon. Cholon is now part of the city of Saigon but was then a separate commercial city with a large Chinese population.

Combining his Chinese and Vietnamese experiences, in 1863 Garnier proposed to the Governor of Cochin China the idea for an expedition up the Mekong River, on which Saigon is located, into the interior of China to see whether it could serve as a way of opening up a vast trade hinterland for French commercial firms in Saigon. He also wrote two brochures on this subject, which were read with approval in Paris, especially by the Minister of the Marine, the Marquis de Chasseloup-Laubat. The expedition was approved, but because of Garnier's junior rank the title of commander was given to Ernest Doudart de Lagrée with Garnier as second in command. He was given responsibility for the astronomical, meteorological, and geographical observations that they intended to make.

The expedition left Saigon on June 5, 1866 in two gunboats with eight Frenchmen, two interpreters, and 12 Vietnamese soldiers and servants. It stopped for a while in Cambodia to get necessary documents and set out again on July 7. One of the gunboats was left behind in Phnom Penh, and the other one was used for only six days when it proved to be too large for the river. They transferred to canoes made out of tree trunks with a straw roof to protect them from the sun.

The expedition visited the ruins of Angkor Wat, the former capital of the Khmer kingdom, and then continued up the Mekong into Laos where it was halted by the Khon rapids. This was just the first of a series of rapids that interrupted the flow of the Mekong, and each time the French expedition was obliged to travel around them through the surrounding forest. They did this so often that they wore their boots out and had to walk barefoot. In southern Laos, Garnier left the expedition to return to Saigon with reports of their progress and to pick up the mail. He returned and caught up with Doudart de Lagrée and the others at the former Laotian capital of Vientiane on April 1, 1867. They traveled on to the royal capital of Luang Prabang, which they reached on April 20 and where they were well received.

By this time the French expedition had suffered greatly—Garnier had almost died of typhus—and they realized that the Mekong could never serve as a gateway to China. However, they continued on, much of the time overland since they could not travel along the river. They reached the northeastern limits of Burma on September 30 and were received by Chinese officials at the small town of Simao, in the province of Yunnan, on October 7. Several great river systems come together in that part of southern China, and Garnier heard that the upper course of the Red River was nearby. The Red River flows into northern Vietnam past the city of Hanoi to empty into the Gulf of Tonkin. With that information, Garnier conceived the idea that the Red River could serve as the French route to the interior rather than the Mekong. However, Tonkin, or northern Vietnam, was then still in the control of the Emperor of Annam.

The French explorers proceeded to the capital of Yunnan province, Kunming, which they reached on December 23, 1867. Their passage through Yunnan revealed that it was a vast, well-populated province with much natural wealth, but with very difficult communications over the mountains to the rest of China. This whetted Garnier's desire to open it up to French exploitation even more. By this time Doudart de Lagrée was very ill, and

Francis Garnier. The Granger Collection, New York.

Garnier took charge of the expedition. He led a small party to the city of Dali, which was then in the control of Chinese Muslims rebelling against rule from Beijing. He stayed only a short while because the city's inhabitants were very hostile. He returned to Kunming to find that Doudart de Lagrée had died on April 7, 1868.

Garnier and the remainder of the expedition left Kunming on April 7 and traveled overland to the headwaters of the Yangtse River. They then traveled by Chinese junk to the great city of Hankow. There Garnier met a French arms merchant named Jean Dupuis, and he told Dupuis about his ideas concerning the Red River. From Hankow the members of the French expedition went by steamer to Shanghai, which they reached on June 12, 1868, having traveled almost 7,000 miles, about 2,500 of that on foot. Garnier returned to France in October 1868, where he was received as a hero. He was given the gold medals of both the British and French geographical societies, and the first international geographical congress gave him one of its two special medals of honor—the other went to **David Livingstone**. Garnier was received by the French Emperor Napoleon III and was given a special assignment to write up the story of his expedition, which was published in 1869.

When the Franco-Prussian War broke out in 1870, Garnier served in the defense of Paris. However, he strongly criticized the French decision to capitulate to the Germans, and this led to his being placed in an obscure post. He decided to take a leave of

absence from the French Navy, and traveled with his wife back to China. (He had married a young Englishwoman in February 1869 upon his return to France.) He financed the trip partly out of his own resources, partly from money donated by French supporters, and partly as a correspondent for a leading French newspaper. The Garniers arrived in Shanghai in November 1872. From there, Garnier traveled to Hankow and Beijing and then traveled through central China as far as Kweichow in the southwest. He returned to Shanghai to meet up with his wife in July 1873.

Back in Shanghai Garnier received an urgent telegram from Admiral Dupré, the Governor of Cochin China. Garnier's acquaintance in Hankow, Jean Dupuis, had pursued his advice about following the Red River to the sea. After notable adventures, he had collected a force of Chinese mercenaries and traveled down the Red River to Hanoi, where the Vietnamese government was holding them hostage. Dupré wanted Garnier to lead a mission to Hanoi to secure the release of Dupuis and to negotiate with the Vietnamese to open up the Red River to commerce. Garnier accepted the assignment and arrived in Saigon on October 5, 1873, setting out for Hanoi with a small escort of French marines on October 11. He arrived at Haiphong, the port of Hanoi, on October 23 and traveled up the Red River to Hanoi, where he arrived on November 5. He immediately started making demands of the Vietnamese commander. When these were not met, he stormed the Vietnamese fortress with 110 men in the early morning of November 20, while it was bombarded by the French gunboats. The fortress capitulated, and the French took 2,000 prisoners. The Vietnamese commander himself was mortally wounded. In the two following weeks, Garnier sent out his small band of troops and received the surrender of all the neighboring towns and forts.

The largest Vietnamese force was at the town of Son-tay, upriver from Hanoi. It was reinforced by a band of Chinese mercenaries and pirates called the Black Flags. On the morning of December 21, 1873 a combined Chinese and Vietnamese force appeared under a huge black flag at the walls of the Hanoi citadel. The French cannons were easily able to beat them off. Then Garnier did something very reckless. He personally led a small party of only 12 men out of the gates of the fortress to pursue the retreating Black Flags. Garnier fell into a ditch and was killed by a volley of spears. Hours later his body was recovered minus its head and heart.

This disaster eventually led the French to abandon Hanoi after signing a favorable treaty with the Vietnamese. The French did not return to take final possession of Hanoi until 1882. Garnier was blamed by the French government for the disaster. They refused to award his widow, left behind in Shanghai, a pension.

Where to learn more

The best source in English about the history of Garnier, on which this account is based, is Henry McAleavy, *Black Flags in Vietnam* (New York: Macmillan, 1968). It includes a bibliography.

Sir Humphrey Gilbert

(1539-1583)

Sir Humphrey Gilbert was an English nobleman who promoted the search for a Northwest Passage and founded the first English colony in North America, in Newfoundland.

S ir Humphrey Gilbert was a member of the English nobility. He was a step-brother of **Sir Walter Raleigh** through his mother's second marriage. Gilbert joined the English army at an early age and fought in France and in Ireland.

In 1566 Gilbert presented a petition to Queen Elizabeth I requesting support for a voyage to look for the Northwest Passage around North America. This was turned down, but he was put in charge of an expedition to settle Englishmen in Ireland (as a way of putting down a rebellion). He continued to fight the Irish for the next three years until he returned to England where he married and was elected to Parliament.

In 1572 Gilbert was sent to the Netherlands to help the Dutch Protestants who were rebelling against Spain. The troops he was leading were defeated by the Spanish, and Gilbert returned to England and lived five years in retirement. During this period he continued to think of schemes for reaching China by sailing west around North America. As a result of Gilbert's lobbying, **Sir Martin Frobisher** was given a license by the government to explore the northern seas around North America in 1575, and, finally, in 1578 Gilbert himself was given a charter by the Queen to look for the passage.

With the assistance of Sir Walter Raleigh, Gilbert fitted out an expedition that left England on September 23, 1578. It was attacked by Spaniards near the Cape Verde Islands off the coast of West Africa, and the survivors had to return to England in May 1579. Gilbert lost all of his money in this failure and went back to his old employment in the army in Ireland. After he returned to England, he spent his time trying to raise funds for a new expedition before his charter expired in 1584. He was successful and left England with a fleet of five ships on June 11, 1583.

Although Gilbert left with five ships, one of them was leaky and had to return to port and the other four got separated. Gilbert reached the northern coast of Newfoundland on July 30, 1583 and sailed south along the east coast where he met up with the other ships. On August 5 the ships sailed into the harbor at St. John's, now the capital and largest city in Newfoundland, which Gilbert claimed for the Queen of England.

Sir Humphrey Gilbert. The Granger Collection, New York.

Gilbert took his men ashore and proclaimed a government for the new colony at St. John's, the first one that the English established in the New World. However, he only stayed there for two weeks and then went exploring towards Sable Island off the coast of Nova Scotia. It was his intention to return the following year and to occupy the land he had annexed and to control the fishermen (from several European countries) who came to Newfoundland each year.

The largest of the three ships that went with Gilbert south from Newfoundland sank near Cape Breton Island, and Gilbert himself sailed to England on the smaller of the two remaining ones, the *Squirrel*. The members of the expedition begged Gilbert to transfer to the larger ship, the *Golden Hind*, but he refused.

The two ships sailed through stormy weather and encountered each other again near the Azores Islands. Gilbert was seen sitting at the rear of the ship reading a book, and he shouted out his valedictory slogan, "We are as near to heaven by sea as by land." That night, September 9, 1583, the *Squirrel* sank and everyone on board was drowned.

Where to learn more

The documentary sources for Gilbert's voyages are found in David B. Quinn, ed. *The Voyages and Colonising Enterprises of Sir Humphrey Gilbert* (London: Hakluyt Society, 1940). Professor Quinn, of the University of Liverpool, also wrote an extensive and accurate biography of Gilbert in *Dictionary of Canadian Biography*, vol. 1 (Toronto: University of Toronto Press, 1967).

The standard biography, long out-of-print, is William G. Gosling, *The Life of Sir Humphrey Gilbert, England's First Empire Builder* (London: 1911). There is an excellent account in Samuel Eliot Morison, *The European Discovery of America: The Northern Voyages, A.D. 500-1600* (New York: Oxford University Press, 1971).

Ernest Giles

(1835-1897)

Ernest Giles was an Australian explorer who was the first person to cross the continent from east to west and then return.

Ernest Giles was born on July 20, 1835, in Bristol, England, and educated at Christ's Hospital, London. He emigrated to Australia in 1850 to join his parents in Adelaide. He worked in the goldfields of Victoria and as a clerk in Melbourne. Attracted by what he saw as the adventure of exploring, Giles spent the years from 1861 to 1865 investigating the country inland from the Darling River in western New South Wales.

By the time the Overland Telegraph Line was opened in 1872, most of eastern Australia was known, and explorers were concentrating on the virgin country in the west. Sponsored by Baron Ferdinand von Müller, a noted botanist, and several wealthy Victorians, Giles investigated the country to the west of

Ernest Giles. The Granger Collection, New York.

the Overland Telegraph Line between Adelaide and Darwin in 1872. He failed to make it across the continent, as he had hoped, but he did discover one of the great natural wonders of Australia, the monoliths called Mount Olga. He traveled up the Finke River into the Macdonnell Ranges, but lack of water finally forced him to return to the Telegraph Line.

In 1873 Giles tried to make it overland again, this time with only one companion, an illiterate workman named Alfred Gibson. Gibson died in the desert they discovered, and Giles named it in his honor. Giles was left alone in the desert and forced to walk out by himself, carrying a 45-pound keg of water on his shoulders for 60 miles. He often hallucinated and was semiconscious. Just as he was near death, he stumbled upon a small, dying wallaby that weighed about two pounds. In his book about the nightmarish expedition, Giles says that "the instant I saw it I pounced upon it and ate it, living, raw, dying—fur, skin, bones, skull and all."

Finally, in 1875-1876, Giles achieved his cherished dream of an inland eastward crossing of western Australia. By that time he had already been beaten across by **John Forrest**, but Giles pressed on anyway. He left Port Augusta, at the head of Spencer Gulf in South Australia on May 6, 1875 with a party of five men and 22 camels. They took only a little more than five months to cross the 2,500 miles from Port Augusta to Perth, arriving there in mid-November—quite a feat under the circumstances, which included a march of 330 miles without water.

The return journey was even more difficult because he traveled farther north, through the forbidding country just south of the Tropic of Capricorn. Leaving Perth on January 13, 1876 he went north to the Gibson Desert, searching unsuccessfully for traces of his missing friend. At one stage Giles went completely blind, but he and his party reached the Peake telegraph station on August 23, 1876, and Giles became the first person to cross the continent in both directions.

Although honored by the Royal Geographical Society in London for his successful double crossing of Australia, Giles' achievement did not earn him much recognition in his native country because the land he had explored could not be used for livestock or farming. He was turned down for an official position with the South Australian government because it was said that he gambled and drank too much. He worked for a while as a land surveyor and as a prospector. He joined the gold rush to Coolgardie in Western Australia in the 1890s. He eventually got a job as a clerk in Coolgardie and died there from an attack of pneumonia on November 13, 1897.

Where to learn more

Giles wrote several books about his explorations: *Diary of Mr. Ernest Giles's Explorations in Central Australia, 1872* (Adelaide, 1873); *Geographic Travels in Central Australia, 1872-4* (Melbourne: 1875); *The Journal of a Forgotten Expedition* (Adelaide: 1880); and *Australia Twice Traversed: The Romance of Exploration* (London: 1889). There are excerpts from this last-named book in Kathleen Fitzpatrick, *Australian Explorers: A Selection from their Writings* (London: Oxford University Press, 1958).

There is a good recent biography: Geoffrey Dutton, *Australia's Last Explorer: Ernest Giles* (New York: Barnes & Noble, 1970).

John Glenn

(1921 -   )

Astronaut John Glenn was the first American to orbit the earth.

John Glenn was born in New Concord, a small town in southeastern Ohio, on July 18, 1921. His father was a fireman for the B&O Railroad. He attended local Muskingum College from 1939 until after the outbreak of World War II in 1942. He then volunteered for service in the United States Marine Corps and was sent for flight training at the University of Iowa and at the Naval Air Training Center in Corpus Christi, Texas. Before going overseas, he married his high school sweetheart, Anna (Annie) Castor. He fought in the Pacific War against Japan in the Marshall Islands.

Glenn stayed on as a Marine pilot after the war and received advanced training and a variety of assignments. He then flew

John Glenn. NASA.

strafing and bombing missions in Korea in support of Marine ground troops. He sought out an assignment for air-to-air combat over the Yalu River, on the border between Korea and China, and shot down three MiGs during the last few days of the war. As soon as the war ended, he requested to be assigned to the Navy's Patuxent River Test Pilot School in Maryland. He worked as a test pilot for three years and then conceived the idea of making the first flight across North America at supersonic speeds. He was the first pilot to make a coast-to-coast flight at an average speed greater than Mach 1. During the flight, his F8U aircraft was refueled three times by tankers. The flight took place on July 16, 1957, flying from Los Angeles to Floyd Bennett Field in New York in three hours and 23 minutes.

Starting in 1958 Glenn became involved in experiments to test human reaction to being subjected to high gravity, tests that would be necessary if man was to ever fly in space. He volunteered for runs on the Navy's human centrifuge machine in Johnsville, Pennsylvania. In March 1959 he served as a representative of the Navy's Bureau of Aeronautics to review progress of the manufacture of the Mercury space capsule, designed to take humans into space. These assignments helped Glenn to be chosen in April 1959 as one of the "Mercury Seven," the team of military pilots who would be the first Americans in space.

Beginning in April 1959, the team of seven astronauts, as they were dubbed to distinguish them from Soviet "cosmonauts," started training at Langley Air Force Base in Newport News, Virginia, and then later at the Cape Canaveral Space Center on the east coast of Florida where the first manned space flights were to occur. Each of the seven astronauts hoped to be the first into space, and Glenn was keenly disappointed when on January 19, 1961 it was decided that Alan Shepard would pilot the first flight, with Glenn and Virgil I. ("Gus") Grissom as back-up pilots.

The United States was put on the defensive when the Soviet Union sent the first man, cosmonaut **Yuri Gagarin**, into space on April 12, 1961. He made one complete orbit of the earth in one hour and 48 minutes. At 9:30 a.m. on May 5, 1961, Alan Shepard became the first American in space when he took off in a Mercury-Redstone rocket on a 15-minute flight from Cape Canaveral to a spot 40 miles out from Bermuda. He was weightless for only five minutes. On May 25 President John F. Kennedy went before Congress and asked for a commitment for the United States to put a man on the moon before the end of the decade, the beginning of the **Apollo** program. Shepard's flight was repeated on July 21 with Gus Grissom as pilot, with Glenn once again serving as back-up pilot.

On August 6, 1961 the Soviets sent *Vostok 2* into orbit with cosmonaut Gherman Titov aboard. Titov made seventeen complete orbits of the earth and landed on earth in Soviet Central Asia. The United States responded by announcing that it would launch its first orbital flight with John Glenn as pilot.

Glenn's flight was first scheduled for December 20, 1961, but weather over the Cape kept forcing postponements. He was set to go on January 27, 1962, when last-minute difficulties forced an additional postponement for two more weeks, until mid-February. Finally, on February 20, at 9:45 a.m, Glenn's Mercury-Atlas rocket with the space capsule *Friendship* attached took off from Cape Canaveral. As the rocket surged through the earth's atmosphere, Glenn was subjected to 6 g's of gravity before he achieved weightlessness as the space capsule went into orbit 100 miles above the earth traveling at a speed of 17,500 miles an hour. Glenn's first words back to Space Control in Florida were, "Oh, that view is tremendous!" As Glenn headed east around the world and day turned into night, the one clear picture that he got was of the city of Perth, Australia whose inhabitants had stayed up till midnight to turn on all their lights so that he could see them as he went by.

As Glenn headed into his second orbit, all of a sudden the capsule swung about twenty degrees out to the right. It then stopped and swung back in again and then, as though it had hit a little wall, it bounced back. The spacecraft started swaying back and forth. Something had gone wrong with the automatic attitude control, and Glenn had to correct the sway by using manual controls. There was a danger that the malfunctioning control would use up so much fuel that it would endanger the re-entry process. Ground control told Glenn that they were going to have to bring him down after only two orbits. They later gave him the go-ahead for his third and final orbit as he sailed over the United States.

As Glenn flew backward across the United States he could not see anything because of the clouds. It was just like flying at high altitude in an airplane. The clouds began to break, and he could see the Mississippi delta and then saw the Florida peninsula quite clearly. At about that time, ground control radioed to him that there had been an indication that the spacecraft's landing bag had deployed. If so, this would mean that the heat shield that protected the vessel as it re-entered the atmosphere could be loose. In that case, it would be scraped off by the atmosphere, and the capsule would burn up on re-entry. Glenn checked his instruments and everything seemed to be normal.

As Glenn reached California on his final orbit, the spacecraft's retro-rockets were supposed to fire to move it out of orbit and head it down toward the earth. This was the trickiest maneuver of the whole flight: if the angle was too shallow the spacecraft would bounce off the atmosphere and head out into space, if it was too steep the friction of the atmosphere would burn up the capsule. Glenn turned on the automatic controls and found that they worked, although he had to continue to correct the craft's sway manually. At this time Glenn was told that once the retro-rockets

fired that he was to leave the pack that contained them attached to the space capsule and to retract the periscope manually. Although they did not tell Glenn explicitly, this meant that ground control was still worried that the heat shield was loose and hoped that the retropack straps would help to keep it on.

Friendship 7 hit the earth's atmosphere just about the time that Glenn was flying over Cape Canaveral. As he descended, burning chunks of the retro-pack started to fly by the window. At this point he was dropping at the rate of a thousand feet a second with no way to control the swaying of capsule. The parachute blew automatically, just as he was about to hit it manually. The space craft landed one mile away from the target point, which was 300 miles from Cape Canaveral near Bermuda, at 2:45 p.m., five hours after Glenn had left.

While Glenn had been aloft, his wife Annie had been besieged in their Arlington, Virginia home by the media. The success of the flight created enormous enthusiasm and made the suborbital flights of Shepard and Grissom seem minor by comparison. Glenn received a tremendous reception. He was greeted by Vice-President Lyndon Johnson in person as he descended from his helicopter at the Cape. President Kennedy later flew down to Florida to congratulate him personally. He was called upon to address a joint session of the United States Congress, where some members of Congress were seen to be crying openly. He and his wife and the other Mercury Seven astronauts were treated to a ticker tape parade in New York City that rivaled the reception that had been given to **Charles A. Lindbergh**. Glenn had become a national hero.

Following this success, Glenn decided to enter politics and planned to run for United States Senator in 1964. However, before the campaign began, he was injured by a fall in the bathtub at his home that caused middle ear difficulties and grounded him. He retired from the Marine Corps in 1965 and went to work in 1966 for the Royal Crown Corporation as vice-president and president of Royal Crown International. He ran for Senate once again in 1970 but was beaten in the primary election by Howard Metzenbaum, a wealthy Ohio industrialist. Metzenbaum lost the general election to Robert Taft, Jr. Glenn and Metzenbaum faced each other again in 1974, and this time Glenn won the contest. He then easily won the general election and has served in the Senate ever since. He tried to run for President in 1984, but his campaign generated little enthusiasm among Democratic Party regulars, and he soon dropped out. He was mentioned as a possible vice-presidential candidate in 1988.

Where to learn more

Glenn was one of the Mercury Seven astronauts who wrote about their experiences in *We Seven* (New York: Alfred A. Knopf, 1962). The best, and most entertaining, book about the Mercury flights is Tom Wolfe, *The Right Stuff* (New York: Farar, Straus & Giroux, 1979), which is available in a Bantam paperback edition and which was the basis for a movie of the same name (Warner Bros., 1983).

Glomar Challenger

(1968 - 1980)

The Glomar Challenger *was an American oceanographic research ship that pioneered the study of the earth's geology by taking sample cores of the ocean floor.*

The Deep Sea Drilling Project began on August 11, 1968 with the commissioning of the research ship *Glomar Challenger*. The project was an outgrowth of preliminary drilling made during Project Mohole, a scheme proposed by the U.S. National Academy of Sciences in 1957 to drill all the way through the outer crust of the earth. During the Project a hole was drilled thousands of feet below the surface of the water, but the technology was not sufficiently advanced to achieve the Project's goals. Its failure led to the building of the *Glomar Challenger*, a ship constructed especially for underwater drilling.

Glomar Challenger was designed by a California offshore oil-drilling company, Global Marine, Inc. The first part of the ship's name is an acronym for that company. The second part was taken from *H.M.S. Challenger*, the world's pioneer oceanographic vessel. When completed, the *Glomar Challenger* looked like an oil-drilling derrick on top of a ship. From the derrick it was possible to lower up to 20,000 feet of pipe into the open ocean, bore into the sea floor, and then bring up samples (or "cores") of the earth beneath the ocean. One technical problem encountered immediately was that as the pipe was raised out of the ocean, the core fell out and as much as two-thirds of the material collected was lost. One of the geologists came up with an ingenious solution. He designed little plastic fingers that bent outward when the drilling was being done and then folded inward when the core was being pulled out of the ocean. Eventually, upwards of 90 percent of the material was retained by this method. Each plastic finger cost one cent to manufacture.

On its first drilling voyage (or "leg"), the ship traveled from Galveston, Texas to New York. At the second drilling site, it found a salt dome in water 11,750 feet deep. Oil often accumulates inside of salt domes, as in this case, but no one thought that salt domes existed at such great depths. Thus, almost immediately, the *Glomar Challenger* proved that it could be commercially as well as scientifically valuable.

On its third drilling leg, the ship proved something that has become the basis of our theories of the geological structure of the world. The land area of the Earth once formed one great landmass. Over hundreds of millions of years the continents were

formed as this landmass broke up and the pieces moved apart. The continents are still moving. On Christmas Day 1968 in the mid-Atlantic Ocean, *Glomar Challenger* took samples that showed that the ocean floor was youngest at the mid-ocean divide and got progressively older the farther one went from the divide. Later calculations showed that Africa is moving away from South America at the rate of about one inch a year.

Glomar Challenger advanced our ability to test these theories by making it possible to take core samples of bottom sediments at depths no ship could reach before. By dating the fossils of the tiny organisms that constantly rain down on the ocean floor, it is possible to date the formation of the sea floor itself. The *Glomar Challenger* proved that the oldest sea floors—which are about 160 million years old—are much younger than the oldest land rocks—which are estimated to be as much as 4 billion years old.

On Leg 13, which started in August 1970, the *Glomar Challenger* proved that Africa is slowly moving north, closing in the Mediterranean Sea. This gradual movement is folding and displacing the floor of the Mediterranean, and the core samples taken by the *Glomar Challenger* documented this movement. The same movement is pushing the Alps higher. The scientists speculated, however, that the force of erosion would keep the Straits of Gibraltar from closing, thereby creating an inland sea. This same expedition showed that the Mediterranean is an oceanic "desert" compared to the rest of the world's seas. The fossil remains are much more meager.

During the course of other expeditions, the drilling showed that the main geological plate beneath the Pacific Ocean is moving north, which caused the underwater volcanoes that erupted to form the islands of Hawaii and that are still erupting and gradually increasing the size of the islands. The *Glomar Challenger* continued its work until 1980 when it was decommissioned.

Where to learn more

There has not been much non-technical material written about the *Glomar Challenger*. This account is largely based on "This Changing Earth," *National Geographic* (January, 1973) and on Peter Briggs, *200,000,000 Years Beneath the Sea* (New York: Holt, Rinehart and Winston, 1974). The results of one particular voyage are reported in Kenneth J. Hsü, *The Mediterranean Was a Desert: A Voyage of the Glomar Challenger* (Princeton: Princeton University Press, 1983).

The scientific reports of the expeditions, written by the scientists aboard the ship, were published after each voyage as: *Initial Reports of the Deep Sea Drilling Project* (Washington, D.C.: U.S. Government Printing Office).

Isabel Godin des Odonais

(1728 - 1792)

Isabel Godin des Odonais, born in Ecuador, made an epic voyage through the Andes Mountains and down the Amazon River system to rejoin her French husband.

During the expedition of **Charles Marie de La Condamine** to Ecuador, he employed a Frenchman, Jean Godin des Odonais, as a chain-bearer to carry out his scientific measurements. During the expedition's long stay in the Andes, Godin met and married Isabela de Grandmaison y Bruno, the daughter of a local dignitary who was himself of French extraction. When they married in 1735, Jean was thirty years old and Isabel (as she was known in French) was thirteen.

When La Condamine finally left Ecuador in 1743, he decided to leave by traveling eastward over the Andes and then down the Amazon and its tributaries to the port of Belém and then across the Atlantic to France. It was planned that the Godins would accompany him, but Isabel was pregnant at the time and could not leave. Therefore, all along the way La Condamine left word for the inhabitants to be on the lookout for the couple and to help them on their way when they arrived.

In fact, however, Isabel was either pregnant or nursing young children for the next few years. In March 1749 Jean set out alone, promising to scout out the way and return and get her as soon as possible. He followed La Condamine's route and reached Cayenne, in French Guiana, in April 1750. Once there, he seems to have run into some kind of difficulties. Apparently, the Portuguese did not want this Frenchman to travel through their territory to Spanish Quito and back. He wrote to La Condamine and the French government asking for their help. In spite of their efforts, nothing happened. Jean Godin waited in Cayenne until 1763—thirteen years.

He then came up with an idea. Since France had just lost the Seven Years' War and with it its empire in North America, he proposed that his native country expand its Guiana colony into the whole Amazon basin, taking it from the relatively weak Portuguese. He wrote about his scheme to the French Foreign Minister. The Minister got the letter but never bothered to reply. Godin then became convinced that it had been intercepted by the Portuguese.

On the contrary, however, after the war's end, the Portuguese had listened to the French government's requests for assistance, and in 1765 they sent a small boat to Cayenne to take Godin up the Amazon to Quito and then to bring him and his wife back.

Godin was convinced that it was a trap and refused to take the boat. The boat refused to leave. It stayed in Cayenne harbor for a year until the Governor ordered it to leave.

At this point, Godin realized that this was probably his last chance to be reunited with his wife. He still refused to take the boat but hired another man to take it as far up the river as it would go (to the port of Lagunas at the juncture with the Marañon River). He gave the man money and letters to send to his wife telling her to make the journey to Lagunas and to meet him in Cayenne. The messenger stole the money and the letters never reached Isabel, but the boat did travel to Lagunas.

Back in Ecuador, Isabel Godin heard rumors about the boat and sent a trusted servant, Joachim, to Lagunas. It took him two years to make the journey and back. So it was not until 1769, twenty years after her husband had left, that Isabel prepared to go meet him: she was now 40 years old. In the meantime, all of her four children had died, and she lived with her father in the town of Riobamba.

Isabel's father, Pedro de Grandmaison, undertook to travel to Lagunas first and pave the way for her. He sent back letters to her describing the route and making arrangements along the way for her to be boarded and cared for. When she finally left Riobamba at the end of 1769, she traveled with a large party: 31 Native Americans, three servants, Joachim, two of her brothers and a 12-year-old nephew. They were joined at the last minute by three traveling Frenchmen who wanted to get back to France.

From Riobamba they traveled to Canelos, a mission station at the head of Bobonaza River. It took them seven days to travel 60 miles. When they reached Canelos they learned that someone in her father's party had been carrying the smallpox virus, and it had decimated the town. Everyone in it had either died or left. At this news, the 31 Native Americans traveling with Godin left as well. As a result, the canoes that Pedro de Grandmaison had left behind were no longer there.

The party found a canoe and a raft to take them down the Bobonazo River. The morning they set off, the Frenchman steering the raft fell overboard, and he and the raft were lost. The canoe also capsized, but no one drowned. They recovered the canoe although some of the supplies were lost. One of the Frenchmen then offered to take the canoe and Joachim and go to Andoas, the next place along the way, to get help.

The party waited for four weeks for the canoe to return. In the meantime they ran out of food, and the young nephew became ill. They constructed a raft and set off again, but the raft hit a tree almost immediately and fell apart. All of the seven survivors were thrown into the water. Now they had lost all of their supplies. The nephew died that night. He was followed by two of the servant women, and the third one wandered off into the forest. Then the two brothers died, followed by the remaining Frenchman. Godin fell into unconsciousness for two days. When she awoke, she was surrounded by dead bodies.

She then took off into the woods and wandered for nine days having no idea where she was. In the meantime, the servant Joachim returned looking for her. He had traveled to Andoas where the Frenchman had stolen the canoe and left. Joachim had to beg a canoe from the missionaries in order to return. When he reached the spot, he found everyone dead and immediately fled. He traveled back to Andoas and then on to Lagunas where he met Godin's father and told him that all of his family were dead. He then sent the news downriver to Jean Godin in Cayenne, who wrote to La Condamine in Paris.

But Isabel Godin was still alive. After wandering aimlessly in the forest, she encountered two Native Americans who took her to the mission station at Andoas during the first week of January 1770. She rewarded them with two gold chains that she had around her neck. The two priests took the gold away from them, and this so incensed Godin that she told her rescuers to take her away immediately—even though she was wearing nothing but "the soles of the shoes of her dead brothers."

Godin went downstream to another mission station where the priest offered to equip her for a return trip to Riobamba, but she refused, vowing to continue the trip to find her husband. Word was sent to her father who was still at Lagunas as was the Portuguese boat (which had arrived in Cayenne five years before). They headed upstream to meet her and encountered her canoe at the juncture of the Marañon and Pastaza Rivers. They then traveled together down the Amazon system to the Atlantic and on to Cayenne.

In the harbor of Cayenne Jean Godin took a canoe and met his wife on the ship, "On board this vessel, after twenty years' absence and a long endurance on either side of alarms and misfortunes, I again met with a cherished wife whom I had almost given up every hope of seeing again."

The Godins and Grandmaison and Joachim stayed in Guiana for three years — until 1773. They then traveled to France, which Jean Godin had left 38 years before. By this time, the story of Isabel's amazing adventure was well known, and they were celebrities. They went to Jean's family home in the town of Saint-Amand-Mont-Rond (in the department of Cher in the center of France). Some years later the son of one of the dead brothers came to live with them, and he married and stayed in the town, where his descendants still live.

Pedro de Grandmaison died in Saint-Amand in 1780. Jean died on March 1, 1792 and Isabel on September 28, 1792. It is said that the only souvenir of her trip was a pair of soles from her brother's shoes that she kept in an ebony box. It is also said that she always refused invitations for a walk in the woods.

Where to learn more

Godin's incredible odyssey is told in a very effective way in two popular books about South American exploration: Victor Wolfgang von Hagen, *South America Called Them: Explorations of the Great Naturalists* (New York: Duell, Sloan and Pearce, 1955) and Anthony Smith, *Explorers of the Amazon* (New York: Viking, 1990), which was used in writing this account but which does not, unfortunately, have a bibliography.

James Augustus Grant

(1827 - 1892)

James Augustus Grant was a Scottish Army officer who accompanied John Speke on his second expedition to find the source of the Nile River.

James Augustus Grant was born in Nairn, Scotland on April 11, 1827, the son of a Protestant minister and his wife. He entered the British Army at the age of 19 and was sent to India. He fought in several campaigns in the subcontinent and was severely wounded in a famous battle, "The Relief of Lucknow." He went back to England to recover in October 1858.

Grant had been acquainted with **John Hanning Speke** in India. On his return to England, Grant was invited by his old friend to accompany him on an expedition to Africa. Speke had been on a previous expedition to east Africa with **Sir Richard Burton** and had discovered an enormous lake, Lake Victoria Nyanza, that he felt was the source of the White Nile River. Burton disputed this claim, and Speke was being sponsored on an expedition by the Royal Geographical Society to settle the argument.

Grant was the perfect companion for Speke: modest where Burton had been egotistical, a marksman, zoologist, botanist, and painter. They left England in April 1860 for the island of Zanzibar off the east coast of Africa. There they hired **Sidi Mubarak Bombay** to be their caravan leader. The vast expedition, which included more than 200 men and about 40 animals, left from the mainland town of Bagamoyo opposite Zanzibar on October 2, 1860. By the time they reached the town of Tabora (today in central Tanzania) on January 23, 1861, half of their supplies had disappeared along with many of the porters. Bombay had to be sent ahead to hire new porters all along the route. In addition, Grant had become ill with fever.

Grant and Speke left Tabora on March 17, 1861. Within a few weeks Grant was too sick to continue and was forced to stay by himself in the village of Ukuni from May 27 to September 21, 1861. Speke and Bombay continued on, preoccupied with the need to recruit new porters to carry their supplies the rest of the way. Grant was well enough to meet up with the rest of the party in September, but he had to be carried in a litter, and his little party was attacked by bandits along the way. Once rejoined with Speke, the two pushed on to the town of Karagwe on the west side of Victoria Nyanza, which they reached on November 17, 1861.

Grant was forced to stay in the town until April 1862, this time immobilized by an infected leg. He was tended by the Rumanika, the King of Karagwe, and one of the chief interests in the book that he wrote after the expedition was the picture he gave of daily life in the African town.

Grant set out on April 14, 1862 to meet up with Speke who had moved on to Buganda (now part of the country of Uganda), a large African kingdom ruled by King Mutesa. They were the first Europeans to reach this country, and they stayed in the capital of Kampala until July 7. Speke went on to find the spot where the Nile emerges from Lake Victoria Nyanza, while Grant headed off to visit King Kamrasi of Unyoro. However, the King sent word that the expedition was not welcome, and Grant was forced to return to Buganda.

James Augustus Grant. The Granger Collection, New York.

Speke and Grant met up again on August 19, 1862. By then King Kamrasi had had a change of heart, and the two explorers traveled together to Chagasi, the capital of Unyoro, where they stayed until November 9. From Chagasi Speke and Grant went partly by land and partly by water to Karuma Falls. They were not able to follow the river flowing out of Lake Victoria Nyanza all the way because of warring tribesmen. This later gave Burton the chance to claim that they had not proved that the source of the Nile was the Victoria Nyanza. They reached the town of Gondokoro, today in the southern Sudan, where they met **Samuel White Baker** and his wife **Florence**, who were searching for the source of the Nile by traveling in the other direction.

Grant and Speke stayed in Gondokoro until February 26, 1863 continuing up the Nile to Khartoum, which they reached on March 30, and on to Cairo. On June 1, the 18 African followers who had stayed with the two British explorers took their leave to travel back to Zanzibar by boat through the Red Sea and the Indian Ocean. Grant and Speke sailed to England on June 4, but Grant later sent £100 to be shared by the 18 "Faithfuls."

Grant's notes were invaluable to Speke when he wrote his account of the expedition. After Speke's death in September 1864, Grant's wrote his own account, which appeared in December 1864 with the title *A Walk across Africa*. The title was prompted by a remark of Lord Palmerston, the British Prime Minister: "You have had a long walk, Captain Grant."

Grant returned to the Army and served on an expedition to Ethiopia led by Lord Napier in 1868. He then retired to his farm in Scotland and stayed there until his death in 1892.

Where to learn more

Grant's book, *A Walk Across Africa* was published in Edinburgh in 1864. See also John Milner Gray, "Speke and Grant," *Uganda Journal*, vol. 17 (1953). For other sources, see the bibliography under Speke.

Sir Augustus Gregory

(1819 - 1905)

Sir Augustus Gregory was an Australian surveyor who pioneered a route from northern to eastern Australia and was the first person to travel overland from Brisbane to Adelaide.

Augustus Gregory was born in Farnsfield, Nottingham, England, on August 1, 1819. His father was an officer in the British Army who had been wounded in the Napoleonic Wars and was awarded a land grant by the British government in the new colony of Western Australia. The family moved there in 1829. Along with his brothers Frank and Henry, Augustus was trained as a surveyor by the Western Australia Survey Department, where he started working in 1841.

Gregory made his first journey in 1846 from Perth to north of the Murchison River, on the central coast of Western Australia. Along with his two brothers, he explored an extensive area to the north of Perth and discovered coal in the Irwin River. In 1848, while examining the grazing potential of the country inland from Shark Bay, he mapped the Murchison River and discovered lead deposits in the vicinity of the present-day town of Geraldton.

In 1855 Augustus was commissioned by the British government to explore a route from the north to the east coasts of Australia. From a point on the west coast of the Northern Territory where the Victoria River empties into the Timor Sea, he followed the river inland and then proceeded overland where he discovered the Sturt Creek that flows south of the divide with the Victoria and then disappears into the desert. He followed it to the edge of the Great Sandy Desert. He headed back to the Victoria which he followed downstream for about half of its course and then turned eastward to parallel the Gulf of Carpentaria. From there, he followed the Gilbert and Burdekin Rivers to the Great Dividing Range and descended to the east coast south of Rockhampton. His route had paralleled the one that **Ludwig Leichhardt** had taken in 1845, but Gregory covered the same distance in four months while it had taken Leichhardt fifteen. He had also discovered much good grazing land that was quickly taken up by settlers.

In 1857 Gregory set out from Brisbane on the northeast coast with the aim of getting all the way to Adelaide on the south coast.

Along the way, he hoped to find out what had happened to Leichhardt's last expedition. He made it as far as the Barcoo River, where he found traces of the Leichhardt Expedition but was forced to give up the search because of the extreme drought conditions. He followed the Barcoo downstream to Cooper's Creek, thus verifying what others had thought—that the two were part of the same river system. He then traveled between Lakes Frome and Torrens, proving that the lake system did not block the way north of Adelaide. (He demonstrated that many rivers drained into Lake Eyre and thus solved the puzzle of Australia's inland drainage.) He reached Adelaide in July, 1858.

Gregory became Surveyor General of the newly established colony of Queensland in 1859. This was a very important position, and he quickly became allied with the interests of the large stockbreeders and herders as opposed to those of small farmers. In his capacity as Surveyor General and later as a member of the colony's Legislative Council, he was well known for his belief in the most conservative principles of government and society. He was also, however, known for generous gifts to various charities. He was knighted in 1903 for his services to Australian exploration. He died unmarried at his home in Brisbane on June 25, 1905.

Augustus Gregory's brother Frank (1821-1888) was also a notable explorer. Besides the expeditions he went on with Augustus, he made several of his own that opened up fertile and mineral-rich areas in west and northwest Australia.

Where to learn more

Gregory submitted a report of his 1855 expedition, which was published by the British House of Commons in 1857: *Papers Relating to an Expedition Recently Undertaken for the Purpose of Exploring the Northern Part of Australia.* In 1884 the government of Queensland published the collected papers and reports of Augustus and Frank Gregory as *Journals of Australian Explorations.* Excerpts from these can be found in Kathleen Fitzpatrick, *Australian Explorers: A Selection from Their Writings* (London: Oxford University Press, 1958).

An historian of Australian exploration, J.H.L. Cumpston, discusses Gregory's role in understanding the Australian drainage system in *Augustus Gregory and the Inland Sea* (Canberra: Australian National University Press, 1972).

A couple of good books on the exploration of Australia that discuss the role of the Gregory brothers are: Sir Ernest Scott, *Australian Discovery*, vol. 2, *By Land* (London: 1929) and Erwin H.J. Feeken and Gerda E.E. Feeken, *The Discovery and Exploration of Australia* (Melbourne: Nelson, 1970).

Médard Chouart des Groseilliers

(1618 - 1696?)

Médard Chouart des Groseilliers was a Frenchmen who opened up some of the main fur trading areas of North America and was responsible for the founding of the Hudson's Bay Company.

Médard Chouart des Groseilliers was born in northern France on the farm of his parents which was called Les Groseilliers—the Gooseberry Bushes. He went to New France (Canada) at an early age, probably as a soldier. He married in Quebec City and stayed there to raise a family. After his first wife died, he remarried and moved to the town of Trois Rivières. His second wife's half-brother was **Pierre-Esprit Radisson**, who was to become Groseilliers' companion on many of his trips. (The two have been known as "Gooseberries and Radishes" to generations of Canadian schoolchildren.)

Ever since the founding of New France, the French had been at war with the Native American confederation of tribes known as the Iroquois. In the early 1650s the Iroquois destroyed the Huron tribe, who had become Christianized and allies of the French. This victory cut off New France from much of the fur trade of the interior, which was the main economic support of the colony. Following a truce between the French and Iroquois in 1654, Groseilliers headed a two-year expedition to the interior that went around the Iroquois and came back with a large supply of furs.

We do not know Groseilliers' exact route on this trip, but the most interesting result was that he came back claiming that he had found an overland route to Hudson Bay, discovered by **Henry Hudson** in 1610. We also do not know Groseilliers' companions on this trip: many historians have assumed it was with Radisson, but this is probably not true.

In any case, in 1659 Groseilliers set out again, this time definitely accompanied by Radisson. They traveled up the St. Lawrence River to the Ottawa River, and then into the Great Lakes to the south shore of Lake Superior. They spent time among the Sioux tribe, who were practically unknown to Europeans, and traveled to the north shore of Lake Superior. They discovered the Grand Portage, which turned out to be the easiest route for later explorers and traders to travel even farther west. They returned to Quebec in 1660 with reports of their route and of the vast fur fields beyond the reach of the Iroquois.

This trip by Groseilliers and Radisson opened up a new fur trapping and trading area for the French colony and greatly increased its prosperity. But far from being rewarded for their discoveries, Groseilliers was thrown into jail, and they were both fined because they had left the colony without the Governor's permission. This made the two men very bitter, and they vowed to turn over their knowledge to France's enemies.

In April or May 1662, Groseilliers started out to lead an expedition to Hudson Bay by sailing down the St. Lawrence River to the Gulf of St. Lawrence and then up the coast of Labrador. However, the two men got no farther than the Gaspé Peninsula when their plans were disrupted, and they turned south to the English colony at Boston. They tried to lead several expeditions from there to Hudson Bay but were forced to turn back because of bad weather.

However, while they were in Boston they convinced the Governor of Massachusetts of the value of opening a fur trading route to Hudson Bay, and he sent them to England to convince the British government. On the way to England their ship was captured by Dutch pirates and they were put ashore in Spain, where they had to make their way overland to London.

Once in London, Groseilliers and Radisson were able to convince the English King, Charles II, to sponsor a trip to Hudson Bay in 1668. Groseilliers made it to the south shore of the Bay, where he discovered the Rupert River, named after one of the king's sons, and Charles Fort. Radisson did not succeed, however, and returned to London to wait for Groseilliers there.

The value of the fur cargo that Groseilliers brought back to England inspired a group of English investors to found the Hudson's Bay Company on May 2, 1670, and it was given a monopoly on trade to northern Canada. The Company has lasted until today and has always played a major role in Canadian history. Between 1670 and 1675 the two Frenchmen made several trips to Hudson Bay in the employ of the company and founded trading posts and explored the area.

France became very jealous of the success of the Hudson's Bay Company and disputed its rights in Hudson Bay. This long dispute was not resolved until the British finally conquered the French in North America in 1763. In the meantime, a French priest, Father Albanel, who had been captured by the English, was able to convince Groseilliers and Radisson to return to their native allegiance. They went to France in 1675 and then returned to Quebec in 1676.

In 1682 a Frenchmen, Aubert de La Chesnaye, received permission from the French king to found a company, the Compagnie du Nord, to trade in Hudson Bay. He then hired Groseilliers and Radisson to lead the expedition. They arrived in September 1682 at the same time as an expedition from England sponsored by the Hudson's Bay Company and one from Boston sponsored by New England merchants. The two Frenchmen were the most experienced and most clever, and they captured the furs of the other two groups and took them back to France.

In France, however, the French king was trying to stay friends with the English, and he restored the Hudson Bay trading posts to them. Groseilliers returned to Quebec, but Radisson went back to Hudson Bay as an employee of the English company! We do not know what happened to Groseilliers after his return, but circumstantial evidence shows that he died in the town of Sorel sometime around 1696.

Where to learn more

Many of the explorers and voyageurs of New France were romantic figures including Groseilliers. His exploits are chronicled in Grace Lee Nute's *Caesars of the Wilderness: Medard Chouart, Sieur Des Groseilliers and Pierre Esprit Radisson, 1618-1710* (New York: D. Appleton-Century, 1943).

Groseilliers' name also appears many times in the index to the *Jesuit Relations and Allied Documents: Travels and Explorations of the Jesuit Missionaries in North America* (New York: A. & C. Boni, 1925).

Further information on Groseilliers may also be found in the sources listed in the entry for Radisson.

Johann Grüber

(1621 - 1680)

Johann Grüber was an Austrian priest who, together with Albert d'Orville, became the first European to visit Tibet in over 300 years.

Johann Grüber was born in the Austrian city of Linz. He entered a Jesuit seminary where he studied mathematics. In 1656 he volunteered to travel to China to work with the Roman Catholic missionaries there. He started out from Venice and sailed to the port of Izmir in Turkey. He then traveled overland through the Ottoman Empire, Armenia, and Persia to the great port of Ormuz on the Persian Gulf. From Ormuz he took a ship to the port of Surat, north of Bombay in India. He was forced to stay in India for ten months before finding a ship that took him to China. He arrived in the Portuguese colony of Macau on the south coast of China at the end of July 1658. From there he traveled to the court of the Manchu emperor of China in Beijing.

After a couple of years at Beijing, Grüber was put in charge of an important and difficult mission. The Jesuits in China had become involved in a dispute that needed a decision from Rome. Grüber was to take the necessary documents and requests back to Europe. At that time the Protestant Dutch had taken control of the sea routes to China during a war with the Portuguese, and it was thought to be too dangerous to travel by ship. Grüber chose to set out overland and chose another Jesuit, Albert d'Orville, to accompany him.

Grüber and d'Orville set out from Beijing on April 13, 1661. They followed an ancient caravan route to the city of Xining near the great lake of Koko Nor in the modern Chinese province of Qinghai. At the time of their visit it was the westernmost city in China. From there they traveled via the Koko Nor through the Baian Gol plains and then climbed through several mountain ranges, the Burkhan Buddha Range and the Shuga Mountains, to reach the Plateau of Tibet.

The two Jesuit missionaries reached the city of Lhasa, capital of Tibet, on October 8, 1661, 300 years after the city had last been visited by Europeans. It took several weeks for them to find a caravan traveling on to India and in the meantime they had the occasion to observe Tibetan life. At the time the country was ruled by the Fifth Dalai Lama, or supreme religious leader of the Lamaist sect of Buddhism. Grüber was a staunch Catholic and presented many of the local religious practices in a prejudiced way. He did however make drawings of the local scene, including a portrait of the Dalai Lama and the Potala, the hill in Lhasa where the Dalai Lama's palace is located. He was also the first Westerner to write about the prayer wheel, a small cylinder with a prayer written inside that Tibetans twirled to send their prayers to heaven.

Leaving Lhasa in November 1661, Grüber and d'Orville crossed the high passes of the Himalayas into Nepal, where Grüber once again described the local customs in an unfavorable light. From Nepal they traveled south into India, which they reached a month after leaving Tibet. They traveled to the cities of Patna, Benares, and Agra. In Agra Father d'Orville died at the age of 39 on April 8, 1682. Grüber then traveled on alone overland through Persia and Asia Minor to Rome, which he reached in February 1664.

Grüber intended to return to China, but he never achieved his goal. He told of his experiences to another Jesuit scholar, Athanasius Kircher, who wrote about them in a book called *China Illustrata*, published in 1667. Grüber became a chaplain in the Imperial Austrian army and served in Transylvania. He returned to Austria in 1669. Little is known about him after that until his death in the Hungarian town of Saros Patak on September 30, 1680.

Where to learn more

This account is based on a summary of Grüber's travels in John MacGregor, *Tibet: A Chronicle of Exploration* (London: Routledge & Kegan Paul). MacGregor bases his narrative on Grüber's report as told to Athanasius Kircher, *China Monumentis Qua Sacris, Qua Profanis Nec Non Variis Naturae et Artis Spectaculis, Aliarumque Rerum Memorabilium Argumentis Illustrata*, published in Amsterdam in 1667. This was translated and excerpted in French in Thevenot, *Relations de divers voyages curieux*, vol. 4 (Paris, 1672) and in English in Thomas Astley, *New General Collection of Voyages and Travels*, vol. 4 (London: 1747). The most important modern work for the history of the Jesuits in Tibet is C. Wessels, *Early Jesuit Travellers in Central Asia, 1603-1721* (The Hague: Martinus Nijhoff, 1924).

Charles Francis Hall

(1821 - 1871)

Charles Francis Hall was an American adventurer who led two expeditions to search for remains of the Franklin expedition and then mounted an attempt to reach the North Pole that ended in disaster.

Charles Francis Hall was born in Rochester, New Hampshire. He never finished high school before joining the flood of Americans moving west. He worked as a blacksmith, journalist, stationer, and engraver. He finally settled in Cincinnati, Ohio, where he married and had two children and ran a small newspaper, the Cincinnati *News*. He closely followed the events surrounding the search for **Sir John Franklin**, who had disappeared while trying to find the Northwest Passage through the Canadian Arctic. Hall believed that not enough had been done to locate Franklin. When **Sir Francis Leopold McClintock** found the remains of the Franklin expedition in 1859, Hall was still convinced that there were survivors in the Arctic.

Hall decided to act on his beliefs. He sold his newspaper, enlisted the support of philanthropist Henry Grinnell, who had financed Elisha Kent Kane, and headed north. Hall's expedition cost less than $1,000. He sailed out of New London, Connecticut, on May 29, 1860 in a commercial whaling ship. The ship left him ashore at Frobisher Bay on Baffin Island on July 30. There he met two Inuit, Tookolito (called ''Hannah'') and her husband Joe Ebierbing. These two remarkable people had been taken by British whalers from their home in Repulse Bay to England. There they learned to speak English and were presented to Queen Victoria and Prince Albert.

Hall stayed for two years on Baffin Island, living with Hannah and Ebierbing and learning the Inuit language and way of life. He also found relics of the three expeditions that **Sir Martin Frobisher** had made to Baffin Island in 1576-1578. When Hall left Frobisher Bay on August 9, 1862, he brought the Inuit couple and their baby son with him. On his return to the United States, he immediately started out on a lecture tour, with his Inuit friends at his side, in order to earn money for another expedition.

Hall's stay in the United States did not go well. Hannah's son got sick and died on February 28, 1863, sending Hannah into a coma that lasted for four days. Hall himself only stayed two weeks with his own family, spending all of his time fundraising. At this he was very unsuccessful: the country was in the middle of the Civil War and was not interested in Arctic exploration. He wrote a book about his experiences on Baffin Island, but got involved in a lawsuit with his co-author and editor. Trying to escape all this, Hall, Hannah, and Joe caught another whaling ship north, leaving the United States on July 1, 1864.

This time, Hall landed on the west side of Hudson Bay where he planned to used his Inuit contacts to try to find remnants of the Franklin expedition. He spent the winter of 1864-1865 on Depot Island in Roes Welcome Sound. In April 1865 he moved to Repulse Bay at the base of the Melville Peninsula and spent the following winter there. On March 31, 1866 he set out for King William Island where McClintock and John Rae had already found traces of Franklin. Along the way, Hannah's second son died. Hall did find relics from the Franklin expedition and returned to Repulse Bay at the end of May 1866, where he stayed during the winter of 1866-1867.

In the spring of 1867 Hall tried to enlist some sailors from nearby whaling ships to go back with him to King William Island, but they backed out at the last minute, forcing him to spend one more winter at Repulse Bay. In March 1868 Hall along with Hannah and Ebierbing and a sailor traveled up the Melville Peninsula where they heard stories about Europeans who had been there many years before. (It is thought that these were not members of the Franklin expedition but of ones that had preceded it.)

On his return to Repulse Bay, Hall got into an argument with another sailor, Patrick Coleman, and shot him with a revolver. It took Coleman two weeks to die—on August 14, 1868. Hall was never charged with the crime because no one knew who had jurisdiction. In March 1869 Hall and his two Inuit friends went back to King William Island, where he found more traces of the Franklin expedition, including the skeleton of one of the officers. Hall left the Arctic on a whaling ship on August 13, 1869, taking Hannah and Ebierbing with him.

Back in the United States, Hall realized that he had probably found as much information about Franklin as he was likely to discover. He then changed his goals—he decided that he would be the first man to reach the North Pole. By then, the Civil War was over, and the public was much more receptive to his ideas. He lobbied Congress and paid a visit to President Ulysses S. Grant. In July 1870 Congress approved a grant of $50,000 to sponsor a Polar expedition. Hall spent the winter of 1870-1871 refitting a U.S. Navy ship, which he renamed the *Polaris*, and selecting a crew.

Because of a misunderstanding, Hall ended up with two captains for his ship, Sidney Budington and George Tyson.

Tyson agreed to serve under Budington. Hall chose a 24-year-old German doctor, Emil Bessels, to be the expedition's chief scientist; eventually, half of the crew was German, most of whom could not speak English. Of course, Hannah and Ebierbing were on board as well. The *Polaris* left from the Brooklyn Navy Yard on June 29, 1871.

Hall and his expedition steamed up the west coast of Greenland to Upernavik, where Hans Hendrik, an Inuit who had accompanied many previous expeditions came on board. Because of favorable conditions, Hall decided to continue north up Smith Sound to Kane Basin, named for Elisha Kent Kane. Hall made it 200 miles farther north than Kane and set a new northern record, for the western hemisphere, of 82°11′. On August 28, 1871, the ship could go no farther and turned south to winter at a small harbor that was named Thank God Harbor.

On October 10, Hall led a small party out on sledges to investigate sea conditions north of where they had sailed. On his return two weeks later, he asked for a cup of coffee. He almost immediately became sick to his stomach. He remained sick for the following week, sometimes suffering from hallucinations and running a high fever. On November 6, 1871 he was well enough to walk around but almost immediately suffered a relapse. He died on the morning of November 8. In the later inquiry into his death, the U.S. Navy ruled that, in spite of certain mysterious circumstances, he had died of a stroke. In 1968 the author Chauncey Loomis traveled to Greenland and dug up Hall's body. The analysis of his hair and nails showed that he had a toxic amount of arsenic in his body. No one knows for sure, but the most likely suspect in the poisoning is Dr. Bessels, who was known to detest Hall but had no particular motive for killing him.

Following Hall's death, the expedition fell apart. Both Budington and Tyson seem to have been drunk most of the time. The *Polaris* was not able to leave Thank God Harbor until August 12, 1872. Three days later, Budington ran it into the pack ice, and it was stuck on an ice floe that gradually carried it south. On October 13 there was a fierce storm that broke up the ice, and it looked as though a large iceberg was going to sink the ship.

Budington ordered all of the supplies unloaded onto the ice. Tyson and some of the crew went onto the ice to move the supplies to a safer place. Suddenly, the ice separated from the ship, leaving Tyson and the two Inuit families, the steward, the cook, and six German sailors stranded.

The nineteen people with Tyson's party floated south on their ice floe along the east coast of Baffin Island for many months. Experiencing some amazing adventures and suffering great hardships, they all managed to survive thanks to the hunting skills of Ebierbing and Hendrik. They were picked up by a Newfoundland whaling ship on April 30, 1873, after being at sea for six and a half months. The crew that had been left on the *Polaris* abandoned the ship the day after Tyson's party had been separated and made it to the shore of Greenland where they stayed until they were picked up by a rescue ship in July 1873.

Where to learn more

Hall wrote about his first expedition in *Life with the Esquimaux*, 2 vols. (London: 1864; reprinted, Edmonton: Hurtig, 1970), which was published in the United States with the title *Arctic Researches, and Life Among the Esquimaux*, 2 vols. (New York: Harper & Brothers, 1866). Hall took his notes from the second expedition with him on the *Polaris*, planning to spend his spare time in editing them for publication. By some strange premonition, he left them behind in the care of a Danish official in Godhavn. These were later recovered and edited by J.E. Nourse as *Narrative of the Second Arctic Expedition Made by Charles F. Hall* (Washington: Government Printing Office, 1879).

Hall's records from the *Polaris* expedition have never been found. There are three eyewitness accounts: Euphemia Vale Blake, editor, *Arctic Experiences, Containing Captain George E. Tyson's Wonderful Drift on the Ice Floe* (New York: Harper Brothers, 1874); C.H. Davis, *Narrative of the North Polar Expedition: U.S. Ship Polaris* (Washington: Government Printing Office, 1876); and Emil Bessels, *Die Amerikanische Nordpol Expedition* (Stuttgart: 1879).

As indicated above, Chauncey C. Loomis's fascinating book, *Weird and Tragic Shores: The Story of Charles Francis Hall, Explorer* (New York: Alfred A. Knopf, 1971), solves the mystery of Hall's death.

Leslie H. Neatby's *Conquest of the Last Frontier* (Athens: Ohio University Press, 1966) has an extensive chapter on Hall as does Pierre Berton, *The Arctic Grail: The Quest for the North West Passage and the North Pole, 1818-1909* (New York: Viking, 1988; paperback edition, New York: Penguin, 1989), which is particularly good for the harrowing story of Tyson and his party adrift on the ice floe.

Hanno

(500 B.C.?)

Hanno was a Carthaginian who made a trip down the west coast of Africa and back around 500 B.C.

Hanno was an inhabitant of the city of Carthage in modern-day Tunisia (founded by Phoenicians from Lebanon). Sometime around the year 500 B.C. he made a voyage to West Africa, traveling farther than Europeans were to do for another 2,000 years. His story was often referred to by geographers and historians of the classical world. He himself wrote a narrative of his voyage, which was found in a Greek transcription from the 10th century A.D. What follows is the story he told with the most likely modern locations placed in parentheses after:

1. The Carthaginians commissioned Hanno to sail past the Pillars of Hercules (the Straits of Gibraltar) to found Libyo-Phoenician (Phoenicians living in Africa: Carthaginians) cities there. He set sail with sixty ships of fifty oarsmen each and a total of 30,000 men and women, together with provisions and other equipment. (The figure of 30,000 must be a transcription error—that many people won't fit on 60 Phoenician ships.)

2. When we had set sail and passed the Pillars, we sailed beyond them for two days. Here we founded our first city, which we named Thymiaterium (Mehdia on the northern coast of Morocco). Below it lay a great plain.

3. We journeyed from here to the west and came to Soloeis, a promontory in Libya that is covered with trees (Cape Cantin).

4. There we built an altar to Poseidon and then journeyed on for half a day to the east until we came to a marshy region full of tall, dense reeds that was lying not far from the sea (the marshes of the Tensift River). Here there were elephants and large numbers of other grazing beasts.

5. Having journeyed on for a day beyond the marshy region, we placed new inhabitants in cities by the sea that we called Carian Fort (Mogador), Gutta, Acra (Agadir), Melitta, and Arambys.

6. Passing on from there we reached a big river flowing from Libya, Lixus (the Oued Draa). Lixite nomads pastured their flocks on its banks. We made friends with them and stayed with them for a time.

7. Beyond these dwelt inhospitable Ethiopians who inhabit a country full of wild animals. This is broken off by high mountains where it is said that the river Lixus rises (the Anti-Atlas Mountains). But people of a different appearance, the Troglodytes, are said to live in the mountain gorges, who are said by the Lixites to run faster than horses.

8. Then we journeyed two days to the south past desert land, taking with us Lixite interpreters, and then a farther day to the east. There, in a silted-up bay of the sea, we came across a small island, five stadia (half a mile) in circumference. Here we founded a colony named Cerne (probably Herne Island in the Western Sahara). From our journey, we came to the conclusion that it lay directly opposite Carthage, since the voyage from Carthage to the Pillars was as long as from the Pillars to Cerne.

9. From that point we sailed through a delta of a big river named the Chretes (the Senegal River), and to a lake. In this lake there are three islands, larger than Cerne. After a day's journey from here we came to the end of the lake, beyond which rose great mountains (a problem: there are no mountains behind the Senegal). These were inhabited by forest dwellers who were attired in the skins of animals and who sought to stop us from landing by hurling stones at us.

10. Sailing on from there, we came to another deep and wide river, which was infested with crocodiles and hippopotami (another mouth of the Senegal?). Then we turned around and went back to Cerne.

11. From Cerne we sailed south for twelve days, skirting the land. This was peopled all the way with Ethiopians, who ran away from us and did not stay. Their tongue was unintelligible to us and to the Lixites in our company.

12. On the last day of the twelve we came in sight of great, wooded mountains, with varied and fragrant trees (Cape Verde).

13. We doubled the cape in two days' sail, after which we came into a vast ocean bay (the Gambia estuary), the opposite mainland shore of which was level country. Every now and then during the night we saw fires, at times in fair numbers, at other times only a few of them.

14. We took on water and journeyed on for five days along the coast until we came to a large bay which according to our interpreters was called the Western Horn (Bijagos Bay in modern Guinea-Bissau). In it there was a large island, and in the island a marine lake containing another island (Orang Island). Landing on the smaller island, we could see nothing but forest, but at night we saw many fires. We heard the sound of pipes and cymbals and the

rumble of drums and mighty cries. We were seized with fear, and our interpreters told us to leave the island.

15. We left in a hurry and coasted along a country with a fragrant smoke of blazing timber, from which streams of fire plunged into the sea. We could not go ashore because of the heat. (This is thought to be large grass fires.)

16. So we sailed away in fear from this place also. On the four following nights we saw land covered in flames. In the center a leaping flame towered above the others and appeared to reach the stars. This was the highest mountain which we saw: it was called the Chariot of the Gods. (This presents a problem. Hanno's description seems to be of a volcano erupting. If so, the closest volcano, and the highest mountain in West Africa would be Mount Cameroun, which is much farther than Hanno appears to have gone. Many authors claim that it was Mount Cameroun. Others think it was Mount Kakulima, the Lion Mountain, in Sierra Leone, which is a much smaller peak.)

17. We journeyed on from here for three days past streams of fire and came to a bay that is called the Southern Horn (Sherbro Bay in Sierra Leone). In the gulf lay an island like the previous one, with a lake, and in it another island (Macauley Island).

18. This island was full of wild people. By far the greater number were women with hairy bodies. Our interpreters called them Gorillas (probably chimpanzees and not gorillas). We chased the men but could not catch any, for they all scrambled up steep rocks and pelted us with stones. We captured three women, but they bit and scratched their captors and would not go with them. But we killed and skinned them and took the hides to Carthage with us.

19. We did not journey any farther than this because our supplies were running low.

Where to learn more

The text of Hanno's narrative is in M. Cary and E.H. Warmington, *The Ancient Explorers* (London: Methuen, 1929; reprinted in paperback, Baltimore, Maryland: Penguin, 1963).

Samuel Hearne

(1745 - 1792)

Samuel Hearne was an English employee of the Hudson's Bay Company who was the first European to travel across the interior of Canada's Northwest Territories. He discovered the Coppermine River and reached the Arctic Ocean.

Samuel Hearne was born in London, England, the son of an engineer who died three years after Hearne's birth. He became a servant on a Royal Navy ship at the age of 11 and stayed in the Navy until 1763. He then became mate on a trading ship to the fur-trading post of Churchill, Manitoba.

The post at Churchill was run by the Hudson's Bay Company, which was interested in increasing its profits by developing other activities besides fur trading. There had long been persistent rumors of valuable deposits of copper in the unknown interior to the northwest of Hudson Bay. When the governor of the post at Churchill received permission from the directors of the Company to send an exploring expedition to try to find the copper deposits, it was probably a surprise to Hearne that he was chosen to go.

Hearne made his first trip in November 1769 but was forced to turn back when his Native American guide abandoned him. He tried again in February 1770, but after wandering lost for several months turned back again, returning to Churchill in November.

On his next attempt, Hearne chose a new guide, the Chipewyan chief Matonabbee who had greater experience in the lands Hearne planned to visit. Hearne joined Matonabbee's band, and they left Churchill on December 7, 1770. The way led over a great barren desert. Hearne survived by learning to adapt himself to the way of life of his guides, who followed the wanderings of buffalo and caribou, the only source of food in the wasteland. Proceeding this way they made it to the Coppermine River on July 14, 1771.

Along the way, they encountered a band of Inuit, the eternal enemies of the Chipewyans and Crees, and Hearne witnessed a massacre of the Inuits. Traveling down the Coppermine River, Hearne reached the Arctic Ocean, the first European to have reached it overland. From there he went back upstream to the area of the reported copper deposits, but was disappointed to find only one lump of copper. Actually, there are large copper deposits in the area, but Hearne was not able to stay long enough to find them.

Hearne headed south with Matonabbee's band and became the first European to see and cross the Great Slave Lake. They returned to Churchill on June 30, 1772. Hearne had not found the hoped-for copper mines, and his navigational calculations were inaccurate so that he placed the Coppermine River farther north than it actually is. However, his explorations tended to reinforce the growing knowledge that there was no practicable Northwest Passage between the Atlantic and the Pacific.

Following his return, Hearne was chosen to open the Hudson's Bay Company first inland trading post. He founded Cumberland House in the winter of 1774-1775, the first European settlement in what is now the Canadian province of Saskatchewan. He was then appointed head of the post at Churchill. During the American Revolution the post was attacked by the French allies of the Americans on August 8, 1782, and Hearne was forced to surrender to a French naval captain, the **Comte de la Pérouse**. He returned the following year and rebuilt the fort on the site of the present town of Churchill. He retired to England in 1787.

During his retirement in London, Hearne wrote a book that recounted his trip to the Coppermine River. It was not published until three years after his death in 1792, but it served to increase his reputation. His observations about the land and inhabitants have served as a valuable resource ever since.

Where to learn more

Hearne's own narrative of his journeys was first published in London in 1795: *A Journey from Prince of Wales's Fort in Hudson's Bay to the Northern Ocean Undertaken by the Order of the Hudson's Bay Company for the Discovery of Copper Mines, a North West Passage, etc. in the Years 1769, 1770, 1771 & 1772*. This was edited by Joseph Barr Tyrrell and published in 1911 by the Champlain Society in Toronto, which publishes original documents on Canadian exploration. This edition was reprinted in New York in 1968. Another edition was edited by Richard G. Glover, who is the foremost modern scholar on Hearne (Toronto: Macmillan of Canada, 1958).

Tyrrell also edited the *Journals of Samuel Hearne and Philip Turner Between the Years 1774 and 1792* (Toronto: Champlain Society, 1934).

Glover has written several articles dealing with Hearne, including: "Sidelights on Samuel Hearne," *The Beaver* 277 (March 1947), pp. 10-14; "La Pérouse on Hudson Bay," *The Beaver* 281 (March 1951), pp. 42-46; and "Matonabbee (ca. 1736-1782)," *Arctic*, vol. 35, no. 3 (1983), pp. 206-207. Other articles are J. Tuzo Wilson, "New Light on Hearne," *The Beaver* 280 (June 1949), pp. 14-18; and Eric W. Morse, "Modern Maps Throw New Light on Samuel Hearne's Route," *Cartographica*, vol. 18, no. 4 (1981), pp. 23-35.

Older books about Hearne include Agnes Laut, *Pathfinders of the West* (New York: 1904; reprinted, Freeport, N.Y.: Books for Libraries Press, 1969) and Laurence J. Burpee, *The Search for the Western Sea*, 2 vols. (New York: Macmillan, 1936). A recent book, but hard to find, is Gordon Speck, *Samuel Hearne and the Northwest Passage* (Caldwell, Idaho: Caxton Printers, 1963).

There are many histories of the Hudson's Bay Company that include discussions of Hearne and his explorations. The most recent, and one of the most lively and readable, is Peter C. Newman, *Company of Adventurers* (New York: Viking, 1985; also available in paperback.)

Sven Hedin

(1865 - 1952)

Sven Hedin was a Swedish explorer who made five important expeditions into central Asia.

Sven Hedin was born in Stockholm on February 19, 1865. As a student at a private high school, Hedin became interested in geography and map-making. He was asked to make a map for the Swedish Geographical Society to illustrate a lecture on the expeditions of **Nikolai Przhevalsky**. He was complimented on his work by the famous Arctic explorer **Nils Adolf Erik Nordenskjöld**.

At the age of 20 Hedin was hired to tutor the son of a Swedish engineer working in the oil fields of Azerbaijan. He left in August 1885 and stayed in Baku on the Caspian Sea until April 1886. During that time he took up the study of Farsi (the language of

Sven Hedin. Bettmann/Hulton.

Iran) and Turkish. Using the money he had saved from his employment, he traveled alone for 2,000 miles through Iran and Iraq, part of the time in a merchants' caravan. On his return to Sweden he wrote his first book about his experiences. In 1889 he went to the University of Berlin for post-graduate studies in geography. He only stayed for five months, but he had the opportunity to study under Ferdinand von Richthofen, a prominent Asian explorer, who recognized Hedin's talents as a map-maker and linguist. He left the university to serve as interpreter on a diplomatic mission to Iran (then known as Persia). The mission left Stockholm in April 1890 and carried out its assignment without incident. When it came time to leave Tehran, however, Hedin telegraphed the King and received permission to explore Russian Central Asia and Chinese Turkestan.

Hedin left Tehran on September 9, 1890 and traveled via the cities of Mashhad and Tashkent across the Pamir Mountains to Kashgar, the westernmost town in the Chinese Empire. On his return he traveled over the Tien Shan Mountains to Lake Issyk-Kul, where he visited Przhevalsky's gravesite. He returned to Stockholm in the spring of 1891 and wrote books about the mission to Persia and his own journey through Central Asia. He was also invited by Richthofen to address the Berlin Geographical Society. In July 1892 he received his doctorate in geography from the University of Halle in Germany.

Hedin now set about making plans for his first scientific expedition. Financial backing included support from King Oscar II. He was delayed by the recurrence of an old eye problem, which caused him to lose the sight in one eye. This did not deter him, however, and he set out on October 16, 1893. He went to Tashkent and then crossed over into China in January 1894. He explored around Kashgar and south and west into the Pamirs.

In February 1895 Hedin headed east with his local guide into the great Takla Makan Desert. Starting in April near the town of Khotan, he crossed the Takla Makan from south to north. He and his four guides and porters ran out of water along the way, and one of the guides died. The rest would have died as well, but they found a well at the edge of the desert on May 5 just as they were about to collapse. In later years, Hedin became a well-paid lecturer, and his story about crossing the Takla Makan was always his most popular.

Returning to Kashgar to recover, Hedin set out again in January 1896. He headed east through part of the Takla Makan to the Tarim Basin, another great desert. Near Khotan he found traces of ancient cities with art objects that clearly showed the influence of Persia and India. His reports stirred archeologists into investigating the sites, and their studies re-shaped views on the history of the area. He continued to the western shore of the desert lake of Lop Nor, where he tried to solve the riddle of why the lake was constantly shifting its size and location. On November 15, 1896, he reached the town of Tankar where he met the Canadian missionary **Susie Carson Rijnhart** and her husband, the first Westerners he had seen in ten months. He continued on to the Chinese capital of Beijing and then turned north and crossed the eastern end of the Gobi Desert to Mongolia and the Russian border town of Kyakhta. He reached the Trans-Siberian Railroad and traveled to St. Petersburg, where he had an audience with the tsar in May 1897.

In 1899, Hedin set out on another journey. This time he got backing not only from the Swedish king but from the Russian tsar as well, who gave him an escort of four Cossacks. He traveled via Kashgar and Yarkand to the Tarim River, which he sailed down to explore the region of Lop Nor. From there, he turned south, crossing the Astin Tagh mountains onto the Plateau of Tibet. In March 1901 he found the remains of a ruined city named Lou Lan. At this point, Hedin adopted the disguise of a Mongol, hoping that this would enable him to enter Lhasa, the capital of Tibet, which was forbidden to Westerners. On August 5, 1901, when he was still more than 150 miles from Lhasa, Tibetan officials forced him to turn back. He headed west to Leh, the capital of Ladakh, the region on the border of Tibet and Indian Kashmir. Once in India he went to Calcutta and met with Lord Curzon, the viceroy. He then retraced his steps to Kashmir and returned home by way of Russian Central Asia and St. Petersburg. On his return home, he was awarded a title of nobility, the last one ever granted in Sweden.

Hedin set out once more in October 1905. Russia was in the middle of turmoil, so he chose to travel by way of Persia and India. His aim was to go back to Tibet, this time by way of the southern border with India. He traveled back to Leh, and then in mid-August 1906 he slipped across the border into western Tibet. Hedin explored much unmapped territory and reached Shigatse, the second largest city in Tibet. Hedin mapped a previously uncharted mountain range—the Kailas—and reached the source of the Brahmaputra River. He also confirmed the sources of the Indus and Sutlej Rivers, which were known but had never been visited by Westerners. He returned to India in April 1908 and traveled home by way of Japan, where he was received by the Emperor, and the Trans-Siberian Railway through Russia. When he got off the boat in Stockholm, on January 17, 1909, the king and his family and the prime minister and all of his cabinet were there to meet him.

In the following years, Hedin became more deeply involved in Swedish politics. Profoundly conservative, he supported Swedish ties to Germany and warned against the dangers of Russian expansionism. Following the end of World War I, Hedin became less involved in political matters. He spent his time writing and lecturing. In 1923 he made a trip around the world that included a visit to the newly-formed Soviet Union. In 1925 he went to

Germany at the invitation of Hugo Junkers, an airplane manufacturer, to discuss the possibility of setting up regular air service between Europe and Asia. Junkers hired Hedin to travel to Asia to survey sites for weather stations and to propose routes. The Chinese Republican government was very skeptical of this plan. At its insistence, Hedin's mission was called the Sino-Swedish Scientific Expedition and several restrictions were placed on its activities.

This expedition was very different from Hedin's previous, one-person operations. Essentially, he was the leader of a large group of scientists and specialists who traveled widely over Central Asia, many times to places that he himself did not visit. He was often away in Europe or North America, fundraising and taking care of administrative tasks. In 1927 he traveled through Inner Mongolia for six months to Urumchi in far northwestern China. The Sino-Swedish Expedition ended in 1933, after accomplishing an enormous amount of work in a wide variety of fields. It has been counted as Hedin's greatest success. After returning to Stockholm in April 1935, he began editing the scientific reports of the expedition, which reached 54 volumes by 1982. Hedin himself wrote three of them.

In order to get money to publish these reports, Hedin made a lecture tour of Europe. Adolf Hitler invited Hedin to make one of the opening speeches at the 1936 Olympic Games in Berlin. Hedin accepted, the only foreigner who did. During the war, Hedin maintained close ties to the Nazis and had several meetings with Hitler. He wrote two books favorable to the Germans. These ties did, however, allow him to save the lives of 13 Norwegian Resistance fighters and of a Jewish colleague at a German university.

In the years after the war, Hedin wrote five more books, including one about his wartime missions to Germany and a memoir about famous people he had met. Remarkably, an operation allowed him to regain the vision he had lost in his eye 60 years before. He died on November 26, 1952.

Where to learn more

Hedin was an astonishingly prolific writer. His books that have appeared in English and deal with his explorations include: *Through Asia*, 2 vols. (London: 1898); *Central Asia and Tibet: Towards the Holy City of Lhasa*, 2 vols. (New York: Charles Scribners Sons, 1903); *Transhimalaya: Discoveries and Adventures in Tibet*, 3 vols. (London: 1909-1913); *Southern Tibet: Discoveries in Former Times Compared with My Own Researches*, 9 vols. (Stockholm: 1917-1922); *My Life as an Explorer* (New York: Boni & Liveright, 1925); *Across the Gobi* (London: G. Routledge and Sons, 1931); *Jehol: City of Emperors* (New York: E.P. Dutton & Co., 1933); *A Conquest of Tibet* (New York: E.P. Dutton & Co., 1934); *The Wandering Lake* (New York: E.P. Dutton & Co., 1940); and *The Silk Road* (E.P. Dutton & Co., 1940).

There is a very good biography and summary of Hedin's career, although it neglects his personal life, by geographer George Kish: *To the Heart of Asia: The Life of Sven Hedin* (Ann Arbor: University of Michigan Press, 1984). It served as the main source for this account.

Louis Hennepin

(1626 - 1705?)

Louis Hennepin was a native of Belgium who went with French explorer La Salle on his trip to the Mississippi and claimed to be the first person to travel to its mouth. He wrote the first accounts of two great North American waterfalls.

Louis Hennepin was born in the town of Ath, in what is now Belgium, the son of a butcher. He studied at the classical school there and then became a novice (student priest) of the Franciscan order. He entered the priesthood, made a journey to Rome and then preached in Belgium and northern France. From 1672-1674 he nursed the sick and wounded of the war between France and Holland and became ill himself.

In May 1675 Father Louis Hennepin was sent by his superiors to be a missionary in New France (Canada). He took the same ship from Europe as **René-Robert Cavelier de La Salle**. On his arrival in Quebec he made a preaching tour of the colony. In 1678 La Salle requested that Hennepin accompany him on his voyage of exploration to the Mississippi.

Hennepin traveled to Fort Frontenac (Kingston, Ontario) where La Salle was commander and then continued with an advance party that went to the Niagara River. He left Fort Frontenac on November 18, 1678 and arrived at Niagara Falls on December 6. He is the first person to write a description of the Falls: "the most beautiful and altogether the most terrifying waterfall in the universe." While on the Niagara River, Hennepin's party built a fort and a boat, the *Griffon*, to sail the Great Lakes.

Hennepin sailed with La Salle on August 7, 1679 and went with him all the way to Fort Crèvecoeur, the base that La Salle built on the Illinois River in January 1680. On February 29 La Salle sent Hennepin and two others ahead to reconnoiter the upper Mississippi. In the subsequent books that he wrote about the expedition, Hennepin claimed that he sailed all the way down to the mouth of the Mississippi between February 29 and March 25: in other words, that he beat La Salle down the Mississippi by two years. Scholars since then have tended strongly not to believe Hennepin, but he insisted that it was true until his death.

In any case, by April 11, 1680, Hennepin and his companions were (back?) on the upper Mississippi above the point where it is joined by the Illinois River. They were suddenly attacked by 33 canoes of the Sioux tribe, who took the Frenchmen prisoner. They were taken up the Mississippi as far as St. Anthony Falls (near St. Paul, Minnesota), becoming the first Europeans to see it.

They then traveled overland to the Sioux village in the Thousand Lakes region, which they reached on April 21, 1680.

While with the Sioux Hennepin joined an expedition to the Wisconsin River, where he had a chance meeting with the Frenchman Daniel Greysolon Dulhut (after whom Duluth, Minnesota is named) who had been sent by Governor Frontenac to visit the Sioux. They all returned to the Sioux village, where in September they received permission to depart. They spent the winter of 1680-1681 at the French post at Michilimackinac. They left for Quebec in April 1681, and Hennepin traveled on to Europe and was in Paris before the end of the year.

On his return to Europe, Hennepin wrote of his adventures in a famous book, *Description de la Louisiane*, published in January 1683. It was an immediate success and became a bestseller in several languages. As a result, Hennepin's career flourished, and he received several important posts. That all ended in 1687 when he was expelled from his monastery and forced to travel north to Holland. We do not know why this happened. Hennepin blamed it on a plot by La Salle, who allegedly feared what the priest could tell about the discovery of the Mississippi.

From that point on Hennepin's life was in turmoil. He became involved in various religious and other disputes in Holland, France, and Rome. In the meantime, he published two other books about his travels in North America, *Nouvelle découverte* and *Nouveau voyage*. He was last heard of in Holland in 1702, and we do not know how or where he died.

Where to learn more

Hennepin's three famous works have appeared in different editions and manifestations over the years. *Description de la Louisiane, nouvellement découverte au sud-ouest de la Nouvelle-France* was first published in Paris (Chez la Veuve Sebastien Huré) in 1683. The first English translation was by John Gilmary Shea, a pioneer historian of the French exploration of North America: *A Description of Louisiana* (New York: John G. Shea, 1880; reprinted, Ann Arbor: University Microfilms, 1966). A later version is *Description of Louisiana Newly Discovered to the Southwest of New France by Order of the King* by Marion E. Cross, with an introduction by Grace Lee Nute (Minneapolis: University of Minnesota Press, 1938).

Nouvelle découverte d'un très grand pays situé dans l'Amérique entre le Nouveau-Mexique et la mer glaciale was published in 1697 (Utrecht: Guillaume Broedelet). *Nouveau voyage d'un pays plus grand que l'Europe* appeared in 1698 (Utrecht: Antoine Schouten). They were translated and edited together in a 1698 English version (known as the "Tonson" version after one of the publishers). This was reprinted and edited by historian Reuben G. Thwaites as *A New Discovery of a Vast Country in America*, 2 vols. (Chicago: A.C. McClurg & Co., 1903). It includes a bibliographical history of Hennepin's works.

For a discussion of Hennepin see Jean Delanglez, *Hennepin's Description of Louisiana: A Critical Essay* (Chicago: Institute of Jesuit History, 1941) and the biographical essay on Hennepin by Jean-Roch Rioux in the *Dictionary of Canadian Biography*, vol. 2 (Toronto: University of Toronto Press, 1969).

Prince Henry the Navigator

(1394 - 1460)

Prince Henry the Navigator was a member of the Portuguese royal family who used his own private fortune to sponsor expeditions of discovery in the Atlantic Ocean and down the coast of Africa.

Prince Henry was the third son of the Portuguese king John I and his wife, Philippa of Lancaster, a member of an English noble family. In 1415 Henry took part with his father and brothers on an assault on the port of Ceuta in northern Morocco. This trip inspired him with the idea of discovering what lay to the south in Africa. In reward for his services his father made him governor of the southern Portuguese province of the Algarve.

In the Algarve Henry constructed a school for navigation on a promontory, Sagres, that sticks out into the sea between Cape St. Vincent and the Bay of Lagos. He surrounded himself with scientists and experts on navigation and began to formulate a plan for systematically exploring the west coast of Africa. He wanted to find the sources of gold that were carried by Saharan caravans, locate the legendary Christian kingdom of Prester John and see if he could reach Asia by a means other than the overland route through the Middle East.

The first results of Henry's efforts were obtained in 1419 when João Gonçalves Zarco rediscovered the island of Madeira. In 1427 and 1432 two expeditions succeeded in reaching the Azores. For 12 years starting in about 1420 Henry sent out 14 expeditions with the aim of rounding Cape Bojador on the coast of what is now the Western Sahara. This was the big sticking point—Portuguese sailors were afraid to go any farther because of legends that there was only a churning sea beyond. This psychological block was finally removed when **Gil Eannes** rounded the cape in 1432.

Following Eannes' achievement Henry's ships advanced over 250 miles farther down the coast in the next two years. But Henry was disappointed when the Pope granted the Canary Islands to Spain in 1436. In 1437 he took part in an unsuccessful attempt to rescue his brother Ferdinand who had been captured by Muslims and imprisoned in the Moroccan city of Tangier. After that, Henry returned to Sagres for good and continued to direct his voyages. He was able to finance them by revenues he received as governor of the Catholic Order of Christ. This was never enough to meet his ambitions, however, and he was always in debt.

In the following years Henry's ships reached Cabo Blanco in 1441 under Nuno Tristão. Also in 1441, Antão Gonçalves reached the Rio de Oro and brought captives back to Portugal. This started the trade in slaves from the fort that Gonçalves built on the island of Arguim in 1443. During 1444 and 1445 Dinis Dias (brother of **Bartolomeu Dias**) reached as far as the Senegal River and Gorée Island off the present-day city of Dakar.

In 1445 Henry sent out a large fleet to attack and destroy the Moroccan fort at Tider. After the victory, one ship under Alvaro Fernandes continued on to reach the "Cape of Masts" near the Gambia River. In 1456 **Alvise da Cadamosto** discovered the Cape Verde Islands. The last voyage sponsored by Henry in 1460 Pedro de Sintra reached as far as Sierra Leone, 1,500 miles down the coast of Africa.

Diogo Gomes, one of Henry's captains recorded his death: "In the year 1460 the lord Infant Henry fell ill in his town at Cape St.

Prince Henry the Navigator. The Granger Collection, New York.

Vincent and died of the illness on the 13th November . . . and on the night of his death, he was taken to the Church of St. Mary at Lagos and there honorably buried. And the King Afonso . . . was very saddened, both he and his people, by the death of so great a lord, because he spent all his revenues and all he got from Guinea in war and in continual fleets at sea against the Saracens for the faith of Christ."

Where to learn more

There are numerous biographies of Henry and studies of his work. Many of these are, of course, in Portuguese as are the original documentary sources. The following works in English are recommended: Richard Henry Major, *The Life of Prince Henry of Portugal Surnamed the Navigator and Its Results, from Authentic Contemporary Documents* (London: 1868; reprinted, London: Frank Cass 7 co., 1967); C. Raymond Beazley, *Prince Henry the Navigator: The Hero of Portugal and of Modern Discovery, 1394-1460 A.D.* (London: 1895; reprinted, New York: Burt Franklin, 1968); J.P. Oliveira Martins, *The Golden Age of Prince Henry the Navigator*, trans. by J.J. Abraham and W.E. Reynolds (London: 1914); Edgar Prestage, *The Portuguese Pioneers* (London: 1933; reprinted, London: Adam & Charles Black, 1966); Elaine Sanceau, *Henry the Navigator: The Story of a Great Prince and His Times* (New York: W.W. Norton & Co., 1947); Ernle Bradford, *A Wind from the North: The Life of Henry the Navigator* (New York: Harcourt, Brace & Co., 1960; oddly enough, the English edition is entitled *Southward the Caravels*); Christopher Bell, *Portugal and the Quest for the Indies* (New York: Harper & Row, 1974); John Ure, *Prince Henry the Navigator* (London: Constable, 1977).

Matthew A. Henson

(1866 - 1955)

Matthew A. Henson was an American who accompanied Robert Peary on his Arctic explorations and was with him on the first expedition to reach the North Pole.

Matthew A. Henson was born in Charles County, Maryland, south of Washington, D.C. on August 8, 1866. Henson was an African-American, but both of his parents had been born free. When he was young, he moved with his parents to Washington. Both of his parents had died by the time he was seven. He was raised by an uncle and attended a segregated school in Washington for six years. At the age of 13, he went to Baltimore and found a job as a cabin boy on a ship bound for China. He was befriended by the ship's captain, Captain Childs, and worked his way up to being an able-bodied seaman. During that period he sailed to China, Japan, the Philippines, North Africa, Spain, France, and Russia. Childs died when Henson was 17, and he left the sea to look for work on land.

In 1888 Henson was working in a clothing store in Washington when he met a young U.S. Navy lieutenant, **Robert Edward Peary**, who had come in to buy a tropical helmet. Peary offered to hire him as a valet. Henson did not like the idea of becoming a personal servant, but he thought it would be worthwhile to accompany Peary to Nicaragua where he was headed to survey for a possible canal across Central America. They spent a year together in Nicaragua and then Henson worked as a messenger when Peary was stationed at League Island Navy Yard. Peary was interested in the possibilities of Arctic exploration and had made a first trip to Greenland in 1886 with the intention of being the first to cross the Greenland ice cap. He was beaten by **Roald Amundsen** and he then set himself the goal of being the first person to reach the North Pole.

Peary returned to northern Greenland in June 1891, and Henson accompanied him along with Peary's wife, Josephine, and other assistants, including **Frederick Albert Cook**. During this first trip Henson started to learn about the way of life of the Inuit who lived at the northern end of Greenland, to learn to speak their language and to learn how to use their knowledge of survival in the Arctic. Henson became very popular among the Inuit where he was credited with learning their language and adapting their customs better than any other outsider. He was nicknamed Maripaluk—"kind Matthew."

Henson returned with Peary to Greenland in June 1893, at which time he adopted a young Inuit orphan named Kudlooktoo

Matthew A. Henson. The Granger Collection, New York.

and taught him to speak English. On this expedition Peary and Henson crossed the northern end of Greenland from their base at Etah to the northeastern corner of the island at Independence Bay in "Peary Land." Henson later wrote, "The memory of the winter and summer of 1894 and 1895 will never leave me . . . the recollections of the long race with death across the 450 miles of the ice-cap of North Greenland in 1895 . . . are still the most vivid." They returned to the United States in September 1895, and Henson vowed never to return.

But he did return—in the summers of 1896, 1897, 1898, 1900, and 1902. In July 1905 Peary and Henson went back north to Greenland again, this time with the intention of traveling over the polar ice cap to the North Pole. Starting in early 1906 they traveled by dog sled over the frozen sea, but it turned out to be an unusually warm winter and early spring, and they encountered too many stretches of open water to be able to continue.

They got to within 160 miles of the Pole, the farthest north any one had reached to that time.

Peary and Henson set out again on July 6, 1908 on a ship named after the U.S. president, the *Roosevelt*, with an expedition that included 21 members. They sailed to Etah in Greenland and took on board 50 Inuit who were to help set up the supply bases on the route to the Pole. They then went to Cape Columbia at the northern end of Ellesmere Island. Peary and Henson set out from there on the morning of March 1, 1909. They were accompanied by or met up with various advance teams along the way. One of these support teams was headed by Professor Ross Marvin of Cornell University. It set up its last supply depot 230 miles from the Pole and then headed back for Cape Columbia. Marvin never made it. One of the Inuit in the party, Kudlukto, said that he had fallen into a stretch of open water and drowned. Years later Kudlukto confessed that he had shot Marvin and dumped his body in the water when he refused to let one of Kudlukto's young cousins ride on a dog sled.

On March 31 Peary and other members of the expedition were at 87°47′, the farthest north any man had reached—about 150 miles from the Pole. At that point Peary told Captain **Bob Bartlett**, commander of the *Roosevelt*, to return to Cape Columbia. He would make the last dash to the Pole accompanied by Henson. Bartlett was bitterly disappointed, and the next morning walked alone to the north for a few miles as though he would try to make it on his own. He then turned around and headed south. It made sense for Peary to take Henson: he had much more Arctic experience and was an acknowledged master with the dog teams. But there have always been suggestions that Peary sent Bartlett back because he did not want to share the honor of reaching the Pole with anyone else. Given the racial prejudice at the time, Henson and the four Inuit—Ootah, Seegloo, Ooqueah, and Egingwah—did not "count."

A couple of days later, on April 3, Henson was crossing a lane of moving ice, and one of the blocks of ice that he was using for support slipped and he fell into the water. Fortunately one of the Inuit was next to him and was able to pull him out immediately or he would have frozen and drowned. The normal day's procedure was for Peary to leave the night's camp early in the morning and push ahead for two hours breaking the trail ahead. The others would pack up the camp and then catch up with Peary. Then Peary (who at the age of 52 was already suffering from the leukemia that would later kill him) would ride in one of the dogsleds while Henson went ahead and broke trail. They would not see each other until the end of the day.

On April 6, 1909 Henson arrived at a spot that he, just by calculating the distance traveled, thought must be the North Pole. When Peary arrived 45 minutes later, Henson greeted him by saying, "I think I'm the first man to sit on the top of the world." Peary was furious. Peary then attached an American flag to a staff, and the whole expedition went to sleep. At 12:50 p.m. there was a break in the clouds, and Peary was able to take a reading of their location. It showed that they were 3 miles short of

the Pole. After another nap, Peary took another reading and then set out with Egingwah and Seegloo to where he thought the Pole must be—without telling Henson. They then spent 30 hours in the vicinity of the Pole, and Henson officially raised the flag over what Peary's calculations told him was the North Pole. (Whether it really was the Pole or not has been a source of controversy ever since.)

Peary and Henson and the four Inuit arrived back at the spot where they had left Bartlett at midnight on April 9, an incredible speed—and reached Cape Columbia on April 23. They stayed there until July 17 when the ice had melted enough for the *Roosevelt* to steam into open water. They telegraphed news of their triumph from Labrador on September 6, 1909. But by that time, the world already thought that Frederick Cook had been the first one to reach the Pole. Peary spent the next few years defending his claims and was eventually vindicated.

By the time Henson got back to the United States he weighed 112 pounds (his normal weight was 155 pounds), and he was forced to spend several months recovering. For a while, he accompanied Peary on his lecture tours, where he would be exhibited in his Inuit clothes. In 1912 he wrote a book about his experiences (*A Negro at the North Pole*). However, the book died quickly, and Henson was forced to take a job as a porter working for $16 a week. Thanks to some politically influential friends he was later given a job as a messenger at the United States Customs house in New York at a salary of $20 a week, which was later raised to $40 a week. He retired in 1936, at which time there was an effort to have him awarded the Congressional Medal of Honor, but nothing came of it.

As racial attitudes in the United States changed, Henson began to receive more recognition. He was elected a full member of the Explorers Club in New York in 1937, the first Black member. In 1945 all of the survivors of the North Pole expedition received the Navy Medal, but Henson's was awarded in private. When he went to attend a banquet in his honor in Chicago in 1948, none of the downtown hotels would allow him to register because of his race. In 1950, however, he was introduced to President Truman and in 1954 was received by President Eisenhower in the White House. He died in New York in 1955 at the age of 88 and was buried in a private cemetery there. Years later, in 1988, when news of his achievements received more publicity, he was reburied at Arlington National Cemetery with full military honors in a plot next to Peary's.

Since Peary and Henson were both married at the time of their Arctic expeditions, it is not surprising that there was no public knowledge that both of them had liaisons with Inuit women. Dating from the 1905 expedition, they both fathered children—

Peary had two sons and Henson had a boy named Anaukaq. This information came to light in 1986 when it was revealed that the small Greenland village of Moriussaq was largely made up of Henson's descendants, who had prospered as traders and hunters.

Where to learn more

Henson's autobiography, *A Negro Explorer at the North Pole* was first published in 1912 (New York: 1912). It was reprinted in 1969 with a slightly different title: *A Black Explorer at the North Pole* (New York: Walker and Company). This edition was reprinted as a paperback by the University of Nebraska Press in Lincoln in 1989.

There are two biographies of Henson: Bradley Robinson, *Dark Companion* (New York: Robert M. McBride & Co., 1947) and Floyd Miller, *Ahdoolo!: The Biography of Matthew A. Henson* (New York: E.P. Dutton & Co., 1963).

The story of Henson's descendants is told in ''The Henson Family'' by S. Allen Counter in the 100th anniversary edition of the *National Geographic* magazine (September 1988, pp. 422-429).

Wally Herbert

(1934 -   )

Wally Herbert, a British explorer, made the first surface crossing of the frozen Arctic Ocean from North America to Spitsbergen.

Wally Herbert was born in Sussex, England on October 24, 1934, the son of a British Naval captain. He joined the Royal Engineer Corps in 1953 and was stationed on the Suez Canal in Egypt. He left the Army in 1955 and spent a year traveling throughout the Middle East on his own. He then got a job as a surveyor with the Falkland Islands Dependencies Survey, which was responsible for mapping British claims in the Antarctic region. He spent the years 1955 through 1958 at the British base at Hope Bay, Antarctica.

After he left Antarctica the first time, Herbert traveled on his own through South America and then was chosen to be a member of a scientific expedition to Lapland in northern Scandinavia and to Spitsbergen in the Arctic Ocean north of Norway in 1960. He made a trip to Greenland and then signed on as a member of a New Zealand Expedition to Antarctica at the end of 1960. He was chosen to be the leader of the expedition's "Southern Party" and was put in charge of mapping 26,000 square miles of the Queen Maud Range. On the 50th anniversary of the event in 1962, Herbert re-traced **Roald Amundsen**'s route to the South Pole.

At this point in his life Herbert wanted to achieve one of the great explorations along the lines of the great polar explorers of the early 20th century. He decided that the last great unmade trip in the world was across the Arctic Ocean from one end to the other by land. He thought the trip could be made in 130 days, traveling at an average of 14 miles a day. He presented his ideas in 1965 and received the backing and financial support of Britain's Royal Geographic Society. In preparation for such a journey, he dog sledded 1,400 miles from Greenland to Canada in 1967.

Herbert's Trans-Arctic Expedition started out from Point Barrow, Alaska on February 21, 1968. It consisted of Herbert and three companions, each driving a team of dogs. Herbert and his team trekked the 3,700 miles from Point Barrow, Alaska to Spitsbergen by way of the North Pole. They reached the Pole, supported by air drops, on April 6, 1969. The trip had taken 407 days, and Herbert sent a telegram to Queen Elizabeth II via an American relay post that was stationed at the Pole.

From the North Pole the expedition traveled the last part of the journey "downhill" to Spitsbergen, which they reached on June 11, 1969, 476 days after they had left Alaska. The last part of the trip was a nightmare, a series of desperate forced marches over disintegrating sea ice as summer crept up on the Arctic.

After the success of this expedition, Herbert returned to the Canadian Arctic and Greenland to study the Inuit people that he had met during the course of his Arctic explorations. He filmed the Inuit of Thule in far northwest Greenland in 1971 to 1973 and went to Lapland in 1975. From 1978 through 1982 he led another expedition to Greenland in which he tried to travel all the way around the world's greatest island by dog sled and kayak. In 1986 and 1987 he worked on research and a book about **Robert Edward Peary**'s expedition to the North Pole in which he reached the conclusion that Peary had faked his results and had never made it to the Pole at all. Herbert knew Peary's Inuit family well and had traveled with them on several hunting expeditions. In 1987 he returned to northwestern Greenland, Ellesmere Island, and the North Pole to make another movie. He has become one of the world's foremost spokesmen for Arctic conservation and the preservation of the culture of the Inuit.

Where to learn more

Herbert has written several books about the Arctic. The one that deals with his trip across the frozen ocean is *Across the Top of the World* (London: Longmans, 1969), which was published in the United States as *The Last Great Journey on Earth* (New York: G.P. Putnam's Sons, 1971). Other books about the Arctic are *The North Pole* (London: Sackett and Marshall, 1979) and *Polar Deserts* (London: Collins, 1971). His study of the Peary controversy is *The Noose of Laurels: Robert E. Peary and the Race to the North Pole* (New York: Atheneum, 1989).

Herbert has written two books about the Inuit: *Eskimos* (London: Collins, 1976) and *Hunters of the Polar North* (London: Time-Life Books, 1981).

Herodotus

(485? B.C. - 425? B.C.)

Herodotus, the most famous classical Greek historian, gave an accurate geographical account of the places he wrote about and apparently visited many of them.

Herodotus was born at Halicarnassus (near modern-day Bodrum on the west coast of Turkey), a Greek colony on the coast of Asia Minor. He was the son of Lyxes and Dryo, who seem to have been substantial citizens of the town. At the time of Herodotus' birth Halicarnassus was ruled by Queen Artemisia, an ally of the Persians. Following the defeat of the Persians in Ionia in 478 B.C., which is part of the story of Herodotus' famous *History*, the throne passed to her son Lygdamis, who became involved in a civil war that resulted in the death of Herodotus' uncle.

Herodotus left his native city and traveled to the Aegean island of Samos. He may have returned to Halicarnassus following the defeat of Lygdamis, but if so he left shortly thereafter and went to Athens. He then traveled widely throughout the Greek world—Asia Minor, the Aegean islands, Greece, Macedonia, Thrace, the coast of the Black Sea as far as the Crimean Peninsula, Persia, Tyre (in Lebanon), Egypt, and Cyrene (in modern-day Libya). These travels seem to date from the years 454 B.C.-447 B.C. In 447 B.C. he returned to Athens, the intellectual center of the Greek world. He had already written a good portion of the *History* and gave public readings from it.

In 443 B.C. the colony of Thurii was founded by Athens on the Gulf of Taranto in southern Italy, and Herodotus joined it. From Thurii he visited Sicily and southern Italy. Civil strife broke out in Thurii in later years, and it is possible that Herodotus traveled back to Athens in his final years. It is thought that he finished writing his history in the final years of his life, when he was in his fifties, since they mention the beginning of the Peloponnesian War, which started in 431 B.C.

On his extensive travels Herodotus collected historical, geographical, ethnological, mythological, and archaeological material for his great history which was not only a history of the wars between the Greeks and their neighbors, but also an explanation of the causes. His history begins with the conquest of the Greek colonies in Asia Minor by the Lydian king Croesus, continues with a history of Lydia, and passes to Persia, Babylon, and Egypt. It then gives a history of the two wars between Persia and the Greeks.

Herodotus had a very clear view of the geography of that part of the world that he knew. He rejected the traditional view that the world was divided into three equal parts—Asia, Europe, and Africa (which he called Libya). He did, however, think that Europe was as wide as the other two continents. He knew nothing about northwestern Europe—Britain and Scandinavia—and his view of Asia went only as far east as the Indus River. He was the first geographer to realize that the Caspian Sea was a great inland sea rather than a gulf of an ocean circling the world.

Herodotus thought that Africa was surrounded by water because he described a supposed voyage by the Egyptian king Necho that circumnavigated the continent around the year 600 B.C. However, he made two major mistakes. He thought that the Nile River rose in the Atlas Mountains and then flowed eastward through what would be the Sahara Desert before turning northwards and watering Egypt. His other error is more surprising. He was aware of the voyage of **Scylax of Caryanda** who had sailed down the Indus River into the Arabian Sea and then around Arabia to Egypt. But Herodotus still talked about the Indus flowing southeastward.

Herodotus. The Granger Collection, New York.

All of these observations are interspersed throughout the *History*, attesting to the fact that the author, who gives the most complete and accurate account of classical geography, had visited many of the places he wrote about.

Where to learn more

There are many editions of Herodotus' *History*. Two recent ones that can be recommended are Herodotus, *The History*, translated by David Grene (Chicago: The University of Chicago Press, 1987) and Herodotus, *The Histories*, translated by Walter Blanco and edited by Walter Blanco and Jennifer Tolbert Roberts (New York: W.W. Norton, 1992), which contains several introductory essays, including "The Shape of Herodotus' World," by James Romm.

Another interesting edition is Joseph C. Farber, editor and photographer, *Democracy's First Struggle: Herodotus' Histories* (Barre, Mass.: Barre Pub-lishing, 1975), which is an abridged version that contains photographs of the sites mentioned in the text.

A recent book-length study of Herodotus with an extensive bibliography is Charles W. Fornara, *Herodotus: An Interpretive Essay* (Oxford: Oxford University Press, 1971). A shorter study can be found in Michael Grant, *The Ancient Historians* (New York: Charles Scribner's Sons, 1970).

For the specifically geographical aspects of Herodotus' *History*, see M. Cary and E.H. Warmington, *The Ancient Explorers* (London: Methuen, 1929; revised paperback edition, Baltimore: Pelican Books, 1963) and H.F. Tozer, *History of Ancient Geography*, 2nd edition (Cambridge: Cambridge University Press, 1935).

Sir Edmund Hillary

(1919 -   )

Edmund Hillary is a New Zealander who was the first person to climb Mount Everest, the highest peak in the world, and led an expedition to the South Pole.

Edmund Hillary was born in Auckland, New Zealand on July 20, 1919. He grew up on a farm in the small town of Tuakau, 40 miles south of Auckland. He attended Auckland Grammar School while commuting to his family's farm. He saw a mountain and snow for the first time when he took a school trip to Mount Ruapehu on the North Island of New Zealand at the age of 16. He went to university for two years and then dropped out of school to work full-time as a beekeeper on his father's farm. At the outbreak of World War II he decided not to volunteer to fight in the New Zealand armed forces because of religious convictions. He then took a trip to the high mountains known as the Southern Alps on the South Island of New Zealand to mull over his decision. There, he developed the enthusiasm for mountain climbing that was to guide his later life.

When conscription was introduced into New Zealand later in the war, Hillary decided to go ahead and volunteer for the Royal New Zealand Air Force. He was accepted into a training program. Finding that it was not too demanding, he spent much of his time climbing mountains around the air base. While there, he climbed his first tall mountain, Mount Tapuaenuku at 9,465 feet. While at navigation school he climbed Mount Egmont (8,260 feet), New Zealand's "Mount Fuji." Hillary spent the last part of the war as a navigator on planes flying in the islands of the South Pacific, where he was seriously injured when his plane crashed in the ocean near a small atoll.

Following the war, Hillary returned to New Zealand and took a few months off to climb in the Southern Alps, where he met a famous mountaineer, Harry Ayres, who gave him formal training in the techniques of mountain climbing that Hillary had previously only read about or picked up on his own. Together they climbed Mt. Cook, at 12,349 feet New Zealand's highest peak and then, a few years later, climbed up its southern face, the first persons to do so. Hillary returned to the family's bee farm, which he eventually bought from his father. When the family traveled to Europe for his sister's wedding, Hillary climbed in the Austrian and Swiss Alps for the first time.

Following Hillary's return to New Zealand from Europe, he was asked to take part in the first all-New Zealand expedition to the Himalayas. He and three colleagues traveled to India in May

Sir Edmund Hillary and Tenzing Norgay. The Granger Collection, New York.

1951 and traveled to Nepal. They conquered Mukut Parbat (23,760 feet) on the Nepal-Tibet border in August 1951. On their return to India, Hillary and one of his companions were invited to join a British expedition led by Eric Shipton that was making a reconnaissance of Mount Everest, which at 29,028 feet is the highest mountain in the world. In October they made several climbs up various faces of the mountain to try to determine the best approach. Hillary returned to New Zealand in December 1951. Shortly after, he received an invitation from Shipton to join an expedition in 1952 to climb Cho Oyu (26,870 feet) in preparation for a full-scale Everest expedition in 1953.

The British expedition ran into impassable ice fields and was not able to reach the summit of Cho Oyu. However, it gained much valuable experience, and many of the members, including Hillary, were included in the 1953 expedition, which was headed by Colonel John Hunt of the British Army. Also included in the 1953 expedition were several Sherpa guides and porters. These were Nepalese who lived in the Himalayas near Mt. Everest and knew the mountains well. Among them was Tenzing Norgay, an experienced climber who had been part of two Swiss expeditions in 1951 and 1952.

Hillary took charge of setting up the base camp on Khumbu Glacier, at 17,900 feet, which he completed on April 12, 1953. Hillary and Tenzing started climbing together, and Tenzing saved Hillary's life when a piece of overhanging ice that he was standing on collapsed and he fell into a deep crevasse. Six days after that incident, Hillary and Tenzing went from the Base Camp to set up an advance base, experimenting with the expedition's oxygen system. They were given three days to accomplish this task but completed it in one. On May 7 the assault on Everest began in earnest. On May 26 two members of the expedition left from Camp VIII and reached 28,700 feet, the highest ever climbed, but were unable to get to the top because of the lateness of the day and their insufficient oxygen supply. These two climbers were so exhausted by the effort that they had to be sent down the mountain.

On the morning of May 28, 1953, five climbers made it up to 27,900 feet where they set up a tent and some supplies. Hillary and Tenzing spent the night in the tent. They went to bed at 6 p.m. and awoke at 3:30 a.m. on the morning of May 29. After eating and preparing their equipment, they took off at 6:30 a.m. Hillary fell at one point and suggested turning back, but without further discussion they went on. They reached the South Peak of Mt. Everest at 9 a.m. and then followed along a descending ridge that then led up to the peak of the mountain itself. At the end they had to climb up a "chimney" 40 feet high that led to the summit. They reached the summit at 11:30 a.m, Hillary first followed by Tenzing. They stayed on the peak for about one half hour. Hillary took a picture of Tenzing at the top, but Tenzing did not know how to work the camera so there is no picture of Hillary. It took them the rest of the day to make it back to the other climbers at the farthest advance camp. The following day they climbed down to the rest of the expedition, and news of the triumph was radioed to the world.

On June 2, 1953 Queen Elizabeth II was crowned in London, and one of the highlights of the celebration was that a British team had conquered the highest point in the world, a feat that had first been attempted in 1924. As one of her first official acts, the Queen knighted Hillary for his achievement. The local Nepalis proclaimed Tenzing a hero, and Hillary was besieged by members of the world press to tell his story. In Kathmandu they were greeted by the King and Queen of Nepal. Hillary then went on to London where he was received by the Queen in a private ceremony. He returned to New Zealand in August 1953, stopping in Sydney to propose to Louise Rose, who was the daughter of the president of the New Zealand Alpine Club. They were married in September. After the wedding Hillary began a lecture and personal appearance tour that took him across Europe and throughout the United States.

In 1954 Hillary led a New Zealand expedition to the Himalayas that ended in disaster. One of the members of the expedition fell into a crevasse and Hillary broke three ribs trying to rescue him. Then, as he reached a camp at 22,000 feet he came down with pneumonia and had to be evacuated to a hospital. He returned to New Zealand and his bee farm.

In June 1955 Hillary was invited to join **Vivian Fuchs'** expedition to cross Antarctica by way of the South Pole. He reached Scott Base on the Ross Ice Shelf in January 1956. He helped to establish this New Zealand base during the next few months and then returned to New Zealand to get further supplies. He went back to Antarctica in December 1956 and spent the following months setting up supply depots for the trip across the continent.

In the original plan for the expedition, the New Zealanders under Hillary were to serve as a support team for the British. Fuchs and his team members were to reach the South Pole from the opposite side of the continent at Shackleton Base, and then use the supply depots set up by Hillary to continue across Antarctica. As it happened, Hillary made much better progress than the British, and he arrived at the South Pole on January 4, 1958, two weeks before Fuchs. He was the first person to reach the Pole by using gas-powered vehicles and the first one there since **Robert Falcon Scott** in 1912. Hillary and Fuchs then traveled on together to Scott Base in time to catch the supply ship on March 2 before it was forced to leave by encroaching ice.

In 1960 Hillary led an expedition to Nepal to search for Yeti—the mythical (?) Abominable Snowman—and to carry out other research in the Himalayas. During that time he built a school for the local Sherpa population, the first of 17 schools and two hospitals that he was to build in northern Nepal. The money was supplied by corporations for whom Hillary endorsed products or by the proceeds from his lecture tours or writings. In 1967 Hillary led an expedition to Antarctica in which two New Zealand climbers scaled Mount Herschel, at 11,000 feet one of the highest mountains on the continent. The expedition also collected geological samples that were later used to support the theory that Antarctica had once been linked to Australia. Hillary continued to travel extensively and returned every year to Nepal to build a new hospital or school. On one trip, in 1975, his wife and teenage daughter were killed in an airplane crash. In 1977 Hillary led an expedition that traveled up the Ganges River from its mouth to its headwaters in the Himalayas. He then retired and lives on his bee farm outside of Auckland.

Where to learn more

Hillary wrote the story of his adventurous life in *Nothing Venture, Nothing Win* (New York: Coward, McCann & Geoghegan, 1975).

Friedrich Hornemann

(1772 - 1801)

Friedrich Hornemann was a German who was hired by a British scientific society to travel to the Niger River. He became the first European to cross the Sahara but did not live to write about his experiences.

Friedrich Hornemann was the son of a German pastor, born in the town of Hildesheim. In 1791 he entered the University of Göttingen to study theology and oriental languages. His father died while he was at the university. His widowed mother was left with several children to support, and Hornemann was forced to leave the university in 1794 to take a teaching job. He went back to Göttingen the following year to talk with Professor J.F. Blumenbach, an early anthropologist. He wanted an introduction from Blumenbach to **Sir Joseph Banks**, the Secretary of the Association for Promoting the Discovery of the Interior Parts of Africa. Hornemann wanted funding from the Association for a trip to the Niger River.

Blumenbach was impressed with the young man and furnished a letter of recommendation. He sent it off in May 1796 along with Hornemann's detailed proposal as to how he would accomplish his goal. The two documents impressed the selection committee, and, at meeting on June 3, 1796, they hired him for £200 a year plus expenses. The Association proposed to send Hornemann to try to find the Niger from the east, by way of Egypt. At the same time, **Mungo Park** was trying to reach the same goal from the west coast of Africa. Hornemann was to follow a plan originally drafted by an American, John Ledyard, who had died in Egypt in 1788 before beginning his trip.

Hornemann spent the following months in Göttingen learning some rudimentary medicine and perfecting his Arabic. He left for London in February 1797 and met members of the Association at a meeting on March 20. His final instructions were issued on June 23, 1797, and he left the following week. At the time England and France were at war, and it was only through the influence of Banks that he was able to get a safe passage through France. In Paris he met various men of science and a Turkish diplomat who gave him letters of introduction to people in Cairo.

Hornemann traveled via Marseilles and Cyprus to the port of Alexandria in Egypt and then on to Cairo, which he reached at the end of September 1797. In Cairo Hornemann met Joseph Frendenburgh from the German city of Cologne who had been living in Egypt for a number of years and had converted to Islam. Inspired by Frendenburgh, Hornemann decided to make his trip disguised as a Muslim and engaged Frendenburgh to accompany

him as his servant. They were the first known European travelers in North Africa to disguise themselves successfully as Muslims. Hornemann was able to convince questioners that he was a Mameluke, a native of Turkey's European provinces who were forcibly converted to Islam and who served in the Caliph's army.

Hornemann had hoped to set out with a caravan of merchants who were traveling to the Fezzan in what is now southern Libya in the spring of 1798. He was prevented from doing so by an outbreak of plague in April and then, in July, by Napoleon's invasion of Egypt in July 1798. Hornemann was interned with other Europeans until Napoleon's arrival in Cairo at the end of July. He no longer had access to money from England and did not have the funds to continue on his trip. He was, however, able to meet several scientists who were traveling with Napoleon, and he was even introduced to the future Emperor himself. Napoleon gave Hornemann a safe conduct through the French lines and helped him raise the money he needed. He even offered to forward Hornemann's reports back to London.

Hornemann and Frendenburgh started out for the oasis of Marzuq in the Fezzan at the beginning of September 1798. They traveled via the oasis of Siwa on what is now the border between Egypt and Libya. Along the way, members of the caravan and, especially, the townspeople of Siwa began to suspect that Hornemann was not who he claimed to be. He was in danger several times but finally put an end to the suspicions by displaying his knowledge of the Koran. In one such encounter, however, Frendenburgh had a servant bury Hornemann's notebooks, and they were never found.

They reached Marzuq on November 17, 1798, where Frendenburgh became ill with fever and died. Hornemann wrote to his mother back in Hildesheim that Frendenburgh had been "led astray by wine and women." Hornemann stayed alone in Marzuq for seven months collecting information on the people and geography of the Fezzan. Unable to find a caravan headed south, Hornemann went north to the coastal city of Tripoli, which he reached in August 1799. He wrote a letter to Banks telling him that he planned to travel to Bornu, in what is now northern Nigeria, and then to Timbuktu, which had never been visited by a European.

Hornemann left Tripoli on December 1, 1799 and arrived back in Marzuq on January 20, 1800—"after a long but happy Travel. I am in the best health in few words very well," he wrote to Banks. On April 6 he wrote a letter to the Association. He announced that he was leaving that day on a caravan bound for Lake Chad (then unknown to Europeans) and hoped to reach the

Gulf of Guinea by way of the city of Katsina in northern Nigeria. This was the last word that the Association had from Hornemann. In 1802 it published Hornemann's diary of his trip from Egypt to Marzuq, and Banks sent a copy to Napoleon.

Hornemann's fate was not learned until 1819. In that year, two British explorers, Joseph Ritchie and George Lyon, reached Marzuq. They met a man who had been in the caravan that Hornemann had joined. He had gone to Bornu, where he spent a few months, and then traveled to Katsina and to the Kingdom of Nupe just short of the Niger River at Bokani, where he died of dysentery. He was the first European to cross the Sahara since Roman times and the first to see Lake Chad. It was reported to Ritchie and Lyon that he had been greatly admired by the people of Bornu as a skillful doctor and a Muslim holy man.

Where to learn more

The African Association published *The Journal of Frederick Hornemann's Travels from Cairo to Mourzouk, the Capital of the Kingdom of Fezzan, in* *Africa in the Years 1797-8* in 1802. It was later reissued by the Hakluyt Society in E.W. Bovill, ed. *Missions to the Niger*, vol. 1 (Cambridge: Cambridge University Press for the Hakluyt Society, 1964). The records of the African Association pertaining to Hornemann can be found in Robin Hallett, ed. *Records of the African Association, 1788-1831* (London: Thomas Nelson & Sons for the Royal Geographical Society, 1964). Lyon's report on Hornemann is in his *A Narrative of the Travels in Northern Africa, 1818-1820* (London: 1821), also included in Bovill's collection.

There is a German biography of Hornemann: A. Pahde, *Der Erste Deutsche Afrikaforscher* (Hamburg: 1895). There is also a biography of Blumenbach that discusses his influence on exploration: H. Plischke, *Johann Friedrich Blumenbachs Einfluss auf die Entdeckungsreisenden seiner Zeit* (Göttingen: 1937).

Several of the books dealing with the attempt to reach the Niger discuss Hornemann: A. Adu Boahen, *Britain, the Sahara, and the Western Sudan, 1788-1861* (Oxford: Clarendon Press, 1964); Robin Hallett, *The Penetration of Africa: European Enterprise and Exploration Principally in Northern and Western Africa up to 1830*, vol. 1 (London: Routledge & Kegan Paul, 1965), which served as the main source for this account; and E.W. Bovill, *The Niger Explored* (London: 1968).

Daniel Houghton

(1740 - 1791)

Daniel Houghton was an Irish explorer who searched for the source of the Niger River and died along the way.

In 1788 a group of English gentlemen, led by **Sir Joseph Banks**, formed a new organization called the Association for Promoting the Discovery of the Interior Parts of Africa. At its first meeting on June 9 the group decided that its major priority would be the discovery of the Niger River and the fabled city of Timbuktu. Europeans knew about both of these places from stories they had heard at their trading posts on the west coast of Africa. However, no Westerner had ever actually seen either.

The Association sent out two explorers within the first year of its operation. Simon Lucas set out from Tripoli on the north coast and traveled 500 miles into the desert before turning back. John Ledyard, an American, proposed to get to the Niger via Cairo and the Nile River, but he died in Egypt before he could start out.

The Association then hired Daniel Houghton, an Irishman who had served in the British Army. Houghton had joined the Army in 1758 at the age of 18 and had fought in the Caribbean during the Seven Years' War. In 1772 he had been stationed in Gibraltar on the south coast of Spain and had undertaken a diplomatic mission to the court of Morocco. He accepted the post of engineer to the ruler of one of the Indian states and was on his way to India in 1778 when war broke out between Britain and France during the American Revolution. The ship he was on stopped at Gorée, an island off the coast of Senegal, which had recently been evacuated by a French garrison. Houghton accepted the job of commander of the fort and stayed there for three years. During that time he learned Mandingo, one of the major trading languages of West Africa.

At the end of the war, Gorée was returned to the French, and Houghton went back to England without any means of support. He married, but his wife's assets were seized by his creditors. He tried to capitalize on his African experience by getting the British government to support an expedition to West Africa to investigate its mining resources. The government was not interested. Therefore, Houghton was very pleased to learn that the African Association was looking for men to travel to the Niger. He proposed himself to the Association and offered to work on a very small budget. His offer was accepted on July 5, 1790, and he was given instructions "to ascertain the course and if possible the rise and termination of that mysterious river (the Niger)."

Houghton reached the mouth of the Gambia River at the beginning of November, 1790. He traveled to a small British trading post called Pisania about half-way up the course of the Gambia River. He sent reports along the way back to Pisania. Unfortunately, his mission was ill-fated from the beginning. In the town of Medina he was caught in a fire that destroyed most of his equipment, including his gun. The gun he bought to replace it exploded in his hands and wounded him very badly. While he was recovering, his guide stole most of his pack animals and remaining equipment. He was not able to leave Medina until May 8, 1791.

In spite of his difficulties, he made it as far as the town of Sinbing, about 500 miles from his starting point. From there, he wrote a letter back to Pisania dated September 1, 1791 that reported that although he had not yet reached the Niger he had learned that it flowed eastward and was navigable. He also reported that the country he had traveled through presented great opportunities for trade: "gold, ivory, wax, and slaves, may at all times be had here for the most trifling articles; and a trade, the profit of which would be upwards of eight hundred per cent can be carried on at Fattatenda without the least trouble."

That letter was the last word from Houghton. Later, it was found that he had joined a group of Muslim tribesmen headed north and that they had taken everything from him and left him to die. However, his reports back encouraged the Association to keep searching for the Niger, and were the motivating force behind the expedition of **Mungo Park**, who was to succeed where Houghton had failed. It was also Park who learned about Houghton's ultimate fate.

It was a year after his disappearance before the African Association gave up hope of Houghton's reappearance. His death left his wife and three children destitute. At first the Association was only willing to give his wife the princely sum of £10. She was thrown into debtor's prison in 1794. Eventually, a private subscription was taken to get her out and to provide for her sons' education. She was later granted a government pension of £30 a year.

Where to learn more

The original records of Houghton's trip can be found in Robin Hallett, ed. *Records of the African Association, 1788-1831* (London: Thomas Nelson and Sons, for the Royal Geographical Society, 1964). These later served as the basis for Hallett's narrative history, *The Penetration of Africa: European Enterprise and Exploration Principally in Northern and Western Africa up to 1830* (London: Routledge & Kegan Paul, 1965).

Cornelius Houtman

(1540 - 1599)

Cornelius Houtman was a Dutch merchant who led the first Dutch trading expedition to what is now Indonesia.

Cornelius Houtman was a merchant from the Dutch province of North Holland. His father was a brewer from the famous cheese-making town of Gouda. In the summer of 1592 Houtman went to Lisbon in the employ of his wealthy cousin Reynier Pauw. It has long been thought by historians that he was sent there specifically to serve as a commercial spy: to bring back maps and sailing instructions on the Portuguese route to the East Indies (modern Indonesia) in order to break the Portuguese monopoly on the spice trade. Other historians have claimed, however, that he was in Lisbon on legitimate business and that any information he brought back was incidental. The Dutch had many other relations with Portugal, and men such as **Jan Huyghen van Linschoten** had also brought back much valuable data. In any case, Houtman returned to Holland in 1594 with a plan to sail to the East.

On Houtman's return, seven wealthy Amsterdam merchants invested in a new enterprise called the Compagnie van Verre. This was an example of Dutch financial innovation that was later to spread throughout the world: each person invested a certain amount and then was subject to risks or got rewards in relation to how much had been invested. It was the beginning of the joint stock company, or corporation. The Compagnie van Verre, which eventually became the famous Dutch East India Company, bought four ships and outfitted them and hired 248 crew members. The head of navigation was Pieter de Keyzer while Houtman was the "chief merchant" and sailed on the *Mauritius*. Houtman's younger brother, Frederik, was given the title of "junior merchant" and sailed on the *Hollandia*.

The little fleet sailed from Texel, at the northern tip of the province of Holland, on April 2, 1595. At first, they made good time: by April 19 they had passed the Canary Islands off the coast of the western Sahara and reached the Cape Verde Islands on April 26. Then the Dutch ships ran into what are called the "doldrums," when the wind and sea are both still. They did not sight the coast of Brazil, where Portuguese ships altered course to the east, until June 27. Many of the men were sick with scurvy, and the navigators had a hard time steering by the unfamiliar constellations of the southern hemisphere. They sighted the island of Tristan da Cunha, and that helped them adjust their course towards the Cape of Good Hope at the southern tip of Africa. They landed at the Cape on August 2, 1595. It then took

another two months to reach the island of Madagascar. By the time they arrived, there were 71 corpses on the ships. They were buried in a little bay that was named Holland Cemetery.

The four ships stayed in the bay for several months while the men recovered. They were forced to set sail in February 1596 when the local inhabitants grew tired of their constant depredations and drove them away. By this time, the Dutchmen were in constant battle with each other. It did not help that they had set sail after the favorable monsoon winds had passed, and it took them four months to cross the Indian Ocean. When the fleet sighted some of the outlying islands of the Indonesian archipelago, Houtman had the chief merchant on one of the other ships arrested for mutiny.

The four Dutch ships, with what was left of their crews, anchored off the port of Bantam on the northwest coast of Java on June 23, 1596, 15 months after they had left Holland. Bantam was the chief port in the East Indies at the time, and the sultan was happy to have new trading partners. He welcomed the Dutchmen and gave them a house to use as a headquarters in the town. Houtman, who fancied himself a clever trader, quickly alienated the townspeople by refusing to pay the going price for spices. The Portuguese, naturally, tried to eliminate their rivals by claiming that they were pirates. When the Dutch ships began to take soundings of the harbor, the sultan began to think they were spies. He ordered that all supplies, including water, be cut off.

Houtman and some of the Dutch merchants stayed in the town, while the ships under de Keyzer sailed across the Sunda Strait to Sumatra in order to get food and water. During the trip, de Keyzer died under mysterious circumstances, and many said he had been poisoned. Moreover, when the ships returned to Bantam they found that Houtman and the other Dutchmen had been arrested. The ships bombarded the town and some of the boats in the harbor in retaliation. Houtman was released, and relations were restored. This did not last long, however, and soon word was sent along the whole coast of Java that the Dutch were thieves and pirates.

Houtman refused to deal for spices in Bantam and headed east along the coast of Java, with the aim of reaching the Moluccas, which were the actual source of the spices being traded. At the port of Sidayu, near what is the modern city of Surabaya, open hostilities broke out between the two sides and 12 men from one of the ships were killed, including the captain and one of the merchants. When the Dutch reached the island of Madura off the east coast of Java, one of the local kings came out to greet them. The nervous Europeans mistook his intentions and fired on his canoes, killing several people including the king. This ruined their welcome elsewhere as well.

By then, only 94 of the men who had started on the voyage were still alive. Many wanted to turn back. Houtman wanted to continue on to the Moluccas. When one of the captains opposed him, he was soon found dead. "A child could tell he had been poisoned." Houtman was accused of murder and was arrested. He was released when he finally agreed to lead the ships back to Holland. They burned one of the ships and divided up the crew among the remaining three. They stopped at the island of Bali, which they considered to be an island paradise, thus contributing to a reputation that continues to this day. It was so appealing that two of the sailors deserted. One particularly leaky boat was burned.

The three Dutch ships left Bali on February 26, 1597. They sailed along the south coast of Java, which as far as is known had never been done by another European ship. The return trip was much easier, and they returned to Holland on August 14, 1597. Only 89 men were still alive, and seven of them died a short time after the return. Because of Houtman's stubbornness, the cargo of spices was quite small and apparently did not even sell for enough to cover expenses. In spite of all this, Houtman and the three ships were received enthusiastically. They had pioneered the route to the East Indies and had shown that it was possible to break the Portuguese stranglehold on the spice trade.

Soon after Houtman's return the Amsterdam investors equipped a larger fleet of eight ships and sent it east. Other investors soon followed, and in 1598 a total of 22 Dutch ships left Holland headed for the East. Nine of the ships tried to get to Indonesia by sailing west through the Straits of Magellan. One of them, under Captain Oliver van Noort, succeeded and became the first Dutch ship to circumnavigate the world. Some of the ships that made it as far as Java did much better than those of Houtman and returned with cargoes that earned enormous profits.

Amazingly, Houtman and his brother Frederik were chosen to command two of the ships that sailed east in 1598. They were employed by a group of merchants from the town of Middelburg in the southern province of Zeeland. Also in their small fleet was an Englishman, **John Davis**, who had been sent out to spy on the Dutch. The two Houtman brothers sailed from Middelburg in mid-March 1598. Once again, they got stuck on the coast of Madagascar, where memories of their previous visit were still vivid. Rather than going back to Java, where they knew they would not be welcome, Cornelius and Frederik Houtman sailed to the large island of Sumatra.

The Houtmans had better luck in Sumatra and were able to trade profitably for pepper, for which the island was renowned. They arrived in the Kingdom of Atjeh, at the northern end of Sumatra, the stronghold of Islam in Indonesia, in June 1599. The sultan welcomed them and asked them to take part in a campaign against his enemy the sultan of Johore across the Straits of Malacca in what is now Malaysia. When the Dutch captains refused, their ships were stormed and Cornelius Houtman was killed. Frederik Houtman was captured and put in prison for two years, where he was continually threatened with being executed. While in prison, he wrote the first Malay-Dutch dictionary and composed a prayer-book in Malay. The two ships wandered aimlessly for a while and then returned to Zeeland in July 1600.

Where to learn more

Houtman's voyage to the East Indies is always called "The First Voyage" because it was the beginning of the Dutch East India Company and the Dutch empire in Indonesia. There are several collections in Dutch of the records of the voyage. The most complete is G.P. Rouffaer and J.W. Ijzerman, *De eerste schipvaart der Nederlanders naar Oost Indië*, 3 vols. (The Hague: 1915-1929). Parts of this are translated as "The Description of a Voyage Made by Certain Ships of Holland into the East Indies" in Richard Hakluyt's famous book on early explorations, *Hakluyt's Collection of the Early Voyages*, which is available in several editions. An excellent modern book about the early years of Dutch imperialism in Indonesia, which was the main source for this account, is George Masselman, *The Cradle of Colonialism* (New Haven: Yale University Press, 1963).

Hsüan-Chuang

(602 - 649)

Hsüan-Chuang was a Chinese Buddhist monk who made an overland trip to India and then traveled throughout the subcontinent.

Hsüan-Chuang was born in the town on Chin-liu, the youngest of four sons. His father was a member of the Mandarin class of officials who governed China. It is said that Hsüan-Chuang started reading the sacred Buddhist texts at the age of eight. One of his older brothers was a Buddhist monk who was impressed by Hsüan-Chuang's studiousness and had him brought to his monastery in the city of Luo-yang on the Yellow River. He did so well that he was one of only 14 students nationwide who were selected to study at the monastery on a full scholarship.

At the fall of the Sui dynasty in 618, China experienced a period of strife and upheaval. In order to escape this, Hsüan-Chang went to the new capital of the T'ang dynasty (618-906) at

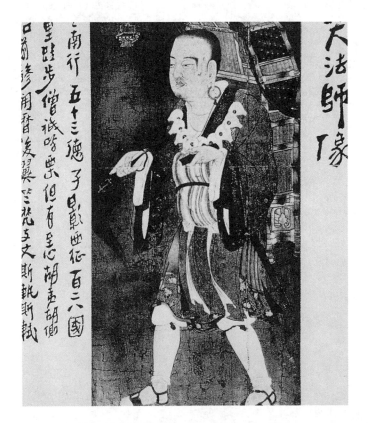

Hsüan-Chuang. The Granger Collection, New York.

Ch'ang-an. Unable to find the peace he sought, he traveled on to Ch'eng-tu, where he found the calm and prosperity he had been searching for. He was ordained a full monk at the monastery at Ch'eng-tu at the age of 20. He then returned to Ch'ang-an. Taking advantage of the improved conditions in the country as the T'ang Emperor established control, Hsüan-Chuang decided that he wanted to follow the example of **Fa-Hsien** and travel to Western countries to discuss Buddhist texts with learned men abroad. In the account that he wrote years later, he said that his aim was to "travel to the countries of the west in order to question the wise men on the points that were troubling his mind."

Hsüan-Chuang started his trip from the city of Sian in 629. He traveled to Liang-chou, where he served as a "guest lecturer" at a monastery. Told by the governor that he could not travel to the West, he ignored the order and slipped out of town with the aid of two monks. At the frontier he was stopped by border guards on several occasions, but each time they allowed him to pass and told him of a detour around the last and most dangerous guard post. This detour sent him and his horse into the southern Gobi Desert. In the desert he lost his way and then dropped his water bag. According to the chronicles, he traveled four nights and five days without water until his horse found his way to a spring. They made it safely to the caravan town of Hami.

From Hami, Hsüan-Chuang was escorted by an honor guard sent by the King of Turfan, in what is now Chinese Turkestan. The King of Turfan was a devout Buddhist and wanted to keep the eminent monk at his court. When Hsüan-Chuang declined the offer, the King supplied him with horses, provisions, money, and letters of introduction to the countries he was going to visit. Traveling by way of the oases of Kharashahr and Kucha, the following spring Hsüan-Chuang crossed the Tien Shan Mountains and descended to the Issyk-Kul lake in what is now the Republic of Kyrghyzstan. There he met the Khan of the Western Turks, who was pleased to receive the Chinese monk. He traveled through the Khan's capital of Tashkent and the city of Samarkand and then through the Iron Gates to Bactria (modern Afghanistan). He visited the city of Balkh, where there were many famous relics of the Buddha.

Crossing the Hindu Kush Mountains, Hsüan-Chuang arrived in Bamian, where he saw a Buddha 140-150 feet high, carved out of stone. During the summer of 630, he traveled down the Kabul River through the city of Peshawar to Taxila (now ruins near the Pakistani capital of Islamabad). He went to Srinigar, the capital of Kashmir, where the chronicle says that the King and his minsters and 1,000 monks came out to meet him. He stayed in

Srinigar and studied Buddhist texts with nine monks, each expert in a different field, until early 633.

In eastern Punjab, Hsüan-Chuang and his party were assaulted by 50 bandits, and only escaped because Hsüan-Chuang was able to slip away to get help. He traveled on to the headwaters of the Ganges, the sacred river of India. Stopping at Kannauj, he stayed there for three months studying with a famous Buddhist master. Sailing down the Ganges to Kanpur, his boat was captured by pirates who wanted to sacrifice Hsüan-Chuang to their god. As he was preparing to die, the pirate boats were hit by a cyclone and destroyed, and they released him before even worse things happened.

In the vicinity of Allahabad and Varanasi, Hsüan-Chuang visited the sacred sites where the historical Buddha had lived in what had once been the Kingdom of Magadha. At the village of Kasia, he saw the place where the Buddha had entered Nirvana (a kind of heaven). At the great monastery of Nalanda, Hsüan-Chuang stayed for five years from 633 to 637 studying the sacred texts.

After leaving the monastery, Hsüan-Chuang continued down the Ganges to the port of Tamralipti. From there he sailed down the east coast of India and visited south India and Maharastra. He returned north and stopped at Nalanda again and then spent some time nearby studying non-religious subjects, such as mathematics and geography, with a famous teacher. He was sent to Gauhati, the capital of Assam, to convert the King to Buddhism. Back in Nalanda he took leave of the monks and headed back to his native country in 643. He crossed the Thar Desert to reach the Indus River. Crossing the Indus, he made it across

safely on the back of an elephant, but the monk following him who was carrying many of his manuscripts and a collection of rare seeds was swept away. The monk survived but not his cargo.

Crossing the high mountains into central Asia, Hsüan-Chuang faced many hazards. He survived blizzards and storms and the death of his elephant, who drowned while fleeing an attack of bandits. Hsüan-Chuang succeeded in reaching Kashgar in what is now the westernmost part of China and Hetien, the capital of the Buddhist kingdom of Khotan. The King of Khotan came out to greet him, and he spent seven or eight months there lecturing on what he had learned during his pilgrimage. He finally arrived back in Sian in the spring of 645.

Hsüan-Chuang had arrived back in China with 150 Buddhist relics, six statues and more than 650 religious texts after a journey of 40,000 miles. The Emperor ordered him to write about his experiences. He had completed this book, *Ta-T'ang Si-Yu-Ki* (Memoirs on Western Countries), by the time he died in 649.

Where to learn more

The original texts on Hsüan-Chuang's journey can be found in Shaman Hui Li, *The Life of Hiuen-tsang* (London: 1911) and Samuel Beal, translator and editor, *Buddhist Records of the Western World, Translated from the Chinese of Hiuen Tsiang (A.D. 629)* (London: Kegan Paul, Trench, Trübner & Co., 1906; reprinted, New York: Paragon, 1968). These two sources are combined in Jeannette Mirsky, *The Great Chinese Travelers* (New York: Random House, 1964).

There are studies of Hsüan-Chuang in Sir Aurel Stein, "The Desert Crossing of Hsüan-tsang, 630 A.D." *Indian Antiquary*, vol. 50, pp. 15-25 and Arthur Waley, *The Real Tripitaka* (London: George Allen & Unwin, 1952).

Evariste Régis Huc

(1813-1860)

Evariste Régis Huc was a French missionary who traveled with a fellow priest from Beijing to Tibet.

In the fall of 1844 two French Catholic missionaries who were working in China, Father Evariste Régis Huc and Father Joseph Gabet, decided to extend their mission into Tibet. They disguised themselves as Mongolian lamas (they spoke both Chinese and Mongol) and headed west from Beijing.

On the way they went through the Great Imperial Forest, where only the Emperor was allowed to hunt, and which, as a consequence was a kind of wildlife preserve with a large population of tigers, panthers, bears, and wolves. They traveled through the Ordos Desert in Inner Mongolia and lived with Mongols and "Tartars" before reaching the great lake of Koko Nor in far western China. The two missionaries stayed there until October 1845 when they joined the great ambassadorial caravan traveling from China to Tibet.

The caravan traveled through great mountain ranges stopping to rest at Buddhist monasteries along the way. They crossed the frozen Yangtze River where they saw yaks frozen in the ice. Father Gabet almost died from the extreme cold, but they reached Lhasa, capital of Tibet, safely on January 29, 1846.

Once in Lhasa, Huc and Gabet were given a house in which to live where they set up a small chapel. They were not allowed to teach their religion however, and within two months the Chinese ambassador, worried about their influence, was able to have them expelled. They left Lhasa in March 1846 with a Tibetan escort and traveled through the high mountains of eastern Tibet and western China. They had difficulty crossing the upper courses of the great Salween and Mekong rivers and an exciting time crossing a high glacier: "We seated ourselves carefully on the edge of the glacier, we stuck our heels together on the ice, as firmly as possible, then using the handles of our whips by way of helm, we sailed over these frozen waters with the velocity of a locomotive."

After crossing the Yangtze, they entered China proper and made their way to the Portuguese colony of Macau on the south coast of China in October 1846. Huc traveled on his own from

Evariste Régis Huc. The Granger Collection, New York.

Macau to Beijing in the years 1848-1849. He then wrote an account of his travels that was translated into English by a famous author, William Hazlitt, as *Travels in Tartary, Thibet and China*. This book was the source of most of the information and misinformation that Europeans had about Tibet until the end of the nineteenth century.

Where to learn more

Huc wrote two books pertinent to his Tibet adventures: *Christianity in China, Tartary and Tibet*, 2 vols. (Peking: Lazarist Press, 1857) and *Travels in Tartary, Thibet and China, 1844-1846*, translated by William Hazlitt and edited by Paul Pelliot, 2 vols. (London: 1928).

A modern narrative of Huc's travels can be found in John MacGregor, *Tibet: A Chronicle of Exploration* (London: Routledge & Kegan Paul, 1970).

Henry Hudson

(? - 1611)

Henry Hudson was an English navigator who led two expeditions to North America to search for the Northwest Passage and explored the Hudson River and Hudson Bay.

Nothing is known about the early life and career of Henry Hudson. In 1607 he was hired by the Muscovy Company of England to search for the Northeast Passage around the north coast of Siberia to China. He explored the coast of the Svalbard Islands and rediscovered Jan Mayen Island east of Greenland but did not find a sea passage to the east. He was sent out again in 1608 but this time had to turn back because of heavy ice without making any new discoveries.

In 1609 Hudson was hired by the Dutch East India Company to look for the Northeast Passage once again. He sailed the *Half Moon* with a mixed crew of English and Dutch. Beyond North Cape in Norway the ship ran into heavy ice, and the crew refused to go any farther. Instead of returning to Holland, Hudson

Henry Hudson.

decided to try to find the Northwest Passage to Asia instead and he headed for the coast of North America. It is said that he headed there because his friend **John Smith** had told him of a large bay that might lead to a Northwest Passage.

The *Half Moon* reached the coast of Nova Scotia in July 1609 and headed south as far as Chesapeake Bay. It then turned north and explored Delaware Bay. Heading back north, Hudson sailed to Sandy Hook at the entrance to New York harbor on September 12, 1609. **Giovanni da Verrazzano** had already discovered the entrance to the harbor in 1524 but had not explored any farther. Hudson sailed up the large river that now has his name as far as the site of Albany, and some of his crew members rowed a boat even farther north. By a coincidence the Frenchman **Samuel de Champlain** was exploring Lake Champlain at the same time and the two great explorers came close to meeting.

On his voyage up and down the Hudson River the explorer noted how rich the land was and how much opportunity there would be for a prosperous fur trade. His report inspired the Dutch to form a new company, The Dutch West India Company, which founded the colony of New Netherland in 1614. Hudson had a couple of uneasy encounters with Native Americans, and one of his crew members was killed by an arrow through the throat. Relations improved, however, when Hudson started trading European goods for food. The *Half Moon* stayed for several days in New York Harbor on "that side of the river that is called Manna-hata" before heading back across the Atlantic.

On its return to Europe, the *Half Moon* stopped in the English port of Dartmouth on November 7, 1609. The English authorities took Hudson and all the English crew members off the ship, and they were forbidden to work for a foreign country again. As a result, Hudson interested a group of English investors in supporting an expedition to the north of his previous voyage to find the Northwest Passage.

Hudson sailed on his next voyage of exploration on April 17, 1610 in the ship *Discovery*. Almost immediately there were signs of trouble among the crew members, and Hudson does not seem to have been able to control the discord. In June they sighted Resolution Island which separates Davis Strait, discovered by **John Davis**, from what is now called Hudson Strait. In fact, the strait had already been discovered by **Sir Martin Frobisher** in 1578. But Hudson was the first one to sail through it—a voyage that took six weeks.

Hudson and his crew rounded Cape Wolstenholme, named after one of the voyage's backers, and entered into Hudson Bay.

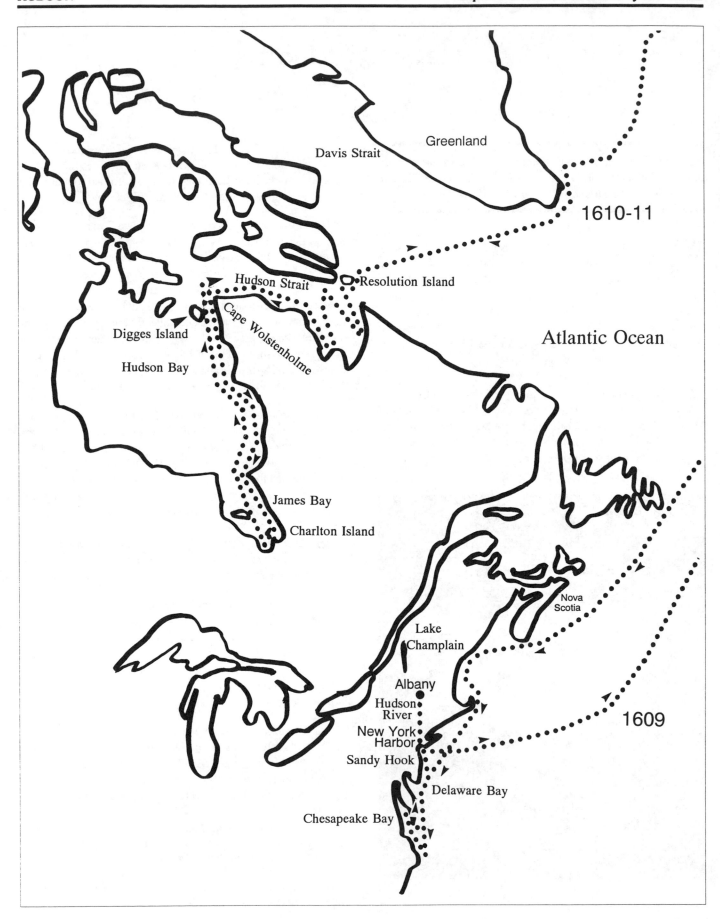

Hudson's voyages to New York and upper Canada.

The optimistic Hudson thought that like Magellan he had sailed from the Atlantic to the Pacific and headed enthusiastically to the south. However, he ended up in the dead-end now known as James Bay. By this time, it was October and the Bay was beginning to ice up so that the Englishmen were forced to spend the winter there. Because of Hudson's lack of foresight, they did not have enough provisions, and they spent a very difficult season. Although they made contact with some nearby Native Americans, they were unable to trade with them. The crew members spent the winter of 1610-1611 fighting among themselves.

On June 12, 1611 the ice had melted enough for the *Discovery* to sail towards home. It had only gotten as far as Charlton Island in the southern part of James Bay on June 23 when the crew members mutinied against Hudson. On the morning of June 24 they put Hudson, his 19-year-old son John and six of the weaker crew members on a small boat and set them adrift. They were never seen or heard of again.

The *Discovery* sailed north through Hudson Bay piloted by **Robert Bylot**. It anchored at Digges Island at the entrance to Hudson Bay. There they fought with a party of Inuit, and the mutiny's ringleader, Henry Greene, and several others were killed. The remainder were able to make it to southern Ireland where they were rescued and taken to London. Of the eight survivors none were ever convicted of any charges.

Where to learn more

The records of Hudson's voyages are found in G.M. Asher, ed. *Henry Hudson the Navigator: The Original Documents in Which His Career is Recorded, Collected, Partly Translated, and Annotated* (London: Hakluyt Society, 1860). There is one complete biography of Hudson in English: Llewellyn Powys, *Henry Hudson* (New York, 1928). There are chapters on Hudson in: Jeannette Mirsky, *To the Arctic!: The Story of Northern Exploration from Earliest Times to the Present* (New York: Alfred A. Knopf, 1948; Leslie Neatby, *In Quest of the Northwest Passage* (Toronto: 1958); and Ernest S. Dodge, *Northwest by Sea* (New York: 1961).

Alexander von Humboldt

(1769 - 1859)

Alexander von Humboldt, a German scientist, made an expedition to South America with his companion Aimé Bonpland that included a trip up the Orinoco River and across the Andes and that collected a wealth of scientific information.

Alexander von Humboldt was born in Berlin, then the capital of Prussia, on September 14, 1769. Humboldt's father was a nobleman and a major in the army of Frederick the Great, King of Prussia. His mother came from a wealthy family that was descended from French Huguenots who had escaped from France during the persecutions of Protestants by King Louis XIV.

Humboldt's father died in 1779. His education was in the hands of his cosmopolitan mother who hired private tutors and then sent him to the best school in Berlin. He attended the University of Frankfurt-an-der-Oder for six months and then

Alexander von Humboldt. The Granger Collection, New York.

transferred to the University of Berlin, where he developed a passionate interest in botany. After a year in Berlin, he joined his older brother Wilhelm (later a famous linguistics scholar) at the University of Göttingen. He studied under Georg Forster, who had been a naturalist on Captain **James Cook**'s second expedition around the world. While at Göttingen he made his first scientific expedition, a field trip up the Rhine River. He also accompanied Forster on a trip to England where he met the most famous political and scientific men of the day.

In 1790 Humboldt entered the School of Mines in Freiburg in southern Germany. Even though he did not graduate, he was able to get a job in the Mining Department of the Prussian Government where he worked for five years. One of his assignments was to travel to the Alps and the Carpathians and write reports on the mining industries of other countries. He also spent his time studying other fields of science, carrying out experiments with electricity and making the acquaintance of such luminaries as Johann Wolfgang von Goethe and Friedrich Schiller.

At the beginning of 1797, Humboldt's life reached a crisis. He was devastated when a fellow student, to whom he had a passionate attachment, got married and when, shortly after, his mother died of breast cancer. Left with a large fortune, Humboldt decided to use the money to travel, and he wandered rather aimlessly around Europe. He ended up in Paris and twice planned to make trips to Egypt but was stopped by Napoleon's invasion of that country in 1798. Determined to get there one way or another, Humboldt accidentally met Aimé Bonpland, a young French doctor who was an amateur botanist. Bonpland also wanted to got to Egypt. Together the two set out for the Mediterranean seaport of Marseilles.

Once in Marseilles they were unable to board the ship. (Britain and France were at war, and the Royal Navy was blockading French ports.) They then decided to walk to Spain, where they hoped they would have better luck in getting transportation. In Madrid they made use of various of Humboldt's connections to meet Spanish officials. Humboldt even had an audience with the Spanish King in March 1799. King Carlos IV authorized them to travel to Spanish America and commanded all royal officials to come to their assistance. The Spanish overseas empire was still generally closed to foreigners and, despite the expeditions of **Charles-Marie de La Condamine** and **Hipólito Ruiz**, there was little scientific knowledge of the area.

Humboldt and Bonpland sailed from the Spanish port of La Coruña on June 5, 1799. On July 16, 1799 they landed at Cumaná east of Caracas on the coast of Venezuela. In Cumaná

Expeditions of Humboldt and Bonpland in South America, 1799-1800 and 1801-1802.

they waited until the end of the rainy season. They spent their time collecting specimens of plant and animal life and examining traces of a recent earthquake. In November 1799 they went to Caracas, where they prepared for their expedition to the Orinoco River. Their aim was to travel to the Orinoco and see just how it connected to the Amazon river system, a phenomenon that La Condamine had reported on.

The two scientists left Caracas on February 7, 1800. To reach the Orinoco it was necessary to cross the llanos, a tropical grassland that was practically a desert during the dry season and was covered with water during the rainy season. The annual mean temperature on the llanos is 90°F, one of the highest in the world. Despite the heat and discomfort, Humboldt and Bonpland encountered many natural phenomena that they found fascinating. In the little cattle town of Calabozo, Humboldt investigated an electric fish, *Eletrophorus electricus*, that can produce currents of up to 650 volts, enough to kill a horse. Electricity had always been a subject of interest to Humboldt, and he was fascinated by the animals. He accidentally stepped on one of the fish after it had been taken from the water, and he got a jolt that produced "a violent pain in the knees, and in almost every joint" for the rest of the day.

In March 1800 the travelers reached the little town and mission station of San Fernando de Apuré on the Apuré River, a tributary of the Orinoco. On March 30 they set sail down the Apuré in a large dugout canoe furnished by the Capuchin monks from the mission. It took them six days to reach the Orinoco and then they started rowing up river. They suffered terribly from hordes of insects that pursued them, but they also saw much exotic wildlife.

On April 6, they reached one of the three islands in the Orinoco where turtles lay their eggs in the sand. They were in time to see the turtle eggs being harvested by several hundred Native Americans, who came from great distances to collect the eggs in order to make turtle oil. Humboldt estimated that there were about 500,000 female turtles laying eggs along the Orinoco, and each one laid about 100 eggs.

On April 17, 1800 Humboldt and Bonpland reached the mission station of La Concepción de Urbana. By then the river had narrowed, and their guides no longer knew the way. They purchased a new canoe and took on board Father Bernardo Zea, a missionary who knew the Orinoco well and was quite happy to accompany the explorers. From that point on, the trip was increasingly difficult, with more and greater rapids. In May they reached the mission of San Antonio de Yavita. There they hired Native Americans to drag their canoe across the narrow neck of land that separated the Orinoco river system from that of the Rio Negro, a tributary of the Amazon. On their way back, Humboldt and Bonpland used the 180-mile-long Casiquiare Canal to return to the Orinoco. This is the only place in the world where two great river systems are joined by a natural canal.

Once back on the Orinoco, they traveled upstream to the mission station of Esmeralda, the farthest reach of Christianity. Bonpland and Humboldt both became ill with typhoid fever, and they started back down the river on May 23, 1800. By the time they reached Angostura (source of Angostura bitters and now called Ciudad Bolivar) on June 13, Bonpland's life was threatened. He was sick for a month. On his recovery he fell in love with a mestiza woman and left Humboldt for a while to pursue her into the interior. The two were reunited in November. This was the end of the Orinoco expedition. Besides confirming and mapping the Casiquiare Canal, they had disproved age-old rumors of the vast Lake Parima in the interior and had collected 12,000 plant specimens, although a third of them had been ruined by the humidity.

Humboldt and Bonpland returned to Cumaná, where they boarded a ship to take them to Cuba at the end of November 1800. They had planned to travel from there to North America, but changed their minds and headed back south again in April 1801. From the port of Cartagena in Colombia, Humboldt and Bonpland set off up the Magdalena River in April 1801. It took them six weeks to reach Bogotá. When they reached the point where the boat could go no farther, they rode mules and horses to climb the Andes to Bogotá. There, their main goal was to visit the famous Spanish naturalist **José Celestino Mutis**, who showed them some of the items in his collection of 20,000 plants and gave Humboldt 100 botanical drawings.

On September 8, 1801 they were on their way to Quito, via the snow-covered Quindiu Pass. They reached Quito on January 6, 1802 and spent several months there. Humboldt developed the desire to climb to the top of Mount Chimborazo, a volcanic mountain south of Quito that had never been climbed. Chimborazo is 20,577 feet above sea level and was practically impossible to climb in the days before oxygen equipment existed.

Humboldt prepared for the climb by climbing Pichincha, 15,672 feet. He left for Chimborazo on June 9, 1802 and started the climb on June 23, accompanied by Bonpland and the son of the provincial governor. The first 6,000 feet of the climb were not too difficult, but thereafter the path became steeper and more dangerous. At the snowline, 7,000 feet from the summit, their porters left them, and the three Europeans (and a mestizo boy) were left to finish the climb themselves. Their progress was impeded by snow, ice, and low-lying clouds. In addition, the climbers began to suffer from soroche or mountain sickness—nausea and dizziness, and bleeding from the eyes, lips, and gums. They kept going until, little more than 1,000 feet from the

summit, they found themselves on the brink of a vast ravine that was impossible to cross. Although they did not reach the top, Humboldt calculated that they had climbed to 19,286 feet—which remained a world record for nearly 30 years. On the way back down they were hit by a hailstorm and then a blizzard. Many years later, just before his death at the age of 90, Humboldt sat for a last portrait. He asked that the background be Mt. Chimborazo.

On their return from the mountain-climbing excursion, Humboldt and Bonpland decided to leave Quito and head for Lima in Peru in order to observe the transit of the planet Mercury across the sun. Along the way, they stopped to investigate Inca ruins at Cañar, and Humboldt made the first accurate drawings of them, so becoming the earliest archeologist of South America.

Near Loja, Bonpland spent his time collecting specimens of the bark of the cinchona tree, which is the source of the medicine quinine, the only known remedy for malaria at the time. The plant was a valuable local commodity, and local hunters collected it in the wild. Humboldt recognized that if this trade was allowed to continue without regulation the plant might one day disappear, and a major natural medicine would no longer be available. This was one of the first recognitions of the need for biodiversity and the protection of species in the tropical rainforest. Fortunately, 50 years later **Richard Spruce** was able to gather specimens and cultivate them.

From the mountains around Loja, Humboldt and Bonpland descended to the little town of Jaén on the Marañon River, the upper course of the Amazon. Humboldt used the occasion to improve on the map La Condamine had made more than 50 years before. After 17 days on the upper Amazon the two men climbed the mountains to Cajamarca where the Inca Atahualpa had surrendered to **Francisco Pizarro**. When they descended to the coast at Trujillo they encountered the desert that makes up the narrow coastal plain of Peru in front of the Andes. Humboldt started investigating the reasons why the coast was so dry. He established that it was caused by the cold current that flows north along the shores of Peru, which was named the Humboldt Current in his honor. He also identified guano, the remains of bird droppings that were to become the world's main source of phosphate fertilizers.

Humboldt and Bonpland arrived in Lima on October 22, 1802. Two weeks later they observed the transit of Mercury. On January 2, 1803, Humboldt and Bonpland boarded a ship bound for Acapulco, Mexico. They stayed in Mexico until March 1804 when they sailed to Cuba. From Cuba they sailed to the United States, where they spent three months as the guests of President Thomas Jefferson at Monticello. They sailed for France in July 1804.

On their arrival in Europe, they were received as heroes, having caught the popular imagination through the descriptions of South America that Humboldt had written in letters to friends in Europe. After their return, Bonpland got a job as the superintendent of the gardens of Napoleon's wife Josephine. After her death in 1814, he went to Buenos Aires and became the director of a museum. While on a collecting expedition, he was captured by soldiers of the Paraguayan dictator José Francia and held captive for nine years. He was finally released after numerous entreaties by Humboldt and others and retired to a small town in Uruguay where he raised a family with a local woman.

Humboldt lived in Paris for many years after his return, working on the vast amount of data he had brought back from South America. He interrupted his work for a short time in 1815 to serve as a representative to the Congress of Vienna, where treaties were negotiated to end the Napoleonic Wars. Humboldt wrote 30 volumes using his South American material. Having spent much of his fortune on the South American expedition and in publishing his books, he accepted a court appointment and returned to Berlin in 1827. He organized one of the world's first international scientific congress in 1828. In 1829, at the age of 60, he made an expedition across Russia and Siberia to the Yenisei River. In 1845, at the age of 76, he started work on a book called *Kosmos*, which was supposed to be a comprehensive account of the physical structure of the universe. Four volumes of *Kosmos* had appeared by the time he died at the age of 90 in May 1859, and one was published after his death. He never married.

Where to learn more

Humboldt was an enormously prolific writer. Of his many volumes, several have direct bearing on his South American experiences. The first volumes to appear were written in French. The English translation by Helen Maria Williams appeared a few years later as *Personal Narrative of Travels to the Equinoctial Regions of the New Continent During the Years 1799-1804*, 6 vols. (London: 1814; Philadelphia: M. Carey, 1815; reprinted, London: Bohn's Library, 1850). The main body of the Andean researches is included in *Researches Concerning the Institutions and Monuments of the Ancient Inhabitants of America*, 2 vols. (London: Longmans, 1814). *Views of Nature, or Contemplation on the Sublime Phenomena of Creation*, translated from the German by E.C. Otté and H.G. Bohn (London: George Bell & Sons, 1828) contains Humboldt's later reflections on his journey and *Examen critique de l'histoire de la géographie du nouveau continent*, 5 vols. (Paris: 1836-1839) is an attempt to come up with a systematic natural history of the Americas.

In addition to the books he published, a later volume, E.T. Hamy, ed. *Lettres américaines d'Alexandre d'Humboldt (1787-1807)* (Paris: Librairie Orientale et Américaine, 1905) is said to be "indispensable" for anyone wanting to study the South American journey in depth.

During the 19th century, there were numerous biographies written about Humboldt. The one that is considered the best and most useful is Karl C. Bruhns, *Life of Alexander von Humboldt*, 2 vols. (London: 1873). More recent biographies that are recommended are: Helmut de Terra, *Humboldt: The Life and Times of Alexander von Humboldt, 1769-1859* (New York: Alfred A. Knopf, 1955), written by a geologist; Charlotte Kellner, *Alexander von Humboldt* (London: Oxford University Press, 1963), written by a physicist; Douglas Botting, *Humboldt and the Cosmos* (New York: Harper & Row, 1973), a shorter biography; and Val Gendron, *The Dragon Tree: A Life of Alexander von Humboldt* (New York: Longmans, 1961), which is intended for young readers.

A very useful book for the non-specialist is Victor Wolfgang von Hagen, *South America Called Them: Explorations of the Great Naturalists* (Boston: Little, Brown & Company, 1955). The chapters on Humboldt served as the main source for this account.

Alexander Hamilton Hume

(1797-1873)

Alexander Hamilton Hume was an Australian explorer who was one of the first to pioneer the country outside of Sydney. He discovered the Murray River and explored the overland route between Sydney and Melbourne.

Alexander Hamilton Hume was the eldest son of one of the superintendents who governed the British convict colony of New South Wales. Hume was born at Parramatta, New South Wales, on June 19, 1797, just nine years after the colony had been founded. The British were frustrated in their attempt to expand the colony because it was surrounded by very rugged terrain that made it difficult to expand. It was only in 1813 that **Gregory Blaxland** found a trail through the rugged terrain surrounding Sydney.

Hume began exploring at the age of 17 from the family's home at Appin, south of Sydney and about 20 miles from the coast. On his first few trips, Hume went southwest to an area about 50 miles from his home. In 1818 the colony's Governor asked him to become an official government guide for the various expeditions the Governor was sponsoring. Hume traveled 95 miles southwest of Sydney with James Meehan in 1817, went to Goulburn and Lake Bathurst with Meehan and Charles Throsby in 1818, and to Jervis Bay, on the south coast of New South Wales, with **John Oxley**, Meehan, and Throsby in 1819. In 1821 he explored the Yass Plains, near the present Australian capital of Canberra, and followed this in 1822 with an examination of the land bordering the Clyde River, south of Port Jervis.

By this time, the Governor had decided that there was no major access route to the interior and sharply cut back his support for exploration. Hume settled down on his farm in Appin and made the acquaintance of retired sea captain William Hovell. The two came up with a scheme to travel overland to Spencer Gulf, the large body of water that cuts into the interior of South Australia. Hovell and Hume shared the costs, and the government furnished them with some second-hand camping equipment.

Hume and Hovell left from the farthest of Hume's outstations on October 17, 1824. They traveled for sixteen weeks, and made many important discoveries, including the Murray River, the largest river in interior Australia. As a result of a quarrel, they changed their course along the way so that they were no longer headed for Spencer Gulf. They also disagreed about most other aspects of the expedition, and this quarrel lasted long after the expedition was over. They came upon salt water on December 16 at Corio Bay, the site of the present-day city of Geelong, not far from Melbourne. They returned to New South Wales and reported back on the fine pasture land they had found. Unfortunately, through a navigational error, they thought they had reached the sea at Westernport, which is actually about 50 miles east of Corio Bay. When the government sent settlers to Westernport, they found it to be a very desolate area and they blamed Hume and Hovell for their travails.

Hume received a grant of 1,200 acres for his efforts, but he was forced to sell it to pay for the accumulated expenses of the expedition. He then withdrew to his pastoral property near Yass, briefly coming out of retirement to blaze a new road over the Blue Mountains in 1828 and to act as assistant to **Charles Sturt** in 1828-1829 on the expedition that discovered the Darling River in the State of Queensland.

Hume increased his holdings over the years and became a very wealthy landowner in New South Wales. In his later years he got involved in a very lengthy quarrel with Hovell over who did what and who was responsible for what in their joint 1824 expedition to what is now the State of Victoria. Hume died at Yass on April 19, 1873, by which time almost all of Australia had been explored. The main highway between Sydney and Melbourne, which follows his route south, is named the Hume Highway.

Where to learn more

The records of Hume and Hovell's expedition are found in W. Bland, ed. *Journey of Discovery to Port Phillip* (Sydney: 1831). Excerpts can be found in Kathleen Fitzpatrick, *Australian Explorers: A Selection from Their Writings* (London: Oxford University Press, 1958).

There is no full-length biography of Hume. The best accounts are two articles in the *Journal of the Royal Australian Historical Society*: Ernest Scott, "Hume and Hovell's Journey to Port Phillip," vol 7 (1921) and F. O'Grady, "Hamilton Hume," vol. 49 (1963), pp. 337-359.

Wilson Price Hunt

(1782 - 1842)

Robert Stuart

(1785 - 1848)

American Wilson Price Hunt and Canadian Robert Stuart were two employees of John Jacob Astor's fur company who pioneered the route through the northwestern United States that was to become known as the Oregon Trail.

Wilson Price Hunt was born in Hopewell, New Jersey and moved to St. Louis in 1804. He went to work for John Jacob Astor in 1809. Astor was a rich New York businessman who was trying to organize the fur trade with the Pacific Northwest. In 1810 Astor sent Hunt to Montreal to engage fur trappers for an expedition to the Columbia River to trap for furs. Hunt then returned with his men to Missouri and spent the winter of 1810-1811 at a camp near present-day St. Joseph, Missouri. On April 21, 1811 they left the camp and headed up the Missouri River.

At the head of his "Overland Astorians" Hunt reached the villages of the Arikara tribe in June 1811. There he traded for horses with the Spanish trader Manuel Lisa and headed out on July 18, accompanied by 61 men and 82 horses. Avoiding the dangerous Blackfoot country to the north, Hunt and his men headed due west through what is now South Dakota, southeast Montana, and across Wyoming to the Wind River and then across the Rocky Mountains near Jackson Hole to the headwaters of the Snake River in Idaho.

When he reached the Snake, Hunt decided to let the horses go and to float down the river. But it proved impossible because of the numerous rapids and obstructions and the party was forced to walk overland, splitting up into smaller groups along the way. They almost starved as a result and had to live on skins and roots. The first of the party reached Astoria at the mouth of the Columbia River on January 18, 1812 and Hunt himself did not show up until February 15. In spite of their difficulties, however, they had pioneered the western part of what was to become the Oregon Trail.

Hunt became involved in trading ventures by sea with the Russians to the north in Alaska and with Hawaii and China. He returned to St. Louis in 1814 and went into business and politics

there until his death in 1842. In the meantime, another employee of Astor's, Robert Stuart, had reached Astoria by sea. Stuart was a native of Scotland who had moved to Montreal in 1807. He traveled to Astoria on board the *Tonquin*, which arrived in March 1811 and was chosen to lead the trip back overland at the head of what was called the "Returning Astorians."

Stuart left Astoria with six men on June 29, 1812. They went over the Blue Mountains of eastern Oregon to the Snake River, which, like Hunt, they found very difficult to navigate. They then crossed the Grand Tetons to Jackson Hole in the reverse direction that Hunt had taken. They almost starved until they stumbled upon a stray buffalo that they were able to shoot and kill. They then traveled south of where Hunt had gone and on October 23, 1812 came upon South Pass which was to become the eastern half of the Oregon Trail.

From South Pass Stuart and his party rested by the Sweetwater River and then traveled in December to the Platte River in western Nebraska where they spent the rest of the winter. They arrived in St. Louis on April 30, 1813 where they received a heroes' welcome. They were the first Americans to cross North America after Lewis and Clark. Stuart reported back to Astor in New York, and then was put in charge of fur-trading posts in northern Michigan. He settled in Detroit where he became one of the city's most influential residents until his death in 1848 following a sudden illness.

Where to learn more

The book that made Hunt and Stuart famous was Washington Irving's story of their adventures as part of his book *Astoria, or Anecdotes of an Enterprise Beyond the Rocky Mountains*, 2 vols. (Philadelphia: 1836; reprinted, Norman: University of Oklahoma Press, 1964). There are a couple of editions of Robert Stuart's reports: Philip Ashton Rollins, ed. *Discovery of the Oregon Trail, Robert Stuart's Narratives* (New York: 1935) and Kenneth Spaulding, ed. *On the Oregon Trail: Robert Stuart's Journey of Discovery* (Norman: University of Oklahoma Press, 1953).

There is a good account of Hunt and Stuart in an excellent history of the exploration of the American West: William H. Goetzmann, *Exploration and Empire: The Explorer and the Scientist in the Winning of the American West* (New York: Alfred A. Knopf, 1966). There is a short biography of Hunt by William Brandon in LeRoy R. Hafen and Harvey L. Carter, eds. *Mountain Men and Fur Traders of the Far West* (Lincoln: University of Nebraska Press, 1982).

Abu Abdallah Ibn Battuta

(1304 - 1369)

Ibn Battuta, a native of Morocco, was the greatest traveler of the Middle Ages, eventually covering some 75,000 miles in Africa and Asia.

Abu Abdallah Ibn Battuta was a Berber, born in the city of Tangier, Morocco, on February 25, 1304. He was born into a family of Muslim legal scholars. A very devout Muslim himself, he left his birthplace at the age of 22 soon after finishing his studies. On June 14, 1325 he set out to make the *hajj*, the pilgrimage to Mecca and Medina that is required of Muslims who can afford it. "I set out alone, with neither companion to delight in nor caravan to accompany, my sole inspiration coming from an uncontrollable impulse and a desire long-cherished in my bosom to visit the holy places," he wrote in his memoirs.

It took Ibn Battuta ten months to cross North Africa, passing through what are now Algeria, Tunisia, and Libya, before arriving in Alexandria, the main port of Egypt. There he saw the Pharos at Alexandria, a giant lighthouse in the harbor that was one of the Seven Wonders of the Ancient World. He traveled to the nearby retreat of a famous mystic where he had a dream that he was on the wing of a giant bird that took him to Mecca and then flew him on to the east to a "dark and greenish" country.

From Cairo, Ibn Battuta traveled up the Nile River to Aswan and then overland to the port of Aidhab on the Red Sea. From there, he had planned to take a ship across the Red Sea to the Arabian port of Jeddah. However, he arrived at a time when a local rebellion in progress, and none of the ships were leaving the harbor. He was forced to return to Cairo and from there set out across the Sinai Peninsula to Jerusalem.

At the time of Ibn Battuta's visit, Jerusalem was a small city of 10,000 people that subsisted by catering to pilgrims of the three great monotheistic religions—Jews, Christians, and Muslims. After seeing the main sights of the Holy Land, Ibn Battuta went to Damascus, where he arrived on August 9, 1326. He studied with some of the famous Islamic scholars in the ancient city and married, apparently for the second time. In the course of his travels he married several times, but his wives drop out of the narrative almost as quickly as they enter it.

Ibn Battuta joined the main pilgrim caravan in September 1326. They journeyed south through Arabia by the Derb-el-Haj, the pilgrim road to Medina and Mecca, on a trip that took 55 days. Ibn Battuta devotes only a short section in his narrative to the performance of the traditional rites in these two cities because they were well known to his Muslim audience. He left Medina in mid-November. Rather than returning home, he headed off to Iraq with a group of pilgrims who were returning to Baghdad.

Ibn Battuta left the caravan and stopped in Najaf in southern Iraq, a holy city for the Shi'ite sect of Islam. From there, he went south to the port of Basra, which had once been a center of Islamic learning but had sadly declined. He made a sidetrip to Persia, visiting the cities of Shiraz and Isfahan. Back in Iraq he went on to Baghdad, which had long been the center of the Islamic world but was then still in ruins after having been sacked by the Mongols in 1258. While waiting for the next *hajj* caravan, he went to Mosul on the Tigris and to the walled city of Diyarbakir in what is now southeastern Turkey. He then returned to Baghdad and joined a caravan headed south for Mecca.

Ibn Battuta stayed in Mecca from September 1327 to the fall of 1330, studying Islamic law. He used this knowledge to finance his future travels: he became an itinerant *qadi*, or Muslim legal scholar. Leaving Mecca, he went to Jeddah where he took a ship sailing down the Red Sea to Yemen and traveled in the interior of that country to Ta'iz and the capital at Sana'a. From the port city of Aden he sailed as a trader across the Gulf of Aden to Zeila in Somalia, which he said was "the dirtiest, most disagreeable, and most stinking town in the world." He sailed down the east coast of Africa to Mombasa and as far south as Kilwa, 600 miles south of the equator in what is now Tanzania.

From east Africa, Ibn Battuta sailed to Oman in Arabia and then went back to Mecca for a third pilgrimage in 1332. From there he wanted to go to India, but went about it from the "back door." He took a ship from Jeddah to Egypt and then traveled up the eastern coast of the Mediterranean to Anatolia (Turkey). He traveled across the Anatolian plateau by an unknown route that included a stay in the trading city of Konya. From Sinope on the Black Sea, he sailed to the Genoese port of Kaffa in the Crimean Peninsula, one of his rare sojourns among Christians.

From the Crimea, Ibn Battuta headed inland through the steppes of what are now southern Russia, entering the domains of the Mongol Özbeg Khan (whose name was later taken by the people of Uzbekistan). At the request of one of the Khan's wives, he accompanied her back to her native city of Constantinople, where he met the Byzantine Emperor Andronicus III. Ibn Battuta stayed in that great city for five weeks and then returned to the Khan's capital at New Sarai on the Volga River. (Today, New Sarai is an archeological site not far from the Russian city of Volgograd, formerly Stalingrad).

By this time, Ibn Battuta had become a wealthy man. Everywhere he went he was welcomed by the princely courts and given presents, including, in many cases, slaves and concubines. He and the entourage he had accumulated along the way traveled across the steppes to Khwarizm south of the Aral Sea. From there they went by camel to Bukhara and Samarkand and stayed with the Khan of Chagatay, another of the Mongol rulers of central Asia. Leaving Samarkand, he and his party went south across the Amu Darya River to Meshed in Persia and then into Afghanistan. They passed through the Hindu Kush Mountains, Ibn Battuta being the first to record their name. He reached the Indus River in September 1335.

Visiting Multan in present-day Pakistan, Ibn Battuta sent word ahead to the court of the great Mughal Emperor in Delhi of his impending arrival. The Emperor, Muhammad Tughluq, was noted for his capriciousness, and Ibn Battuta wrote that "there was no day that the gate of the palace failed to witness alike the elevation of some subject to affluence and the torture and murder of some living soul." The Emperor was, however, also a patron of scholars and Islamic learning, and Ibn Battuta remained at his court for seven years in the capacity of judge and was paid a large salary. Spending lavishly, he fell into debt and was rescued by the Emperor. But he fell out of favor with Tughluq when he visited a local mystic who had offended the Emperor.

Ibn Battuta was put under house arrest for five months and was then called to the Emperor's court—where he was named the head of a mission to travel to the court of the last Mongol ruler of China with 15 returning Chinese emissaries. Unfortunately, the junk carrying the envoys and gifts was wrecked by a violent storm at Calicut, on the south coast of India. Ibn Battuta was left destitute, having lost a child in the disaster. Afraid of returning to Tughluq, he sailed for the Maldive Islands in the Indian Ocean, 400 miles southwest of Sri Lanka, where he was befriended by Queen Khadija. He was given an official post and married and divorced six times in the eight months that he stayed there. He became involved in local politics, however, and was forced to leave in August 1344 for Sri Lanka.

In Sri Lanka Ibn Battuta visited Adam's Peak, a mountain with a large imprint on its summit that Muslim legend says is the footprint of Adam, the first man, as he took his first step on Earth after being cast out of heaven. Traveling up the coast of India, Ibn Battuta's ship was attacked by pirates, and he was once again left destitute. He eventually made it to Bengal and then sailed on board a Chinese junk to Sumatra. He was well received by the Muslim ruler of Samudra on the northeast coast of Sumatra, who gave him a junk and supplies to travel on to China. He left Sumatra in April 1346 and went to Zaiton, or Quanzhou, on the Fujian coast of China, and from there to Sin-Kalan, the Arabic name for Canton.

Ibn Battuta was impressed by Chinese civilization but deplored its "paganism." His itinerary in China is not clear, but he left Canton in the fall of 1346 and returned to the West by way of Sumatra, India, Arabia, Persia, and Damascus, where he saw the results of the great epidemic known as the Black Death. He made another pilgrimage to Mecca in November 1348 and then went back to Egypt. He took a boat along the North African coast and reached Fez in Morocco on November 8, 1349. He returned to his hometown of Tangier, where he learned that his mother had died a few months previously. He was 45 years old and had been away for 24 years.

Soon after his return, Ibn Battuta went to the northern city of Ceuta (now part of Spain) and then joined a military expedition that was being sent to defend the Muslim fortress of Gibraltar from a Christian army. Following the successful defense, he traveled in southern Spain, which was still a Muslim kingdom, and visited the cities of Malaga and Granada.

In 1352 Ibn Battuta set out with a camel caravan that was headed southwards through the Atlas Mountains across the Sahara Desert. It took them 25 days to reach the salt mines of Terhazza, in what is now Mali. From there, he visited the trading center of Timbuktu and left one of the earliest written records of its growth, about 100 years before it reached the peak of its prosperity. On his return, Ibn Battuta went eastward into what is now Niger and then turned north to the Al-Haggar Mountains of southern Algeria. He arrived back in Fez in January 1354. It is estimated that in the course of his lifetime he had traveled at least 75,000 miles, not counting detours.

On Ibn Battuta's return to Morocco, the Sultan provided him with a secretary to help him write down and edit the narrative of his travels. This took about two years, and the *Rihla*, or travel book, was ready in December 1355. In it he proclaimed that of all the lands that he had seen, his native Morocco was superior to all others. Ibn Battuta spent the rest of his life as a judge somewhere in the region of Fez. He died in 1369 at the age of 64.

Where to learn more

Ibn Battuta's *Rihla* has the formal name of *A Gift to the Observers Concerning the Curiosities of the Cities and Marvels Encountered in Travels*. Five manuscript copies (none of them complete) were found in the middle of the 19th century by French soldiers in Algeria. They are now housed in the Bibliothèque Nationale in Paris. Using these as a source, two French scholars, C. Défrémery and B.R. Sanguinetti, published an Arabic text and French translation in four volumes between 1853 and 1858, *Voyages d'Ibn Battuta*. These have recently been reprinted (Vincent Monteil, ed. (Paris: 1979)). Using this version as the base, translations have been made into several other languages. The first English translation was an abridged edition made by H.A.R. Gibb, *Ibn Battuta: Travels in Asia and Africa* (London: 1929; reprinted, London: 1983). Gibb then started work on a complete English translation, of which the first three volumes have appeared, while four more are in preparation: *The Travels of Ibn Battuta A.D. 1325-1354* (Cambridge: Cambridge University Press for the Hakluyt Society, 1958, 1961, 1971). Other sections of the book have appeared in: Said Hamdun and Noel King, translators and editors, *Ibn Battuta in Black Africa* (London: 1975) and Agha Mahdi Husain, translator and editor, *The Rihla of Ibn Battuta* (Baroda, India: 1976).

There is an extensive bibliography of works about Ibn Battuta. Highly recommended is a book that was one of the sources for this account and which gives a summary of Ibn Battuta's travels and puts them into historical context for the general reader: Ross E. Dunn, *The Adventures of Ibn Battuta: A Muslim Traveler of the 14th Century* (Berkeley: University of California Press, 1986; paperback edition, 1989). It includes a very complete bibliography. Also of interest is Thomas J. Abercrombie, "Ibn Battuta: Prince of Travelers," *National Geographic*, December 1991, which gives a summary of the travels and includes current photos of many of the places that Ibn Battuta visited.

Ahmad Ibn Fadlan

(10th century)

Ahmad Ibn Fadlan was an Arab theologian and traveler in the service of the Caliph of Baghdad who made one of the first recorded trips into what is now southern Russia.

Nothing is known about the life of Ahmad Ibn Fadlan other than the account that he wrote about a diplomatic mission from the court of the Arab caliph north into what is now Russia. From indirect evidence in his account it appears as though Ibn Fadlan was himself not an Arab. Ibn Fadlan left Baghdad on June 21, 921 as a member of a mission sent by the Abbasid Caliph al-Muktadir to the King of the Volga Bulgars, a Turkish tribe then living on the east bank of the Volga River. Ibn Fadlan was not the leader of the mission but appears to have been its religious adviser, and he later wrote the account of the trip. His role as theologian was important because one of the purposes of the mission was to explain the laws of Islam to the Bulgars who had recently been converted to Islam. The mission was actually headed by Susan al-Rassi, a eunuch in the service of the Caliph.

Following its departure from Baghdad, the mission traveled by well-known caravan routes to Bukhara in central Asia. Then it headed west to Khwarizm (modern-day Khiva) and Gurgan in what is now Iran near the Caspian Sea. They left Gurgan on March 4, 922 and crossed the country of the Oghuz Turks (ancestors of the modern Turkmens living east of the Caspian Sea), the Petchenegs (a Turkish tribe living along the Ural River), and the Bashkirs (another subdivision of the Turks now in central Russia). He also wrote about the Khazars, a Turkish tribe on the southern end of the Volga River, whom he describes as Jews. In fact, the Khazars had started converting to Judaism at the beginning of the ninth century, one of the few examples in history of mass conversion to Judaism. Ibn Fadlan wrote some of the first accounts that we have about all of these peoples, and his work remains a valuable ethnographical resource on the history of the steppes of central Asia.

Ibn Fadlan and the Arab mission arrived at the capital of the Bulgars on May 12, 922. When presented to the King of the Bulgars, it was Ibn Fadlan's job to present the gifts sent to him by the Caliph and to read a letter that he had composed for the occasion. Here the Arabs met members of the Rus, Vikings from the Baltic who were in the process of mixing with local Slavs to form the first Russian state. The Rus had trading posts along the Volga River. They had not yet converted to Christianity, and Ibn Fadlan writes very disapprovingly of their idol worship and animal sacrifices. In the best-known part of his text, Ibn Fadlan describes a Viking ship burial. The dead chief's property was divided into three parts. One part was kept by the family, but the rest was sold in order to finance the burial. The funeral ceremony itself involved the sacrifice of a female slave who was first forced to take part in a ritual orgy. She was then stabbed to death and placed along with the dead chief on a Viking boat that was set afire and launched into the river.

Ibn Fadlan's text is full of descriptions of customs such as these, which seemed very strange to an educated Muslim from Baghdad, one of the centers of world civilization. He also recounts some miraculous tales, such as those of the legendary giants Gog and Magog, but he is careful to point out that he did not witness these fantastic things himself but only heard about them from others. Unfortunately, the last part of Ibn Fadlan's text has been lost, and we know nothing about how the Arabs returned to Baghdad or about Ibn Fadlan's fate. The text that we do have became known in Europe only in 1823 when a Russian scholar, C.M. Fraehn, translated it from Arabic into German as a source on the history of the early Russians.

Where to learn more

C.M. Fraehn's books on Ibn Fadlan are *Ibn Foszlan's und anderer Araber Berichte über die Russen älterer Zeit* (St. Petersburg: 1823) and *Die ältesten arabischen Nachrichten über die Wolga-Bulgharen aus Ibn Foszlan's Reiseberichte* (St. Petersburg: 1832). Ibn Fadlan's text has also been published in French: M. Canard, "La relation du voyage d'Ibn Fadlan chez les Bulgares de la Volga," *Annales de l'Institut d'Etudes Orientales de l'Université d'Alger*, vol. 16 (1958).

There is no complete English translation. D.M. Dunlop in *The History of the Jewish Khazars* (Princeton: Princeton University Press, 1954) includes the passages related to the Khazars on pp. 109-114. Two studies, which unfortunately are to be found in rather obscure academic journals, are: R.P. Blake and R.N. Frye, "Notes on the Risala of Ibn Fadlan," *Byzantina Metabyzantina*, vol. 1, no. 2 (1949) and D. M. Dunlop, "Zeki Validi's Ibn Fadlan," *Die Welt des Orients*, vol. 4 (1949) is a review of a German translation by A. Zeki Velidi Togan that appeared in Leipzig in 1939.

Abu al-Kasim Ibn Ali al-Nasibi Ibn Hawkal

(920? - 990?)

In the year 943 Ibn Hawkal of Baghdad set out on a long journey that lasted 30 years and took him to all parts of the Muslim world.

Ibn Hawkal was born in Nisibis in Upper Mesopotamia (present-day Iraq). According to his own account, he left Baghdad on Thursday, 7 Ramadan 331 (May 15, 943) with the intention of learning about other lands and peoples and of engaging in trade. He then spent the next thirty years traveling. He later wrote about his experiences in a book called *On the Shape of the World*.

Ibn Hawkal reached Mahdiya on the east coast of Tunisia in the year 947 and traveled across North Africa to Morocco. From there, he sailed across the Strait of Gibraltar to Spain in 948. At that time Spain was ruled by the Muslim Umayyad dynasty, and had been united by the Caliph Abd al-Rahman III from his capital at Cordoba. Ibn Hawkal gives a long description of Cordoba, which at the time was a great cultural and intellectual center and was probably the largest city in Europe. Ibn Hawkal tells how rich Spain was and how weak it was militarily. From these reports there has been speculation that he was sent there as a spy for the Fatimids, a North African Shi'ite dynasty that was then in the process of military expansion.

From Spain Ibn Hawkal went back to North Africa and reached Sijilmasa at the southern edge of Morocco in 951. From there he headed south to the ancient African kingdom of Ghana in what is now Mali. He stayed in the commercial center of Awdaghost, which he says was fabulously rich. He reported seeing a check there made out in the sum of 42,000 dinars to a merchant in Sijilmasa. He gave the first account of Kumbi, the capital of Ghana, on the edge of the Sahara. He also saw the Niger River. Since it was flowing to the east, he came to the conclusion that it was the upper course of the Nile. Ibn Hawkal then returned north to Egypt. He says that the most direct route from Ghana to Egypt had been interrupted by Berber raiders. He was in Egypt at a time when it was being invaded by the Fatimids, which is another source of the idea that he was a Fatimid spy. (Egypt was finally captured by the Fatimids in 969 who founded the city of Cairo and made it their capital.)

From Egypt Ibn Hawkal continued eastward and traveled to the northernmost reaches of Islam at the time—Armenia and Azerbaidjan, which he reached in 955. He complains about the lack of Islamic fervor on this religious frontier. He then went to El-Jezira in western Syria. He was in Basra in southern Iraq in 961.

From there he headed east to Khuzistan and Fars in southern Iran. He was at Gurgan in northern Iran in 969 and from there crossed the Amu Darya (Oxus) River into central Asia. He went as far as the city of Samarkand and describes the gardens of the city where the gardeners practiced the topiary arts (trimming bushes and trees to look like animals). He discusses the way in which irrigation water at Samarkand was strictly regulated and gives the salary scale for public officials. From Samarkand Ibn Hawkal returned in 969 to Basra and Khuzistan. The last of Ibn Hawkal's trips that we know about was to Sicily—he writes that he was in Palermo on April 16, 973, having been there since the previous year. Sicily had been conquered by the Arabs starting in the year 825 and remained Muslim until it was taken by the Christian Normans in 1061.

The first edition of Ibn Hawkal's book seems to have been written about the year 967 and was called *Of Ways and Provinces*. A second edition seems to date from 977, while the final and definitive work, *On the Shape of the Earth*, was composed in 988. Ibn Hawkal copied some of his geographic descriptions from the work of another famous Arab geographer, al-Istakhri, but he seems to have corrected al-Istakhri's work with his own observations of the various places that he visited. In his book Ibn Hawkal recounts how he met al-Istakhri, who asked him to correct the errors in his book. Ibn Hawkal then went beyond that and replaced some of the original maps and some of al-Istakhri's descriptions with his own. His goal seems to have been to update the body of knowledge that then made up Arab geography. The point was not to compose an individual work but to pass on a corrected version of accumulated information.

Ibn Hawkal took care to state the situation in a country or region at the time that he himself visited. Therefore, his book has great value to historians. He was also the first Arab geographer to discuss the basic facts of the production and economy of the places he visited. In the course of his work he discusses such diverse subjects as the market for vegetable oils in the Mediterranean, the difficulties of handicraft producers in Egypt, the price of pens in Spain, the decline of Armenian bakeries, trade in coral and in dates, and the monopoly of tar in Cyrenaica.

Where to learn more

On the Shape of the Earth was presented in its original Arabic text by two noted Dutch scholars of Arab travelers: M.J. De Goeje (Leiden: 1873) and J.H. Kramers (Leiden: 1938), and their books contain introductions that discuss the voyages of Ibn Hawkal. Kramers worked on a translation that was revised and published by Gaston Wiet, in French, *Configuration de la terre* (Paris: 1964), which contains a very helpful introduction. There are two other studies in French: H. Darmaun, *Extraits des principaux géographes arabes du Moyen Age* (Paris: 1957) and A. Miquel, *La Géographie humaine du monde musulman jusqu'au milieu du XIeme siècle* (Paris: 1967).

Abu al-Hasan Muhammed Ibn Jubayr

(1145 - 1217)

Ibn Jubayr was a Muslim scholar from Spain who made three trips to the Middle East and wrote an important account of his travels.

Ibn Jubayr was a Muslim born in the Spanish city of Valencia at a time when it was ruled by Arabs from their great center of Cordoba in Andalusia in southern Spain. His father worked in the royal administration, and Ibn Jubayr received the best education of the time, studying the Koran and Arabic language and literature. As a result of his brilliant studies, he was appointed secretary to the Governor of Granada. According to his account, one day the Governor told him to drink a cup of wine. Ibn Jubayr protested, saying that as a good Muslim he could not touch alcohol. The Governor then told him that he would not only drink it but would drink it seven times. Ibn Jubayr dared not protest any more, but when the Governor filled the cup up the seventh time it was not with wine but with gold coins to pay him for his obedience. Ibn Jubayr then resolved to use the money to finance a pilgrimage to Mecca.

Ibn Jubayr set off from Spain in 1182. Along the way he stopped at various places in the Mediterranean including the islands of Sardinia and Crete. He landed at Alexandria in Egypt and then traveled to Cairo and from there to Mecca. He stayed in Arabia for nearly a year and spent a great deal of time measuring the holy places of Islam, and his writing has served as a major historical reference ever since. During this time the famous Islamic warrior Saladin was in the process of trying to drive the European Crusaders out of the Holy Land. Ibn Jubayr mentions him favorably several times when commenting on events in the Middle East. Ibn Jubayr returned to Spain by way of Iraq and Sicily, arriving home in 1185.

One of the most interesting parts of Ibn Jubayr's travels is the account that he gives of the Muslim population of Sicily, which had once been ruled by Arabs but was now part of a Norman Christian kingdom ruled by the descendants of Scandinavian Vikings. According to Ibn Jubayr, the Muslims of Sicily lived in some apprehension of their rulers, but seem to have had a fairly good status. Many of them were employed by the Norman rulers as ministers and court officials as well as cooks and other servants. Ibn Jubayr wrote that the Muslim female servants at the court were so numerous that they were able to convert the Christian women of the court. The King himself could both read and write Arabic.

On his return to Spain, Ibn Jubayr wrote about the experiences of his trip in a book called a *Rihla* ("Journey"). It has been the source of much information about the Mediterranean world at the end of the 12th century. It also is an important sourcebook on the methods of navigation at the time. It contains a harrowing description of a storm that Ibn Jubayr encountered on his return to Spain.

In 1187 Saladin conquered Jerusalem from the Crusaders. News of this victory so inspired Ibn Jubayr that he set off to Mecca again in 1189 and traveled in the Middle East until 1191. He attempted the journey once again in 1217 but died along the way, in the autumn of that year.

Where to learn more

There are a couple of English translations of Ibn Jubayr's *Rihla* into English: W. Wright and M.J. De Goeje, editors, *Travels of Ibn Jubayr* (London: 1907) and R.J.C. Broadhurst, *The Travels of Ibn Jubayr* (London: Jonathan Cape, 1952).

I-Ching

(634 - 712?)

I-Ching was a Chinese Buddhist monk who went to Indonesia and India and provided valuable accounts of both places.

The great Buddhist pilgrim **Hsüan-Chuang** returned to China from his epic trip to India in 645. His example inspired many other devout Buddhists, including a young monk named I-Ching. Along with 37 other monks, he resolved to make the trip to India, the homeland of the Buddha, himself. The group traveled to the southern port city of Canton in order to find a ship to take them on the sea, or southern, route to India. (Hsüan-Chuang had traveled overland through northern China and Mongolia.) At the last minute, the other monks changed their mind, but I-Ching decided to proceed alone. He found a Persian ship headed for Indonesia and left his homeland in 671.

The ship sailed by way of Poulo Condore off the southern coast of Vietnam. It reached the trading center of Palembang on the southeast coast of the island of Sumatra. I-Ching stayed there for six months, and then traveled around the island to Atjeh on its northern tip. From there, he took a Sumatran ship to the Nicobar Islands and on to the great port of Tamralipti in the delta of the Ganges River, not far from the modern city of Calcutta. His route from the Nicobar Islands to Tamralipti is not clear: either by way of Sri Lanka and Negapatam on the south Indian coast or via the Arakan coast of southwestern Burma.

At Tamralipti, I-Ching stayed in the Buddhist temple of Varaha for three years in order to learn Sanskrit, the language of the Buddhist scriptures. He then went up the Ganges to the great Buddhist center of Nalanda, also visited by Hsüan-Chuang. He stayed there for 10 years, studying the holy texts and collecting a great library to take back to China. One account said that he acquired 10,000 books.

I-Ching visited thirty different kingdoms or principalities in India before leaving the country. He went back to Sumatra and stayed there for several years working on the translations of his texts. Some stories say that he made a brief visit to Canton in 689 to recruit monks to help him with his translation work. He arrived back in his native province of Honan in China in either 693 or 694. It is said that from then until 712 he translated 56 different Buddhist texts into Chinese. He wrote a book telling the story of 56 other Buddhist monks or converts who made the long voyage to India. He also wrote a book that discussed the religious practices of the people of India and of Sumatra.

Where to learn more

Books in English about I-Ching are scanty. This account is largely based on an important book that is long out of print: Samuel Beal, translator, *The Life of Hiuen-Tsiang* by the Shaman Hwui Li (London: Kegan Paul, Trench, Trübner & Co., 1911; reprinted, 1914).

Abu Abd-Allah Muhammed al-Sharif al-Idrisi

(1100 - 1166)

Idrisi was an Arab traveler and geographer who produced what is probably the most important geographical work of the Middle Ages.

Idrisi was born in the city of Ceuta in North Africa on the coast of Morocco (the city is now ruled by Spain). He was a member of the Idrisid family that ruled North Africa and southern Spain. He himself was a direct descendant of the prophet Muhammed through his daughter Fatima (the origin of the Fatimid dynasty that ruled Egypt). He studied at the great Muslim center of Cordoba in southern Spain. He then appears to have traveled throughout the Middle East between North Africa and Anatolia and may have traveled as far north as Denmark and England.

Idrisi was invited to the court of the Christian King Roger II of Sicily, the descendant of the Norman conquerors who had taken Sicily from the Arabs. The reasons that he accepted this appointment, which made him appear to be a renegade to Islamic scholars of the time, are unknown. Shortly before Roger's death in 1154, Idrisi produced for the King a famous globe and map of the world engraved on silver. He wrote a book to explain the globe and to give a description of the known parts of the world. The book has been known by several titles, including the *Kitab al-Rujar* ("The Book of Roger") and the *Nuzhat al-Mushtak fi Khtirak al-Nafs* ("The Would-Be Traveler's Promenade Across the Horizons of the Globe").

There are only six original copies of this important work in existence, and the text of the book has never been fully translated from the Arabic. It is generally recognized to be the fullest and most accurate account of the known world in the 12th century. It includes significant information about the ethnic groups of the world and their cultures. It also discusses economic life and commerce. The text also contains 71 maps (some of them in color) that are thought to be the most accurate produced in the Middle Ages, whether in Europe or the Islamic world.

The *Book of Roger* was followed by what seems to be an even larger work that was written for Roger's successor William I. But this work is only known through an extract preserved in a library in Istanbul. The circumstances of Idrisi's death are not known.

Where to learn more

The most complete translation of the *Book of Roger* into a Western language is P.A. Jaubert, *Géographie d'Edrisi traduite de l'arabe en français d'après deux manuscrits de la Bibliothèque du Roi et accompagnée de notes*, 2 vols. (Paris: 1836-1840). Various parts of the book have been translated into other languages, generally dealing with a specific country. Examples are: R. Blachère, *Extraits des principaux géographes arabes du Moyen Age* (Paris: 1932); A.F.L. Beeston, "Idrisi's Account of the British Isles," *Bulletin of the Society of Oriental and Asian Studies*, vol. 13 (1950); D.M. Dunlop, "The British Isles According to Medieval Arabic Authors," *Islamic Quarterly*, vol. 4 (1957); D.M. Dunlop, "Scotland According to al-Idrisi," *Scottish Historical Review*, vol. 26 (1947); W. Hoenerbach, *Deutschland und seine Nachbarländer nach der Geographie des Idrisi* (Stuttgart: 1955); A.S. Marmardji, *Textes géographiques arabes sur la Palestine* (Paris: 1951); S. Maqbul Ahmad, *India and the Neighbouring Territories as Described by the Sharif al-Idrisi in His Kitab Nuzhat al-Mushtaq fi 'khtiraq al-afaq* (Leiden: 1960); H.M. Elliot and J. Dowson, *Early Arab Geographers* (Calcutta: 1956).

There are brief descriptions of the contents of the *Book of Roger* in J.H. Kramers, "Geography and Commerce" in *The Legacy of Islam* (Oxford: Oxford University Press, 1931) and D.M. Dunlop, *Arab Civilization to A.D. 1500* (New York: 1971).

Thomas James

(1593 - 1635)

Thomas James was an English lawyer who led an expedition to Hudson Bay to search for the Northwest Passage and explored and named James Bay.

Thomas James was the son of the mayor of Bristol, the leading port of western England at the time of his birth in 1593. James became a prosperous lawyer in that city.

In 1629 the navigator **Luke Fox** convinced King Charles I to sponsor an expedition to Hudson Bay to search for the Northwest Passage. The merchants of Bristol were worried that if this venture coming from London were successful, they would be at a disadvantage. They therefore used the lawyer Thomas James to argue before the king about their rights as well. King Charles agreed that if Bristol mounted an expedition as well then both groups would share in any eventual profits.

As a result, James led an expedition to northern Canada at the same time as Fox. James left Bristol on May 3, 1631, a couple of days before Fox set sail. James traveled in the *Henrietta Maria*, named after the queen of England, with a crew of 22 men, none of whom had any experience in Arctic navigation. They reached Davis Strait, named after **John Davis**, between Greenland and Baffin Island on June 5.

From Davis Strait, James went into Hudson Strait and followed it into Hudson Bay, which he reached on July 16, after a difficult passage. He then headed to the western shore and explored it at the same time as Fox. James discovered and named the Severn River on July 26 and then met up with Fox from July 29-30. He then went north to the present-day town of Churchill, which he reached on August 11.

On September 3, 1631 James sighted and named Cape Henrietta Maria at the northwest entrance to James Bay. This enormous bay is the southernmost part of Hudson Bay. James was the first one to explore it, and it is named in his honor. He hoped that it would continue south and lead to a way to the St. Lawrence River. This passage did not exist, and in October he anchored off Charlton Island in the southern part of the bay to spend the winter. Fox had already headed back to England, and James and his crew were the first Europeans to deliberately spend the winter in northern Canada.

During the long winter that they spent on Charlton Island, the Englishmen suffered greatly from illness and lack of food. Four of them died. The ship sank, and it took most of the spring to raise it

out of the water and repair it enough so that they could sail again. On June 24, 1632 James claimed Charlton Island in the name of King Charles I. They left on July 1 and the next day they saw remnants of a European ship that may have been left by **Henry Hudson** 20 years before.

It took a long time to cross Hudson Bay in the injured ship, and it was only on August 24 that the expedition reached Nottingham Island at the entrance of Hudson Bay. James tried to travel farther north but the condition of the *Henrietta Maria* made it impossible for him to go as far as Fox had done the previous year. He therefore set sail for England, which he reached on October 22. The crew thought it was a miracle that they did not sink on the way.

The combined results of the expeditions led by James and Fox showed that there was no Northwest Passage by way of Hudson Bay. So discouraging was this that there were no further European trips to the bay until 1668 when **Médard Chouart des Groseilliers** led an expedition there with an entirely different purpose—to open it up for the fur trade. The next attempt to find a Northwest Passage north of the Canadian mainland was not made until 1819.

James wrote a book about his voyage called *The Strange and Dangerous Voyage of Captaine Thomas James . . ..* It became a great success, and its tales of hardship are said to be the basis for Samuel Taylor Coleridge's famous poem *The Rime of the Ancient Mariner*. As a result of this voyage James was appointed to command the Bristol Channel squadron of the Royal Navy. He died in unknown circumstances within three years of his return from Hudson Bay.

Where to learn more

The main source for James and Fox's voyages is Miller Christy, ed. *The Voyages of Captain Luke Foxe of Hull, and Captain Thomas James of Bristol in Search of a North-West Passage, in 1631-32* (London: Hakluyt Society, 1894). It includes "The Strange and Dangerous Voyage . . ." mentioned above.

Several books that discuss the role of Bristol in opening up European exploration and trade with North America include discussions of James, including: J.W. Damer Powell, *Bristol Privateers and Ships of War* (Bristol: 1930) and P. McGrath, ed. *Records Relating to the Society of Merchant Venturers of the City of Bristol in the Seventeenth Century* (Bristol Record Society, 1952).

There are discussions of James' voyage in: Sir Clements Markham, *The Lands of Silence* (Cambridge: Cambridge University Press, 1921); Jeannette Mirsky, *To the Arctic!: The Story of Northern Exploration from Earliest Times to the Present* (New York: Alfred A. Knopf, 1948); Ernest S. Dodge, *Northwest by Sea* (New York: 1961); and Tryggvi J. Olesen, *Early Voyages and Northern Approaches 1000-1632* (Toronto: McClelland and Stewart, 1963).

Willem Janszoon

(1570 - ?)

Willem Janszoon was a Dutch sea captain who was the first European to sight Australia.

I n 1595 the Dutch sent out their first great trading expedition to the East Indies under the command of **Cornelius Houtman.** The expedition was made up of four ships that were built in Amsterdam. The fourth and smallest was a "yacht" of 50 tons, very small indeed. It was named the *Duifken* (Little Dove), and it was destined to play a big role in history.

Yachts were never a distinct type of vessel as far as shape or rigging was concerned. The *Duifken* was in fact a miniature three-master. With the other ships it left Amsterdam in 1595 and returned on August 14, 1597. The voyage was such a commercial success for the Dutch merchants that they sent out a second fleet in 1598. They formed the Dutch East India Company in 1601, which sent out two expeditions under its control before 1605. The *Duifken* went along on all of these voyages, and in a battle with the Portuguese off Bantam, on the west coast of Java, had distinguished itself by capturing a much larger galley.

The second East India Company voyage was commanded by Admiral Van der Hagen, who returned to Holland by the end of July 1606. However, he left behind the two small yachts in his fleet and gave them special missions: one was the *Delft*, which was sent on a reconnaissance mission to the east coast of India; the other was the *Duifken*.

The *Duifken* sailed from Bantam on November 28, 1605 under skipper Willem Janszoon, with instructions to explore the south coast of New Guinea. It sailed through the Banda Sea past the Kai and Aru islands and sighted New Guinea at its southwest corner at Dolak Island. It then sailed into what we now call the Torres Strait where it ran into shallow water. The ship headed south, rather than sail into what was believed to be a cul-de-sac.

On this southern course the Dutch ran down the west coast of the Cape York Peninsula on the east side of the Gulf of Carpentaria. In other words, they had discovered Australia. The *Duifken* joined the small number of European ships, including Columbus's *Niña* and *Pinta*, that sailed to an unknown continent for the first time.

The Dutch had discovered Australia although they did not know what they had found. They thought they were traveling down the coast of New Guinea. Janszoon's men were also the first Europeans to see the Australian Aborigines. This first encounter ended badly; the Dutch went ashore to trade and nine crew members were killed.

A few months after the *Duifken* had been in these waters the Spaniard **Luis Vaez de Torres** sailed through the straits between Australia and New Guinea, which were later named in his honor. But the Spaniards did not sight Australia and were unaware that they had sailed between two great landmasses.

When Janszoon got back to Java, he made a report that indicated that the land he had found was desolate, with no opportunities for trade, which is what the Dutch were interested in. Seventeen years later another captain, Jan Carstenszoon, retraced Janszoon's route and came back with an equally unfavorable report that kept the Dutch away from Australia except for accidental landings. The most important of these occurred in 1616 when Captain Dirk Hartog sailed too far east in the Indian Ocean and landed on the west coast of Western Australia. As a result, the Dutch knew that there was a great landmass south of New Guinea that they named New Holland. But it was to be many, many years before anyone knew whether it was attached to New Guinea or not.

As for the *Duifken*, it continued to sail for the Dutch East India Company until it finally rotted away and was abandoned.

Where to learn more

Two books were helpful in writing this narrative of Janszoon and the *Duifken*: Arthur Jose, *Builders and Pioneers of Australia* (London: J.M. Dent & Sons, 1928) and George Masselman, *The Cradle of Colonialism* (New Haven: Yale University Press, 1963). Masselman's information is largely based on Jan E. Heeres, *The Part Borne by the Dutch in the Discovery of Australia, 1606-1765* (London: 1899).

Anthony Jenkinson

(? - 1611)

Anthony Jenkinson was an English merchant who took the Arctic route to Moscow and then explored central Asia.

After **Richard Chancellor** had secured trading rights with Russia for the Muscovy Company, the English merchants were anxious to exploit their new privileges immediately. In order to do so, they hired Anthony Jenkinson who had spent seven years as a merchant in the Middle East to become Captain-General in Moscow. Jenkinson went to Russia in 1557, the year following Chancellor's last voyage. His specific instructions were to explore the possibility of developing trade with China via the new Moscow connection.

Jenkinson took the Arctic route via Arkhangelsk to Moscow and was well received by Tsar Ivan IV (the Terrible) who gave him letters of introduction to help him to continue his travels into central Asia. In Moscow he noted the splendor of the tsar's court in contrast with squalor and drunkenness of the common people. From Moscow Jenkinson went to Nizhni Novgorod, where he visited the annual fair, and then sailed down the Volga River in the company of the new governor of the city of Astrakhan on the Caspian Sea.

From Astrakhan, Jenkinson and his small party bought a boat to sail down the east coast of the Caspian Sea. Landing on the Mangishlak Peninsula, they joined a caravan of 1,000 camels that traveled 20 days through the desert to the town of Urgench. On December 9, 1558 they were attacked by a gang of thieves who took a large part of their belongings, and they lived for three days without food or water until they reached the Oxus River.

Jenkinson and his two English companions and Tatar interpreter finally reached the great trading city of Bukhara on December 23, 1558. Now in Uzbekistan, Bukhara had long been one of the crossroads of trade in Asia. At the time of Jenkinson's visit, Bukhara was an independent Persian-speaking state but, to his chagrin, no longer a wealthy trading city. However, the King of Bukhara was friendly, and he sent a party of soldiers to capture and punish the thieves that had attacked Jenkinson.

Learning that the country he planned to travel through was in the middle of a war, Jenkinson went no farther than Bukhara. In fact, only ten days after he left the city it was attacked by forces from the neighboring city of Samarkand. On hearing Jenkinson's report, the Muscovy Company abandoned trying to open this route to China.

Jenkinson left Bukhara with another trade caravan in March 1559. Reaching the Caspian Sea, he made a dangerous crossing in a small boat, from which he flew the Cross of St. George, the flag of England at the time. Back in Moscow, he was well received by the Tsar, who invited him to dinner.

After returning to London to report on his trip to Bukhara, Jenkinson went back to Moscow in 1561. His object on this second trip was to try to find a trade route to another great empire—that of Persia, which was then ruled by the powerful Shi'ite Safavid Dynasty. The cohesive and dynamic Persian state presented opportunities for trade by Westerners, but they were difficult to exploit. Jenkinson once again went down the Volga River to Astrakhan and across the Caspian, this time landing in Derbent on the western shore. The Governor of Derbent was friendly and gave him an introduction to the Shah of Persia, whose court was at Qazvin. The Shah was less friendly, however, and Jenkinson had to return without winning any trading rights. He made two further trips to Russia, in 1566 and 1571, and then retired to England, where he died on February 26, 1611.

Where to learn more

Jenkinson's accounts of his travels have been published in collections by other authors. Included in Richard Hakluyt's *Collection of Voyages* (London: 1809) is Jenkinson's *Voyage from the Citie of London Toward the Land of Russia, 1557* and *Voyages and Travels of Mr. Anthony Jenkinson, from Russia to Bogher, or Bokhara in 1557*. Other accounts by Jenkinson are included in John Pinkerton's *A General Collection of the Best and Most Interesting Voyages and Travels* (London: 1808-1814). The best source is E. Delmar Morgan and C.H. Coote, eds., *Early Voyages and Travels to Russia and Persia by Anthony Jenkinson and Other Englishmen* (London: Hakluyt Society, 1886), with an introduction by Morgan that includes all the information known about Jenkinson's life.

Gonzalo Jiménez de Quesada

(1501? - 1579?)

Gonzalo Jiménez de Quesada traveled into the interior of Colombia, where he led the conquest of the Chibcha, the last of the great Andean civilizations to be subdued by the Spanish.

Gonzalo Jiménez de Quesada was born in the southern Spanish city of Córdoba sometime around the year 1501. He became a lawyer and was attached to the staff of Don Pedro Fernández de Lugo, who was governor of the Spanish colony of Santa Marta on the northern coast of Colombia in South America. In 1536 the governor sent Jiménez de Quesada on an expedition into the interior to find "El Dorado." One of the main motives for the Spanish conquests in the Americas was the search for gold. This became mixed up with legends they heard about a fabulous king, El Dorado—the Golden One—who lived in his rich capital of Manoa on the shores of Lake Parima.

Jiménez de Quesada left Santa Marta in April 1536 and traveled south up the Magdalena River, the great waterway that rises in the Andes of southern Colombia and flows into the Caribbean. While the main part of his force marched overland, ships sailed up the Magdalena River carrying supplies. The first fleet of ships was caught in a bad storm, and the ships were either wrecked or turned back. The land force almost starved to death, and many became sick and died.

In spite of this disaster, Jiménez de Quesada refused to turn back. Four more ships were then sent upriver with supplies. The voyage was difficult, and one ship was partially wrecked, but the survivors did eventually meet the land force. By December 1536 the Spanish were again short of food and raided a deserted Native American village and stole the supplies of corn they found there. At this point many of the Spaniards wanted to turn back, but Jiménez de Quesada insisted on continuing. He was spurred on by growing signs of civilization: woven fabrics and trade goods.

In April 1537, Jiménez de Quesada and his force reached the first of the large mountain valleys where the advanced cultures of Colombia were centered. By that time only 166 out of the original 900 Spaniards were still alive. In August 1537 Jiménez de Quesada and his small army defeated the King of Tunja, in the mountains north of Bogotá. The King was made a prisoner in his own palace and forced to turn over all his gold and precious metals to the Spanish. At the end of 1537 and the beginning of

Gonzalo Jiménez de Queseda. The Granger Collection, New York.

1538, Jiménez de Quesada conquered the petty rulers of Cundinamarca, the region surrounding Bogotá.

On the plateau of Bogotá, Jiménez de Quesada encountered the Kingdom of the Chibchas. These Native Americans, like the Incas in Peru and the Aztecs in Mexico, had founded a strong state that produced beautiful ornaments made of gold, emeralds, and semi-precious stones. This was the wealth that the Spanish had been looking for. During an encounter with the Spanish, the King of Bogotá was killed, and Jiménez de Quesada appointed the dead ruler's cousin as King with the understanding that he would turn over all the royal treasure to the Spanish. When this was completed, the man was killed.

Jiménez de Quesada founded the new town of Santa Fé on the site of the old Chibcha capital. Later called Santa Fé de Bogotá, it is today the capital of Colombia. Soon after that, Europeans coming from different directions arrived in the new town. One was a German, Nicholas Federmann, who had been sent by a German financial house to try to find the great wealth that was rumored to exist in South America. Forbidden by the Spanish to travel up the Magdalena, he arrived overland from what is now Venezuela. At almost the same time, another Spanish *conquistador*, Sebastián de Benalcázar, arrived from Quito in Ecuador to the south. Both were dismayed to find that Jiménez de Quesada had beaten them to Bogotá and to the wealth of the Chibchas.

Occupied with plundering the Chibchas, Jiménez de Quesada abandoned his search for El Dorado. However, even though he had been responsible for opening up the Magdalena route from the coast and for conquering the mountain kingdoms, Jiménez de Quesada was soon replaced by royal officials. His only reward was to be named much later to be a royal councilor at Santa Fé de Bogotá, a post that he assumed in 1565. In 1569-1571, he led another expedition into the interior to try to find El Dorado. This time he traveled as far as the Orinoco River in Venezuela but found no gold mines or rich civilizations. He returned to Bogotá, where he died in unknown circumstances.

Where to learn more

There are three "classic" biographies of Jiménez de Quesada by eminent historians of the old school who tell the story with much dramatic incident and action: Sir Clements Markham, *The Conquest of New Granada* (London: Smith, Elder & Co., 1912); R.B. Cunninghame Graham, *Conquest of New Granada: Being the Life of Gonzalo Jimenez De Quesada* (reprinted, New York; Cooper Square Publishers, 1967); Germán Arciniégas, *The Knight of El Dorado*, translated by Mildred Adams (New York: Viking, 1957; reprinted, New York: Greenwood, 1968).

A more recent book, with lots of illustrations, is John Hemming, *The Search for El Dorado* (New York: Dutton, 1979).

John of Marignolli

(14th century)

John of Marignolli was an Italian Catholic priest who made an extensive trip to the Far East between the years 1338 and 1353.

John of Marignolli was a member of a patrician family from Florence who entered the Catholic priesthood. Nothing much is known about his early life until he was placed in charge of a diplomatic mission from the Pope to the Great Khan in China following a request from the Khan. John left Avignon, in the south of France, which was then the seat of the Popes, in December 1338 with a party of 32 men, including three other bishops. They did not get to Constantinople until May 1339 and from there crossed the Black Sea and traveled to the court of the Tartars, a Turkic-speaking tribe allied with the Mongols, who had been given control over the Russians. They stayed until the spring of 1340 at that court and then moved on to the Ili River in western Sinkiang where they stayed until the end of 1341.

John's party did not reach Beijing until 1342, where they made quite a stir by presenting the Emperor with a large Western horse, which inspired several poems and a painting of the Emperor on his new steed. These Catholic emissaries found that the Franciscan mission started by **John of Monte Corvino** was prospering and that the monks were supported in high fashion by the imperial court, where they had a cathedral, several other churches, and residences and celebrated their rites in the presence of the emperor.

John of Marignolli stayed three years in Beijing and then set out with his companions to return to Europe by the southern route that had been used by Marco Polo. In Amoy they found three thriving Catholic churches and were able to have two bells cast and erected in the heart of the Arab quarter, so that the Muslims would have to listen to the Christian call to mass.

Taking to the sea, the papal delegation sailed on to southern India where they reached Malabar in April 1347. John stayed among the St. Thomas Christians for 16 months where he had a church constructed in the Latin fashion with more bells and embellished with the papal insignia. He traveled on via Sri Lanka (which he named as the closest place on earth to paradise), Ormuz, Babylon, Baghdad, Mosul, Nineveh, Aleppo, Damascus, Jerusalem and Cyprus before returning to Rome in 1353.

John completed a narrative about his journey that is full of interesting details, but is also replete with various miraculous happenings and is difficult to read because the author keeps losing his train of thought. A contemporary archbishop called him "a poor old wheezing hound, without repute for eloquence or learning." In any case, the success of his eastern mission earned him an archbishopric, appointment as secretary to the Holy Roman Emperor, and a reputation as the "Apostle of the East."

Where to learn more

John's own account can be found in Sir Henry Yule, *Cathay and the Way Thither: Being a Collection of Medieval Notices of China*, 4 vols. (London: Hakluyt Society, 1913-1916) and Christopher Dawson, ed. *The Mongol Mission: Narratives and Letters of the Franciscan Missionaries in Mongolia and China in the 13th and 14th Centuries* (London: Sheed and Ward, 1955); reprinted as *The Mission to Asia* (Toronto: University of Toronto Press, 1986).

Other sources are C. Raymond Beazley, *The Dawn of Modern Geography*, vol. 3 (Oxford: Clarendon Press, 1906); Alfred Percival Newton, *Travel and Travellers of the Middle Ages* (New York: Alfred A. Knopf, 1930); Leonardo Olschki, *Marco Polo's Precursors* (Baltimore: The Johns Hopkins Press, 1943); and I. de Rachewiltz, *Papal Envoys to the Great Khans* (Stanford: Stanford University Press, 1971).

John of Monte Corvino

(1247? - 1328)

John of Monte Corvino was an Franciscan friar from Italy who spent several years as a missionary at the court of the Great Khan in Beijing.

John of Monte Corvino was born in about 1247, the year that **Giovanni di Piano Carpini** had returned from the first Western trip to the Mongols. He became a Franciscan friar and started his life's work as a missionary in the Middle East.

In 1291 he went to Rome and asked the Pope to send him on a mission to the courts of the Mongol Khans.

Leaving Rome in 1291, John traveled overland to Tabriz in Persia and then down to the great port of Ormuz. He embarked on a dhow, a small sailing vessel, and sailed to the south coast of India, near Madras. This part of India had (and still has) an ancient colony of Christians, called the St. Thomas Christians because of the legend that they had been converted by one of the twelve apostles, St. Thomas.

The Franciscan missionary stayed among these Indians for about a year and in a manuscript dated December 20, 1292 wrote an account of south India that he sent back to Rome. He was not heard from again until the reception of a second letter dated January 8, 1305 from Khanbaligh, or Beijing, the capital of the Great Khan. By that time, **Marco Polo** had left China thirteen years before and Kublai Khan had been dead for eleven.

Piecing together the story of how this and following letters got back to Rome is not easy. Apparently, they were handed from one Mongol outpost to another all across central Asia and Persia, where the Franciscans had a mission at Tabriz, the capital of the Il-Khans. Several were passed on by a Brother Thomas of Tolentino who worked in Armenia and India.

John's letters tell of the ups and downs of his missionary efforts. In his early years, he was able to convert one of the Nestorian princes to Catholicism and with his aid built a church and translated the liturgy. On the death of this prince, however, he lost his main protector and was subject to the jealous attacks of the Nestorian clergy. But John struggled on and was rewarded by the help of a Brother Arnold of Cologne, who had made it to China by unknown means. With his aid, John built a second church in Beijing and translated the New Testament and the Psalms.

John's letters back to Rome created a great deal of enthusiasm for the mission in China. Pope Clement V named John the Archbishop of Khanbaligh and sent out seven bishops to help him—only three of whom made it to China, in 1308. These bishops helped to establish a church in the port city of Amoy, which soon became a Christian center. Christianity continued to prosper in China even after John of Monte Corvino's death in 1328 until the fall of the Mongol dynasty in 1367.

Where to learn more

John's own letters about his mission in China can be found in Christopher Dawson, ed. *The Mongol Mission: Narratives and Letters of the Franciscan Missionaries in Mongolia and China in the 13th and 14th Centuries* (London: Sheed and Ward); reprinted as *The Mission to Asia* (Toronto: University of Toronto Press, 1976).

Other books that discuss the mission of John of Monte Corvino include: C. Raymond Beazley, *The Dawn of Modern Geography*, vol. 3 (Oxford: Clarendon Press, 1906); Arthur Percival Newton, *Travel and Travellers of the Middle Ages* (New York: Alfred A. Knopf, 1930); Paul Stanislas Hsiang, *The Catholic Missions During the Middle Ages (1294-1368)* (Washington, D.C.: Catholic University of America Press, 1949); Paul Herrmann, *Conquest by Man* (New York: Harper & Brothers, 1954).

One very interesting book about the history of the relations between the Pope and the Great Khan is I. de Rachewiltz, *Papal Envoys to the Great Khans* (Stanford: Stanford University Press, 1971).

Amy Johnson

(1903 - 1941)

Amy Johnson was a British pilot who was the first woman to fly from Britain to Australia and who then set speed records from London to Tokyo and London to South Africa.

Amy Johnson was born in the northern English seaport of Hull, where her father was a well-to-do fish merchant. She attended Sheffield University for three years. After an unhappy romance with a fellow student from Switzerland, she took a typing course and moved to London in 1927, where she got a job as a sales clerk and then took a position as a secretary in a lawyer's office. In 1928 she rented a room near an airfield at Stag Lane. In order to receive reduced tuition for flying lessons, she became the volunteer secretary for the British Air League.

Johnson began her flying lessons in September 1928. It took her twice as long as the usual student to get her license, and her instructor told her she had no aptitude for flying. She got lost on her first solo flight. In the meantime, she had taken to hanging around the flight school's hangar, and she started learning to take care of aircraft engines. She became the first woman in Great Britain to qualify as a ground engineer in December 1929. As a result of this accomplishment, she began to get some publicity in the popular press, where aviation was a matter of intense interest at the time. In one article she announced that she was going to fly solo to Australia—much to the astonishment of her fellow flyers.

Johnson then began badgering well-known British personalities who were interested in flying to put up the money for her proposed expedition. She convinced her father to put up the first £500 and Lord Wakefield, an oil magnate, to advance an additional £500. She bought a secondhand Gipsy Moth, painted it bottle green and wrote the name *Jason* (a legendary Greek figure) in silver on its side. She took off from Croydon Airfield on May 5, 1930. She had had a total of only 75 hours in the air, her longest flight was 147 miles, and she had never flown over water. "The prospect did not frighten me, because I was so appallingly ignorant that I never realized in the least what I had taken on."

From England, it took Johnson two days to fly to Istanbul. She almost turned back then because she became nauseous when she had to manually pump gasoline from the storage tank to the tank in the upper wing. Throughout the entire flight she had to pump 50 gallons of fuel every hour, each gallon requiring forty strenuous strokes. On the fourth day, she ran into a sandstorm in the Iraqi desert and was forced to land. She used her luggage to brake the plane's wheels, covered the engine and fuel tanks with canvas to keep the sand out, and sat on the wing for three hours with a revolver in hand in case she was attacked by wild animals. When she was able to take off again, she flew on to Baghdad, where she broke one of the wheel struts landing. It was repaired overnight, but she broke it again the next day when she landed in Oman.

Johnson reached Karachi, Pakistan on the sixth day. There had been only one previous solo flight from Britain to Australia. An Australian pilot, Bert Hinkler, had flown the distance in 1928 in 15 days. Johnson's goal when she set out was to beat Hinkler's time and set a new record. By the time she reached Karachi, she was two days ahead of his schedule. She had left London with little publicity, but the news that she had made record time to Karachi was telegraphed around the world. Suddenly, all the world's media were interested in the British pilot.

Setting out from Karachi, Johnson ran out of fuel in the town of Jhansi and landed on a parade ground at a British military post, scattering the marching soldiers across the field and stopped by wedging the plane between two barracks. Once again, the damage was repaired overnight. Between Calcutta and Rangoon she ran into monsoon storms and, unable to see, landed in a ditch and tipped the plane over, nose down. She landed near the Burmese Technical Institute and the students helped her repair the plane in their machine shop. However, this took two days, and she fell hopelessly behind Hinkler's schedule. Flying from Bangkok to Singapore, she got lost and found out that she had been making circles in the air. She was forced to land in Songkhla. The next day she landed in Singapore, where the whole British colony turned out to welcome her.

Flying over Java, clouds parted just in time for Johnson to see that bamboo stakes were tearing off the bottom part of her wings. At Surabaya she had engine trouble. Landing in Timor, she missed the airfield and landed in a field of ant mounds. On May 24, 1930, however, Johnson landed in the northern Australian town of Darwin, having taken 19½ days, four days longer than Hinkler. Knowing that she had not broken the record, she thought that the flight was a failure. On the contrary, the world thought she was a heroine. She was greeted by an ecstatic crowd and received congratulatory telegrams from all over the world, including the King and Queen of England, the British Prime Minister, and famed aviator **Charles A. Lindbergh**. The London *Daily Mail* announced that it was awarding her £10,000.

After only one night's rest in Darwin, Johnson started out on a triumphal air tour of Australia. However, she was physically and emotionally drained. She cried uncontrollably when she was out of public view. The crowds would not leave her alone, however, until she crashed the *Jason* when she tried to land in the Australian city of Brisbane.

Johnson returned to England by sea. The amount of publicity built up by her flight was intense. There was a spate of popular songs written about her—"Queen of the Air," "Aeroplane Girl," "The Lone Dove," and "Amy, Wonderful Amy." It is estimated that a million people turned out to greet her when she arrived in London on August 5, 1930. The *Daily Mail* then sent her on a tour of the country. However, she lasted only a week before her health and nerves collapsed, and she had to give it up. Never having had to deal with the public before, she now only wanted to escape from her fans. She conceived the idea of flying solo across Siberia to Japan. Setting out in January(!) 1931, she was forced to give up the idea when she crash landed in a potato field in Poland.

In the summer of 1931 Johnson set out again with fellow pilot Jack Humphreys, and the two of them set a record of flying the 7,000 miles from London to Tokyo in 10 days. The flight was so uneventful that it received little publicity, much less than that of pilot Jim Mollison who set a new record for flying from London to Australia at the same time. On her return to England, Johnson had a serious operation and then went to South Africa to recover. She was introduced to Mollison there, and they met again in London in May 1932. He proposed to her, and they were married in July. They became known as the "Flying Sweethearts" and the "Air Lovers" in the popular press.

The Mollisons then began trying to outdo one another. He set a record for flying east to west across the Atlantic in 1932. She then flew solo to Cape Town and beat his previous record time by 11 hours. She was given an award for the most meritorious flying achievement in 1932. He won it in 1933 for flying solo across the South Atlantic. In 1933 they tried to make their first joint flying venture by setting a world long-distance record. This ended with a crash landing in Bridgeport, Connecticut that put both of them in the hospital. During Johnson's recovery, she became a close friend of **Amelia Earhart**'s.

In 1934 the Mollisons entered another race to Australia but were forced to abandon it because of engine trouble. He then went on his own to America. They separated and eventually divorced in 1938. In 1936 Johnson set a second world's record in flying from London to South Africa. This once again brought her a great deal of popular fame, but she was experiencing money problems. She took a job flying for an air ferry company. As Britain re-armed for World War II, she was hired by the Air Transport Auxiliary of the Royal Air Force. She seems to have enjoyed her work even though she was paid less than a man would have been for doing the same work. She was on a routine flight, delivering an aircraft from Scotland to an airfield near London, on January 5, 1941, when the plane crashed and she died in the Thames River.

Where to learn more

Johnson only wrote one book about her adventures: *Sky Roads of the World* (London: W. & R. Chambers, 1939). She also contributed a chapter on her early life in Countess of Oxford and Asquith, ed. *Myself When Young by Famous Women of Today* (London: F. Muller, 1938), pp. 131-156.

A couple of books were written about Johnson when she was at the height of her fame: Charles Dixon, *Amy Johnson—Lone Girl Flyer* (London: Sampson Low, Marston & Co., 1930) and Hubert S. Banner, *Amy Johnson* (London: Rich and Cowan, 1933). Since then, there has been one full-scale biography: Constance Babington Smith, *Amy Johnson* (London: Collins, 1967).

There are several good books on the role of women as aviation pioneers that include chapters on Johnson: Pauline Gower, *Women With Wings* (London: John Long Ltd., 1938); Edward Jablonski, *Ladybirds: Women in Aviation* (New York: Hawthorn Books, 1968); Wendy Boase, *The Sky's the Limit: Women Pioneers in Aviation* (New York: Macmillan, 1979); Valerie Moolman, *Women Aloft* (New York: Time-Life Books, 1981); and Judy Lomax, *Women of the Air* (New York: Dodd, Mead & Co., 1987).

Louis Jolliet

(1645 - 1700)

Louis Jolliet was a Canadian-born Frenchman who was the first European to travel down the Mississippi River and also made expeditions to Hudson Bay and the coast of Labrador.

Louis Jolliet was born in the new colony of New France in 1645, the son of a craftsman who died while Jolliet was still a child. His mother was widowed twice before she married a farmer and settled down in the town of Beauport near Quebec City.

At the age of 11, Jolliet entered the Jesuit college in Quebec where he studied philosophy and prepared to enter the priesthood. He also studied music and played the organ at the cathedral of Quebec for many years. In 1666 he defended a thesis before Bishop Laval of Quebec and other learned men. His work impressed the Bishop, who became one of his patrons in the years to come.

In 1667 Jolliet gave up his seminary studies and borrowed money from Laval to spend a year in France. On his return to Quebec he decided to enter the fur trade—the main business in New France. In that capacity he made at least one trip to the west, in 1670-1671, and was one of the signers of a document in which the French claimed possession of the Great Lakes region.

In 1672 Jolliet was chosen by the two highest officials in French Canada, the Intendant, Jean Talon, and the Governor, the Count de Frontenac, to lead an expedition to discover the Mississippi River. The French knew of the river from reports from their Native American trading partners, but they wondered if it emptied into the Gulf of Mexico or farther west, into the Gulf of California. This was what Jolliet was instructed to discover.

On October 4, 1672, Jolliet left Quebec with his party and made it to the mission and trading post at Michilimackinac (on the strait between Lake Huron and Lake Michigan) on December 6. There he stayed for the winter and made the acquaintance of the priest in charge of the mission, Father **Jacques Marquette**. Jolliet had brought instructions that Marquette was to accompany him on his voyage in order to preach among the tribes they encountered. This Marquette was very pleased to do.

The exploring party left Michilimackinac in May, 1673 with seven men in two canoes. The only names we know of for sure are those of Jolliet and Marquette. Both Jolliet's and Marquette's logs of the journey were lost, and we do not know their exact route. However, it is supposed that they traveled westward along the north shore of Lake Michigan to Green Bay and then up the Fox River. They then made a portage overland to the Wisconsin River and descended that to the Mississippi, which they entered on June 15, 1673. They traveled down the Mississippi past the Missouri and Ohio Rivers.

Jolliet and Marquette stopped about 450 miles south of the mouth of the Ohio River, just north of the present boundary between the states of Arkansas and Louisiana. There they stayed among the Quapaw tribe, where they heard reports of the Spanish approaching the same area from the west. The unfriendliness of the Quapaws and the knowledge that the Mississippi must run into the Gulf of Mexico convinced the explorers to turn back without having reached the mouth of the river.

The expedition started upriver on the Mississippi in mid-July 1673. On the return they paddled up the Illinois River and made the portage at Chicago into the southern part of Lake Michigan. Jolliet and Marquette split up at Saint Francis Xavier mission on Green Bay in the state of Wisconsin. Jolliet spent the winter of 1673-1674 at Sault Ste. Marie writing and copying his journal and making maps, all of which were lost in a boating accident on the return to Quebec, which he reached in the fall of 1674.

Once back in Quebec, Jolliet married and settled down as a fur merchant. He requested permission from the French government to settle a colony in the Illinois country, but this was refused because it was felt that New France was spreading its meager resources over too large an area. Jolliet devoted himself to the fur trade on the North Shore of the St. Lawrence River.

In 1679 Jolliet was entrusted with a mission to explore an overland route to the rich fur-trading regions of Hudson Bay, which were being exploited by the English. He left Quebec on April 13, 1679 and traveled up the Saguenay River to Lake Saint John, then to the Mistassini River and Lake Mistassini, to Marten River and the Nemiskau River, into Rupert Bay at the south end of Hudson Bay. There he encountered English traders and learned about the extent of their activities. On his return to Quebec, he wrote a report saying that the French risked losing the fur trade to the English if they were allowed to continue their activities.

On his return from this trip Jolliet was given trading rights and land on the North Shore and obtained the large island of Anticosti that sits in the middle of the Gulf of St. Lawrence. Although we do not know many of the details, he had a successful career in the fur and fish trades of the St. Lawrence. He made several trips, including one in 1689 to the coast of Labrador. He wanted to return and in 1694 was commissioned to lead an expedition to map that unknown coastline.

Jolliet left Quebec on his last expedition on April 28, 1694 and sailed along the North Shore and the coast of Labrador during the summer until he reached the site of the present settlement of Zoar, Labrador in July. He drew the first maps of that area and wrote about the landscape and the Inuit inhabitants. He noted that the only economic resources were whale oil and seal oil, which could be traded with the Inuit. He returned to Quebec in October 1694.

In 1692 Jolliet was made official hydrographer of New France and taught at the Jesuit college. He died during the summer of 1700 in unknown circumstances.

The Jolliet-Marquette route to the Mississippi River.

Where to learn more

The major chronicler of Louis Jolliet was Jesuit priest Jean Delanglez, who wrote a series of articles on the explorer that notably include: "The Discovery of the Mississippi—Primary sources," *Mid-America*, vol. 16 (1945), pp. 219-231; "The Discovery of the Mississippi—Secondary Sources," *Mid-America*, vol. 17 (1946) pp. 3-29; "The Jolliet Lost Map of the Mississippi," *Mid-America*, vol. 17 (1946), pp. 67-144; "Louis Jolliet: Early Years, 1645-1674," *Mid-America*, vol. 16, (1945) pp. 3-29; "Louis Jolliet: The Middle Years, 1674-1686," *Mid-America*, vol. 16 (1945), pp. 67-96.

The fruits of this work were summarized in *Life and Voyages of Louis Jolliet (1645-1700)* (Chicago: Institute of Jesuit History, 1948), published a year before Delanglez' death. It appeared in Canada as Jean Delanglez, S.J. *Louis Jolliet: vie et voyages, 1645-1700* (Montreal: 1950).

A French-Canadian historian, Ernest Gagnon, published his *Louis Jolliet, découvreur du Mississippi et du pays des Illinois, premier seigneur de l'Ile d'Anticosti* (Montreal: Beauchemin, 1946) at about the same time.

There is an excellent biographical essay on Jolliet by André Vachon in the *Dictionary of Canadian Biography*, vol. 1 (Toronto: University of Toronto, 1967), which served as the basis for this account.

The 1673 exploration was linked to two men: Jolliet and Louis Marquette. The extensive bibliography listed in the Marquette entry also necessarily includes a great deal of information about Jolliet as well, particularly concerning the controversy over the exact role that Marquette played in the trip to the Mississippi.

Jordanus of Séverac

(1290 - 1354)

Jordanus of Séverac was a French Catholic missionary who traveled to and wrote about India in the 14th century.

John of Monte Corvino was the first Roman Catholic missionary known to have worked among the Christians of south India. Following his departure in 1292, there appears to be no further missionary activity until 1321 when a French Dominican friar, Jordanus of Séverac, led a group of four others to Thana near the present-day city of Bombay.

This group had intended to land further south on the Malabar coast where the St. Thomas Christians lived. However, they were blown off course after leaving Ormuz in Persia. When they landed at Thana, a group of Nestorian Christians persuaded Jordanus, who spoke Persian, to go off and visit a group of Christians farther north near the city of Broach in Gujarat. While he was away, local Muslims set upon the remaining missionaries and killed them on April 7, 1321.

Jordanus returned and gathered up the remains of his colleagues and took them to Suali near the city of Surat, which is where St. Thomas was reputed to have landed on his mission to India. During his trials Jordanus wrote two letters to the Franciscans and Dominicans who maintained a mission in Tabriz in Persia, one dated October 12, 1321 and one dated January 24, 1323. In both of them he tells of his misery, loneliness, poverty, illness, and the treachery of the people who surrounded him.

In any case, Jordanus persevered, and in 1330 the Pope named him bishop of Columbum, or Kulam, at the southern tip of India. In the following years he wrote his *Description of Marvels*, which is his claim to fame as one of the world's great travellers. In this book Jordanus gives descriptions of Armenia, Persia, and various parts of India that show that he had visited all of those places, and he gives some of the first descriptions of plants and animals native to those regions.

His book also contains accounts of the marvels of the East Indies and Indochina, but it is clear that he never visited these places but is repeating tales, some true, some not, that he had heard from other voyagers. He does, however, give a prolonged account of the land of Abyssinia and its Christian king, Prester John. The myth of Prester John had long fascinated Christian visitors to the East, and they had tried to pin down the location of the monarch. Jordanus was the first to connect that story with the accounts he heard of the Christian kingdom in the mountains of northeastern Africa.

Where to learn more

The best book to read about Jordanus is the one he wrote himself, *Description of Marvels* (London: Hakluyt Society, 1863). The bulk of work on medieval explorers was done in the first part of the 20th century. There is, for example, a chapter on Jordanus in C. Raymond Beazley, *The Dawn of Modern Geography*, vol. 3 (Oxford: Clarendon Press, 1906), and he is mentioned in A.P. Newton, *Travel and Travellers of the Middle Ages* (New York, 1926).

The standard work on early Catholic missionaries in Asia is J. Richard, *La papauté et les missions d'Orient au moyen age (XIIIe-XV siècles)* (Rome: Ecole Française de Rome, 1977). Also helpful for understanding the context of early European-Asian contacts is *The Medieval Expansion of Europe* by J.R.S. Phillips (Oxford University Press, 1988), but it is organized thematically rather than by personality or chronologically.

Edmund Kennedy

(1818-1848)

Edmund Kennedy was a native of the island of Guernsey who explored the interior of Queensland, Australia, and was killed on an expedition to the Cape York Peninsula.

Edmund Kennedy was born on September 5, 1818 in Guernsey in the Channel Islands, the son of a retired British colonel. He went to Sydney in 1840 where he became a land surveyor for the colonial government. Kennedy found that surveying work was dull, and he was happy when he was chosen to join **Thomas Livingstone Mitchell**'s expedition to the interior of Queensland in November 1845.

The aim of Mitchell's expedition was to find an overland route to the Gulf of Carpentaria on Australia's north coast. The expedition did not get that far, but they did find a stream, which Mitchell called the Victoria, that seemed to flow north to the sea. After the Mitchell expedition arrived back in Sydney in January 1847, Kennedy volunteered to lead an expedition north to investigate the Victoria and to follow it to the Gulf.

Kennedy left on this trip on March 13, 1847 and went north to the Victoria. Following it for some distance, it changed course and headed south where it met Cooper's Creek. Cooper's Creek is the main stream in central Australia, but it gradually disappears into the desert. Finding "Victoria" to be much too pretentious a name for the little stream he found, Kennedy renamed it the Barcoo. He returned to Sydney on February 7, 1848 with his negative information.

The government then decided to attack the problem of getting to the Gulf of Carpentaria from the other direction. It sent Kennedy north to the east side of the Cape York Peninsula in the far north of Australia with a plan to travel up the east coast to the tip and then down the west coast. Once he reached the head of the Gulf he was to travel overland to Sydney. Kennedy set out on this ambitious plan on April 28, 1848.

After Kennedy and his party landed on the coast, they found that the terrain was almost impossible to cross, being made up of mangrove swamps with mountains just behind. After two months he had only made it 20 miles into the interior. After pushing on through the difficult countryside, on November 13 Kennedy decided to leave the main part of his party behind and to take a small group north to the tip where there was a supply ship waiting. In the end, the group that was left behind wasted away from starvation, and by the time it was found only two out of the eight men were still alive.

Along the way north, one of the men shot himself accidentally, and Kennedy left two others behind to take care of him. They all died. Kennedy continued on with an Aborigine boy named Jackey Jackey. Sometime in December, when they were only 20 miles from the supply ship, they were attacked by Aborigines. Kennedy died in Jackey Jackey's arms. In his testimony at the investigation of the expedition, Jackey Jackey said: "I asked him, 'Mr. Kennedy, are you going to leave me?' and he said, 'Yes, my boy, I am going to leave you . . . I am very bad, Jackey.'" Jackey Jackey made it alone to the waiting supply ship on December 23, 1848.

Where to learn more

The biographer of Kennedy is Edgar Beale, who has written about him in the *Australian Dictionary of Biography*; in an article entitled "Edmund Besley Court Kennedy" in the *Journal of the Royal Australian Historical Society*, vol. 35 (1949): and in a full-scale biography, *Kennedy of Cape York* (Adelaide: Rigby Limited, 1970).

Yerofey Pavlovich Khabarov

(1610? - 1670?)

Yerofey Pavlovich Khabarov was a Russian entrepreneur who pioneered a route to the Amur River and who established Russian claims to that river valley.

Yerofey Pavlovich Khabarov was born in the town of Ustyug in the northern part of European Russia. Sometime around 1636 he joined the ranks of Russian pioneers then opening up the vast lands to the east: he migrated to Siberia and started a farm on the Yenisei River. Khabarov made a success of this as well as other enterprises, which led him to become involved in trading activities in eastern Siberia. He heard about the richness of the Amur River Valley, which had been discovered by **Vasili Danilovich Poyarkov** in 1644.

In 1649 Khabarov organized a private expedition (with no government funds) to explore the Amur. His force of 150 men left the important Russian fort of Yakutsk and traveled upstream along the Lena, Olekma, and Tungir rivers until they reached the height of land in the Yablonovy Range. They then traveled down one of the small tributaries into the great Amur River in January 1650. This proved to be the most accessible overland route to the Amur and was used by subsequent Russian expeditions.

When Khabarov got to the Amur he found the villages of the native Daurians deserted: Russian bootleggers had warned them away, hoping to get the valuable trade for themselves. Khabarov learned that the Daurians already paid tribute to the Chinese and that any Russian encroachment meant possible war with China.

Khabarov returned to Yakutsk in May 1650 to report these findings to the governor. He told the governor that it would take a Russian army of 6,000 to hold the Amur region but told the governor that it would be worth it. This report was forwarded to Moscow.

In the meantime, Khabarov organized a return expedition to the Amur that left Yakutsk in the fall of 1650. This time the Daurians were definitely hostile, and Khabarov was forced to fight. He took the village of Albazin and made that his headquarters. In the spring of 1651 he started down the Amur fighting the local inhabitants along the way. He built a fort at Achansk, about halfway down the river, where he wintered in 1651-1652. In 1652 the Chinese court ordered Manchu soldiers to attack the Russian intruders, and they did so in March of that year. The Russians were able to fight off the Manchus, and this increased their prestige among local tribesmen enormously.

But Khabarov knew that more Chinese would follow, so he headed back up the Amur. In spite of desertions, Khabarov stabilized his position and built a fort at the site of the present-day Russian city of Blagoveshchensk. In the meantime, many Russians heard about the possibilities along the Amur and took the route pioneered by Khabarov along the Olekma into the river valley. The Russian government sent a new official, Dmitri Ivanovich Zinoviev, to try to control these Russians, and he replaced Khabarov, accusing him of misconduct. His accusations led to a full-fledged trial that was fought between the two men in Moscow in 1654. Khabarov was exonerated and was appointed manager of a fort west of Lake Baikal, where he lived out the rest of his life.

In the following years, the Russians and Chinese became involved in a more serious struggle for control of the Amur. The upper hand switched back and forth for several years until the two countries negotiated a treaty at the Russian post of Nerchinsk in 1689 that gave control of the Amur to the Chinese. The Russians returned many years later—in the 1850s. While China was going through a period of inner turmoil and weakness, the Russians were able to reassert control of the north bank of the Amur River and the entire course of the lower river. This has remained the boundary between the two countries since then.

When the Russians returned in the 1850s, they built a new headquarters on the Amur in 1858. This place they named Khabarovsk after the man who had led the Russians into the river valley. It is now the largest city in the Russian Far East.

Where to learn more

The best book on English on the expansion of the Russians into Siberia, and the one on which this account is largely based, is George V. Lantzeff and Richard A. Pierce, *Eastward to Empire: Exploration and Conquest on the Russian Open Frontier, to 1750* (Montreal: McGill-Queen's University Press, 1973. Two older accounts of the conquest of the Amur valley are E.G. Ravenstein, *The Russians on the Amur: Its Discovery, Conquest and Colonisation* (London, 1861) and Frank A. Golder, *Russian Expansion on the Pacific, 1651-1850* (Cleveland, 1914). For the history of Russian-Chinese diplomatic negotiations, see Mark Mancall, *Russia and China, Their Diplomatic Relations to 1728* (Cambridge: Harvard University Press, 1971).

Mary Kingsley

(1862 - 1900)

Mary Kingsley was an Englishwoman who made two pioneering trips to West Africa and became a well-known writer on African subjects.

Mary Kingsley was born in Cambridge, England on October 13, 1862, four days after her parents had married. Her father, George, was a doctor and the younger brother of Charles and Henry Kingsley, two well-known writers. After the marriage, George spent most of his time traveling abroad. Kingsley's mother was an invalid, and Mary was forced to take charge of the household from a very early age. She later wrote, "The whole of my childhood and youth was spent at home, in the house and garden." The family spent a great deal of money on her brother's education but refused to give her any formal schooling at all. She was taught to read at home and then turned loose in the library.

In 1892, when Kingsley was 30 years old, her mother and father both died. She later wrote, "dead tired and feeling no one

Mary Kingsley. The Granger Collection.

had need of me any more, when my Mother and Father died within six weeks of each other in '92, and my Brother went off to the East, I went down to West Africa to die." In fact, she took a vacation in the Canary Islands, and there she saw cargo vessels loaded for the West African coasts. Finding the idea exotic, on her return to England she started planning her own trip there.

Kingsley made her first trip to West Africa in 1893 when she traveled for four months on a local cargo ship down the coast from Freetown in Sierra Leone to Luanda in Angola. She was one of two women on the boat and took the time to learn about navigation and piloting. On her second trip at the end of 1894 she stayed for 11 months. This time she went to Gabon and traveled up the Ogowe River to the land of the Fan tribe, who were reputed to be one of the most hostile to Europeans in West Africa. Kingsley quickly made friends there and was received with great hospitality.

In order to finance this trip, Kingsley had decided to operate as a trader, and she brought along a supply of cloth that she traded for ivory and rubber. During all her trips, she wore a Victorian shirtwaist dress with stays, a long skirt and a cap. "You have no right to go about Africa in things you would be ashamed to be seen in at home." She had many adventures during her trip and faced down two leopards and was attacked by crocodiles.

While in West Africa, Kingsley undertook one expedition that was simply for the thrill of discovery. She climbed Mt. Cameroun, which at more than 13,000 feet is by far the tallest peak in West Africa. She climbed it alone through a rainstorm and was disappointed that the rain blocked the view once she got to the top. She claimed to be "the third Englishman to ascend the Peak, and the first to have ascended it from the south-east face."

On Kingsley's return to England in 1895, she wrote a book about her experiences called *Travels in West Africa*, published in 1897, plus a large number of articles on African subjects. She immediately became the center of controversy because she was very much opposed to the methods that the British and other Europeans were using to colonize Africa. This made her a hero among certain interest groups and a target for others.

Kingsley wanted to return to West Africa, but in 1899 the Boer War broke out between Great Britain and the Afrikaner republics of South Africa. She went to South Africa as a journalist and a nurse, but soon came down with typhus. She died in the port of Simonstown near Cape Town on June 3, 1900. In her honor, the Mary Kingsley Hospital was founded in Liverpool to treat tropical diseases, and the African Society was established to study African anthropology.

Where to learn more

Kingsley wrote two books about her experiences in West Africa: *Travels in West Africa* (London: Macmillan, 1897; reprinted in paperback, Boston: Beacon Press, 1982) and *West African Studies* (London: Macmillan, 1899; reprinted, London: Cass, 1964).

There have been several books written about Kingsley. The best early biography was by a friend of hers who based his book partly on personal knowledge: Stephen Gwynn, *The Life of Mary Kingsley* (London: Macmillan, 1932). The famous English writer Rudyard Kipling was an admirer of Kingsley's and wrote a book about her, *Mary Kingsley* (Garden City, N.Y.: Doubleday, 1932).

Other biographies are: Rosemary Glynn, *Mary Kingsley in Africa* (London: Harrap, 1956); Kathleen Wallace, *This Is Your Home: A Portrait of Mary Kingsley* (London: Heinemann, 1956); Olwen Campbell, *Mary Kingsley, a Victorian in the Jungle* (London: Methuen, 1957); Cecil Howard, *Mary Kingsley* (London: Hutchinson, 1957); Jean Hughes, *Adventurous Miss: The Adventures of Mary Kingsley* (London: Macmillan, 1968); Katherine Frank, *A Voyager Out: The Life of Mary Kingsley* (Boston: Houghton Mifflin, 1986); and Valerie Grosvenor Myer, *A Victorian Lady in Africa: The Story of Mary Kingsley* (Southampton, England: Ashford Press, 1989).

All of the books discussing women explorers and travelers include chapters on Kingsley. These include: Winifred Holmes, *Seven Adventurous Women* (London: Bell, 1953); Mary Cathcart Borer, *Women Who Made History* (New York: Warner, 1963); Dorothy Middleton, *Victorian Lady Travellers* (London: Routledge & Kegan Paul, 1965); Leo Hamalian, ed. *Ladies on the Loose: Women Travellers of the 18th and 19th Centuries* (New York: Dodd, Mead, 1981); Catherine Barnes Stevenson, *Victorian Women Travel Writers in Africa* (Boston: Twayne, 1982); Dea Birkett, *Spinsters Abroad: Victorian Lady Explorers* (London: Basil Blackwell, 1989); and Marion Tinling, *Women into the Unknown: A Sourcebook on Women Explorers and Travelers* (New York: Greenwood Press, 1989), which has been very helpful in writing this account.

Kintup

(1849? - ?)

Kintup was one of the Indian "pundits" who tracked the source of the Brahmaputra River.

Kintup was, like **Nain Singh**, one of the "pundits"— Indians who were used by the British rulers of India to explore Tibet, where it was impossible for Europeans to travel. Unlike the other pundits, however, Kintup was a completely untrained and illiterate native of Sikkim, a kingdom bordering India in the Himalayas. His code name was K.P.

Kintup had made his first expedition into Tibet as the assistant to another pundit, Nem Singh. He had proven to be a hard worker and very reliable and was clearly suited for greater responsibility. However, because he could not record his field observations, it was decided to team him up with a Mongolian lama whose servant he pretended to be. Their assignment was to travel to the Tsangpo River, which runs from west to east in southern Tibet, to find out if it was in fact the same as the mighty Brahmaputra River, which flows through Assam in India. Previous explorations, including one by Nain Singh, had indicated that the Tsangpo was the only river large enough to be the Brahmaputra, but no one knew what course it took or how it descended from 10,000 feet to 500 feet during the 120 miles that were still unexplored. Did it drop sharply in what could be the world's greatest waterfall (it does not), or were there a series of rapids?

Efforts to investigate the river northward from Assam had been stopped by hostile hill tribes. Therefore, Kintup was instructed to travel to the Tsangpo in Tibet and attempt to follow it downstream. If this proved to be impossible, he was supposed to send a message to the British Survey in Assam and then float specially marked logs down the river. Workers would be stationed at the point where the river entered Assam to look for the logs as they came downstream.

Kintup and the Mongolian lama left Darjeeling in northern India near the Sikkim border in the summer of 1880. They crossed into Tibet by way of the Donkya Pass and made their way to a monastery near Lhasa. After various delays, they reached Gyala Sindong in March 1881, the farthest point that had been surveyed along the Tsangpo. At the small village of Pemaköchung, Kintup saw a series of waterfalls. His report on this got garbled, and for many years it was thought that there was one gigantic waterfall.

The two explorers could not go any farther in that direction and detoured into a totally unknown region called Po Me. At a town named Tongkyuk Dzong, on May 24, 1881, the Mongolian lama announced that he was going to take care of some business and would return in two or three days. In fact, he returned home to Mongolia and was never seen again. Before leaving, however, he had sold Kintup to the headman of the village. The pundit was forced to work as a domestic servant and was not able to escape until March 7, 1882.

Kintup headed back for the Tsangpo in order to continue his investigations. In the town of Marpung he was apprehended by agents sent out by his former master. He threw himself on the mercy of the head lama of the local monastery who agreed to rescue him if Kintup would stay and work. After four and a half months, he got permission to make a pilgrimage down river to the holy mountain of Kondü Potrang. Kintup used his time to prepare some 500 logs that he intended to send down the Tsangpo. He then returned to the monastery at Marpung. Now he had to alert the Survey of India staff to look out for the logs. He was given two months' leave to make another pilgrimage. Instead, he went to Lhasa (probably in December 1882) where he managed to find someone to carry a message back to India. The message did reach the Survey, but either it was not delivered to the right people or it was ignored.

Kintup returned to Marpung and his life of servitude. He stayed there for nine more months. Finally, the head lama was so impressed with Kintup's piety that he released him from his contract. He stayed at the monastery for another month in order to earn some money. He then traveled to the place where he had hidden his logs. He had lost the drill he was supposed to use to insert metal tubes into the logs so he tied the tubes to the logs with bamboo strips instead. He then released the logs down the river at the rate of 50 logs a day.

Kintup then tried to follow the river downstream himself. He got to within 40 miles of the border of British territory but was forced to turn back by hostile tribesmen. He then returned the way he had come and went back to Sikkim by way of Lhasa. He finally reached the offices of the Survey on November 17, 1884, four years after he had left. On his return, nobody paid much attention to him. He learned that no one had followed up on his message from Tibet, and his logs had floated down the river unnoticed. It was two years before anyone even bothered to take down his story. When it was finally published, people learned that Kintup had investigated more of the Tsangpo than any previous explorer and had established its connection to the Brahmaputra.

Kintup was finally given a reward for his work and served in a minor role on one further expedition. He then returned to his native village and took up his work as a tailor.

Where to learn more

The original sources for the explorations of the Pundits were in reports of the British Survey of India, and many of them were published by the Royal Geographical Society. A complete listing of these reports can be found in a recent book that tells the whole fascinating history of the Pundits: Derek J. Waller, *The Pundits: British Exploration of Tibet and Central Asia* (Lexington: The University Press of Kentucky, 1990).

There are good summaries of the activities of the Pundits in two books about the exploration of Tibet: John MacGregor, *Tibet: A Chronicle of Exploration* (London: Routledge & Kegan Paul, 1970) and Peter Hopkirk, *Trespassers on the Roof of the World: The Race for Lhasa* (London: John Murray, 1982).

Ludwig Krapf

(1810 - 1881)

Ludwig Krapf was a German missionary who was the first European to see Mt. Kenya. His explorations in East Africa paved the way for the explorers who found the source of the Nile River.

Ludwig Krapf, the son of a farmer, was born in the village of Derendingen near the south German city of Tübingen on January 11, 1810. When he was 11 years old, the village tailor beat him so badly, apparently without any reason, that he was forced to stay in bed for six months. During that time he occupied himself by reading the Bible and other religious works. From then on, his family said he was destined to become a preacher. Later, he was attracted by an essay that he read on the work of missionaries. At the age of 16 he went to Basle in Switzerland and applied to a missionary training school. He was accepted the following year. However, he was caught reading forbidden books and was kicked out. He studied theology at the University of Tübingen briefly but was then successful in being readmitted to the school in Basle.

After completion of his studies, Krapf wrote to the Church Missionary Society in London and asked to be sent on a mission to Ethiopia. He was accepted and traveled there at the beginning of 1837. He stopped for a while in Cairo, where he showed his amazing talent for languages by quickly learning to speak Arabic. In Ethiopia he met a fellow missionary, C.W. Isenberg, and traveled with him to Adua, the capital of the province of Tigre. In 1839 he went to the province of Shoa, the center of Ethiopia (or Abyssinia as it was then called). He was well received by the king of Shoa and accompanied him on a campaign against the Galla tribe (now generally called the Oromo), a non-Christian people who were perennial enemies of the central government. He was immediately attracted to the Gallas as a fruitful field for missionary work and set up a mission station among them. He wrote the first grammar of the Galla language and translated part of the Bible. He also developed the idea, which was incorrect, that the Galla were spread throughout East Africa.

In 1842 Krapf left his work in the Kingdom of Shoa. Attacked and robbed along the way, he reached the port of Massawa in May 1842. He sailed to Aden on the south coast of Arabia and from there to Egypt, where he married a German woman named Rosine Dietrich who had been sent out by the Basle missionary school. They returned to Aden where Krapf laid out his future plans. He thought that if he traveled to the coast of East Africa he could go northward into the interior and once again encounter members of the Galla tribe. The theory was good, but in actuality it proved impossible.

Krapf reached Zanzibar in January 1844, after stopping briefly in the port of Mombasa (now in Kenya), which impressed him as a good place to start his missionary work. Krapf and his wife settled in Mombasa in May 1844, where he started to learn the Swahili language. Soon after their arrival the German couple both came down with malaria. Krapf's wife gave birth to a baby girl on July 9, 1844. Both of them died within a week. Krapf stayed at his post however and began to translate the Bible into Swahili.

Krapf traveled in the vicinity of Mombasa to try to find a site to build his mission station. He finally settled on the village of Rabbai Mpia, which was only a few miles inland from Mombasa. It was situated on the top of a hill about 1,000 feet high and commanded a wide view of the port of Mombasa and the Indian Ocean. On June 10, 1846, a fellow missionary, **Johannes Rebmann**, arrived, and they started work on the mission station at Rabbai Mpia.

In the following years Krapf traveled throughout East Africa looking for possible mission sites. His plan was to penetrate into the interior by establishing a chain of mission stations that would support each other and provide a link to the coast and the outside world. In July 1848 he left for Usambara, an area south of Mombasa, with a guide and seven porters. He met Kmeri, "the only true lion," king of Usambara, on August 10. He had feared that he might get a bad reception, but in fact the king welcomed him and told him that he would be pleased to have Christian missionaries among his people.

In October 1849 Krapf traveled to Ukambani, the country of the Wakamba. When he reached the first of their villages on November 17, 1849, they looked at him as though he were a "being from another world." He reached Kitui, the village of the king, Kivoi, on November 26. The king told him that he had been to the Chagga country and had seen the white mountain of Kilimanjaro, which Rebmann had reported on. He also added, however, that there was another snow-capped mountain a six days' journey from Kitui. He told Krapf to climb the top of a nearby hill to look at it. It was too cloudy and rainy, however, for him to see anything. On December 3, 1849, however, as Krapf was leaving the town, he was able to get a good view of the two white peaks of Mount Kenya, 17,058 feet high. He was the first European to see the mountain.

In 1850 Krapf made a voyage down the east coast of Africa in a small Swahili boat. He traveled as far as Cabo Delgado in what is now Mozambique and there heard stories of Lake Nyasa (Malawi) in the interior. On his return, he left for England to make a report in person to the Church Missionary Society about his efforts. The Society endorsed his work, and he was authorized to found a mission in the Ukambani country. He also visited Germany and discussed his explorations with such well-known scientists as **Alexander von Humboldt** who were all interested to hear his stories of snow-covered mountains in tropical Africa. He returned to Rabbai Mpia in April 1851. In July he headed into the interior with the aim of setting up a mission station in the highlands beyond the Athi River.

Abandoned by his porters, he decided to push on to Kitui, where King Kivoi had been so helpful. The king said that he would do all that he could to help him but first he must accompany him on a journey to the Tana River. They set out on August 24. After some days the party was set upon by robbers. Kivoi himself was killed, and Krapf had a miraculous escape from the arrows of his attackers. During his flight into the forest, Krapf came face to face with two rhinoceroses. His discovery of the upper reaches of the Tana River was virtually an accident: he stumbled upon it while looking for water. He took the opportunity to explore the Tana for a short distance. He saw a tall mountain on the other side of the river, which he named Mount Albert in honor of Queen Victoria's husband, who was a supporter of missionary activities. Another mountain he named Mount William in honor of the king of Prussia.

The Wakamba people blamed Krapf for the death of their king, Kivoi, and he faced much hostility. Realizing that it was not possible to set up a mission in Ukambani, he returned to Usambara and received permission from Kmweri to establish a mission station there. By this time, however, his health was failing, and Krapf was unable to lead this mission himself. He returned to Rabbai Mpia and then left for Europe in September 1853. He traveled by way of Cairo where he met **Sir Richard Burton**, who was in the city at the same time. Burton was intrigued with his tales of the Tana River, which he thought might be the source of the Nile River.

Krapf stayed in Germany for a year and then headed back to Africa. He only got as far as Ethiopia when he ran into difficulties and realized that his health would not allow him to continue. He went back to Germany in September 1855 and settled in the village of Korntal near Stuttgart. He remarried, and he and his second wife had a daughter. He outlived his second wife and married for a third time in 1869. Krapf spent his time writing up his notes on his experiences and pursuing his studies of African languages, publishing several grammars. He returned to East Africa for a few months in 1862 to found a mission for the United Methodist Free Church and again in 1867. Ill-health prevented him from staying very long either time. He died in Korntal on November 26, 1881.

Where to learn more

Krapf's narratives of his years in East Africa are told in: *The Journals of C.W. Isenberg and J.L. Krapf Detailing Their Proceedings in the Kingdom of Shoa and Journeys in Other Parts of Abyssinia in the Years 1839, 1840, 1841 and 1842* (reprinted, London: Cass, 1968) and *Travels, Researches, and Missionary Labours During an Eighteen Years' Residence in Eastern Africa* (London: Trübner & Co., 1860; reprinted, New York: Johnson Reprint Corp., 1968). There is one biography in English: Charles Granston Richards, *Ludwig Krapf, Missionary and Explorer* (London: 1958).

Charles-Marie de La Condamine

(1701 - 1774)

Charles-Marie de La Condamine was a French mathematician who was sent to Ecuador in South America to measure the earth at its equator.

Charles-Marie de La Condamine was the son of a high French official who, at the age of 18, fought in the battles of the War of the Spanish Succession. At the age of 20 he took up the study of mathematics. He became particularly interested in geodesy, earth measurement. At the age of 29 he was elected to the prestigious French Academy of Sciences.

During this time a controversy about the earth's shape started in European scientific circles. One group held that the earth is flattened—wider around the equator than around the poles—while the other held that it was elongated—wider at the poles. In order to determine locations accurately, this controversy needed to be resolved. The king of France proposed sending two expeditions to test the theories. One was to go north to Lapland, the other south to the equator. La Condamine was put in charge of the South American expedition, which was to head for Quito in Ecuador.

La Condamine left in May 1735 with a group of fellow scientists. The expedition landed at the port of Cartagena in Colombia where it was joined by two Spanish naval officers, sent along to watch over the French scientists. From Cartagena they traveled on land across the Isthmus of Panama and then sailed from Panama City to Ecuador. Most of the participants traveled to Guayaquil, the chief port in Ecuador, while La Condamine stopped in the town of Manta to begin his measurements.

From Manta La Condamine headed north along the coast in order to reach the equator as quickly as possible. Along the way he was met by Pedro Vicente Maldonado, the governor of the Ecuadoran province of Esmeraldas, who was an amateur mathematician and scientist. He offered to accompany La Condamine to Quito by a little-known route up the Esmeraldas River. La Condamine accepted, and the two spent the month of May 1736 traveling through the heavy rainforest. It is said that during this trip La Condamine was introduced to natural rubber and carried it back with him to Europe.

The two men traveled up the Andes Mountains and reached Quito on June 4, 1736, a short time after the main party. Once in Quito the French scientists started taking measurements immediately. They set up their instruments in the plains of Yarqui a few miles northeast of Quito. By June 1739, nearly four years after they had left France, La Condamine's party had completed the series of measurements from which they could calculate the shape of the earth. At that very moment, however, a letter arrived from Paris telling them that the expedition to Lapland had long since completed its work and had proved that the world is flattened. In spite of this great disappointment, La Condamine stayed in Ecuador for four more years carrying out scientific observations.

La Condamine left Ecuador in March 1743. Accompanied once again by Maldonado, he decided to do something extraordinary: to travel back to Europe by climbing over the Andes and sailing down the Amazon River. Although not the first European to do this, he was the first scientist, and his map remained the most accurate until the 20th century. He was also the first person to pass on the stories he heard about a connection between the Amazon and Orinoco River systems, which was later investigated by **Alexander von Humboldt**. La Condamine did not return to Paris until the spring of 1745—ten years after his departure.

Back in Europe, La Condamine continued his scientific investigations. He is credited with developing the idea of vaccination against smallpox, later perfected by Edward Jenner. In 1760 he was elected to the Académie Française. However, he was almost constantly ill and died in 1773, deaf and completely paralyzed.

Where to learn more

La Condamine's complete account of his journey to South America is contained in *Journal du voyage fait par l'ordre du roi à l'équateur* (Paris: 1751). A shorter version of this appeared a few years earlier: *Relation abrégée d'un voyage fait dans l'intérieur de l'Amérique méridionale* (Paris: 1745). This version was translated into English as *A Succinct Abridgement of a Voyage Made Within the Inland Parts of South-America* (London: E. Withers, 1747). The other major primary source is the account given by La Condamine's Spanish colleagues, Antonio de Ulloa and Jorge Juan y Santacilla, *Relación histórica del viaje a la América meridional hecho de orden de Su Majestad*, 4 vols. (Madrid: Antonia Maria, 1748). An English version of this appeared several years later as *A Voyage to South America*, translated by John Adams, 2 vols. (London: Lockyer Davis, 1772).

A good, if somewhat dry, summary of La Condamine's expedition can be found in Edward J. Goodman, *The Explorers of South America* (New York: Macmillan, 1972). Livelier accounts are available in Victor Wolfgang von Hagen, *South America Called Them: Explorations of the Great Naturalists* (Boston: Little, Brown & Company, 1955), which served as the main source for this account, and Anthony Smith, *Explorers of the Amazon* (New York: Viking, 1990).

(Alexander) Gordon Laing

(1793 - 1826)

Gordon Laing was a Scottish army officer who traveled across the Sahara to find the source of the Niger River and was the first European to reach Timbuktu, but he did not return.

Gordon Laing was born in Edinburgh, Scotland on December 27, 1793. His father had opened the first classical secondary school in Edinburgh, and Laing was educated there and at the University of Edinburgh. He joined the British Army and in 1822 was stationed in Sierra Leone, a colony the British had recently established as a refuge for freed slaves. While there, he made a short expedition from April to October 1822 into the interior from the port of Freetown. Laing returned to England and wrote a book about his experiences that earned favorable comment.

At this time, the leading British official in and expert on North Africa was Colonel Hamner Warrington, consul in the North African city of Tripoli on the Mediterranean coast in what is now Libya. Warrington was convinced that the best way to find the source of the Niger River (a major goal of British geographers) was to attack it from the north—through the Sahara Desert. He was able to convince the British Colonial Secretary, Lord Bathurst, to have the government pay for such an expedition. Laing wrote to Bathurst asking to be given the assignment.

Laing arrived in Tripoli in May 1825. While waiting to get the necessary permission from the ruler of Tripoli, the Bashaw, to travel into the interior, Laing made the acquaintance of the consul's daughter, Emma Warrington. The two fell in love. In spite of Warrington's initial objections, he finally agreed to marry the two of them in the consular office. However, he made them agree that they would not live together until after the wedding had been regularized in a church. Two days after the civil ceremony, on July 18, 1825, Laing started out to try to reach the Niger.

Laing traveled south into the Sahara into the Fezzan and then turned back north to the caravan rendez-vous of Ghadames, now in southern Tunisia. Laing joined a caravan of Arabs heading south for Timbuktu from Ghadames. They traveled west around the Ahaggar Mountains to the oasis at In Salah and then southwestward to Timbuktu. The Arabs were the enemies of the fierce Tuareg tribesmen, who attempted to control the trade routes of the Sahara. Laing wrote that the Tuareg were so feared "that I shall consider myself as fortunate if I get through their territories with the loss of half my baggage."

In fact, Laing was not so lucky. One night they were attacked by the Tuareg while asleep in their camp. In the report that was given afterward to Warrington in Tripoli, Laing's camel driver told what happened: "They entered Laing's Tent, and before he could arm himself He was cut down by a sword on the thigh, He again jumped up and received one cut on the Cheek and Ear, and the other on the right arm above the wrist which broke the arm, he then fell on the Ground where he received seven cuts the last being on his neck." Laing was not killed, but the members of the caravan had run away during the Tuareg attack. He had to be carried by his servants to catch up with the rest of the party.

In spite of his injuries, Laing reached Timbuktu on August 18, 1826. He recovered in a mud house in the city that is alleged to still be standing. When he was able, he walked around the famous city openly in his Western clothes and was constantly accused of being a Christian spy. He left the city on September 26, 1826 with a caravan headed north. Two days later he was stopped by a Tuareg sheikh. The sheikh ordered one of his supporters to kill the foreigner. The man refused, and so the sheikh had two slaves hold him down while he plunged a spear in Laing's chest. All of his papers were burned.

Where to learn more

Laing's book about his Sierra Leone explorations is *Travels in Timmannee, Kooranko, and Soolima, Countries of West Africa* (London: 1825).

Laing's fate was not learned until 1910 when a French army officer investigated the incident and talked to people who had heard stories about the death. The officer, A. Bonnel de Mezières, also found documents relating to Laing's visit to Timbuktu. He wrote about the results in *Le Major A. Gordon Laing* (Paris: 1912).

There is a good summary of the Sierra Leone travels in Christopher Hibbert, *Africa Explored: Europeans in the Dark Continent, 1769-1889* (London: Allen Lane, 1982) and of the trip to Timbuctu in Sanche de Gramont, *The Strong Brown God: The Story of the Niger River* (Boston: Houghton Mifflin, 1975).

Richard Lander

(1804 - 1834)

Richard Lander was an Englishman who made three expeditions to West Africa and was the first European to sail down the Niger River to the ocean.

When **Hugh Clapperton** returned to Africa on his second attempt to reach the Niger River, he brought with him as his servant and assistant a young man named Richard Lander from Cornwall in the west of England. Having had no formal education at all, Lander had developed a desire to travel at an early age and had made a trip with a merchant to the West Indies at the age of 11, had stayed there for three years, and then returned to England where he found work as a servant for men traveling to Europe and South Africa.

After he had been hired by Clapperton, the two traveled to the port of Badagri near the present-day city of Lagos, Nigeria, which they reached in November 1825. They were accompanied by four other Europeans who all died within a short while after they headed inland. They traveled to the town of Badagri on the Niger and then headed north to the great emporium of Sokoto in northern Nigeria. Along the way Lander became ill and was physically carried by Clapperton for part of the distance.

Once Lander and Clapperton reached Sokoto in March 1827, 15 months after they had left Badagri, it was Clapperton's turn to become sick. Lander nursed him for six weeks, but he died on April 18, and Lander was left alone to bury him. He headed back to the coast at Badagri, which he did not reach until December 1827. There he was accused of witchcraft and forced to drink a poisonous liquid—if he died it would prove that he was guilty. He survived. He was picked up by a British ship and taken to Cape Coast in what is now Ghana. From there he finally managed to get passage back to England, where he arrived in July 1828.

Clapperton and Lander's trip had been a failure: they were supposed to have traveled down the Niger to its mouth. However, the English sponsors of the voyage were so impressed with Lander's resourcefulness in making the journey that they sent him back again two years later to try again. This time he traveled with his brother John. The two brothers left from Badagri in February 1830 and reached Bussa on the Niger on June 17. They then traveled 100 miles upstream where they found traces of **Mungo Park**'s expedition of 1806. They then went down the Niger in leaky, locally-made canoes.

They were captured and robbed by the King of the Ibos. He demanded a ransom that they could not pay, but they were rescued by another monarch, King Boy of Brass, who agreed to pay their ransom if they would see to it that he was rewarded by the British. King Boy took them to his capital, Brass Town, at the mouth of the Niger. Eventually a British ship showed up, but the captain fired at King Boy and drove him away and only reluctantly agreed to take the Lander brothers on board. He dropped them almost immediately on the nearby island of Fernando Po. From there they got passage to Rio de Janeiro and then back to England.

At long last Europeans had followed the course of the Niger to the sea and now knew which of the many streams along the coast led to the great river to the interior. For this feat Richard Lander was given a prize by the Royal Geographical Society.

Richard Lander returned to the Niger in 1833 on an expedition financed by Liverpool merchants. This time his luck did not hold. He was attacked by African tribesmen and died along the Niger River shortly before his thirtieth birthday in April 1834.

Where to learn more

The two original sources for Lander's explorations are Richard Lander, *Records of Captain Clapperton's Last Expedition to Africa*, 2 vols. (London: Henry Colburn & Richard Bentley, 1830; reprinted, London: Frank Cass and Company, Ltd. 1967) and Richard and John Lander, *Journal of an Expedition to Explore the Course and Termination of the Niger, with a Narrative of a Voyage Down the River to its Termination*, 3 vols. (London: 1832). This second volume was edited by Robin Hallett as *The Niger Journal of Richard and John Lander* (London: 1965).

Books discussing the exploration of the Niger include A. Adu Boahen, *Britain, the Sahara, and the Western Sudan, 1788-1861* (Oxford: Clarendon Press, 1964); Christopher Lloyd, *The Search for the Niger* (London: Collins, 1973); Sanche de Gramont, *The Strong Brown God: The Story of the Niger River* (Boston: Houghton Mifflin Company, 1975; reprinted in paperback, 1991); and Christopher Hibbert, *Africa Explored: Europeans in the Dark Continent, 1769-1889* (London: Allen Lane, 1982).

Jean François de Galaup, Comte de la Pérouse

(1741-1788)

The Comte de La Pérouse was a French naval officer who led a major expedition to the Pacific following those of Cook. He disappeared in the South Pacific.

Jean Francois de Galaup, Comte de La Pérouse was born at Guo near Albi in southern France. He entered the navy at 15. He was wounded and captured by the British while serving on board the *Formidable* during a naval battle off the coast of Brittany in November 1759. Sent home from England, he served off the east coast of North America and in the Indian Ocean during the rest of the Seven Years' War (the French and Indian War in North America).

He was promoted to lieutenant in April 1775 and captain in 1780 after France became allied with the newly-formed United States during the American Revolution. During that war, he distinguished himself by commanding an attack that took British forts in Hudson Bay in August 1782. He demonstrated his

Comte de La Pérouse. The Granger Collection, New York.

humanity by leaving the remnants of the settlements enough arms and provisions to enable them to survive during the oncoming winter. He also arranged for the release of one of his British prisoners, **Samuel Hearne**, so that Hearne could go back to England to publish an account of his trip to the Arctic Ocean in 1770-72.

In 1783 the French government decided to send an expedition to the Pacific to follow up on the work of Captain Cook, and in particular to explore the passage to the Bering Sea, which had been a mystery to Europeans since the sixteenth century. King Louis XVI himself helped to draw up the proposal for this voyage of exploration and, when La Pérouse, was selected to lead the fleet, gave him an audience before he sailed.

In command of two ships, *La Boussole* and *L'Astrolabe* (captained by Paul-Antoine de Langle), La Pérouse left Brest on August 1, 1785 bound for Brazil. After passing south of Cape Horn he went to Chile for reprovisioning, sailed to the Sandwich Islands (as Hawaii was then called) and then went north to Alaska. He landed at Yakutat Bay near Mount St. Elias in Alaska. From there he went south along the coast as far as California, proving that there was no northwest passage in that region. After a short time in Monterey, the capital of Spanish California, he sailed across the Pacific, finding several islands unknown to Europeans. He reached Macau, a Portuguese colony on the south coast of China on January 2, 1787.

After six weeks of reprovisioning and making repairs, La Pérouse left Macau on April 10, 1787 and headed for the Sea of Japan and the Sea of Okhotsk in the northwest Pacific. He sailed up the Tatar Straits, naming several points on both its shores, and, without going all the way around it, speculated that Sakhalin must be an island, not a peninsula attached to the Asian mainland. In September he put in to the Russian port of Petropavlovsk on the Kamchatka Peninsula, and sent one of his officers, Baron Jean de Lesseps, overland across Siberia to report on his discoveries thus far.

La Pérouse then turned south for Australia. In December 1787 he reached Tutuila, in what is now American Samoa, which had been discovered by **Louis Antoine de Bougainville** in 1767. A party from *L'Astrolabe* including the Captain, Langle, went ashore to look for water and were killed by the Samoans. La Pérouse left without taking reprisals and sailed via Tonga and Norfolk Island to Botany Bay, near present-day Sydney, Australia. He landed there on January 26, 1788 just eight days after the first British convict ships arrived to found the new colony of New South Wales. Captain Arthur Phillip, the new

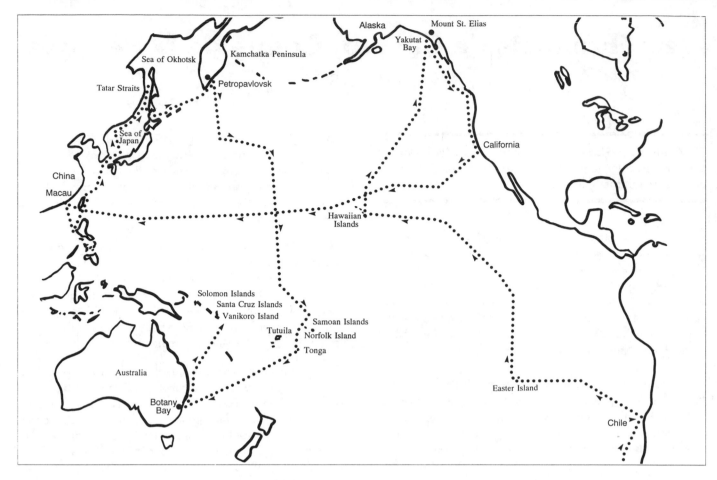

La Pérouse's Pacific route.

governor, had already gone north to Sydney to look for a more favorable site. Most of the British ships were still at Botany Bay, however, and they helped La Pérouse to anchor. He set up a camp on the northern shore, at a spot that is now called La Perouse, and maintained good relations with the English during his six-week stay.

He left Botany Bay on March 10, 1788 and headed into the Pacific and was never heard from again. When the French government realized that La Pérouse was missing, it immediately equipped and expedition under **Joseph-Antoine Raymond Bruni d'Entrecasteaux** to look for him, but without success.

As Franco-British relations deteriorated during the French Revolution, rumors spread in France blaming the British for having killed La Pérouse in order to keep him out of their new colony in Australia. It was not until 1828 that the mystery was solved, when **Jules-Sébastien-César Dumont d'Urville** found the remains of the two ships on Vanikoro Island in the Santa Cruz group to the south of the Solomon Islands.

Fortunately the records of most of La Pérouse's discoveries were saved because they had been sent back to Paris from Kamchatka.

Where to learn more

La Pérouse's original French account appeared in Paris in three volumes in 1797: *Voyage de La Pérouse autour du monde.* It was translated into English and was published in London in 1798 and in the United States in 1801 as *A Voyage Round the World, Performed in the Years 1785, 1786, 1787, 1788, by M. de la Pérouse* (Boston: Joseph Bumstead). (Of course, the title of the book is wrong because La Pérouse never made it around the world!) An abridgement of the French edition appeared in Tours in 1840, edited by F. Valentin. This version was translated by Julius S. Gassner as *Voyages and Adventures of La Pérouse* (Honolulu: University of Hawaii Press, 1969).

The best summary in English of La Pérouse's voyage is John Dunmore, *French Explorers in the Pacific,* vol. 1: *The Eighteenth Century* (Oxford: Oxford University Press, 1965). Other books about La Pérouse in English include: Charles N. Rudkin, *The First French Expedition to California: La Pérouse in 1786* (Los Angeles: Glen Dawson, 1959) and Edward Weber Allen, *The Vanishing Frenchman: The Mysterious Disappearance of Lapérouse* (Rutland, Vermont: Charles E. Tuttle Co., 1959).

René-Robert Cavelier de La Salle

(1643 - 1687)

René-Robert Cavelier de La Salle was a French adventurer who was the first European to sail down the Mississippi to its mouth and later led a disastrous French expedition to Texas.

René-Robert Cavelier de La Salle was born into a well-to-do family in Rouen, the capital of the French province of Normandy. He studied at a Jesuit school in his hometown and then became a novice, or student for the Catholic priesthood, at a Jesuit seminary in Paris. He showed an aptitude for mathematics and taught that subject to secondary school students while pursuing his own studies. La Salle was not a successful seminarian, however—the Jesuits thought he was too adventurous and unstable. After being turned down twice for a chance to be a missionary, he quit the seminary in 1667.

La Salle had family connections in New France (Canada) and went there soon after leaving the seminary. He arrived at Quebec sometime before November, 1667. He was granted a gift of land

René-Robert Cavelier de la Salle. The Granger Collection, New York.

on the island of Montreal and sold it two years later for a profit. With this money La Salle determined to lead an expedition to find the Ohio River, which he felt would lead to the South Seas and eventually to China.

This expedition, which left Montreal in July 1669, attracted the attention of a Catholic order, the Sulpicians, who sent two of their members to serve as missionaries along with La Salle. Since none of these travelers had any experience, the trip was pretty much a disaster. They crossed Lake Ontario and then were forced to spend a month in the village of the hostile Seneca tribe. They were rescued by an Iroquois who offered to guide them to the Ohio by way of Lake Erie. But before they got as far as Lake Erie, La Salle became sick with fever, and the two missionaries were lured away to visit the Potawotomi tribe, who had never been evangelized.

Because of his illness, La Salle told his companions that he was going to return to Montreal. However, he did not turn up there again until the fall of 1670. We do not know where he went during 1669-1670, but many later supporters claimed that he discovered the Ohio and/or the Mississippi Rivers during this period. Evidence shows that this is almost certainly not true and that the Mississippi was not found until 1673 by **Louis Jolliet** and **Jacques Marquette**.

La Salle made unknown trips during the period 1671-1672 and again in 1672-1673. In the fall of 1673 he returned to Montreal where he allied himself with Governor Frontenac of New France in a dispute that was then going on in the colony. As a result, La Salle was given a title of nobility (which is why he is often called Sieur de La Salle) and command of a French fort at what is now Kingston, Ontario. In 1677 he went back to France, and on May 12, 1678 he received permission from the King to explore the western part of North America between New France, Florida, and Mexico.

La Salle started his explorations by constructing a fort on the Niagara River between what is now Ontario and New York in September 1678. He was accompanied by several men who were to gain fame as well—Dominique La Motte, **Henri de Tonty**, Father **Louis Hennepin** and Father de La Ribourde. La Salle was forced to spend the winter of 1678-1679 at Fort Frontenac at Kingston. When he returned his men had built a sailing ship, the *Griffon*, to explore the Great Lakes. They sailed on August 7, 1679.

The explorers traveled through Lake Erie into Lake Huron and then to Michilimackinac that separates Lake Huron from Lake

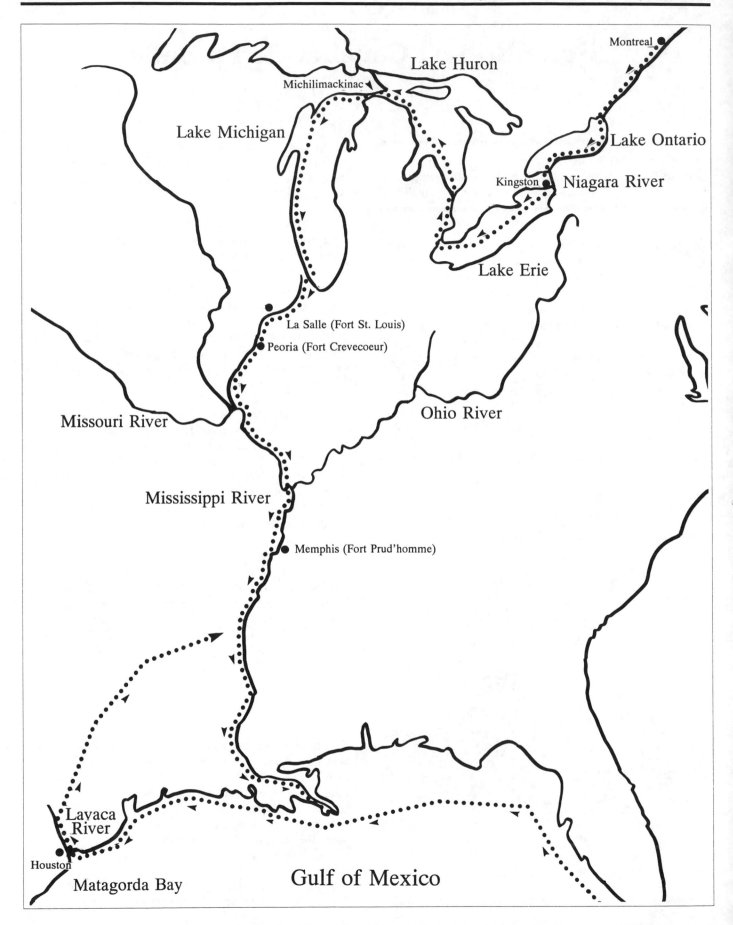

La Salle's voyage through the Great Lakes and down the Mississippi River, 1678-1682, and his voyage through the Gulf of Mexico, 1684-1687.

Michigan. They left the *Griffon* there and went south on Lake Michigan in canoes. In the middle of winter they reached a village of the Illinois tribe near the present city of Peoria. Discouraged by the Native Americans from continuing, several of La Salle's men deserted. He built a fort that he called Crèvecoeur in the area to serve as a supply center for future explorations. La Salle then sent Hennepin to lead an advance party to the Mississippi while he headed back to Canada.

La Salle's return was full of disappointments: the *Griffon* had been lost, the fort on the Niagara had been burned down, and a supply ship had sunk. He reached Montreal in June 1680 and turned around immediately and headed back. At Fort Frontenac he learned that Fort Crèvecoeur had been burned and that many of his men had deserted and were returning to Canada, robbing his supply posts along the way. La Salle set an ambush for them and captured them at the beginning of August. He then retraced his steps and went all the way back to Fort Crèvecoeur, hoping to find his lieutenant, Henri de Tonty, whom he had left in charge. Tonty was not among the corpses left behind at the burned fort, but it was not until May 1681 that the two explorers met up again, Tonty having rowed a canoe back to Michilimackinac.

La Salle returned once again to Montreal in the spring and summer of 1681, where he tried to calm down his creditors as well as other enemies who were spreading rumors about his mismanagement. He headed back into the wilderness in the fall and winter of 1681 and reached Fort Crèvecoeur in January 1682 at the head of a party of about 40 men. From there they reached the Mississippi on February 6, 1682. They built canoes and headed down the river, passing the mouth of the Missouri River, the Ohio River that La Salle had been looking for for so long, and the site of Memphis, Tennessee, where he built a fort called Prud'homme.

In March La Salle and his men were almost attacked by a party from the Arkansas tribe, but he was able to make peace and took possession of the country in the name of the King of France. He passed the farthest point reached by Jolliet and Marquette and spent time among the Tensas and Natchez tribes and then reached the Gulf of Mexico on April 9, 1682. There he erected a great cross and led ceremonies proclaiming these new discoveries to be part of France.

La Salle and Tonty and their men started back upriver the next day. They were attacked by Native Americans along the way, and La Salle became seriously ill and had to rest at Fort Prud'homme. He sent Tonty on ahead to report back to the Governor of New France on their discoveries. Following his recovery, La Salle made it as far as Michilimackinac in September, 1682 where he met up with Tonty and wrote dispatches on his adventures to Quebec and to France.

In the winter of 1682-1683 La Salle went back to the Illinois River and built a fort near the present-day town of La Salle, Illinois. In the meantime, a new governor had arrived in New France, and he was quickly influenced by La Salle's enemies. On his orders, La Salle was sent to France in December 1683 to report on his conduct.

Once back in France, La Salle found that there was very little support for his ideas on developing the Mississippi Valley. However, there was an influential party that was trying to interest the French government in the idea of sending an expedition to the mouth of the Rio Grande in the Gulf of Mexico in order to conquer New Mexico and/or New Spain (Mexico) and take over their valuable mines. In order to fit into these schemes, La Salle purposely falsified his discoveries and made a map that showed the Mississippi River much farther west than it actually is, showing it to empty into the Gulf of Mexico in what is now Texas, rather than Louisiana.

La Salle was able to convince the King and rich French merchants to back an expedition to the Gulf of Mexico. He left France at the end of July 1684 at the head of an expedition of four ships and 320 men and women. As a result of bad planning and La Salle's ongoing quarrel with the ships' captain, the boats were overloaded and there was not enough water. They were forced to put into the French colony of Haiti, where they got word that one of the ships, which was carrying most of the expedition's supplies, had been captured by the Spanish.

The three remaining ships left Haiti on November 25, 1684 and headed toward the Mississippi delta. On December 27 and 28 they saw the muddy waters that indicated they were near the mouth of the great river. However, La Salle had made miscalculations in his navigation and chose to believe unreliable old Spanish charts. Therefore, he decided he was much farther east than he actually was and headed west rather than investigating the immediate area.

By the time La Salle realized his mistake, the ships were off Matagorda Bay south of what is now the city of Houston. In trying to get into the Bay one of the ships ran aground. Local Native Americans tried to take some of the goods from the wrecked ship and were shot at by the Frenchmen. From then on the two groups were enemies. In March the naval captain returned to France with one of the ships and many men who had become discouraged. La Salle was left behind with one boat and a very unhappy expedition.

In May 1685 the Frenchmen began construction of a fort at the mouth of the Lavaca River. From there, La Salle and other members of the expedition made exploring trips into the surrounding countryside. In April 1686 the remaining ship was wrecked when its pilot became drunk, and the little colony was left without any means of escape. La Salle decided that the only way was to travel overland to find the Mississippi and then to head up the river to the Great Lakes where he could find French missions and traders. He left Fort St. Louis at the end of April with 20 men, but through various mishaps this was reduced to eight by October, and he was forced to return.

La Salle set out again on January 12, 1687 with 17 companions, leaving 25 behind at the fort. By this time the men hated La Salle, who had caused them such misery, and on the night of March 18/19, 1687 a group of five of them killed La Salle's nephew, servant and guide. The next morning, a little north of the modern town of Navasota, Texas, they shot La Salle in cold blood and left his body for wild animals to eat. What was left of La Salle's party made it to Montreal on July 13, 1688. The group that had been left behind at Matagorda Bay was attacked by the Karankawa tribe and destroyed except for two small boys who were taken by a Spanish raiding party.

Where to learn more

The first collection of original documents relating to La Salle was made by French archivist Pierre Margry in the 19th century: *Mémoires et documents pour servir à l'histoire des origines françaises des pays d'outre mer: Découvertes et établissements des Français dans l'ouest et dans le sud de l'Amérique septentrionale*, 6 vols. (Paris: Maisonneuve, 1876-1886). It is said that Margry took some liberties with the documents in order to bolster La Salle's reputation.

I.J. Cox, ed. *The Journeys of René Robert Cavelier, Sieur de La Salle*, 2 vols. (New York: 1905; reprinted, Austin: Pemberton Press, 1968) contains translations of original accounts by various associates. Another such account is Jean Delanglez, trans. and ed., *The Journal of Jean Cavelier: The Account of a Survivor of La Salle's Texas Expedition, 1684-1688* (Chicago: Institute of Jesuit History, 1938), which includes a critical analysis of the sources relating to La Salle. One such associate has received a biography of his own: Marion A. Habig, *The Franciscan Père Marquette: A Critical Biography of Father Zénobe Membré, O.F.M. La Salle's Chaplain and Missionary Companion* (New York: Joseph Wagner, 1934), which also discusses the source material critically.

Robert S. Weddle, ed. *La Salle, the Mississippi, and the Gulf* (College Station: Texas A&M University Press, 1987) contains translations of and essays about some previously obscure documentary material.

Henri Joutel, a survivor of the Matagorda Bay expedition, wrote a narrative that was published in Paris in 1713. The English translation appeared the following year: *A Journal of the Last Voyage Perform'd by Monsr. de la Sale to the Gulph of Mexico, to Find Out the Mouth of the Mississippi River* (London: 1714, facsimile reprint, Ann Arbor: University Microfilms, 1966). Another edition was published as *A Journal of La Salle's Last Voyage*, edited and with an introduction by Henry Reed Stiles (New York: Corinth, 1962).

An important question concerning this expedition was investigated by Herbert E. Bolton, a well-know historian of the West: "The Location of La Salle's Colony on the Gulf of Mexico," *Mississippi Valley Historical Review*, vol. 2 (September 1915), pp. 171-189. Another book looks at the expedition from the point of view of the Spanish, who considered La Salle an interloper and wanted to throw him out: Robert S. Weddel, *Wilderness Manhunt: The Spanish Search for La Salle* (Austin: University of Texas Press).

The most famous history of La Salle's explorations is Francis Parkman's *La Salle and the Discovery of the Great West*, 2 vols. (originally published Boston: 1869; many subsequent editions). It is now noted more for its literary than its historical qualities.

Many of Parkman's biases are corrected by Jean Delanglez, S.J. in *Some La Salle Journeys* (Chicago: Institute of Jesuit History, 1938). Delanglez also wrote an important chronology of La Salle's activities: "A Calendar of La Salle's Travels, 1643-83," *Mid-America*, vol. 22 (1940). A French perspective is given in Paul Chesnel, *Histoire de Cavelier de La Salle, exploration et conquête du bassin du Mississippi* (Paris: 1901), which was translated into English by Andrée Chesnel Meany as *History of Cavelier de La Salle, 1643-1687* (New York: G.P. Putnam's Sons, 1932). A more recent biography that is considered to be judicious and well-rounded is E.B. Osler, *La Salle* (Toronto: Longmans Canada, 1967). Patricia K. Galloway, ed. *La Salle and His Legacy: Frenchman and Indians in the Lower Mississippi Valley* (Jackson: University Press of Mississippi, 1982) is a collection of monographs on different aspects of La Salle's explorations and their ramifications. Galloway's own essay concerns the primary source material for the 1682 expedition.

There is an excellent biographical essay on La Salle, which was very helpful in writing this account, by Céline Dupré in the *Dictionary of Canadian Biography*, vol. 1 (Toronto: University of Toronto Press, 1967).

Pierre de La Vérendrye

(1685-1749)

Pierre de La Vérendrye was a Canadian explorer who tried to find a way across North America to the Pacific and traveled farther west than any previous European.

Pierre de La Vérendrye was born to a prosperous family in the Quebec town of Trois-Rivières. He received some education at the Seminary of Quebec and then joined the army. He fought in some of the North American campaigns of the War of Spanish Succession (1699-1713). He was then sent to Europe in 1708 where he fought in the great battle of Malplaquet and was seriously wounded. He was promoted to lieutenant but after a few years in France requested to be sent back to Canada.

On his return to Quebec, La Vérendrye married and settled down as a farmer and fur trader. He was the father of four sons and two daughters, and his sons were also to become famous as explorers. His quiet life lasted until 1726 when his brother was given the rights to the fur trade in the vast country north of Lake Superior. La Vérendrye joined his brother and became leader of the operation after his brother returned to Quebec in 1728.

At this point, La Vérendrye became obsessed with finding a way across the continent of North America to the "Western Sea" (Pacific Ocean). He and his contemporaries thought that the continent was much smaller across than it actually is, and they believed it could be crossed relatively easily. At that time, the farthest west that Europeans had traveled was to Rainy Lake in western Ontario.

After talking to Native Americans at his trading post at what is now Thunder Bay, Ontario, La Vérendrye felt that the ocean could be reached by way of a river to the northwest, probably the Saskatchewan. In 1730 he got permission and money from the government in Quebec to establish a fort at Lake Winnipeg in northern Manitoba not too far from the headwaters of the Saskatchewan. On June 8, 1731 La Vérendrye set out from Montreal on an expedition that included three of his sons.

In spite of the refusal of many of the expedition to go all the way, La Vérendrye reached Rainy Lake in the fall of 1731 and built a fort there. In the spring of 1732 he went on to the Lake of the Woods (now on the border between the United States and Canada) and built another fort, which became La Vérendrye's headquarters. From there, he tried to push on to Lake Winnipeg but found that he was short of supplies and had to send back to Montreal to ask for additional money. This appeal was success-

ful, and he was able to send members of the expedition to build Fort Maurepas on the shores of Lake Winnipeg.

In the meantime La Vérendrye became involved in disputes between different tribes in the area. After a short trip to Montreal in 1734-1735, he returned to Lake of the Woods to face an attack by Sioux in June 1736, in which many important members of the expedition, including one of his sons, were killed.

Following the defense against the Sioux, La Vérendrye traveled to Fort Maurepas, arriving there in February 1737, almost six years after he had first set out from Montreal. At this point he became convinced that if he could find the Saskatchewan River it would prove to be the way to the Pacific. He returned to Quebec in 1737 to seek support for this. He was given more money but only on the condition that he find the Mandan tribe, who were thought to be the key to the west.

After returning to Fort Maurepas in September 1738, La Vérendrye and his sons traveled southwestward to the country of the Mandans, who actually lived on the Missouri, not the Saskatchewan. He reached the largest Mandan camp on December 3, 1738 in what is now western North Dakota. From there, his son Louis-Joseph traveled a little farther to the Missouri River. They returned to Lake of the Woods in January 1739.

La Vérendrye remained at Lake of the Woods until 1744, when he returned to Quebec and lived off of the profits he had made in the fur trade. He was planning another expedition to try to find the Saskatchewan when he died on December 5, 1749.

In the meantime, La Vérendrye's son Louis-Joseph traveled to the headwaters of the Saskatchewan River at Cedar Lake, Manitoba, in 1739. In 1742 he undertook another expedition to the Mandan country and then continued farther west to the foothills of the Rocky Mountains in modern Wyoming. In March 1743 he and the members of his expedition were in a camp of the Pawnee tribe opposite present-day Pierre, North Dakota. They buried a lead plaque there with the names of members of the expedition that was found in 1913. This was as far west as Europeans were to get on continental North America for many decades. Louis-Joseph's expedition had shown that there was no way to the Western Sea to the south. It was this discovery that motivated La Vérendrye's plans for an expedition to the Saskatchewan that was cut short by his death.

Where to learn more

La Vérendrye's activities were forgotten for many years. He was rescued from obscurity by discoveries made in the Archives of France by archivist Pierre Margry starting in 1852, who published the documents he found in *Découvertes et établissements des Français* (Paris: 1856). This was the beginning of several books about the fur-trader and explorer. Agnes Laut included La Vérendrye among her *Pathfinders of the West* (New York: 1904; reprinted, New York: Books for Libraries Press, 1969) and Lawrence Johnstone Burpee wrote about him in two books: *The Search for the Western Sea* (London, 1908; 2nd edition, Toronto: 1935, New York: Macmillan, 1936) *Pathfinders of the Great Plains: A Chronicle of La Vérendrye and His Sons* (Toronto: Glasgow, Brook & Co., 1914).

The most complete book in English is Nellis M. Crouse, *La Vérendrye: Fur Trader and Explorer* (Ithaca: Cornell University Press, 1956), which has a French-language counterpart in Antoine Champagne, *Les La Vérendrye et le poste de l'ouest* (Quebec: Presses de l'Université Laval, 1968). There is a more recent book about the explorations in the Great Plains: G. Hubert Smith, *The Explorations of the La Vérendryes in the Northern Plains, 1738-43* (Lincoln: University of Nebraska Press, 1980).

Michael J. Leahy

(1901 - 1979)

Michael J. Leahy was an Australian miner who explored large areas of New Guinea while searching for gold.

In the years of the late nineteenth and early twentieth century, the great island of New Guinea came under the political control of various European powers. The Dutch claimed the western half and ruled it as part of its vast East Indian empire. The British claimed the southeastern quarter and then turned it over to the Australians when they formed a self-governing dominion. German traders on the islands and mainland of the northeast eventually induced the German Kaiser to take over that section. But this territory was quickly conquered by the Australians and British during the early days of World War I.

Following the end of the First World War, the Australians extended their control over the coastal region of the eastern half up to the mountain spine that ran through the length of the island. By the 1930s, they had established that the island was rather sparsely populated by different tribes along the coast and in the main river valleys and that the immense mountains in the center were impenetrable and had almost no inhabitants. This view was entirely wrong.

In fact, the high mountains hid enormous valleys where agricultural tribes had developed a complex social system and very dense populations, much greater than those of the lowlands. It was one of the great shocks to contemporary knowledge of the world when the first Westerners stumbled upon these "Shangri-las" in the years immediately before the outbreak of the Second World War. It was also an enormous surprise to the Papuan tribes, who were still dependent on stone tools (they used copper for ornaments but had no other use for metal), were probably the last humans to learn about tobacco, and had no inkling of the great world outside their valleys.

The lure that led men into the mountainous interior was the discovery of gold. In 1922 an important gold find was made on the Bulolo River in the hills southwest of the large coastal town of Lae. Many prospectors rushed to the area and about $75 million dollars worth of gold was exported during the 1930s. One of these miners was Michael J. ("Mick") Leahy, born in Toowoomba in the Australian state of Queensland in 1901. He was the fourth of nine children of an Irish immigrant. When news of the gold strike a gold strike at Edie Creek reached Australia in 1926, Mick left his "T-model Ford on the side of the road" and quit his job as a railway clerk to seek his fortune in the New Guinea bush.

In 1930 Leahy and a fellow miner, Michael Dwyer, went upstream on one of New Guinea's river systems, the Ramu, and, without knowing it, crossed over the divide and started to follow another stream. This stream eventually became the Purari River, one of the main rivers emptying out into the *south* coast. By following this route, they became some of the first Westerners to traverse the island.

In the headwaters of the Ramu and Purari, the two Australians had noticed what seemed to be promising mineral deposits. In 1931 they mounted a prospecting expedition to explore this area. It turned out to be a disaster. They had hired an airplane to reconnoiter the area they were exploring on foot: it crashed into a mountain wall and was only discovered because the pilot's severed head rolled down the mountain onto a Papuan hunting trail. The land expedition was attacked by the hostile Kukukuku tribe, and Mick Leahy was clubbed in the head and his brother Patrick ("Paddy") was shot in the arm and shoulder with arrows. Another miner nearby was clubbed to death.

This did not deter Leahy, and in 1932 he went back inland to an area called Bena Bena with his 18-year-old brother Dan. They built an airfield that served as the western base for penetration of the interior by both government officials and gold prospectors. Several gold claims were staked out in the area. The Leahy brothers used this field as their base for further exploration, and on March 8, 1933, they flew into the first of the great mountain valleys—Mount Hagen. "What we saw," wrote Mick Leahy, "was a great flat valley, possibly twenty miles wide and no telling how many miles long, between two high mountain ranges, with a very winding river meandering through it. Below us were evidences of a very fertile soil and a teeming population—a continuous patchwork of gardens laid off in neat squares like chessboards, with oblong grass houses in groups of four or five dotted thickly over the landscape. Except for the grass houses, the view below us resembled the patchwork fields of Belgium as seen from the air."

Ground expeditions followed, usually led by Jim Taylor, the Australian government's representative to the area. Using a combination of aerial reconnaissance and land exploration, several other valleys were discovered and opened up—the Goroka, Chimbu, Wabag, and Wahgi. In each case, the explorers were the first white men the Papuans had ever seen. When the planes first flew over the valleys, the inhabitants threw themselves on the ground in terror. In later accounts to anthropologists, they told of how among themselves they had said, "If we look at this thing, we shall surely die."

Mick Leahy continued his explorations in 1933 and 1934, eventually coming out of the mountains and meeting Papuans who were already in touch with Europeans from the north coast. As it happened, none of the lands they opened up proved to have any gold. Even the initial claims at Bena Bena were not commercially worthwhile. In 1934 another expedition led by Tom and Jack Fox went almost to the border of Dutch New Guinea without finding any trace of gold. When they got back to Mt. Hagen and told Mick Leahy, he records his reaction—"When we had heard it all, Danny and I walked back to the base camp in almost complete silence, both of us feeling that we had been robbed of our principal interest in life."

The Australian government continued its explorations. Jim Taylor reached the last of the great valleys, Telefomin, in 1939 right before the outbreak of World War II. On the Dutch side of the border, the mountain valleys were actually discovered during the war. The largest, the Grand Valley of the Baliem River, was accidentally discovered by a U.S. Army Air Force pilot in 1944 when he flew into a gap in the mountains. It was promptly named "Shangri-La" by war correspondents who were thinking of a mythical valley in the Himalayas in James Hilton's novel *Lost Horizon*.

Leahy himself continued an adventurous career. In 1935 he traveled to London to claim priority for his discoveries before the Royal Geographical Society. He became the center of an international incident in 1936 when the Italian government condemned his methods in "pacifying" Papuan tribes before the League of Nations as justification for their actions in Ethiopia. When World War II broke out, he was offered the rank of sergeant by the Australian Army, and he turned it down to become a lieutenant for the U.S. Air Force. He was awarded the U.S. Medal of Freedom in 1948.

In the meantime, Leahy had married a childhood sweetheart back in Queensland in 1940, with Jim Taylor as his best man. They had five children, but Leahy never acknowledged the three illegitimate sons that he had with New Guinea women; they lived with his brother Dan. After the war, Leahy acquired an agricultural property at Zenag in the eastern highlands of New Guinea. It prospered, especially after the independence of Papua New Guinea, which he had opposed. In 1971 the Explorers' Club in New York awarded him its highest medal at the same time as **Neil Armstrong**, for being the man to open up the last-known places on Earth. He died in Zenag on March 7, 1979.

Where to learn more

Leahy collaborated with writer Maurice Crain to write the story of his highlands adventures in *The Land that Time Forgot* (London: Hurst & Blackett, 1937). The story of the contact between the Australians and the Papuans is told in Colin Simpson, *Plumes and Arrows* (Sydney: Angus & Robertson, 1962). The history of the exploration of New Guinea, which talks about the explorations of the Leahy brothers and Jim Taylor, can be found in Gavin Souter, *New Guinea: The Last Unknown* (New York: Taplinger Publishing Co., 1966). There is an award-winning documentary film about the first European encounters with the highlanders of New Guinea that includes footage taken by Leahy: *First Contact* (Sydney, 1983). There is a good biographical essay on Leahy by James Griffin in the *Australian Dictionary of Biography*.

Ludwig Leichhardt

(1813 - 1848)

Ludwig Leichhardt was a German explorer who led an expedition from Brisbane to a place near Darwin on the north coast of Australia.

Ludwig Leichhardt was born at Trebatsch near Frankfurt-on-Oder in Prussia in Germany on October 23, 1841, the son of a well-to-do farmer. He was educated at the Universities of Berlin and Göttingen. He had started out as a student of philosophy and language but switched to the study of the natural sciences, which he also pursued in England and France. He never graduated but was often called "Dr." in later life because of his encyclopedic knowledge. He evaded military service in Prussia and went to Australia, arriving in Sydney on February 14, 1842.

While in Sydney, Leichhardt gave lectures on botany and geology and made some walking expeditions into the country-side, including a trip from Newcastle in New South Wales to Moreton Bay in Queensland, a distance of 480 miles. At that time, the government of New South Wales was interested in finding a route from Sydney to Port Essington, a harbor on the very northernmost part of Australia, that a naval expedition had

Ludwig Leichhardt.

said would make a fine place to serve as the gateway between Australia and Asia. Leichhardt offered his services but was turned down as being too inexperienced. He then went out and got private financing and mounted the expedition on his own.

Leichhardt's expedition left Sydney in August 1844 and sailed to Moreton Bay, the site of Brisbane. They left Moreton Bay in October 1844 and headed aimlessly north, with Leichhardt often getting separated from the rest of the party. By February 1845 Leichhardt calculated that they had covered one quarter of the distance but had eaten three-quarters of the provisions. They therefore quickened the pace and reached the Gulf of Carpentaria in June 1845. Here, they were attacked by Aborigines, and one man was killed and two were wounded. Hampered by the wounded men, Leichhardt was still able to travel around the Gulf and to reach Port Essington (the site of present-day Darwin) on December 17, 1845. They were picked up by a ship and returned by sea to Sydney on March 25, 1846. They were treated as heroes, and Leichhardt was pardoned by the King of Prussia for his desertion.

Leichhardt then decided on a more ambitious project: to travel from Moreton Bay all the way across the continent to Perth on the coast of Western Australia. He left Brisbane in December 1846 with seven other men. They were delayed by heavy rains; the animals they were driving along to use as food strayed off; and the party became ill with fever. They were forced to return to Brisbane in June 1847, after having traveled about 500 miles. After resting for two weeks, Leichhardt set out on his own and traveled about 600 miles exploring the Condamine River. By then it was generally known that Leichhardt did not have the skills to lead an expedition. The success of his first expedition had been mainly the result of luck and the skill of his Aborigine guides. Therefore, he had a difficult time trying to get backing for another attempt to get to Perth. This did not deter him, however, and he set out with six companions from the Darling Downs intending to travel to the Upper Barcoo River (discovered by **Thomas Livingstone Mitchell** in 1845) and from there north to the Gulf of Carpentaria. From there he would follow the coast all the way around to Perth. He left a settlement on the Condamine River just west of Cunningham's Gap in the Great Dividing Range on April 3, 1848 and was never seen or heard of again. No conclusive traces of the expedition have ever been found.

Where to learn more

Leichhardt wrote about his excursions around Sydney in *Scientific Excursions in New Holland, 1842-44* (London: 1845) and of the expedition to Darwin in *Journal of an Overland Expedition in Australia, from Moreton Bay to Port Essington, a Distance of Upwards of 3000 Miles, During the Years 1844-1845* (London: 1847). Excerpts can be found in Kathleen Fitzpatrick, *Australian*

Explorers: A Selection from Their Writings (London: Oxford University Press, 1958). The results of Leichhardt's investigations were presented by John Dunmore Lang in *Cooksland in North-Eastern Australia* (London: Longman, Brown, Green, and Longmans, 1847; reprinted, New York: Johnson Reprint Corporation, 1970).

There have been several collections of Leichhardt's letters over the years, including: L.L. Politzer, ed. *Dr. Ludwig Leichhardt's Letters from Australia* (Melbourne: 1945) and M. Aurousseau, *Letters of F.W. Ludwig Leichhardt* (Cambridge: University of Cambridge Press, 1968). Among biographies are:

C.D. Cotton, *Ludwig Leichhardt and the Great South Land* (Sydney: 1938) and A.H. Chisholm, *Strange New World* (Sydney: 1941; 2nd revised edition published as *Strange Journey: The Adventures of Ludwig Leichhardt and John Gilbert* (Adelaide: 1973).

The noted Australian writer Patrick White (the only Australian to win the Nobel Prize for Literature) based his famous novel *Voss* on the quixotic life of Leichhardt.

Meriwether Lewis

(1774 - 1809)

William Clark

(1770 - 1838)

Meriwether Lewis and William Clark led the first official United States expedition across North America to the Pacific Ocean.

Meriwether Lewis grew up on a farm near Charlottesville, Virginia, where his family was friends with Thomas Jefferson, whose famous estate, Monticello, is just outside Charlottesville. He was an officer in the local militia and was called to active duty in 1794 during the Whiskey Rebellion. He then joined the U.S. Army and served as a captain in the First Infantry under General Anthony Wayne in the wars against the Native Americans in the "Old Northwest Territory." When Jefferson became President in 1801 he chose Lewis to be his personal secretary (comparable to today's chief of the White House staff).

In 1803 Jefferson negotiated a treaty with Napoleon Bonaparte by which France turned over its claims to the western basin of the Mississippi River (recently re-acquired by France from Spain) to the United States for $15 million. The treaty was signed on April 30, 1803, with the formal cession to take place the following year. In his budget request to Congress in January 1803 Jefferson had already requested funds to send an exploring party to the West to find an overland route to the Pacific. Following intensive lobbying by Lewis, he was chosen to lead the expedition.

Jefferson sent Lewis to Philadelphia for several weeks to study botany and astronomy so that he would be prepared to carry out the scientific investigations that so interested the President. With Jefferson's approval, Lewis invited William Clark to be co-leader of the expedition. The Clark family had been neighbors of the Lewises outside of Charlottesville before joining the pioneers traveling across the Appalachian mountains into Kentucky. The boyhood friends had later served together in the frontier wars. Clark was the younger brother of George Rogers Clark, a Revolutionary War hero.

Jefferson's instructions for the expedition were to find "the most direct and practicable water communication across the continent for the purposes of commerce." This "commerce" explicitly included the fur trade, which Jefferson hoped to divert from the British Hudson's Bay Company into the hands of Americans. The expedition was supposed to travel up the Missouri River, cross the Rocky Mountains, and then descend the western slope by the most practicable river, "whether the Columbia, Oregon, or Colorado, or any other river" to the Pacific Ocean.

Lewis left Philadelphia in early July 1803 and headed to Pittsburgh. He floated down the Ohio River, where he was joined by Clark and his African-American servant York in Louisville. The expedition spent the winter of 1803-1804 on the east bank of the Mississippi River, in American territory. The formal cession of the Louisiana Territory had not yet taken place. Clark took charge of training the men they had recruited along the way in military drill, building boats, and making preparations for the trip. Lewis spent a good deal of his time in St. Louis, where he gathered information from fur traders who were familiar with the upper reaches of the Missouri River. On March 9, 1804 Lewis was an official witness to the transfer of Upper Louisiana from Spain to France and then, on the following day, of the same territory from France to the United States.

The expedition set out on May 14, 1804. There were a total of 45 men in three boats. Of these, 29 were to travel all the way to the Pacific while the others were to turn back at approximately the halfway point. The first part of the journey up the Missouri was through well-traveled country. They passed Femme Osage, the last European settlement and home of the famous frontiersman **Daniel Boone** on May 25. In late July, a little beyond the mouth of the Platte River, they met members of the Oto and Missouri tribes and informed them that their territory had been taken over by the United States. In August the expedition's only death occurred: Sergeant Floyd died suddenly of a "bilious colic" and was buried on a bluff near the site of Sioux City, Iowa. The Floyd River was named in his honor.

The party met with the Omaha tribe and with various bands of Sioux. They were threatened only once: on September 25 near present-day Pierre, South Dakota, a group of Teton Sioux made threatening movements. The expedition countered with a show

Meriwether Lewis. The Bettmann Archive.

from what is now the state of Idaho. Sacajawea had been captured in a raid and sold to Charbonneau. She was pregnant and gave birth to a baby boy—Pompey— on February 11, 1805. Lewis and Clark hired Charbonneau and his wife as interpreters and guides.

The winter was spent hunting and bartering for supplies for the coming trip. In the spring, 13 of the men headed back to St. Louis. The rest of the expedition set out again on April 7, 1805, this time into unknown country. Clark wrote in his journal: "I could not but esteem this moment of my departure as among the most happy of my life." They reached the junction with the Yellowstone River (in what is now Montana) on April 25.

Along this stretch of the trip, Clark usually took charge of managing the canoes, while Lewis, accompanied by his big Newfoundland dog, Scannon, kept to the shore, exploring, hunting, and gathering specimens. On June 3, 1805 they reached a place where "the river split in two." Lewis followed the northern fork for a while, which he decided was not the main course. He named it the Marias River, in honor of his cousin, Maria Wood. He then turned around and caught up with Clark. They cached a large amount of supplies at the juncture of the two rivers in anticipation of the return.

Heading up what they had decided was the main stream, they were stopped by the great falls of the Missouri (at Great Falls, Montana). They were forced to build crude wagons and haul the boats and all their supplies around the rapids. It took them one month to make the 18-mile portage. On July 25, they reached the place where three smaller streams come together to form the Missouri. The three rivers were named after Jefferson, James Madison, and Albert Gallatin (the Secretary of the Treasury). Following Sacajawea's advice, they followed the southwest branch, which they had named after Jefferson. The river quickly narrowed and the angle of descent grew steeper. Lewis took three other men (but not Sacajawea) and went ahead to see if he could reach a Shoshoni village. On August 12 he reached the source of the Missouri and crossed over the Continental Divide to the source of the Lemhi River, a tributary of the Columbia.

The next day Lewis stumbled upon a group of Shoshoni. They were initially hostile, but he was able to reassure them about his peaceful intentions. He took the Native American chief and some of his warriors back to meet with Clark and the rest of the expedition. When they entered the camp, Sacajawea recognized them as her own people. One of the women was a childhood friend who had been captured with her and then escaped. The chief was her brother. The Lemhi was unnavigable so the explorers had to continue on land. They bought 29 horses from the Shoshoni, and the chief agreed to go with them part way as guide. From that point on the trip was very difficult. The trail was steep, crooked, and dangerous, and it took them 50 days to cover 300 miles. The explorers were often hungry and had to eat horse meat and dog meat. On September 5, 1805 the group reached a village of the Flathead tribe, where they were able to get food and more horses. They passed through the Bitterroot

of force and then talked to the Native Americans in a conciliatory way, and a confrontation was avoided. Lewis and Clark wrote in their journals that the Americans had broken the Sioux blockade of the Missouri and opened it up for free movement. This turned out to be a little optimistic in that the United States and the Sioux fought each other until the Battle of Wounded Knee in 1877.

On October 8, Lewis and Clark reached the territory of the Arikara tribe. Several French traders were in the village and could serve as interpreters. One of the Arikara chiefs agreed to accompany the Americans upstream to the encampments of the Mandan tribe. The Mandans lived near the modern city of Bismarck, North Dakota. Their territory was the farthest point about which the Americans had any definite knowledge, and Lewis and Clark had planned to spend the winter there.

The expedition reached the small cluster of Mandan villages at the end of October and spent three weeks building a small stockade about three miles downstream that they named Fort Mandan. They were 1,600 miles from St. Louis and had traveled an average of about nine miles a day. The Americans spent five months at Fort Mandan. During that time they were visited by various groups of Native Americans and fur traders. One of the visitors was Toussaint Charbonneau. He had a Native American wife named Sacajawea, who was a member of the Shoshoni tribe

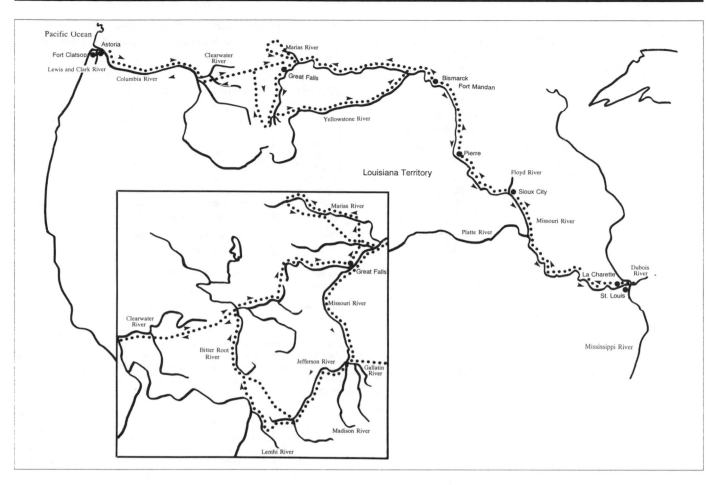

The Lewis and Clark expedition of 1804-1806.

Range by way of Lolo Pass and descended the mountains into the valley of the Clearwater River on September 20. Now in the territory of the Nez Percé (Pierced Nose) tribe, the expedition made it to a Nez Percé camp where they were fed so generously that they all got sick.

The expedition built five canoes to float down the Clearwater River. They arrived at the Snake River on October 10 and at the Columbia on October 16. Along the way they bartered for food with the Native Americans, but by that time they had very little left to trade and so they often performed in order to get their supper. One of the men played his violin while York danced, and Lewis showed off his watch, telescope, and compass. After making the portage around Cascade Falls on November 2, they found that the river was subject to tidal flows and knew that they must be close to the Pacific. They got their first view of the ocean on November 7, 1805.

Lewis and Clark and the rest of the expedition constructed winter headquarters at a place they named Fort Clatsop in honor of the local tribe. It was on the Lewis and Clark River near the mouth of the Columbia, not far from modern Astoria, Oregon. Unlike the previous winter when they had been at Fort Mandan, they were short of supplies and the local Native Americans were

not especially cooperative. They lived principally on elk that they shot and preserved in sea salt.

Leaving behind letters for any European traders who might travel along the coast, Lewis and Clark headed back east on March 23, 1806. Rowing upstream on the Columbia, they had difficulty getting food. Lewis and Clark sold their services as doctors to the villages they passed along the way in return for dog meat. When they reached the Clearwater they recovered horses they had left behind. The party split up at the Bitter Root River in June. Lewis found a short cut and was able to make it to the great falls of the Missouri only six days after crossing the Continental Divide. He then spent some time exploring the Marias River. Along the way, he had a minor skirmish with members of the Blackfoot and Gros Ventre tribes. He was shot in the leg by one of the hunters, who was nearsighted and thought he was a bear. He was disabled for a month.

Clark and the rest of the party, including Sacajawea, followed the route they had taken out as far as the Three Forks area. From there they went through a pass, now known as Bozeman Pass, pointed out by Sacajawea, that led to the Yellowstone River. When they reached the Yellowstone, a Native American raiding party slipped in one night and took half of their horses. As they followed the river downstream, they passed a gigantic rock, which Clark climbed and into which he carved his name and the date July 25, 1806. He named the rock Pompey's Rock in honor of Sacajawea's little boy.

The two parties met up again on the Missouri River. They reached the Mandan villages on August 14, 1806 and persuaded Chief Big White to come with them back to Washington. They returned to St. Louis on September 23, 1806. "We were met by all the village," wrote Clark, "and received a hearty welcome from its inhabitants." From St. Louis, Lewis and Clark traveled on to Washington to report personally to the President.

The expedition had been a great success. Both Lewis and Clark were awarded large land grants in the West. In 1806, Lewis was appointed Governor of the Louisiana Territory. He headed back to Washington in 1809 to carry out some official business when he stopped in an isolated cabin in Tennessee to spend the night. He was later found dead with a gunshot wound in his head. It was never clear what happened, but there is evidence that Lewis, who was subject to depressive moods, shot himself.

Clark entered the fur-trading business and became a partner in **William Henry Ashley**'s Missouri Fur Company. He was appointed Governor of the Missouri Territory and served in that capacity until it became a state. He was then appointed Superintendent of Indian Affairs and held that position until his death in 1838.

Clark had adopted Pompey, Sacajawea's son, and educated him at the best schools on the East coast. When he was 18, Pompey met a German prince who was traveling in the United States, went back to Europe with him, and spent six years touring the continent. He returned to the United States and became an important fur dealer and guide. He moved to California and became the mayor of San Luis Rey. He died in 1866 on his way to Oregon. Sacajawea is thought to have died from fever in December 1812.

Where to learn more

There are several editions of the records and papers of the Lewis and Clark expedition: Meriwether Lewis and William Clark, *History of the Expedition Under the Command of Captains Lewis and Clark*, edited by Elliott Coues, 3 vols. (New York: Allerton Book Co., 1922); Reuben Gold Thwaites, ed., *Original Journals of the Lewis and Clark Expedition*, 8 vols. (New York: 1904-1905; reprinted, New York: Antiquarian, 1959); Bernard De Voto, ed., *The Journals of Lewis and Clark* (Boston: 1963); Ernest S. Osgood, ed., *The Field Notes of Captain William Clark, 1802-1805* (New Haven: Yale University Press, 1964); and Donald Jackson, ed., *Letters of the Lewis and Clark Expedition with Related Documents* (Urbana: University of Illinois Press, 1962).

Worthwhile books about the great expedition include: Noah Brooks, *First Across the Continent* (New York: Charles Scribner's Sons, 1901); John Bakeless, *Lewis and Clark: Partners in Discovery* (New York: 1947); and David Freeman Hawke, *Those Tremendous Mountains: The Story of the Lewis and Clark Expedition* (New York: 1980).

There are also several specialized studies on different aspects of the expedition: Eldon G. Chuinard, *Only One Man Died: The Medical Aspects of the Lewis and Clark Expedition* (2nd edition, Glendale: Arthur H. Clark Co., 1980); Raymond Darwin Borroughs, ed. *The Natural History of the Lewis and Clark Expedition* (East Lansing: Michigan State University Press, 1961); Paul Russell Cutright, *Lewis and Clark: Pioneer Naturalists* (Urbana: University of Illinois Press, 1969); and Cutright, *A History of the Lewis and Clark Journals* (Norman: University of Oklahoma Press, 1976)

The major participants also have been given a great deal of attention. There is a full-scale biography of Lewis, Richard Dillon, *Meriwether Lewis: A Biography* (New York: 1965), as well as an interesting study on the question of his death, Howard I. Kushner, "The Suicide of Meriwether Lewis: A Psychoanalytic Study," *William and Mary Quarterly*, vol. 38 (July 1981) pp. 464-481. Arguments about the exact role that Sacajawea played in the expedition—whether she was indispensable or whether her contribution has been overrated—are presented in Grace Raymond Hebard, *Sacajawea* (Glendale: Arthur H. Clark Co., 1933) and C.S. Kingston, "Sacajawea as Guide: The Evaluation of a Legend," *Pacific Northwest Quarterly*, vol. 35 (January 1944), pp. 3-18. For a discussion of other featured players, see Charles G. Clarke, *The Men of the Lewis and Clark Expedition* (Glendale: Arthur H. Clark Co., 1970).

Charles A. Lindbergh

(1902 - 1974)

Charles A. Lindbergh was the first person to fly across the Atlantic Ocean.

C harles A. Lindbergh was born in Detroit, Michigan on February 4, 1902. His father was an immigrant who came from a distinguished Swedish family. He moved to Little Falls, Minnesota when Charles was two months old and farmed and practiced law there. He was elected to Congress in 1907 and served there until 1917, where he was a leading isolationist.

Lindbergh attended public and private schools in Washington, D.C. and Minnesota. He entered the University of Wisconsin in 1920 but dropped out after two years and entered flying school in Lincoln, Nebraska. He made his first flight on April 9, 1922 as a passenger. After less than eight hours of instruction, he began flying barnstorming flights with a stunt aviator in Nebraska. He made his first parachute jump in June 1922. He bought his first plane for $500 and made his first solo flight in April 1923. In 1924 he signed up to take flight training at Brooks Army Base in San Antonio, Texas and a year later was commissioned in the United States Air Service Reserve. He began flying air mail service flights between Chicago and St. Louis on April 15, 1926.

During one of these routine flights, Lindbergh decided that he wanted to win the $25,000 Orteig Prize that a wealthy financier was offering to the first person flying non-stop from New York to Paris. Trying to scrape together the money to buy a plane and finance the flight, Lindbergh made a presentation to a group of St. Louis businessmen, who agreed to come up with the money in order to promote St. Louis as a future site of aviation. He thereupon decided to name his plane the *Spirit of St. Louis.*

Lindbergh traveled to San Diego, California to the Ryan Air Craft Factory, where he had his airplane constructed according to his specifications. During this period, he began making detailed plans for the solo flight, including sleep deprivation training. He started out by staying awake 24 hours at a stretch, then 30, then 35, and finally 40 hours at a time. When the plane was ready, he took off from San Diego on May 10, 1927, stopped in St. Louis, and then flew on to Curtiss Field on Long Island in New York. He made the flight in 21 hours and 20 minutes, a new record. After resting and getting his equipment ready, Lindbergh took off from Curtiss Field at 7:52 a.m. on May 20, 1927. He had been so nervous the night before that he had been unable to sleep, thereby prolonging his hours of sleeplessness.

Lindbergh's flight plan took him up the coast of New England and Nova Scotia and then over the Gulf of St. Lawrence to the island of Newfoundland. The last land he saw in North America was at Cape Race on the eastern tip of Newfoundland. As he flew across the North Atlantic, eating only sandwiches, he was constantly assailed by the need to sleep. He dozed off several times and once awoke to find that he was skimming the waves of the North Atlantic. There was no radio aboard the plane, and no one knew if he was alive or not. He also had to make all of his own navigational calculations with the chance that any error would push him far off course. He knew that he was safe when he flew over the southern coast of Ireland during the day on May 21, 1927.

When Lindbergh reached the coast of Normandy, it was nearing nightfall. He found his way to Paris by following the

Charles Lindbergh. AP/Wide World Photos.

course of the Seine River upstream. Unknown to him, his progress was reported by telephone and radio by watchers who passed the news on to Paris. As he got closer to the city, Parisians began pouring out of the city and heading for Le Bourget Field where he was scheduled to land. More than a million Parisians were on hand when he reached Le Bourget, having caused the greatest traffic jam in French history. As Lindbergh began to land at the airfield, he could not understand what the large crowds were doing and thought something was wrong. When he touched ground and the crowds surged toward his plane, he could not believe that they had turned out for him. He had made the first flight across the North Atlantic from New York to Paris, a distance of 3,610 miles, in 33 hours, 29 minutes, and 30 seconds.

Lindbergh instantly became a world hero. He was received by royalty and heads of state throughout Europe and was awarded several medals. There were numerous awards in the United States as well as ticker-tape parades in New York and St. Louis. He made an air tour of the United States that traveled to 75 cities. At the invitation of the President of Mexico, he made a non-stop flight from New York to Mexico City that took 27 hours and 10 minutes in December 1927. At a reception at the American Embassy, he met the daughter of the American ambassador, Ann Morrow. They were married on May 27, 1929.

Lindbergh was an intensely private person who was put off by the degree of his popular fame. After his marriage, he took a job as technical adviser to several of the new commercial airline companies. He bought a large estate in New Jersey outside of New York City and lived there quietly. This peace was shattered in 1932 when his only child, a one-year-old boy, was kidnapped. The kidnapping soon became the world's biggest media event, labeled as the "crime of the century." After several months, the boy's body was found, and an unemployed German immigrant, Bruno Hauptmann, was found guilty of the crime and executed. As a result of the notoriety of the case, federal law was changed to make kidnapping a federal crime.

The Lindberghs had other children, but they and their children were constantly harassed by the press. As a result, they left the United States and moved to England in December 1935. Lindbergh later moved to France and worked with a famous botanist, Dr. Alexis Carrel. He designed a perfusion pump used in zoological experiments and published a scientific book in collaboration with Dr. Carrel. In 1938 and 1939 Lindbergh traveled to Germany and the other countries of Europe and commented favorably on the state of the German Luftwaffe and the corresponding lack of preparation by the democracies. When he returned to the United States in 1939 he spoke out forcefully in favor of his father's isolationism. The combination of these actions led to much unfavorable comment. When World War II broke out, Lindbergh tried to volunteer to serve in the United States Army Air Corps but was rejected because of his prior "treasonable" statements.

In 1943 Lindbergh was hired by Henry Ford, and he traveled to the South Pacific in 1944 to help in planning aircraft operations there. After the war, it was revealed that he had been employed as an unpaid consultant to the Air Force on secret projects during the last two years of the war. The combination of this news and the popularity of his wife's books about flying and their life together led to Lindbergh's restoration in the public's esteem. He spent the following years speaking out on various topics and writing books, especially about the spiritual aspects of life and environmental concerns. He and his wife built a house on a remote part of the Hawaiian island of Maui where he died on August 26, 1974.

Where to learn more

One of the reasons for Lindbergh's enormous influence was his great skill as a writer. He wrote several books that had a large readership. The first was *"We"*: *The Famous Flier's Own Story of His Life and His Transatlantic Flight* (New York: G.P. Putnam's Sons, 1927). This was followed by *Of Flight and Life* (New York: Charles Scribner's Sons, 1948); *The Spirit of St. Louis* (New York: Charles Scribner's Sons, 1953), the best history of the famous flight, it won the Pulitzer Prize and was made into a movie starring James Stewart (Warner Brothers, 1957); *The Wartime Journals of Charles A. Lindbergh* (New York: Harcourt Brace Jovanovich, 1970); *Boyhood on the Upper Mississippi: A Reminiscent Letter* (St. Paul: Minnesota Historical Society, 1972); and *Autobiography of Values* (New York: Harcourt Brace Jovanovich, 1977).

Likewise, Anne Morrow Lindbergh was a notable author. The books that she wrote about their life together include: *Listen! The Wind* (New York: Harcourt, Brace, 1938); *North to the Orient* (New York: Harcourt, Brace, 1938; reprinted, 1963); *The Wave of the Future* (New York: Harcourt, Brace, 1940); *Gift from the Sea* (London: Chatto & Windus, 1955); *Bring Me a Unicorn: Diaries and Letters 1922-28* (London: Chatto & Windus, 1972); *Hour of Gold, Hour of Lead: Diaries and Letters 1929-32* (New York: Harcourt Brace Jovanovich, 1973), which tells the story of the famous kidnapping; *Locked Rooms and Open Doors: Diaries and Letters 1933-35* (New York: Harcourt Brace Jovanovich, 1974); and *The Flower and the Nettle: Diaries and Letters 1936-* (New York: Harcourt Brace Jovanovich, 1976).

Several biographies of Lindbergh, of varying quality, appeared during the height of his fame in the 1930s. A more recent book that tries to assess the impact of his whole career is Leonard Mosley, *Lindbergh: A Biography* (London: Hodder & Stoughton, 1976). A good book about the famous flight, which includes many family and other photos, is Brendan Gill's *Lindbergh Alone* (New York: Harcourt Brace Jovanovich, 1977).

Jan Huyghen van Linschoten

(1563 - 1611)

Jan Huyghen van Linschoten was a Dutch traveller, whose famous book about Asia, the Itinerario, *encouraged the Dutch to explore the East Indies, and who went with Barents on two of his voyages to the Arctic Ocean.*

Jan Huyghen van Linschoten was born in Haarlem, in Holland, and moved with his family to another commercial town, Enkhuizen, at an early age. Preceded by two older brothers, he went to Spain at the age of 16 and from there to Portugal, where he got a job as clerk to an archbishop who was on his way to Goa, a Portuguese trading post on the west coast of India. Linschoten left Lisbon in April 1583 and stayed in Goa until 1589. On his way back to Europe, he stopped over in the Azores and finally returned to Enkhuizen in September 1592.

Back in Holland, Linschoten became friends with a learned doctor who had made many travels of his own. This man, known by his Latin name of Bernardus Paludanus, collaborated with

Jan Huygen van Linschoten. Taken from a portrait in his work *Navigatio in Orientalem sive Lusitanorum Indiam* (1599).

Linschoten on an account of his voyages, which was published under the title of *Itinerario, Voyage, or Passage by Jan Huyghen van Linschoten to East or Portugal's India.* The enormous work, in several volumes, recounted not only what he had actually seen traveling to and from Goa but also all that he heard from Portuguese voyagers sailing out of the port.

Linschoten's book gave extremely valuable information to the Dutch merchants who at that moment were planning to challenge the Portuguese monopoly on trade with the East. His descriptions of the Indies, and the maps illustrating his text, provided the necessary spur for the Dutch to send an expedition to the East Indies. On April 2, 1595 a great Dutch expedition under **Cornelius Houtman** sailed eastward and began the history of Dutch colonialism in the East Indies (now called Indonesia) that was to last until 1949.

Linschoten, however, was not part of Houtman's expedition. He had instead gone north. His colleague Paludanus had convinced Dutch merchants that it was theoretically possible to reach the East by sailing north around the Eurasian continent. Linschoten sailed aboard one of two Dutch ships that left Holland in June 1594; the other one was commanded by **Willem Barents**. The ships separated, and the one with Linschoten on board attempted a more southerly route. He got as far as the Kara Sea, east of the large island of Novaya Zemlya. At the time he was there, the sea was open, and Linschoten thought he had found the way to the East.

In 1595, therefore, Barents and Linschoten set out on another expedition to explore the route that Linschoten had seen. This time, when they sailed into the Kara Sea, it was filled with ice, and the expedition hung around aimlessly for five weeks before returning to Amsterdam. Linschoten did not sail on Barents' third, and fatal, voyage but remained as a wealthy merchant in his home town until his death in 1611.

Where to learn more

Linschoten's complete *Itinerario* has been published in Dutch in The Hague in 8 volumes by the Linschoten Vereeniging, an effort that took from 1910 to 1957. The only English edition is Arthur C. Burnell and Pieter A. Tiele, eds. *The Voyage of John Huyghen van Linschoten to the East Indies*, 2 vols. (London: Hakluyt Society, 1884). A good summary of the influence of the work can be found in George Masselman, *The Cradle of Colonialism* (New Haven: Yale University Press, 1963). Less specifically tuned to Linschoten's contribution, but a must for understanding Dutch colonialism in the East Indies is C.R. Boxer, *The Dutch Seaborne Empire, 1600-1800* (London: Hutchinson, 1965; paperback edition, 1977). For the role of Linschoten in the search for the Northeast Passage, see Gerrit de Veer, *The Three Voyages of Willem Barents to the Arctic Regions* (London: Hakluyt Society, 1876) and a good summary in Jeannette Mirsky, *To the Arctic!: The Story of Northern Exploration from Earliest Times to the Present* (New York: Alfred A. Knopf, 1948).

David Livingstone

(1813 - 1873)

David Livingstone was a Scottish missionary who became the first European to cross Africa and led several expeditions to explore the lake system of central Africa.

David Livingstone.

David Livingstone was born in the town of Blantyre near Glasgow, Scotland, on March 19, 1813, the second son of a traveling tea salesman. He started working in a local cotton mill at the age of 10. After working from 6:00 a.m. until 8:00 p.m., he studied for two hours at night school and then read when he got home. When the night school was forced to close, he read at work by "placing the book on a portion of the spinning jenny, so that I could catch sentence after sentence as I went by." By dint of this tireless self-application, he taught himself Latin, Greek, and mathematics. He was admitted to the University of Glasgow to study Greek and theology. He then went to the University of London to get a medical degree. During this time he became a member of the London Missionary Society and was ordained as a minister in 1840.

Livingstone's original intention had been to go to China as a medical missionary. This possibility was cut off by the outbreak of the Opium War between Britain and China in 1839. So he chose Africa instead. He sailed to Cape Town, spending a month there before sailing to Algoa Bay, where he arrived on March 15, 1841, just four days before his 28th birthday. He then made a 10-week, 700-mile journey by ox cart to Kuruman, a mission station among the Tswana people established by Dr. Robert Moffat.

From the beginning, Livingstone was not satisfied working for someone else and wrote that he wanted to "preach the gospel beyond every other man's line of things." By August 1843 he had founded his own mission station at Mabotsa, 250 miles north of Kuruman. While there, he was attacked and almost killed by a lion. He was saved by a companion who distracted the lion's attention, but for a while it was not clear whether he would survive or not. His left shoulder was broken in several places, and he never fully regained the use of his left arm.

Livingstone went back to the mission station at Kuruman to recuperate. During his stay he married Mary Moffat, the daughter of the mission head, having decided that it was time to enter "into the marriage relation." They went back to Mabotsa, but Livingstone quarreled with a colleague and left to be on his own once again. He went first to a place 40 miles to the north, and then in 1847 he moved his family to Kolobeng on the eastern edge of the

Kalahari Desert. Within a couple of years, however, Livingstone once again became restless.

North of the Kalahari Desert is Lake Ngami, which Livingstone had heard about but which no European had ever visited. Livingstone wanted to go there, partly because he wanted to look into the possibilities of establishing a mission among the Makololo people, a Tswana tribe ruled by the renowned chief Sebituane who lived north of the lake. Livingstone was able to finance his expedition by enlisting the support of a wealthy young big-game hunter named William Colton Oswell and his friend Mungo Murray.

Livingstone set out with the two English sportsmen on his first exploring expedition on June 1, 1849. They were guided by an African named Ramotobi who knew the Kalahari very well. The expedition consisted of 80 oxen, 20 horses, and 30 to 40 porters and drivers. This large troupe often ran out of water, and it was only because Ramotobi knew where to dig for it that they survived. They saw mirages several times along the way and ran ahead thinking they had arrived at Lake Ngami. At one point, even Ramotobi got lost, but they were saved when Oswell saw a Bushman woman running away and was able to catch up with her and persuade her to lead them to a large pool eight miles away. On July 4, 1849 they reached a previously unknown river, the Zouga (now called the Botletle). The local people confirmed that it led to Lake Ngami, and they followed it for 280 miles, reaching the lake on August 1, 1849.

The Makololo lived another 200 miles to the north. The local ruler refused to supply guides in order for the Europeans to make the trip, and they were forced to return to Kolobeng. On his return, Livingstone sent an account of the expedition, barely mentioning Oswell and Murray, to the Royal Geographical Society in London. As a result, he received his first recognition as an explorer, being awarded one-half of the 1850 royal grant for geographical discovery.

In 1850 Livingstone tried to reach the Makololo once again. This time he took his pregnant wife and three small children with him. The animals were attacked by tsetse flies, who carry the parasites that cause sleeping sickness, and two of the children became ill with malaria. Oswell, who happened to be in the area, helped them make it back to Kolobeng. Soon after their return, Mary Livingstone gave birth to a baby girl, who also caught malaria and died six weeks later.

Livingstone refused to give up, however. He wrote in his diary: "I mean to follow a useful motto and *try again*." Mary's mother pleaded with him not to take the family along, but he insisted. This time he asked Oswell to come with them and proposed taking a different route from the disastrous trip of the previous year. They set out in April 1851. Oswell, the hunter, supplied them with fresh game, but often there was nothing to shoot. Their guide, Shobo, turned out to be quite inexpert, getting lost several times, and he finally deserted them altogether. The spare water in one of the wagons was lost in an accident. At one point south of the Chobe River, they went for four days without any water. Livingstone wrote about his children: "The less there was of water, the more thirsty the little rogues became." They did, however, face the real prospect of watching the three children "perishing before our eyes." They were saved when they found the Mababe River on the fifth day.

The Mababe, however, was infested with tsetse flies, and 43 of the oxen died. Four days later they reached the Chobe (or Linyanti) River, a tributary of the Zambezi. Livingstone and Oswell went ahead in a canoe to meet Sebituane. The chief had traveled 400 miles and was waiting on an island in the middle of the river "with all his principal men around him, and engaged in singing when we arrived." Sebituane wanted guns from the Europeans, but he also seemed well disposed to the idea of setting up a mission station in his country. Unfortunately, he died from an infection in an old wound less than a month after meeting Livingstone.

Livingstone and Oswell traveled northeast through the Makololo country looking for a good site for a mission station, which they did not find. However, at the end of June 1851 at the village of Sesheke in what is now Zambia, they saw a great river—the Zambezi—whose course that far in the interior of Africa was unknown to Europeans. At that point, Livingstone conceived the idea of continuing on to reach the west coast of Africa. Oswell wrote: "He suddenly announced his intention of going down to the west coast. We were about 1,800 miles off it. To my reiterated objections that it would be impossible—'I'm going down. I mean to go down,' was the only answer." Livingstone wrote in his own journal: "I at once resolved to save my family from exposure to this unhealthy region by sending them home to England, and to return alone, with a view to exploring the country in search of a healthy district that might prove a centre of civilization, and to open up by the interior a path to either the east or west coast."

Livingstone and Oswell returned to the Chobe River to get Mary and the three children and then headed back to Kolobeng; Mary gave birth to another child in the middle of the desert. From there they went to Cape Town where they arrived in April 1852, and Livingstone packed his family onto a ship and sent them to England, where he entrusted them to the care of the London Missionary Society.

When Livingstone got back to Kolobeng, he found that his mission station had been destroyed by Boer raiders, with whom he had been in conflict for years. The Boers felt that the missionaries were getting in the way of their efforts to drive the Africans off the land and to use them as laborers for their own farms. Livingstone continued north and reached the Makololo country May 23, 1853, where he was greeted by Sebituane's son and successor, Sekelutu. Sekelutu accompanied him on a trip up the Zambezi to look for a site for a mission station. Taking leave of Sekelutu at his headquarters at Linyanti on November 11, 1853, Livingstone traveled into the land of the Barotse people, accompanied by 27 porters and guides supplied by Sekelutu.

Livingstone and his supporters went north around Lake Dilolo and through a swampy plain as far as the Kasai River, a tributary of the Congo, which he reached at the end of February 1854. Livingstone was sick with malaria for most of the time but was well cared for by the men in his caravan. At one point, a local chief demanded that he sell some of the men as slaves in return for food. Livingstone refused, and the expedition was on the verge of starvation. On March 30, 1854 they stood on a height of land and looked down on the valley of the Cuango River in what is now northeastern Angola. They were arguing with the people of a nearby village, who refused to give them food, when a sergeant in the Portuguese militia appeared and directed them to a nearby military outpost.

Traveling by way of Kasange, they reached the city of Luanda, capital of Angola, on May 31, 1854. In four months they had covered over 1,500 miles of unmapped country. Livingstone was housed in the home of the British consul, and his men found

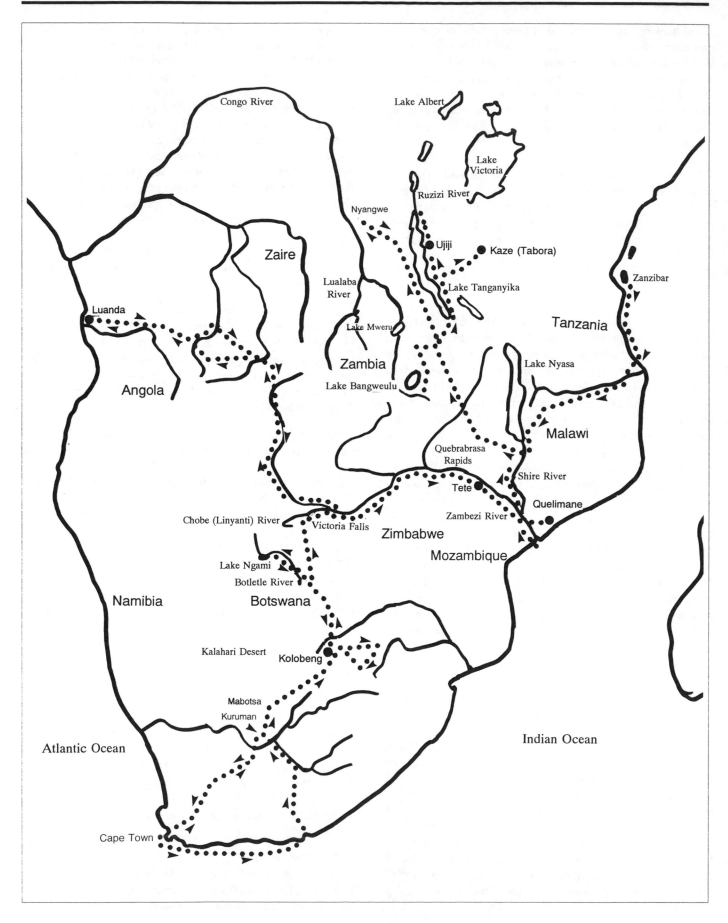

Livingstone's expeditions in south and central Africa from 1841-1873.

remunerative work on the docks of Luanda. But Livingstone had not found what he was looking for—a site free from fever among receptive people where he could start a new mission. So, rather than finding a ship to sail back to England, he turned around and on September 20, 1854 headed back inland.

The return by a different route proved to be more difficult, and it took a year before they reached Linyanti, arriving there on September 11, 1855. As he crossed the Kasai River on his way back, Livingstone recorded that he suffered his 27th bout of fever. He also almost died from rheumatic fever. Livingstone stayed in Linyanti for seven weeks before setting out to travel downstream on the Zambezi on November 3, 1855. Sekelutu accompanied him for part of the way and furnished him with an even larger retinue of porters and guides. Within a couple of weeks after setting out, they came upon the great falls that the Africans called *Mosi-Ao-Tunya* ("smoke that thunders") and which Livingstone named Victoria Falls in honor of his Queen. "It had never before been seen by European eyes; but scenes so lovely must have been gazed upon by angels in their flight."

Continuing eastward, on November 30 the expedition crossed the Kalomo River into territory inhabited by enemies of the Makololo. From then on they often encountered hostility from the tribes they visited. Livingstone cut across a loop of the Zambezi River, thereby missing seeing the Quebrabasa Falls. They were saved from starving to death by a party of men sent out from the Portuguese outpost of Tete in what is now western Mozambique. The expedition reached the port of Kilimane (Quelimane) on the Indian Ocean on May 20, 1856. Livingstone was the first European known to have traveled across the continent.

Livingstone's exploit immediately became widely known. A Royal Navy ship was sent out to bring him back to England. When he arrived there in December 1856, he was showered with honors and prizes. The President of the Royal Geographical Society said that he had achieved "the greatest triumph in geographical research . . . in our times." He resigned from the London Missionary Society, which found his explorations to be only remotely related to practical mission work. The British Government, however, appointed him Consul for the East Coast of Africa and provided him with £5,000 and several European assistants, including his brother Charles, to explore new regions. He was also given a steamer, which he named the *Ma-Robert*—the Africans' named for Mary Livingstone.

The *Ma-Robert* arrived at the mouth of the Zambezi in May 1858 and steamed up the Zambezi past Tete. Livingstone's plans for using the Zambezi as a quick way into the interior were stopped, however, by the Quebrabasa Rapids that he had missed on his previous journey. The rapids stretched for 40 miles and had waterfalls as high as 30 feet, making the river impassable. Livingstone next tried a northern tributary of the Zambezi, the Shire River, but was once again blocked by impassable rapids. Trying once again, he traveled as far as Lake Shirwa and then,

leading a small party, found the much larger Lake Nyasa (Lake Malawi) on September 16, 1859. They also discovered one of the busiest slave routes from the interior to the coast.

The following year Livingstone traveled back to the Makololo country. When he got there, however, he found that Sekelutu was suffering from leprosy and had gone into seclusion. He did not live long after Livingstone left on September 17, 1860, and his kingdom fell apart. When Livingstone returned to the coast, he found a large contingent of missionaries and helped them get established in two stations. These were not a success, however, and they eventually had to be abandoned. Livingstone explored Lake Malawi during September and October 1861.

On January 30, 1862, a British ship arrived at Kilimane with Mary Livingstone on board. She had, however, changed greatly since he had seen her last. She had become a heavy drinker. She soon came down with fever and died at the end of April. Livingstone became very despondent after her death, writing "I feel as if I had lost all heart now." He made a trip up the Rovuma River (which now forms the boundary between Tanzania and Mozambique) and found that it only led 160 miles into the interior before it was blocked by rapids. By that time, all of Livingstone's European assistants had either died or returned to England. In July 1863 he himself was recalled and he returned to London the following year. The government was dissatisfied with the results of his mission, and the general public ignored him.

Livingstone retired to a country estate that was the home of a big-game hunter he had known in Africa where he wrote up the results of his latest explorations. He was unhappy, however, and was thrilled when the Royal Geographical Society commissioned him to travel back to Africa to continue the search for the source of the Nile. **Sir Richard Burton** and **John Hanning Speke** had traveled to East Africa in 1857-1858 and had come away with differing opinions. Speke had returned in 1861-1863 and had shown that the Nile almost certainly flowed from Lake Victoria. Not everyone, including Burton, accepted that conclusion. Livingstone thought they were all wrong. He felt that one of the sources for Lake Victoria could be found to the south in Lake Tanganyika and that the ultimate source was a river and a lake the local people called Bangweulu. (He was wrong: Lake Bangweulu does discharge into Lake Tanganyika, but it ultimately flows into the Congo River system. This was finally elucidated by **Henry Morton Stanley**.)

In 1865 Livingstone left England for what proved to be the last time. He went via Bombay in India, where he engaged **James Chuma**, who had been with him at Lake Malawi. He then went to Zanzibar where he hired another freed slave named Susi. He was able to find only 60 porters willing to travel inland with them. Everywhere they went they saw the depredations of the slave trade: "village after village all deserted and strewn with corpses and skulls." There was little food to be found, and Livingstone had only 11 half-starved men with him when he reached Lake Malawi on August 8, 1866.

From Lake Malawi they traveled slowly inland to Lake Tanganyika. The journey became a series of disasters: a porter dropped the chronometer so that Livingstone could not make accurate observations of his position. Another porter deserted, taking Livingstone's medicine chest with him. By January 1867 the whole party became ill, and Livingstone came down with rheumatic fever in February. He wrote in his journal: "I feel as if I had now received sentence of death."

He was rescued by a party of Arab slave traders, with whom he traveled to Lake Mweru, which he reached on November 8, 1867. He left them to search for Lake Bangweulu. Only four men would accompany him on the journey. They reached the lake on July 18, 1868. In his desperate situation, his only choice was to go to Ujiji and catch up with the Arabs. "I am nearly toothless and in my second childhood," Livingstone wrote. Along the way, he came down with pneumonia. When he reached Ujiji on March 4, 1869 he found that all his supplies had been stolen. For the next year Livingstone was sick for most of the time and traveled little. During this period he read the Bible through four times.

In March 1871 Livingstone and three faithful attendants, Susi, Chuma, and Garner, reached the Lualaba River at Nyangwe. The Lualaba flows north (to eventually become the Congo), and Livingstone wanted to believe that it was part of the Nile system. Nyangwe was a major slave trading post, and Livingstone witnessed a massacre when some Arab slave traders fired into a crowded market, killing many innocent people. No longer wishing to depend upon the Arabs and wanting to tell the outside world of the horrors of the slave trade, he set out with his three faithful companions for a 350-mile walk to Ujiji "almost every step in pain."

When Livingstone reached Ujiji, he had no money and nothing to trade for food. He was destitute and in despair. But help was at hand. "Susi came running at the top of his speed and gasped out: 'An Englishman! I see him!' and off he darted to meet him. The American flag at the head of the caravan told me the nationality of the stranger." Henry Morton Stanley had arrived.

The medicine and food that Stanley had brought with him were sufficient to restore Livingstone's health. The two men set off together to explore the north end of Lake Tanganyika. The two men went farther up the lake than Burton and Speke had been able to do in 1858. They were able to settle one question about the source of the Nile by finding the Ruzizi River at the north end of the lake, which, contrary to Burton's belief, flowed into and not out of the lake. Unfortunately, this led Livingstone to believe even more firmly that the Lualaba River had to be the upper course of the Nile.

Livingstone and Stanley traveled together to the major trading center of Tabora (Kazeh) in what is now central Tanzania, 300 miles away. There, Livingstone hired porters in order to make an investigation of the Lualaba, and Stanley headed for the coast. He promised to obtain porters and supplies in Zanzibar to send back to Livingstone. Historians have often speculated about why

Livingstone did not return to England with Stanley, but there is no definitive answer. In any case, he waited at Tabora for five months until supplies arrived from the coast.

On August 25, 1872 Livingstone began his last journey around the south shore of Lake Tanganyika. He crossed the Kalongosi River, which flows into Lake Mweru and headed south towards Lake Bangweulu. He got hopelessly lost and became ill again. He suffered from dysentery and started bleeding profusely from hemorrhoids on March 31, 1873. A month before his death, he wrote in his journal: "Nothing earthly will make me give up my work in despair. I encourage myself in the Lord my God, and go forward." By April 22, he could no longer walk and had to be carried in a litter. "It is not all pleasure, this exploration," he wrote in his diary. The sad little expedition stopped at a village called Chitambo's in the district of Ulala. He made his last diary entry on April 27, 1873. At midnight on April 30 he said to Susi, "All right, you can go now." During the night, one of his companions looked in and saw him kneeling by his cot in prayer. The next morning he was still in the same position, dead.

Livingstone's companions, led by Susi and Chuma, embalmed his body with raw salt after they had cut out his heart and other internal organs. They buried his heart under a tree and then wrapped the body in cloth and bark and slung it on a pole. For eight months they carried it across East Africa until they reached Tabora on October 20, 1873. There they met an expedition commanded by **Verney Lovett Cameron** that had been sent out to look for Livingstone. They turned the body over to the Englishmen, but traveled with it to the coast and ultimately to England, where there was a large public funeral preceding his burial at Westminster Abbey on April 18, 1874.

Where to learn more

Livingstone's own books are the primary source for his travels: *Missionary Travels and Researches in South Africa*, 2 vols. (London: John Murray, 1857); and, in collaboration with Charles Livingstone, *Narrative of an Expedition to the Zambesi and Its Tributaries: And of the Discovery of Lakes Shirwa and Nyassa, 1858-1864*, 2 vols. (London: John Murray, 1865). Chuma and Susi carried his diary to England where it was published: Horace Waller, ed. *The Last Journals of David Livingstone*, 2 vols. (London: John Murray, 1874; New York: Harper & Brothers, 1875).

Livingstone left behind a significant number of papers that have been published over the years: J.P.R. Wallis, ed. *The Zambezi Expedition of David Livingstone, 1858-1863* (London: 1956); I. Schapera, ed. *David Livingstone: Family Letters, 1841-1856* (London: 1959); I. Schapera, ed. *Livingstone's Private Journals, 1851-1853* (London: 1960); I. Schapera, ed. *Livingstone's Missionary Correspondence, 1841-1856* (Berkeley: University of California Press, 1961); I. Schapera, ed. *Livingstone's African Journal, 1853-1856* (London: 1963);

There have been a large number of biographies over the years. Two that can be recommended are George Seaver, *David Livingstone: His Life and Letters* (London: Butterworth Press, 1957) and Jack Simmons, *Livingstone and Africa* (London: Hodder & Stoughton, 1955), which presents a good, brief summary of his career in its historical context. Others include: James I. MacNair, *Livingstone's Travels* (London: 1954); Frank Debenham, *The Way to Ilala: David Livingstone's Pilgrimage* (London: 1955); Elspeth Huxley, *Livingstone and His African Journeys* (London: 1974); Judith Listowel, *The Other Livingstone* (New York: 1974), which presents a less favorable view of Livingstone's accomplishments; and Tim Jeal, *Livingstone* (New York: 1974).

There are also more specialized studies of various aspects of Livingstone's career: Reginald Coupland, *Livingstone's Last Journey* (London: Collins, 1945);

Michael Gelfand, *Livingstone the Doctor* (Oxford: Oxford University Press, 1957); David Shepperson, ed. *David Livingstone and the Rovuma* (Edinburgh: 1965); George Martelli, *Livingstone's River* (London: 1970).

A useful interpretive essay is Norman Robert Bennett, "David Livingstone: Exploration for Christianity," in Robert I. Rotber, ed. *Africa and Its Explorers: Motives, Methods, and Impact* (Cambridge: Harvard University Press, 1970).

The overview presented in Christopher Hibbert, *Africa Explored: Europeans in the Dark Continent, 1769-1889* (London: Allen Lane, 1982) served as the main source for this account.

The important story of the Africans who accompanied Livingstone is told in D.H. Simpson, *The Dark Companions* (New York: Barnes & Noble, 1976).

Stephen Long

(1784 - 1864)

Stephen Harriman Long was an American mathematician and explorer who led four important expeditions to the western United States.

Stephen Long was born in Hopkinton, New Hampshire on December 30, 1784. He graduated from Dartmouth College in 1809 and became a professor of mathematics at the U.S. Military Academy. He then became one of the first officers in the newly-formed Army Corps of Engineers. He was chosen to lead an expedition in 1817 to search out sites for possible Army forts west of the Mississippi River. His small party traveled up the Arkansas River and went as far up the Mississippi as the Falls of St. Anthony (at present-day St. Paul). Following this expedition, the U.S. Army built Fort Smith on the Arkansas River and Fort Snelling at the juncture of the Mississippi and Minnesota Rivers.

In 1817 the Secretary of War, John C. Calhoun, proposed to build a fort in the Far West on the Yellowstone River as a way of keeping out the British Hudson's Bay Company. This led to the organization of the Yellowstone Expedition of 1819, under the overall command of General Henry Atkinson and a group of engineers commanded by Long. This expedition marked the first use of of steamboats on the Missouri River. The military expedition camped at Council Bluffs in what is now Iowa, where all the soldiers became ill with fever and scurvy. The expedition had to be abandoned.

In Washington, the War Department changed Long's instructions. On his return to the Missouri, he was to head southwestward. Long and his scientific and military colleagues left Council Bluffs on June 6, 1820. They reached the Front Range of the Rocky Mountains on June 30. They sighted and named Long's Peak. The following week they passed the site of the future city of Denver, and on July 18 one of the members of the party became the first American to climb Pike's Peak. On July 24 the expedition divided into two parties. One descended the Arkansas River: it was harassed by Native Americans, and three of its members disappeared with weapons, horses, and the expedition's records. Long led the other party to find the Red River, which was then the boundary between the United States and Spanish Mexico. They did find a large river that they thought was the Red and followed it downstream, but it turned out to be the Canadian, a tributary of the Arkansas.

The official report of Long's 1820 expedition was written by one of his colleagues, Dr. Edwin James, a botanist. In it he repeats the views of **Zebulon Pike** that the Great Plains were the "Great American Desert," not suitable for settlement. Although this was not an original view, many later authors have held Long responsible for spreading this myth and thereby slowing down the advance of Americans into the West.

In 1823 Long was sent to the northern United States to investigate the land between the Mississippi and Missouri Rivers and to find the source of the Minnesota River. He traveled as far as Fort Snelling overland and then went up the Minnesota River to its headwaters and across the small portage to the headwaters of the Red River of the North, which is in the Hudson Bay drainage basin. He went to the 49th parallel, where he surveyed the border between the United States and Canada, just north of what is now Pembina, North Dakota. He continued north to Lake Winnipeg in Canada and then returned to the eastern United States via Lake Superior and the other Great Lakes. The expedition had been a success, and he was acclaimed on his return to Philadelphia on October 26, 1823.

In the following years, Long became interested in the new engineering challenges posed by the development of the railroad. In 1827 he was assigned by the War Department to find a route for the Baltimore & Ohio Railroad. He worked as a consulting engineer for different railroads while still serving as an active officer in the Army. He wrote several books on railroad and bridge construction and patented a method of building wooden bridges. He was called to Washington at the outbreak of the Civil War in 1861 and promoted to Colonel. He retired in 1863 and died in Alton, Illinois on September 4, 1864.

Where to learn more

Long wrote about his first expedition in an article, "Voyage in a Six-Oared Skiff to the Falls of St. Anthony in 1817," *Collections of the Minnesota Historical Society*, vol. 2 (1860). Edwin James's account of the following two expeditions is *Account of an Expedition from Pittsburgh to the Rocky Mountains, Performed in the Years 1819 and '20*, 3 vols. (Philadelphia: 1822-1823; reprinted, Barre, Mass.: Imprint Society, 1972). The fourth expedition was reported in W.H. Keating, *Narrative of an Expedition to the Source of the St. Peter's River, Lake Winnepeek, Lake of the Woods ... Performed in the Year 1823*, 2 vols. (Philadelphia: 1824; reprinted, Minneapolis: Ross & Haines, 1959).

There are a couple of biographies of Long: Richard G. Wood, *Stephen Harriman Long, 1784-1864* (Glendale, CA: Arthur H. Clark Co., 1966) and Roger Nichol, *Stephen Long and American Frontier Exploration* (Newark: University of Delaware Press, 1980).

A very good book about the exploration of western America, which served as a main source for this account, is: William H. Goetzmann, *Exploration and Empire: The Explorer and the Scientist in the Winning of the American West* (New York: Alfred A. Knopf, 1967).

Luna

(1959-1972)

The Soviet Luna spacecraft were the first man-made objects to travel to the moon.

The Soviet Union launched Luna 1 on January 2, 1959. The name "Luna" was taken from the Latin word for "Moon." The first Luna was nicknamed Mechta ("Dream"). Luna 1 was a small object, only 40 inches in diameter. It was chiefly designed to measure the Moon's magnetic field, which it discovered to be almost non-existent. It flew by the Moon at a closest distance of 4,660 miles and then entered into orbit around the Sun, broadcasting data for a total of about 34 hours.

On September 12, 1959, the Soviets launched Luna 2. It was much larger than its predecessor—it weighed 3,000 pounds and carried 858 pounds of instruments and transmitting equipment. Luna 2 was the first man-made object to hit the Moon: it crashed between the craters Archimedes and Autolycus in the Mare Imbrium on September 14. Signals stopped at the precise moment when it had been predicted to hit the surface.

Luna 3 was a much more significant flight. It had been designed to fly around the Moon and give humans their first view of the satellite's "dark" side. The spacecraft weighed 3,300 pounds, of which 614 pounds was something called the Automatic Interplanetary Station that allowed it to operate even when it could not be reached by signals from the Earth. It was launched on October 4, 1959, exactly two years after the first flight of **Sputnik**. It went behind the Moon, approaching within 4,372 miles of the lunar surface on October 10. The quality of the photographs it sent back was not very good, but it allowed the first view of several important features, including the Mare Crisium, or Sea of Crises.

Lunas 4 through 8 were unsuccessful. The Soviets were finally successful with Luna 9, which made the first soft landing on the Moon's surface on February 3, 1966. It landed in the Oceanus Procellarum and sent back its first pictures to the Earth within the next few minutes. Luna 9 showed that the Moon's surface was hard, not covered with a heavy layer of dust as some scientists had thought. This confirmed that the surface could support a spacecraft carrying humans. Luna 9 is still standing.

Luna 10 achieved another first by entering into lunar orbit. Launched on April 3, 1966 and weighing 3,500 pounds, it maintained contact with the Earth for 460 orbits. Its instruments studied micrometeoritic particles and gamma radiations coming from the Moon's surface.

Lunas 11 and 12 both entered lunar orbit successfully during the latter half of 1966. Luna 12 got within 62 miles of the Moon's surface. Luna 13 landed successfully in the Ocean of Storms, while Zond 5 and 6, part of a parallel Soviet program, were the first spacecraft to circle the Moon and then return to Earth. Luna 14 orbited the Moon in April 1968. These programs were designed to lead to the next accomplishment: landing a craft on the Moon and then returning it safely to Earth. The first attempt, Luna 15, launched on July 13, 1969, crash landed a few days after the arrival of **Apollo** 11 with **Neil Armstrong** aboard.

Luna 16 was launched on September 12, 1970. It descended from lunar orbit and recovered 101 grams of soil samples by using a hollow drill bit at the end of a boom designed to bend like a human arm. On November 17, 1970 Luna 17 landed on the Moon and launched a mobile unit called the Lunokhod 1. This vehicle traveled around the surface of the Moon for 10 months, covering 6 miles. It transmitted 20,000 photos back to Earth from two television cameras located in portholes at the front of the vehicle. The instruments eventually froze, and the Lunokhod ceased to function.

Luna 18 was launched on September 2, 1971 but crash landed. Luna 19 followed less than a month later and made a total of 1,000 orbits before contact was lost. Luna 20 landed successfully in the Mare Fecunditatis, the Sea of Plenty, in February 1972. It drilled for soil samples and returned to Earth on February 25. The Soviets donated slightly more than 2 grams of Luna 20's samples for use by American scientists as part of a U.S.-Soviet scientific exchange program.

Luna 21 was launched on January 8, 1973 and carried Lunokhod 2. The Moon vessel traveled over 23 miles and took 80,000 pictures. Luna 22, setting out on May 29, 1974, made over 4,000 orbits of the Moon. Luna 23 soft-landed on the far side of the Moon and transmitted for about a week in November 1974. Launched on August 9, 1976, the last Luna spacecraft—Luna 24—landed as planned in the Mare Crisium on the far side of the Moon and took soil samples that it safely returned to Earth.

Where to learn more

A good overall introduction to space flights can be found in Wernher von Braun and Frederick I. Ordway III, *Space Travel: A History* (4th edition, New York: Harper & Row, 1985). It includes an extensive bibliography. More specific information on Soviet achievements in space can be found in Brian Harvey, *Race Into Space: The Soviet Space Programme* (New York: John Wiley & Sons, 1988).

Sir Alexander Mackenzie

(1764 - 1820)

Alexander Mackenzie was a Scot who discovered the Mackenzie River in the Canadian Arctic and was the first person to cross North America north of Mexico.

Alexander Mackenzie was born in Stornoway in the Outer Hebrides off the northwest coast of Scotland in 1764. In 1774 his widowed father took Alexander and sailed to New York. Shortly after their arrival the American Revolution broke out, and Mackenzie's father joined forces fighting on the Loyalist side. He died from illness while in service in 1780. In the meantime, Mackenzie had been sent to Montreal to go to school.

In 1779 Mackenzie was employed to work as a clerk in one of the main Montreal fur-trading companies. In 1784 he was entrusted with his first trading mission—the delivery of supplies to the company's post in Detroit. He carried that out so successfully that he was made a partner in the company and sent to Grand Portage, the post at the end of Lake Superior that served

Sir Alexander Mackenzie. The Granger Collection, New York.

as the link to the interior of Canada. When the partners had their annual meeting at Grand Portage in June 1785, Mackenzie was chosen to head the region of the Churchill River, with headquarters at Ile-a-la-Crosse in what is now northern Saskatchewan.

In 1787 Mackenzie's company was merged with the much larger North West Company. This made him a colleague of Peter Pond, a trader who had explored widely in the interior. Using information that he had gained from Native Americans that he did business with, Pond had gotten a general idea of the river system of the northwest. He learned of a large river (the Slave) that flowed into Great Slave Lake from the south and of a second river that flowed out of the western end of the lake and flowed to the Arctic. About this time, Pond became aware of the discoveries of Captain **James Cook** who had found Cook Inlet on the south coast of Alaska. Pond then came up with the theory that the river that flowed out of the Great Slave Lake flowed westward into Cook Inlet rather than north. If so, this would provide the much-sought-after route to the Pacific.

After Pond's retirement in 1788, it was left to Mackenzie to test his ideas. He set out on June 3, 1789 with a large party of traders and Native Americans from Fort Chipewyan on Lake Athabasca in what is now far-northern Alberta. The large number of rapids on the Slave River made travel slow and difficult, and they were delayed by ice on Great Slave Lake. However, once they entered the river flowing out of the lake (which has since been named the Mackenzie River after the explorer), they traveled very rapidly, averaging 75 miles a day. For the first few days the river continued westward, and Mackenzie thought he had found the way to the Pacific. But then it turned north, and after going several days downstream, he realized that it must flow into the Arctic Ocean.

Mackenzie followed the river all the way to its mouth in the Arctic Ocean and stayed four days on an island in the ocean. He started back upstream on July 16, 1789 and reached Fort Chipewyan on September 12. He had discovered one of the world's great rivers, but he came back disappointed because it did not offer any practical use for the fur traders who were looking for a way west. Mackenzie determined to make another expedition to see if he could find another route. In the meantime, he went to London during the winter of 1791-1792 to learn more about navigation and surveying so that he could make more accurate measurements of locations. He returned with a supply of rudimentary measuring instruments that he was to put to good use.

Mackenzie set off on his second great expedition from Fort Chipewyan on October 10, 1792. This time he followed another river emptying into Lake Athabasca, the Peace, as far as its juncture with the Smoky River. He built a base there to spend the winter. He set out again on May 9, 1793. By the end of May, he reached the point where the Parsnip and Finlay rivers come together, in northeastern British Columbia, to make the Peace. Following the advice of local Native Americans, Mackenzie canoed up the Parsnip River and then made a portage over the height of land to McGregor River, which led him to the Fraser River (named after **Simon Fraser** who would follow it to its mouth a few years later).

Mackenzie thought that he had come upon the headwaters of the Columbia River. He headed down the river as far as the site of the town of Alexandria, B.C. (named after him), where the Native Americans advised him to go no farther—the river course was too difficult, with numerous falls and rapids. He then turned back as far as the West Road River. He started up the West Road on July 4, 1793. He crossed Mackenzie Pass at 6,000 feet and then headed down the Bella Coola River. On July 17 he reached the houses of members of the Bella Coola tribe set on stilts. "From

Mackenzie's expeditions in western Canada.

these houses, I could perceive the termination of the river, and its discharge into a narrow arm of the sea." He was the first person to cross North America north of Mexico.

Mackenzie spent a few days exploring the fjords that make up that part of the British Columbia coast. At Dean Channel he learned that Europeans had been there very recently: he just missed meeting the navigator **George Vancouver** who had arrived by sea on June 2. On the morning of June 22, Mackenzie painted a famous inscription on a large rock in Dean Channel: "Alex Mackenzie from Canada by land 22d July 1793." It is preserved today in a provincial park. Mackenzie started his return on July 23 and reached Fort Chipewyan on August 24, an amazing speed given the means of transportation and the obstacles encountered.

Following the winter of 1793-1794, which he spent in Fort Chipewyan, Mackenzie headed back east with big ideas about uniting the two largest fur-trading companies, the Hudson's Bay Company and the North West Company, and together they would cooperate with the East India Company to open a new trade route to China. He continued to advocate these ideas for years although they never materialized in quite that form. On his return to Montreal, Mackenzie became a director of a trading company and traveled every year to the annual meeting in Grand Portage until he left for England in November 1799.

Once in England, Mackenzie wrote the account of his expeditions, which was published in December 1801. As a result, he was knighted and became Sir Alexander Mackenzie in 1802. He returned to Canada in 1802 and was elected to the colonial legislature in 1804. He went back to London in 1805 and then retired to Scotland in 1812, where he married a girl of 14 (he was 48). He died on his way home from Edinburgh, where he had gone to seek medical advice, on March 12, 1820.

Where to learn more

The original records of Mackenzie's travels are found in several places: Alexander Mackenzie, *Voyages from Montreal Through the Continent of North America to the Frozen and Pacific Oceans in 1789 and 1793* (Toronto: The Radisson Society, 1927). Walter Sheppe, ed. *First Man West: Alexander Mackenzie's Journal of His Voyage to the Pacific Coast of Canada in 1793* (Berkeley: University of California Press, 1962); T.H. McDonald, ed. *Exploring the Northwest Territory: Sir Alexander Mackenzie's Journal of a Voyage by Bark Canoe from Lake Athabaska to the Pacific Ocean in the Summer of 1789* (Norman: University of Oklahoma Press, 1966); and W. Kaye Lamb, ed. *The Journals and Letters of Sir Alexander Mackenzie* (Cambridge: Cambridge University Press for the Hakluyt Society, 1970).

There are two great storytellers of North American exploration who include Mackenzie in their books: Agnes Laut, *Pathfinders of the West* (New York: 1904; reprinted, Freeport, N.Y.: Books for Libraries Press, 1969) and Laurence J. Burpee, *The Search for the Western Sea*, 2 vols. (New York: Macmillan, 1936). Two other out-of-print works make interesting reading: M.S. Wade, *Mackenzie of Canada* (1927) and A. Woollacott, *Mackenzie and His Voyageurs* (1927).

A more recent book, which gives the story clearly and concisely, is Roy Daniells, *Alexander Mackenzie and the North West* (New York: Barnes & Noble, 1969). Peter C. Newman in *Company of Adventurers* (New York: Viking, 1985) puts Mackenzie's explorations in the context of the activities of the Hudson's Bay and North West Companies.

Ferdinand Magellan

(1480? - 1521)

Ferdinand Magellan was a Portuguese who entered the service of Spain to lead an expedition around the world. He was killed in the Philippines, and Juan Sebastián de Elcano continued on to become the first person to circle the globe.

Ferdinand Magellan was a member of the Portuguese nobility, born in about 1480, whose name in Portuguese is Fernão de Magalhaes. He grew up in the household of the Portuguese Queen. Magellan had sailed with Portuguese fleets on several voyages to the East Indies, the first in 1505, sailing around the Cape of Good Hope. As a result, he knew the places where spices were to be obtained, and the relation of those places to the line of demarcation between the Spanish and Portuguese spheres that the Pope had established.

On his return from the Indies, Magellan fought with the Portuguese in Morocco in an expedition against the town of Azemmour in which he suffered a leg wound that left him lame for the rest of his life. Upon his return to Portugal, he was falsely accused of corruption. Even though he was later acquitted, King Manoel II refused to reward him for his services. The king not only turned him down but suggested that he would be better off working for another sovereign.

As a result of this snub, Magellan moved to Spain with his friend the astronomer Ruy de Falero in order to make an offer to King Charles V to organize an expedition to sail to East Asia by sailing westward around the southern tip of South America. He insisted that this would take him to the Moluccas Islands, which were known to be one of the main sources for spices, but had not yet been visited by the Portuguese. He also felt that these islands lay to the east of the "Line" between the Spanish and Portuguese domains.

Magellan began his arguments in favor of such an expedition with the Spanish officials in Seville who were responsible for trade with the new empire that was opening up in the Americas. These officials were not impressed, and he was forced to start lobbying the king's advisors directly, again without success. Finally, he approached the king himself, who immediately realized the advantages to Spain if Magellan's ideas should turn out to be true.

After much negotiation, in which Magellan had to fight off Portuguese intrigues against him, an agreement was signed on March 22, 1518, which gave to Magellan and Falero the titles of Governor and Captain-General for all time of any lands that they

Ferdinand Magellan.

discovered plus the exclusive right for ten years to trade along any routes they pioneered. The King undertook to equip five ships to carry out the expedition, which would be under Magellan and Falero's command, but would be staffed by officials appointed by the King.

It took a year for the expedition to be equipped and staffed. It consisted of five ships: *Trinidad*, the flagship, *San Antonio, Concepción, Victoria,* and *Santiago.* It had a total of 560 men and enough supplies to last two years.

Just before the fleet was ready to leave, Magellan's friend Ruy de Falero turned down the offer to sail with him as co-commander. At the same time, King Charles V also appointed the captains of the other four ships, including Juan de Cartagena as captain of the *San Antonio,* which was the largest of the five vessels. Cartagena was also made second-in-command of the expedition

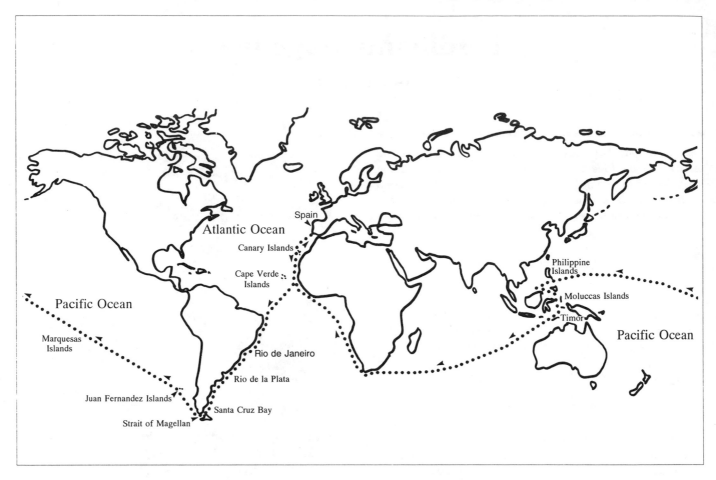

Magellan's circumnavigation of the world.

to replace Falero. On May 8, 1519 Charles V issued a set of instructions to Magellan that contained 74 items on how the expedition should be conducted and what it should achieve. These rules include instructions on what the ships should do if they were separated at sea, how they should treat the inhabitants of places they landed, and what records they should keep of the voyage.

Magellan's fleet left the city of Seville on September 8, 1519 and sailed down the Guadalquivir River to the port of Sanlúcar de Barrameda at its mouth. They set out to sea on September 20, 1519. The fleet stopped at the island of Tenerife in the Canary Islands and then crossed the equator on November 5 and sailed into the harbor of Rio de Janeiro on December 13. From there they headed south along the coast of South America to the estuary of the Río de la Plata. Magellan spent some time investigating that great river system to see whether it connected somehow with the Pacific, either because he had not heard of or did not believe the explorations that **Juan Díaz de Solis** had made in the area in 1516.

Finding no outlet at the Río de la Plata Magellan headed south, closely investigating every bay and cove that he came to. He arrived at the Bay of San Julián on March 21, 1520, where the cold and ice forced him to spend the winter to wait for better weather and to repair the damage of six months of navigation. The ships were there for four months, and it was there that the Spaniards encountered a group of Native Americans dressed in guanaco skins and with coverings on their feet that led Magellan to call them, in Portuguese, "patagoes" (big feet), from which the name of the region, Patagonia, is derived.

During this stay in southern Argentina the members of the expedition broke into open quarreling. The four Spanish noblemen who had been appointed captains of the four ships were unhappy with the way Magellan had changed route throughout the voyage without ever consulting them or asking their advice on any of the other decisions that he made. Magellan then took it upon himself to stop the criticism by removing the four men from their posts. They rebelled and in the ensuing fighting three of them were killed.

The expedition continued with a complete change in command of the accompanying ships. They left San Julián in the month of August, 1520 and headed south again to sight land in the area of the Bay of Santa Cruz. They stayed there until October 18 and then sighted three days after that the passage west that they had been searching for. The entrance to what was to be known as the "Strait of Magellan" starts at the Cabo de las Virgenes (Cape of the Virgins) at about 52° south latitude. Magellan sailed into it with only four ships, the *Santiago* having been wrecked on the bluffs of Santa Cruz.

It took Magellan more than a month to traverse the strait that now opened up to his view. He divided his ships up so that each one could inspect the numerous channels of the passage to see if they led to the west. It was not until November 27, 1520 that they reached the western ocean, which they named the Pacific because the waters seemed so much quieter after the stormy passage through the strait. When the fleet reached the ocean there were only three ships left. The *San Antonio* had decided, without consulting Magellan, that it did not have sufficient supplies to cross the Pacific and turned back and headed for Spain.

The route that Magellan took was mainly to the north, passing between the coast of Chile and the Juan Fernández Islands. From there he turned to the northwest and passed one of the outlying islands of the Marquesas group, crossing the equator at 153° west longitude, to reach the island of Guam in the Marianas, on March 7, 1521.

It took five long and difficult months to make this crossing, in which they went from 52° S and 70° W to 14° N and 144° E. During this time many of the crew members died and many more became ill from scurvy, caused by the lack of fresh vegetables and fruits, and others died simply from hunger and thirst. In Guam they were able to provision the ships and to care for the sick men with fresh food and to continue the journey. By March 16 they reached the island of Samar in the archipelago that they named after Saint Lazarus and which was later to be called the Philippines in honor of King Philip II of Spain.

From Samar the Spanish ships sailed into the Philippine archipelago and reached the island of Cebu, where they rested for several days, taking on provisions and repairing the ships, after their voyage of 13,000 miles. In Cebu, they were welcomed and helped by the inhabitants, and the king undertook to become a vassal of the King of Spain. But Magellan ignored one of the instructions that he had been given and took a force of 60 men to the nearby island of Mactan, in order to get the local leader to recognize the chief of Cebu as their ruler. They were set upon by a group of 1,000 warriors who killed Magellan and eight of his men and wounded many more. Magellan died on April 27, 1521 without completing his objective of reaching the Moluccas Islands.

On the return of the survivors of the Mactan disaster to Cebu, Duarte Barbosa was chosen as successor to Magellan and captain of the fleet. Barbosa then violated another one of the instructions given by King Charles V and accepted an invitation from the leader of Cebu to take part in a banquet on May 1 with about thirty of his men. In the middle of the banquet the Cebuanos turned on the Spaniards and killed all of them.

Magellan was killed near the island of Cebu in the Philippines.

Left with a much smaller number of men, the survivors decided to burn the *Concepción* and to continue on with the *Trinidad* and the *Victoria*. Gonzalo Gómez de Espinosa was chosen as captain general of the *Trinidad* and Juan Sebastián de Elcano was chosen to command the *Victoria*.

From Cebu the two ships sailed through the Philippines touching at several islands, including Negros and Mindanao and the northeastern corner of Borneo, and several of the smaller islands north of Sulawesi to reach the island of Tidore in the Moluccas on November 8, 1521. This had been the goal of the expedition when it left Spain more than two years before. In Tidore they were greeted warmly by the ruler, Sultan Almanzor, who swore to be a vassal of the King of Spain and not to trade with any other European nation. They loaded their ships with cloves, one of the most highly valued spices.

When they left Tidore the *Trinidad* was so weighted down with goods and was in such bad condition that it began to take on water. It was necessary to turn back in order to make repairs. Since it looked like these repairs would take some time, it was decided that Espinosa would remain behind with the ship with the intention of sailing back home to the east across the Pacific to Panama, while Elcano would continue westward with the records of the voyage. Therefore, Elcano and the *Victoria* set out alone from Tidore on December 21, 1521.

Elcano headed first for the island of Timor. Then, in order to avoid any Portuguese ships, who were very jealous of keeping the route to the Indies to themselves, he crossed the Indian Ocean as far to the south as possible in order to avoid the African coast. He did not touch land until he reached Santiago Island in the Cape Verde Islands on July 13, 1522. In order to avoid difficulties with the Portuguese who owned the islands, he pretended that he was returning from a voyage to the Americas. He needed their help in resupplying his ships which had traveled for 150 days straight, more than Magellan had taken in going from America to Guam. On Cape Verde Elcano discovered an amazing fact: the journals of the voyage were off by one day from the real date. In traveling around the world from east to west (opposite to the direction of rotation of the earth) he had "lost" a day. The reason for this is that when you are traveling "against" the sun, every sunrise to sunrise is a little longer than 24 hours and the difference is exactly one day in a complete circle of the globe. Elcano, the first man to travel around the world, was obviously the first man to have experienced this. This discrepancy was later adjusted by establishing the International Date Line along 180° of longitude.

The *Victoria* arrived at Sanlucar on September 6, 1522 and went on to Seville a few days later. Only 18 of the original 270 men survived the voyage that had lasted 14 days short of three years. The news of its arrival and of the first circumnavigation of the globe traveled quickly across Spain and the rest of Europe. The sale of the cargo brought back from the Moluccas earned a large profit, part of which went to the 18 returning men. Elcano was received with great honor by King Charles V and a globe was erected in his home village of Guetaria, with the legend "The First One to Circle Me."

Meanwhile, Gonzalo Gomez de Espinosa had been left behind with the *Trinidad* in Tidore. He spent several months traveling among the islands of the Moluccas signing treaties of friendship and commerce with the local rulers in order to assure Spanish control over the major source of spices in the East. Fearful of carrying the large cargo across the Pacific with him, he built a warehouse on Tidore and left some of his men to guard it. He then set out with 54 men on April 6, 1522. He sailed to the northeast and discovered the Palau Islands in western Micronesia and some of the Marianas farther north. Espinosa sailed east at around latitude 40° N, which in time was to become the route for Spanish ships coming from the Philippines. However, he ran into so many storms and contrary winds that he was forced to turn back, after 32 men had already died of scurvy.

Six months after his departure, Espinosa returned to Tidore. There he found that the Portuguese had attacked and captured the island as well as the Spaniards he had left behind. They captured Espinosa and the *Trinidad*, which served out its days in Portuguese service in the East Indies. Espinosa was held in captivity on different islands for several years until he was finally released and forced to make his way back to Spain alone and overland.

Where to learn more

The main primary source for the Magellan-Elcano voyage is by Antonio Pigafetta, one of the members of the crew. Sources for this include: Lord Stanley of Alderley, ed. *The First Voyage Around the World* (London: Hakluyt Society, 1874); Antonio Pigafetta, *Magellan's Voyage Around the World*, translated by James Alexander Robertson, 2 vols. (Cleveland: A. H. Clark Company, 1906); Antonio Pigafetta, *The Voyage of Magellan*, translated by Paula Spurlin Paige (Englewood Cliffs, N.J.: Prentice-Hall, 1969); Antonio Pigafetta, *A Narrative Account of the First Circumnavigation*, translated and edited by R.A. Skelton (New Haven: Yale University Press, 1969). It is one of three accounts included in Charles E. Nowell, ed. *Magellan's Voyage Around the World: Three Contemporary Accounts* (Evanston, Illinois: Northwestern University Press, 1962).

There are numerous biographies of Magellan. One from the 19th century, the first complete biography in English, is often cited as being the best and most complete: F.H.H. Guillemard, *The Life of Ferdinand Magellan* (London: George Philip & Son, 1890). Another that appeared later is easier to read and more vivid: Arthur Sturges Hildebrand, *Magellan* (New York: Harcourt, Brace & Co., 1924). A famous German author, Stefan Zweig, wrote a biography that was translated into English a few years later: Stefan Zweig, *Conqueror of the Seas: The Story of Magellan* (New York: Viking Press, 1938). It is quite readable, as is Edward Frederic Benson, *Ferdinand Magellan* (New York: Harper & Brothers, 1930), although neither includes information not found in the Guillemard book.

Highly recommended, even though the account is somewhat fictionalized, is Charles McKew Parr, *So Noble a Captain: The Life and Times of Ferdinand Magellan* (New York: Crowell, 1953), which was republished, even though essentially the same, as *Ferdinand Magellan, Circumnavigator* (New York: 1964). Edouard Roditi, *Magellan of the Pacific* (New York: McGraw-Hill, 1972) is also very good.

There is only one biography of Elcano in English: Mairin Mitchell, *Elcano: The First Circumnavigator* (London: Herder, 1958).

General histories of Pacific exploration inevitably devote considerable attention to Magellan. The two best are J.C. Beaglehole, *The Exploration of the Pacific* (Stanford: Stanford University Press, 1966) and O.H.K. Spate, *The Spanish Lake* (Minneapolis: University of Minnesota Press, 1979).

There is a complete bibliography of works on Magellan up to that date in M. Torodash, "Magellan Historiography," *Hispanic American Historical Review*, vol. 51 (May 1971).

Ella Maillart

(1903 -   )

Ella Maillart is a Swiss woman who made an overland trip with one companion through China and Sinkiang into Kashmir in the 1930s.

Ella Maillart was born in Geneva, Switzerland on February 20, 1903 into a prosperous family. She excelled in sports as a young woman and was on the Swiss sailing team at the 1924 Olympic games. Not being able to settle on a career, she went on an extended visit to Russia in the late 1920s to see the results of the 1917 Revolution. This whetted her appetite for travel.

On her return from Russia, Maillart wrote a book about her travels that was sufficiently popular to pay for a trip to Soviet Central Asia in 1932. She visited Kirghizia and the cities of Tashkent, Samarkan, Bukhara, and Turktol as well as taking a barge trip down the Amu Darya River and crossing Kyzyl Kum Desert in midwinter in a cart. She returned home and wrote another book about her adventures.

Maillart then conceived the trip that would make her famous. She decided that she wanted to travel all the way across Asia from west to east. While she was making her plans she met a young Englishman, Peter Fleming, at a cocktail party who was also planning a trip to China. They ran into each other again in China and discovered that they both had the same idea about crossing Asia. They decided to combine efforts and make the trip together.

China at that time was in a state of turmoil. Following the revolution of 1911 the central government was very weak and large parts of the country were controlled by local "warlords." Chinese Turkestan, or Sinkiang, where Maillart and Fleming proposed to travel had not been visited by foreigners for four years, and no one knew who was in charge. They were fortunate to find a Russian emigré family who had a house in the Sinkiang city of Tsaidam and wanted to return. They agreed to act as translators and guides.

It was very difficult to get permission to travel in China at the time, and Maillart was forced to bribe officials and even falsify documents before she could set off. They left Beijing in February 1935, traveling by train and truck as far as the city of Lan-chou, the capital of Gansu, the farthest west part of China "proper." There Maillart and Fleming were allowed to continue but their White Russian friends were forced to stay behind.

Maillart and Fleming set out alone with one mule driver and a mule to carry supplies. At first, they rented and then bought horses to ride. As they came into Sinkiang they found that conditions were peaceful, and they crossed parts of the province where they did not encounter any other people. Two days outside of the far western city of Kashgar the mule slipped in a stream and all of their possessions were soaked and in some cases ruined. They entered Kashgar looking very shabby but were met by the British vice-consul in the city and were able to recuperate in his home.

From Kashgar Maillart and Fleming traveled south over the Pamir, Hindu Kush and Karakorum Ranges into the Indian province of Kashmir, then ruled by Great Britain. It had taken them 6½ months to cover 3,500 miles at a total cost of £150. On their return to Europe, Maillart and Fleming remained friends although they rarely saw each other, and they both wrote books about their expedition.

In 1939 Maillart set out again on an expedition, this time traveling by car from Paris to Afghanistan. She then spent the years during World War II in India and Tibet. In the 1950s she went hiking in the Himalayas of Nepal. She is now retired and lives in Geneva.

Where to learn more

Maillart has written several books about her travels, including: *Turkestan Solo: One Woman's Expedition from the Tien Shan to Kizul Kum* (New York: G.P. Putnam's Sons, 1935); *Forbidden Journey* (London: Heinemann, 1937; reprinted, London: Century, 1983); *Cruises and Caravans* (London: Dent, 1942); *Gypsy Afloat* (London: Heinemann, 1942); *The Cruel Way* (London: Heinemann, 1947; reprinted in paperback, Boston: Beacon Press, 1985); *"Ti-Puss": A Travel Book* (London: Heinemann, 1951; *The Land of the Sherpas* (London: Hodder & Stoughton, 1955).

An excellent book about women travelers contains a chapter on Maillart: Marion Tinling, *Women into the Unknown: A Sourcebook on Women Explorers and Travelers* (New York: Greenwood Press, 1989). It was the main source for this account.

S.S. Manhattan

(1969)

The Manhattan *was a large oil tanker that was converted into an ice breaker and sent on a voyage through the Northwest Passage to see if it was possible to use the Passage commercially for the transport of oil from Alaska.*

In 1968 large oil fields were discovered on the Arctic seacoast of Alaska, on the North Slope. In addition to the enormous problems that were involved in exploring and drilling the petroleum, there was the gigantic task of getting the oil to refineries and markets. One solution that was proposed was that of using gigantic ice-breaking tankers to sail through the Northwest Passage that had finally been traversed by **Roald Amundsen** in 1903-1906. In order to test whether this was a practical venture or not, the Humble Oil & Refining Company paid $39,000,000 to modify an oil tanker and to pay for its trip through the Arctic to Alaska. Later, the Atlantic Richfield Company and BP Oil, both corporations with interests in Alaskan oil, contributed $2,000,000 each.

The ship chosen for conversion was the *S.S. Manhattan*, the largest U.S. tanker then afloat. It was so big that in order to convert it to an icebreaker, it was cut into smaller pieces. Two sections were towed to shipyards in Virginia and Alabama where extra rudder guards were installed, a heavy "girdle" was put around the midsection and the forward section was given extra beam. The armored prow was designed and manufactured at Bath, Maine. The parts were reassembled at a shipyard in Chester, Pennsylvania. Nine foot wide armored "blisters" were placed around the ship's hull to protect the thin inner hull. When complete, the ship displaced 150,000 tons and was 1,005 feet and 5 inches long. It had 43,000 horsepower, twice as much as any other tanker then afloat and was nine times larger than the next largest icebreaker.

The ship left Chester on August 24, 1969. There were 126 people on board—a volunteer crew, scientists to study the waters the *Manhattan* passed through, and journalists to record the event. The first icebergs were sighted on September 1, 1969 off the west coast of Greenland. There it was joined by a Canadian icebreaker escort, the *John A. Macdonald*. On September 2 the *Manhattan* plowed into a sheet of ice 60 feet thick and a mile wide to test its ability to break up pack ice. Water shot 60 feet over the ship's bow, but it shattered the giant floe, the biggest piece of ice ever torn apart by a ship. The crew members heard giant pieces of ice popping against the propellers and the captain slowed the ship down for fear of injuring them.

The *Manhattan* sailed into Lancaster Sound north of Baffin Island, which was largely ice free that year. Off Bathurst Island it passed near the North Magnetic Pole, which was far from its usual position because of a giant solar storm then in progress. The subatomic particles generated by the storm interfered with the ship's radios. The nearness of the magnetic poles made the magnetic compasses spin uselessly, and even the gyroscopic compasses were affected and position had to be determined by celestial sighting.

Entering Viscount Melville Sound the ship ran into multi-year ice—ice that had been frozen, melted and refrozen over the years so that the salt had drained out, and it was rock-hard freshwater ice. Forced to stop, the scientists aboard the ship descended and went out onto the pack ice to study its characteristics. The *Manhattan* then revealed its most serious flaw as an icebreaker. It was so constructed that the engines could only muster one-third of its power in reverse. In the meantime, ice that had previously been broken had refrozen and could not be broken up. The ship's captain had to call on the escort ship, the *John D. Macdonald*, to break the ice pack for it.

The *Manhattan* then reached M'Clure Strait (named after discoverer **Robert McClure**), the toughest part of the voyage. Winds from the west drove the ice in M'Clure Sound and made it into a 220-mile-long ice plug of jumbled ridges as much as 20 feet high and 100 feet deep. No vessel had ever passed through it traveling from east to west. And the *Manhattan* did not succeed either—encountering an ice floe three miles wide it was forced to turn south and travel through Prince of Wales Sound and Amundsen Gulf off the mainland of Canada. On September 14, 1969 the helicopter reconnaissance reported that there were only ten miles of ice between the ship and the open sea. It broke through at 2:34 a.m. on the 15th.

The ship then sailed through the 1,000 miles of open sea to Barrow, Alaska. At Barrow it took on board a symbolic barrel of oil. It then headed back to the east coast of the United States by the same route that it had come, taking four weeks to cross Viscount Melville Sound. During the transit through Lancaster Sound in the eastern part of the Arctic, a piece of ice knocked out a large panel of steel in the ship's hull, spilling 15,000 barrels of ballast oil into the sea, thus revealing the environmental dangers of transporting oil through the Arctic. The *Manhattan* sailed into New York Harbor on November 12, 1969.

The voyage of the *Manhattan* had shown that it was theoretically possible for large tankers to travel through the Northwest Passage. However, it turned out that it was economically and environmentally too risky. The oil companies decided to build an oil pipeline from the North Slope to Valdez on the south coast of Alaska and then ship the oil by tanker from there. The *Manhattan*'s pioneering route has never been used commercially.

Where to learn more

One of the passengers on board the *Manhattan*, Bern Keating, wrote about the voyage in "North for Oil: *Manhattan* Makes the Historic Northwest Passage," *National Geographic*, vol. 137 (March 1970) pp. 374-391, and *The Northwest Passage—From the Matthew to the Manhattan: 1497-1969* (Chicago: Rand McNally & Co., 1970).

Thomas Manning

(1772 - 1840)

Thomas Manning was the first Englishman to travel to the "forbidden" city of Lhasa in Tibet.

Thomas Manning was born in the English county of Norfolk on November 8, 1772, the son of a clergyman. He enrolled at Cambridge University in 1790 and studied mathematics there until 1795 but never received a degree. He stayed on in Cambridge as a private tutor until 1800, when he went to Paris to learn Chinese. Manning stayed there for three years studying the language under an eminent scholar of the day. When war broke out between Great Britain and France in 1803, Manning was given a pass signed by Napoleon to return home.

Manning decided that he wanted to travel to China to continue his studies. He acquired a basic knowledge of medicine and, with the support of **Sir Joseph Banks**, was appointed as a doctor at the British East India Company's post at Canton. He traveled to Canton in 1807. From there, he went to Calcutta in 1810, the center of the East India Company's operations. He asked the Company to sponsor him on an expedition to Tibet, but they turned down his request and he set out on his own.

Accompanied only by his Chinese servant, Manning traveled to Rangpur in what is now northern Bangladesh. He entered the remote Himalayan Kingdom of Bhutan in September 1811 and reached the Tibetan border on October 20. Using his medical knowledge, he was able to cure a Chinese general who was at the border post. On his recovery, the general agreed to let Manning travel with him to Lhasa, the capital of Tibet. Since entry into Tibet was forbidden to Westerners, Manning tried to disguise himself in some of his Chinese robes. His disguise proved to be inadequate for the cold Himalayan winter, and he was forced to barter it for something warmer. Manning reached Lhasa in December 1811, the first Englishman to do so.

Once in Lhasa, Manning was impressed by the Potala, the great stone palace where the spiritual and political leader of Tibet, the Dalai Lama, lived. But his view of Lhasa was different: "If the palace exceeded my expectations the town as far fell short of them. The habitations are begrimed with smut and dirt. The avenues are full of dogs, some growling and gnawing bits of hide which lie about in profusion, and emit a charnel-house smell; others limping and looking livid; others ulcerated; others starved

and dying, and pecked at by ravens, some dead and preyed upon. In short, everything seems mean and gloomy, and excites the idea of something unreal. . . ."

Manning was, however, impressed by the ninth Dalai Lama, even though at the time he was only seven years old. Manning was allowed an audience with the ruler and performed the traditional kowtow and presented him with gifts. The Dalai Lama, seated on a high throne, blessed Manning's head, which had been shaved for the occasion, and offered him a cup of buttered tea, the traditional Tibetan drink. Manning commented in his diary: "This day I saluted the Grand Lama! Beautiful youth. Face poetically affecting. Very happy to have seen him and his blessed smile. Hope often to see him again."

In April 19, 1812, Manning was forced to leave Lhasa because of the ill-will of the Chinese officials who advised the Dalai Lama. Manning was the last Englishman to visit Lhasa until the arrival of **Sir Francis Younghusband** in August 1904.

Manning did not get back to Calcutta until the summer of 1813. Having received no official encouragement to make his trip, he refused to give the authorities any information about his journey. He returned to Canton and stayed there until 1816 when he was taken to Beijing to serve as the interpreter for a British embassy that was being sent to the Chinese Emperor.

Following his return to England in 1818, Manning became known as the foremost Chinese scholar in Europe. He was also famous for his beard, which reached down to his waist. He lived in a small country house with no furniture, surrounded by Chinese books. He had a stroke in 1838 that paralyzed his right hand and moved to the town of Bath in order to take advantage of its famous medicinal springs. Before leaving, however, he plucked out the hairs of his beard, one by one. Manning died in Bath on May 2, 1840.

Where to learn more

Manning's diary of his trip to Tibet, first published in London in 1876 by Sir Clements R. Markham, the Secretary of the Royal Geographical Society, is included in *Narratives of the Missions of George Bogle to Tibet and of the Journeys of Thomas Manning to Lhasa* (New Delhi: Manjusti Publications, 1971). Two good books about Western penetration of Tibet that include accounts of Manning are: John MacGregor, *Tibet: A Chronicle of Exploration* (London: Routledge & Kegan Paul, 1970) and Peter Hopkirk, *Trespassers on the Roof of the World* (London: John Murray, 1982). The quotations from Manning's diary come from Eric Newby, *A Book of Travellers' Tales* (New York: Viking, 1986).

Jean-Baptiste Marchand

(1863 - 1934)

Jean-Baptiste Marchand was a French soldier who led an expedition from the Atlantic coast of Africa to the Nile River in order to expand French territory. He was confronted by the British at the Sudanese town of Fashoda and forced to retreat.

Jean-Baptiste Marchand was born in the little French town of Thoissey in eastern France north of the city of Lyons. His family was poor, and he was forced to quit school after the first year of high school (lycée). He was apprenticed to a notary at the age of 13 and worked there until the death of his mother when he was 20. He enlisted in the French Army on October 1, 1883. He was promoted to corporal on April 1, 1884 and then progressed to sergeant. His superiors thought so highly of him that he was sent to officer training school in 1886 and returned to his former regiment as a second lieutenant in March 1887.

In January 1888 Marchand was sent to serve in France's colony of Senegal in west Africa. At that time France was engaged in a colonial war to expand its empire throughout west Africa. In what is now Mali, there was a war going on with the Tukulors. Marchand distinguished himself in his first combat, helping to capture the Tukulor stronghold of Koundian in early 1889. In April 1890 he took part in the capture of the fortress of Segu, was promoted to lieutenant and awarded the Legion of Honor. On February 21, 1891 he was wounded in the assault on the Tukulor capital of Jenné.

Following the defeat of the Tukulor, Marchand joined the campaign against another foe of French imperialism, Samori Turé, in Guinea. He fought in battles against Turé from April 1891 to the end of 1894. He was wounded in the Battle of Bonua in November 1894 in which Turé's forces defeated the French in spite of the notable bravery of Marchand. Marchand returned to France on June 14, 1895.

On Marchand's return to France, he almost immediately began agitating for a plan that he had conceived with his French colleagues in Africa. He proposed to lead an expedition from France's settlement of Brazzaville on the Congo River across Africa to the Nile, thereby winning for France control of the upper Nile and eventually linking it with France's outpost on the Red Sea at Djibouti by forming an alliance with Ethiopia.

The upper Nile had been originally explored by British explorers such as **John Hanning Speke** and **Samuel Baker**. An

Anglo-Egyptian government had been imposed on the Sudan that reached as far south as the sources of the Nile in what is now Uganda. That government had been led by Charles "Chinese" Gordon and had used such agents as **Charles Chaillé-Long** and **Emin Pasha** to control the upper Nile. But all of that had been wiped out by the Muslim forces of "El-Mahdi" in 1885. Marchand now proposed to step into the confused situation along the Nile by replacing British power with French. In effect, it was a French imperialist design to control the sources of the Nile by taking over a band stretching from the Atlantic on the west to the Red Sea on the east. This would counter, and derail, British attempts to control Africa from north to south: from "the Cape to Cairo."

Marchand presented his ideas at a meeting with the French Foreign Minister on July 18, 1895. He then submitted a detailed proposal to the Ministry of Colonies on September 11, 1895. During this period, governments in France changed frequently. One of the main political divisions was between the colonialist faction that thought that France should make itself stronger following its defeat by Germany in the Franco-Prussian War of 1870 by expanding outside of Europe—in Africa and Asia. The other side thought that France should not weaken itself by using its forces overseas while the main struggle was in Europe. Marchand happened to make his proposals at a time when the imperialists were in control and when they were not too worried about offending the British, who they knew were trying to defeat the Mahdi and return to the upper Nile. On February 24, 1896, therefore, Marchand's proposal was tentatively agreed to, and this was approved by the Prime Minister on April 7.

In the meantime, Marchand had been making preparations, and the first of four detachments of officers and supplies left France on April 24, 1896. Marchand himself sailed on June 25. They traveled to the small port of Loango in the French Congo, where Marchand arrived in August. The governor of the French Congo at the time was **Pierre Savorgnan de Brazza**, a native Italian who had explored the Congo and had founded France's colony along the great river.

When Marchand reached Loango, he found that it was impossible to move his supplies inland to the Congo River port of Brazzaville because there was a revolt by the Basundi and Bakongo tribes against the French. Marchand was in a hurry, and on August 18, 1896 he convinced Brazza to declare martial law in the Congo with Marchand in control. He then organized his French officers and Senegalese soldiers into a campaign against the rebels. Some of the rebel leaders were captured and executed on October 17. The last resistance to Marchand ended on

December 12, by which time he was in Brazzaville. The rest of his men and supplies caught up with him by the end of February 1897.

Marchand was now faced with a problem. The French had no transport adequate to carry the supplies up the Congo. They requested help from the Belgians who ruled the other side of the river from Léopoldville (now Kinshasa). The Belgians initially refused, but new orders came from Brussels and the use of the steamship *Ville de Bruges* was approved. It made two trips with Frenchmen and supplies up the Congo as far as it was possible to navigate. The first one left Brazzaville on January 13, 1897, and the second followed with Marchand, sick with malaria, on board on March 10, 1897. They were deposited in the village of Zinga and then had to proceed up the Ubangi River to Bangui (now the capital of the Central African Republic) in 72 dugout canoes. They reached Bangui in early April.

From Bangui the expedition traveled 450 miles to Ouango, the last outpost before the Mbomu Rapids. At this point, Marchand seized a small riverboat, the 50-foot long *Faidherbe* to take with him to the Nile with the plan of floating it down the Nile with the French flag flying. Since they had reached the limit of navigation, the *Faidherbe* had to be totally disassembled and hauled overland by the African porters, each carrying a 55-pound load. This considerably slowed down the progress of the expedition. Fortunately, along the way the French discovered two other streams, the Mboku and the Méré, by which the *Faidherbe* could be sailed 160 miles farther. At that point, Marchand had a road 100 miles long built to carry the pieces of the boat from Méré to Khojali. Once they reached Khojali in November, they realized they would have to wait until the spring rains before they would be able to proceed any farther. In the meantime Marchand sent part of the force ahead to build a French post near the present Sudanese city of Wau.

While they were waiting for the rains to come, Marchand and other members of his force went exploring in different directions throughout the southern Sudan. It was not until June 4 that the boat reached the new French outpost, and it was possible to continue on the Sué River, a tributary of the Nile. After sailing for seven days they reached a vast swamp, the Sudd, and it took them until June 25 before they could fight their way out onto the Bahr-el-Ghazal, a bigger river flowing into the White Nile. They reached the little village of Fashoda on the Nile on July 10, 1898. Later that day the French force took possession of a fort a little ways outside of the town that had been abandoned by Egyptian troops years before.

The next day, Marchand had a formal ceremony raising the French flag over the fort of Fashoda and thereby claimed that part of the Nile valley for France. Significantly, on their first attempt to raise the flag, the flagpole broke. They were then able to celebrate Bastille Day, July 14, in their new outpost. On August 25 they were surprised by an attack of Mahdist forces, but the French easily drove them away with no loss of life. They were

soon faced, however, with a much more serious challenge. The British arrived on September 19.

A joint Anglo-Egyptian force under the command of Lord Kitchener had been fighting the Mahdists since 1896. At the Battle of Omdurman on September 2, 1898, they had destroyed the power of the Sudanese in their capital and restored the country to Anglo-Egyptian control. Kitchener had immediately headed up the Nile after his victory to oust the French from Fashoda. At a famous meeting on September 19, 1898, Kitchener demanded that Marchand withdraw. Marchand refused. The matter was then referred to the two governments in London and Paris.

The news of the confrontation at Fashoda drove the newspapers of both countries into a nationalistic frenzy. The British began threatening the French with recriminations. In the midst of this, the French government sent a message to Marchand by way of a British Nile steamer that reached him on October 9. It announced his promotion to major and ordered him to send an officer to Paris to report on the expedition. When that officer reached Paris on October 27, he found the French government in the midst of backtracking. It realized that it did not have the wherewithal to confront the British government nor the means of supplying Marchand by his impractical overland route. Marchand himself took a British steamer down the Nile to Cairo, where he arrived on November 3 to communicate with his government by telegram. The next day, he received instructions from Paris to evacuate.

A furious Marchand spent the next several days arguing with his superiors in Paris. He was then ordered to return to Fashoda and carry out his instructions. The only concession granted was that he was not required to accept the humiliating offer of the British to evacuate the French soldiers on British steamships down the Nile. They were allowed to continue their march eastward through Ethiopia to the French port of Djibouti. Marchand arrived back in Fashoda on December 4, 1898. The French troops played the "Marseillaise" and struck the tricolor flag on the morning of December 12 and marched out of the fort of Fashoda.

They reached Addis Ababa on March 9, 1899. They arrived in Djibouti on May 16 and embarked for France on a steamship sent to pick them up. On their return to Paris at the end of May, they were met by enormous crowds who cheered the French heroes. The popular sentiment was used by French nationalists to try to bring down the government. This attempt failed, and Marchand and his force marched together for the last time on the parade to celebrate Bastille Day, 1899. Marchand then was reintegrated into the French Army where he continued to make a name for himself. He was promoted to general and fought with notable success in World War I. He died in Paris in 1934.

The "Fashoda Incident" was one of the major turning points in modern European history. The failure at Fashoda taught the French that they would never be able to achieve their goals without the support of Great Britain. The country's leaders therefore started a conscious policy of befriending the government in London and quickly settled all the major problems it had with the British. The two countries signed a treaty of friendship, the "Entente Cordiale" in 1904. This eventually led to a military alliance that pitted France and Britain against Germany in World War I.

Where to learn more

There is a very good summary in English of the Marchand expedition and the Fashoda crisis, based largely on secondary sources: David Levering Lewis, *The Race to Fashoda: European Colonialism and African Resistance in the Scramble for Africa* (New York: Weidenfield & Nicolson, 1988; also available in paperback.) A very detailed study in French, based on primary sources is Marc Michel, *La Mission Marchand, 1895-1899* (Paris: Mouton, 1972). For the diplomatic repercussions of the Fashoda Incident, see William L. Langer, *Diplomacy of Imperialism, 1890-1902*, 2nd edition (New York: Alfred A. Knopf, 1965) and Charles Andres, *Théophile Delcassé and the Making of the Entente Cordiale* (London: Macmillan, 1968).

Mariner

(1962-1975)

The United States' ten-launch Mariner space program was designed to explore and gather information about other planets in the solar system.

The United States made its first effort to send a spacecraft to another planet in 1962. *Mariner 1* was designed to travel to the planet Venus. Unfortunately, an error in the computer programming (there was a missing minus sign) caused the mission to fail, and the spacecraft plunged into the Atlantic Ocean shortly after take-off on July 22, 1962. A back-up, *Mariner 2*, was quickly launched on August 27 and became the first space mission to reach another planet.

Mariner 2 took three and a half months to fly the 35 million miles to Venus, which it reached on December 14. It got as close as 22,000 miles to the Earth's "sister planet." The 447-pound *Mariner 2* sent back an enormous amount of information, confirming that the planet suffered from a "super greenhouse"

The planet Venus, from a mosaic of pictures taken by Mariner 10 in 1974.
NASA/Jet Propulsion Laboratory.

effect: it is surrounded by dense layers of gases that keep heat from escaping so that temperatures reach almost 900°F. It also discovered that, unlike Earth, Venus had no detectable magnetic field or radiation belts. *Mariner 2* lost contact with Earth on January 3, 1963.

The next Mariner was designed to go to Mars. Launched on November 5, 1964, *Mariner 3* followed its designated trajectory with no problems. However, it proved to be impossible to jettison the cover that protected the spacecraft during launch, and the mission had to be cancelled. *Mariner 4* was launched on November 28, 1964. It took a little more than seven and a half months to travel the 325 million miles to Mars and got as close to the Red Planet as 6,118 miles on July 14-15, 1965. As it made a loop around Mars, the camera on the spacecraft took 22 pictures. Only 19 were usable; the rest were taken on the dark side of the planet. The photos showed a pock-marked surface with no especially exciting or unusual features. Later probes found that this was far from the truth, but *Mariner 4* offered a rather disappointing view of the planet that had fueled science fiction stories for so long. The second American probe to Venus, *Mariner 5*, was launched on June 14, 1967, two days after the Soviet Union's *Venera 4*. *Mariner 5* made its closest approach to Venus on October 19, 1967 at a distance of 2,480 miles. It transmitted excellent pictures of the planet's upper atmosphere but nothing about its surface. The previous day, however, the Soviet spacecraft had landed and sent back invaluable data.

The next American missions to Mars were the twin *Mariner 6* and *Mariner 7* probes. *Mariner 6*, launched on February 24, 1969, flew by the planet on July 31. *Mariner 7* was launched on March 27, but it was programmed for a shorter trajectory and made its closest approach less than a week later, on August 5, 1969. The two spacecraft both weighed 910 pounds and carried the same instrumentation. *Mariner 6* flew by the Martian equator and came within 2,120 miles of the surface. *Mariner 7* flew over the southern hemisphere slightly farther out. Their photographic equipment was better than that of *Mariner 4*, and some of the distinctive features of the planet became apparent: the polar ice, giant craters, and evidence of erosion by wind and water. All of these things indicated that Mars may once have been more earthlike, with flowing water and volcanic activity.

The United States sent another set of twin probes to Mars in May 1971 to take advantage of the period when Earth and Mars were closest to each other. The rocket carrying *Mariner 8* malfunctioned on take-off and plunged back to Earth. *Mariner 9*, however, launched on May 30, 1971, was one of the most successful of all the Mariner flights. It traveled to Mars in only 167

The planet Mercury, photographed by Mariner 10 as it was leaving orbit. NASA.

days, arriving there on November 13. After traveling 248 million miles, it arrived 4.4 seconds ahead of schedule. It entered Martian orbit, the first spacecraft to orbit another planet. The Soviet's *Mars 2* spacecraft followed two weeks later.

Mariner 9 reached Mars in the middle of a giant dust storm. It was not until January 1972 that the storm subsided, and the spacecraft's cameras were able to transmit pictures of the surface. *Mariner 9* orbited Mars for 349 days, rather than the originally-planned 90 days. It made 698 orbits and sent out its last signal on October 27, 1972. During that time, it took 7,329 photographs and was able to map the entire surface of the planet. It found a giant crater 10 miles high and a 2,500-mile canyon much deeper than the Grand Canyon, which was named Valles Marineris in honor of the spacecraft. *Mariner 9* confirmed that water had once flowed on the planet but found no signs of recent geological activity. The spacecraft also took photos of Mars' two small moons—Deimos and Phobos.

After the success of *Mariner 9*, the next launch was directed towards the inner planets of the solar system—Venus and

Mercury. *Mariner 10* took off from the Kennedy Space Center on November 3, 1973. It weighed 1,108 pounds, of which 170 pounds were measuring devices and instruments. These included two television cameras equipped with ultraviolet filters and instruments to study infrared and ultraviolet radiations and magnetic fields. These cameras took a total of 3,500 photographs of Venus, the first ones ever made.

En route to Venus, *Mariner 10* had been commanded to make two midcourse corrections, allowing it to get within 3,600 miles of the planet at its closest approach on February 5, 1974. Photos of the atmosphere of Venus revealed that the clouds that cover the planet are layered and have an unusual circulation pattern. Unlike the *Mariner 2* spacecraft, *Mariner 10* was able to detect a slight magnetic field around Venus. A previous Soviet discovery—that the Venusian atmosphere consists largely of carbon dioxide—was confirmed.

As it flew by Venus, *Mariner 10* was speeded up by the planet's gravitational field. The flight was designed to send it around the Sun at the exact speed needed to meet Mercury in the same spot every time the planet completed one revolution. This required incredible precision because at their nearest approaches, the Earth and Mercury are 57.5 million miles apart. Theoretically, these rendezvous may last forever, but *Mariner 10* stopped transmitting signals after meeting Mercury on March 29, 1972, September 21, 1974, and March 16, 1975, and we have no way of knowing its fate.

Mariner 10 began taking photographs of Mercury when it was still 3 million miles away. It took a photo every 42 seconds during the time it approached and then sped away from the planet, eventually making almost 2,000 pictures. *Mariner 10* revealed that the surface of Mercury is riddled with craters of all sizes, which were created by collisions with meteors. There is no evidence that there was ever any volcanic activity or atmosphere, although there are a few helium atoms. The most obvious feature was a gigantic basin surrounded by tall mountains. The basin was named Caloris, from the Latin word for "heat," because it is in the hottest part of the planet. *Mariner 10* completed the Mariner program with spectacular photos of a small planet so distant that it is hard to find with a telescope on Earth.

Where to learn more

General information on the Mariner flights can be found in: Wernher von Braun, *Space Travel: A History* (New York: Harper & Row, 1985); Bruce Murray, *Journey into Space: The First Three Decades of Space Exploration* (New York: W.W. Norton & Co., 1989); and William E. Burrows, *Exploring Space: Voyages in the Solar System and Beyond* (New York: Random House, 1990).

There are more specialized books on the exploration of different planets and on specific flights in: Jet Propulsion Laboratory, NASA, *Mariner: Mission to Venus* (New York: McGraw-Hill, 1963); Irl Newlan, *First to Venus: The Story of Mariner II* (New York: McGraw-Hill, 1963); Oran W. Nicks, *A Review of the Mariner IV Results* (Washington, D.C.: NASA, 1967); and Bruce Murray and Eric Burgess, *Flight to Mercury* (New York: Columbia University Press, 1977).

Beryl Markham

(1902 - 1986)

Beryl Markham was a pioneer aviator who was the first person to fly solo across the Atlantic Ocean from London to North America.

Beryl Markham was born in England, but at the age of three she moved with her parents to Kenya in East Africa. Kenya had become a British colony in 1886, and in the early 1900s many Englishmen established farms in the highlands, which had lots of available land, a pleasant climate, and a productive soil for growing such tropical crops as coffee.

Markham's father cleared land and started a farm at Njoro, about 70 miles from the new capital of Nairobi. After trying to raise various crops, he discovered his true talent as a horse breeder and trainer who furnished horses for racing in Nairobi,

Beryl Markham. The Granger Collection, New York.

which was very popular as a sport and social activity for the colonists. Markham spent her entire childhood on this farm and learned to speak several African languages from the families her father employed; she also learned to hunt wild game with a spear and, from her father, how to ride. In the course of her adventurous childhood she was attacked by a "pet" lion and killed a deadly black mamba snake with a stick.

The European farmers in Kenya prospered over the years and, as more and more settlers arrived, they were able to create a leisurely and comfortable lifestyle. Some of this story is told in a famous book, *Out of Africa*, by the Danish author Karen Blixen. Blixen was a good friend of Markham's who helped her get out of an unhappy early marriage—she married a man of 32 when she was 16. Following her divorce, Markham started a career of her own as a horse trainer.

Markham was so successful as a horse trainer that one of her horses won the most prestigious racing prize in Kenya when she was only 24. This success helped her to become one of the most socially prominent young women in Nairobi and to meet her second husband, a wealthy young Englishman named Mansfield Markham. They were married in 1927, with Karen Blixen as part of the wedding party, and she used his family name for the rest of her life.

In 1928 the Markhams went to England where Beryl gave birth to her only child and where she became notorious in society for having a romantic relationship with Prince Henry, the Duke of Gloucester, second son of the King of England. This affair caused a scandal that destroyed her marriage and forced her to return to Kenya without her husband or her young son.

Considered to be the most beautiful woman in the colony, Markham began a relationship with Denys Finch Hatton, a famous "great white hunter" and the man loved by Karen Blixen. Finch Hatton took Markham flying several times in his airplane, and Markham was so thrilled by the experience that she decided to learn how to fly herself. Soon after she began her lessons, Finch Hatton was killed in a crash, which seems to have increased her determination to become an aviator. She also transferred her emotional feelings to her flying instructor, Tom Campbell Black.

Following a few months' training, Markham got her pilot's license in July, 1929. She later became the first woman in Kenya to get a commercial pilot's license and began a second career as a bush pilot. This meant that she flew alone delivering supplies, passengers, and mail to the remote, or "bush", parts of the country. There were no airfields—she landed on small clearings in the forests or fields.

In April 1930 Campbell Black flew to England on business, and Markham followed him all alone without telling him of her plans. She left Nairobi in a single-engine, 120-horsepower airplane that had no radio, direction-finding equipment, or speedometer. On her first day, she flew to Juba in the Anglo-Egyptian Sudan (now the Sudan) and was forced down short of the airport by a storm and engine trouble. The next day she flew to Malakal on the Nile River. She tried to reach the capital city of Khartoum on the following day but made it only halfway when her engine conked out, and she had to make a forced landing in the desert. She worked on the engine and convinced the local people to push the plane to harder sand where she took off again and made it to a nearby airfield. The next morning she flew on to Khartoum, even though the engine died on her twice. In Khartoum it was discovered that the engine had a cracked piston ring. She was unable to get spare parts so she continued on to Atbara where she replaced the piston.

The engine continued to malfunction, and she was forced to land outside of Cairo in the middle of a dust storm so bad that she could not see the ground as she was landing. The British Royal Air Force helped her out and repaired the engine for good. She then flew on across the Mediterranean, with an inner tube around her neck, to Italy and France, where she ran into bad weather. She landed in London 23 days after she had set out from Kenya and went and knocked on Campbell Black's hotel door.

Following years of bush flying and scouting big game for safaris, Markham returned to England in 1936 with the aim of winning one of the big prizes that were being offered for record-breaking aviation achievements. She had originally thought of competing in a race to South Africa with Campbell Black but decided instead to try for the prize of flying solo from London to New York. This had never been accomplished because it meant flying against the prevailing winds. In the northern hemisphere the jet stream travels from west to east, so that when **Charles Lindbergh** made his solo flight he had the wind pushing him on. Other people had attempted to do the opposite, but had fallen short of the mark. Jim Mollison (the husband of **Amy Johnson**) had flown from western Ireland to eastern Canada in 1932. John Grierson had flown the whole distance in 1934, but he stopped at four places along the way and it had taken him six weeks.

Markham's aim was to travel all the way non-stop from London to New York to show that commercial air service between the two cities was possible. She flew a borrowed airplane—a single-engine Vega Gull with a 200-horsepower engine that could fly at up to 163 miles per hour. It was fitted with extra tanks so that it could fly 3,800 miles, but it had no radio equipment. After her plane was ready, Markham waited several days for good weather and then left London at 8 p.m. on September 4, 1936, with a strong head wind, low clouds and blustery weather. She was seen over Ireland at 10:25 p.m.; at 2 p.m. the next day she was spotted by a ship in the Atlantic; and then at 4:35 p.m. she flew over the tip of Newfoundland, the easternmost part of North America. Then she disappeared.

The next news was a telephone call from a small town in Nova Scotia where Markham had crash landed. With the nose stuck in a peat bog, she climbed out of the plane and greeted two fishermen—"I'm Mrs. Markham. I've just flown from England." Along the way, she had almost crashed in the ocean as the fuel line to one of her tanks froze, but it warmed up and the gasoline started to flow just before she reached the sea. It was another frozen fuel line that caused her to crash where she did.

She was disappointed that she had missed her goal of reaching New York and was afraid that the flight would be thought a failure. In fact, news services carried reports throughout the world, and she was considered a heroine. A U.S. Coast Guard plane met her in Nova Scotia, and she co-piloted it to New York City where she was met by Mayor Fiorello LaGuardia and rode in a motorcade through the city. While in New York, she heard that Tom Campbell Black had been killed in the race to South Africa that she had once set out to enter.

Markham returned to England, where she had become a celebrity, and spent the next few years of her life there, talking about entering another of the great air races. However, after the death of Campbell Black her interest in flying seems to have died as well. She made several trips, including one around the world by steamship. She moved to America in 1939, just before the beginning of World War II.

Markham stayed in California for a number of years, remarried and ran an avocado ranch. In 1952 she returned alone to Kenya and after a few difficult years and a major illness took up the career she had started thirty years before—raising and training horses. From 1958 to 1972 she was the most successful trainer in Kenya, winning all of the major prizes and becoming a local legend. Unlike many Europeans, she stayed on in Kenya after the country became independent in 1964. In her final years, she was gratified to once again become a well-known personality when her book was republished and she was the subject of a television documentary.

Where to learn more

Markham wrote about her own life in *West with the Night* (London: Harrap & Co., 1943; reprinted in paperback, San Francisco: North Point Press, 1983). An excellent biography by Mary S. Lovell, *Straight on till Morning* (New York: St. Martin's Press, 1987) includes interviews with the pilot just before her death. During the same period, PBS produced a documentary about her life called *World without Walls*.

Markham's aviation exploits are discussed in many surveys including *Women of the Air* by Judy Lomax (New York: Dodd, Mead & Co., 1987).

The lives of the European settlers in Kenya have produced a number of interesting books such as *Flame Trees of Thika* (Baltimore, Maryland: Penguin, 1984) by Elspeth Huxley and *Out of Africa* (New York: Modern Library, 1952) by Karen Blixen, which was made into a popular movie. A much more sensational account was written by James Fox in *White Mischief* (New York: Random House, 1983).

Jacques Marquette

(1637 - 1675)

Jacques Marquette was a Jesuit missionary from France who founded a mission in northern Michigan and accompanied Louis Jolliet in the discovery of the Mississippi River.

Jacques Marquette was the son of a distinguished French family from the town of Laon in the north. He studied to become a Jesuit priest and developed the desire to become a missionary. He was sent out to Canada in 1666 and arrived at Quebec on September 20 of that year.

Marquette showed a great aptitude for languages, and it is said that he became fluent in six Native American tongues. His first mission was at Trois-Rivières, midway between Quebec and Montreal. From there he went to Sault Ste. Marie, and then in September 1669 he was sent to found a mission at the end of Lake Superior. In 1671 he founded another mission at Saint Ignace on the north shore of the straits of Michilimackinac.

Jacques Marquette.

On December 8, 1672 the voyageur **Louis Jolliet** arrived at Marquette's mission with instructions to find the Mississippi River. Marquette decided to accompany him, and they set out in the middle of May 1673. A month later, they entered the Mississippi and were greeted by members of the Peoria tribe at a place in present-day Iowa. From there they sailed down the Mississippi to a place near the border of Arkansas and Louisiana. They turned around in mid-July and paddled back upstream through the Chicago River to Lake Michigan, which they reached in September. Jolliet went on to Montreal to report on the discoveries, but Marquette was ill and stayed at a mission near present-day De Pere, Wisconsin.

In the summer of 1674 Marquette had recovered, and he set out to fulfill a promise he had made to the Kaskaskia tribe to set up a mission there. However, his illness returned, and he was forced to spend the winter at a camp that is now in suburban Chicago. On March 30, 1675 he decided to continue his journey and traveled to a village on the Illinois River. There he preached a sermon on the Thursday before Easter to a gathering of 2,000 members of the Illinois nation. By this time he was very ill and set out to try to reach the mission at St. Ignace. He died along the way on May 18, 1675 and was buried at the mouth of a river that was named for him at the site of Ludington, Michigan.

Where to learn more

Marquette's reports back to his superiors in France can be found in Reuben G. Thwaites, ed. *The Jesuit Relations and Allied Documents: Travels and Explorations of the Jesuit Missionaries in New France, 1610-1791*, 73 vols. (Cleveland: Burrows, 1896-1901). Marquette's reports are in vols. 50-60. Included is a document called the *Récit*, which is a first-person account of the 1673 expedition.

Thwaites also wrote an early biography of Marquette: *Father Marquette* (New York: Appleton, 1902). This biography accepted that Marquette was the author of the *Récit* and had played a major role in the Mississippi expedition. This viewpoint was accepted by other authors such as Agnes Repplier, *Père Marquette: Priest, Pioneer and Adventurer* (New York: Doubleday, 1929).

This conventional wisdom about the role of Marquette was called into question by Franciscan friar Francis Borgia Steck in a series of publications: *The Jolliet-Marquette Expedition, 1673* (Quincy, Illinois: Franciscan Fathers, 1928; distributed by The Arthur H. Clark Co., Glendale, California) and *Essays Relating to the Jolliet-Marquette Expedition, 1673* (Quincy, Illinois: privately printed, 1953). This latter book was edited by August Reyling and published as *Marquette Legends* (New York: Pageant Press, 1960).

Steck's opinions caused immediate controversy: after all, Marquette was one of two Wisconsin statues in the Statuary Hall of the U.S. Capitol. They were met by a counterfire from Gilbert J. Garraghan: *Marquette: Ardent Missionary, Daring*

Explorer (New York: America Press, 1937). The noted historian of French exploration, Jean Delanglez, examined all the evidence and came out in favor of the view that Marquette did not write the *Récit*, with the corollary that his role was less than some supporters had thought. His arguments are summarized in *Life and Voyages of Louis Jolliet, 1645-1700* (Chicago: Institute of Jesuit History, 1948).

There are two more recent biographies of Marquette. Joseph P. Donnelly in *Jacques Marquette* (Chicago: Loyola University Press, 1968) largely contents himself with drawing a traditional portrait of Marquette. Raphael N. Hamilton in *Marquette's Explorations: The Narratives Reexamined* (Madison: University of Wisconsin Press, 1970) argues against the Delanglez evidence. He also published a shorter biography: *Father Marquette* (Detroit: William B. Eerdmans Publisher, 1970).

Meanwhile, there was a lesser controversy as to whether Marquette was an ordained priest or merely a catechist, a religious teacher. This fight was carried out in the pages of Catholic and historical academic journals. One view is presented in J.C. Short, "Jacques Marquette, Catechist," *Revue de l'Université Laval*, vol. 3 (1948-1949). The opposing argument is in Jerome V. Jacobson, "Attempted Mayhem on Père Marquette," *Mid-America* vol. 31 (1949), pp. 109-115. The arguments are summarized in Claude Corrivault, "Le Père Jacques Marquette," *Bulletin des Recherches historiques*, vol. 56 (1950).

Al-Mas'udi

(895? - 956?)

Al-Mas'udi was an Arab scholar who traveled extensively in the Muslim world and gave one of the first accounts of the Caspian Sea and Aral Sea and the lands north of the Caucasus Mountains.

Al-Mas'udi was a descendant of the prophet Mohammed who was born in Baghdad. From indirect evidence we believe he was born between the years 893 and 898. The earliest date in his own writings is 912, a date he mentions when telling an anecdote about meeting an official of the Abbasid dynasty in Baghdad. He was traveling in Persia by the year 915. In that year he traveled east through the provinces of Khuzistan, Ahwaz, Fars, where he visited Persepolis, the ancient Persian capital, Qumis, Khurasan, and Sistan. Unlike most Muslim travelers of this period, he showed his intellectual curiosity by visiting the temples of the Zoroastrians, the ancient religion of Persia before its conquest by the Muslims.

Later in 915 al-Mas'udi went to India and stayed there until the following year. Although his exact route is not known, there is some evidence that he took the caravan route from Khurasan to the Indus Valley. The Indus Valley (now part of Pakistan) was already settled by Muslims, but he went beyond that to the western Deccan, the central plateau of India, in what is now the region of Bombay. He visited the ports of Chaul and Kanbaya and discussed the effect of the monsoon on that part of the subcontinent. He also wrote about the plants, including oranges and coconuts, and animals of the area, such as elephants, peacocks, and parrots. In discussing his visit to India, al-Mas'udi talks about China and Sri Lanka ("Sarandib"), but it is obvious that he did not visit those places but reported on what he heard from others.

Al-Mas'udi returned from India in late 916 or early 917. He then went from Oman on the east coast of Arabia to an island on the east coast of Africa. Trade relations between Oman and East Africa date from ancient times, but al-Mas'udi talks about the difficulty of travel between the two places and gives a long list of shipwrecks and drowned persons. On his return from Oman al-Mas'udi went back to Baghdad and seems to have stayed there for several years. There is no record of his activities until 918, but for the following ten years he seems to have traveled in Iraq, Syria, and the Arabian Peninsula. He was in the Syrian city of Aleppo in 921 and from there went to the Mediterranean. In 925 he was in northern Iraq in Tikrit (the hometown of Saddam Hussein).

In 926 al-Mas'udi went back to Syria and then traveled to its southern part, or Palestine. He states that he was in Nazareth (the place where Jesus Christ grew up) and also went to Jerusalem and Nablus as well as to the Jordan Valley and the Dead Sea. While in Palestine al-Mas'udi visited Christian churches and talked with Jewish and Christian scholars. He also learned about the Samaritans, a small Jewish sect who remained in Palestine through the centuries while rejecting much of modern Jewish tradition, including the Torah.

In 927 al-Mas'udi went to Damascus in Syria and to the ruins of the great cities of Palmyra and Ba'albek. There he met the Sabians, another ancient Middle Eastern sect bypassed by modern Judaism and Islam. On his return to Iraq in 928, al-Mas'udi sailed down the Euphrates River from Syria. In February 928 he witnessed the siege of the western Iraqi city of Hit by the Carmathians. He then returned to Baghdad and in 930 went back to Ahwaz and Fars in Iran.

At about this time—sometime after 932 and before 941—al-Mas'udi traveled to the Caspian Sea and Armenia. He was the first person to give a written description of the Aral Sea, and he sailed across the Caspian and was able to state that unlike what some believed it was not part of the Black Sea. He collected a great deal of information about the non-Muslim peoples who lived in the Caucasus Mountains and to the north. He passed on some of the first knowledge that we have about the Khazars, Bulgars, and Russians.

In about 941 al-Mas'udi went back to Arabia, probably as part of the pilgrimage to Mecca that Muslims try to perform during their lifetime. He visited both Medina and Mecca and went as far south as San'a in Yemen. In January 942 he was in Egypt where he described the Christian festival of the Epiphany celebrated by the Coptic Christians of Egypt. In 942 he was in Antioch in northern Syria and in 946 was in Damascus. Starting from the time he was in Egypt, he began drafting his great work of travel and geography, *Meadows of Gold and Mines of Precious Stones*, and he also drafted a map of the world that shows the Atlantic and Indian Oceans connected to the south of Africa, the Nile Valley in its correct position, India with the Indus and Ganges Rivers in their proper positions, Sri Lanka off the southeast coast of India and the two great inland seas—the Caspian and the Aral. In his last years, al-Mas'udi traveled back and forth between Syria and Egypt and died in Egypt in about 956.

Where to learn more

There is one recent book in English devoted to al-Mas'udi: Ahmad M.H. Shboul, *Al-Mas'udi and His World: A Muslim Humanist and His Interest in non-Muslims* (London: Ithaca Press, 1979).

Douglas Mawson

(1882 - 1958)

Douglas Mawson was an Australian scientist who was a member of the first expedition to reach the South Magnetic Pole and then led two Australian expeditions to Antarctica.

D ouglas Mawson was born in the English city of Bradford in Yorkshire in 1882. His family emigrated to Australia when he was a young child, and he grew up there. He earned a degree in geology from the University of Adelaide.

In 1907 Mawson applied for and was accepted as a scientist on **Ernest Shackleton**'s expedition to Antarctica. Shackleton had announced that the aim of the expedition was to reach both the South Pole and the South Magnetic Pole. While Shackleton headed off with a team of four others in an unsuccessful attempt to make it to the Pole, Mawson joined Australian professor Edgeworth David and British naval surgeon Alistair Mackay on the expedition to the Magnetic Pole. They left the base on Ross Island on September 26, 1980.

During the trip to the South Magnetic Pole, the three men suffered various mishaps and hazards. On December 11, David fell into a crevasse, and the following day Mawson fell through a patch of ice into the water. On December 20 Mawson fell into a very deep crevasse and was suspended by the harness tied to his sledge until his companions could pull him up. They reached the South Magnetic Pole, which was then at 72°25'S, 155°16'E, on January 16, 1909. They carried out a little ceremony and proclaimed all of the surrounding territory for the British Empire. (It now lies in the sector claimed by Australia, but all Antarctic claims are in abeyance following a 1959 agreement.) Returning to the base, the three men were constantly in danger of starvation and were forced to live on half rations. They met up with the expedition ship, the *Nimrod*, on February 5 while it was on its way to the Ross Island base.

Following this success, Mawson was asked by British explorer **Robert Falcon Scott** to take part in his 1910 expedition to reach the South Pole. Mawson was not, however, interested in the race for the Pole but asked Scott if he could lead a team to do scientific research during the expedition. This was not practical, and Mawson then interested the Australasian Association for the Advancement of Science in sponsoring him on his own expedition. Mawson's ship, the *Aurora*, set sail from Hobart, Tasmania, on December 2, 1911. The expedition's first order of business was to establish a base on sub-Antarctic Macquarie Island. Australia has maintained a weather and radio station on the island ever since.

On January 8, 1912 Mawson established his base at a place he named Commonwealth Bay on the Adélie Coast, first seen by **Jules-Sébastien-César Dumont d'Urville** in 1840. Mawson called this hut on Cape Denison the "Home of the Blizzard" because of the constant winds. The winds that swept Cape Denison were exceptionally strong even compared to the rest of Antarctica. There were recorded gusts of up to 200 miles per hour (a very strong hurricane has winds of 140 m.p.h.), and there were ceaseless snow storms. In spite of this, the Australians were able to maintain meteorological observations for 10 months.

After setting up the base at Camp Denison, the *Aurora* sailed westward with part of the expedition to explore the Shackleton Ice Shelf under the command of Frank Wild, a veteran of Scott's and Shackleton's expeditions. In November 1912, Mawson divided the remaining part of the expedition into five teams. Mawson, accompanied by the English lieutenant B.E.S. Ninnis and the Swiss Dr. Xavier Mertz, a mountaineer and skiing champion, set out on November 17 to the unexplored territory between Cape Denison and Oates Land, about 350 miles to the east. They took three sledges and 18 dogs.

At the end of November one of the sledges fell into a crevasse. They were able to pull it out, but it was so badly damaged that they eventually had to transfer the supplies to one of the other two. On December 14, Ninnis was bringing up the rear with the heavily-laden sledge. Mertz was skiing in front to scout out the route. He signaled a crevasse ahead covered by an ice bridge. Mawson made it across, but Ninnis and his sledge fell through the ice. Looking down, Mawson and Mertz saw only two dogs on an ice shelf 150 feet below. One of them was dying, and the other was already dead. For three hours, they shouted below and tried to make a rope long enough to reach to the ice shelf. Unsuccessful, they were forced to give up. In addition to Ninnis's death, this meant that they faced a 300-mile return trip with no tent and only enough food for 10 days for themselves and nothing for the six remaining dogs.

The two men improvised as best they could. They made a makeshift tent out of a tent cover and broken sledge parts. Mertz carved two spoons out of the wood of a broken sledge. They fed the dogs wornout mittens and rawhide straps. As each dog got weaker, they were successively killed and eaten. The last dog died on Christmas Day, December 25, 1912, when they were still 160 miles from their base. On January 1, Mertz collapsed, and Mawson had to haul him on the sledge. Mertz died on January 7, 1913 in his sleep, huddled close to Mawson in the flimsy little tent. For a while, Mawson thought about staying where he was and dying along with his companion. The next day, however, he rallied and buried his friend in his sleeping bag and set out on his own.

By then, Mawson was suffering from severe frostbite. The soles had separated from his boots, and he had to tie a rag around them to keep them together. He averaged about five miles at first, but on January 15 he only covered one mile. On January 17, crossing the Mertz Glacier, named after his dead friend, he fell into a crevasse. He was left dangling at the end of a 14-foot-long sledge rope. The sledge stuck in the snow, and Mawson managed to climb up the rope. Just as he reached the edge, he fell back in and had to do it all over again. He got out on the second try and lay in the snow, not able to move for an hour.

On January 27 he was stopped by a blizzard. On January 29 he ran out of food. That day he stumbled on a cairn with a bag of food that had been left by a search party just hours before his arrival. In it was a message saying that there were further supplies 23 miles ahead. He reached the second cairn on February 1, but a blizzard pinned him down there for a week. On the morning of February 8, he stumbled into the camp at Cape Denison just as the *Aurora* was disappearing over the horizon.

Fortunately, however, five volunteers had stayed behind in the hope that Mawson and his two companions would show up. Since Mawson's was the first expedition to be equipped with a radio, they were able to signal to the ship to return. But the weather conditions were so bad that the captain was unable to turn back. In spite of his condition, Mawson was forced to spend another winter in Antarctica. By the following summer, in November 1912, he was well enough to make a sledge trip to carry out some observations. The *Aurora* returned on December 12, 1912 and, after further exploring along the coast, returned to Adelaide on February 26, 1913. Mawson was given a tumultuous welcome and was awarded a knighthood, becoming Sir Douglas Mawson.

On his return to Australia, Mawson took up his duties as professor of geology at the University of Adelaide. During the following years, he was a main advocate for continued Australian exploration and involvement in Antarctica. Following World War I, other countries, especially France and Norway, began to push forward territorial claims in Antarctica based upon previous activities of their citizens. Mawson urged that the British Commonwealth countries should do the same thing. In 1929 he was chosen to lead a joint expedition financed by the governments of Great Britain, Australia, and New Zealand.

Mawson's ship, the *Discovery*, sailed from Cape Town, South Africa, on October 19, 1929. On January 5, 1930 Mawson flew in the expedition's seaplane over a previously-unseen coast and named it MacRobertson Land. On January 30 a small party went ashore on tiny Proclamation Island and proclaimed British sovereignty over a large stretch of the coast between 45°E and 70°E. The ship spent the winter in Australia and then headed south again on November 22, 1930. The *Discovery* sailed along the coast of Antarctica and stopped at various points to proclaim British possession. Mawson returned to his old base at Cape Denison on January 4, 1931. The expedition made its last flag-raising at Cape Bruce on February 14, 1931 and then returned to Australia on March 19. The British government ratified the claims to sovereignty of over 2 million square miles of territory in 1933 and turned them over to Australia in 1936. Mawson returned to the University of Adelaide, where he taught until his retirement in 1952. He died in 1958.

Where to learn more

Mawson wrote about his second trip to Antarctica and his incredible overland trek in *The Home of the Blizzard: The Story of the Australian Antarctic Expedition, 1911-14* (London: Heinemann, 1915). Frank Hurley wrote about the same expedition in *Argonauts of the South* (New York: G.P. Putnam's Sons, 1925).

Two studies of Mawson's explorations are: C.F. Laseron, *South with Mawson* (London: Harrap, 1947) and Paquita Mawson, *Mawson of the Antarctic* (London: Longmans, 1964).

A good general history of the record of Australia in Antarctica, Mawson in the forefront, is R.A. Swan, *Australians in the Antarctic* (Melbourne: Melbourne University Press, 1961). For other general histories of Antarctic exploration during the "Heroic Age," see the bibliography under Ernest Shackleton.

Sir Francis Leopold McClintock

(1819 - 1907)

Sir Francis Leopold McClintock was a British naval officer who was sent on several parties to try to find the remains of Sir John Franklin's expedition and was the man who finally solved the mystery.

Leopold McClintock was born in Dundalk, Ireland on July 8, 1819, the son of a retired Army officer. His family was not wealthy, and he was one of 12 children. He joined the Royal Navy as a volunteer in June 1831 at the age of 12. He served as a non-commissioned officer on ships in South America, England, and North America. He returned to England in 1841 to pass his examinations to be promoted to lieutenant. He then went to Brazil in 1843 and was sent on a two-year cruise of the Pacific.

McClintock was engaged in studies at the British naval station of Portsmouth in 1848 when the British Admiralty decided to send an expedition to the Canadian Arctic to try to find what had happened to the expedition of **Sir John Franklin**. He served on the *Enterprise* commanded by **Sir James Clark Ross**. The *Enterprise* and its companion ship the *Investigator* were frozen in on the north shore of Somerset Island at a place called Port

Sir Francis Leopold McClintock. The Granger Collection.

Leopold for 11 months during 1848-1849 on Somerset Island. McClintock was put in charge of sledge trips to the interior in the spring of 1849 to try to find Franklin. He came within 180 miles of the spot where Franklin had died, but at a great cost to his men: all of them had to be put in the sick bay on their return to the ship. It was during this period that McClintock developed his interest in sledges as a way of traveling over the frozen tundra. Over the years, he developed many techniques and pieces of equipment for making such travel more efficient.

McClintock was selected to be first lieutenant on board the *Assistance*, one of the ships on another expedition to search for Franklin, this one commanded by Horatio Austin. They sailed from England in May 1850 with enough provisions to last three years. They anchored in Barrow Strait during the winter of 1850-1851, and McClintock set up six sledge teams to explore the interior. On one trip, McClintock set an Arctic record by traveling 875 miles in 80 days exploring parts of Bathurst and Melville Islands. He left a message on the southern shore of Melville Island that was later found by **Robert McClure**, who had entered the Arctic from the west and was stranded. There were, however, no traces of the Franklin expedition. On the return of the expedition to England, McClintock was promoted to commander on October 11, 1851.

Spurred on by Franklin's wife, the British government did not give up the search for the missing explorer. It outfitted an expedition under Sir Edward Belcher that consisted of five ships, two of which had auxiliary steam power for the first time. The expedition set sail in February 1852. McClintock received his first command, the *Intrepid*. He also took charge of setting up the sledge teams. One of them found and rescued McClure and his men from Banks Island in March 1853. McClintock himself made one of the great sledge trips of all time. Starting out on April 4, 1853, he and his men hauled a ton of supplies over 1,328 miles for 106 days. The British at the time did not believe in using dogs and continued to rely on manpower. One man died during the trip. During the course of their journey they discovered Prince Patrick and Eglinton Islands. The *Intrepid* was iced in and could not move. In the summer of 1854 Belcher ordered that it be abandoned, and the men were put on other ships and returned to England. McClintock was promoted to captain in October 1854.

The return of the Belcher expedition was the end of the attempts by the British Admiralty to find out what had happened to Franklin. In the spring of 1854, however, Dr. John Rae, traveling overland in the service of the Hudson's Bay Company found evidence of Franklin's expedition on the mainland opposite King William Island. Franklin's widow was unwilling to give up the search but could not get official backing. She was able to get enough private financial support to fit out one more expedition. McClintock volunteered to lead it for free.

McClintock sailed from England in a yacht, the *Fox*, in July 1857. He was not able to reach King William Island until 1859. Once there, however, his sledge teams soon found traces of the Franklin expedition. A member of McClintock's expedition, Lieutenant William R. Hobson, even found two notes that confirmed that Franklin had died there on June 11, 1847. McClintock and his party then found traces of the survivors all along the western and southern coasts of King William Island, including several graves and skeletons. He had discovered the fate of the Franklin expedition.

On McClintock's return to England in 1860 the British Admiralty gave him his pay for the time he had been away, and he was awarded a knighthood in honor of having solved the mystery of Franklin's disappearance. He went back to the Arctic very briefly in 1860 while surveying for a route for a telegraph line across the North Atlantic. In the following years, he commanded various ships in the Mediterranean, English Channel, and North Sea and was then put in charge of Royal Navy ships in Jamaica.

McClintock returned to Ireland in 1868 and ran for a seat in the British Parliament. As the representative of the Anglo-Irish aristocracy, he was not popular with Catholics and had to withdraw his candidacy because of rioting. He married another member of the Irish aristocracy, Annette Dunlop, in 1870 at the age of 51. They had one son, who also became a naval officer. McClintock was promoted to captain in 1871 and served as superintendent of the Portsmouth Naval Base from 1872 to 1877. He became vice-admiral in 1877 and was put in charge of the British fleet in North America and the Caribbean in 1879. In 1884 he was promoted to full admiral one day before his retirement. He lived for several more years, dying in London on November 17, 1907.

Where to learn more

McClintock's story of the 1857-1860 expedition is told in *The Voyage of the Fox in the Arctic Seas: A Narrative of the Fate of Sir John Franklin and His Companions* (Philadelphia: Porter & Coates, 1859; reprinted, Edmonton, Alta.: Hurtig, 1972). McClintock's biography was written by his admirer Sir Clements R. Markham, sometime Secretary of the Royal Geographical Society: *The Life of Admiral Sir Leopold McClintock* (London: John Murray, 1909). A graphic retelling of the search for Franklin can be found in Pierre Berton, *The Arctic Grail* (New York: Viking, 1988).

Sir Robert McClure

(1807 - 1873)

Sir Robert McClure was a British naval officer who was sent on the search for Sir John Franklin and discovered the Northwest Passage north of the American continent.

Robert McClure was born in Wexford, Ireland and educated at Eton (an English private school) and Sandhurst (the British military academy). He entered the Royal Navy in 1824. He first traveled to the Arctic in 1836-1837 as mate on the *Terror* under the command of **Sir George Back** on an expedition that went to Hudson Bay and explored the Melville Peninsula. He was promoted to lieutenant on his return to England in September 1837. He then served on British ships in the Great Lakes and in the Caribbean.

In 1848 McClure was chosen to be an officer on the first ship sent out to look for the missing expedition of **Sir John Franklin**, serving under **James Clark Ross**. They returned to England in the fall of 1849 without finding any trace of Franklin. McClure was then appointed to command the *Investigator* under the general command of Captain Richard Collinson in the *Enterprise* on a second attempt to find Franklin. This time they proposed to solve the mystery of Franklin's disappearance by attacking the problem from the opposite side—from the Pacific and Alaska.

They sailed together from England on January 10, 1850 but were separated by a storm in the Pacific Ocean soon after they had passed through the Straits of Magellan. As McClure's ship headed through the Pacific, it was hit by a sudden storm that knocked down all three masts. The *Investigator* arrived in Honolulu on July 1, 1850, only to find that Collinson had sailed the day before.

By cutting through the Aleutian Islands rather than following his instructions and sailing west of them, McClure reached Bering Strait between Alaska and Siberia before Collinson. For unknown reasons that have since caused much speculation, he did not wait for his superior but set out on his own. McClure's goal was to reach Melville Island in the northwestern Arctic, which had been visited by **William Edward Parry** as long ago as 1819. He rammed the ship through one patch of pack ice and then had to use five rowboats to tow the *Investigator* past Point Barrow. Forced by the pack ice of the Beaufort Sea to travel eastward along the coast of Alaska to the Mackenzie delta, McClure turned northwards east of the Mackenzie and reached the south shore of Banks Island, which had been spotted from the north by Parry, who named it in honor of **Sir Joseph Banks**.

Off the east coast of Banks Island, McClure saw a channel, later named Prince of Wales Strait, with a clear stretch of water leading to the northeast. As he sailed up it, he realized that if this body of water connected with Melville Sound, already sailed by Parry, he would have found the long-sought-after Northwest Passage.

By then, however, it was getting late in the year. On September 17, 1850, at a point about 30 miles from Melville Sound, McClure was forced to stop by increasing ice and rising winds. Wind pushed the *Investigator* 30 miles farther back down the channel. The growing ice toppled the ship on its side and threatened to crush it against some rocks. The men on the ship were convinced they were doomed and broke out the store of alcohol. On September 28, however, the storm died, the ship righted itself and was iced in for the winter.

On October 21, 1850, McClure took seven companions and headed north over the ice in sledges. On the fifth day, they reached the north end of Banks Island. On October 27, 1850, they climbed a small mountain and looked out on Melville Sound—McClure and his men had found the Northwest Passage. On the return trip, McClure ran ahead of the rest of his crew, got lost, and arrived barely alive after a sleepless night fighting his way through a storm.

The *Investigator* stayed locked in the ice during the winter of 1850-1851. During that time, McClure sent out three land parties to try to find traces of the Franklin expedition, without any success. In the summer of 1851 he tried to sail through Prince of Wales Strait into Melville Sound once again. This time he was stopped by ice 25 miles short of his goal. He then decided to sail south and try to get around Banks Island from the west side. Initially, he made very good time—300 miles in three days. Then, on August 20, 1851, the ship got caught in the ice once again. It was wedged in a small channel of open water too narrow to turn around in—so McClure continued north for another week. Once he had sailed around the northern end of Banks Island into Melville Sound he was once again stopped by ice.

McClure found a small harbor on the north coast of Banks Island, which he named Mercy Bay, and spent the winter of 1851-1852 there. While his men spent their time hunting, McClure took a small party north to Melville Island, hoping to find another one of the ships sent out to search for Franklin. He did find a note from **Francis McClintock** who had been there the previous June but who had long since left.

During the summer of 1852, McClure tried to get the *Investigator* free from the ice that blocked Mercy Bay but to no avail. By September when it became obvious that they were going to have to spend another winter in the Arctic, food supplies were dangerously low. Two of the junior officers showed signs of insanity, and 20 men were ill with scurvy. The following spring, McClure proposed to split up his crew into three different groups to try to get help overland.

In the meantime, the British government had sent out ships to look for McClure and Collinson, who had also disappeared. In September 1852 Captain Henry Kellett found a note on Melville Island that McClure had left five months previously indicating his location. Also iced in by the winter, Kellett could not go look for McClure until the following year. On April 6, 1853, shortly before he was to send out his land parties, McClure and his first officer were walking on the beach discussing the burial of a crew member who had died of scurvy. They looked up to see a strange man running down the beach towards them. It was Lieutenant Bedford Pim, an officer from Kellett's ship sent to fetch them.

At first, McClure refused to abandon the *Investigator*, and three more men died while waiting for supplies. When only four men volunteered to stay with him, McClure was forced to give up and leave the *Investigator* in Mercy Bay. Once his men reached Kellett's ship and crowded on board, it was too late in the year to depart. The following year, on the orders of Sir Edward Belcher, they abandoned Kellett's two ships and used supply ships to sail back to England via Baffin Bay, arriving home in September 1854.

McClure was given credit for discovering the Northwest Passage, even though he had not been able to navigate it. He was promoted to captain, knighted, and given a reward of £10,000. The journal of his voyage was edited and published in 1856. He then served in the Pacific Ocean from 1856 to 1861. After that, he returned to the Admiralty Office in London. He was promoted to rear admiral in 1857 and vice admiral in 1873 shortly before his death.

Where to learn more

There are three original accounts of the *Investigator* expedition by participants in it. There is also an account by the ship's doctor, Alexander Armstrong: *A Personal Narrative of the Discovery of the North-West Passage* (London: Hurst & Blackett, 1857) and by a Moravian missionary, Johann August Miertsching, who served as interpreter with the Inuit: Leslie H. Neatby, editor, *Frozen Ships: The Arctic Diary of Johann Miertsching, 1850-5420*(Toronto: Macmillan of Canada, 1967).

There are two fairly recent studies of the expedition: J.H. Nelson, "The Last Voyage of H.M.S. *Investigator*, 1850-53 and the Discovery of the North West Passage," *Polar Record*, vol. 13 (1967), no. 87 and Leslie H. Neatby, *The Search for Franklin* (London: Arthur Barker, 1970).

Other histories of Arctic exploration have good summaries of McClure's voyage: Jeannette Mirsky, *To the Arctic! The Story of Northern Exploration from Earliest Times to the Present* (New York: Alfred A. Knopf, 1948); George Malcolm Thomson, *The Search for the North-West Passage* (New York: Macmillan, 1975); and Pierre Berton, *The Arctic Grail: The Quest for the North West Passage and the North Pole, 1818-1909* (New York: Viking, 1988; paperback edition, New York: Penguin, 1989).

Alvaro de Mendaña

(1541 - 1595)

Alvaro de Mendaña led a Spanish expedition that found the Solomon Islands in the southwest Pacific and then returned 25 years later to attempt to found a colony there.

Pedro Sarmiento de Gamboa was a historian, mathematician, astronomer, and sea captain in the Spanish colony of Peru in the mid-16th century. He had become convinced after listening to Inca legends that there was a vast and wealthy land westward off the coast of South America. This was one more manifestation of the belief in a Great Southern Continent, Terra Australis. Sarmiento was able to convince the Spanish governor to sponsor an expedition to find this mythical land. When the expedition was put together, Sarmiento was appointed captain of the flagship, but overall leadership was given to the young and inexperienced nephew of Governor Garcia de Castro, 25-year-old Alvaro de Mendaña de Neyra.

The two ships of the expedition, *Los Reyes* and *Todos Santos*, left the Peruvian port of Callao on November 19, 1567. For about three weeks they sailed to the west and then, in a decision criticized by Sarmiento, turned toward the northwest. This course took the Spanish expedition across the ocean

Alvaro de Mendaña. The Granger Collection, New York.

without spotting any of the numerous islands and atolls until they saw the small island of Nui in what is now Tuvalu on January 15, 1568. A navigational error prevented them from landing on that one island sighted, and they did not see land again until they reached the large island of Santa Isabel in the Solomon Islands on February 1, 1568, 82 days after sailing from Callao.

Mendaña believed he had reached the shores of the sought-after southern continent, but soon found that it was an island. It was he who named the group the Solomon Islands, thinking that they held the wealth of the ancient king of Israel. They traveled around the islands, naming Guadalcanal, San Cristobal, Florida, Ramos (Malaita), San Marcos (Choiseul), and Arrecifes (New Georgia). In spite of Mendaña's efforts, relations with the native Melanesians deteriorated, with Sarmiento being most at fault. He burned down a village and took hostages, which led to retaliation in which nine Spaniards were killed. After a council of all the sailors, it was decided to return to Peru. The islands remained unvisited for another 200 years.

Mendaña sailed for home on August 11, 1568, passing Namu in the Marshall Islands, where they found evidence of a previous Spanish visit but no water. They passed by Wake Island (which was not seen again until 1796). They made a passage of 4,000 miles that took 131 days from the Solomons, and were so thirsty and hungry that they were forced to eat cockroaches. They sighted Baja California on December 19, 1568 where they went ashore to get water. They reached the port of Colima, near Acapulco on the coast of Mexico, on January 23, 1569. There, Mendaña had Sarmiento arrested for insubordination before sailing for Callao, which they reached on September 11, 1569.

Back in Peru, Mendaña became obsessed with the idea of returning to the Solomons and converting the islanders to Christianity and founding a colony. He went with his uncle, the Governor, back to Spain in 1569 to sell his idea there. He was not granted permission to found his colony until 1574. When he reached Peru again in 1577, he found the current Governor unwilling to carry out his instructions. It was not until another Governor was appointed in 1594 that Mendaña was able to realize his dream.

Mendaña set sail once again with four ships from Callao, Peru on April 9, 1595 with 378 people on board, 100 of them women. With Mendaña sailed his wife, Doña Ysabel Barrato, who turned out to be a very difficult personality, and three of her brothers and a sister. From the start of the voyage family disputes became frequent, and Mendaña was not able to put a stop to them.

On July 21, the ships spotted a group of beautiful islands to which Mendaña gave the name by which they are still known today, Las Islas Marquesas de Mendoza, in honor of the Peruvian governor, the Marques de Cañete, whose family name was Mendoza. Mendaña and the chief pilot of the expedition, **Pedro Fernandez de Quiros**, thought that the islanders were very handsome and friendly, but disputes soon arose as the Polynesians tried to leave the ships with various items and fighting broke out every time the ship anchored at one of the islands. Quiros estimated that 200 Polynesians were killed in the three or four days that they were there.

The ship continued to the west after leaving the Marquesas but several weeks passed in which only a few small atolls were seen— Pukapuka in the Cook Islands and Niulakita in Tuvalu. On September 7, 1595 the ships ran into dense fog. When it cleared one of the ships had disappeared and was never seen again. In 1970-1971, however, excavations on the north coast of the island of San Cristobal found remnants of Spanish pottery that indicated that the ship had run aground there, and the survivors had camped out on the shore.

On that same evening, a large and beautiful island was sighted near a smoking volcano. The islanders who headed toward the Spanish ships resembled the people that Mendaña had seen in the Solomons, and he thought that he had once again reached those islands. In fact, he had reached the island of Ndeni, which Mendaña called Santa Cruz, which is now part of the Republic of the Solomon Islands but lies about 300 miles east of the main part of the archipelago.

The Melanesians of the island were initially friendly, but relations quickly went downhill when the Spanish tried to build a settlement. The Spanish also began to fight among themselves. Doña Ysabel, who was much hated by the Spanish sailors and settlers, gained the upper hand over her husband who was ill with malaria and refused to give up the idea of building a settlement although almost everyone else wanted to return to Peru. She had some of those who disagreed with her executed. Within a short while, there were only 15 healthy soldiers left. The islanders attacked the survivors with poisoned arrows and quickly learned to attack after a rainfall when the Spanish guns were wet and would not fire. Mendaña died of malaria on October 18, 1595. Following his death, Quiros took over command and was finally able to talk Doña Ysabel into leaving and heading for the Spanish colony in the Philippines.

Where to learn more

The original account of the Mendaña expedition can be found in the *The Discovery of the Solomon Islands*, edited by Lord Amherst of Hackney and Basil Thomson, 2 vols. (London: Hakluyt Society, 1901)

The most complete recent history is in Colin Jack-Hinton, *The Search for the Islands of Solomon, 1567-1838* (Oxford: Clarendon Press, 1969). Other books about Pacific exploration, especially J.C. Beaglehole, *The Exploration of the Pacific* (Stanford: Stanford University Press, 1966) and O.H.K. Spate, *The Spanish Lake* (Minneapolis: University of Minnesota Press, 1979), have considerable information on Mendaña.

Daniel Gottlieb Messerschmidt

(1685 - 1735)

Daniel Gottlieb Messerschmidt was a German scientist who worked for the Russian Tsar and is credited with being the first person to make a scientific study of Siberia.

Daniel Gottlieb Messerschmidt was born on September 16, 1685 in the Prussian port of Danzig on the Baltic coast. (It is now the Polish city of Gdansk.) He attended the University of Halle, where he studied mathematics and physics and then went to medical school. He received his M.D. degree in May 1713 and returned to Danzig to practice medicine.

In 1716 Peter the Great, the Tsar of All the Russias, traveled to Danzig as part of his program of visiting Western Europe to learn the latest technologies. He asked one of Danzig's eminent scientists if he could recommend a young man who would be willing to undertake a scientific study of Siberia. Messerschmidt was recommended and traveled to St. Petersburg, then the capital of Russia, at the end of 1717. On November 15, 1718 he signed a contract with the Russian government to go to Siberia and study its geography, natural history, medical conditions, ethnology, ancient ruins, and anything else that he thought was important. He was to be paid 500 rubles a year for his work.

Messerschmidt left St. Petersburg in the summer of 1720 and went to Moscow and then to the city of Tobolsk in western Siberia, where he spent the winter of 1720-1721. There he met a Swedish officer named Philipp Tabbert (who later became Count Strahlenberg). Tabbert was a prisoner of war: Russia and Sweden fought the Great Northern War from 1700 to 1721. Although a Swedish officer, he was actually from the northern German province of Pomerania (not far from Danzig), which was ruled by Sweden until 1815. He and Messerschmidt became friends, and Tabbert was assigned to work with him. When Messerschmidt left Tobolsk on March 1, 1721, Tabbert accompanied him.

Their itinerary took them down the Irtysh River to Tara and then to Tomsk on the Ob River as far as Kuznetsk and over the divide to the Yenisei River valley where they spent the winter of 1721-1722 in the town of Krasnoyarsk. In the following years their travels took them as far as the Amur River in the Far East. Between 1720 and 1727 Messerschmidt's travels took him across all of Siberia from the far north into central Asia and as far as Lake Dalai Nor in what is now Chinese Manchuria.

Messerschmidt carried out all of the instructions that he had been given in St. Petersburg. He collected botanical and zoological specimens and studied the customs of the various native peoples that he met. He mapped many of the most prominent landmarks of Siberia. He collected religious statues, and old manuscripts. He collected words from the languages of the various Siberian peoples, and was the first person to try to understand the relationships between them. On the Tom River he found the bones of the hairy mammoth, an extinct species related to the elephant. East of Lake Baikal he discovered and described extensive mineral deposits. He was the first person to give a description of permafrost, the condition in polar regions in which the ground remains frozen throughout the year but a small layer thaws out in the summer.

Messerschmidt collected enormous amounts of valuable information, but by the time he returned to St. Petersburg Peter the Great was dead and the new Tsar was not interested in his discoveries. His achievements were hardly noticed. He returned to Danzig, hoping for better recognition, but without success. He returned to Russia where he married in St. Petersburg and lived in poverty until his death in 1735.

The ten volumes that he wrote in Latin describing his discoveries have never been translated or published. They are still, along with his collections, in the Academy of Sciences in St. Petersburg.

Where to learn more

Many of Messerschmidt's writings are available only in their original German. There is brief mention of Messerschmidt, however, in J.N.L. Baker, *A History of Geographical Discovery and Exploration* (New York: Cooper Square Publishers, 1969).

S.S. Meteor

(1925 - 1927)

The S.S. Meteor was a German scientific research ship that made the first systematic survey of one part of the world's oceans.

Following the Peace Treaty at Versailles that ended World War I, Germany was made to pay a large sum of money to the Western Allies as "reparations." This was very difficult for the Germans to do because of the country's difficult economic situation after the war. A German geologist at the University of Heidelberg, Alfred Merz, had studied samples of the water from the south Atlantic Ocean and proposed the theory that gold and silver must exist in sufficient strength on the ocean floor to enable extraction in commercial quantities. If so, this would help Germany pay off its debt. With the support of the German government a research ship, the *Meteor*, was outfitted to go to the South Atlantic to test Professor Merz's theories. It sailed from Hamburg on April 13, 1925.

Merz died on board the ship in August 1925, and the expedition was taken over by the ship's captain, Wilhelm Spiess. Merz's ideas turned out to be wrong, but in attempting to prove them the expedition made a valuable contribution to the study of the ocean. The German scientists on board the *Meteor* made numerous observations, measuring the depth, temperature, and the various properties of seawater, and studying the features of the ocean floor, and the blanket of sediments that covers it. Through their work, they contributed more to basic understanding of the ocean than any expedition before. The *Meteor's* comprehensive survey of the South Atlantic was the only example of this kind of work, necessary for understanding the world's oceans, until the 1950s.

Part of the problem in comprehending the ocean is that observations need to be taken at a series of closely related points in order to study variations in currents, temperature, and geological structure. Given the vast size of the ocean and the difficulty of taking such measurements, the task has proven to be daunting. Measurements need to be taken repeatedly so that sequences of charts can be compared and changes in currents and water characteristics followed over time. The *Meteor* was the first ship to make a very intensive effort in a limited area. It conducted its survey in the South Atlantic off the west coast of Africa for the two years from 1925 to 1927. This survey was the only one of its kind until the International Geophysical Year in 1956. In fact, an important project of the International Geophysical Year was to reoccupy the old *Meteor* stations so that measurements could be compared with those made three decades previously.

One of the most important discoveries made by the *Meteor*, and one that eventually led to a complete change in opinion on how the earth's crust was formed was that the sea floor surface is not smooth. It has mountains, valleys, and plains just like the earth's surface. This was largely unsuspected until the *Meteor* began running lines of echo soundings. At that time the submarine topography could not be worked out in more than a generalized way because the echo sounder would only record one depth each time it was used. It was only after World War II that continuous-recording echo sounders were developed that kept a running depth record of the surface beneath a ship.

Meteor also pioneered in taking the first cores of the soil and rock beneath the ocean bottom. These cores were only about a foot long and scarcely penetrated the upper layers beneath the sediment. No really long cores were taken until after World War II. Because of this inability to penetrate deeply, the pre-war interest in coring was relatively slight. The *Meteor* expedition accounted for most of the cores taken before World War II. Even with heavy weights attached coring tubes could penetrate no more than a few feet with only gravity to help punch into the sediments, and it took the development of new technology to make coring under the ocean floor really valuable.

Where to learn more

The *Meteor* expedition is referred to in *Exploring the Ocean World: A History of Oceanography* (New York: Thomas Y. Crowell, 1969). More extensive coverage of the expedition including a photograph of the *S.S. Meteor* can be found in Susan Schlee's *The Edge of an Unfamiliar World: a History of Oceanography* (New York: E.P. Dutton & Co., 1973).

Thomas Livingstone Mitchell

(1792-1855)

Thomas Livingstone Mitchell was a Scottish-born explorer who made four expeditions in interior of Australia that were largely responsible for establishing the nature of the interior river system.

Thomas Livingstone Mitchell was born at Craigend, Stirlingshire, in Scotland and served in the British army in the Peninsular War against Napoleon, where he gained experience mapping the battlefields. In 1827 he and his wife emigrated to Sydney, Australia where he was appointed Assistant Surveyor-General of New South Wales, and in 1828 he succeeded **John Oxley** as Surveyor-General.

When **Charles Sturt** was sent out in 1829 to explore the interior river systems of Australia, Mitchell felt slighted; he felt that as a professional surveyor he should have been given the responsibility. In 1831, therefore, he proposed an expedition to outdo Sturt: search out a great river flowing north that the Aborigines called the Kindur. Leaving Sydney in November 1831, he crossed the Liverpool Plains in northern New South Wales and then traveled to the Namoi River, then continued north over the Gwydir to the Macintyre and down the Barwon. To his great disappointment all of these rivers turned out to be tributaries of the Darling, the river that Sturt had discovered. Mitchell was forced to give up and turn back to Sydney in February 1832 when Aborigines attacked his party, killing two men and taking all of their supplies.

In his next expedition Mitchell set out to prove that Sturt had been wrong in thinking that the Darling River flowed southwest into the Murray. Maybe it flowed to the northwest instead. Mitchell and his party set out in the March 1835. The expedition's botanist, Richard Cunningham, brother of **Allan Cunningham**, wandered off and was killed by Aborigines. Mitchell reached the Darling on May 25 but found that he could not sail down it. He was forced to walk through the rough terrain along its shore. He followed the river for 300 miles to the southwest until it turned south near the present-day town of Menindee. Mitchell had to admit that he was wrong; by all appearances the Darling flowed south into the Murray. However, threatened by increasingly hostile Aborigines, he turned back before he reached the place where the two rivers met.

Mitchell was sent out again in March 1836 to prove that the Darling flowed into the Murray by attacking it from the other angle—from the Murray. This time he went downstream along the Lachlan, Murrumbidgee, and Murray Rivers, and he established their relationship, and that of the Murray to the Darling. Along the way, Mitchell continued his tradition of bad relations with the Aborigines. On May 24, 1836 he encountered a group of Aborigines that he thought were the same ones that had threatened his 1835 expedition. He set an ambush for them at a place called Mount Dispersion and killed seven of them before the rest were able to escape.

Returning up the Murray, past its junction with the Murrumbidgee, Mitchell disobeyed his instructions and, rather than heading east for Sydney, turned south down one of the tributaries of the Murray. Here he made his greatest discovery—a very large expanse of fertile land that is now the rich sheep-raising and wheat-growing districts of western Victoria state. Mitchell was so pleased with his discovery that he named it Australia Felix ("Blessed Australia").

Mitchell continued south and discovered and crossed the Grampian Mountains and descended the Glenelg River that flows into the Indian Ocean in western Victoria. He then made his way eastward to Sydney, arriving there in November 1836. Along the way, he saw the first squatters who were beginning to settle in what became the state of Victoria. As a result of his discoveries he was knighted in 1839, although the award was held up for a while to investigate the Mount Dispersion massacre. (The Board found that he had shown "a want of coolness and presence of mind" but brought no charges.)

In later years, the focus of Australian exploration turned to the north. While **Ludwig Leichhardt** was making his first expedition to Queensland, Mitchell also decided to attempt to find a way to the Gulf of Carpentaria on the northern coast. He set out in December 1845 with the largest expedition in Australian history up to that point. Exploring the rivers of central Queensland, he discovered one that appeared to be heading north. He named it the Victoria after the Queen and went back to Sydney telling everyone that he had found the way north. In 1847 Mitchell's assistant, **Edmund Kennedy**, found that in fact the river was a small stream, the Barcoo, that quickly turned south and was a tributary of Cooper's Creek.

Following this expedition, Mitchell went to London and wrote up the record of his last expedition. On his return to Sydney, he wrote the first school textbook on Australian geography and worked on a new design for ships' propellers. Mitchell became involved in various disputes with the colony's governors, and in 1855 a Royal Commission was appointed to investigate the way in which he ran the Survey Department. Before it was able to make its report (which was very unfavorable), Mitchell caught pneumonia while out surveying a new road and died at home in Sydney on October 5, 1855.

Where to learn more

Mitchell himself wrote two books about his explorations: *Three Expeditions into the Interior of Eastern Australia* (London, 1839) and the *Journal of the Expedition into the Interior of Tropical Australia in Search of a Route from Sydney to the Gulf of Carpentaria* (London, 1848). There are extracts from these in Kathleen Fitzpatrick, *Australian Explorers: A Selection from Their Writings* (London: Oxford University Press, 1958).

There is one full-length biography of Mitchell: J.H.L. Compston, *Thomas Mitchell, Surveyor General and Explorer* (London and Melbourne: 1954). A good survey of the field of Australian exploration that contains interesting material on Mitchell is E.H.J. Feeken and Gerda E.E. Feeken, *The Discovery and Exploration of Australia* (Melbourne: Nelson, 1970).

Robert Moffat

(1795 - 1883)

Robert Moffat was a British missionary in South Africa who traveled throughout Botswana and pioneered the route from South Africa to western Zimbabwe.

Robert Moffat was born in Scotland near the city of Edinburgh on December 21, 1795. He apprenticed as a gardener and then hired out as a horticulturist on different estates in Scotland and England. While working in the county of Cheshire in England, he was converted to Methodism by some local lay missionaries. He then determined to devote himself to religion and then went to study to become a missionary in Manchester, England. There he met his future wife Mary who was the daughter of the owner of the estate he was working on.

In 1816 Moffat was accepted as a missionary by the Methodists and on October 18 of that year he left England to travel to South Africa, arriving in Cape Town on January 13, 1817. He spent a year learning Dutch in the town of Stellenbosch and was then sent to Namaqualand on the west coast of the Cape Province. There he converted the chief to Christianity and traveled in his company to the north and across the arid lands to the west to Griqualand. In December 1819 Mary arrived from England, and they were married in Cape Town.

In 1820 Robert and Mary Moffat were sent to the outpost of Lattakoo on the northern edges of the British colony to work among Tswana-speaking Africans. These tribes were threatened by Matabele tribesmen (as the Ndebele-speakers were called by the British) moving westward. Moffat was able to organize the Tswanas to fight off the Ndebele, with a resulting increase in his prestige among the Africans. In 1825 he moved his mission station to Kuruman, more centrally located to work among the Botswana. In 1829 he was able to achieve a mass conversion of the Botswana people. He also began his great work of translating the Bible into Tswana.

Meantime, Moffat paid several visits to the Matabele people and was able to help in establishing an American mission among them. In 1837, however, the Dutch farmers of the Cape Colony, hating British rule, started their great migration, the Boer Trek, to the north. They came into conflict with the Matabele who were pushed off of their own lands and were ultimately driven to settle in what is now western Zimbabwe.

In 1838 Robert and Mary Moffat returned to England with their family to oversee the publication of the parts of the Tswana Bible that they had translated. There they met **David Livingstone** who was one of several young missionaries who returned with them to "Bechuanaland" in 1843. Livingstone was injured by a lion while on his remote station and returned to Kuruman where he was nursed by the Moffats' daughter Mary. They fell in love and were married in 1844.

For the next several years the Moffats were busy with their missionary and translating activities. In the meantime, David Livingstone began his exploring trips into central Africa. In May 1854 Robert Moffat set off to find his wandering son-in-law. On this trip he went across the edge of the Kalahari Desert to the town of Shushong and then walked 18 days through unknown country to the northeast until he came into the new lands of the

Robert Moffat. The Granger Collection, New York.

Matabele, where he met the aged chief Mosilikatse whom he had known years before. He did not find Livingstone but left supplies that eventually made their way to him.

By 1857 Moffat had finished the translation of all the Bible into Tswana and was ordered by the missionary society to travel back to Matabeleland to obtain permission for opening a new mission there. This he did, and returned once again, in October, 1859, to open the new station at Inyati.

The Moffats retired to England in 1870, where Mary died in January, 1871. Robert lived on until 1883 and spent most of his time collecting honors and reminiscing about his fifty years in Africa.

Where to learn more

Moffat's missionary activities and explorations in southern Africa are told in his *Missionary Labours and Scenes in Southern Africa* (New York: Johnson Reprint Corp., 1969).

There are two biographies of Moffat, *Robert Moffat: The Story of a Long Life in the South African Mission Field* (London: National Sunday School Union, 1883, 1925) and Cecil Northcott's *Robert Moffat: Pioneer in Africa, 1817-1870* (London: Lutterworth Press, 1961).

Muhammed ibn-Ahmad al-Muqaddasi

(945 - 1000)

Al-Muqaddasi was an Arab traveler in the tenth century who used his personal knowledge of the Islamic countries to write an important geographical study of them.

A l-Muqaddasi was born in Jerusalem in the middle of the tenth century. Both of his grandfathers were prominent architects and builders who were responsible for several famous constructions, including the fortifications of the port city of Acre. In the year 966 al-Muqaddasi undertook the pilgrimage to Mecca that is an obligation of devout Muslims. He made the pilgrimage, or *hajj*, again in 977 and 987. Each time, he used the opportunity to visit other lands, and so he spent twenty years of his life traveling throughout the various Muslim countries of his time. He did not, however, travel into neighboring non-Muslim countries, thinking it not worth the effort. In fact, he noted the presence of Jews or Christians in Muslim cities as flaws in their make-up.

It is not known what prompted al-Muqaddasi to make his journeys although there is some speculation that he was a traveling propagandist for the Fatimid rulers of Egypt. He discussed all the various sects and schools of Islam but seemed to have a preference for the Shi'ites, who claim that the biological descendants of Muhammed are the rightful rulers of Islam and who are now the dominant sect in certain Islamic countries as opposed to the "orthodox" Sunnis.

We do not know in what order al-Muqaddasi made his various trips. We know that he sailed all the way around the Arabian Peninsula from the Red Sea to Abadan on the south coast of Iran at the head of the Persian Gulf. He went to such places in Iran and central Asia as Shiraz, Khorasan, Bukhara, and Gurgan. He said that he spent a year in Yemen on the southern coast of Arabia. He spent 70 days crossing Persia and traveled across the Arabian Desert several times, visiting it from the north, south, east, and west. He wrote that he visited every Muslim country except "al-Sind" (Pakistan) and "al-Andalus" (southern Spain).

Throughout all his journeys, al-Muqaddasi took great care to obtain accurate information about the climate, the products, the state of trade, the coinage, weights and measures, and the general characteristics of the inhabitants of the countries he visited. He mixed with persons of every class. He wrote that on some occasions he had audiences with different rulers and mixed familiarly with the great, while at other times he earned a living by hawking in the bazaar or by bookbinding. He also worked as a teacher, scribe, courier, doctor, lawyer, paper-maker, and *muezzin* (the man who calls the faithful to prayer). He was thrown into prison as a spy and was robbed many times by highwaymen and other thieves. Sometimes he traveled in a sedan chair and sometimes he had to walk through desert sands and mountain snows.

As a result of these wide travels and experiences, al-Muqaddasi sat down in 985 and wrote a geographical description of the world of Islam, called the *Ahsan at-takasim fi ma'rifat al-Akalim* ("The Best Division for Knowing the Provinces"). He had clear and fairly accurate ideas about the geographical conditions of all the countries of Islam, especially Mesopotamia, Syria, Samarkand, and Bukhara. The information supplied by him is very authentic and reliable because it reflects the knowledge he gained on his own travels.

Where to learn more

The sources for this account were: S.M. Ziauddin Alavi, *Arab Geography in the Ninth and Tenth Centuries* (Aligarh, India: The Department of Geography, Aligarh Muslim University, 1965) and Basil Anthony Collins, *Al-Muqaddasi: The Man and His Work* (Ann Arbor, Michigan: Department of Geography, University of Michigan, Michigan Geographical Publication No. 10, 1974). See also Sir T.W. Arnold, "Arab Travellers and Merchants, A.D. 1000-1500" in Arthur Percival Newton, *Travel and Travellers of the Middle Ages* (New York: Alfred A. Knopf, 1930; reprinted, Freeport, N.Y., 1967).

George Chaworth Musters

(1841 - 1879)

George Chaworth Musters was a British naval officer who was the first European to travel across the length of Patagonia, the southernmost part of South America.

George Chaworth Musters was born in Naples, Italy on February 13, 1841 the son of English parents who were traveling in Europe. Both of his parents died by the time he was three years old, and he was raised by an uncle who had been an officer on the *Beagle* that carried **Charles Darwin** around the world.

Musters joined the Royal Navy and spent the years from 1861 to 1866 on a ship that sailed the coast of South America. In Rio de Janeiro in 1862 he and another young officer climbed up to the top of Sugar Loaf mountain, which overlooks the city, and planted the British flag; it took the Brazilians a long time to pull it down.

After Musters left the Navy, he resolved to return to South America to make a journey across the length of Patagonia, the southern end of the continent. He sailed from the British colony of the Falkland Islands (Malvinas) to the Chilean outpost of Punta Arenas on the Strait of Magellan in April 1869. He joined a group of Chilean soldiers that went out looking for prisoners who had escaped from the prison colony at Punta Arenas. This took him as far as the Argentine settlement of Río Gallegos at the mouth of the Gallegos River in the far south of mainland Argentina.

At Río Gallegos Musters met up with a band of Tehuelche Indians. These Native Americans were the southernmost of all the original inhabitants of the Americas. They were nomadic, roaming the dry plains of Patagonia hunting the guanaco, a relative of the llama. They were noted for the minimal nature of their material culture; visitors were always amazed to see how they were able to thrive in their cold climate wearing nothing but a cloak of animal skins. The band that Musters encountered was led by a man with the improbable name of Sam Slick—he had spent some time in the Falkland Islands where he learned English and acquired his nickname.

Musters joined Sam Slick's band and started out across the interior of Patagonia. He spent the winter of 1869 in their camp (in the southern hemisphere the winter starts in June) and then headed north in September, where he first saw the Andes. They crossed the Río Chico on September 1 and reached an Indian settlement that is now the village of Tamel Aike on September. There was still ice blocking the rivers at this date.

During his entire journey, Musters was able to retain the trust of his Native American guides and was the first European to write about the customs and way of life of the Tehuelches. He was invited to attend the coming of age ceremony of a young Tehuelche girl, which was considered a great honor. In his book about the trip, he explained his success: "Never show distrust of the Indians . . . as you treat them, so will they treat you."

In October 1869, Musters discovered a large lake in the middle of Patagonia. It later turned out to be two separate bodies of water—Lago Colhue Huapi and Lago Musters. In November as they journeyed into the warmer and better-watered northern part of Patagonia, they encountered more and more Native Americans. Musters served as a kind of diplomat between the various bands. They even ran into a group of Araucanians, these were the "cowboy" tribesmen of the Argentine pampas who were on a hunting mission to the south. By April 1870, the weather had started to turn cold again, and fever had spread among his band, killing several children. So it was with great relief that Musters reached the European settlement of Carmen de Patagones on the Río Negro, where he was taken in by Welsh settlers, who had been brought over to settle this part of Argentina by the Argentine government.

After Musters returned to England, he wrote about his experiences in a book called *At Home with the Patagonians* published in 1871. As a result, he was given an award by the Royal Geographical Society. He also brought back several habits that he acquired in South America: he preferred to sleep in his garden wrapped up in a blanket rather than in his bed. He continued to travel: to Vancouver Island in British North America, to Venezuela, and to Bolivia, where he married. He died unexpectedly on January 25, 1879 in London while preparing to travel to Mozambique in East Africa, where he had been appointed British consul.

Where to learn more

Musters wrote about his explorations in an article for the *Journal of the Royal Geographical Society*, "A Year in Patagonia," vol. 41 (1871), pp. 59-77, and in his book *At Home with the Patagonians* (London: J. Murray, 1873). A summary of his trip can be found in Edward J. Goodman, *The Explorers of South America* (New York: Macmillan, 1972).

José Celestino Mutis

(1732 - 1808)

José Celestino Mutis was a Spanish botanist who spent many years investigating the plant life of Colombia and was responsible for the discovery of many valuable species.

During the 18th century, European monarchs and governments were influenced by the ideas of the Enlightenment to sponsor systematic investigations of the natural sciences. Convinced of the value of these scientific explorations, King Charles III of Spain sent out three expeditions to his American colonies of New Spain (Mexico), New Granada (Colombia), and Peru. The man he chose for the expedition to what is now Colombia was a Spanish priest, Father José Celestino Mutis, who was also a physician. He was sent out at the same time that **Hipólito Ruiz** was sent to Peru.

Mutis left Spain on September 7, 1760. He arrived at the Colombian port of Cartagena on October 29. He then took a boat up the great Magdalena River to the Colombian capital of Bogotá. Along the way, he took care of the medical problems of the boat's crew and collected biological specimens. They arrived at Bogotá on February 18, 1761.

Mutis spent the rest of 1761 and 1762 traveling throughout the area around Bogotá and collecting specimens and examining other natural phenomena. He climbed the nearby Cerro de Guadalupe in February 1762. He started a correspondence with the famous Swedish botanist Linnaeus, who was working on his system for classifying life forms. Mutis also took on the duties of a local doctor, and it was not until 1777 that he was able to make an extensive trip away from Bogotá.

On October 1, 1777 Mutis left Bogotá and went to the settlement of Minas del Sapo, where he spent a year collecting plant specimens, but also writing about flying ants, termites, worms, carnivorous flies, armadillos, and anteaters. He saw his first rubber tree, whose existence had first been reported to Europe by **Charles-Marie de La Condamine** and described how latex was extracted. He discovered the saffron plant and investigated the native American cinnamon plant. In Minas del Sapo he also received news of the death in February 1778 of Linnaeus—"the saddest news I have received in my life."

Returning to Bogotá, Mutis finally received authorization and a grant from a new Governor-General to make an extensive trip into the interior of the country to find new species. He left Bogotá on April 29, 1782 heading down the mountains to the village of Honda on the Magdalena River. Along the way he discovered the chinchona tree, the source of quinine, which was to be the major weapon against malaria until very recent years. He also discovered the *aristoloquia* plant, which is used as a remedy against snakebite. He traveled through the Magdalena valley, making his headquarters at a place called Mariquita, where he had assistants to help him preserve and document his collections. He stayed there until 1792 when he returned to Bogotá and then eventually made his way back to Spain, where he died in 1808.

Most of Mutis's work remains unpublished, but he was brought to the attention of the world by the German scientist **Alexander von Humboldt** who called him the "patriarch of botany in the New World."

Where to learn more

Mutis's record of his explorations and observations can be found in Guillermo Hernández de Alba, ed. 2 vols. *Diario de observaciones de José Celestino Mutis* (Bogotá: Editorial Minerva, 1958). There is a good summary of his work in Edward J. Goodman, *The Explorers of South America* (New York: Macmillan, 1972).

Gustav Nachtigal

(1834 - 1885)

Gustav Nachtigal was a German doctor who traveled through North Africa to Lake Chad and from there to the Nile; he later helped found the German Empire in Africa.

Gustav Nachtigal was born in the small German town of Eichstedt, in the region of Brandenburg, on February 23, 1834. His father was a Lutheran minister who died when Gustav was quite young. He attended the medical schools of several German universities. After getting his medical degree, he became a military surgeon in Cologne. In 1863, he became ill with a lung problem, and one of his former professors suggested that he move to a warm, dry climate in order to recover.

Nachtigal decided to go to North Africa. He went first to Bône in Algeria and then settled in Tunis. He stayed there for several years and was employed as physician to the Bey of Tunis. In the warm, dry climate of Tunisia, he regained his health. In his position at the court in Tunis, he also acquired a great knowledge of the Arabic language and of Arab life.

Nachtigal was on the point of returning to Germany, when **Gerhard Rohlfs** arrived in Tunis with some presents that the King of Prussia wished to be given to the ruler of Bornu (now in northern Nigeria) in recognition of the help given to German explorers in the area. Rohlfs himself was unable to make the trip, and Nachtigal offered to make the journey in order to satisfy his curiosity about Africa. He left Tunis on February 19, 1869 with a small expedition of five guides and servants, including Muhammad el-Qatruni, who had served as guide for **Heinrich Barth**, and an Italian pastry chef, and eight camels.

The expedition reached Marzuq, the capital of the Fezzan in what is now southern Libya, on March 27. While there, Nachtigal met the Dutch explorer **Alexine Tinné** and was the last European to see her before she was killed by Tuareg tribesmen in the desert. He was delayed in traveling on to Bornu and took advantage of the time to explore the region. Nachtigal went south through the oases of Qatrun and Tajarhi. The little caravan almost perished from lack of water but discovered a lone well and were able to keep going. They reached the Tibesti Massif, a large mountainous region in the northern part of Chad; Nachtigal was the first European to visit there.

In the Tibesti region Nachtigal and his companions were looked upon suspiciously by the Tubu tribesmen. They were forced to pay "taxes" in every town they passed through in order to proceed. In the main town of Bardai they were kept prisoner

Gustav Nachtigal. The Granger Collection, New York.

for two months while the local ruler tried to decide whether to send them back to Fezzan or allow them to go on. Finally Nachtigal decided that his only safety was in escape, so he and his companions bribed one of the guards in order to sneak out of their tent in the middle of the night and head back to the Fezzan.

Nachtigal made it back to Marzuq on October 8, 1869. However, there was still no caravan headed for Bornu so he was forced to spend a miserable Christmas in a leaky hut. He spent some time trying to ascertain the circumstances of Tinné's death. It was not until April 18, 1870 that he was able to leave to travel south to Kukawa, the center of Bornu, where he arrived on July 6, 1870. He met the Sultan, Sheikh Muhammad el-Kanemi and presented his gifts. He "was delighted with the artistically written royal covering-letter, which I presented to him in an elegant case with an Arabic translation attached to it. I had to read it in out in German at least half a dozen times, seeking by vigorous intonation and declamatory delivery to make good what the hearer lacked in understanding." At the court he found that the Sultan's soldiers dressed in extraordinary costumes that ranged from near nakedness to suits of armor and yellow, green and red costumes like those of harlequins.

From Bornu, Nachtigal made a long excursion from March 1871 to January 1872 with a group of Arab nomads northeastward as far as Borku just south of Tibesti, returning to Kukawa. He then traveled west to Timbuktu and then back east through the regions of Wadai (now in eastern Chad) and Darfur (in the Sudan) to the Nile River. Then he traveled downstream to Cairo, where he arrived in November 1874. He was the first person to have traveled overland between the Lake Chad region and the Nile. In all, his journey lasted for over five years and covered over 6,000 miles.

As a result of this journey, Nachtigal became recognized as one of the foremost German authorities on Africa. He joined the *Kolonialverein*, an organization agitating for the establishment of German colonies in Africa and the South Pacific. In 1876 he attended the Brussels Conference called by King Leopold that led to the formation of the Congo Free State. He was appointed German consul in Tunis. There, on May 19, 1884, he received a telegram from the German Chancellor, Otto von Bismarck, telling him to embark on the gunboat *Möwe* to travel to the west coast of Africa. Nachtigal used threats of bombardment and exploited local political disputes to force the local chiefs to turn their land over to the Germans. Treaties were signed on the coast of Togo on July 4-6, 1884, and with the Duala tribe of Cameroon on July 14. Togo and Cameroon became German colonies until after World War I. In September 1884 Nachtigal traveled to Southwest Africa where he signed similar treaties that established a German colony in what is now the country of Namibia.

Nachtigal then headed back to Germany, having established a new German empire. However, he died on board ship off Cape Palmas, Liberia, on April 21, 1885.

Where to learn more

Nachtigal's book about his African travels was published as *Sahara und Sudan: Ergebnisse sechsjähriger Reisen in Afrika*: vol. 1 (Berlin: Weidmannsche Buchhandlung, 1879); vol. 2 (Berlin: Verlagshandlung Paul Parey, 1881); vol. 3 (Leipzig: F.A. Brockhaus, 1889). The English version, *Sahara and Sudan*, translated and edited by Allan G.B. Fisher and Humphrey J. Fisher, appeared between 1971 and 1980 in 4 vols.: (London: C. Hurst & Co.; Berkeley: University of California Press, 1971).

There is an interesting retelling of the first part of Nachtigal's journey to Bornu in Christopher Hibbert, *Africa Explored: Europeans in the Dark Continent, 1769-1889* (London: Allen Lane, 1982), which was helpful in writing this account. The biography of Nachtigal in the *Allgemeine Deutsche Biographie* gives quite a lot of detail about his later diplomatic activities.

Fridtjof Nansen

(1861-1930)

Fridtjof Nansen was a Norwegian explorer who led the first expedition across Greenland and made a famous voyage to the Arctic that came closer than any previous attempt to reach the North Pole.

Fridtjof Nansen was born in the Norwegian capital of Oslo, then known as Christiania. His mother, Adelaide, was a baron's daughter who had eloped with a baker's son and had had five children. When he died, she married a lawyer, Baldur Nansen, and had two more sons, of whom Fridtjof was the older. Nansen grew up on the couple's farm outside of Christiania and loved the outdoors, spending much of his free time camping and skiing. He attended the University of Christiania and majored in zoology. One of his professors there suggested that a trip to the Arctic in a sealing ship would be a worthwhile experience. Nansen sailed aboard the *Viking* for six months in 1882. For 24 days the ship was caught in the icepack off the east coast of Greenland, and Nansen developed the desire to explore the great island.

Returning home, Nansen became the curator of natural history at the Bergen Museum in Norway's second-largest city. He

Fridtjof Nansen. UNHCR.

took some time off to study marine zoology in Naples, Italy in 1886. On his return from Italy, he came up with a scheme to cross Greenland from east to west. he traveled to Stockholm to consult with the explorer **Adolf Erik Nordenskjöld** who had attempted the Greenland crossing in the opposite direction in 1883. Nansen got the financial backing of a Danish financier and recruited a small crew made up of two Lapps and three young Norwegians, including Otto Sverdrup. They trained during the winter of 1887-1888 in the mountains outside of Bergen. A few days before departing, Nansen defended his doctoral thesis at the University, and then the expedition set out for Greenland in May 1888. They traveled in a sealing schooner that spent most of its time hunting seals, and they did not reach the east coast of Greenland until July 17.

The sealing ship left Nansen and his colleagues off at sea two miles from Cape Dan. As they rowed their small boats ashore, they were hit by storms and ice floes that forced them 300 miles south over the next two weeks. Once they made it ashore, they rowed 200 miles back north, which took them another two weeks. They reached Umivik Fjord on August 12, 1888 and set out inland from there on August 15. The first part of the trip was the worst—they had to climb up the rocky mountain that rings the east coast of Greenland to an altitude of 7,930 feet before they reached the interior plateau.

By the time Nansen and his men made it over the coast ranges, they had used up all of their water. Their only supply was what they had at the end of each day from melting snow in tin flasks they had put under their clothing to warm with their own body heat. Once they headed across the inland plain, the going was easier, especially after they were able to start using their skis on September 2. In the middle of September, they reached their highest point, 8,920 feet, and on September 19 they sighted the peaks of Greenland's west coast. As they ran down the mountain in their excitement, they almost fell into a giant snow crevasse, and their progress was slowed by a large field of such crevasses. They reached the edge of the icefield on September 25. Nansen and Sverdrup built a small boat to float down the Ameralik Fjord 60 miles to the Danish settlement of Godthaab. The rest of the expedition walked along the shoreline. When Nansen reached Godthaab on October 3, 1888, the Danish official in charge greeted him by saying, "Allow me to congratulate you on taking your doctorate."

Nansen and the members of his expedition were the first Europeans to cross Greenland (and perhaps the first humans to do so). During the course of the expedition, he invented the Nansen sledge, a kind of sled on narrow runners, that was used in many later Polar explorations, as well as the Nansen cooker, an efficient alcohol-fueled stove. Nansen was able to send word of his accomplishment back to Europe, but it was too late in the year to travel back themselves. They spent the winter in Godthaab, where Nansen used the occasion to study the local Inuit. When they returned to Christiania, they were welcomed as national heroes. Nansen proposed to Eva Sars, an opera singer and the daughter of one of his zoology professors, and she accepted. They were happily married for many years.

While he was in Greenland, Nansen had noted that the native Inuit made tools from driftwood that came from Siberia and Alaska. This observation led him to think about the forces of the currents in the Arctic Ocean. In 1881 the American ship *Jeannette*, commanded by **George Washington De Long**, broke up in the ice north of Siberia. Three years later wreckage from the ship came ashore in southwestern Greenland. Nansen used this as evidence for his idea that the currents in the Arctic would be strong enough to carry a ship to the North Pole simply by drifting.

Nansen's plan was supported in Norway, and he was able to get money to test his theory from many supporters including the King of Norway. With this money he built a ship called the *Fram* ("Forward") that was designed to resist the pressure from the ice that covered the northern ocean. The *Fram* left Norway on June 24, 1893. It rounded North Cape (the northernmost tip of Europe) and headed east along the Siberian coast. It stopped briefly to take 34 Siberian dogs on board and then headed north.

The *Fram* ran into the ice pack on September 20 and by September 27 was completely frozen in and remained that way for the next 35 months. By December the pressure of the ice threatened to crush the little ship, but its ingenious design allowed it to lift itself out of danger. Later a large chunk of ice raised above the surface threatened to override it and force it down below the surface, but once again it escaped. During this long period the men on board occupied themselves making scientific observations, but life was inevitably very boring.

In the spring of 1895 the ship was still about 350 miles away from the Pole and started heading west. Nansen decided that he would never reach his goal by depending on the currents alone. He then set off on March 14, 1895 with teams of dogs and one companion, Hjalmar Johansen, planning to travel overland to the North Pole in 50 days. They traveled until April 8 when the long ridges of ice prevented them from going any farther. They had reached 160 miles farther north than any previous explorer and were only 240 miles from the Pole.

Once Nansen and Johansen turned back, they headed for the group of islands known as Franz Josef Land. However, a navigational error took them off course. As they went farther south and summer came on, the ice began to break up and it was increasingly difficult to travel. They were forced to kill their dogs and became progressively weaker. On July 24 they saw the north coast of Franz Josef Land and on August 7 they reached the edge of the ice and were able make a boat and sail through the open seas.

Nansen and Johansen made a camp at the end of August and then were forced to spend the whole winter in their small hut living only on bear meat that they were able to shoot. As it happened, an English expedition under the command of Frederick Jackson was also camped out on the same island during the winter. On June 17, 1896 Nansen heard dogs barking and set out to follow the sound. As he reports in his book, *Farthest North*, he heard a shout. "Soon I heard another shout and saw a man. . . .We approached one another quickly. I waved my hat; he did the same. I heard him speak to the dog, and I listened. It was English. . . .It was sometime before the English explorer, Frederick Jackson, said: 'Aren't you Nansen? . . . By Jove! I am glad to see you!'"

On August 7, 1896 the two Norwegians sailed in one of the English ships back to Norway and reached there a week before the *Fram* turned up as well. It had continued to float west and was finally freed from its ice trap north of Spitsbergen. They returned to Christiania to a tumultuous welcome, including Nansen's 3-year-old daughter Liv (whom he had never seen), and were honored at a state banquet by King Oscar of Sweden and Norway.

Nansen became famous for his exploits, and he was able to set up a foundation to continue his scientific research. He continued to study oceanography and made several important scientific expeditions to the North Atlantic. When Norway separated from Sweden in 1905, he became his country's first ambassador to Great Britain. During World War I he worked to help famine victims in Russia and to help prisoners of war return to their countries after the war. He was influential in setting up the League of Nations and was awarded the Nobel Peace Prize in 1922.

Where to learn more

Nansen wrote several books about his Arctic explorations that remain classics of exploration: *First Crossing of Greenland* (London: Longmans, Green & Co., 1890); *Farthest North*, 2 vols. (New York: Harper & Brothers, 1898); and *The Norwegian North Polar Expedition 1893-6* (London: Longmans, Green & Co., 1900-1906).

Nansen also wrote a history of the Vikings in Iceland, Greenland, and North America: *In Northern Mists: Arctic Exploration in Early Times* (New York: F.A. Stokes, 1911; reprinted, New York: AMS Press, 1969) and a book about the Inuit entitled *Eskimo Life*.

There are good surveys of Nansen's work in Jeannette Mirsky, *To the Arctic!: The Story of Northern Exploration from Earliest Times to the Present* (New York: Alfred A. Knopf, 1948); L.P. Kirwan, *A History of Polar Exploration* (New York: W.W. Norton & Company, 1960); and John Maxtone-Graham, *Safe Return Doubtful: The Heroic Age of Polar Exploration* (New York: Charles Scribner's Sons, 1988).

Interestingly, there is no modern biography of Nansen in English. His daughter wrote a memoir of her family life: Liv Nansen Hoyer, translated by Maurice Michael, *Nansen: A Family Portrait* (New York: Longmans, Green & Co., 1957). There is a short biographical essay in Helen Acker, *Four Sons of Norway* (New York: 1948; reprinted, Freeport, N.Y.: Books for Libraries Press, 1970) and a biography in French: René Ristelhueber, *La Double aventure de Fridtjof Nansen* (Montréal: Les Editions Variétés, 1945).

U.S.S. *Nautilus*

(1958)

The U.S.S. Nautilus was a nuclear-powered submarine that made the first trip under the Arctic Ocean and the North Pole.

The *U.S.S. Nautilus* was the world's first atomic-powered submarine, commissioned at the U.S. Navy's submarine base at Groton, Connecticut in 1955. From a defense point of view, the great advantage of nuclear-powered submarines was that they could remain submerged much longer than conventional diesel-powered submarines, thus making it easier to go undetected. In order to test the *Nautilus*'s ability to travel for long distances undersea, the Navy set it on a mission of traveling all the way under the polar ice of the Arctic Ocean.

The first attempt was made in August 1957 when the ship entered the Greenland Sea between Greenland and Spitsbergen and then made three probes toward the North Pole. It reached within 180 miles of the Pole before being forced to turn back because an electrical power failure closed down the master gyroscope, which was needed for navigation.

The *Nautilus* tried again in June 1958, entering from the Pacific side, which is more difficult because there are thick ice jams in the bottleneck between Alaska and Siberia. The submarine had to submerge in fairly shallow water, only 160 feet deep, because ice had formed in the Chukchi Sea. The average depth of the ice was only 10 feet so there was plenty of room for the ship to maneuver. However, they unexpectedly encountered a tongue of ice reaching 62 feet deep, which they cleared by only 8 feet. The captain, Commander William R. Anderson, then lowered the submarine to a depth of 140 feet, only 20 feet off the ocean's bottom. Suddenly they encountered another ice tongue that was 85 feet deep, which given the size of the sub, cleared the top of the ship by a mere 5 feet. Since there were 300 miles of shallow seas ahead of them, the captain decided to turn the submarine back rather than risk disaster.

The *Nautilus* returned to its base at Pearl Harbor in Hawaii. A month later, when ice conditions were more favorable, it set out once again, on July 22, 1958. Its mission was secret, and the family of the crew members thought they were headed on a routine training run to Panama. After pulling out of port, the ship submerged and headed north. Traveling at more than 20 knots, it reached the Aleutian Islands on July 26. Once it entered the Bering Sea the water became much more shallow, as little as 80 feet, and the ship had to slow down to 10 knots. It crossed the Arctic Circle at 6:25 a.m. on July 29. It passed the point where it

had run into ice the month before and came up to periscope depth so that the officer in charge of the watch could search for ice. The first ice was encountered early on the morning of July 30, and the ship surfaced to get a better look. Crew members went on deck and took a chunk of the ice as a souvenir.

The ship then began a 24-hour search for a passage under the ice, looking for water that was deep enough, at least 300 feet, for the submarine to stay safely submerged under it. Not finding a passage, it turned east along the northern coast of Alaska as far as Point Barrow. There it found a tongue of the Barrow Submarine Canyon, where there were depths of 420 feet. This was the ship's passageway to the north. It submerged and headed north at 5:00 a.m. on August 1. On August 2 it crossed a 9,000-foot submerged mountain range that had never been recorded before. At 10 a.m. on August 3 the submarine passed 87°N, the farthest ever reached by a ship before. The *Nautilus* reached the North Pole at 11:15 p.m. on August 3, 1958. The crew celebrated and deposited mail in the shipboard post office to be stamped "North Pole."

From the North Pole, the *Nautilus* headed south toward the channel between Greenland and Spitsbergen, where the Gulf Stream pushes the ice much farther north. It reached the edge of the ice at 5:12 a.m. on August 5. From there it sent radio messages back to the United States to say that the mission had been successfully completed. Near Iceland a helicopter took Captain Anderson off the ship to report back to Washington. The ship sailed on to England, where the crew was greeted with much fanfare. The trip had been one of the major experiments in proving the value of the nuclear submarine.

A few days after the *Nautilus* left the North Pole, a sister ship, the *Skate*, arrived from the Greenland Sea and spent 10 days carrying out observations and experiments. It reached the North Pole twice. Unlike the *Nautilus*, it surfaced several times in the leads, or clear water, that are features of the Arctic sea.

Where to learn more

The voyage of the *Nautilus* is described in Lt. William G. Lalor, Jr., "Submarine Through the North Pole," *National Geographic*, vol. 65, no. 1 (January 1959), pp. 1-20. The voyage of the *Skate* is in Comdr. James F. Calvert, "Up Through the Ice of the North Pole," *National Geographic*, vol. 65, no. 7 (July 1959).

In some ways, the voyage of the *Nautilus* under the polar ice cap was a stunt to promote the idea of nuclear submarines. In any case, the ship cannot be separated from the history of the nuclear navy. A good narrative of that subject can be found in Francis Duncan, *Rickover and the Nuclear Navy* (Annapolis: Naval Institute Press, 1990).

Nearchus

(360 B.C. - 312 B.C.)

Nearchus was a Greek commander under Alexander the Great who explored along the coast of Pakistan and Iran to open up a trade route from the Euphrates River to the Indus River.

Nearchus was a commander in the army of **Alexander the Great**. After Alexander had conquered the Indus Valley and headed back toward the Mediterranean, he put Nearchus in charge of a fleet that was supposed to parallel the march of the army along the coast. Nearchus was charged with finding a sea route between the Euphrates and Indus Rivers.

Nearchus left from the mouth of the Indus in late September 325 B.C. He was delayed for 24 days at Crocola (Karachi) because of unfavorable winds. It took five days to sail to the mouth of the Hab River. Sailing from there three ships were capsized in a storm, but the crew members were saved. The fleet anchored at Ras Kachari and met up with part of Alexander's troops and was able to take on supplies.

At the mouth of the Hingol River, Nearchus and his men were attacked by 600 of the native inhabitants of whom he wrote: "They were hairy over their heads as well as the rest of their persons, and had nails like wild beasts; at least they were said to use their nails like iron tools, and to kill fish by tearing with them, and to cut up soft wood with them." Nearchus defeated them and took several captives.

He sailed from there to Cape Malan, and then it took him twenty days to coast along the waterless coast of Gedrosia (now called Makran), which was inhabited by "savage" fish-eaters. Anchoring by the small river Kalami, he saw the island of Astola, which was a religious center for the inhabitants of the coast who worshiped the sun. Nearchus sailed out and landed on the sacred island to prove that he would not be harmed by violating the local taboos.

Sailing from there the expedition began to run short of supplies and had to hunt wild goats on the shore. However, they reached the port of Mosarna (Pasni) and were able to re-stock. The land from that point on was more fertile. They put in at the port of Cophas (Kappar) where Nearchus remarked that the people paddled canoes rather than rowing the way that the Greeks did.

Nearby, they were surprised to see great towers of water blowing in the air. When they asked their guides what was happening, they were told that they had run into a fleet of whales. At the port of Gwadar they were once again in need of supplies. Rather than bartering with the inhabitants who seemed willing to trade, Nearchus attacked the town. After a stalemate, he accepted what the townspeople had to offer in the way of food: fishmeal.

From Gwadar, Nearchus sailed along the coast into Persia (Iran) to Cape Jask in the region of Kerman, where it was easier to get provisions. Farther along the coast he was able to see Cape Musandam, the tip of the Arabian Peninsula that divides the Gulf of Oman from the Persian Gulf. Nearchus rejected the suggestion of his second in command that they cross over and explore the other coast. Instead, he continued on to the mouth of the Minab River.

Nearchus went inland along the Minab and met up with Alexander at the Persian town of Golashkerd, with much rejoicing on both sides. He returned to his ships and sailed past Ormuz Island (which was to become the main port for the Persian Gulf for many centuries) to put in at the larger Qeshm island. The ships ran aground on the sandbanks off the island, and it took three weeks to repair them and start out again. Traveling up the Persian Gulf, Nearchus and his ships made it to the port of Diridotis at what was then the mouth of the Euphrates River.

Nearchus traveled up the Karun River to rejoin Alexander in the Persian capital of Susa. His report enabled the Greeks to see that the Persian Gulf led into the Indian Ocean and that it was possible to trade with India by that route.

Where to learn more

The voyage of Nearchus is basically a subsidiary tale to that of Alexander the Great, and many of the sources listed in that entry also deal with Nearchus. See also M. Cary and E.H. Warmington, *The Ancient Explorers* (London: Methuen, 1929; reprinted in paperback, Baltimore, Md.: Penguin Books, 1963); Walter Woodburn Hyde, *Ancient Greek Mariners* (New York: Oxford University Press, 1947); and Rhys Carpenter, *Beyond the Pillars of Heracles* (New York: Delacorte Press, 1966).

Gennady Ivanovich Nevelskoy

(1814 - 1876)

Gennady Ivanovich Nevelskoy was a Russian naval officer who was responsible for Russia's taking control of the Amur River in the Far East.

In 1805 the Russian navigator Adam Johann von Krusenshtern, as part of his circumnavigation of the globe, made a brief foray along the northern Pacific coast of Asia. He agreed with what the **Comte de La Pérouse** had concluded in 1787: that Sakhalin was an island and not part of the Asian mainland. Neither one of these men, however, actually sailed through the strait between the two. Krusenshtern also concluded that the mouth of the Amur River was unnavigable because of silting.

Other Russian naval officers referred back to old maps and traveler's records and decided that the mouth of the Amur might well be navigated and, in view of the important position of the river in opening up the Far East, felt that this ought to be investigated. One such officer was Captain Lieutenant Gennady Ivanovich Nevelskoy. In 1848-1849 he commanded the ship *Baikal* on a voyage from Kronshtadt, the main naval base near St. Petersburg around Cape Horn to the Kamchatka Peninsula. In 1849 he went to the mouth of the Amur River and showed that the river was accessible to ships from the sea. From the Amur he sailed south to the Sea of Japan, going through the narrow straits between the mainland and the island. He thereby proved that Sakhalin was an island, and the straits were named after him— Proliv Nevelskogo.

Nevelskoy traveled overland by way of Siberia in the winter of 1849-1850 to return to St. Petersburg. Gaining the approval of the Tsar for his explorations, in 1850 Nevelskoy was appointed commander of an expedition to establish a post "on the south-west coast of the Okhotsk Sea." Acting on his own initiative, he raised the Russian flag at the mouth of the Amur and founded a Russian post, which is today the city of Nikolayevsky-na-Amure. He also claimed as Russian territory all the Amur region and the island of Sakhalin, an action that violated Russia's 1689 treaty with China.

Between 1851 and 1855, as commander of the Amur Expedition, he directed the work of several assistants who explored the Amur region and Sakhalin, mapped the Tatarsky Proliv (Tatar Strait) between the mainland and Sakhalin, and discovered several harbors. Nevelskoy left the Far East in 1855 and returned to St. Petersburg, but he spent the last 20 years of his life in voluntary exile in Paris, in protest at the oppressive rule of the Russian Tsar.

Nevelskoy's action in claiming the Amur region was ratified by the Chinese at the treaty of Aigun in 1858, which they were forced to negotiate because of the threats they were getting from all sides by the Western imperialist powers.

Where to learn more

The history of the Russians in the Amur River valley can be found in E.G. Ravenstein, *The Russians on the Amur: Its Discovery, Conquest and Colonisation* (London: 1861) and Frank A. Golder, *Russian Expansion on the Pacific, 1651-1850* (Cleveland: The Arthur H. Clark Company, 1914).

Jean Nicollet

(1598 - 1642)

Jean Nicollet was a Frenchman who lived among the Native Americans of what is now Ontario and was the first European to travel through the Great Lakes to the states of Wisconsin and Illinois.

Jean Nicollet was born in the French port of Cherbourg in the province of Normandy, the son of a postman. He went to Canada in 1618 in the employ of one of the French trading companies that was developing the fur trade with Native Americans. It was intended that he would live among them long enough to learn their language so that he could serve as an interpreter for his employers.

Nicollet went with **Samuel de Champlain** up the St. Lawrence and Ottawa Rivers to a place called Allumette Island in the middle of the Ottawa. He stayed there for two years and learned the Huron and Algonkin languages as well as the customs of those tribes. He was accepted into their society and served as a negotiator in their dealings with the Iroquois tribes, who were enemies of the Hurons as well as the French.

In 1620 Nicollet returned to Quebec and was then sent out to live among the Nipissing tribe who lived along the lake of the same name and to direct their fur trade to the French. He stayed there for nine years. In 1629 Quebec was captured briefly by the English, and Nicollet took refuge among his friends the Hurons.

Nicollet returned to Quebec in 1633 and was then sent out on an important mission. The tribe that lived along the shores of Green Bay in the present-day state of Wisconsin were not friendly with the Algonkins, and it was feared that they would direct their trade to the English. Nicollet was sent out to deal with these people, known in English as the Winnebagoes. It was also thought that by following the Great Lakes he might also find the route to China, so he set off wearing a Chinese robe embroidered with flowers and birds.

Nicollet left Quebec in mid-July 1634 and traveled up the Ottawa River and then to Lake Nipissing and down the French River to Lake Huron then to the straits of Michilimackinac, Lake Michigan, and into Green Bay. He was the first European to follow this route, which was to become the main route for French fur traders to the west. One of the great scenes of North American exploration is Nicollet coming ashore in Green Bay dressed in his flowery Chinese robe. Nicollet overawed the tribesmen with his elaborate costume and was able to conclude a treaty of peace with them. He did some exploring in the area along the Wisconsin and Illinois Rivers.

After his return to Canada in the fall of 1635, Nicollet became a respected merchant of the town of Trois-Rivières. He was drowned in 1642 in a boating accident near the town of Sillery, now a suburb of Quebec City.

Where to learn more

The original knowledge that we have about Nicollet comes from a biography that was written the year after his death, in 1643, by Father Vimont, the Jesuit Superior of New France. It is published in volume 23 of the *Jesuit Relations*, edited by Reuben G. Thwaites (Cleveland: Burrows, 1898). It is reprinted in Louise P. Kellogg, *Early Narratives of the Northwest, 1634-1699* (New York: Scribner's, 1917). He also figures in Gabriel Sagard, *The Long Journey to the Country of the Hurons*, translated and edited by George M. Wrong (Toronto: The Champlain Society, 1939).

An early American biographer of Nicollet was C.W. Butterfield, *History of the Discovery of the Northwest by Jean Nicolet, with a Sketch of His Life* (Cincinnati: 1881). There is a good summary of his explorations in Louise P. Kellogg, *The French Régime in Wisconsin and the Northwest* (Madison: University of Wisconsin Press, 1925; reprinted, New York: Cooper Square Publishers, 1968). Another summary by Jean Hamelin, which was used as a source for this account, is in the *Dictionary of Canadian Biography*, vol. 1 (Toronto: University of Toronto Press, 1967).

Carsten Niebuhr

(1733-1815)

Carsten Niebuhr was a German surveyor and mathematician who was the only survivor of a Danish expedition to Arabia.

Carsten Niebuhr was born in the Duchy of Lauenburg in northern Germany. He came from a humble family but was able to educate himself to be a surveyor. At the age of 22 he entered the University of Hamburg to study mathematics and then transferred to the University of Göttingen, where he got a scholarship to study astronomy.

In 1758 King Frederick V of Denmark decided to send out the first scientific expedition to explore Arabia. He asked Professor Kästner at Göttingen to recommend a mathematician to accompany the expedition. Kästner asked Niebuhr if he would be interested, and Niebuhr is said to have replied, "Why not?". The

Carsten Niebuhr. The Granger Collection, New York.

other members of the expedition were Friedrich von Haven, a Danish linguist; Peter Forrskål, a Swedish botanist; Christian Kramer, a Danish physician and zoologist; and George Baurenfeind, a German artist. There was also a Swedish ex-soldier named Berggren, who was supposed to act as a servant for the others. Niebuhr's job was to serve as surveyor and cartographer. It turned out to be a very odd combination of people, and the members of the expedition did not get along with each other.

It took more than two years to select the members of the expedition and to collect the necessary scientific equipment and supplies. King Frederick issued his final instructions in December 1760, and the group set out from Copenhagen on January 4, 1761. They spent a year in Egypt where they bought appropriate clothes in order to "disguise" themselves as Muslim pilgrims. They boarded a pilgrim ship at the port of Suez in October 1762 bound for Jeddah, on the west coast of Arabia.

Rather to their surprise, they encountered no hostility in Jeddah and stayed there six weeks while Forrskål collected botanical and zoological specimens to send back to Europe. They then traveled down the Red Sea coast of Arabia in a "tarrád," an open boat, to Yemen. Each evening along the way the stopped so that Niebuhr could go ashore to make astronomical observations for his maps and Forrskål could continue his collecting. On December 29, 1762, they landed at Luhaiya, the northernmost port of Yemen, where they were well received and stayed for two months.

They left Luhaiya on February 20, 1763 and set off on donkeys for Bait-al-Faqih, an inland trading town on the way to Sana'a. Along the way and once established in the town, Niebuhr spent his time making observations that led to the first modern map of Yemen, one that was in use for more than a century. Niebuhr and Forrskål took a week-long trip to Taiz, where Forrskål found specimens of a balsam tree that was famous for its healing properties.

At Bait-al-Faqih Niebuhr and von Haven both came down with malaria. They were incapacitated for two weeks before the expedition could continuing the journey to the port of Mocha. In order to make their observations, they traveled during the day when temperatures sometimes reached 100°F. On reaching Mocha, their previous genial experiences with the Arabs changed for the worse. Forrskål's specimens, preserved in alcohol, were poured from their jars by customs officials who then complained about the smell and locked up all of their belongings. They were kicked out of the house they were renting. Fortunately a resident English merchant and a helpful local judge were able to mediate and restore friendly relations. But von Haven suffered a relapse of malaria and died on the night of May 25, 1763. His passing does not seem to have been much regretted by his companions.

On June 9, 1763, the five survivors set off for Sana'a, a large walled city in the interior of Yemen, which is now the national capital. They traveled by way of Taiz, which Niebuhr had already visited. Once again they ran into difficulties with the local authorities but were allowed to continue on June 28. Along the way, Forrskål came down with malaria, and he died at Yarim on July 11.

On July 13, the remainder of the party continued on to Sana'a, where on July 19 they were conducted into the city to the palace of the Imam of Yemen, who received them graciously. Niebuhr had had a relapse of malaria, and his map of the route to Sana'a is marked with blank spaces. He was also sick while they were in the city. They left on July 26, having received a generous present of money from the Imam. They then made a forced march on camels back to Mocha in order to meet up with an English ship that was to take them on to India. If they missed it, they would have to wait until the following year. They reached the port on August 5 and were relieved to find that the ship was still there. In fact, it was delayed for a couple of weeks and did not sail until August 23. During that time the remaining members of the expedition all became ill. During the voyage to Bombay, Baurenfeind died on August 29 and Berggren on the following day.

Niebuhr and Kramer arrived in Bombay on September 13, 1763. Kramer died in India in February 1764. Niebuhr was the only survivor of the Danish Arabian expedition. He stayed in India until December 1764, working on the notes he had taken and recuperating from his illness. From India he sailed in a small English warship to the port of Muscat on the Persian Gulf, the present-day capital of Oman. He then took a dhow up the Persian Gulf to the port of Bushire and then traveled overland through Iraq and Syria to the city of Aleppo, where he was aided by the Dutch consul. He spent another year traveling in the Middle East and Turkey.

Niebuhr returned to Copenhagen via Poland and Germany on November 20, 1767. The first volume of his book about his travels came out in 1772. His books were remarkably full of facts and information that have been a major source on the history of Arabia ever since. They are particularly important because he traveled to Arabia just before the Al-Sa'ud family in alliance with the Islamic fundamentalist movement of the Wahhabis gained power. As a result of the maps that he drew and the many notes that he took, he is considered one of the greatest scientific travelers. He lived to the age of 82.

Where to learn more

Niebuhr's multi-volume book *Reisebeschreibung nach Arabien und andern umliegenden Ländern* appeared in Copenhagen starting in 1772. The first English edition was published in London as *Travels in Arabia* in 1792. Selections from the German original can be found in *Arabien: Dokumente zur Entdeckungsgeschichte* (Stuttgart: 1965). Niebuhr's son, Barthold Georg Niebuhr, who later became a famous historian of ancient Rome, wrote a German-language biography of his father that was published in 1817.

For modern works, see D.G. Hogarth, *The Penetration of Arabia* (London: 1904; reprinted, Oxford: Clarendon Press, 1922); R.H. Kiernan, *The Unveiling of Arabia* (London: Harrap, 1937); Thorkild Hansen, *Arabia Felix* (London: Gregg International, 1964); Robin Bidwell, *Travellers in Arabia* (London: Hamlyn, 1976); and Zahra Freeth and H.V.F. Winstone, *Explorers of Arabia: From the Renaissance to the End of the Victorian Era* (London: George Allen & Unwin, 1978), which served as the main source for this account.

Umberto Nobile

(1885 - 1978)

Umberto Nobile was an Italian specialist in dirigibles who piloted Roald Amundsen's airship across the Arctic and then captained another airship that crashed on the ice.

Umberto Nobile was the son of a modest Italian bureaucrat born near Naples on January 21, 1885. He studied engineering at the University of Naples and then went to work for the Italian public railways in Rome. He studied aviation in his spare time, and in 1915 was transferred to the Ministry of War and put in charge of a project to develop lighter-than-air ships, or dirigibles. He developed the prototypes for the most advanced airships and became recognized as a world expert in the field.

In July 1925 Nobile was contacted by the Norwegian explorer **Roald Amundsen** who wanted him to develop an airship for flight over the North Pole. Financed in part by the American explorer **Lincoln Ellsworth**, Nobile built the airship which was

Umberto Nobile. The Granger Collection, New York.

named the *Norge* (Norwegian for Norway) and flew the Norwegian flag although it was captained by Nobile and most of the crew was Italian. Nobile flew the *Norge* from Rome to Spitsbergen Island off the northern coast of Norway, reaching King's Bay, Spitsbergen on May 7, 1926. Two days after his arrival, **Richard Byrd** left Spitsbergen in his airplane to become the first person to fly over the North Pole.

The goal of Amundsen's expedition was not simply to fly to the Pole and back but to fly across it to the other side of the Arctic Ocean in Alaska. They set off from Spitsbergen in the early morning of May 11. On the trip Amundsen and Ellsworth had no formal duties but spent their time observing the polar landscape and making notes; Nobile and his crew navigated and flew the airship. The flight to the Pole was relatively easy although the airship was constantly icing up, and a large chunk of ice had to be pulled from the air intake to keep the ship from crashing. They reached the North Pole 15 hours after leaving Spitsbergen and dropped Norwegian, American, and Italian flags over it.

It was the remainder of the trip from the Pole to Alaska that turned out to be the most difficult. They were constantly bombarded by ice that formed on the propellers and was then flung loose. One large chunk cut a hole in the hull of the airship. When they reached the Alaskan shore, there was heavy fog and they could not see the outline of any mountains so that Nobile had to urge the airship to its maximum height in order to fly over unseen obstacles. They were knocked around by two heavy storms and at one point they climbed so high that there was danger of the airbag exploding or leaking. They finally landed at the small settlement of Teller not far from Nome. The *Norge* was in such bad shape that it had to be scrapped. They had traveled 3,180 miles on a voyage that took 70 hours and 40 minutes at an average ground speed of 45 miles per hour. During that time Nobile had gotten almost no sleep.

Almost as soon as they landed, Nobile and Amundsen quarreled over who deserved the most credit for the flight. Nobile headed back to Rome where he received a hero's welcome from the Italian people and the new Fascist government of Benito Mussolini. Nobile resolved to carry out an entirely Italian flight over the pole. He commissioned a sister ship to the *Norge*, which he named the *Italia*.

The *Italia* arrived in Spitsbergen on May 5, 1928. Nobile planned to make three flights to parts of the Arctic that were previously unknown. After an initial failure, the first one was made on May 15-18 to the tip of Severnaya Zemlya, an island group north of Siberia. On May 23 Nobile and his crew set out for the North Pole. They reached it, but because of bad weather were unable to achieve their goal of landing there. On the return, the storm intensified, and 20 hours after leaving the Pole they were forced to crash land on the polar ice. One crew member was killed, and six others were carried off in the main hull never to be seen again. Nobile and eight companions escaped, but some, including Nobile, were injured. They were able to set up the portable camp they had brought with them, including a famous "red tent" that they hoped would be seen from the air.

It turned out that they had crashed only 50 miles north of Spitsbergen. They sent out radio messages but received no acknowledgment. They heard broadcasts that indicated that the search was going on in the wrong area. Three of the men started out over the ice to try to reach land. In the meantime, an international rescue effort was begun, and the Italians saw the first plane fly over them on June 17, but it did not see them. Roald Amundsen joined the rescue efforts, but his plane disappeared on June 18 on the flight from Norway to Spitsbergen. On June 20 an Italian aircraft spotted the survivors and dropped supplies that day and the next.

Finally, on June 22 a Swedish seaplane was able to land at Nobile's camp. It could only carry one of the men, and after much argument it was agreed that Nobile would go. The plane would return later to pick up the other two. On its return, the Swedish plane crashed although the pilot survived. When he reached Spitsbergen, Nobile found that he was being blamed in Italy for the disaster and criticized for being rescued first. In the meantime, the weather had deteriorated, and the spring thaw had begun. It was not until July 12 that a Russian ice-breaker was able to reach the remainder of the party. It also rescued two of the three men who had set out over the ice. But the third, a Swedish meteorologist named Malmgren, had been abandoned to die along the way.

In 1929 an Italian commission of inquiry found Nobile responsible for the disaster. He then quit his native country and went to work in the Soviet Union designing and making warships. He spent World War II in the United States helping with the war effort against the Axis powers. On his return to Italy after the fall of the Fascist state, a new court of inquiry found that his original condemnation had been motivated by political reasons, and he was acquitted of all charges. He died in Rome in 1978.

Where to learn more

Nobile's own story of his two flights over the Arctic is in *My Polar Flights* (London: Muller, 1961). A book about his controversial flights was published soon after they took place: Elisabeth Dithmer, *The Truth About Nobile* (London: Williams & Norgate, 1933). Nobile later wrote his memoirs, but they are not available in English: *Il Destino di un uomo: Pagine autobiografiche* (Milano: U. Mursia, 1988).

See chapters about Nobile in George Simmons, *Target Arctic: Men in the Skies at the Top of the World* (Philadelphia: Chilton Books, 1965) and John Grierson, *Heroes of the Polar Skies* (New York: Meredith Press, 1967).

There is a feature-length movie about Nobile, an Italian-Soviet co-production starring Peter Finch and Sean Connery, *The Red Tent* (1970, released in the United States by Paramount).

(Nils) Adolf Erik Nordenskjöld

(1832-1901)

Adolf Erik (A. E.) Nordenskjöld was a Swedish explorer who was the first person to make the northeast passage between the Atlantic and Pacific by way of the Arctic Ocean north of Siberia.

Adolf Erik (A. E.) Nordenskjöld was born in Helsinki, Finland, on November 18, 1832. His prominent family was part of the Swedish-speaking minority in Finland. Finland at that time was part of the Russian Empire, and Nordenskjöld was in conflict with that oppressive regime. After graduating from university, therefore, he emigrated to Sweden and became a Swedish citizen. He became head of the Division of Mineralogy of the Swedish National Museum of Natural History in Stockholm.

A. E. Nordenskjöld. The Granger Collection, New York.

In 1858, 1861, and 1864 Nordenskjöld participated in expeditions to Svalbard, a group of Arctic islands north of Norway. In 1868 he traveled from Svalbard on a small Swedish boat to a point farther north than man had ever been before. As a result of these expeditions, he began to get a worldwide reputation as an Arctic explorer.

In 1870 Nordenskjöld went to Greenland with the aim of trying to cross the ice cap that covers much of the world's largest island. He set out from the town of Godthaab in July with a fellow Swedish scientist and two Inuit. They only made it to as far inland as 35 miles and reached an altitude of 2,000 feet before they were forced to turn back. However, this was one of the first scientific investigations of the Greenland ice cap, which is of crucial importance in studying world weather and the history of glaciation.

In 1872 Nordenskjöld set out once again to try to reach the North Pole from Svalbard. He lost the reindeer he had planned to use as pack animals, and his ship was frozen in during the winter of 1872-1873 so there was no hope of making it to the Pole. He did, however, take advantage of the delay to make further scientific investigations on Svalbard.

After this attempt, Nordenskjöld gave up trying to reach the North Pole and instead decided to devote himself to making the Northeast Passage through the Arctic Ocean to eastern Asia. In 1875 and 1876 he made preliminary trips proving the navigability of the Kara Sea, the place where **Willem Barents** had come to grief in 1597.

Nordenskjöld received the backing of the King of Sweden and wealthy Swedish and Russian businessmen for his epic voyage along the north coast of Siberia. He set out in a steam- and sail-driven ship, the *Vega*, which had been converted from use as a whaling ship, on July 21, 1878 from the northern Norwegian port of Tromsö. For the first part of the voyage, three Russian merchant ships sailed with him, but they pealed off at various stages to trade at ports in the Russian Arctic.

The weather conditions were favorable and without much difficulty the *Vega* reached Cape Chelyuskin, the northernmost point in Asia on August 19, 1878. No ship had ever passed Cape Chelyuskin before. The expedition reached the mouth of the great Lena River on August 28, where the last of the Russian merchant ships landed. Nordenskjöld tried to turn north from there but was forced back by pack ice. As he continued east, the ice became thicker as the year advanced. The ship passed North Cape on September 28, the point that Captain Cook had reached coming from the Pacific in 1779. There the *Vega* was stopped by the frozen seas, only 120 miles from Bering Strait.

The *Vega* expedition spent the winter of 1878-1879 trapped in the ice. Nordenskjöld used this time to make scientific observations of the region and to establish relations with the Chukchis, the native peoples of the far northeast corner of Asia. In his book about the expedition, Nordenskjöld tells about a breakfast served in a Chukchi household: "first seals' flesh and fat, with a sort of sauerkraut of fermented willow-leaves, then seals' liver, and finally seals' blood—all frozen."

The ship was not able to get free of the frozen sea until July 18, but then it only took two days to sail into the Pacific Ocean. The expedition sailed south to Yokohama, Japan, which was reached on September 2, 1879. From there, Nordenskjöld telegraphed back to Sweden to tell the world that after three centuries of trying the first navigation of the Northeast Passage had been made. It had also been accomplished without any loss of life or even any major sickness on the part of the four officers, four scientists, and twenty sailors who made up the crew.

When Nordenskjöld sailed into Stockholm harbor on April 24, 1880, he was acclaimed a national hero, and that date is a holiday in Sweden—Vega Day. Nordenskjöld spent the next three years writing up the narrative of his voyage as well as a five-volume work on the scientific findings of the expedition.

Nordenskjöld made another expedition to the Greenland ice cap in 1883. He was convinced that in the interior of the island, somewhere beyond the ice, there was open pastureland. He tried to push as far as he could into the interior to test his theory. On this occasion, his expedition of 10 members made it 73 miles inland and reached an altitude of 5,000 feet. All they found was more ice.

On his return to Sweden, Nordenskjöld gave advice to the young Norwegian explorer **Fridtjof Nansen**, who made the first crossing of Greenland in 1888. In later years, he endorsed the failed effort of Swedish balloonist Salomon Andrée to fly a lighter-than-air craft over the North Pole in 1897. Nordenskjöld himself did no more exploring but wrote important works on geology, mineralogy, and cartography.

Where to learn more

Nordenskjöld's account of the trip through the Northeast Passage, *The Voyage of the Vega Round Asia and Europe*, (London: Macmillan, 1883) was translated by Alexander Leslie, who was also responsible for popularizing his earlier accomplishments in *The Arctic Voyages of Adolf Eric Nordenskiöld, 1858-1879* (London: Macmillan, 1879).

Good summaries of the explorations of Nordenskjöld can be found in Jeannette Mirsky, *To the Arctic!: The Story of Northern Exploration from Earliest Times to the Present* (New York: Alfred A. Knopf, 1948); L.P. Kirwan, *A History of Polar Exploration* (New York: W.W. Norton, 1959); and John Maxtone-Graham, *Safe Return Doubtful: The Heroic Age of Polar Exploration* (New York: Charles Scribner's Sons, 1988).

Odoric of Pordenone

(1286? - 1331?)

Odoric of Pordenone was a Christian missionary who traveled to the court of the Great Khan and remained there for three years.

Over the years, the Christian mission in China that was started by **John of Monte Corvino** in 1305 received several missionaries sent out from Europe. One of the first of these was Odoric of Pordenone, who was from the town of that name in the Friuli region of northeastern Italy. The year of his birth is traditionally given as 1286. Ordained a brother in the Franciscan order, he left Venice in 1314 and went to the great Greek trading center of Trebizond on the north coast of Asia Minor. From there he moved to Tabriz in Persia.

In about 1317 or 1318 Odoric embarked with his companion Friar James at the Persian port of Ormuz and sailed to the south coast of India and then via Sumatra, Java, and Borneo to Indochina and on to Canton in south China. He traveled overland to the port city of Amoy and then to Beijing (Khanbaligh as it was then called). He arrived there in 1325 and preached for three years.

During all this time, Odoric kept a careful narrative of his voyage, which has since been one of our main sources for understanding those parts of the world during the early 14th century. His descriptions of the Christians of south India, of the things he saw in Sumatra, to which he was one of the first Western visitors, and of the state of Champa in Indochina are especially valuable. He reported that Canton was three times the size of Venice and that Amoy was twice the size of Bologna.

Odoric gave a detailed description of the great city of Hang-chow, which had also been visited by **Marco Polo.** He told of a city that was 100 miles around, with 12,000 bridges, where the citizens used paper money to purchase all of the luxuries known to man. He also related that Hang-chow had four Franciscan friars who had converted one of the great magnates of the city.

Odoric was also the first Westerner to report on the habit of the Chinese mandarins, or ruling elite, of allowing their fingernails to grow, of binding the feet of women, and of fishing by using cormorants (a kind of bird) to trap the fish in their beak while rope was tied to their throats to keep them from swallowing.

During Odoric's three years in Khanbaligh, he and some fellow monks arranged to be on the roadside while the Great Khan was traveling from his summer to his winter palace. When the Khan's cortege approached, they put on their priestly robes and started singing a Latin hymn. The Khan stopped and asked his attendants what was going on; they told him that it was the Frankish teachers. He leaned over and kissed the cross when it was presented to him. He also accepted the apples that the friars had brought as gifts. This incident shows that the Catholics were well known in court circles but, as it turns out, their efforts were never to have much effect.

After he left Khanbaligh in 1328, Odoric returned to Europe by a route that was unique among Westerners during the Middle Ages. He traveled west through the great Chinese provinces of Shensi, Kansu, and Szechuan, and then into Tibet, where he appears to have been the first Westerner to see the Tibetan capital of Lhasa and its Buddhist monasteries. He crossed the mountains and traveled on to Persia.

From Persia, Odoric's route is uncertain, although it may have taken him through Iraq, Syria and Palestine before he returned to Venice at the end of 1329 or the beginning of 1330. His request for more missionaries was received and acted upon by Rome. On his return, he dictated his account to another friar, William de Solanga, in 1330 in Udine in Friuli. Friar William wrote that he transcribed the stories not "in difficult Latin or in an eloquent style, but just as Odoric himself told them, to the end that men might the more easily understand the things reported."

Where to learn more

The complete version of Odoric's travels can be found in Sir Henry Yule, ed. *Cathay and the Way Thither, Being a Collection of Medieval Notices of China*, 4 vols. (London: Hakluyt Society, 1913-1916; reprinted, Kraus Reprints, 1967). The most accessible version is Manuel Komroff, ed. *Contemporaries of Marco Polo* (New York: 1928; reprinted, New York: Dorset Press, 1989).

There is one full-length modern study of Odoric: Anselm M. Romb, *Mission to Cathay: The Biography of Blessed Odoric of Pordenone* (Paterson, N.J.: St. Anthony Guild Press, 1956).

The most comprehensive account of the Christian missions to the Mongols is I. de Rachewiltz, *Papal Envoys to the Great Khans* (Stanford: Stanford University Press, 1971). Other sources include: C. Raymond Beazley, *The Dawn of Modern Geography*, vol. 3 (Oxford: Clarendon Press, 1906); Arthur Percival Newton, *Travel and Travellers of the Middle Ages* (New York: Alfred A. Knopf, 1930); Leonardo Olschki, *Marco Polo's Precursors* (Baltimore: The Johns Hopkins Press, 1946); Björn Landström, *The Quest for India* (Garden City, N.Y.: 1964).

Peter Skene Ogden

(1790 - 1854)

Peter Skene Ogden was a Canadian fur trapper and trader who made five extensive expeditions throughout the American West.

Peter Skene Ogden was born in Quebec City in Canada. His father was a native of the United States who had left during the American Revolution because he supported the British King. When Peter was four years old, his father was appointed a judge in Montreal, and the family moved there. Montreal at that time was the center of the fur trade in North America. There was bitter competition between the Hudson's Bay Company (HBC), controlled from London, and the Montreal-based North West Company. Unlike his brothers who followed their father into the legal profession, Peter entered the fur trade as an employee of the North West Company in 1809.

Ogden quickly gained a reputation for being one of the most violent and ruthless of all the traders engaged in a notoriously cut-throat business. He was accused of a number of crimes that culminated in March 1818 when he was indicted for the murder of a Native American who traded with Ogden's rival, the Hudson's Bay Company. In order to put him out of the reach of the law, the North West Company sent Ogden to its most remote posts in what is now the Pacific Northwest of the United States.

Unfortunately for Ogden, the two rival fur companies decided that their competition was only helping their American rivals and in 1821 they decided to unite under the name of the Hudson's Bay Company. Ogden was so hated by the directors of the HBC that one of the provisions of the agreement was that he was not to be employed by the joint company. Ogden now had no way to support himself so he traveled to Montreal and then to London to try to convince the Company to rehire him.

At about this time, the HBC sent out George Simpson to take charge of its posts in what are now Oregon, Washington, Idaho, and British Columbia. This was an area that was claimed by both Great Britain and the United States, and the dispute was not to be settled until 1846. South of this was Spanish territory that was just then coming under the control of the new Republic of Mexico. Simpson felt that if Britain was to prevail it would have to make use of its most ruthless men, including Ogden. Under his influence, the Company agreed to re-employ Ogden in 1823, and he was instructed to travel to the Snake River country in present-day Idaho in the spring of 1824.

On December 20, 1824 Ogden left Flathead House at Flathead Lake in northern Montana with a party of 58 people. He met up with the famous American trapper **Jedediah Smith** near present-day Missoula, Montana, and they joined forces for the next two months trapping as far south as the Bear River in southeastern Idaho. They then split up and Ogden went farther south where one of his men sighted the Great Salt Lake from a mountain peak, probably the second time it had been seen by Westerners. Ogden's party camped at Mountain Green east of the Great Salt Lake. On May 23, 1825 a larger party of American trappers showed up at the camp and persuaded most of Ogden's trappers to leave with them. They attacked Ogden and took all the furs he had collected. He then returned to the British post near Walla Walla, Washington, which he reached on November 2, 1825.

In the winter and spring of 1825-1826 Ogden trapped in the Snake River country as far east as the Portneuf River in eastern Idaho near present-day Pocatello. He then returned to Walla Walla (Fort Nez Percé). After only two months' rest, he headed out again in September 1826. This time he went south through eastern Oregon to Malheur Lake and Klamath Lake in northern California. He saw and named Mount Shasta, the tallest peak in the Cascade Range before turning back north. In the region around Goose Lake on the California-Oregon border, the only thing that was available to drink was liquid mud, and Ogden wrote, "this is certainly a most horrid life."

In August 1827 Ogden went back to the Portneuf River in Idaho. During the next season of 1828-1829 he went south into Nevada and was the first Westerner to see the Humboldt River that rises on the western slope of the Rockies and disappears in the Humboldt Sink east of Reno. This was later to be one of the main routes west for American pioneers headed for California. In his diary at this point Ogden made the cryptic but disturbing notation: "280 Indians camp attacked."

Ogden's widest-ranging expedition was his last. Leaving the Columbia River in October 1829 he went south to the Humboldt Sink where he had been the previous year and had a clash with the local Native Americans. He then turned south until he reached the Colorado River, probably the first Westerner to have approached it from the north. He visited the Mojave tribe where Jedediah Smith had been in 1827 near present-day Needles, California. He marched his men across the desert, forcing them to eat their dying horses for food and drink their blood to keep from dying of thirst. In a clash with the Mojave, Ogden and his men killed 26. From this point, Ogden and his party followed the Colorado south all the way to the Gulf of California. They were the first Westerners to cross the American West from north to south.

Heading back north, Ogden led his men through Cajon Pass near San Bernardino, California and then into the San Joaquin Valley. Avoiding the Mexican mission stations, he made it to northern California and then took his previous trail north from Klamath Lake. As he was crossing the Columbia River near The Dalles, Oregon, one of his boats was capsized, drowning nine men, and all of Ogden's records of his monumental last trip were lost.

On his return to Fort Nez Percé in July 1830 he was ordered to head north to what is now British Columbia. He established a Hudson's Bay Company post at the mouth of the Nass River, near what is now the southern border of Alaska. There he fought off competition from Americans and Russians and was made the director of all of mainland British Columbia for the HBC in 1834. It was about this time that George Simpson wrote of him that he was "one of the most unprincipled Men in the Indian Country . . . madness to which he has a predisposition will follow as a matter of course." However, this seemed to be what was required on the fur-trading frontier because Ogden continued to prosper and to be promoted.

Ogden spent a year's furlough in England in 1844 and returned with a secret British surveying team that was tracing a route from eastern Canada to the Columbia River as part of the negotiations between Britain and the United States over the Oregon Country. This all came to naught in 1846 when the boundary settlement continued the 49th parallel boundary all the way to the Pacific, thereby giving Washington and Oregon to the United States.

Ogden and the Hudson's Bay Company remained in what was now American territory pending the arrival of an effective American government. In December 1847 Ogden led a team that negotiated the release of American prisoners taken by members of the Cayuse tribe who had attacked a mission station near Walla Walla. Ogden spent his last years at Fort Vancouver, Washington. In August 1854 he became ill and traveled to the American settlement of Oregon City to seek medical help. He died there at the age of 64.

Where to learn more

Ogden's journals of his trips have appeared in different places at different times: T.C. Elliott, ed. "The Peter Skene Ogden Journals," *Oregon Historical Society Quarterly*, vol. 11 (1910); W.N. Sage, ed. "Peter Skene Ogden's Notes on Western Caledonia," *British Columbia Historical Quarterly*, vol. 1 (1937); John Scaglione, ed, "Ogden's Report of His 1829-1830 Expedition," *California Historical Society Quarterly*, vol. 28 (June 1949); and David E. Miller, ed. "Peter Skene Ogden's Journal of His Expedition to Utah, 1825," *Utah Historical Quarterly*, vol 20 (April 1952).

The Hudson's Bay Record Society has published three volumes of *Peter Skene Ogden's Snake Country Journals:* vol. 1, 1824-1825 and 1825-1826, edited by E.E. Rich (London: Hudson's Bay Record Society, vol. 13, 1950); vol. 2, 1826-1827, edited by K.G. Davies (London: Hudson's Bay Record Society, vol. 23, 1961); and vol. 3, 1827-1828 and 1828-1829, edited by Glyndwr Williams (Hudson's Bay Record Society, vol. 28, 1971).

Ogden wrote an anonymous book about his exploits (the author was listed as "A Fur Trader"), recounting 16 colorful incidents, in *Traits of American-Indian Life and Character* (London: Smith, Elder & Co., 1853).

There is a chapter on Ogden by Ted J. Warner, professor at Brigham Young University in LeRoy R. Hafen, ed. *Mountain Men and Fur Traders of the Far West* (Lincoln: University of Nebraska Press, 1982) and a section on Ogden in William H. Goetzmann, *Exploration and Empire: The Explorer and the Scientist in the Winning of the American West* (New York: Alfred A. Knopf, 1966). Also see Gloria Griffen Cline, *Exploring the Great Basin* (Norman: University of Oklahoma Press, 1963).

Alonso de Ojeda

(1468? - 1515?)

Alonso de Ojeda was a Spanish adventurer who explored along the northern coast of South America and founded a colony in Colombia.

Alonso de Ojeda was born in the Spanish city of Cuenca in the province of Castille. He came from an aristocratic family and served in the household of an important nobleman, the Duke of Medina Celi. He fought with the Duke in the last campaign to drive the Muslims out of Granada in southern Spain. Ojeda commanded one of the ships in **Christopher Columbus**'s second expedition to America in 1493. During this expedition Ojeda took part in campaigns against the Native Americans and in exploring expeditions into the interior of the island of Hispaniola.

Upon his return to Spain, Ojeda became associated with Juan de la Cosa, who produced one of the first maps of the Americas, and with **Amerigo Vespucci**. Ojeda was able to get the financing to support a small fleet of four ships to sail to South America. Cosa served as pilot, and Vespucci commanded two of the ships. They left Cadiz sometime between May 16 and 20, 1499. This voyage violated the monopoly that the Spanish king had granted to Columbus, and the expedition even used a copy of Columbus's map. It is thought that the ships reached land in what is now Suriname. Vespucci then headed to the southwest towards Brazil while Ojeda traveled north and westward.

Ojeda made his first landing on Trinidad where he encountered the Caribs who inhabited many of the islands of the Caribbean. The two sides clashed. He sailed through the Gulf of Paria and landed on the mainland. He visited Margarita Island and realized the potential value of the pearl fishery there. He touched at the island of Curaçao. From Curaçao Ojeda went to Lake Maracaibo on the mainland, where the Native American villages on stilts reminded him of Venice. He named the area "Venezuela," meaning little Venice. He went as far as the Guajira Peninsula in what is today Colombia before sailing to Hispaniola, where he arrived on September 5, 1499. He returned to Spain in the summer of 1500 with a cargo of pearls, brazilwood (used for making dyes), and Native American captives to be sold as slaves.

In 1501 Ojeda requested permission to make another voyage to the Western Hemisphere. The king gave his assent and named him Governor of Coquivacoa, the local name for the area around Lake Maracaibo. He was authorized to take as many as ten ships to America to cut brazilwood. In the end, he was only able to raise enough money to outfit four. They sailed from Cadiz in early January 1502 and reached the Gulf of Paria in early March. One of the ships was wrecked and another went to Jamaica to get supplies.

Once reunited, the Spaniards decided to set up a base by attacking and capturing a Native American village. They established the first Spanish colony on the mainland of America on the Guajira Peninsula. The colony was a failure, and in May or June 1502 Ojeda's partners arrested him on charges that he had cheated them and brutalized the Native Americans. The Spaniards abandoned their settlement and went to Santo Domingo, where Ojeda was tried and found guilty. The sentence was overturned, however, on November 8, 1503, after he had returned to Spain.

In 1504 the king of Spain authorized Ojeda to establish a colony in the Gulf of Urabá in northwestern Colombia near the Darien Peninsula, although it is unclear whether he made a voyage there in 1505. In 1508 he was named Governor of the Province of Nueva Andalucía, the coastline that stretched from the Guajira Peninsula to the Gulf of Urabá. Stopping in Santo Domingo, he recruited 220 Spaniards, including **Francisco Pizarro**, and they sailed from there in November 1509.

Ojeda initially tried to establish his colony on the site of the modern city of Cartagena, Colombia's main port. However, he once again became involved in a fight with Native Americans, and Juan de la Cosa, among others, was killed on February 28, 1510. Ojeda moved on to the Gulf of Urabá. Attacked by Native Americans, Ojeda was wounded with poisoned arrows. He saved his life by taking hot irons and applying them to the wounds. The colony was soon faced with starvation, and Ojeda went back to Santo Domingo to get supplies. In his absence, the colony was taken over and rescued by **Vasco Núñez de Balboa**, who relocated it to Panama.

Meanwhile, Ojeda was shipwrecked on the island of Cuba while trying to get back to Santo Domingo. He undertook an epic journey along the south coast of Cuba and then over the sea to Jamaica. By the time he reached Santo Domingo, he was destitute. It is said that he lived in Santo Domingo in extreme poverty until his death in 1515. One source, however, claims that he joined a monastery.

Where to learn more

The best source in English is Samuel Eliot Morison, *The European Discovery of America: The Southern Voyages, A.D. 1492-1616* (New York: Oxford University Press, 1974). A readable earlier account is Washington Irving, *Voyages and Discoveries of the Companions of Columbus* (New York: 1831; reprinted, New York: Frederick Ungar, 1960).

Diego de Ordaz

(1480? - 1532)

Diego de Ordáz was a Spanish conquistador who took part in the conquests of Cuba and Mexico and then led an expedition that discovered the Orinoco River.

Diego de Ordáz was born in the village of Castroverde de Zamora in the old Spanish province of León. Like many of the conquistadors, he came from a humble family. He made his first trip to the Americas as a member of **Alonso de Ojeda**'s expedition to the northern coast of Colombia in 1509. He then took part in the conquest of Cuba in 1511 under the command of Diego Velázquez. From Cuba he went to Yucatan with Juan de Grijalva in 1518 and then joined **Hernán Cortés** when he set off for Mexico in 1519.

Ordáz commanded one of the ships in Cortés's expedition. He fought in many of the early battles as a leader of the infantry. It is said that he tried to incite opposition to Cortés's leadership until the two had a famous confrontation and Ordáz was converted into a loyal follower. Along the route to Mexico City, Ordáz stopped long enough to climb the volcanic peak of Popocatepetl. Later, he was granted a coat of arms by the Spanish King that had a volcano in the background. He accompanied Cortés on his first visit to Montezuma. Although wounded, he escaped from Mexico City during the "Sad Night" when the Spaniards were forced to retreat from the city.

In 1521 Cortés sent Ordáz back to Spain to report on the conquest to King Charles and to take back some of the spoils to present to him. There, he became Cortés's principal defender in the Spanish court. He also had to defend himself against charges that he had smuggled a large quantity of pearls into Spain. He returned to Mexico while Cortés was on an expedition to Honduras. Ordáz tried to meet up with him but was unsuccessful and returned to Mexico and passed on rumors that Cortés had died. This added more confusion to the chaos caused by Cortés's absence. However, when Cortés did return, he rewarded Ordáz with a large land grant that made him one of the richest men in Mexico.

In 1530 Ordáz received permission to conquer and settle a stretch of the coast of South America from the Gulf of Paria in Venezuela to the mouth of the Amazon River. He sailed from Sanlucar de Barrameda in Spain on October 20, 1530 with three ships and nearly 500 men to take over his new possessions.

Unable to land at the mouth of the Amazon River, Ordáz sailed northwestward to the Gulf of Paria between Trinidad and the mainland of Venezuela. He took over an abandoned fort and founded the settlement of San Miguel de Paria in 1531. There he heard tales of a rich land to the south that was called Guiana and a large river that flowed out of the center of the continent called the Huyapari (it is now known as the Orinoco).

Ordaz set out to explore the Orinoco in June 1531 with a force of 350 men. After experiencing many hardships, he made it up the river past its juncture with the Meta River, which now forms part of the boundary between Colombia and Venezuela. He was stopped by a series of rapids and forced to turn back. Although he himself never found any riches whatsoever, his reports back to Spain began the myth of the wealthy kingdom of Guiana.

On his return to the Gulf of Paria, Ordáz tried to move his colony to the small island of Cubagua off the island of Margarita, where there were already some Spanish settlers. They disputed his rights to rule over them. They arrested him and sent him to Santo Domingo. The governor of Santo Domingo freed him, but he died (some said of poisoning) in 1532 on board the ship that was taking him back to Spain so that he could argue his rights at court.

Where to learn more

The two main modern sources for the life of Ordaz are available only in Spanish: Florentino Pérez Embid, *Diego de Ordás, compañero de Cortés, y explorador del Orinoco* (Seville: Escuela de Estudios Hispano-Americano, 1950) and Casiano García, *Vida del Comandador Diego de Ordaz, descubridor del Orinoco* (Mexico: Editora Justicia, 1952). Information on Ordaz is also available in: Leonard Dalton, *Venezuela* (New York: Charles Scribner's Sons, 1912); Bernal Diaz del Castillo, *The True History of the Conquest of New Spain* (London, Hakluyt Society, 1912); J.N.L. Baker, *A History of Geographical Discovery and Exploration* (New York: Cooper Square Publishers, 1967).

Francisco de Orellana

(1511? - 1546)

Francisco de Orellana was a Spanish conquistador *who was the first European to travel down the Amazon River.*

Francisco de Orellana was born in the town of Trujillo in the Spanish province of Extremadura. He was a relative of **Francisco Pizarro**. Orellana probably went to America in about the year 1527 when he was 16 years old, possibly to Panama and then to Nicaragua. Orellana accompanied Pizarro when he set out to conquer Peru and participated in battles at Lima, Trujillo, and Cuzco. He was injured in a skirmish with the Incas and lost one eye. After the conquest, he was awarded an estate at Puerto Viejo in what is now Ecuador.

When Orellana heard that Pizarro was being besieged in Lima by a force of Native Americans, he collected a group of 80 men and rode to help defeat them. When civil war broke out between Pizarro and **Diego de Almagro** in 1538, Orellana took part in Pizarro's victory. As a reward for his services, he was made lieutenant governor of Guayaquil and refounded the city of Puerto Viejo on the site of the present-day city of Guayaquil.

Late in 1540, Pizarro's brother Gonzalo left Quito with a large force of Spaniards and Native Americas in search of cinnamon, a valuable spice that was rumored to grow on the eastern slopes of the Andes. When Orellana heard about the expedition, he resigned his office in Guayaquil and gathered a group of 23 men to join Gonzalo Pizarro. By the time they reached Quito, Pizarro had already left. Orellana and his men caught up with the larger force in Zumaco in March 1541, and Orellana was named second in command.

By the time that Gonzalo Pizarro's expedition discovered the Napo River in eastern Ecuador, one of the headwaters of the Amazon River, they were lost, exhausted, and hungry. As a chronicle of the time put it, the difficulties were "such that anyone but Gonzalles Pizarre would have abandon'd such an Enterprize as seem'd to be opposed by both Heaven and Earth."

Pizarro decided to build a boat to carry the weaker members of the party and to look for food farther downstream. The work took two months. When the boat was completed, it was launched on the Napo River, and Orellana was put in charge. According to the accounts left by both parties, this was done by mutual consent, and Orellana clearly planned to return when he took leave of Pizarro on January 1, 1542. However, the fast-flowing rivers quickly took him downstream through an area where there were no signs of human habitation, and at a certain point he and his men realized that they would never be able to row back up the river. When the remainder of Pizarro's expedition realized that they were stranded, they had no choice but to return overland to Quito, where the survivors arrived in June 1542. Pizarro wrote a letter to the King of Spain, bitterly accusing Orellana of desertion.

Meanwhile, Orellana had sailed down the Napo to where it met the Aguarico River, which he reached on February 2, 1542. Along the way he and his companions had stopped in Native American villages where they were well received and were given food to eat. They continued on until they reached the main stream of the Amazon River on February 11. They stayed for a while in a village called Aparia where they had plenty to eat and started work on a new, bigger boat.

The records of Orellana's journey were kept by Gaspar de Carvajal, a Dominican friar. He recorded that one day while they were in Aparia four very tall and light-skinned men, dressed in gold, arrived in the village. They stayed for a short while and then left. It was the first mention in European literature of "White Indians," about whom there were to be persistent rumors over the centuries but of whom no trace has ever been found.

Leaving Aparia on April 24, the Spaniards entered the domain of the Machiparo. These people were not friendly, and from that point on Orellana and his men had to fight many battles as they made their way down the river. On June 3, they passed the point where another large river joined the Amazon, and its dark waters did not mingle with the brown Amazon for many miles. They named it the Rio Negro, which is the name it still has today. Shortly after passing the confluence of the Madeira River, the Spaniards were once again attacked. This time the Native American warriors included women. Carvajal immediately labeled them "Amazons," the name given by the ancient Greeks to the mythical women warriors of Scythia. Carvajal described the Amazons as being light-skinned and very tall and robust and armed with bows and arrows. This story created quite a stir when it was published in Europe, and within a few years the world's greatest river became known as the "River of the Amazons."

Orellana reached the mouth of the Amazon on the Atlantic Ocean on August 26, 1542. From there, the Spaniards in their two boats headed northwestward along the coast of Guiana and eventually reached the island of Cubagua near Margarita off the coast of Venezuela. Many of them returned to Peru, but Orellana went back to Spain where he arrived in May 1543.

Orellana made a personal report of his expedition to King Carlos I. He asked to be made Governor of the territories that he

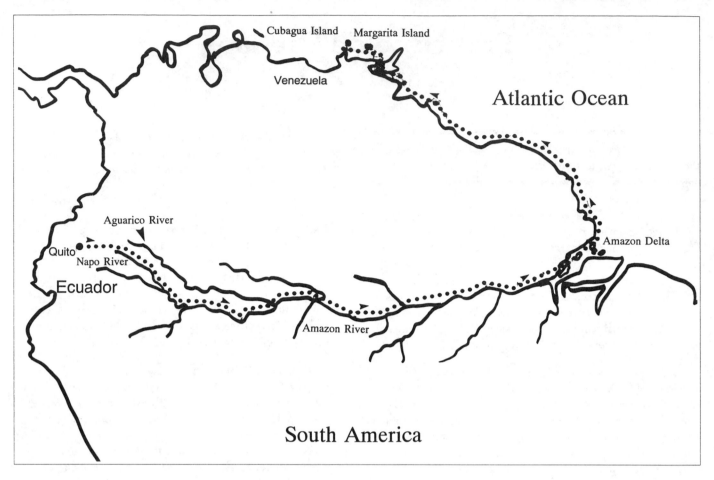

Orellana's trip down the Amazon River.

had found. He was granted that title on February 13, 1544 and was authorized to lead a colonizing expedition to the Amazon, but he was required to finance the venture himself. While in Spain, Orellana, who was in his early thirties, married Doña Ana de Ayala, who came from a good family but had no money. Her lack of a dowry did not help Orellana, who was having difficulty in finding the money he needed to finance his expedition.

On May 11, 1545 Orellana left Spain for the Amazon with a fleet of four vessels and about 300 to 350 men. The ships were in poor condition, and there were fewer men than he had wanted. They stopped in the Canaries and the Cape Verde Islands along the way and did not reach the Amazon until the end of December. Along the way, half of the men had either died or deserted, and one of the ships had disappeared in the mid-Atlantic.

Once on the Amazon, Orellana went upstream with one of the ships and a boat. The ship was wrecked, and the survivors divided up into smaller groups, some of whom made it to Cubagua.

Orellana himself died from fever while traveling in the complicated waterways of the Amazon's delta sometime during the month of November 1546.

Where to learn more

The major documentary source for Orellana's journey is Gaspar de Carvajal's account. It was rescued from the archives and published with an introduction by Chilean scholar José Toribio Medina in 1894. This version was translated into English by Bertram T. Lee and edited by H.C. Heaton as *The Discovery of the Amazon According to the Account of Friar Gaspar de Carvajal, and Other Documents* (New York: American Geographical Society, 1934).

There are good summaries of Orellana's voyage in Frederick A. Kirkpatrick, *The Spanish Conquistadores* (London: Adam & Charles Black, 1934) and Edward J. Goodman, *The Explorers of South America* (New York: Macmillan, 1972). For a discussion of the relationship between Gonzalo Pizarro and Orellana, see Philip A. Means, "Gonzalo Pizarro and Francisco de Orellana," *Hispanic American Historical Review*, vol. 14 (1934), pp. 275-295.

There is an entertaining retelling of the trip down the Amazon based on Carvajal's account in Anthony Smith, *Explorers of the Amazon* (New York: Viking, 1990), but it suffers because it does not detail its sources.

John Oxley

(1785? - 1828)

John Oxley was a British explorer who followed two major rivers trying to find an access route into Australia's interior.

John Oxley was born in the English county of Yorkshire, the son of landed gentry. He joined the Royal Navy as a midshipman in 1799. In 1801 he was transferred to a ship sailing to Australia, where the British had founded a colony at Sydney in 1788. Oxley arrived in October 1802, and during the following years he was employed doing coastal survey work. He commanded a ship to Tasmania in 1806.

Oxley returned to England in 1807 but sailed back to Australia the following year with two very large land grants. He applied to become Surveyor-General of the colony of New South Wales and was appointed to that position in 1812 after retiring from the Navy in 1811. Governor Lachlan Macquarie was anxious to find a way into the interior of the colony so that it could expand beyond the small area around Sydney. In earlier exploring expeditions, a surveyor on Oxley's staff, George Evans, had found the headwaters of two rivers, the Lachlan and Macquarie, that flowed westward. Macquarie sent Oxley out to find where they went.

Oxley left Bathurst, the westernmost British post, on April 28, 1817 and headed for the Lachlan River. His party included the earlier explorer, Evans, and the botanist **Allan Cunningham**. Within a week they made it to the farthest point that Evans had reached. They headed down the Lachlan, but this quickly became an impenetrable swamp. The expedition abandoned their boats and headed due west to try to find firmer ground. Once they achieved this, they turned southwestward thinking they would intersect a river that flowed to the south. Before they could reach the Murrumbidgee, they gave up and headed back north to the Lachlan. Once again in swampy territory they headed east to Bathurst, which they reached on August 29, 1817.

Oxley's report was very disappointing to Governor Macquarie who had hoped that the Lachlan would serve as the way west. He was, however, pleased with Oxley's work and recommended him for an award of £200. Hoping for better luck, he sent Oxley out again—this time to investigate the Macquarie River. Leaving Bathurst in April 1818 Oxley sailed down the Macquarie for 220 miles until it, like the Lachlan, became a swampy morass, since named the Macquarie marshes, in the northern interior of New South Wales. He then turned east and crossed a range of mountains and discovered a great grassy area that he named the Liverpool Plains. This fertile region is in the southern part of a section of New South Wales known as New England, centered around the town of Tamworth. It is one of the richest agricultural regions of Australia.

Oxley continued east, crossing the Great Dividing Range and finally reached the Pacific on September 23, 1818 which he said he was as happy to see as Balboa had been for the first time. When he made his report to Macquarie, the governor was once again disappointed that the Macquarie was not a viable route to the interior, but he was happy to learn about the Liverpool Plains, which could serve as a major settlement area if a more practical route could be found.

These were Oxley's only two inland exploring expeditions. For the next few years he occupied himself with coastal surveys. In September-October 1819 he went to Jervis Bay on the south coast of New South Wales, which is now part of the Australian Capital Territory and site of the Australian Naval Academy. Earlier that year and in 1820 he surveyed Port Macquarie on the north coast of New South Wales. In October 1823 he surveyed and named the site of the future city of Brisbane, which was first settled the following year.

Oxley received a government salary as well as fees for doing private surveying work. He also had several large land grants that he developed in addition to other business interests. However, he lived in a very grand style and was a pillar of the colonial society. When he died at the young age of 42 (partly, it is said, from maladies he caught exploring), he was so much in debt that the government granted special assistance to his wife and children.

Where to learn more

Oxley wrote about his explorations in *Journals of Two Expeditions into the Interior of New South Wales, Undertaken by Order of the British Government 1817-18* (London: 1820). Excerpts can be found in Kathleen Fitzpatrick, *Australian Explorers: A Selection from Their Writings* (London: Oxford University Press, 1958). There is one full-length biography: E.W. Dunlop, *John Oxley* (Melbourne: 1960). See also E.C. Rowland, "The Life and Work of John Oxley," *Journal of the Royal Australian Historical Society*, vol. 28 (1942).

Pedro Paez

(? - 1622)

Pedro Paez was a Spanish missionary who was taken captive and spent several years in southern Arabia and then reached the kingdom of Ethiopia, where he converted the Emperor and was the first European to see the source of the Blue Nile.

Pedro Paez was a Spanish Jesuit who was serving as a priest in the Portuguese trading center of Goa on the southwest coast of India when he was chosen in 1587 to go with a colleague, Anthony de Monserrate, on a mission to Ethiopia. The Portuguese had been in contact with Ethiopia ever since the journey of **Pero da Covilhão** one hundred years before. The Ethiopians were Christians but belonged to a division of the Church that did not recognize the authority of the Pope. Rome, and Portugal, hoped to make Catholics out of the Ethiopian Christians.

Paez and Monserrate were unable to find a ship that could carry them across the Indian Ocean to the horn of Africa. Therefore, they disguised themselves as Armenian merchants and traveled to the port of Diu in the Indian region of Gujerat. Unable to find transportation there, they stayed at Diu until they accepted the offer of an Armenian merchant to carry them to Basra (in southern Iraq). They sailed on his ship as far as Muscat, the present-day capital of Oman.

From Oman they visited the great Persian port city of Ormuz, which was then in the hands of the Portuguese. They then left on an Arab *dhow* headed for Zeila on the coast of Somaliland. But the ship was wrecked off the Kuria Muria islands off the south coast of Arabia. The two priests managed to make it to shore and obtained a small boat. They then sailed along the coast of Hadramawt (now in Yemen), but were discovered by a Turkish ship. The Turks were doing everything possible to keep the Portuguese out of what they considered their domain, and they immediately seized the two priests.

Paez and Monserrate were thrown in prison "stripped almost naked, and shut up in an old house of mud walls where they had little to eat by day, and abundance of vermin to break their rest at night." The commander of the town they were in decided to send the Christians off to his ruler. They were taken in a boat and then forced to walk overland for ten days through the desert to Tarin where the inhabitants "spit on their faces, and had they not been put into a house would have stoned them to death."

Five more days of walking brought them to the capital of King "Hunor" where they were put in cages so the crowds could view

them. Yemen had been called Arabia Felix or "Happy Arabia" by the Romans in contrast to the deserts to the north. In his narrative, Paez commented, "though that part of Arabia is called the Happy it is to be supposed the ancients gave it the name by the rule of contraries or else through a mistake."

In June and July 1589 they were sent to Canaan, a city 60 leagues from the port of Mocha, which had once been the capital of the Kingdom of Saba (Sheba). There they joined 25 other Portuguese and 5 Christian Indians as prisoners. They stayed in that jail for six years while the ruler tried to obtain ransom for their release. That did not happen so they were sent to Mocha to be sold as slaves to Indian merchants; no one would buy them. They were then sent on board a Turkish ship to be galley slaves. They stayed there for another year.

In the meantime, a Syrian youth that had known them in Canaan was released and went to India. In Goa he told the Portuguese viceroy about the capture of the two priests and their misfortunes. At the end of 1595 the viceroy then sent an Indian merchant to Mocha with the money to purchase their release. They then returned to Diu where Monserrate died in 1600. Paez continued to plan how to get to Ethiopia.

Paez persuaded the viceroy to provide ships, and on March 22, 1603 he set off, once again disguised as an Armenian merchant. This time he was successful and arrived at the port of Massawa on the Red Sea and made his way to Debaroa, the headquarters of the Bahr Negash ("sea province" or Eritrea) and then to Fremona on May 15, 1603. There was then a struggle going on for the Ethiopian throne. Both sides wanted to enlist the aid of the Portuguese, and the Emperor started introducing reforms to bring his church closer to that of Rome. He was very impressed with Paez, who became an important adviser at his court.

The influence of the Portuguese created turmoil at the Ethiopian court, and the Emperor was deposed. The new Emperor, Susenyos, was, however, also interested in what the Portuguese had to say, and he called for Paez to come to his court, which was then north of Lake Tana in the Ethiopian highlands. Paez traveled across the lake by boat, which was almost sunk by a hippopotamus. Paez then accompanied the Emperor to his coronation in the ancient city of Axum, which took place on March 23, 1609.

After this, Paez set up his mission at Gorgora on a peninsula that sticks out into Lake Tana. He was near to the Emperor's court and was always available for theological discussions. The

Emperor came more and more under the influence of the Catholics, and this led to conflict with more traditional believers. In 1618 he was forced to lead a campaign against one of the religious leaders, and Paez went with him. On April 21, 1618 Paez walked outside the Emperor's camp to two little springs, which were the source of the Blue Nile River, one of the two main tributaries of the Nile. He preceded the next European visitor, **James Bruce**, by 150 years.

Following the successful campaign Paez helped the Emperor build a new palace, which became the wonder of all Ethiopia because it was two stories tall: "a house upon a house." He also built a second church at Gorgora, which is still standing. There, early in 1622, the Emperor formally converted to Catholicism.

Paez, however, soon after became ill with fever and died on May 23, 1622.

Where to learn more

The collected documents of all the Jesuit priests who went to Ethiopia are contained in *Rerum Aethiopicarum Scriptores Occidentales inediti a saeculis XVI ad XIX*, 15 vols. (Rome: Beccari, 1903-1915). Paez wrote a history of his own experiences and that of the other Portuguese in Ethiopia. There is a modern Portuguese-language version of this work: Pêro Pais, *História da Etiópia*, 3 vols. (Porto: Livraria Civilização, 1945).

There are two main English-language studies: Charles F. Rey, *The Romance of the Portuguese in Abyssinia* (London: H.F. & G. Witherby, 1929; reprinted, New York: Negro Universities Press, 1969) and Elaine Sanceau, *The Land of Prester John: A Chronicle of Portuguese Exploration* (New York: Alfred A. Knopf, 1944).

John Palliser

(1817 - 1887)

John Palliser was an Irishmen who led an expedition to the Canadian West for the British government to investigate its economic potential.

John Palliser was a member of a prominent Anglo-Irish family. The Anglo-Irish were Protestants who settled in Ireland during the long period of British rule and who made up the aristocracy, and governing elite, until the twentieth century. The famous Victorian novelist William Makepeace Thackeray wrote a series of novels about such a family, called the Pallisers, that very much resembled that of John Palliser himself.

John Palliser was born in Dublin on January 29, 1817. He studied for a while at Trinity College in Dublin but never took his degree. He held several honorary local offices in the area of his family's estate in County Waterford and served from time to time as an officer in the militia. His real interests, however, were in travel and big-game shooting.

Palliser made his first trip to North America in 1847 when he went hunting for buffalo, antelope, and grizzly bear on the prairies of the Missouri Valley and the foothills of the Rocky Mountains. He returned to England by way of New Orleans and Panama and wrote about his adventures in a book called *Solitary Rambles and Adventures of a Hunter in the Prairies*, which was published in 1853.

Following this trip Palliser came up with the idea of leading an expedition to British North America (Canada) to investigate the possibilities of settlement in the Prairies and to explore the best ways to travel west. At this time, what is now the Canadian West was occupied by Native Americans and a few European trappers and traders. The only area of agricultural settlement was along the Red River of southern Manitoba where a group of *Métis* (mixed Native Americans and Europeans) had formed a colony starting in the 1830s. In the meantime, the Americans farther south were rapidly expanding westward, and the British feared they would lose their territorial claims if they did not match the Yankees.

After several years of lobbying, Palliser was able to get support for his plan from the British Colonial Office and the Royal Geographical Society. As finally constituted, the expedition included a geologist, botanist, magnetic observer, and astronomer, with Palliser as the head. They traveled with a wide range of scientific instruments.

These men left England on May 16, 1857 and sailed to New York. From there they traveled to Sault Ste. Marie on Lake Superior. They traveled from there on canoes all the way to Fort Garry on the Red River, which they reached in July. On July 21 the expedition started on its journey across the plains, heading south on the Red River to the U.S. border where they made observations with an American surveyor that they encountered there. From Pembina, North Dakota, they went west along the border as far as what is now eastern Saskatchewan and then headed north to the South Saskatchewan River and the North Saskatchewan River to Fort Charlton, a fur-trading post. While the party wintered there, Palliser returned to New York via St. Paul, Minnesota (with a side trip to New Orleans) to apply to the Colonial Office in London for more time and more money. He arrived back in Saskatchewan to head out again in the spring of 1858.

The expedition headed west and then split up northwest of the modern city of Calgary to explore various possible routes through the Rocky Mountains. Palliser went south to the North Kananaskis Pass and returned farther north through the North Kootenay Pass. The expedition's geologist and physician, Dr. James Hector, discovered Kicking Horse Pass, which was named when his horse threw him and kicked him in the head. His Native American guides thought he was dead and had lowered him into a grave when he managed to wink his eye at them. Kicking Horse Pass later became the route of the Canadian Pacific Railroad through the Rockies.

The members of the expedition met up again at Fort Edmonton (now Edmonton, Alberta) and spent the winter of 1858-1859 there. In the spring of 1859, they headed south and then split up once again. Hector went north to investigate Howse Pass. Palliser traveled through the North Kootenay Pass and then downstream down the Kootenay River to the Columbia as far as present-day Colville, Washington. He then pushed overland to the site of Midway, B.C. He traveled down the Columbia to its mouth, went by boat to Victoria on Vancouver Island, then to San Francisco, Panama, Montreal and arrived in Liverpool, England, on June 16, 1860.

The expedition's reports appeared over several years until 1863, and the map of its explorations was published in 1865. Palliser's report told future settlers of a fertile belt of land lying along the North Saskatchewan River. However, he thought that the more arid lands of southern Alberta and Saskatchewan would not be suitable for agriculture. This area eventually came to be called "Palliser's Triangle" (and is today a major farming region). His most controversial recommendation was that it would not be possible to build a railroad across the continent entirely through British territory—the land north of the Great Lakes was too rugged and construction costs in the Rockies would be too expensive. Ten years later when Canadian entrepreneurs set out to build the Canadian Pacific they had to find answers to these difficulties posed by Palliser.

After his return, Palliser inherited his father's estates in 1862. Also in 1862 he was sent to the West Indies on a secret mission for the British Government that seems to have involved negotiations with the Confederate States of America. In 1869 he made another expedition to explore and shoot game on the large island of Novaya Zemlya in the Russian Arctic. All of these ventures cost a great deal of money. By the time he died in 1887, he had spent most of the family's fortune, and the estate was heavily mortgaged.

Where to learn more

The main student of Palliser and his expedition has been Irene M. Spry who wrote a biographical essay about him in volume 11 of the *Dictionary of Canadian Biography*, edited *The Papers of the Palliser Expedition* (Toronto: Champlain Society, 1968), and then wrote a history of his travels in *The Palliser Expedition* (Toronto, 1973).

See also John Warkenton, ed. *The Western Interior of Canada: A Record of Geographical Discovery, 1612-1907* (Toronto: 1967).

Mungo Park

(1771-1806)

Mungo Park was a Scottish doctor who was the first European to see the Niger River and return to tell about it. He died on a second expedition.

In 1788 the Association for Promoting the Discovery of the Interior Parts of Africa was founded in London by the famous scientist **Sir Joseph Banks**. The Association's immediate goal was to reach the Niger River and determine which way it flowed. The Association sent out two explorers in its first year, Simon Lucas and John Ledyard, but they both died within a short time of their arrival in North Africa. In 1791 **Daniel Houghton** was killed in what is now eastern Senegal. Following Banks's recommendation, the Association selected a Scottish doctor, Mungo Park, to make the next attempt.

Park was born in the village of Foulshiels near the town of Selkirk in Scotland on September 10, 1771. He was the seventh of thirteen children of a small farmer, called a "crofter" in

Mungo Park. The Granger Collection, New York.

Scotland. Park took courses in anatomy and surgery at the University of Edinburgh but never graduated. Leaving school, he went to London where he stayed with a sister and her husband, James Dickson. Dickson was an amateur botanist who was acquainted with Banks. Through that contact, in 1792 Park got a job as a ship's doctor on a trading vessel bound for Sumatra in the East Indies. Park was very interested in natural history and brought back a collection of botanical specimens that he presented to Banks. Impressed, Banks nominated Park to be the next explorer sent out to find the Niger.

Park was interviewed and accepted by the Selection Committee (Banks and one other member) on July 23, 1794. He intended to leave immediately for the Gambia River on the west coast of Africa in the company of the new British consul. But that official kept delaying his departure so long that Park finally set out on his own in May 1795, reaching the Gambia in June. He spent the second half of 1795 at the trading post of a Dr. Laidley upriver at Pisania learning Mandingo, the local language. At the beginning of the dry season, Park left Pisania on December 2, 1795, accompanied by a guide, a servant, and four porters.

His initial route pretty much followed that of Houghton, taking him northeast to Medina, the capital of the Kingdom of Woolli, where he was well received by the King. The King of Bondou, however, was more suspicious, and Park appeased him by presenting him with his umbrella. As he entered lands that were more Islamic, Park, as a Christian, began to experience outright hostility. He passed through the town of Simbing where Houghton had written his last letter. At the nearby town of Jarra, he learned about the circumstances of his predecessor's death. Also at this point, all of his attendants except for a young slave named Demba deserted him. On his way through the town of Deena, where he arrived on March 11, 1796, he was spit at on the streets.

Park continued on alone, heading north. At the town of Benown he was imprisoned by the local King, Ali, for a month in a mud hut. Attacked by neighbors, Ali and his men left the town, taking Park with them. Along the way, he was subject to more mistreatment. His captors would not even give him water, and he was forced to drink out of the cattle trough. At the end of June 1796 Park was able to escape alone with his horse in a crowd of refugees fleeing the fighting. Robbed of his cloak by a gang of robbers, he had to beg to survive. He almost perished of thirst on several occasions. Once he was saved by a rain squall: he drank the water that he wrung out of his clothes.

Eventually Park reached the Bambara country, where the people were friendlier. As he approached the capital of Segou, he saw "with infinite pleasure the great object of my mission—the long-sought-for, majestic Niger, glittering to the morning sun, as broad as the Thames at Westminster, and flowing slowly *to the eastward*." Park had found one of the great missing links in European knowledge of Africa.

Park visited the city of Segou, which had 30,000 inhabitants and impressed him with its magnificence. The King of Segou refused to receive him but gave him 5,000 cowrie shells, the local medium of exchange, to help him on his way. From Segou Park wanted to continue down the Niger to the fabled city of Timbuktu. He was only able to make cover a short distance—to Sansanding and Silla. There, sick and with no resources, on July 29, 1796, he decided he would have to turn back. Returning via Bamako, the present-day capital of Mali, which he passed on August 25, Park was attacked by robbers who left him with nothing but a shirt, a pair of trousers, and the hat where he had stuffed his notes. At that point, he almost gave up. However, his strong religious faith kept him from despair: "I started up, and disregarding both hunger and fatigue, travelled forwards, assured that relief was at hand: and I was not disappointed.

In the next town, Park was treated with kindness and recovered part of his clothes. On September 16 he met a slave trader named Kafra who agreed (for a price to be paid on arrival) to take Park with him along with the column of slaves he was leading to the coast. They waited for the end of the rainy season, leaving the town of Kamalia on April 19, 1797. There were 35 slaves in the column, bound together by ropes around their necks and fetters on their feet. During the march, two of the women committed suicide by eating clay. They reached Pisania on June 11, 1797, and Park paid Kafra with cloth he got from Dr. Laidley. He then found passage to the Caribbean as the ship's doctor on an American slave ship. During the crossing of the Atlantic, 11 of the 130 slaves died.

In Antigua, Park was able to get a ship back to England, arriving in London on December 25, 1797. No one in England even knew that he was still alive. Since he did not want to disturb anyone on Christmas morning, he wandered the empty streets. He came to the gardens of the British Museum and found one gate open. Going inside, he stumbled upon Dickson, his brother-in-law, who was out tending to some gardening chores.

Park was warmly received in London and wrote a book about his African experiences that became a bestseller. On May 25, 1799, he attended a meeting of the African Association at which Banks proposed that Great Britain should take advantage of Parks's journey to send an army to conquer the Niger. It was the first public call for British imperialism in Africa. In the summer of 1799 Park returned to Scotland and took up residence in the small town of Peebles, where he started a medical practice and married the daughter of one of his college professors. He became the neighbor and friend of the famous writer Sir Walter Scott. He was troubled by recurring illnesses from his trip to the Niger and nightmares about being captured and tortured.

Park grew bored with his medical practice, telling Scott that "he would rather brave Africa and all its horrors, than wear out his life in long and toilsome rides over the hills of Scotland, for which the remuneration was hardly enough to keep body and soul together." The British government wanted to send out an expedition to show the flag as a counter to the French in Senegal and to further explore the Niger. When offered the chance to lead this expedition, Park accepted and was given the temporary rank of lieutenant in the British Army.

Park arrived on the Gambia on April 6, 1805 with a force of about 40 Europeans, including 30 soldiers from a British garrison at Goree, an island off the coast of Senegal that had been taken from the French. Park hired an English-speaking Mandingo named Isaaco to serve as guide. The expedition set out from Pisania on May 4, just before the start of the rainy season. By the time the rains started on June 10, two men had already died, and half of the others were sick. When they reached the Niger at Bamako on August 19, only seven Europeans were still alive. The rest had died from malaria and dysentery.

In spite of this disaster, Park insisted on continuing. He hired canoes at Bamako to take the rest of the expedition downstream. On August 26 he came down with dysentery himself. At Sansanding he was met by emissaries of the King of Segou. Park told them that he planned to sail all the way down the Niger to the sea. If he found the way, then he would open up direct trade relations with the Africans, bypassing the Arab middlemen. With this news, the King sent two (broken) canoes for the Europeans. After working 18 days to repair them and join them together, Park launched it as His Majesty's Schooner *Joliba* (an African name for the Niger). While he was doing this, his wife's brother, Alexander Anderson died, leaving Park with four soldiers, three slaves, and a new guide, Ahmadi Fatouma. Park wrote a letter home from Sansanding on November 19, 1805 and sent it back to the coast with Isaaco.

That was the last word that was ever heard from Park. Five years later, the British government hired Isaaco to go into the interior to try to find out what had happened to him. In Sansanding, Isaaco met Fatouma and got the story. Park and his men had proceeded on their way by using their firearms to force their way down the river, rather than negotiating passage with the local rulers. They passed Kabara, the river port five miles from Timbuktu, but were not allowed to proceed up the canal to the famed trading center. Park sailed around the great 300-mile bend of the Niger past the city of Gao.

In March or April 1806, Park and his remaining men reached the small Hausa state of Yauri, about 600 miles from the Gulf of Guinea and 1,500 miles from Bamako, his starting point. Park sent Fatouma to the local king with a number of gifts. According to Fatouma, the king found the gifts inadequate, and the next morning he ordered his men to attack the *Joliba* at the Bussa rapids. When they were fired upon and realized they could not prevail, Park and the remaining soldiers jumped into the river and were drowned. Only one slave survived and made it to Yauri to tell the story to Fatouma.

Although there are discrepancies in Fatouma's story, it is the most complete account anyone has ever been able to get. Isaaco brought this story back to the coast, and it made its way to England. Park's wife refused to believe it, however, and died in 1840 thinking her husband might still be alive in Africa. One of their three sons, Thomas, a midshipman in the Royal Navy, was given three years' leave in 1827 to search for his father. He died of fever on his way into the interior from the port of Accra. **Hugh Clapperton** and **Richard Lander** traveled to Bussa and Yauri in 1825 and heard stories about Park's death. Lander returned in 1830 and recovered a gun and a robe that had belonged to Park. He lost them during his own adventurous journey. He also saw a nautical almanac that contained Park's writing. This was recovered in 1857 by Lieutenant John Glover and is now in the museum of the Royal Geographical Society in London.

Where to learn more

Mungo Park, *Travels in the Interior Districts of Africa Performed under the Direction and Patronage of the African Association, in the Years 1795, 1796, and 1797* (London: 1799; many subsequent editions, the latest is in Everyman's Library). The parts of Park's journal of his second expedition that he sent back to England were printed as the *Journal of a Mission to the Interior of Africa in 1805* (London: 1815). It contained a biographical sketch of Park's life by J. Wishaw and an appendix with Isaaco's story of his death. Excerpts from these can be found in Margery Perham and J. Simmons, *African Discovery: An Anthology of Exploration* (London: Faber & Faber, 1942; reprinted, Chicago: Northwestern University Press, 1963) and C. Howard and J.H. Plumb, *West African Explorers* (London: Oxford University Press, 1951). Park's correspondence with the African Association is in Robin Hallett, *Records of the African Association, 1788-1831* (London: Thomas Nelson & Sons, 1964).

There are three biographies of Park that are usually cited: one is by the African explorer Joseph Thomson, *Mungo Park and the Niger* (London: 1890). Of the other two, Stephen Gwynn, *Mungo Park and the Quest of the Niger* (London: 1890; reprinted, 1934) is considered to scholarly and straightforward while Lewis G. Gibbon, *Niger: The Life of Mungo Park* (Edinburgh: 1934) is a romanticized version of the explorer's life.

There are several general histories of African exploration that devote considerable space to Park: A.Adu Boahen, *Britain, the Sahara, and the Western Sudan, 1788-1861* (Oxford: Clarendon Press, 1964); Robin Hallett, *The Penetration of Africa: European Enterprise and Exploration Principally in Northern and Western Africa up to 1830*, vol. 1 (London: Routledge & Kegan Paul, 1965); Christopher Lloyd, *The Search for the Niger* (London: Collins, 1973); and Sanche de Gramont, *The Strong Brown God: The Story of the Niger River* (Boston: Houghton Mifflin, 1975). Of these, Hallett is the best and most complete, while Gramont's is quite readable.

Sir (William) Edward Parry

(1790 - 1855)

Edward Parry was a British Arctic explorer who was the first person to find the entrance to the Northwest Passage and then set a record for traveling farthest north.

Edward Parry was born in Bath, England, the son of a doctor. After an education in a private grammar school, he joined the Royal Navy on June 30, 1803 as a volunteer on the *Ville de Paris*. He served on several ships that saw active duty during the Napoleonic Wars, including the protection of British whaling ships north of Norway. He was promoted to lieutenant on January 6, 1810. In 1813 he was assigned to *La Hogue*, stationed at Halifax, Nova Scotia. He remained in North America, serving on different ships, until 1817.

On his return to England, Parry, who came from an influential family, arranged to meet **Sir Joseph Banks**, the president of the Royal Society, Britain's major scientific association. He also cultivated an official in the British Admiralty, John Barrow, who was the leading proponent of Arctic exploration at the time. Parry presented him with a volume on navigational astronomy that he had written. As a result of these contacts, in 1818 he was given command of the *Alexander* on an expedition led by **Sir John Ross** to find the Northwest Passage.

Ross's expedition was not a success, and he and Parry quarreled. Parry had wished to explore farther in Lancaster Sound, but Ross had turned back. The Admiralty preferred Parry's view and sent him to investigate further. He left England on May 4, 1819 with two ships, the *Hecla* and the *Griper* under his command. At the same time, **Sir John Franklin** was sent out to travel overland through northern Canada to try to find the Northwest Passage from the landward side.

Parry and his two ships arrived at the entrance to Lancaster Sound on July 30, 1819. The expedition was very lucky—weather conditions were unusually warm and the ice was abnormally thin. The ships made it through Lancaster Sound and proved that it did in fact lead westward. Parry turned south and sailed 100 miles through Prince Regent Inlet to the west of Baffin Island. He then returned to the north and pushed his way westward through the channel he named after his patron—Barrow Strait. Entering Viscount Melville Sound the two ships were faced with pack ice, but a lookout on the *Hecla* was able to spot an area of thinner ice that the ships could break through. On September 4, 1819 the *Hecla* made it to 110°W longitude. As a result of this accomplishment, the crew was eligible for a £5,000 bounty that had been established by the British Parliament.

By now the Arctic winter had set in, and Parry found a small harbor on the south coast of Melville Island. It took three days for the crew to saw a channel through the ice so that the two ships could enter the haven, which Parry named Winter Harbour. Parry had stocked up on lime juice and tinned vegetables so that his men would not suffer from scurvy, and he organized work projects as well as amateur theatricals, sporting events, and a ship newspaper to keep them occupied. As a result of this foresight the crew stayed relatively well disciplined and healthy in spite of the bitter cold, which they were not well equipped to handle.

As the weather began to improve, on June 1, 1820 Parry led an expedition to the north coast of Melville Island to a place that he named Hecla and Griper Bay. On August 4 the ships were able to leave Winter Harbour, and Parry sailed westward, hoping to make it all the way through the Northwest Passage. However, ice conditions were much less favorable than they had been the

Sir Edward Parry. The Granger Collection, New York.

previous year, and he was forced to turn back on August 23. It was not until 30 years later that **Sir Robert McClure** was to find the way out of Melville Sound via the southwest, thereby completing the Northwest Passage. In any case, Parry had sailed 600 miles farther west than any previous navigator and set a distance record for a sailing vessel entering the Passage from the east that has never been equaled. The two ships returned to England at the end of October with the loss of only one life. Parry became a national hero.

Following this success, Parry set out again the following year. This time he wanted to test his theory that the Northwest Passage could be found farther south, on the northwest corner of Hudson Bay. He left England on May 8, 1821 with two ships, the *Fury* and the *Hecla*. He sailed to Foxe Basin, west of Baffin Island, which had been found by **Luke Fox** 200 years previously. He went to the west side of the basin to investigate Frozen Strait and Repulse Bay, first seen by Europeans in 1742, which seemed to offer the most likely way west. He quickly found that they are dead ends. He then headed up the east coast of the Melville Peninsula (once again named for the First Lord of the Admiralty) until he was forced to stop on October 8, 1821 to put in at Winter Island.

During the winter the Englishmen became friendly with a band of Inuit, and Parry learned some of their Arctic survival techniques. He also looked carefully at their maps to see if he could figure out a way west. He sent out land expeditions starting in May, but without success. It took three weeks to cut a passage through the ice out of their anchorage, before the two ships could leave on July 2, 1822. They sailed to the north of the Melville Peninsula to a small island named Igloolik. There is a narrow passageway between Baffin Island and the mainland, which Parry named Fury and Hecla Strait. He waited all summer for the ice to clear so that he could sail through it. It never did, and he was forced to anchor for the winter at Igloolik.

Parry and his crew were forced to spend 11 months at Igloolik, where they got to know the Inuit very well and wrote some of the first anthropological descriptions of these people. When the summer came, the ice still did not break up, and by then the crew was sick and provisions were low. Parry was forced to give up and left Igloolik and sailed back to Europe on August 12, 1823. He reached the Shetland Islands off the coast of Scotland on October 10.

On his return to London, Parry was ill for several weeks and depressed when he learned that his fiancée had left him for someone else during his absence. But he continued to be highly favored by the Navy and was given the post of Chief Hydrographer. He discussed the results of Franklin's expeditions, who had made it down the Coppermine River all the way to the Arctic Ocean. Parry realized that the narrow Fury and Hecla Strait was always likely to be blocked by ice, and that the only answer was to sail around the north end of Baffin Island through Prince Regent Inlet on the west side of the Melville Peninsula. This is in fact the only navigable way for a small ship and was the route that was taken

by **Roald Amundsen** when he actually navigated the Northwest Passage in 1903-1905.

The British Admiralty sponsored Parry on an expedition to test this new theory. He set out once again with the *Fury* and *Hecla* on May 8, 1824. Ice was very heavy that year, and he made slow progress. He was only able to make it into Lancaster Sound by the second week in September. He forced his way into Prince Regent Inlet and then anchored in a small harbor on the northwest coast of Baffin Island at the end of September. The two ships were able to leave the harbor on July 20, 1825. At first things went well, and it looked as though the warm weather would break up the ice. But on July 30 they were hit by a storm that grounded the *Fury* on a beach. It was possible to re-float it, but the ship was severely damaged. After being hit by further storms and traveling ice floes that also damaged the *Hecla*, the *Fury* had to be abandoned on August 23. Parry was forced to return to England, reaching London on October 16, 1825.

Back home, Parry went through another period of depression but this was relieved when he married Isabella Stanley, the daughter of a wealthy and socially prominent family in October 1826. In the meantime, Parry had proposed another expedition—this time to the North Pole—in order to compensate for the relative failures of his previous two expeditions. He took the *Hecla* to the Spitsbergen Islands north of Norway, accompanied by **James Clark Ross**. The two men left Spitsbergen on June 21, 1827 traveling on a boat with runners pulled by 12 crew members. This turned out not to be a practicable means of travel, and he only made it 178 miles north, returning to the *Hecla* on August 21. However, this still set a polar record of 82°45′ that was not beaten for another 50 years. During this and other Arctic voyages, Parry was responsible for inventing and devising several pieces of equipment and techniques that benefited other explorers for generations.

As a result of his expeditions, Parry received many awards and medals. He was promoted to Commander on November 4, 1820 and to Captain on November 8, 1821. Following his return from Spitsbergen, he was knighted on April 29, 1829. In May 1829 he resigned his commission in the Navy to become head of the company that was promoting British emigration to the Australian colony of New South Wales. He returned to England in 1834. In 1837 he returned to work with the British Admiralty, becoming "Comptroller of Steam Machinery." In 1847 he was appointed superintendent of a hospital in London and then was appointed lieutenant governor of Greenwich Hospital shortly before his death. He was given an honorary promotion to Rear Admiral on June 4, 1852.

Where to learn more

The place to start in following Parry's Arctic explorations is with his own books: *Journal of a Voyage for the Discovery of a North-west Passage from the Atlantic to the Pacific Performed in the Years 1819-20 in His Majesty's Ships Hecla and Griper* (London: John Murray, 1821-1824); *Journal of Second Voyage for the Discovery of a North-west Passage from the Atlantic to the Pacific Performed in the Years 1821-23 in H.M. Ships the Fury and Hecla* (London: John Murray, 1826); and *Journal of a Third Voyage* (London:

John Murray, 1826). Later in life, Parry published his autobiography: *Memoirs of Rear-Admiral Sir W. Edward Parry* (London: Longman, Brown, Green, Longmans & Roberts, 1858).

The doctor on the first expedition, Alexander Fisher, wrote *A Journal of a Voyage of Discovery to the Arctic Regions in His Majesty's Ships Hecla and Griper* (London: Longman, Hurst, Rees, Orme & Browne, 1821) while George F. Lyon, the captain of the *Fury* during the second expedition, wrote *The Private Journal of Captain G.F. Lyon During the Recent Voyage of Discovery under Captain Parry* (Boston: Wells and Lilly, 1824). Parry's mentor, John Barrow, wrote a history of the voyages he had sponsored: *Voyages of Discovery and Research within the Arctic Regions* (London: John Murray, 1846).

Two more recent histories are: W. Gillies Ross, "Parry's Second Voyage," *History Today*, vol. 10 (1960), no. 2; and Ann Parry, *Parry of the Arctic: The Life Story of Admiral Sir Edward Parry, 1790-1855* (London: Chatto & Windus, 1963).

Because of the importance of his voyages, the general histories of Arctic exploration and the search for the Northwest Passage all include lengthy sections on Parry. Recommended are: Jeannette Mirsky, *To the Arctic!: The Story of Northern Exploration from Earliest Times to the Present* (New York: Alfred A. Knopf, 1948); George Malcolm Thomson, *The Search for the Northwest Passage* (New York: Macmillan, 1975); and Pierre Berton, *The Arctic Grail: The Quest for the Northwest Passage and the North Pole, 1818-1909* (New York: Viking, 1988; paperback edition, New York: Penguin, 1989).

Robert Edward Peary

(1856 - 1920)

Robert Edward Peary was an American naval officer who led the first successful expedition to reach the North Pole.

Robert Edward Peary was born in the small town of Cresson, in western Pennsylvania, on May 6, 1856 and entered the U.S. Navy in 1881 after graduating from college as a civil engineer. In 1885 he was appointed to serve on the survey for a proposed canal route through Nicaragua from the Caribbean to the Pacific. The experience seems to have whetted his enthusiasm for exploration. His choice of the Arctic as a field of exploration seems to have been related to reading about the exploits of Elisha Kent Kane and other explorers when he was a boy.

One of the objectives of Arctic exploration in the 1880s was to cross the Greenland Ice Cap, attempted by the Norwegian explorer **Adolf Erik Nordenskjöld** in 1883 (and achieved by **Fridtjof Nansen** in 1888). Peary made his first Arctic expedition in 1886 in the company of Danish Lieutenant Christian Maigaard. They set out from the west coast of Greenland on June 8, 1886, but were only able to travel 125 miles in 24 days before being forced to turn back.

Following his return from Greenland, Peary was again assigned to Central America to work on the proposed canal. Just before leaving Washington, he went to a store to buy a tropical pith helmet to wear on his new assignment. He was waited on by a young African-American man named **Matthew A. Henson**. Peary hired Henson to be his personal valet, and the two were to become inseparable traveling companions for the following 20 years. Peary sailed from New York to Nicaragua on November 30, 1887. On his return the following year, he married Josephine Diebetsch, whom he had met at a dance in Washington in 1882. When news of Nansen's crossing of Greenland reached Peary, he immediately began to plan for a crossing across the north end of the island.

In 1891 Peary returned to Greenland, accompanied by his wife and Henson and four others, including Dr. **Frederick Albert Cook**. They landed on the western Greenland coast of Baffin Bay on July 27, 1891 and spent the following 13 months in a makeshift shelter, making measurements and studying the survival techniques of the Greenland Inuit. In April 1892, Peary traveled with a Norwegian hunter overland to the northeast coast of Greenland. They reached a peak from which they could see the ocean on July 4, 1892, thereby proving that Greenland was an island and did not extend farther north toward the Pole.

Robert Edward Peary.

However, Peary claimed to have seen a channel ("Peary Channel") separating the mainland from another island ("Peary Land"). It was many years before other explorers found out that no such channel exists.

On his return to the United States, Peary began to receive the acclaim that he wanted, and by this time he seems to have been convinced that his destiny was in the Arctic. He returned to the same place in Greenland in 1893, where Josephine Peary gave birth to their daughter, Marie, on September 12, 1893. Peary set off from their base with eight companions on dogsleds in March 1894 to try to cross Greenland once again. To his great frustration, they were forced to turn back by a series of blizzards. Peary tried one more time, starting out on April 2, 1895. This time, he and Henson made it back to Independence Bay on the northeast coast of Greenland after a series of forced marches that almost killed both of them.

During his summer voyages of 1896 and 1897, Peary discovered a group of meteorites in the Cape York area of Greenland. He brought them back to the United States, including one weighing 37.5 tons, which he sold to the American Museum of Natural History for $40,000. He also brought back six Inuit to put on display with the meteor. They all caught pneumonia, and four of them died. One of the two who survived, Minik, stayed in New York and tried to reclaim his father's body to take back home. His story became a *cause célèbre* in the New York newspapers. By this time, however, Peary had set his sights on a new goal—being the first human to reach the North Pole.

In order to do this he needed money. Back in the United States, Peary spent his time fundraising. He was able to interest several important businessmen, notably Morris K. Jessup, who had made a fortune in banking and railroads. These supporters formed the Peary Arctic Club in New York City, which had its first meeting on January 29, 1899. He used the funds supplied by his

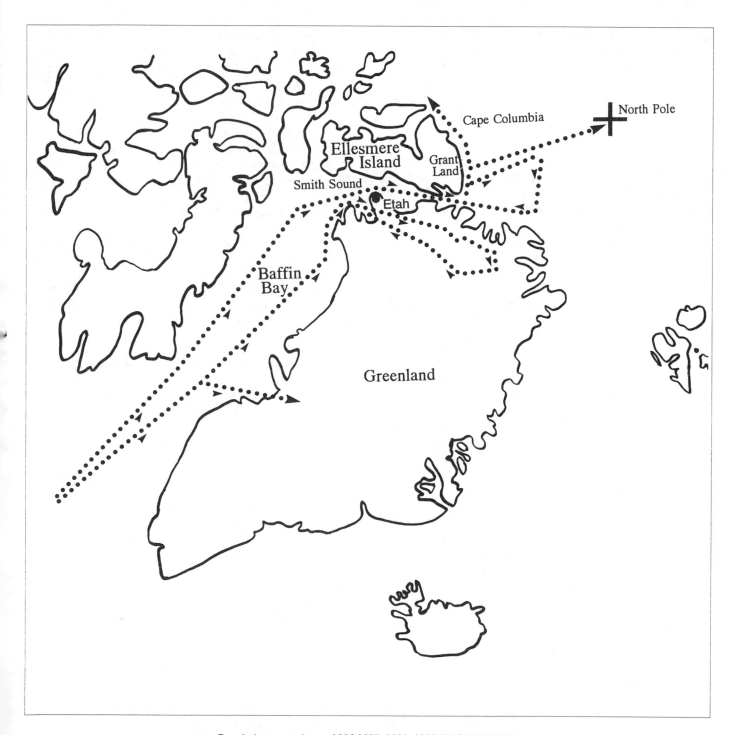

Peary's Arctic expeditions, 1886-1897, 1902, 1905-1906, 1908-1909.

backers to build a base camp at Fort Conger on the northern end of Ellesmere Island in the Canadian Arctic.

Peary traveled to Fort Conger for the first time in January 1899. The rashness of making the trip in mid-winter was revealed when Henson helped Peary take off his boots, and two or three toes snapped off with them. "My God, Lieutenant! Why didn't you tell me your feet were frozen?" asked Henson. Peary replied, "There's no time to pamper sick men on the trail. Besides, a few toes aren't much to give to achieve the Pole." Eventually, parts of seven toes had to be amputated. Peary was in severe pain for weeks and was partially lame the rest of his life. While recuperating on his bed, it is said that he carved the Latin motto "Find a way or make one" on the walls of the cabin. Peary and his men carried 14 tons of supplies to the camp during the following summer, returning with more provisions and equipment in 1900. He made his first trip north in April 1901 but only covered about 40 miles in eight days.

Peary made his first serious attempt to reach the Pole in 1902 accompanied by Henson and several Inuit. They left from Cape Hecla at the northern tip of Ellesmere Island on April 6, 1902 but only traveled 82 miles when they were forced to turn back on April 21. They were faced by heavy blizzards and shifting ice, and two wide channels or "leads" opened up along their route. Peary returned very discouraged, feeling that he was too old to make the trip again and that he would have to give up his ambition. "The game is off," he wrote. But when he learned later that an Italian team had bested the previous farthest north record, his old competitive resolve returned.

Peary learned from his failure. He adapted his equipment to the Arctic conditions that he had experienced, building lighter and broader sledges, for example, so that they could travel better over the rough ice fields. He also worked out what was later called the "Peary system": sending advance parties ahead to lay down supply depots and open up a trail, so that the main party could spend its energy in covering distance. In 1904 he commissioned the building of the ship *Theodore Roosevelt* to his own specifications. Peary hired Newfoundland-born **Bob Bartlett**, who had served on a previous Peary ship, as captain.

Peary's next expedition set sail from New York on July 16, 1905. The *Roosevelt* headed first for Greenland to pick up a party of Inuit men and women and a team of Siberian huskies. The Inuit were crucial to the success of the expedition: the men constructed the igloos to live in, and the women sewed the fur and hide garments that everyone wore. Once the race for the Pole began, it was the Inuit men who bore the brunt of the "Peary system," traveling ahead to break the trail. Also joining the expedition in Greenland was Peary's mistress, Aleqasina, who was the mother of his sons Anaukak, born in May 1900, and Kale, born in May or June 1906.

The *Roosevelt* fought its way through the ice of Smith Sound to Cape Sheridan on the northeast coast of Ellesmere Island, 90 miles from the base camp at Cape Hecla. The first Inuit advance parties set out on February 9, 1906. Peary himself left on March 5. The expedition faced increasingly difficult conditions. Temperatures reached the record low of -60°F, and both the rugged ice surface and the speed and direction of drift were worse than had been expected. On March 26, they reached the "Big Lead"—an uncrossable patch of open water. They waited a week, and the weather turned cold enough to allow ice to form on the lead. With Henson and six Inuit, Peary continued on. Three days later they were hit by a blizzard that kept them in camp for another week.

By then, Peary realized that he would not be able to reach the Pole on that trip. He therefore set out to beat the farthest north record. By his own calculations, he achieved this on April 21, reaching a new high latitude of 87°6'. This was 36 miles farther than the Italian record, but still 174 miles away from the Pole. Peary and his companions turned and headed towards the coast of Greenland, which they reached on May 9. Peary's records of this trip and the supporting evidence are so sketchy that there has always been controversy as to whether he achieved the point he claimed. Henson had no knowledge of celestial navigation and could not confirm Peary's readings. He did, however, attest to the remarkable quality of the 64-day trip across the polar ice.

On their return to the *Roosevelt*, Peary set out along the north coast of Ellesmere Island, making the first trip to its western point and naming geographical features after his financial backers all along the way. At this time he also claimed to have spotted a distant land to the northwest, which he named Crocker Land, after George Crocker, a director of the Southern Pacific Railroad. No such land exists.

On Peary's return to the United States, he was well received, but financing for another polar attempt had dried up. His supporters apparently felt that he had made his last effort and failed. His book about the 1906 expedition only sold 2,230 copies. But when Peary learned that Cook was going to make an attempt on the Pole, he redoubled his efforts and over the next few years was able to scrape together the needed funds.

The *Roosevelt*, once again captained by Bartlett, sailed out of New York harbor one more time on July 6, 1908. It stopped at Etah, Greenland, long enough to take on the usual complement of Inuit and dogs. While there, Peary heard that Cook had already headed north in March. In what later became a great source of controversy, he also seems to have confiscated some of Cook's supplies. The ship sailed once again to Cape Sheridan on the coast of Ellesmere Island in early September. This time the supply base was set up at Cape Columbia, 40 miles west of Cape Hecla to help compensate for the eastward drift of the polar ice.

Bartlett led the first advance party out of the base on February 28, 1909. Henson and three other advance teams left the next morning. Peary set out last. In total, there were 24 men, 19 sledges, and 133 dogs on the ice. The advance teams were scheduled to cover 11 miles a day, which they had great difficulty in doing. On the second day out, they were stopped by an open channel that was a quarter of a mile wide. The next morning the break closed enough for the men to get across by traveling from one floating ice floe to the next. They were stopped again on March 5 by an even wider lead about 45 miles north of Cape Columbia. Peary was forced to wait six days for it to close up.

Meanwhile, the advance teams pushed on to establish the supply camps. They began to head back to the base camp in the middle of March. On March 31, Peary, Henson, Bartlett and some of the Inuit were at the farthest advance base, 133 miles from the Pole. That night Peary told Bartlett that he was sending him back with some of the Inuit. He would continue on with Henson. Bartlett was furious: he thought he had a prior arrangement with Peary to go with him all the way. Peary's decision is highly controversial: Did he send Bartlett back because he did not want him around to verify his positions? Was he unwilling to share credit with another white man? Was it because Henson really was the better dogteam driver? These and other reasons have been suggested. In any case, Bartlett turned back on April 1, and on the morning of April 2, 1909 Peary left for the final assault accompanied by Henson, Egingwah, Seeglo, Ootah, and Ooqueah.

Peary and his companions had five sledges and 40 dogs. They traveled the remaining distance in the amazing time of five days, averaging 29 miles a day, three times faster than any speed attained thus far. Peary wrote that this was because the ice was unusually smooth and easily traveled. Later explorers have not found this to be the case. On the morning (evening according to Henson) of April 6, 1909, Peary announced to his companions that they had reached the North Pole. The party stayed at the Pole for 30 hours. Peary took a picture of Henson and the Inuit standing in front of a large mound of ice with an American flag planted triumphantly on top. Since he was the only photographer, there is no picture of Peary at the Pole.

Leaving the Pole at 4 p.m. on April 7, the six men had an amazingly easy return. They covered the distance back to the base camp in three forced marches of about 45 miles per march, about 48 hours of sledging at an average speed of about 2.8 miles per hour. This is a record no other Arctic or Antarctic traveler has ever come close to reaching. Peary reached Cape Columbia on April 23, only five days after Bartlett. Wasting no time, they returned to the *Roosevelt* two days later. The ship was not able to break out of the ice and steam south until July 17. It reached the first telegraph station on the coast of Labrador on September 6, 1909 to let the world know that the Pole had been reached.

But Peary's triumph was marred. Five days earlier, Cook had announced that he had reached the Pole in April, days before Peary. Peary immediately challenged Cook, and a furious war of words erupted between the two of them and their supporters. Peary's claim was accepted by the National Geographic Society, the Explorers' Club, and the Royal Geographical Society. In 1911 the Naval Affairs Committee of the U.S. House of Representatives also endorsed him and retired him with the honorary rank of Rear Admiral. The Committee's findings were challenged by a Congressman in 1917, but his objections were never pursued.

This dispute has never fully died out, although most people have not believed Cook's claim. In recent years there were two major efforts to discredit Peary's claim to be the first to reach the Pole. In September 1988 the British explorer **Wally Herbert** examined Peary's records and decided that wind-driven ice had pushed him to the west, and that despite Peary's own beliefs, he was not actually at the Pole. In 1989 a Baltimore astronomer made headlines by claiming that Peary had falsified his evidence on purpose and knew that he was not at the Pole. The National Geographic Society then commissioned a study in 1990 that used photographic and other evidence to show that, within the limits of his instruments, Peary actually was at the North Pole.

Following his return, Peary spent most of the following years in publishing his records and in defending his claims. He died of leukemia in Washington, D.C., on February 20, 1920.

Where to learn more

Peary's own books about his polar journeys are: *Northward Over the "Great Ice"* (New York: Frederick A. Stokes, 1898); *Nearest the Pole: A Narrative of the Polar Expedition of the Peary Arctic Club* (New York: Doubleday, 1907); *The North Pole: Its Discovery Under the Auspices of the Peary Arctic Club* (New York: Frederick A. Stokes, 1910); *Secrets of Polar Travel* (New York: Century, 1917).

Peary's wife and daughter both wrote books about their own Arctic experiences: Josephine Peary, *My Arctic Journal* (New York: Contemporary Publishing, 1893) and Marie Ahnighito Peary, *Snow Baby* (London: Routledge, 1935).

In addition to the works listed under the entries for Matthew Henson, Bob Bartlett, and Frederick Cook, others among Peary's companions wrote eyewitness accounts: Eivind Astrup, *With Peary Near the Pole* (London: Pearson, 1898) and *At the Pole with Peary and Cook* (Portland, Maine: Nelson, 1909); George Borup, *A Tenderfoot with Peary* (New York: Frederick A. Stokes Co., 1911); and Donald B. Macmillan, *How Peary Reached the North Pole* (Boston: Hale, Cushman & Flint, 1933).

Peary's obsessive personality practically cries out for psychological interpretation, and there have been no lack of people willing to try. The two best biographies are John Weems, *Peary, the Explorer and the Man* (Boston: Houghton, Mifflin Co., 1967; also available in paperback) and Wally Herbert, *The Noose of Laurels: Robert E. Peary and the Race to the North Pole* (New York: Atheneum, 1989; paperback, New York: Anchor Books, 1989). There is also a good portrait and summation of his career in Pierre Berton, *The Arctic Grail: The Quest for the North West Passage and the North Pole, 1818-1909* (New York: Viking, 1988; paperback, New York: Penguin, 1989). All three of these books have extensive bibliographies that will lead the reader to other sources.

The question of whether Peary and Cook actually achieved the North Pole has spawned an entire sub-branch of literature. Two good books about this question are William R. Hunt, *To Stand at the Pole* (New York: Stein and Day, 1981) and Theon Wright, *The Big Nail: The Story of the Cook-Peary Feud* (New York: John Day & Co., 1970). (The "Big Nail" refers to an Inuit visualization of the Pole as a physical entity with a big iron nail sticking out of the globe.)

The National Geographic Society was always one of Peary's biggest supporters and fans, and its magazine contains numerous articles about him. The recent ones weighing the evidence as to whether he actually reached the Pole or not are: Wally Herbert, "Did Peary Reach the Pole?" *National Geographic*, September 1988, pp. 387-413, and Thomas D. Davies, "New Evidence Places Peary at the Pole," *National Geographic*, January 1990, pp. 44-61. There is also an article on Peary's Inuit descendants in the centennial anniversary edition of the magazine: "Descendants of the Expeditions," September 1988, pp. 414-421.

One of the tragic sidelights of Peary's ruthlessness is told in Kenn Harper, *Give Me My Father's Body: The Life of Minik the New York Eskimo* (Frobisher Bay, Canada: Blacklead Books, 1986).

Annie Smith Peck

(1850 - 1935)

Annie Smith Peck was an American traveler and mountain climber who became the first to climb Mt. Huascarán in Peru and set a record for highest altitude in the Americas.

Annie Smith Peck was born in Providence, Rhode Island on October 19, 1850. She came from a prominent New England family, and her father was a well-to-do lawyer. She became a teacher and then attended the University of Michigan. In 1885 she became the first woman to be admitted to the American School of Classical Studies in Athens.

Following her studies in Europe, Peck tried to earn her living by giving lectures on Greek archeology. This turned out to be not very remunerative and she decided to switch to giving lectures on her hobby—mountain-climbing. In 1895 she had become the third woman to climb the Matterhorn. She followed this up with climbs in other mountains in the Alps, Mt. Shasta in California, and Mt. Orizaba, at 18,700 feet the highest mountain in Mexico.

Annie Smith Peck. The Granger Collection, New York.

She then resolved to climb a mountain that had never been scaled and one that would be higher than any man had climbed.

For this feat Peck chose Mt. Illampu (21,276 feet), north of La Paz in Bolivia. At that time it was thought to be the highest mountain in South America. She traveled to La Paz in July 1903. She had hired two professional guides and had arranged for an American professor of geology to accompany her. The guides proved unreliable, and the professor was uninterested in the climb and got sick along the way. They were only able to reach 15,350 feet before turning back. She then went on to Peru and climbed El Misti at 19,199 feet.

On her return to New York, Peck was depressed by her failure but was determined to try again. She was able to get financial support for another expedition and left again on June 21, 1904. This time she took with her a suit made out of animal skins that *Robert Peary* brought back from the Arctic and that was donated to her by the American Museum of Natural History. This time she took as her male companion an Austrian who had volunteered to go with her. Peck always thought that she needed to be accompanied by a man, although they invariably turned out to be unsuited for the task. This time she reached 18,000 feet before the pleas of the Austrian and her local guides forced her to turn back.

Not one to give up, Peck then traveled to Mt. Huascarán in the Andes north of Lima in Peru. She had heard that Huascarán might be even taller than Illampu. (At 22,205 feet it is actually the second tallest mountain in South America, only 440 feet lower than Mt. Aconcagua.) She traveled to the town of Yungay at the foot of the mountain. This time she took with her a young American miner she met in Yungay as well some young men from the town. She and the miner quarreled about the best way to make the climb, and they ended up going two separate routes. Peck was able to make it to a small ledge at 19,000 feet that overlooked the glacier that divided the mountain into two peaks. She descended just in time to miss being buried by an avalanche. After dismissing the miner, she tried climbing up another face of the mountain with local guides but was forced to turn back.

Peck returned to New York broke and was only able to try again on the basis of a $600 advance she was given by a magazine to write her story. She went back to Peru in 1906 and tried twice more to conquer Huascarán with a local companion she called E-, who turned out to be more useless than her previous partners. She went back to New York to find out that the magazine loved her stories and was willing to help sponsor another attempt.

Peck went back to Yungay in 1908 and there met up with two Swiss guides, Rudolf and Gabriel, that she had hired for the trip. They did make it to the top of Huascarán but only with great difficulty. They lost much of their equipment including the Peary snowsuit and frequently were in danger of sliding down the mountain. At the last minute, Rudolf ran ahead of Peck and reached the peak before her; however, along the way he lost his mittens and later had to have part of one hand, a finger on the hand, and half of one foot amputated.

Peck, at the age of 58, had finally conquered Huascarán. Once she had reached the top she tried to determine its height, but that was impossible under the prevailing conditions. There were estimates that it reached 24,000 feet. If so, then Peck had set a world's record. However, her great rival, *Fanny Bullock Workman*, refused to concede that Peck had beaten her—Workman had climbed to 23,300 feet in the Himalayas. Workman went so far as to hire a team of American engineers to travel to Peru and measure Huascarán. They found that they peak that Peck had climbed, the lower of the two, was "only" 21,812 feet. She had set a record for the highest climb in the western hemisphere but not in the world. It was a record that was to last for 26 years. She was given a medal by the Peruvian government, and the peak she had climbed was named Cumbre Aña Peck.

Peck returned to the United States and wrote about her experiences in a book, *A Search for the Apex of America*, published in 1911. She went on to climb Mt. Coropuna in Peru (21,079 feet) and put a banner that said "Votes for Women" on the peak. She then continued to travel extensively in South America and wrote a guidebook and a statistical handbook of the continent. From 1929 to 1930 she made a tour of the whole continent using all the commercial airlines that were then in operation and wrote a book about the trip.

In January 1935 she started out on a trip around the world but only got as far as Athens. There, in February, she became tired while climbing the Acropolis (she was 84 years old) and returned to New York, where she died on July 18, 1935.

Where to learn more

This account is largely taken from *Women into the Unknown* by Marion Tinling (Westport, Connecticut: Greenwood Press, 1989). Another good source is *Women of the Four Winds* by Elizabeth Fagg Olds (Boston: Houghton Mifflin, 1985).

Peck's own book about her mountain climbing experiences is *A Search for the Apex of America: High Mountain Climbing in Peru and Bolivia* (New York: Dodd, Mead, 1911). The story of her airplane trip is told in *Flying over South America: Twenty Thousand Miles by Air* (Boston: Houghton Mifflin, 1932).

Pethahiah of Regensburg

(late 12th century)

Pethahiah of Regensburg was a Jewish merchant and rabbi from central Europe who made an overland journey through Russia and the Caucasus Mountains to the Middle East.

There were numerous Jewish travelers during the Middle Ages, which is natural enough considering that many Jews worked as itinerant merchants, finding lodging with their co-religionists throughout the Jewish Diaspora. Unfortunately, not many of them left records. Probably the best known of these travelers is **Benjamin of Tudela**, who traveled from Spain to the eastern Mediterranean in the middle of the 12th century. A contemporary of his, Pethahiah of Regensburg, made a trip that was just as remarkable, but we know much less about it. The incomplete records that we do have were heavily edited by the man Pethahiah told his story to—Rabbi Yehuda the Pious of Regensburg.

Regensburg is a city on the Danube River in the German state of Bavaria, which had a large Jewish population during the Middle Ages. Pethahiah was a rabbi and merchant of that city who was living in Prague, in what is now the Czech Republic, before setting out on his voyage. Unlike Rabbi Benjamin of Tudela, who traveled across the Mediterranean to get to the Holy Land, Pethahiah went east and then south to come upon these lands from the "back door." Our best guess is that he made his trip between the years 1180 and 1186.

Pethahiah traveled to Kiev and then through southern Russia in lands that were inhabited by the ancestors of the modern Ukrainians and Russians. In the southern Ukraine he traveled through a country that had once belonged to the Jewish Khazars, and he encountered groups of Karaites, Jews who followed the Old Testament but rejected the teachings of the Talmud.

Pethahiah traversed Georgia and Armenia and the Caucasus Mountains and descended into the Muslim lands south of the mountains. He made his way to Baghdad only about two years after Benjamin of Tudela had been in the same city. He wrote about life in the world's largest Muslim city at that time, of its caliph, and of its important Jewish population. From there he went westward to Damascus and Palestine.

This is of course the most important part of Pethahiah's narrative because he was reporting back to his compatriots in central Europe about the homeland they could never hope to see. His tale is full of miracles of many sorts and much exaggeration. However, reality does intrude, and he truthfully tells that the land of Israel was far from being the vast country of legend. He also reports that the Jewish population of Jerusalem was almost non-existent—he says there was only one Jew living in the city, contradicting Benjamin's estimate of 200.

Pethahiah bribed his way into the Cave of Machpelah, the traditional origin of humankind, even though the Christian rulers forbade this. The fact that Israel was under Christian rulers—it had been conquered by the Crusaders in 1099—meant that Pethahiah was there immediately before the famous Saladin reconquered the country for the Muslims in 1187.

Pethahiah does not record how he returned to Germany from the Holy Land, and we do not know when he related his story to Rabbi Yehuda. The first German version did not appear until 1595 (the original is in Hebrew), and so his knowledge, which could have been of great value to his Christian neighbors at a time when geographical information was quite sparse, had very little impact.

Where to learn more

There are two accessible sources to learn about Pethahiah: C. Raymond Beazley, *The Dawn of Modern Geography*, vol. 2 (London: Henry Frowde, 1901) and Elkan Nathan Adler, ed. *Jewish Travelers: A Treasury of Travelogues from Nine Centuries* (London: George Routledge & Sons, 1930; 2nd edition, New York: Hermon Press, 1966).

Ida Pfeiffer

(1797 - 1858)

Ida Pfeiffer was an Austrian who was one of the first women to travel around the world alone, which she did twice during the 1850s.

Ida Reyer was born into a wealthy Viennese family on October 14, 1797. At the age of 22 she was forced to marry a much older man, Dr. Mark Anton Pfeiffer. Shortly after the marriage, Dr. Pfeiffer became involved in some political difficulties and lost his practice. Ida was forced to work to support her two sons. In 1831 her mother died and left her with a small inheritance. She separated from her husband and returned to Vienna to raise her children alone.

In 1842, after her sons were married and well established, Pfeiffer decided that she wanted to travel—alone. Her first trip of nine months took her to the Holy Land and Jerusalem, and then to Egypt where she crossed the desert from Cairo to Suez. She kept a diary of her trip and published it on her return in 1843. It became quite popular and went through several editions. The proceeds from this book financed a trip to Iceland and Scandinavia in 1845. She then decided she wanted to travel around the world.

She left Europe in 1846 and traveled first to Brazil where she traveled inland from Rio de Janeiro to Petropolis and stayed with the Puri tribe in the tropical forest. From Brazil she went around Cape Horn to Tahiti and then to Hong Kong and Canton in China. In India she traveled inland and went on a tiger hunt. All this time she traveled practically without any money at all and depended upon European strangers taking her in and feeding her.

From India Pfeiffer went to Persia and then up the Tigris River to Baghdad where she joined a caravan to Mosul in what is now Iraq and then on to Tabriz in northern Iran. The British consul in Tabriz was shocked when she showed up at his doorstep having come all that distance totally by herself. She then crossed the Caucasus Mountains into Russia, which she did not care for, and then home to Vienna via Turkey, Greece, and Italy. She arrived home on November 4, 1848 after a voyage that had taken her 35,000 miles by sea and 2,800 miles by land. She wrote a book titled *A Lady's Voyage Round the World*, published in English in 1852.

In 1851 Pfeiffer went to England hoping to find passage to Australia. Unable to pay the fare, she accepted a free offer to travel on a ship to the Dutch East Indies (now Indonesia). She left London on May 24, 1851 and headed to Cape Town in South Africa. There she changed her itinerary and went to Singapore and then decided to visit the land of the "White Rajah" in Sarawak on the north coast of the island of Borneo. Once in Borneo she traveled inland to the land of the Dyak tribe and then floated down the Kapuas River to end up in the Dutch colonial port of Pontianak. From there she went to Sumatra and visited the Batak tribe, which had had little contact with Europeans. Once when threatened by a group of tribesmen that she thought were cannibals, she told them that she was old and tough and would not make good eating. This made them laugh so hard that they soon became friends.

From Sumatra Pfeiffer traveled to remote eastern Indonesia where she visited the Alfora tribe on the island of Ceram. On July 6, 1852 she left the East Indies for San Francisco in California and visited some of the Native American tribes there, who were by then very much Europeanized. She then traveled south around South America stopping at Panama, Ecuador and Peru and the east coast of the United States. She returned to London on June 14, 1855. The book about her travels was called, inevitably, *A Lady's Second Journey Round the World*.

Pfeiffer set out again with the intention of making a third trip around the world. She stopped at the island of Madagascar and traveled to the capital of Antanarivo. She was one of only seven Europeans on the island at the time. While she was there, there was a plot to overthrow the Queen and all of the Europeans were looked upon as spies and ordered to leave the country. It took nearly 50 days to travel from the capital to the coast as prisoners of the Malagasy. During the trip Pfeiffer became quite ill and almost died. When she finally got out of Madagascar she went to the nearby British island of Mauritius to recuperate. Well enough to travel home, she continued to suffer from the liver disease that she had contracted in Madagascar. Back in Vienna, she died during the night of October 27-28, 1858.

Where to learn more

Pfeiffer's own works are: *Visit to the Holy Land, Egypt, and Italy* (London: Ingram, Cooke, 1852); *Journey to Iceland: And Travels in Sweden and Norway* (London: Richard Bentley, 1852); *A Lady's Voyage Round the World* (London: Longman, Brown, Green and Longmans, 1852); *A Lady's Second Journey Round the World: From London to the Cape of Good Hope, Borneo, Java, Sumatra, Celebes, Ceram, the Moluccas, etc., California, Panama, Peru, Ecuador, and the United States*, 2 vols. (London: Longman, Brown, Green and Longmans, 1855). Most of these exist in various other editions.

The main biographical information on for Pfeiffer comes from a book that was edited by her son after her death: *The Last Travels of Ida Pfeiffer: Inclusive of a Visit to Madagascar, with an Autobiographical Memoir of the Author* (London: Routledge, Warne, and Routledge, 1861; New York: Harper & Brothers, 1861).

Harry St. John Philby

(1885 - 1960)

Harry St. John Philby was an Englishman who spent many years exploring in Arabia and was the second Westerner to cross the great desert of the Rub 'al Khali.

Harry St. John Philby was born in Sri Lanka of parents who had been sent there as part of the British colonial administration. Philby's family was not rich, and he was able to attend private schools and Cambridge University only through scholarships. While at the university, Philby studied Asian languages and took the examination to enter the Indian civil service. He was posted to India in 1908 and stayed there until 1915.

In November 1915 Philby was sent to Iraq to be a political officer with the Mesopotamian Expeditionary Force that was engaged in conquering the country from the Turks as part of the Middle Eastern operations of World War I. In 1917 he was sent to Riyadh, the city in central Arabia that was the headquarters of Ibn-Saud who was leading the Arab revolt against the Turks. Once he got to Riyadh, Philby learned that the British representative he had expected to meet there was being held by King Hussein of the Hejaz. Philby traveled on to the Red Sea port of Jeddah, where he hoped to secure the man's release and to cause a reconciliation between Ibn-Saud and Hussein. He was unsuccessful in his second goal, but by making the trip across the peninsula in 44 days, Philby had become the second European to cross Arabia from west to east, the first being an English soldier in 1819. He was awarded a medal for this accomplishment by the Royal Geographical Society.

In 1918 Philby went back to Riyadh and from there traveled south from the port of Jeddah into the region of Arabia known as the Nejd. He got as far south as the oasis of Sulaiyil on the edge of the vast desert known as the Rub' al Khali ("the Empty Quarter"). Looking out over its vast expanses, he developed the desire to cross the desert, something no Westerner had ever done. During his time in Arabia, Philby became associated with T.E. Lawrence ("Lawrence of Arabia") in supporting Arab independence. He also became an admirer of Ibn-Saud.

Following the war, Philby served for three years in Iraq and Jordan. During this ,time he made a trip from Amman, Jordan to the Euphrates and then went south in 1922 to the oasis of Jauf in far northern Arabia and back over the desert to the Iraqi city of Karbala. Philby returned to Arabia and worked for various European companies trying to find markets (and oil) in Arabia. In 1930 he converted to Islam. As a result, Ibn Saud gave him permission to make his wished-for trip across the Rub' al Khali. He was forced to cancel his plans for crossing during the winter of 1930-1931, and did not accomplish the trip in 1932. As a result, he was narrowly beaten in being the first European to cross the great desert by Bertram Thomas. Philby, however, crossed the much more difficult western part of the desert.

Philby began his crossing on January 7, 1932 from the wells of Dulaiqiya, near the town of al-Hofuf west of the peninsula of Qatar. With his party of 19 Bedouins and 32 camels, he crossed the al-Jafurah desert to the oasis of Jabrin in very cold weather. At al-Hadida, in the middle of the Rub' al Khali, he found five large meteorite craters that were supposed to be the site of the legendary city of Wabar. The Arabs believed that Wabar had been destroyed by God because of the wickedness of its inhabitants. Philby went as far south as Shanna, which he reached on February 22. This had been Thomas's starting point. Philby decided to try to duplicate Thomas's achievement. He was forced to cut short his first attempt. He returned to Shanna and rested and then set out with a reduced team on March 5, with only 24 waterskins. Philby went westward across the desert paralleling Thomas's route. He reached the oasis of Sulaiyil on March 11, 1932.

Philby continued exploring and mapping the Arabian Peninsula, and he collected a large amount of biological specimens from all over Arabia. He did this mostly by automobile. He made his last major expedition in 1936 when he traveled throughout the southeastern part of the peninsula from Mecca to the port of Mukalla on the Indian Ocean in what is now Yemen. He also became a close adviser of Ibn-Saud, who was faced with many difficult negotiations with Western companies who were beginning to discover the vast oil deposits of eastern Arabia.

In 1939 Philby returned briefly to England and he ran in a by-election as an anti-war candidate for Parliament. He lost and returned to Arabia. There, he advised King Saud not to become involved in the war. On a short trip to India in 1940, he was arrested by the British government because of his views. He was held in custody for five months and did not return to Arabia until 1945. He became increasingly critical of the way the Saudis were spending the vast wealth flowing to them from the oilfields. Following the death of King Saud in 1953, Philby was exiled to Beirut, where he lived until his death on September 30, 1960. He died before his son, the notorious spy Kim Philby, defected to the Soviet Union in 1963.

Where to learn more

Philby wrote a number of books about Arabia and his own explorations: *The Heart of Arabia*, 2 vols. (London, 1922); *Arabia of the Wahhabis* (London: 1928); *The Empty Quarter: Being a Description of the Great South Desert of Arabia Known as Rub' al-Khali* (London, 1933), which is the history of his greatest expedition; *Sheba's Daughters* (London, 1939); *A Pilgrim in Arabia* (London: 1946); *Arabian Jubilee* (London, 1952), which is the book that got him into trouble with the Saudi government; *Arabian Highlands* (Ithaca, N.Y.: Cornell University Press, 1952), *Sa'udi Arabia* (London: 1955); and *Arabian Oil Ventures* (Washington, D.C.: 1964), which is the story of how Aramco got its vast oil concessions.

There is one full-length biography of Philby: Elizabeth Monroe, *Philby of Arabia* (London: 1973).

Auguste Piccard

(1884 - 1962)

Jacques Piccard

(1922 -   )

Auguste Piccard was a Swiss scientist who conducted experiments in achieving the highest and lowest altitudes reached by man. His underwater research was continued by his son Jacques.

Auguste Piccard was born into a prominent academic family in the Swiss city of Basel. He had a twin brother, Jean, who later became an important chemist. Auguste took up the study of physics and studied at the Zurich Polytechnic School. He became a professor at the Free University of Brussels in 1922. Having read the science-fiction writer Jules Verne as a child, he was inspired to try to carry out some of Verne's predictions. The first of these was to try to reach the highest altitude achieved by man. He achieved this in 1931 when he reached an altitude of more than 50,000 feet in a balloon he had designed and constructed himself. Piccard pioneered the use of a pressurized cabin for human flight, and he was the first person to reach the stratosphere.

Following his exploits in reaching the highest altitudes, Piccard then set himself the goal of reaching the lowest depths. In order to accomplish this he used the same basic idea as his stratospheric balloon to construct a vessel to penetrate the sea. He constructed a free-floating "deep-sea ship" that he named the "bathyscaphe". The pressurized cabin of the bathyscaphe was attached to a float that contained lighter-than-water gasoline while in another compartment there was lead shot to serve as ballast. To descend, gasoline was emptied from the float, and to ascend, the lead shot was released. In 1948 Piccard's first bathyscaphe, the *F.N.R.S. 2* (named after the Belgian scientific foundation that provided the money) descended unmanned to more than 4,500 feet and carried out other experiments with Piccard on board.

There were certain problems with this first bathyscaphe, chiefly that it could not be towed and had to be carried in the hull of a ship. The *F.N.R.S. 2* was damaged in heavy seas, and Piccard set about building a better vessel. He constructed the *F.N.R.S. 3* in June 1953, and it was later acquired by the French Navy. At the request of the citizens of Trieste, Italy, Piccard constructed a similar vessel named the *Trieste*. In 1954 Piccard

and his son Jacques took the *Trieste* to the then-record depth of 10,355 feet in the Mediterranean Sea near Naples, Italy. The *Trieste* was later bought by the U.S. Navy. On January 23, 1960, Jacques Piccard and the American Lt. Donald Walsh piloted the *F.N.R.S. 3* to a record depth of 35,800 feet, where they reported that there were still signs of life.

Jacques Piccard wrote about this experience in the August 1960 edition of the *National Geographic* magazine: "Like a free balloon on a windless day, indifferent to the almost 200,000 tons of water pressing on the cabin from all sides, balanced to within an ounce or so on its wire guide ropes, slowly, surely, in the name of science and humanity, the *Trieste* took possession of the abyss, the last extreme on our earth that remained to be conquered."

Following the success of the bathyscaphe, Auguste and Jacques Piccard then developed the concept of the "mesoscaphe"—a "middle-depth ship" that would operate at depths up to 20,000 feet. If the bathyscaphe could be compared to an underwater balloon, then the mesoscaphe was designed to be an underwater helicopter. In 1969 the Woods Hole Oceanographic Institution in Massachusetts carried out the Gulf Stream Mission using Piccard's mesoscaphe to conduct a series of experiments under the Atlantic Ocean.

During the Mission, Jacques Piccard made a month-long journey from July 14 to August 14, 1969, traveling with the Gulf Stream from West Palm Beach, Florida, to a point 360 miles southeast of Nova Scotia. The six-man crew on the mesoscaphe measured and recorded the physical characteristics of the Gulf Stream and made observations of the rich animal life around them. The Mission also served the experimental needs of the American National Aeronautics and Space Administration (NASA), which wanted to find out how humans would react to confinement in a small space over a fairly long period of time.

Where to learn more

Auguste Piccard wrote about his high-altitude experiences in *Between Earth and Sky*, translated by Claude Apcher (London: Falcon Press, 1950). Jacques Piccard wrote about his underwater explorations in "Man's Deepest Dive," *National Geographic* (August, 1960) and in a book with Robert S. Dietz, *Seven Miles Down: The Story of the Bathyscaph "Trieste"* (New York: G.P.Putnam's Sons, 1950). See also Wilbur Cross, *Challengers of the Deep* (New York: 1965).

Zebulon Pike

(1779 - 1813)

Zebulon Montgomery Pike was an American soldier who led several expedition to the American West and was one of the first Americans to visit New Mexico.

Zebulon Pike was born in what is now part of Trenton, New Jersey on January 5, 1779. His father, who had the same name, was a major in the American Army during the Revolution and continued as a regular officer in the new United States Army. The younger Pike was a cadet in his father's company at an early age and was commissioned a lieutenant in 1799, at the age of 20. He was then assigned to various frontier posts in the West.

In 1805 Pike was instructed by General James Wilkinson to lead an expedition to find the source of the Mississippi River. Wilkinson was the Governor of the newly-acquired Louisiana territory, but was also in the pay of the Spanish government, which still controlled Florida, Texas, New Mexico, and California.

Zebulon Pike.

Pike left St. Louis on August 9, 1805 in a keelboat along with 20 men and enough supplies to last four months. They were forced to build a camp below the Falls of St. Anthony (at what is now St. Paul, Minnesota) by the onset of winter, but in December Pike set out by sledge to try to reach his goal. They reached Leech Lake in northern Minnesota, which Pike took to be the source of the Mississippi. In fact, the farthest reaches of the river are a little bit farther west at Lake Itasca. Pike found several British fur-trading posts in northern Minnesota and informed them that they were trespassing on American territory. He returned to St. Louis on April 30, 1806.

Pike was only in St. Louis for a short time when General Wilkinson sent him out on another mission. He was given instructions to return some members of the powerful Osage tribe who had been taken captive, to try to mediate peace between the Osage and Kansas tribes, and to explore the upper reaches of the Arkansas and Red Rivers. There is also strong evidence that he had secret instructions to investigate a route to the Spanish settlements in New Mexico, centered on Santa Fe. What is less clear is why Wilkinson wanted Pike to travel to the Spanish territory. At the time, the General was involved in a conspiracy with Aaron Burr to separate the West from the rest of the United States. What role Pike was supposed to play is not clear. Even more mysterious, there is reason to believe that Wilkinson betrayed Pike and warned the Spanish authorities that he was traveling into their territory.

Pike left St. Louis on July 15, 1806 with 23 men, including Wilkinson's son and Dr. John Robinson, one of Wilkinson's agents. They followed a route that took them up the Missouri and Osage Rivers in central Missouri through eastern Kansas (where the Osages were returned to their homes) to the Pawnee villages in southern Nebraska. In late September, they turned south towards the Arkansas River, following the trail of a Spanish force that had been sent out to capture them. When they reached the Arkansas, Lieutenant Wilkinson returned to St. Louis with six of the men to report on the results of the expedition thus far.

The rest of the expedition turned west to the Rocky Mountains, which they sighted on November 15, 1806. They reached the site of present-day Pueblo, Colorado about a week later. From there, Pike and three companions set out to try to climb the tall mountain that was later named Pike's Peak. They were unsuccessful, but they did climb Cheyenne Peak, a smaller mountain about 15 miles away. Rejoining the rest of the party, they went up the Arkansas to Royal Gorge (the "Grand Canyon" of the Arkansas). Near the gorge, Pike built a small fort for the men who were too sick to continue. He left the fort on January 14, 1807 with Dr. Robinson and 12 men.

Pike and his men headed through the Sangre de Cristo Mountains in southern Colorado in mid-winter. Six men got gangrene from walking through the snow, two so badly that their feet had to be amputated. They were forced to stop two weeks later and build a small fort on the Rio Conejos, a tributary of the Rio Grande, which ran through the heart of Spanish New Mexico. On February 7, 1807 Dr. Robinson left on his own to travel to Santa Fe, where he claimed to have business. On February 26 a party of Spanish cavalry showed up at the little fort to arrest Pike and his men. Pike insisted that he thought he was on a branch of the Red River, which formed the boundary between the American and Spanish territories. There is general agreement, however, that he knew exactly where he was and was putting on a show for the Spanish authorities.

Pike was taken to Santa Fe and then on to Chihuahua, in what is now northern Mexico, to meet with the Spanish governor. There, he met up with Dr. Robinson and was well treated by the Spanish officers. Although his papers were taken away from him, he carefully memorized his trip so that he could supply important geographical and military information to Wilkinson when he returned to the United States (he also hid some notes in the barrel of his gun). He was escorted out of Spanish territory by way of San Antonio and Nacogdoches in east Texas. He was released on the American side of the border at Natchitoches in Louisiana in early July 1807. By then the Wilkinson-Burr conspiracy had been discovered, and Pike was suspected of collaborating with

them. He protested his innocence to the Secretary of War. His explanations were accepted, and he was promoted to major in 1808.

Following his return, Pike wrote up the results of his expedition in an important book that was published in 1810. In it he said that the Great Plains would never be suitable for settlement by Americans, but he proposed several possible routes through the Southwest to the Pacific Ocean. These views helped shaped the direction of American expansionism in the following years. After the outbreak of the War of 1812 with Great Britain, Pike was promoted to the rank of brigadier general. He was put in charge of the assault on York (now Toronto) in Canada. The attack was a success, but Pike was killed in an explosion on April 27, 1813.

Where to learn more

The official record of Pike's expedition is *An Account of the Expeditions to the Sources of the Mississippi and Through the Western Parts of Louisiana*, 2 vols. (Philadelphia: C. & A. Conrad & Co., 1807; available in Dover paperback). A later edition is Elliot Coués, *The Expeditions of Zebulon Montgomery Pike*, 3 vols. (New York: 1895). The records that were taken from Pike were discovered in the Mexican archives a century later. See Donald Jackson, ed. *The Journals of Zebulon Montgomery Pike*, 2 vols. (Norman: University of Oklahoma Press, 1966).

Two biographies of Pike can be recommended: William Eugene Hollon, *The Lost Pathfinder: Zebulon Montgomery Pike* (Norman: University of Oklahoma Press, 1949) and John Upton Terrell, *Zebulon Pike: The Life and Times of an Adventurer* (New York: Weybright and Telley, 1968).

An excellent source of information on the American West is William H. Goetzmann's *Exploration and Empire: The Explorer and the Scientist in the Winning of the American West* (New York: Alfred A. Knopf, 1966).

Fernão Mendes Pinto

(1509 - 1583)

The first European to visit Japan was Portuguese adventurer Fernão Mendes Pinto, unjustly called the "Prince of Liars" because his book about his travels was so widely disbelieved by his contemporaries.

Fernão Mendes Pinto was born in the Portuguese town of Montemor-o-Velho not far from the ancient university city of Coimbra. At the age of ten or twelve he was taken to Lisbon by an uncle and placed in the household of a rich noblewoman. He stayed there a year and a half until "something happened that placed me in such great jeopardy that I was forced to leave the house at a moment's notice and flee for my life." We do not know what had happened. Mendes Pinto fled to the Alfama section of Lisbon where he caught a ship bound for southern Portugal. Fifteen miles from their destination it was captured by French pirates. Mendes Pinto was eventually put ashore on the coast of Spain and made his way to the Portuguese city of Setubal. He entered the employ of a nobleman there and stayed for a year and a half.

Determined to seek his fortune elsewhere, Mendes Pinto sailed from Portugal on March 11, 1537 bound for India. He sailed around the Cape of Good Hope, stopped in Mozambique, and arrived at the Portuguese fortress of Diu on the northwestern coast of India on September 5, 1537. He then joined an expedition to the Red Sea and delivered a message to the Portuguese soldiers who were fighting on the side of the Christian king of Ethiopia. Leaving Ethiopia, his ship was captured by the Turks and the crew was taken to the port of Mocha in Yemen and sold into slavery. Eventually being bought by a Jewish merchant, Mendes Pinto was taken to the port of Ormuz on the south coast of Persia, where he joined a Portuguese trading ship.

Reaching the Portuguese headquarters of Goa, Mendes Pinto entered the service of the newly appointed captain of Malacca on the coast of Malay. He arrived in Malacca in 1539 and worked for the captain of the fortress there as an emissary to the kingdoms of Sumatra and Malaya. He then went to Patani on the east side of the Malay Peninsula and started a thriving business trading with the Thais in Bangkok. Robbed by pirates, he and his partners got revenge by becoming pirates themselves. He then traded along the coast of Indochina. He was shipwrecked on the coast of China and sold as a slave to work on the Great Wall of China. (Mendes Pinto claimed to have been shipwrecked, captured, and sold into slavery 16 or 17 times.)

Helping Tartar invaders penetrate into China, Mendes Pinto was freed and returned overland to Indochina. Hoping to travel back to India, Mendes Pinto took passage on a Chinese pirate junk that was driven off course during a storm and ended up on the Japanese island of Tanegashima, south of Kyushu in 1542 or 1543, the first European to reach that country. He then returned to Canton in south China and told Portuguese merchants there of the wealth to be gained by trading with Japan. He accompanied a group of them, and they were shipwrecked in the Ryukyu Islands where they were saved by the pleas of the women of the island. He then went back to Malacca.

From Malacca he was sent on a mission to the Burmese who had just captured the Kingdom of Pegu. He was taken prisoner by the Burmese and traveled as far as Luang Prabang in what is now Laos. He escaped and returned to Goa. He then undertook a trading mission to Java where he got involved in a local war and left just in the nick of time. Trying to travel on to China, his ship was attacked by Japanese pirates and was shipwrecked on the coast of Thailand. He and his men built a raft that ended up once again in Java, where they were reduced to cannibalism in order to survive and sold themselves into slavery. Freed again, Mendes Pinto borrowed money to start a trading operation with Thailand. He became involved in Burmese-Thai wars and wrote the first European account of Burmese politics and history.

From Thailand Mendes Pinto made his second trip to Japan where he landed in the port of Kagoshima. On his departure, he brought back a Japanese stowaway whom he handed over to **St. Francis Xavier** in Malacca and thus inspired Xavier's effort to travel to Japan and Christianize the inhabitants. Sometime during these years in Asia, Mendes Pinto had accumulated a large fortune. He was a wealthy merchant when he made his third voyage to Japan in 1551, where Francis Xavier was installed at the court of one of the feudal lords of southern Japan. He gave Xavier the money to build the first Christian church in Japan.

In 1554 Mendes Pinto decided to return with his fortune to Portugal. While waiting in Goa for a ship back to Europe, he underwent a sudden conversion and turned over half of his fortune to the Jesuit missionaries and was accepted by them as a lay brother. He then traveled back to Japan in the company of a group of these missionaries. He was charged by the Portuguese governor in Goa with opening up diplomatic relations between Portugal and Japan, and Mendes Pinto was largely responsible for paying for this mission. At some point following his final departure from Japan in 1557, he voluntarily separated himself from the Jesuits, although he remained on good terms with the Church.

Mendes Pinto returned to Portugal on September 22, 1558. He stayed at court for four years hoping for some reward or recognition for his years of service in the Far East. When this was not forthcoming, he retired to a small estate on the Tagus River opposite Lisbon where he got married and raised a family. Sometime between the years 1569 and 1578 he wrote the book called the *Travels*, which was not published until 1614. It was then translated into most Western languages and became a best-seller throughout Europe. However, it contained so many fantastic stories that it was considered to be a work of fiction. It was only as more information about the exotic lands he visited became available that the book was recognized to be largely (but not totally) factual. Mendes Pinto died on his estate on July 8, 1583, shortly after being awarded a small pension by the Portuguese government.

Where to learn more

Mendes Pinto's *Peregrinação* was first published in 1614. Since then, there have been many versions in many languages. All previous versions in English have now been superseded by a new translation: Rebecca D. Catz, trans. and ed. *The Travels of Mendes Pinto* (Chicago: University of Chicago Press, 1989). Catz includes a long introductory essay that discusses Mendes Pinto's life and the question of the accuracy of his reports. Excerpts from an earlier edition of the book can be found in Charles David Ley, *Portuguese Voyages, 1498-1663* (London: Everyman's Library, 1947; reprinted, 1965).

A previous book, Maurice Collis, *The Grand Peregrination: Life and Adventures of F.M. Pinto* (London: 1949), is also full of exciting tales and makes an interesting contrast to Catz.

Vicente Yáñez Pinzón

(1463? - 1514)

Vicente Yáñez Pinzón was a Spaniard who commanded one of the ships in Columbus's first voyage and then made several voyages to America on his own that included the discovery of Brazil and the Amazon River.

Vicente Yáñez Pinzón was born in the Spanish seaport of Palos. The Pinzón family was one of the three leading shipping families of Palos, a small seaport in southern Spain near the Portuguese border. It was only by enlisting the backing of the Pinzón family that **Christopher Columbus** was able to make his first voyage to America in 1492. As a result of their stake, several members of the family sailed with Columbus. Vicente Yáñez commanded the *Niña*, and his older brother, Martín Alonso, commanded the *Pinta* while another brother, Francisco, was first mate. Martín Alonso deserted Columbus off the north coast of Cuba on November 22, 1492 and spent three weeks searching for gold on his own before rejoining the expedition. Vicente Yáñez, however, stayed loyal to the commander throughout the voyage.

On his return to Spain, Vicente Yáñez was authorized by King Ferdinand and Queen Isabella to make a voyage of his own in 1495, but there is no evidence that this ever took place. A few years later, however, he was able to get the financial support of his family and friends to equip four ships to sail to America. He left Palos in December 1499 and headed to the southwest by way of the Canaries and the Cape Verde Islands, where he took on supplies. Steering south-southwest, on January 20, 1500 he landed at a place that he called Santa Maria de la Consolación at about 8° S latitude on the mainland of South America. This place is usually identified as Cabo São Agostinho near the Brazilian city of Recife. If so, this landing would mean that Pinzón arrived in Brazil three months before **Pedro Alvarez Cabral**, who is usually credited with the discovery of Brazil. Pinzón's claim is disputed by Portuguese and Brazilian historians for nationalistic reasons.

From his landing on the northeastern "hump" of Brazil, Pinzón sailed west and northwest along the coast. As he sailed along the coast, Pinzon noticed that the water had changed color. Dipping a bucket into the sea, he tasted it and found that it was fresh. Thirty leagues from its mouth, the Amazon was strong enough to push fresh water out into the ocean. Because of this, Pinzón named his discovery the Freshwater Sea. He traveled up the giant river for a distance of 20 or 30 leagues and took 36 Native Americans prisoner.

From the Amazon, Pinzón sailed as far up the coast as the Gulf of Paria between Trinidad and Venezuela. He then sailed across the Caribbean to Santo Domingo and the Bahamas, where he lost two ships off Crooked Island. He returned to Palos on September 9, 1500.

Pinzón returned to South America between 1502 and 1504, sailing first to the Gulf of Paria and then eastward and wouthward to a point near Cabo São Roque, the northeastern point of Brazil. He returned to Santo Domingo in July 1504 where he met Columbus who had recently been rescued from Jamaica. Pinzón made two further voyages, both in association with **Juan Diaz de Solís**, but we know very little about either one. Their first joint venture in 1506 took them to parts of the Caribbean coast of Central America and Yucatan that Columbus had explored during the course of his fourth voyage.

The object of the next voyage was to seek a passage around South America. Pinzón and Solís left the port of Sanlúcar de Barrameda on June 29, 1508 and traveled to the Cape Verde Islands. From there, the details of the voyage are vague, but one report said they traveled to Cabo São Agostinho and then followed the coast of South America south past the Rio de la Plata in Argentina as far as the Rio Colorado in Patagonia. If so, they were not too far away from the southern end of South America and the passageway to the Pacific that was actually found in 1520 by **Ferdinand Magellan.**

Where to learn more

The original documents, such as they are, on the voyages of Pinzón can be found in Martín Fernández de Navarret, *Colección de los viajes y descubrimientos*, 5 vols. (Madrid: 1829-1859; reprinted, Madrid: Ediciones Atlas, 1954-1955). Pinzón is also mentioned in the famous contemporary account by the priest Bartolomé de las Casas, which has been published in an abridged edition as *History of the Indies*, translated by Andrée Collard (New York: Harper & Row, 1971).

A good summary of what is known about Pinzón can be found in José L. Hernández-Pinzón y Ganzimotto, *Vicente Yáñez Pinzón: sus viajes y descubrimientos* (Madrid: Ministerio de Marina, 1920) or, more accessibly, in Samuel Eliot Morison, *The European Discovery of America: The Southern Voyages, 1492-1616* (New York: Oxford University Press, 1974).

Much ink has been expended on the question of which European was the first to sight the coast of Brazil. For discussions of this question, Pierre M. Vidal de la Blanche, *La Rivière Vincent Pinzon* (Paris: Félix Alcan, 1902) and Clemente Brandenburger, "O Descobrimento do Brasil por Vincente Yáñez Pinzón," *Revista do Instituto Histórico e Geografico Brasileiro*, vol. 287 (April-June 1970), pp. 439-448.

Francisco Pizarro

(1475? - 1541)

Francisco Pizarro was a Spanish conquistador *who led the first Europeans to Peru and conquered the Inca empire.*

Francisco Pizarro was born sometime around the year 1475 in the town of Trujillo in the Spanish province of Extremadura. He was the illegitimate son of Colonel Gonzalo Pizarro and a peasant woman and had no formal education whatever. He was a soldier of fortune and took part in campaigns in Italy and Navarre. He drifted to Seville, which was the center of Spanish expeditions to the Americas. He sailed to Santo Domingo in 1502. From there, he went with **Alonso de Ojeda** on his expedition to the Gulf of Urabá in Colombia in 1509.

When Ojeda left the struggling colony that he founded on the northern coast of South America to get supplies, he left Pizarro in

Francisco Pizarro.

charge of the garrison. He then went to Panama when **Vasco Núñez de Balboa** moved the settlement there. Pizarro accompanied Balboa on his trip across the Darien Peninsula to the Pacific in 1513, and he is listed in the chronicle of the expedition as being the second European to see the Pacific Ocean. It was Pizarro who later arrested Balboa when he was charged with treason in 1518.

Ever since their arrival in Panama, the Spanish had heard rumors of a rich land to the south, which was called Birú (later corrupted to Peru). Pizarro set up a partnership with two other men, **Diego de Almagro** and Hernando de Luque, to search out these lands. Luque put up the money while the other two led the expedition. They set out in November 1524 and got as far south as Buenaventura on the Pacific coast of Colombia. The men suffered greatly from hunger and the hostility of the Native Americans they met, but they did collect some gold and heard tales of richer kingdoms to the south. They returned to Panama in 1525.

Pizarro and Almagro signed another agreement with Luque on March 10, 1526, in which they agreed to divide any conquered lands between the three of them. They then sailed from Panama with 160 men that it had been difficult to recruit after the hardships of the previous voyage. They sailed once again to the San Juan River that empties into the bay at Buenaventura, and the pilot, Bartolomé Ruiz, was sent ahead to see what he could find. He crossed the equator and came back with stories about a heavily populated land, rich with gold and silver. He was the first European to see Peru.

The entire expedition then sailed southward to the city of Tumbes on the southern shore of the Bay of Guayaquil in Ecuador. This they found to be a large and beautiful seaport, and the inhabitants came out to greet them in boats made from balsa wood. They were brought a wide variety of exotic foods and saw llamas for the first time. Pizarro greeted an Inca nobleman on his ship and sent two of his men ashore. These two Spaniards proceeded 200 miles south where they heard about a great city in the interior that was the capital of a rich and powerful king. They then returned to Panama.

Unable to obtain backing for a voyage of conquest, Pizarro returned to Spain in 1529. He was appointed governor and captain general of a new province stretching 200 leagues south of Panama. He returned to Panama accompanied by his four half-brothers, Almagro, 180 men and 27 horses. They set out from Panama in early January 1531 to conquer Peru.

Pizarro and his men traveled once again to Tumbes, which they found destroyed. He learned about a civil war among the Incas that had resulted in the capture of the legitimate heir, Huascar, by Atahualpa. Atahualpa was camped at the city of Cajamarca, much closer to Tumbes than the distant Inca capital of Cuzco.

Before leaving Tumbes, Pizarro received some reinforcements, and he established a base and supply camp at San Miguel on the Chira River. Five months after landing in Tumbes he set off from San Miguel on September 24, 1532. They had to travel through the cold and mountainous country of the Andes but reached Cajamarca on November 15, 1532. The following day Atahualpa visited Pizarro with a large retinue. While Atahualpa was distracted by a Spanish priest, Pizarro gave a signal for his men to massacre the Inca guards. He then took Atahualpa prisoner.

In order to obtain his release, Atahualpa offered to fill a room 17 feet by 22 feet with gold to a height of 9 feet and to fill two smaller rooms with silver. Pizarro eagerly agreed. When the task was completed, however, Pizarro had Atahualpa put on "trial" and then executed.

By this time, Almagro had arrived in Cajamarca with reinforcements, and the Spanish set off for Cuzco. Along the way they met Manco, a brother of Huascar, and made him the puppet ruler of Peru and had him enthroned in Cuzco in November 1533 so that it was not necessary to conquer the city. By this time the Spaniards had started to quarrel among themselves. **Pedro de Alvarado** landed in Ecuador in order to conquer it, but was persuaded to leave by Pizarro. Almagro was given the lands south of Peru to conquer but returned in 1537 to put down an Inca revolt. He then tried to make himself governor of the city, but was defeated by troops led by Pizarro's brother Hernando in the Battle of Las Salinas in April 1538. Almagro was then executed.

In the meantime, Pizarro was occupying himself with the building of a new capital, Lima, on the coast of Peru, which he founded in January 1535. The antagonisms of the civil war did not die down however. The Almagro faction complained to the King of Spain, and when Hernando Pizarro went back to Madrid to report on his conduct in 1539, he was imprisoned (where he stayed until 1561). The Almagrists formed a faction under the leadership of Francisco Almagro, the son of Diego and a Native American woman from Panama. Pizarro seems to have been unaware of their plots, and on June 26, 1541 he was attacked in his own palace in Lima by 20 Almagro supporters and killed.

Where to learn more

The primary documentary source on the conquest of Peru was written by Pizarro's secretary, Francisco Jérez de Salamanca, *Verdadera relación de la conquista del Perú y provincia de Cuzco* (Seville: 1536). This was translated and edited by Clements R. Markham as *Reports on the Discovery of Peru* (London: Hakluyt Society, 1872). Agustín de Zárate, a Spanish royal official and historian interviewed the participants in the conquest and wrote a contemporaneous account: *Historia del descubrimiento y conquista del Perú* (many editions, the latest is Madrid: Ediciones Atlas, 1946). There is an abridged English translation: *The Discovery and Conquest of Peru*, edited and translated by J.M. Cohen (Baltimore: Penguin, 1968). Pizarro's younger cousin Pedro accompanied him to Peru and wrote his eyewitness account: *Relación del descubrimiento y conquista de los Reinos del Perú* (many editions, the latest is Madrid: Ediciones Atlas, 1964). This was translated by Philip A. Means and published in a limited edition: *Relation of the Discovery and Conquest of the Kingdom of Peru*, 2 vols. (New York: Cortes Society, 1921). One of Pizarro's soldiers also published an account of the expedition: Pedro de Cieza de León, *La crónica del Perú* (latest edition, Madrid: Ediciones Atlas, 1946). This was edited and translated by Clements R. Markham as *The Travels of Pedro Cieza de Leon, A.D. 1532-50* (London: Hakluyt Society, 1864) and by Harriet de Onís as *The Incas of Pedro de Cieza de Leon* (Norman: University of Oklahoma Press, 1959).

The famous American historian William H. Prescott wrote the "classic" account of the Pizarro's conquests: *The Conquest of Peru*, 2 vols. (New York: Harper & Brothers, 1847; many subsequent editions). More recent studies are Frederick A. Kirkpatrick, *The Spanish Conquistadores* (London: Adam & Charles Black, 1934; reprinted, Cleveland: 1962); Jean Descola, *The Conquistadors*, translated by Malcolm Barnes (London: Allen & Unwin, 1954); and James Lockhart, *The Men of Cajamarca* (Austin: University of Texas Press, 1972).

A truly excellent work that tries to present the perspective of the Native Americans as well as of the Spaniards is John Hemming, *The Conquest of the Incas* (New York: Harcourt, Brace, Jovanovich, 1970).

Marco Polo

(1254? - 1324)

Marco Polo was an Italian who traveled overland to the court of Kublai Khan in the 14th century and spent a total of 24 years traveling in Asia.

Marco Polo was born in Venice in about 1254. A few years later, in 1260, his father and uncle, **Nicolò** and **Maffeo Polo**, made a trip all the way to Beijing, which was the capital of Kublai Khan, the Great Khan of the Mongols who had conquered China and most of Asia. The Polo brothers returned to Venice in 1269 and then returned to the East again two years later. While they had been away, Nicolò's wife, Marco's mother, had died. When they set out again, they took Marco, who was then about 15 years old, with them.

The Great Khan had asked the Polo brothers to return with holy oil blessed by the Western Pope. However, at the time the papacy was vacant, and they decided to return without it. At Acre in Palestine, the papal legate, Tebaldo Visconti of Piacenza, gave the Polos letters for the Mongol emperor. They left Acre in November 1271 and reached the city of Ayas on the coast of Cilicia in Little Armenia when they heard that Tebaldo had been elected Pope (Gregory X). On their return to Acre, the new Pope gave them his blessing, and answered Kublai's request for a hundred learned men by sending with them two Dominican friars, who only made it as far as Ayas. But the Polos were able to take Kublai the holy oil.

From Acre, the Polos returned to Ayas and then traveled north to Erzincan, then east by way of Erzurum into Armenia where they saw Mount Ararat, where Noah's ark is supposed to have landed. They then went to Ormuz on the Persian Gulf, where they intended to take a ship for the east. Ormuz was a major port for trade with the east, and Marco describes the bustling scene of merchants from all over Europe and Asia trading goods. However, the ships they saw there looked so flimsy that they decided to make the journey overland instead.

Marco's book describes in detail each region they passed through as well as giving hearsay accounts of places he did not visit. In fact, the book he wrote about his travels is supposed to be a geographical description of the East, and is not strictly speaking an account of his travels, which have been pieced together from his references. One of the few personal stories in the book is of being attacked by bandits on the way to Ormuz and narrowly avoiding capture by running into a walled village nearby.

Marco Polo.

From Ormuz the Polos traveled north through Persia via Kerman to Herat in Afghanistan. In Badakhshan, in what is now Afghanistan, Marco and perhaps other members of the party fell ill. "In those parts I had been ill for about a year, but on visiting the plateau (of Badakhshan) I recovered at once." It is not clear from this reference if Marco's illness delayed the trip for a year and, if so, where it was spent. The whole journey took three and a half years, which is much longer than the time needed for actual travel.

After leaving Badakhshan, the Polos began the ascent into the Pamir Plateau, "climbing so high that it is said that it is the highest place in the world." Marco remarked that because the mountains were so cold it was hard to cook food. The observation he made is correct, but the reason he gave is wrong. The higher the altitude, the lower the atmospheric pressure so that water boils at

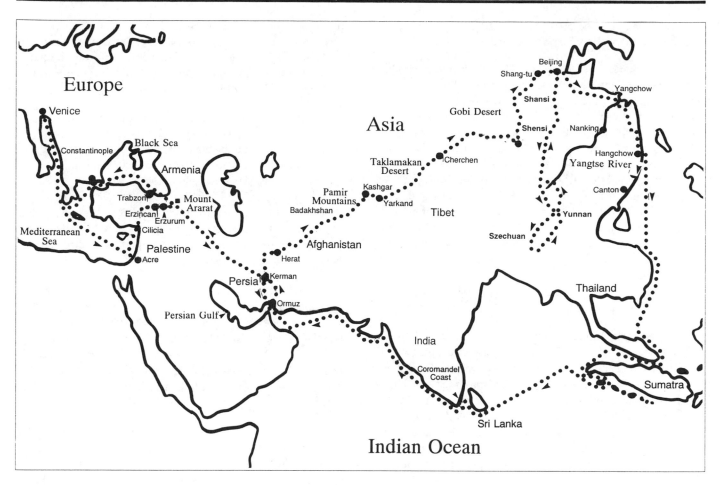

Route of Marco, Nicolò and Maffeo Polo to China and southeast Asia.

a lower temperature, and food takes longer to cook. While in the Pamirs, Marco saw the great mountain sheep that were later given the scientific name of *Ovus poli* in his honor.

After traveling for 40 days over the Pamirs, the Polos descended to the city of Kashgar where there were gardens, and grapes and cotton were cultivated. They skirted the Taklamakan desert, passing through Yarkand, Khotan, and Cherchen to a city Polo called Lop, on the edge of the desert of Lop—the Gobi. Lop was a resting place for travelers, who stayed there for a week to prepare themselves for the desert crossing ahead. It was necessary to carry a month's provisions in order to make the trip across the desert but water was available at waterholes 24 hours' journey apart. Polo says that the desert was inhabited by spirits and that any traveler who lingered behind heard their voices calling out to him.

It took 30 days to cross the desert, a distance of about 300 miles, before arriving at the town of Tun-hwang, which was a center of Buddhism in China. From there, the caravan route headed to the southeast, paralleling the Great Wall, to Lanchow. They then followed the course of the Yellow River into the heartland of China. They were met by emissaries of Kublai Khan who took them on horseback to meet the Great Khan at his summer capital at Shang-tu, or Xanadu, 300 miles north of Beijing. It took them 40 days to make the trip. Curiously enough, Marco does not mention the Great Wall, which he must have seen on this trip.

The Polos reached the court of the Great Khan in May 1275. The Khan was pleased to see the Polos, and he was particularly happy to get the holy oil, which he seems to have assumed had magical qualities. He became particularly fond of Marco Polo, who was to serve him in several capacities in the following years. Likewise, Marco was a great admirer of Kublai, writing that he "is the greatest Lord that is now in the world or ever has been." In his book, Marco describes the Khan and gives a picture of life in his court, including a description of the palace at Shang-tu.

Shang-tu was the site of the Mongol capital during the summer months until the end of August each year. The Polos went with the Khan when he traveled back to Beijing at the end of the season. Marco was even more impressed with the imperial capital, with its famous Forbidden City and its wide avenues. Each of Kublai's four wives maintained a separate court, and their retinues were made up of 40,000 attendants. Marco describes a magnificent banquet at which there were 6,000 guests. "I will say nothing of the dishes, because you can readily imagine that there were a great many of every possible kind."

After their arrival in Beijing, the Polo brothers entered into various trading ventures (at which they made a lot of money), and Marco became an official of Kublai's government. At the time, the government was in the hands of a corrupt official, who was killed in a conspiracy. At the inquest, Marco testified about the official's misdeeds, and this gained him the trust of the Khan. As a result of this confidence, he was sent on a trip to the province of Yunnan in southwestern China. He traveled there by way of Sian, which had been the capital of China during the T'ang dynasty (618-907 A.D.). He then crossed through the provinces of Shensi and Szechuan before reaching the capital of Yunnan at Kunming. Along the way, he passed near the borders of Tibet, and was the first European to write about that remote country. He also wrote about Burma, but it is not clear whether he actually visited that country or not. If he did, it was probably not on this trip but at some later date.

For three years, Marco Polo served as the governor of the city of Yangchow not far from the former capital of Nanking on the Yang-tse River. In his official capacity he traveled to Hangchow, a port south of modern Shanghai that had been the capital of the Southern Sung dynasty from 1135 until its capture by the Mongols under Kublai in 1270. According to Polo, it was "the finest and most splendid city in the world." Modern scholars consider his evaluation to be accurate, and it probably had a population of about one and a half million people at the time he visited it.

During the period that Polo was employed by Kublai, he traveled to India, probably in 1284-1285. He sailed from the port of Zaiton (also visited by **Abu Abdullah Ibn Battuta**) on the Fukien coast of China. It is not clear today which of the Fukien ports was the Zaiton of Polo's time. Along the way he visited the Kingdom of Champa in what is now Vietnam, Thailand, Malaya, and Sumatra. From Sumatra he sailed to the Andaman Islands in the Bay of Bengal, which were untouched by either the Hindu or Buddhist civilizations coming out of India. From there he went to Sri Lanka. It is possible that he was the head of the mission that Kublai sent out at about this time to ask for a major relic of the Buddhist religion—the tooth of Buddha. The Sri Lankans were willing to sell that and other alleged relics at an enormous price, which the Mongol mission was willing to pay.

From Sri Lanka Polo went to the east, or Coromandel, coast of India. There he reported on the practices of the Hindus. He wrote about the *yogi* who "fast all the year round and never drink anything but water" and who were so strict in their practices that they slept naked on the ground, with no covering at all. In his description of the world, Polo also wrote about the east coast of Africa, but it is obvious that he did not travel there.

Polo probably returned to Beijing in 1287. As the years passed, the Polos had became homesick and wanted to return to Europe. Nicolò and Maffeo were by this time elderly men and must have felt that if they delayed their return too long, they might not live to see their native city. But Kublai Khan was reluctant to let his European courtiers go. "He was so fond of them," wrote Marco, "and so much enjoyed their company that nothing would induce him to give them leave."

In 1289, however, an embassy arrived from Kublai's great nephew, the Il-Khan, who ruled over Persia. He requested that a princess be sent out to be his bride. Kublai agreed to the request, and the Polos were able to lobby successfully for the honor of escorting the Princess Kokachin to her new home. They set sail from Zaiton in January 1292. The voyage, involving a fleet of 14 ships, was a two-year ordeal during which it was reported all but 18 of the 600 passengers and crew died. When they finally reached Ormuz, they learned that Arghun had died, but the princess ended up marrying his son.

In Ormuz the Polos also learned that Kublai Khan had died since they left China. They still had, however, his safe conduct, as well as messages for the Pope and the Christian kings of Europe, and the travelers were able to travel through the interior safely. They rode north to Trabzon on the Black Sea coast of Asia Minor and from there to Constantinople and then back home to Venice. They reached their native city in 1295, after an absence of 24 years.

Marco Polo did not sit down on his return to write about all of his marvelous adventures. He took up the family occupation of merchant. In 1298 he was on board a ship that was captured by ships of Venice's great rival port of Genoa. He was captured and put into prison in Genoa. There he met a writer from the Italian city of Pisa named Rustichello. In jail, Polo recounted his stories to Rustichello, who wrote them down in the *Book of Ser Marco Polo*. The book was an immediate popular success, but the readers of the day looked upon it as a book of marvels or legends. Modern scholars agree that Polo was quite accurate in reporting what he saw. He only goes astray when he reports on events and places he only heard about rather than seeing with his own eyes.

Polo eventually got out of the Genoese prison and returned to Venice. He married and had three daughters and worked as a merchant, although he did not leave a particularly big estate behind when he died at the age of 70.

Where to learn more

It has been very difficult to sort out the various manuscript sources of Marco Polo's book (it was written before Europeans started using printing.) An early, scholarly edition in English is: Sir Henry Yule, translator and editor, *The Book of Ser Marco Polo, the Venetian, Concerning the Kingdoms and Marvels of the East*, 2 vols. (London: John Murray, 1902; 2nd edition edited by Henri Cordier, London: John Murray, 1920; reprinted, London: John Murray, 1975).

What is now considered the standard English-language version appeared somewhat later: A.C. Moule and Paul Pelliot, eds. *Marco Polo: The Description of the World*, 2 vols. (London: George Routledge & Sons, 1938; reprinted, New York: AMS, 1976).

There are other more popular versions: N.M. Penzer, ed. *The Most Noble and Famous Travels of Marco Polo* (London: Argonaut Press, 1929); A. Ricci, trans. *The Travels of Marco Polo* (London: 1931); R.E. Latham, ed. & trans. *The Travels of Marco Polo* (London: Penguin, 1958).

For understanding the context and meaning of Polo's observations, a really excellent work is Leonardo Olschki, *Marco Polo's Asia: An Introduction to His "Description of the World" Called "Il Milione"*, translated by J.A. Scott (Berkeley: University of California Press, 1970).

Other good books about Polo are Maurice Collis, *Marco Polo* (London: 1950), which is a concise introduction and served as the major source for this account; G.F. Hudson, *Marco Polo and the Discovery of China* (London: Hodder & Stoughton, 1952); Paul Pelliot, *Notes on Marco Polo*, 2 vols. (Paris: Imprimerie Nationale, 1959; reprinted, Paris: Adrien-Maisonneuve, 1963); Henry H. Hart, *Marco Polo, Venetian Adventurer* (reprinted, Norman: University of Oklahoma Press, 1967).

Polo's adventures lend themselves to illustration and there are several good picture books that include modern-day photos of the sights that Polo saw: C.A. Burland, *The Travels of Marco Polo* (New York: McGraw-Hill, 1970); Richard Humble, *Marco Polo* (New York: G.P. Putnam's Sons, 1975); and R.P. Lister, *Marco Polo's Travels in Xanadu with Kublai Khan* (London: Gordon & Cremonesi, 1976).

Nicolò Polo

(? - 1300?)

Maffeo Polo

(? - 1310?)

The brothers Nicolò and Maffeo Polo were Venetian merchants who traveled to the court of the Great Khan in China and then returned as his envoy to Europe. They later returned to Kublai's court with Nicolò's son Marco.

Nicolò and Maffeo Polo were the middle and youngest sons of Andrea Polo, a nobleman of the San Felice quarter of Venice. (The third son, Marco, gave his name to Nicolò's oldest son, the famous explorer **Marco Polo**.) In the year 1253 they set out on a trading voyage to Constantinople, the Greek capital of the Eastern Roman Empire. Nicolò's wife was pregnant at the time and gave birth the following year to Marco. The Polo brothers stayed in Constantinople for six years.

In the year 1260 the two Venetian merchants decided to move their operations to the Crimean port of Sudak, where there was already a Venetian colony and where the Polo family seems to have had trading interests. There they specialized in trading in

The brothers Nicolò and Maffeo Polo leave Venice with Nicolò's son Marco. The Granger Collection, New York.

precious stones. In order to expand their trade with the Mongol Empire they traveled to Sarai, the headquarters of the Mongol leader Barka Khan on the Volga River, and to Bolgara, another town farther north on the Volga. There they presented jewels to Barka Khan and, according to Marco Polo's later narrative (which is indeed, our source for all the information about his father and uncle), received goods in return that were worth more than twice as much as the jewels. In the year 1262, the Polo brothers proposed to return to Venice but just at that time war broke out between Barka and Hulagu Khan, his cousin and the brother of Kublai Khan. By this time, Nicolò and Maffeo spoke the Mongol language quite well, and they decided to travel east through the Mongol lands hoping to find a roundabout way to get back home.

The Polos left Bolgara and went beyond the Volga at Ukek and proceeded across the steppes to the east of the Caspian Sea and then followed the caravan route south of the Aral Sea. They then took seventeen days to cross the Kara Kum Desert and reached the great caravan city of Bukhara, one of the major commercial cities in Asia. Because the routes west were still cut off by war, the Polos were forced to stay three years in Bukhara.

While the Polo brothers were in Bukhara, an envoy from Kublai Khan to Hulagu Khan passed through the city on his way back to Kublai's court at the city of Khanbaligh. The envoy met Nicolò and Maffeo and proposed that they accompany him back to Khanbaligh (present-day Beijing). For lack of any better alternatives, the Polos accepted the invitation. The brothers set out, directing their steps "eastward and northward" with the Khan's envoys.

It took them a year to cross central Asia to reach the court of Kublai, Great Khan of the Mongols. It is not stated in Marco Polo's later narrative where the Venetians met the Khan because his court moved during the year, and it may not have been at Khanbaligh. He may have been there or at the former capital of Karakorum, in what is now Mongolia, or at the summer palace of Shang-tu, north of Beijing. In any case, Kublai Khan received the two Polos very well and was anxious to hear their accounts of life in the West.

Kublai Khan was especially interested in reports about the Christian religion and the head of its western branch, the Pope of Rome. He offered to sent them back to Italy as his representatives to the Pope. They accepted quickly because they understood that as the Great Khan's envoys, carrying a tablet of gold bearing his seal, they would have no trouble in crossing Asia. Kublai gave them a letter to the Pope requesting that he send one hundred Christian scholars to train his court in their knowledge. He also requested some of the oil that burned above the tomb of Christ in Jerusalem.

We know nothing about the route that Nicolò and Maffeo took to get back to Venice. All that Marco relates is that it took them three years because of the many difficulties they encountered. They arrived at Acre on the east coast of the Mediterranean (now in northern Israel) in April 1269. There they learned that Pope Clement IV had died, and no successor had yet been chosen. They conferred with the Papal Legate, Teobaldo of Piacenza, who advised them to return to Venice until a new Pope was elected. This they did, traveling by way of the Venetian colony of Euboea, off the coast of Greece, and then reached Venice. There they found that Nicolò's wife had died during their absence, and his son Marco was 15 years old.

In 1271, the Polos set out once again for the east, this time taking Marco with them. Their story then becomes part of the narrative that Marco told in his famous book. When Marco returned from his period of captivity in Genoa in August 1299, his father, Nicolò, still seems to have been alive, but is mentioned as having died in Marco's brother Maffeo's will of 1300. Marco's uncle Maffeo seems to have died sometime after 1309 and before 1315.

Where to learn more

The books dealing with Marco Polo inevitably discuss the travels of his father and uncle as well. Books that devote specific attention to the Polo brothers include: Leonardo Olschki, *Marco Polo's Precursors* (Baltimore: The Johns Hopkins University Press, 1943; reprinted New York: Octagon Books, 1972), which is probably the best; C. Raymond Beazley, *The Dawn of Modern Geography*, vol. 3 (Oxford: Clarendon Press, 1906); Percy Sykes, *The Quest for Cathay* (London: 1936); Arthur Percival Newton, ed. *Travel and Travellers of the Middle Ages* (New York: Alfred A. Knopf, 1930); Mary Seymour Lucas, *Vast Horizons* (New York: Viking, 1943); and Björn Landström, *The Quest for India* (Garden City, N.Y.: 1964).

Juan Ponce de León

(1474? - 1521)

Juan Ponce de León was a Spanish soldier and explorer who was the first European to visit Florida.

Juan Ponce de León was born in the village of Santervás del Campo in the northern Spanish province of Valladolid. He had served in various campaigns against the Muslims in southern Spain until they were driven out of the Kingdom of Granada in 1492. He sailed with **Christopher Columbus** on his second journey to America in 1493. Ponce de León then remained in Santo Domingo (today's Dominican Republic).

In 1504 Ponce de León took part in a campaign against the Native Americans in the Dominican province of Higüey in the northern part of the island. Following the success of the campaign he was made governor of the province. In 1508 a Native

Juan Ponce de León. The Bettmann Archive.

American from the neighboring island of Borinquen (later named Puerto Rico by the Spanish) arrived in Santo Domingo with a large nugget of gold. The Europeans were always avid for gold, and Ponce de León led an expedition to investigate the island. He did indeed find traces of the precious metal and returned in 1509 with a larger force to conquer the island. Following the conquest, he was named governor of the new Spanish possession.

Ponce de León was so ruthless in suppressing the Native Americans on Puerto Rico that complaints were made back to Spain. He was removed from office in 1511 when Columbus's son Diego was confirmed as Spanish Viceroy in the Caribbean with the right to make all appointments. By the time he left, however, Ponce de León was a rich man.

In order to make up for this loss, Ponce de León was given the right to find and take possession of Bimini. Today, Bimini is the name of one of the Bahama Islands. In the early 16th century it was the vague name for a region north of Santo Domingo and Cuba that myths said contained the fountain of youth. In fact, there is no reason to believe that the search for this fountain of youth was Ponce de León's main motive in heading north. This was added to his story by two later Spanish writers. He was probably much more interested in the tales of wealth of the new land.

In any case, Ponce de León left the port of San Germán in Puerto Rico on March 3, 1513 with three ships, the *Santa Maria*, *Santiago*, and *San Cristóbal*. They sailed to the northwestward and stopped at the island of Grand Turk. On March 14 they stopped at San Salvador, the first place sighted by Columbus in America, and stayed there for a few days. The ships sailed northwestward again until they sighted land on April 2, 1513, Palm Sunday or a week before Easter. Ponce de León named this new land Florida. In Spanish, the word florida means "flowery." This could have been because of the flowers he saw or as a remembrance of Easter—"la pascua florida." The next day he took possession of the new land in the name of the King of Spain. This was probably at the site of the later Spanish fort and town of Saint Augustine, or it may have been farther down the coast at Daytona Beach at an inlet that is now named for the explorer.

On April 8 Ponce de León and his companions headed south but were slowed down by the heavy current. This was the Gulf Stream, whose discovery by Ponce de León opened up a new route for the Spanish to travel to Europe from North America. The Spaniards approached the land at a place where some Native Americans on shore signaled for them to land but who then tried to take their boat. The two sides started fighting and two of the Spaniards were wounded. A little farther to the south at a place called Santa Cruz (probably Jupiter Inlet), Ponce de León seized one of the local inhabitants as a pilot and hostage.

The Spanish ships stopped again at what is now Lake Worth Inlet and sailed past Miami Bay. On May 8 they rounded the southern tip of Florida and sailed past the Florida Keys to the little group of islands known as the Dry Tortugas before turning north. They sailed up the Gulf coast of Florida as far as the area of Sanibel Island. They turned around at that point and headed back to the Dry Tortugas and to the coast of Cuba, where they landed on June 26. Leaving Cuba, the three ships went north as far as Miami and then headed home via the Bahamas. One of the ships was sent off to continue the search for Bimini and found Andros Island.

After this exploring expedition, Ponce de León returned to Puerto Rico where he once again became involved in putting down Native American rebellions. Once this was more or less accomplished, he went back to Spain to report on his expedition to Florida to King Ferdinand. The King named him Captain General on September 27, 1514 and commissioned him to continue the search for Bimini. On his return to the Caribbean, he led an unsuccessful expedition against the Caribs in the islands south of Puerto Rico. On his return, he stayed in Puerto Rico for five years before setting out once again to find Bimini.

Ponce de León left Puerto Rico in February 1521 with two ships and about 200 men. They landed on the west coast of Florida, probably near Charlotte Harbor. When they went ashore, they were met by a large force of Native Americans who shot a volley of arrows at the intruders. Ponce de León was hit by one of them. He was taken aboard the flagship, which immediately set sail for Cuba. He died in Havana in July 1521. He was buried under the main altar of the Dominican church in San Juan, Puerto Rico. The inscription in Spanish reads, "Beneath this stone repose the bones of the valiant Lion (*león* is Spanish for "lion") whose deeds surpassed the greatness of his name."

Where to learn more

The primary sources relating to Ponce de León's expeditions can be found in John Parry, *New Iberian World: A Documentary History of the Discovery and Settlement of Latin America to the Early 17th Century* (New York: Times Books, 1984).

The definitive biography of Ponce de León is in Spanish: Vicente Murga Sanz, *Juan Ponce de León* (2nd edition, San Juan: Editorial Universitaria, Universidad de Puerto Rico, 1971). Two biographies available in English are Edward W. Lawson, *The Discovery of Florida and Its Discoverer Ponce de Leon* (St. Augustine, Florida: E.W. Lawson, 1946) and *The Fountain of Youth and Juan Ponce de Leon* (Brooklyn: T. Guaus Sons, 1963). See also Samuel Eliot Morison's magisterial *The European Discovery of America: The Southern Voyages* (New York: Oxford University Press, 1974).

Wiley Post

(1899-1935)

Wiley Post was an American aviator who set a speed record for flying around the world and later became the first person to fly solo around the world.

Wiley Post was born on a farm in Grand Saline, Texas, and grew up on a variety of farms in Texas and Oklahoma. He quit school after the eighth grade and worked at various odd jobs. He had decided at an early age that he wanted to be an aviator but could not afford the money to pay for training.

In 1924 he went to a small town flying circus (where people paid an admission to see airplanes do stunt tricks) in Texas and volunteered to substitute for an injured parachute jumper even though he had only been in a plane once before and had never jumped. At 2,000 feet he climbed out on the right wing and jumped. He did so well that the circus hired him, and he began his aviation career by making 99 parachute jumps. Along the way, he picked up some pilot instruction and with a little more training made his first solo flight in 1926.

In order to pay for his flight training, Post worked as an oilfield driller. On October 1, 1926, a fellow worker was using a sledgehammer to drive in a bolt. The bolt came loose and struck Post in his left eye, and eventually he had to have the eye removed. He then trained himself to see almost as well with one eye as he had with two so that he could keep flying. With the workmen's compensation money that he got for his injury, Post bought his first airplane, which he promptly wrecked.

In 1927 Post took on the job of pilot for Oklahoma oilman F.C. Hall. He raced Hall's plane, the *Winnie Mae*, to victory in the Los Angeles-Chicago Bendix Trophy Race in 1930. The $7,500 prize money they gained led Post and Hall to start thinking about other record-breaking flights they might make.

Post took the *Winnie Mae* to California and worked with navigator Harold Gatty in mapping out a route to fly around the world. They also modified the plane, and Post worked to get himself in physical condition for a long-range flight. As he wrote later in his book *Around the World in Eight Days*, "I knew that the variance in time as we progressed would bring on acute fatigue if I were used to regular hours." This seems to be the first appreciation of the effects of jet lag.

After getting permission from various governments to fly over their countries, Post and Gatty took off from New York at 4:55 a.m. on June 23, 1931. They landed first in Newfoundland. They had wanted to go straight on to Berlin, but they were unsure of their position after flying 16 hours solely by instrument with no visibility so they landed in a field in western England. Asked later about this stop, Post said, "I don't think we can honestly say we were lost . . . we just didn't know where we were."

Post and Gatty flew on to Germany, again with no visibility, and put down in the city of Hanover, trying to find Berlin. When they set off for Berlin, they were so tired they forgot to check their fuel supply and had to return to Hanover. When they finally got to the German capital, they were able to get their first sleep in almost 35 hours.

The two Americans reached Moscow in a little less than 8 hours after leaving Berlin, but they were kept awake all night by a Russian welcoming party. They flew along the route of the Trans-Siberian Railroad to Novosibirsk, Irkutsk, and Blagoveshchensk, where the plane got stuck in the mud and had to be pulled out by a detachment of Russian soldiers. They then went on to Khabarovsk, landing there at 1:30 a.m. on June 28; they were forced to wait for 12 hours because of bad weather and necessary engine repairs.

From Khabarovsk, Post and Gatty traveled all the way to Alaska across the Sea of Okhotsk, Kamchatka, and the Bering Sea. This was the longest and most dangerous leg of the trip, and they landed near Nome after 16 hours and 45 minutes with almost no gas left in their tanks. When trying to take off, Post nosed the plane off the runway into soft sand and bent the propeller. While trying to fix the propeller, the engine backfired, and the propeller hit Gatty, badly spraining his back. They made a short three-hour flight to Fairbanks where they had to stop to get medical attention for Gatty and a new propeller for the plane.

They flew through heavy rain over the Canadian Rockies and then landed at the airfield in Edmonton, Alberta. The field had been turned to mud by the rain, so the town officials agreed to let the two men take off down the main street of the city. While Post and Gatty slept, the townspeople took down all the electricity and telephone lines on Portage Avenue so that the *Winnie Mae* could take off. The two stopped in Cleveland and then arrived in New York on July 1, 1931. It had taken them 8 days, 15 hours, and 51 minutes to circle the globe—12 days faster than the previous record.

Post received an enormous amount of attention from the press and public following his record-breaking flight. But it led to a break with his employer, F.C. Hall: Post was doing all of this while he was supposed to be working for him. Post bought the *Winnie Mae* from Hall and then set out looking for financial backing so that he could carry out his next exploit—flying around the world by himself.

While preparing for his solo flight, Post wrecked the *Winnie Mae*. He took some friends up for a flight even though the fuel gauge read empty. Post insisted that he had just filled the tanks—it turned out that some teenagers had siphoned off the gas for their car. The plane crashed, but no one was seriously injured, and Post used the opportunity to make some changes to the *Winnie Mae* that helped it to fly better over long distances.

By 1933 Post had got enough money from a group of businessmen and companies promoting the aviation business to make his flight. He took off from New York at 5:10 a.m. on July 15. This time the plane was equipped with one of the first automatic pilots. The automatic pilot caused him some problems along the way, but without this technological advance Post's flight would have been impossible.

Post planned to take almost exactly the same route that he and Gatty had taken two years before but with fewer stops along the way. Because he had modified the plane (and had one less passenger), this was feasible. He flew straight from New York to Berlin in 25 hours and 45 minutes—the first person to fly that great distance nonstop. He was met in Berlin by a cheering crowd, including Hermann Goering, the head of the German Luftwaffe. Post left Berlin after a rest of only two hours and 15 minutes but had to stop soon afterwards when he realized he had forgotten his maps. The weather turned bad, and he ended up getting six hours of sleep.

Because of persistent trouble with the automatic pilot, Post was forced to land in Moscow, Novosibirsk, Irkutsk, a village called Skovorodino, and Khabarovsk. From Khabarovsk, Post flew to Alaska, where a combination of radio problems, poor visibility and fatigue got him lost, and he circled aimlessly for several hours. He finally was able to find a place to land at a small settlement called Flat in central Alaska. Here the runway was too short, and he ran off into a ditch and bent his propeller. While Post slept, local volunteers salvaged the plane, and a bush pilot flew in a new propeller from Fairbanks.

From Alaska, Post flew to Edmonton, where he landed on a dry field and then on to Floyd Bennett Field in New York. When he arrived, there was a crowd of 50,000 people waiting to greet him. He had flown around the world in 7 days, 18 hours, and 49 minutes. He had beaten his previous record by 21 hours and was the first person to fly solo around the world.

Unfortunately, Post was not able to savor his fame for long. He was killed on August 15, 1935—with his friend and passenger, the humorist Will Rogers—when his plane crashed near Point Barrow, Alaska.

Where to learn more

Post and Gatty collaborated on a book about their flight around the world: *Around the World in Eight Days* (New York, Rand McNally, 1931). See also Chelsea Fraser, *Heroes of the Air* (New York: Thomas Y. Crowell, 1940); Lowell Thomas and Lowell Thomas, Jr., *Famous Flights that Changed History* (Garden City, N.Y.: Doubleday, 1968) and Mark P. Friedlander and Gene Gurney, *Higher, Faster and Farther* (New York: William Morrow, 1973).

A good short biography of Post and history of his career, which served as the main source for this account is in Carroll V. Glines, *Round-the-World Flights* (New York: Van Nostrand Reinhold, 1982).

Vasily Danilovich Poyarkov

(? - 1668)

Vasily Danilovich Poyarkov was a Russian explorer, who was the first European to travel on the Amur River, in far eastern Russia.

Vasily Danilovich Poyarkov was born in the town of Kashin in Russia, north of Moscow. His parents were state-owned serfs. At some point, Poyarkov started working for the Governor of Siberia and went with him in 1638 to construct a fort on the Lena River in eastern Siberia that later became the large city of Yakutsk.

The Russians had traveled to the eastern part of Siberia searching for furs and metal. They heard rumors of a great river valley to the south, which was supposed to be rich in precious metals. In 1643 the commander of the Russian fort sent Poyarkov to investigate these reports.

Poyarkov headed a military detachment of 133 men that traveled up several of the tributaries of the great Lena River, which flows into the Arctic Ocean. These rivers—the Aldan, the Uchur, and the Gonam—were full of rapids, and progress was very slow. (It was a successor to Poyarkov, **Yerofey Pavlovich Khabarov**, who found the easiest route to the Amur.) By the winter of 1643-1644 Poyarkov was only able to make it as far as the height of land to the headwaters of the Zeya River, one of the tributaries of the Amur. He left some of his men behind at a supply camp on the Gonam.

From his camp on the Zeya, Poyarkov sent some of his men on a scouting mission to try to get supplies. They encountered the first Daurians, the local inhabitants of the Amur Valley. The tribesmen reported that their country did not produce any metals—the metal tools they had were obtained in trade with the Chinese. Because of the unreasonable demands of the Russians for tribute and supplies, the Daurians soon became hostile. There

was a pitched battle in which the Russians suffered some casualties. The survivors returned to Poyarkov's camp where the Russian expedition barely survived the winter on very meager rations. Forty of the men died of starvation, and it is said that the others lived only by resorting to cannibalism. In the spring of 1644 the detachment left on the Gonam arrived with supplies, and the expedition was able to continue down the Zeya to the Amur.

The Russians encountered hostility from all of the peoples they encountered along the great river. They were, however, able to reach the mouth of the Amur, where they spent the winter of 1644-1645. Knowing that they were too weak to fight their way back up the Amur, Poyarkov set out in the summer of 1645, when the mouth of the Amur was free of ice, into the Sea of Okhotsk. He saw the coast of Sakhalin Island, and traveled along the coast of the mainland to the Ulya River, which the Russians knew about from an expedition by Ivan Moskvitin in 1639. Poyarkov and his men spent the winter in a camp on the Ulya River. In the early spring of 1646 they headed up the Ulya on skis, crossed over the height of land, and then descended tributaries of the Lena to arrive in Yakutsk on June 12, 1646. In his report, Poyarkov called for a major Russian effort to take over the Amur valley, and this led to the Russian expeditions that were to follow in the next few years.

Poyarkov himself returned to Moscow in 1648, and the last known mention of him was in 1668.

Where to learn more

This account is largely based on George V. Lantzeff and Richard A. Pierce, *Eastward to Empire: Exploration and Conquest on the Russian Open Frontier, to 1750* (Montreal: McGill-Queen's University Press, 1973). Two other sources on Siberian exploration are: F.A. Golder, *Russian Expansion on the Pacific, 1641-1850* (Cleveland: Arthur H. Clark Co., 1914) and Joseph L. Wieczynski, *The Russian Frontier* (Charlottesville, University of Virginia Press, 1976).

Nikolai Przhevalsky

(1839 - 1888)

Nikolai Przhevalsky was a Russian explorer who led four major expeditions to Central Asia and Tibet.

Nikolai Przhevalsky was born in the village of Kimborovo near the city of Smolensk in European Russia on April 12, 1839. He attended secondary school in Smolensk and then joined the Russian army during the Crimean War. After the war, he passed the exams needed to get into officers' training school. While still in school, he wrote a paper on the Russian Far East that got him elected to the St. Petersburg Imperial Geographical Society. In 1863, before his graduation, he was sent to Poland (then part of the Russian Empire) to help suppress a revolt. He taught in a military academy in Warsaw for two years. In 1866 he was assigned to a base in eastern Siberia.

Soon after his arrival in Siberia, in June 1867, Przhevalsky was sent to the Ussuri River, a tributary of the Amur, to make a report on its geography and topography. His work attracted favorable comments from his superiors. He went back to St. Petersburg in January 1870 and raised money for an expedition to central Asia. He received permission from the Army to make the expedition and started out in August with a small Cossack guard for the town of Kyakhta on the Russian-Mongolian border. Although the main purpose of the expedition was scientific, one of the reasons that Przhevalsky was able to get official backing was because it also provided the opportunity to explore regions that were very important for Russia's strategic interests.

From Kyakhta the small Russian party traveled to Urga (now known as Ulan Bator, the capital of Mongolia) in rickety two-wheeled Chinese carts. In Urga they were able to join a caravan headed for Kalgan, north of Beijing. This meant crossing the Gobi Desert in winter, when temperatures dropped to -34°F at night. They reached Kalgan, a Chinese rather than Mongolian city, on May 7, 1871. From there, Przhevalsky made trips to Beijing, Dalai Nor (the Great Lake), and the Ordos Desert in Inner Mongolia. He wanted to go all the way to the Koko Nor but lack of money and the unwillingness of his companions forced him to turn back 400 miles short of his goal. On the return trip, they were robbed of their camels. They reached Kalgan in January 1872.

In March 1872 Przhevalsky and his companions, including two new Cossacks, set out for the Koko Nor once again. This time they had to cross the Ordos Desert in mid-summer. From there, they moved southward across the salt plains of Tsaidam into Tibet, which was the ultimate goal that Przhevalsky had set

Nikolai Przhevalsky. The Granger Collection, New York.

himself. He only got as far as the Dza Chu River in the frontier area between the Chinese province of Tsinghai and Tibet. His camels had died and he had run out of money, and he was forced to turn back. On his return to Russia, he was promoted to lieutenant colonel and given several awards.

Przhevalsky's next expedition had a distinctly political motive. In 1876, he was sent to negotiate with the rulers of one of the states between China and Russia, who seemed ready to transfer his allegiance to Russia. This turned out not to be true, but the ruler did supply Przhevalsky with an escort to take him through Sinkiang, where he explored and described the Tien Shan and the Tarim Basin.

Przhevalsky's major accomplishment on this trip was to reach Lop Nor in December 1876, which no European had visited since **Marco Polo**. This shallow lake is in the area between the

Turfan Depression and the Takla Makan Desert. It had never been accurately located because, in fact, its location changes. Przhevalsky advanced several theories as to how this could happen. From Lop Nor Przhevalsky tried to cross the Astin Tagh Mountains but was forced to turn back. He went to Kuldja, where he became ill and was forced to recuperate while writing the history of his expedition.

The one goal that Przhevalsky had still not attained was Tibet. He was determined to reach the "Forbidden Kingdom" on his next expedition in 1879. At the start of the expedition in the town of Zaysan, he was presented with the skin of a wild horse that had been rumored about but never seen by Europeans. It was named "Przhevalsky's horse" in his honor. From Zaysan, he traveled through the desert of Dzungaria and over the Nan Shan mountains to the Tsaidam Depression, which he skirted. He then turned south into Tibet. At Nagchu, only 170 miles from Lhasa, the capital of Tibet, Przhevalsky was stopped by Tibetan soldiers and forced to turn back. He returned to Russia by a more easterly route that took him back to Kyakhta.

Undeterred, in August 1883 Przhevalsky left St. Petersburg and went back to Kyakhta. He assembled a party of 21 men and crossed into Mongolia in November in another attempt at reaching Tibet. The expedition crossed the Gobi Desert and investigated the headwaters of the Hwang Ho River. He crossed the Nan Shan and went back to the Koko Nor. He went around the southern margins of the Tsaidam Depression. In this area east of the Kun Lun mountains, he saw several mountain ranges that had never been reported on before. He named them after famous explorers; one of them was later named in his honor.

Przhevalsky crossed the Astin Tagh range and spent two months investigating Lop Nor. Once again, he wanted to turn south and enter Tibet, but the authorities prevented him from doing so. Instead, he skirted the southern part of the Takla Makan and went to the oasis and caravan town of Khotan. From Khotan he headed straight across the Takla Makan, crossed the Tien Shan and descended to Issyk Kul on the Russian side of the border in October 1885. He returned to St. Petersburg in January 1886.

This expedition and his writings about it made Przhevalsky one of the most famous explorers of his day, at a time when explorers were major celebrities and heroes. He was promoted to Major General and was given awards by geographical societies from all over Europe. He was still not content, however, because he had not visited Lhasa. He mounted another expedition in the fall of 1888. He only got as far as Issyk Kul when he suddenly became ill and died on November 1, 1888 in the town of Karakol (which was called Przhevalsk by the Soviets). He was only 49 years old.

Where to learn more

Przhevalsky wrote two accounts of his travels in Tibet and other part of Asia: *Mongolia, the Tangut Country and the Solitudes of Northern Tibet, being a Narrative* . . . (London: Samuel Low, Marston, Searle & Rivington, 1876) and *From Kulja Across the Tian Shan to Lob-Nor* (London: Samuel Low, Marston, Searle & Rivington, 1879). There is a good, fairly recent biography by an American scholar: Donald Rayfield, *The Dream of Lhasa: The Life of Nikolay Przhevalsky 1839-1888, Explorer of Central Asia* (Athens: Ohio University Press, 1976). J.N.L. Baker has numerous entries on the Russian explorer in his *History of Geographical Discovery and Exploration* (New York: Cooper Square Publishers, 1967).

A good summary of Przhevalsky's career, which was helpful in writing this account, can be found in Piers Pennington, *The Great Explorers* (New York: Facts on File, 1979).

Pytheas

(380 B.C.? - 300 B.C.?)

Pytheas was a Greek from the city of Massalia in southern France who traveled all the way around Britain and wrote the first account of Scandinavia.

Pytheas was born in the Greek colony of Massalia on the south coast of France (now called Marseilles) in about 380 B.C. Sometime toward the end of the fourth century B.C., he was sent out by the merchants of his native city to find a route to the tin mines of southern Britain, which were the source of that valuable metal for all of Europe and the Mediterranean. The trade in tin was controlled by the Carthaginians (from the city of Carthage in present-day Tunisia), and the Greeks would have been glad to break their monopoly.

At that time, the Pillars of Hercules (the Straits of Gibraltar), the exit from the Mediterranean into the Atlantic, were controlled by the Carthaginians. So Pytheas either avoided them by going overland or he went during a time of Carthaginian weakness: possibly between 310-306 B.C. when Carthage was fighting a war with Syracuse in Sicily. In any case, he made it to the port of Corbilo at the mouth of the Loire River. From there he sailed to the island of Ouessant off the tip of Brittany.

Pytheas sailed from Brittany to Belerium (Land's End) in Cornwall, the southwestern tip of Britain, which was the source of tin. He described what he found: "The inhabitants of Britain who dwell about the headland of Belerium are unusually hospitable and have adopted a civilized manner of life because of their intercourse with foreign traders. It is they who work the tin, extracting it by an ingenious process. The bed itself is of rock but between are pieces of earth which they dig out to reach the tin. Then they work the tin into pieces the size of knuckle bones and carry it to an island that lies off Britain and is called Ictis (St. Michael's Mount, Cornwall); for at the time of ebb tide the space between this island and the mainland becomes dry, and they can take the tin in large quantities over to the island on their wagons."

From Cornwall, Pytheas sailed north through the Irish Sea between Britain and Ireland all the way to the northern tip of Scotland, probably going as far as the Orkney Islands. Along the way, he stopped and traveled for short distances inland and described the customs of the inhabitants. Beyond northern Scotland, Pytheas described another land called the "Island of Thule." (Ever since, the far northern extremes of the earth have had the poetic name of Thule: it is now given to the northernmost town in Greenland.) It is not clear whether Pytheas actually went to Thule or merely reports what he heard about it.

According to Pytheas, Thule is six days' sail north of Britain. In midsummer, the sun retires to its resting place for only two or three hours. The inhabitants lived on wild berries and "millet" (in this case, probably oats) and made mead (a drink) from wild honey. From his description, Thule was probably Norway in the present region of the city of Trondheim, although other locations have been suggested. North of Thule he was told of a land where the sea became solid and the sun never set in summertime. These reports seemed so crazy to the people of the Mediterranean world that his report was not believed and was ridiculed for years later.

From Thule, Pytheas sailed back to Britain and down its east coast and then crossed the North Sea to the North Frisian Islands off the coast of Germany and to the island of Heligoland, which he called Abalus. He said: "In the spring the waves wash up amber on the shores of this island. The inhabitants use it as fuel instead of wood . . . and also sell it to their neighbors the Teutons." From there Pytheas sailed back along the coast of Europe and returned home.

Where to learn more

Pytheas has generated more interest than any other of the ancient explorers. There are those who say that he is the first known explorer in the modern sense of the word. As a result, most histories of exploration have something to say about him, including: Fridtjof Nansen, *In Northern Mists: Arctic Exploration in Early Times*, 2 vols. (London: William Heinemann, 1911; reprinted, New York: AMS Press, 1969); M. Cary and E.H. Warmington, *The Ancient Explorers* (London: Methuen, 1929; reprinted in paperback, Baltimore, Md.: Penguin Books, 1963); Walter Woodburn Hyde, *Ancient Greek Mariners* (New York: Oxford University Press, 1947); Paul Herrmann, *Conquest by Man* (New York: Harper & Brothers, 1954); Björn Landström, *The Quest for India* (Garden City, N.Y.: Doubleday, 1964); Rhys Carpenter, *Beyond the Pillars of Heracles: The Classical World Seen Through the Eyes of Its Discoverers* (New York: Delacorte Press, 1966).

There is one recent monograph devoted to Pytheas: C.F.C. Hawkes, *Pytheas: Europe and the Greek Explorers* (Oxford: Oxford University Press, 1977).

Pedro Fernandez de Quiros

(1565 - 1615)

Pedro Fernandez de Quiros was a Portuguese navigator sailing for Spain who took over Mendaña's expedition to the Solomon Islands after Mendaña's death and then attempted to found a Spanish colony in Vanuatu.

Pedro Fernandez de Quiros was a native of Portugal (his family name was originally Queiroz) who entered the service of Spain in 1580 and eventually ended up in the Spanish colony of Peru. There he was chosen to be the pilot of the expedition led by **Alvaro de Mendaña** to colonize the Solomon Islands, which Mendaña had discovered in 1568. The second Mendaña expedition left Peru in April 1595 and reached the Santa Cruz islands southeast of the Solomons in September. There the Spanish fought among themselves, the native Melanesians tried to drive them away, and Mendaña died in mid-October. Quiros replaced him as head of the expedition.

Quiros decided to abandon the attempt and set sail with three leaky ships on November 18, 1595. Along the way, he had to contend with Mendaña's widow and her family. They were of noble origin and thought that any work was beneath them. They also felt that they should be directing the expedition. History has been particularly unkind to Doña Isabel Barreto de Mendaña who is said to have used precious water to wash her clothes while people were dying of thirst around her and to have kept two pet pigs on leashes near her while they were dying of hunger. The two smaller supply ships were lost during the voyage but the flagship, the *San Geronimo*, made it to Guam on January 1, 1596 and to the island of Samar in the Philippines a couple of weeks later.

The leaking galleon had a hard time making it through the Philippine islands, and the crew was always on the brink of mutiny. They made it into the port of Cavite in Manila Bay on February 11, 1596. Of the 400 who had left Santa Cruz in the three ships, only 100 arrived in Manila. There, Doña Isabel stayed and married the Governor's cousin. Quiros repaired the *San Geronimo* and sailed to Acapulco, which he reached on December 11, 1597, and then went on to Peru.

Back in Peru, Quiros tried to obtain a ship to sail back to the Pacific, specifically to the Marquesas Islands in Polynesia where the Mendaña expedition had stopped and which Quiros thought was a paradise on earth. The governor refused to help him, and he returned to Spain. He made a pilgrimage to Rome in 1600 and got the Pope's blessing to travel to the Marquesas and convert the Polynesians to Christianity. He then went to Spain and in 1603 got the Spanish king to write instructions to the Viceroy of Peru to aid Quiros in his mission. Quiros left Spain in 1604 but was shipwrecked in the West Indies and had to make his way overland via Caracas to Lima. On his arrival there, he presented the Viceroy with the king's instructions.

Quiros was given two ships that held 250-300 people, six Franciscan monks, and supplies for one year. He chose as the captain of his flagship, the *San Pedro y San Pablo*, the navigator **Luis Vaez de Torres**. They left the Peruvian port of Callao on December 21, 1605. In the middle of January, Quiros changed course, thereby missing the Marquesas entirely. Instead they passed isolated Ducie and Henderson Islands and several islands of the Tuamotu archipelago and the small island of Caroline. They landed at Rakahanga in the northern Cook Islands. Although Quiros wanted to stay, the others convinced him to press on. Out to sea again, they made very slow progress, and 94 days after leaving Peru the crew became mutinous.

Fortunately, they soon passed other islands and landed on Taumako, about 100 miles west of the Santa Cruz Islands. There, the chief told the Spaniards about the other islands in the vicinity and how to get to them. Not wishing to return to the ill-fated Santa Cruz group, Quiros turned to the southwest. On the

Pedro Fernandez de Quiros. The Granger Collection, New York.

morning of May 1, 1606 they sailed into a very large bay on the north coast of a large, mountainous island. This island Quiros named Espiritu Santo, ("Holy Spirit"), and that is still its name today. It is the largest island in what is now the country of Vanuatu.

On this island, Quiros set about founding his colony of New Jerusalem. He named the largest river the Jordan and the best harbor, Vera Cruz (the "True Cross"). He also set up an Order of the Holy Ghost to which all the new colonists were to belong. They were also instructed to wear a blue cross over their clothes. On May 25 they celebrated the Catholic feast of Corpus Christi. That evening, Quiros took a walk in the woods and came back and announced that they were abandoning the settlement.

By the time the expedition was ready to leave on May 28, everyone became sick from food poisoning after eating some fish they had caught. They were not able to sail until June 8. Once they sailed out into the bay, they were met by adverse winds. Quiros signaled to the other ship that they were going to return to port at Vera Cruz. The second ship, the *Almiranta*, captained by Torres, sailed into the harbor, but the next morning Quiros's ship had disappeared. It had sailed off alone—no one knows why. Quiros later claimed that the winds had kept him from sailing into the harbor and that he was forced out to sea. Some say there was a mutiny, and the crew forced him to sail away, while others claim that Quiros had a nervous breakdown and purposely abandoned the other ship.

Quiros and his ship sailed to the north, missing Santa Cruz, and after a ship's council it was decided to continue north to hit the prevailing westerly winds and then to sail to Mexico. This they did, reaching Acapulco on November 23, 1606. Quiros eventually made it back to Spain where he bombarded King Philip III with 50 letters and 200 maps urging him to sponsor another voyage to the South Pacific. He traveled back to Peru in 1614 but only got as far as Panama, where he died.

Where to learn more

There are two sources for the original accounts of Quiros's voyages: Sir Clements Markham, ed., 2 vols. *The Voyages of Pedro Fernandez de Quiros* (London: Hakluyt Society, 1904) and Celsus Kelly, ed. *Austrialia del Espiritu Santo: Documents on the Voyage of Quiros to the South Sea, 1605-6* (Cambridge: Cambridge University Press, 1965).

Colin Jack-Hinton gives a very complete account of the voyages of Mendaña and Quiros in *The Search for the Islands of Solomon, 1567-1838* (Oxford: Clarendon Press, 1969).

Two excellent books about Pacific exploration discuss Quiros in some detail: J.C. Beaglehole, *The Exploration of the Pacific* (Stanford: Stanford University Press, 1966) and O.H.K. Spate, *The Spanish Lake* (Minneapolis: University of Minnesota Press, 1979).

Pierre-Esprit Radisson

(1636? - 1710)

Pierre-Esprit Radisson was a Frenchman who explored the area north of Lake Superior, realized the potential of the fur trade in Hudson Bay, and was responsible for founding the English Hudson's Bay Company.

Pierre-Esprit Radisson was born in Avignon in the south of France sometime between the years 1636 and 1640. His half-sister immigrated to Canada, and Radisson either went with her or joined her there later. The first mention of him comes in 1651 when he was captured by Iroquois warriors. His sister's husband was killed, and she remarried **Médard Chouart des Groseilliers** in 1653. Groseilliers was to become Radisson's exploring partner.

Radisson was taken by members of the Mohawk tribe to a village near present-day Schenectady, New York. He was adopted by a family and stayed there until he escaped to the Dutch trading post at Fort Orange (Albany, New York) in 1653. From there he went to Amsterdam and returned to his home in Trois-Rivières, Canada in 1654.

By the time of Radisson's return the French and Iroquois had reached a peace agreement, and Radisson went on a French missionary trip to Onondaga (near Syracuse, New York) as an interpreter in 1657. The Iroquois soon got tired of the missionaries and plotted to kill them, but Radisson learned about what was going on. In the accounts of the time and the legends that grew up afterwards, Radisson is supposed to have convinced the Iroquois to attend a big feast where they were drugged long enough for the Frenchmen to make their escape.

In August 1659 Radisson and Groseilliers left Montreal on a voyage that took them to Lake Superior and on to a smaller lake, Lake Courte Oreille (near the present-day village of Radisson, Wisconsin) where they spent the winter with Huron and Ottawa refugees. These tribes were enemies of the Iroquois, who had defeated them and driven them out of their lands. The two Frenchmen also met members of the Sioux tribe, the first Europeans to do so. In the spring they traveled to the north shore of Lake Superior and learned from Cree tribesmen about the wealth of furs that could be found in the country around Hudson Bay.

Radisson and Groseilliers returned to Trois-Rivières with a large supply of furs and knowledge about a trading route beyond the lands of the Iroquois. Instead of being welcomed, however, the furs were confiscated, Groseilliers was put in jail, and they were both fined. All of this because they had left the colony without permission. The bitterness caused by this treatment was to have major consequences on the history of North America.

In the spring of 1662 Radisson and his brother-in-law set out again. This time their aim was to travel down the St. Lawrence River and then take the sea route to Hudson Bay. Whether by circumstance or pre-arrangement, this did not happen: they ended up in Boston, Massachusetts. From there they made two unsuccessful efforts to trade with Hudson Bay. Then, with the blessing of the Governor, they were sent to England to convince King Charles II of the advantages of opening up the fur trade in the north.

The ship that the two took to England was captured by a Dutch pirate, and they were landed in Spain. They then had to make their way overland to England. After some effort, they were able to convince the King to sponsor an expedition to Hudson Bay. They left in 1668 on board two different ships. Radisson's, the *Eaglet*, was damaged in a storm and had to return to England. While waiting for Groseilliers to return, he wrote his *Voyages*, which is our source for his amazing adventures thus far. Groseilliers made it to Hudson Bay and returned with a valuable cargo of furs. As a result, a private trading company, the Hudson's Bay Company, was chartered on May 2, 1670.

The two brothers-in-law set out again almost immediately, on May 31, 1670, once again on separate ships. Radisson went to the mouth of the Nelson River on the west coast of Hudson Bay in what is now Manitoba. He founded a trading post there and took possession of the land in the name of the King of England. He had to abandon the post, but this claim became the basis for the British possession of the Bay and its tributaries.

During the next few years Radisson and Groseilliers made several trading voyages to Hudson Bay. By this time the French were becoming very alarmed at the encroachments of the English. In 1675 a Jesuit priest, Albanel, who had been captured by the English convinced the two men to return to French allegiance. They sneaked across the English Channel to France and presented themselves to the French court. They were then sent back to Canada. The Governor of New France, the Count de Frontenac, mistrusted the two men and refused to help them. Groseilliers returned to his farm at Trois-Rivières and Radisson went back to France.

In France no one was interested in the schemes of the Canadian trader, and the best job he could get was as a midshipman on a French Navy ship that was part of an expedition to capture Dutch colonies on the west coast of Africa and in the Caribbean. He left in 1677, but most of the ships were wrecked on a hidden reef in the Caribbean, and Radisson barely survived to come back to France in 1678, again without any source of income.

Unhappy with his reception in France, Radisson went back to England in order to try to convince his wife (he had married the daughter of a prominent English businessman) to leave with him for either France or Canada. Her family refused to let her go, and Radisson returned to Paris alone.

This time, Radisson's fortunes improved. The French backers of a new company, the Compagnie du Nord, hired him to lead a French expedition to the Nelson River. Since the Hudson's Bay Company was planning to do the same thing, it is possible that Radisson brought this information back with him from England, spurring the French to action. In any case, when Radisson arrived in Hudson Bay there were ships from England as well as one from Massachusetts. Radisson was joined by Groseilliers, and the two of them outwitted their opponents and captured the trading post and the furs for France.

Once in Quebec, however, they were told they would have to pay taxes on their furs. Radisson disputed this assessment and took his case to Paris. Once there, the French government was unwilling to risk an incident with England and refused to support the two adventurers. Groseilliers went back to Canada and Radisson—to England! He was helped to escape by a French Protestant who was being persecuted for his religion and wanted to get to England; he thought that if he arrived with Radisson it would help his prospects.

In 1684 Radisson went back to work for the Hudson's Bay Company. He was sent back to the Nelson River, where he found his nephew, the son of Groseilliers, in charge of the French post Radisson had founded. He convinced the young man to change sides and to take his great stock of furs to England. As they were leaving the Bay, they just missed being caught by French ships come to foil the plot.

Back in London, Radisson attended the coronation of King James II. Radisson's nephew came to regret his change of allegiance and tried several times to escape to France, but was caught every time. In the meantime, the French put a price on Radisson's head. He made his last trip to Hudson Bay in 1685-1687. Just before leaving England, he married the daughter of the French Protestant who had helped him out of France, his first wife presumably having died.

In 1687 Radisson returned to England for the last time. He settled down in the suburbs of London. He was given stock in the Hudson's Bay Company and an annuity. These payments led to a quarrel with the Company that turned into a law suit, which Radisson won in 1697. His second wife died during delivery of their fifth child, and he married for the third time and had three more children. He made his will on June 17, 1710 and died shortly thereafter.

Where to learn more

The first English edition of Radisson's narrative of his explorations was edited by G.D. Scull as *Voyages of Pierre Esprit Radisson* (Boston: Prince Society, 1885; reprinted, New York: Burt Franklin, 1967). A different version, which rearranges the sequence of documents in order to achieve a more rational chronology, is Arthur T. Adams, ed. *The Explorations of Pierre Esprit Radisson* (Minneapolis: Ross & Haines, 1961).

Historian Grace Lee Nute has contributed "Radisson and Groseilliers' Contribution to Geography," *Minnesota History*, vol. 16 (1935), pp. 414-426, and *Caesars of the Wilderness: Médard Chouart, Sieur des Groseilliers, and Pierre Esprit Radisson, 1618-1710* (New York: Appleton-Century Co., 1943). This latter work has been characterized as "florid," which is easy to understand given the subject matter. Nute also wrote the excellent biographical essays on Radisson and Groseilliers in the *Dictionary of Canadian Biography*, vols. 1 & 2 (Toronto: University of Toronto Press, 1967-1969), which served as the main source for these accounts. Another popular treatment is Walter Stanley Campbell, *King of the Fur Traders: The Deeds and Deviltry of Pierre Radisson* (Boston: Houghton Mifflin, 1940).

General histories of the Hudson's Bay Company necessarily treat the adventures of Radisson and Groseilliers in some detail. These include: Agnes C. Laut, *The Conquest of the Great Northwest: Being the Story of the Adventurers of England Known as the Hudson's Bay Company*, 2 vols. (New York: Outing Publishing Co., 1908; reprinted, Toronto: Musson Book Company, 1918) and *The "Adventurers of England" on Hudson Bay: A Chronicle of the Fur Trade in the North* (Toronto: Glasgow, Brook, 1914); E.E. Rich *Hudson's Bay Company, 1670-1870*, vol. 1 (New York: Macmillan, 1960); and Peter C. Newman, *Company of Adventurers*, vol. 1 (New York: Viking, 1985; reprinted in paperback).

There is a movie about Radisson and Groseilliers entitled *Hudson's Bay* with Paul Muni as Radisson, Laird Cregar as Groseilliers, and Vincent Price as King Charles II of England (Twentieth Century-Fox, 1940).

Sir Walter Raleigh

(1552 - 1618)

Sir Walter Raleigh was an English adventurer who sponsored the first attempted English settlement in North America and led two expeditions to the Orinoco River in South America.

Walter Raleigh (he spelled his name Ralegh) was born in the western English county of Devon, the birth place of many of England's navigators and seamen. He was the half-brother of **Sir Humphrey Gilbert** and sailed with him on a voyage in 1578, which was attacked by the Spanish and had to return without reaching North America in 1579.

Following this failure, Raleigh fought in Ireland with the English army that was trying to put down a rebellion being aided by the Spanish. In 1581 he was sent to London with dispatches from the army to the court of Queen Elizabeth I telling her about the fighting. Once there he immediately caught the Queen's eye and soon became her "favorite" and, it is often assumed, her lover. As a result of this royal connection he was showered with honors and the chance to make a lot of money through various offices that he held. He used this position to foster exploration and settlement by the English in North America.

Raleigh helped supply part of the money that Gilbert needed for his expedition to Newfoundland in 1583. Raleigh wanted to go along as well but was finally forbidden to do so by the Queen. Following Gilbert's death returning from this voyage, Raleigh received a patent (exclusive right) to explore and settle the coast of North America in the Queen's name. In April 1584 he sent out an expedition that sailed to the Caribbean and then north along the coast to North Carolina, which they claimed for England. On the return of this expedition in September the Queen gave the newly claimed area the name of Virginia, named after herself, the "Virgin Queen."

Raleigh now wanted to establish a permanent settlement in Virginia, but once again the Queen refused him permission to lead it himself. He therefore sent out an expedition under the command of his cousin, Sir Richard Grenville, in April 1585. This group quarreled among themselves and with the Native Americans and returned in June 1586. In the summer of 1587 a new expedition was sent out under the command of John White. White returned with the expedition's ships but left 89 men, 17 women, and 2 children behind. The next spring Raleigh sent out a ship to take supplies to the new colony of Roanoke, but it was captured by French ships and had to return to England. It was not until 1589 that another relief expedition was sent out, and by then it was too late. When the ships arrived there was no trace of

Sir Walter Raleigh.

the settlement. Raleigh lost £40,000 in the venture. His patent expired in 1603.

Raleigh was a member of the commission that planned England's defense against the Spanish Armada in 1588. He then quarreled with the Queen's new favorite, the Earl of Essex, and lost some of his influence at court. This was made much worse when the Queen discovered that he had been carrying on a liaison with another woman, Elizabeth Throgmorton, and he was imprisoned in the Tower of London in 1592. On his release, he married Throgmorton and was banished from the court. By this time Raleigh had become fascinated with Spanish stories of a mythical place in South America called Manoa ruled by El Dorado, "the golden one." He sent out an expedition in 1593 under Jacob Whiddon to explore the Orinoco River and try to find Manoa. Whiddon returned at the end of the year without having found the non-existent country.

Raleigh then decided to set out on his own. He left the English port of Plymouth on February 9, 1594 with a fleet of five ships and sailed to Trinidad, where he arrived on March 22. The island was then ruled by the Spanish, and Raleigh attacked the town of San Jose and captured it and the governor. The governor showed him a letter written by a Spaniard, Juan Martinez, who claimed to have traveled up the Orinoco River and to have stayed in the fabulously wealthy country of Manoa.

The Englishmen then set out to find Manoa themselves. Raleigh entered the Orinoco through its westernmost channel, the Manamo, and then rowed with five of the ships' boats and one hundred men upstream. They made it as far as the Caroni River about 125 miles up the river. By then they were nearly out of supplies and had seen no signs of Manoa. Raleigh left two of the men with a group of Native Americans so that they could learn the language and scout out any traces of Manoa, and then he returned downstream to Trinidad. After raiding other Spanish settlements he returned to England with a load of ore that indeed turned out to contain gold (in the nineteenth century gold and other mines were established in the region traversed by Raleigh).

On his return to England Raleigh was criticized by his enemies at court. To justify himself he wrote his book *Discoverie of Guiana* and drew a map of his discoveries in 1596. Guiana is the geographical name of the area between the Orinoco and Amazon Rivers. Raleigh then became involved in preparations for a war against Spain. He did send out another expedition to the Orinoco under his friend Lawrence Kemys, who brought back news that the Spanish had established a fort near the mouth of the Caroni on the Orinoco. Raleigh then took part in an English assault on the Spanish port of Cadiz, where he was wounded and distinguished himself by his bravery. As a result, he was once more in the Queen's favor and returned to court in May 1597. He fought in the Azores in 1597.

In 1600 Raleigh was appointed Governor of Jersey, one of the Channel Islands ruled by the Queen. He stayed there until the Queen's death in 1603. The new King, James I, was convinced by Raleigh's enemies that he was guilty of treason, and he was arrested on July 17, 1603. Raleigh was so upset that he tried to kill himself, but was unsuccessful. He was convicted and sentenced to death and had actually mounted the scaffold to be beheaded when news came that the King had changed the sentence to life imprisonment. He then spent the following 13 years in the Tower of London. During that time he wrote several books, including the first volume of a *History of the World*.

Starting in 1610 Raleigh argued in favor of sending another expedition to Guiana to look for gold mines. He was released in January 1616 in order to lead an expedition, with orders not to attack any Spanish settlement. Raleigh mounted the expedition with his own money as well as the investments of several friends. It left England in June 12, 1617 with a fleet of 14 ships. It immediately ran into a storm in which many of the ships were damaged, and one was sunk. They had to put into to port in Ireland to make repairs and did not leave again until August 19.

Throughout the voyage Raleigh and his ships faced problems: shortage of water, storms, and doldrums that kept them from moving for 40 days. Raleigh became ill with fever, and many of the men died from it. They finally anchored off the coast of what is now French Guiana, and were able to get fresh water and supplies. Raleigh then sent his old friend Lawrence Kemys up the Orinoco River with the main part of the expedition, including his nephew and his son. He stayed behind with the ships to guard against a Spanish attack. Kemys and his men attacked the fort that the Spanish had established on the Orinoco, San Tomás. During the fighting Raleigh's son was killed. The Spanish then abandoned the town. Kemys did not follow them through the heavy forest. Upon his return to Raleigh's ship, he was so reproached that he committed suicide.

Raleigh wanted to pursue the possibility of rich mines in the interior, but at this point none of his men would follow him. The ships parted company, and Raleigh himself headed north to Newfoundland where he took on a cargo of fish in order to have something to help pay for the costs of the voyage. He returned to Plymouth in the middle of June 1618. By then news of the attack on San Tomás had reached England, and the Spanish ambassador insisted that Raleigh should be punished. He was arrested by his cousin, Sir Lewis Stukeley, and failed in an attempt to escape to France. He was put on trial, condemned to death and executed on October 29, 1618. As he was about to be beheaded, the executioner wanted him to turn his head another way. His last words were, "What matter how the head lie, so the heart be right?"

Where to learn more

Raleigh's own account of his voyage to South America (*The Discoverie of the Large, Rich and Beautifull Empire of Guiana*) was contained in volume 10 of Richard Hakluyt's famous book, *Principall Navigations of the English Nation*, of which there are several editions. This account was later by Vincent T. Harlow, *The Discoverie of the Large and Bewtiful Empire of Guiana* (London: Argonaut Press, 1928) with a useful introduction on the history of the quest for El Dorado. A recent volume includes excerpts with extensive footnotes of Raleigh's account: Philip Edwards, *Last Voyages: Cavendish, Hudson, Raleigh—The Original Narratives* (New York: Oxford University Press, 1988).

There are many biographies of Raleigh. One that is entertaining to read is Donald Barr Chidsey, *Sir Walter Raleigh: That Damned Upstart* (New York: The John Day Company, 1931).

John Hemming has written an interesting and important book on the El Dorado legend that includes a good summary of Raleigh's voyages: *The Search for El Dorado* (New York: E.P. Dutton, 1978).

Hari Ram

(19th century)

Hari Ram was an Indian "pundit" who made four expeditions in the area of Mt. Everest and added much new territory to Western maps.

Hari Ram was one of the "pundits," who like **Nain Singh** were hired by the British government to penetrate areas of Asia where Europeans were not allowed. Hari Ram had as his code names "M.H." and "No. 9." Although nothing certain is known, he probably made his first expedition in 1868 to the area of Nepal north of Mt. Everest.

Probably because of his previous experience, in 1871 Hari Ram was sent to the same area. He left Darjeeling in the foothills of the Himalayas in the summer of 1871 and went to the little kingdom of Sikkim. He tried to cross the border into Tibet but was refused admission because he looked suspicious to the officials at the border. Fortunately, he met a Sikkimese official and they became friends. The wife of the Sikkimese was ill, and Hari Ram used some of the Western medicines he had been provided with to treat her, and she recovered. The Sikkimese then used his influence to get the Indian across the border. He reached the Tibetan city of Shigatse on September 17, 1871. He then traveled southwest to the town of Dingri, which served as the main trading center between Tibet and Nepal.

In order to get across the Himalayas before winter set in, Hari Ram traveled through the Kuti Pass, 60 miles west of Mt. Everest. At some places the path was only 9 inches wide with a drop of 1,500 feet. Hari Ram arrived in Kathmandu in January 1872 and then went back to Darjeeling. He thus made the first recorded trip completely around Mt. Everest and surveyed 844 miles that were completely unknown to Western geographers.

Hari Ram set out again on July 1, 1873, masquerading as a physician. This time he entered Nepal from the west and traveled to the city of Jumla and then to the trading center of Mustang on the Tibet border. He was able to cross the border and intended to head east to the Mt. Everest area again when he was arrested and put in jail at Tradom. He was then escorted back to the Nepali border and then followed the Gandak River back to India.

Because he had not achieved the purposes of his mission, Hari Ram was laid off work by the government of India. However, others who attempted his route were also forestalled and he was re-hired in April 1885. He returned to Nepal and was stopped once more. This time he cured a Nepali governor's daughter-in-law of goiter and was allowed to travel with the governor's son on a caravan to Tibet. The caravan traveled through the Pangu La Pass at 20,000 feet and got within 15 miles of Mt. Everest, the closest that any of the pundits were to go. They reached the town of Dingri in early October 1885. He was able to bribe his way back across the border into Nepal. During this trip he traced the course of the Dudh Kosi River at the base of Mt. Everest and added 420 miles to the survey of the Indian government.

Where to learn more

This account is based on an excellent book that gives a complete history of the pundits: Derek J. Waller, *The Pundits: British Exploration of Tibet and Central Asia* (Lexington: University Press of Kentucky, 1990). Hari Ram's travels in Tibet are briefly mentioned in *Geographical Discovery and Exploration* by J.N.L. Baker (New York: Cooper Square Publishers, 1967).

Antônio Raposo Tavares

(1598 - 1659)

Antônio Raposo Tavares was a Brazilian slave trader who made an early trip across South America.

Antônio Raposo Tavares was born in the Portuguese town of Beja in 1598 and went to Brazil in 1622 with his father who was appointed captain-major (governor) of the colony of São Vicente (now in the state of São Paulo) in 1622. There he became a leader of *bandeiras*. *Bandeiras* were Portuguese slave-hunting expeditions that raided Native American villages and took their inhabitants captive. In particular, they attacked the Spanish Jesuit "reductions" in Paraguay, where the Guaraní tribe had been Christianized and had settled into to permanent farming villages.

Raposo Tavares led his first *bandeira* in 1629. It was made up of four companies of soldiers—900 mixed race African-Portuguese and 2,200 Native Americans. They attacked the settlement of Encarnación on the Paraná River until they were driven back by a force of 1,200 Guaranís led by two Jesuit priests. From there, they went to San Antonio where they captured a great many prisoners.

In January 1636 Raposo Tavares left São Paulo at the head of 150 Portuguese and mixed race soldiers and 1,500 Tupis. This time he headed south to the Taquari River in the present Brazilian state of Rio Grande do Sul, where the Jesuits had taken refuge. He took the settlement of Jesús María in December and then San Cristóbal and San Joaquín, defeating a force of 1,600 Spanish and Guaranís along the way. He returned to São Paulo and then went back south in mid-1638.

In May 1648 Raposo Tavares set out on his greatest trip: so great that much of it is legendary, and we do not really know where he went. He started out with 200 Portuguese and mixed race soldiers and more than 1,000 Native Americans. The *bandeira* first attacked the Jesuit post at Itatim at the juncture of the Paraguay and Apa rivers, now on the border of Brazil and Paraguay. It then went up the Paraguay River and crossed over the height of land to the Guaporé River (now the boundary between Brazil and Bolivia) and then down the Guaporé to the Madeira River and then to the Amazon.

Once he reached the Amazon Raposo Tavares is alleged to have traveled up it to the Spanish city of Quito, high in the Andes, reaching it in 1651. He then traveled down the tributaries of the Amazon until he reached the Rio Negro, which he then explored. He traveled down the Amazon to the Portuguese port of Belém at its mouth and from there took a ship back to São Paulo, where he arrived sometime in 1652. By the time he got back home, it is said that the *bandeira* had only 59 soldiers left and Tavares was so disfigured by the hazards of the journey that his family did not recognize him. If he had made the trip as he had claimed, he had covered about 8,000 miles.

Where to learn more

Unfortunately, there is very little available in English about the bandeiras. The only general work is a collection of essays, which contains a chapter on Raposo Tavares: Richard McGee Morse, ed. *The Bandeirantes: The Historical Role of the Brazilian Pathfinders* (New York: Alfred A. Knopf, 1965).

The best book in Portuguese is Jaime Cortesão, *Raposo Tavares e a formação territorial do Brasil*, 2 vols. Lisbon: Portugália, 1966.

Johannes Rebmann

(1820 - 1876)

Johannes Rebmann was a German missionary who explored the interior of East Africa and was the first European to see Mt. Kilimanjaro.

Johannes Rebmann was born in the town of Gerlingen in southern Germany near the city of Stuttgart on January 16, 1820. His father owned a vineyard. From his youth Rebmann was very pious and decided he wanted to be a missionary at an early age. After training in Basel and London, he went out to join his compatriot **Ludwig Krapf** at the port of Mombasa on the east coast of Africa, arriving there on June 10, 1846.

After his arrival, Rebmann helped Krapf establish a mission station at Rabai about 15 miles inland from Mombasa. On October 14, 1847 Rebmann set out on his first journey to evaluate the prospects for evangelization among the nearby peoples and to look for places to establish missions. The trip only lasted about two weeks and took him to the country of the Wateita tribe on the edge of the inland plateau that rises up from the coastal plain where Mombasa and Rabai are located. He saw that the plateau stretched on for as far as the eye could see and put off further exploration until another time.

On April 27, 1848 Rebmann set out to visit the Chagga, who lived beyond the Wateita in what is now the border region between Kenya and Tanzania. He retraced his steps to the Wateita country. On May 11 as he traveled into the lands of the Chagga, he saw a tall mountain that looked like it was covered by a large, white cloud. His guide said that it was "beredi," meaning "cold," and Rebmann realized that it must be capped with snow. It was in fact the snow-covered peak of Mt. Kilimanjaro, which, at 5,895 feet, is the highest mountain in Africa. Rebmann was the first European to see it.

From May 13 to May 29, Rebmann stayed in the village of Masaki, one of the chiefs of the Chagga tribe, recovering from his journey and trying to explain his religion to the Africans. On May 25 he climbed 2,000 feet of a nearby mountain, hoping to get a better view of Kilimanjaro, but it was covered with clouds. He reached Mombasa on June 11, 1848, noting along the way how beautiful and rich the land was.

On November 14, 1848 Rebmann started out on a more ambitious journey. He planned to travel to the land of the Kikuyu people in what is now central Kenya not far from the capital in Nairobi. He went as far as the town of Bura, but unspecified "circumstances" forced him to turn back. He returned to the Chagga country, reaching Masaki's village on December 7. He had learned that Masaki was not a particularly important chief, and he wanted to travel on to meet King Mankinga. Masaki, on the other hand, did not want him to leave because it was to his advantage to serve as the intermediary between his tribe and the Europeans. However, some troops of Mankinga forced him to release Rebmann, and they escorted the missionary out of the village on January 4, 1849.

On the way to visit King Mankinga, Rebmann passed along the lower slopes of Kilimanjaro and saw the "majestic snow-clad summit" by moonlight. He wrote that the night was as cold as Germany in November. He had a pleasant visit with King Mankinga, who seemed quite receptive to the idea of allowing the Christians to establish a mission station in his country. Taking his leave on January 29, Rebmann traveled back past Kilimanjaro. He learned that unlike what his guide had led him to suppose, the Chagga had a word for "snow" and understood its properties. The Swahilis from the coast, however, thought that the mountain was capped with silver.

Rebmann sent reports of Mt. Kilimanjaro back to Europe. There the armchair geographers of the time said that he must be quite mistaken. It was impossible that snow could exist on the equator in Africa. W.D. Cooley, an eminent geographer who had never been to Africa, wrote in his book *Inner Africa Laid Open* in 1852 that what Rebmann had thought was snow was actually a light-colored, quartz-like rock that existed on equatorial mountains. Rebmann, who was of course quite correct, stuck to his story.

Rebmann left on his third journey to the Chagga country on April 6, 1849, hoping to go as far as the land of the Wanyamwezi. He traveled once again via the lands of Masaki to the headquarters of King Mankinga. This time it was Mankinga who did not want Rebmann to travel any farther, and he kept him in his village for two weeks while each day he relieved him of more and more of his trade goods. When Rebmann started to cry at this thievery, the King said he would reimburse him with tusks of ivory. When, however, Rebmann prepared to leave on June 6, the King's brother arrived to inform him that it would not be possible to supply the ivory after all. Since Rebmann had nothing left, they gave him one old broken tusk to trade for enough food to get him home. As he left the village, the inhabitants lined up to spit on him, which was their usual departure ceremony, meaning this as a sign of peace. On the return trip, the expedition had barely enough to eat, and Rebmann wrote ahead on July 26 asking Krapf to send him "a bottle of wine and some biscuits."

During Rebmann's trip to the Chagga country, two new missionaries arrived in Rabai, Jakob Erhardt and Johannes Wagner. Immediately after their arrival, they both came down with fever, and Wagner died on July 30, 1849. In the spring of 1850, Krapf went to Europe for a vacation and to promote the mission. While he was away, Rebmann and Erhardt bought a plot of land at Kisulidini farther south on the coast, opposite the island of Zanzibar, where they started building another mission station. After Krapf's return in September 1851, Rebmann traveled to Cairo where he married an Englishwoman recently widowed by the death of one of Rebmann's missionary colleagues. They returned together to East Africa in April 1852 and moved to Kisulidini.

After moving to Kisulidini, Rebmann continued to make trips into the interior. Using these journeys and the reports he gleaned from the Africans he had talked with, he and Erhardt drew a map that was published in 1856 in Krapf's book about their travels. It showed the interior to be occupied by one gigantic lake, shaped like a slug. This body of water (which does not exist) was assumed to be the source of the Nile River. Therefore, when **Richard Burton** and **John Hanning Speke** arrived in Africa in January 1857 to search for the Nile sources, their first stop was to consult with Rebmann.

Rebmann's wife died in November 1866. He stayed and maintained the mission post at Kisulidini until 1875. By then, he was prematurely aged and had lost the sight in one eye and was partially blind in the other. He went back to Germany and saw his native village for the first time in 31 years. However, he caught pneumonia in the cold climate and lost what little sight he had left. Krapf was living in the nearby village of Kornthal, and he took Rebmann in to take care of him. He hired a nurse, who had known Rebmann as a youth, and after he recovered they got married. They went on a honeymoon to a health spa, but Rebmann suffered a relapse. They returned to Kornthal, where he died on October 4, 1876.

Where to learn more

The major source is Krapf's book, *Travels, Researches, and Missionary Labours During an Eighteen Years' Residence in Eastern Africa* (London: Trübner & Co., 1860; reprinted, New York: Johnson Reprint Corp., 1968), which also includes narratives of Rebmann's journeys. There is a summary of these trips in Christopher Hibbert, *Africa Explored: Europeans in the Dark Continent, 1769-1889* (London: Allen Lane, 1982). There is a biographical essay on Rebmann in *Allgemeine Deutsche Biographie*, vol. 27 (Leipzig: Duncker & Humblot, 1888).

Sally Ride

(1951 -)

Sally Ride was the first American woman to fly into space, on board the seventh space shuttle mission in June 1983.

Sally Ride was born in Encino, California on May 26, 1951. Her father was a professor of political science at a local community college, and her mother later worked as a vocational counselor. Her sister is a Presbyterian minister. Ride had natural athletic ability and at about the age of 10 took up tennis. She became a member of the United States junior tennis circuit and eventually ranked 17th nationally. Because of her tennis skills, she received a partial scholarship to a private prep school in Los Angeles, the Westlake School for Girls. There she was influenced by a favorite teacher, Dr. Elizabeth Mommaerts, to take up the study of science.

Ride entered Swarthmore College in Pennsylvania in 1968, intending to study physics. She dropped out after three semesters with the intention of becoming a professional tennis player.

Sally Ride. NASA.

However, after a few months she decided that she would never become a top-ranked pro and returned to college at Stanford University in 1970. There she took a double major in physics and English literature, with a specialization in Shakespeare. She received a joint B.A./B.S. degree in 1973 and then returned to Stanford to do graduate work in x-ray astronomy and free-electron lasers. She wrote her doctoral dissertation on the theoretical behavior of free electrons in a magnetic field.

In 1977, Ride read an advertisement in a newspaper from the National Aeronautics and Space Administration (NASA) requesting applications from young scientists to serve as "mission specialists" on future space flights. She was one of more than 8,000 to apply. Because of her qualifications, she was one of 208 finalists. She was then flown to Houston, Texas, in October 1977 to take psychiatric evaluation exams, physical fitness tests, and several personal interviews. She was chosen with five other women, the first selected by NASA, to be members of the astronaut class of 1978.

Ride then entered a year-long training program that included parachute jumping, water survival, acclimatization to gravitational pull and weightlessness, and radio communications and navigation. She also got a pilot's license and learned how to fly jet airplanes. She found this so enjoyable that she then took up flying as a hobby. Following the first-year training program, Ride was assigned to an engineering team that was charged with designing a remote mechanical arm to be used in deploying and retrieving space satellites. She also spent hundreds of hours flying in facsimile spacecraft, or "simulators." During the second and third flights of the space shuttle *Columbia*, in November 1981 and March 1982, Ride served as the ground-based communications officer who radioed messages back and forth between the shuttle crew.

In April 1982 Robert Crippen, who had been named as commander of the seventh space shuttle flight, chose Ride to be one of the four other crew members. Crippen's announcement that Ride would be the first American woman in space generated a lot of publicity. Both Crippen and Ride attempted to downplay this aspect of the flight by insisting that she had been chosen because she was the best-qualified mission specialist available and that no thought had been given to the historic nature of her flight. After the announcement of the crew members, they all began several months of intensive training to prepare them for the flight. During this period, Ride also got married to fellow astronaut Steven Hawley in July 1982.

The seventh space shuttle flight, with Ride on board, took off in the spacecraft *Challenger* at 7:33 a.m. on June 18, 1983 from Cape Canaveral, Florida. (On a later flight, in January 1986, *Challenger* was to explode on take-off, killing all crew members aboard including schoolteacher Christa McAuliffe.) After the shuttle achieved earth orbit, Ride's duties aboard the flight were to deploy two communications satellites, to conduct trials of the mechanical arm that she had helped design, and to perform and monitor about 40 scientific experiments.

Ride launched Anik-C, a Canadian communications satellite, on the first day of the flight. The next day she successfully deployed Palapa B, an Indonesian communications satellite. She then turned her attention to the various scientific experiments, which included making metal alloys, growing crystals, and producing drugs in conditions of weightlessness. On the fifth day of the flight, Ride took part in experiments with the mechanical arm in which a German satellite was launched and then retrieved several times. The aim of the experiments was to test the possibility of capturing defective spacecraft and repairing them on board the shuttle.

The shuttle mission ended on June 24, 1983. It had been planned that the *Challenger* would touch down at the Cape Canaveral, where a large crowd was waiting, but bad weather forced it to land at Edwards Air Force Base in California instead. Ride immediately became the focus of press and public attention. In her post-flight press conference, she said, "I'm sure it was the most fun I'll ever have in my life." However, she refused to make any public appearances or press statements without the other members of the crew present.

After three weeks of debriefings, Ride took another assignment at NASA—acting as liaison officer between NASA and private companies doing work on the space program. She flew on another space shuttle mission, on board the *Challenger*, from October 5-13, 1984. Following her landmark flight, a number of other women have flown on U.S. space shuttle missions.

Where to learn more

Ride told her own story in *To Space and Back* (Lothrop, Lee & Shepard Books, 1986). There are three biographies: Karen O'Connor, *Sally Ride and the New Astronauts: Scientists in Space* (Franklin Watts, 1983); Carolyn Blacknall, *Sally Ride* (Dillon Press, 1984), and, designed for young readers, Jane Hurwitz and Sue Hurwitz, *Sally Ride: Shooting for the Stars* (New York: Fawcett Columbine, 1989).

More general books about the space shuttle include: Robin Kerrod, *Space Shuttle* (New York: Gallery Books, W.H. Smith Publishers, 1984); Andrew Wilson, *The Shuttle Story* (New York: Hamlyn Publishing, 1986); and Mary Virginia Fox, *Women Astronauts Aboard the Shuttle* (Julian Messner, 1987).

Susie Carson Rijnhart

(1868 - 1908)

Susie Carson Rijnhart was a Canadian missionary who traveled through eastern Tibet in an attempt to reach the Tibetan capital of Lhasa.

Susie Carson was born in the small town of Strathroy in Ontario, Canada where her father was the Methodist minister. She decided at an early age that she wanted to be a medical missionary and graduated from the Woman's Medical College in Toronto in 1888. In 1894 she met Petrus Rijnhart, a Dutch missionary who had just returned from China. They married and then left immediately for China to continue his work together. They were not sponsored by any church but were financed by donations from friends and their own savings.

The Rijnharts planned to go to Kumbum on the China-Tibet border where no Christians had ever worked and from where it might be possible to travel to Tibet, where no Christian missionaries had been allowed since the 17th century. They landed in Shanghai and traveled up the Yangtze River to Sining, the capital of the province of Tsinghai. From there, they went to the small town of Lusar, the trading center for the great Buddhist monastery of Kumbum. They stayed there for two years. While at Kumbum the Muslim inhabitants of the neighboring province of Gansu revolted, and there were many casualties. To their surprise the Rijnharts were invited to the Buddhist lamasery to set up a hospital. As a result, they were able to learn Tibetan and study the Buddhist religion.

The Rijnharts then settled in another trading town, Tankar. There they were visited by several explorers who were traveling through central Asia, including **Sven Hedin**. The Rijnharts themselves made an exploring expedition with their newborn baby boy, Charlie, to Koko Nor (Lake). On this trip they decided that they wanted to travel to Lhasa and see if they could continue their missionary work. They knew this would be difficult because the city was closed to all foreigners, and no Western woman had ever been there.

Susie and Petrus Rijnhart left Tankar with Charlie, their dog Topsy, and three servants on May 20, 1898 and traveled into Tibet. They celebrated Charlie's first birthday on June 30 with a birthday cake. His mother wrote, "How thoroughly baby enjoyed those days, when he made the tents ring with joyousness from his musical laughter, his shouts and the beating of our Russian brass wash-basin which he used as a drum. Then from sheer weariness he would fall asleep, leaving the camp pervaded by a stillness, made sweet by the fact that he was still there."

After three months they were within 200 miles of Lhasa. Then, their two guides deserted them. One of their horses, which they depended on for transport, died and five others were stolen. Then, on "the darkest day in our history," baby Charlie simply stopped breathing and died without any warning. "The very joy of our life, the only human thing that made life and labour sweet amid the desolation and isolation of Tibet—the child of our love" was dead. They buried him that night in a medicine box, "in his hand was placed a little bunch of white asters and blue poppies," and continued on their way the next day.

At Nagchuk (Nagqu) they were told they could not proceed any farther and were turned back. They were, however, supplied with fresh horses and supplies. Along the road, the Rijnharts stopped and had a picnic to celebrate their fourth wedding anniversary on September 15, 1898. There they were ambushed by a gang of robbers. The thieves took those horses they could and shot the ones they could not, including one in the spine so she would be crippled, to prevent pursuit. They stole Topsy as well. After the attack, the porters said they would go to get help, and then they disappeared. The Rijnharts were left with one old gray pony and some of their supplies.

By this time, they were assailed by winter blizzards and were unable to carry very much. They loaded themselves with a minimum of provisions and set off. On the third day, they reached a wide river and saw an encampment on the other side. That night they pitched camp in a snowstorm. The next morning, Petrus crossed the river and headed to the encampment to get help. He disappeared behind a rock and was never seen again.

Susie was left alone in the middle of Tibet. She was able to get only the smallest amount of assistance and experienced the treatment that Tibetan women were subjected to. She was not allowed to enter a tent and had to spend several nights sleeping outside in the snow. Her possessions were taken or she had to use them to pay for guides. She had to sell her Bible and her baby's fur coat and boots in order to eat. Finally, two months after her husband disappeared, she arrived, starving and with frostbitten feet, at the Christian mission station of Ta-chien-lu in western China and announced, "I am Dr. Rijnhart."

Rijnhart stayed at the mission station for six months recuperating. There, she found out that her husband had been killed by robbers, probably the same ones who had attacked them on the road. When she was well, she returned to Canada and wrote about her experiences and lectured to Christian audiences. In 1902 she returned to Ta-chien-lu to work. In 1905 she married a fellow missionary, a Mr. Moyes. She became ill in 1907 and went back to Canada where she died on February 7, 1908, leaving a three-week-old son.

Where to learn more

Rijnhart's heartbreaking story has been told by several writers. Her own account, on which all the others are based, is *With the Tibetans in Tent and Temple: Narrative of Four Years' Residence on the Tibetan Border, and of a Journey into the Far Interior* (Chicago: Revell, 1901; Edinburgh: Oliphant, Anderson and Ferrier, 1901).

Rijnhart's story is recounted in the context of women explorers by Marion Tinling, *Women into the Unknown* (New York: Greenwood Press, 1989) and Jane Robinson, *Wayward Women: A Guide to Women Travellers* (New York: Oxford University Press, 1990). Carlotta Hacker in *The Indomitable Lady Doctors* (Toronto: Clarke, Irwin, 1974) investigated Rijnhart's school and church records. Isabel S. Robson, *Two Lady Missionaries in Tibet* (London: Partridge, 1909) is an account designed to inspire future missionaries with the courage of Rijnhart and her contemporary, **Annie Royle Taylor**.

As part of the history of Western exploration of Tibet, the narrative of Rijnhart's odyssey is told by John MacGregor in *Tibet: A Chronicle of Exploration* (London: Routledge & Kegan Paul, 1970) and Peter Hopkirk in *Trespassers on the Roof of the World* (London: John Murray, 1982).

Jacob Roggeveen

(1659-1729)

Jacob Roggeveen was a Dutch navigator who made a trip to the Pacific to find the "great southern continent" and was the first European to visit Easter Island.

One of the great legends and mysteries of world exploration was that of a vast southern continent that extended from the South Pole far into the South Seas, or the Pacific Ocean. The history of the discovery of Australia, as well as of much of the South Pacific, was the attempt to find this continent. Various expeditions whittled away at its contours until it was finally realized that Antarctica was not connected to Australia or to any other great land mass. One such expedition was that of the Dutch explorer Jacob Roggeveen. Roggeveen's father had interested the Dutch West India Company in looking for the southern continent, but he died before he was able to mount the expedition. Jacob worked for a competing company, the Dutch East India Company, from which he retired with a large fortune. In 1721 he took up his father's work, with the West India Company providing three ships.

Roggeveen left Holland on August 21, 1721 and went south through the South Atlantic to the Falkland Islands and around Cape Horn into the Pacific. He sailed north and reached the Juan Fernandez Islands, which had been discovered by **Willem Schouten** and **Jacob Le Maire** in 1616 and on which Alexander Selkirk had been marooned, serving as the basis for Daniel Defoe's *Robinson Crusoe*. Roggeveen thought that these small islands would serve as the ideal base for a Dutch colony from which to explore the southern continent.

Roggeveen headed east, fully expecting to land shortly on the as-yet-undiscovered continent. Instead, he stumbled upon a small island on April 5, 1722—Easter Sunday. He named the island after the day. Easter Island is the farthest east of the islands of Polynesia. Isolated as it is, its Polynesian inhabitants developed a distinctive culture—its most remarkable feature being the carving of large stone statues of heads that were then worshiped as gods. The Dutchmen under Roggeveen were the first Europeans to see these Easter Island carvings, and there were no further visitors from the West for another fifty years. By that time, the population was much smaller because of continuous warfare between rival clans, and the people had lost the knowledge of how the carvings were made. It is unfortunate that Roggeveen did not take more time to find out about this culture and its achievements, which are now considered so remarkable and so mysterious.

Roggeveen stayed only one week on Easter Island, and he considered the islanders to be friendly even though they tended to take the Europeans' possessions without asking, and some of the Polynesians were killed in initial contacts. Roggeveen left quickly, convinced that he would shortly reach his goal. He sailed generally northwestward but often changed his course, thinking the southern continent was just over the horizon. The three ships sailed 800 leagues without seeing any land at all. In May, they came upon the northern Tuamotus, islands that are now part of French Polynesia, which had also been discovered by Schouten and Le Maire. Here things did not go well—one of the ships was wrecked on a coral reef. In a confrontation with the inhabitants of the island of Makatea, some of the islanders were shot and ten Dutchmen were stoned to death.

At this point, the leaders of the expedition held a council and decided that since they had not yet found the southern continent, they should head directly for Batavia, the capital of the Dutch East Indies, and from there take the usual route back to Holland. On their way westward, they passed the island of Bora Bora, which is part of the Society Islands, and the Samoan Islands, where they went ashore to get fresh water and fruit. The Dutch ships passed between the island groups of Tuvalu and Kiribati and headed north of New Guinea to the Moluccas, which were part of the Dutch East Indies. From there, they went to Java and the great port of Batavia, now called Jakarta, which they reached in September 1722.

Roggeveen was not welcomed in Batavia. The Governor and other officials all worked for the East India Company, which had a monopoly on Dutch trade east of Holland. Since Roggeveen worked for the West India Company, he had now trespassed into the other company's domain. His ships were confiscated, and he and his men were sent back almost as prisoners on ships of the East India Company. When he got back to Holland, Roggeveen started legal proceedings, that he eventually won, to get the value of his ships back. He died within a few years of his voyage.

Where to learn more

The most complete documentation of Roggeveen's voyage is in Dutch: F.E. Baron Mulert, *De Reis van Mr. Jacob Roggeveen* (The Hague: 1919). Roggeveen's journal has since been edited in English by the eminent Pacific historian Andrew Sharp, ed. *The Journal of Jacob Roggeveen* (Oxford: Clarendon Press, 1970). Two of the general histories of Pacific exploration give valuable information on Roggeveen: J.C. Beaglehole, *The Exploration of the Pacific* (Stanford: Stanford University Press, 1966) and O.H.K. Spate, *Monopolists and Freebooters* (Minneapolis: University of Minnesota Press, 1983).

Friedrich Gerhard Rohlfs

(1831 - 1896)

Gerhard Rohlfs was a German adventurer who was the first European to cross West Africa from the Mediterranean to the Gulf of Guinea.

Gerhard Rohlfs was born near Bremen in Germany in 1831, the third son of a doctor. He was educated at home until he was 15. Once he got to school, he hated it and ran away to Amsterdam, but his parents caught up with him and brought him back home. At the age of 18 he quit school and joined the army in order to fight in the war between the German Confederation and Denmark over Schleswig-Holstein. At the end of the war, he spent some time at different universities as a medical student. Giving that up, he enlisted in the Austrian Army, from which he deserted to join the French Foreign Legion in North Africa.

Rohlfs arrived in Algeria in 1855 and fought in the Kabylia campaigns of 1856 and 1857. He was promoted to sergeant

Gerhard Rohlfs. The Bettmann Archive.

(and acting surgeon!) and stayed in the Foreign Legion until 1861. He then headed for Morocco where he hoped to get a job as a doctor in the army of the Sultan of Morocco. Setting out from Tangier on the Mediterranean coast, he disguised himself as a Muslim because he thought it would be easier to travel that way. He was soon robbed of all his money, and no one was fooled by the disguise. This did not stop him, however, and he reached Ouezzane where he was given a letter of recommendation by the Grand Sherif. From there he went to Meknès where he was hired as a physician in the court of the Sultan.

Rohlfs stayed in the Sultan's court for a while but in 1862 he left in order to travel to the south. He went as far south as Tafilelt in the southern Atlas Mountains. He was the first European to visit the city since **René Caillié** in 1828. In the oasis of Bouanane, north of Tafilelt, he was attacked by robbers and left for dead. He had been shot through the thigh, and his left arm and right hand were almost cut off. These wounds bothered him for the rest of his life. Two passersby found him and took him to the oasis of Hadjui, where he recuperated for two months. He then headed across the border to the French outpost of Géryville in Algeria.

Rohlfs traveled to Oran and Algiers in order to try to regain his health and then, in 1864, made a visit to the region of Tuat in southern Algeria, the first European to travel there, but he did not make it to Timbuktu, which had been his objective. By this time he had sent some of his reports to a German geographical magazine, and he was beginning to become well known as an African explorer. On a visit to Germany in 1865 he was persuaded by **Heinrich Barth** to try to discover the relationship between the rivers flowing into Lake Chad and the Niger-Benue system.

On this expedition, Rohlfs left Tripoli in May 1865, crossed the Sahara by way of Marzuq to Kukawa, arriving there on July 22, and then went on to Bornu. He reached the Benue at Lokoja on March 28, 1867 and sailed down it and the Niger to the Gulf of Guinea near Lagos. In making this trip, he became the first European to cross western Africa from the Mediterranean to the Gulf of Guinea. On his return to Germany he was given many honors and met personally with the Prussian King and Chancellor Otto von Bismarck to tell them about his trip.

Rohlfs was sent as an official observer on Sir Robert Napier's military expedition to Ethiopia in 1868. He went back to Tripoli at the end of 1868 and was entrusted with some gifts from the King of Prussia to the King of Bornu. He turned them over to

Gustav Nachtigal and sent him off into the Sahara. In the following years, Rohlfs went as far east as the Nile and then explored the fringes of the highlands of Ethiopia. He attended the conference sponsored by King Leopold of Belgium on African exploration in Brussels in 1876. Following that, he traveled from Benghazi to Aujila and then across the desert to Kufra, covering over fifty miles a day for five days.

Rohlfs was sent on a diplomatic mission to the court of the Emperor of Ethiopia in 1879. In 1884 he was named German consul in Zanzibar but got into conflict with the British consul and was quickly recalled. He then refused offers of consulates in other places and went back to a life of semi-retirement in Germany, writing about his adventures in a series of popular books that earned him a great deal of money. He led a prosperous and leisurely life until his death from a heart condition in June 1896.

Where to learn more

Almost all of the available material on Rohlfs is in German. Only one of his books appeared in English, *Adventures in Morocco and Journey Through the Oases of Draa and Tafilet* (London: 1874), which is about his early travels in Morocco. The books about his major explorations are: *Land und Volk in Afrika* (Bremen: 1870); *Kufra: Reise von Tripolis nach der Oase Kufra* (Leipzig: 1881); *Quer durch Afrika: Reise vom Mittelmeer nach dem Tschadsee und zum Golf von Guinea* (Leipzig: 1874-1875); and *Reise durch Marokko* (Norden: 1884).

There is one full-scale biography, which was written by his nephew and is based on his personal papers: Konrad Günther, *Gerhard Rohlfs: Lebenbilds eines Afrikaforschers* (Freiburg: 1912). There is a good biographical sketch in one of the standard German biographical dictionaries: Viktor Hansch, "Gerhard Rohlfs," in *Allgemeine Deutsche Biographie*, vol. 53, pp. 440-449.

The best source in English, and the one on which this account is based is Wolfe W. Schmokel, "Gerhard Rohlfs: The Lonely Explorer" in Robert Rotberg, *Africa and Its Explorers: Motives, Methods, and Impact* (Cambridge: Harvard University Press, 1970).

Cândido Rondon

(1865 - 1958)

Cândido Rondon was a Brazilian army engineer who spent many years exploring in the Brazilian forests of Mato Grosso and the Amazon River basin.

C ândido Rondon was born in the Brazilian state of Mato Grosso in 1865. His father was of Portuguese origin, and his mother was Native American. They both died when he was a small child, and he was raised by an uncle. After finishing high school, he became a primary school teacher for two years and then joined the Brazilian army.

In 1883 he entered the Brazilian military academy where he graduated with honors in 1888. He then went on to a post-graduate school for army officers, and became influenced by the fashionable philosophy of positivism, which he retained all his life. He joined the army officers who overthrew the Emperor of Brazil (the only monarchy in the Americas) in 1889. In 1890 he started his career as an army engineer by helping to build a telegraph line across the state of Mato Grosso.

This line was completed in 1895, and Rondon started construction of a road between Rio de Janeiro and Cuiabá, the capital of Mato Grosso. (Until the road was completed, the only transport between the two cities was by river through Argentina.) From 1900 to 1906 he was in charge of building telegraph lines across Brazil to Bolivia and Paraguay. During this time he opened up new territory, collected important biological specimens for the National Museum, and served as intermediary with the warlike Bororo tribe of western Brazil.

As a result of Rondon's success, he was put in charge of extending the telegraph line from Mato Grosso to the Amazon in 1906. In the course of doing so, he discovered the Juruena River in northern Mato Grosso, an important tributary of the Tapajós, one of the main rivers flowing into the Amazon. He also established the first contact with the Nambikwara tribe, who had maintained a policy of killing all Europeans they encountered.

On May 3, 1909, Rondon began his longest and most important expedition. He left the tiny settlement of Tapirapuã in northern Mato Grosso state heading northwest to meet up with the Madeira River, a major tributary of the Amazon. By August the party had eaten all of its supplies and had to live for the next four months on food it could scavenge from the forest. They reached the Jiparaná River with no supplies, and some of the men were so weak they could only crawl, not walk. Along the way, they had picked up a man who been lost for four months.

They were able to build canoes and float down the Jiparaná to the Madeira, which they reached on Christmas Day, 1909. During the course of their walk through the forest, Rondon had come upon a large river flowing to the northwest between the Juruena and the Jiparaná that had never been mapped or heard of by the Brazilians. He named it the River of Doubt, since nothing was known about it.

Following Rondon's arrival in the Amazon city of Manaus in early 1910, he came down with a bad case of malaria and was forced to return to Rio de Janeiro where he was received with popular acclaim and became an overnight celebrity: people had thought he had disappeared in the dense forest.

In June 1910 the Brazilian government created the first agency to protect and defend its Native American population from the ongoing exploitation of Brazilian settlers and business-men. Rondon became the agency's first director. In March 1911, he resolved a dispute between the Caingangue tribe and settlers in São Paulo state and another involving the Parintins in Amazonas state in 1912.

At the end of 1913, Rondon joined former U.S. president **Theodore Roosevelt** in the Roosevelt-Rondon Scientific Expedition, which was designed to explore the River of Doubt. They left Tapiripuã in January 1914 and reached the River of Doubt on February 27. They did not reach the mouth of the river until April 26, after much suffering. During the course of the expedition, Rondon renamed the river the Roosevelt.

Between 1915 and 1919, Rondon worked on mapping the state of Mato Grosso, during which time he traced the courses of several unknown rivers and established first contact with several Native American tribes. In 1919 he became chief of the Brazilian army's engineering corps as well as the head of the telegraph commission. In 1924 and 1925 he led army forces against a rebellion in the state of São Paulo.

From 1927 to 1930 Rondon returned to his exploring activities, being put in charge of surveying the boundaries between Brazil and all of the neighboring countries. During this work, he encountered many tribes that had had little or no contact with Brazilians: Wapixana, Yanomami, Maku, Mayongong, Pianokotó, Tiriyó, and Wayaná. In 1930 he was on the wrong side in a coup d'état, but was pardoned and spent four years writing about his trips to inspect the boundary surveys. From 1934-1938 he was in charge of a commission to mediate the dispute between Peru and Colombia over the Amazon river town of Leticia, which was finally awarded to Colombia. As recognition for this work, the Brazilian composer Hector Vila-Lobos composed a symphony in his honor.

During the remaining years of his long life, Rondon was showered with many honors and tributes, including having a territory (now a state) named after him—Rondônia. His advancing age, however, did not stop him from continuing his work: he was responsible for increasing the power and resources of the Native American protection service, established the National Indian Museum, and established Brazil's first national park along the Xingu River. He died in Rio de Janeiro in 1958 at the age of 93.

Where to learn more

There is not much available about Rondon in English. He figures in two important books by the historian John Hemming about the decimation of the Native Americans of Brazil: *Red Gold: The Conquest of the Brazilian Indians* (Cambridge: Harvard University Press, 1978) and *Amazon Frontier: The Defeat of the Brazilian Indians* (Cambridge: Harvard University Press, 1987). There is a discussion of Rondon in Edward Goodman, *The Explorers of South America* (New York: Macmillan, 1972). The books about **Theodore Roosevelt**'s expedition necessarily deal with Rondon as well.

The most comprehensive studies of Rondon in Portuguese have been done by Edilberto Coutinho: *Rondon e a integração amazônica* (Rio de Janeiro: 1968) and *Rondon, o Civilizador da Ultima Fronteira* (Rio de Janeiro: Instituto Nacional do Livro, 1975). Shortly before his death, Rondon recounted his life to author Ester Viveiros: *Rondon conta sua vida* (Rio de Janeiro: 1958).

Theodore Roosevelt

(1858 - 1919)

Theodore Roosevelt was an American who led an adventur-ous life that included ranching, big game hunting in Africa, serving as President of the United States, and exploring an unknown part of Brazil.

Theodore Roosevelt was born in New York City on October 27, 1858, the descendant of a Dutch family that had achieved wealth and social standing in New York society. He was unhealthy during his childhood, suffering from asthma and bad eyesight, but developed a mystique of activity and sportsmanship that stayed with him throughout his life.

After graduating from Harvard University in 1880, he married Alice Hathaway Lee. He wrote a history of the War of 1812 and then was elected to the New York State Assembly in 1882. During the summer of 1883 he suffered badly from asthma and took a trip to the western United States to seek relief. He ended up in the small town of Moffit, North Dakota not far from Bismarck. He convinced some local ranchers to take him on a buffalo (bison) hunt, and this launched his career as a "big game hunter." He was so excited by his experience that he bought a ranch in the Bad Lands of North Dakota.

Theodore Roosevelt.

His young wife died in childbirth in 1884 (his daughter was Alice Roosevelt Longworth who later gained notoriety on her own), on the same day that his mother died. These setbacks slowed him down for a while, but then he continued his involvement in Republican politics and wrote several books. He became Commissioner of the United States Civil Service in 1889 and police commissioner in New York City in 1895.

When William McKinley was elected President of the United States in 1896, he chose Roosevelt as Assistant Secretary of the Navy. In this post he was partly responsible for the outbreak of war with Spain in 1898. During the war he organized a volunteer cavalry regiment, the Rough Riders, which he led in battle in Cuba. He gained such fame from his exploits that he was elected Governor of New York State in November 1898.

Roosevelt only served two years as Governor when he was chosen to be vice-presidential candidate during President McKinley's second campaign. They won, but McKinley was assassinated, and Roosevelt became President on September 14, 1901, at the age of 43. During his term of office he was noted for various progressive and reform policies and was renominated and won the office again in 1904. He decided not to run again in 1908, but helped in the campaign of fellow Republican William Howard Taft.

Out of office this energetic man had to find adventures to keep himself occupied. A month after his successor was inaugurated he headed off with his elder son Kermit on a hunting safari in East Africa. They arrived in Mombasa, Kenya on April 21, 1909. They then went by train from Mombasa to the Kapiti Plains in northwestern Kenya where they started their hunting expedition. Roosevelt killed specimens of many of the great predatory mammals that live in that part of Africa, and was almost trampled by a rhinoceros when his first shot missed.

Roosevelt slowly followed a route northwest and then north from Nairobi to Kijabi and then on a trek through waterless country to Lake Naivasha, where he shot several hippopotami. He also came down with fever and was sick for several days. He then went to Mt. Kenya and Mt. Elgon. From Kenya he took a steamer across Lake Victoria Nyanza to Entebbe in Uganda. From there he took his safari across Uganda to Lake Albert; along the way he was almost trampled by an elephant.

From Lake Albert Roosevelt and his party took steamers across the lake and then up the White Nile. For a while they stopped and hunted in the Lado country in far northwestern Uganda, which had rarely been visited by Europeans. They traveled to Gondokoro in the southern Sudan and then on to Khartoum, which they reached on March 14, 1910. He wrote about his experiences in a popular book, *African Game Trails.*

From Africa Roosevelt traveled to Europe where he met with the kings and prime ministers of various countries and was always welcomed by large crowds. He went to Oslo to accept the Nobel Peace Prize, which he had won for his efforts to end the Russo-Japanese War. He represented the United States at the funeral of King Edward VII of Great Britain. He returned to New York on June 18, 1910.

On his return to the United States, Roosevelt became involved once more in politics and broke with President Taft to become the leader of the progressive wing of the Republican Party. He lost the Republican nomination for President in 1912 and chose to run as the candidate of a new Progressive Party. During a campaign speech in Milwaukee, Wisconsin on October 12, 1912, he was shot and wounded by a would-be assassin. He recovered in time to finish the campaign but lost the election.

Following this defeat, Roosevelt started out on his greatest adventure and the one that gives him claim to be a noteworthy explorer in addition to all his other occupations. He had planned a speaking trip to Argentina and Brazil to be followed by a steamer trip on the Amazon and other rivers. The Brazilian government proposed a much more adventurous journey—to accompany the Brazilian explorer **Cândido Rondon** on a trip to the "River of Doubt" in Mato Grosso state that Rondon had recently found.

Roosevelt started on the expedition with Rondon at the border between Paraguay and Brazil on the Paraguay River. They took a steamboat up the river as far as the little town of Cáceres, where the Sepotuba River flows into the Paraguay. Along the way Roosevelt killed a peccary, a kind of wild boar, with a spear. They traveled by canoe up the Sepotuba River, where he shot a jaguar and a tapir. They reached the settlement of Tapirapuã, which was where Rondon had started out on his expedition that first saw the River of Doubt and was the last place inhabited by Brazilians before the forest.

From Tapirapuã they traveled to the northwest through dense forests, then up to the top of the Parecís plateau, across the divide into the Amazon basin. They then continued on with horses, pack-mules, and oxen. They rode through many heavy rains, across "endless flats of grass and of low open scrubby forest." There were many enormous ant hills inhabited by leaf-carrying ants, which could also cut up and carry away items of clothing; poisonous black ants; and fire ants. They also saw the telegraph line that Rondón had constructed. The road ended at a Native American village at Salto Belo, the thunderous falls of the Rio Sacre. They then traveled on through pouring rain to the falls of Utiariti, almost as big as Niagara Falls, where the river dropped from a great shelving rock three hundred feet to the gorge below.

On February 3, 1914 the expedition traveled through territory inhabited by the Nambikwara tribe with a mule train and six oxcarts, driving a dozen steers ahead of them to use as food. On February 24 they reached a camp that one of Rondon's lieutenants had set up on a small stream that flowed into the River of Doubt. The expedition then divided, with part of them taking the Jiparaná River to the Madeira.

On the afternoon of February 27 Roosevelt and his party started down the river. "It was interesting work," he wrote, "for no civilized man, no white man, had ever gone down or up this river or seen the country through which we were passing." By March 5 they had chopped their way through the jungle around the first rapids safely, and found that their main problem was insects; ants took part of the lining out of Roosevelt's helmet and termites chewed a leg off his underwear.

After 15 days they had passed three more rapids, lost two canoes, and had to cut a tree to make a large canoe to replace two that had sunk. Their work was completed in a rainstorm. At that point, they had enough food for 35 more days, but they had only covered about a tenth of their route during the first 15 days. The next day, one of the canoes was overturned in a whirlpool, and Roosevelt's son Kermit was almost drowned; in addition, a large part of the food supplies were lost. While they were trying to salvage their goods, one of the dogs wandered off and was shot by Native Americans who resented the intrusion. The trip was becoming less fun.

In the next few days, a new river was discovered that was named the Rio Kermit, and Rondon announced that the Brazilian government was renaming the River of Doubt the Rio Roosevelt. They built two new dugouts to replace the lost ones and set out again on March 22. On March 27 Roosevelt bruised his leg badly against a boulder in the water while trying to keep one of the canoes from capsizing. This injury became infected, and he was also plagued with fever and dysentery. For 48 hours he was very near death and afterwards could only travel a short distance each day. The trip was becoming a disaster—all the more so since they were almost out of food.

During the remainder of the trip, one of the Brazilian porters killed another one and was then abandoned on the shore. Kermit Roosevelt became ill with a very high fever, and his father even offered to stay behind so that he would not hold up the rest of the party from reaching safety. But by April 13 the river became smoother, and it was possible to travel farther and faster without having to make so many difficult portages. On the 15th they reached the first house they had encountered in seven weeks. The pioneer farmer who lived there told them about the rest of the course they were to take. The health of the two Roosevelts improved somewhat, and they were able to reach the mouth of the Rio Roosevelt where it flowed into the Aripuanã River, a tributary of the large Madeira River whose course was already known. They reached the little hamlet of São João at the end of April.

Roosevelt's voyage down the River of Doubt.

Roosevelt traveled by steamer to the Amazon river town of Manaus, where one observer said, "he had wasted to a shadow of his former self; but his unbounded enthusiasm remained undiminished." The expedition had collected a large number of animal and insect specimens and had mapped a great river that had previously been unknown. Roosevelt wrote a book about his experiences, which was quite popular.

Soon after his return to the United States, World War I broke out. At first, he supported American neutrality but later urged intervention on the side of Great Britain and France. He died at his home of Sagamore Hill on Long Island on January 6, 1919 at the age of 61. His early death was partly caused by the injuries and disease he suffered during his Brazilian explorations.

Where to learn more

The best introduction to the life of Theodore Roosevelt is *Theodore Roosevelt: An Autobiography* (New York: G.P. Putnam's Sons, 1913; several subsequent editions). This can be supplemented by his *Collected Works, the National Edition*, 20 vols., edited by Hermann Hagedorn (New York: 1926) and *Letters of Theodore Roosevelt*, 8 vols., edited by E.E. Morison (New York: 1951-1954). Hagedorn also wrote an entertaining biography for young people: *The Boys' Life of Theodore Roosevelt* (New York: Harper & Bros., 1922). Two good biographies of Roosevelt that include extensive bibliographies are G.W. Chessman, *Theodore Roosevelt and the Politics of Power* (New York: Harper & Row, 1968) and David McCullough, *Mornings on Horseback* (New York: Alfred A. Knopf, 1977) about his early life.

Works that specifically relate to Roosevelt's South American adventure are: Theodore Roosevelt, *Through the Brazilian Wilderness* (New York: Charles Scribner's Sons, 1914); George K. Cherrie, *Dark Trails: Adventures of a Naturalist* (New York: G.P. Putnam's Sons, 1930), by one of the participants, who was a notable explorer in his own right; Leo Miller, *In the Wilds of South America* (New York: Scribner's, 1919), by another participant; and John Augustine Zahm, *Through South America's Southland* (New York: Appleton, 1916), a Catholic missionary who traveled to many remote parts of South America and whose original idea spurred Roosevelt to make the expedition.

James Clark Ross

(1800 - 1862)

James Clark Ross was a British naval officer who was a member of several expeditions to the Arctic, where he discovered the North Magnetic Pole, and who made three trips to Antarctica, where he came close to the South Magnetic Pole.

James Clark Ross was the nephew of a well-known British Arctic explorer, **Sir John Ross**. In 1818 John Ross was sent to continue the search for a Northwest Passage around North America. James Ross was on board as a junior officer. The expedition entered Lancaster Sound north of Baffin Island, but Sir John almost immediately ordered it to turn around claiming to have seen mountains barring the way.

In fact, Sir John had been deceived by the fog, and in the following year the British Admiralty sent out another expedition under the command of **Sir Edward Parry** with James Ross again as a member of the crew. This expedition went as far as Melville Island, hundreds of miles farther west than any ship had sailed that far north. James Ross sailed on Parry's other expeditions as well.

In 1829 Sir John Ross was put in command of an Arctic expedition financed by private interests. He commanded the ship *Victory* and put his nephew in command of the expedition's second ship, the *Erebus*. The two ships became trapped in ice off an area of land that was named the Boothia Peninsula in honor of Sir Felix Booth, one of the backers of the expedition. They remained trapped by this ice for three winters and both of the Rosses made expeditions to visit and report on the Inuit peoples who lived in that part of the Arctic.

During this period James Clark Ross was able to compute the location of the North Magnetic Pole and to travel overland to it. (The magnetic pole is not stable and has moved since Ross first visited it.) He wrote, "Nature had erected no monument to denote the spot which she had chosen as the centre of one of her great and dark powers."

After three winters it became apparent that the ships were hopelessly stuck. In May 1832 the members of the expedition abandoned them and made an extremely difficult overland crossing 300 miles to Lancaster Sound. They were forced to spend the next winter there until, on August 26, 1833, they were rescued by a passing British whaling ship. On their return to England they were treated as heroes.

James Clark Ross. The Granger Collection, New York.

In 1839 James Ross was chosen to lead a British expedition to search for the South Magnetic Pole. At about the same time a French expedition under **Jules-Sébastien-César Dumont d'Urville** and an American expedition under **Charles Wilkes** set off with the same goal. However, Ross's ships were better equipped to deal with the harsh environment. He left England on September 30, 1839 and reached Hobart, Tasmania in August 1840.

Having heard about the French and American expeditions, Ross decided to head farther east, and on January 1, 1841 he crossed the Antarctic Circle. He broke through the ice into an open area of water that is called the Ross Sea. Ross steered for the South Magnetic Pole and sighted land on January 10, which he named Victoria Land after the Queen of England. On January 27 he discovered an active volcano, which he named Mount Erebus after his ship. Soon after that his progress was stopped by the great mass of ice known as the Ross Ice Shelf. He was about 160 miles away from the South Magnetic Pole. This was the farthest south that anyone was to go for the next 60 years.

Ross returned to Tasmania and spent the southern winter there. He left again on November 23, 1841 and spent 137 days skirting various parts of the continent. He then returned to England.

The following year Ross received permission from the British government to make a third expedition to Antarctica. His aim was to survey the east coast of Graham Land, the long peninsula that points toward South America and to set a new record for traveling farthest south in the Weddell Sea. The weather became very bad and Ross reached his farthest point on February 14, 1843, 550 miles north of where James Weddell had traveled. He was able to explore the east coast of the peninsula and discovered James Ross Island.

On his return to England James Ross was knighted, and in 1847 he published the story of his adventures, *Voyage of Discovery*.

Following the disappearance of **Sir John Franklin**, Ross was chosen to lead one of the expeditions to the Arctic to search for him. He was to search in the area of Melville Sound, Banks Island, and the Wellington Channel. However, the ice was so bad that he was forced to stop much farther east at Somerset Island. In fact, he was only 70 miles away from Franklin's first winter camp, but all of his efforts to find the missing men (sledge trips overland, sending foxes out with engraved collars, and firing off guns and rockets) failed. After this voyage Ross returned to England and retired. He died at Aylesbury in 1862.

Where to learn more

Ernest Dodge's dual biography *The Polar Rosses* covers the exploits of both James and John Ross. It was published by Barnes & Noble Books (New York: 1973). Ross' narrative of his experience in Antarctica was published under the title *A Voyage of Discovery and Research in the Southern and Antarctic Regions During the Years, 1939-43* (New York: A.M. Kelly, 1969).

Sir John Ross

(1777 - 1856)

John Ross was a British naval officer who led an unsuccessful search for the Northwest Passage in 1818 and then returned several years later and spent four winters in the Canadian Arctic.

John Ross was born in Wigtown in Scotland. He entered the Royal Navy at the age of 12 as a volunteer and served for three years in the Mediterranean. He then joined the merchant marine and traveled to the Caribbean and the Baltic. In 1794 he joined the East India Company. He returned to the Royal Navy in 1799 as a midshipman. He then served in the navy during the following wars with Napoleon and reached the rank of commander in February 1812 when he took command of a ship in the Baltic.

In 1818 Ross was put in charge of two ships to sail to the north of Baffin Island to see if it were possible to find the elusive Northwest Passage. Ross left England in April 1818 and reached the west coast of Greenland in the middle of June. There are three straits leading out of the northern part of Baffin Bay. One, Smith Sound, goes to the north separating Ellesmere Island from Greenland. Ross initially headed in this direction but was forced to turn back. He missed the second exit, Jones Sound, and headed into the most southerly one, Lancaster Sound. In fact, Lancaster Sound is the only practical way west.

Ross sailed into Lancaster Sound for about 50 miles. Then, he claimed to see mountains, which he named the "Croker Mountains" surrounding the strait and became convinced that it was a bay—that is, it did not lead anywhere. The only problem was that there were no such mountains, and no one else on his ships saw them. Ross insisted, however, and returned to England.

Ross's description of the Croker Mountains was disputed by his second-in-command, **Sir Edward Parry**, and they became involved in a public argument on their return to England. As a result, Parry was sent out on an expedition to Lancaster Sound in 1819 and returned with the news that it led west in 1820. Ross wanted to lead a new expedition there, but the British Admiralty had lost confidence in him and refused to sponsor the voyage.

After several years of trying, Ross was able to obtain private backing for his voyage from Sir Felix Booth, a gin merchant. Ross set out in May 1829 on a paddle steamer called the *Victory*. His crew included his nephew **James Clark Ross**, who was to gain fame as an explorer in his own right. They traveled through Lancaster Sound and then into Prince Regent inlet, where they found traces of Parry's ship *Fury*, which had been wrecked on North Somerset Island. From there he turned south where he landed on a large peninsula that Ross named the Boothia Peninsula after the sponsor of his expedition.

Having reached land, Ross and his party were forced to stay there for the winter. To keep his men occupied Ross gave lectures and taught lessons. They were visited by the native Inuit people of the area, who were able to draw accurate maps of the peninsula and the surrounding area. They also taught the Englishmen how to build sledges and Ross's nephew James used these to make several expeditions into the interior. On one of these he discovered the North Magnetic Pole.

The Ross expedition was stuck on the Boothia Peninsula for the winters of 1829/30, 1830/31, and 1831/32. Realizing they would never be able to get away in the *Victory*, they abandoned it in May 1832 and traveled through the open water in one of the ship's boats. They reached the spot where Parry's *Fury* had gone aground and were able to find some of its

Sir John Ross. The Granger Collection, New York.

supplies, which was all they had to keep them alive. They tried to reach Lancaster Sound but were forced to spend the following winter ashore before setting out again. At 4:00 a.m. on August 26, 1833 they met a whaler in Lancaster Sound and were rescued. By an amazing coincidence it was the same ship that Ross had commanded in the 1818 expedition.

The results of this expedition restored Ross's reputation, and he was knighted and received several rewards. However, he was still not given a Navy ship to command. He was, however, appointed British consul to Stockholm, where he served from 1839 to 1846. In the meantime, **Sir John Franklin** headed off on his ill-fated expedition to find the Northwest Passage. When he was lost, Ross wanted to command one of the ships sent to search for him.

Unable to get government backing, Ross organized a private expedition on a small ship called the *Felix*. This expedition spent the winter of 1850/51 in Barrow Strait, but was too ill-equipped to help very much in the search for Franklin. This was Ross's last exploring expedition.

Where to learn more

The Polar Rosses by Ernest Stanley Dodge (New York: Barnes & Noble Books, 1973) covers the lives and explorations of both John and James Ross.

John Ross wrote *Narrative of a Second Voyage in Search of a Northwest Passage, and of a Residence in the Arctic Regions During the Years 1829, 1830, 1831, 1832, 1833* (Paris: Baudry's European Library, 1835).

An interesting book on Arctic explorers in search of the Northwest Passage is Douglas Wilkinson's *Arctic Fever: The Search for the Northwest Passage* (Toronto: Clarke, Irwin, 1971).

Hipólito Ruiz

(1752 - 1808)

Hipólito Ruiz was a Spanish botanist who led an expedition to Peru and Chile that was one of the first to systematically investigate the plant life of those two countries.

In 1774, the government of France requested permission from the King of Spain to send a botanist to investigate unknown botanical species in the Spanish colony of Peru. Permission was granted with the stipulation that Charles Joseph Dombey, the French nominee, should take with him two young Spanish botanists, Hipólito Ruiz and José Pavón. Ruiz was appointed leader of the expedition. At the time, he was a 22-year-old student of natural sciences who had come to Madrid to serve as an assistant to his pharmacist uncle.

According to King Charles III's directive, the purpose of the expedition was to "undertake the methodical examination and identification of the products of nature of my American dominions . . . not only in order to promote the progress of the physical sciences, but also to banish doubts and adulterations that are found in medicine, painting, and the other important arts, and to increase commerce and to form herbaria and collections of natural products."

The three scientists left Spain in 1777 on the ship *El Peruano* and arrived in Callao in Peru on April 8, 1778. Ruiz and his companions traveled through a variety of climatic zones in Peru and then headed south to Chile. They collected specimens from each ecological region. They started in the vicinity of Lima and then went to the Chancay, Jauja and Tarma valleys. From these valleys, they climbed into the surrounding mountains. They sent 53 boxes of botanical specimens back to Spain on the boat *San Pedro de Alcantara*, but it sank off the coast of Portugal. Fortunately, they had kept duplicates of their specimens.

They returned to Juanuco and established themselves in the house of Matias Tranco, but a fire destroyed much of what they had collected. They then made new collections and left in April 1778. They arrived back in Spain on September 12, 1778. They proceeded to publish two works on their researches. Some of the material they collected had medicinal properties, including quinine (to treat malaria) and coca (from which cocaine is made) and agave (whose leaves cured ulcers and whose roots were a treatment for rheumatism).

Where to learn more

The most recent edition of Ruiz's narrative of the expedition is *Relación del viaje hecho a los reynos del Perú y Chile por los botánicos y dibuxantes enviados para aquella expedición, extractado de los diarios por el orden que llevó en estos su autor* (Madrid: Tipográfico Huelves y Co., 1931). The records of the expedition were translated by B.E. Dahlgren as *Travels of Ruiz, Pavón, and Dombey in Peru and Chile (1777-1788)* (Chicago: Field Museum of Natural History, 1940).

There is an excellent book in English about the Ruiz-Pavón expedition with many beautiful illustrations: Arthur R. Steele, *Flowers for the King: The Expedition of Ruiz and Pavón and the "Flora of Peru"* (Durham: Duke University Press, 1964).

A good short account of the expedition can be found in Edward J. Goodman, *The Explorers of South America* (New York: Macmillan, 1972).

Dick Rutan

(1939 -   )

Jeana Yeager

(1952 -   )

Dick Rutan and Jeana Yeager are two American airplane pilots who flew an experimental plane around the world without stopping or refueling.

Dick Rutan was born in Loma Linda, California, near Los Angeles in 1939. After World War II, his father, a dentist, moved the family to the small town of Dinuba, near Fresno. Rutan started taking flying lessons at the age of 15 and made his first solo flight and got his pilot's license on his 16th birthday, the earliest legal age. After graduating from high school, he enlisted in the U.S. Air Force and trained to become a navigator. After serving in Viet Nam, he was accepted for fighter pilot training and then returned to Viet Nam in 1967. On his last assigned combat flight he had to eject from a burning airplane. He was then assigned to Europe and resigned from the Air Force when he failed to get a sought-after promotion. After he left the Air Force he separated from his wife and went to work for his brother, Burt, an airplane designer, as a test pilot.

Jeana Yeager grew up in Texas where her father was an engineer for a defense contractor. She ran on the track team in high school and then became a horse trainer. She married a deputy sheriff and moved to Rosenberg, Texas, near Houston, in 1972. After five years of marriage she left her husband and moved to California, where she got a job drafting and surveying for a geothermal energy company in Santa Rosa, California. She got her pilot's license in 1978. She met Rutan at an airshow in Chino, California, where the Rutan Company was demonstrating its experimental aircraft.

Yeager went to work with the Rutan Aircraft Factory and broke several speed records with the specially-designed Rutan planes. Over lunch one day in 1981, the two Rutan brothers and Yeager came up with the idea of trying to break existing records by designing and flying a plane around the world with no stops or refueling. It took five years to build the plane that Burt Rutan designed, and it became Rutan and Yeager's obsession to build it and fly it. They spent much of their time trying to raise money and lived a barely subsistence life in order to finance the plane.

Burt Rutan's problem was to build a very light airplane large enough to carry all the fuel that would have to be used to power a round-the-world flight. His design was an H-shape with the main wing toward the rear and the stabilizing wing in front. The wingspan was 111 feet, longer than a 727 jetliner. There is very little metal in the plane, and the body itself was made of a composite material consisting largely of epoxy. It had two engines, a rear one of 110 horsepower that could power cruising speeds of 80 miles per hour and a more powerful engine in front for take-offs and landings.

In July 1986 Rutan and Yeager took the plane, the *Voyager*, on a test flight that lasted 4½ days flying up and down the California coast. This flight set a world record for distance and endurance. During the flight one of the two would sit up at the controls while the other would stretch out in the narrow 3-foot wide space and rest. It was difficult to eat and drink under the conditions, and Yeager consumed less than a gallon of water during the flight and fainted during the post-flight press conference.

Following this and other test flights, the round-the-world trip was planned for mid-September 1986. However, during one flight, part of the front propeller was broken off, and this forced a postponement. They decided to go ahead in December in spite of the fact that they would be flying around the northern hemisphere in winter. They left Edwards Air Force Base in California on December 14, 1986. It was the first time the plane had been flown with its full load of fuel, and the weight caused the tips of the wings to dip and to scrape off the winglets at right angles to the wings. Rutan, who piloted the plane then and through most of the trip, was able to shake off the damaged material and continue the flight.

They flew into the Pacific. Near the Philippines they ran into Typhoon Marge with 80 mile-per-hour winds. In spite of the danger, the typhoon's tail winds pushed them along so that they reached the fastest speed of the trip, 147 miles per hour. They slept for two or three hours at a time, and ate pre-cooked meals and took food supplements. From the time they reached Malaysia, all the way across the Indian Ocean and across Africa, they ran

Jeana Yeager and Dick Rutan. UPI/Bettmann Newsphotos.

into storms that forced them to fly higher than planned, at less-fuel efficient altitudes, and sometimes to use both engines in order to avoid turbulence. Yeager was badly bruised when the plane was tossed around by strong winds. The two pilots suffered alternating mood swings from euphoria to despair depending on the weather and the flight's progress.

Off the west coast of Africa, they ran into an unexpected storm, and Rutan lost control of the plane for a short time. A little farther along, the oil warning light came on and one engine almost overheated because they were so tired they forgot to check the oil level. They flew over Central America in the dark with Yeager at the controls. In spite of all their difficulties, they landed at Edwards Air Force Base on December 23, 1986, a day ahead of schedule, with Yeager cranking down the landing gear by hand. When the plane landed, it had only about 10 gallons of

fuel left of the 1,200 gallons it had started with. The 9-day flight had covered 25,012 miles, more than twice as much as the previous record for an unrefueled flight.

Rutan and Yeager were received by enthusiastic crowds as they traveled around the United States after the flight. They were presented with a medal by President Ronald Reagan. Corporate sponsorships and a royalty advance on the book about the flight enabled them to pay off the large debt they still had from constructing the plane. The *Voyager* itself was placed in the Smithsonian's National Air and Space Museum in Washington, D.C.

Where to learn more

Jeana Yeager and Dick Rutan wrote about their flight with the help of professional writer Phil Patton in *Voyager* (New York: Alfred A. Knopf, 1987).

Alvaro de Saavedra y Cerón

(? - 1529)

Alvaro Saavedra led the first Spanish expedition to cross the Pacific from Mexico to the East Indies. He was defeated twice trying to sail back in the opposite direction.

Following the conquest of Mexico by **Hernán Cortés** in 1521 and the return of **Ferdinand Magellan**'s expedition around the world in 1522, King Charles V of Spain decided to see whether he could open up a trade route between Mexico and the Molucca Islands (the "Spice Islands") in Indonesia. He sent a letter to Cortés dated June 20, 1526 instructing him to send out an exploratory expedition.

Cortés chose for this task his cousin Alvaro de Saavedra. While Saavedra was getting his expedition together, a ship, the *Santiago*, arrived in the Mexican port of Mazatlan. It was a survivor of the Spanish expedition around the world of which **Andrés de Urdaneta** was a member. Saavedra was able to use some of the equipment and crew, including a Portuguese pilot familiar with the East Indies, from the *Santiago* to equip his own ships. Saavedra put together a small fleet of three ships and 110 men, with the *Florida* as flagship. After a "shakedown" cruise of three weeks, they sailed from the port of Zihuatanejo on October 31, 1527.

Soon after the voyage started, the *Florida* was leaking badly, but Saavedra refused to transfer to one of the other ships. This was just as well because they were both lost in a storm in mid-December. Saavedra sailed past some small islands in the northern Marshalls, Utirik and Rongelap, and sighted Guam but did not land there. He reached Mindanao in the southern Philippines on February 1, 1528. There he found a Spanish sailor left behind by the Urdaneta expedition who directed them southward. Saavedra reached the island of Tidore on March 27, 1528 where he found the other remaining survivors of the Urdaneta expedition.

Once on Tidore, Saavedra helped the Spanish there to fight off the Portuguese who were trying to drive them out of their trading grounds. He made a map of the islands to take back to Mexico and loaded a cargo of cloves on board the *Florida*. He then set out to head back to Mexico on June 12, 1528. He sailed north of the island of Manus, the first European to see the

Admiralty Islands of New Guinea, and into the Caroline Group. However, by now Saavedra was in trouble. By chance, the route he had taken from Mexico to Guam was the one best suited for a sailing ship. He had left at the time of the year when the prevailing winds went from east to west, and this enabled him to make the crossing relatively easily. But now, on his return, he was facing the same winds and could make no headway. He was forced to return to Tidore, reaching there on November 19, 1528, after having sighted the mainland of the island of New Guinea.

Saavedra's return to Tidore was deeply disappointing to the Spanish there. They had hoped that he would be able to find a route for supplying the Moluccas from Mexico and would thus take the trade from the Portuguese who controlled posts in India and Malaya. Saavedra's return convinced them to give in to the Portuguese, who thereby gained control of the spice trade until it was, in turn, taken from them by the Dutch in the following century.

In Tidore Saavedra repaired the *Florida* and built another small ship. He left once again on May 3, 1529. He insisted once again in trying the same route back to Mexico. This was self-defeating. This time he sailed through the Carolines and discovered the islands of Ponape, Ujelang, and Eniwetok. The Spaniards got as far as 31°N before they realized that they could not make any further headway west by following that course. They then turned north and got as far as the northern outliers of the Hawaiian Archipelago. There, after a long illness, Saavedra died.

After Saavedra's death, the ship's crew was forced to turn back. They reached the Moluccas on December 8, 1529 with only 22 survivors. It was not for another 37 years that the Spanish, in an expedition once again led by Urdaneta, were to discover the way to get across the Pacific back to Mexico.

Where to learn more

The best source for the early Spanish explorers of the Pacific is O.H.K. Spate, *The Spanish Lake* (Minneapolis: University of Minnesota Press, 1979), which includes extensive footnotes of original sources and a lengthy bibliography. Also useful is Carlos Prieto, *El Océano Pacífico: navegantes españoles del siglo XVI* (Madrid: Alianza Editorial, 1975).

See also Andrew Sharp, *The Discovery of the Pacific Islands* (Oxford: Oxford University Press, 1960) and Herman R. Friis, ed. *The Pacific Basin: A History of Its Geographical Exploration* (New York: American Geographical Society, 1967).

Sir Robert Hermann Schomburgk

(1804 - 1865)

Robert Hermann Schomburgk was a German who was employed by the British government to explore Guyana and northern Brazil.

Robert Hermann Schomburgk was born in the town of Freiburg-an-der-Unstrut in the Prussian province of Silesia, now part of Poland, on June 5, 1804. He started in business in Germany and then went to New York and Virginia as a tobacco trader. He moved to the West Indies in 1830, where his interest in natural history led him to survey the coasts of the island of Anegada in the British Virgin Islands. The results were published in the *Journal of the Royal Geographical Society.*

Schomburgk's article was well received and in 1834 he was hired by the Royal Geographical Society to explore the colony of British Guiana (now the country of Guyana) in South America. British Guiana had been acquired from the Dutch over a period of years and was made up of three separate colonies, Essequibo, Demerara, and Berbice. In actuality these three colonies were thin strips of plantations along the Atlantic coast, and nothing was known about the interior. Schomburgk's task was to explore the great rivers and find out what economic possibilities the colony had.

Schomburgk began his first expedition on October 1, 1835 by traveling up the Essequibo River. His expedition of 22 members all became ill with dysentery, and they had to spend the month of November at a camp trying to recover. The Essequibo, like all the rivers of the Guianas, is broken up by many waterfalls and rapids that make travel very difficult. Schomburgk was the first European to reach many of these, and he named the largest King William's Cataract after the king of England. By February, 1836 they had reached the confluence with the Rupununi River, the Essequibo's largest tributary, and continued on until March 5. They then turned back to Georgetown, the capital, but along the way one of the canoes was overturned and all the biological specimens that Schomburgk had collected were lost.

In September 1836 Schomburgk started out again, this time traveling up the Courantyne River, the easternmost in Guyana, which now forms the boundary with Suriname. He reached the major falls of that river on October 18, but could find no way around and headed back to the coast. He set out on November 25, 1836 to explore the third great river, the Berbice. During this expedition he suffered many difficulties: his Native American

guides abandoned him, he narrowly escaped being attacked by thousands of ants, a herd of wild hogs charged him and he survived only by climbing a tree, he ran out of supplies and was forced to live off the land.

On January 28, 1837 Schomburgk found a path through the forest to the Essequibo River and a little later he found a way to the Courantyne and was able to continue his exploration of that river. By this journey he was able to map out the courses of all the great rivers of Guyana. He was not satisfied with this, and in early 1838 he entered what is now the Brazilian territory of Roraima by way of the Tacutú River (which forms part of the border between Guyana and Brazil).

Schomburgk traveled down the Tacutú toward the main Brazilian post in the area, Fort São Joaquim. Along the way he encountered Brazilian slave traders who raided the Native American villages and stole the inhabitants to sell as laborers. "They brought away little children of 5 and 6 years old, and showed us that even *they* had been tied with their hands to their backs." From Fort São Joaquim Schomburgk traveled up the Surumu River to Mount Roraima, a flat peak that rises far above the surrounding forest and is now the point where Guyana, Brazil, and Venezuela come together. Along the way he encountered members of the Wapixana, Arekuna, Purukotó, and other tribes, most of whom had never seen a European before.

From Mount Roraima, Schomburgk traveled back down the Surumu and Tacutú Rivers to the Uraricoera and Parima Rivers which took him to the headwaters of the great Orinoco River. He crossed over the Casiquiare Canal to the upper Rio Negro. The Casiquiare is a unique natural feature: in the lowlaying areas of the Amazon forest it is a natural canal between two river systems—the Orinoco and the Amazon. It had been discovered by **Alexander von Humboldt** in 1800, and Schomburgk was the second European to visit it. Following the Rio Negro, Schomburgk traveled down it to the Rio Branco and then up that river to Fort São Joaquim and back to Georgetown by way of the Essequibo.

Following this expedition, Schomburgk went to England in 1840 where he was awarded a gold medal by the Royal Geographical Society for his work. He also brought back many botanical specimens including a lily that he named Victoria Regia after the new queen, which was quickly adopted by European gardeners. He discussed with the British government the necessity of mapping the boundaries of British Guiana and was sent out on a new expedition to do just that in 1841.

During 1841 Schomburgk marked the northwestern boundary of Guyana. He then traveled to the post of Pirara on the Tacutú River that was claimed by both Brazil and the British. He went back to Fort São Joaquim and Mount Roraima and then up the Rupununi where he visited the Wapixana tribe. He went up the Essequibo to its source, and then in June and August 1843 he crossed over the watershed of the Essequibo River to the unexplored Brazilian side, where he explored tributaries of the Trombetas River. There he met tribes unseen by Europeans: the Tarumá, the Carib-speaking Wai-Wai, the Tiriyó, and the Arawak-speaking Mawakwa. He then went back over the divide to the Courantyne River to the coast. As a result of this work, he became a British subject and was knighted in 1844.

Schomburgk became British consul in Santo Domingo in 1848 and then was appointed consul in Bangkok, Thailand in 1857. While in Thailand, he explored in the northern part of the kingdom as far as Chiengmai and then went to the Isthmus of Kra in the south to see whether it was practical to dig a canal there. He retired in 1864 and returned to Germany, where he died in Berlin in 1865.

Where to learn more

Schomburgk wrote about his explorations in a series of articles for the *Journal of the Royal Geographical Society* in London. They appeared in volumes 6 (1836), pp. 224-284; 7 (1837), pp. 285-301, pp. 302-350; and 15 (1845), pp. 1-104. It was published as a book in German as *Reisen in Guiana und am Orinoko während der Jahre 1835-39* (Leipzig: G. Wigard, 1841).

Robert Schomburgk's brother, Moritz Richard Schomburgk, was also a notable explorer and wrote a book about his own explorations that was published as *Richard Schomburgk's Travels in British Guiana, 1840-1844*, in 2 volumes, in Georgetown, Guyana in 1922-1923.

There is information about Schomburgk in John Hemming, *Amazon Frontier: The Defeat of the Brazilian Indians* (Cambridge: Harvard University Press, 1987) and Edward Goodman, *The Explorers of South America* (New York: Macmillan, 1972).

Willem Schouten

(1567 - 1625)

Jacob Le Maire

(1585 - 1616)

Willem Schouten and Jacob Le Maire were Dutch navigators who set out to end the monopoly of the Dutch East India Company on trade with the East Indies and who discovered Cape Horn and several island groups in the Pacific.

I n 1595 the Dutch made their first trip to the East Indies, where the valuable trade in spices was at that time controlled by the Portuguese. Within a few years the Netherlands, which was rapidly becoming an important maritime and trading country, displaced Portugal as the major power in southeast Asia. In 1602 the Dutch East India Company was formed and was given a monopoly on all trade with the East Indies.

This powerful new company was not loved by every Dutchman, and one man, Isaac Le Maire, tried to get the States-General, or Dutch parliament, to end the monopoly of the East India Company. He lost. Not giving up, Le Maire tried to get around the restrictions another way. The East India company monopoly was based on the provision that it had control of trade going to and from the East either around the Cape of Good Hope in Africa or through the Straits of Magellan at the tip of South America.

The Straits of Magellan, discovered by Magellan in 1520, are a passageway from the Atlantic to the Pacific between the mainland of South America and the large island of Tierra del Fuego. At that time, the Europeans did not know whether Tierra del Fuego was an island or the northern part of the mythical great southern continent. Le Maire took a gamble that it was in fact an island and that it would be possible to sail south of it and reach the Pacific.

Le Maire collaborated with a famous navigator, Willem Correliszoon Schouten, to convince the rich citizens of the Dutch town of Hoorn to invest in an expedition to prove this theory correct. In May 1615 the expedition set out from Hoorn with two ships, the *Eendracht*, commanded by Schouten, and the *Hoorn*, commanded by Jan Schouten, Willem's brother. The overall command of the expedition was given to Isaac Le Maire's son Jacob.

When the expedition reached the region of Patagonia, in what is now southern Argentina, it suffered a series of accidents and the *Hoorn* was lost. All of its men were transferred to the *Eendracht*. This ship left the Patagonian coast on January 13, 1616 and headed south. After several days' sailing they saw a passage to the west and were able to head towards the Pacific. The southernmost point of land that they passed on January 29 was named after the town that had financed the trip and from which they had sailed. In English the land is called Cape Horn (even though it is actually a small island).

Once the *Eendracht* entered the Pacific and headed northwestward, it had to endure a month of storms before they reached the Juan Fernandez islands in March. By that time most of the crew had become sick, and on March 9 Jan Schouten died.

The ship sailed on to the northwest among the islands of the Tuamotu Archipelago and the Tonga islands. The Polynesians that they met in these places had a hard time understanding what the Europeans wanted, while the visitors were very nervous. The islanders were excited to see the new material goods that the Dutchmen brought and often carried things away without asking permission. This "thievery" angered the crew members, and the meetings inevitably turned into confrontations in which weapons were used and many islanders killed by the Europeans' greater firepower.

In May the Dutchmen came to the islands of Futuna and Alofi (now part of the French territory of Wallis and Futuna), where they were able to maintain better relations. They were invited to participate in a feast held by a local king and had a better opportunity to see some of the complex social relationships that made up Polynesian culture.

At this point Schouten and le Maire argued about the best course to follow. Le Maire wanted to sail due west to see if they could find Mendaña's almost legendary Solomon Islands and the great southern continent. Schouten, the practical navigator, wanted to head to the northwest along the north coast of New

Guinea, which was a known route and would lead to Batavia, the capital of the Dutch East Indies. His view prevailed.

The Dutchmen sailed along the coasts of New Ireland and New Guinea and stopped occasionally to get fresh water and food. They reached the Dutch outpost of Ternate on September 17, 1616, where they were well received. Their reception in Batavia, where they landed on October 28, was not so friendly. The new governor, sent out by the East India Company, refused to believe that they had found a new passage into the Pacific and confiscated the ship and all its goods. Schouten and Le Maire were sent home as prisoners on a Company ship, and Jacob le Maire died during the trip.

Back in Holland, Jacob's father, Isaac, took the East India Company to court over the confiscation. After two years of litigation, the Dutch courts accepted the claim of a passage south of the Straits of Magellan and ordered the East India Company to return the ship and to pay all costs and interest that had accumulated.

Where to learn more

The return of Willem Schouten and the journal of his voyage around Cape Horn was immediately news throughout Europe. Translations were published in the major languages, including in French in Paris in 1618 (*Journal du voyage de Guillaume Schouten dans les Indes*) and English in London in 1619 (W. Phillip, translator and editor, *The Relation of a Wonderful Voyage by William Cornelison Schouten of Horne*).

The most complete modern documentation is unfortunately only available in Dutch: W.A. Engelbrecht and P.J. van Herwerden, *De Ontdekkingsreis van Jacob Le Maire en Willem Cornelisz Schouten in de jaren 1615-1617: Journalen, documenten en andere bescheiden* (The Hague: 1945). Some of these documents were published early in the century in English by the Hakluyt Society: "Australian Navigations Discovered by Jacob Le Maire," in *The East and West Indian Mirror*, edited by J.A.J. de Villiers (London: Hakluyt Society, 1906).

There are chapters on Schouten and le Maire in: J.C. Beaglehole, *The Exploration of the Pacific* (Stanford: Stanford University Press, 1966); Colin Jack-Hinton, *The Search for the Islands of Solomon, 1567-1838* (Oxford: Clarendon Press, 1969); and Derek Wilson, *The Circumnavigators* (New York: M. Evans & Company, 1989).

Georg August Schweinfurth

(1836 - 1925)

Georg August Schweinfurth, a German botanist, was the first European to cross the watershed between the Nile and Congo Rivers.

Georg August Schweinfurth was born in the Baltic city of Riga in 1836, the son of a merchant. A botanist and zoologist, who became famous for the drawings he made of the plants he studied, he spent 2 years exploring the Red Sea coast of Africa, when he applied for and received a grant from the Humboldt Institute to continue his botanical explorations in the equatorial districts to the west of the Nile. He returned to Egypt in July 1868, stopping in Khartoum, and then going south from there in December 1868 to study the plants along the rivers that run into the White Nile River.

One of the first tribes that he encountered were the Shilluks, who are famous for being very tall and for never wearing any clothes. They oiled their hair into fanciful shapes and were amazed when the German was able to take his own hat off. Schweinfurth began his explorations of the watershed between the Nile and Congo Rivers by traveling up the marshy reaches of the Bahr el-Ghazal, a western tributary of the White Nile. He reached the last river port at Mashra ur-Raqq and then headed towards the southwest into the unknown.

In November 1869, Schweinfurth crossed the Tondy River. Once across the divide between the Nile and Congo river systems he found himself in forest that was typical of the rainforests of West Africa. On March 19, 1870, he became the first European to see the Uele River, which flows into the Congo. He was also the first European to see pygmies, in the dense Ituri Forest in what is now northern Zaire. He tried to bring one of them back with him to Europe, but the African died along the return route. Schweinfurth saw and reported on many cultural groups, each with distinctly different societies. He tended to describe the various customs in sensationalistic terms, accepting, for example, the pejorative Arab term Niam-Niam for one tribe. The name was supposed to imitate the sound they made when eating human flesh.

The German explorer headed out of the Congo basin in the summer of 1870, recrossing the Tondy River on June 24. At year's end, he was back in the southern Sudan. A fire broke out in

Georg August Schweinfurth. The Granger Collection, New York.

his camp on December 1 and destroyed all his records and most of his insect collection. He then decided to leave Africa and headed toward the coast. He returned to Europe in November 1871, where he was recognized as one of the leading authorities on central Africa. In September 1876 when King Leopold II of Belgium convened an international conference to discuss the future of the exploration of central Africa, Schweinfurth was one of the German delegates. He argued for the creation of independent African states that would be protected by the Great Powers of Europe. He died at the age of 90 and was buried in a botanical garden he had helped to establish.

Where to learn more

Schweinfurth published the story of his African trip in *Heart of Africa* (New York: Harper & Brothers, 1874). There is an interesting section on him in Christopher Hibbert, *Africa Explored: Europeans in the Dark Continent, 1769-1889* (London: Allen Lane, 1982).

Robert Falcon Scott

(1868 - 1912)

Robert Falcon Scott was a British naval officer who led two expeditions to Antarctica and just missed being the first person to the South Pole. He died on the return from the Pole.

Robert Falcon Scott was born in the English naval port of Devonport and joined the Royal Navy in 1881. Although he had no Arctic experience, in 1901 the 32-year-old lieutenant was put in command of the National Antarctic Expedition sponsored by the Royal Geographical Society and the Royal Society. It was provided with a specially-designed ship, the *Discovery* (the latest of a line of ships of that name first used by *Henry Hudson*). Included among the ships's officers was another man who was to become a famous Antarctic explorer—**Ernest Shackleton**.

The *Discovery* entered Antarctic waters on January 21, 1902 at McMurdo Sound and then traveled east along the north shore

Robert Falcon Scott.

of Ross Island to the base of Mount Terror. Scott sailed eastward past the point that a previous British explorer, **Sir James Ross**, had reached and sighted a new land stretching off to the northeast. Scott named it King Edward VII Land after the reigning king of the United Kingdom and Emperor of India. The build-up of pack ice stopped Scott from going any farther and he retraced his path and anchored in a small bay. There Scott sent up a balloon tied to the ship with himself aboard on February 4, 1902. It was the first aerial ascent in Antarctica.

Scott and his expedition spent the winter of 1902 in huts built at a place named Hut Point on Ross Island. On November 2, 1902 Scott and two companions tried to cross the giant Ross Ice Shelf on sledges pulled by 19 dogs. They traveled for 59 days until they became so ill with scurvy that they had to turn back. On their return to camp, they found a British rescue ship waiting and part of the expedition was sent back to England in March 1903. Scott himself stayed until the following year, exploring the ice shelf. He returned to England on September 10, 1904.

On Scott's return he was welcomed as a great popular hero, and his book, *The Voyage of Discovery* was a bestseller. He was promoted to full captain in 1906. In April 1907, he heard about Shackleton's plans to return to Antarctica and to reach the South Pole. This inspired him with the desire to do the same, and he asked Shackleton not to use the two camps that Scott had established at McMurdo Sound and the Bay of Whales so that they would be available for his own future use. Shackleton returned in 1909 without having reached his goal, and Scott set out on June 1, 1910 in the *Terra Nova* with a naval crew that had been given special leave and a team of scientists.

When Scott reached Melbourne, Australia on October 12, 1910 he received word that the Norwegian **Roald Amundsen** was leading his own expedition to try to reach the South Pole. So began the race between the two men to see who could get there first. On January 4, 1911 the *Terra Nova* reached Ross Island. During the following autumn and winter they set up supply depots across the Ross Ice Shelf. Scott's party set off on November 1, 1911 for the South Pole itself; Amundsen had left his base 600 miles to the east two weeks earlier. Scott's supplies were carried by dogs, Siberian ponies and motor vehicles on tracks. The ponies and motor sledges gave out within a couple of days.

Scott drove himself and his men too hard trying to equal the speed that Shackleton had made a couple of years earlier on much the same route. They had to spend many days climbing and traversing Beardmore Glacier. They were still on it on December

21, 1911 when Amundsen actually reached the Pole. On January 4, 1912 Scott sent back the last of his support teams of men, but in addition to the three men accompanying him he added one of the support team members to his own. This cut into his supplies.

Scott and his men began the assault on the Pole from the edge of Beardmore Glacier, a distance of 178 miles. On January 7 they reached 10,560 feet, their highest point and started the descent to the pole. They got there on January 18, only to find the little tent with the Norwegian flag that Amundsen had erected. They took a photograph at the Pole that shows their strain and disappointment. Scott wrote in his journal, "Great God! This is an awful place, and terrible enough for us to have laboured to it without the reward of priority."

Starting back to their base on Ross Island all five of the men were suffering from scurvy, frostbite and exhaustion. They reached Beardmore Glacier on February 7 during a windstorm. They then took time to collect rock samples, including some with plant impressions that showed that Antarctica had once been forested. On February 17, Seaman Edgar Evans died a short distance from the last supply camp that they had established on the glacier.

By this time, the nighttime temperatures were down to -40°F, and Army Captain Lawrence Oates was suffering from severe frostbite. "In the morning, with the blizzard still at its height and with the words 'I am just going outside and may be some time,' he left the tent and was never seen again." Scott set up his final camp on March 21, eleven miles from One Ton Depot where there were plenty of supplies. However, a raging blizzard kept them from going any farther. Scott's last journal entry was on March 29, 1912. "Every day now we have been ready to start for our depot eleven miles away, but outside the door of the tent, it remains a scene of swirling drift. I do not think we can hope for any better things now. We shall see it to the end, but we are getting weaker, of course . . . It seems a pity, but I do not think I can write more. For God's sake look after our people."

Scott and his two companions were found dead in their sleeping bags by a search party on November 12, 1912. Nearby were the rock samples they had taken from Beardmore glacier.

Where to learn more

In some ways, Robert Scott has been seen as the very model of an English explorer—always the gentleman, always playing by the rules, and ready to sacrifice himself for a higher cause. The fact that he ultimately failed has even enhanced the legend. Indeed, there are analyses of what the hero worship of Scott reveals about the British character, as opposed to the coldly efficient operation of Amundsen, which achieved its goal and returned safely. In any case, this has meant that there is an enormous literature on Scott.

Scott himself wrote *The Voyage of the Discovery* (London: Smith, Elder & Co., 1905; New York: Charles Scribner's Sons, 1928), and his journals were edited by Leonard Huxley to provide an account of the fatal attempt to get to the South Pole and back: *Scott's Last Expedition*, 2 vols. (London: Smith, Elder & Co., 1913). A participant on the expedition who did not take part in the race to the Pole, R.E. Priestley, published his story after returning to England: *Antarctic Adventure—Scott's Northern Party* (London: Fisher Unwin, 1914) as did E.R.G.R. Evans in *South With Scott* (London: Collins, 1922).

One of the most memorable books about Antarctic exploration was written by another member of the "Northern Party": Apsley Cherry-Garrard, *The Worst Journey in the World* (London: Constable, 1923). It has been called a classic of the literature about exploration.

Biographies of Scott or histories of the Scott-Amundsen rivalry include: J. Gordon Hayes, *The Conquest of the South Pole* (London: Butterworth, 1932); Stephen Gwynn, *Captain Scott* (London: Allen Lane, 1939); John Grierson, *Challenge to the Poles* (London: Foulis, 1964); Elspeth Huxley, *Scott of the Antarctic* (London: Weidenfeld, 1977); David Thomson, *Scott's Men* (London: Allen Lane, 1977); and Roland Huntford, *Scott and Amundsen* (London: Hodder and Stoughton, 1979).

More general books that include extensive information about Scott are: E.R.G.R. Evans, *British Polar Explorers* (London: Collins, 1943); Gerald Bowman, *Men of Antarctica* (New York: Fleet Publishing Corp., 1959); and L.P. Kirwan, *A History of Polar Exploration* (New York: W.W. Norton & Co., 1960). A recent book, John Maxtone-Graham, *Safe Return Doubtful: The Heroic Age of Polar Exploration* (New York: Charles Scribner's Sons, 1988), has a dramatic chapter on the Scott-Amundsen race.

Scylax of Caryanda

(end of 6th century B.C.)

Scylax, a Greek commander in the Persian navy, was the first person known to have sailed down the Indus River and across the Arabian Sea.

There have probably been trade routes along and across the Arabian Sea between India and Arabia since the time of the first civilizations in Sumeria and maybe even before. However, Scylax, the first person whose account of crossing the sea that we know about, came much later.

Scylax was an ethnic Greek from the town of Caryanda in Asia Minor (today's Turkey). He was a naval commander in the fleet of the great Emperor Darius I of Persia. After ascending to the Persian throne in 521 B.C., Darius set out to expand his empire in several directions. He wanted to invade India so he sent Scylax out to visit the mouth of the Indus River and find the best sea route from the Persian Gulf to India.

To accomplish his goal, Scylax started out from the reverse direction—at the source of the Indus River in the Hindu Kush Mountains of Afghanistan. Some historians have said that he started from as far upstream as Kabul, the capital of modern Afghanistan. But the river is not navigable at that point, and he probably started out from near the confluence of the Kabul and Indus Rivers not far from the modern town of Attock in Pakistan.

Scylax sailed down the Indus River to its mouth near present-day Karachi and then followed the coastline of Pakistan to the Gulf of Oman and crossed it to Arabia. He did not travel up the Persian Gulf since that was already known to the Persians. He followed the southern coast of Arabia to the Red Sea and sailed up it to the Sinai Peninsula. He was able to sail through to the Mediterranean because Darius had cleared the old canal of the Pharaohs that linked the Mediterranean and Red Seas, where the Suez Canal is today.

It took Scylax 30 months to complete his trip. The length of time is explained by the fact that he probably traded along the way and may have run into unfavorable monsoons. Darius made use of the information that Scylax brought back to him: he conquered Sind, the region through which the Indus flows.

Where to learn more

The best source for the history of ancient exploration is M. Cary and E.H. Warmington (London: Methuen, 1919; reprinted Penguin Books, 1963). Other good books are: Walter Woodburn Hyde, *Ancient Greek Mariners* (New York: Oxford University Press, 1947); Björn Landström, *The Quest for India* (Garden City, N.Y.: 1964); and Rhys Carpenter, *Beyond the Pillars of Heracles* (New York: Delacorte Press, 1966).

Sir Ernest Shackleton

(1874 - 1922)

Ernest Shackleton was a British explorer who made four voyages to Antarctica. On his second one he came within 100 miles of the South Pole.

Ernest Shackleton was born in Ireland on February 17, 1874, the son of a doctor. His family moved to London when he was 10, and he was educated at Dulwich College, later part of the University of London. He left school at the age of 16 determined to become a sailor and joined the merchant marine. In 1901 he was able to get the position of third lieutenant on board the ship *Discovery* that **Robert Falcon Scott** was outfitting to take to Antarctica. This was the first scientific expedition to carry out extensive land exploration on the continent of Antarctica.

During the course of the Scott expedition, Shackleton was chosen to accompany Scott and the zoologist Dr. Edward Wilson on a journey by sledge across the Ross Ice Shelf to the farthest point south yet reached, 82°17'S. On the return journey all three suffered severely from scurvy, Shackleton in particular. He was therefore sent home on the supply ship *Morning* in 1903. He was determined to come back and continue his explorations.

Once back in Britain, Shackleton went to work as a journalist and then was able to get himself appointed to the post of secretary of the Scottish Geographical Society in Edinburgh. After taking time out to run a losing campaign for Parliament in 1906, he used his post at the Geographical Society to lobby wealthy patrons for his own expedition to Antarctica. In 1907 he announced plans to lead an expedition financed entirely by private contributions whose goal would be to reach both the South Pole and the South Magnetic Pole. He planned to get there by using dogs, ponies, an automobile modified to pull sledges and to record the whole thing on a movie camera. Before he left, he received an unexpected letter from Scott saying that he intended to make another assault on the South Pole and asking Shackleton not to use his base on Ross Island at McMurdo Sound.

Shackleton's expedition, which included the Australian **Douglas Mawson**, sailed from England on the *Nimrod* on August 7, 1907. They stopped in New Zealand and left from there to Antarctica on January 1, 1908. Shackleton had agreed to Scott's request, but when he got to the edge of the Ross Ice Shelf he found that the only place his ship could land was at the western end of Ross Island near Scott's old base. Scott later accused Shackleton of bad faith. Shackleton (whose men had nicknamed him "The Boss") set up his hut at Cape Royds on Ross Island on February 3, 1908. Three members of the expedition climbed Mt. Erebus, an active volcano on Ross Island, in March.

Shackleton and his men began setting up supply depots on the Ross Ice Shelf at the end of the Antarctic winter in September. The main team consisting of Shackleton and three companions, using ponies as transport, started out from Cape Royds at the end of October, and the last advance party turned back on November 6, 1908. On November 26, Shackleton passed (with a little celebration) Scott's farthest point south. At the beginning of December, they reached the end of the ice shelf and the beginning of the continental landmass. They discovered Beardmore Glacier, which Shackleton named in honor of his principal financial backer. They climbed the glacier and reached the central plateau of Antarctica on December 25. By then all the ponies were dead (and eaten), and rations were short. On January 7, 1909 Shackleton realized that he could not go any farther and

Ernest Shackleton. The Granger Collection, New York.

ordered his men to turn around and head back. They had traveled to within 97 nautical miles of the South Pole. On their return, they had trouble spotting their supply depots and almost starved to death.

While Shackleton was trying to get to the South Pole, another member of the expedition, Edgeworth David (50 years old), led a party to the South Magnetic Pole, which they reached on January 16, 1909. On their return to the base at Cape Royds, they met the *Nimrod*. On February 26, the ship, fearing the approach of winter, left the base. Shackleton and his men did not arrive until February 28, to find themselves abandoned. They signalled wildly, and the next morning the *Nimrod* returned to pick them up. They reached England in June 1909.

On his return, Shackleton became a popular hero and was knighted by King Edward VII. The British government gave him £20,000 to help pay off his debts from the expedition, and he was

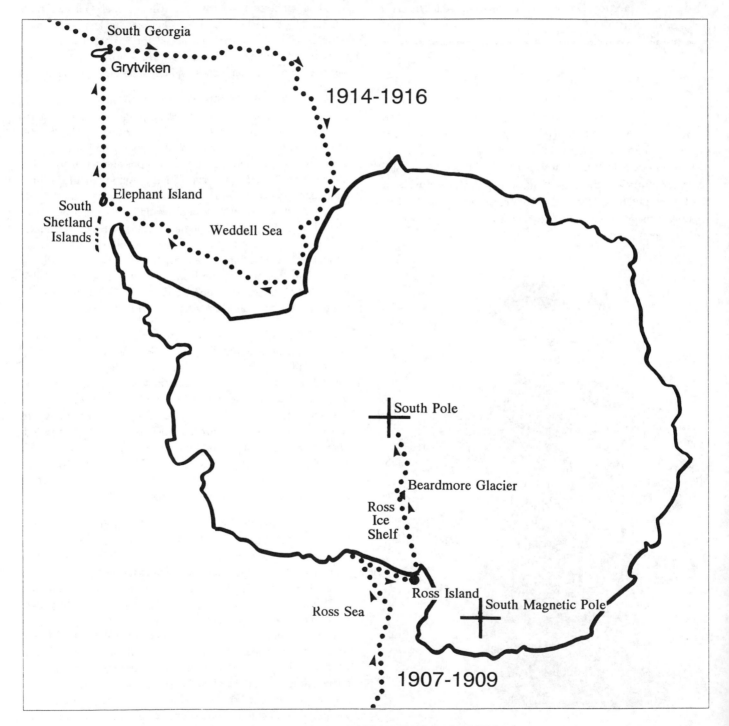

Shackleton's Antarctic expeditions, 1907-1909 and 1914-1916.

awarded a gold medal by the Royal Geographical Society. In the next few years the South Pole was reached by **Roald Amundsen** and by Scott (who did not return alive). Shackleton, ever anxious for glory, then came up with an even more ambitious scheme—to travel all the way across Antarctica from the Weddell Sea to the Ross Sea. Using his formidable fundraising skills, he was able to get enough money to buy and equip two ships. He was ready to sail from England on one of them, the *Endurance*, on August 1, 1914, when World War I broke out. Without consulting anyone, Shackleton offered the ship to the British government. The First Lord of the Admiralty, Winston Churchill, turned down the generous offer and told him to sail on to Antarctica. He left port on August 8, 1914.

The *Endurance* reached the pack ice of the Weddell Sea on December 7. It threaded its way through and came close to the mainland of Antarctica at a stretch of the coast known as Coats Land. The ship headed west looking for a safe anchorage. On January 19, 1915 it became trapped in the ice and could not move. They were trapped there throughout the long Antarctic winter. The sun set on May 1 and did not reappear until July 26, by which time the ice began to break up. It was impossible to free the *Endurance*, however, and it was badly battered by the pressure of the cracking ice. On October 24, 1915 the ship began to leak badly, and the men had to take their supplies off of it. They set up a camp on a large ice floe 1½ miles from the *Endurance*, which sank on November 21.

Shackleton's plan was to walk over the ice field to Paulet Island, 350 miles away, where he knew there was a hut and a supply depot. They set out on December 20, dragging their boats with them. On January 1, 1916 they were adrift on a large ice floe. The drifting ice carried them north, and by March 17 they were 60 miles from Paulet Island. However, the ice conditions were such that it seemed unattainable, so Shackleton set his sights on reaching Elephant Island at the tip of the Palmer Peninsula. They had to abandon the ice floe and take to their boats on April 9. Resting on a floe one night, it split in two, and Shackleton had to pull one man out of the water by grabbing his sleeping bag. They reached Elephant Island on April 15, 1916.

Realizing they could not live long on the desolate, ice-covered island, Shackleton took five companions and headed out in a boat on April 24 to try to get help. On the second day they were hit by a blizzard, and on the tenth day by a gigantic wave that almost sank them. On the 16th day, they reached South Georgia Island and were almost wrecked on the shore by a sudden storm. Once ashore, on May 15, 1916 Shackleton set out with two men to travel across the island to the small whaling station of

Grytviken on the north shore: the rest of the men were too sick to move. They walked for 24 hours straight to Grytviken, the first time the island had ever been crossed.

After they had rested and eaten, one of Shackleton's party led a rescue team to the other side of the island to pick up the men there. Shackleton himself headed out in a whaling ship to reach the remnants of his expedition on Elephant Island. The ship was not able to make its way through the pack ice. The Uruguayan government lent a ship, which was also forced back. Shackleton then chartered a British ship, but its engine broke down along the way. It was not until August 20, 1916 that the Chilean steamer *Yelcho* reached the stranded men. They were all still alive.

After his return to England, Shackleton served in the British expeditionary force that went to northern Russia in 1919. After the end of the war, he was determined to achieve his goal of crossing Antarctica. He set out again in 1921 accompanied by many of his former colleagues and **George Hubert Wilkins**, who would later attempt to fly across Antarctica. They set sail in September 1921. Shackleton became ill during the voyage. On January 4, 1922 the ship anchored in Grytviken Harbor on South Georgia Island. Shackleton died of a massive heart attack during the early morning hours of January 5, 1922. He was buried on a hill above the whaling station, where his grave still stands. The rest of the expedition tried to carry on but got caught in the ice and was forced to turn back in April 1922.

Where to learn more

Shackleton wrote a book about his attempt to reach the South Pole, *The Heart of the Antarctic* (London: Heinemann, 1909), and another about the boat trip to South Georgia that has been called one of the most dramatic of all the stories of exploration, *South* (London: Heinemann, 1919).

Two of the participants in the epic boat journey also published accounts: Frank Hurley, *Shackleton's Argonauts* (Sydney: Angus & Robertson, 1948) and F.A. Worsley, *The Great Antarctic Rescue* (London: Times Books, 1975).

The record of Shackleton's last trip to Antarctica is told by a close associate of his, Frank Wild, who was his second-in-command and had been on the two previous trips: *Shackleton's Last Voyage: The Story of the Quest* (London: Cassell, 1923).

There are two biographies of Shackleton. One was written right after his death: H.R. Mill, *The Life of Sir Ernest Shackleton* (London: 1923). The other is more recent and has the advantage of greater distance from its subject, Margery and James Fisher, *Shackleton* (London: 1957).

More general books that include accounts of Shackleton's expeditions are: E.R.G.R. Evans, *British Polar Explorers* (London: Collins, 1943); Gerald Bowman, *Men of Antarctica* (New York: Fleet Publishing Corp., 1959); L.P. Kirwan, *A History of Polar Exploration* (New York: W.W. Norton & Co., 1960); John Maxtone-Graham, *Safe Return Doubtful: The Heroic Age of Polar Exploration* (New York: Charles Scribner's Sons, 1988); and *Antarctica: Great Stories from the Frozen Continent* (Sydney: Reader's Digest, 1988).

May French Sheldon

(1847 - 1936)

May French Sheldon was an Englishwoman of American origin who was one of the first women to explore in East Africa, leading an expedition there in 1891.

May French was born near Pittsburgh, Pennsylvania on May 10, 1847. Her mother was a doctor and her father an engineer.

She was educated in Europe and used her family's money to found a publishing house in London. In 1876 she married a fellow publisher, Eli Sheldon, and they went into business together, publishing her novel *Herbert Severance* and the first English translation of Gustave Flaubert's novel *Salammbô*. In 1890 Sheldon met **Henry Morton Stanley**, the famous American journalist and explorer of Africa who had "found" **David Livingstone**.

Sheldon was so excited by Stanley's stories of Africa that she decided to make an expedition there herself. Everyone except for her husband tried to dissuade her. When she arrived at the port of Mombasa in Kenya, the British authorities thought she was crazy and refused to give her any help. Sheldon went to the offshore island of Zanzibar and was able to convince the Sultan that she was serious. He enlisted porters for her and gave her an official letter telling the local chiefs to provide her with assistance.

Sheldon returned to Mombasa and set out from there with a party of about 100 porters and an elaborate set of supplies including a silk court dress with long train that she intended to wear when presented to local chiefs and several thousand finger rings engraved with her name that she intended to give as gifts. Sheldon learned Swahili in order to be able to carry on most negotiations herself and administered medicine to her porters along the way. Only one member of the expedition died: killed by a lion when he strayed from the path. Sheldon herself walked most of the way, was injured in one eye by a thorn, and awoke one night to find a python in her bed.

Sheldon left Mombasa in March 1891 and traveled inland to the town of Taveta (now on the Kenya-Tanzania border) and from there to Mount Kilimanjaro. She then went to Lake Chala, which was inside an ancient volcanic cone. It had rarely been visited because of the steep descent into the lake. She climbed down the precipice by holding on to vines. Once down, she constructed a makeshift boat and traveled around the lake putting up American flags and markers with her name on them. She visited the Rombo tribe, who were reported to be very ferocious, but encountered no problems. In her memoirs, however, she remarked that a German explorer, Carl Peters, followed six weeks after her and "felt obliged to turn his guns on these Rombos, . . . and kill a hundred and twenty of them before breakfast one morning."

As they traveled farther inland, Sheldon encountered many tribes that had not seen a European woman before. Her fame preceded her, and many people came from all the surrounding countryside to look at her and hear her talk. At one point, she was threatened by a Masai warrior but scared him off by shooting a gun into the air. On her return to the coast, she was seriously injured at the Tanzanian town of Pangani when the litter she was in fell into a stream twenty feet below and she was then dropped once again by her porters as they tried to rescue her. She was able to make it back to Mombasa, where she recovered.

Following her return to Europe in late 1891, Sheldon wrote a book about her experiences, *Sultan to Sultan*, that was published in December 1892. Its publication made her famous, and she was asked to speak at many conferences and meetings. Her husband died while she was speaking to the Congress of Women at the World's Columbian Exposition in Chicago in 1893.

In 1903 Sheldon traveled to the Belgian Congo where she wrote favorably about the authoritarian colonial rule of the Belgians. She traveled to the independent African nation of Liberia in 1905. She worked as a fundraiser for the Red Cross during World War I. An outspoken feminist, she spent the 1920s traveling and lecturing. She died at her home in West Kensington, London on February 10, 1936.

Where to learn more

Sheldon told about her East African expedition in *Sultan to Sultan: Adventures among the Masai and Other Tribes of East Africa* (London: Saxon, 1892; Boston: Arena, 1892). Short biographies of her can be found in Dea Birkett, *Spinsters Abroad: Victorian Lady Explorers* (London: Basil Blackwell, 1989) and Marion Tinling, *Women into the Unknown: A Sourcebook on Women Explorers and Travelers* (New York: Greenwood Press, 1989).

Kishen Singh

(1850 - 1921)

Kishen Singh was one of the Indian "pundits" who made a remarkable journey through Tibet and then around its northern and eastern borders.

Rai Bahadur Kishen Singh Milamwal, often known by his code name Krishna, or sometimes by his code initials, A-K, was, like his cousin **Nain Singh**, a "pundit," one of the Indian agents trained by the British to explore Tibet.

Kishen Singh was the youngest pundit when he was put in charge of four assistants in the fall of 1872 to travel to Koko Nor, near the Chinese border with Tibet. They were attacked by robbers near Lake Tengri in central Tibet. Left without any possessions, they were able to make it to Lhasa on March 8, 1873. They rested there and then returned to headquarters in India to report on their failure.

Singh made one other expedition before setting out in 1878 on the trip that would ensure him a place as one of the greatest pundits. He left Darjeeling, accompanied by one servant, on April 24, 1878 and arrived in Lhasa on September 5. His aim was to find a Mongolian caravan headed north and to attach himself to it so that he could travel to Koko Nor. He was forced to wait a year until he could find a suitable caravan. During the long wait, he spent his time mapping the city and environs of Lhasa and studying Mongolian. He finally connected with a group of traders headed in his direction and left Lhasa in September 1879.

The caravan traveled north through the high plateau country of central Tibet for several weeks. They were suddenly attacked by a large force of Golok tribesmen while trying to cross the Chang Tang desert in northern Tibet. The bandits were beaten off, but Kishen Singh lost his personal possessions and the trade goods that he intended to sell in order to live. The only things he had left were his survey instruments. However, he persisted on his mission. At times he was forced to become a domestic servant in order to earn enough money to eat. He spent five months as a goatherd.

In the spring of 1880 Kishen Singh reached the trading center of Tunhwang in western China. Singh wanted to go on to Lop Nor, but the local governor had become suspicious that he might be a spy and arrested him and held him captive in the town of Sachu for seven months. However, a Tibetan lama, or priest, that Singh had known in Tunhwang passed through the town and vouched for the pundit's innocence. The lama, who was headed south, agreed to take Singh along with him as his servant.

Singh (always accompanied by his own servant) and the lama traveled for 600 miles through Kham province in eastern Tibet. At the town of Tachienlu, or Batang, on the border between Tibet and China, Singh made his way to a Catholic missionary station and revealed his identity to the French missionaries. The missionaries gave him money to continue his journey and also sent word back to India, where he had long since been given up for lost, that he was still alive. Traveling through the wild country of the Atak Gangla Range and the upper Salween River, where Tibet, India, Burma, and China all meet, Singh and his servant were twice arrested on suspicion of being thieves and spies. In the first case the authorities could find no evidence to keep them, and in the second they were once again vouched for by an influential traveler they had met along the way.

The two Indians traveled through southern Tibet and crossed over the border into India, where they arrived at Darjeeling in early 1883, four and a half years after they had started. Kishen Singh had kept an accurate count of the many steps he had made during his 2,800-mile trip. At one point, he was forced to ride a horse for 230 miles while he was traveling through bandit country, and he calculated the distance by comparing the horse's stride with his own. Years later, when his calculations were checked over a 120-mile distance, they were found to be off by only one mile.

Kishen Singh did not have a happy homecoming. In his absence his son had died, and his family had been forced to split up. His superiors at the Geographical Survey of India were very impressed with his achievement and praised him lavishly and wrote of his exploits to the Royal Geographical Society. The Society presented him with a gold watch, but it was stolen before it got to him.

Where to learn more

The original sources for the explorations of the pundits were in the reports of the Survey of India, and many of them were published by the Royal Geographical Society. A complete listing of these reports can be found in a recent book that tells the whole fascinating story of the pundits: Derek J. Waller, *The Pundits: British Exploration of Tibet and Central Asia* (Lexington: The University Press of Kentucky, 1990).

The two books that served as the chief sources for this account give good summaries of the exploits of the pundits: John MacGregor, *Tibet: A Chronicle of Exploration* (London: Routledge & Kegan Paul, 1970) and Peter Hopkirk, *Trespassers on the Roof of the World: The Race for Lhasa* (London: John Murray, 1982).

Nain Singh

(1830? - 1882?)

Indian explorer Nain Singh, the first of the British-trained "pundits," made three trips into Tibet.

Thomas George Montgomerie was an engineer in the British Army in the India. In 1852 he joined the Great Trigonometrical Survey, which was charged with mapping all of India. He was sent to Kashmir in the far north, where he calculated the height of K2, the second highest mountain in the world. By 1864 he had completed the mapping of all the domains of the Maharajah of Jammu and Kashmir and was awarded a gold medal by the Royal Geographical Society in London. At this point, he was stymied. The small states in the Himalayas and the Buddhist kingdom of Tibet were afraid of British power and absolutely prohibited any Westerners from entering their countries. Montgomerie wanted to know what was on the other side of the mountains he was surveying.

In 1863 Montgomerie sent a Muslim clerk in his office named Abdul Hamid from Ladakh to Yarkand in Chinese Turkestan. Hamid stayed there for six months and accurately calculated the location of Yarkand in addition to spying on the activities of the Russians in the area. He died traveling back to India, but his notes made their way to Montgomerie. Buoyed by this success, Montgomerie proposed to his superiors that a regular training school be set up to train Indians to penetrate Tibet and bring back information to the British in India. His idea was accepted, and he was put in charge of training these "pundits," at his headquarters at Dehra Dun in the foothills of the Himalayas in northern India.

Montgomerie began his training in 1863 with two cousins named Nain Singh and Mani Singh. They were the sons of two brothers who had helped the explorer William Moorcroft in 1812. Nain Singh was the headmaster of a village school, and both cousins had accompanied a German expedition to the Himalayas some years before. Under Montgomerie's supervision, they were trained for two years in the use of surveying instruments, navigational astronomy, and methods for calculating altitude. They were also trained to be spies, traveling with luggage that had secret compartments and clothes with hidden pockets. Blank paper was put in Tibetan prayer wheels on which coded notes could be written. They also learned how to make accurate measurements of distance by perfecting their walk so that each pace was exactly the same length. They then kept track of how many paces they walked using Buddhist prayer beads that had been shortened from the usual length of 108 beads to 100 beads.

The pundits were given code names to conceal their true identities. The first one, Nain Singh, was simply known as "the Pundit" or the "Chief Pundit." He set out with his cousin on their first mission in January 1865, reaching Kathmandu on March 7. At the Tibetan frontier town of Kyirong they were turned back by a suspicious governor who found their story unconvincing. They then returned to Kathmandu, where they split up. Nain Singh joined a caravan posing as a merchant from the region of Ladakh. This time he crossed the border successfully into Tibet, where he soon split up from his original caravan.

Nain Singh joined another Ladakh trading caravan that eventually took him to Shigatse, the second largest town in Tibet. There he visited the nearby Tashilhunpo monastery, the headquarters of the Panchen Lama. He was summoned to an audience with the Panchen Lama, the second highest religious authority in Tibet, who turned out to be a boy of eleven.

Nain Singh arrived in Lhasa on January 10, 1866, one year after he had left Dehra Dun. He had counted every step of the way. During the three months that he was in Lhasa, he carried out a number of duties: By making a total of twenty solar and stellar observations, he was able to come very close to calculating the exact latitude of Lhasa for the first time in history. He made sixteen thermometer readings every day for almost two weeks. He used the boiling point of water to calculate Lhasa's altitude at 11,700 feet above sea level, very close to what is generally accepted today. He also went to the great palace of the Potala for a group audience with the twelfth Dalai Lama, at that time 13 years of age, and received his blessing.

After three months, Nain Singh was beginning to get nervous. His disguise had been detected by two Muslim merchants from Kashmir, but they did not report him to the authorities. He heard that the governor of Kyirong, who had stopped him before, was in town. He knew that if he were discovered he would be executed. When he learned that the caravan he had traveled with was preparing to leave, he asked to rejoin it.

He traveled with the caravan along the main east-west trade route of Tibet as far west as Lake Manasarovar. He then turned south and headed on his own into India. Along the way he was attacked and held captive for a short while. He returned to Dehra Dun in July 1867. He had walked 1,200 miles and had counted 2½ million steps. Montgomerie wrote a letter to the Royal Geographical Society praising his efforts.

One of Nain Singh's major accomplishments was to chart the Tsangpo River from its source at Lake Manasarovar to its junction with the Kyi-Chu. His observations allowed Montgomerie to calculate the discharge of the Tsangpo after joining the Kyi-Chu. This led him to theorize that the Tsangpo was the upper part of the Brahmaputra River that flowed through Assam in eastern India. He was later to test this theory by sending out **Kintup**, another pundit.

Nain Singh had brought back reports of large golden Buddhas and other gold objects in Tibet. Tibet had long been reputed to be rich in gold, and Nain Singh was next sent on a mission to investigate the gold fields at Thok Jalung in western Tibet. He also was instructed to plot the location of Gartok, Tibet's largest western city.

On May 2, 1867, Nain Singh set out for Thok Jalung from the town of Mussoorie accompanied by his cousin Mani Singh and his brother Kalian Singh. They arrived at the 8,570-foot Mana Pass on the border with Tibet on June 3, only to find it still blocked with snow. They had to wait until July before it was opened. They passed safely across the Tibetan frontier and traveled to the Sutlej River, a tributary of the Indus, crossed by a 76-foot suspension bridge across a high gorge. Bypassing Gartok, they came to a camp of Tibetan nomads, whose headman spotted the travelers for what they were. They had to bribe him in order to proceed and left Mani Singh behind as a hostage. By prior arrangement, Kalian Singh headed out on his own. Nain Singh had to climb the Chomorong Pass and travel to the gold fields by himself.

After traveling through three days of blizzards, Nain Singh reached Thok Jalung on August 26, 1867. Thok (meaning goldfield) Jalung was on a bleak and desolate plain, 16,000 feet high, possibly the highest inhabited place in the world. The gold mine itself was a mile-long trench about 25 feet deep. Streams were diverted from nearby hills to flow through the trench, and the miners used sluices to wash the soil from the heavier gold.

The chief of the goldfield met Nain Singh in his tent while sipping tea and smoking his water-pipe. He was suspicious of the Indian from the start. He looked curiously at Nain Singh's well-constructed wooden box that contained a secret compartments to hide his surveying instruments. The headman thought it was too elegant for such a simple traveler. Nain Singh, however, was able to make up a story to the chief's satisfaction and bribed him with some coral jewelry for his wife. He got permission to stay in the camp for five days. He reported back that it was a rich mine: he saw one nugget that weighed two pounds.

Nain Singh returned to pick up his cousin and his brother. Kalian Singh had traveled up a branch of the Sutlej River that was called the Gartang. He learned that it was the larger of the two, and therefore the main source for the Indus River. He got almost to the headwaters of the Gartang but was stopped by bandits. The source was finally traced by **Sven Hedin** in 1907. As the three pundits headed home, Nain Singh took a detour through the town of Gartok but left hurriedly when he heard that people

were saying he was a British spy. Nain Singh and his two companions returned to India in November 1867.

Nain Singh traveled with Sir Thomas Douglas Forsyth on a diplomatic mission to Yarkand in Chinese Turkestan in 1873-1874. On his return he was asked to make one last expedition— to follow a route from Leh in Ladakh through central Tibet to Lhasa. If possible, he was to join a Chinese caravan there and travel all the way to Beijing. Nain Singh left on this assignment shortly after returning from Yarkand. He left Leh on July 15, 1874 with four companions. They were disguised as Buddhist monks and drove a flock of sheep with them.

Nain Singh and his party went first to Lake Pangong, where he mapped its eastern side for the first time. They headed eastward across the great central plateau of Tibet north of the previous route that Nain Singh had taken along the Tsangpo. This area is studded with mountain lakes, none of which had been mapped before Nain Singh's visit. Nain Singh and his companions traveled across a vast region with an average altitude of 14,000 feet that has very few human inhabitants. They marched parallel to a large mountain range to the south, which is now called the Nain Singh Range. Nain Singh investigated goldfields at Thok Daurakpa and reported how difficult it was to extract the ore there. At the eastern end of the plateau is a large lake, Tengri Nor. Prior to Nain Singh, the only reports of this lake had been made by Nain Singh's compatriot, **Kishen Singh**, who had traveled there three years previously.

From Tengri Nor, Nain Singh headed south for the 80 miles to Lhasa. He reached the capital on July 15, 1875. He only stayed there for two days. The money he was expecting to be sent by another route had not arrived. The city was full of rumors about an approaching British agent, and he was actually recognized on the street by a merchant from Ladakh. Fearing exposure, Nain Singh sent two of his men back to Leh with all his astronomical surveys, and then he quickly headed south by the quickest route to India.

Nain Singh traveled south across the Tsangpo and crossed the Himalayas at Karkang Pass, 16,000 feet above sea level. He entered the small Himalayan state of Tawang on December 24, 1875 and was held prisoner there until February 17, 1876. He managed to escape and reached British territory on March 1. The notice of his arrival was immediately telegraphed back to Leh. He traveled down the Brahmaputra by boat to Calcutta and from there went home.

News of Nain Singh's brilliant achievements were published in the *Geographical Magazine* of the Royal Geographical Society in 1876. In 1877 the British government granted him a patch of land and a pension. He was presented with a gold watch from the Paris Geographical Society and was awarded the gold medal of the Royal Geographical Society. These were presented to him by the Viceroy of India in a ceremony on January 1, 1878. Colonel Henry Yule of the Royal Geographical Society said at the time the award was announced, "His observations have added a larger amount of important knowledge to the map of Asia than those of any other living man." Nain Singh returned for a while to Dehra Dun to help instruct other pundits. He then retired to the piece of land granted to him by the government. *The Times* of London reported his death in 1882 from cholera, although there is another report that says he died in 1895 from a heart attack.

Where to learn more

The original sources for the explorations of the pundits were in reports of the British Survey of India, and many of them were published by the Royal Geographical Society. A complete listing of these reports can be found in a recent book that tells the whole fascinating history of the pundits: Derek J. Waller, *The Pundits: British Exploration of Tibet and Central Asia* (Lexington: The University Press of Kentucky, 1990).

There are good summaries of the activities of the pundits in two books about the exploration of Tibet: John MacGregor, *Tibet: A Chronicle of Exploration* (London: Routledge & Kegan Paul, 1970) and Peter Hopkirk, *Trespassers on the Roof of the World: The Race for Lhasa* (London: John Murray, 1982).

Jedediah Smith

(1799 - 1831)

Jedediah Smith was an American trapper and fur-trader who was the first American to travel overland to what is now the southwestern United States and was then part of Mexico.

Jedediah Smith was born on January 6, 1799 in New York state of parents who had come from New Hampshire. The family moved to western Pennsylvania in either 1810 or 1811. Smith went to St. Louis, Missouri in the spring of 1822. He was hired by **William Henry Ashley**, a Virginia businessman who had founded a fur-trading company in St. Louis in 1819. He went on Ashley's first expedition to the West in 1822-1823 and proved himself to be a natural leader and resourceful frontiersman.

In September 1823 Smith was put in charge of an expedition that left Fort Lookout on the upper Missouri River with plans to trap in the central Rockies and Columbia River areas. Smith led 11 men across the Great Plains via the White River and through the Badlands of the Dakotas and the Black Hills. Crossing the Badlands, they nearly died of thirst. In the Black Hills, Smith was attacked by a wounded grizzly bear that almost crushed his head between his jaws. One of Smith's men sewed up the wounds with a needle and thread and reattached his ear. It took him 10 days to recover, during which time his men explored the Black Hills. Smith always wore his hair long after that to cover up the scars.

Traveling across the Belle Fourche River, Smith and his men continued on into the Powder River Valley, over the Bighorn Mountains through Granite Pass, and into the basin of the Bighorn River. They spent the winter of 1823-1824 at a Crow village in the Wind River Valley near present-day Dubois, Wyoming. They left in late February 1824 and crossed the Continental Divide into the Green River valley in mid-March. The pass through the mountains that they pioneered was named South Pass; it later became the main passageway for Americans moving west. Once they reached the Green River, they found it to be rich in beaver and divided up into two parties to go trapping upstream and downstream.

In September 1824 Smith encountered a party of native Americans working for the British Hudson's Bay Company. He and seven of his men traveled with them and their leader, Alexander Ross, to the Company's Flathead Post (present-day Eddy, Montana), on the Clark Fork of the Columbia River, where they arrived on November 26, 1824. The Americans spent the winter there as unwelcome guests of the Hudson's Bay Company.

Smith had sent word back to Ashley of his discoveries and of the rich fur country he had found. Ashley traveled up the Missouri from St. Louis and met up with Smith on the Green River around the first of July 1825. This was the first big rendezvous of fur trappers and traders that was to become an annual event. Smith and Ashley then took their large supply of furs back down the river to St. Louis, arriving there on October 4, 1825. In St. Louis, Smith concluded an agreement with Ashley to become his partner and headed back toward the Rocky Mountains a month later. He only got as far as the Platte River in western Nebraska when winter set in, and he was forced to winter in a village of the Pawnee tribe.

Ashley again met up with Smith in the spring of 1826. At this meeting he sold his interest in the fur-trading company he had founded to a partnership that included Smith. Following the conclusion of this agreement, Smith headed toward the Great Salt Lake, which he had seen in 1824, in order to investigate reports that it emptied into the Pacific Ocean. He set out to find the legendary (and non-existent) Buenaventura River that was supposed to be its link with the sea. He had already sent out David Jackson and a few men to investigate the area north and west of the lake, but they failed to find the Buenaventura.

In August 1826 Smith led a party of sixteen out of the Cache Valley to the Great Salt Lake and then to Utah Lake. They followed the Virgin River downstream to the Colorado River, where they stayed for two weeks as guests of the Mojave tribe. They then crossed the Mojave Desert by following the course of the Mojave River, which Smith named the Inconstant. They reached Mission San Gabriel in what is now a suburb of Los Angeles on November 27, 1826. They were the first Americans to travel overland to California. Smith left his men and went to report to the Mexican governor of California in San Diego. The governor was not at all happy to see him and made him promise to return the way he had come. Smith got passage on an American trading ship from San Diego in January 1827. He was let off at San Pedro Bay, south of present-day Los Angeles, where he rejoined his men.

The Americans did not follow their original route. They went north over the Tehachapi Mountains into the San Joaquin Valley in central California, where they were gratified to find the furs they had been looking for but did not find the Buenaventura River. They tried to make it over the Sierra Nevada by following the American River (near Sacramento) in early May 1827, but the snow was still too deep in the mountains and they were forced to turn back. Smith got word that the Mexican governor had sent troops after him, and he headed up the Stanislaus River, farther south, in late May and was able to make it over the mountains to Walker Lake in what is now Nevada. Smith and his men then traveled across the Great Basin in time to reach the trappers' rendezvous at Bear Lake on July 3, 1827. They were welcomed with cannon fire because they had long since been given up for lost.

Smith rested for only nine days and then headed back west. He reached the Mojave villages again on August 18, 1827. At first, the Mojaves were quite friendly, as they had been on his previous visit. But as the fur trappers tried to cross the Colorado on August 18, the Native Americans attacked and killed half of the men in Smith's party. The remainder escaped down the river on a raft and eventually made it back to their former camp on the Stanislaus River. This time Smith was arrested and taken to Monterey, the capital of the province of Alta California. He was held for two months but was finally released. He and 20 companions left San José mission in late December 1827. They reached the Umpqua River in southern Oregon in mid-July 1828.

Smith's aim was to reach the Willamette River, which he knew flowed into the Columbia. Smith left with two companions on the morning of July 14 to scout the best route. While they were away, a band from the Kelwatset tribe attacked the others and killed all of them but one, who was able to escape into the woods. The four survivors made their way to the Hudson's Bay Company's headquarters at Fort Vancouver (Vancouver, Washington, across the Columbia from Portland, Oregon) in early August. The British sent out a party to punish the Native Americans and bought the furs that Smith had been able to salvage. Smith stayed at Fort Vancouver until March 12, 1829. He did not get back to the Rockies in time to take part in the 1829 rendezvous.

During the winter of 1829-1830 Smith trapped in the Blackfoot country of what is now western Montana. He went to the fur rendezvous along the Wind River in July 1830. At that rendezvous he and his partners sold out their interests in their fur-trading business to a new group of traders, who also called themselves the Rocky Mountain Fur Company.

Using the profits from the sale to buy a farm and a townhouse, Smith returned to St. Louis. There he got involved in schemes to open up a trading route between the United States and Santa Fe in New Mexico. Smith led a wagon train that left St. Louis on April 10, 1831. On May 27, they were in the dry stretch of land between the Arkansas and Cimarron Rivers in southern Kansas and had gone three days without water. Smith went ahead to look for a water hole. He was never seen again. When the rest of the wagon train got to Santa Fe, they found pistols and a rifle that had belonged to Smith. These had been traded by a group of Comanches who had mistaken Smith's intentions and fired on him at the water hole. He was only 32 when he died.

Where to learn more

Smith left only fragmentary accounts and journals of his travels. His journal of the first trip to California has been edited as *The Southwest Expedition of Jedediah S. Smith: His Personal Account of the Journey to California: 1826-1827* by George R. Brooks (Glendale, California: Arthur H. Clark Co., 1977; reprinted in paperback, Lincoln: University of Nebraska Press, 1989). Our knowledge of his first expedition in 1824-1825 is based entirely on the account of one of Smith's colleagues, which can be found in Charles L. Camp, ed. *James Clyman, Frontiersman* (Portland, Ore.: Champoeg Press, 1960). Other documents can be found in Harrison C. Dale, *The Ashley-Smith Exploration and the Discovery of a Central Route to the Pacific, 1822-1829* (Glendale, California: Arthur H. Clark Co., 1941).

The definitive biography of Smith is Dale L. Morgan, *Jedediah Smith and the Opening of the West* (New York: Bobbs-Merrill Co., 1953; also available in paperback). Morgan also published, along with Carl I. Wheat, *Jedediah Smith and His Maps of the American West* (San Francisco: California Historical Society, 1954).

Other biographical studies of Smith include John Neihardt, *Splendid Wayfaring: The Story of the Exploits of Jedediah Smith and His Comrades the Ashley-Henry Men* (original edition, 1920; reprinted, Lincoln: University of Nebraska Press, 1970); Maurice S. Sullivan, *The Travels of Jedediah Smith* (Santa Ana, California: 1934) and *Jedediah Smith: Trader and Trail Breaker* (New York: 1936); and Alson J. Smith, *Men Against the Mountains* (New York: 1965).

John Smith

(1580 - 1631)

John Smith was an English adventurer who took part in the first English colony in Virginia and led expeditions to explore the Chesapeake Bay and the coast of New England.

John Smith was born in the little town of Willoughby in the English county of Lincolnshire. He was baptized by his parents on January 9, 1580. On his father's death in 1596, Smith went off to fight in the French army against Spain. He then fought with the Dutch who were revolting against their Spanish rulers. After a short visit to England, he returned to the Continent in 1600 and joined the army of Austria who were fighting the Ottoman Turks in eastern Europe.

Smith's own account of his many adventures have not always been believed, but there is no proof that they did not happen.

John Smith.

According to him, he was responsible for two great Austrian victories and then fought three Turkish warriors in successive single-handed combats. His bravery so impressed Prince Sigismund Bathori, the prince of Transylvania (now part of Romania), that he was granted a coat of arms and a pension of 3,000 ducats a year.

In subsequent fighting in Transylvania, Smith was taken prisoner by the Turks and was sent to Constantinople (now Istanbul) as a present for the Turkish pasha's wife, Tragabigzanda. According to Smith, she fell in love with him, and she sent him to her brother in the port of Varna on the Black Sea for safekeeping. There he was enslaved and had to kill his master in order to escape. He went back to Transylvania where he got a safe-conduct from Prince Sigismund. After various wanderings, he ended up in Morocco, where he met up with an English naval ship and returned to his native country in 1605.

Back in England, Smith decided to set out with a group of colonizers who were going to Guiana on the northeastern coast of South America. This scheme fell through, however, and he ended up traveling with a group of 105 men who left England on December 19, 1606 to found the first British colony in Virginia. When they arrived on April 26, 1607 and opened up their sealed instructions, it was found that Smith had been chosen to be one of the seven leaders of the colony even though he had caused trouble on the way over and had been accused of mutiny.

Once the colonists established themselves at Jamestown on May 24, 1607, Smith quickly became the leader of the group. He took charge of exploring the neighboring territory and hunting for supplies. On his first trip he went up the James River as far as the site of present-day Richmond. On others he went down the James and up the Chickahominy River. On his second trip to the Chickahominy in December 1607 he was captured by members of what the English called the Powhatan tribe. He was taken north to the main camp of King Powhatan (whose given name was Wahunsonacook). Condemned to death by having his brains beat out, he was saved at the last minute by Powhatan's young daughter, Pocahontas. This famous story may or may not be true, but Pocahontas (whose real name was Matoakah) was a real person who went on to marry another English settler, John Rolfe. She died in England from smallpox.

In addition to his efforts in guiding the colony through its first difficult years (when 80 percent of the colonists died), Smith was responsible for two major exploring expeditions during the summer of 1608. He had been instructed from London to see

515

whether there was a passage westward to the Pacific through the Chesapeake Bay.

On the first trip, Smith left Jamestown on June 2, 1608. He and his companions traveled up the coast of the Chesapeake Bay as far as the Patapsco River (where Baltimore is today). On their return, they went up the Potomac River as far as the site of present-day Washington, D.C. Smith reached that point the same day (July 3, 1608) that **Samuel de Champlain** landed at Quebec to found a new French colony. On the way south, Smith and his men took a detour up the Rappahanock River. They speared fish to eat, and Smith was stung by a stingray he had caught. His body became so swollen and he ran such a high fever that his companions thought he was going to die. He recovered, and the spot has been called Stingray Point ever since. The expedition returned to Jamestown on July 21, 1608.

Accompanied by almost the same party of men, Smith set out again almost immediately, on July 24. This time the goal was to travel all the way up the Chesapeake. They made it back up to the Patapsco in a couple of days. From there they explored the mouth of the Susquehannah and the other rivers that flow into the north end of the Bay. They met two previously unknown groups of Native Americans, the Massawomekes and the Tockwoughs. Smith found a waterfall on the Susquehannah that he named after himself. He met up with a party of Susquahannock traders, from an Iroquois tribe unrelated to the Algonkins he had previously encountered. They had European goods that Smith rightly guessed they had obtained by trading with the French. On the way south he stopped to explore the Patuxent, Rappahannock (going as far as present-day Fredericksburg, Virginia), and Nansemond Rivers. He arrived back in Jamestown on September 7, 1608.

Smith sent back his accounts of these explorations in a work called the *True Relation . . .*, written in July 1608, and *A Map of Virginia*, drawn in 1612, that gave the English their first knowledge of what were to become Virginia and Maryland. During the winter of 1608-1609 Smith served as president of the Council that governed Virginia and saved the colony by bartering for corn with the Native Americans. In August 1609 a new ship with more settlers arrived, and there was much argument about who was supposed to be in charge. In September, Smith was badly hurt in an accidental explosion of gunpowder, and he returned to England in October 1609. During his recovery he continued to

argue in favor of settling North America, but he never returned to Virginia.

In March 1614 Smith was hired by a group of London merchants to explore the region north of Virginia and to report back on its prospects for settlement. He returned to England with a valuable cargo of furs and fish, and he used his knowledge to write *A Description of New England* in 1616. This was the first English work to show the contours of New England. In fact, it was in this work that Smith gave the region its name as well as several others, including Plymouth, that were kept by the later Puritan settlers.

Impressed by Smith's work, a wealthy English merchant, Sir Ferdinando Gorges, sent him out on two further voyages of exploration in 1615. On the first of these, he was forced to turn back when his ship lost its mast in a storm. He set out again and was captured by pirates and then by a French naval ship. He helped the French to fight the Spanish and was released in the port of La Rochelle in November 1615. He tried to sail to America once more in 1617, but was forced to give up because of bad weather. After that he stayed in London and wrote maps and pamphlets telling Englishmen about North America and recounting his adventures. He died in June 1631.

Where to learn more

Smith's major works are: *A True Relation of Such Occurrences and Accidents of Noate as Hath Hapned in Virginia since the First Planting of that Collony* (London: 1608); *A Map of Virginia. With a Description of the Countrey, the Commodities, People, Government and Religion* (Oxford: 1612); *A Description of New England: Or the Observations, and Discoveries of Captain John Smith* (London: 1616); *New Englands Trials* (London: 1620; second edition, 1622); *The True Travels, Adventures, and Observations of Captaine John Smith, In Europe, Asia, Affrica, and America, from Anno Domini 1593 to 1629* (London: 1630).

These works are included in Edward Arber, ed. *Travels and Works of Captain John Smith*, 2 vols. (Edinburgh: 1910).

A recent book gathers together all of Smith's writings: Philip L. Barbour, ed. *The Complete Works of Captain John Smith (1580-1631)*, 3 vols. (Chapel Hill: University of North Carolina Press, 1986).

There are many, many works on the life of John Smith. The preeminent Smith scholar is Philip Barbour, who, in addition to the collected works cited above, has written what is probably the best biography of Smith: *The Three Worlds of Captain John Smith* (Boston: Houghton Mifflin, 1964). It includes what is close to being a definitive bibliography. Also good is Bradford Smith, *Captain John Smith: His Life and Legend* (Philadelphia: J.B. Lippincott Co., 1953). A very recent work is J.A. Leo Lemay, *The American Dream of Captain John Smith* (Charlottesville: University Press of Virginia, 1991).

Juan Díaz de Solís

(1470 - 1516)

Juan Díaz de Solís was a Spanish explorer who took part in expeditions along the coast of Central and South American and then led one that discovered the Río de la Plata.

J uan Díaz de Solís was born in the town of Lebrija in the southern Spanish province of Andalucia. Very little is known about his early life. Some historians include him on a hypothetical first voyage to America made by **Amerigo Vespucci** in 1497-1498 in the company of **Vicente Yáñez Pinzón**, who had been one of **Christopher Columbus**'s captains in the 1492 voyage. Most historians do not believe that this voyage ever took place. According to some accounts, Solís then participated in a voyage that Vespucci made to Brazil in 1503-1504.

Solís did make two documented voyages in the company of Pinzón. Their first joint venture took them to the coast of Central America in 1506. It is possible that this was the first Spanish expedition to reach the Yucatan Peninsula in Mexico. Pinzón and Solís left again from the port of Sanlúcar de Barrameda on June 29, 1508 with instructions to find a passage around the Americas. Our knowledge of the voyage is very hazy, but at least one report said that they traveled as far south as Patagonia in southern Argentina.

When Vespucci died in 1512 Solís was named to replace him as the Pilot Major of Spain. On November 12, 1514 King Ferdinand commissioned him to take three ships for a period of two years in another attempt to find a passage westward to the Spice Islands. After he entered the Pacific, his instructions were to sail northward as far as the Isthmus of Panama and then follow that latitude westward to his destination. Solís sailed from the port of Sanlúcar de Barrameda at the mouth of the Guadalquivir River on October 8, 1515. After a brief stay in the Canary Islands he proceeded southwestward to the general area where he and Pinzón had been in 1509. As a result he reached the mouth of the Río de la Plata in February 1516.

Solís named his discovery the Freshwater Sea because it was so large. It was not renamed Río de la Plata (the Silver River) until 1527. It seemed like a good passageway into the interior so Solís traveled up it for some distance. In August 1516 he rowed ashore to what is now Uruguay and was killed by Native Americans on the shore. The rest of the expedition then left immediately for Spain under the command of Solís's brother-in-law, Francisco de Torres. They reached Spain on September 4, 1516. One of the people they told their story to was **Ferdinand Magellan**, who was inspired to go look for a passageway to the west.

Where to learn more

The best source in English for the activities of Solís is Samuel Eliot Morison, *The European Discovery of America: The Southern Voyages, 1492-1616* (New York: Oxford University Press, 1974), which contains an extensive bibliography. The most complete information can be found in José Toribio Medina, *Juan Díaz de Solís, estudio histórico*, 2 vols. (Santiago de Chile: 1897).

John Hanning Speke

(1827 - 1864)

John Hanning Speke was a British Army officer who accompanied Richard Burton on two expeditions to Africa and then led one of his own that found the source of the Nile River in Lake Victoria in east Africa.

John Hanning Speke was born in the town of Ilminster in Somerset County in England on May 4, 1827, the son of an Army officer. Speke himself was educated for the Army from an early age. He entered the British Army in India in 1844 and fought in several campaigns that the British colonialists led against the Indians. He was promoted to lieutenant in 1850 and captain in 1852.

During his time in India, Speke developed an interest in exploring and spent his leaves hunting and exploring in the

John Hanning Speke and James Augustus Grant. The Granger Collection, New York.

Himalayas and Tibet. At the conclusion of his ten-year tour of duty in India in 1854, he traveled to the British colony of Aden on the south coast of Arabia. He apparently intended to arrange a trip from there to Africa. Coincidentally, he met up with the already well-known explorer **Sir Richard Burton**. Burton was in Aden organizing an expedition to Somaliland on the northeastern coast of Africa. Speke signed up to join the expedition.

Speke's job on the expedition was to travel in advance of the main party and scout out some of the territory and then to report his findings to Burton in the seaport of Berbera. He left Aden on October 18, 1854 but was unable to reach his goal and was forced to return to Aden on February 15, 1855. He then traveled to Berbera on March 21, arriving there on April 3. Soon after his arrival, however, Burton's party was attacked by Somalis. Burton was injured in the mouth by a javelin, and Speke was captured and tied to the ground where he was beaten with clubs. He managed to escape even though he had eleven major injuries.

Speke returned to England to recover from his wounds and then volunteered for service in Russia during the Crimean War, which Great Britain had entered in 1854. After the war, Speke was thinking about further explorations when he was invited by Burton to join him on new expedition to East Africa to try to find Lake Nyasa. They left Bombay together on December 3, 1856 and arrived on the island of Zanzibar off the coast of Africa on December 21. They spent the next six months reconnoitering the coast before setting off for the interior on June 27, 1857 accompanied by a great caravan of porters and supplies, led by **Sidi Mubarak Bombay**.

Burton and Speke's caravan proceeded very slowly, and both Englishmen came down with malaria. By July 25 they reached the important caravan station of Zungomero where they rested for two weeks. They joined an Arab caravan at Ugogo and traveled with it to Kazeh—the modern Tanzanian city of Taborà —which they reached on November 7. There they learned that the "Lake Nyasa" they were searching for was actually one of three great interior lakes. They were led to believe that one of these lakes was the source of the Nile River.

The two explorers were very excited by the prospect of locating the long-sought-after source of the Nile and set out again on December 5 even though Burton was so ill with fever that he had to be carried in a litter and Speke was half-blind with an eye infection. They reached the Arab trading center of Ujiji on the eastern shore of Lake Tanganyika on February 13, 1858. They set out on April 10 to try to reach the northern end of the lake to see whether in fact the Nile flowed out of it. Before they got there they learned that the northern river flowed into Lake Tanganyika and so they turned back. (In fact, the lake drains to the west into Zaire.)

Speke and Burton returned to Kazeh, which they reached on June 20. By that time, they were no longer on speaking terms. They disagreed and Speke set out on his own to investigate the most northerly of the lakes they had heard about. On August 3 he reached the vast lake that he named Lake Victoria after the Queen. He immediately became convinced that this was the source of the Nile. He returned to Kazeh to meet Burton on August 25, 1858. Burton refused to believe that his partner had found the much-sought-after source of the Nile, and their arguments became even more intense. On the return trip to England, Speke left Burton in Aden to recuperate and traveled on his own to report his discovery.

Speke's news was enthusiastically received in England, and the Royal Geographical Society immediately made plans to send him out again to confirm his discovery. He left on April 27, 1860 this time accompanied by **James Augustus Grant**. They left the east coast of Africa for the interior in early October. The last communication from Speke back to England was dated September 30, 1861, and then there was no more news from him for more than a year. In the meantime, the Royal Geographical Society sent the British consul at Khartoum south down the Nile with a load of supplies to meet him from the north. The consul, John Petherick, was also not heard from for several months and was thought dead.

Speke in fact traveled from Kazeh back to Lake Victoria and then traveled around its western end, carefully mapping the northwestern shore. Along the way, he met the rulers of the several African kingdoms that had developed in that part of the continent—Karagwe, Buganda, and Bunyoro. He had found the Nile flowing out of the lake and followed in north for a great distance. Unfortunately, he was not allowed by the King of Bunyoro to travel all the way down the Nile and was forced to travel overland for part of the distance. He rejoined the river at a place called Afuddu. He then joined an Arab ivory and slave-trading expedition down the Nile to Gondokoro, the last Arab outpost coming from the north.

Speke expected to meet Petherick there but instead was greeted by **Samuel Baker** and his future wife Florence on February 15, 1863. Much to Speke's anger, Petherick had been sidetracked by becoming involved in a trading expedition. From Gondokoro, Speke and Grant took the relatively well-traveled route down the Nile to Khartoum, Cairo and Alexandria. Upon his return to England, he was welcomed as a hero. However, this was soon overshadowed by the continuing dispute with Burton. Burton proclaimed that by not following the river for all of its distance Speke had not proven that the river that flowed out of Lake Victoria was actually the Nile. Speke was in fact correct, but the British Association for the Advancement of Science scheduled a public debate on September 16, 1864 for the men to argue their positions. Burton and the audience were already assembled when it was announced that Speke had died that afternoon in a hunting accident. Since he was alone at the time and was an experienced hunter, there was a great deal of speculation then and later that he had committed suicide. However, the weight of the evidence seems to be that the death was accidental.

Where to learn more

Speke wrote two books about his explorations: *What Led to the Discovery of the Source of the Nile* (Edinburgh: William Blackwood & Sons, 1864) and *Journal of the Discovery of the Source of the Nile* (Edinburgh: William Blackwood & Sons, 1863; reprinted, London: 1969).

There is only one complete biography: Alexander Maitland, *Speke* (London: 1971). There is a good interpretive essay by Roy C. Bridges, "John Hanning Speke: Negotiating a Way to the Nile," in Robert I. Rotberg, ed. *Africa and Its Explorers: Motives, Methods and Impact* (Cambridge: Harvard University Press, 1970).

The earliest history of the search for the source of the Nile was by an English explorer who had himself spent many years in East Africa: Harry H. Johnston, *The Nile Quest* (London: Lawrence & Bullen, 1903). More recent studies of the same theme are Alan Moorehead, *The White Nile* (New York: Harper & Brothers, 1960) and Frederick Bradnum, *The Long Walks: Journeys to the Sources of the White Nile* (London: 1970).

There is a recent feature film about Burton and Speke: *Mountains of the Moon* (Carolco Pictures, 1989).

Richard Spruce

(1817 - 1893)

Richard Spruce was an English botanist who spent 15 years collecting plant specimens from all across the different biological regions of South America.

Richard Spruce was born in the northern English county of Yorkshire. He became a mathematics teacher at the Collegiate School in York, but developed a strong interest in botany and spent ten months in the Pyrenees Mountains of northern Spain collecting specimens. He published the results of that trip and then moved to London in 1848. There he learned about the success that **Alfred Russell Wallace** and **Henry Walter Bates** were having collecting specimens in the Amazon rain forest. He decided to go there himself and left England on June 7, 1849, accompanied by Robert King and Wallace's brother Herbert.

They arrived at the port of Belém on July 12 and spent the next three months collecting specimens in the area. They then traveled up the Amazon to the river port town of Santarém where they made their headquarters at the end of October. He met Alfred Wallace during his stay there. He then made an expedition to the Trombetas River, which flows into the Amazon from the north. There he and King were rained upon every day, and King got lost in the forest and suffered greatly from rheumatism as a result. They returned to Santarém where they stayed until October 8, 1850.

From Santarém Spruce and his companions continued up the Amazon to Manaus, the largest town in the Amazon basin where they stayed until November 14, 1851. Without traveling more than five miles out of town he was able to add 750 specimens of new plants to the 110 he had already collected. In November Spruce headed up one of the main branches of the Amazon, the Rio Negro, and he explored that and the Uauapes River as far as the frontier with Colombia until March 1853.

Spruce next decided to travel up the Rio Negro to see the Casiquiare canal that connected the Amazon River system to that of the Orinoco. This unusual geographic feature had been discovered by **Alexander von Humboldt** in 1800. There were still Native Americans alive who remembered Humboldt at the time of Spruce's visit. He explored up to the source of the Orinoco and collected many valuable specimens, which he packed at the little village of San Carlos de Rio Negro in Venezuela. In June 1854 he went downstream on the Orinoco as far as San Fernando de Atabapo. He became ill from fever and was forced to seek refuge with a Venezuelan woman who didn't want him for three weeks while he was near death. Back in San Carlos he overheard some of the inhabitants plotting to kill him and had to spend the night in his canoe with his gun at hand before he could escape.

Following his adventures along the Orinoco, Spruce returned to Manaus on December 22, 1854 and then headed upstream to the Peruvian port of Iquitos on March 14, 1855. From Iquitos he traveled by canoe up the Amazon and its tributaries to the western slope of the Andes where he then spent two years collecting specimens in the Huallaga River valley and near the town of Tarapoto. He collecting many species of mosses and 1,094 species of flowering plants and ferns. At one point the canoe with all his specimens was almost lost in a storm until his Native American guides stayed in it all night holding onto the branches of riverside plants to keep it from being swept away.

By this time Spruce had traveled up the Bombonaza River in Ecuador. He had to build his own bamboo bridge to cross the Rio Topo and in order to get down to the Pastaza River had to climb down a 150-foot notched pole leaning against a rock. This led him to the forest of Canelos where **Isabel Godin des Odonais** had been lost in the previous century.

From July 1857 to September 1860 Spruce wandered throughout the Andes of Ecuador and climbed Mount Pichincha. He suffered greatly from the cold and was almost attacked by condors when he passed out from exhaustion at one point. He lost his hearing in one ear and became partly paralyzed in his back and legs but continued to explore, "partly dragging myself about by the aid of a long staff." On October 28, 1860 he left the mountains and headed for the Pacific port city of Guayaquil. He continued to collect specimens although he was in poor health and he lost almost all of his money when a bank in Guayaquil went bankrupt. In 1861 he went to Peru and stayed there collecting the unusual plants of the Peruvian coastal desert. Finally forced by ill health to quit, he returned to England in 1864 on a ship via Panama.

On his return to England, Spruce spent the following years writing up the results of his long stay in South America. He died at the age of 76 in 1893.

Where to learn more

Spruce's journals, as edited by Alfred Russell Wallace, were published as *Notes of a Botanist on the Amazon and Andes*, 2 vols. (London: Macmillan, 1908). Two good books that put Spruce's travels in the context of the other naturalists of the 19th century are: Paul Russell Cutright, *The Great Naturalists Explore South America* (New York: Macmillan, 1940) and Victor Wolfgang von Hagen, *South America Called Them: Explorations of the Great Naturalists* (Boston: Little, Brown & Company, 1955).

Sputnik

(1957 - 1958)

The Soviet Sputnik spacecraft were the first manmade objects to orbit the Earth.

I n 1955 the Soviet Union began construction of the Baikonur Space Center in Kazakhstan near the small town of Tyuratam. One of the first priorities at the new base was the launching of the first intercontinental ballistic missile (ICBM)—the A-1. This was achieved on August 3, 1957 with a flight that took it 5,000 miles. With this success, it then became possible to launch the first artificial satellite, which had already been announced as a project in September 1955. It had also already been named "Sputnik," but there was no public announcement of this.

Both the A-1 and Sputnik were designed by the Soviet Union's premier space engineer, Sergei Korolov. At the time there was no publicity about Korolov at all, and the envious Americans called the unknown man the "Chief Designer." He had been imprisoned twice during Stalin's rule but had survived to become the moving force behind the Soviet space program under Nikita Khrushchev. It was not until his death in January 1966 that his name was announced to the public.

Following the successful launching of the A-1 missile, Radio Moscow announced on September 18, 1957 that a satellite would soon be launched. The event took place on October 4, 1957, one of the great dates in history because it marked the first time that humans were able to leave their planet. It was the beginning of the "Space Age."

Sputnik 1 was essentially a radio transmitter encased in a steel case with four antennas sticking out of it. It weighed 184 pounds.

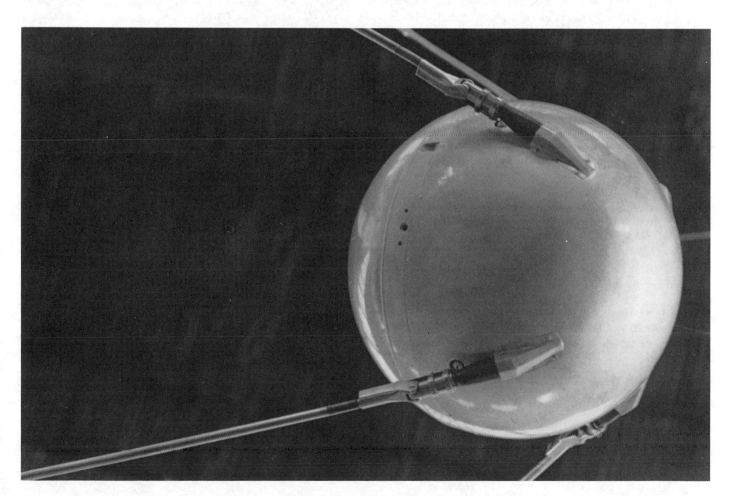

Sputnik 1. NASA.

The instruments on board were designed to study the density, temperature, and concentration of electrons in the upper atmosphere and to transmit the results back to Earth. It took 95 minutes to circle the Earth in an elliptical orbit whose altitude varied from about 140 to 560 miles. *Sputnik 1* made about 4,000 trips around the Earth before it gradually lost altitude and then disintegrated as it re-entered denser atmosphere on January 4, 1958.

The world reaction to the launching of Sputnik was intense. Everyone was impressed with the Soviets' accomplishment, especially since much of the country had been devastated by the Stalinist years and World War II. The space program had only started after the "Great Patriotic War," as the Second World War was called in the Soviet Union. The reaction in the United States was especially agitated. The launch occurred at the height of the Cold War, and Americans saw it as a major victory for the other side. There was a Congressional investigation as to why the United States had fallen behind, and public opinion demanded results quickly. Perhaps the two major effects were the formation of the National Aeronautics and Space Administration (NASA) in July 1958 and a renewed emphasis on teaching science in U.S. schools.

The relatively simple technology of *Sputnik 1* was quickly followed by something much more sophisticated. The Soviets launched *Sputnik 2* less than a month later, on November 3, 1957. It was much bigger, weighing 1,120 pounds, and flew at a much higher altitude. More impressively it carried a passenger— a female dog named Laika. Obviously, Laika's flight was intended to test the possibility of sending humans into space. Laika suffered no ill effects from weightlessness and was able to move about and take food. Unfortunately, the oxygen in her cabin gave out after a week and she died. *Sputnik 2* stayed in orbit for 163 days before disintegrating in April 1958.

Sputnik 3 was launched on May 15, 1958. It was much larger than its two predecessors, weighing a ton and a half. It contained various instruments for measuring such things as the pressure and composition of the upper atmosphere, the incidence of micro-meteoroids, and solar and cosmic radiation. In effect, it was a miniature science lab and even had an on-board computer. It stayed in orbit for 691 days.

The Soviet space program was now geared towards putting a human into space. This was clearly indicated by *Sputnik 4*, which was launched on May 15, 1960. The spacecraft was the first of the Vostok series, which contained a cabin and an ejector seat for the cosmonaut pilot on board. *Sputnik 4* only carried a dummy passenger, which was fortunate because it went off course four days after launching and swung into a high orbit that lasted until it disintegrated in October 1965.

The aim of the flights at this time was to successfully send a spacecraft into orbit (which had now been achieved several times) and then to change its path and bring it safely back to Earth (which had not). This was accomplished by *Sputnik 5*, launched on August 19, 1960. On board were two dogs named Belka and Strelka as well as two rats and 28 mice. The spacecraft made 18 orbits. The day after launch, the descent cabin separated and headed back to Earth. Two cabins containing the two dogs were ejected and came down to ground, slowed by parachutes. They were recovered by a group of wary farmers in a field. Strelka and Belka were both alive and well.

It seemed clearly possible to send a human into space safely. One last trial was made: *Sputnik 6*. It was launched on December 1, 1960 with two dogs, Pchelka and Mushka, on board. Two days later the rockets fired to change the orbit, but the angle of descent was too steep and the spacecraft burned up. More test flights would be needed. *Sputnik 7* and *8* were actually the first of the Venus probes, later known as Venera. *Sputnik 7* reached Earth orbit, but ground control failed to redirect it towards Venus. *Sputnik 8* headed into the proper orbit but its communications equipment failed, and all contact was lost.

Sputnik 9, sent up on March 9, 1961, and *Sputnik 10*, launched on March 25, were both successes. They both sent dogs (Chernushka on the former, Zvedochka on the latter) into orbit and returned them safely to Earth. It was now time to send the first human into space. This was achieved on April 5, 1961, when **Yuri Gagarin** made his historic flight.

Where to learn more

A good starting-point for information on Sputnik and its place in the history of Soviet space exploration is Brian Harvey's *Race Into Space: The Soviet Space Program* (New York: John Wiley & Sons, 1988), which served as the main source for this account. See also James E. Oberg, *Red Star in Orbit* (New York: Random House, 1981) and Evgeny Riabchikov, *Russians in Space* (London: Weidenfeld and Nicolson, 1972). Books that deal specifically with the Sputnik program are mostly of Soviet origin and tend to have a propagandistic flavor: Mikhail Vasilev, *Sputnik Into Space* (London: Souvenir Press, 1958) and *Soviet Sputniks, Based on Material Published by Soviet Scientists* (London: Soviet News, 1958).

Lady Hester Stanhope

(1776 - 1839)

Lady Hester Stanhope was an English noblewoman who left her native country behind and spent most of her life traveling through the Middle East.

Lady Hester Stanhope was born on an estate in the English county of Kent on March 12, 1776. Her father was the third Earl Stanhope and her mother was the favorite sister of Sir William Pitt, who became Prime Minister of Great Britain in 1783 at the age of 24. Stanhope's mother died when she was four years old, and her father, a political radical and inventor, paid no attention to his numerous children. She went to live with her grandmother until her death in 1803. In August 1803 Pitt, who was a bachelor, asked her to come live with him and manage his household.

Pitt soon became very attached to his niece, and she got herself involved in the highest political affairs of the country, making several enemies with her sharp tongue. She was very happy managing Pitt and his house, but this came to an abrupt end on January 23, 1806 when Pitt suddenly took ill and died at the age of 46. He left Stanhope with a small inheritance but no other prospects. When a friend once remarked to Pitt that his niece would marry when she had found a man as clever as herself, Pitt replied, "Then she will never marry at all." This turned out to be true.

Stanhope began a courtship with John Moore, one of the most prominent generals in the British army, which was then engaged in fighting France under Napoleon. Moore went off to fight the Napoleonic army in northern Spain and was killed during the Battle of La Coruña in 1808, dying in the arms of Stanhope's brother James. His last words were "Stanhope, remember me to your sister." Later the same day, Stanhope's favorite brother Charles was shot through the heart and killed. Stanhope was overwhelmed with grief and retreated to an isolated cottage in Wales. She soon decided to leave England altogether and set sail for the Mediterranean on board the frigate *Jason*.

After visiting her brother James in Gibraltar, Stanhope and her entourage (which included her doctor Charles Meryon who kept an account of all Stanhope's doings) sailed to Malta. There she met a young Scottish nobleman named Michael Bruce. They quickly became lovers; he was 23, she was 34. Since Bruce was dependent on his family for an income, Stanhope proposed writing to his father and asking for his approval of their arrangement. The senior Bruce's reply to Stanhope began, "Our correspondence has certainly started off on a very extraordinary footing." But he accepted the liaison and, in effect, agreed to finance it, thinking that his son could learn a great deal from Stanhope.

From Malta Stanhope decided that she wanted to go to Constantinople where she had a plan to meet the French ambassador and get his help in setting up a meeting with Napoleon. Along the way, she stopped in Athens and met the poet Lord Byron. She and her party reached Constantinople on November 3, 1810, where she quickly became a celebrity. She shocked Turkish society when she showed up in a pair of overalls to inspect a Turkish warship. She left Constantinople in October 1811 headed for Alexandria in Egypt. But the ship was wrecked in a storm along the way, and she and her friends were thrown up on the island of Rhodes, after having almost drowned. Arriving without any clothes, Stanhope adopted the dress of a Turkish gentleman, which was the costume she wore for the rest of her life.

Lady Hester Stanhope. The Granger Collection, New York.

Stanhope and her entourage traveled on to Egypt, where they arrived in February 1812. There she was received by the Khedive of Egypt at his palace in Cairo and visited the pyramids. She continued on to the Holy Land, arriving in Jaffa on May 16, 1812. From there she traveled to Jerusalem and then went in a magnificent caravan north to Acre. Along the way she met **Jean Louis Burckhardt** on his way to Arabia. Once in Acre, Stanhope received an unexpected invitation to travel into the mountains of Lebanon to meet the Emir of the Druses, at that time a mysterious Islamic sect that was isolated in their mountain fastnesses where they kept out all strangers. Stanhope was the first European admitted to the Emir's palace.

By this time Stanhope's travels were beginning to become a burden on Bruce's father. He had paid the modern-day equivalent of $100,000 for their expenses over the previous eight months. Her extravagance eventually led to a breach with Michael Bruce who returned to England and became a lawyer and member of Parliament.

On September 1, 1812 Stanhope entered the gates of Damascus in Syria. She rode into the Muslim city on a horse, not only not veiled but dressed in a man's clothes. She had been warned that she would be stoned if she attempted this, but, on the contrary, she was cheered, many thinking that she was a queen come from a foreign land. She was invited to visit a harem and was one of the first to give a description of one—European men, of course, were never allowed inside.

From Damascus Stanhope accepted an invitation to ride into the desert to visit Bedouin tribes. Then she determined that she wanted to visit the ruins of the city of Palmyra in the desert of what is now Jordan. This famous city had been a main caravan stop in the days of the Roman Empire and had many beautiful buildings in the Roman as well as earlier styles. From the year 267 Palmyra was ruled by the famous Queen Zenobia, who had defeated Roman armies and had ruled Egypt for a short while. She was defeated in 270, and Palmyra was laid waste. Stanhope saw herself as a modern Zenobia and insisted upon visiting the city in spite of the warnings that she received from all sides that it was too dangerous. She went there in January 1813, the first European woman to visit the ruins. The nearby residents came out to see her, and a child hung down from an arch and dropped a wreath on her head as though she were a latter-day Zenobia herself.

From Palmyra Stanhope went to the Mediterranean coast where she settled in the Syrian port of Latakia in May 1813. She and Dr. Meryon (who had stayed with her through all her travels) were there when an epidemic of plague broke out. They both became ill but survived. In the following years Stanhope and Meryon traveled throughout what was then called the "Levant." They visited Roman ruins in Baalbek and Ascalon and other archeological sites. In January 1817 Meryon returned to England, and Stanhope bought a castle on a mountain top in the Druse country opposite that of the Emir. There she set up her own feudal court with retainers and ruled over the nearby countryside. She was in constant conflict with her former host, the Emir.

Stanhope lived out the rest of her life at her retreat at Djoun. She was occasionally visited by touring Westerners, and the faithful Dr. Meryon came frequently from England. Her last European servant died, however, in 1828. She became more and more isolated but still ruled over her little kingdom. She was seriously in debt when she died alone on June 23, 1839.

Where to learn more

The major primary source for Stanhope's travels in the Middle East are two books by her companion, Dr. Charles Meryon: *The Memoirs of Lady Hester Stanhope*, 3 vols. (London: Henry Colburn, 1845) and *Travels of Lady Hester Stanhope*, 3 vols. (London: Henry Colburn, 1846).

Given Stanhope's romantic life, it is inevitable that there should be a large number of biographies. The best, early biography was written by her niece, the Duchess of Cleveland, who had access to her correspondence: *The Life and Letters of Lady Hester Stanhope* (London: John Murray, 1914). Others include: Frank Hamel, *Lady Hester Stanhope* (London: Cassell, 1913); Joan Haslip, *Lady Hester Stanhope* (New York: Frederick Stokes, 1936); Ian Bruce, *The Nun of Lebanon: The Love Affair of Lady Hester Stanhope and Michael Bruce* (London: Collins, 1951); Jean Gordon Hughes, *Queen of the Desert: The Story of Lady Hester Stanhope* (London: Macmillan, 1967); and John Watney, *Travels in Arabia of Lady Hester Stanhope* (London: Gordon Cremonesi, 1975).

Books about Palmyra and Queen Zenobia include: Kazimierz Michalowski, *Palmyra* (New York: Praeger, 1968); Horst Klingel, *The Art of Ancient Syria* (New York: A.B. Barnes, 1972); Agnes Vaughan, *Zenobia of Palmyra* (New York: Doubleday, 1976); Malcolm Colledge, *The Art of Palmyra* (London: Westview, 1976); Iain Browning, *Palmyra* (Princeton, New Jersey: Noyes, 1979).

A good summary of Stanhope's life, which served as the source for this account, is in James C. Simmons, *Passionate Pilgrims: English Travelers to the World of the Desert Arabs* (New York: William Morrow & Co., 1987).

Henry Morton Stanley

(1841 - 1904)

Welsh-born Henry Morton Stanley began his career as an explorer by heading an expedition that "found" David Livingstone. He went on to lead three expeditions that traced the course of the Congo River and the great lakes of central Africa.

Henry Morton Stanley's real name was John Rowlands, and he was born in Denbigh, Wales in 1841. He was an illegitimate child, and he spent the years from 1847 to 1856 in the St. Asaph Union Workhouse, a Dickensian institution run by a sadistic schoolmaster. When he got big enough, he beat up the schoolmaster and ran away. After going to sea as a cabin boy, he was adopted by a New Orleans cotton merchant named Henry Morton Stanley in 1859, and he took this man's name and nationality. When the American Civil War broke out,

Henry Morton Stanley.

he served as a volunteer in the Confederate army. Captured by Union forces, he then switched sides and fought in the U.S. Navy, from which he deserted at the end of the war.

He drifted into journalism, beginning his career as a reporter for a St. Louis newspaper. He covered the invasion of Ethiopia by a British force under Sir Robert Napier in 1867 for the New York *Herald*. Impressed with his work, the paper's owner, James Gordon Bennett, decided to send him on the hunt to find the famous explorer **David Livingstone**. Livingstone had set out on an expedition in 1866 to continue the search for the sources of the Nile River. By 1868 there had been no word from him, and it was feared that he might be dead. The Royal Geographical Society in London prepared an expedition to search for him. Then letters written by Livingstone from the shores of Lake Nyasa arrived in Zanzibar, and the search was called off. Several months followed in which there was no further word—very unlike Livingstone who was noted for sending news of his progress back on a continual basis. Bennett decided that news of the whereabouts of Livingstone would give a boost to the circulation of his newspaper, and he sent Stanley out to try to find him. "If he is dead bring back every possible proof of his death," Bennett said.

Stanley arrived in Zanzibar off the coast of East Africa at the beginning of 1871. He had been provided by the newspaper with unlimited funds, and he used the money lavishly to equip the most expensive expedition that had ever traveled to the interior of Africa. He hired the veteran **Sidi Mubarak Bombay** to be his caravan leader. They set out on February 6, 1871. In spite of his preparations, Stanley had a very difficult time. He had two British companions who died along the way. Stanley himself became ill with fever and was sometimes unconscious. It took him two months to cover the 212 miles to the trading center of Kazeh (modern Tabora in central Tanzania). West of Kazeh, he became involved in fighting between Arab slave dealers and African tribes and was forced to make a wide detour to the south. He began to doubt whether he would ever achieve his goal and at one point carved on a tree, "Starving: H.M.S."

In spite of these difficulties, Stanley pushed ahead ruthlessly, exhibiting the characteristics that were to mark all his expeditions. If he encountered the slightest opposition, he ordered his men to take out their guns and shoot. If any of his porters shirked their duties, he had them whipped or even hanged. If anyone left the caravan, he had the deserter tracked down and punished and chained for the rest of the journey. Using these methods, Stanley reached a hill overlooking the town of Ujiji on Lake Tanganyika on November 10, 1871. He had heard reports of an elderly

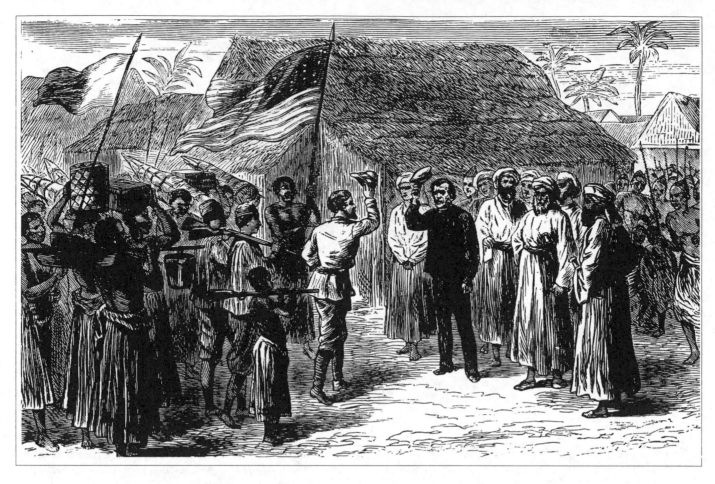

"Dr. Livingstone, I presume." Stanley's famous meeting with David Livingstone.

European in Ujiji. Stanley ordered the American flag unfurled at the front of the caravan and marched his column into the town, firing 50 guns simultaneously. He was met by Susi, one of Livingstone's African supporters, who guided him to where the famous doctor was staying.

"As I advanced slowly toward him," Stanley wrote in his book, "I noticed he was pale, looked wearied, had a gray beard, wore a bluish cap with a faded gold braid round it, had on a red-sleeved waistcoat, and a pair of gray tweed trousers. I would have run to him, only I was a coward in the presence of such a mob—would have embraced him, only, he being an Englishman, I did not know how he would receive me. So I did what cowardice and false pride suggested was the best thing—walked deliberately to him, took off my hat, and said:

" 'Dr. Livingstone, I presume?'

" 'Yes,' said he, with a kind smile, lifting his cap slightly.

"I replace my hat on my head, and he puts on his cap, and we both grasp hands, and then I say aloud:

" 'I thank God, Doctor, I have been permitted to see you.'

"He answered, 'I feel thankful that I am here to welcome you.'"

The two spent the next five months together and developed a close relationship—almost like father and son—in spite of their very different personalities. For Stanley the event marked the turning point in his life. They traveled together around Lake Tanganyika and found out that, contrary to the beliefs of **Sir Richard Burton**, the Ruzizi River flowed into and not out of the lake and was not, therefore, the source of the Nile. The two men traveled together back to Tabora, where they separated. Livingstone headed back to interior to investigate the Lualaba River, which was his own favorite candidate to be the Nile source. (The Lualaba does flow north from the river flowing out of Lake Tanganyika but is actually a part of the Congo River system.) Stanley went back to Zanzibar to gather supplies to send to the British explorer.

When Stanley arrived in England with news of the famous meeting, the reception was not what he had expected. At first, many people disbelieved his reports. When the Livingstone family confirmed the authenticity of the letters he brought back, he was still looked down upon as a boorish American. He

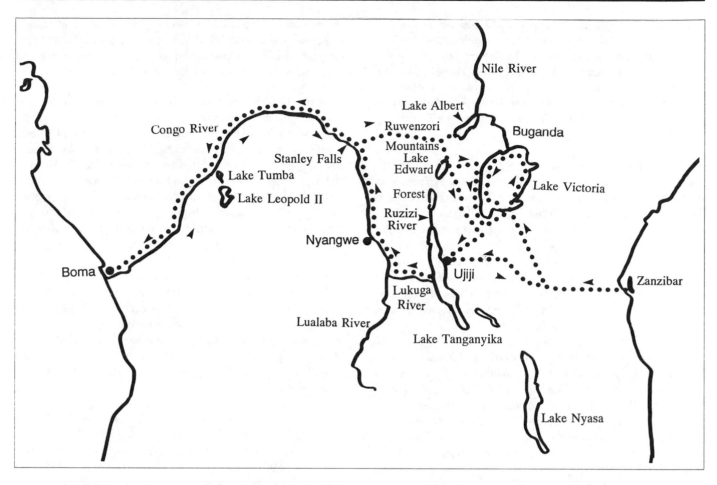

Stanley's expeditions in Africa, 1871-1872, 1874-1877, 1879-1883, and 1888-1889.

stormed out of one testimonial dinner because he thought he was being condescended to. When he got back to New York, he received a much better welcome, but some newspapers printed unflattering portraits, mentioning, for example, his desertion from the Navy. Stanley remained bitter about his reception for the rest of his life. In many ways, his decision to return to Africa was an attempt to prove that his critics were wrong.

Livingstone died in Africa on April 27, 1873, and his body was brought back to England for burial. Stanley served as one of the pall-bearers at his funeral at Westminster Abbey in London. On hearing of his death, Stanley wrote, "May I be selected to succeed him in opening up Africa to the shining light of Christianity!" He then proposed to the London *Daily Telegraph* that it sponsor him on another expedition to Africa in which he would continue Livingstone's explorations. The newspaper agreed, and he left for Africa on August 15, 1874.

The Great Congo Expedition included 356 porters, gun bearers, and camp followers. Stanley had chosen as his companions two brothers, Frank and Edward Pocock, sons of an English fisherman, and Frederick Barker, a London hotel clerk. None of them had ever been out of England before. The expedition had three objectives: to sail around Lake Victoria, to explore and map

Lake Tanganyika, and to follow the Lualaba River to see where it led. In order to accomplish these goals, Stanley brought along a 40-foot boat that he had designed himself, the *Lady Alice*, which could be taken apart in five sections to make it easier to carry.

The expedition experienced difficulties from the time it left Bagamoyo on the east African coast. Porters deserted, the column was wracked by disease that killed many, including Barker and Edward Pocock, and they were faced by open hostility from the Africans they encountered, which led to armed warfare. Stanley persevered, however, and reached Lake Victoria on February 27, 1875. As he sailed around the lake in the *Lady Alice*, he fired at a group of Africans on Bumbire Island with his rifle and shotgun, killing several of them. "The savage only respects force, power, boldness, and decision," he wrote. These and similar actions led to a great deal of criticism when he returned to Europe. He did, however, make a complete circumnavigation of the lake and proved that it was one body of water and that it was drained at the north by the Victoria Nile, just as **John Hanning Speke** had said.

From Lake Victoria Stanley wanted to go north to Lake Albert but was blocked by hostile tribes. He therefore had the *Lady*

Alice carried over to Lake Tanganyika. He sailed all the way around the lake and established that its only outlet was the Lukuga River on the west shore. He also established that the Lukuga was a tributary of the Lualaba. He started down the Lualaba and reached the town of Nyangwe on October 17, 1876. This was the headquarters of the famous African-Arab trader Tippu Tib and the farthest point yet reached by Europeans.

In return for a substantial payment, Tippu Tib agreed to accompany Stanley with a force of 700 men, and they set off on November 5, 1876. They soon split up, however, with Stanley floating downstream in the *Lady Alice* while Tippu Tib followed on land. The trip lay through a vast tropical rainforest, and the land party suffered numerous casualties from sickness and starvation. On November 24, Stanley was attacked by a party of Africans in war canoes, and according to his account hardly a day went by after that when they did not have to fight off "murderous" Africans. In December, Tippu Tib and his party turned back to Nyangwe, but Stanley urged his men to continue.

A few miles upstream from the modern city of Kisangani (once known as Stanleyville), they came to the first of a chain of seven cataracts that were named Stanley Falls. All of the supplies had to be unloaded, the *Lady Alice* disassembled and everything had to be carried through the forest jungle and over rocks and cliffs. They were attacked along the way by Africans who feared that they were the precursors of Arab slave traders. Below the falls the river turned to the west, and Stanley surmised correctly that the Lualaba was the upper course of the Congo River.

From there there was a stretch of 1,000 miles of almost unobstructed waterway. They reached cataracts again before coming to a large body of water known as Stanley Pool, where the cities of Kinshasa and Brazzaville now stand. Below the Pool they came to an even wilder series of cataracts that Stanley named Livingstone Falls. At Massassa Rapids, Frank Pocock, the only surviving European besides Stanley, was drowned on June 3, 1877. His death deeply depressed Stanley. "I am weary, oh so weary, of this constant tale of woes and death," he wrote.

At the end of July they abandoned the *Lady Alice* on a cliff and set out overland for Boma, a European trading post on the Atlantic coast. The expedition was reduced to 115 people including three mothers with newborn children; 277 people had either deserted or died along the way. On August 9, 1877, exactly 999 days after leaving Zanzibar, Stanley led the expedition into Boma. They had traced the entire course of the Congo River. Stanley fulfilled his promise to his porters and took them back to Zanzibar in November 1877 before proceeding to England at the end of the year, where he was condemned in newspapers and Parliament for the ruthless way in which he had conducted the expedition.

In 1879 Stanley was back on the Congo River on an expedition sponsored by King Leopold II of the Belgians to open up access to the interior, and he traveled upstream as far as Stanley Falls. He spent most of the succeeding years working for Leopold. In 1883, he discovered two major lakes—Tumba and Leopold II—on a tributary of the lower Congo.

All of this work gave Stanley the reputation as being the preeminent African explorer of his time. Therefore, in spite of the constant criticism of his methods, he seemed the obvious choice to lead the "Emin Pasha Relief Expedition." **Emin Pasha** was a German who had converted to Islam and worked for the Khedive of Egypt as the Governor of the Equatoria Province in Sudan. When the Sudanese under the Mahdi revolted against Egyptian rule, Emin Pasha was cut off from contact with the outside world. Over £20,000 was raised to pay for an expedition to go to his rescue.

Stanley's plan for the rescue was to use his Congo experience and cut through the unknown Ituri Forest to reach Emin Pasha, then headquartered on Lake Albert in what is now Uganda, from the west rather than approaching from the more obvious, and much easier, route from the east. This would have the advantage of exploring new territory to King Leopold's "Congo Free State." Accordingly, Stanley arrived at the mouth of the Congo River on March 18, 1887.

The expedition consisted of 700 African employees of Stanley commanded by eight European officers and 800 of Tippu Tib's supporters. It was divided into two groups—an advance column and a rear column. Stanley led the advance column up the Congo and then the Aruwimi River. In the upper reaches of the Aruwimi they had to fight their way through the Ituri, one of the densest, darkest, and most impenetrable forests on Earth. It is also the home of the Pygmies, who were very adept at maintaining their sanctuary by shooting poison arrows at intruders. The death toll from these attacks and from disease and hunger was very high. In one place, 52 men who were too sick to carry on were abandoned to die. At another place, Stanley had a man who had stolen a rifle hanged. The survivors reached the edge of the forest on December 2, 1887. Stanley built a small fort for the rear column and brought up his boat so that he could sail down to Lake Albert.

When Stanley finally met up with Emin Pasha and his companion **Gaetano Casati** on April 29, 1888, he was dismayed to discover that they did not feel particularly threatened and did not want to be rescued. Stanley argued with them for a period of time and then returned to his fortified camp to meet up with the rear column. On the way back he got his first glimpse of a great snowcapped range of mountains in the distance. The clouds on the upper slopes parted long enough to reveal peaks rising to nearly 17,000 feet. This is the Ruwenzori Range, which have been identified with the legendary Mountains of the Moon that the Greek geographer Ptolemy had written 1,900 years before. They were supposed to be the source of the Nile, and, in fact, some of the water draining the mountains flows into Lake Edward and Lake Victoria and so to the White Nile.

When Stanley got back to his camp, he found that the rear column had not arrived. He traveled 90 miles into the Ituri Forest before finding the missing men. They had been decimated by dissension and disease, and only 98 out of the original 258 were still alive. He gathered up the remnants and traveled back with them to Emin Pasha's headquarters. By the time they arrived, some of Emin Pasha's troops had rebelled, and there was news that the Mahdists were making gains to the north. In spite of this, Emin Pasha could not make up his mind what he wanted to do. In one final angry confrontation, Stanley convinced the German to go with him to Zanzibar. Along the way they explored the land south of Lake Albert. They found another large lake that Stanley named Albert Edward Nyanza after Britain's Prince of Wales. It is now called Lake Edward. One of Stanley's officers tried to scale one of the peaks of the Ruwenzori and got two-thirds of the way up.

They reached Zanzibar in December 1889. Emin Pasha had decided that he did not want to go back and returned to the interior, where he was killed in 1892. Stanley returned to England where he married the artist Dorothy Tennant in 1890. He was naturalized as a British subject in 1892 and served as a Member of Parliament for the London constituency of Lambeth from 1895 to 1900. He died on May 9, 1904.

Where to learn more

Being a journalist, Stanley wrote profusely and vividly about his African adventures. *How I Found Livingstone* (London: Sampson Low, 1872; New York: Scribner, Armstrong & Co., 1872) is the story of the search for Livingstone and contains the famous "Dr. Livingstone, I presume" scene. Excerpts can be found in S. Newson-Smith, ed. *Quest: The Story of Stanley and Livingstone Told in Their Own Words* (London: 1978) and the newspaper articles in Norman Bennett, ed. *Stanley's Dispatches to the New York Herald* (Boston: 1970).

Through the Dark Continent (London: 1878) is the history of the trip across Africa and down the Congo River. His efforts in support of King Leopold are in *The Congo and the Founding of Its Free State* (London: 1885), and *In Darkest Africa*, 2 vols. (London: Sampson Low, 1890; New York: Charles Scribner's Sons, 1891) tells the story of the Emin Pasha Relief Expedition. For other histories of that costly expedition see the bibliography under Emin Pasha.

Following Stanley's death, his wife edited and published his autobiography: Lady Dorothy Stanley, ed. *The Autobiography of Sir Henry Morton Stanley* (London: 1909), which is very unreliable about the actual events of his life. The story of his youthful adventures in America are told in a book that has recently been re-issued: *My Early Travels and Adventures in America* (Lincoln: University of Nebraska Press, 1982). Other writings are in Richard Stanley and Alan Neame, eds. *The Exploration Diaries of H.M. Stanley* (London: 1933; reprinted, 1961) and Albert Maurice, ed. *H.M. Stanley: Unpublished Letters* (London: 1957).

There have been numerous biographies: J. Wasserman, *H.M. Stanley, Explorer* (London: 1932); A.J.A. Symons, *H.M. Stanley* (London; 1933); Frank Hird, *H.M. Stanley: The Authorized Life* (London: 1935); Ian Anstruther, *I Presume: Stanley's Triumph and Disaster* (London: 1956); Byron Farwell, *The Man Who Presumed: A Biography of Henry M. Stanley* (New York: 1957); and Richard Hall, *Stanley: An Adventurer Explored* (Boston: 1975).

Eric Halladay presents a balanced assessment in "Henry Morton Stanley: The Opening Up of the Congo Basin," in Robert I. Rotberg, ed. *Africa and Its Explorers: Motives, Methods and Impact* (Cambridge: Harvard University Press, 1970). Christopher Hibbert, *Africa Explored: Europeans in the Dark Continent, 1769-1889* (London: Allen Lane, 1982) was useful in writing this survey.

Vilhjalmur Stefansson

(1879-1962)

Vilhjalmur Stefansson was a Canadian who spent long years living among and studying the Inuit of the Canadian Arctic.

Vilhjalmur Stefansson was born in Arnes, Manitoba of Icelandic parents on November 3, 1879. They moved to the United States when Stefansson was two. He attended the State University of North Dakota and graduated in 1903. He got a scholarship to Harvard Divinity School but quickly changed his studies to the field of anthropology. He was recommended to serve as anthropologist on an Arctic expedition led by the Danish explorer Ejnar Mikkelsen in 1906. They traveled to Herschel Island in the Arctic Ocean west of the Mackenzie delta. There, Stefansson met **Roald Amundsen** at the end of his passage through the Northwest Passage. He also took up the study of the Inuit language and heard about a light-skinned group of Inuit who lived near the Coppermine River.

Stefansson returned to Arctic Canada in 1908. He did not reach Herschel Island until August 1909. From there, he traveled over land to Cape Parry and then crossed to the south side of Victoria Island. There he encountered a group of Copper Inuit (named because of their use of copper tools) for the first time. This was also the first time they had ever seen a Westerner, although they had heard about them and their strange ways. Stefansson stayed among these people until 1912. Some of them had what he considered to be European features and a few had blue eyes. On his return to the United States, he propounded the sensational theory that the Copper Inuit were the result of the mixture of Norsemen from Greenland and the Inuit. The theory was greeted with incredulity at the time and has never gained many adherents. It did earn him a lot of publicity however.

Stefansson wanted to return to the Arctic and was able to get himself appointed scientific head of the first Canadian Arctic Expedition in 1913. This expedition was seriously underfunded but was able to buy an old sealing ship in Seattle, the *Karluk*, which was captained by **Bob Bartlett**. The ship was stopped by ice in August 1913 north of Alaska. It could not get free. Stefansson left the ship in September at the head of a hunting party that included **Sir Hubert Wilkins**. After they left, the ship was pushed to the west by the Arctic currents until it was crushed off the coast of Siberia. Thanks to Bartlett, most of those left on board were saved. Stefansson never returned to the ship. Instead, he and his party drifted deliberately on ice floes through the islands of the Canadian Arctic until 1918 when they returned to Alaska.

In the following years Stefansson spent his time writing and lecturing, spreading his ideas that the Arctic was not a wasteland but an area of great potential. In 1921-1924 he organized an expedition (in which he did not participate) to Wrangel Island off the coast of Siberia and tried to claim it for Canada. The Canadian government objected, and there was an international incident. In addition, all of the members of the expedition died. Following that, Stefansson spent most of his time in New York City. He was appointed director of a polar studies program at Dartmouth College in New Hampshire and lived there from 1947 until his death on August 26, 1962.

Where to learn more

Stefansson was a prolific author. His most important books were probably: *My Life with the Eskimo* (New York: Macmillan, 1913); *The Friendly Arctic* (New York: Macmillan, 1921); and his autobiography, *Discovery* (New York: McGraw-Hill, 1964). There are two recent biographies: Richard J. Diubaldo, *Stefansson and the Canadian Arctic* (Montreal: McGill-Queen's University Press, 1978) and William R. Hunt, *Stef: A Biography of Vilhjalmur Stefansson* (Vancouver: University of British Columbia Press, 1986).

Will Steger

(1944 -   )

Will Steger is an American who led the first overland expedition to the North Pole since 1909 that was not furnished with supplies by airplaines and then led an international expedition across Antarctica.

Will Steger was born in Richfield, Minnesota, near Minneapolis, in 1944. His interest in exploration was kindled at the age of 12 when he was one of many American schoolchildren who volunteered to participate in science projects as part of the International Geophysical Year (IGY) in 1957-1958. He made sky observations nightly and reported on displays of the northern lights that he could see from his home, including one of the biggest recorded in the twentieth century. He also read about the crossing of Antarctica by **Sir Vivian Fuchs** and **Sir Edmund Hillary** as part of the IGY activities and decided that he too would visit Antarctica.

In 1963 at the age of 19 he and a school friend made a trip to Alaska and kayaked down the Yukon River. The next summer he

Will Steger. AP/Wide World Photos.

kayaked 3,000 miles down the Mackenzie River in Canada to the Arctic Ocean. After graduating from college Steger taught high school science classes. In 1969 he made another trip down the Yukon and in 1970 hitchhiked from Minnesota to Fairbanks, Alaska. In the 1970s he bought a piece of land near Ely in northern Minnesota and built himself a small cabin there and lived on less than $2,000 a year, growing or hunting most of his own food. He earned his living by leading canoe trips into the wilderness and by teaching winter camping and outdoor skills to tourist groups. In the following years he kayaked more than 10,000 miles, dogsledded another 15,000, and hitchhiked over 100,000 miles. In 1985 he dogsledded from his cabin in Minnesota to Point Barrow on the northern coast of Alaska.

Starting in 1983, Steger began planning a trip over the ice to the North Pole with Paul Schurke, a fellow wilderness instructor. Steger's aim was to reach the North Pole entirely by dogsled without any resupply by airplanes. This was something that had not been accomplished since **Robert Edward Peary** made the first trip to the Pole in 1909. The Steger International Polar Expedition consisted of seven men and one woman, Ann Bancroft, a schoolteacher from Minnesota. They left from the northern tip of Ellesmere Island in Canada on March 8, 1986.

They had five sleds, each of which carried an initial load of 1,350 pounds. Since it was impossible for the total of 49 dogs that made up their teams to carry such a large weight all at once, at first they had to make relays—delivering part of a load to a camp and then going back and getting the rest. That is why it took three weeks to travel the first 80 miles of the 478 miles from Ellesmere Island to the Pole. Along the way as the team members and the dogs consumed the food and fuel they had brought along the load got lighter. Gradually they cut off parts of the sled and made fires from the leftover wood. That also meant that they needed fewer and fewer dogs to pull the sleds (and less food to feed them). On earlier expeditions the dogs had been killed along the way and then either fed to the other dogs or eaten by the humans. On Steger's expedition he arranged for planes to pick up the excess dogs at various points along the way, although in keeping with his groundrules these planes did not bring in any supplies or give the expedition any navigational or meteorological help.

The expedition suffered various mishaps along the way. The dogs broke out one night and ate a good deal of their supplies. One member injured his ribs in an accident with one of the sleds and had to be airlifted out. Another one suffered severe frostbite and had to fly back as well. Bancroft fell into a lead, an open stretch of water in the ice, and almost drowned as well as almost freezing to death although she suffered no serious injuries and was able to continue. She became the first woman to travel to the Pole overland. The sextant that was being used for navigation was slightly damaged, and this led them slightly off course until the discrepancy was spotted.

Along the way, Steger and his team members had an interesting encounter. A Frenchman, Jean-Louis Etienne, left from another spot on Ellesmere Island the day after Steger, skiing alone all the way to the Pole (he was supplied by air). Although they were following different routes and were not coordinating their travel, their paths crossed on April 8. Etienne spent a day in Steger's camp, and there the two of them talked of their dreams of crossing Antarctica. Steger and the remaining members of his party reached the North Pole after 56 days of travel on May 1, 1986. Etienne made it there 10 days later. Steger and his colleagues were taken off the polar ice by aircraft and flown back to Canada.

In 1988 Steger made a south-to-north crossing of the ice cap of Greenland. This helped him to prepare for his next great expedition, which had been suggested by his chance encounter with Etienne—an international team to cross Antarctica on land across the continent's greatest length. The team that made up the International Trans-Antarctica Expedition was Steger, Etienne, Victor Boyarsky of the Soviet Union, Qin Dahe of China, Geoff Somers of Great Britain, and Keizo Funatsu of Japan. It was purposely designed to include men of different nationalities, none of whom had worked together before. They left from some rocky outcrops of the Antarctic Peninsula called the Seal Nunataks on July 27, 1989. Their route took them across the mountainous Antarctic Peninsula, the first time it had ever been crossed in winter. The day they left it was a warm 28°F, but by the eleventh day it had dropped to zero, and they were caught in a storm with winds as high as 75 miles per hour.

The expedition depended for supplies on caches that had been airdropped along the way the previous year. There were twelve of them, but three were never found, sometimes leading to shortages of food for both the men and dogs. They were also supplied by airdrops along the way. During their trip they carried out scientific experiments and observations and took samples of the snow, which told much about weather history, all across the continent. The expedition reached the American Amundsen-Scott Base at the South Pole on December 11, where they were greeted by about 60 people.

From the South Pole Steger's expedition entered the "area of inaccessibility," so named because it was equally remote from all coasts of Antarctica. The 800-mile-wide area had never been crossed on foot before. This was the most difficult part of the trip. They had to climb to altitudes up to 11,400 feet where oxygen was thin and they were bombarded with ultraviolet rays. They also crossed it during a period of solar storms that made radio communications almost impossible. It took them a month to cross this region, reaching the Soviet base of Vostok on January 18. They were now in the coldest part of the continent and temperatures got down to -54°F, with a wind chill factor of -125°. As they got near the coast temperatures increased, but two days away from their goal of the Soviet base of Mirnyy, they ran into heavy storms.

On March 1, 1990 Funatsu left the tent at 4:30 p.m. to feed his dogs. He got lost in a blinding snowstorm. At 6:00 p.m. the other team members went out to search for him, but had to give up at 10:30 p.m. They started again at 4:00 a.m. the next morning. At 6:00 a.m. Funatsu, who had sat down in a snow ditch and let the blowing snow cover him, heard the calls. He was able to stand up and shout out to them. After this dramatic rescue, the snows calmed, and all six members walked into Mirnyy Base on March 3, 1990, after a journey of 3,741 miles that had taken them 220 days to complete.

Where to learn more

Steger's first account of the North Pole expedition appeared in the *National Geographic* magazine ("North to the Pole," September 1986, pp. 289-317). He then wrote a book, with co-author Paul Schurke, that gave the complete story: *North to the Pole* (New York: Random House, 1987; paperback edition, New York: Ballantine Books, 1989).

Likewise, the first story about the Trans-Antarctica expedition was published in the *National Geographic* ("Six Across Antarctica," November 1990, pp. 67-93), followed by Will Steger and Jon Bowermaster, *Crossing Antarctica* (New York: Alfred A. Knopf, 1992).

Sir Aurel Stein

(1862 - 1943)

Aurel Stein, a Hungarian who emigrated to England, made several important archeological expeditions in Central Asia.

Aurel Stein was born in Budapest, Hungary on November 26, 1862. His well-to-do family sent him to schools in Hungary and Germany, where he got his Ph.D. in archeology in 1883. He went to Oxford University in England for post-graduate studies in 1884. While he was in England, his parents died. He accepted a position at Punjab University in Lahore, India and went there in 1888.

Stein stayed at his post in the city of Lahore until 1899. During his vacations he made archeological expeditions into Kashmir and the Pamir and Gilgit mountain ranges and published several important works on early India and Persia. He accepted another job in Calcutta in 1899, but his great ambition was to investigate the archeological sites of central Asia. With support from the Indian government, he set out on his first expedition in March 1900.

Sir Aurel Stein. The Granger Collection, New York.

Stein's first expedition was inspired by the Swedish explorer **Sven Hedin**'s discovery of the ruins of an ancient city in the Takla Makan Desert of western China. During his expedition of 1900-1901, Stein excavated part of the city, which had perished when its water supply from the Kun Lun Mountains dried up. He also investigated other sites near the city of Khotan and discovered a large number of documents in ancient languages.

Stein's second expedition started in 1906 with a return to the area around Khotan. He went as far as the shifting desert lake of Lop Nor. He excavated at Lou-lan, a Chinese outpost from the 2nd century that had also been discovered by Hedin. Stein's greatest discoveries were at Tun-huang where he found the "Caves of the Thousand Buddhas," which contained an incredible store of manuscripts and frescoes. The caves had served as a storehouse from the 5th to the 10th centuries but had been walled off since the 11th century. Stein's discovery is said to be the greatest archeological find ever made in Asia.

During 1907 Stein's expedition explored the Nan Shan range and made a mid-winter crossing of the Takla Makan. He suffered from severe frostbite while exploring the Kun Lun Mountains in the summer of 1908. He had to return to India, and the toes of one foot were amputated. Stein was appointed head of the Archeological Survey of India in 1910. The Survey sponsored him on his longest expedition, which began in 1913. He circled the Takla Makan and explored the Turfan Depression and far northwestern China. Between 1913 and 1915 Stein made further great discoveries. At Kan-chou he found a hoard of manuscripts in the Tangut and Tibetan languages, and while he was in the region his Indian assistant surveyed the headwaters of the Kan-chou River. In 1915 he found the Sassanian wall paintings in Sistan, having traveled to Persia from Kashgar by way of the Pamirs, Bukhara, and the Amu Darya River. From Sistan the expedition reached the Indus by way of Afghanistan. He crossed the Pamir Mountains into Russian Turkestan and returned to India by way of Persia and Baluchistan in what is now Pakistan.

Because of the instability caused by the Russian and Chinese revolutions, there was no access to central Asia for several years. In the meantime, Stein made journeys in Baluchistan and Persia. Stein shifted his interest to the Middle East and traced the routes of **Alexander the Great**. He had always wanted to investigate the ancient sites of Afghanistan, but political conditions prevented it. In 1943 he was granted permission to travel there. A few days after his arrival in Kabul, he became ill and died on October 26, 1943.

Where to learn more

Stein's books, which blend archeology with exploration, include: *Ruins of Desert Cathay: Personal Narrative of Explorations in Central Asia and Westernmost China* (London: Macmillan, 1912; reprinted, New York: Benjamin Blom, 1968) and *On Ancient Central-Asian Tracks* (London: Macmillan, 1933). An eminent historian of exploration, Jeannette Mirsky, wrote *Sir Aurel Stein, Archeological Explorer* (Chicago: University of Chicago Press, 1977).

Karl von den Steinen

(1855 - 1929)

Karl von den Steinen was a German anthropologist who was the first European to contact many of the Native American tribes of central Brazil and was the first person known to travel the length of the Xingu River.

Karl von den Steinen was born in the German city of Mülheim in the industrial Ruhr region. He studied medicine and psychiatry at the Universities of Berlin and Vienna. From 1879 to 1881 he made a trip around the world during which he studied under a German professor, Adolf Bastian, who was doing work in the new science of anthropology. Bastian and Steinen studied the Marquesas Islanders in French Polynesia. After his return to Germany Steinen took part in a German expedition to South Georgia Island off the coast of Antarctica in 1882 and 1883.

In 1884 Steinen started out on his own expedition to the forests of Mato Grosso in western Brazil to study the Native American tribes of the region, many of whom had had minimal or no contact with Europeans. He left the city of Cuiabá in May 1884 accompanied by his cousin Wilhelm von den Steinen and a military escort of 29 soldiers. They visited the Bakairi tribe, who had a history of contact with other Brazilians, on the Paranatinga River, and crossed over to the Batovi River, one of the tributaries of the great Xingu River. They sailed down the Batovi for 17 days without seeing any humans. On August 11 they had their first contact with a previously unknown tribe, the Bakairi. Steinen wrote movingly about this encounter in his book *Through Central Brazil* (published only in German, unfortunately).

Steinen's expedition traveled all the way down the Xingu River to the port city of Belém, which they reached in October 1884, after passing a great stretch of rapids (which Steinen named the Von Martius Rapids after another German scientist), which was the effective boundary between contacted and uncontacted tribes. They were the first Europeans to descend the river for its full length. Along the way they made initial contact with several tribes: Waurá, Trumäi, Kustenáu, and Suyá as well as other tribes that had already been contacted. These tribes all spoke different languages but years of contact with each other had given them very similar cultures, which Steinen was the first to write about. Steinen's writings showed that he was sympathetic to the Native Americans and particularly to the cultural shock that they experienced when faced with expanding Brazilian civilization.

The Native Americans were not of course always as happy to see Steinen as he was to see them: "They propelled their canoes hastily to the bank, snatched up their children, and with the smallest infants on their left hips, ran shrieking into the forest to reach their huts overland."

Steinen returned to Brazil in 1887 accompanied by anthropologist Paul Ehrenreich, a geographer, and his cousin Wilhelm once again. They left Cuiabá in July and traveled once again to the Batovi River and from there to the Culiseu. They revisited the tribes that Steinen had seen earlier plus the Kalapalo, Mehinaku, Auetí, Kamayura, and Yawalapiti. They made extensive ethnological observations, which were published in the story of the expedition, *Among the Native Peoples of Central Brazil*. They were forced to return to Cuiabá at the end of 1887 by lack of food and illness. Steinen then went to visit the Bororo tribe in western Mato Grosso, where he wrote about the corruption and alcoholism that the tribe suffered as a result of their association with Europeans. He also noted that no provision was made for their education.

Upon his return to Germany, Steinen was appointed professor of anthropology at the University of Marburg and then at the University of Berlin, where he set up the South American section of the ethnological museum. He died at the resort town of Cronberg in the Taunus Mountains at the age of 74.

Where to learn more

Steinen's own accounts were published in German: *Durch Zentralbrasiliens* (Berlin: 1886) and *Unter den Naturvölkern Zentralbrasiliens* (Berlin: 1884).

The best accounts in English of Steinen's explorations can be found in John Hemming, *Red Gold: The Conquest of the Brazilian Indians* (Cambridge: Harvard University Press, 1978) and *Amazon Frontier: The Defeat of the Brazilian Indians* (Cambridge: Harvard University Press, 1987).

John McDouall Stuart

(1815-1866)

John McDouall Stuart was a Scottish-born Australian explorer who explored the center of Australia. He was the first person to travel across the continent from south to north and return.

John McDouall Stuart was born in Fifeshire in Scotland on September 7, 1815. He migrated to South Australia in 1838 and worked as a surveyor for the colonial government. He served as draftsman on **Charles Sturt**'s expedition from 1844-1846 into central Australia.

Between May and August 1858 Stuart explored the country between Lake Torrens and Streaky Bay at the eastern end of the Great Australian Bight. In 1859 he found good grazing country west of Lake Eyre in the center of South Australia.

In order to end their isolation, the Australian colonists decided that they needed to build a telegraph line to connect with the rest of the world through Darwin on the north coast. The South Australian government offered a prize of £2,000 to the first person who could survey a route across the continent from south to north. Stuart set out to win it in January 1860, leaving Adelaide with two other men and 13 horses. Suffering from scurvy, they reached a point 125 miles east of Alice Springs on April 22, which their calculations told them was the exact center of the continent of Australia.

Stuart wrote about the event in his journal: "Today I find from my observations of the sun, 111°00'30, that I am now camped in the center of Australia. I have marked a tree and placed the British flag there. There is a high mount about two miles and a half to the north-north-east. I wish it had been in the center; but on it tomorrow I will raise a cone of stones and plant the flag there, and name it 'Central Mount Stuart'." He wrote that he planted the flag to show "the natives that the dawn of liberty, civilization and Christianity was about to break on them." The name of the mountain was later changed to Central Mount Stuart in honor of the first European explorer to see it.

In this part of the continent, Stuart found well-watered and well-grassed country, but as he and his companions headed north the creeks dried up. They were dying of thirst when they reached Tennant Creek, and they ignored gold lying on the ground to dig for water. At Attack Creek on June 26 Aborigines began to menace the party and set fire to the brush in order to force the Europeans away. This threat and the fact that they were extremely short of provisions forced Stuart to give up: "I have

John McDouall Stuart. The Granger Collection, New York.

most reluctantly come to the determination to abandon the attempt to make the Gulf of Carpentaria. Situated as I now am, it would be most imprudent." In fact, Stuart was almost blinded from scurvy. "The days are now become very hot again, and the feed for the horses as dry as if it were the middle of summer. The poor animals are very much reduced in condition, so much so that I am afraid of their being longer than one night without water." He returned to Adelaide.

The South Australian government then gave Stuart £2,500 to equip an even larger expedition. He left Adelaide on November 29, 1860 and reached Attack Creek on April 25, 1861. He continued to Newcastle Creek about 175 miles farther north. The burning hot plain and thick scrub proved "as great a barrier as if there had been an inland sea or a wall." Shortage of supplies forced him to turn back to Adelaide on July 12, which he reached on September 23, 1861. By this time **Robert O'Hara Burke** and **William John Wills** had reached the north coast, but no one knew about their fate.

Stuart's next expedition left Adelaide in December 1861, following the same route as before. He was back at Attack Creek on March 28, 1862. After much searching, a path was found through the brush. Daly Waters was reached on May 28, the headwaters of the Roper River on June 26, and on July 24 they arrived safely at the sea by the mouth of the Adelaide River near present-day Darwin. In his journal Stuart wrote: "I did not inform any of the party that I was so near the sea, as I wished to give them a surprise. . . .Thring, who rode in advance of me, called out, 'The Sea!' which so took them all by surprise, and they were so astonished, that he had to repeat the call before they fully understood what was meant. Then they immediately gave three long and hearty cheers." Later Stuart adds: "I dipped my feet, and washed my face and hands in the sea, as I promised the late Governor Sir Richard McDonnell I would do if I reached it."

The 2,000-mile return journey in 1862 was the most difficult of all Stuart had made, since by this time he was seriously weakened with exhaustion and illness. By the time he reached Chambers Creek he was almost blind, was suffering from scurvy, and was living on a little boiled flour which was all he could manage to swallow. When he started to bleed heavily, the others rigged up a litter slung between two horses. Three months later, ten gaunt and ragged men "leading a string of limping, emaciated horses, came riding slowly, wearily, triumphantly out of the mirage that filled the empty north. The Commander of the South Australian Great North Exploring Expedition, along with his faithful companions, had returned."

On his return to Adelaide on December 18, 1862, Stuart was rewarded with a government land grant and £2,000 and the Gold Medal of the Royal Geographical Society, but his health was completely broken. In April 1864 he returned to Scotland to visit his sister and then moved to London. He died in London, in some poverty, on June 5, 1866, almost blind and with his memory gone.

The greatest legacy left by Stuart's exploration was the Overland Telegraph Line connecting Adelaide in the south with Darwin in the north that was opened in 1872 along the trail that Stuart had blazed. Today the main highway through central Australia follows his trail and is appropriately called the Stuart Highway.

Where to learn more

Stuart wrote two books about his explorations: *Exploration of the Interior: Diary of J.M. Stuart from March 2 to September 3, 1860* (Adelaide: 1860) and *The Journals of John McDouall Stuart During the Years 1858, 1859, 1860, 1861, and 1862, edited from Mr. Stuart's manuscript by William Hardman* (London: 1864). Excerpts can be found in Kathleen Fitzpatrick, *Australian Explorers: A Selection from Their Writings* (London: Oxford University Press, 1958).

There are two fairly recent biographies of Stuart; both were published in the same year, in the same place, and with the same title: M.S. Webster, *John McDouall Stuart* (Melbourne: 1958) and D. Pike *John McDouall Stuart* (Melbourne: 1958). See also T.G.H. Strehlow, *Comments on the Journals of John McDouall Stuart* (Adelaide: 1967) and *The Heroic Journey of John McDouall Stuart* (Sydney: 1968).

The excellent book by Alan Moorehead, *Cooper's Creek* (New York: Harper & Row, 1963), about the exploration of central Australia contains much interesting information.

Charles Sturt

(1795-1869)

Charles Sturt was an Englishman who discovered the great interior river systems of Australia and penetrated almost to the center of the continent.

Charles Sturt was born in India on April 28, 1795, one of 13 children of a judge in the service of the East India Company. He returned to England at age 5 and was raised by relatives. Unable to afford the cost of going to university, he obtained an officer's commission and entered the British army in 1813. He served in Spain during the Peninsular War against Napoleon and then went to Canada, France, and Ireland. He was sent to the Australian colony of New South Wales in 1827 as part of the garrison guarding a detachment of convicts being sent to the penal colony. He arrived in Sydney on May 23, 1827.

Charles Sturt. The Granger Collection, New York.

Sturt had only been in New South Wales a short time when Governor Darling put him in charge of an expedition into the interior to try to fix the courses of the main interior rivers, which had been reported on, but never mapped. Sturt chose the experienced Australian explorer **Hamilton Hume** to accompany him. Their party set out from Sydney on November 10, 1828 and traveled northwestward over the Great Dividing Range to the Macquarie River, which had already been discovered, and then down that river to a vast swampy region that led to the Darling River (named after the Governor). This very large river, with its salty water, was thought to lead into a great inland sea. Sturt and Hume returned with this news to Sydney in April 1829.

On his return, Sturt requested permission to lead an expedition to follow the Darling to its outlet. Instead, he was sent southwestward to the Murrumbidgee River to see if it flowed into the Darling. Leaving Sydney on November 3, 1829 he followed the Murrumbidgee until it flowed into the Murray River and then followed the Murray past where it was joined by the Darling all the way to the sea. To his great disappointment he discovered that it emptied into the sea at a great salt marsh, Lake Alexandrina, that was impossible to navigate. This meant that the Murray River system, the greatest in Australia, could not serve as an easy access to the interior. Sturt and his men were forced to row back up these rivers in order to get back to Sydney, which they reached on May 25, 1830. The return trip was so difficult that Sturt went temporarily blind, and his health was permanently impaired.

After being sent to Norfolk Island to recover, Sturt returned to England and married the daughter of a family friend and resigned his commission in the army. He petitioned the government for a land grant as a reward for his explorations and returned to Australia in 1834, having been given 5,000 acres in New South Wales. The ranch went bust, however, and in 1839 he accepted a post in the South Australia Survey Department. He quarreled with the governor in 1841 and was demoted. Deeply in debt, in 1843 he presented a grandiose plan for exploring all of the interior of Australia in order to redeem himself. This was thought to be too ambitious, but he was given command of an expedition to try to find a mountain range west of the Darling River, a great continental divide like the one in North America. No such divide existed, nor did the great inland sea that Sturt expected to find.

At the age of 48, Sturt led his last expedition north from Adelaide on August 10, 1844. North of the Darling River in what is known as the Sturt Desert, the expedition ran into heat and drought so severe that it is said the men's hair stopped growing: thermometers burst, and the ink in their pens dried up faster than they could write. The heat dried up all the water in the area, and

Sturt was forced to wait out the drought for six months, from January 27, 1845 to July 16. Sturt's second-in-command died from scurvy during this period.

When the drought finally broke, Sturt and his party traveled 450 miles northwestward to the Great Stony Desert and came close to reaching the center of the continent. When he could not find an inland sea or a dividing range, Sturt finally turned back to Adelaide, which he reached on January 19, 1846.

Sturt did no more exploring. His old enemy the governor had moved on to another post, and Sturt's position improved considerably. He was appointed colonial treasurer in South Australia in 1846. In 1847 he took a leave of absence to return to London, but arrived too late to attend the ceremony where he was awarded the Gold Medal of the Royal Geographical Society. He returned to Adelaide in 1849 and was appointed colonial secretary. He was forced to retire by failing eyesight in 1851 but was granted a pension from the first South Australian parliament. He retired to Cheltenham, England, in 1853 and stayed there until his death on June 16, 1869.

Where to learn more

Sturt wrote two books about his explorations: *Two Expeditions into the Interior of Southern Australia, During the Years 1828, 1829, 1830, and 1831* (London: 1833) and *Narrative of an Expedition into Central Australia, Performed under the Authority of Her Majesty's Government, During the Years 1844, 5, and 6*, 2 vols. (London: Boone, 1849). Excerpts from these can be found in Kathleen Fitzpatrick, *Australian Explorers: A Selection from Their Writings* (London: Oxford University Press, 1958).

An early biography of Sturt was published by his daughter-in-law: Mrs. Napier George Sturt, *Life of Charles Sturt* (London: Smith Elder, 1899). J.L. Cumpston, a historian of Australian exploration, has written the only other full-length biography: *Charles Sturt* (Melbourne: 1951).

There is a fascinating book on the exploration of central Australia that includes a good deal of information on Sturt: Alan Moorehead, *Cooper's Creek* (New York: Harper & Row, 1963).

Sir Percy Sykes

(1867 - 1945)

Percy Sykes was a British army officer who led several expeditions through Iran and central Asia.

Percy Sykes was born in the English town of Canterbury on February 28, 1867, the son of an army chaplain and of the daughter of an army officer. He was sent to private school at Rugby and then to the British military academy at Sandhurst, where he graduated in 1888. He was assigned to a British regiment in India and served there until 1893.

As part of the contest that was then going on between Great Britain and Russia for control of Iran (then called Persia), Sykes was sent in 1893 to travel from the shores of the Caspain Sea to the city of Kerman in east central Iran and then on to London to report back to the British government on the state of defenses of the country. The government was pleased with his report, and he was appointed British consul for Kerman and Baluchistan in the southeastern part of the country, which had been assigned to the British "sphere of influence," but which had no British official in charge.

Sykes invited his sister, Ella, to accompany him to Iran, and she wrote an account of their travels. They traveled via the Mediterranean and Black Seas to southern Russia, crossed the Caucasus by land and then sailed on the Caspian Sea to the Iranian port of Enzeli. They then traveled on horseback over the Elburz mountains to the Iranian capital of Tehran. They stayed seven weeks in Tehran before traveling on to Kerman to open the British legation. Sykes and his sister were the only European residents of the city.

In 1896 Sykes was appointed to the commission that was supposed to draw the boundary between Persian Baluchistan and that part that was to become part of the Indian Empire (now in Pakistan). In order to do so he traveled by camel for 600 miles across the desert to the border, at the little town of Kuhak on the Ruhtuk River. From there he went to the city of Quetta, the capital of British Baluchistan. Upon leaving Quetta Sykes got news that the Shah of Iran had been assassinated and was ordered to the head of the Persian Gulf to take care of the interests of British citizens who had been injured in the resulting riots. He traveled as far as the provincial capital of Khuzistan,

Shushtar, where he became ill. He returned to London in March 1897.

During the Boer War in South Africa, which broke out in 1899, Sykes worked in British military intelligence and commanded a regiment. He was wounded and received several medals. At the end of the war he returned to India and Iran and served as consul-general at Khorasan in the northeastern part of the country.

In 1915, after World War I had broken out, Sykes was appointed consul-general in the city of Kashgar, in the far western part of Chinese Turkestan, or Sinkiang Province. He took a train across Russian Central Asia as far as it went and then traveled by horse across the Tien Shan Range into China. While there he made an expedition to the Pamir Mountains and Lake Karakul in what is now Kirghizia. He explored the glacier of Mustagh Ata and crossed the Ulughat Pass on a yak at 12,000 feet. He also traveled east to the Takla Makan Desert and the city of Khotan. He left Kashgar at the end of 1918 and traveled through Russia back to England.

At this time the Germans were trying to replace British influence with their own in Iran. The country was in a state of anarchy. With the consent of the British government, the government of Iran requested the services of Sykes in leading an army to restore order. He landed at the port of Bandar Abbas in March 1916 with a small number of British officers and proceeded to raise a force of 8,000 men called the South Persia Rifles. This force prevailed in southern and western Iran in spite of shifting loyalties and alliances until the end of the war. Sykes left Iran in 1918 and retired from the army in 1920.

During his retirement years Sykes wrote several scholarly works about Iran and Afghanistan and received many honors. He died in 1945.

Where to learn more

Sykes entitled his Persian narrative *Ten Thousand Miles in Persia: or, Eight Years in Iran* (London: J. Murray, 1902). Sykes also wrote *A History of Persia* (London: Macmillan and Co., Limited, 1921), *A History of Afghanistan* (London: Macmillan & Co., Ltd., 1940), and *A History of Exploration from the Earliest Times to the Present Day* (New York: The Macmillan Company, 1936). Sykes is also referred to in J.N.L. Baker's *A History of Geographical Discovery and Exploration* (New York: Cooper Square Publishers, 1967).

Abel Janszoon Tasman

(1603 - 1659)

Abel Janszoon Tasman was a Dutch navigator who was the first European to visit the islands of Tasmania, New Zealand, Tonga, and Fiji.

A bel Janszoon Tasman was born in a small village in the Dutch province of Groningen in 1603. He went to the Dutch East Indies for the first time in 1633 and then spent the next ten years of his life sailing the ships of the East India Company back and forth between Holland and Batavia, the capital of the East Indies, now called Jakarta.

In 1642, under the instigation of the governor of the East Indies, Anthony van Diemen, Tasman was charged with making a great voyage. He was to determine if the great southern continent which had been talked about for so long actually existed. He was to take as his pilot Frans Jacobszoon Visscher who had written a book hypothesizing about where the continent could be found.

The expedition left Batavia on August 14, 1642 with two ships, the *Heemskerck* and the *Zeehaen*. They sailed southwestward to the island of Mauritius in the southern part of the Indian Ocean, which at that time was a base for the Dutch East India Company. When they left Mauritius, they did something unusual—rather than sailing northeastward, which was the well-known route to the East Indies, they sailed due west hoping that they would bump into the great southern continent.

The Dutch knew about the northwest coast of Australia because many of their ships had been blown off course and had sighted land there before turning north to go to Batavia. But they had no idea how far south this land extended. As it happened, Tasman's course was too far south to touch the southern coast of mainland Australia, and he sailed on until November 24, when he first sighted land. This was the southern coast of the island of Tasmania, which is the southernmost part of the country of Australia. A party of Dutchmen went on land and, although they saw evidence of humans, they did not encounter any. Tasman actually named the island Van Diemen's Land after the Dutch governor. It kept this name for two centuries and then was renamed after its European discoverer.

From Tasmania, the Dutch ships turned northward as they continued to sail east. They thus traveled the Tasman Sea (also named for the explorer) and came to the northern tip of the South Island of New Zealand (named after one of the Dutch provinces). There Tasman met a Maori tribe, but the two sides were very suspicious of each other and started hostilities. Tasman was forced to withdraw.

At this point, Tasman and Visscher wanted to find a passage to the east and to sail on to Chile—one of their goals had been to open a way for the Dutch to trade with that Spanish colony. A passage did exist in this area, between the North and South Islands, but it was complicated by small islands, heavy currents, and adverse winds, and the Dutch were not able to find a way through. They therefore sailed north and on January 4, 1643 reached the northernmost point of New Zealand, which they named after the governor's wife—Cape Maria van Diemen.

As they sailed north, they eventually reached the Polynesian islands of Tonga, where the inhabitants proved to be friendly, and the Dutch were able to go ashore and get fresh water and food. They stayed about a week and were able to meet with a chief and to trade European metal products for food and curiosities made by the islanders. On February 1 they sailed on to the west and came upon some of the Fiji islands, but they did not stop.

At this point Tasman and Visscher chose the same path that so many later explorers took. Rather than sailing due west where they would have come upon the eastern side of the continent of Australia, they sailed north and then west along the north coast of New Guinea into the East Indies and then to Batavia, where they landed on June 14, 1643.

Although it would seem to us that Tasman had completed a great voyage, the directors of the East India Company were not pleased. They had hoped to open a trade route to Chile or at least to find a land that produced valuable products for trade. Neither happened. Hoping to do better, they sent Tasman out on another voyage.

This time the goal was to see whether there was a passage between the coast of New Holland (Australia) and New Guinea that might lead out into the Pacific and on to Chile. Tasman sailed from Batavia in February 1644 and went to the northwest coast of Australia and along it to Arnhem Land, a large peninsula in the north of Australia, and the Gulf of Carpentaria. He did not, however, find the opening, which did exist. It had been discovered in 1605 by the Spaniard **Luis Vaez de Torres** but his records had not been made known. Tasman did not fulfill his mission.

After this trip, Tasman went back to captaining ships between Holland and the East Indies, fought the Spaniards in the Philippines, lost his position because of drunkenness, was reinstated, became a large landowner in Batavia, and died there in 1659.

Where to learn more

Tasman's early role in the exploration of Australia caused much interest on the part of Australian historians, who did considerable research in the archives of the Dutch East India Company in order to reconstruct his voyages. Australian archivist and historian J.B. Walker published the first results of this in *Discovery of Van Diemen's Land in 1642* (London: 1888-1899) and in *A Collection of Papers Relating to Abel Janszoon Tasman and His Voyages* (Canberra: National Library, 1896). At about the same time, A Dutch historian, J.E. Heeres was also conducting significant research and published two important books: J.E. Heeres, ed. *Abel Janszoon Tasman's Journal* (Amsterdam: 1898) and *The Part Borne by the Dutch in the Discovery of Australia* (London: 1899).

The most valuable modern research on Tasman has been done by Australian historian Andrew Sharp, who is the author of three extensive works: *The Discovery of the Pacific Islands* (Oxford: Oxford University Press, 1960); *The Discovery of Australia* (Oxford: Oxford University Press, 1963); and *The Voyages of Abel Janszoon Tasman* (Oxford: Clarendon Press, 1968).

Also see T.D. Mutch, "The First Discovery of Australia," *Journal of the Royal Australian Historical Society*, vol. 28 (1942) pp. 303-352.

Three important books on Pacific exploration include accounts of Tasman: J.C. Beaglehole, *The Exploration of the Pacific* (Stanford: Stanford University Press, 1966); Colin Jack-Hinton, *The Search for the Islands of Solomon, 1567-1838* (Oxford: Clarendon Press, 1969); and O.H.K. Spate, *Monopolists and Freebooters* (Minneapolis: University of Minnesota Press, 1983).

Annie Royle Taylor

(1855 - ?)

Annie Royle Taylor was an English missionary who was the first European woman to travel in Tibet, at a time when the country was forbidden to all Westerners.

Annie Royle Taylor was born in the English county of Cheshire. She was one of 10 children of a prosperous businessman. She was born with a heart condition and as a child was coddled by her parents and nannies. At the age of 16, she underwent a religious conversion that led her to do mission work in the slums of east London. This led to a growing rift with her family, and her father begged her to give up her work and "go into Society like your sisters." Instead, at the age of 28 she sold her jewelry to finance a medical missionary course.

In 1884 Taylor became a missionary for the China Inland Mission, an evangelical Protestant society founded in 1865 that recruited single men and women to carry their brand of Christianity into remote areas of China. Taylor was determined to introduce Christianity into Tibet, where Westerners had been forbidden since the journey of **Evariste Régis Huc** and Joseph Gabet in 1846. Taylor worked for seven years on the borders of Tibet, either in Sikkim to the south or in China to the east. In 1887 she visited the great Buddhist monastery of Kumbum in China.

In the fall of 1892 Taylor learned that a Chinese Muslim named Noga and his Tibetan wife were traveling to Lhasa, the capital of Tibet. Noga agreed to take Taylor with them if she would pay for all the expenses. Taylor set out from her post at Tao-chou in the Chinese province of Szechuan on September 2, 1892 accompanied by her servant Pontso, a Tibetan whom she had converted to Christianity, and two other servants. One of these two died along the way ("We buried him at noon"), and the other deserted and turned back to China.

Taylor experienced an extraordinarily difficult journey that she endured only because of her strong faith. No matter what dangers or problems she encountered, she always felt that God would take care of her. "Quite safe here with Jesus" was the constant refrain in her diary. "He has sent me on this journey, and I am his little woman." Recent commentators on Taylor's remarkable diary have tended to denigrate it because she was not interested in the geography of the country she traveled through ("she tells us no more than that the country is cold, the rivers wide, and the mountains high") or in the deep cultural traditions of the Tibetan people ("Poor things, they know no better; no one has ever told them about Jesus"). However, she was the first Western woman to have ever traveled to Tibet and came very close to making it to Lhasa—"the Forbidden City."

During the trip to Lhasa, Taylor and her party were set upon by bandits, her horse died from exhaustion while she was still riding it, they ran out of food, and the yaks they were bringing with them ate the travelers' clothes. She had to cross rivers ringed with ice floating on bullock skins that had been blown up. On Christmas Day she boiled a plum pudding that she had brought with her from England but was too sick from altitude sickness to eat it.

Noga, the guide, turned out to be a treacherous companion. He kept threatening to expose her to the authorities and one time threw a cooking pot at her and raised his sword to kill her. He was stopped by a friendly Tibetan, who offered to kill Noga for her. She declined the offer. Noga then stole two horses and rode ahead to tell the Tibetan officials that he was traveling with an Englishwoman. She and Pontso were left with practically nothing and had to barter their last tent in order to get food. They were forced to sleep 20 nights in the open air in mid-winter.

On January 3, 1893, only three days out of Lhasa, Taylor was stopped by Tibetan soldiers and put under arrest (in a narrow, coffin-shaped hole in the ground). In spite of her pleas, she was told that she would have to return the way she came. She stood her ground, however, and said that she could not go back until Noga returned her stolen goods. Noga was brought to the magistrate's office and denied all her charges. ("I had never heard such lying," she wrote.) The magistrate at first ruled in Noga's favor, but she refused to give up. After six days he provided her with two horses and some money and supplies.

In spite of this assistance, the return trip was even worse than the trip in. Taylor and Pontso traveled alone for 1,300 miles in a journey back to China, arriving back in Tau-chou seven months and ten days after they had left. On her return to the mission station, Taylor sent the diary of her journey to mission headquarters in London, and it was published in 1894. This achieved some fame, and she went back to England to lecture and to recruit more missionaries for her Tibetan Pioneer Mission.

She set up the headquarters of her Tibetan mission in the border town of Yatung in Sikkim, which was opened to trade with Tibet in 1893. She named her house there the "Lhasa Villa" and stayed there, assisted by Miss Ferguson and Miss Foster, until sometime between 1907 and 1909, when she returned to England. It is not known when or in what circumstances she died.

Where to learn more

Taylor's diary was published as *Pioneering in Tibet* (London: Morgan and Scott, 1894). This served as the basis for other edifying accounts such as William Carey, *Travel and Adventure in Tibet: Including the Diary of Miss Annie R. Taylor's Remarkable Journey from Tau-Chau to Ta-Chien-Lu through the Heart of the Forbidden Land* (London: Hodder and Stoughton, 1902) and a chapter entitled ''A Heroine of Tibet'' in John C. Lambert, *The Romance of Missionary Heroism: True Stories of the Intrepid Bravery and Stirring Adventures of* *Missionaries with Uncivilized Man, Wild Beasts and the Forces of Nature in All Parts of the World* (London: Seeley & Co., 1907).

More recent summaries of her trip can be found in Peter Hopkirk, *Trespassers on the Roof of the World* (London: John Murray, 1982) and Jane Robinson, *Wayward Women: A Guide to Women Travellers* (Oxford: Oxford University Press, 1990).

Pedro de Teixeira

(1587 - 1641)

Pedro de Teixeira made the first trip upstream on the Amazon by a European and claimed the whole Amazon basin for Portugal.

Pedro de Teixeira was born in Portugal and went to Brazil in 1607. He became a captain in the colonial forces and took part in an expedition in 1615 that expelled French occupiers from the town of São Luís on the northern coast of Brazil. (São Luís is now the capital of the Brazilian state of Maranhão.) He then helped found Fort Presépio on January 12, 1616 near one of the mouths of the Amazon River. This was to grow into the city of Belém, capital of the state of Pará and the largest city in the Amazon basin.

In the following years Teixeira helped clear the Amazon region of foreign traders and to secure the area for Portugal. In 1637 six Spanish soldiers and two Spanish priests arrived in Belém, having traveled down the Amazon River from one of its tributaries, the Napo, now in Ecuador. At that time Spain and Portugal were ruled by the same king and were allies. However, they still maintained different governments and jealously guarded their colonial possessions. The Portuguese, in particular, were afraid of being swallowed up by the more powerful Spanish state. Therefore, the Governor of Maranhão was worried that the presence of the Spanish might mean that they would seek to control the Amazon from their possessions in the Andes, the Vice-Royalty of Peru. He sent out Teixeira to forestall them.

Teixeira set out from the village of Cametá on the Tocantins River on October 28, 1637 at the head of an enormous expedition made up of 70 Portuguese soldiers and 1,200 Native American men plus a multitude of women and children in 47 large canoes holding the soldiers and some twenty-odd other ones carrying the supplies and families. This was the first European expedition *up* the Amazon: previous ones of **Francisco de Orellana** and other Spaniards had all floated down the river from its sources in the Andes. This one was much more difficult because they had to row against the current and, because of the expedition's large size, had to spend a great deal of time hunting for food.

It took Teixeira's expedition eight months to travel up the Amazon and its tributaries to reach the first Spanish settlements on the eastern slopes of the Andes. He and his companions went as far by river as they could and then traveled overland to the city of Quito, which they reached a year after starting out. The Spanish were dismayed to have their Portuguese allies in Quito,

but welcomed them to the city, where they stayed for about four months.

Teixeira left Quito on February 16, 1639. He was accompanied on his return by the brother of the Spanish Governor of Quito, a Jesuit priest, who was instructed to report on the journey to Spain. At a place he named Franciscana at the junction of the Napo and Aguarico Rivers (now the eastern boundary of Ecuador), Teixeira "according to his instructions" took possession in the name of Portugal of all the lands and rivers "that enter from the east". This was the basis for the Portuguese, and later Brazilian, claim to control of the Amazon.

Along the way down the river, they encountered a group of Native Americans who had taken refuge on a large island in the river. This tribe, the Tupinambá, had fled from the Portuguese in Pernambuco, in northeastern Brazil, to Mato Grosso and Bolivia and then from the Spanish they had met there to the Amazon, only to encounter Europeans once again in the form of the Teixeira expedition.

Teixeira returned to Belém on December 12, 1639, where he received a rapturous welcome. The following year Spain and Portugal split up again, this time permanently, and Brazil and the Amazon went to Portugal, thanks to Teixeira's expedition.

As a reward for his services, Teixeira was named governor of Belém on February 28, 1640. He was forced to give up that position because of ill-health and died shortly thereafter on June 4, 1640.

Where to learn more

The only original documentary source available in English is a translation of the account by the Spanish Jesuit who accompanied Teixeira back from Quito, Cristóbal de Acuña, "A New Discovery of the Great River of the Amazons," in Clements R. Markham, ed. *Expeditions Into the Valley of the Amazons* (London: Hakluyt Society, 1859). Other original documents, including Teixeira's own account, are included in Spanish translation in "Viaje del capitán Pedro Teixeira (1638-1639)," *Boletín de Historia y Antigüedades* (Bogotá, Colombia), vol. 29 (1942), pp. 287-307. Additional documents are printed in Jaime Cortesão, "O significado da expedição de Pedro Teixeira a luz de novos documentos," in *Anáis* of the Instituto Histórico e Geográfico Brasileiro, Fourth National Congress (Rio de Janeiro: Imprensa Nacional, 1950).

There is one full-length 19th-century book on the Teixeira expedition: Marcos Jiménez de la Espada, *Viaje del Capitán Pedro Teixeira a aguas arriba del río de las Amazonas, 1638-1639* (Madrid: 1889). As with all the major South American explorers, there is a good, brief, scholarly account in Edward J. Goodman, *The Explorers of South America* (New York: Macmillan, 1972). There is a readable chapter on Teixeira in Anthony Smith, *Explorers of the Amazon* (New York: Viking, 1990), which unfortunately does not include any references or bibliography.

The important subject of Portuguese-Native American relations is dealt with in Mathias C. Kiemen, *The Indian Policy of Portugal in the Amazon Region, 1614-1693* (Washington: Catholic University Press, 1954).

Valentina Vladimirovna Tereshkova

(1937 -   )

Valentina Vladimirovna Tereshkova, a Soviet cosmonaut, was the first woman to fly in space.

Valentina Vladimirovna Tereshkova was born on March 6, 1937 in the small village of Maslennikovo near the Russian city of Yaroslavl. Her father was a tractor driver on a collective farm who was killed in action during World War II. Her mother moved to Yaroslavl, where she found work in a textile factory. Tereshkova started school in Yaroslavl in 1945. She went to work at age 16 in the Yaroslavl tire factory, while studying at night school. In 1955 she took a job as a loom operator at the Red Canal Cotton Mill and took correspondence courses at a technical school. She also took up parachuting as a hobby and founded a parachute club at her factory. She made her first jump in May 1959. On one jump she landed in the Volga River and almost drowned but went on to make 126 successful jumps. By 1961 she had become a spinning machinery technician and secretary of the local Communist Youth League.

Following the Soviet Union's first successful unmanned space launch, the Vostok I, in May 1960, Tereshkova became interested in the idea of space flight. When **Yuri Gagarin** made the first manned space flight in April 1961, Tereshkova was so enthusiastic that she wrote a letter to the Soviet Space Commission asking to be considered for cosmonaut training. The Space Commission filed her letter along with several thousand others that it had received. In early 1962, however, Nikita Khrushchev, the Soviet leader, came up with the idea that the U.S.S.R. could score an important public relations coup against its space rival, the United States, by sending a woman into space. (The United States did not accept women for astronaut training for another 20 years.) At his urging, the Space Commission reviewed the letters it had received in April 1961. Tereshkova and four other Soviet women were chosen for cosmonaut training on February 16, 1962.

Khrushchev had wanted to choose an ordinary Russian worker to be the first woman in space, not one of the many highly skilled Soviet women scientists or airplane pilots. When Tereshkova was chosen, she was told not to tell her friends or family what she was going to be doing. She told them that she had been selected for training in a program for a women's precision sky-diving team. She immediately entered an intensive training program at the Baikonur space center—working in a centrifuge, isolation chamber, weightless conditions, and making parachute jumps in a space suit. She was also given jet pilot training. Tereshkova, who had had no scientific training, found the intricacies of space technology difficult to master, but it is said that she applied herself to the course and mastered it.

There has been speculation that Tereshkova was not the first choice for the flight that she made: that she was originally intended to be the back-up pilot but that the other woman cosmonaut was disqualified for medical reasons. In any case, Tereshkova took off aboard the Vostok 6 rocket shortly after noon on June 16, 1963. The Vostok 5 rocket with Valeri Bykovsky on board had been launched on June 14. This was the second joint space flight. In August 1962 Andrian Nikolayev and Pavel Popovich had flown in two rockets, one trailing the other a few miles behind. In the case of Bykovsky and Tereshkova, they were launched into two totally separate orbits that at one point were only three miles apart but this widened to as much as several thousand miles. The reason for the orbits chosen is not known.

While in space, Bykovsky and Tereshkova conversed with each other and relayed television pictures back to earth. Tereshkova carried out a series of physiological tests to continue the effort to learn about the effects of weightlessness and space travel on humans. She experienced some sea sickness, and this was expanded by members of the Western press to say that she had been violently ill. In fact, she reacted so well that the flight, which had originally been scheduled for one day, was expanded to three days. She landed after two days, 22 hours and 50 minutes in space. To return to earth Tereshkova fired the retro-engine to brake the rocket. As the space capsule re-entered the atmosphere, flames caused by atmospheric friction surrounded the capsule. It then stabilized under a small parachute, and Tereshkova was ejected through the side hatch. She landed in a regular aviation parachute.

Following her successful space flight, Tereshkova entered into a taxing round of personal appearances. Almost immediately after landing, she was flown to Moscow to address an International Women's Peace Congress. She then traveled around the world and made speeches on space flight and the role of women throughout the world. During her training program, Tereshkova had become friendly with fellow cosmonaut, Andrian Nikolayev, the only unmarried male cosmonaut. In November 3, 1963 they were married in a ceremony in Moscow that was presided over by Khrushchev and broadcast nationwide. Tereshkova and Nikolayev had a daughter, Valentina, born in June 1964. However, the couple grew apart, and in June 1983 it was announced that they had divorced.

Tereshkova continued her round of publicity appearances and official functions. She was elected as member for Yaroslavl to the Supreme Soviet in 1967, and served on the Council of the Supreme Soviet from 1966 to 1970 and from 1970 to 1974. In 1974, she was elected to the Presidium of the Supreme Soviet, an important position. She served briefly in the national government during the rule of Yuri Andropov in 1983.

Where to learn more

In addition to the books on the Soviet space program listed under Yuri Gagarin, also see *Red Star in Orbit* (New York: Macmillan, 1977) by James E. Oberg, which gives a sympathetic account of Tereshkova and her flight.

Wilfred Thesiger

(1910 -   )

Wilfred Thesiger was an English explorer who made several trips into the interior of the Arabian peninsula right after World War II.

Practically the last place on earth that was visited by Europeans was the Rub 'al Khali, or Empty Quarter, of Arabia. The first crossing was only made in 1931 by an Englishman, Bertram Thomas. He only made one crossing. More systematic exploration had to wait until after World War II when another Englishman, Wilfred Thesiger, made several journeys into this enormous desert.

Thesiger was an English soldier, writer, and photographer who had made a trip from the highlands of Ethiopia to the Red Sea coast in 1934. After the war Thesiger was assigned to the Middle East Anti-Locust Unit, which was designed to destroy the hordes of locusts that threatened agricultural production. In 1945 he made a trip from the Oman coast westward into what was then the British colony of Aden.

In 1946 Thesiger left from the port city of Salala on the south coast of Oman into the interior. He used as his guides a group of Bedouin Arabs who had never seen a European before. Following a route farther to the east than the one Thomas had taken, he traveled to the town of Mughsin on the eastern edge of the Rub 'al Khali. He collected a group of four tribesman who had guided Thomas and headed north through the desert to the Liwa Oasis. He then went along the entire eastern edge of the sands back to his starting point at Salala, which he reached in early 1947.

During this arduous journey Thesiger and his Arab companions ran out of water several times, but the knowledgable Bedouin were able to find wells of murky water that saved their lives on each occasion. In his book about his adventures, *Arabian Sands*, Thesiger wrote, "To others my journey would have little importance. It would produce nothing except a rather inaccurate map which no one was ever likely to use. It was a personal experience, and the reward had been a drink of clean, nearly tasteless water. I was content with that."

Thesiger's second crossing was made from the well at Manwakh, north of the region of the Hadramaut, west of Oman. This time he traveled all the way around the eastern and northern edges of the Rub 'al Khali to reach the shores of the Persian Gulf in what is now the United Arab Emirates. He made one final journey from 1948-1950, in which he traveled in the interior of Oman and the United Arab Emirates. By this time the great petroleum wealth of the Arabian peninsula was starting to be exploited. Thesiger's accounts of traditional life were the last ones before the great transformation in Arabian society, caused by the new oil industry took place.

Where to learn more

Thesiger described his travels in *Arabian Sands* (New York: Penguin, 1984). He is also included in Timothy Green's *The Restless Spirit: Profiles in Adventure* (New York: Walker, 1970. This title was published in London as *The Adventurers: Four Profiles of Contemporary Travellers* (1970). Thesiger has writen an autobiography of his exciting life entitled *The Life of My Choice* (New York: W.W. Norton & Co., 1987).

David Thompson

(1770 - 1857)

David Thompson was an Englishman who went to Canada at an early age and explored much of northwestern Canada. He was the first person to travel through the Rocky Mountains to the Columbia River and down it to its mouth.

David Thompson was born in London in 1770 and attended a charity school there. At the age of fourteen the school apprenticed him to the Hudson's Bay Company, the largest fur trading company in British North America (now Canada). In September 1784 he arrived at the Company's post of Churchill on the coast of Hudson's Bay in what is now the province of Manitoba.

During his first year Thompson worked for **Samuel Hearne**, who had been the first European to travel to the Arctic Ocean overland. In the following year Thompson was sent to another trading post, York Factory, which was about 150 miles to the south. He made the trip at the beginning of winter with only two local guides, and this was to be the start of his many trips. In 1786 he went on a trading expedition to the North Saskatchewan River, and the next year farther west to the region of the present-day city of Calgary. He spent the winter of 1787-88 with the Piegan Indians and began to learn the language and customs of that people.

For the next two years Thompson traded for furs in the northern parts of the present provinces of Saskatchewan and Manitoba. During these years, he began to develop his skills and interests in surveying and to keep meteorological records. In 1790 he was ordered to return to York Factory, and he took

Thompson's expeditions through the Canadian northwest.

advantage of the opportunity to survey his return route of 750 miles.

In 1792 Thompson left York Factory to begin a series of trips into the far north of what is now Saskatchewan. The aim of these expeditions was to try to find a way to capture the valuable fur trade of this region, which was being exploited by the rival to the Hudson's Bay Company—the Northwest Company, headquartered in Montreal. In 1796 he made it to his goal and northernmost point—Lake Athabaska. By this time, however, the local bosses of the Hudson's Bay Company had decided that his surveying expeditions were taking up too much time and told him to stop.

Thompson felt that his efforts were not getting the recognition they deserved, so he quit the Hudson's Bay Company, walked to the nearest Northwest Company post and offered his services there. They were, naturally, delighted to have him and were willing to employ him solely as a surveyor without any trading duties. In 1797 he was instructed to survey the new boundary with the United States at 49°N and to travel as far west as the camps of the Mandan Indians along the Missouri River in present-day North Dakota. During this expedition Thompson made it as far as the Assiniboine River before winter. However, he was still a long way from the Missouri, but he decided to push on ahead, often without a guide. He reached the Missouri River and the Mandan villages on December 29, 1797 where he stayed until January 10, 1798.

On the way back he was faced with frigid winter weather and then by the thaws of spring which made travel even more difficult. However, on April 27 he was able to reach Turtle Lake, one of the sources of the Mississippi river in northern Minnesota. He then traveled to Lake Superior by way of the site of Duluth and surveyed its shores to Grand Portage and then north to Lake of the Woods, Lake Winnipeg, and Lake Manitoba.

Thompson spent the rest of 1798 and 1799 in the country in the area between the North Saskatchewan and Athabaska rivers in what is now Saskatchewan and Alberta. In June, 1799 he married a young woman whose father was a Scottish trader and whose mother belonged to the Chippewa tribe. They had numerous children, and from that time Thompson traveled with

his family. In 1801 he made an attempt to cross the Rocky Mountains, but could not find a pass that would take him through. He then went back to his trading operations in the Muskrat Country. In 1806 the Northwest Company sent him and his family back to the North Saskatchewan River to prepare for another attempt at crossing the mountains.

In 1807 Thompson and his family made it through the Howse Pass and reached the Columbia River. For the next three years they traveled back and forth across the Rocky Mountains and in the Columbia River valley. He founded Fort Kootenay, the first fur-trading post on the Columbia River as well as surveying the whole area for future traders. The pass that Thompson had first used was the scene of rivalry between the Piegan and Kootenay tribes so Thompson searched for another one. On January 10, 1811 he discovered the Athabaska Pass farther north, and it became the usual route across the mountains until the railroad was built many years later. In 1811 Thompson traveled all the way down the Columbia to its mouth, but he found American fur traders sent out by John Jacob Astor already there.

In 1812 Thompson retired from the Northwest Company and went to live in Montreal. He completed a map of western Canada based on his explorations, and he served until 1826 on the Boundary Commission set up to survey the boundary between the United States and Canada. He had a long life—he died in Montreal on February 10, 1857 at the age of 87.

Where to learn more

Thompson's own accounts of his travels can be found in J.B. Tyrrell, *David Thompson's Narrative of His Explorations in Western America* (Toronto: Champlain Society, 1916) and Richard Glover, ed. *David Thompson's Narrative 1784-1812* (Toronto: Champlain Society, 1962). Glover has also written an overview of Thompson's career in "The Witness of David Thompson," *Canadian Historical Review* vol. 31 (1950), pp. 25-38).

The histories of the Canadian fur trade and of the Hudson's Bay Company all included summaries of Thompson's explorations. These include: Agnes Laut, *The Conquest of the Great Northwest* (New York: Outing Publishing Co., 1908); E.E. Rich, *The History of the Hudson's Bay Company, 1670-1870*, vol. 2 (London: Hudson's Bay Record Society, 1959); George Woodcock, *The Hudson's Bay Company* (Toronto: Collier-Macmillan Canada, 1970); and Peter C. Newman, *Company of Adventurers*, vol. 1 (New York: Viking, 1985).

Joseph Thomson

(1858 - 1895)

Joseph Thomson was a Scottish geologist who made three expeditions to East Africa, during which he became the first European to travel to the land of the Masai people in Kenya.

Joseph Thomson was born in the small village of Penpont in Scotland on February 14, 1858 in the stone house his father had built. Later his father moved to a nearby farm and bought a stone quarry. As a teenager, Thomson spent much of his time in the quarry. This experience got him interested in geology, and he wrote several papers on the quarry rocks for a local scientific society. He attended the University of Edinburgh and graduated in 1877 with an honors degree in geology and natural science.

As a result of these accomplishments, Thomson was chosen to be the geologist on an expedition led by Keith Johnston to East Africa sponsored by the Royal Geographical Society. The expedition arrived in Zanzibar on January 5, 1879. After collecting its supplies and hiring a team of porters, including the experienced **James Chuma** as caravan leader, it headed for the interior on May 19, 1879. Johnston died of malaria on June 28, and Thomson was suddenly in charge of the expedition.

Guided by Chuma, Thomson decided to continue, even though he had no African experience and was only 21 years old. He reached the northern end of Lake Nyasa (Malawi) on September 20, 1879, the first European to travel overland to that part of the lake. He continued on to Lake Tanganyika even though he had become ill with fever and arrived there on November 3. He reached the Lukuga River on Christmas Day and confirmed that it was the only outlet for the lake. Thomson headed for the Lualaba River in what is now Zaire but was forced to turn back because of unstable conditions in the area. He turned to the northeast and visited Lake Rukwa (Leopold), the first European to see it. He then took the old Arab trade route to Tabora (Kazé) and returned to the coast and Zanzibar on July 10, 1880. Only one of the African porters had died along the way, an unprecedented record.

The success of Thomson's first African expedition gave him a considerable reputation. In June 1881 he was hired by the Sultan of Zanzibar, who was the nominal ruler of the mainland as well, to travel to the Rovuma River to investigate reports of coal deposits. He reached the Rovuma on August 3 to find that the mineral deposits were shale, which had no commercial value. He took a roundabout route to return to Zanzibar and report to the Sultan. He went back to Scotland at the end of the year.

In June 1882 Thomson was hired by the Royal Geographical Society to travel to Mount Kenya, which had been sighted from a distance by **Ludwig Krapf** in 1849 but had never been visited by a Westerner. Traveling to Mount Kenya meant penetrating the land of the Masai people, who had a reputation for being very warlike and hostile to outsiders. When Thomson reached Zanzibar in January 1883, he found that Chuma had died, and he chose another experienced man, Manua Sera, to be caravan leader.

Thomson left the coast in March 1883, taking with him a Maltese sailor named James Martin, 130 porters under Manua Sera's command, and a few donkeys. During the first part of the expedition he was following the route of German explorer Gustav Adolf Fischer, who had reached Mount Kilimanjaro the previous year and who had had an armed fight with Masai warriors. Thomson reached Mount Taveta at the foot of Mount Kilimanjaro on May 5. He climbed nearly 9,000 feet up the mountain.

By this time, Thomson was in Masai territory. He had several nervous encounters with the Masai but always stood his ground and did not resort to firearms. At one point, he caught their attention by putting some bicarbonate of soda into a glass of water to make it fizzle. As an additional safeguard he joined forces with a Swahili caravan in July and traveled with it as far as Lake Naivasha, where Fischer had been forced to turn back. At Lake Naivasha, in September, his party was attacked by members of the Kikuyu tribe, and two porters were killed.

Thomson then crossed a 14,000-foot-high range of mountains, which he named after Lord Aberdare, the President of the Royal Geographical Society. He saw Mount Kenya, but the hostility of the Masai forced him to give up his hopes of climbing it. He reached the northeast shore of Lake Victoria on December 10, 1883, but the unfriendliness of the inhabitants forced him to leave three days later.

Heading back to the coast, he made a detour and became the first European to see the 14,094-foot Mount Elgon, an extinct volcano on the present borders of Uganda and Kenya. He also visited the remarkable prehistoric caves on the mountain's southern slopes. On December 31, 1882 he was badly gored by a buffalo. Shortly after, he became seriously ill from dysentery and spent six weeks semi-conscious in a grass hut. His party was being threatened by the Masai once again. They were able to hook up with the same Swahili caravan and resumed their journey in April 1884, with Thomson being carried in a litter. They reached Rabai, inland from Mombasa, on May 24 after a journey of 3,000 miles. Thomson celebrated by getting out of his litter and walking into the town.

Thomson returned to London in poor health, but he was well received for his exploits. He was given a gold medal by the Royal Geographical Society, and his book about his experiences with the Masai was a bestseller.

In 1885 Thomson offered to lead the Emin Pasha Relief Expedition, but **Henry Morton Stanley** was chosen instead. Thomson returned to Africa on behalf of the National African Company. This time he went to West Africa with the aim of forestalling Germans coming from Cameroon who were penetrating into what the British saw as their preserve. He landed on the coast of Nigeria in March 1885 and went up the Niger to what is now northeastern Nigeria and carried out diplomatic negotiations with the leaders of the region. He returned to England in September.

Thomson's health was now seriously impaired, and he spent the following three years recuperating. In 1888 he traveled to Morocco at his own expense and climbed some of the highest peaks in the Atlas Mountains. In 1890 he was hired by Cecil Rhodes' British South African Company to travel to what are now Malawi and Zambia to sign treaties with the chiefs of the region that placed them under British protection. He became

seriously ill and barely made it back to London in October 1891. He suffered from lung problems during the following year and traveled to Cape Town in 1893, hoping that the climate would be better for his health. He did improve, but he became ill again on his return to England. He died in London on August 2, 1895, at the age of 37.

Where to learn more

In addition to numerous articles in various periodicals, especially the *Geographical Journal* of the Royal Geographical Society, Thomson wrote three books about his explorations: *To the Central African Lakes and Back: The Narrative of the Royal Geographical Society's East Central Africa Expedition, 1878-1880*, 2 vols. (London: 1881; reprinted, London: Frank Cass, 1968); *Through Masai Land: A Journey of Exploration Among the Snowclad Volcanic Mountains and Strange Tribes of Eastern Equatorial Africa* (London: Sampson Low, Marston, Searle & Rivington, 1885; revised edition, 1887; reprinted, London: Frank Cass & Co., 1968); *Travels in the Atlas and Southern Morocco* (London: 1889). There are excerpts from these works in Charles Richards and James Place, editors, *East African Explorers* (London: Oxford University Press, 1960). Thomson also wrote a history, *Mungo Park and the Niger* (London: 1890), and a novel about Africa, *Ulu* (London: 1888).

The first biography of Thomson was written shortly after his death by his brother, James Baird Thomson: *Joseph Thomson: African Explorer* (London: 1896). The definitive study is Robert I. Rotberg, *Joseph Thomson and the Exploration of Africa* (New York: Oxford University Press, 1971). Rotberg also wrote an evaluative essay on Thomson, "Joseph Thomson: Energy, Humanism, and Imperialism," in *Africa and Its Explorers: Motives, Methods, and Impact*, edited by Robert I. Rotberg (Cambridge: Harvard University Press, 1970).

Alexine Tinné

(1835 - 1869)

Alexine Tinné was a wealthy Dutch woman who organized several trips up the Nile River and was killed while attempting to be the first European woman to cross the Sahara.

Alexine Tinné was baptized Alexandrina Petronella Francina Tinné on her birth in The Hague, Netherlands, on October 17, 1835. Her father was a wealthy Dutch merchant and her mother, Harriet, was his second wife, 26 years younger than he was. Alexine's father died when she was nine years old, leaving her a large fortune.

When Alexine was 20 she suffered from an unhappy love affair. She had become engaged to a baron who, it turned out, was deeply in debt. She learned that he was planning to use her money to pay off his debts after their marriage. She broke off the engagement. Her mother then persuaded her that they should undertake an extended tour of Europe and the Middle East as a means of forgetting her unhappiness.

During their travels, they went to Egypt and rented a large boat, luxuriously furnished, which they sailed up the Nile River as far as Aswan, visiting the ancient Egyptian monuments along the way. They then went back to Cairo, traveled from there to the Holy Land as far as Beirut in Lebanon and returned to Cairo to celebrate Christmas 1856. By this time Alexine had decided that she wanted to travel up the Nile as far as Khartoum in the Sudan. They set out again in their luxurious boat but could only get as far as the Second Cataract of the Nile before being forced to turn back.

After this disappointment they returned to Cairo and spent the rest of 1857 traveling to Beirut, Turkey, Italy, and Vienna before returning to the Netherlands. Alexine had not given up her desire to travel farther up the Nile, and she organized a much larger expedition in 1860, this time including her mother's sister, Adriana, "Aunt Addy," who had been a lady-in-waiting at the Dutch court. They went to Cairo in the summer of 1861 and rented a large house where they had china and silver sent from Europe and a grand piano installed for Alexine, and they designed uniforms for the servants.

The enormous household set out in January 1862 in three boats containing numerous servants and pets. When Tinné's intentions were known, she was dubbed "Queen of the Equator" by the numerous Europeans in Cairo, including Ferdinand de Lesseps who took her to visit the Suez Canal he was building.

Alexine Tinné. The Granger Collection, New York.

This time they made it all the way to Khartoum where they met **Samuel Baker** and his companion Florence. At that time, everyone was waiting for news of **John Hanning Speke** and **James Augustus Grant** who were expected to be coming up the White Nile from central Africa. This news made Tinné change her mind about traveling up the Blue Nile into Ethiopia, and she decided to head south to meet Speke.

Tinné hired a steamer to take her farther up the river and to tow the odd assortment of boats that she had by now collected. In case she wanted to build a house along the way, she took along a supply of building materials and an Italian mason. They left Khartoum on May 11, 1862 and traveled to Jebel Dinka, a slave trading post. There Tinné was so overwhelmed by the misery she saw that she bought a family of six and set them free. Upriver they ran into a tangled mess of swamps and streams, and it took three weeks to travel 150 miles.

When they reached Gondokoro, the last navigable spot on the Nile and a major slave depot, they found that Speke had not yet arrived. Tinné became ill, and they were forced to return to Khartoum. In Khartoum Tinné made plans to head south again, this time determined to reach the equator. This time she took along two German scientists, a traveling Dutchman, and her mother as well as the usual array of servants, soldiers, animals, and luggage. Her aunt decided to stay in Khartoum.

The expedition did go into territory that had never been visited by Westerners, but otherwise it was a total disaster. Tinné's mother died on July 22, 1863, followed by her maid and then Tinné's maid. One of the German scientists died, and the other German and the Dutchman were so ill they had to be carried in litters. Aunt Addy became worried after the expedition had been gone for eight months. She organized a rescue party of 75 and headed after them. They met up in the south Sudanese town of Wau, but Aunt Addy became ill during the trip back and died in Khartoum.

Faced with these tragedies, Tinné did not wish to return to Europe. Her half-brother bought her a yacht named the *Seagull*, and she traveled throughout the Mediterranean on it with the crew dressed in Arab uniforms that she had designed herself. For a while she lived in Cairo. In 1867 she settled in Algiers, capital of the French colony of Algeria. There she decided to become the first European woman to cross the Sahara to visit the city of Timbuktu.

She organized an expedition made up of two Dutch soldiers and her large retinue of servants. They set out from the port of Tripoli in what is now Libya in January 1869. They reached Marzuq, in the Fezzan region of southern Libya in March. Tinné was ill, and they stayed in Marzuq until the middle of July. Once recovered, she chose a Tuareg chief to guide her across the desert. Her expedition left with a band of Tuareg headed for Ghat. At the small oasis of Aberjoudj, on August 1, 1869, the Tuareg fell upon Tinné and killed her and most of her entourage. Word of her death did not get back to Tripoli until September 20. The Turkish governor organized an expedition to track down the killers, which was also able to recover part of her possessions.

Where to learn more

There is one fairly recent biography of Tinné in English: Penelope Gladstone, *Travels of Alexine: Alexine Tinné, 1835-1869* (London: John Murray, 1970).

Tinné has received considerable attention in the collective biographies of women explorers of the 19th century: Mignon Rittenhouse, *Seven Women Explorers* (Philadelphia: J.B. Lippincott, 1964); Dea Birkett, *Spinsters Abroad: Victorian Lady Explorers* (London: Basil Blackwell, 1989); and Marion Tinling, *Women into the Unknown: A Sourcebook on Women Explorers and Travelers* (New York: Greenwood Press, 1989).

Henri de Tonty

(1650? - 1704)

Henri de Tonty was a Frenchman who accompanied La Salle on his trip down the Mississippi River, made several trips on the river himself, and led expeditions throughout the Mississippi Valley.

Henri de Tonty was born in Italy. His father was forced to leave Italy after an unsuccessful revolt against Spain and settled in France. In 1668-1669 Tonty served as a cadet in the French army and then spent four years as midshipman on French naval vessels. He lost his right arm in a battle with the Spanish. At the end of the Dutch war in 1678 he returned to the French court and received an appointment to serve as lieutenant to **René-Robert Cavelier de La Salle** who had been charged with exploring the Mississippi River.

Having arrived at La Salle's headquarters at Fort Frontenac (Kingston, Ontario) in the fall of 1678, Tonty was sent to the Niagara River to take charge of building a boat for the expedition and a supply post (Fort Conti). He was then sent out to hunt down some of La Salle's men who had not returned from a trading mission and caught up with them at Michilimackinac on August 27, 1679.

Tonty left Sault Ste. Marie on October 5, 1679 to meet up with La Salle at the St. Joseph River in southern Michigan. There he helped him to construct Fort Miami. They then went to the Illinois River on the other side of Lake Michigan and started construction of Fort Crèvecoeur near Peoria, Illinois in January 1680. From there La Salle went back east, leaving Tonty in charge with instructions to build another fort upstream at Starved Rock. While there the men at Fort Crèvecoeur mutinied, and Tonty was forced to take refuge in a village of the Illinois tribe with five supporters. The village was attacked by Iroquois warriors on September 10, 1680, and Tonty was wounded and forced to leave the area.

On their way back north Tonty rediscovered the portage between the Chicago River and the Des Plaines River that was to be a main passage for traders for many years and was the site of the city of Chicago. It had been seen by **Louis Jolliet** and **Jacques Marquette** seven years earlier. While traveling up Lake Michigan, Tonty's canoe was wrecked on November 1, 1680. He and his men survived on "wild garlic" from under the snow for two weeks until they stumbled upon a village of the Potawatomi tribe, where they spent the winter.

In early June 1681, La Salle and Tonty were reunited at Michilimackinac. They traveled together to Montreal to get further support for their expedition. They then returned to Fort Miami on the St. Joseph River. On December 27 Tonty set out with most of the expedition across the Chicago portage. They were joined by La Salle on January 6, 1682 and started out on their trip down the Illinois and Mississippi Rivers. They reached the mouth of the river in the Gulf of Mexico on April 7.

On the return trip up the Mississippi, La Salle became ill and Tonty traveled on ahead to take care of supplies. He reached the Chicago portage by the end of June and Michilimackinac on July 22. La Salle arrived there in September; he went back to Canada and sent Tonty to Fort Miami to build a new fort farther up the St. Joseph River. Tonty ignored his instructions and went instead to Starved Rock on the Illinois where he built Fort St. Louis. He traveled throughout the surrounding country persuading the Native Americans to bring their furs to trade with the new French post. He fought off an Iroquois attack in the spring of 1684.

In the meantime, La Salle had run into political difficulties in Quebec and France. Tonty left Fort St. Louis on May 23, 1684 to go back to Montreal to help sort out the problems. By the time he got to Quebec La Salle was back in favor, and Tonty was ordered west once more. In November, 1685 he heard that La Salle had started out on his large expedition to find the mouth of the Mississippi from the sea. On February 16, 1686 Tonty left Fort St. Louis with a party of 25 Frenchmen and 4 Native Americans to meet up with La Salle at the mouth of the Mississippi.

When Tonty arrived on the Gulf of Mexico during the second week of April, there was no sign of La Salle. However, certain of the local Native Americans reported seeing European ships sailing west along the coast. Tonty sent canoes along the coast but could not find La Salle's ships—they had sailed on to Matagorda Bay in Texas. At that point, Tonty wanted to sail along the coast to New York and then up the Hudson to Montreal. His men convinced him, however, to return the way they had come: up the Mississippi.

Years later, in 1699, members of the French expedition to found Louisiana were shown a letter in French by one of the chiefs of the Taensas tribe. It was dated April 20, 1686 and had been left by Tonty for La Salle.

On his return, Tonty was instructed to go to Montreal where he was put in charge of a campaign against the Iroquois. He went back to Fort St. Louis, gathered a war party of Illinois and then went up to Michilimackinac where he met up with his cousin, the

Sieur Dulhut. Together they led a party east to Niagara where they captured 60 Englishmen and some of their Iroquois allies who had been on the way to attack Michilimackinac.

For the next two years, Tonty managed his trading post at Fort St. Louis. Then in September 1689 one of the survivors of the Matagorda Bay colony arrived to tell about La Salle's failed expedition and the murder of the explorer. Tonty immediately set out to try to reach the survivors of the colony in Texas. He did this on his own initiative and was the only one who concerned himself with their fate. Neither the government in France or in Canada tried to rescue them. However, Tonty never made it—starving and short of ammunition he was forced to turn back not far from the present-day town of Crockett in East Texas.

For the next few years, Tonty occupied himself with his fur-trading business. He was granted La Salle's trading concessions and built a new fort near Peoria, Illinois. In 1695 he was granted permission to trade with the Assiniboin tribe north of Lake Superior. He left Michilimackinac on August 8, 1695 and traveled far to the north into what is now Manitoba. He heard about the victory of Iberville over the English in Hudson Bay in June 1696 and may have gotten as far as Hudson Bay himself.

In 1698 King Louis XIV decided to found a colony on the Gulf of Mexico and to control the Mississippi from its mouth. This was the beginning of Louisiana. Tonty was told to cooperate in its founding and guided a party of Jesuit priests as far as the Arkansas River on Christmas, 1698. The following year he left the Illinois country and settled at Fort Mississippi (near Phoenix, Louisiana, downstream from New Orleans). In 1700 he went on an expedition up the Red River as far as present Natchitoches. In March 1702 he led the French side in trade talks with the Choctaw and Chickasaw tribes north of Mobile, Alabama (the first capital of French Louisiana). He led a campaign against the Alabamon tribe in 1703.

In 1704 a French ship arrived in Mobile carrying young unmarried French girls who were to be married to the new colonists in Louisiana. Tonty was on hand to meet the ship and contracted yellow fever, which it turned out was also being carried on the ship. He died from the disease in Mobile on September 6, 1704.

Where to learn more

Because of Tonty's close association with La Salle, all of the references for that entry include much information on Tonty as well. In addition, see Louise Kellogg, *Early Narratives of the Northwest* (New York: 1917); E.R. Murphy, *Henry de Tonty, Fur Trader of the Mississippi* (Baltimore: The Johns Hopkins University Press, 1941); and "The Voyages of Tonty in North America, 1678-1704" *Mid-America*, vol. 26 (1944), pp. 255-297. The famous American historian Francis Parkman gives a very vivid history of the French exploration of North America in *Pioneers of France in the New World* (Boston: 1897, with many subsequent editions), although many of his prejudices and attitudes now seem old-fashioned.

Luis Vaez de Torres

(? - 1613?)

Luis Vaez de Torres was a Spanish navigator who was the first to sail through the strait named after him that separates Australia and New Guinea.

Luis Vaez de Torres was a Spanish navigator. Nothing is known about his life until he was signed up to serve as captain of the second of two ships that **Pedro Fernandez de Quiros** took with him to found a Spanish colony in the Marquesas Islands in 1605. In fact, that expedition missed the Marquesas entirely and ended up on the north coast of the large island of Espiritu Santo in Vanuatu. They landed there on May 1, 1606 and stayed until the first week of June. Then Quiros abruptly decided to abandon the colony and announced an immediate departure. The two ships set sail on June 8 with Quiros in command of the flagship and with Spanish nobleman Don Diego de Prado y Tovar as nominal captain of the second ship, the *Almiranta*. In fact, Torres was the real sailor and took command.

After trying for a couple of days to sail out of the great bay, Quiros signaled to Torres that they would return to harbor and wait for better winds. The next morning when Torres woke up he found that Quiros was gone. (He sailed alone to Mexico.) There was no explanation for this sudden desertion. He stayed there for fifteen days waiting for Quiros to return. During that time he sailed around a good deal of Espiritu Santo and established that it was an island and not part of a continental landmass.

When it became clear that Quiros was not going to return, Torres opened up the sealed orders that he had received from the Viceroy of Peru to find out what he was supposed to do on his return trip. These commanded the members of the expedition to try to make for the island of New Guinea and from there to head for the Philippines, where there were Spanish settlements. Torres sailed out into the Coral Sea and then turned northwest until he encountered the islands of the Louisiade Archipelago off the southeastern tip of New Guinea. His aim was to sail along the northern coast of New Guinea, which would, he knew, take him to the Moluccas Islands and from there to the Philippines. But, he later wrote, "I could not weather the east point, so I coasted along to the westward on the south side."

No European had ever sailed along this coast before, and no one knew whether New Guinea was an island or part of a much larger continent. Beyond that, Torres was sailing in very danger-ous seas, the land between New Guinea and the northern tip of the Cape York Peninsula of Australia is full of reefs, small islands and shifting currents. But Torres was lucky, there is a 90-mile-wide passage between New Guinea and Australia, and Torres made his way through it. At 11°S Torres spotted "some very large islands and more were seen to the south." This is now generally taken to mean that he saw the mainland of Australia. If so, that means that he was the second European to have done so, following **Willem Janszoon** who had spotted it farther west about five or six months before Torres.

Torres sailed along the south coast of New Guinea, which he named "Magna Margarita" stopping at various points to take possession of the land in the name of the King of Spain. He was able to get directions for sailing to Ternate, one of the chief islands of the Moluccas, or "Spice Islands." From there he turned north and reached Manila in the Philippines on May 22, 1607.

It appears that Torres died in Manila no later than 1613: in that year there is a letter from his companion Diego de Prado referring to his death. Before his death, however, Torres wrote an account of his voyage to send back to the King of Spain and, interestingly, to Quiros, who had made his way back to Spain. In these reports, Torres told them that New Guinea was an island and that it was possible to sail around it from the south. The Spanish government did not want the rest of the world to know this valuable information and kept it hidden. However, from some maps that appeared over the next hundred years it would appear that Quiros did pass the information along to certain persons.

This information was, however, never put to practical use, and Torres himself was forgotten. He was resurrected in 1762 when the British hydrographer Alexander Dalrymple found a copy of Torres's report in Manila. He then publicized it and named the channel between Australia and New Guinea Torres Strait. The next European to sail through Torres Strait was **James Cook** on his first voyage to the South Pacific in 1769.

Where to learn more

Torres' own journals have been published in English: Henry N. Stevens, ed. *New Light on the Discovery of Australia As Revealed by the Journal of Captain Don Diego Prado y Tovar* (London: Hakluyt Society, 1930).

An excellent book that presents pretty much all the information known about Torres and his voyage is: Brett Hilder, *The Voyage of Torres: The Discovery of the Southern Coastline of New Guinea and Torres Strait by Captain Luis Vaez de Torres in 1606* (St. Lucia, Queensland: University of Queensland Press, 1980). Three other books that include extensive material on Torres are: J.C. Beaglehole, *The Exploration of the Pacific* (Stanford: Stanford University Press, 1966); Colin Jack-Hinton, *The Search for the Islands of Solomon, 1567-1838* (Oxford: Clarendon Press, 1969); and O.H.K. Spate, *The Spanish Lake* (Minneapolis: University of Minnesota Press, 1979).

Andrés de Urdaneta

(1508 - 1568)

Andrés de Urdaneta was a Spaniard who took part in the second voyage around the world and then, many years later, pioneered the sailing route between the Philippines and Mexico.

Following the return of the Spanish expedition that had started out under **Ferdinand Magellan** and had eventually sailed all the way around the world, the Spanish king Charles V sent out another expedition to follow its route. This was led by Garcia Jofre de Loaysa with Sebastian de Elcano (who had commanded the first expedition following Magellan's death) as chief pilot. Also aboard was del Cano's assistant or servant, Andrés de Urdaneta, then aged 17 years, from the little Basque town of Villafranca de Oria.

Loaysa's expedition was a disaster. Of the seven ships that left Spain on August 24, 1525, two deserted in the Atlantic, one was wrecked at the southern tip of South America, and the rest were separated once they reached the Pacific. Of these four, one was disabled and traveled to the west coast of Mexico, one was wrecked in the Tuamotu Islands, and another on Mindanao. Only the flagship, *Santa Maria de la Victoria*, survived. However, aboard it, Loaysa died on July 30, 1526 and del Cano died five days later.

The *Santa Maria* reached Guam on July 30, 1526, where it found a cabin boy left from Magellan's expedition. Two other commanders died, but the ship finally made it to Tidore, in the "Spice Islands" on January 1, 1527. There, the Spanish sailors immediately began warring with the Portuguese who were established on the neighboring island of Ternate. The Spanish were aided by the arrival of the *Florida* sailing from New Spain, under the command of **Alvaro de Saavedra**, and were able to hold on to their position on Tidore. Saavedra left, however, in May 1529, leaving Urdaneta and some of the Spanish behind. They eventually realized that they would never prevail and surrendered to the Portuguese at the end of 1529. By this time, there were only 17 surviving Spaniards.

Urdaneta continued trading under the auspices of the Portuguese until February 1534 when word was received that Charles V had sold his rights in the Moluccas (the "Spice Islands") to the Portuguese. Urdaneta then set out for Europe via Java, Malacca, and Cochin in south India. He reached Lisbon in mid-1536, from where he was summoned by the King of Spain back to his native country. He wrote an account of the expedition and presented it to the king. He was one of only a handful of survivors of the Loaysa expedition that had left Spain 11 years previously. This small group was the second to have traveled around the world.

In the following years, Urdaneta went to New Spain where he occupied several government positions. In 1553 he had a spiritual crisis and retired to an Augustinian monastery in Mexico, away from the world. In 1556 Philip II ascended to the throne of Spain and again decided to see if there were some way for the Spanish to get a part of the spice trade by sailing west from Mexico. Until that time the various expeditions of Loaysa, Saavedra, and Lopez de Villalobos had been unable to find a return route in face of the prevailing easterly winds. The King wrote a letter dated September 24, 1559 to Urdaneta asking him, as the leading Spanish expert on the Pacific crossing, if he would give up the monastic life and help with a new expedition. Urdaneta agreed.

At Urdaneta's recommendation, the leader of the new expedition was Miguel Lopez de Legazpi, a former mayor of Mexico City. Because of various difficulties, the fleet of four ships put together under Urdaneta's overall control was not ready to leave Mexico for five years. It sailed from Acapulco on November 21, 1564. It was Urdaneta who decided on Acapulco as the port for the expedition, thereby making it the center of the Pacific trade for another 250 years. The expedition was made up of 150 sailors, mostly Mexicans, 200 soldiers, and five Augustinian monks.

One hundred miles out of port, the ships' instructions were opened. They were directed to go to the Philippines and found a Spanish colony there. Once this was done, Urdaneta was instructed to return as quickly as possible to Mexico. The Philippines were chosen because the Spanish had made several landings there already, and they were not under the control of the Portuguese, as were the Moluccas. In early January 1565, they sailed by some of the islands of the northern Marshalls and reached the Marianas on January 22. Urdaneta took possession of them for Spain on January 26.

The Spanish fleet arrived in the Philippines on February 13, 1565 and traveled to Samar, Bohol, and Cebu. On April 27, 1565 the Spanish anchored off the island of Cebu and bombarded it with cannons. After the local residents fled, they went ashore and took possession of it in the name of the King of Spain and founded the city of San Miguel, today Cebu City, the second largest in the Philippines. Legazpi took charge of the conquest of the Philippines for Spain and became its first governor.

Meanwhile, Urdaneta was charged with finding the return route to Mexico. Three weeks after the founding of San Miguel, he sailed from there on June 1, 1565 in the *San Pedro*. In order to avoid the northeast trade winds (which are adverse winds when sailing the northern Pacific in this direction), he sailed farther north than his predecessors through an area known for variable winds and typhoons. He sailed past the small island of Parece Vela in the Philippine Sea, going as far north as 42°N, where westerlies predominate and used these winds to sail across the Pacific. He sighted the Channel Islands off the coast of California on September 18 and then sailed down the coast to Acapulco, which he reached on October 8, 1565.

The route pioneered by Urdaneta was to be the route of the famous "Manila galleons," which traveled to and from Mexico and the Philippines during the entire period of Spanish rule in Mexico until 1821. Upon his return, Urdaneta retired once again to his monastery where he died a few years later in 1568.

Where to learn more

The main source for this account of Urdaneta is O.H.K. Spate, *The Spanish Lake* (Minneapolis: University of Minnesota Press, 1979), which contains extensive footnotes and bibliography. A good study of the Spanish exploration of the Pacific in the 16th century, with helpful maps, is Carlos Prieto, *El Océano Pacífico: navegantes españoles del siglo XVI* (Madrid: 1985).

Pedro de Valdivia

(1500? - 1553)

Pedro de Valdivia was a Spanish conquistador who established a colony in Chile and explored most of the country.

Pedro de Valdivia was born in the Spanish province of Extremadura, home of many of the *conquistadores*, in either 1500 or 1501. He fought in the Spanish army at the Battle of Pavia in 1525 and then served under **Francisco Pizarro** in the conquest of Peru, taking Pizarro's side in the civil war with **Diego de Almagro**. As a reward for his services, Pizarro named him lieutenant-governor of Chile and sent him to conquer the coast south of Peru. Valdivia had to dispute this grant with Pedro Sanchez de la Hoz, who had been granted the same concession by King Charles V of Spain.

Valdivia led a Spanish expedition into Chile in January 1539. He crossed the Andes and descended down to the deserts at Arequipa, Moquegua, Tacna, and Tarapacá. Upon reaching the large and very dry Atacama Desert, Valdivia met Sanchez de la Hoz and his supporters, and the two struggled for control. Valdivia won and his adversary agreed to serve under him. The Spaniards crossed the Atacama with the loss of only one man and then entered the fertile valleys of Copiapó and Coquimbo. Farther to the south, they came upon a bay and a beautiful valley with flowering almond trees. Valdivia named this the Valley of Paradise, Valparaíso, which is now the site of Chile's chief seaport.

South of Valparaíso is the Maile River, and Valdivia followed it inland to reach its tributary, the Mapocho. There on February 12, 1541, on the rock of Santa Lucia that formed a natural fortress, he founded the city of Santiago del Nuevo Extremo, which was to be the center of his colony and is today Chile's capital. The Native Americans were hostile to the Spanish and did everything they could to drive them away.

In August 1541, Valdivia left the city to lead an expedition into the surrounding countryside. While he was away, Native Americans attacked Santiago on September 11, 1541. There were only 50 Spaniards in the town but under the leadership of Valdivia's lieutenant Alonso de Monroy they were able to fight off the attack. It is said that one of the major reasons for the victory was Inés Suarez, the only Spanish woman in the colony and Valdivia's mistress. She is reported to have slain six captive chieftains single-handedly and thrown their heads back at the attackers. She then led a counterattack by Spanish cavalry dressed in a knight's coat of mail.

On his return, Valdivia sent Monroy back to Peru in January 1542 to try to get reinforcements. Soon after he left, Monroy was captured by Native Americans, and four of his five companions were killed. He was allowed to live on condition that he teach the local chief how to ride on one of the two horses that the Spaniards had with them. Monroy and his companion had managed to smuggle a knife in their clothes and took the opportunity of the equestrian lesson to use it to kill the chief and make their escape. Even though they had no supplies, they were able to cross the Atacama and make their way to Cuzco. There, Monroy obtained supplies and returned to Valparaíso in a ship along the coast.

This and further reinforcements allowed Valdivia to expand his colony. In 1544-1546 he traveled to and conquered all of the country north of the Maule River. During this time, the Spanish both in Chile and Peru were fighting among themselves to see who would possess the spoils of their victories. On one such

Pedro de Valdivia. The Granger Collection, New York.

occasion, Valdivia returned by ship to Peru in 1548 and did not get back to Chile until April 1549. On his return, he mounted an expedition to the south in January 1550. Having crossed the Maule River, which was the Spanish line of defense, he was confronted by the fierce Araucanian tribe who jealously guarded their independence. In the bloody Battle of Andalien on February 22, 1550, every Spanish soldier was either killed or wounded but managed to drive off a much larger army of Araucanians.

Soon after, at the harbor of Talcahuano, Valdivia founded the city of Concepción, Chile's second-largest. He used this as a base to continue south, founding small Spanish posts all along the way—Imperial, Villarica, Arauco, Osorno, Tucapel, and Puren. The last one, and largest, was named after himself, Valdivia, founded in February 1552. Also in 1552 Valdivia sent an expedition from Concepción under the command of Francisco de Villagra to see if he could find a way to the tip of the continent, to the Straits of Magellan, discovered in 1520 by **Ferdinand Magellan**. Villagra traveled over the Andes and saw either the Río Negro or the Río Colorado, in what is now the Patagonia region of Argentina, but was forced to turn back because of lack of food.

In the meantime, the Araucanians took advantage of the dispersal of the Spanish forces to rise up and destroy the fortress at Tucapel. They then organized themselves around Lautaro, a young Araucanian who had been a slave to Valdivia but had escaped. When Valdivia returned at the head of the Spanish forces at the end of December 1552, Lautaro and the Araucanians were waiting for them. In overwhelming numbers they fell upon the Spanish and killed all of them. Valdivia himself was captured and tortured to death, some say by pouring molten gold down his throat to indicate the disdain the Indians felt for the Spanish passion for the precious metal. Warfare between Spanish and Araucanians continued for another 250 years.

Where to learn more

There is a very good biography of Valdivia from a number of years ago: R.B. Cunninghame Graham, *Pedro de Valdivia: Conqueror of Chile* (London: William Heinemann, 1926). This has now been superseded by two more recent studies, both of them excellent: H.R.S. Pocock, *The Conquest of Chile* (New York: Stein and Day, 1967) and Ida Stevenson Weldon Vernon, *Pedro de Valdivia, Conquistador of Chile* (Austin: University of Texas Institute of Latin American Studies, 1946).

George Vancouver

(1757 - 1798)

George Vancouver was a British naval officer who was in charge of an expedition that explored and mapped the coast of northwestern North America.

George Vancouver was born in the town of King's Lynn in Norfolk, England on June 22, 1757, the son of a customs official. He entered the Royal Navy in 1772 at the age of 13 as a "young gentleman" or midshipman candidate. Through family connections he was able to get an appointment to serve with Captain **James Cook** on the *Resolution* on Cook's second voyage to the Pacific from 1772 to 1775. It was during this voyage that Cook approached the continent of Antarctica, and the teenaged Vancouver hung off the front of the ship so that for years he could truthfully claim to have been farther south than any other person.

Vancouver sailed as midshipman on board the *Discovery* during Cook's third and last voyage, which left England in July 1776 at just the time that the United States was declaring independence. Vancouver was a party to the events that resulted in Cook's death on February 14, 1779 on the island of Hawaii. The day before he had helped rescue another crew member who was attacked by a group of Hawaiians. He was a member of the crew that was sent on shore to retrieve Cook's body after he was killed. Vancouver returned to England on the *Discovery* in October 1780 and was promoted to lieutenant on October 19, 1780.

During the Napoleonic Wars between Britain and France, Vancouver carried out various assignments in the North Sea and the Caribbean. He fought in a sea battle in the West Indies in April 1782. In 1789 he left active duty in the navy but was then appointed to be second in command of an expedition to the South Pacific. He took charge of the ship being built for the expedition, which was named the *Discovery*.

At about this time, word reached England that several British ships had been taken by the Spanish in Nootka Sound on the west coast of what is now Vancouver Island in British Columbia. However, at the conclusion of hostilities between Spain and Great Britain, Spain signed the Nootka Convention in which it gave up its claims to the northwestern coast of North America to the British. Rather than going to the South Pacific, Vancouver was sent to the Pacific Northwest to take formal possession for the British and to make a survey of the coast. He sailed from England in the *Discovery*, accompanied by the *Chatham*, on April 1, 1791.

George Vancouver. The Granger Collection, New York.

Vancouver sailed eastward from England, going around the Cape of Good Hope in South Africa and crossing the Indian Ocean to Australia. He explored along the western coast of Australia and discovered and named King George's Sound, Mount Gardner, and Cape Hood. He then went on to New Zealand and filled in information about that coast that Captain Cook had left out. From New Zealand, Vancouver went to Tahiti, which he reached on December 30, 1791.

Sailing north from Tahiti, Vancouver stopped in Hawaii in March 1792. He arrived at a time when there was a war going on between the islands, which later resulted in all of them being united under the rule of King Kamehameha. Vancouver sailed on to the coast of California, arriving about 110 miles north of San Francisco Bay on April 18. His instructions indicated that he was

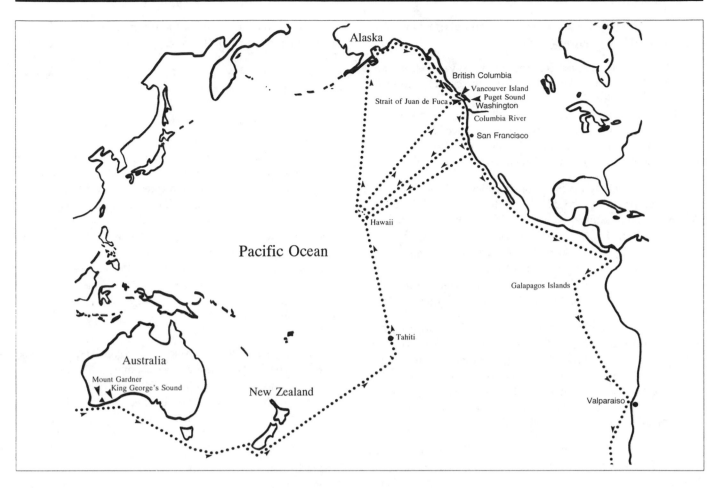

Vancouver's travels in the Pacific Ocean, 1791-1795.

to continue the search for the western entrance to a Northwest Passage between the Atlantic and Pacific.

As Vancouver made his way north along the west coast of North America, he noted the discharge from a large river off a point that had been named Cape Disappointment. He did not stop to investigate and thereby missed being the first European to see the Columbia River. Two days later he encountered an American ship, the *Columbia*. Its captain, Robert Gray, reported that he had just visited the large river that he named after his ship. This was later used as justification for American claims to what are now the states of Washington and Oregon.

On May 1, 1792, Vancouver entered the Strait of Juan de Fuca that separates Vancouver Island from the mainland. In the following months he and his men carefully surveyed the coasts of what are now Washington state and British Columbia, including the complex waterways of Puget Sound (named after an officer on his ship) and the Strait of Georgia. He also saw and named Mount Rainier after an officer he had served with in the West Indies. At the end of May, Vancouver claimed formal possession of the Pacific Northwest for Great Britain, naming the country New Georgia in honor of King George III.

Vancouver headed north through the Strait of Georgia, stopping at a large bay that he named Burrard Inlet after a fellow officer. This is the site of the city of Vancouver, British Columbia. On the afternoon of August 6, 1792, near the northern end of Vancouver Island, the *Discovery* ran aground in the fog. It was possible to float it off during high tide that night with only minimal damage. The next day the *Discovery* entered Queen Charlotte's Sound, thereby showing that Vancouver Island was an island and having been the first European ship to negotiate the treacherous waters between it and the mainland.

On August 28 Vancouver sailed into Nootka Sound where there was a small Spanish fort commanded by Don Francisco de la Bodega y Quadra. Quadra and Vancouver soon developed friendly relations but came to a stalemate over the manner in which Vancouver was to carry out his instructions—to take possession of the Spanish settlement. Vancouver sent a ship back to London to ask for further directions. In the meantime, Quadra proposed that they mark their friendship in some manner. Vancouver thereupon proposed naming the large island he had just circumnavigated "Quadra and Vancouver Island." This was the name that it was known by until the mid-19th century when it was shortened to its present name. There is now a smaller Quadra Island in the Strait of Georgia.

While waiting for instructions from England, Vancouver continued his explorations. Going south along the coast he stopped at Gray' Harbor, first visited by his American competitor. At the mouth of the Columbia, he sent a party ashore under Captain William Broughton to investigate, and they traveled 100 miles upstream to the site of Vancouver, Washington. Broughton also named Mount Hood after a British admiral.

Vancouver anchored in San Francisco Bay on November 14, 1792, and proceeded to Monterey, the capital of Spanish California, where negotiations continued for the next two months. Vancouver then set out to find the Los Majos Islands that had been reported by earlier Spanish navigators. These were probably early sightings of the Hawaiian Islands, and that is where Vancouver landed in February 1793. He was visited by the great King Kamehameha, who took him to the site of Cook's murder.

Vancouver returned to America in April 1793. Traveling up the coast of British Columbia he sailed into Bella Coola inlet just seven weeks before **Alexander Mackenzie** reached the same spot on July 20 by traveling overland from Canada. The combined results of the Vancouver and Mackenzie expeditions showed that there was no Northwest Passage around or through North America south of the Arctic.

During the next several months, Vancouver charted the islands and waters of northern British Columbia, the Inside Passage of Alaska, and the Queen Charlotte Islands. At Revillagigedo Island in southern Alaska, he got involved in a quarrel with a group of Native Americans and turned his guns on them, killing as many as ten. He then returned south, stopping at Monterey, where he was not well received by the Spanish viceroy, José de Arrillaga, and going as far as Baja California.

In early January 1794 Vancouver returned to Hawaii. During this visit, on February 25, 1794, he accepted the offer of King Kamehameha to turn his country over to the British (which was never acted upon by the British government). He then headed north and spent the following months charting Cook Inlet (site of Anchorage) and the southern coast of Alaska. He completed his survey on August 18, 1794. On the way south he stopped at Nootka and Monterey, where he learned that the Nootka dispute

had once again been settled in the European capitals. He then returned home by way of Valparaiso, Chile, Cape Horn, and St. Helena Island in the South Atlantic. He joined a British convoy in the Atlantic because France and Britain were once again at war. He reached England on October 15, 1795.

In his absence Vancouver had been promoted to captain, and he took advantage of the opportunity that his increased pay gave him to spend the next few years writing about his voyage. He retired to the village of Petersham a few miles up the Thames from London. These years were marred by a public dispute with one of his former junior officers, Baron Camelford, a relative of the British Prime Minister, William Pitt. Camelford accused Vancouver of unjustly punishing him during the Pacific voyage and of general charges of brutality and tyranny. He challenged Vancouver to a duel, which he refused. The two ran into each other on a London street in September 1796, and the younger man beat Vancouver severely with a cane. There appears to have been an investigation, but its results are not known.

Vancouver had been suffering from some kind of chronic illness for a while. Modern investigators think it may have been Graves' disease, a hyperthyroid condition. He had just corrected the last proofs of his book when he died on May 10, 1798 in Petersham, England. The book appeared a few months after his death.

Where to learn more

As noted, Vancouver wrote a book about his circumnavigation of the globe: *A Voyage of Discovery to the North Pacific Ocean and Round the World*, 3 vols. (London: C.J. and J. Robinson and J. Edwards, 1798). Other original sources for the same expedition are: Bern Anderson, ed. "The Vancouver Expedition: Peter Puget's Journal of the Exploration of Puget Sound, May 7-June 11, 1792," *Pacific Northwest Quarterly*, vol. 30 (April 1939), pp. 195-295; William R. Broughton, *A Voyage of Discovery to the North Pacific Ocean* (London: T. Cadell and W. Davies, 1804); and C.F. Newcombe, ed. *Menzies' Journal of Vancouver's Voyage, April to October, 1792* (Victoria, B.C.: W.H. Cullin, 1923).

Later studies include: Edmond S. Meany, *Vancouver's Discovery of Puget Sound* (New York: Macmillan, 1907); George Godwin, *Vancouver: A Life* (New York: D. Appleton & Co., 1931); Henry R. Wagner, *Cartography of the Northwest Coast of America to the Year 1800*, 2 vols. (Berkeley: University of California Press, 1937); and Bern Anderson, *Surveyor of the Sea: The Life and Voyages of Captain George Vancouver* (Seattle: University of Washington Press, 1960). The last named is quite complete but seems to want to justify every one of Vancouver's actions.

Ludovico di Varthema

(early 16th century)

Ludovico di Varthema was a Italian adventurer who was the second European to enter Mecca and traveled throughout Arabia and south Asia.

Ludovico di Varthema was an Italian native of the city of Bologna, although he liked to refer to himself as a "Gentleman of Rome." We do not know when he was born or anything about his early life. Our knowledge of his adventures comes from the history he wrote later, *The Travels of Ludovico di Varthema.*

In 1503 Varthema and a certain number of companions left Rome and traveled across the Mediterranean to Egypt. He stayed for a short time in Alexandria and Cairo and then traveled on to Beirut and the Syrian capital of Damascus. He seems to have parted company with his fellow travelers and was able to join a caravan of pilgrims headed for the Muslim holy city of Mecca. He disguised himself as a Mameluke, a European soldier in the army of the Ottoman Caliph, and pretended to be a Muslim, since only believers in Islam are allowed to enter Mecca.

Varthema's caravan left Damascus on April 8, 1503. He traveled through the Arabian peninsula via Meda'in Salih, Khaibar, where he went through a settlement of Jews, and Medina. He reached Mecca on May 18, 1503, making him the second non-Muslim European to see the city after **Pero da Covilhão**'s visit in 1492. Varthema's description of the city corresponds to that of later travelers and proves that he did see the sights that he reported on. He described the Great Mosque, which contained the Kaaba, "The Cube," the holiest place in Islam.

After remaining in Mecca for 20 days, Varthema deserted from the Mameluke guard. He was risking exposure as a Christian but happened upon an Arab merchant, who wanted Varthema's help in smuggling spices without paying the required taxes. He hid Varthema in his house until he was able to escape to the port city of Jeddah. From there he found a ship on its way to Persia. In Aden in what is now Yemen on the south coast of Arabia, he and the ship's company got involved in a fight with the local inhabitants that landed him in irons for 55 days. From there he was taken to the town of Rada in the interior to be interrogated by the Sultan.

After a 160-mile camel journey to Rada that took eight days, Varthema was unable to convince the Sultan that he was not a Christian spy. The Sultan ordered Varthema to recite the Muslim creed ("There is no God but God, and Mohammed is His Messenger") in Arabic. Unfortunately, "whether such was the will of God, or through the fear which has seized me," he was unable to reply. He was put into prison; a short while later the Sultan left with his troops to attack the city of Sana'a, the present-day capital of Yemen.

In prison Varthema pretended to be insane and was able to capture the interest of one of the wives of the Sultan. She did not believe in his madness. "The following day she had prepared for me a bath according to their custom, with many perfumes, and continued these caresses for twelve days. Afterwards, she began to come down to visit me every night at three or four o'clock." However, Varthema wrote that he resisted the woman's offers, saying, "I am already in chains. I do not want to lose my head."

After the Sultan's return, his wife helped Varthema to escape by arranging a trip to Aden on a pretext. While waiting for a ship to travel on to India, he wandered through the mountainous interior of southwest Arabia, going as far as the walled city of Sana'a, 7,500 feet up in the mountains.

Leaving from Aden, Varthema's ship was blown off course, and he landed on the coast of Ethiopia. From there he went to Persia, where he became the traveling companion of a wealthy Persian merchant, Khadhar Djauher. They journeyed together through western India and touched on Burma, Thailand and the East Indies. He left the merchant in India and joined the Portuguese who had just established a fort at Goa. He joined in an assault on a town near Calicut and then served as a business agent in Cochin.

Varthema returned to Europe in 1508, landing first in Lisbon. In November 1508 he gave a public lecture on his travels in Venice. The warm response he received encouraged him to write his famous travels, which first appeared in 1510. A second edition was published in Milan in 1519, with an introduction by a prominent Italian noblewoman. That is the last word we have of Varthema, and we do not know when or where he died.

Where to learn more

There have been several English-language editions of Varthema's story of his travels. Probably the most accessible is G.P. Badger, editor, *The Itinerary of Ludovico di Varthema of Bologna*, translated from the 1510 Italian edition by John Winter Jones (London: The Argonaut Press, 1928). There is another version in an appendix to Sir Richard Burton's *Pilgrimage to Al-Medinah and Meccah* (1st edition, London: 1893). Burton was an adventurer much in the mold of Varthema.

There are entertaining accounts of Varthema in Paul Herrmann, *The Great Age of Discovery* (New York: Harper & Brothers, 1956) and Zahra Freeth and H.V.F. Winstone, *Explorers of Arabia: From the Renaissance to the End of the Victorian Era* (London: George Allen & Unwin, 1978).

Giovanni da Verrazzano

(1485-1528)

Giovanni da Verrazzano was a native of Italy who sailed for the King of France and was the first European to describe the east coast of North America.

Giovanni da Verrazzano came from an aristocratic family of the Chianti region of Tuscany in Italy. In about 1506-1507 he moved to Dieppe, a port on the northwest coast of France, in order to begin a career as a mariner. From there, he sailed to the eastern Mediterranean and may have traveled to Newfoundland in 1508. In 1523 a syndicate of Italian merchants in the French cities of Lyons and Rouen convinced the French king, François I, to sponsor a voyage to North America with Verrazzano as commander. The aim was to explore the coast from Florida to Newfoundland to see if the elusive passage to Asia could be found in these unexplored regions.

Verrazzano sailed from Dieppe in early 1524 in the ship *La Dauphine* accompanied by his younger brother Girolamo, a

Giovanni da Verrazzano. The Granger Collection, New York.

map maker. Verrazzano crossed the Atlantic and sighted land on March 1, 1524 at or near Cape Fear, North Carolina. After a short voyage southward, he turned back north and landed near Cape Hatteras on the Outer Banks of North Carolina. The Outer Banks form a sand bar separated from the mainland by Pamlico Sound. From his vantage point, Verrazzano could not see the mainland, and he gave way to some very wishful thinking—he imagined that the body of water on the other side of the narrow piece of land was the Pacific Ocean and the way to China. On the maps prepared by Girolamo, North America is a vast continent that tapers to a tiny narrow strip of land right at the coast of North Carolina.

Without finding a passage through what he thought was a narrow isthmus, Verrazzano continued his way north along the coast, probably stopping at Kitty Hawk, where he encountered a group of Native Americans and kidnapped a child. He continued north but missed the entrance to both the Chesapeake and Delaware Bays. On April 17, however, Verrazzano sailed into the Upper Bay of New York harbor, which he described in his Journal: "We found a very pleasant place, situated amongst certain little steep hills; from amidst the which hills there ran down into the sea a great stream of water (the Hudson River), which within the mouth was very deep, and from the sea to the mouth of same, with the tide, which we found to rise 8 foot, any great vessel laden may pass up." He anchored at the Narrows that were later named after him (as is the great suspension bridge that crosses from Brooklyn to Staten Island).

From New York harbor, Verrazzano sailed to the entrance of Narragansett Bay and named one of the islands Rhode Island because it had the shape of the Greek island in the eastern Mediterranean. Years later, Roger Williams, the founder of an English colony took up Verrazzano's name. Verrazzano anchored in the harbor that is today Newport and gave his crew a rest for a couple of weeks. Exploring parties from the ship went as far inland as the site of Pawtucket.

From Rhode Island Verrazzano sailed up the coast of Maine, sailed around Nova Scotia and made it as far north as Newfoundland before returning to Dieppe on July 8, 1524.

Verrazzano's report of his expedition, written for François I immediately after returning to France, is important because it gives us the first firsthand information we have about the eastern coast of North America and the Native Americans who lived there.

Verrazzano's next expedition, in 1527, was sponsored in part by Philippe de Chabot, admiral of France, because King François I was preparing for war in Italy and could not spare any ships. On this trip Verrazano traveled to the coast of Brazil and brought back a valuable cargo of logwood, which is used for making textile dyes.

Verrazzano's third voyage was designed to go back to the area of his original landfall in North America and search for a passage to the Pacific south of Cape Fear. He left France in the spring of 1528 and apparently ended up in the West Indies where he followed the chain of islands northward. He stopped at one of the islands, probably Guadeloupe, where he was taken by members of the hostile Carib tribe and killed. His ships then turned south and headed for Brazil where they obtained another cargo of logwood to take back to France.

Where to learn more

Verrazzano's letters telling of his discoveries were published by the Hakluyt Society in London in 1874. The book that has been called the "last word" on Verrazzano is L.C. Wroth, *The Voyages of Giovanni da Verrazzano* (New Haven: Yale University Press, 1970). An excellent and very readable account of Verrazzano's voyages is given by the great American historian Samuel Eliot Morison in two books *The European Discovery of America: The Northern Voyages* (Oxford University Press, 1971) and a shorter version in *The Great Explorers: The European Discovery of America* (Oxford University Press, 1978).

Amerigo Vespucci

(1451-1512)

Amerigo Vespucci was an Italian merchant who mounted two expeditions to the Americas, which were later named in his honor.

Amerigo Vespucci was born in Florence in 1451. He served as secretary to the Florentine ambassador to France, and then returned to Florence, where he became the manager of a trading firm owned by the Medici family, the rich and powerful rulers of Florence. In 1493 he set up a business for the Medici in Seville and then took it over himself. His business was to supply the provisions for the Spanish ships that were then sailing out of Seville on their great voyages of discovery. He is thought to have supplied the provisions for at least one, and maybe two, of the expeditions led by **Christopher Columbus**.

Vespucci was able to interest the court in his own expedition to the newly-found lands across the Atlantic and sailed from Cadiz

Amerigo Vespucci.

in southern Spain on May 18, 1499 with four ships. The expedition itself was commanded by **Alonso de Ojeda**, who had sailed with Columbus on his second voyage. Vespucci, who was not a mariner himself, was there as the representative of the financial interests backing the voyage.

When they reached the northern coast of South America after a very quick crossing of 24 days, Ojeda and Vespucci split up, and Vespucci headed south, allegedly being the first person to sight the coast of Brazil on June 27, 1499 and the first to sail into the mouth of the Amazon. He then sailed north to Trinidad and the coast of Venezuela. From there he went to the Spanish colony of Santo Domingo to replenish his supplies and then northward to the Bahamas, where he kidnapped 200 Native Americans to take back to Spain as slaves. He arrived in Cadiz in June 1500.

Vespucci was convinced that there was still a way to Asia, and he sailed again, this time in the service of Portugal, on May 13, 1501. During his crossing he met the ships of Pedro Cabral returning from their trip to Brazil and India. On this second trip, Vespucci is thought to have reached land near the eastern tip of Brazil, entered the harbor of Rio de Janeiro in the first week of January 1502, and then headed south. In Vespucci's account he claims to have gone as far south as what is now southern Argentina, but this is not generally believed, nor are reports of two other voyages he made to the Americas. The question as to whether Vespucci made two or four voyages to the "New World" has long kept scholars occupied.

Vespucci returned to Lisbon in June 1502 and proclaimed that he and his fellow voyagers had not explored outlying islands of Asia but had, in fact, discovered a continent previously unknown to Europeans lying between Europe and Asia. This was something that Columbus never wanted to admit.

In 1505 Vespucci was naturalized as a Spanish subject and from 1508 till his death in 1512 was pilot-major of the kingdom, in charge of compiling all the information about the new geographical knowledge.

Vespucci's name was given to two continents (North and South America) because of an inaccurate account of his travels published at St. Dié in Lorraine in France in 1507, in which he is represented as having discovered and reached the mainland in 1497. If that had been true he would in fact have beaten Columbus, who did not land on the mainland, on the Paria Peninsula of Venezuela, until August 1498. But Vespucci did not

actually land until 1499. By the time anyone realized this, the name had already stuck.

Whatever the truth about Vespucci's voyages, his accounts of them were widely believed in his own time. It even led the geographer Waldseemüller to regard him, rather than Columbus, as the discoverer of the great land mass in the west, and to suggest that it should be called America in honor of his expeditions.

Where to learn more

The controversial career of Amerigo Vespucci has generated a lot of scholarly studies. Original narratives can be found in *The First Four Voyages of Amerigo Vespucci, Reproduced in Facsimile, with a Translation* (London: Bernard Quantsch, 1893) and Sir Clements Markham, ed. *The Letters of Amerigo Vespucci and Other Documents Illustrative of His Career* (London: Hakluyt Society, 1894). These books accept Vespucci's claims to have made four voyages as does Germán Arciniegas in *Amerigo and the New World: the Life and Times of Amerigo Vespucci*, translated by Harriet de Onis (New York: Alfred A. Knopf, 1955), which is a good, popular biography.

More recent scholarly research tends to reject the claim of four voyages in favor of two. This includes Frederick Pohl, *Amerigo Vespucci: Pilot Major* (New York: Columbia University Press, 1944); and Arthur Davies, "The 'First' Voyage of Amerigo Vespucci in 1497-98," *Geographical Journal*, vol. 108 (September 1952). A summary of the arguments in favor of the two viewpoints can be found in G. Caraci, "The Vespucian Problems—What Point Have They Reached," *Imago Mundi*, vol. 18 (1964).

Viking

(1975 - 1980)

The U.S. Viking program landed two spacecraft on Mars that searched for signs of life on that planet.

The success of the *Mariner 9* mission in orbiting Mars encouraged American scientists to work on the Viking program with the aim of actually landing a spacecraft on the red planet.

The Viking probes consisted of an orbiter, much like those used in the Mariner program, and a lander. The orbiter carried two television cameras and infrared instruments for mapping the planet's thermal characteristics and for detecting atmospheric pressure. Most of the scientific instruments were in the lander. These were squat spacecraft powered by two radioactive heat sources set on three legs. A robot arm with a scoop for a hand was provided to pick up soil samples to be dropped in an analysis unit where life forms would be cultivated and detected by chemical means. A mini weather station was mounted on a short boom. An antenna provided direct contact with Earth, although most pictures and data were relayed through the orbiters.

The entire space craft fitted inside a shell for entry through the atmosphere. After supersonic braking, the shell was split and a parachute slowed the lander until an altitude of 4,000 feet where three mutinozzle rockets took over. The whole contraption had to be sterilized in hot nitrogen gas in order to make sure that no Earthly life forms contaminated Mars.

After a brief delay in which the two spacecraft had to be swapped because of technical problems, *Viking 1* and *2* were

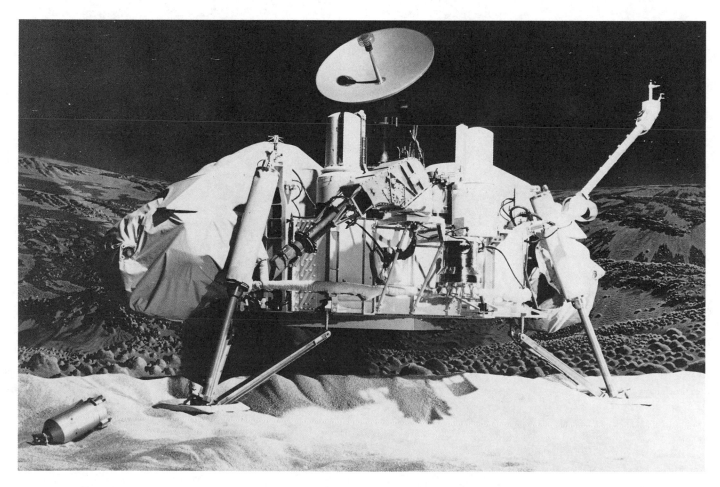

Viking lander. NASA.

launched on August 20 and September 9, 1975, respectively. They arrived at Mars on June 19 and August 7, 1976. During its flight Viking 1 broadcast a signal to a duplicate of its soil arm to cut the ribbon on the opening of the National Air and Space Museum in Washington, .D.C on July 1.

The original landing site was found to be too rough when surveyed by the *Viking 1* orbiter and another site was selected to the north. On July 20 the lander was deployed and settled onto the surface of the Chryse Planitia (Golden Plains). Within minutes it began sending black and white photos back to Earth. *Viking 2* was landed farther north on the Utopia Planitia (Plains of Utopia). Scientists were amazed that they were able to land both craft successfully, especially when the first photos showed that they had both landed in the middle of large rocks that could have toppled them or broken their legs.

The immediate aim of both landers was to search for signs of life. Their scoopers picked up soil samples to be analysed for signs of carbon-14 and gases given off by life. The consensus was that there was some inorganic chemistry at work in the soil that mimicked aspects the organic chemistry that the scientists were looking for. Such reactions have since been duplicated by science labs on Earth. In other words, there was no evidence of life.

Although designed for six-month missions, the spacecraft operated for far longer than that. Orbiter 2 had to be shut down when its thruster gas rout out on July 24, 1978; the same happened to Orbiter 1 on August 8, 1980. Lander 1 operated the longest, transmitting weather data and photos until March 8, 1983. Plans for a Viking 3 mission were never carried out.

Where to learn more

Viking was one of America's most successful space programs and much has been published on it in both the poplar and technical press.

The Viking Mission to Mars (Washington: Scientific and Technical Information Office, National Aeronautics and Space Administration, 1974) by William R. Corliss and Bevan M. French's *Mars: The Viking Discoveries* (Washington: National Aeronautics and Space Administration, 1977) are two government publications. A title from the popular press is Eric Burgess' *To the Red Planet* (New York: Columbia University Press, 1978).

Fans of extraterrestrial mapping will especially appreciate *Viking Lander Atlas of Mars* (Washington: National Aeronautics and Space Administration, Scientific and Technical Information Office, 1982) compiled by the United States Office of Space Science and Applications.

Voyager 1 & 2

(1977 - 1990)

Voyager 1 & 2 were unmanned American spacecraft that took an unprecedented "Grand Tour" of the four large planets of the solar system beyond the Earth's orbit.

In 1965 an engineer, Gary Flandro, working for the Jet Propulsion Laboratory of the United States' National Aeronautics and Space Administration (NASA) did calculations that showed that during the late 1970s the outer planets of the solar system would be in a rare configuration that would make it possible for an Earth-launched spacecraft to fly by the four biggest planets. This configuration happens only once every 175 years. The scientists who wanted to carry out such a mission called it the "Grand Tour."

Scientists proposed building four spacecraft to take advantage of this opportunity. However, because of budgetary problems caused by the cost of building the space shuttle, it was only possible to construct two. The project was approved for the United States government's 1972 fiscal year and officially launched on July 1, 1972. The two spacecraft that were constructed were named *Voyager 1 and 2*. They weighed 1,808 pounds each, had a 12-foot antenna, and on-board computers (with back-ups) that were loaded with instructions for the mission before they took off so that they could function by themselves, if necessary, for years. Also included on the spacecraft were gold-plated copper records that included greetings in 60 languages, a series of Earth sounds, selections of music, and 115 pictures, including a map of DNA structure. It would be millions of years before *Voyager* ever encountered a possible planet outside the solar system, let alone one with intelligent life.

Voyager 2 was launched on August 20, 1977. *Voyager 1* left later, on September 6, but was scheduled to reach Jupiter 4 months ahead of *Voyager 2* because it was on a different trajectory. There were some problems along the way. *Voyager 1*'s scan platform, which turned the cameras and other sensors in various directions, was jammed and would not move but was eventually fixed. *Voyager 2* had a malfunctioning valve that resulted in a lot of fuel loss until it was repaired. *Voyager 2* lost its main radio receiver.

Voyager 1 took its first photographs of Jupiter on December 10, 1978 and then began a month of photographing from distant observations in January 1979. It crossed the orbit of Sinope, the most distant of Jupiter's moons on February 10, 1979. It then took pictures of two other satellites, Callisto and Ganymede. Pictures of the satellite Io showed it to be very active geologically with one currently active volcano, Prometheus. *Voyager 1* came closest to Jupiter on March 5, 1979 at 216,800 miles away, traveling at 62,000 miles an hour. It photographed the Great Red Spot, a 25,000-mile-wide structure of gas. *Voyager 2* reached its closest approach to Jupiter on July 9. It took photos of Ganymede and Europa and then was re-programmed to get closer to Io, which had turned out to be the most fascinating of the Jovian moons. The two spacecraft took a total of 31,000 photographs. They also confirmed the existence of rings around Jupiter, like those of Saturn but invisible from Earth.

Voyager 1 reached Saturn in November 1980, followed by *Voyager 2* in August 1981. Saturn is almost twice as far from Earth as Jupiter and receives about 1 per cent of the solar energy that hits Earth. *Voyager 1* made its closest approach on November 12. It found spokes coming out of the planet's "B" ring and discovered three new satellites. Both spacecraft took numerous

Scale model of a *Voyager* spacecraft. NASA.

pictures of Saturn's rings, which sometimes appeared braided or wavy, in defiance of the known laws of physics. They also were able to penetrate the atmosphere of the moon Titan, which is covered with a mixture of nitrogen and methane that is thought to be similar to the early atmosphere of Earth. Saturn's moons of Enceladus, Dione, and Rhea all showed signs of volcanic activity, and Mimas had an impact crater that had chewed out one-third of its size. The flights also confirmed that Saturn gave off more heat than it absorbed, showing that it may have been a "failed" star.

When the two *Voyagers* had set off on their trip, the plan was to send them only to Jupiter and Saturn because it was thought that the "Grand Tour" would be too expensive. However, the spectacular success convinced the scientists that a further effort had to be made. *Voyager 1* was directed off into another trajectory while *Voyager 2* was aimed at Uranus and Neptune. When Ronald Reagan was elected President in 1980, *Voyager 2* was almost scrapped in a budget-cutting measure but was salvaged at the last minute. *Voyager 2* had to be extensively re-programmed in order to achieve its Uranus rendez-vous. Five days before its closest approach, a piece of binary code in the processor switched from "0" to "1" and an all-night effort was made to route data around it. It worked.

The closest approach to Uranus came on January 24, 1986. *Voyage 2* took incredible close-up pictures of the planet, which is on a different axis from all the other planets in the solar system—the poles are on the equator and the planet's rings circulate north to south. *Voyager 2* took pictures of the five known moons of Uranus—Titania, Ariel, Umbriel, Oberon, and Miranda—and discovered ten new ones. Miranda, a small satellite nearest Uranus, was found to be one of the most bizarre features in the solar system, with characteristics like Mercury and Mars as well as some of the moons of Jupiter and Saturn. *Voyager 2* photographed the nine known rings of Uranus and found two new ones.

Voyager 2 reached its closest approach, 3,048 miles, to Neptune on August 25, 1989. Neptune is three billion miles from the sun. It was discovered by mathematical deduction in 1846 and has not yet made a complete trip around the sun since its discovery—that takes 165 years. At the time of *Voyager 2*'s visit, it was the farthest known object in the solar system; the small planet Pluto has an orbit that sometimes brings it closer to the sun. *Voyager 2* discovered six moons around Neptune in addition to the two that were already known and found Neptune to be a large mass of violent, swirling storms with an atmosphere of high white clouds, probably made up of methane. The planet also contains a Great Dark Spot, made up of a great storm of gases, on its surface. A set of at least four rings was also discovered around Neptune. Some of the rings appear to have arcs, areas where there is a higher density of material than at other parts of the ring. Pictures of the satellite Triton showed it to be slightly smaller than the Earth's Moon, with two great color bands of salmon and blue. It is one of the brightest and coldest points in the solar system, and its peculiar orbit indicated that it had been captured by Neptune relatively recently.

On August 29, 1989 *Voyager 2* was 2,758,530,928 miles from Earth and headed out of the solar system, the first manmade object to be sent out into the universe. Its cameras were turned off in order save energy, but it will be sending data back to Earth about interstellar space for years to come. On February 14, 1990 *Voyager 1*, still climbing after having been separated from *Voyager 2* at Saturn, sent back one last photo, a snapshot from 3.7 billion miles that showed all of the planets except Pluto lined up in their orbits.

Where to learn more

Two general histories of recent space exploration that discuss the *Voyager* journeys are Bruce Murray, *Journey Into Space: The First Thirty Years of Space Exploration* (New York: W.W. Norton, 1989) and William E. Burrows, *Exploring Space: Voyages in the Solar System and Beyond* (New York: Random House, 1990).

An excellent, specialized book, although it was written before the Neptune encounter, is Joel Davis, *Flyby: The Interplanetary Odyssey of Voyager 2* (New York: Atheneum, 1987).

Joseph Reddeford Walker

(1798 - 1876)

Joseph Reddeford Walker was an American fur trader who pioneered the main emigrant trail to California.

Joseph Reddeford Walker was born in Virginia shortly before his parents migrated to Roane County in eastern Tennessee. In 1819 he moved to Independence in western Missouri, then the farthest west of all American settlements and the center for the Western fur trade and what was to become the Santa Fe Trail.

Walker became a fur trapper and trader and took part in the first attempt that the Americans made to travel to Santa Fe and open trade with what was then a Spanish colony. For a while Walker was sheriff of Jackson County, Missouri. On May 1, 1832 Walker set out with **Benjamin Bonneville** on a fur-trading expedition to the West. After a year of trapping, Walker met up with Bonneville in July 1833 at the annual fur rendez-vous on the Green River in eastern Utah. Bonneville then sent Walker west to look for furs and/or find a trail to the Pacific Ocean.

Walker and his party traveled for a month over the desert west of the Great Salt Lake before reaching the Humboldt River in northern Nevada that had been found by **Peter Skene Ogden** in 1828. They followed the river to the Humboldt Sinks, a series of marshy lakes in the desert where the Humboldt River disappears. There, Walker and his group of 60 men were approached by a band of curious Digger tribesmen. The Americans opened fire and killed "several dozen" of them within a few minutes. From there, Walker traveled up the Walker River to Walker Lake and then crossed over the Sierra Nevada Mountains at Mono Pass between the Merced and Tuolumne Rivers. They entered what is now Yosemite National Park and were the first Westerners to see its famous waterfalls.

Traveling through California, Walker and his party were amazed by the redwood forests they saw, experienced a major earthquake, and witnessed a meteor shower. They traveled to San Francisco Bay and then down the coast to Monterey, the capital of Mexican California. The Americans were well received and stayed there from November 1833 until January 13, 1834. On the return east, Walker went down to the southern end of the San Joaquin Valley and traveled through Walker's Pass, which was to be one of the main gateways for Americans moving into California.

The Americans then turned north through the desert where they almost died of thirst before reaching the Humboldt Sinks once again. Again, they fired on defenseless Digger Indians, this time killing 14 of them and wounding many more. From there, the Americans headed north from the Humboldt River to the Snake River in southern Idaho, thereby avoiding the desert west of the Great Salt Lake. Walker and his men met up with Bonneville on the Bear River on July 12, 1834. The route that Walker had found was to become the main trail to California in following years.

Walker continued to trap and trade in the Rocky Mountains for the next nine years, making one trip to Los Angeles to buy horses in 1841. In 1843 he led a group of American settlers to California via Walker's Pass and met up with **John Charles Frémont** on his return. He then served as guide for Frémont's 1845-1846 expedition to California. In 1849 he joined the flood of Americans heading west during the Gold Rush and went into business selling cattle to the miners as well as leading several prospecting expeditions. He led a group of prospectors to Arizona in 1861 and finally retired and settled down with his nephew in Contra Costa County near San Francisco in 1868, where he died eight years later.

Where to learn more

There are several biographies of Walker by Western historians: D.S. Watson, *West Wind: The Life Story of Joseph Reddeford Walker* (Los Angeles: 1934); Joel P. Walker, *Pioneer of Pioneers* (Los Angeles, 1953); and D.E. Conner, *Joseph Reddeford Walker and the Arizona Adventure* (Norman: University of Oklahoma Press, 1956).

A very good general history of the opening of the American West by fur trappers and traders is Bernard DeVoto, *Across the Wide Missouri* (Boston: 1957, with several subsequent editions). There is a good biographical summary of Walker by Ardis M. Walker in LeRoy R. Hafen, ed. *Mountain Men and Fur Traders of the Far West* (Lincoln: University of Nebraska Press, 1982).

Alfred Russell Wallace

(1823 - 1913)

Alfred Wallace was a British naturalist who made two important scientific expeditions to South America and Indonesia and formulated the modern theory of evolution at the same time as Charles Darwin.

Alfred Wallace was born in the town of Usk in Monmouthshire in England near the Welsh border on January 8, 1823. He attended only grammar school and then was apprenticed to a watchmaker. In 1839 his older brother William took him along to Herefordshire to help out on a surveying job. There, he became interested in the natural sciences and started studying astronomy, agriculture, and botany on his own. In 1844 he took a job as a schoolmaster in the city of Leicester. There he met **Henry Walter Bates** another amateur student of biology. They went on several trips together collecting specimens, and in 1848 they decided to go to the Amazon River to investigate the rich botany of that part of the world.

Alfred Russell Wallace. The Granger Collection, New York.

Wallace and Bates left England in April 1848 and sailed to the Brazilian port city of Belém near the mouth of the Amazon River. During 1848 and 1849 they collected near Belém, and in late 1849 they traveled up the Amazon to the city of Manaus, visiting the former missions at Parintins and Serpa. In March 1850 Wallace and Bates split up, and in August of that year Wallace traveled up the Rio Negro, a major tributary of the Amazon, on his own. He traveled as far as the headwaters of the Rio Negro and stayed among the Baniwa tribe in southern Venezuela.

Returning from the Rio Negro, Wallace traveled up the Uaupes River in June and July 1851 into Colombia. He returned to Manaus in September and then headed back up the Negro and Uaupes, reaching the Brazilian border at the village of Yavaraté in early 1852. While in the area, he came down with malaria and dysentery and recovered in a Native American village where they had never seen a European before. He sailed back down the Uaupes, Negro, and Amazon to Belém and left for England in July 1852. During the return voyage the ship was destroyed by fire. After ten days in a lifeboat with other survivors, Wallace was rescued, but the notes and specimens he had with him (some had already been sent back) were lost.

On his return to England, Wallace spent his time writing about his discoveries and attending scientific meetings, making the acquaintance of such famous scientists as **Charles Darwin**. In 1854, he decided that the best field for continued investigation of the multiplication of species was in the East Indies—what is today Malaysia and Indonesia. He traveled there and spent the following eight years visiting every major island in the archipelago. While in Southeast Asia he made several major discoveries. One of these was the "Wallace Line": an imaginary boundary between the islands of Bali and Lombok. East of the line the plants and animals are like those of Asia, west of it they resemble Australian and New Guinea species.

Already in 1855, Wallace had written his first book about evolution. In 1858 while he was ill with fever on the island of Ternate in eastern Indonesia, he had a sudden brainstorm: species evolved by the process of natural selection. This meant that haphazard genetic changes are perpetuated if they serve to enable a species to adapt to its natural environment. Darwin was working on the same idea separately, and Wallace wrote him a letter describing his theories. As a result, Darwin presented a paper listing himself and Wallace as authors on July 1, 1858 to the Linnaean Society in London. It was the world's introduction to the modern theory of evolution. Darwin went on to write his famous book *On the Origin of Species*, for which Wallace had great admiration. Wallace himself wrote a volume entitled *Contributions to the Theory of Natural Selection* in 1870.

Wallace left Singapore in early 1862 to return to England. There he wrote about his travels in a book called *The Malay Archipelago*, which is still a major sourcebook for information about the natural and human life of the islands of southeast Asia. He continued to write about many subjects during the remaining years of his long life, including socialism, space travel, geographical dispersion of species, vaccination, and human evolution. He

died at his country house in Dorset on November 7, 1913 at the age of 90.

Where to learn more

Wallace wrote several books on a large variety of subjects. The one that deals with his South American journeys is *A Narrative of Travels on the Amazon and Rio Negro* (London: Macmillan, 1870; revised edition, London: Ward, Locke & Co., 1911). On this aspect of his career, also see Paul Russell Cutright, *The Great Naturalists Explore South America* (New York: Macmillan, 1940).

For the role of Wallace in the development of modern theories of evolution, see A. William-Ellis, *Darwin's Moon: A Biography of Alfred Russell Wallace* (London: Blackie, 1966) and Lewis McKinney, *Wallace and Natural Selection* (New Haven: Yale University Press, 1972).

Samuel Wallis

(1728-1795)

Samuel Wallis was an English navy captain who made a circumnavigation of the world and was the first European to visit the island of Tahiti in the South Pacific.

Samuel Wallis was born in the English county of Cornwall, where he was baptized on April 23, 1728. He went to sea as a young boy. He fought in the Royal Navy during the War of the Austrian Succession (1740-1748) and was promoted to lieutenant on the conclusion of the war on October 19, 1748. He rose in rank during the succeeding years and got his first command on June 30, 1756. He commanded various ships in North America and the English Channel during the Seven Years' War (1756-1763) between Great Britain and France.

In May 1766 Commodore **John Byron** returned from his trip around the world. His ship, the *Dolphin*, was almost immediately commissioned for another voyage around the world, and Wallis was chosen to be its captain. The *Dolphin* sailed from the English port of Plymouth on August 22, 1766. Wallis's orders were to sail to the South Pacific and try to find the great southern continent that was thought to extend northward from Antarctica.

Philip Carteret sailed with Wallis at the same time in the *Swallow*, which was almost totally unseaworthy. The *Dolphin* had to go slowly in order not to lose the *Swallow*, but after an incredibly difficult passage through the Straits of Magellan that took four months, the two ships were separated. Carteret later charged that Wallis left him behind on purpose so that he would not be burdened with the slower ship.

Wallis continued in the *Dolphin* and sailed northwestward across the Pacific, where he encountered numerous storms. Many of the ship's crew, including Wallis, became sick. On June 10, 1767 the ship came in sight of some of the small outlying islands of the Tuamotu Archipelago in what is now French Polynesia. Wallis stopped briefly and took on fresh water and coconuts. The *Dolphin* sailed west, and on June 18 Wallis and his crew were rewarded with the sight of the large island of Tahiti. At twilight, they anchored offshore of the mountainous island.

The next day the crew of the *Dolphin* was surprised to see their ship surrounded by hundreds of canoes manned by the Tahitians, who had come to see the first Europeans who had landed at their island. After Wallis's men indicated that they were friendly a few of the Tahitians came on board, but one of them was butted by a goat: "the appearance of this animal, so different

from any he had ever seen, struck him with such terror, that he instantly leaped overboard; and all the rest, upon seeing what had happened, followed his example."

After a few days of hostile gestures on both sides, including firing a cannon at a Tahitian chief in his canoe, the two groups decided that it was to their mutual advantage to trade. The Englishmen got all the fresh fruit and other provisions they needed by bartering with nails: these were the first metal tools the Tahitians had ever seen. In fact, the Tahitians were so anxious to get the nails, and the crew so willing to trade, that they started pulling the nails out of the ship itself. Wallis had to control the number of men who could go on shore, and the supply of nails they took, or the ship would have fallen apart.

Wallis was received by one of the local queens during an audience in which the English officers were massaged by young Tahitian women until the ship's doctor took off his wig and frightened them all away. Different parties made trips into other parts of the island, and they came back with enthusiastic tales about the wealth and fertility of the island and the beauty and friendliness of the people. Thus, almost from the day it first became known to Westerners, Tahiti gained the kind of favorable publicity that ever since has led many people to think of it as paradise on earth.

Even though Wallis would have liked to have stayed and the queen begged him not to leave, he felt it was his duty to continue his explorations. He weighed anchor on July 26 and sailed to the northwest, where he passed many of the islands of Polynesia and discovered the group of islands that were later named for him—the Wallis Islands, which are now a French territory.

The *Dolphin* did not stop at any of these places until he reached the island of Tinian in the Marianas on September 19, 1767. This island was a Spanish possession and the seas from that point on had been well charted. The ship sailed on to Batavia in the Dutch East Indies. Although Wallis tried to keep the visit as short as possible, many of the crew members came down with smallpox and dysentery while the ship was at Batavia, and the Indian Ocean crossing was very difficult. The ship had to spend a month at the Cape of Good Hope in order for the crew to recuperate. The *Dolphin* reached England on May 20, 1768, after a voyage of one year and nine months.

Wallis had carried out his instructions creditably, although he did not show the kind of curiosity as an explorer that was to distinguish his successor, **James Cook**, a few years later. He was rewarded with the command of several ships and in 1782 was appointed to a high administrative position in the Royal Navy. He remained in that post until his death at his home in London on January 21, 1795.

Where to learn more

The first notice of Wallis's discoveries appeared in a famous book that included information on all the Pacific voyages made by Royal Navy officers in the years following the Seven Years' War: John Hawkesworth, 3 vols. *An Account of the Voyages . . . by Commodore Byron, Captain Wallis, Captain Carteret and Captain Cook* (London: 1773). Much later, the Hakluyt Society published a volume with another contemporary account of Wallis's voyage: Hugh Carrington, ed. *The Discovery of Tahiti: A Journal of the Second Voyage of H.M.S. Dolphin Round the World, under the Command of Captain Wallis, R.N., Written by Her Master, George Robertson* (London: Hakluyt Society, 1948).

General histories of Pacific exploration that include useful material on Wallis include: J.C. Beaglehole, *The Exploration of the Pacific* (Stanford: Stanford University Press, 1966); O.H.K. Spate, *Paradise Found and Lost* (Minneapolis: University of Minnesota Press, 1988); and Derek Wilson, *The Circumnavigators* (New York: M. Evans & Co., 1989).

Peter Warburton

(1813-1889)

Peter Warburton was an Australian explorer who was the first person to cross the central part of the continent from east to west.

Peter Warburton was born in Cheshire, England on August 16, 1813. His father was an Anglican clergyman. Peter entered the Royal Navy as a midshipman candidate at the age of 12. At the age of 16 he entered the training academy of the British Army in India. After graduating from the academy, he went to India and served in the Army there for the next 22 years. On one of his leaves in England, he married Alicia Mant from the town of Bath.

Warburton retired with the rank of major from the Indian Army in 1853. He took his wife, daughter, and two sons to the new British colony of South Australia, founded in 1836, where he was appointed Commissioner of Police in the capital city of Adelaide. In 1857 he made the first of a series of expeditions into the interior of South and Western Australia to fill in some of the gaps in the map of the continent.

In one expedition in 1858 Warburton traveled north of Adelaide and discovered the route between two great salt lakes—Lake Torrens and Lake Eyre—in the interior desert of South Australia. This disproved the theory that there was a continuous ring of lakes in the central part of Australia. In 1865 Warburton discovered a river, named after him, that flows into Lake Eyre from the northeast. For unknown reasons, Warburton was investigated by a secret board of inquiry and fired from his job as Police Commissioner in 1867. A later investigation said that he had been treated unjustly and recommended his reinstatement.

In 1873 Warburton set out to fill in the largest gap remaining in man's knowledge of Australia—the area west of the north-south route opened up by **John McDouall Stuart** through central Australia. This same feat was attempted by **Ernest Giles** in 1872 who was stopped by the Gibson Desert and by William Gosse in 1873 who discovered Ayers Rock before being forced to give up.

In his attempt at crossing central Australia from east to west, Warburton was the first explorer to depend entirely on camels for transportation across the desert. In April 1873, having already covered more than a thousand miles from Adelaide, he set off from the small post of Alice Springs, which is almost exactly in the center of Australia. He traveled with his son, a cook, a surveyor, two Afghan camel drivers, an Aborigine boy called Charley, and 17 camels.

Warburton had planned to travel to Perth, the capital of Western Australia in the southwestern part of the state, but lack of water repeatedly forced him to turn northward. He traveled north of the MacDonnell Ranges and then entered a rugged plain covered with spiny plants that tore at the feet of both men and camels. On June 18, 1873 they found some waterholes that were full of dead rats. They named the spot Waterloo Wells since it was the anniversary of the Battle of Waterloo.

From the desolate plain they traveled into the even worse conditions of the Great Sandy Desert, where the camels began to die from eating poisonous plants. Each camel that died immediately became food for the starving and thirsty men. At one point, when the party was down to its last supply of water, Charley, the Aborigine, set off without telling anyone and was able to find a band of Aborigines to which he guided the desperate men. At the point when they thought they could go no farther, on December 11, 1873, they reached the Oakover River, which is the first stream south of the Great Sandy Desert flowing into the Indian Ocean. When they arrived, Warburton was unconscious and strapped to his camel. The main body of the expedition stayed there while the surveyor, who was the strongest, took the remaining two camels to find help. He returned just in time to save the dying Warburton.

From the Oakover River, the group continued their trek, finally reaching the Indian Ocean on January 21, 1874 after covering 2,000 miles in ten months, the first expedition to cross central Australia from east to west. In his account of the expedition Warburton wrote, "no exploring party ever endured such protracted suffering . . . nor did anyone ever cross so vast an extent of continuous bad country."

For this exploit, Warburton was awarded a medal by the Royal Geographical Society during a visit to England in 1874 and was given an award of £1,000 by the South Australian government. In 1877 he retired from his position as head of the militia and retired to his wine-growing estate outside of Adelaide. He died there on November 5, 1889.

Where to learn more

Warburton wrote a book about the crossing of western Australia: *Journey Across the Western Interior of Australia* (London: 1875). The South Australian Parliament also published his diary: *Diary of Colonel Warburton's Expedition to Western Australia, 1872-74* (Adelaide: 1875). Excerpts from these can be found in Kathleen Fitzpatrick, *Australian Explorers: A Selection from Their Writings* (London: Oxford University Press, 1958). See also B. Threadgill, *South Australian Land Exploration, 1856 to 1880* (Adelaide: 1922) and Sir Ernest Scott, *Australian Discovery*, vol. 2, *By Land* (London: 1929).

James Wellsted

(1805 - 1842)

James Wellsted was a British naval officer who explored along the south coast of Arabia and was the first European to bring back information about the Himyarites, an early pre-Arab civilization.

James Wellsted was born in England in 1805. As a young man he got a job as secretary to the head of the Bombay Marine, the naval arm of the East India Company, which controlled Britain's possessions in India. In 1830 he obtained an appointment as second lieutenant on board the East India Company's ship *Palinarus*. The *Palinarus* was stationed off the coast of Arabia in order to survey its shores and to control the pirates that preyed on British shipping.

Following a rest period in Bombay, the *Palinarus* returned to Arabia at the end of 1833 in order to find suitable sites for coaling stations for East India Company ships. In January 1834 it anchored at the island of Socotra off the northeastern tip of Africa. Wellsted went ashore and spent two months traveling around the island and sent an article about his explorations to the Royal Geographical Society in London.

In April 1835, as the *Palinarus* sailed along the southern coast of the Arabian Peninsula, Wellsted heard about some ancient ruins in the interior. In the company of his friend Lieutenant Charles Cruttenden, he traveled 50 miles inland from the little port of Bal Haf on the south coast of the Hadhramaut, the rocky plateau that makes up the eastern part of Yemen. There the two English officers found the ruins of the city of Naqab-al-Hayar in the Wadi (dry river bed) Meifa'a. Naqab-al-Hayar, built in the 2nd century B.C., was the largest city of the Himyarites, the pre-Arab inhabitants of the southern part of the Arabian Peninsula. Wellsted transcribed the inscriptions that he found on the ruins, the first European knowledge of the Himyarite script.

In November 1835, the *Palinarus* docked at Muscat, the capital of Oman. Wellsted received permission from the Imam to explore the interior of the country, which was practically unknown to Westerners. He left from the small port of Sur south of Muscat on November 28, 1835 and traveled into the mountainous country of the Jebel Akhdar. From there he became the first European to see the vast Rub 'al Khali, or Empty Quarter, the desert that makes up most of southeastern Arabia. He did not try to explore the desert because, as he said, "even the hardy Bedouin scarcely dares to venture there." It was not until the 20th century that **Harry St. John Philby** and Bertram Thomas became the first Europeans to venture into the Rub 'al Khali. In spite of an attack of fever, Wellsted's travels lasted until March 1836.

Wellsted went back to Muscat in April 1837. He suffered so badly from fever that he became delirious and shot himself in the mouth with a gun. He did not die but was seriously hurt, with two large wounds in his upper jaw. He was invalided out of his job and sent back to England. He traveled around Europe for a while, in great pain and sometimes out of his mind. He died in his father's house in London on October 25, 1842.

Where to learn more

Wellsted wrote a book about his explorations: *Travels in Arabia*, 2 vols. (London: John Murray, 1838; reprinted, Graz, Austria: Akademische Druck, 1978). He is also the author of *Travels to the City of the Caliphs, Along the Shores of the Persian Gulf and the Mediterranean*, 2 vols. (London: H. Colburn, 1840), which, although he does not make it clear, are not about his own travels, but of those of a fellow officer, Lieutenant Ormsby.

Two books that devote considerable attention to Wellsted's explorations are: David Hogarth, *The Penetration of Arabia* (New York: F.A. Stokes Co., 1904; reprinted, Westport, Conn.: Hyperion Press, 1981) and R.H. Kiernan, *The Unveiling of Arabia* (London: 1937).

Charles Wilkes

(1798 - 1877)

Charles Wilkes led an important American scientific expedition to the Pacific and was one of the discoverers of the continent of Antarctica.

Charles Wilkes was born in New York City, the son of a prosperous businessman. He received an education in mathematics and navigation and joined the merchant marine in 1815. He was appointed a midshipman in the U.S. Navy in 1818. He continued to study navigation and astronomy and in 1833 was appointed head of the Navy's Depot of Charts and Instruments, which later became the Naval Observatory and the Hydrographic Office.

For many years, the U.S. government had discussed the idea of sending an exploring expedition to make a scientific study of the world's oceans. On May 14, 1836 President Andrew Jackson signed a bill that created the U.S. South Seas Surveying and Exploring Expedition. After many false starts, Wilkes was appointed to head the expedition in 1838 although he was only a lieutenant.

Wilkes set out in the middle of August 1838 in the flagship *Vincennes* and five other aged and not very seaworthy ships.

Charles Wilkes. The Granger Collection, New York.

The expedition included naval officers charged with oceanography and several civilian scientists who were to study the natural history of the lands they visited. Most of the first year was spent at sea, and these scientists had little opportunity to carry out their work.

In January 1839, Wilkes' squadron sailed around Cape Horn at the tip of South America and entered the oceans near Antarctica for the first time. They then sailed among the Pacific islands (a total of 280 islands were surveyed) until they reached Sydney, Australia in November 1839. The natural scientists stayed ashore, and Wilkes went south to visit Antarctica, leaving Sydney on December 26, 1839. He was able to navigate through the ice that surrounded the continent and saw an outlying island of Antarctica on January 16. He sailed into a deep bay and definitely sighted land on January 19, 1840. This was the very same day that the French explorer **Dumont d'Urville** saw the mainland of Antarctica for the first time. These were the first two confirmed sightings of the mainland of Antarctica. Unconfirmed sightings had been made by **Fabian von Bellingshausen** and American and British whaling captains in 1819 and 1829, and **John Biscoe** had gone ashore on an inshore island in 1832.

On January 30, 1840 Wilkes was able to sail the *Vincennes* through a maze of icebergs into a bay in the mainland and to get within a half-mile of the coast. He named the place Piner's Bay after a member of his crew. This part of the coast of Antarctica is known as Wilkes Land. By this time, Wilkes' crew was near mutiny and wanted to sail away, but he pressed on as far as 100°E, discovering what is known as the Knox Coast. He was stopped by a large ice barrier later named the Shackleton Ice Shelf and turned north on February 16.

From Antarctica, Wilkes headed north through the Pacific Islands to Hawaii, where one of the scientists set up an observatory on the volcanic peak of Mauna Loa. They then sailed to the Pacific Northwest and charted 800 miles of streams and coasts. The expedition returned to Hampton Roads, Virginia in July 1842. It had sailed more than 80,000 miles and had collected materials on zoology, botany, anthropology, geology, meteorology, and hydrography.

Soon after his return, Wilkes was court-martialed for mistreating his crew. He was acquitted of most of the charges. He then spent the years until 1861 in Washington preparing the reports from the expedition for publication. His *Narrative* in five volumes was published in 1844, and he was also responsible for several of the scientific volumes. Congress authorized the publication of these works, but only budgeted enough money to print 100 copies of each.

During the Civil War, Wilkes had a checkered career. By the time war broke out, he was a captain and commanded a ship designed to keep Confederate traders from reaching port. On November 8, 1861 he stopped a British ship and removed two Confederate representatives, James Mason and John Slidell. Although this action made Wilkes a hero in the United States, it caused an international incident and the two men were released. In September 1862 he was made a rear admiral and put in charge of U.S. operations in the Caribbean. He failed to capture any Confederate ships but offended several foreign governments and was recalled and demoted. In 1864 he was court-martialed for insubordination and suspended from duty. He retired in 1866 and spent the last years of his life in Washington, D.C.

Where to learn more

Wilkes spent several years writing up the results of the expedition. This was first published in 5 volumes as the *Narrative of the United States Exploring Expedition During the Years 1838, 1839, 1840, 1841, 1842* (Philadelphia: American Philosophical Society, 1845). In 1854 the U.S. government published a 3-volume edition of the work in Washington, D.C. This was reprinted in a very fine edition in 1968 (Monticello, N.Y.: Lubrick & Cramer). Wilkes published a one-volume edition: *Synopsis of the Cruise of the United States Exploring Expedition* (Philadelphia: American Philosophical Society, 1848).

There are two fairly recent books that give admirable histories of the expedition: David B. Tyler, *The Wilkes Expedition* (Philadelphia: American Philosophical Society, 1968) and William Stanton, *The Great United States Exploring Expedition* (Berkeley: University of California Press, 1975).

There are good chapters on Wilkes in L.P. Kirwan, *A History of Polar Exploration* (New York: W.W. Norton & Co., 1960) and Ernest S. Dodge, *Beyond the Capes: Pacific Exploration from Captain Cook to the Challenger, 1776-1877* (Boston: Little, Brown and Co., 1971). An excellent book on Antarctic exploration, which gives details of Wilkes' visit to the southern continent, is *Antarctica: Great Stories from the Frozen Continent* (Sydney: Reader's Digest, 1988).

Sir (George) Hubert Wilkins

(1888 - 1958)

Sir Hubert Wilkins was a native of Australia who pioneered flying in both the Arctic and Antarctic.

George Hubert Wilkins was born in the Australian outback on a sheep "station" about 100 miles north of the city of Adelaide on October 31, 1888. He left Australia at the age of 20 when he hid on a ship sailing out of Adelaide that took him to Algiers in North Africa. He worked as a smuggler until he reached England where he became one of the first film photographers. He learned how to fly in 1910 and then was sent by his employers to film the Balkan Wars for newsreel cameras.

In 1913 Wilkins was sent by *The Times* of London to cover the Canadian Arctic Expedition led by **Vilhjalmur Stefansson**. He spent two years in the Arctic and saved Stefansson's life at one point when he got lost. He returned to Europe in 1915 and photographed action on the Western Front during World War I. He was wounded by bullets nine times, buried by bomb blasts on several occasions, and was gassed. After the war he was navigator on a plane that tried to be the first to fly from England to Australia. The engine on the plane failed, and it crashed into the

Sir George Hubert Wilkins. UPI/Bettmann.

wall of a mental institution on the island of Crete in the Mediterranean.

Following these experiences Wilkins was chosen to be the naturalist on **Ernest Shackleton**'s 1920 expedition to Antarctica. Shackleton died on the trip, but Wilkins' work collecting specimens was favorably noted. He then returned to Europe to make a documentary about the famine in Russia that was then going on as a result of the Russian Revolution and Civil War. From 1923 to 1925 he led an expedition to Northern Australia for the British Museum to study its mammals and to record on film the life of the Aborigines there.

In 1926 Wilkins was chosen to lead the Detroit Arctic Expedition. This was sponsored by American automobile manufacturers to send two airplanes to the Arctic Ocean and to fly over it to search for new land, including the reported (but non-existent) Keenan Land. The expedition traveled from Seattle, Washington to Fairbanks, Alaska where both planes crashed (although with only slight damage and no human injuries) and one of the accompanying reporters was killed when he walked into a propeller. Wilkins, however, repaired one of the aircraft and then flew north to Point Barrow, flying over 150 miles of the Arctic Ocean. He made several flights to and from Point Barrow but was constantly being thwarted by problems with the two planes.

Wilkins returned to Alaska in February 1927 with a new airplane. This time he flew 500 miles out over the Arctic Ocean when he was forced to land on an ice floe because of engine problems. There he took depth soundings that showed the ocean to be about 16,000 feet deep at that point, much deeper than anyone had thought. Wilkins and his pilot, Carl Eielson, tried to repair the engine and took off once but landed almost immediately. They took off again at sunset and ran into a snowstorm. After running out of fuel, they were forced to land in a snowbank on an ice floe 65 miles northwest of Point Barrow. They then traveled overland for thirteen days, falling in the water more than once. Wilkins could not swim and was almost carried away on one occasion but survived thanks to an air pocket in his backpack. Both men made it back to Point Barrow alive.

Wilkins and Eielson returned to Point Barrow in 1928 with a Lockheed Vega, this time with the intention of flying across the Arctic from Alaska along the northern edge of the Canadian Arctic islands and Greenland to Spitsbergen off the northern end of Scandinavia. They left Point Barrow on April 5, 1928 and flew according to their flight plan until they ran into a storm near Spitsbergen. They flew over a small, isolated island but could find no place to land and turned back to try to find the island again. After several attempts, they located it and were able to land in a snowbank. They were kept on the ground for four days until the storm broke. When they tried to get underway again, they found that the skis at the bottom of the plane froze so quickly that Wilkins had to stay on the ground and push while Eielson flew the plane. The first time after Eielson got off the ground he threw a rope to Wilkins who tried to catch it in his mouth and thereby loosened all his teeth before being hit by the airplane's tail and knocked into the snow. He made it on the third try, and the two landed successfully at Green Harbor in Spitsbergen.

This flight was the first in a heavier-than-air craft across the Arctic. **Roald Amundsen** and **Umberto Nobile** had flown across the North Pole in the dirigible *Norge* in 1926. After Wilkins' flight Amundsen said, "No flight has been made anywhere, at any time, which could be compared with this." He was knighted by the British government and received a medal from the Royal Geographical Society.

Following this accomplishment, Wilkins became the first person to fly an airplane in Antarctica. He and Eielson headed south at the end of 1928 on an expedition sponsored by the Hearst newspapers—"the Wilkins-Hearst Expedition." Wilkins and Eielson made their first take-off on November 16, 1928. Four days later, they flew 600 miles over the continent from their base on Deception Island. These were the first flights in Antarctica although Wilkins did not try to fly over the South Pole, a feat that **Richard Byrd** accomplished about a week later. Weather conditions did not allow Wilkins to continue flying. He returned in December 1929 and made a limited number of flights over the Graham Peninsula and west of Peter I Island, but was again forestalled by bad weather.

On his return from Antarctica in 1930, Wilkins was able to convince his fellow explorer **Lincoln Ellsworth** to help subsidize him in his next scheme—sailing a submarine under the ice at the North Pole. Wilkins was able to purchase a surplus World War I submarine from the U.S. Navy, which he named the *Nautilus*,

and to have it refitted. The ship sailed for Spitsbergen on August 18, 1931 for a trial run under the ice. However, the submarine had mechanical problems, and the crew was very apprehensive about sailing under the ice, going so far as to sabotage the *Nautilus*. It sailed for a few hours under the ice, but the attempt was abandoned on September 8, 1931. It was some 25 years later before a second submarine named the **Nautilus** finally accomplished the feat envisaged by Wilkins.

In the following years, Wilkins went to Antarctica twice with Ellsworth and in the winter of 1937-1938 organized a four-month effort to find a Russian pilot lost over the Arctic. These flights furnished valuable information on the climate and ice movements of the Arctic Ocean north of Siberia. At the end of 1938, Wilkins went back to Antarctica on an expedition sponsored by Ellsworth and set off in January 1939 on his own to put out markers claiming the area of the Vestfold Hills as Australian territory.

During World War II Wilkins worked for the U.S. government in supplying aircraft for the war effort. During the early part of the war, he was aboard two different aircraft that were shot down, one over France and one over the Mediterranean, but he escaped unharmed both times. After the war he became an adviser to the U.S. military on Arctic warfare and on camouflage. He died of a heart attack in a hotel in Framingham, Massachusetts on November 30, 1958. In response to a request he had made several times, his ashes were scattered near the North Pole in March 1959, when the U.S. submarine *Skate* surfaced in the Arctic Ocean.

Where to learn more

Wilkins told some of his many tales in *Flying the Arctic* (New York: G.P. Putnam's Sons, 1928). There are two biographies of the intrepid explorer: John Grierson, *Sir Hubert Wilkins: Enigma of Exploration* (London: Hale, 1960) and Lowell Thomas, *Sir Hubert Wilkins: His World of Adventure* (New York: 1961). There is also a long section on Wilkins in John Grierson's *Heroes of the Polar Skies* (New York: Meredith Press, 1967).

William of Rubruck

(1215? - 1270?)

William of Rubruck was a Franciscan friar who was sent on a diplomatic mission to the court of the Great Khan by King Louis IX of France.

Faced with the threat of the Mongols, the leaders of Western Europe came up with all sorts of stratagems to contain the menace from the East. One continuing hope was that the nomadic tribesmen could be converted to Western Christianity. At the time of their greatest conquests, the Mongols practiced their native tribal religion. But, as they came into contact with the rest of the world, they were subject to attempts at conversion by Buddhists, Nestorian Christians, and Muslims.

Hoping to make such a conversion, King Louis IX (Saint Louis) dispatched a Franciscan monk, William from the Flemish town of Rubruck, to the court of the Great Khan. At the time, Louis was in Palestine attempting to reconquer the Holy Lands for the Christians following their loss to the Muslims under Saladin in 1187. William set off on his mission in 1252 from the port of Acre in northern Palestine.

From Acre he traveled to Constantinople where he stayed a year and then set out with a companion, Friar Bartholomew of Cremona, and a mysterious personage called "Homo Dei Turgemanus," who served as translator and guide. The party sailed across the Black Sea to the Crimea and then went overland by wagon into southern Russia.

It is here that William met the Mongol tribesmen for the first time. It was a classic case of culture shock. The good friar was horrified at the ways of the nomads who had no fixed abode, but lived in tents made of felt, ate all kinds of revolting food, painted their faces, and who seemed to embody all that a European meant by barbaric—insolent, suspicious, greedy, and cruel. In this, William was like so many explorers throughout the ages who easily succumbed to the temptation to see everything unfamiliar as being evil.

William and his entourage traveled eastward across the steppes of Russia, which had been made barren by the Mongol warriors. They reached an encampment of the Mongols at Sartach, a three days' march west of the Volga River. An Armenian in the camp was able to read their documents from King Louis, which had been translated into Arabic and Syriac. The Mongols then sent them on to the camp of the great general Batu, but not without relieving them of some of their worldly goods, including their priestly vestments.

The camp of Batu was reached after several days of marching and of sailing down the Volga. William was embarrassed that he had to face the chief in his simple friar's robes, but he summoned the courage to address Batu and his court and he urged them all to accept Christian baptism. At this, the court broke out in uproarious laughter. Batu did, however, give him permission to proceed to the Great Khan. He was not able to leave his host for another five weeks, during which time he and his party were never given anything to eat. They would have starved but for the generosity of some Hungarian captives in the camp.

Just before the beginning of winter, on September 15, 1253, they left Batu's camp and continued their trip eastward. They traveled on horses with a Mongol guide, changing mounts at different camps along the way. They ate only one meal a day—mutton or meat broth at the end of the day, with some millet gruel for breakfast. It took them seven weeks to cross the vast steppe in this manner until they came to the great Tien Shan mountain range, probably in the region of the present-day city of Alma-Ata. They crossed the Ili River near the present-day city of Kuldja. In this region, William came into contact with Lamaist Buddhists, whom he labeled idolaters. He had equally unfavorable things to say about the Nestorians he encountered—calling them ignorant drunkards, polygamists, and sorcerers.

Finally, on December 27, 1253, they reached the court of the Great Khan, where they were housed in a miserable little hut until presented to the Great Khan Möngkhe on January 3, 1254. As he approached, the Great Khan said, "Fear not." "If I had been afraid, I would not have come," replied Rubruck. The meeting itself turned out to be rather unfortunate in that their guide and interpreter quickly became drunk, and the Great Khan himself seemed to be none too sober. Moreover, his interest in his visitors seemed to be chiefly in finding out military information about France and ascertaining how difficult it would be to conquer. William was forced to give evasive answers.

William's party was invited to accompany the Great Khan to the capital city of Karakorum. In the great travelling march he encountered many other Westerners who had either been captured in various Mongol campaigns or who had attached themselves to the court. In particular, Friar William was aided by a goldsmith, William Buchier of Paris, who had become wealthy by fashioning ornaments for Möngkhe and his court.

As part of the competition among various religious parties, William was allowed to sing Latin psalms at the court along with the Nestorian hymns, the prayers of the Muslims, and the chants of the Buddhists. This competition was reflected in Karakorum where there was a Nestorian church, two mosques, and 12 "idol temples," along with the royal palace and buildings for the court secretaries. In spite of this, William rated the town as being only the size of the Paris suburb of Saint Denis.

In a final audience with the Khan on May 31, 1254, William was allowed to present his case for staying at the court and instructing its members on the virtues of Latin Christianity. Möngkhe rejected this and offered to send an emissary back with him to the King of France. William delicately turned this offer down but did accept a letter from the Great Khan to King Louis, which said, in part, "If you will obey us, send your ambassadors, that we may know whether you wish for peace or war. But if you say, Our Country is far, our mountains are strong, and our sea is wide, then you shall find what we can do."

On his departure, William left behind his companion Brother Bartholomew, who was judged too sick to travel. He returned by a route similar to his outward voyage except that it was more northerly. He returned to the camp of Batu on November 15, 1254, where he met up with members of his party who had been left behind and who were on the verge of being enslaved by the Mongols. At this point, the party turned south, crossing the Caucasus Mountains to Mount Ararat. On February 15, 1255, William and his companions entered Asia Minor near the city of Kars and then made their way to the Mediterranean (in May) and

back to Acre. King Louis had left the city by then and the Franciscan Superior forced William to wait there several months before he was allowed to present his report to the King.

William went on to Paris, and it is known that he met with the famous philosopher Roger Bacon there in 1257. After that, there is no further word of him.

Where to learn more

William of Rubruck's own history of his journey was printed by the Hakluyt Society, which publishes the original narratives of voyages of exploration: W. Woodville Rockhill, translator, *The Journey of William of Rubruck to the Eastern parts of the World, 1253-55, as Narrated by Himself* (London: Hakluyt Society, 1900). A new edition translated by Peter Jackson and edited by David Morgan has appeared recently: *The Mission of Friar William of Rubruck: His Journey to the Court of the Great Kahn Mönkhe, 1253-1255* (London: Hakluyt Society, 1990). The narrative of William's travels can also be found in Christopher Dawson, ed. *The Mongol Mission: Narratives and Letters of the Franciscan Missionaries in Mongolia and China in the 13th and 14th Centuries* (London: Sheed and Ward, 1955); reprinted as *The Mission to Asia* (Toronto: University of Press for the Mediaeval Academy of America, 1986). The most accessible version is Manuel Komroff, ed. *Contemporaries of Marco Polo* (New York: 1928; reprinted, New York: Dorset Press, 1989).

Other books that discuss Rubruck include: C. Raymond Beazley, *The Dawn of Modern Geography*, vol. 2 (London: John Murray, 1901); Arthur Percival Newton, *Travel and Travellers of the Middle Ages* (New York: Alfred A. Knopf, 1930); Leonardo Olschki, *Marco Polo's Precursors* (Baltimore: The Johns Hopkins Press, 1943); Björn Landström, *The Quest for India* (Garden City, N.Y.: Doubleday, 1964); and I. de Rachewiltz, *Papal Envoys to the Great Khans* (Stanford: Stanford University Press, 1971).

Fanny Bullock Workman

(1859 - 1925)

Fanny Bullock Workman was an American who traveled with her husband by bicycle in North Africa and Asia in the early 1900s. She then became a mountain climber and set two altitude records for women.

Fanny Bullock was born in Worcester, Massachusetts on January 8, 1859. Her mother was the daughter of a wealthy Connecticut businessman, and her father was a politician who was elected Governor of Massachusetts in 1866. In 1881 Fanny married Dr. William Hunter Workman who was twelve years older than she was. They had one daughter who spent most of her years in boarding schools while her parents traveled.

In 1889 Dr. Workman gave up his practice in Worcester because of ill health, and he and Fanny moved to Germany, which they used as their base for making a series of travels by bicycle throughout Europe. In 1895 they took a long bicycle trip to Spain and then to Morocco where they crossed the Atlas Mountains into the Sahara Desert in Algeria. The Workmans traveled by bike, Fanny dressed in the long skirts that were the Victorian fashion. They carried twelve to twenty pounds of luggage on their bicycles and stopped at inns to eat and sleep, averaging 50 miles of travel a day. They were often nearly run off the road by mule trains and got into several arguments with mule drivers. They wrote about their adventures in two books — *Algerian Memories* (1895) and *Sketches Awheel* (1897).

Pleased with the success of their North African trip, the Workmans next tackled a more difficult terrain—India. They traveled, always on bicycle, from the extreme south of India into Kashmir in the north and then from the east coast to the west and from there went to Burma, Sri Lanka, Java, and Indochina. They kept rigidly to a schedule during all of their travels, and, when some of their photographs were lost in a flood in Kashmir, they revisited the spots they had seen in order to take the same photos over again. They spent three years covering the length and breadth of India and South Asia.

While in Kashmir, the Workmans had taken time to climb some of the mountains in Karakorum Range. In 1899 Fanny set a world altitude record for women by climbing Mt. Koser Gunge to a height of 21,000 feet. This first experience of climbing thrilled the Workmans, and they then became serious mountain climbers, making expedition to the Himalayas in 1898, 1899, 1902, 1903, 1906, 1908, 1911, and 1912. In 1906 Fanny set a new world record by climbing Pinnacle Peak in the Nun Kun Range to an altitude of 22,815 feet. When **Annie Smith Peck** claimed to have bettered that record by climbing a higher peak in the Andes in 1908, Fanny hired scientists to measure it and proved that it was not quite as tall as the one she had climbed. The Workmans used their expeditions to map and measure the Himalayan terrain they crossed and were not deterred, for example, when one of their porters fell into an icy crevasse and was killed. One of their photos shows Fanny on the top of one of the peaks in the Karakorums reading a paper titled "Votes for Women."

These travels made the Workmans famous, and Fanny was the second woman (**Isabella Bird** was the first) to address the Royal Geographic Society and was the first American woman to lecture at the Sorbonne (University of Paris). During World War I, the Workmans lived at Cannes in the south of France. She was ill for many years after the war and died in Cannes on January 22, 1925. Her husband took her ashes back to Worcester, Massachusetts, where he stayed until 1937. There is a memorial to the two of them in Worcester that reads, "Pioneer Himalayan Explorers."

Where to learn more

Workman wrote a number of books and articles about her experiences: *Algerian Memories: A Bicycle Tour over the Atlas to the Sahara* (London: Unwin, 1895; New York: A.D.F. Randolph, 1895); *Sketches Awheel in Fin de Siècle Iberia* (London: Unwin, 1897), published as *Sketches Awheel in Modern Iberia* in the United States (New York: G.P. Putnam's Sons, 1897); *In the Ice World of Himálaya . . . Among the Peaks and Passes of Ladakh, Nubra, Suru, and Baltistan* (London: Unwin, 1900; New York: Cassell, 1900); *Through Town and Jungle: Fourteen Thousand Miles A-Wheel Among the Temples and People of the Indian Plain* (London: Unwin, 1904); *Ice-Bound Heights of the Mustagh: An Account of Two Seasons of Pioneer Exploration and High Climbing in the Baltistan Himálaya* (London: Constable, 1908; New York: Scribners, 1908); *Peaks and Glaciers of Nun Kun . . . A Record of Pioneer Exploration and Mountaineering in the Punjab Himalaya* (London: Constable, 1909; New York: Scribners, 1909); *The Call of the Snowy Hispar: A Narrative of Exploration and Mountaineering on the Northern Frontier of India* (London: Constable, 1910; New York: Scribner's, 1911); and *Two Summers in the Ice-Wilds of Eastern Karakorum: The Exploration of Nineteen Hundred Square Miles of Mountain and Glacier* (London: Unwin, 1917; New York: Duttons, 1917).

The rivalry between Workman and Peck can be seen in a series of letters entitled "Miss Peck and Mrs. Workman" in the *Scientific American*, vol. 102 (1910). Workman fired off the first salvo on February 12 on p. 143; Peck replied on February 26; and Workman got in the last word on April 16, p. 319.

Several of the books about women explorers include chapters about Workman: Mignon Rittenhouse, *Seven Women Explorers* (Philadelphia: J.B. Lippincott Co., 1964); Dorothy Middleton, *Victorian Lady Travellers* (London: Routledge & Kegan Paul, 1965); Leo Hamalian, ed. *Ladies on the Loose: Women Travellers of the 18th and 19th Centuries* (New York: Dodd, Mead & Co., 1981); Dea Birkett, *Spinsters Abroad: Victorian Lady Explorers* (London: Basil Blackwell, 1989); and Marion Tinling, *Women into the Unknown: A Sourcebook on Women Explorers and Travelers* (New York: Greenwood Press, 1989), which was of most help in writing this account.

St. Francis Xavier

(1506 - 1552)

One of the first Europeans to travel to Japan and to travel in Japan, St. Francis Xavier was a Roman Catholic missionary.

Francis Xavier was born in his family's castle of Xavier near the town of Sanguesa in the Basque Country of northern Spain on April 7, 1506. His father, Juan de Jasso, was an important official in the court of the King of Navarre. He went to study at the University of Paris in 1525 and graduated with a Master of Arts degree in 1530 and then lectured at one of the colleges of the university. While at the university Francis Xavier became an associate of Ignatius Loyola, the founder of the Society of Jesus—the Jesuits. Francis Xavier took the vows of poverty and chastity in August 1534 and studied theology until 1536 when he went to Italy and was ordained a priest on June 24, 1537.

Francis Xavier was sent to Lisbon in 1540 by the Pope with a recommendation to King João III of Portugal that he be sent as a missionary to the Far East where the Portuguese were the leading European trading nation. He left Portugal on April 7, 1541, spent the following winter in Mozambique, and arrived at the Portuguese city of Goa in India on May 6, 1542. He made a trip

St. Francis Xavier. The Granger Collection, New York.

to Travancore in southern India in 1543 and is credited with baptizing 10,000 Indians into Christianity while there. On his return to Goa he was appointed the chief of all Catholic missions east of the Cape of Good Hope in southern Africa.

In 1545 Francis Xavier traveled to Portuguese posts in southern India and then went to the great trading center of Malacca in what is now Malaysia. In 1546 he traveled to the "Spice Islands" of the Moluccas in eastern Indonesia. He returned to Malacca in July 1547. There he heard for the first time about the distant islands of Japan, where three Portuguese traders had landed in 1542 after having been shipwrecked while on a voyage to northern China. As news of Japan filtered back to the Portuguese trading stations, Francis Xavier determined to go there himself. First, however, he returned to India.

Francis Xavier left from Goa bound for Japan on April 15, 1549 with two Jesuit companions and three young Japanese who had come with a Portuguese trader to Malacca and had been converted to Christianity. They arrived at the port of Kagoshima on the southern Japanese island of Kyushu on August 15, 1549. Francis Xavier stayed in Japan for two years. During that time he traveled to the port of Hirado on a small island off the west coast of Kyushu. He then went to the castle town of Yamaguchi, which was the headquarters of Ouchi clan, the feudal rulers of western Japan. There he argued matters of theology with Buddhist monks of the Lotus and Zen sects. He traveled to the capital of the Emperor of Japan at Kyoto, where he found things in turmoil, and then returned to Yamaguchi. He then went to Bungo, the center of the Otomo clan where he found a warm welcome. The head of the Otomo clan converted to Christianity and welcomed Francis Xavier's successors.

As a result of Francis Xavier's visit, a Roman Catholic mission was founded in the southern island of Kyushu, which had a great deal of success over the following decades. By the year 1615 there were an estimated 500,000 Christians in Japan. By that time, however, the centralizing Tokugawa shogunate had started to persecute Christians and to cut Japan's ties with the rest of the world. The Portuguese were expelled in 1639, and contact with Europe was limited to a small Dutch trading post in the southern city of Nagasaki, which had been founded by Christians in the 1560s and was sometimes ruled by Jesuits.

Francis Xavier left Japan from Bungo in November 1551 and reached Goa in the middle of February 1552. By this time he had decided to set up missions in China. At this time the great Chinese empire was becoming wary of foreign influence and power and zealously guarded admission to its domains. A Portuguese ambassador was sent out to try to get permission for Francis Xavier to travel to China and to secure the release of some Portuguese who were being held in Canton. The Chinese refused to even talk to the ambassador. By this time Francis Xavier was in Malacca, having left Goa on April 17, 1552. He then decided to enter China on his own without official permission. He left Malacca with this intention on July 15, 1552. Francis Xavier reached the small island of Sanchuan in the Pearl River estuary near Canton at the end of August; the Portuguese had been allowed to set up a small trade fair there. He became ill in November and died at Sanchuan on December 3, 1552. He was made a saint of the Roman Catholic Church in 1622.

Where to learn more

St. Francis Xavier's letters have been edited and published by J. Broderick, 2 vols. (London: 1932). By far the best book on Xavier and the Catholic missionaries in Japan is C.R. Boxer, *The Christian Century in Japan, 1549-1650* (Berkeley: University of California Press, 1951; 2nd edition, 1967, reprinted, 1974). Another book by Boxer, *Fidalgos in the Far East, 1550-1770* (The Hague: Martinus Nijhoff, 1948; reprinted, Hong Kong: Oxford University Press, 1968) discusses early Portuguese-Japanese relations. See also Theodore Maynard, *The Odyssey of St. Francis Xavier* (London: 1936).

Xenophon

(435? B.C. - 355? B.C.)

Xenophon was a Greek soldier who led a Greek army across Asia Minor in an epic march and then wrote about it in a famous travel book.

Xenophon was born in the Greek city-state of Athens. He became a pupil and companion of the famous Greek philosopher Socrates. Following the death of King Darius II of Persia, his two sons fought over the succession to the Persian Empire. The elder son Artaxerxes became king, but the younger son Cyrus coveted the crown for himself. In 401 B.C. Prince Cyrus attempted to overthrow his brother with the aid of a Greek mercenary army, known as the Ten Thousand. Xenophon was one of the Greeks who signed on to this force. He wrote about his experiences in a famous book, the *Anabasis* ("The March into the Interior"), composed about twenty years after the events it narrates.

In his book Xenophon tells about how the Greeks marched into Persia and then took part in the great battle of Cunaxa, 45 miles from Babylon, in what is now Iraq. Cyrus was defeated and killed in this battle, and the 24 Greek mercenary generals were captured and put to death. That left the large Greek force stranded in a foreign and hostile land without any leadership. They thereupon elected their own generals. Xenophon was chosen to be second in command after the Spartan Cheirosophus.

Xenophon became the inspiring force for this refugee army on its march of 1,500 miles back home. Marching out of the Persian Empire they were harassed by the Persian army until they reached the mountains of Kurdistan. They had to fight their way through the mountains against the hostile Kurdish tribes until they reached the border of the Kingdom of Armenia at the Centrites River, a tributary of the Tigris in eastern Turkey. When they got to Armenia they were met by a force under the command of Tiribazus, the ruler of Armenia. Pursued by the Kurds, they had to promise Tiribazus that they would not live off of his land on their way through it in order to get him to agree to let them pass. By now it was December 401 B.C. and the highlands of Armenia were covered in the ice and snow of winter. The way led through mountainous country that they now had to cross in the dead of winter depending upon their own meager resources. The Greeks suffered greatly from frostbite and snow blindness, in addition to hunger and exhaustion, and many of them died during this part of the journey. The territory they passed through was so rugged that it was little known until modern times.

Xenophon and what remained of the Ten Thousand marched northwestward toward what is now the city of Erzurum. They then entered the territory of the warlike Chalybes, but were fortunately well received. They arrived at the city of Gymnias, which was the center of a rich silver-mining district. There they learned that they were only five days' march from the city of Trapezus (modern-day Trabzon) on the Black Sea. Xenophon wrote a famous passage about this part of the trip:

"When the men in front reached the summit and caught sight of the sea there was great shouting. Xenophon and the rearguard heard it and thought there were some more enemies attacking in front. . . . However, when the shouting got louder and drew nearer, and those who were constantly going forward started running towards the men in front who kept on shouting, and the more there were of them the more shouting there was, it looked then as there was something more serious. Xenophon galloped forward to the front with his cavalry. When he got near he heard what the cry was—The Sea! The Sea! (*Thalassa! Thalassa!*). Then they all began to run, the rearguard and all, and drove on the pack animals and horses at full speed; and when they had all got to the top, the soldiers, with tears in their eyes, embraced each other and their generals and captains."

Trapezus was a Greek colony, and the soldiers were welcome there even if the citizens where a little worried about what such a large, unruly band of men might do. At this point Xenophon thought of capturing a nearby native city and settling the Greeks there and starting a new colony. But the soldiers were not interested—they only wanted to get back home. At this point Cheirosophus died, and Xenophon became the sole leader. He was able to keep the men together in spite of their tendency to divide into smaller bands depending on their native cities.

Xenophon evacuated the Ten Thousand (now reduced to about 6,000) by land and sea to the city of Chalcedon, on the Asian shore opposite Byzantium (Constantinople or Istanbul) in 399 B.C. With some difficulty Xenophon kept his men from sacking the palace at Byzantium and then he hired them out to the Thracian prince Seuthes, who used them to put down some rebellious tribes. Seuthes cheated them out of their pay, and then they were enlisted by the Spartans to help them in a war with the Persians along the coasts of Asia Minor. They were able to pillage and sack and obtained a large amount of plunder. Xenophon then turned command over to someone else and returned to Athens.

On his return to Athens he found that his old master, Socrates, had died and he did not find his native city congenial. He returned to fight the Persians, but then Athens allied itself with the Persians against Sparta. Xenophon was banished from Athens and went into exile in Sparta. There he was given a country estate at the town of Scillus, not far from Mt. Olympus. He stayed there for more than twenty years and wrote the *Anabasis* as well as the *Greek History*, which told the story of his native land from 411 B.C., the time left off by his predecessor Thucydides. He lost his estate and retreated to the city of Corinth. In the meantime, Athens restored his citizenship, but it is thought that Xenophon never returned there but died in Corinth sometime around the year 355 B.C. His *Anabasis* was the world's first travelogue.

Where to learn more

The only place to get the real flavor of Xenophon is by reading the *Anabasis*, which is available in many editions, including in Penguin paperback (1986).

Charles E. Yeager

(1923 -   )

Charles E. Yeager was a test pilot for the United States Air Force who was the first person to fly a plane faster than the speed of sound.

Charles ("Chuck") E. Yeager was born in Myra, West Virginia on February 13, 1923. His father was a driller for natural gas in the West Virginia coal fields. As the United States began mobilizing for World War II, Yeager enlisted in the Army Air Force in 1941 at the age of 18. In 1943 he became a flight officer, a non-commissioned officer who could pilot aircraft. He went to England where he flew fighter planes over France and Germany during the last two years of the war.

In his first eight missions, at the age of 20, Yeager shot down two German fighters. On his ninth mission he was shot down over German-occupied France, suffering flak wounds. He bailed out of the plane and was rescued by members of the French resistance who smuggled him across the Pyrenees Mountains into Spain. In Spain he was jailed briefly but made his way back to England where he flew fighter planes in support of the Allied invasion of Normandy.

On October 12, 1944 Yeager took on and shot down five German fighter planes in succession. On November 6, flying a propeller-driven P-51 Mustang, he shot down one of the new jet fighters the Germans had developed, the Messerschmidt-262, and damaged two more. On November 20 he shot down four FW-190s. By the end of the war, at which time he was 22 years old, he was credited with having shot down 13½ German planes (one was also claimed by another pilot).

In 1946 and 1947 Yeager was trained as a test pilot at Wright Field in Dayton, Ohio. He showed great talent for stunt-team flying and was chosen to go to Muroc Field in California, later to become Edwards Air Force Base, to work on the top-secret XS-1 project. At the end of the war, the U.S. Army had found that the Germans had not only developed the world's first jet fighter but also a rocket plane that had tested at speeds as fast as 596 miles an hour. Just after the war, a British jet, the Gloster Meteor, had raised the official world speed record to 606 miles per hour. The next record to be broken was to attain the speed of sound, Mach 1, which was what the XS-1 project was designed to do.

The measurement for the speed of sound was named after the German scientist Ernst Mach, who had discovered that sound traveled at different speeds at different altitudes, temperatures,

and wind speeds. On a calm day at 60°F at sea level it was about 760 miles an hour. This speed decreased at higher altitudes. Airplane pilots who had come close to the speed of sound in dives reported that their controls froze and the structure of the plane shook uncontrollably. A British test plane disintegrated as it approached the speed of sound. Because of these experiences, Mach 1 became known as the "sound barrier."

The Army had developed an experimental plane called the X-1 to break the barrier. Built by the Bell Aircraft Corporation, it was a rocket shaped like a bullet that was launched from another plane once they were airborne. The idea was to send up the X-1 on a number of flights, each time getting a little closer to Mach 1. A top commercial test pilot had been making these flights and had reached .8 Mach, where the plane shook violently. The pilot demanded a large bonus to fly the plane up to Mach 1. The Army refused to pay the bonus, and Yeager was given the job of piloting the X-1 at his usual salary.

In his test flights Yeager was able to get the plane to fly at .9 Mach and still keep control of the plane. It was his personal belief that the heavy vibration of the plane would actually calm down after reaching Mach 1. The date of October 14, 1947 was set for breaking the "sound barrier." On the night of October 12, Yeager went horseback riding and fell off the horse. The next day his right side was in a great deal of pain. Afraid of being taken off the flight, he drove to a local town and saw the doctor there who told him that he had broken two ribs.

Yeager went ahead with the flight without telling anyone of his injury. Because of his injury, he was unable to close the plane's right side door, but he solved the problem by taking the handle of a broomstick with him and using it to close the door with his left hand. Early on the morning of October 14, Yeager went up in the B-29 bomber that carried the X-1. He entered the X-1 and locked himself in at 7,000 feet. The B-29 released the X-1 at 26,000 feet. At .87 Mach the violent vibrations began, but Yeager continued to push the aircraft faster. Just as he had predicted, at .96 Mach the aircraft steadied and he passed Mach 1. At that moment a giant roar was heard on the desert at the experimental test site—the first man-made sonic boom. Yeager reached Mach 1.05 and stayed above Mach 1 for seven minutes. On his way back to the field he performed victory rolls and wing-over-wing stunts.

As soon as Yeager landed safely, the results were telephoned to the head of Army aviation, who ordered the base not to give

Chuck Yeager. UPI/Bettmann Newsphotos.

out any information about the flight. Rumors of the flight appeared in the aviation press in December 1947, but the Air Force (as the Army Air Force became) did not confirm it and release Yeager's name until June 1948.

Yeager continued to test planes at Edwards Air Force Base. In December 1953 he set a new record by flying the X-1A to Mach 2.4. He left Edwards in 1954 and then went to Okinawa where he flew Soviet planes captured in the Korean War in order to test their performance. He returned to the United States in 1957 to lead an air squadron, and flew on training operations and readiness maneuvers at Air Force bases in the United States and abroad. In 1961 he was appointed director of test flight operations at Edwards Air Force Base and the following year was made commandant of the Aerospace Research Pilot School at Edwards.

In 1963 Yeager tested an experimental plane designed for high altitude flying, the NF-104, to see if it could beat the record set by a Soviet military plane of 113,890 feet. Yeager reached 108,000 feet when the plane spun out of control, and he was forced to eject from the plane. He was severely burned on the left side of his face and left hand. He spent a month in the hospital but was able to return to flying duties and as head of the experimental test pilot school.

Yeager was promoted to brigadier general in 1969, by which time he had flown more than one hundred missions in Southeast Asia in B-57 tactical bombers. Yeager had become the most famous pilot in the United States, and the Air Force called upon him increasingly for its public relations and recruiting efforts. He served in a variety of Air Force positions until his retirement in 1975. He is the recipient of numerous military awards and was awarded the Presidential Medal of Freedom in 1985.

Where to learn more

Yeager has written a couple of autobiographies. The first was entitled simply *Yeager* and published in New York by Bantam Books in 1985. This was followed by *Press On: Further Adventures of the Good Life*, Bantam Books, 1988. An interesting account of Yeager's life was written by William Lundgren and published as *Across the High Frontier* (New York: Morrow, 1955; paperback edition, New York: Bantam Books, 1987). There is an exciting retelling of Yeager's flights in the X-1 in Tom Wolfe, *The Right Stuff* (New York: Farrar, Straus & Giroux, 1979; paperback edition, New York: Bantam, 1980), which served as the main source for this account. Wolfe's book was later made into a movie (Warner Brothers, 1983), with Sam Shepard playing the role of Yeager.

Yermak Timofeyev

(1540?-1585?)

Yermak Timofeyev was a Russian Cossack who conquered the Siberian khanate, beginning the expansion of Russia to the east.

The Cossacks were a people of Turkish origin living along the Volga River. They were organized along military lines and were used as mercenary soldiers by the Russian tsars. Of uncertain origin, Yermak Timofeyev was first heard of as a leader of one of many Cossack bands plundering on the Volga River and robbing Russian merchants, Persian ambassadors, and the Tsar's ships.

In 1579, Yermak went to work for the great Stroganov family, who were the leading fur traders in the Ural Mountains. It is not clear whether this was at the request of the Stroganovs or whether Yermak and his men showed up at the Stroganov camp while escaping from Russian troops and were put to use by the Stroganovs. In any case, the Cossacks helped the Stroganovs defend their property from attacks by the local inhabitants.

In 1581 the Stroganovs outfitted Yermak with supplies for a force of 840 men with the aim of driving back the Tatar raiders who had cut off fur supplies from the east. This expedition traveled east on the Chusovaya River up into the Ural Mountains into areas unknown by the local guides. It spent the winter in the mountains, and then boated down the Tura River in the spring. Once over the mountains, the Russians encountered the first representatives of the Tatars, Muslims who were ruled by the Khan of Siberia.

The Russians learned that the Khanate (the area ruled by the Khan) was much weaker than they had supposed, and they were able to launch a major attack against the capital of Sibir and to defeat the forces of the Khan Kuchum. The Tatar forces dissolved, and Yermak found himself the ruler of Sibir.

He then sent envoys to Moscow with tribute from the new territory to Tsar Ivan IV (the Terrible). The Tsar was quite happy to accept rule of the newly-conquered territory, and in 1584 he sent reinforcements to help Yermak hold on to his conquests. These reinforcements were welcome because Yermak was busy trying to subdue the local inhabitants. But when they arrived in Sibir, there was not enough food to feed them. The Russian forces spent the winter of 1584-1585 in near-starvation conditions in the fort at Sibir. They were besieged in the spring by Tatars but were able to break out and to drive off their attackers.

In August 1585 Yermak set out to plunder a caravan of traders coming from the central Asian city of Bukhara when he was ambushed by Tatars and drowned trying to escape. Following his death, the Russians evacuated Sibir but returned four years later to establish themselves permanently. Sibir then became the base for their great march east across Siberia, the name of which comes from the city conquered by Yermak.

Where to learn more

The documentary sources for Yermak's career can be found in Terence Armstrong, ed. *Yermak's Campaign in Siberia: A Selection of Documents* (London: Hakluyt Society, 1975). There is a chapter on Yermak, based on Russian sources, in George V. Lantzeff and Richard A. Pierce, *Eastward to Empire: Exploration and Conquest on the Russian Open Frontier, to 1750* (Montreal: McGill-Queen's University Press, 1973). See also Joseph L. Wieczynski, *The Russian Frontier* (Charlottesville: University of Virginia Press, 1976).

Sir Francis Younghusband

(1863 - 1942)

Sir Francis Younghusband was a British officer and official who explored widely in the Himalayas and led an important expedition into Tibet.

Francis Younghusband was born in northern India in the foothills of the Himalayas. His father was a major in the British Army in India. Younghusband was educated at Sandhurst, the British military school, and then returned to India as an Army officer. His uncle had been an explorer in the Himalayas, and Younghusband developed an interest in following in his footsteps.

In 1884 Younghusband made the first of his trips to the Himalayas and then did reconnaissance work for the Army on the border with Afghanistan and in Kashmir. He worked as an intelligence officer in the "Great Game"—the struggle between Britain and Russia for control of Afghanistan and Central Asia. In 1886 he was chosen to go on a British mission to Manchuria. On his return from there to Beijing he met a Colonel Mark Bell who had decided to return to India overland. Younghusband received permission to accompany him. They left Beijing on April 4, 1887 and split up for part of the journey.

Sir Francis Younghusband. The Granger Collection, New York.

Younghusband traveled more than 1,250 miles through the Gobi Desert, the first European to cross it, to the town of Hami. When he got there, he found that Bell had gone on alone so he set out by himself across the northern edge of the Taklamakan Desert, south of the Tien Shan Mountains passing through the towns of Turfan, Aksu, and Kashgar. He crossed the Karakorum mountains by way of the Mustagh Pass, the first European to do so, and then down the slopes of the Himalayas to Rawalpindi in northern India. His journey had lasted seven months.

Promoted to captain, in 1889 Younghusband returned to the Karakorum Range to investigate attacks on trade caravans by local tribesmen and to explore the passes between Yarkand north of the mountains in the Taklamakan and Hunza Mountains in northern Kashmir. During these expeditions he met up with a Russian exploring party who were moving down from Central Asia. This competition between the British and the Russians fueled the exploration of the region for many years.

In 1889, Younghusband became an official of the Indian Foreign Department concerned with stopping the advance of the Russians. In 1890 he traveled with Sir George Macartney on a diplomatic mission into Central Asia. On his return, he went through the Pamir Mountains in what is now the border region between Tadzhikistan and Afghanistan. He ran into a party of Russian troops who arrested him and escorted him out of the region. He wrote about his experiences in 1896 in his book *Heart of a Continent*. In the following years, he served as a government official administering areas in the border regions of northern India. He took time out for various Army duties and to write about the Boer War in South Africa.

In 1903 Younghusband was chosen to lead a British mission to Tibet to counter the growing influence of the Russians in Lhasa, the capital. He was accompanied by a force of 3,000 soldiers commanded by Sir James Macdonald. The mission did important geographical work along the way, exploring the Brahmaputra and Sutlej Rivers. They had a couple of military encounters with the Tibetans but were able to make their way to Lhasa and to negotiate a treaty giving Britain certain political rights in Tibet. In 1906, however, the British gave up these rights to the Chinese, which began the modern period of Chinese intervention in Tibetan affairs.

After his return to India, Younghusband became the top British official in Kashmir until his retirement in 1910. On his return to England he became president of the Royal Geographical Society, and he actively encouraged the climbing of Mount

Everest, about which he wrote several books. He also wrote about Hinduism and Buddhism and worked to reconcile the world's great religions.

Where to learn more

Younghusband's books include *India and Tibet* (London: John Murray, 1910) and *The Epic of Mount Everest* (London: 1926). An extensive obituary appeared in the *Geographical Journal* vol. 100 (1942).

There is an interesting history of the Younghusband mission to Tibet: Peter Fleming, *Bayonets to Lhasa* (London: Rupert Hart-Davis, 1961) and a complete biography of Younghusband: George Seaver, *Francis Younghusband: Explorer and Mystic* (London: 1952).

Two books on the history of the exploration of Tibet give good summaries of Younghusband's mission: *Tibet: A Chronicle of Exploration* (London: Routledge & Kegan Paul, 1970) and Peter Hopkirk, *Trespassers on the Roof of the World: The Race for Lhasa* (London: John Murray, 1982).

EXPLORERS
and
DISCOVERERS
of the
WORLD

Glossary

African Association: officially, the Association for Promoting the Discovery of the Interior Parts of Africa. It was organized by **Sir Joseph Banks** and other English gentlemen in a London tavern in 1788. It set as its first goal the discovery of the course of the Niger River and sponsored several expeditions, including those of **Mungo Park**, for that purpose. The African Association declined with the death of Banks in 1820 and merged with the newly-founded **Royal Geographical Society** in 1831.

caravel: a small, fast ship first used by the Portuguese in about 1440. It had three triangular, or lateen, sails and a center rudder. It was used for the voyages down the west African coast sponsored by **Prince Henry the Navigator**. Not large enough for oceanic voyages, it developed into the nau or carrack that was used by **Christopher Columbus** and **Vasco da Gama**. These ships had large square sails. They later developed into the galleon of the 16th and 17th centuries.

chronometer: any instrument for measuring time (chronos in Greek). However, it has come to be applied more specifically to very accurate time-keeping instruments that are used for navigation, for determining longitude. The principle is that if you set the timepiece at the place you leave from (say, Greenwich, England, which later became the "prime" meridian for everybody), you can calculate your longitudinal distance from that spot by comparing the time on the chronometer with your observed time (say, at "high noon" when the sun reaches the highest point in your sky). In order to work, however, the timepiece has to be extremely accurate because even slight variations will be greatly magnified by distance. The first timepiece that met these standards was invented by an English carpenter named John Harrison and was first used on a voyage in 1763. He was given a reward of £20,000 by the British government.

conquistador: the Spanish word for "conqueror." It is particularly applied to the Spaniards, such as **Hernando Cortés** and **Francisco Pizarro**, who conquered Mexico and Peru in the 16th century.

cutter: a small boat used to transfer goods and passengers between a ship and the shore, or from ship to ship.

Dalai Lama: the chief priest and spiritual head of Lamaism, the religion of Tibet and Mongolia.

dhow: a sailing vessel common along the coast of the Indian Ocean, having one mast and a triangular, or lateen, sail.

hadj, hajj: the pilgrimage to Mecca, birthplace of Muhammad, that is a religious duty of all Muslims who can afford it at least once in a lifetime. The great journeys of the medieval Arab travelers often started out as a hadj. The first Europeans who penetrated Mecca in disguise joined hadj caravans to make the trip.

khan: the supreme ruler of the Turkish, Tatar and Mongol tribes of Central Asia. The word comes from Turkish kan, meaning lord. The first great Mongol ruler, Genghis, who conquered much of Asia was the first of the "Great Khans." His grandson Kublai was visited by **Marco Polo**.

lama: a priest or monk of Lamaism, the religion of Tibet and Mongolia. It is a variety of Buddhism modified by Hinduism and native shamanistic beliefs and practices. The chief lama and spiritual head of Lamaism is known as the Dalai Lama.

latitude: the angular (that is, in terms of degrees rather than kilometers or miles) distance north or south of the equator. Humans developed methods, such as the sextant, for calculating latitude at a fairly early date.

Line of Demarcation: a line established by Pope Alexander VI in 1493 to settle the claims of Portugal and Spain to the "new" lands they had discovered. The north-south line ran 100 leagues west of the Azores and Cape Verde Islands. The Treaty of Tordesillas in 1494 moved the line 270 leagues further west. According to the terms of the treaty, all lands west of the line (the New World) belonged to Spain; territory east of the line (Africa, India, the Far East) was Portugal's. The easternmost part of Brazil is east of the line. This gave Portugal its toehold in the New World. Its colony in Brazil gradually moved westward. Today Brazil still retains the Portuguese language and culture while the rest of Latin America is Spanish-speaking.

longitude: the angular distance east or west of a standard meridian. In the modern world, the standard meridian has been set at the location of the Greenwich Observatory near London. Calculating longitude has always posed a great problem for navigators and was not solved until the invention of the **chronometer**.

magnetic poles: two points near the North and South Poles that are the focus of the Earth's magnetic field. Using a magnetic compass, the needle will point towards the magnetic pole. It was probably **Christopher Columbus** who first realized that the north magnetic pole was not due north, that is, that it was not the same as the North Pole. **Sir James Ross** was the first person to reach the north magnetic pole. When it was next visited, it was not in the same place; the Earth's magnetic field, and therefore the two magnetic poles, moves.

the Mahdi: a Muslim term for messiah, the title was assumed by Muhammad Ahmad ibn as-Sayyid 'Abd Allah (1844-1885), a Sudanese religious and nationalist leader. In 1881 he announced that he had been divinely appointed to purify Islam and drive out the tyrannical Egyptian forces which were occupying the Sudan. He and his followers besieged the capital city of Khartoum in October 1884 and took it in January 1885, massacring the defenders, including British General Charles Gordon (1833-1885), and many of the inhabitants.

malaria: an acute infectious disease endemic to tropical and subtropical regions. It is caused by single-celled organisms called plasmodia which are transmitted by the bite of the female *Anopheles* mosquito.

Symptoms include chills, fever, headache, sweating, and muscle pain. Untreated primary attacks can last from a week to a month or longer; relapses often occur sporadically for several years. Quinine, a drug derived from the bark of the cinchona tree, was one of the first treatments for malaria and is still used in extreme cases, although it has generally been replaced by the drug chloroquine.

meridian: an imaginary circle passing through the poles, therefore a "meridian" of longitude.

New World: name given to the lands of the Western Hemisphere. The term was first used by Italian historian Pietro Martire d'Anghiera (1457-1526) in *De Rebus Oceanicis et Novo Orbe*, the first account of the European discovery of America.

North Pole, South Pole: two imaginary points that represent the places where the Earth's axis of rotation crosses the surface. The Inuit, having heard about the North Pole from Europeans, visualized it as a real place they called the "Big Nail."

Northwest Passage: a sea route between the Atlantic and Pacific Oceans along the northern coast of North America. It was the object of Arctic exploration for many years. **Roald Amundsen** was the first to successfully navigate it.

Pundit: a Hindi word meaning learned expert or teacher. It was adopted by the British as a nickname for the Indians and Nepalese who were trained in geography, cryptography, measurements, etc. in order to map the Himalayas and Tibet.

Royal Geographical Society: founded in London in 1830 as a private association to promote geographical knowledge and exploration, it was the sponsor of many of the great expeditions of the 19th and 20th century. It awards annually a number of prizes for geographical accomplishment, including the most prestigious, the Founders' Gold Medal, which was earned by several of the explorers in this book. The other European countries imitated the British by establishing their own national geographic societies, all of which awarded prizes. The U.S. counterpart is the American Geographical Society. The National Geographic Society, founded in 1888, is a somewhat different kind of institution that has remained in the control of the Grosvenor family. It has grown rich from the sales of its famous magazine, which has allowed it to sponsor many expeditions, including those of **Robert Edward Peary** and **Jacques-Yves Cousteau**.

scurvy: a disease caused by lack of vitamin C. It is the result of a diet that lacks fresh vegetables and was a common affliction of anyone making long journeys, especially voyages at sea. Its symptoms are swollen and bleeding gums, spots on the skin, and weakness, and it can eventually lead to death. Traditionally, the British Royal Navy is supposed to have solved the problem by having its sailors drink lime juice, hence the slang word "Limeys" for British sailors or the British in general. In fact, the British and other navies experimented with a large number of foodstuffs and sanitary measures to try to stop the disease. **James Cook** made the first voyage around the world in which none of the men on his ship died of scurvy. He accomplished this with a wide variety of measures, not just lime juice, and was given a special award by the Royal Geographical Society for his achievement.

sextant: a navigational instrument that was developed in the 18th century. It had an arc of 60 that was divided into degrees, minutes, and seconds. By measuring the angle made by the sun or other celestial body with a sextant, it was possible to determine latitude. Prior to the use of the sextant, other less sophisticated instruments such as the astrolabe, quadrant, and cross-staff were used to make the same measurements, but less accurately.

sledge: a vehicle on runners for going over the snow. The more common American term is "sled." In the history of Polar exploration, experiments were made pulling sledges by manpower, horses, ponies, reindeer, and dogs. Dogs turned out to be the most effective.

transit: When viewed from Earth, the apparent passage of a celestial body across the meridian, which can be used as a means of determining location. Also, the apparent passage of one of the inner planets across the Sun. **James Cook** made his first visit to the South Pacific to observe the rare occurrence of the transit of Venus.

triangulation: the basic technique of surveying and mapping. Measurements are made by subdividing an area into ever-smaller triangles with known base lengths and base angles.

voyageur: literally, a "traveler." In the context of North American exploration, it came to be applied to a French-Canadian boatman who was employed to transport goods (usually furs) and passengers in canoes between trading posts.

Bibliography

There have been several general histories of the exploration of the world that have focused on different aspects of the subject and/or have had varying scopes. Leonard Outhwaite, *Unrolling the Map: The Story of Exploration* (New York: The John Day Company, 1935; 3rd edition, 1972) includes the major trends and the better known explorers in a generally impressionistic survey of the field. It is quite good for young people. J.N.L. Baker, *A History of Geographical Discovery and Exploration* (New York: Houghton Mifflin, 1931, 2nd edition, 1937, reprinted, New York: Cooper Square Publishers, 1967) is more detailed, while Sir Percy Sykes, *A History of Exploration from the Earliest Times to the Present Day* (London: George Routledge & Sons, 1934) tends to concentrate on a few of the most famous explorations.

Piers Pennington, *The Great Explorers* (London: Aldus Books, 1979; New York: Facts on File, 1979) gives quite complete biographical sketches of the most famous explorers and is well illustrated. Its usefulness is hampered by the lack of references or bibliography. Eric Newby, *The World Atlas of Exploration* (London: Mitchell Beazley Publishers, 1975; New York: Crescent Books, 1975) has a wider scope and includes detailed accounts of some voyages as well as treatment of some lesser-known figures. Newby's *A Book of Travellers' Tales* (New York: Viking, 1986) includes the original documentary sources for many of the personages he wrote about in *The World Atlas*. All three of these books were very useful to the present author in writing the sketches that are found in the current volume.

The accounts that appear in Helen Delpar, ed. *The Discoverers: An Encyclopedia of Explorers and Exploration* (New York: McGraw-Hill, 1980) vary considerably. Some are very general while others contain more useful and detailed information. It includes some information, on Russian exploration, for example, that is not found in other general surveys. Probably the most useful sections are the comprehensive accounts of a particular topic, such as "Siberia." The bibliographies are helpful but rather sketchy.

The *Atlas of Discovery* (New York: Gallery Books, 1989). with a preface by Sir Francis Chichester, contains some very valuable and accurate maps of explorers' routes. The explanatory text is minimal.

A very interesting book is Richard A. Van Orman, *The Explorers: Nineteenth Century Expeditions in Africa and the American West* (Albuquerque: University of New Mexico Press, 1984). It deals with the subject of exploration in its 19th century heyday in a topical manner, examining such questions as the motivation of explorers and the consequences of their explorations. It goes beyond the simple mechanics of what the explorers did in trying to find the meaning of their actions.

Ancient and Medieval

The best general survey on early exploration is hard to find: C. Raymond Beazley, *The Dawn of Modern Geography*, vol. 1, which covers the period up to the early Middle Ages, (London: John Murray, 1897; reprinted, New York: Peter Smith, 1949); vol. 2, to the 13th century (London: Henry Frowde, 1901); vol. 3, from the late Middle Ages to 1420 (Oxford: Clarendon Press, 1906), vols. 1-3 reprinted, Freeport, N.Y.: Books for Libraries Press, 1967.

There are two good books on ancient exploration: M. Cary and E.H. Warmington, *The Ancient Explorers* (London: Methuen & Co., 1929; reprinted, London: Penguin, 1963) and Walter Woodburn Hyde, *Ancient Greek Mariners* (New York: Oxford University Press, 1947). See also Rhys Carpenter, *Beyond the Pillars of Heracles: The Classical World Seen Through the Eyes of Its Discoverers* (New York: Delacorte Press, 1966).

Arthur Percival Newton, ed. *Travel and Travellers of the Middle Ages* (New York: Alfred A. Knopf, 1926), is a series of essays by specialists on various aspects of the topic, including useful accounts of the Arabs and Vikings. Paul Herrmann, *Conquest by Man*, translated from the German by Michael Bullock (New York: Harper & Bros., 1954), is the first of two volumes by the author, covering the period up to the era of Prince Henry the Navigator. Herrmann has a very readable style but his inclusion of material is rather capricious.

I. de Rachewiltz, *Papal Envoys to the Great Khans* (Stanford: Stanford University Press, 1971) is an academic survey of the important contacts between Western Europe and the Mongol Khans.

J.R.S. Phillips, *The Medieval Expansion of Europe* (Oxford: Oxford University Press, 1988) is a topical study that refers to journeys made by individual explorers in order to illuminate the author's points.

Björn Landström, *The Quest for India* (Garden City, New York: Doubleday, 1964) is a very popularly written book that leads up to the period of the great maritime explorations of the 15th and 16th centuries—the period known as the Great Age of Discovery.

The Great Age of Discovery

Boies Penrose, *Travel and Discovery in the Renaissance, 1420-1620* (Cambridge: Harvard University Press, 1952) is a very good academic survey of the period. The best overall evaluation of the important role played by the Portuguese is Edgar Prestage, *The Portuguese Pioneers* (London: Adam & Charles Black, 1933; reprinted, 1966). For other works see the bibliographies under **Prince Henry the Navigator** and **Vasco da Gama**.

Paul Herrmann's *The Great Age of Discovery*, translated from the German by Arnold. J. Pomerans (New York: Harper & Bros., 1958) is fun to read but very selective in its coverage.

For an overall understanding of all the great voyages, there are no better works than those of the great American historian, Samuel Eliot Morison: *The European Discovery of America: The Northern Voyages, A.D. 500-1600* (New York: Oxford University Press, 1971) and *The European Discovery of America: The Southern Voyages* (New York: Oxford University Press, 1974). These two were abridged and combined in *The Great Explorers: The European Discovery of America* (New York: Oxford University Press, 1978), which unfortunately lacks the bibliographies of its two predecessor volumes.

Africa

There is one recent book that covers the whole field of African exploration: Christopher Hibbert, *Africa Explored* (London: Allen Lane, 1982). It is a good general survey, and the author has gone beyond merely re-hashing the stories of the most famous explorers. Also important is Robert I. Rotberg, ed. *Africa and Its Explorers: Motives, Methods and Impact* (Cambridge: Harvard University Press, 1970), which is a collection of essays on the most important explorers with assessments of their careers.

There were two main themes in the history of African exploration: the effort to trace the course of the Niger River and to reach Timbuktu and, secondly, the search for the sources of the Nile River. The first is dealt with in several books, including Robin Hallett, *The Penetration of Africa: European Enterprise and Exploration Principally in Northern and Western Africa up to 1830*, vol. 1: to 1815 (London: Routledge & Kegan Paul, 1965); E.W. Bovill, *The Niger Explored* (London: 1968); Christopher Lloyd, *The Search for the Niger* (London: Collins, 1973); and Sanche de Gramont, *The Strong Brown God: The Story of the Niger River* (Boston: Houghton Mifflin, 1975). The book by Sanche de Gramont, who later changed his name to Ted Morgan, is probably the most accessible and enjoyable to read.

The search for the Nile sources was first written about by an East African explorer, Harry Johnston in *The Nile Quest* (London: Lawrence & Bullen, 1903). Alan Moorehead has written two books about the search: *The White Nile* (New York: Harper & Brothers, 1960) deals with the southern approaches from Lake Victoria Nyanza while *The Blue Nile* (New York: Harper & Row, 1962) discusses the Ethiopian highlands. Other books on this subject can be found in the bibliographies for **Sir Richard Burton** and **John Hanning Speke**.

An important topic that is only beginning to be investigated is the role of native peoples in either helping or obstructing exploration by outsiders. In the case of Africa there is an interesting work by Donald Simpson: *Dark Companions: The African Contribution to the European Exploration of East Africa* (New York: Barnes & Noble, 1976). No comparable work has been done on the role of Native Americans, Pacific Islanders, Inuit, West Africans, etc.

Arabia

The history of European penetration of the Arabian Peninsula and the Middle East are covered in: Zahra Freeth and H.V.F. Winstone, *Explorers of Arabia: From the Renaissance to the End of the Victorian Era* (New York: Holmes & Meier, 1978); Kathryn Tidrick, *Heart-Beguiling Araby* (Cambridge: Cambridge University Press, 1981); James C. Simmons, *Passionate Pilgrims: English Travelers to the World of the Desert Arabs* (New York: William Morrow & Co., 1987).

Arctic and Antarctic

There are two overall surveys of the field of Polar exploration, both of the Arctic and Antarctic. The first was written by a President of the Royal

Geographical Society, Sir Clements Markham, who was instrumental in sponsoring many of the explorations that he wrote about: *The Lands of Silence* (Cambridge: Cambridge University Press, 1921). It retains the author's personal flavor, as well as his prejudices, but has been superseded by later works. This includes L.P. Kirwan, *A History of Polar Exploration* (New York: W.W. Norton, 1959). Kirwan was a Secretary of the Royal Geographical Society and was involved in planning many of the expeditions. His survey is quite useful even if it seems to lack the excitement that the subject would seem to generate. A more dramatic account can be found in John Maxtone Graham, *The Great Age of Polar Exploration*

Jeannette Mirsky's *To the Arctic! The Story of Arctic Exploration from Earliest Times to the Present* (New York: Viking, 1934; 2nd edition, New York: Alfred A. Knopf, 1948) is full of information and very well written. George Malcolm Thomson, *The Search for the North-West Passage* (New York: Macmillan, 1975) is also quite useful even if it lacks the élan of the Canadian author Pierre Berton's *The Arctic Grail: The Quest for the North West Passage and the North Pole, 1818-1909* (New York: Viking, 1988; paperback edition, New York: Penguin, 1989).

Leslie H. Neatby's *Conquest of the Last Frontier* (Athens: Ohio University Press, 1966) covers some of the lesser known Arctic and sub-Arctic explorations, many of which are also covered in J.M. Scott, *Icebound: Journeys to the Northwest Sea* (London: Gordon & Cremonesi, 1977).

A valuable chronology, with a minimum of narrative of the history of Antarctic exploration is R.K. Headland, *Chronological List of Antarctic Expeditions and Related Historical Events* (Cambridge: Cambridge University Press, 1989). A book that is highly recommended both because it covers many Antarctic voyages that are skimped on elsewhere and because it is enjoyable to read is *Antarctica: Great Stories from the Frozen Continent* (Sydney: Reader's Digest, 1988).

John Grierson, *Challenge to the Poles: Highlights of Arctic and Antarctic Aviation* (Hamden, Connecticut: Archon Books, 1964) gives a well-nigh complete history of Polar aviation.

Chinese and Arab Explorers

There is a compendium of texts on several of the Chinese voyagers that is both interesting and valuable: Jeannette Mirsky, *The Great Chinese Travelers* (New York: Random House, 1964). However, it has only a minimal amount of historical background and does not include a bibliography. The history of the subject needs to be written. This is even more true of the great Arab travelers. There is no overall survey of the field, and much of the information on individual explorers is taken from the *Encyclopedia of Islam*.

North America

For the early history of the exploration of the North American continent, see John Bartlet Brebner, *The Explorers of North America, 1492-1806* (London: Adam & Charles Black, 1933).

The exploration of the American West is covered, very successfully, in William H. Goetzmann, *Exploration and Empire* (New York: Alfred A. Knopf, 1966) while LeRoy R. Hafen, W. Eugene Holton, Carl Coke Rister, *Western America: The Exploration, Settlement and Development of the Region Beyond the Mississippi* (Englewood Cliffs, N.J.: Prentice-Hall, 1970) is a textbook that covers the material in a systematic, but interesting, manner.

The important role of the Hudson's Bay Company in fostering the exploration of the northern part of North America can be found in the works listed under **Samuel Hearne** and **David Thompson**.

The Pacific and Australia

By far the best book on European exploration in the Pacific is by the leading specialist in the field: J.C. Beaglehole, *The Exploration of the Pacific* (Stanford: Stanford University Press, 1966). Beaglehole does, however, limit himself to the most well-known explorations. Others can be found in Ernest S. Dodge, *Beyond the Capes: Pacific Exploration from Captain Cook to the Challenger, 1766-1877* (Boston: Little, Brown & Co., 1971) and O.H.K. Spate, *The Pacific Since Magellan*, 3 vols. (Minneapolis: University of Minnesota Press, 1979, 1983, 1988). John Dunmore, a student of Beaglehole's, has expanded on the field in *French Explorers in the Pacific*, 2 vols. (Oxford: Clarendon Press, 1965, 1969).

There is no recent general survey of the field of Australian exploration. Sir Ernest Scott's *Australian Discovery*, 2 vols. (London: 1929) is probably the most complete. A very good book is Alan Moorehead, *Cooper's Creek* (New York: Harper & Row, 1966), but it covers only a limited time span.

There is one general survey of the exploration of New Guinea. It is quite detailed and accurate but could be more exciting: Gavin Souter, *New Guinea: The Last Unknown* (New York: Taplinger Publishing Co., 1966).

South America

There is a very good survey of the whole field of South American exploration from the earliest years until the early 20th century: Edward J. Goodman, *The Explorers of South America* (New York: Macmillan, 1972). It is very complete and detailed, if sometimes a little dry. It is complemented by Goodman's extensive bibliography: *The Exploration of South America: An Annotated Bibliography* (New York: Garland Publishing, 1983).

Victor Wolfgang von Hagen, *South America Called Them: Explorations of the Great Naturalists* (New York: Duell, Sloan and Pearce,

1955) is a popularly written account of the four greatest scientists who explored South America in the 19th century.

Tibet

Tibet, which was the focus of much of the exploration of central Asia is covered in John MacGregor, *Tibet: A Chronicle of Exploration* (London: Routledge & Kegan Paul, 1970) and Peter Hopkirk, *Trespassers on the Roof of the World: The Race for Lhasa* (London: John Murray, 1982).

Women

The active role of feminists, as well as historians in general, in re-evaluating the role of women in all fields of human endeavor has extended to the history of our geographical knowledge of the world, i.e., the field of exploration. Not unsurprisingly, new studies have found many women who made remarkable journeys or had extensive careers as travelers but never got the credit that was their due. General surveys include: Mignon Rittenhouse, *Seven Women Explorers* (Philadelphia: J.B. Lippincott Co., 1964); Marion Tinling, *Women Into the Unknown: A Sourcebook on Women Explorers and Travelers* (New York: Greenwood, 1989); Dea Birkett, *Spinsters Abroad: Victorian Lady Explorers* (London: Basil Blackwell, 1989); and Jane Robinson, *Wayward Women: A Guide to Women Travellers* (Oxford: Oxford University Press, 1990).

One field in which women have had pioneering roles comparable to those of men has been in the area of aviation. There are two surveys of this subject, which often seem to mirror each other: Wendy Boase, *The Sky's the Limit: Women Pioneers in Aviation* (New York: Macmillan, 1979); and Judy Lomax, *Women of the Air* (New York: Dodd, Mead & Co., 1987).

List of Explorers by Area Explored

Explorers are listed alphabetically under their major areas of exploration.

Afghanistan

Scylax of Caryanda
Sir Aurel Stein

Africa   *See also* North Africa, South Africa, individual countries

Hanno

Air Travel

Amelia Earhart
Amy Johnson
Charles A. Lindbergh
Beryl Markham
Wiley Post
Dick Rutan
Charles E. Yeager
Jeana Yeager

Alaska

Alexander Andreyevich Baranov
James Cook
Jean François de Galaup, Comte de la Pérouse

Algeria

Henri Duveyrier
Paul-Xavier Flatters
Fernand Foureau
Friedrich Gerhard Rohlfs
Alexine Tinné
Fanny Bullock Workman

Angola

Pedro João Baptista
Diogo Cão
Hermenegildo de Brito Capelo
Roberto Ivens
Amaro José

Antarctica

Roald Amundsen
Fabian Gottlieb von Bellingshausen
John Biscoe
Richard Evelyn Byrd
Jean-Baptiste Charcot
Frederick Albert Cook
James Cook
Jules-Sébastien-César Dumont d'Urville
Lincoln Ellsworth
Sir Vivian Fuchs
Sir Edmund Hillary
Douglas Mawson
Robert Falcon Scott
Ernest Shackleton
Will Steger
Charles Wilkes
Sir (George) Hubert Wilkins

Arabia

Gertrude Bell
Lady Anne Blunt
Sir Wilfred Scawen Blunt
Jean Louis Burckhardt
Sir Richard Burton
Charles Montagu Doughty
Aelius Gallus
Abu Abdullah Ibn Battuta
al-Mas'udi
Muhammed ibn-Ahmed al-Muqaddasi
Carsten Niebuhr
Pedro Paez
Harry St. John Philby
Scylax of Caryanda
Lady Hester Stanhope
Wilfred Thesiger
Ludovico di Varthema
James Wellsted

Arctic

Roald Amundsen
Louise Arner Boyd
Richard Evelyn Byrd
Jean-Baptiste Charcot
Frederick Albert Cook
Lincoln Ellsworth
Sir Martin Frobisher
Charles Francis Hall
Matthew A. Henson
Wally Herbert
Anthony Jenkinson
Fridtjof Nansen
U.S.S. Nautilus
Umberto Nobile
(Nils) Adolf Erik Nordenskjöld
Robert Edward Peary
Will Steger
Sir (George) Hubert Wilkins

Argentina

Alvar Nuñez Cabeza de Vaca
Sebastian Cabot
Charles Darwin
Ferdinand Magellan
George Chaworth Musters
Juan Díaz de Solis

Armenia

Abu al-Kasim Ibn Ali al Nasibi Ibn Hawkal

Asia   *see* Central Asia, individual countries

Australia

Gregory Blaxland
Robert O'Hara Burke
James Cook
Allan Cunningham
William Dampier
Joseph-Antoine Raymond Bruni d'Entrecasteaux
Edward John Eyre
Matthew Flinders
John Forrest
Ernest Giles
Sir Augustus Gregory
(Alexander) Hamilton Hume
Willem Janszoon
Edmund Kennedy
Ludwig Leichhardt
Thomas Livingstone Mitchell
John Oxley
John McDouall Stuart

Charles Sturt
Abel Janszoon Tasman
Luis Vaez de Torres
George Vancouver
Peter Warburton
William John Wills

Bahamas

Christopher Columbus

Bolivia

Percy Fawcett
Annie Smith Peck

Botswana

Carl Johan Andersson
David Livingstone
Robert Moffat

Brazil

Henry Walter Bates
Pedro Alvarez Cabral
Percy Fawcett
Isabel Godin des Odonais
Charles-Marie de La Condamine
Francisco de Orellana
Vicente Yáñez Pinzón
Antônio Raposo Tavares
Cândido Rondon
Theodore Roosevelt
Sir Robert Hermann Schomburgk
Richard Spruce
Karl von den Steinen
Pedro de Teixeira
Giovanni da Verrazzano
Amerigo Vespucci
Alfred Russell Wallace

Burma

Fernão Mendes Pinto

Cameroon

Mary Kingsley

Canada

Sir George Back
Etienne Brûlé
Robert Bylot
John Cabot
Sebastian Cabot
Jacques Cartier
Samuel de Champlain
John Davis
Leif Eriksson
Luke Fox
Sir John Franklin
Simon Fraser
Sir Martin Frobisher
Sir Humphrey Gilbert
Médard Chouart des Groseilliers
Charles Francis Hall
Samuel Hearne

Louis Hennepin
Henry Hudson
Thomas James
Louis Jolliet
René-Robert Cavelier de La Salle
Pierre de la Vérendrye
Alexander Mackenzie
S.S. Manhattan
Jacques Marquette
Sir Francis Leopold McClintock
Sir Robert McClure
Jean Nicollet
Peter Skene Ogden
John Palliser
Sir (William) Edward Parry
Robert Peary
Pierre-Esprit Radisson
James Clark Ross
Sir John Ross
Vilhjalmur Stefansson
David Thompson
Henri de Tonty
George Vancouver
Giovanni da Verrazzano

Cape Verde

Alvise da Cadamosto

Central African Republic

Pierre Savorgnan de Brazza
Jean-Baptiste Marchand

Central Asia

Giovanni di Piano Carpini
Chang Chi'en
Ella Maillart
Sir Percy Sykes
William of Rubruck

Chad

Hugh Clapperton
Fernand Foureau
Gustav Nachtigal

Chile

Diego de Almagro
Charles Darwin
Hipólito Ruiz
Pedro de Valdivia

China

Isabella Bird
Giovanni di Piano Carpini
Francis Garnier
Sven Hedin
John of Marignolli
John of Monte Corvino
Ella Maillart
Maffeo Polo
Marco Polo
Nicolò Polo
Odoric of Pordenone
Nikolai Przhevalsky

Susie Carson Rijnhart
Sir Aurel Stein
William of Rubruck
Sir Francis Younghusband

Colombia

Alexander von Humboldt
José Celestino Mutis
Gonzalo Jiménez de Quesada
Alonso de Ojeda

Congo

Pierre Savorgnan de Brazza
Jean-Baptiste Marchand

Cuba

Christopher Columbus

Dominican Republic

Christopher Columbus

Ecuador

Charles Darwin
Isabel Godin des Odonais
Alexander von Humboldt
Charles-Marie de La Condamine
Richard Spruce
Pedro de Teixeira

Egypt

Alexander the Great
Jean Louis Burckhardt
Herodotus
Friedrich Hornemann
Abu al-Hasan Muhammed Ibn Jubayr

Ethiopia

James Bruce
Pero da Covilhão
Pedro Paez

Europe

Rabban Bar-Sauma
Abu Abd-Allah Muhammed al-Sharif al-Idrisi

Falkland Islands

Louis Antoine de Bougainville
John Byron
John Davis

French Guiana

Jules Crevaux
Sir Walter Raleigh

Gabon

Pierre Savorgnan de Brazza
Paul Du Chaillu
Mary Kingsley

Gambia

Alvise da Cadamosto
Daniel Houghton
Mungo Park

Great Britain

Pytheas

Greenland

William Baffin
Louise Arner Boyd
Jean-Baptiste Charcot
John Davis
Erik (the Red)
Leif Eriksson
Charles Francis Hall
Fridtjof Nansen
(Nils) Adolf Erik Nordenskjöld
Robert Edward Peary

Guadeloupe

Giovanni da Verrazzano

Guatemala

Pedro de Alvarado

Guyana

Sir Robert Hermann Schomburgk

Hawaii

Isabella Bird

Holy Land

Benjamin of Tudela
Abu al-Hasan Muhammed Ibn Jubayr
Pethahiah of Regensburg
Lady Hester Stanhope

India

Afonso de Albuquerque
Alexander the Great
Pedro Alvares Cabral
Cheng Ho
Pero da Covilhão
Vasco da Gama
Fa-Hsien
Hsüan-Chuang
I-Ching
John of Marignolli
John of Monte Corvino
Jordanus of Séverac
Jan Huygen van Linschoten
al-Mas'udi
Nearchus
Fanny Bullock Workman

Indonesia

Cheng Ho
Cornelius Houtman
I-Ching

Ida Pfeiffer
Andrés de Urdaneta
Alfred Russell Wallace

Iran

Alexander the Great
Rabban Bar-Sauma
Isabella Bird
Herodotus
al-Mas'udi
Muhammed ibn-Ahmed al-Muqaddasi
Nearchus
Ida Pfeiffer
Sir Percy Sykes

Iraq

Pethahiah of Regensburg
Xenophon

Italy

Abu al-Hasan Muhammed Ibn Jubayr

Ivory Coast

Louis-Gustave Binger

Japan

Isabella Bird
Fernão Mendes Pinto
St. Francis Xavier

Jupiter

Voyager 1 & 2

Kenya

Delia Akeley
Ludwig Krapf
Johannes Rebmann
Theodore Roosevelt
May French Sheldon
Joseph Thomson

Kyrgyzstan

Hsüan-Chuang

Lebanon

Lady Hester Stanhope

Libya

Henri Duveyrier
Friedrich Hornemann
(Alexander) Gordon Laing
Gustav Nachtigal
Friedrich Gerhard Rohlfs

Malaysia

Ida Pfeiffer
Fernão Mendes Pinto

Mali

Heinrich Barth
Rene Caillié
Daniel Houghton
Abu al-Kasim Ibn Ali al Nasibi Ibn Hawkal
(Alexander) Gordon Laing
Mungo Park

Mars

Mariner
Viking

Mauritania

Alvise da Cadamosto
Gil Eannes

Mercury

Mariner

Mexico

Pedro de Alvarado
Alvar Núñez Cabeza de Vaca
Hernán Cortés

Mongolia

Sven Hedin
Nikolai Przhevalsky
Sir Aurel Stein
Sir Francis Younghusband

Moon

Apollo
Neil Armstrong
Luna

Morocco

Hanno
Abu al-Kasim Ibn Ali al Nasibi Ibn Hawkal
Friedrich Gerhard Rohlfs
Fanny Bullock Workman

Mozambique

Pedro João Baptista
Hermenegildo de Brito Capelo
Vasco da Gama
Amaro José
David Livingston

Namibia

Carl Johan Andersson
Diogo Cão
Bartolomeu Dias

Nepal

Sir Edmund Hillary
Hari Ram
Nain Singh
Fanny Bullock Workman

Neptune

Voyager 1 & 2

New Guinea

Evelyn Cheesman
Luigi Maria D'Albertis
Willem Janszoon
Michael J. Leahy
Willem Schouten
Luis Vaez de Torres

New Zealand

James Cook
Abel Janszoon Tasman
George Vancouver

Newfoundland

Gasper Corte-Real
Miguel Corte-Real

Nigeria

William Balfour Baikie
Heinrich Barth
Hugh Clapperton
Samuel Adjai Crowther
Richard Lander
Gustav Nachtigal

North Africa

Abu Abd-Allah Muhammed al-Sharif al-Idrisi

North America   *see* individual countries

North Pole   *see* Arctic

Oceans

Challenger
Jacques(-Yves) Cousteau
Glomar Challenger
S.S. Meteor
August Piccard
Jacques Piccard

Pakistan

Hsüan-Chuang
Scylax of Caryanda

Panama

Vasco Nuñez de Balboa
Sir Francis Drake

Paraguay

Alvar Núñez Cabeza de Vaca

Peru

Diego de Almagro
Hiram Bingham
Alexander von Humboldt
Francisco de Orellana
Annie Smith Peck
Francisco Pizarro
Hipólito Ruiz
Richard Spruce

Puerto Rico

Christopher Columbus
Juan Ponce de León

Russia

Willem Barents
Vitus Bering
Giovanni di Piano Carpini
Richard Chancellor
Sven Hedin
Henry Hudson
Ahmad Ibn Fadlan
Anthony Jenkinson
Yerofey Pavlovich Khabarov
Jean François de Galaup, Comte de la Pérouse
Jan Huygen van Linschoten
Ella Maillart
Daniel Gottlieb Messerschmidt
Pethahiah of Regensburg
Maffeo Polo
Nicolò Polo
Vasily Danilovich Poyarkov
Nikolai Przhevalsky
William of Rubruck

Sahara Desert

Heinrich Barth
Rene Caillié
Henri Duveyrier
Paul-Xavier Flatters
Fernand Foureau

Saturn

Voyager 1 & 2

Scandinavia

Pytheas

Siberia

Vladimir Vasilyevich Atlasov
Semyon Ivanovich Dezhnev
Yerofey Pavlovich Khabarov
Daniel Gottlieb Messerschmidt
Gennady Ivanovich Nevelskoy
Vasily Danilovich Poyarkov
Yermak Timofeyev

Sierra Leone

Hanno
(Alexander) Gordon Laing

Sikkim

Alexandra David-Neel

Solomon Islands

Alvaro de Mendaña
Pedro Fernandez de Quiros

Somalia

Sir Richard Burton

South Africa

Carl Johan Andersson
Bartolomeu Dias
Vasco da Gama
Robert Moffat

South America   *see* individual countries

South Pacific

Louis Antoine de Bougainville
John Byron
Philip Carteret
Evelyn Cheesman
James Cook
Sir Francis Drake
Jules-Sébastien-César Dumont d'Urville
Joseph-Antoine Raymond Bruni d'Entrecasteaux
Jean François de Galaup, Comte de la Pérouse
Ferdinand Magellan
Alvaro de Mendaña
Ida Pfeiffer
Pedro Fernandez de Quiros
Jacob Roggeveen
Alvaro de Saavedra y Cerón
Willem Schouten
Abel Janszoon Tasman
Luis Vaez de Torres
Andrés de Urdaneta
George Vancouver
Samuel Wallis
Charles Wilkes

South Pole   *see* Antarctica

Space

Neil Armstrong
Explorer
Yuri Gagarin
John Glenn
Luna
Mariner
Sally Ride
Sputnik
Valentina Vladimirovna Tereshkova
Viking
Voyager 1 & 2

Spain

Abu al-Kasim Ibn Ali al Nasibi Ibn Hawkal

Sri Lanka

Fa-Hsien

Sudan

Florence Baker
Samuel White Baker
Jean Louis Burckhardt
Charles Chaillé-Long
Emin Pasha
Jean-Baptiste Marchand
Georg August Schweinfurth
Alexine Tinné

Syria

Benjamin of Tudela
Jean Louis Burckhardt
Lady Hester Stanhope

Tanzania

Sir Richard Burton
Verney Lovett Cameron
Emin Pasha
James Augustus Grant
Ludwig Krapf
David Livingstone
Johannes Rebmann
May French Sheldon
John Hanning Speke
Henry Morton Stanley

Thailand

Fernão Mendes Pinto

Tibet

Antonio de Andrade
Francisco de Azevado
João Cabral
Alexandra David-Neel
Ippolito Desideri
Johann Grüber
Sven Hedin
Evariste Régis Huc
Kintup
Thomas Manning
Nikolai Przhevalsky
Hari Ram
Susie Carson Rijnhart
Kishen Singh
Nain Singh
Annie Royle Taylor
Sir Francis Younghusbnad

Turkey

Pethahiah of Regensburg
Xenophon

Uganda

Florence Baker
Samuel White Baker
Emin Pasha
James Augustus Grant
John Hanning Speke
Henry Morton Stanley

United States of America

William Henry Ashley
Jim Beckwourth
Benjamin Louis Eulalie de Bonneville
Daniel Boone
Etienne Brûlé
Alvar Núñez Cabeza de Vaca
John Cabot
Sebastian Cabot
Juan Rodriguez Cabrillo
Samuel de Champlain
William Clark
John Colter
Francisco Vázquez de Coronado
Hernando de Soto
Sir Francis Drake
Estevanico
John Charles Frémont
Louis Hennepin
Wilson Price Hunt
Louis Jolliet
René-Robert Cavelier de La Salle
Pierre de La Vérendrye
Meriwether Lewis
Stephen Long
Jacques Marquette
Jean Nicollet
Peter Skene Ogden
Zebulon Pike
Juan Ponce de León
Pierre-Esprit Radisson
Sir Walter Raleigh
Jedediah Smith
John Smith
Robert Stuart
David Thompson
Henri de Tonty
George Vancouver
Giovanni da Verrazzano
Joseph Reddeford Walker

Uranus

Voyager 1 & 2

Vanuatu

Evelyn Cheesman
Pedro Fernandez de Quiros
Luis Vaez de Torres

Venezuela

Christopher Columbus
Alexander von Humboldt
Alonso de Ojeda
Diego de Ordaz
Sir Walter Raleigh
Richard Spruce
Amerigo Vespucci

Venus

Mariner

Vietnam

Cheng Ho
Francis Garnier

Western Sahara

Gil Eannes

Yemen

Muhammed ibn-Ahmad al-Muqaddasi
Carsten Niebuhr
Pedro Paez

Zaire

Delia Akeley
Verney Lovett Cameron
Diogo Cão
Hermenegildo de Brito Capelo
Emin Pasha
Roberto Ivens
Jean-Baptiste Marchand
Georg August Schweinfurth
Henry Morton Stanley

Zambia

Hermenegildo de Brito Capelo
Robert Ivens
David Livingstone

Zimbabwe

Pedro João Baptista
Amaro José
David Livingstone

List of Explorers by Place of Birth

If expedition(s) was sponsored by a country other than the explorer's place of birth,
the sponsoring country is listed in parentheses after the explorer's name.

Angola

Pedro João Baptista (Portugal)
Amaro José

Australia

John Forrest
(Alexander) Hamilton Hume
Michael J. Leahy
Douglas Mawson
Sir Hubert Wilkins
William John Wills

Austria

Johann Grüber
Ida Pfeiffer

Belgium

Louis Hennepin
William of Rubruck

Brazil

Cândido Rondon

Canada

Bob Bartlett
Louis Jolliet
Pierre de la Vérendrye
Peter Skene Ogden
Susie Carson Rijnhart
Vilhjalmur Stefansson

Carthage

Hanno

China

Rabban Bar-Sauma
Chang Ch'ien
Cheng Ho
Fa-Hsien
Hsüan-Chuang
I-Ching

Denmark

Vitus Bering (Russia)

Ecuador

Isabel Godin des Odonais

England

Sir George Back
William Baffin
Samuel White Baker
Sir Joseph Banks
Henry Walter Bates
Gertrude Bell
Isabella Bird
John Biscoe
Gregory Blaxland (Australia)
Lady Anne Blunt
Sir Wilfrid Scawen Blunt
Sir Richard Burton
Robert Bylot
John Byron
Verney Lovett Cameron
Philip Carteret
Challenger
Richard Chancellor
Evelyn Cheesman
James Cook
Allan Cunningham
William Dampier
Charles Darwin
John Davis
Charles Montagu Doughty
Sir Francis Drake
Edward Eyre
Percy Fawcett
Matthew Flinders
Luke Fox
Sir John Franklin
Sir Martin Frobisher
Sir Vivian Fuchs
Sir Humphrey Gilbert
Ernest Giles (Australia)
Sir Augustus Gregory (Australia)
Samuel Hearne
Wally Herbert
Daniel Houghton

Henry Hudson (Netherlands)
Thomas James
Anthony Jenkinson
Amy Johnson
Edmund Kennedy
Mary Kingsley
Richard Lander
Thomas Manning
Beryl Markham (Kenya)
George Chaworth Musters
John Oxley
Sir (William) Edward Parry
Harry St. John Philby
Sir Walter Raleigh
Robert Falcon Scott
John Smith
John Hanning Speke
Richard Spruce
Lady Hester Stanhope
Charles Sturt
Sir Percy Sykes
Annie Royle Taylor
Wilfred Thesiger
David Thompson
George Vancouver
Alfred Russell Wallace
Samuel Wallis
Peter Warburton (Australia)
James Wellsted
Sir Francis Younghusband

Estonia

Fabian Gottlieb von Bellingshausen (Russia)

France

Louis-Gustave Binger
Louis Antoine de Bougainville
Etienne Brûlé
René Caillié
Jacques Cartier
Francis de la Porte, Comte de Castelnau
Paul Du Chaillu (United States)
Samuel de Champlain
Jean-Baptiste Charcot
Jacques(-Yves) Cousteau
Jules Crevaux

Alexandra David-Neel
Jules-Sébastien-César Dumont d'Urville
Henri Duveyrier
Joseph-Antoine Raymond Bruni
    d'Entrecasteaux
Paul-Xavier Flatters
Fernand Foureau
Francis Garnier
Médard Chouart des Groseilliers
Evariste Régis Huc
Jordanus of Séverac
Charles-Marie de La Condamine
Jean François de Galaup, Comte de la
    Pérouse
René-Robert Cavelier de La Salle
Jean-Baptiste Marchand
Jacques Marquette
Jean Nicollet
Pierre-Esprit Radisson

Germany

Heinrich Barth (Great Britain)
Emin Pasha (Egypt)
Friedrich Hornemann (Great Britain)
Alexander von Humboldt
Ludwig Krapf
Ludwig Leichhardt
Daniel Gottlieb Messerschmidt (Russia)
S. S. Meteor
Gustav Nachtigal
Carsten Niebuhr (Denmark)
Johannes Rebmann
Pethahiah of Regensburg
Friedrich Gerhard Rohlfs
Sir Robert Hermann Schomburgk (Great
    Britain)
Georg August Schweinfurth
Karl von den Steinen

Greece

Alexander the Great
Herodotus
Nearchus
Pytheas
Scylax of Caryanda
Xenophon

Hungary

Sir Aurel Stein (Great Britain)

Iceland

Leif Eriksson

India

Kintup
Hari Ram
Kishen Singh
Nain Singh

Iraq

Ahmad Ibn Fadlan
Abu al-Kasim Ibn Ali al Nasibi Ibn Hawkal
al-Mas'udi

Ireland

Robert O'Hara Burke (Australia)
Daniel Houghton
Sir Francis McClintock
Sir Robert McClure
John Palliser
Ernest Shackleton

Italy

Luigi Maria D'Albertis
Pierre Savorgnan de Brazza (France)
John Cabot (England)
Sebastian Cabot (England, Spain)
Alvise da Cadamosto (Portugal)
Giovanni di Piano Carpini
Gaetano Casati
Christopher Columbus (Spain)
Ippolito Desideri
John of Marignolli
John of Monte Corvino
Umberto Nobile
Odoric of Pordenone
Maffeo Polo
Marco Polo
Nicolò Polo
Henri de Tonty (France)
Ludovico de Varthema
Giovanni da Verrazzano (France)
Amerigo Vespucci (Spain, Portugal)

Malawi

James Chuma (Great Britain)
Sidi Mubarak Bombay (Great Britain)

Morocco

Abu Abdallah Ibn Battuta
Abu Abd-Allah Muhammed al-Sharif al-
    Idrisi
Estevanico

Netherlands

Willem Barents
Cornelius Houtman
Willem Janszoon
Jacob Le Maire
Jan Huygen van Linschoten
Jacob Roggeveen
Willem Schouten
Abel Janszoon Tasman
Alexine Tinné

New Zealand

Sir Edmund Hillary

Nigeria

Samuel Adjai Crowther (Great Britain)

Norway

Roald Amundsen
Erik (the Red) (Iceland)
Fridtjof Nansen

Palestine

Muhammed ibn-Ahmad al-Muqaddasi

Portugal

Afonso de Albuquerque
Antonio de Andrade
Francisco de Azevado
João Cabral
Pedro Alvares Cabral
Juan Cabrillo (Spain)
Diogo Cão
Hermenegildo de Brito Capelo
Gaspar Corte-Real
Miguel Corte-Real
Pero da Covilhão
Bartolomeu Dias
Gil Eannes
Vasco da Gama
Prince Henry the Navigator
Roberto Ivens
Ferdinand Magellan (Spain)
Fernão Mendes Pinto
Pedro Fernandez de Quiros (Spain)
Antônio Raposo Tavares
Pedro de Teixeira

Romania

Florence Baker

Rome

Aelius Gallus

Russia   *see also* Union of Soviet Socialist Republics

Vladimir Vasilyevich Atlasov
Alexander Andreyevich Baranov
Semyon Ivanovich Dezhnev
Yerofey Pavlovich Khabarov
Gennady Ivanovich Nevelskoy
Vasily Danilovich Poyarkov
Nikolai Przhevalsky
Yermak Timofeyev

Scotland

William Balfour Baikie
James Bruce
Hugh Clapperton
James Augustus Grant
(Alexander) Gordon Laing
David Livingstone
Sir Alexander Mackenzie
Thomas Mitchell
Robert Moffat
Mungo Park
James Clark Ross
Sir John Ross
John McDouall Stuart

Robert Stuart (United States)
Joseph Thomson

Spain

Diego de Almagro
Pedro de Alvarado
Vasco Nuñez de Balboa
Benjamin of Tudela
Alvar Núñez Cabeza de Vaca
Francisco de Coronado
Hernán Cortés
Hernando de Soto
Abu Al-Hasan Muhammed Ibn Jubayr
Gonzalo Jiménez de Quesada
Alvaro de Mendaña
José Celestino Mutis
Alonso de Ojeda
Diego de Ordaz
Francisco de Orellana
Pedro Paez (Portugal)
Vicente Yáñez Pinzón
Francisco Pizarro
Juan Ponce de León
Hipólito Ruiz
Alvaro de Saavedra y Cerón
Juan Díaz de Solís
Luis Vaez de Torres
Andrés de Urdaneta
Pedro de Valdivia
St. Francis Xavier

Sweden

Carl Johan Andersson
Sven Hedin
(Nils) Adolf Erik Nordenskjöld

Switzerland

Jean Louis Burckhardt (Great Britain)
Ella Maillart
Jacques Piccard
Auguste Piccard

Union of Soviet Socialist Republics

Yuri Gagarin
Luna
Sputnik
Valentina Vladimirovna Tereshkova

United States of America

Delia Akeley
Apollo
Neil Armstrong
William Henry Ashley
Jim Beckwourth
Hiram Bingham
Benjamin Louis Eulalie de Bonneville
Daniel Boone
Louise Arner Boyd
Richard Evelyn Byrd
Charles Chaillé-Long
William Clark
John Colter
Frederick Albert Cook
George Washington De Long
Amelia Earhart
Lincoln Ellsworth
Explorer
Simon Fraser (Canada)

John Charles Frémont
John Glenn
Glomar Challenger
Charles Francis Hall
Matthew A. Henson
Wilson Price Hunt
Meriwether Lewis
Charles A. Lindbergh
Stephen Long
S.S. Manhattan
Mariner
U.S.S. Nautilus
Robert Edward Peary
Annie Smith Peck
Zebulon Pike
Wiley Post
Sally Ride
Theodore Roosevelt
Dick Rutan
May French Sheldon
Jedediah Smith
Will Steger
Viking
Voyager 1 & 2
Joseph Reddeford Walker
Charles Wilkes
Fanny Bullock Workman
Charles E. Yeager
Jeana Yeager

Wales

Henry Morton Stanley (United States)

Place of Birth List

Index

Bold-faced numbers refer to inclusive pages in which
explorer is featured.

Index